Nineteenth-Century Literature Criticism

Guide to Gale Literary Criticism Series

For criticism on	Consult these Gale series
Authors now living or who died after December 31, 1999	*CONTEMPORARY LITERARY CRITICISM (CLC)*
Authors who died between 1900 and 1999	*TWENTIETH-CENTURY LITERARY CRITICISM (TCLC)*
Authors who died between 1800 and 1899	*NINETEENTH-CENTURY LITERATURE CRITICISM (NCLC)*
Authors who died between 1400 and 1799	*LITERATURE CRITICISM FROM 1400 TO 1800 (LC)* *SHAKESPEAREAN CRITICISM (SC)*
Authors who died before 1400	*CLASSICAL AND MEDIEVAL LITERATURE CRITICISM (CMLC)*
Authors of books for children and young adults	*CHILDREN'S LITERATURE REVIEW (CLR)*
Dramatists	*DRAMA CRITICISM (DC)*
Poets	*POETRY CRITICISM (PC)*
Short story writers	*SHORT STORY CRITICISM (SSC)*
Literary topics and movements	*HARLEM RENAISSANCE: A GALE CRITICAL COMPANION (HR)* *THE BEAT GENERATION: A GALE CRITICAL COMPANION (BG)*
Asian American writers of the last two hundred years	*ASIAN AMERICAN LITERATURE (AAL)*
Black writers of the past two hundred years	*BLACK LITERATURE CRITICISM (BLC)* *BLACK LITERATURE CRITICISM SUPPLEMENT (BLCS)*
Hispanic writers of the late nineteenth and twentieth centuries	*HISPANIC LITERATURE CRITICISM (HLC)* *HISPANIC LITERATURE CRITICISM SUPPLEMENT (HLCS)*
Native North American writers and orators of the eighteenth, nineteenth, and twentieth centuries	*NATIVE NORTH AMERICAN LITERATURE (NNAL)*
Major authors from the Renaissance to the present	*WORLD LITERATURE CRITICISM, 1500 TO THE PRESENT (WLC)* *WORLD LITERATURE CRITICISM SUPPLEMENT (WLCS)*

ISSN 0732-1864

Volume 155

Nineteenth-Century Literature Criticism

Criticism of the
Works of Novelists, Philosophers, and Other
Creative Writers Who Died between 1800
and 1899, from the First Published Critical
Appraisals to Current Evaluations

Jessica Bomarito
Russel Whitaker
Project Editors

THOMSON
GALE

Detroit • New York • San Francisco • San Diego • New Haven, Conn. • Waterville, Maine • London • Munich

Nineteenth-Century Literature Criticism, Vol. 155

Project Editors
Jessica Bomarito and Russel Whitaker

Editorial
Kathy D. Darrow, Jeffrey W. Hunter, Jelena O. Krstović, Michelle Lee, Thomas J. Schoenberg, Noah Schusterbauer, Lawrence J. Trudeau

Data Capture
Francis Monroe, Gwen Tucker

Indexing Services
Synapse, the Knowledge Link Corporation

Rights and Acquisitions
Peg Ashlevitz, Lori Hines, Sheila Spencer

Imaging and Multimedia
Dean Dauphinais, Robert Duncan, Leitha Etheridge-Sims, Lezlie Light, Michael Logusz, Dan Newell, Kelly A. Quin, Denay Wilding

Composition and Electronic Capture
Kathy Sauer

Manufacturing
Rhonda Dover

Associate Product Manager
Marc Cormier

LIBRARY OF CONGRESS CATALOG CARD NUMBER 84-643008

ISBN 0-7876-8639-5
ISSN 0732-1864

Printed in the United States of America
10 9 8 7 6 5 4 3 2 1

Contents

Preface vii

Acknowledgments xi

Literary Criticism Series Advisory Board xiii

Preface

Since its inception in 1981, *Nineteeth-Century Literature Criticism* (*NCLC*) has been a valuable resource for students and librarians seeking critical commentary on writers of this transitional period in world history. Designated an "Outstanding Reference Source" by the American Library Association with the publication of is first volume, *NCLC* has since been purchased by over 6,000 school, public, and university libraries. The series has covered more than 450 authors representing 33 nationalities and over 17,000 titles. No other reference source has surveyed the critical reaction to nineteenth-century authors and literature as thoroughly as *NCLC*.

Scope of the Series

NCLC is designed to introduce students and advanced readers to the authors of the nineteenth century and to the most significant interpretations of these authors' works. The great poets, novelists, short story writers, playwrights, and philosophers of this period are frequently studied in high school and college literature courses. By organizing and reprinting commentary written on these authors, *NCLC* helps students develop valuable insight into literary history, promotes a better understanding of the texts, and sparks ideas for papers and assignments. Each entry in *NCLC* presents a comprehensive survey of an author's career or an individual work of literature and provides the user with a multiplicity of interpretations and assessments. Such variety allows students to pursue their own interests; furthermore, it fosters an awareness that literature is dynamic and responsive to many different opinions.

Every fourth volume of *NCLC* is devoted to literary topics that cannot be covered under the author approach used in the rest of the series. Such topics include literary movements, prominent themes in nineteenth-century literature, literary reaction to political and historical events, significant eras in literary history, prominent literary anniversaries, and the literatures of cultures that are often overlooked by English-speaking readers.

NCLC continues the survey of criticism of world literature begun by Thomson Gale's *Contemporary Literary Criticism* (*CLC*) and *Twentieth-Century Literary Criticism* (*TCLC*).

Organization of the Book

An *NCLC* entry consists of the following elements:

- The **Author Heading** cites the name under which the author most commonly wrote, followed by birth and death dates. Also located here are any name variations under which an author wrote, including transliterated forms for authors whose native languages use nonroman alphabets. If the author wrote consistently under a pseudonym, the pseudonym will be listed in the author heading and the author's actual name given in parenthesis on the first line of the biographical and critical information. Uncertain birth or death dates are indicated by question marks. Single-work entries are preceded by a heading that consists of the most common form of the title in English translation (if applicable) and the original date of composition.

- The **Introduction** contains background information that introduces the reader to the author, work, or topic that is the subject of the entry.

- A **Portrait of the Author** is included when available.

- The list of **Principal Works** is ordered chronologically by date of first publication and lists the most important works by the author. The genre and publication date of each work is given. In the case of foreign authors whose works have been translated into English, the list will focus primarily on twentieth-century translations, selecting those works most commonly considered the best by critics. Unless otherwise indicated, dramas are dated by first performance, not first publication. Lists of **Representative Works** by different authors appear with topic entries.

- Reprinted **Criticism** is arranged chronologically in each entry to provide a useful perspective on changes in critical evaluation over time. The critic's name and the date of composition or publication of the critical work are given at the beginning of each piece of criticism. Unsigned criticism is preceded by the title of the source in which it appeared. All titles by the author featured in the text are printed in boldface type. Footnotes are reprinted at the end of each essay or excerpt. In the case of excerpted criticism, only those footnotes that pertain to the excerpted texts are included. Criticism in topic entries is arranged chronologically under a variety of subheadings to facilitate the study of different aspects of the topic.

- A complete **Bibliographical Citation** of the original essay or book precedes each piece of criticism.

- Critical essays are prefaced by brief **Annotations** explicating each piece.

- An annotated bibliography of **Further Reading** appears at the end of each entry and suggests resources for additional study. In some cases, significant essays for which the editors could not obtain reprint rights are included here. Boxed material following the further reading list provides references to other biographical and critical sources on the author in series published by Thomson Gale.

Indexes

Each volume of *NCLC* contains a **Cumulative Author Index** listing all authors who have appeared in a wide variety of reference sources published by Thomson Gale, including *NCLC*. A complete list of these sources is found facing the first page of the Author Index. The index also includes birth and death dates and cross references between pseudonyms and actual names.

A **Cumulative Nationality Index** lists all authors featured in *NCLC* by nationality, followed by the number of the *NCLC* volume in which their entry appears.

A **Cumulative Topic Index** lists the literary themes and topics treated in the series as well as in *Classical and Medieval Literature Criticism, Literature Criticism from 1400 to 1800, Twentieth-Century Literary Criticism,* and the *Contemporary Literary Criticism* Yearbook, which was discontinued in 1998.

An alphabetical **Title Index** accompanies each volume of *NCLC*, with the exception of the Topics volumes. Listings of titles by authors covered in the given volume are followed by the author's name and the corresponding page numbers where the titles are discussed. English translations of foreign titles and variations of titles are cross-referenced to the title under which a work was originally published. Titles of novels, dramas, nonfiction books, and poetry, short story, or essay collections are printed in italics, while individual poems, short stories, and essays are printed in roman type within quotation marks.

In response to numerous suggestions from librarians, Thomson Gale also produces an annual paperbound edition of the *NCLC* cumulative title index. This annual cumulation, which alphabetically lists all titles reviewed in the series, is available to all customers. Additional copies of this index are available upon request. Librarians and patrons will welcome this separate index; it saves shelf space, is easy to use, and is recyclable upon receipt of the next edition.

Citing *Nineteenth-Century Literature Criticism*

When citing criticism reprinted in the Literary Criticism Series, students should provide complete bibliographic information so that the cited essay can be located in the original print or electronic source. Students who quote directly from reprinted criticism may use any accepted bibliographic format, such as University of Chicago Press style or Modern Language Association style.

The examples below follow recommendations for preparing a bibliography set forth in *The Chicago Manual of Style,* 14th ed. (Chicago: The University of Chicago Press, 1993); the first example pertains to material drawn from periodicals, the second to material reprinted from books:

Guerard, Albert J. "On the Composition of Dostoevsky's *The Idiot.*" *Mosaic: A Journal for the Interdisciplinary Study of Literature* 8, no. 1 (fall 1974): 201-15. Reprinted in *Nineteenth-Century Literature Criticism.* Vol. 119, edited by Lynn M. Zott, 81-104. Detroit: Gale, 2003.

Berstein, Carol L. "Subjectivity as Critique and the Critique of Subjectivity in Keats's *Hyperion.*" In *After the Future: Postmodern Times and Places,* edited by Gary Shapiro, 41-52. Albany, N. Y.: State University of New York Press, 1990. Reprinted in *Nineteenth-Century Literature Criticism.* Vol. 121, edited by Lynn M. Zott, 155-60. Detroit: Gale, 2003.

The examples below follow recommendations for preparing a works cited list set forth in the *MLA Handbook for Writers of Research Papers,* 5th ed. (New York: The Modern Language Association of America, 1999); the first example pertains to material drawn from periodicals, the second to material reprinted from books:

Guerard, Albert J. "On the Composition of Dostoevsky's *The Idiot.*" *Mosaic: A Journal for the Interdisciplinary Study of Literature* 8. 1 (fall 1974): 201-15. Reprinted in *Nineteenth-Century Literature Criticism.* Ed. Lynn M. Zott. Vol. 119. Detroit: Gale, 2003. 81-104.

Berstein, Carol L. "Subjectivity as Critique and the Critique of Subjectivity in Keats's *Hyperion.*" *After the Future: Postmodern Times and Places.* Ed. Gary Shapiro. Albany, N. Y.: State University of New York Press, 1990. 41-52. Reprinted in *Nineteeth-Century Literature Criticism.* Ed. Lynn M. Zott. Vol. 121. Detroit: Gale, 2003. 155-60.

Suggestions are Welcome

Readers who wish to suggest new features, topics, or authors to appear in future volumes, or who have other suggestions or comments are cordially invited to call, write, or fax the Associate Product Manager:

Associate Product Manager, Literary Criticism Series
Thomson Gale
27500 Drake Road
Farmington Hills, MI 48331-3535
1-800-347-4253 (GALE)
Fax: 248-699-8054

Acknowledgments

The editors wish to thank the copyright holders of the criticism included in this volume and the permissions managers of many book and magazine publishing companies for assisting us in securing reproduction rights. We are also grateful to the staffs of the Detroit Public Library, the Library of Congress, the University of Detroit Mercy Library, Wayne State University Purdy/Kresge Library Complex, and the University of Michigan Libraries for making their resources available to us. Following is a list of the copyright holders who have granted us permission to reproduce material in this volume of *NCLC*. Every effort has been made to trace copyright, but if omissions have been made, please let us know.

COPYRIGHTED MATERIAL IN *NCLC*, VOLUME 155, WAS REPRODUCED FROM THE FOLLOWING PERIODICALS:

Afro-Hispanic Review, v. 14, fall, 1995 for "Nineteenth Century Autobiography in the Afro-Americas: Frederick Douglass and Juan Francisco Manzano" by Luis A. Jiménez. Copyright © 1995 by Afro-Hispanic Review. All rights reserved. Reproduced by permission of the publisher and the author.—*Bulletin Baudelairien*, v. 37, April-December, 2002 for "Baudelaire's Province" by Kalliopi Nikolopoulou. Copyright © 2002 by Bulletin Baudelairien. All rights reserved. Reproduced by permission of the author.—*Bulletin of Latin American Research*, v. 20, January, 2001. Copyright © 2001 Basil Blackwell Ltd. Reproduced by permission of Blackwell Publishers.—*English Studies*, v. 57, June, 1976. Copyright © 1976 by Swets and Zeitlinger B. V. All rights reserved. Reproduced by permission.—*French Forum*, v. 27, no. 3, 2002. Copyright © 2003 by French Forum, Inc. All rights reserved. Reproduced by permission of the University of Nebraska Press.—*French Studies: A Quarterly Review*, v. 55, July, 2001 for "Superfluous Intrigues in Baudelaire's Prose Poems" by Maria Scott. Copyright © 2001 by the Society for French Studies. All rights reserved. Reproduced by permission of the publisher and the author.—*Genre*, v. 10, winter, 1977 for "Jane Eyre and Genre" by Jerome Beaty. Copyright © 1977 by The University of Oklahoma. All rights reserved. Reproduced by permission of Genre at the University of Oklahoma, and the author.—*Latin American Literary Review*, v. 16, July-December, 1988. Copyright © 1988, by the Latin American Literary Review. All rights reserved. Reproduced by permission of the publisher.—*Mosaic*, v. 21, fall, 1988. Copyright © 1988, by Mosaic. All rights reserved. Acknowledgment of previous publication is herewith made.—*Narrative*, v. 4, January, 1996. Copyright © 1996 by The Ohio State University Press. All rights reserved. Reproduced by permission.—*Nineteenth-Century French Studies*, v. 13, summer, 1985; v. 25, spring-summer, 1997; v. 26, spring-summer, 1998; v. 27, spring-summer, 1999. Copyright © 1985, 1997, 1998, 1999 by Nineteenth-Century French Studies. All rights reserved. All reproduced by permission.—*Papers on Language & Literature*, v. 4, summer, 1968. Copyright © 1968 by The Board of Trustees of Southern Illinois University. All rights reserved. Reproduced by permission.—*Renascence*, v. 37, 1984. Copyright © 1984, Marquette University Press. All rights reserved. Reproduced by permission.—*Revista de Estudios Hispánicos*, v. XXI, 1994. Copyright © 1994, by Seminario de Estudios Hispánicos and Federico de Onís. All rights reserved. Reproduced by permission./v. XXVIII, October, 1994. Copyright © 1994, by Washington University. All rights reserved. Reproduced by permission.—*South Central Review*, v. 13, winter, 1996 for "Heads and/are Tails: Eccentric Conjunctions in Baudelaire's *Spleen de Paris*" by Margaret Miner. Reproduced by permission of the author.—*Studies in the Novel*, v. 28, nos. 1 and 4, 1996; v. 34, winter, 2002. Copyright © 1996, 2002 by The University of North Texas. All rights reserved. Reproduced by permission.—*SubStance: A Review of Theory and Literature Criticism*, v. 22, 1993. Copyright © 1993 by the Board of Regents of the University of Wisconsin System. All rights reserved. Reproduced by permission.—*Victorian Newsletter*, v. 30, fall, 1966; v. 90, fall, 1996. Copyright © 1966, 1996 by The Victorian Newsletter. All rights reserved. Reproduced by permission of The Victorian Newsletter.

COPYRIGHTED MATERIAL IN *NCLC*, VOLUME 155, WAS REPRODUCED FROM THE FOLLOWING BOOKS:

Bailly, Jean-Christophe. From "Prose and Prosody: Baudelaire and the Handling of Genres," in *Baudelaire and the Poetics of Modernity*. Edited by Patricia A. Ward. Translated by Jan Plug. Vanderbilt University Press, 2001. Copyright © 2001 by Vanderbilt University Press. All rights reserved. Reprinted by permission.—Barbaret, John R. From "Baudelaire: Homoérotismes," in *Articulations of Difference: Gender Studies and Writing in French*. Edited by Dominique D. Fisher and Lawrence R. Schehr. Stanford University Press, 1997. Copyright © 1997 by the Board of Trustees of the Leland Stanford Junior University. All rights reserved. Reprinted by permission.—Bock, Carol. From *Charlotte Brontë and the Storyteller's*

Thomson Gale Literature Product Advisory Board

The members of the Thomson Gale Literature Product Advisory Board—reference librarians from public and academic library systems—represent a cross-section of our customer base and offer a variety of informed perspectives on both the presentation and content of our literature products. Advisory board members assess and define such quality issues as the relevance, currency, and usefulness of the author coverage, critical content, and literary topics included in our series; evaluate the layout, presentation, and general quality of our printed volumes; provide feedback on the criteria used for selecting authors and topics covered in our series; provide suggestions for potential enhancements to our series; identify any gaps in our coverage of authors or literary topics, recommending authors or topics for inclusion; analyze the appropriateness of our content and presentation for various user audiences, such as high school students, undergraduates, graduate students, librarians, and educators; and offer feedback on any proposed changes/enhancements to our series. We wish to thank the following advisors for their advice throughout the year.

Charles Baudelaire
1821-1867

French poet, critic, translator, novelist, and diarist.

This entry presents Baudelaire criticism from 1985 to 2002. For further information on Baudelaire's career, see *NCLC*, Volumes 6 and 29; for discussion of the work *Les fleurs du mal*, see *NCLC*, Volume 55.

INTRODUCTION

Baudelaire is best known as the author of *Les fleurs du mal* (1857; *The Flowers of Evil*). Considered shocking because of its amoral tone and explicit portrayal of such topics as prostitution, sexual perversion, urban lowlife, and the poet's own tortured and conflicted psyche, *The Flowers of Evil* was neither a popular nor a critical success upon its publication. While only a few nineteenth-century reviewers recognized Baudelaire's highly individual talent, today he is widely appreciated for his style, daring subject matter, and distinctly modern point of view.

BIOGRAPHICAL INFORMATION

Baudelaire was born in Paris to financially secure parents. His father, who was three decades older than his mother, died when Baudelaire was six years old; Baudelaire's mother remarried seven years later. Exceptionally close to his mother, Baudelaire deeply resented his stepfather and, as he grew older, became rebellious, neglecting his studies in favor of a dissipated lifestyle. His parents sent him on a two-year trip to India in hopes of reforming him, but Baudelaire returned much the same. It was during this trip, however, that he began experimenting with writing verse and wrote some of the poems that would later become part of *The Flowers of Evil*. When he returned to Paris, Baudelaire received an inheritance that allowed him to live for a brief time as a dandy intent on challenging the norms of what he viewed as the corrupt bourgeois society around him. He fell in love with Jeanne Duval, a Parisian woman of African descent, who inspired his "Black Venus" cycle of love poems. Their highly sensual and volatile relationship eventually ended, leaving Baudelaire introspective and disillusioned. He began to experiment with opium and hashish—which also inspired his interest in the work of Thomas De Quincey—and eventually published several poems in the journal *Revue de deux mondes*.

Except for a few literary figures, notably Victor Hugo and Algernon Charles Swinburne, reviewers roundly condemned his work as scandalous.

Baudelaire was similarly attacked upon the publication of *The Flowers of Evil* in 1857, when even his close friend Charles Sainte-Beuve, an author and critic, refused to praise the book. Shortly afterward, Baudelaire and his publisher, Auguste Poulet-Malassis, were prosecuted and convicted of immorality. Six poems deemed morally offensive were removed from the book and published later the same year in Belgium as *Les épaves*. These poems scandalized Paris with their graphic eroticism and depiction of lesbianism and vampirism. For both the 1861 and the posthumously published 1868 editions of *The Flowers of Evil*, some poems were added and others revised, but the ban on the suppressed poems was not lifted in France until 1949. After the publication of the 1861 edition, Baudelaire's publisher went bankrupt. In an attempt to regain both his reputation and his financial solvency, Baudelaire traveled to

Belgium on a lecture tour. The tour was unsuccessful and Baudelaire returned to Paris in 1866, where he suffered a severe stroke. He died in 1867.

MAJOR WORKS

Critics agree that *The Flowers of Evil* is Baudelaire's masterpiece. Written and revised over a number of years, the poems of this collection combine his passionate Romanticism, fervent striving for stylistic perfection, and his religious quest. In his desire to depict the horror and ecstasy of life, Baudelaire explored the beautiful as well as the ugly and the sinful as well as the repentant. Many critics have called attention to these polar opposites, which drive the themes of *The Flowers of Evil.* Pervaded with satanic themes, the poems also attest to Baudelaire's search for spiritual perfection amid a life of temporal pleasure, culminating in his search for peace in death. Baudelaire's most controversial poems in *The Flowers of Evil* are his love pomes, written for his three mistresses (Duval, Apollonie Sabatier, and Marie Daubrun). Their raw, sometimes brutal sensuality testifies to what many scholars regard as Baudelaire's conflicted feelings toward women.

Baudelaire is also acknowledged as one of the first French poets to delineate the plight of the urban underclass. Unlike his artistic predecessors who located beauty in art, Baudelaire discovered artistic possibilities among the outcasts of Parisian society. The beauty and cruelty of Parisian existence, Baudelaire contended, mirrored the complicated and irrational nature of all humanity. Scenes of the Parisian underworld are vividly depicted in his *Petits poèmes en prose: Le spleen de Paris* (1869, *Poems in Prose from Charles Baudelaire*). Comparable in lyrical imagery and language to *The Flowers of Evil,* this work conveys in melancholy tones a desire to escape the misery of earthly existence. Critics note that the stylistic innovations of Baudelaire's prose poems strongly influenced the poetry of Stéphane Mallarmé, Paul Claudel, and Arthur Rimbaud.

CRITICAL RECEPTION

Despite his dismissal by reviewers in his own era, Baudelaire's reputation in the twentieth century is secure. Critics consistently rank *The Flowers of Evil* among the greatest works of Western poetry and they fully acknowledge Baudelaire's influence on Symbolist poetry and such later modern poets as T. S. Eliot and W. B. Yeats. For the most part, scholars have focused on Baudelaire's transformation of Romantic themes, the religious elements in his work, his rigorous concern for the formal aspects of his verse, and his emphasis on emotion and the senses. Toward the end of the twenti-

eth century and the beginning of the twenty-first, scholars expanded their exploration of Baudelaire's poetry. While critics like Margaret Miner, Nicolae Babuts, James R. Lawler, Peter Broome, Maria Scott, and Rosemary Lloyd continue the tradition of close stylistic study of Baudelaire's work, other critics have probed, for example, the influence of caricature on Baudelaire's style (Ainslee Armstrong McLees), the poet's handling of the metaphor of surgery in his work (Cheryl Krueger), and Baudelaire's technique of writing about prostitution as an intermediary for homoeroticism. Sonya Stephens and Jean-Christophe Bailly discuss Baudelaire's blurring of the boundaries between the genres of poetry and prose in the context of modernism, while Ross Chambers and Kalliopi Nikolopoulou comment on his attitude toward the city, with Chambers pointing out that noise and disorder become incorporated into Baudelaire's poetic style. Baudelaire's political ideas have also attracted critics' attention, and Beryl Schlossman, Geraldine Friedman, Timothy Raser, and Dabarati Sanyal chart the effects of revolution and its aftermath in some of his works.

PRINCIPAL WORKS

Salon de 1845 (poetry) 1845

La fanfarlo (novel) 1847

Histoires extraordinaires [translator; from the short stories of Edgar Allan Poe] (short stories) 1856

Les épaves (poetry) 1857

Les fleurs du mal [*The Flowers of Evil*] (poetry) 1857; revised enlarged edition, 1861

Nouvelles histoires extraordinaires [translator; from the short stories of Edgar Allan Poe] (short stories) 1857

Aventures d'Arthur Pym [translator; from the novel *The Narrative of Arthur Gordon Pym* by Edgar Allan Poe] (novel) 1858

Les paradis artificiels: Opium et haschisch [*Artificial Paradises: On Hashish and Wine as a Means of Expanding Individuality*] (autobiography and poetry; includes Baudelaire's translation of Thomas De Quincey's *Confessions of an English Opium Eater*) 1860

Curiosités esthétiques (criticism) 1868

L'art romantique (criticism) 1869

Petits poèmes en prose: Le spleen de Paris [*Poems in Prose from Charles Baudelaire*] (prose poems) 1869; also published as *Paris Spleen*

Journaux intimes [*Intimate Journals*] (diaries) 1887

Lettres: 1841-1866 (letters) 1905

Oeuvres complètes de Charles Baudelaire. 19 vols. (poetry, criticism, essays, novel, letters, journals, autobiography, and translations) 1922-53

The Letters of Charles Baudelaire (letters) 1927

Baudelaire on Poe; Critical Papers (criticism) 1952

CRITICISM

Ross Chambers (essay date summer 1985)

SOURCE: Chambers, Ross. "Baudelaire's Street Poetry." *Nineteenth-Century French Studies* 13, no. 4
(summer 1985): 244-59.

[*In the following essay, Chambers describes the poems
of the "Tableaux Parisiens" section of* The Flowers of
Evil *as being about Paris street life, and as stylistically
reflecting the concept of disorder inherent in their subject.*]

When, in the 1861 edition of the **Fleurs du Mal,** Baudelaire introduced a new section entitled "Tableaux Parisiens," he included in it a series of eight poems (from
"Le Soleil" to **"Le Squelette Laboureur"**)[1] which constitute the "diurnal" sequence of the section, corresponding to a "nocturnal" sequence which runs from
"Le Jeu" to **"Rêve parisien."**[2] One unifying feature of
the eight diurnal poems is that they are all set in the
street; and my first purpose here is to show that in these
texts the street should be understood as the place in
which the "I" subject of the poems encounters the conditions of "modernity." For the street is a metonym of
the city, but its very metonymic status is what makes it
a metaphor of urban existence, the "chaos des vivantes
cités" (of **"Les petites vieilles"**) which is also "la forêt
où mon esprit s'exile" (of **"Le Cygne"**). *Pars pro toto,*
when the "whole" is itself elusive, indefinable, chaotic—a jumble of unrelated parts—becomes an experience of fragmentation and disconnectedness: it produces enigma and poses the problem of meaningfulness.
Thus Baudelaire uses synecdoche, not to reconstitute a
missing unity, but to express its disintegration. The
Baudelairean street is a place in which encounters occur
but their finality is obscured, in which knowledge of
their origin and certainty as to their end are unavailable:
"Car j'ignore où tu fuis, tu ne sais où je vais" ("A une
passante"); a place which thus comes to signify that
disconnectedness of experience which, since Marx, we
have learned to call alienation.[3]

However, the street is not only the place in which the
"action" of the poems occurs, their setting; it serves
also, within the poems, as a figure of poetic discourse
itself. By this means, the poems describe themselves as
places of encounter for the reader—of encounter with
beauty, the bizarre, the fantastic, the grotesque, the absurd, the enigmatic; of encounter, as I shall suggest,
with figures of death. And by extension of the analogy,
they define themselves also—*pars pro toto*—as fragments of some chaotic and ungraspable discursive whole
from which they are disconnected but through which
moments of human communication can occur and the
questions of significance they raise can be posed. Like
the street, the Baudelairean poem is a "cana/l/étroit du
colosse puissant" in which one encounters a fantastic
proliferation of sameness, as in **"Les sept vieillards,"**[4]
or through whose meandering verses, like "les plis
sinueux des vieilles capitales," one may "follow" little
old women and reconstruct their lives. Like the Baudelairean street, the poem is often fluvial, whether after
the manner of Andromache's "Simoïs menteur"[5] or, like
the *faubourg* of **"Les sept vieillards,"** leading to the
"mer monstrueuse et sans bords" of absurdity. Of the
poems, as of the experience they are concerned with, it
can be said that "tout . . . devient allégorie" (as in **"Le
Cygne"**) and that "tout, même l'horreur, tourne aux en-
chantements" (as in **"Les petites vieilles"**), so true is it
that this is poetry which simultaneously raises the question of meaning and posits the proximity of horror and
enchantment, beauty and death.

But the beauty and death one encounters in the street or
in the street-poem are of an untraditional kind. Death
does not necessarily put an end to life, as is shown in
the final poem of the series by the anatomical engravings one encounters in the streets that border the river,

> Qui traînent sur les quais poudreux
> Où maint livre cadavéreux
> Dort comme une antique momie.
>
>   (**"Le squelette laboureur"**)

The digging skeleton suggests that "tout, même la Mort,
nous ment" and that there is no end to the labor and
questioning of existence. In the poet's book, too, death
is not an escape from life so much as what we encounter in life itself, "sur les quais poudreux": it is death-in-
life—life defined as death-in-life—which is the subject
of these poems. And in them, too, as in the drawings,

>   . . . auxquels la gravité
> Et le savoir d'un vieil artiste,
> Bien que le sujet en soit triste,
> Ont communiqué la Beauté,

death appears with a strangely enhanced quality—a
quality of beauty.

But if we go back now to the first poem of the sequence,
"Le Soleil," we can see that beauty, although it is attributed to the work of an artist, his "fantasque escrime"
in the street, appears in a way which itself differs mark-

edly from conventional conceptions. If, like the sun, it "embellit le sort des choses les plus viles,"[6] beauty is here the chance result of an inefficient performance which contrasts with the strength and precision of the sun's action, an aleatory act indistinguishable, in the domain of language, from the poet's stumbling progress along a street:

> Le long du vieux faubourg, . . .
> Je vais m'exercer seul à ma fantasque escrime,
> Flairant dans tous les coins les hasards de la rime,
> Trébuchant sur les mots comme sur les pavés,
> Heurtant parfois des vers depuis longtemps rêvés.

It seems, indeed, if the suggestions of these two framing poems can be extrapolated, that beauty, inasmuch as it results from poetic performance, has now less to do with "la gravité / Et le savoir d'un vieil artiste" than with the modern artist's grotesque grappling with the forces of chance *in language*. And similarly, it is the poet's encounters *in the street,* which, posing the question of their meaning like the skeletal diggers:

> Dites, quelle moisson étrange,
> Forçats arrachés au charnier,
> Tirez-vous, et de quel fermier
> Avez-vous à remplir la grange?

raise the spectre of death in life to which his poetry seeks to give its strange beauty. If so, what I have called the question of meaning (the presence of death in life) and the question of beauty (the proximity of horror and enchantment) are not separate questions but aspects of a single problematics which has at its core the random quality of the encounters that make up city life. And it is the street, as locus of such encounters (without which they could not take place, but in which they can only occur randomly) which consequently lies at the heart of a poetics of modernity. For the street stands both for the question of the meaningfulness of urban experience, and for a language in which poetic meaning is subject to chance.

Philippe Jaccottet has defined poetry somewhere as "la voix donnée à la mort." Baudelaire's street poetry defines itself both as a place in which death walks in the guise of beauty (it is a street-walker), and as a discourse whose beauty is regained from chance; so that here the place and the discourse are one in their apprehension of the presence, in beauty, of the forces of disorder, disharmony and destruction. In surveying briefly the remaining six poems of the street sequence—framed, as we have seen, by a poem which establishes the equivalence of street and poem and a poem which makes the street (-poem) a place of encounter with death-in-life—I will need to examine both a thematics and a poetics, and I shall do so sequentially. But the discontinuity between them is not great if one accepts that disorder is what underlies both; for the thematics is

a thematics of encounter—but of encounter with "bizarre" forms of beauty whose strangeness is the sign of the presence of death[7]—and the poetics (presented already in **"Le Soleil"** as a poetics of encounter) is that of a language traversed by death in the form of communicational disorder, or noise.

For where, as Jonathan Raban points out,[8] English city-writers identify it as a place of dirt (Baudelaire's "quais poudreux"), the Baudelairean street manifests the phenomenon of entropy most obsessively in the form of noise. Indeed, it is as a place of noise—"Le faubourg secoué par les lourds tombe-reaux" of **"Les sept vieillards"**—that the street achieves its fundamental unity as a place where death makes itself manifest and poetic language becomes problematic; such, at least, is the case I wish to make. But this means that a certain question of communication is of the essence: the thematics of encounter explores the relationship between the lonely poet, the *flâneur* "I," and the beings he fleetingly meets; while the poetics of noise makes of his voice that "voix donnée à la mort" which, speaking in solitude, dramatizes as clumsy gesticulation the need to communicate through art. Death's most pervasive manifestation, in "life" as in "art," is as that which problematizes human communication.

. . . . .

A complex network of motifs connects the six "inner" poems: I cite at random those of widowhood, the river of tears, the shock of eye-contact. . . . But the major themes can be allowed to emerge by pursuing the "coupling" technique I have already adopted. Proceeding inwards from the two frame poems, one can link **"A une mendiante rousse"** and **"A une passante"** as explorations of the ambivalence of beauty, **"Le Cygne"** and **"Les Aveugles"** as treatments of exile in an alienating world, and finally **"Les petites vieilles"** and **"Les sept vieillards"** as exemplifications of the enveloping theme of encounter itself, in its dual aspect (the establishment of human contact, the brush with absurdity and death).

"A une mendiante rousse" concerns the proximity, in modern times, of poverty and beauty. The fantasy of Renaissance splendor suggested by the beggar-woman is not incompatible with the sordid reality of her prostitution in the present:

> —Cependant tu vas gueusant
> Quelque vieux débris gisant
> Au seuil de quelque Véfour
> De carrefour.

She is a Muse entirely appropriate to the poet, himself a sickly figure ("poëte chétif"); and her "jeune corps maladif" adorned only by its own "maigre nudité" (since the poet cannot afford to buy her the tawdry jewelry she covets) fittingly represents a form of beauty allied with misery and death. Yet it simultaneously suggests that in beauty there is something timeless, since the beggar's rags might, in another age, have been a "robe de cour." So the contrast with the splendidly and fashionably dressed widow (I presume her mourning is for a spouse) of **"A une passante"** is, in the last analysis, only apparent. She, too, in her modern clothes, allows a glimpse of a timeless element, to which the poet responds, behind her contemporary exterior; so that both of these female figures can be seen as exemplifications of Baudelaire's theory of the double composition (eternal and contemporary, relative and absolute) of beauty.

But it is clear that something has changed between these two poems; and that the change affects the value attached to the two components of beauty. Whereas the present appearance of the beggar is one of poverty, sickness and death, while the underlying timelessness is suggested by the fantasy of a "superbe robe de cour" and the context of courtly lovers and poets that accompanies it, it is the classical nobility of the passerby in her magnificent mourning (a contemporary reprise of Renaissance splendor) that makes her a manifest figure of death, while what is glimpsed, through her eye— "ciel livide où germe l'ouragan"—is an eternity of chaos, disorder and tempest. Whereas, in the first case, the poet is moved to rival in some sense the sonnets of "maître Belleau," he is left "crispé comme un extravagant" in the second: struck electrically, and deprived of his means. In each poem, then, death walks the street in the guise of feminine beauty, but the timelessness it suggests is, in one instance, a form of continuity (that of the wretched present with the noble past), but in the other a vision of cosmic disorder capable of plunging the present into impotence, and the absurdity of problematized communication:

> Car j'ignore où tu fuis, tu ne sais où je vais,
> O toi que j'eusse aimée, ô toi qui le savais![9]

The poems are suggesting, I think, that there has been a historical change, not in the dual nature of beauty nor in its essential affinity with death, but in the nature of the timeless component, which once was a matter of splendor, majesty and nobility but in which a rupture of continuity has occurred—some historic break—so that it has now become a matter of disorder and tempest. That, it would seem, is why modern art can no longer be a matter of "gravité" and "savoir," but has become rather an unhealthy business of spastic gesticulation (as in **"A une passante"**) and clumsy stumbling (as in **"Le Soleil"**).

So it is that **"A une mendiante rousse"** anticipates **"Le Cygne,"** in which the grotesque swan in the contemporary Parisian gutter recalls—as the beggar recalls the courtly lady—Andromache and "l'immense majesté de

/ ses / douleurs de veuve." But here the theme of widowhood, of course, similarly foretells the "douleur majestueuse" of **"A une passante,"** and it does so most interestingly, I would say, because in **"Le Cygne"** the nobility of this ancient widow is seen as being already, in the past, fatally tinged with the first signs of *déchéance*:

> Vil bétail . . .
> Veuve d'Hector, hélas! et femme d'Hélénus!

The plunge from former splendor into the mud of urban exile is what widowhood (and the consequent history of remarriage which in this case it entails) seems to connote: it not only exemplifies the proximity of the sublime and the grotesque (an essential theme of **"Le Cygne,"** as Wolfgang Fietkau has pointed out, in another connection),[10] but it suggests that the slippage from one to the other results from a manifestation of death. But of a death which has not, like Hector's, brought about an end to life: it is a death which, like Andromache, one survives. The death of the hero seems rather to be the historic event that has brought about a disruption in the serenity of the world of the eternal and produced a slippage there—from the sublime to the grotesque—which is responsible for the modern situation. This is a new disorder in the order of timelessness which requires of the artist that beauty be a beauty of death, and that it be regained from randomness and chance: these are the conditions of exile which define— as they do for the Swan—the heroism of modern life.

Just as **"A une mendiante rousse"** looks forward to **"Le Cygne,"** then, so too the "I" of **"A une passante,"** "crispé comme un extravagant," looks back to **"Les Aveugles,"** where the subject of the poem already described himself as "plus qu'eux hébété." There, too, the sky to which the blind raise their sightless eyes, "d'où la divine étincelle est partie," has something in common—as the place where the determining event of modernity has occurred—with the "ciel livide" of **"A une passante"** as well as with the sky, "ironique et cruellement bleu" which the swan implores, "comme l'homme d'Ovide," in the earlier poem. And similarly, with their spastic gesturing and "pareils aux mannequins," the blind not only anticipate the crispation of **"A une passante,"** but they also recall the swan, with its "gestes fous," **"Comme les exilés, ridicule et sublime."**

Thus the sense of exile in all these poems is attributed to a loss occurring originally in a transcendant and irrecuperable beyond which is at the origin of disorder, "où *germe* l'ouragan." The city, in **"Le Cygne,"** is a place of entropic disorder:

> Ces tas de chapiteaux ébauchés et de fûts,
> Les herbes, les gros blocs verdis par l'eau des flaques,
> Et, brillant aux carreaux, le bric-à-brac confus

in which only human work (the "voirie" perhaps, but it too is a noisy and "sombre ouragan," and certainly the ordering activity of the poetic mind, working with association and memory) represent negentropic forces, opposing *change* ("Paris change! mais rien dans ma mélancolie n'a bougé"). And the city, in **"Les Aveugles,"** is a place of noise, whose din is the structural equivalent of the silence of eternity:

> Ils traversent ainsi le noir illimité,
> Ce frère du silence éternel. O cité!
> Pendant qu'autour de nous tu chantes, ris et beugles,
>   . . . . .
> Vois! je me traîne aussi!

and where the futile gesturing of the blind, "Dardant on ne sait où leurs globes ténébreux," designates them as lost souls in the hell of the living.

Exile, then, is at bottom a matter of disconnectedness. The disconnectedness of spastic gesture reflects the disconnectedness of a world cut off from heaven, or from "le beau lac natal" of the past. Such gesticulation, "ridicule et sublime," figures also the disconnectedness of a world in which chance encounters and the chance associations they arouse pose the question of meaning ("tout pour moi devient allégorie") and leave the observer as much or more "hébété" than those whose exile he observes. For there is also the ultimate loneliness which, in these poems, is that of the poetic "I," the *flâneur* who, while emphathizing with the exiled beings he meets and sharing their pain, experiences in addition a kind of exile of the mind ("Ainsi dans la forêt où mon esprit s'exile . . .") which separates him from them. For it is he who, as poet, asks the question of meaning: "Je dis: Que cherchent-ils au Ciel, tous ces aveugles?"—a line which is an unmistakable *mise en abyme* of the poem itself, as communicational act.[11]

Indeed, as an exile himself, the *flâneur*-poet experiences disconnectedness in a quite particular way, as a problem in communication. Or, like the other lonely and disconnected individuals he encounters, he must himself be logically a figure of death, stalking the streets; and we have seen his sense of affinity with them increase as their quality as exiles becomes more explicit. The two central poems, **"Les sept vieillards"** and **"Les petites vieilles,"** confirm this affinity with figures of death, the old women by the sympathy (and empathy) they extract from him, the old men by the way their fantastic resemblance attacks the poet's own sense of identity and brings him up against a sense of absurdity expressed in the now familiar meteorological metaphor of the storm:

> Vainement ma raison voulait prendre la barre;
> La tempête en jouant déroutait ses efforts,
> Et mon âme dansait, dansait, vieille gabarre
> Sans mâts, sur une mer monstrueuse et sans bords!

But the poet, as exile and death-figure, has a special privilege or responsibility, which is to speak—to speak a language, we must now realize, which has the qualities of "bizarre" beauty: a beauty expressive of death. What can such a language be? To whom can it be addressed, in a disconnected world? How can the poet's speech (the *dire* of **"Les Aveugles"**) be heard amid the din of the street-world, of the city? These are the questions we must now turn to.

Fellow-feeling, and hence communication, is possible for the poet only with his "congénères," the people of the street: beggars, widows, the blind, "petites vieilles," "fantôme(s) débile(s) / Traversant de Paris le fourmillant tableau," or "Débris d'humanité pour l'éternité mûrs." We may extrapolate that the readership his poems presuppose must also be a readership of exiles (but we know, from the enumerative passages of **"Le Cygne,"** that that category subsumes a vast number of people, if not all people). However, if poetic communication is a negentropic activity opposing disorder and entropy, and seeks to counter disconnectedness by establishing contacts and community, it is itself a problematic and indeed dangerous activity, as the two central poems suggest, for what is at stake in poetic activity is individual identity itself.

It is true that, for the "I" subject, the "petites vieilles" are the occasion to move outside of himself in identification with the lives of others, an experience which the poem presents as near-euphoric (and it does dramatize a gift which is part of every city-dweller's survival equipment: the power to reconstruct the lives of others from the most immediately perceptible signs).

> Je vois s'épanouir vos passions novices;
> Sombres ou lumineux, je vis vos jours perdus;
> Mon cœur multiplié jouit de tous vos vices!
> Mon âme resplendit de toutes vos vertus!

But such power of identification, depending as it ultimately does on the similarity of self and others, is in the final analysis a function of the sameness of city people, of the city as ant-bed ("de Paris le fourmillant tableau")—and it is precisely the threat posed by the "fourmillante cité," the hostility to the individual soul of its similarity and repetition, which forms the subject of **"Les sept vieillards,"** whose eerily multiplying old men pose the problem of indifferentiation and anonymity. In this poem, the "I" subject must finally retreat in self-defence from the street, and shut himself up in a room:

> Exaspéré comme un ivrogne qui voit double,
> Je rentrai, je fermai ma porte, épouvanté,
> Malade et morfondu, l'esprit fiévreux et trouble,
> Blessé par le mystère et par l'absurdité!

—a reaction which confirms both the Baudelairean sense of the street as a place of metaphysical danger and the fragility of a conception of the self, as autonomous being, so threatened by the phenomenon of communication, whether it be as euphoric multiplication and enhancement of the soul, or dysphoric dissolution in the undifferentiated sea of sameness.[12]

For **"Les sept vieillards"** is readable, as I have suggested elsewhere,[13] as a poem that allegorizes poetic language itself: the language of metaphor which, for example, causes a street to "simulate" a river, the repeated equivalences which, line by line and strophe by strophe, multiply like the old men and produce the sense of sameness we call poetic unity. If this is so, then poetic language thus becomes itself a manifestation of death, the exact equivalent for the reader of what the encounter with the fantastic old men signifies for the narrative "I" in the poem, that is, "le spectre en plein jour raccroch / ant / le passant" (note, incidentally, that here again death is figured as a prostitute). The reader is thus defined him or herself as a "passant"—a street-person passing on the way to death—the poem as a phantom, plucking at our sleeve with its proliferating discourse like the proliferating sameness of the old men. And, just as the old men are, in some sense, emanations of the street (fluid like a river, angular like urban landscape), so the poem in the final analysis shows itself to be, not just a poem *of* the street, but a poem that shares the characteristics of the street. In its fluidity, it recalls the street-river:

> Les mystères partout coulent comme des sèves
> Dans les canaux étroits du colosse puissant.

But in its threatening hostility as a place of repeated sounds connoting death, it is exactly like the place of its own setting: "Le faubourg secoué par les lourds tombereaux"—that is, this text is producing an equivalence between street-noise and poetic sameness, as the language of death. For these "tombereaux"—metaphors, I take it, for the omnibuses whose "fracas roulant" startles the "petites vieilles"—have a name which speaks death doubly (suggesting both the tomb and revolutionary terror), and their shaking of the street is the image of an insistent, disruptive, repetitive force. If the poet's speech has its place, then, and can be heard amid the din of the city, it can only be as a form of noise itself. And the speech which seems such a threat to the poetic subject is no less a threat to the reader. That is the price set, in the world of exile, on the achievement of communication.

Modern information theory, an outgrowth of thermodynamics, treats noise as an impediment to communication and permits us to see its kinship, as a form of entropy, with the disorder in Baudelaire's streets (the "quais poudreux" of **"Le squelette laboureur"** or the "Palais neufs, échafaudages, blocs" of **"Le Cygne"**); its kinship, also, with the gestural clumsiness of certain exile-figures ("I" in **"A une passante,"** or the blind

men, or the swan); and finally, of course, with that of the poet in **"Le Soleil,"** whose stumbling gait in the street metaphorizes poetic creation itself as a matter of disorder, chance and accident. But Baudelaire, then, does not present noise as an impediment to communication so much as he sees noise-traversed communication as the only mode available to modern poetic speech; and the problem for him is not to exclude noise from poetic beauty but to find a means of producing poetry which incorporates noise into its texture, just as modern beauty incorporates death. The din of the city, with its songs, laughter and bellowing ("Pendant qu'autour de nous tu chantes, ris et beugles"), with its "fracas roulant," and everything, in short, that constitutes the "rue assourdissante" (**"A une passante"**), is a dangerous rival to poetic speech, but also its model.

Not that the poem is to become sheer noise: the models of poetic speech the poems produce tend to be dual, incorporating the flow of the river and the hostile angularity of the street (**"Les sept vieillards"**), the entropy of change and the negentropy of thought (**"Le Cygne"**), the grace and control of equilibrium ("Soulevant, balançant le feston et l'ourlet") but with a hurricane at its heart. Here, too, the double character of beauty is the ultimate reference. But, in seeking to incorporate noise into poetic beauty, Baudelaire is taking a step whose daring, in the contemporary context, becomes evident by contrast with the poetic mood of the period.

When he published *Emaux et Camées* in 1852—a short time after the *coup d'état*—Gautier took care, in a liminal poem, to emphasize the exclusion of noise from his poetics:

> Sans prendre garde à l'ouragan
> Qui fouettait mes vitres fermées,
> Moi, j'ai fait *Emaux et Camées.*

The political motivation was evident: Gautier is asserting the apolitical character of verse, its autonomy with respect to the turbulent events of the recent past. The esthetic effect—if Michel Serres is correct in suggesting that codification is what drives out "noise" from discourse[14]—was to declare poetry a matter of purely formal beauty: thus, in Gautier's poem, Goethe—the Goethe of the *Westöstlicher Diwan,* "pour Naisimi quittant Shakespeare"—exemplifies the choice of purely conventional expression, in the manner of Persian poetry, over the drama of life, represented by Shakespeare. Gautier's lead, as we know, was in general followed by the poets of the Second Empire period, who took refuge in doctrines of esthetic autonomy ("l'art pour l'art") and impassiveness (the Parnasse)—even though this poem itself demonstrates the futility of an enterprise which does not so much exclude noise as it dramatizes the gesture of excluding it.

However, in opting for a poetry of the street, for a poetic discourse which incorporates the "hurricane" instead of attempting to exclude it, Baudelaire is quite deliberately taking an oppositional course, whose esthetic and political implications are inextricably intertwined, but whose first effect is to redefine the street which we have seen is his poetic model so that, in addition to denoting "la rue où l'on passe," it comes to connote also "la rue où l'on descend": the street which is the scene of barricades and attempted revolution. (My distinction between denotation and connotation is an attempt to characterize the duplicitous mode of discourse made necessary by a régime of censorship such as existed under Napoléon III.) For the liminary poem of "Tableaux Parisiens," "Paysages," explicitly picks up the theme of Gautier's own liminary:

> L'Emeute, tempêtant vainement à ma vitre,
> Ne fera pas lever mon front de mon pupitre;

but it does so in a clearly ironic and distanced fashion. The irony is readable within the poem itself[15]—indeed, I would read the wretchedly halting metric structure of the second line just quoted as a way of smuggling noise into the very line that talks of its exclusion—but it becomes inescapable when one realizes that the very next poem, the first of the street series, shows the poet responding to the invitation and example of the sun, and emerging from the protection of his mansard-room into the street (and more specifically, a lower-class street, the "faubourg" with its "masures").

> Le long du vieux faubourg . . .
> Quand le soleil cruel frappe . . .
> Je vais m'exercer seul à ma fantasque escrime.

This emergence is not only, by obvious implication, a *descente dans la rue,* from the "mansarde" of **"Paysage"** to the "pavés" of **"Le Soleil"** (the word "pavés" not being itself an entirely innocent one), but its impulse, in following the lead of the sun, goes clearly in the direction of a revolutionary democracy. For,

> Quand, ainsi qu'un poète, il descend dans les villes,
> Il ennoblit le sort des choses les plus viles,
> Et s'introduit en roi, sans bruit et sans valets,
> Dans tous les hôpitaux et dans tous les palais.

The poet, less privileged in this and other ways, must operate—like the revolutionary crowds of 1848—"*avec bruit*"; but he is here indicating the political relevance of a street-poetry whose significance is not limited to, or exhausted by its esthetic and metaphysical ramifications. In Haussmann's Paris, experienced by the contemporaries as a place of imposed order and "alignement," Baudelaire's twisting streets, with their litter and noise and scurrying passersby, are haunted, not simply by an abstract and philosophical figure of death, but also by something more historically specific, the spectre of the barricades. (That, for example, is why the "voirie," signifying negentropy, can also signify noise, "à

l'heure où sous les cieux / Froids et clairs le Travail s'éveille. . . .")[16] The suggestion is, then, that the historic event responsible for the slippage that has produced the conditions of modernity can be called *revolution.*

For the street is the place of exile of those who, like Baudelaire, knew themselves "physiquement dépolitiqué"[17] by the coming to power in 1851 of the new régime. That is perhaps the meaning of the dedication of three major street-poems to Victor Hugo, the most prominent political exile of the period. Baudelaire's street people, including the "I" of the poems, are victims—unlike Hugo—of internal exile, but their exile, like his, shows itself as a kind of surrogate of the death-sentence (a death-in-life), which does not suppress political activity so much as it obliges it to change its form. For "dépolitiqué" not only does not mean "apolitical" (a very over-hasty, if frequent, reading), but also the restrictive "physiquement" leaves open the possibility of recourse to *other,* non-physical forms of political action (as Hugo's example verifies): spiritual action, perhaps, or esthetic. And there is in Baudelaire's work at least one recognizable figure of the *physiquement dépolitiqué,* and that is the buffoon Fancioulle in **"Une mort héroïque."** Condemned to death (physically depoliticized) for political opposition, reduced to silence as a mime (his name, cf. Italian "fanciullo," means "infant"—one who cannot speak), yet closely identified with the Prince himself, the buffoon *lives his condemnation in the form of an esthetic performance,* one so beautiful (it is a "parfaite idéalisation") as to lead his audience, and the artist himself, to forget "les terreurs du gouffre," but which *the Prince himself ensures is traversed by an ear-splitting noise.* The "sifflet" signals the failure of art as a euphemization of death, but simultaneously raises Fancioulle to a new and higher *favor* (Baudelaire italicizes the word)—as an artist, in conjunction with the Prince, of death, who does not "voiler les terreurs du gouffre" but manifests them.

With these ideas and associations in mind, it is perhaps disappointing to re-read the actual poems of Baudelaire's street-series, which to the reader of today appear to subscribe to a poetics scarcely distinguishable from that of classical French verse. But a study of their rhetorical and metric structure—the irregular *coupes* and enjambments, the strategically placed dashes and suspension points which introduce breaks and angularities into the flow of verse and ideas—would show one way in which Baudelaire introduces disorder and communicational noise into his poetic practice.[18] More basic, however (for clearly there is little or no real attempt—at least by our contemporary standards—to imitate noise in the actual structure of the verse) is the subtle use of self-reference as a mode of illocutionary re-definition of these more-or-less conventional verse forms. The last line of **"Les Aveugles,"** with its flat diction, irregular rhythmic schemes and clearly anticlimactic "Je dis," shows how such a redefinition by *mise en abyme* can function. But another, and more striking case in point is the use of the verb "hurler" in **"A une passante."**

It is used of street noise, which it curiously humanizes: "La rue assourdissante autour de moi hurlait"—and what it suggests, as a consequence, is the possibility of this howl "autour de moi" becoming internalized into a howl *within* the throat of the poetic "I"—a subject who is in a state, one must remember, of muscular spasm ("crispé") and has lost control of the means of expression ("comme un extravagant," one who divagates). This state is further attributed to the vision of disorder—"ciel livide où germe l'ouragan"—in the eye of the passing stranger, who in other ways (her rhythmic walk, her "jambe de statue") figures a work of art and hence refers back to the poem itself. The sonnet is not out of control, like a howl; nor does it imitate a howl: its topic, indeed, is not lack of control but the subtle alliance of control ("balançant le feston et l'ourlet") and disorder ("ciel livide où germe l'ouragan"—"crispé comme un extravagant") in the one conjoined experience of beauty and death. But it does suggest that at its very heart there is disorder, and that it emanates from, has its point of origin ("germe") in communicational as well as metaphysical disorder, that is a cry which is perhaps silent in the poem but nevertheless traverses its texture like the Prince's "sifflet" in Fancioulle's performance (which is why one might see some equivalence between "I" 's spastic seizure here and Fancioulle's convulsive death). The implied howl in the verbal poem, like the implied revolution in the noisy street, is the silent cry of the *physiquement dépolitiqué;* it signals the death of the sublime and the coming of the grotesque, in poetry or in politics. Modern beauty can only be the bizarre beauty of death.[19]

Notes

1. The complete list is: "Le Soleil," "A une mendiante rousse," "Le Cygne," "Les sept vieillards," "Les petites vieilles," "Les aveugles," "A une passante," and "Le squelette laboureur."

2. I am treating "Paysage," "Le Crépuscule du Soir" and "Le Crépuscule du Matin" as liminary poems having a mainly intersequential function. See on this point my essay "Trois paysages urbains: les poèmes liminaires des *Tableaux Parisiens,*" *Modern Philology,* 80, 4 (May 1983), 372-389.

3. The seminal reference on Baudelaire and urban experience is of course Walter Benjamin, *Charles Baudelaire. Ein Lyriker im Zeitalter des Hochkapitalismus* (Frankfurt am Main: Suhrkamp, 1969). I have learned much also from Richard D. Burton, *The Context of Baudelaire's "Le Cygne"* (University of Durham: Modern Languages Se-

ries, 1980), and from the work of Edward J. Ahearn, especially "The Search for Community: The City in Hölderlin, Wordsworth and Baudelaire," *Texas Studies in Literature and Language,* 13 (Spring 1971), 71-89 and "Confrontation with the City. Social Criticism, Apocalypse and the Reader's Responsibility in Poems by Blake, Hugo and Baudelaire," *Hebrew University Studies in Literature,* 10, 1 (Spring 1982), 1-22.

4. I have studied this poem as an allegory of itself in "Are Baudelaire's *Tableaux Parisiens* About Paris?" in M. Issacharoff and A. Whiteside, eds., *On Referring in Literature* (to appear).

5. On the "Simoïs menteur" as a figure of the poem, see my article "'Je' dans les *Tableaux Parisiens* de Baudelaire," *Nineteenth-Century French Studies,* IX, 1-2 (Fall-Winter 1980-81), 59-68.

6. There is room for doubt as to whether this achievement is attributed to the poet or to the sun alone, for the syntax is ambiguous. See my "Baudelaire et l'espace poétique: à propos du 'Soleil,'" in *Le lieu et la formule. Hommage à Marc Eigeldinger* (Neuchâtel: La Baconnière, 1978), 111-120.

7. The word "bizarre" is, of course, Baudelairean. It figures in the slogan of *Exposition Universelle, 1855*: "Le beau est toujours bizarre," which encapsulates the doctrine that beauty escapes order and classification—a doctrine from which it is only a step to the view that beauty is a manifestation of disorder. See *Oeuvres complètes,* II (Paris: Pléiade, 1976), p. 578.

8. *Soft City* (London: Hamish Hamilton, 1974), p. 25. Raban, to whose discussion of synecdoche as a necessary response to the city as a jumble of unconnected parts I owe much, does not see that synecdoche can itself be metaphoric of that jumble when it identifies manifestations of fragmentation, disconnectedness and entropy.

9. I have proposed more extended readings of "A une passante" in "Pour une poétique du vêtement," *Michigan Romance Studies,* 1 (1980), 18-46, and "The Storm in the Eye of the Poem: A Reading of 'A une passante'" (to appear).

10. See *Schwanengesang auf 1848* (Reinbek bei Hamburg: Rowohlt, 1978). The "other connection" is political: the poem is seen as an oblique comment on the Second Empire in the light of Napoleon I's famous remark, at the retreat from Moscow: "Du sublime au ridicule il n'y a qu'un pas."

11. Cf. my article, "Seeing and Saying in Baudelaire's 'Les Aveugles,'" in R. L. Mitchell, ed., *Pre-text/ Text/Context: Essays on Nineteenth-Century*

French Literature (Columbus: Ohio State University Press, 1980), 147-156.

12. The two poems thus reproduce, not only the problematics of the Baudelairean "bain de multitude," but of the sense of identity he encapsulated in the key-pronouncement of *Mon Cœur mis à nu*: "De la vaporisation et de la centralisation du Moi. Tout est là," a statement of which Georges Poulet's essay in *Les Métamorphoses du Cercle* (Paris: Plon, 1961), 397-432, remains perhaps the best commentary.

13. See "Are Baudelaire's *Tableaux Parisiens* About Paris?" op. cit.

14. I am thinking specifically of his essay from *Hermès II* (L'Interférence) (Paris: Minuit, 1972), translated as "Platonic Dialogue" in M. Serres, *Hermes. Literature, Science, Philosophy* (Baltimore: Johns Hopkins University Press, 1982), 65-70. Cf. especially, p. 68: "to formalize . . . means to eliminate noise" and p. 70: "To isolate an ideal form is to render it independent of the empirical domain and of noise. Noise is the empirical portion of the message."

15. See "Trois paysages urbains," op. cit.

16. The seminal reading of "Le Cygne" as the poem of nostalgia for the revolution is Dolf Oehler, "Ein hermetischer Sozialist. Zur Baudelaire-Kontroverse zwischen Walter Benjamin und Bert Brecht," *Diskussion Deutsch*, 26 (Dezember 1975), 569-584.

17. Cf. his letter to Ancelle of March 5, 1852 (*Correspondance*, t. I, p. 188) (Paris: Pléiade, 1973). The expression is characteristically ambivalent: the neologism "dépolitiqué" can be taken—by contrast with *dépolitisé*—to mean "cured of meddling in political matters" (with a pejorative view of political action which is itself the object of strong irony), while "physiquement" has at once the strength of "radically" and of "brutally, by main force."

18. See G. Chesters, "Baudelaire and the Limits of Poetry," *French Studies*, XXXII, 4 (October 1978), 420-434.

19. For a political reading of "A une passante," see Dolf Oehler, "Art-névrose. Sozio-psychanalyse einer gescheiterten Revolution bei Flaubert und Baudelaire," *Akzente*, 2 (April 1980), 113-130. Richard Stamelman's important and suggestive article "The Shroud of Allegory: Death, Mourning and Melancholy in Baudelaire's Work," *Texas Studies in Literature and Language*, 25, 3 (Fall 1983), 390-409, unfortunately appeared too late for me to refer to it in the body of my text.

A shorter version of this paper was read at the Nineteenth-Century French Studies colloquium held at Harvard University, October 27-29, 1983.

Ainslie Armstrong McLees (essay date fall 1988)

SOURCE: McLees, Ainslie Armstrong. "Baudelaire's 'Une charogne'": Caricature and the Birth of Modern Art." *Mosaic* 21, no. 4 (fall 1988): 111-22.

[*In the following essay, McLees links Baudelaire's poetry to the flowering of graphic caricature in his era, and suggests that like many French painters, Baudelaire recognized in the medium a new kind of beauty that signaled modernism.*]

Of all the poems in Charles Baudelaire's **Fleurs du mal,** the one which has most disturbed critics is **"Une charogne."** Similar on the surface to baroque poems with a memento mori theme, the poem is radically unconventional in its attitudes toward and treatment of the subject—as its title in itself suggests. To register his disapproval of Baudelaire's innovations, Lemercier de Neuville, a contemporary critic for *Le figaro*, wrote a witty review entitled "*La cuisiniere bourgeoise—physiologie de esprit*," wherein he reduced the poem to a recipe: "*Découpez un cadavre faisandé et déjà en décomposition, en autant de parties que vous pourrez, bourrez de vers bien faits et d'originalité, saupoudrez de paradoxes, parez de* Fleurs du Mal *et servez raide—(Echauffant).*"

Nor have critical attitudes toward the piece greatly altered in the twentieth century. In their studies of Baudelaire, Yvonne Rollins and Lydie Krestovsky develop Sainte-Beuve's view of the poem as "*pétrarquisant sur l'horrible*" (1: 219-22) while to René Galand, Martin Turnell and J. D. Hubert it is an atrocious piece. Jean Prévost concludes that only those who value a "*chef d'oeuvre de l'art funèbre*" will laud this poem (291).

My purpose in the following essay is to suggest that the reason critics find **"Une charogne"** so unsettling is that they have failed to recognize what it is that Baudelaire is attempting to do in this poem: namely, to adapt the esthetics of caricature to poetic expression, and specifically the strategies of caricature as they were articulated by Diderot and graphically pioneered by Goya. Arguing in this way that caricature has a long tradition in which the visual and the verbal are combined, I will conclude by observing that just as Baudelaire was inspired by Goya, so Cézanne and Manet were inspired by Baudelaire. The development of caricature, in short, is also the development of modern art.

* * *

As a graphic form, caricature has existed since the late sixteenth century when it was restricted to the studio, a sort of parlor game shared among artists. Historians generally credit Agostino and Annibale Caracci, refined artists of the Bolognese School, for originating the form. They were the first artists to distort their models playfully rather than academically. In medieval grotesques playful distortion decorated texts and adorned buildings, but the process involved imaginary figures rather than distortions of models. Academic distortion as a means of studying the degrees of expressiveness achieved through variation of features had been a serious method of instruction since the time of Leonardo. The Caracci's playful distortions were more than stylistic exercises, however. They commented upon the Bolognese society of their period: taking models from life, they distorted the salient features to reveal an underlying character flaw.

Annibale Caracci called his distorted portraits *ritrattini carichi.* Although he may have been punning on his own name, the coinage also reflects the combination of the Italian verb *caricare* (to load or charge) and the Italian noun *carattere* (character or type), and in doing so conveys the essence of caricature: exaggeration as a means to unmasking character. The French equivalent for *carichi* is *chargés,* which like its Italian counterpart, is derived from the verb to load or exaggerate. In sixteenth-century usage *chargés* applied to loaded weapons and to a state of intoxication, as well as to a "loaded" or exaggerated portrait. As such, these early meanings foreshadow both the role of caricature as a political weapon and the type of heightened perception it involves in serious art. Significantly, too, the French noun, *charge,* remains a synonym for caricature.

The earliest literary use of the word in France is in d'Argenson's *Mémoires* (1740), where it is defined as *"une reproduction grotesque par le dessin ou la peinture."* A decade later both caricature and *charge* became dictionary entries in Diderot and d'Alembert's *Encyclopédie ou dictionnaire raisonné des sciences, des arts et des métiers* (1751). Caricature, the term which has endured, was paradoxically the shorter of the two entries:

> Caricature. *ff (Peinture). Ce mot est francifié, de l'Italien caricature, & c'est ce qu'on appelle autrement* charge. *Il s'applique principalement aux figures grotesques & extremement disproportionnées, soit dans le tout, soit dans les parties qu'un peintre, un sculpteur ou un graveur fait exprès pour s'amuser & pour faire rire. Callot a excellé dans ce genre. Mais il en est du burlesque en peinture comme en poésie c'est une espèce de libertinage d'imagination qu'il ne faut se permettre tout au plus que par délassement.*

In this entry the principles of exaggeration and intent to provoke laughter dominate. The final sentence, a warning against taking burlesques too seriously, further anticipates the power of caricature when applied seriously to a specific purpose. The author of this entry is not sympathetic to the form. He senses in it the potential danger of the liberated imagination.

The entry for *charge,* written by Diderot, is considerably longer and more analytic. Several important ideas emerge from it. Caricature, asserts Diderot, is not limited to portraiture; its subjects can be objects and actions, just as it may involve the use of color. Nor is caricature limited to visual art: it is equally appropriate in prose and poetry. Purposeful exaggeration is the requirement for a work to be classified as caricature, with the purpose being to pass moral judgment on the subject. Excessive exaggeration must thus be avoided, as must invention of elements not present in the subject. As such, caricature differs equally from burlesque (which is gratuitous exaggeration) and the grotesque (which is an imaginative creation of deformed figures) and satire (which lacks the concern with unmasking essences and the playful use of distortion to these ends). Caricature, in short, is the distinctive form which emerges from the combination of the burlesque and satire, just as it marries the visual and verbal—the caption or "moral" in the case of the graphic form and the pictorial element in the written form.

* * *

In the area of the visual arts, no figure was ultimately as influential as Francisco Goya (1746-1828) in advancing the development of caricature as a serious art form. Louis-Philippe's *Gallérie espagnole,* a wing of the Louvre devoted to Spanish art including Goya's *Duchesse d'Albe,* attests to the Spanish art's importance in setting fashion (Schlumberger 56-65). As a court portraitist Goya produced works which seem like those of van Dyke or Reynolds in terms of both color and composition. Beneath the grandeur of their poses, however, the faces of the court figures reveal their pettiness and vanity, their greed and their ugliness—both physical and spiritual. Separating himself sharply from the past conventions of the court painter in this way, Goya also was innovative in his choice and treatment of subjects in his etchings. Rather than illustrating an historical, biblical or literary subject, he depicted his own private vision. Several groups of his works demonstrate this break with tradition, and reveal the emerging esthetic of distortion in art.

Goya's *Caprichos, Disparates* and *Desastres de la guerra* unmask the follies of human behavior. Although each series utilizes the same technical devices (etchings in aquatinta; distortion, composition, shading) they reflect the evolution of Goya's understanding of the comic and its ability to convey serious content. The *Caprichos* (1799) is a series of eighty etchings. The first prints communicate the traditional theme of reason and imagination in conflict and use the human form haunted by fantastic figures to express the malaise of the model. Goya subsequently substituted allegorical depictions of people in animal form, recalling the tradition of the bestiary and fable. The final etchings of the *Caprichos* depict human forms vastly distorted. The stylistic development through the series shows that the comic— that is, deviation from the classical norm in both theme and style—as a means of treating serious and tragic themes was central to Goya's conception of art. It demonstrates, too, a new role for imagination. Instead of threatening reason, imagination assumes a visionary role in the final etchings of the series. The distance between what is seen (appearance) and what is known (essence) is expressed by means of distortion.

With enigmatic captions like those of the *Caprichos,* the *Disparates* rely heavily on formal distortion. In this series, Goya gives free rein to the frightening and fantastic visions of a dream-like state. For example, to depict the caption, "She who is ill-wed never misses a chance to say so" (the *Disparate matrimonial*), he depicts man and woman, joined as androgynous halves. The male is human; the woman is a monster with female breasts. Onlookers, a group of monsters and people, watch as the two struggle to stand.

Goya's series on the disasters of war chronicles the atrocities of the Napoleonic campaigns in Spain between 1808 and 1814. To appreciate Goya's treatment of this subject, it is helpful to recall that modern warfare first surfaced at this time. Napoleon's campaign into Spain was consistently ruthless, forcing the Spanish to respond in an innovative way. Their solution was to attack at night with irregulars who vanished back into the hills after their raids. French officers coined the term "guerrilla" or "little wars" to describe the new form of attack. Goya's series similarly deviates from the traditional heroic treatment of war and victory in presenting death and pain as a corollary to the triumph of armies. These etchings, with their ironic captions, depict the corpses of the slain, peopling a countryside and cluttering the path of unsuspecting lovers who happen upon them during a stroll. The allegorical figure of Truth, in the form of a full-breasted woman, lies murdered, shines on her deathbed, and finally rises to address a farmer and suggest that perhaps the Spanish countryside, also ruined by the ravages of war, will flourish again. In treating the shocking and realistic aspects of the effects of war, Goya is startlingly modern in his vision.

During the nineteenth century, Goya's works were classified as caricatures because of their reliance upon distortion—a device which placed them within the category of non-serious art. Goya himself calls certain works in his Madrid and Sanlucar notebooks caricatures (Lopez-Rey 55). His use of the word, however, refers to

the form (etching with caption), the technique of distortion, and most important of all, the self-conscious expression of meaning.

* * *

Baudelaire's admiration for Goya's art is first evident from his remarks in the *Salon de 1846,* where he finds the only commendable aspect of Manzoni's *La rixe des mendiants* to be its resemblance to Goya's ferociously violent sketches. More extensively, in a critical essay entitled *"Quelques caricaturistes étrangers"* (1857), he cites Goya's work as an example of artistic caricature. As Baudelaire summarized aptly in *"Quelques caricaturistes étrangers"*: *"Goya est toujours un grand artiste, souvent effrayant. Il unit à la gaieté, à la jovialité, à la satire espagnole du bon temps de Cervantes, un esprit beaucoup plus moderne, ou du moins qui a été beaucoup plus cherché dans le temps moderne, l'amour de insaisissable, le sentiment des contrastes violents, des épouvantements de la nature et des physiognomies humaines étrangement animalisées par les circonstances"* (2: 568). Baudelaire here emphasizes the hallucinatory quality of Goya's works, tracing it to the play of light and shadow made possible through the technique of the aquatinta. Light bathes the grotesque scenes and shadow augments their mysterious and troublesome nature. Similarly, in **"Les phares,"** a poem which signals the importance of seven artists' work to Baudelaire's poetics, he devotes a stanza to Goya. In a letter dated 14 May 1859, he asked Nadar to go to Moreau's commercial gallery and make a photographic reproduction of Goya's *Duchesse d'Albe* for him. He further recommends to Nadar that if he has the money he should invest in some Goya prints. As poet and collector Baudelaire valued Goya's art. It is perhaps no coincidence that in the same letter he writes that it grieves him to have been called the *"Prince des charognes"* by unsympathetic critics.

As Jean Prévost has noted, poems such as **"Duellum," "Voyage à Cythère"** and **"Danse macabre,"** all of which figure in Baudelaire's poetic collection *Les fleurs du mal* (1857), put Goyesque themes in poetic form. The grotesque elements of the affinity have been explored by Yvonne Bargues Rollins; however, the broader application of caricature as model in Baudelaire's poetry is an area which has been overlooked by critics. Yet one cannot help wondering if **"Une charogne"** may have been an early attempt by Baudelaire to incorporate the elements of graphic caricature in poetic form.

* * *

Baudelaire ushers in the startling content of **"Une charogne"** with a deceptive rhythm of alternating Alexandrine and octosyllabic lines. Like other poems in *Les fleurs du mal* which alternate these meters, **"Une** charogne" weaves together the themes of woman, pleasure, death and horror. The combination of Alexandrine, traditionally reserved for tragedy, with the octosyllablic line replicates the contrast between the theme of death and the incongruous thoughts of ideal beauty which the contemplation of the carcass inspires. A benign atmosphere arises from the rapidity with which the shorter line completes the longer one, just as in conversation one often cancels out a serious statement with a light closing remark.

Individual sonorities augment the musicality of the stanza's ebbing and flowing rhythm and accentuate the incongruity of that rhythm with its content. For example, the swarming flies and oozing maggots appear first in stanza 7, approximately half-way through the poem. However, the great number of sibilants throughout the poem creates a rasping undercurrent which enhances the motif of disintegration and contributes to the scene's whispered obscenity. The staccato of stops provides a sonorous counterpart for the poet's footsteps and the activities of the winnower. In addition, it beats out a steady reminder of mortality.

Baudelaire was sensitive to the exaggeration generated by combining incongruous elements, as he reveals in *Les paradis artificiels*:

> *Un grand malheur, un malheur irréparable qui nous frappe dans la belle saison de l'année, porte, dirait-on, un caractère plus funeste, plus sinistre. . . . "Il se produit alors une antithèse terrible entre la profusion tropicale de la vie extérieure et la noire stérilité du tombeau. Nos yeux voient l'été, et notre pensée hante la tombe; la glorieuse clarté est autour de nous, et en nous sont les ténèbres. Et ces deux images, entrant en collision, se prêtent réciproquement une force exagérée."*

(1: 500)

Baudelaire's comments on and quotation from Rousseau's *Confessions* are applicable to the scene he presents in **"Une charogne,"** just as they describe a source of the powerful emotions inspired by Goya's art. Baudelaire heightens each element's affective force by juxtaposing rhythms which emit ambiguous messages and by setting a scene of death in the bright summer sun. He achieves a similar effect when he unites images which are physically antithetical to each other, but which share a common movement. In stanza 3, for example, the lines, *Et de rendre au centuple à la grande Nature / Tout ce qu'ensemble elle avait joint,* ironically suggest that decay is a form of multiplication rather than of disintegration. The process is as mysterious as that which in mathematics allows the multiplication of two negatives to produce a positive.

A similar network of antitheses is created through end rhymes. The dialectic of spleen and ideal which Baudelaire associated with both spirit and nature emerges from the exaggeration created through the juxtaposition of opposites in different esthetic categories. The transformation of carcass into flower in stanza 4 hinges upon the visual similarity between spreading flesh and opening petals. The element upon which the comparison rests is movement. Baudelaire does not explain; he simply presents the two images and allows the reader to draw his own conclusions. The cognitive process is similar in reading a graphic caricature's meaning through gesture and implied movement.

In stanzas 5 and 6 the illusion of movement surrounding the carcass conflicts with one's usual expectation of *rigor mortis*. Fascinated by the sight before him, Baudelaire analyzes the strangely vital aspect of the dead body. The *"ventre plein d'exhalaisons"* of stanza 2 becomes a theater of movement: buzzing flies hover over it, larvae ooze forth from it. The carcass itself is hidden from view. In this stanza the extreme busyness of the insects creates a comic tone which undermines the obscene and serious implications.

Distorted visual perception offers an alternate scene in stanza 6. As if the poet had taken several steps back, lost sight of the component parts of the previous stanzas, and instead perceived the moving outline of the whole, this stanza marks a shift from objective analysis into the mind of the poet. The scene is unfocused. It appears that the insects' movement belongs to the carcass. The corpse seems perversely alive. For Baudelaire, the carcass is now a microcosm: life begins, is lived and ends in a cycle of procreation and death. What one would expect to symbolize death and decay is instead a symbol of life and immortality. The insects' movement, misperceived, offers the poet a mysterious revelation which parallels the insight into character revealed through graphic caricature.

In stanza 7 he projects into the flies' buzzing and the larvae's crawling a sort of music of the spheres. The sound of their movements expands to the cosmic level touching both nature (*eau courante, vent*) and man (*vanneur*), implying that all levels of life and elements are intimately related. Although the synesthetic vision seems uncannily naive, it is highly sophisticated. Running water, wind and man break down matter as effectively as insects do. Deconstruction gives way to a new vision. Imagination allows the artist to perceive hidden relationships without the limitations imposed by logic, as Baudelaire explains in his *Salon de 1859.*

In a similar leap of imagination Baudelaire equates the reduction of matter to the process of artistic creation. In stanza 8 he describes how, from a raw sketch, the artist reconstructs the whole by relying on memory and imagination. It is a slow process. Until brought to life, memories, the raw material, lie dormant in the subconscious (*"sur la toile oubliée"*). Memory distorted through time allows the artist to complete and interpret the picture. The image of reality thus engendered is a subjective one, much like scenes depicted by Goya. By affirming the role of memory rather than model, Baudelaire defies the traditional beauty associated with verisimilitude and adopts the Romantic preference for improvisation and personal expression. This stanza summarizes the preceding seven stanzas' activity and draws the parallel between poetry and art.

After a transitional stanza in which the poet's movements rather than the carcass's are the focal point, the speaker aggressively addresses his mistress and applies the harsh lesson of disintegration to her. While the preceding stanzas framed a visual memory, these shift to predictions of the future. In stanzas 10 and 11 the fate of animal carcass and beautiful woman are united: the physical beings will be eaten by worms, will decay until nothing remains. Both are equally subject to mortality. These stanzas are peppered with a mixture of clichés of feminine beauty ("*Etoile de mes yeux,*" "*la reine des grâces*") and cruel invectives of death and decay ("*ordure,*" "*Infection*") which exaggerate the woman's beauty and her vulnerability. Stanza 12 offers immortality through verse, a conventional solution, as a panacea to decay.

Although this solution, paradoxically reserved for the last two lines of the poem, seems to permit Baudelaire to escape from the powerful subject he has introduced, the final lines of **"Une charogne"** contain a significant thematic twist. Throughout the eleven previous stanzas, the poem appears to be a variation of the *carpe diem*. Various elements support this notion: the innocent walk, the sexual connotations inherent in the vocabulary, and the increasingly ecstatic tone of the first eight stanzas, even the lesson of mortality which the carcass provides as did Ronsard's wilted rose. Instead of a Ronsardian closing, however, Baudelaire introduces the concept of immortality through verse, a separate Renaissance theme, which he devalues and makes quite unconvincing by relegating it to just two lines in a poem forty-eight lines long. The ironic tone conveys the poet's self-mockery. He has, after all, chosen a decaying carcass to symbolize woman in the sexual act and Poetry.

In this way Baudelaire articulates an esthetic dilemma which reflects the anguish of modern man. Can poetry immortalize an insect-ridden, stinking mass of flesh, even if that flesh was once a beautiful woman? He sees the weakness in the traditional poetic device and mocks both himself—as poet—and it. In theme, technique and attitude, Baudelaire is grappling with his own poetics in which a new vision of beauty and of reality emerge from the most unlikely scenes. As in Goya's works, mortality takes on immense proportions in **"Une charogne,"** for the hope of immortality through verse is put ironically in question.

Despite its gruesome title, the poem combines many comic elements. As in the graphic equivalent, distortion is a key element. In addition, when Baudelaire reduces the carcass to an ensemble of insect life, he crosses the boundary between two levels in the hierarchy of life. His perception of the scene is realistic, and yet highly original. The incongruity of making a carcass the source of beautiful insights gives the poem a mysterious quality. As he dissects the movements which the carcass envelops, attributing to them the mechanical aspect of soldiers carting off the loot from a pillaged city, he assumes a posture of naïveté, allowing imagination to distort the physical scene before him without imposing restraints of logic.

When he addresses his love, telling her almost cheerily that she, too, will be in that disgusting condition some day, he is emphasizing the bestial side of humanity (a traditional source of low comedy) and moving into the realm of black humor. Throughout the poem he registers primitive perceptions without concern for (or perhaps in clear defiance of) the social attitudes which would prohibit the equation of woman and carcass, and which would frown severely upon the blasphemous idea that insects' movement could be equated to the life force known in Christianity as the spirit. In the choice of theme and tone in **"Une charogne,"** Baudelaire looks at his model, the carcass, in a manner no poet before him would have dared. His use of objective analysis, his changes in perspective and his incorporation of comical elements enable him to enhance what exists in nature and to surpass it. Intentional, comical distortion to convey meaning, rather than idealization to create an illusion of perfection, separates Baudelaire's esthetic from the *grande tradition* and places it firmly within the domain of caricature.

Also allying **"Une charogne"** with caricature is the graphic layout of the poem's two thematic parts. The first nine stanzas are descriptive, sketching the scene and suggesting its curious effect on the observer. The final three stanzas function as a caption which delivers the ironic punchline.

That **"Une charogne"** should take the form of caricature is not surprising, given Baudelaire's theoretical interest in the genre. Indeed, in **"Quelques caricaturistes français"** he describes a creative process parallel to the one which governs **"Une charogne."** The case he cites is that of Philipon, publisher and editor of *Le charivari,* a satirical journal. Demonstrating before the tribunal how, through a process of reduction and subsequent reconstruction through memory, he had happened upon the image of the pear-head to represent Louis-Philippe, Philipon explained the creative technique of caricature. As Baudelaire describes the incident:

> *Cette fantastique épopée est dominée, couronnée par la pyramidale et olympienne* Poire *de processive mémoire. On se rappelle que Philipon, qui avait à chaque instant*

maille à partir avec la justice royale, voulant une fois prouver au tribunal que rien n'était plus innocent que cette irritante et malencontreuse poire, dessina à l'audience même une série de croquis dont le premier représentait exactement la figure royale, et dont chacun, s'éloignant de plus en plus du terme primitif, se rapprochant davantage du fatal: la poire. "Voyez, disait-il, quel rapport trouvez-vous entre ce dernier croquis et le premier?" . . . Le symbole dès lors suffisait. Avec cette espèce d'argot plastique, on était le maître de dire et de faire comprendre au peuple tout ce qu'on voulait.

(2: 549-50)

This demonstration illustrates the steps through which the artist moved before arriving at the appropriate symbol for the model. Taken independently, the relationship between the first and the last is one of reduction and abstraction, which is what Baudelaire does in **"Une charogne"**—but in reverse. Baudelaire introduces the carcass, his *terme fatal* in the title and first stanza. The carcass is the concrete form given to his poetry, but this becomes clear only at the end of the process. In the intervening stanzas he traces the steps by which he arrived at his symbol. Moving backward through the image of lascivious woman and artistic creation, he depicts the gradual distortion through which he developed it metaphorically. The *terme primitif* is hidden in the last two lines of the poem. Poetry's boast to immortality is no different than that decaying hunk of flesh; thus poetry and carcass are effectively united in the oxymoron: *mes amours décomposés.* The possessive reveals the poet's intense emotional involvement in this caricature. It marks the solitary nature of Baudelaire's experience and suggests that the preceding memory was not shared with another person, but was rather an interior dialogue between poet and alter ego (*"mon âme"*). Equating poetic inspiration with sexual intercourse, a parallel which coincides with his definition of art as prostitution, Baudelaire strips poetry of its transcendent power and reduces himself, the poet, to human stature.

"Une charogne" offers a compelling example of the adaptation of graphic caricature's esthetics to poetic form. A rich critical model, caricature entertains alternate readings, tempered by successive and recessive resonance. In this early poem, which Claude Pichois dates from 1846, Baudelaire's esthetic of distortion parallels Goya's. Baudelaire, however, went beyond Goya's personal vision to open up a field of future development in both art and poetry. In **"Une charogne"** Baudelaire went beyond the grotesque into the realm which he calls "artistic caricature" in **"De l'essence du rire,"** his essay on the esthetics of the comic: *"[les caricatures artistiques] contiennent un élément mystérieux, durable, éternel, qui les recommande à l'attention des artistes. Chose curieuse et vraiment digne d'attention que l'introduction de cet élément insaisissable du beau jusque dans les oeuvres destinées à représenter à*

l'homme sa propre laideur morale et physique! Et, chose non moins mystérieuse, ce spectacle lamentable excite en lui une hilarité immortelle et incorrigible" (2: 526). The similarity between Baudelaire's fascination with caricature and Diderot's is clear. The paradox at the root of caricature unites esthetics and morality.

The interplay of critical model, comic theory, and traditional poetics in Baudelaire's works has had far-reaching effects. Writing half a century after Baudelaire's death, poet Rainer Maria Rilke summarized the importance of Baudelaire's break with traditional poetics:

> I could not help thinking that without this poem the whole development toward objective expression, which we now think we recognize in Cézanne, could not have started; it had to be there first in its inexorability. Artistic observation had first to have prevailed upon itself far enough to see even in the horrible and apparently merely repulsive that which is and which, with everything else that is, is *valid.* The creator is no more allowed to discriminate than he is to turn away from anything that exists: a single denial at any time will force him out of the state of grace, make him utterly sinful. . . . You can imagine how it moves me to read that Cézanne in his last year still knew this very poem—Baudelaire's **"Charogne"**—entirely by heart and recited it word for word.

(181)

To the same effect, Dore Ashton has discussed the extent to which **"Une charogne"** inspired several of Cézanne's sketches, just as it is the esthetic of irreconcilable opposites which links Baudelaire and Manet.

In **"Une charogne"** Baudelaire anticipated concerns central to the works of modern artists and poets. In this poem Cézanne and Rilke recognized a modern esthetic in which visual and verbal expression are inextricably intertwined. It was Baudelaire who moved this vision from the graphic, introduced by Goya, into the verbal plane. Unlike his contemporaries, Baudelaire saw in the poetic adaptation of the form much more than a means of ridicule as social corrective. Beyond the traditional theme of the memento mori, beyond **"Une charogne"**'s strange versification, diction, obscene vocabulary and banter, lies an esthetic statement which ushers in modernity.

Works Cited

Ashton, Dore. *A Fable of Modern Art.* London: Thames, 1980.

Baudelaire, Charles. *Oeuvres complètes.* Ed. Claude Pichois. 2 vols. Paris: Gallimard, 1976.

Diderot et d'Alembert. *Encyclopédie ou dictionnaire raisonné des sciences, des arts et des métiers.* Tome 1. Lausanne: Société Typographique, 1751.

Galand, René. *Baudelaire: poétiques et poésie.* Paris: Nizet, 1969.

Hubert, J. D. *L'esthétique des Fleurs du mal.* Geneva: Cailler, 1953.

Krestovsky, Lydie. *Le problème de la beauté et de la laideur.* Paris: Presses universitaires de France, 1948.

Lopez-Roy, José. *Goya's Caprichos.* Princeton: Princeton UP, 1953.

Prévost, Jean. *Baudelaire: essai sur la création et l'inspiration poétique.* Paris: Mercure de France, 1964.

Rilke, Rainer Maria. *Letters I.* Trans. Jane Greene and M. D. Herter Norton. New York: Norton, 1948.

Rollins, Yvonne Bargues. *Baudelaire and the Grotesque.* Washington: UP of America, 1980.

Sainte-Beuve. *Correspondance: 1822-1865.* 2 vols. Paris: Charpentier, 1877-78.

Schlumberger, Eveline. "*La gallérie espagnole de Louis-Philippe.*" *Connaissance des arts* 115 (1961): 56-65.

Turnell, Martin. *Baudelaire: A Study of His Poetry.* New York: New Directions, 1972.

Wittkower, Rudolf. *The Artist and the Liberal Arts.* London: H. K. Lewis, 1952.

Beryl Schlossman (essay date 1993)

SOURCE: Schlossman, Beryl. "Baudelaire: Liberté, Libertinage, and Modernity." *SubStance* 22, no. 1 (1993): 67-80.

[*In the following essay, Schlossman discusses Baudelaire's role as a modernist by focusing on his attitude toward revolution and libertinism as seen in his poetry.*]

POLITICS AND POETICS

"Le modern style" in french literature ranges from Baudelaire's reading of Poe to the Modernism of Beckett, and the transition between these two phenomena might be located in Walter Benjamin's critique of literary modernity. Benjamin's work constitutes a double articulation that allows him to move between "revolutionary criticism" (political ideology, the Russian Revolution, Marx, Brecht, Lukacs, revolutionary art) and a critique of Proust and Valéry, who deliberately distanced their works and aesthetics from political concerns. The intersection between Benjamin's two fields of focus can be located in his framework of "modernity." This conceptual frame arises at the crossroads of history, sociology, economics, urban architecture and politics. Their paths, passageways, and arcades map

what he calls capitalism, filtered into the idiom of poetry. Benjamin's reading of modernity can best be seen in his analysis of the poetic *oeuvre* of Baudelaire.

Benjamin's text begins with an image of Baudelaire. The poet appears in the guise of a bohemian revolutionary, described by Marx as a "conspirateur de profession." In two articles published in 1850,[1] these revolutionaries were characterized by anger, provocation, mystification, a taste for playing devil's advocate, and a penchant for improvising strategies. Benjamin draws a parallel between Baudelaire and Auguste Blanqui, the archetypal revolutionary of the day, who enjoyed considerable prestige and spent many years in prison. In 1886, in *Die Neue Zeit,* Marx and Engels described professional conspirators as black-gloved artists of revolution. They wrote:

> They are the alchemists of the revolution and they completely share with the earlier alchemists their confusion of ideas and their limitation/stubbornness of obsessive ideas.
>
> (Quoted in Benjamin, 519)[2]

Marx's opinion of the conspirators is echoed in Benjamin's account of Baudelaire's limited political intuitions ("Il faut aller fusiller le général Aupick!")[3]

However, Benjamin opens up Marx's comment to include Baudelaire's enigmatic storehouse of allegory: "With this Baudelaire's image presents itself as if automatically: the enigmatic bric-à-brac of allegory in the one, the mystery-mongering of the conspirator in the other" (Benjamin, 519). Where did Benjamin learn how enigmas and secrets articulate the correspondences between poetry and politics? The connection may have been an overdetermined one, but it is certain that he discovered it in the German *Trauerspiel* as well as in trans-Romantic French poetry. German mourning-plays and Baudelairean poetics became the ground of his interpretation of allegory, and represent the two modes of allegory that inform his writing: baroque and modern.

BAUDELAIRE'S REVOLUTIONARY RHETORIC: CONTRADICTIONS AND EROTICISM

> Mais moi, je ne suis pas dupe! je n'ai jamais été dupe! Je dis *Vive la Révolution!* comme je dirais: *Vive la Déstruction! . . . Vive la Mort!*
>
> —Baudelaire, *OC* II, 961.

Baudelaire's equation of "vive la révolution!" with "vive la mort!" is echoed in his declared desire to be both victim and executioner: "Non seulement je serais heureux d'être victime, mais je ne haïrais pas d'être bourreau" (961). The Sadian *noirceur* of his remarks springs from two calculated rhetorical excesses: the oxymoron "long live death" petrifies the political enterprise and contemplates it as a death mask; the avowed discourse on "démocratisation" is subverted by a vocabulary of violent eroticism. Happiness and hatred—the conditional "je serais heureux" paralleled by the quasi-classical "je ne haïrais pas"—are applied to "victime" and "bourreau"—the roles played by a subject of revolution. Baudelaire uses "victim"/"executioner" to deny the ideological premises of revolutionary politics, and to reduce the content of ideology to eroticized subjectivities. These subjectivities are interchangeable; the artist/bohemian/conspirator/flaneur sees revolution as a stage for allegorical representation. The remarks quoted above may be Baudelaire's most explicit discussion of revolution, and they occur beyond the borders of French territory, in a racist dossier entitled *Pauvre Belgique!*

Baudelaire's evocations of revolution cannot be separated from the eroticism that informs them. Through happiness and unhappiness associated with playing the role of "victime" and "bourreau," the question of *jouissance* infiltrates the statement that begins: "Je dis: *Vive la révolution!*" The voice proclaiming "je ne suis pas dupe!" announces that the rhetoric of revolution cannot be separated from Romantic fantasies of mastery. Baudelaire's poetry subverts this fantasy with a vocabulary of erotic violence.

"L'HÉAUTONTIMOROUMÉNOS": FROM CONSPIRATORIAL RHETORIC TO IRONY

"L'Héautontimorouménos," one of the *Fleurs du Mal,* displays the negating and theatrical power of Baudelaire's technique of pairing images. Polarized, parallel, or one to one, the significations generated by comparisons and oppositions are the effect of rhetorical "correspondences." In Baudelaire's poetry, correspondence often brings together three (or more) elements in the "divine symphonie" to which the poem alludes:

"L'Héautontimorouménos"

à J.G.F.

Je te frapperai sans colère
Et sans haine, comme un boucher,
Comme Moïse le rocher!
Et je ferai de ta paupière,

Pour abreuver mon Sahara,
Jaillir les eaux de la souffrance.
Mon désir gonflé d'espérance
Sur tes pleurs salés nagera

Comme un vaisseau qui prend le large,
Et dans mon coeur qu'ils soûleront
Tes chers sanglots retentiront
Comme un tambour qui bat la charge!

Ne suis-je pas un faux accord
Dans la divine symphonie,
Grâce à la vorace Ironie
Qui me secoue et qui me mord?

Elle est dans ma voix, la criarde!
C'est tout mon sang, ce poison noir!
Je suis le sinistre miroir
Où la mégère se regarde!

Je suis la plaie et le couteau!
Je suis le soufflet et la joue!
Je suis les membres et la roue,
Et la victime et le bourreau!

Je suis de mon coeur le vampire
—Un de ces grands abandonnés
Au rire éternel condamnés,
Et qui ne peuvent plus sourire!

As in the sonnet **"Correspondances,"** the "comme" of Baudelaire's similes plays a decisive role in the mysterious **"L'Héautontimorouménos."** The rhetorical and stylistic elements of simile, metaphor, and correspondence engage the reader with the equally mysterious figures of the narrative voice, the interlocutor, the personification of irony, the shrew, and the vampire.

The poem's ostensible subject is suffering, sadistic evil, irony, and eroticism. "Je te frapperai . . ." is echoed by the fourth line, "Et je ferai . . ." The two anticipated acts of violence will be perpetrated in the future against a "tu" whose identity constitutes one of the gaps that challenges Baudelaire's readers. The "tu" neither appears nor speaks within the poem; only its anticipated sobs can be heard resonating in the heart of the narrator. The reader knows only that the object is desired by the speaker and that some sentimental value has been assigned to its "sanglots." This sentimental value is undercut by the complete disappearance of the object after the evocation of "her" sobs, imagined and interiorized by the speaker.

In a letter to Victor Mars, Baudelaire described a projected Epilogue to a series of the *Fleurs du Mal* published in the *Revue des Deux Mondes.* This projected Epilogue resembles **"L'Héautontimorouménos"** so closely that some critics have seen it as the source of the poem.[4] In the paraphrased Epilogue, the "tu" is characterized as "une dame." Through a series of adjectives, the narrator ascribes to her a certain consistency: "Si vous voulez me plaire et rajeunir les désirs, soyez cruelle, menteuse, libertine, crapuleuse, et voleuse" (*OC* 985). However, this explicitness vanishes in **"L'Héautontimorouménos."** The erotic object, "tu," disappears from the poem at the moment of "her" tears and imagined sobs. The sadistic image of the speaker's desire "gonflé d'espérance" sailing away on the tears of his object, as in **"Le Voyage,"** includes an image of the object as a "rocher" with its water and a "paupière" with the "pleurs salés" that intoxicate the narrator's heart. The image expands: her tears have become an ocean, and somewhere in between subject and object, the "rocher" of the violated object has become the narrator's intimate desert, "mon Sahara." The subject is "like a butcher," "like Moses," "like a sailing ship;" his object's imagined sobs are "like a drum."

When the fragile presence of the object evaporates, the personification of *l'Ironie* becomes the alibi for the speaker's challenge to correspondance; the power that turns sadism into masochism produces an intimate doubling of the self. "Je suis" is two rather than one. The rhetoric of "victime et bourreau" that appears in *Pauvre Belgique!* offers its negative power to this poem; it infiltrates Romantic subjectivity and explodes it from inside the "intoxicated heart" where its "dear sobs" resound. The conspiratorial rhetoric, the discourse of infiltration, is allegorized as Irony, who turns the initial roles around. The passive weeping virtual object has faded out; like his blood, the voice of the speaking subject is literally infiltrated by the voracious vampire:

> Elle est dans ma voix, la criarde!
> C'est tout mon sang, ce poison noir!
> Je suis le sinistre miroir
> Où la mégère se regarde.

Irony, Baudelaire's black vampire, turns the tables on the narrator: her tortures replace the "chers sanglots" of Romanticism and the desired "tu" with the dark image ("le sinistre miroir") of the speaker's "rire éternel." The anticipated future tense vanishes (into the past, into the future of prophecy, or into the thin air of fantasy) with the sadistic scenarios that irony is supposed to explain. Beginning with the first line of the fourth stanza, the verbs shift to a present tense that intensifies the mysterious union of opposites in the oxymorons of the penultimate stanza. Thanks to the allegorical goddess of Irony, the speaker who says "je suis" describes himself as a series of images that include both subject and object of violent acts. These oppositions culminate in the paradox of the speaking subject who is not only possessed from the inside—voice, blood, and image—but is also the vampire who consumes his own heart. The beating of the speaker's heart is rendered as the object's sobs, before the beating of the drum invades the rhythm of the poem in the penultimate stanza, when the "self-tormenter" of the title turns on himself the violence originally inflicted on the "tu."

In the final stanza, *l'Ironie* is no longer the narrator's alibi. Like the virtual beloved, she seems to have been incorporated into the speaker's heart. His blood is black poison; the "sinistre miroir" reflects her dark image. Although many poems in "Spleen et Idéal" use darkness and light to form paradoxical pairs and oxymorons, there is no light in **"L'Héautontimorouménos."** As in **"Le Coucher du Soleil Romantique," "La nuit irré-sistible établit son empire"** (*OC* 149). The similes of a projected and fantastic voyage of desire disappear into the "sinistre miroir" where violence is turned against

the speaker and internalized as an agent of destruction. In the deceptive symmetry of this stanza, the oppositions between torturer and tortured harbor secret complicities of rhyme and rhythm. Violence infiltrates the present tense and the harmony of the divine symphony.

"L'Héautontimorouménos" indicates the basis of Baudelaire's provocative dismissal of revolution and his understanding of it as a structure of reciprocal violence. This limits political ideology to a relationship of victim and executioner. The "faux accord" the speaker evokes makrs a kind of conspiracy against romantic discourse; the black violence of allegory inserts a moment of dissonance in the divine harmony of correspondence.

VOLUPTUOUS REVOLUTIONARIES

In his *Notes sur Les Liaisons dangereuses,* Baudelaire writes: "la Révolution a été faite par des voluptueux" (*OC* II, 68). Although the tone of the *Notes* is somewhat enigmatic, Baudelaire had an avowed "sympathie pour le livre." Who are the voluptuous revolutionaries? They may have something in common with the images of opposites that permeate Baudelaire's **"Vive la Révolution!"** These images are inscribed with the transgressions that are central in Baudelairean scenarios of *jouissance.* The reciprocal identities, the roles exchanged, construct *volupté* as an enigmatic contract between violence, suffering, and desire. **"L'Héautontimorouménos"** circles around the inarticulable knot of *jouissance* at its center. It illustrates the explosion named in the **"Coucher du Soleil Romantique"**—an attack on the sentimental views of pleasure avowed by some of Baudelaire's predecessors and contemporaries.

The speaker in Baudelaire's **"Epilogue"** demands that his mistress please him by being cruel, false, and so on. He implores her: "soyez . . . libertine!" (*OC* 985) This imperative would have no relation to **"Vive la Révolution!"** were it not for the voluptuous revolutionaries associated with *Les Liaisons dangereuses.* Both inside and outside of literature, the late eighteenth century adds a specifically political and revolutionary dimension to the religious and philosophical connections that were made in the seventeenth century between *libertinage* and *liberté.*

In *1789: Les Emblèmes de la raison,* Jean Starobinski writes:

> . . . pour ceux qui le condamnent et qui veulent l'abolir, le monde finissant prend le visage du mal: c'est l'expression d'une volonté qui refuse activement le bien universel.
>
> (14)

The *noirceur* that stylizes the blackness of night with pre-Baudelairean eroticism, suffering and evil finds its most privileged representatives in the Vicomte de Valmont and Mozart-Da Ponte's Don Giovanni. It is this *noir-ceur* of eroticism that returns in Baudelaire's poetry; if Benjamin's parallel between Blanqui and Baudelaire is pursued, the return to the baroque and its violent mysteries might be seen as a compensation for Baudelaire's absence of revolutionary consciousness.

The reciprocal identification of victim and executioner takes place on the stage where Valmont and Don Giovanni allegorize unlimited *jouissance* and ironic distance from morality and religion. In a world of Venetian masks, carnivals and eroticized illusion, the women who are their victims have interiorized and combined the evil of transgression, the delights of seduction, and the images of an idealized object. This deadly combination of beauty, corruption and its funereal consequences, and an idealized love might be described as the *poison noir,* the blood of **"L'Héautontimorouménos."** Its sublimity belongs to the baroque, resurrected by *Les Fleurs du Mal.*

"Correspondances": Valmont and Don Giovanni

In Mozart-Da Ponte's "Don Giovanni," written and performed in 1787, the blackness of *libertinage* is overwritten with a revolutionary *liberté* in several scenes. The most explicit of these moments of moral and political subversion occurs in the finale of Act I. Interrupting the nocturnal *noirceur* that colors much of the opera's atmosphere, Don Giovanni's illuminated ballroom parallels the final festive scene and the flames that will end the opera. When the Trio of Masks arrives in the "sala illuminata e preparata per un gran festa di ballo," Don Giovanni greets them:

> *E aperto a tutti quanti,*
> *Viva la libertà!*
> *(It is open to all*
> *Long live liberty!)*

Revolutionary fervor does not enter explicitly into Don Giovanni's exclamation, "Viva la libertà!"[5] His ball recreates a Venetian carnival atmosphere of intrigue and disguise, illusion and artifice; the masked figures are free to conceal their identity. Revolutionary undertones enter Don Giovanni's exclamation when the score returns to it following the thanks uttered by the Trio of Masks. The exclamation is taken up in ensemble form by five voices, accompanied by the orchestra. Its grandeur interrupts the minuet that was heard while Don Giovanni's servant, Leporello, gave his master's instructions to the Trio. Following the sweeping chorale of "Viva la libertà!" the minuet will be played again.

The exclamation of "Viva la libertà!" interrupts the course of both the music and the narrative account of the festivities; unlike many other elements of the text, it seems to originate with the Mozart-Da Ponte score. Its

repetition by the ensemble appears as a mysterious anacoluthon, since the freedom that Don Giovanni incarnates is contested by the other members of the ensemble.

In a ballroom filled with peasants, Leporello is the only non-aristocrat to sing: "Viva la libertà!" His identification with his master lends him an aura of libertinage, in contrast to the Trio (Donna Elvira, Donn'Anna, Don Ottavio), who wear disguises in the name of the law. A deliberate pause takes carnival license out of context and into the revolutionary period, where it emerges like a symptom: "Viva la libertà!" Don Giovanni suddenly holds up a mirror to the late eighteenth century.

Baudelaire's Modernism—Revolt against Romanticism

Laclos used the epistolary novel to turn libertinage and its forms of seduction into a secret theater of conspiracy. Its pages unfold in boudoirs filled with mirrors; they form a network of *croisements,* the labyrinth of a Baudelairean Paris of Modernism. The strange figure of the voluptuous revolutionary who emerges from Baudelaire's aphoristic notes on Laclos seems to evoke the figure in black, Auguste Blanqui, before his entry onto the scene of history.[6]

In other appearances, Baudelaire wears the black gloves of aesthetic artifice in order to maintain a distance from the personal and political sentiment (reactionary, revolutionary, progressive, etc.) displayed by figures like Lamartine and Hugo. Their writing was Baudelaire's inheritance and his intimate adversary; for this reason, his invention of Modernism was both essentially Romantic and irreducibly distanced from Romanticism.

How did Baudelaire's "modern style" become a voyage to the ends of Romanticism? The new form of writing constitutes a transgression of the parameters of Romanticism. In Baudelaire's terms, Night has fallen on the Romantic Sun. The historical label of "L'Art pour l'Art" is a point of entry; it is impossible to conceive of the Baudelairean enterprise without it. On the other hand, "Art for Art's Sake" cannot account for the banishment of sensibility, for the new interiority of memory and image, and the new relation between sensation and style, life and art.

Baudelaire takes the Romantic ideal of infinity and turns it into an artificial form of the sublime—an excess of language or style. The new "modern style" detached writing from sentiment and textual decorum—rhetorical coherence, the etiquette of appropriate subject matter, and the anti-allegorical, organic form of the Romantic symbol. Although this excess led Baudelaire before a court of law, the violence of his work has more to do with its form than with obscenity.

According to history, philology, and contemporary criticism, this explosive interruption of Romanticism marks a turning point in literary style. Although Modernism is central to contemporary criticism, it remains elusive and perhaps indefinable. Its effects, however, have been felt from the latter half of the nineteenth century and through the twentieth century, in such writers as Joyce, Pound, Woolf, Proust, and Rilke.

The polemics against Baudelaire indicate that the adversaries of Modernism had a clearer understanding of what was at stake than some of the poet's defenders. During Baudelaire's trial in 1857, the prosecutor made the following remarks:

> Charles Baudelaire n'appartient pas à une école. Il ne relève que de luimême. Son principe, sa théorie, c'est de tout peindre, de tout mettre à nu. Il fouillera la nature humaine dans ses replis les plus intimes; il aura, pour la rendre, des tons vigoureux et saisissants . . . il la grossira outre mesure, afin de créer l'impression, la sensation. Il fait ainsi, peut-il dire, la contrepartie du classique, du convenu.
>
> (*OC* I, 1206)

Although this description was uttered as an accusation, it offers an accurate account of Baudelaire's aesthetic in his own terms, including the "mise à nu," the ambition to "paint everything," the use of bold color tones, the deployment of excess for the purpose of creating impression and sensation (rather than the didactic declaration and sentiment associated with earlier generations). Beyond the "convenu" of Romantic codes, in an arena of representation that Benjamin recognized as baroque, these terms characterize the founding aesthetic of Modernism.

Precisely because of the Modernist transgression of the "convenu," some of Baudelaire's defenders took on the ill-fated task of denying the new aesthetic. They attempted to assimilate the writing of *Les Fleurs du mal* to the mode of the symbol (versus allegory), by highlighting the image of literature as organic, idyllic, and rooted in nature. Edouard Thierry portrayed Baudelaire as a gardener cultivating "la nature meurtrière," following on the heels of the more conventional nature principle in literature:

> La nature pacifique a donné depuis longtemps ses plus riches échantillons . . . Le maître du lieu a réalisé un Eden de l'enfer . . . Dans un temps où la littérature indiscrète a raconté au public les moeurs de la vie de bohême . . . il est venu après les amusants conteurs dire à son tour l'idylle à travers champs.
>
> (*OC* 1187-88)

It is difficult to recognize Baudelaire and his poetics in a valorization of nature, a nostalgia for pastoral idyll, or the redemption of Hell in a triumph of heavenly innocence. Thierry's defense stages a denial of Modernism in the reactionary terminology of the adversary.

In more contemporary judgments, Baudelaire's literary explosion still resonates as subversive, obscene, and conspiratorial. In a tone that recalls the justificatory articles written in Baudelaire's defense, Erich Auerbach defends his "entirely new and consummate style." In "The Aesthetic Dignity of the 'Fleurs du Mal,'" he writes that Baudelaire's poems

> . . . gave this age a new poetic style: a mixture of the base and contemptible with the sublime, a symbolic use of realistic horror, which was unprecedented. . . . The form, not only of modern poetry but also of the other literary genres of the century that has elapsed since then, is scarcely thinkable without "Les Fleurs du Mal."
>
> (225)

Auerbach's statement is particularly significant in light of his attempt to apologize for the horror in Baudelaire's poems. His apologetic impulse originates in his reading of the work as a straightforward rendering of the poet's personality.

CROSSROADS AND ARCADES

Baudelaire's poem, **"Le Coucher du Soleil Romantique,"** acknowledges the Modernist explosion of Romanticism. The idyllic mode of the first line is immediately undercut by the conspiratorial irony and the brusque slang of "la vie moderne" in the second line:

"Le Coucher du Soleil Romantique"

Que le Soleil est beau quand tout frais il se lève,
Comme une explosion nous disant son bonjour!
—Bienheureux celui-là qui peut avec amour
Saluer son coucher plus glorieux qu'un rêve!

Je me souviens! . . . J'ai vu tout, fleur, source, sillon,
Se pâmer sous son oeil comme un coeur qui palpite
—Courons vers l'horizon, il est tard, courons vite,
Pour attraper au moins un oblique rayon!

Mais je poursuis en vain le Dieu qui se retire;
L'irrésistible Nuit établit son empire,
Noire, humide, funeste et pleine de frissons;

Une odeur de tombeau dans les ténèbres nage,
Et mon pied peureux froisse, au bord du marécage,
Des crapauds imprévus et de froids limaçons.

The Romantic celebration of nature is no longer possible; the explosion that undermines the beauty of the sun sounds more like modernity. The world of *Les Fleurs du Mal* is the empire of "l'irrésistible Nuit"— "Noire, humide, funeste et pleine de frissons"—allegorized in the poem. This sonnet, which was supposed to serve as the epilogue for Asselineau's *Mélanges tirés d'une petite bibliothèque romantique,* may be read as the epilogue to Romantic subjectivity: the narrator's ravishment includes a vision of strangely detached natural objects ("fleur, source, sillon") in the guise of the quivering heart of Romanticism. Removed from their Romantic coherence as elements of an idyllic Nature, these objects play new roles, as hieroglyphs of subjectivity. The exclamation of memory inscribes this poem with the aesthetic of Modernism. Transfigured by the vision of "Je me souviens!" the fragmented and distanced objects have become images in a new style.

In the preface to *Le Spleen de Paris,* Baudelaire gives an account of style that takes lyricism out of the domain of sentimentality and into a new idiom of "poetic prose," located within the frame of the modern city. The poetics of the Modernist sublime that unfold in *Les Fleurs du Mal* becomes a modern architecture of form and content:

> Quel est celui de nous qui n'a pas . . . rêvé le miracle d'une prose poétique, musicale sans rythme et sans rime, assez souple et assez heurtée pour s'adapter aux mouvements lyriques de l'âme, aux ondulations de la rêverie, aux soubresauts de la conscience?
>
> (*OC* 275-276)

The new idiom is miraculous, musical, and inseparable from the structure of "correspondance" that originates near the beginning of the *Fleurs du mal* and plays an important role throughout Baudelaire's poetic *oeuvre*. In the poet's commentary, the verb "s'adapter" links the triad of oxymorons characterizing literary form to the spiritual, imaginative, and ethical faculties of content. Baudelaire maintains the distance between the two triads in order to affirm the artifice of art: "s'adapter" cannot be assimilated to natural or organic expression. Like "correspondance," it maintains the entities that mysteriously mingle together. The "fondu" of these opaque, differentiated entities cannot be assimilated to the organic "translucence" of the symbol that Coleridge evokes in his polemic against allegory. Like "correspondance," the "fondu" evoked at key moments in Modernist poetics maintains aesthetic artifice. It prefigures the vocabulary of "Prägung"—cast, imprint, coinage, stamp, and seal—that characterizes Benjamin's discussions of allegory and some of Lacan's polemics for a psychoanalysis beyond the positivist body of psychology.

Like Flaubert writing *Madame Bovary,* Baudelaire places his project in the frame of "la vie moderne, ou plutôt d'*une* vie moderne" and criticizes the traditional "subject" of the novel. He provocatively dismisses it as "le fil interminable d'une intrigue superflue" (*OC* 275). The crossings of modern life are as decisive for *Le Spleen de Paris* as they were for *Les Fleurs du Mal*; they run parallel to the allegorical painting of Rouen in *Madame Bovary* that sets the stage for the recreation of Carthage, Paris, and so on, in later works. Baudelaire writes:

> C'est surtout de la fréquentation des villes énormes, c'est du croisement de leurs innombrables rapports que naît cet idéal obsédant.
>
> (*OC* 276)

This remark could serve as an epigraph for Benjamin's writings on the nineteenth century: at the crossroads or "croisements" of history, sociology, economics, urban architecture, and politics, the artifices of modernity shape the arcades and passageways of allegory.

Baudelaire's remark locates modernity in the "croisements" of writing that link the image, correspondence, synaesthesia, and signification with the allegorical effects of the city. Modern subjectivity provides the interior passageway or subterranean transfer ("correspondance") where the cityscape of the *flâneur* takes shape in a poetic voice. The *croisement* of *rapports* in the modern city gives rise to the effects represented in many of Baudelaire's poems and Benjamin's writings. Benjamin wrote in *Zentralpark,*

> If it is imagination that offers the correspondences to memory, then it is thought that dedicates the allegories to it. Memory brings the two together.

In Baudelaire's **"Le Cygne,"** monuments and disguises go underground; they live on in the sanctum of memory. Evanescence is made permanent in the effects of style: "Tout pour moi devient allégorie" marks the spot where the poet has transformed the promise of authorial consistency that shaped French Romantic discourse, into the poetic voice of modernity, prefiguring Barthes's "mort de l'auteur." This death marks a decisive turn in the economy of textuality; the reign of the authorial self is declared to be over. In its place is the monument of absence, the transformed carnival, necropolis, or the *Passagenwerk*—the looped and labyrinthine arcades of writing. Who reigns, now that the imperial author is dead? Barthes's "empire des signes" approaches representation from the other side of psychological consistency; like the Japanese brushstrokes and theatrical masks that emblematize Barthes's understanding of Modernism, the image of the artist emerges from Benjamin's reading of Baudelaire, along with the vision of allegory that is central to the new cityscape of Modernism. The paradise of memory, the temporal artifices of its representation as a paradise lost or a *champs elysées,* take us through the transfers of *correspondance* to the enigmatic and unfinished *Zentralpark* of allegory.

Notes

1. *Les Conspirateurs,* by Adolphe Chenu, and *La Naissance de la République en février 1848,* by Lucien de la Hodde, both published in Paris in 1850.

2. Unless otherwise indicated, all translations into English are my own.

3. General Aupick was Baudelaire's stepfather.

4. Claude Pichois, editor of Baudelaire's *Oeuvres Complètes.* See notes to the poem.

5. References to the score of "Don Giovanni" are taken from the *Neue Mozart Ausgabe (Neue Ausgabe samtlicher Werke,* ed. Wolfgang Plath and Wolfgang Rehm. (Kassel: Barenreiter, 1968), Serie II: Buhnenwerke, vol. 17. See also *Don Giovanni: Texte, Materialien, Kommentare,* ed. Attila Csampai and Dietmar Holland (Reinbek bei Hamburg: Rowohlt Taschenbuch Verlag, 1981).

6. The concept of Baudelaire's prose poetry as a reflection of a revolutionary aesthetic is developed by Barbara Johnson in *Défigurations du langage poétique* (Paris: Flammarion, 1982). Johnson's emphasis on a rupture between the poet's verse and his prose poems contrasts with Paul De Man's reading of the continuity of central concepts (e.g. correspondence) in Baudelaire's poetics. See *The Rhetoric of Romanticism* (New York: Columbia University Press, 1983).

Abbreviations Used

OC *Oeuvres Complètes,* Charles Baudelaire.

Works Cited

Auerbach, Erich. *Scenes from the Drama of European Literature.* Minneapolis: Univ. Minnesota Press, 1984.

Baudelaire, Charles. *Oeuvres Complètes.* Ed. Claude Pichois. Paris: Pléiade, 1975 and 1976.

Benjamin, Walter. *Gesammelte Schriften.* Ed. Rolf Tiedemann and Hermann Schweppenhauser. Frankfurt: Suhrkamp Verlag, 1974.

————. *Zentralpark.* In *Gesammelte Schriften.* Band I, 2.

de Laclos, Pierre Choderlos. *Les Liasions dangereuses.* Paris: Flammarion, 1981.

Starobinski, Jean. *1789: Les Emblèmes de la raison.* Paris: Flammarion, 1973.

Margaret Miner (essay date winter 1996)

SOURCE: Miner, Margaret. "Heads and/Are Tails: Eccentric Conjunctions in Baudelaire's *Spleen de Paris.*" *South Central Review* 13, no. 4 (winter 1996): 38-53.

[*In the following essay, Miner discusses Baudelaire's contortions of grammar and juxtapositions of beauty and ugliness in his* Le Spleen de Paris.]

In critical pairings of Baudelaire and Mallarmé, it is generally Mallarmé who receives attention for productively tinkering with grammar, for connecting altered or ambiguous syntax with interrogations of truth, subjectivity, and referential language. Baudelaire's writing is also held to pursue such interrogations, of course, but most often by other routes; its grammar and syntax usually seem just correct or conventional enough to remain on the fuzzy periphery of the reader's interest. To stay on the periphery is not to drop out of sight, however, and details of grammar in Baudelaire's texts sometimes expand into pressing questions about the linguistic and social construction of the subject. What I want to explore here is an exemplary instance of this expansion, involving portions of *Le Spleen de Paris.* The grammatical nicety in question makes its first, unobtrusive appearance in the letter of dedication that accompanied twenty of Baudelaire's prose poems when he sent them in 1862 to Arsène Houssaye, literary editor of *La Presse.* At the start of this now famous letter, one finds an initial image and some suggestions on what to do with it:

> Mon cher ami, je vous envoie un petit ouvrage dont on ne pourrait pas dire, sans injustice, qu'il n'a ni queue ni tête, puisque tout, au contraire, y est à la fois tête et queue, alternativement et réciproquement. Considérez, je vous prie, quelles admirables commodités cette combinaison nous offre à tous, à vous, à moi et au lecteur. Nous pouvons couper où nous voulons, moi ma rêverie, vous le manuscrit, le lecteur sa lecture; car je ne suspends pas la volonté rétive de celui-ci au fil interminable d'une intrigue superflue. Enlevez une vertèbre, et les deux morceaux de cette tortueuse fantaisie se rejoindront sans peine. Hachez-la en nombreux fragments, et vous verrez que chacun peut exister à part. Dans l'espérance que quelques-uns de ces tronçons seront assez vivants pour vous plaire et vous amuser, j'ose vous dédier le serpent tout entier.[1]

As an opening paragraph, this leads to sweeping problems; it helps *Le Spleen de Paris* eventually open not only into the transgressive space where poetry merges with prose, but also into the dense field of relations between language and the modern city.[2] But the specific problems that concern me are points of grammar raised by the coordinate conjunctions in the first sentence: "tête *et* queue," "alternativement *et* réciproquement." One difficulty is that these conjunctions do not necessarily coordinate very well. Although each may join the elements immediately surrounding it (two nouns or two adverbs), the sentence is arranged so that the resulting pairs remain somewhat at odds with one another: "*à la fois* tête et queue" fights a little with "*alternativement* et réciproquement," as if the comma between the two were a sign that the harmonizing conjunction within each couple could not successfully appear between them. This first difficulty is related to a second one, because if the coordinating power of the two conjunctions is weakened by the intervening comma, it is also slightly soured by the preceding copula: "tout . . . y *est* à la fois tête et queue." That is, the deceptive homophony of *est* and *et* is not quite enough to drown out the clash of meaning when "tout," "à la fois," and "alternativement" collide. How can everything be any two things both simultaneously and alternatively—or even in alternation? It's as if someone were making the conventional call for heads *or* tails while demanding, at exactly the same time, both heads *and* tails: in other words, heads I win, tails you lose.

With its initial image, however, the letter of dedication evokes not so much a mixed-up gambler as a chopped-up snake. Like Houssaye, readers of **Le Spleen de Paris** are invited to take an ax to this fantastic serpent, which will either (both?) reunite its segments or set them all wriggling on their own. Such a temptation to connect reading with mutilation leaves the prose poems in a precarious position, writhing along the tenuous line between violent death and vibrant rebirth, between the bestial and the miraculous, between sordid realism and poetic convention.[3] The temptation similarly opens the readers' position to question, since it will rarely be clear whether the primary effect of their reading is to conjoin textual fragments or disperse them, to promote extraordinary animation or inflict haphazard damage. Moreover, at least five prose poems draw instant attention to this question because their titles all feature two elements prominently linked with a conjunction: **"Le Fou et la Vénus," "Le Chien et le flacon," "La Femme sauvage et la petite-maîtresse," "La Soupe et les nuages," "Le Tir et le cimetière."** Even the most cursory review of this list shows that the central *et* does not always work to coordinate, or at any rate that it coordinates in a number of divergent ways. One could imagine, for instance, a flat-footed editor's campaign to join the titles more tightly to their texts by replacing *et* with something else: "La Soupe *ou* les nuages," "Le Chien *contre* le flacon," "Le Fou *avec* la Vénus," "La Femme sauvage *est* la petite-maîtresse." With differing degrees of savagery, moreover, this last substitution or mutilation (the homophonous *est* for *et*) lurks within reach of all five titles. It is enticingly easy to misread the conjunction as a copula, or else to read either as a supplement for the other, simultaneously and alternatively.[4] What is more, such reading or misreading would seem to help readers follow the ambulant writer of the prose poem **"Les Foules"** (1: 291) in pursuit of identities that shift and merge and split,[5] turning modes of being and parts of speech into "termes égaux et convertibles pour le poète actif et fécond," so as to take—at once and in alternation—a "bain de multitude" and a sort of "bain de grammaire."

But if one resists the temptation to bathe the conjunctions in copulas, there remains the problem of reading the conjunctions as such. Especially beside the striking nouns in some of the prose poem titles, the *et* seems so neutral as to fade toward invisibility. Its ordinariness discourages specific scrutiny: having formed a discreet and unassuming link between the nouns in the title, it leaves the text apparently free to elaborate and complicate their relation. Yet the *et* also forms a midpoint that separates as effectively as it joins: one could argue that an important function of each *et* in the five titles is to hold its adjoining nouns apart, thereby preventing its own role as connector from being stifled by their fusion.[6] Taken thus as a connection that divides, the *et* is no more stable in its functioning than when it is (mis)taken for a copula; in any of the titles, the conjunction might variously seem to accentuate the deliberate opposition or the random juxtaposition or the unexpected complementarity of the two substantives. Further, by virtue of its presumed versatility as a mediator, the conjunction raises the question of whether the linked nouns are interchangeable—whether the operation by which they are added together is commutative—to such a degree that neither has priority and their ordering is a matter of indifference. As a result of this unsettling malleability, the conjunction can generate potential friction between the titles and their texts, threatening any secure juncture between the title's pairing of nouns and the text's development of their rapport. At once bland to the verge of transparency and volatile to the point of explosiveness, the *et* in Baudelaire's prose poems often does much more or (and) less than simply conjoin.

The slippery centrality—the in-betweenness—of *et* is particularly hard to ignore in **"Le Fou et la Vénus."** One might suppose that the conjunction's intended rôle is to remain as neutral as possible, to provide the minimum amount of linguistic glue needed to set "le fou" (a term that connotes, among other things, erratic singularity, crazy eccentricity) beside "la Vénus" (whose definite article suggests not just classical regularity, but also mass-produced, lawn-ornament uniformity). Beyond facilitating juxtaposition, one might guess, the conjunction's only active task is to hint that the text may well follow the title's lead, amplifying its division into two contrasting, minimally joined parts. This is, in fact, the hint that Robert Kopp implicitly takes in his commentary on **"Le Fou et la Vénus"**: "ce poème . . . offre la forme d'un diptyque aux volets savamment équilibrés qui sont reliés par une phrase-pivot."[7] Much like the title, in other words, the text would seem to be constructed from two equally weighted groupings on either side of a connector. First would come a three-paragraph description of colorful but impersonal exuberance, as manifested in a sun-drenched park:

> Quelle admirable journée! Le vaste parc se pâme sous l'œil brûlant du soleil, comme la jeunesse sous la domination de l'Amour.
>
> L'extase universelle des choses ne s'exprime par aucun bruit; les eaux elles-mêmes sont comme endormies. Bien différente des fêtes humaines, c'est ici une orgie silencieuse.

On dirait qu'une lumière toujours croissante fait de plus en plus étinceler les objets; que les fleurs excitées brûlent du désir de rivaliser avec l'azur du ciel par l'énergie de leurs couleurs, et que la chaleur, rendant visibles les parfums, les fait monter vers l'astre comme des fumées.

(1: 283)[8]

This is followed by a pivotal sentence,

Cependant, dans cette jouissance universelle, j'ai aperçu un être affligé,[9]

which conjoins the opening section with a three-paragraph evocation of intimate sadness and longing, as revealed in a pitiful jester:

Aux pieds d'une colossale Vénus, un de ces fous artificiels, un de ces bouffons volontaires chargés de faire rire les rois quand le Remords ou l'Ennui les obsède, affublé d'un costume éclatant et ridicule, coiffé de cornes et de sonnettes, tout ramassé contre le piédestal, lève des yeux pleins de larmes vers l'immortelle Déesse.

Et ses yeux disent:—"Je suis le dernier et le plus solitaire des humains, privé d'amour et d'amitié, et bien inférieur en cela au plus imparfait des animaux. Cependant je suis fait, moi aussi, pour comprendre et sentir l'immortelle Beauté! Ah! Déesse! ayez pitié de ma tristesse et de mon délire!"

Mais l'implacable Vénus regarde au loin je ne sais quoi avec ses yeux de marbre.

(1: 283-84)[10]

This manner of linking title to text through their structural similarity—two segments with a centered pivot—is not inaccurate, but it overlooks some provocative reshuffling and rejoining. Whereas the jester precedes the Venus in the title, the text presents the two at nearly the same moment and only *after* the pivot-sentence: "Aux pieds d'une colossale Vénus, un de ces fous artificiels . . ." says the second half of the prose poem, first presenting the statue, then appending the jester. This upsets the title's juxtaposition not only because it gives the Venus top billing by a slender margin, but also because its emphasis on her gigantic size lends her a certain eccentric singularity, while the jester now appears as merely another "one of those" fake fools, manufactured in uniform batches like cheap garden statuary. In its final paragraph, moreover, the text gives additional priority to the Venus by highlighting her silent gaze ("Mais l'implacable Vénus regarde au loin je ne sais quoi avec ses yeux de marbre"), a maneuver that links her more closely to the opening description of the park's "orgie silencieuse" than to the jester's subsequent lament. With a stark sentence that recalls the pivot at its midpoint, the text ends by reconnecting the Venus to its beginning. In order to view this text as the narrative expansion of its title, therefore, the latter might have to read

something like "La Vénus et le fou et la Vénus et . . .", as if the prose poem's actual title had been chopped at random out of a repeating loop.

Faced in this way with the *et*'s potential for endless, redundant proliferation, one might attempt instead an interpretation of **"Le Fou et la Vénus"** that substitutes a copula for the conjunction. From many points of view, admittedly, the jester and the statue are anything but identical, or even remotely interchangeable: the Venus is towering, beautiful, and speechless, while the jester is prostrate, ridiculous, and above all voluble. But it is only the jester's tearful eyes that do the talking, and those eyes are contagiously addicted to coordinate conjunctions, which seep from its discourse into the narrator's report:

Et ses yeux disent:—"Je suis le dernier *et* le plus solitaire des humains, privé d'amour *et* d'amitié, *et* bien inférieur en cela au plus imparfait des animaux. Cependant je suis fait, moi aussi, pour comprendre *et* sentir l'immortelle Beauté! Ah! Déesse! ayez pitié de ma tristesse *et* de mon délire!"

(1: 284; emphasis added)[11]

Oddly verbose, the eyes are never content with a single word if two can be squeezed in; they double every nuance ("privé d'amour et d'amitié," "ma tristesse et . . . mon délire"), piling up descriptors that ironically detail both the jester's numerous deficiencies and his growing desire. It is almost as if the jester were trying to build up his stature by the sheer accumulation of classically symmetrical attributes and by the grandiose pairings chosen ("le dernier et le plus solitaire," "comprendre et sentir," etc.). Although this strategy may not succeed entirely, it does suggest that the jester's highly articulate, rhetorically enriched eyes may to some extent counterbalance the superbly uncommunicative gaze of "l'implacable Vénus" with her blank "yeux de marbre." The equal-but-different power of the jester's eyes in the text goes some way toward justifying his leading position in the title and makes it conceivable that he and the Venus are, if not identical or interchangeable, at least evenly matched. Further still, it is imaginable that the jester's purely visual eloquence—here made vocal only because the narrator intrudes on it—may eventually entitle him to full participation in the silent joy of Venus's park, where "l'extase universelle des choses ne s'exprime par aucun bruit." Presumably accustomed by his profession to constant rôle-playing, that is, the jester may be able to turn the volubility of his eyes into a multiplicity of I's. The jester would thus come to speak (or gaze) from various subject positions, including even Venus's: **"Le Fou est la Vénus."**

It is doubtful, however, that the narrator of **"Le Fou et la Vénus"** would agree with such an analysis. While translating and quoting the jester's expressive gaze, the narrator underlines his pitiable, yet overdone and some-how reprehensible abjection: this is "un être affligé," re-dundantly "affublé d'un costume éclatant *et* ridicule, coiffé de cornes *et* de sonnettes," cringing before Venus in a servile posture. Rebuffed by the statue's unyielding eyes, the jester finds himself excluded from the whole surrounding garden of eros, with its comforting promise of vitality and regeneration. As the only silly, suffering creature to be seen among the magnificently mingled flowers and fountains and perfumes of the park, the jester is set sharply off from the other, almost undiffer-entiated participants in the celebration over which Ve-nus presides. The narrator further makes it hard to know whether the jester, as "un de ces fous *artificiels,* un de ces bouffons *volontaires,*" has simply been rejected or has also voluntarily, perversely excluded himself from "cette jouissance universelle." It is at least certain that the jester remains on the edge of expulsion from the nondiscursive, prelinguistic "orgie silencieuse" around him, since his eyes do not remain wholly outside lan-guage like the marble gaze of Venus, but obsessively enter into symbolic discourse that the narrator claims to have no trouble transcribing.

For the narrator, one might say, the jester embodies the abject. As explored in Kristeva's *Pouvoirs de l'horreur,* abjection forms a precarious limit zone where the I, in the process of emerging into clear-eyed separation from the mother, wavers on the brink of expulsion. Repulsive because of his laughable appearance and subservient at-titude, the jester is above all a "jeté," a throw-away ab-jected from the generative, ultimately maternal space of the park, but a throw-away whose extravagant, jagged-edged costume—as intensely colored as the park's "fleurs excitées"—suggests how incompletely he has torn away from the zone of jouissance around the statue: he is an "exclu" who nonetheless lingers at Venus's feet, on the borderline between her speechless ecstasy and the rigors of language.[12] The narrator himself would seem to feel both horrified and fascinated by his en-counter with the jester, as if obscurely aware that he cannot produce any representation of this comical and afflicted creature that will not make his own narrating voice, as Kristeva says, "à la fois juge *et* complice de l'abject" (23; emphasis added). Suggestively, the narra-tor admits his own participation only in the pivot-sentence *between* sections ("dans cette jouissance uni-verselle, j'ai aperçu un être affligé") and in the "false" pivot that loops back from the text's end to its opening evocation of the silent, sun-soaked park ("Mais l'implacable Vénus regarde au loin je ne sais quoi"). Like the poet of **"Le Soleil"** in *Les Fleurs du Mal,* this narrator partly identifies himself on one hand with the sun, "œil brûlant" that animates and purifies the quasi-sacred space of "l'immortelle Déesse." On the other hand, the narrator also animates the jester's teary eyes, juxtaposing their pathetic discourse with the unreadable "je ne sais quoi" of the statue's gaze. If the narrator

shares in the abjection he portrays, then, it's because he supports *and* condemns all sides at once: he scorns the self-loathing jester and lends him eloquence; he cel-ebrates the Venus's colossal indifference and refuses to read her implacable gaze.[13] As part of the all-animating "œil brûlant," the abject narrator both gives and with-holds discourse, simultaneously and alternatively, in the most mixed-up and humiliating ways available. He thereby makes it possible and maybe necessary to read the prose poem's title in those same ways, with a garbled syllable in the middle serving as a conjunction to keep the cringing jester beside the majestic Venus *and* as a copula to ensure the amorphous identity of jester and Venus under the narrator's burning, language-giving eye. The *et* in the title would thus be quaver-ingly insecure in its place and function, and, as the ma-jor locus of abjection in the prose poem, it would call for Kristeva's much-quoted summary: "Ce n'est donc pas l'absence de propreté ou de santé qui rend abject, mais ce qui perturbe une identité, un système, un ordre. Ce qui ne respecte pas les limites, les places, les règles. L'entre-deux, l'ambigu, le mixte" (12).

A review of the four other prose poems with a central *et* in their titles suggests that they work in ways similar to **"Le Fou et la Vénus."** One might even say that they map out with surprising exactness the primary condi-tions and situations in which, according to Kristeva, the subject confronts and is confronted by the abject.[14] For example, in her introductory "survol, en somme phénoménologique, de l'abjection" (39), Kristeva claims that "le dégoût alimentaire est peut-être la forme la plus élémentaire et la plus archaïque de l'abjection" (10). This brings to mind **"La Soupe et les nuages,"** which is about, among other things, a fascinatingly mixed-up and repulsive meal:

> Ma petite folle bien-aimée me donnait à dîner, et par la fenêtre ouverte de la salle à manger je contemplais les mouvantes architectures que Dieu fait avec les vapeurs, les merveilleuses constructions de l'impalpable. Et je me disais, à travers ma contemplation: "—Toutes ces fantasmagories sont presque aussi belles que les yeux de ma belle bien-aimée, la petite folle monstrueuse aux yeux verts."
>
> Et tout à coup je reçus un violent coup de poing dans le dos, et j'entendis une voix rauque et charmante, une voix hystérique et comme enrouée par l'eau-de-vie, la voix de ma chère petite bien-aimée, qui disait: "—Allez-vous bientôt manger votre soupe, s . . . b . . . de marchand de nuages?"
>
> (1: 350)[15]

This typically Baudelairean narrator is attracted and disgusted by his "bien-aimée," who makes the dinner and becomes sickeningly blended in with the other more or less consumable items in the text. The narrator indi-cates that her eyes are as beautiful and presumably as vaporous as the cloud formations, but he also insinuates that her voice—raucous *and* charming, as if drenched in hysteria and brandy—is a liquid, somewhat toxic composite, probably rather like the soup. Sandwiched in this uncertain way between the soup and the mistress, the clouds form an indistinct border zone in danger of dissolution, since the sacred "architectures que Dieu fait" in the pure space beyond the dining-room window seem ready to melt into the soup being eaten by a "s[acré] b[ougre] de marchand de nuages" in notably impure company. This would imply that the *et* of the title is likewise in danger of liquefaction: unless it can resist the tendency of "la soupe" and "les nuages" to spill into one another, the conjunction that in fact slightly disjoins the two will slop over into a copula. Should this happen, the narrator would likely be washed away in an unspeakable flood of soupy clouds and cloudy soup, melting at once into desire and disgust for the "bien-aimée" whose half-motherly cooking stirs up such half-monstrous mixtures.

Beyond the elementary forms of abjection bound up with food, Kristeva notes, "l'abject nous confronte . . . à ces états fragiles où l'homme erre dans les territoires de l'*animal*" (20). As a thumbnail sketch of **"Le Chien et le flacon,"** this is reasonably accurate, if limited: Jérôme Thélot has recently shown how numerous are the forms of violence inflicted in and by this text.[16] But one could still argue that its narrator is mainly concerned with what fascinates and appalls him as a revolting conflation of the reading public with the animal kingdom:

> «—Mon beau chien, mon bon chien, mon cher toutou, approchez et venez respirer un excellent parfum acheté chez le meilleur parfumeur de la ville.»
>
> Et le chien, en frétillant de la queue, ce qui est, je crois, chez ces pauvres êtres, le signe correspondant du rire et du sourire, s'approche et pose curieusement son nez humide sur le flacon débouché; puis, reculant soudainement avec effroi, il aboie contre moi, en manière de reproche.
>
> «—Ah! misérable chien, si je vous avais offert un paquet d'excréments, vous l'auriez flairé avec délices et peut-être dévoré. Ainsi, vous-même, indigne compagnon de ma triste vie, vous resseblez au public, à qui il ne faut jamais présenter des parfums délicats qui l'exaspèrent, mais des ordures soigneusement choisies.»
>
> (1: 284)[17]

The narrator thus takes a dog, who barks to show its preference for excrement over perfume, to be a good representation of the undiscriminating reader, who raucously prefers pulp to poetry. In elaborating this representation, though, the narrator stages above all the scene of his own abjection. His desire to repulse (repel and/or cause repulsion in) the dog bursts out only when he has himself been repulsed (also in both senses) by the creature's reproachful barking, and this ambivalent repulsion by no means guarantees that he will part company from the "indigne compagnon de [sa] triste vie." Fascinated and disgusted, the narrator takes no unambiguous position; the language with which he tries to express the dog's symbolic relation to the public slides disconcertingly between furious, overstated speeches ("Ah! misérable chien, si je vous avais offert un paquet d'excréments . . .") and fawning, nonsensical baby talk ("—Mon beau chien, mon bon chien, mon cher toutou . . ."). Given this slipperiness of address, it is revealing that the prose poem's title conjoins neither the dog and the public, nor the dog and the poet, but rather the dog and the perfume bottle. What the narrator can neither accept nor reject without nausea, it would appear, is the mingling of his own perfumed language with the inarticulate "aboiement" of the public. Abjectly hesitating, the narrator neither throws away the flask nor kicks out the dog; he merely stands between the two and keeps talking, as if trying to make of himself a conjunction that both links and separates, but never conflates or confuses them. The narrator stations himself on the fragile border between "le chien" (smelly, public, prosaic) and "le flacon" (fragrant, intimate, poetic), a border that wavers at the least sign that the title's *et* might contain a central *s*.

The unnerving phantom of such an *s* hovers even more insistently over the conjunction in "La Femme sauvage et la petite-maîtresse." There are in fact several indications that the speaker in this prose poem thinks the conjunction really ought to be a copula and is doing his best to make its phantom *s* visible. Although he pedantically lists differences between the "femme sauvage" and his "petite-maîtresse," as though to reinforce the *et* that separates them on the page, he also pointedly hints that their cries, however different in sound, are much the same in their effects; the "petits soupirs" and "*précieuses* pleurnicheries" of the one are as provoking as the shrieks of the other "hurlant comme un damné" (1: 289-90). As a result, the speaker feels he can discard niceties of vocabulary, since terms as heterogeneous as "monster," "angel," "beast," and "woman" all apply equally and simultaneously to the creatures in question: "'Ce monstre est un de ces animaux qu'on appelle généralement 'mon ange!' c'est-à-dire une femme,'" he claims, referring soon afterward to the "'dents de la bête féroce, de la femme, veux-je dire.'" The better to underscore this ironic identification, the speaker also relies on the cumulative force of (what else?) numerous coordinate conjunctions, aligning phrases like "vous me fatiguez sans mesure *et* sans pitié" (about the "petite-maîtresse"), "vos soupirs . . . ne traduisent que la satiété du bien-être *et* l'accablement du repos" (also about the "petite-maîtresse"), and "elle déchire des lapins vivants *et* des volailles piaillantes" (about the "femme sauvage"). Not only does this wild woman inhabit the horrifying, indefinite frontier between the human and the bestial, but she also horribly imitates the devouring mother, chewing up little crea-tures and swallowing them live instead of nurturing them. The speaker's repeated *et*, by working to form a zone of indiscriminate pairs and parallels, collapses the vaporous mistress into the voracious mother.

But the speaker conforms at the same time to the per-verse logic of abjection, in which he cannot condemn the abject without also sanctioning it. For with his re-lentless, increasingly strident insistence that the mis-tress's whine blurs into the wild woman's cry, the speaker himself becomes harder and harder to distin-guish from "l'autre monstre, celui qui crie à tue-tête" beside his wife's cage. Mixed into this latter indistinct-ness, moreover, there is another form of blurring: as is emphasized by the quotation marks that open every paragraph, some other narrator is reporting—or at least overhearing—what the speaker says, so that this already hybrid lover/husband/animal trainer also hovers in an indeterminate zone between the voice directly talking to the mistress and the all-but-inaudible voice indirectly narrating the prose poem to the reader. It is toward the end of the text that the speaker's profound in-betweeness approaches the unbearable:

> "A vous voir ainsi, ma belle délicate, les pieds dans la fange et les yeux tournés vaporeusement vers le ciel, comme pour lui demander un roi, on dirait vraisem-blablement une jeune grenouille qui invoquerait l'idéal. Si vous méprisez le soliveau (ce que je suis mainte-nant, comme vous savez bien), gare la grue *qui vous croquera, vous gobera et vous tuera à son plaisir!*"
>
> (1: 290; emphasis in original)[18]

Voluptuous and revolted, the speaker proposes ulti-mately to dissolve himself into the conjoining operation begun in the prose poem's title. That is, treating his "petite-maîtresse" as if she is at once an abject "femme sauvage" and an even more bestial "grenouille," he will abject himself in the same manner: he will imitate not only the wild woman's husband, but also the brutal "grue" (who will eat the "grenouille" alive), in a double attempt to free himself from the maternal threat by de-vouring it. Or at least, that is what he *says* he will do; he is after all only talking in rhetorical flourishes bor-rowed from La Fontaine's poem, "Les Grenouilles qui demandent un roi."[19] The speaker's ultimate attempt to repulse the flesh-tearing mother requires that he tear off and chew on snippets of someone else's poetic lan-guage, spitting back a half-assimilated mixture. Such linguistic goo, however, cannot give much control over the title's potential for slippage between copula and conjunction, a slippage that threatens the speaker as much as his mistress. This prose poem's *et* joins the others as a locus of abjection, particularly supporting Kristeva's claim that "l'abject nous confronte . . . à nos tentatives les plus anciennes de nous démarquer de l'entité *maternelle* avant même que d'ex-ister en dehors d'elle grâce à l'autonomie du langage" (20).

Tangled in the fringes of the speaking subject's ragged separation from the maternal and the regenerative, ac-cording to Kristeva, is a correspondingly horrifying confrontation with the dead and the decaying: "le ca-davre . . . , ce qui a irrémédiablement chuté, cloaque et mort, bouleverse plus violemment encore l'identité de celui qui s'y confronte comme un hasard fragile et fal-lacieux" (11). And it is apparently by just such a "frag-ile chance" that a signboard comes into view at the be-ginning of **"Le Tir et le cimetière"**:

> —*À la vue du cimetière, Estaminet.*—"Singulière enseigne,—se dit notre promeneur,—mais bien faite pour donner soif! À coup sûr, le maître de ce cabaret sait apprécier Horace et les poètes élèves d'Épicure. Peut-être même connaît-il le raffinement profond des anciens Égyptiens, pour qui il n'y avait pas de bon fes-tin sans squelette, ou sans un emblème quelconque de la brièveté de la vie."
>
> (1: 351)[20]

As the strolling protagonist rightly observes, this bar owner seems to have capitalized on the double happen-stance of his bar's strange location and its resulting connection to a poetic tradition. One wonders, though, if it can be by mere chance that the word *estaminet* on the signboard starts with *est* and ends with *et,* both join-ing and separating them, so that one can't tell whether the middle letters flesh out the skeleton of a conjunc-tion or the bones of a copula. In any event, sandwiched as it is between a shooting range and a cemetery, the "estaminet" itself forms what Kristeva has called "[un] espace . . . divisible, pliable, catastrophique" (16), in which celebrations of life and practices of death flow together. The bar thus lives up to the paragrammatic ambiguity of its signboard: it is a midpoint or divider, but only in a sliding continuum that joins vitality with mortality, the differentiated signs of language with the amorphous decomposition of corpses.

The *promeneur* is not the only visitor who lingers here. While giving light to the shooting range, the sun also looks in at the *estaminet* and its adjacent graveyard:

> En effet, la lumière et la chaleur y faisaient rage, et l'on eût dit que le soleil ivre se vautrait tout de son long sur un tapis de fleurs magnifiques engraissées par la destruction. Un immense bruissement de vie remp-lissait l'air,—la vie des infiniment petits,—coupé à in-tervalles réguliers par la crépitation des coups de feu d'un tir voisin, qui éclataient comme l'explosion des bouchons de champagne dans le bourdonnement d'une symphonie en sourdine.
>
> (1: 351)[21]

Like a lover and a cadaver, the sun lies down across the lawn, almost unable to distinguish whether the soft and violent sounds in the cemetery come from buzzing in-sects, firing rifles, and/or popping champagne corks. Himself close to melting into this "soleil qui lui chauffait le cerveau," the *promeneur* makes out a voice mingled in with the other noises. Seeping along the indeterminate borderline between the tombs and the flowers, the voice predictably uses both conjunctions and copulas in mixed profusion:

> "Maudites soient vos cibles *et* vos carabines, turbulents vivants, qui vous souciez si peu des défunts *et* de leur divin repos! Maudites soient vos ambitions, maudits soient vos calculs, mortels impatients, qui venez étudier l'art de tuer auprès du sanctuaire de la Mort! Si vous saviez comme le prix *est* facile à gagner, comme le but *est* facile à toucher, *et* combien tout *est* néant, excepté la Mort, vous ne vous fatigueriez pas tant, laborieux vivants, *et* vous troubleriez moins souvent le sommeil de ceux qui depuis longtemps ont mis dans le But, dans le seul vrai but de la détestable vie!"

> (1: 351-52; emphasis added)[22]

The *promeneur* who listens to this has nothing to answer, even though he talked readily enough through the first paragraph of the prose poem. His words there were a response to what he saw written on the signboard of the *estaminet,* which assured him, however speciously, that *est* and *et* could be kept tangibly apart, coupled but also disjoined by the inscription. At the end of the prose poem, when the *promeneur* sits instead in the cemetery among the "fleurs engraissées par la destruction," material distinctions and tangible separations are harder to come by. When he then hears the "bourdonnement" of such fragments as "et combien tout est néant, excepté la Mort," sense-making grammar begins to decay as the conjunction blurs not just into the copula, but into the homophonous phonemes of "néant" and "excepté": all that keeps *et* and *est* and *é* separate is a voice that sounds as much like the deadly "crépitation des coups de feu" as like the lively "explosion des bouchons de champagne." In other terms, all that holds them apart is practically nothing, an almost imperceptible exception to the surrounding process of undifferentiation. Even without articulation, the mere timbre of this voice would threaten the boundary separating cold death from the listener's overheated brain, and the last words the voice whispers strengthen its limit-violating power: in those words, the neatly separated *et* and *est* of *estaminet* collapse into the messy confusion of *é* and *et* and *est* in "dé*test*able vie."[23] Just barely excluded—abjected— from this "sanctuaire de la Mort," the *promeneur* can by now hardly distinguish, much less use, the language dissolving around him.[24]

Given the ambiguous effects of the sunlight in **"Le Tir et le cimetière,"** one might recall that Baudelaire proposed at an early stage to entitle his projected collection of prose poems *La Lueur et la Fumée.*[25] Had this title been retained, the central *et*—and its virtual *s*—would have foregrounded the collection's gray zones, in which a seductive and terrifying homophony breaches the frontier between the bright regions of grammar and the un-

nameable dark beyond them. Even without the help of his rejected title, though, Baudelaire still sneaks toward this frontier when he asks, in a preliminary draft of his dedication to Houssaye: "Quel est celui de nous qui n'a pas rêvé une prose particulière et poétique pour traduire les mouvements lyriques de l'esprit, les ondulations de la rêverie, et les soubresauts de la conscience?" (1: 365). With its conjunction—conflation?—of "particulière" and "poétique," this draft sets Baudelaire's prose poems in a half-light where particular details of history shade into general truths of poetry, a shading already apt to induce a kind of abject horror in readers looking for the clarity of Aristotelian categories. But the final version of Baudelaire's dedication points to a still more indistinct border zone occupied not by "une prose particulière et poétique," but rather by "le miracle d'une prose poétique, musicale sans rythme et sans rime, assez souple et assez heurtée" (1: 275). Along this insecure border, a subject trying to speak must waver between grammatical articulation and nongrammatical sonority, unsure whether two lacks ("sans rythme et sans rime") can meaningfully conjoin or whether two half-plenitudes ("assez souple et assez heurtée") can either oppose or merge into each other. The final version of the dedication further insists that if the subject is desperately driven to ransack this in-between zone, it is in search of a language adapted both to the "mouvements lyriques de l'âme" and to "la fréquentation des villes énormes" (1: 275-76). With its own process of constitution at stake, that is, the borderline subject must attempt to manipulate a grammar adequate to what Baudelaire might call the poetic intimacy of "Symboles et moralités,"[26] as well as to the prosaic sprawl—the "innombrables rapports" (1: 276)—of urban living. Yet the operation of such a grammar entails high risk, since it continually pushes the speaker toward limit zones in which "tout . . . est à la fois tête et queue, alternativement et réciproquement": to pursue this "miracle d'une prose poétique," the subject must risk slithering into an unarticulatable nonzone in which "tête *é/et/est* queue." It is a pursuit of this kind, I think, that is launched in the title of **"Le Tir et le cimetière"** or in the phrase "particulière et poétique." The chancy attraction of *é/et/est* is not wholly absent even from "safer" pairings such as "poème en prose" or "prose poétique": it stays buried under the half-disintegrated ground of all such pairs whenever the wavering subject attempts to narrate them.

It may be, however, that the rustling cadavers by the *estaminet* do not quite stage the limit case of abjection in ***Le Spleen de Paris.*** I would argue instead that these prose poems play out their culminating confrontation with the abject in the piece originally called "L'Idéal et le réel," but later entitled **"Laquelle est la vraie?"** This too is a text about a corpse and its fascinating, repulsive refusal to respect sacred borders; it is also a text about the narrator's effort to read eyes, decipher voices, and respond with language. The narrator carefully divides his story into two distinct parts, one devoted to the lovely, ideal Bénédicta who dies because she is "trop belle pour vivre longtemps," the other given to the grotesque little creature, also named Bénédicta, who materializes on the dead woman's grave and shouts "C'est moi, la vraie Bénédicta!" (1: 342). The narrator manifestly wishes to hold the two Bénédicta as far apart as possible, since the disturbing sameness of their names threatens to blur the reassuringly sharp line between their identities. But since the narrator's leg is caught in the one Bénédicta's freshly dug grave, upon which the other Bénédicta is trampling, it seems unlikely that he will be able to separate the two very well.

As if to emphasize the narrator's dilemma, the text of this prose poem is pointedly not structured around a pivot-sentence that would keep its two parts slightly disjoined. Nor is the title likely to help effect this separation: rather than hesitating between two elements tenuously linked, this title is composed of a single question, firmly launched so as to get at the truth: **"Laquelle est la vraie?"** The problem, of course, is that in the end the narrator can't or won't answer the question and that his text probably doesn't represent the truth. There is surely nothing very reliable about the discourse of a narrator who has sunk—although as yet only partway—into a decomposing ideal ("enfonc[é] jusqu'au genou . . . , je reste attaché, pour toujours peut-être, à la fosse de l'idéal" [1: 342]). Considering that this narrator, stuck half in and half out of a grave, is quickly reduced to yelling "Non! non! non!" in semi-articulate panic, it seems doubtful that he will ever use language with enough subtlety to make true distinctions between an ideal Bénédicta and a real one, between a living woman and a dead body, between a desired idol and a threatening mother. And since the stuttering of *é/et/est* permeates so many other segments of **Le Spleen de Paris,** one wonders whether the abject narrator of this prose poem can prevent it from seeping into his title question: what if "Laquelle est la vraie?" were really—alternatively and reciprocally—"Laquelle *et* la vraie?" Like the grotesque little Bénédicta, "Laquelle et la vraie?" would trample—"avec une violence hystérique et bizarre"—on the ideal grammar of the question half buried beneath it, churning *est* into *et* until the true syllable became difficult to distinguish.[27] In Bénédicta's grave, where all parts will decompose together, one is tempted to suppose that the copulas and conjunctions of a questioning title can remain no more stable than the fragments of a mutilated serpent. By conjoining my voice to Kristeva's one last time, then, I might observe that the temptation of this abjectly deformed title "me tire vers là où le sens s'effondre. . . . À la lisière de l'inexistence et de l'hallucination, d'une réalité qui, si je la reconnais, m'annihile" (9-10). Or, in other words, what appears here as profoundly abject is the eccentric conjunction of the grammatical and the true.

Notes

1. The original reads:

    My dear friend, I am sending you a small work about which one could not say, without injustice, that it has neither tail nor head, since everything in it, on the contrary, is at once head and tail, alternatively and reciprocally. Consider, I pray you, what admirable conveniences this combination offers to everyone, to you, to me and to the reader. We can cut where we want to—me my reverie, you the manuscript, the reader his reading; for I do not string the latter's restive willpower along the interminable thread of a superfluous plot. Remove a vertebra, and the two pieces of this tortuous fantasy will join together with no trouble. Chop it into numerous fragments, and you will see that each one can exist separately. In the hope that some of these segments will be lively enough to please and amuse you, I venture to dedicate to you the entire serpent.

    (Charles Baudelaire, *Œuvres complètes,* ed. Claude Pichois, 2 vols., Bibliothèque de la Pléiade [Paris: Gallimard, 1983-85], 1:275)

    All further references to page numbers in this edition will appear parenthetically in the text; all translations given in the notes are my own.

2. See, among other studies of this letter of dedication, Barbara Johnson, *Défigurations du language poétique: la seconde révolution baudelairienne* (Paris: Flammarion, 1979), 24-29; Marc Eli Blanchard, *In Search of the City: Engels, Baudelaire, Rimbaud,* Stanford French and Italian Studies, no. 37 (Saratoga, Calif.: ANMA Libri, 1985), 73-77; Margery A. Evans, *Baudelaire and Intertextuality: Poetry at the Crossroads,* Cambridge Studies in French, no. 38 (Cambridge: Cambridge University Press, 1993), 8-11; and Edward Kaplan, *Baudelaire's Prose Poems: The Esthetic, the Ethical, and the Religious in "The Parisian Prowler"* (Athens, Ga.: The University of Georgia Press, 1990), 9-12.

3. In his notes to the letter of dedication, Claude Pichois observes that the mutilated serpent was a frequently recycled image in French poetry from the first half of the nineteenth century; Hugo, Sainte-Beuve, Nerval, Lamartine, and Latouche all used it for various purposes before Baudelaire appropriated it in *Le Spleen de Paris* (Baudelaire, *Œuvres complètes,* 1: 1308).

4. See Jacques Derrida, "Le Supplément de copule: la philosophie devant la linguistique," in *Marges de la philosophie* (Paris: Les Éditions de minuit, 1972), 209-46.

5. For an excellent discussion of identity-splitting in the narrator of Baudelaire's prose poems, see Eugene W. Holland, *Baudelaire and Schizoanalysis: The Sociopoetics of Modernism* (Cambridge: Cambridge University Press, 1993), 177-257.

6. For Richard Terdiman, the notion that a connector must disjoin as well as join is fundamental to the modernism exemplified in the writings of Baudelaire and Freud: "We think of relations as providing cognitive grasp on the phenomena they relate, but the modern period has subverted such a logic and produced a paradoxical paradigm of linkage whose function is to *disconnect*" (*Present Past: Modernity and the Memory Crisis* [Ithaca, N.Y.: Cornell University Press, 1993], 326). I am grateful to an anonymous reader for signaling this reference.

7. See Charles Baudelaire, *Petits Poëmes en prose,* edited with notes by Robert Kopp (Paris: Corti, 1969), 205. Marie Maclean points out (in *Narrative as Performance: The Baudelairean Experiment* [London and New York: Routledge, 1988], 57) that this prose poem evokes one of Deburau's pantomimes at the Théâtre des Funambules; the organization of Baudelaire's text may therefore at least partly reflect that of the performance that inspired it.

8. The original reads:

    What an admirable day! The vast park swoons under the burning eye of the sun, like youth under the domination of Love.

    The universal ecstasy of things does not express itself by means of any noise; even the water is as if asleep. Very different from human celebrations, this is a silent orgy.

    One might say that an ever growing light gives objects more and more sparkle; that the excited flowers burn from desire to compete with the azure of the sky by the energy of their colors, and that the heat, in rendering fragrances visible, makes them rise toward the day star like wisps of smoke.

9. The original reads, "However, in the midst of this universal pleasure/excitement [jouissance], I perceived an afflicted being."

10. The original reads:

    At the feet of a colossal Venus, one of those artificial fools, one of those voluntary clowns charged with making kings laugh when Remorse or Boredom obsesses them, decked out in a flashy and ridiculous costume, with horns and bells for headgear, all

huddled against the pedestal, raises eyes filled with tears toward the immortal Goddess.

And his eyes say:—"I am the lowest and the most solitary of humans, deprived of love and friendship, and in that way inferior to the most imperfect of animals. However, I am made, I as well, to understand and to feel immortal Beauty! Oh! Goddess! take pity on my sadness and my delirious longing!"

But the implacable Venus looks far away at I don't know what with her eyes of marble.

11. The original reads: "*And* his eyes say:—'I am the lowest *and* the most solitary of humans, deprived of love *and* friendship, *and* in that way inferior to the most imperfect of animals. However, I am made, I as well, to understand *and* to feel immortal Beauty! Oh! Goddess! take pity on my sadness *and* my delirious longing!'"

12. See Julia Kristeva, *Pouvoirs de l'horreur: Essai sur l'abjection* (Paris: Seuil, 1980), 9-16. All further references to this edition will be given parenthetically in the text.

13. See Holland, 202-03. Although it does not touch directly on "Le Fou et la Vénus," Holland's discussion suggests an alternative way to view the narrator's rôle in this prose poem. Holland might argue that the narrator's staging of a confrontation between the jester and the statue shows "a keen awareness of primitive splitting as a basic psychic structure and a crucial defense mechanism," which "operates by projecting violence onto other characters or into the scenes described by the narrator"; the result of such projection is generally that "the absent narrator is not implicated in the violence at all" (202). If I prefer to consider the narrator in terms of his abjection, however, it is precisely because any split allowing him to project violence away from himself appears here as uncertain; since he both takes and avoids responsibility for the violence, his distance from it is difficult to establish.

14. Kristeva, 20. In the midst of enumerating and briefly analyzing these conditions, Kristeva summarizes them by saying that the abject confronts society with the border zone where the human blurs into the animal, while it confronts the individual with the early, indistinct attempts of the subject to constitute itself by separation from the mother.

15. The original reads:

    My crazy little beloved was fixing me dinner, and through the open window of the dining room I was contemplating the moving architectures that God makes with vapor, marvelous constructions of the impalpable. And I was saying to myself, through my contemplation: "—All these phantasmagorias are almost as beautiful as the eyes of my beautiful beloved, the crazy little monster with green eyes."

And all of a sudden I received a violent punch in the back, and I heard a raucous and charming voice, a voice that was hysterical and as if hoarse from brandy, the voice of my dear little beloved, which said: "—Are you ever going to eat your soup, you f . . . cloud pusher?"

16. Jérôme Thélot, *Baudelaire: violence et poésie* (Paris: Gallimard, 1993), 19-38.

17. The original reads:

> "—My beautiful dog, my good dog, my dear woofwoof, approach and come breathe in an excellent perfume purchased from the best perfume shop in town."
>
> And the dog, wagging its tail, which is, I believe, for these poor creatures, the sign corresponding to the laugh and the smile, comes up and curiously puts its wet nose on the uncapped bottle; then, recoiling suddenly with terror, he barks at me, by way of reproach.
>
> "—Ah! miserable dog, if I had offered you a packet of excrements, you would have sniffed it with delight and perhaps devoured it. Thus, even you, unworthy companion of my sorrowful life, you resemble the public, to whom one must never present delicate perfumes that exasperate them, but rather meticulously chosen garbage."

18. The original reads, "'To see you that way, my delicate beauty, your feet in the mud and your eyes turned vaporously toward the sky, as if to ask it for a king, one would really take you for a young frog invoking the ideal. If you scorn the log (which is what I am now, as you very well know), beware of the crane *that will chew you, swallow you, and kill you at its pleasure!'*"

19. In their editorial notes on "La Femme sauvage et la petite-maîtresse," Kopp (Baudelaire, *Petits Poëmes en prose,* 220) and Pichois (1: 1315) both remark on Baudelaire's somewhat altered rendering of three lines from La Fontaine's fable: "Le monarque des dieux leur envoie une grue, / Qui les croque, qui les tue, / Qui les gobe à son plaisir."

20. The original reads, "—*Cemetery View, Tavern.—* 'Singular sign,—said our stroller to himself,—but

certainly made to give one a thirst! For sure, the proprietor of this cabaret knows how to appreciate Horace and the poets who studied under Epicurus. Perhaps he even knows about the profound refinement of the ancient Egyptians, for whom no feast was good without a skeleton, or without some emblem of life's shortness.'"

21. The original reads, "In fact, the light and the heat raged there, and one might have said that the drunken sun wallowed full length on a carpet of flowers magnificently fertilized by destruction. An immense rustling filled the air,—the life of the infinitely small,—punctuated at regular intervals by the crackling of gunshots from a shooting range next door, shots that burst like the explosion of champagne corks in the buzzing of a muted symphony."

22. The original reads:

> "A curse on your targets *and* [*et*] your rifles, you turbulent living people, who care so little about the dead *and* [*et*] their divine rest! A curse on your ambitions, a curse on your calculations, impatient mortals, who come to study the art of killing near the sanctuary of Death! If you knew how easy it *is* [*est*] to win the prize, how easy it *is* [*est*] to hit the bull's-eye, *and* [*et*] how everything *is* [*est*] nothingness, except Death, you would not tire yourselves so, laborious living people, *and* [*et*] you would trouble less often the sleep of those who have long since hit the Bull's-eye / but the dust [mis dans le But], the only real bull's-eye / goal of detestable life!"

23. I am grateful to Mary-Kay F. Miller for helping me see this relation between the *estaminet* that opens the prose poem and the "détestable vie" that closes it.

24. Pointing out the possible association of a "tirage" with a "tir," Evans suggests that what is at stake here is not only the integrity of the *promeneur*'s language, but also the narrator's, author's, and publisher's combined production of the prose poem as a printed inscription (54).

25. Pichois reviews the succession of titles that Baudelaire considered from 1857 onward (1: 1298-99); *La Lueur et la Fumée* is mentioned as a possibility in a letter Baudelaire wrote to Arsène Houssaye, dated 20 December 1861 (see Charles Baudelaire, *Correspondance,* ed. Claude Pichois, 2 vols., Bibliothèque de la Pléiade [Paris: Gallimard, 1975], 2: 197).

26. This is a subtitle that Baudelaire planned at one stage to use for a part of his collection; it was to

contain a number of prose poems that were never written (see *Œuvres complètes,* 1: 367, 369, 1299-1300).

27. As Johnson (76) and Evans (28) have noted, the name Bénédicta means "la Bien Dite" or "fine words." Between them, one might say, the two Bénédictas half bury the distinction between a well-spoken and an ill-spoken question.

Nicolae Babuts (essay date spring-summer 1997)

SOURCE: Babuts, Nicolae. "Baudelaire's 'Le Voyage': The Dimension of Myth." *Nineteenth-Century French Studies* 25, nos. 3-4 (spring-summer 1997): 348-59.

[*In the following essay, Babuts analyzes "Le Voyage" in terms of both its differences from and its incorporating of classical Western mythology.*]

"Le Voyage," Baudelaire's longest poem, ranks among his most complex and enigmatic. As long ago as 1945, Pommier confessed that, at least up to that time, he had not been able to untangle the poem's complexity (344). And Leakey begins his analysis by describing its structure as "elaborate, even devious" (294). Complexity and enigma surround not only the structure but the principal figures and symbols as well. While asserting their inalienable difference, their uniqueness in a modern context, the poem's figures, Circe, the drunken sailor, Time, Electra, and Pylades, nevertheless weave intricate echoes of their traditional epic sources. And one way to interpret them is to situate them in relation to their mythological counterparts.

Critics have assumed that such a relation is justified but have not pursued its implications. In his compelling study, Burton acknowledges that "'**Le Voyage**' deploys a wide range of mythological, historical and literary allusion . . ." (*B. in 1859* 72), but sees it "as an anti-*Odyssey*" (73), which "preserves the movement and energy of epic while undermining their teleological justification" (153). He thus stresses the contrast with the classical epic. I focus instead on the resemblance, on the way the relation to traditional structures discloses the mythic attributes of Baudelaire's symbols. This strategy proves helpful in solving a crucial difficulty of interpretation and in accounting for the difference between the voyage in section vii and the one in section viii.

The Victory of Time

The difficulty occurs after two stanzas in which human efforts to escape Time are shown to be futile: "Lorsque enfin il mettra le pied sur notre échine . . ." (line 121).[1] Calling this "the dramatic turning-point of the poem,"

Austin begins his analysis by identifying Time with death: "When at last Time, now identified with death, has laid us low . . . what then?" (29) Expressing a similar view of this line, Adam comments: "Ce sera la Mort, la Mort qui n'est elle-même qu'un dernier voyage" (431n25). But are critics justified in believing that death intervenes at this moment? They acknowledge with Austin the "entirely new and original note" (Austin 30) of the last two quatrains but believe section vii and viii speak of the same voyage. Thus when Burton notes a shift in meaning, he points to the contrast between section vi and the "concluding stanzas" (*B. in 1859* 86) and not between section vii and those stanzas. The question that arises is this: If the voyage that follows the victory of Time signifies Death, why would the speaker need to call on Death in the last section and ask for a new voyage?

To say that the last section, which clearly marks a new departure, continues the previous one without a break, that the two constitute only one voyage, is not satisfactory. The only answer that is consistent with the organization of the poem is that after the victory of Time there are two voyages, one in section vii, one in section viii, and that the first does not signify the death of the speaker. The two-voyage interpretation explains why during the first voyage the voices the travelers hear have a familiar accent (line 133) whereas in the second voyage they seek "du *nouveau*" (line 144).

Intertextual evidence corroborates the view that the victory of Time does not signify death. At the end of **"La Chambre double,"** Time reappears and resumes his dictatorship telling the speaker, "Vis donc, damné!" (Kopp 16). In **"Chacun sa chimère,"** the image of several men, the narrator calls travelers ("voyageurs"), walking with chimeras on their backs and being condemned always to hope is dynamically similar to the one of the travelers in **"Le Voyage,"** who, now that Time is on their backs, can hope and cry, "En avant!" In both cases they are very much alive although moving in an intermediary space between life and death, a Baudelairean Underworld or twilight zone. How then can we explain the fact that in **"Le Voyage"** though they are old, they remain young at heart? Is their joy in accepting the consequences of Time's reign another form of Baudelairean irony? Above all, if the new voyage does not represent death, why are they embarking on the Sea of Darkness? And what is the significance of the voices they hear?

Ulysses's Last Voyage

The first two question have already been answered by Austin and Leakey, who stress that the "child, with his vast appetite, has never died within us" (Austin 30) and that at this point of the poem "the prospect lightens, paradoxically, to one of joy and hope" (Leakey 306). I will attempt to answer the other two. In Crépet's opinion, the reference to the Sea of Darkness has its source in Baudelaire's translation of Poe's *Une Descente dans le Maelstrom,* and "La *Mer des Ténèbres* c'est l'Atlantique" (12: 448). If it does designate the Atlantic, it does not necessarily imply death. I argue, instead, that the voyage on the Sea of Darkness is in fact a modern version of Odysseus's journey to the Underworld and of his subsequent encounter with the Sirens.

As has been pointed out by many (see Kopp 297-98), the dynamic pattern of the afternoon without end comes from "The Lotos-Eaters," but in some ways this section resembles the last voyage of Ulysses invented by Dante and taken up by Tennyson in "Ulysses." The journey is undertaken before the death of the speaker and explores a transitional zone that marks the limits of human power to probe the Unknown. Although apparently Dante did not read Homer and Tennyson did not follow him, the structures of their narratives recall the archetype: Odysseus's visit to the Underworld that occurs long before his death.

In Tennyson's poem, Ulysses and his mariners contemplate embarking on a last voyage and sailing "beyond the sunset" (line 60) at a moment in their lives when they, like Baudelaire's travelers, are old and Time has made them weak in body but "strong in will" (line 69). The sea that awaits them resembles the Sea of Darkness: "There gloom the dark, broad seas" (line 45) and the possibility of reaching "the Happy Isles" and seeing Achilles points to the land of the dead. In Dante, Ulysses sails past the Pillars of Hercules to the Atlantic, the Sea of Darkness, and, almost instinctively, attempts to break the barrier separating this world and the next. His attempt fails because unlike Homer's hero, he has no divine guidance. Yet his ambition is to go beyond the sun and to reach the land of the dead (the mountain of Purgatory).

Ulysses begins his account with the words "When I left Circe" (*The Inferno* 26.86), even though the implication appears to be that he saw his family before leaving. This initial allusion to Circe resembles the dynamics of Baudelaire's reference to Circe at the beginning of the poem, which is clearly intended to mark the departure of a whole category of travelers. Circe's presence in **"Le Voyage"** and in canto 26 of *The Inferno* foreshadows the need to undertake a journey similar to the one Odysseus accomplishes in *The Odyssey* when he leaves Circe, on her advice, to visit the Underworld. Functioning as a catalyst to facilitate the reader's entry into the metaphoric field of the two newer texts, Circe's image betrays the master pattern of *The Odyssey*. (In **"Le Voyage"** the other catalyst is the child with its maps and prints, who prefigures the passion for knowledge and the desire to explore the world.)

Baudelaire's Circe is, of course, stylized in a modern version of the ancient goddess. As Burton says, she "is no daughter of the Sun and Sea but an all-too-human woman" (*B. in 1859* 73). Yet the metamorphosis does not erase the traces of the ancient pattern or the source of her power. Her perfume is dangerous and she still has the capacity to transform men into beasts. The marks of her kisses can be effaced with time, but her appeal and the prestige of the tradition she exemplifies may never be lost. Baudelaire's insight, confirmed by Pound (whose first canto begins with a reference to Circe and summarizes Odysseus's journey to the Underworld), Stevens, Bonnefoy, and others, is that mythical models are susceptible of being transformed to fit a modern context.

THE SIREN-LIKE VOICES

With the victory of Time, the expressions "En avant," "Les yeux fixés au large," "Par ici," and "là-bas" simulate a decisive voyage, a movement in time. But a second and stronger impression is that the travelers are moving not on an empty sea but in a space peopled with familiar figures and voices:

> Nous nous embarquerons sur la mer des Ténèbres
> Avec le cœur joyeux d'un jeune passager.
> Entendez-vous ces voix, charmantes et funèbres,
> Qui chantent: «Par ici! vous qui voulez manger»
>
> «Le Lotus parfumé! c'est ici qu'on vendange
> Les fruits miraculeux dont votre cœur a faim;
> Venez vous enivrer de la douceur étrange
> De cette après-midi qui n'a jamais de fin?»
>
> À l'accent familier nous devinons le spectre;
> Nos Pylades là-bas tendent leur bras vers nous.
> «Pour rafraîchir ton cœur nage vers ton Électre!»
> Dit celle dont jadis nous baisions les genoux.
>
> (lines 125-36)

What these voices offer to the travelers is not something new but the fulfillment of the desires they have always had: the desire to be intoxicated with some impossible fruit that suggests the preoccupations with "artificial paradises" and the need to find Electra, the ideal wife, mother, sister, and mistress. The gesture resembles the temptation of the Sirens in *The Odyssey*. By singing about the hero's exploits in the Trojan war (see Lattimore 12.189-90), the Sirens offer Odysseus knowledge about everything that happens on earth, but the appeal to the memories of his past is the essence of their temptation. Similarly, Baudelaire's travelers are tempted with highlights of their own past. And the quoted stanzas define the metaphoric field of the poem as *a mnemonic sea, where alluring voices tempt the travelers with their own memories.*

THE ELECTRA MYSTIQUE

In **"Le Voyage,"** as in the dedication to **"Les Paradis artificiels,"** the poet's relation to Electra, implying the couple Orestes-Electra, is symptomatic of "la prédisposition de Baudelaire à s'identifier avec un modèle littéraire" (Babuts 4). And Electra is not simply Orestes's sister, but the ideal wife as she is defined by De Quincey in his *Confessions,* translated by Baudelaire in *Les Paradis artificiels.* After comparing his state to that of Orestes, De Quincey addresses his wife Margaret and tells her that she was kind and humble enough "to refresh [his] lips when parched and baked with fever" (153). Baudelaire picks up the verb 'to refresh' both in the dedication and in the text, translating it with the French "rafraîchir" (1: 400 and 463). In the dedication, Baudelaire addresses the woman for whom he writes the translation and after speaking of the consoling role of De Quincey's Electra, he adds: "et tu devineras la gratitude d'un autre Oreste dont tu as souvent surveillé les cauchemars, et de qui tu dissipais, d'une main légère et maternelle, le sommeil épouvantable" (1: 400). In the Greek drama and tradition, Electra may have been fanatic and savage in her vengeance, but her devotion to Orestes was not in doubt. And it is around this trait of her character that a whole romantic tradition converges to transform her into the woman who brings compassion and love to the suffering hero.[2]

If De Quincey's wife is maternal in her affection, she is also like a sister, not only because Electra is Orestes's sister, but also because there is contamination already in *The Confessions* with the "noble minded Ann" (136), an orphan companion, a street walker, who helped him when he was sick, and whom he loved "as if she had been [his] sister" (144). In the dedication to *Les Paradis artificiels,* the affinity between De Quincey's two heroines, Ann and Margaret-Electra, increases and Baudelaire's J. G. F.-Electra unites both maternal and sisterly attributes. And if one accepts that J. G. F.-Electra in the dedication is Jeanne, one will not be surprised that in **"Le Balcon"** dedicated to Jeanne, the poet calls her "mother of memories" and, with the expression "my fraternal hands," suggests a brother-sister relationship. Nor should one be surprised that the image of nestling on the knees of the beloved in **"Le Balcon"** resembles embracing Electra's knees in **"Le Voyage"**: both suggest a strong sexual worship tempered by the need for maternal and sisterly compassion.

The elements of worship are reinforced by a transfer of Circe's divine attributes to the image of Electra. In telling his story, Homer's Odysseus explains that eager to return home, he approached the goddess begging her to keep her promise: "but I, mounting the surpassingly beautiful bed of Circe, / clasped her by the knees and entreated her . . ." (Lattimore 10.480-81). The affinity between the pose of the Homer's hero as a suppliant and the position of Baudelaire, the traveler, embracing Electra's knees shows once again that the strength of the Electra model resides in its mnemonic associations.

The Ghosts of the Underworld

It is true that as a consequence of various strata and mnemonic deposits, Baudelaire's images are no longer in their pure classical state. Yet as myth is filtered through personal memories, it is reinvested with magic powers and the voices in **"Le Voyage,"** having regained their Siren modulations, become attractive, irresistible. And for the travelers they are also elusive, since the danger here is not so much in being lured to death, but in always remaining just on this side of the outstretched hands, in dealing not with real people but with specters. Thus, like the impotent dead crowding around Odysseus, the shades, who drink the sacrificial blood to be able to speak, Pylades, faint at first, needs the infusion of creative energy to stretch out his arms toward the individual traveler. It is not even certain whether his outstretched hands offer welcome or ask for help. Beyond his symbolic function, Pylades does not have any attributes that would permit us to identify him with one of Baudelaire's friends.[3] And Electra-J. G. F. is now stylized as the essence of the beloved wife and sister whose knees the poet embraces in a distant, purified, and stylized "long ago." The use of the possessive adjectives, "nos Pylades" and "ton Électre," is perhaps a reminder that they are not the Greek friend and sister but our friends and our Electra. Despite their "spectral" character or perhaps because of it, these images become vivid markers of a glorified past and have the aura of what has been chosen from a long experience to be preserved in the archives of discourse.

Like the ghosts in the Underworld of *The Odyssey,* the specters dwell in a mnemonic space that is not beyond the reach of the living, in a transitional region between life and death,[4] and function as symbols or emissaries carrying messages. Their voices, however, are not "les signes qui parfois semblent venir de l'Inconnu" (Galand 427).[5] Nor are they demons of a completely uncharted world. Like Homer's Sirens, they are figural representations of the traveler's own desires and identity and their temptation does not suggest "the Forbidden Knowledge of Genesis" or "the occult knowledge of the Faust legend" (Clarke 64); rather it offers certain coordinates to locate the point where one's own life and myth converge.

The Search for Knowledge

The mythic imagination has always invited the question: Why do heroes have to make this visit to the Underworld?[6] The basic goal of the voyage, the search for knowledge, allows for variations. In a leitmotiv older than *The Odyssey,* Gilgamesh, grieving for his dead companion, Enkidu, begins a journey to "cross the waters of death" (Sandars 104), to see Utnapishtim, and "to question him concerning the living and the dead" (Sandars 98). Similarly Odysseus, in the land of the

Kimmerians, consults with Teiresias and others about his destiny and his return home. Dante's hero undertakes his voyage "to seek virtue and knowledge" (*The Inferno* 26.120); Tennyson's hero is enticed by the appeal of the act of striving and seeking.

As the expression "Amer savoir" indicates, in **"Le Voyage,"** the travelers also seek knowledge but Baudelaire's text redesigns the issue: it substitutes implied inquiry and unstated alternatives to overt questions and clear-cut responses. Yet these differences, I suggest, pale before the palimpsestic need to weigh the value of life against the thought of death. The task is all the more urgent because his travelers journey with the burden of Time on their backs. At this crucial stage the imperative is to move along in a space where tasting the miraculous fruit and reaching the land of the inoperative Time become mirror-like patterns of the experience the self has always sought. However, the permanent quality of the illusion/disillusion sequence foredooms any hope of success and the overall tone remains ironic, inconsolable.

The differences in the way the heroes make the final decision to opt for life or for death is also revealing. After his visit to the Underworld, Odysseus is steeled, by what he learns from the ghosts of his friends, Achilleus in particular, and he resolves to live and return home, to his wife and son. Aeneas too is more determined after his stint in the Underworld where he sees his father's shade and has a glimpse of the future of Rome. Their experiences simply reinforce their original intentions. In appreciating the decision made by Baudelaire's travelers, one has to take into account the negative dynamics of their drive, the fact that they began their voyage to flee "une patrie infâme." As a consequence when during the contact with the voices from their past, they understand that the charm of the afternoon without end, friendship, and love are all deception, vanity, and disillusion, they are ready to make the decision to seek the Unknown. There is no one with the wisdom of Teiresias to advise them how to get home because, one senses, there is no home to return to.[7] These travelers have no choice but to summon Death and get ready for another departure.[8]

LO CONOCIDO / ES LO DESCONOCIDO (PABLO
ANTONIO CUADRA, "EL MAESTRO DE TARCA"
III)

And it is at this point that the fundamental theme of the poem stands at epiphanic alignment. The travelers now realize that the only "unknown" that is within human grasp is in Time, in their own past. However, while the past can be explored and better understood, it does not in any ontological sense of the word disclose "something new." This proposition is mirrored in the textual surface. Looking back at what we have read, we can

see that all the previous images of exploration, Icaria, Eldorado, Americas, the drunken sailor and other references, are all part of a past familiar to Baudelaire and his generation and do not represent the unexplored but the explored. Because they are here stylized, downgraded, and wholly traversed by irony, they are not always easy to identify. Columbus, for example, the Admiral of the Ocean Sea, becomes a "drunken sailor, inventor of Americas" (line 43).[9] A few silhouettes and short exclamations condense a whole literature of explorers, conquistadors, and three-masted caravels driven by storms against Caribbean reefs, a whole mythical past as it is preserved in memory.

And it is the resilience of the engram, the richness of its associations, that helps the poet establish the dynamics of the new epic. In the mnemonic context, the new allegories, the foolish lookout on the foremast, the dreamer, the drunken sailor, and the vagabond acquire some of the symbolic prestige of heroes. And although it does not reinscribe in its development a historical chronology,[10] the poem organizes historical fragments into new myths that reflect what must have appeared to Baudelaire's contemporaries as the familiar side of history. The expression "aux yeux du souvenir" 'in the eyes of memory' appearing in the first stanza is a forewarning to the reader: The poem is about memory and its creative and "resurrectionist" prerogatives (see "Le Peintre de la vie moderne" 2: 699). In the eyes of memory the Mediterranean Sea and the Atlantic become the *mare nostrum* of a tradition. Unlike Rimbaud's "Le Bateau ivre," which begins with the unexplored and ends up in familiar surroundings, Baudelaire's voyage of exploration recalls the familiar figures of the past throughout and only in the conclusion allows a confrontation with the unknown.

THE SECOND VOYAGE

Exacting the death of the speakers, the last voyage begins on a sea that has no buoys, no seamarks, no pillars of Hercules, and no voices. The only reality is the rays of light in their hearts, the inner reality then, no longer available for further differentiation. When they set their new course, the travelers see the Unknown in its purest version, without contours or characteristics.[11] The description is minimal, its chronology compressed, and its visions hidden in the last enigma: "pour trouver du *nouveau*!" (line 144) This new reality marks, by definition, the far side of the boundaries of human power and is not open to human understanding.

Clearly the two voyages are related. The first voyage sanctions a commerce between the living and the shades of the Underworld as a basis for making a decision about life and death; the second uses the lesson of this commerce to justify its new ambitions involving the death of the speaker. At times the distinction between the two voyages is ambiguous. Dante's Ulysses, for example, cannot reach the Underworld without dying, but Dante and Virgil do and obtain knowledge. In Tennyson the distinction, though not clearly stated, remains in effect.

The second voyage marks the point of greatest separation between ancient epics and **"Le Voyage."** In the first the arrow of orientation points toward life; in the second toward death. Death, true Death, is the only release from the dimension of Time, and in contemporary terms, the only way to reach the outside of the Western discourse. Thus "Enfer ou Ciel, qu'importe?" (line 143) may not mean that the choice between the two does not matter, but that neither of them matters.

Although thus a tabula rasa may appear as a precondition for the discovery of the new, caution is needed here lest we interpret the poet's desire in terms of a total rejection of life. Baudelaire insists that, before embarking on the journey into the Unknown, his travelers take some rays of light with them, carry a small baggage of memories from this world to the other. In their hearts, no less. All the bitterness and irony of the previous sections are gathered in a powerful élan, a synthesis of desire, which, like a favorable wind that fills the ship's sails, drives the poem to its inevitable end. And though far-reaching pessimism permeates the textual fabric, the impression one has in reading the poem is one of forward momentum, vigor, light, and beauty that overcome pain and despair. These qualities and the tension of the complex metaphoric field, its mythic power and mnemonic depth, all create an appeal to counterbalance the pull of the poem's dark message.

An all-encompassing scope, a far-flung mythic vision, and pessimism then. But a pessimism that is not outside the scope of the western tradition. The paradox is that the poet has to attempt to go beyond the experience of the past, in order to produce a final assessment of it. The implications of Baudelaire's critique of human societies and of the belief in progress reverberate on social, political, philosophical, religious, and historical levels; but the poem's reorganization of signs is neither an attempt at deconstruction nor a politically motivated intention to subvert the bourgeois society even though he loathed its power and nefarious effect on the artist. The need that the text releases is to submit a tradition to the filter of memory for the purpose of rewriting it, to humble it then resurrect it in a form that can belong to his generation and our own. There are many approaches to Baudelaire's poem and many ways to appreciate it. A most profitable one is to replace it in the perspective of the tradition it seeks to define, demoralize, deny and ultimately, in the written text, reaffirm. There is no myth and no history without a witness, without a singer of tales, and no poem without memory. "Aux yeux du souvenir" Troy has to be destroyed for

the tale to begin; one has to leave Circe to obey her commands; one has to resist and leave behind the seductive voices of memory to immortalize them; country and communal beliefs have to be abandoned so that some ultimate hope be reinscribed in the poem's vertiginous trajectory of bitterness and despair.

Notes

1. Baudelaire, *Œuvres complètes* 1: 133. Subsequent references to "Le Voyage" in parentheses will be limited to line numbers. For almost all Baudelairean texts, I have used Pichois's Pléiade edition of *Œuvres complètes*. The exception is that in quoting from Baudelaire's prose poems, I refer to Kopp's edition of *Petits poëmes en prose*.

2. Here are some judgments on Electra's character: "Except for her loyalty and devotion to her brother, Electra is a piece of complete viciousness, stubborn in spite and malice with the bitterness born of envy and resentful virginity" (Arrowsmith, "Introduction to *Orestes*" 109). In speaking about Sophocles's Electra, Banks writes: "The only thing that qualifies this harsh impression [of Electra] is her love for Orestes. He is not merely her instrument of vengeance but the child she tenderly remembers nursing" (xiv).

3. See, however, the intriguing suggestions put forward by Burton about the identity of Pylades and several other figures. He sees Poulet-Malassis "standing as an improbable Pylades-figure to Baudelaire's decidedly unheroic Orestes" (*B. in 1859* 28).

4. In this context, it is instructive to recall the text of Baudelaire's prose poem, "Le Joueur généreux," cited by several critics for its resemblance to the stanzas of the enticing voices. In that passage, the narrator is invited by the devil to a house in the middle of Paris. He compares the atmosphere of "somber beatitude" in the house to the happiness of the lotus-eaters living in the light of an eternal afternoon.

5. Galand takes his cue from Campbell, who speaks of "night visitants from the mythological realm that we carry within" (8). Campbell's claim that this realm is the Unconscious erases the distinction between myth and dreams and is incompatible with a cognitive view.

6. In speaking about Odysseus's trip to the Underworld, Tracy calls the journey "a well-established metaphor for the acquisition of self-knowledge" (55). Although general in scope, this is perhaps the best answer we have. Another way to answer the question is to invoke the imperatives of a tradition. Clarke points out that the protagonists of all great myths, Gilgamesh, Odysseus, Theseus,

Heracles, Orpheus, Christ, Aeneas, and Dante and Virgil make the trip to the Underworld. And he adds: "Perhaps, then, it is pointless to talk of why Odysseus goes to the Underworld": "Odysseus goes because all heroes go" (60). Yet Clarke's excellent discussion of this matter (58-60) promotes a strategy which only postpones the question, nudges it to the end of the list.

7. Underlining the differences between "Le Voyage" and Nerval's *Voyage en Orient,* Betz concludes: "Unlike Nerval, Baudelaire's hero will never return home" (406).

8. Ruff offers a religious interpretation. In his view the travelers' "joy" at the end can be explained by "l'espoir de la vie future, «de cette après-midi qui n'a jamais de fin», et où nous retrouverons les êtres aimés . . ." (348).

9. The original: "Faut-il le mettre aux fers, le jeter à la mer, / Ce matelot ivrogne, inventeur d'Amériques" (lines 42-43). In an ironic twist, Columbus, who "invented" America and was at one point brought back to Spain in irons, is assimilated to the profile of a lowly sailor. For another interpretation of the figure of the drunken sailor, see Burton *B. and Republic* 274.

10. In defining the affinity between Baudelaire and Conrad, Putnam points out that both in "Le Voyage" and in *Heart of Darkness,* "Time will be no more chronological than space will prove geographical" (334).

11. Perhaps Poulet goes too far when he concludes that Baudelaire is "incapable of a clear conceptualization of any future whatever" (14). But in quoting "Elévation," Poulet formulates an assessment that should not surprise us: "Thus the elsewhere and the future are above all centrifugal in function; a pure *beyond* (*au-delà*), characterized by the total absence of characteristics" (14).

Works Cited

Adam, Antoine, ed. *Les Fleurs du mal.* By Charles Baudelaire. Paris: Garnier Frères, 1961.

Alighieri, Dante. *The Inferno.* Trans. John Ciardi. New York: Mentor-New American Library, 1954.

Arrowsmith, William, trans. *Orestes. Euripides-IV.* By Euripides. Eds. David Grene and Richmond Lattimore. Chicago: U of Chicago P, 1958.

Austin, L. J. "Baudelaire: Poet or Prophet?" *Studies in Modern French Literature.* Presented to P. Mansell Jones. Eds. L. J. Austin, Garnet Rees, and Eugène Vinaver. Manchester: Manchester UP, 1961. 18-34.

Babuts, Nicolae. "Baudelaire et J. G. F." *Bulletin Baudelairien* 14.2 (1979): 3-6.

Banks, Theodore Howard, trans. *Electra. Four Plays by Sophocles.* New York: Oxford UP, 1966.

Baudelaire, Charles. *Œuvres complètes.* Ed. Claude Pichois (Pléiade). 2 vols. Paris: Gallimard, 1975-76.

———. trans. *Histoires Extraordinaires par Edgar Poe.* Ed. acques Crépet. Paris: Conard, 1932. Vol. 12 of *Œuvres complètes de Charles Baudelaire.*

———. *Petits poëmes en prose.* Ed. Robert Kopp. Paris: Corti, 1969.

Betz, Dorothy M. "Nerval's *Voyage en Orient* and Baudelaire's Imagined Orient." *Romance Quarterly* 38 (1991): 399-406.

Burton, Richard D. E. *Baudelaire in 1859: A Study in the Sources of Poetic Creativity.* Cambridge: Cambridge UP, 1988.

———. *Baudelaire and the Second Republic: Writing and Revolution.* Oxford: Clarendon Press, 1991.

Campbell, Joseph. *The Hero with a Thousand Faces.* Bollingen Series XVII. 2nd ed. Princeton: Princeton UP, 1968.

Clarke, Howard W. *The Art of* The Odyssey. Englewood Cliffs, NJ: Prentice-Hall, 1967.

Crépet, Jacques, ed. *Histoires Extraordinaires par Edgar Poe.* Trans. Charles Baudelaire. Paris: Conard, 1932. Vol. 12 of *Oeuvres complètes de Charles Baudelaire.*

Cuadra, Pablo Antonio. *Songs of Cifar and the Sweet Sea.* New York: Columbia UP, 1979.

De Quincey, Thomas. *Confessions of an English Opium-Eater and Selected Essays.* New York: A. L. Burt, [1856?].

Galand, René. *Baudelaire: Poétique et poésie.* Paris: Nizet, 1969.

Kopp, Robert. *Petits poëmes en prose.* By Charles Baudelaire. Paris: Corti, 1969.

Lattimore, Richmond, trans. *The Odyssey of Homer.* New York: Harper and Row, 1965, 1967.

Leakey, F. W. *Baudelaire and Nature.* Manchester: Manchester UP, 1969.

Pichois, Claude, ed. *Oeuvres complètes.* By Charles Baudelaire. Pléiade ed. 2 vols. Paris: Gallimard, 1975-76.

Pommier, Jean. *Dans les Chemins de Baudelaire.* Paris: Corti, 1945.

Poulet, Georges. *Exploding Poetry: Baudelaire/ Rimbaud.* Trans. Françoise Meltzer. Chicago: U of Chicago P, 1984.

Putnam, Walter C. "Baudelaire's 'Le Voyage' and Conrad's *Heart of Darkness*." *Revue de Littérature Comparée* 63 (1989): 325-39.

Ruff, Marcel A. *L'Esprit du mal et l'esthétique baudelairienne.* Paris: Armand Colin, 1955.

Sandars, N. K. *The Epic of Gilgamesh: An English Version with an Introduction.* New York: Penguin Books-Harmondsworth, 1972.

Tennyson, Alfred Lord. "Ulysses." *Selected Poetry.* Ed. Douglas Bush. New York: Random House, 1951. 88-90.

Tracy, Stephen V. *The Story of* The Odyssey. Princeton: Princeton UP, 1990.

Virgil. *The Aeneid.* Trans. Robert Fitzgerald. New York: Vintage Books-Random House, 1990.

John R. Barberet (essay date 1997)

SOURCE: Barberet, John R. "Baudelaire: Homoérotismes." In *Articulations of Difference: Gender Studies and Writing in French,* edited by Dominique D. Fisher and Lawrence R. Schehr, pp. 52-63. Stanford, Cal.: Stanford University Press, 1997.

[*In the following essay, Barberet examines Baudelaire's use of prostitution as an intermediary of homoerotic love in his poetry.*]

> Lysander: You have her father's love, Demetrius;
> Let me have Hermia's: do you marry him.
>
> —*A Midsummer Night's Dream*

INTRODUCTION

The erotic triangle was never quite as stable as folk wisdom, or for that matter René Girard, would have it: there is always more going on than two men competing for the affections of a woman, each keeping one eye on the other over his shoulder, and the other on the object of their mimetic desire. Since Hegel, this scenario of rivalry, wherein two men stare each other down until one looks away, as in the master/slave dialectic, has encouraged a confrontational notion of homosociality that Girard elevates to a status rivaling passionate love, if not superseding it. Eve Sedgwick, in her critique of Girard in *Between Men* (21-27), points out the "gender assymmetry" implicit in his approach: male homosocial rivalry is not necessarily the same sort of "love" as heterosexual or lesbian "love," a fact that becomes quite obvious once gendered barriers are displaced. Lysander, whose requited love for Hermia is blocked by her father's endorsement of the rival Demetrius, knows this: homoeroticism is one of the trump cards that can be played against the patriarch, and the "truth" of this "love" becomes all the more demystifying when Egeus

unabashedly acknowledges it: "Scornful Lysander! true, he hath my love" (I.i.95). To be sure, where patriarchal domination greatly restricts the mobility of women such a demystification seems to accomplish very little: "And what is mine my love shall render him" (I.1.96). Lysander's remark does, however, add a nuance to the patriarchal control of women by suggesting that a woman can become the vehicle of another's, and specifically a man's, love for another man. What is more, Lysander suggests that the homoeroticism linking the patriarch to his favorite would be more directly and honestly expressed if Hermia no longer served as its mediating linkage, and proposes homosexual marriage as a resolution to the patriarch's intervention into the "eternal triangle." With the rise of relations dominated by the commodity form, more desires are brought into play around the coveted object; and the more rivals there are, the more libidinal economies come into play, and the more connections are established between desiring gazes. Imagine a group of men looking at a woman on a busy street corner, then turning their gazes onto each other in a modernist version of the story of the woman taken in adultery in John 8:1-11.[1] Suddenly, homoeroticism becomes less of a trump card, and more of a generalized situation. A horizon appears wherein the vehicle of desire could be autonomized and homoeroticism could appear unmediated. Let us imagine, then, Baudelaire heading east, towards this, his Orient.

PROSTITUTION AND HOMOEROTICISM

In mid-nineteenth-century France, the body, specifically the urban body, was being configured by the capitalist phenomenon, through the combined effects of manipulations and resistances, to such an extent that the ideological binarisms which held the body in place (production/consumption, self/other, need/desire, male/female) were beginning to be put into play or disrupted. Emergent, experimental selfhoods, including the dandy, the flâneur, and so on, first discovered on the street what utopian socialisms imagined for mankind: a social body, what Baudelaire in **"Les Foules" ["Crowds"]** calls "this universal communion" (1:291).[2] The erotics of this social body appear as fundamentally excessive and transgressive, especially with respect to the heterosexual restriction of eroticism to male/female relations: "what men call love is quite restricted and quite weak, compared to this ineffable orgy" (1:291). As a counterbalance to such a notion of "love," which restricts eroticism to heterosexual partners, Baudelaire's works are infused with homosocial forms of address and a concomitant homoerotics linking the poet to male Others. Whereas, in romanticism, the idealized woman mediated man's relationship to Nature, in Baudelaire's modernism the idealized prostitute mediates man's relationship to urban artifice. The "divine" prostitute is the communicating vessel linking the poet to other men: "The most prostituted of all beings is the ultimate being, God Himself, since for each individual he is the supreme friend; since he is the common, inexhaustible source of love" (***Mon coeur mis à nu*** [***My Heart Laid Bare***] in 1:692). He becomes connected to other men through her, and when she loses this transparency her body becomes problematic, material, "infâme." Thus the nudity of La Fanfarlo becomes disturbing to Samuel Cramer because he can no longer see, through her stage dress, other men seeing her: her unadorned body has become interference, noise.

"Les Foules" initially describes an erotic relationship with both sexes as entertained by the poet's soul in the guise of the prostitute, whereby he identifies erotically (this ability to identify with others is a "privilege" which causes him "jouissance") with her sexual relations with "the passing stranger." The prostitute as figure—or the act of (self-)prostitution as performed under her aegis—facilitates and mediates the narrator's connection to other men, a connection that, despite the close proximity of the crowd, would otherwise involve crossing gendered barriers. Indeed, the men to whom this text is addressed (or at least who are posed as most capable of understanding it), the "founders of colonies, pastors of peoples, missionary priests," are "exiled at the edges of the world" (1:292) and lead a "very chaste life" only with respect to a restricted notion of "love," since they still experience "these mysterious intoxications" which exceed it. The figure of the prostitute is all the more powerfully a mediating one, since it is capable of retrieving their presence and their experiences from the "edges of the world."[3] The figure of the prostitute becomes the localized site of relations between men, much like the intersection of a busy street that is her defining context.

It is through the figure of the prostitute, and more literally through the prostitute's body itself, that men are brought together in what is ultimately a homoerotic situation: through her, they are entertaining homosexual relations with each other, once removed. Yet if the debasement of the prostitute's body (the classic example is Zola's Nana) represents men's denial of this situation while revealing the patriarchal underpinnings of it, the pluralization and universalization of the prostitute's "soul" work to affirm a new form of "love" or "communion" that is more inclusive and polymorphous. Baudelaire's prostitutes are already no longer such because their venality is no longer their defining characteristic: instead, it is their "generosity" and their "charity" that define them, since no money could possibly compensate them for the gift they make of their souls. The prostitute is no longer in Baudelaire the object of an exchange, but the site of an exchange, of a communication that occurs through her: what he obtains from her signifies his connections with other men. Traces of this connection, such as syphilis, acquire a phatic function, linking the client/artist to the public at large: "The

day a young writer corrects his first proof, he is as proud as a schoolboy who has just earned his first syphilitic lesion" (***Mon coeur*** 1:694). The prostitute is the locus of the (male) crowd's self-eroticization because she reflects back to them the intersection of their desires; as Benjamin puts it, "only the mass [of urban inhabitants] makes it possible for the sexual object to become intoxicated with the hundred stimuli which it produces" (57). Much like the prose poem itself, she would have no existence outside of the "frequenting of enormous cities" and the "intersections of their innumerable relationships" (**"Dédicace,"** in *Le Spleen de Paris* 1:276). Literally and figuratively, the prostitute embodies multiple male interpenetrations: she is indistinguishable from her context, the street corner. She is ostensibly a substitute for other women, but also a homoerotic alibi, whose commodified and policed existence places her on the threshold between the enforcement of compulsory heterosexuality and the homophobia inherent in partiarchy. She might vanish (she is already, in Baudelaire, traversed, transcoded, and to a certain extent transcended) once these dogmas—and the ideology that supports them—wither away.

BAUDELAIRE TRAUMATOPHILE

It is to Walter Benjamin, who read ***Les Fleurs du mal*** alongside Freud's *Beyond the Pleasure Principle,* that we owe our understanding of the crucial role that "shock defenses" play in Baudelaire's poetry. Eugene Holland has depicted with great insight the oscillations between an acquiescing vulnerability to shock effects, and the defensive postures intended to repel or absorb them, that regulate Baudelaire's relations to the urban masses. This dual response to urban stimuli bears a striking resemblance to the tension between homoeroticism and the compulsory heterosexuality and homophobia that make of the prostitute a homoerotic alibi. Seen in this light, the prostitute allows the performance of homoeroticism within the constraints imposed by ideology on the performance of gender in particular, and on the social distribution of power among gendered sites in general. In order to think the prostitute in this way, Baudelaire must radically reimagine anatomical differences.

Baudelaire retrospectively advances his theory of anatomy in conjunction with his theory of the "beautiful" in the 1869 version of **"Morale du joujou,"** couching both in semiautobiographical language. The narrator/child is confronted with an expansive mother-figure, the dame Panckoucke, "the toy-fairy" ["la Fée du joujou"], which thrusts his own mother into a restrictive, mediocritizing role whereby the child is forced to accept the "happy middle" instead of his first choice, the "most bizarre toy." Fecund with an array of artificial and imaginary beings who are presumable sexed, yet described in the same gender-neutral terms (e.g. "beautiful costumes, eyes as pure as diamonds, cheeks aglow with makeup" [1:582]) that are characteristic of the descriptions of "la foule"—this expansive mother-figure possesses one unforgettable feature: "I distinctly recall that this woman was dressed in velvet and fur" (581), she is "the lady dressed in velvet and fur" (582). This simple, metonymic displacement of the fur for orifice, the fur being what conceals an orifice, eventually becomes, for "most brats," a desire to "see the soul [voir l'âme]," to open up and to penetrate the body of the other: where do you cut to find the soul? In *Fusées* we find the following: "The precocious taste for women. I confused the smell of fur with the smell of a woman" (1:661). This originary confusion, now presumably a corrected error, seems to state that in actuality the two belong to separate realms: yet read another way, it could mean that the child/narrator had assumed that only women possessed orifices or the promise of an orifice (one may recall this remark from *Le Peintre de la vie moderne*: "Woman is without a doubt . . . an invitation to happiness" [2:714]). This assumption reveals itself to be doubly false: not only is "Celle qui est trop gaie," discussed below, lacking such an orifice, but it will be the poet's goal to open up a multiplicity of orifices in those of both genders who surround him, including the reader. This is, after all, the Poet's motto in **"Les Foules"**: "For him alone, all is vacant" (1:291). The purpose of this "orificealization" is to enter into a communicative and erotic relationship to the other—and, thanks to his epidermal sensitivity and the bustling crowds, the wounder is also wounded in turn, in the act of wounding, thereby completing the communicative circuit or, as described in **"Les Foules,"** ultimately creating a "universal orgy" (1:291). The fact that all this bears a resemblance to the transmission of syphilis should be kept in mind, especially because Baudelaire brings it up himself in the one poem most clearly devoted to this wounding, **"A celle qui est trop gaie"** [**"To One Who Is Too Cheerful"**]. This poem describes the urbanization of a woman who is initially described, in the first two stanzas, as too closely tied to nature's attributes:

> Ta tête, ton geste, ton air
> Sont beaux comme un beau paysage;
> Le rire joue en ton visage
> Comme un vent frais dans un ciel clair.
>
> Le passant chagrin que tu frôles
> Est ébloui par la santé
> Qui jaillit comme une clarté
> De tes bras et de tes épaules.
>
> Your head, your air, your every way
> Are scenic as the countryside;
> The smile plays on your lips and eyes
> Like fresh winds on a cloudless day.
>
> The gloomy drudge, brushed by your charms
> Is dazzled by the vibrancy
> That flashes forth so brilliantly

Out of your shoulders and your arms.

(1:156)

The final three stanzas depict one of the most violent agendas of *Les Fleurs du mal*:

> Ainsi je voudrais, une nuit,
> Quand l'heure des voluptés sonne,
> Vers les trésors de ta personne,
> Comme un lâche, ramper sans bruit,
>
> Pour châtier ta chair joyeuse,
> Pour meurtrir ton sein pardonné,
> Et faire à ton flanc étonné
> Une blessure large et creuse,
>
> Et, vertigineuse douceur!
> A travers ces lèvres nouvelles,
> Plus éclatantes et plus belles,
> T'infuser mon venin, ma soeur!
>
> So I would wish, when you're asleep,
> The time for sensuality,
> Towards your body's treasury
> Silently, stealthily to creep,
>
> To bruise your ever-tender breast,
> And carve in your astonished side
> An injury both deep and wide,
> to chastize your too-joyous flesh.
>
> And, sweetness that you dizzy me!
> In these lips so red and new
> My sister, I have made for you,
> To slip my venom, lovingly!

(157)

Ultimately, however, and despite the title, **"A celle qui est trop gaie"** was not (to be) addressed to a woman at all, but instead to a group of presumably male judges, as the reader learns in the "note" included in the *Epaves*:

> The judges believed they discovered a meaning both bloody and obscene in the last two stanzas. The seriousness of the Anthology excludes such *jokes*. The possibility that *venom* might signify spleen or melancholy was too simple an idea for these criminalists.
>
> May their syphilitic interpretation remain on their conscience. (*Publisher's note.*)

(1:157)[4]

This addendum compels a radical rereading of the poem, which is henceforth inserted in a circuit linking a fictional "éditeur" to a group of judges, who saw in this poem "an assault on public morality." The reader is invited to judge the judges, while the "éditeur" stands in for both the prosecutor, with the judges as defendants, and the defending attorney, with the poet as defendant. Thus the original address to/of the woman turns out to be—and/or to have been—a series of addresses to many men, which is the figure of the homoerotic alibi. It is according to a chiasmus (that figure which presents two parallel structures while reversing one of them, creating a kind of intersection or street-corner which, as it were, is the locus of the prostitute) that the "injury both deep and wide" is made: for just as "the gloomy drudge, brushed by your charms / is dazzled," so the next stranger who brushes up against her will be rendered melancholic by the "spleen" she now carries within her body. This "melancholy" arises from the "bad faith" implicit in the channeling of homoeroticism through a woman's body. The mediating figure of the prostitute appears as the emblem of this homoerotic detour: the humiliating path the poet takes toward the "body's treasury" retraces the "stealthy" or cowardly ("comme un lâche [like a coward]") passage through the money-form that this mediation entails.

Inflicting a wound, "une plaie" is indeed one of the dominant modes of interpersonal communication in *Les Fleurs du mal* and especially in *Le Spleen de Paris*: examples abound, but the theme of vampirism in the collection is especially deserving of the kind of analysis I am proposing. And whereas the curious child in **"Morale du joujou"** is disappointed by the end result of the wounding procedure ("Here lie the beginnings of stupor and sadness" [1:587]) because nothing is communicated to other bodies, the narrator of **"A celle qui est trop gaie"** is overjoyed to have attained his goal: "Et, vertigineuse douceur! / A travers ces lèvres nouvelles /. . . . / T'infuser mon venin, ma soeur!" (1:157). It is the knowledge that his "venom" will be distributed to other passers-by who brush up against her that causes his delight. Heightened epidermal sensitivity is a prerequisite to this kind of communicative agenda, which must bypass "traditional" erogenous zones in favor of those that can be stimulated by the more discrete bodily encounters that occur among a crowd. Indeed, the poet, as it turns out, is remarkably well-prepared to carry out this program, because his masculinity was tempered by the world of women, because he has become "androgynous" and "complete," because he received a special initiation into sensitivity:

> Indeed, men who have been brought up by women and among women do not completely resemble other men . . . the soothing rocking of the wetnurse, maternal caresses, the playful attentions of sisters, especially older sisters, those diminutive mothers, all transform by kneading, as it were, the masculine dough. The man who, from his earliest infancy, was bathed in the soft atmosphere of woman . . . thereby contracted an epidermal sensitivity and a distinctive inflection, a kind of androgyny, without which the most trenchant and virile genius will remain, with respect to artistic perfection, an incomplete being.
>
> (*Un mangeur d'opium,* **"Chagrins d'enfance,"** 1:499)

It is this "epidermal sensitivity" which characterizes the poet, be it Baudelaire, Thomas de Quincey, or Edgar Allan Poe, because this heightened sensitivity makes their wounding all the easier; the fact that this sensitivity is "contracted" from women, from the *mundi muliebris,* reveals the interpersonal and therefore "contagious" nature of erotic stances—and, further, that the stances most valuable to the Poet are those that happen (due to ideological and social constraints) to be situated under the rubric "femme" at this point in time (Wing 19-40). In a significant parallel to the role of the prostitute as communicating vessel between men, this passage describes how a man must pass through or undergo a certain feminization in order to attain the heightened sensitivity required to experience the homoerotics of the urban crowd.

THE HOMOEROTICIZATION OF EVERYDAY LIFE

Yet such a "sensitivity" can exist apart from or beyond its feminine origins, as is revealed by the excesses of hashish intoxication. In **"Du vin et du hachisch [On Wine and Hashish]"** (1851), the state of "kief" provokes a return to a Sadean erotics of multiplicity, which the narrator calls "a frenzied libertinage": "In this supreme state, love, for gentle and artistic minds, takes the most unusual forms and lends itself to the most baroque combinations" (1:394-95). In the version of 1860, however, this heightened sensitivity produces a more social and urban eroticism, and serves to reveal an everyday, habitually repressed homoeroticism:

> I will simply beg the reader to consider to what extent the imagination of a sensitive man, intoxicated with hashish, is extended to a prodigious degree . . . and his senses honed to a point just as difficult to define. It is thus possible to believe that a simple caress of the most innocent kind, a handshake for example, can have its value multiplied a hundredfold by the current state of the soul and the senses, and can lead them perhaps, and very quickly, to that swoon considered by vulgar mortals to be the apogee of happiness.
>
> (1:433)

Baudelaire's definition (at the fantasy level) of intense erotic experience is clearly moving beyond the erotic yet enclosed world of Sadean combination, into the more generalized erotics of the crowd as expressed in the smallest of gestures, such as brushing up against someone, or shaking someone's hand.

Paneroticism is the erotics of the crowd, although Sade described it first as the erotics of the interpersonal *combinatoire* discussed by Roland Barthes (*Sade* 33). The *combinatoire* is the sum total—if this totality can ever be reached—of the possible interpenetrations available to a human being given an admittedly limited number of orifices and/or coupling appendages (not to mention the erotic detachment of the voyeur, or the use of tools such as the whip). Sade, in his defense of sodomy, mocked those who would seek to establish a hierarchy among the bodily orifices according to which some would be "pure" and others "soiled." As Sade writes in *La Philosophie dans le boudoir*: "What crime is there in this? Surely it is not that of placing oneself in such and such a place, unless one wants to claim that all parts of the body do not resemble each other, and that some are pure while others are soiled; but . . . it is impossible to propose such absurdities" (232).

Charles Fourier, the utopian who actually read Sade, also advocated radical sexual exploration ("the exception is just as useful as the norm"), arguing that "culture cannot function according to the laws of attraction if there are not . . . all kinds of loves [des amours de tout genre]" (27-28; 203). Fourier announced an eventual "libéralisme amoureux," and even suggested that children receive an education in voluptuousness—much like the one Baudelaire, Poe, and de Quincey share—to prepare them for furthering the permutations of such a "combinatoire." Such an education would aim to "methodically refine the passions so as to render them more disposed to sample the innumerable pleasures which the new social order will offer" (43). Thus it would seem that Baudelaire is (re)enacting Fourier's program (or, as it were, taking it to the streets) in his description of the poet's childhood eroticism, as well as through his exploration of hashish effects. Yet it should be clear that, for this program to be realized, urban homoeroticism must eventually dispense with recourse to the prostitute as homoerotic alibi in favor of the more direct anatomical permutations of the Sadean combinatoire. The following anecdote, which reflects the performative nature of Baudelaire's homoeroticism and which can be read as a commentary on the erotics of the handshake, describes one way to "walk away" from the scene of prostitution:

> The brown-skinned Jeanne did not limit herself to Baudelaire's company. She had even been seen dancing at a public ball with a stranger, and leaving with another stranger.
>
> These events were brought to the attention of her lover, who merely observed, with a sigh:
>
> —Poor girl! That's her job. She has to make a living.
>
> Shortly thereafter, the same friend who brought the news to him, and received this response, overheard Baudelaire presenting himself as a man of strong passions, and ventured:
>
> —But wait! when I told you that Jeanne was carrying on . . .
>
> Baudelaire cut him off.
>
> —You see, I know how to contain myself. Listen up! and you'll see. I know how to contain myself so well, that the other night, as I prepared to enter Jeanne's apartment, as I was about to put the key into the lock, here's what I did when I heard two voices, one of which I knew to be Jeanne's, and one belonging to a man . . . Jeanne was with someone . . . Do you understand? with someone . . . Well! . . . I had the courage . . . to leave!

> And the poet, grabbing the hand of his friend, gave it a heartfelt squeeze, with an emotion he seemed willing to share.

(Maillou 139-40 quoted in Bandy and Pichois 121)

Written by a man for a presumably male audience, this anecdote involves three male characters, in addition to the poet himself, and of course the prostitute (and Baudelaire's mistress) Jeanne Duval. We should note the paradoxical inclusion of two "premiers-venus" (literally, "first-comers") which suggests that there are more in the wings, or perhaps that the "friend" could have been one of them. The "ami" is, in any case, standing in for one of these "premiers venus" when he receives Baudelaire's warm handshake, which could just as well be given to the "other man" himself. This handshake is the bodily performance of the inner "courage" displayed by the poet who has managed to overcome the notion of the male Other as usurper of his "property": it acknowledges his reconciliation with male Others, with whom he can now "bond" directly without the intermediary and facilitating figure of the prostitute. In fact, he owes his ability to share his emotions with other men to the prostitute's ability to share her "love" with the "premier venu." It is in this manner that the poet internalizes the prostitute's availability: she has caused Baudelaire to share a strong emotion with another man, and through him with the many "premiers venus" that brush up against him every day in the crowd. The handshake connects two men in a homoerotic gesture all the more powerful because it is no longer blocked by the body of the prostitute. And if "la clef" never makes it into "la serrure," it is because Baudelaire has chosen to remain outside, in the crowd, where there are no locks because "tout est vacant."

POSTSCRIPT

Baudelaire's homoeroticism is closely tied to his attitude toward women who stand out, as it were, from the crowd: prostitutes, actresses, and lesbians. Marcel Proust noted the important role of the latter in *Les Fleurs du mal*; in a conversation with André Gide, recorded by the same in his *Journal*, Proust draws the following conclusions:

> He spoke of his conviction that Baudelaire was a uranist. "The way he speaks about Lesbos, and even the very need to speak of it, would alone suffice to convince me," and since I protested:
>
> "In any case, if he was a uranist, it was almost without his knowing it; and you can't believe that he ever practiced . . ."
>
> "Say what!" he exclaimed. "I am convinced of the contrary; how can you doubt that he practiced? He, Baudelaire!"
>
> And, from the sound of his voice, it seemed that by doubting I was attacking Baudelaire. But I'm willing to believe that he is right, and that uranists are even more numerous than I had thought.

(Gide, *Journal* 692)

Like Baudelaire, Proust has difficulty detaching a generalized and autonomized homoeroticism from its insertion in a mediating scenario involving women who are (posed as) the objects of a male gaze. Baudelaire's lesbians are, of course, more than that: Hippolyte, one of the "Femmes Damnées" in the poem of the same title, describes herself as ontologically evacuated: "Je sens s'élargir dans mon être / Un abîme béant; cet abîme est mon coeur! [I can feel, widening in my being, a gaping abyss; this abyss is my heart]" (1:154). And the narrator of the poem concludes with an apostrophe to them: "Et fuyez l'infini que vous portez en vous! [Flee the infinite that you carry within!]" (155). Even in Proust's and Gide's time, an intermediary and facilitating figure, coded as a vacant, ghostlike alibi, still stands in the way (and in the place) of such a generalized ("more numerous") homoeroticism.

Notes

1. The reference is to the story of the woman taken in adultery, which the New English Bible gives as John 7:53-8:11. As Tony Tanner shows in his discussion of this New Testament account (18-24), Jesus "disperses the social stare that petrifies the wrong-doer" (22). It is but a short leap from this primal scene—already no longer primal, since the original scene presumably resulted in stoning—to the scene of prostitution: etymologically, the prostitute stands out in the marketplace, just as the adultress is "set in their midst" (John 8:3).

2. With the exception of "A celle qui est trop gaie," translated by James McGowan, all translations are my own.

3. Although I am indebted to Nathaniel Wing's discussion (*Limits of Narrative,* 39-40) of this prose poem, which he argues "is about those libidinal exchanges which disrupt opposition," I am suggesting that the prostitute is both a disruptive and a recuperative (or mediating) figure with respect to male others.

4. "A celle qui est trop gaie" was one of the six poems condemned for "outrage à la morale publique" in Baudelaire's trial on these charges in 1857. The "Publisher's note" was actually written by Baudelaire himself, and was appended to the poem when it was included in *Epaves* in 1866.

Works Cited

Bandy, W. T. and Claude Pichois, eds. *Baudelaire devant ses contemporains.* Paris: Editions du Rocher, 1957.

Barthes, Roland. *Sade, Fourier, Loyola.* Paris: Seuil, 1971.

Baudelaire, Charles. *The Flowers of Evil.* Trans. James McGowan. Intro. Jonathan Culler. Oxford: Oxford University Press, 1993.

———. *Oeuvres complétes.* Paris: Gallimard (Pléiade), 1975. 2 vols.

———. *Correspondence.* Paris: Gallimard (Pléiade), 1973.

Baudrillard, Jean. *De la séduction.* Paris: Galilée, 1977.

———. *Oublier Foucault.* Paris: Galilée, 1977.

———. *Les Stratégie fatales.* Paris: Grasset, 1983.

———. *Le Systéme des objets.* Paris: Grasset, 1983.

———. *La Transparence du Mal. Essai sur les phénomèmes extrêmes.* Paris: Galilée, 1990.

Benjamin, Walter. *Charles Baudelaire: A Lyric Poet in the Era of High Capitalism.* London: Verso, 1983.

Fourier, Charles. *Vers la liberté en amour.* Ed. Daniel Guérin. Paris: Gallimard, 1975.

Gide, André. *Journal (1889-1939).* Paris: Gallimard [Pléiade], 1959 [1951].

Sedgwick, Eve Kosofsky. *Between Men: English Literature and Male Homosocial Desire.* New York: Columbia University Press, 1985.

Tanner, Tony. *Adultery in the Novel: Contract and Transgression.* Baltimore: The Johns Hopkins University Press, 1979.

Wing, Nathaniel. *The Limits of Narrative: Essays on Baudelaire, Flaubert, Rimbaud and Mallarmé.* Cambridge: Cambridge University Press, 1986.

James R. Lawler (essay date 1997)

SOURCE: Lawler, James R. "Conclusion." In *Poetry and Moral Dialectic: Baudelaire's "Secret Architecture,"* pp. 173-81. London: Associated University Presses, 1997.

[*In the following essay, Lawler discusses the overarching structure and themes of Baudelaire's poetry, concluding that the individual poems are shaped through a dialectic of contrast.*]

In a letter dated 1 January 1861, barely a month before the publication of the second edition of **Les Fleurs du mal,** Baudelaire told his mother that he had just finished reading the final proofs: "Pour la première fois de ma vie je suis presque content. Le livre est *presque bien.*"[1] The plan allowed for the possibility of adding still further poems, and he continued to work with a view to a third edition in the way that would also be that of Marcel Proust: for him, as for Proust, art and life were consubstantial. Fifteen poems were collected in 1866 under the title "Nouvelles Fleurs du mal," while the posthumous edition of 1868 comprises one hundred and fifty-one poems (excluding the unnumbered **"Au lecteur"**) instead of the one hundred and twenty-six of 1861. The pity is that the order was established without Baudelaire's guidance so that the new pieces appear in haphazard fashion. If we are grateful for splendid additions such as **"Recueillement," "Le Gouffre,"** and **"L'Examen de minuit,"** the elegance of the original conception is lost. The second edition remains his book.

The method is admirably suited to his ends. It enables him to combine regularity with nonuniformity. Baudelaire, Georges Poulet once observed, is the most mathematically intuitive of the great French poets,[2] and he takes the measure of his own sensibility from one end to the other of *Les Fleurs du mal.* By his arrangement he establishes an urgent insistence, like a heartbeat, that combines mathematics and music—"chaque mouvement du rythme marquant un mouvement de votre âme, chaque note se transformant en mot."[3] Each poem offers an aspect of the subsection to which it belongs, and stands in tension with the poems that accompany it; at the same time, each subsection has a role in the large Pythagorean plan. Numbers are beautifully exact—"childlike" as Baudelaire says—and recur over and again. On the other hand, monotony is avoided in an entirely effective way. Baudelaire does not underline the pattern by subheadings or typographical ploys; he presents the book in sections of different lengths that appear at first sight to give the lie to order. Exceptionally diverse, the prosodic forms modulate traditional schemes, remake styles and tones. There are critics who have reproached him for his indebtedness to the past, but one of the most striking virtues of his art is his ability to pastiche the individual manners of sixteenth-, seventeenth-, eighteenth-, and nineteenth-century French poets, as well as medieval Latin, English (Shakespeare, Gray, Byron), and American (Longfellow, Poe) authors like so many voices heard and answered. Though we understand that in a sense all writers respond to a predecessor with each of the works they write, nothing of the scope of this self-aware multiple utilization of the tradition had previously occurred in French lyricism. Baudelaire shows prodigious intertextual virtuosity that surprises the reader at every turn, while yet adhering to the sustaining numbers of his work.

I would also point to what seems to me a second paradox of this arrangement: the impetus is sure, but nonlinear. Birth at the beginning ("Lorsque, par un décret des puissances suprêmes, / Le Poète apparaît . . .") and death at the end ("O Mort, vieux capitaine . . .") anchor the "history" of one man, which is the potential history of all in its moral breadth. **"Spleen et Idéal"** espouses the ternary movement of vocation, love, destiny—"mon irrémédiable existence," Baudelaire elsewhere calls it[4]—which concludes with time's ironic victory; **"Tableaux parisiens"** breaks with this solitude, yet finds collective existence generating an analo-

gous "history" and leading to dark resignation; the four shorter parts, no less directed towards a goal through wine, lust, revolt, advance to the ultimate recognition of mortality. The progression thus merits the importance Baudelaire gave to the notions of "commencement," "fin," "histoire," "suite." Yet we need to emphasize that this is no ordinary line, since it has regular countermoves that qualify it. I think of **"Le Vin,"** in which a dream paradise seems to be won; likewise, **"Révolte,"** which dismisses **"Fleurs du mal"** with the pride of a soul that will not bow to shame. These two sections signal dramatic reversals, but we know that they are not isolated cases. From start to finish the book inscribes a complex dialectical series in a manner that reminds us of the Portuguese proverb relished by Claudel: "Deus escreve direito por linhas tortas" [God writes straight with curved lines]. Exclusion takes issue with election, self-indulgence with selfless desire, nontranscendence with transcendence in this sequence of a man who must proceed by way of constant negations. He stands in the company of the great moralists.

. . . . .

Some readers will no doubt be reluctant to accept the interpretation I have advanced. They may not give credence to Baudelaire's statement that he wrote his poems to fit a frame (we recall: "Tous les poèmes nouveaux ont été faits pour être adaptés à un cadre singulier que j'avais choisi");[5] they may feel that the evidence has been weighted with respect to my readings; they may judge that I have put before them a poet they do not, or cannot, recognize. My own conviction, which I would of course wish to share, is that this poet-philosopher is still greater than we believed and that he traces a marvelous unitary scheme.

Can further testimony be adduced? I think of famous occasions, in particular in the *Journaux intimes,* when duality shows itself to be the poet's prime epistemological instrument in a parallel way to its use in *Les Fleurs du mal.* The remarks concern subjects that range from the poet himself ("Tout enfant, j'ai senti dans mon cœur deux sentiments contradictoires, l'horreur de la vie et l'extase de la vie")[6] to all mankind ("Il y a dans tout homme, à toute heure, deux postulations simultanées, l'une vers Dieu, l'autre vers Satan").[7] Feeling, thought: the sweep is wide. An observation on the rule of complementary forces ("Car il y a des choses dans l'homme qui se fortifient et prospèrent à mesure que d'autres se délicatisent et s'amoindrissent . . .")[8] is pithily echoed with respect to sexual powers ("Plus l'homme cultive les arts, moins il bande");[9] a general comment on extreme emotional states ("Cruauté et volupté, sensations identiques comme l'extrême chaud et l'extrême froid")[10] resurfaces provocatively in personal terms ("Il serait peut-être doux d'être alternativement victime et bourreau");[11] an aphorism on self-contradiction as a mode of learning ("Apprendre c'est se contredire")[12] recurs subversively on a concrete level that covers many a sociopolitical and moral issue ("Je comprends qu'on déserte une cause pour savoir ce qu'on éprouvera à en servir une autre").[13] Truth can only be understood in its full implications by way of its opposite (Baudelaire quotes with admiration a sentence he ascribes to the minor nineteenth century novelist Adolphe de Custine: "[I]l y a un degré de conséquence qui n'est qu'à la portée du mensonge");[14] literature must similarly incorporate polar elements ("Deux qualités littéraires fondamentales: surnaturalisme et ironie");[15] the thinker and poet must balance immersion in sensibility on the one hand, volition on the other ("De la vaporisation et de la centralisation du Moi. Tout est là").[16] Marvelously, over and again, negation guides reflection.

Readers can perhaps agree in general terms, but there are those who do not admit that Baudelaire applied such an approach in a creative and methodical fashion to the structure of his book. As we have seen, some give exceptional emphasis to disorder inasmuch as they are more than content with a random arrangement and maintain that the poet had neither the desire, nor the will, nor perhaps the capacity to order his poems. To respond to these comments I wish to point to a feature that seems to me pertinent to the discussion. *Le Spleen de Paris* has been held by commentators, with greater unanimity even than *Les Fleurs du mal,* to be an omnium-gatherum collection. Baudelaire, however, spoke of it in terms that suggest the reverse, claiming self-awareness ("le résultat d'une grande concentration d'esprit"),[17] taking pride in calculation ("j'espere que je réussirai à produire un ouvrage singulier, plus singulier, plus volontaire du moins que *Les Fleurs du mal*").[18] His aim, as he told it, was to represent the melancholy of a man wandering through the streets of Paris whose observations are bound to his reverie, his reverie to his philosophy, his philosophy to his dreams, his dreams to his anecdotes. An 1865 letter to his mother provides a definition of the project: "[J]'associerai l'effrayant avec le bouffon et même la tendresse avec la haine."[19] In conformity with the law of contrasts, he formulates the idea of *Le Spleen de Paris* by emphasizing the "association" of contradictory states. I cannot but think of the interpretation I have here sought to advance for *Les Fleurs du mal*; and Baudelaire himself points to the interconnectedness of his two books, even as he underscores the larger freedoms of the prose: "En somme, c'est encore *Les Fleurs du mal,* mais avec beaucoup plus de liberté, et de détail, et de raillerie."[20]

In the standard critical edition Robert Kopp uses the term "aleatory" to describe the order of *Le Spleen de Paris.*[21] Yet we know that Baudelaire drew up a list of fifty titles that was faithfully respected when the original posthumous edition appeared. We also remember his prefatory letter to Arsène Houssaye, which speaks of a sequence of a special kind: there is no novelistic

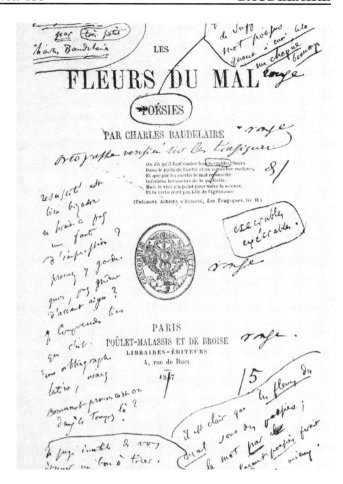

A page of corrections to the title page from Les fleurs du mal, *1857.*

plot and no organic unity—"Enlevez une vertèbre, et les deux morceaux de cette tortueuse fantaisie se rejoindront sans peine. Hachez-la en nombreux fragments et vous verrez que chacun peut exister à part"[22]—though the pieces are part of a single project. His statement is as assured as it is tantalizing: "Mon cher ami, je vous envoie un petit ouvrage dont on ne pourrait pas dire, sans injustice, qu'il n'a ni queue ni tête, puisque tout, au contraire, y est à la fois tête et queue, alternativement et réciproquement."[23] I find the indication that duality has been observed and that, if a piece or section were taken away, the antagonisms would continue to operate.

It would require more pages than I have at my disposal to argue the case with appropriate care, but I wish to sketch out the extraordinary solution Baudelaire appears to me to have found. I think it useful at least to outline the case, since it may throw additional light on *Les Fleurs du mal.* For I would suggest that the prose poems are not fortuitously placed but obey the simplest of patterns—not threes or fives or a combination of each, but abrupt twos in which one text plays directly off the other by a sudden turn of the screw or a twist of the ka-leidoscope (the two images are Baudelaire's). Tail an-swers head, head answers tail: the pairings seem to me compelling.

Thus we read the two opening poems together. "L'Etranger" is a dialogue with a man unable to sub-mit to the ordinary ways of the world—conventions of family, friends, beauty, financial gain—who seeks the fugitive wonder he glimpses in the clouds: "J'aime les nuages . . . les nuages qui passent . . . là-bas . . . là-bas . . . les merveilleux nuages!"[24] The word "aimer," which occurs four times in this short prose poem, sig-nals a love forever dissatisfied with the world and obliged to look beyond. The second piece, "Le Dés-espoir de la vieille," is an abrasive variation on the same theme: love is impossible for the old woman who would wish to caress an infant, but the infant is afraid and cries out loudly so that the hag must return to her loneliness. She frightens those she loves ("nous faisons horreur aux petits enfants que nous voulons aimer").[25] The literary kind changes from dialogue to anecdote, but we are held by the pathetic connection/disconnection of the twin faces of desire. Read together, the pieces enrich each other by the ironies of language, tone, atti-tude—the first, otherworldly aspiration sighed rather than proclaimed, the second, a narrative of the thirst for human affection that will "eternally" be frustrated.

The second two pieces form a similar pair. "Le *Confit-eor* de l'artiste" adopts the manner of a dramatic mono-logue that proceeds in four graduated paragraphs from the poet's initial delight in contemplating a sunset to climactic suffering and despair: he will be vanquished by the very ideal he has chosen ("L'étude du Beau est un duel où l'artiste crie de frayeur avant d'être vaincu").[26] The other text also treats beauty, though in a mode gratingly different: "Le Plaisant" is an anecdote concerning a dandy who pokes fun at an ass and thereby encapsulates the inglorious vulgarity of French wit. The lines are bitter irony aimed at intellectual smugness that does not realize its own ridicule. The dandy is "un beau monsieur ganté, verni, cruellement cravaté et empris-onné dans des habits tout neufs"; he is "ce beau plai-sant," "ce magnifique imbécile."[27] No longer the artist's high yet tragic goal, beauty is trivialized by a falsely sophisticated public, reduced to a ludicrous caricature of itself in the shape of a fool lovely in his eyes alone. We read unfathomable wryness in the self-qualifying interaction of the two texts.

The law of contrasts continues to unfold. After love and beauty, the third group is devoted to the poet's destiny. "La Chambre double" puts before us his room of dreams in which harmony, voluptuousness, and eternity reside but which, in a moment, reveals itself to be nau-seous reality. "Cette vie suprême" of the ideal is fol-lowed by "la Vie, l'insupportable, l'implacable Vie":[28]

existence is both ideal and spleen like the two-pronged goad ("double aigillon") that pricks the bullock, or this textual diptych. The companion piece is allegory: "Cha-cun sa chimère" depicts several men bent under the charge of chimeras who advance in ignorance of their destination. They do not protest or despair but ironi-cally, as if hopeful, march past the poet, who soon yields to the same fatal chimera of unthinking indifference. The key to the enigma is only half-revealed, since man-kind chooses not to look at life; nor does the poet take full cognizance of his own destiny, and that of others, as damnation. In the first poem the shock of dream and reality is conveyed in emotional terms; in the second the tragic dimension opens vistas that are not pursued, like an essential question unceasingly deferred. Suffer-ing becomes a habit we no longer question, let alone contest. Each piece, in gravely conflictual—that is, self-qualifying—terms, problematizes each.

Poems VII and VIII turn on the notion of art in a paral-lel way. "Le Fou et la Vénus" is composed in the two parts of rhapsody and plaint: first, the idyllic evocation of a park in which pools, light, flowers, and perfumes form a pervasive voluptuousness, then the lament of a solitary clown who implores a statuesque Venus to al-low him to feel and understand beauty. But Venus has marble eyes . . . The emblem is that of the artist alien-ated and scorned who nonetheless sacrifices his all to a transcendent ideal. Counterfoil to this portrait, "Le Chien et le Flacon" proposes a sarcastic epigram: the poet lets his dog sniff a costly perfume, which it dis-dains, and he concludes that the dog resembles the pub-lic that wants excrement rather than perfumes. A noble conception is linked to a vulgar one: art is both the most demanding of loves and—as interpreted by the crowd—bad taste. Duality enables the endless subver-sion of ideal by spleen, spleen by ideal.

So, following the order of the book, we go from pair to pair. We encounter next perhaps the most famous of all French prose poems which nevertheless gains splen-didly, I believe, when considered with its accompany-ing piece. "Le Mauvais Vitrier" and "A une heure du matin" explore two faces of evil, the former by a medi-tation, the second by an examination of conscience. "Il y a des natures purement contemplatives et tout à fait impropres à l'action qui cependant . . . ," we read.[29] Baudelaire first adopts the abstract style of a philoso-pher to present his theme of perversity, just as Poe, his model in this page, so frequently does. ("The mental features discoursed of as the analytical, are, in them-selves, but little susceptible of analysis" is the opening sentence of "The Murders in the Rue Morgue.") In the first half he puts the paradox of those who suddenly act in a demonic fashion that nothing in their characters seems to prepare or justify; in the second, he recounts his surge of inexplicable hatred for a passing glazier, and his subsequent shattering of the man's panes of glass. He concludes defiantly without sorrow or guilt: "Mais qu'importe l'éternité de la damnation à qui a trouvé dans une seconde l'infini de la jouissance?"[30] Sadism is flaunted. But **"A une heure du matin"** gives voice to an entirely opposite—indeed, I take it, purposely antagonistic—attitude. The poet finds refuge in the darkness of his home at the end of the day. He recalls his experiences in the past hours—the silliness of other men, his own hypocrisy, his self-contradictions, his pettiness. He prays for the help of those he has loved so as to gain new strength; he prays to God that he be allowed to write some poetry by which to redeem himself in his own eyes. The two pieces summon us to take them together by reason of a treatment that qualifies crime by repentance and satanic bravado by prayer, telling the tensions of mad pride and countervailing humility.

Thus the first ten poems of *Le Spleen de Paris* are arranged in this regular fashion by which the poet cuts against the grain of his every attitude. I shall not labor the point but underline, by a final example, what appears to me to constitute the observance of the rule from one end to the other of the fifty pieces. For this purpose I shall turn to **"Un Hemisphère dans une chevelure"** and **"L'Invitation au voyage"** (Poems XVII and XVIII), both of which have frequently been commented on for their own sakes as well as for the reflections they inspire when placed alongside the parallel verse treatments in *Les Fleurs du mal.* Yet interaction imposes itself, since each text asks to be read with and against the other. Not only do they bring the correspondingly titled verse poems into question, as Barbara Johnson finely showed,[31] but they make us hold in mind the immediately contrasting treatments of the identical motif of dream. The first takes the form of an intimate request by which the poet begs the woman to allow him to pursue his erotic reverie. He is not the artist of **"La Chevelure"** who wills his way ("J'irai là-bas . . .") but a voluptuary ("Laisse-moi respirer longtemps, longtemps . . .")[32] who, if he has difficulty in finding the exact words for sensual pleasure ("Si tu pouvais savoir tout ce que je vois! tout ce que je sens! tout ce que j'entends dans tes cheveux! . . ."),[33] realizes that his dream contains everything he cherishes. He abandons himself to analogies—the waltz of Weber's "Invitation to the Dance," the voyage of his own title—that allow him to glimpse rather than see, to savor rather than analyze, to receive rich mnemonic and submnemonic associations carried on the tips of his senses rather than bestow jewels as he does in **"La Chevelure."** On the other hand, **"L'Invitation au Voyage"** plays with dreams in a mode we cannot confuse with that of the companion piece. No longer a voluptuary, the poet discourses: his beloved is a "vieille amie," a "cher ange" to whom he speaks without amorous intensity, his vision of a far-off land is "honest," his manner passionless; he prizes middle-class clichés more than

fresh metaphors ("Un vrai pays de Cocagne, te dis-je, où tout est riche, propre et luisant, comme une belle conscience, comme une splendide orfèvrerie, comme une bijouterie bariolée).[34] When he speaks of the country of dream he uses the conditional tense because, though he understands he should set out ("il faudrait aller"), he will not. The notion of any future departure is undercut by doubt ("Vivrons-nous jamais, passerons-nous jamais . . . ?"),[35] then turned into a voyage already over. He becomes an allegorist whose imagination loses all force of action ("c'est toi," "c'est encore toi," "ce sont mes pensées," "ce sont encore mes pensées enrichies")—indeed, dissolves its own amorous dream.[36] The emotional commitment of the first piece ("Tes cheveux contiennent tout un rêve . . .") is answered by the emotional detachment of the second ("Des rêves! toujours des rêves! . . .").[37] In this way, the two pieces establish the dialogue of poeticity and prosiness, the one critical of the other, neither triumphant.

Baudelaire tells us he had planned to write the description of life—*one* life—as led in the modern city, but found himself unable to carry out his plan. To think of *Le Spleen de Paris* as a succession of isolated vignettes like the poems of Aloÿsius Bertrand's *Gaspard de la Nuit* would be, he suggests, to go astray. What he did was "singularly different." I take it that he was brought, as if despite himself, to write his poems according to the principle of negation and thereby to make his every theme the occasion for testing the same against the other. Whether he deals with love, art, destiny, beauty, perversity, dream, or any other of his successive motifs, he changes the simple into the complex, the univocal into the dialogical, by his regular homologous pairing of adversarial points of view.

The order may be reversed, for it is not progression that matters but interface: the pieces may be either head or tail, "alternately and reciprocally." Yet those of us who take up the volume in a sequential manner cannot, I think, fail to be sensitive to the connections/disconnections to which the poet commits himself, even if we may at first not fully grasp the precise corrosive pattern at work.[38]

. . . . .

Thus *Les Fleurs du mal* and *Le Spleen de Paris* correspond by a parallel application of the law of contrasts. The special achievement of the book of poems becomes, nevertheless, all the more apparent with respect to the disjunctions of the prose. Dualities in the verse run their course interconnectedly from beginning to end: the argument is not reversible but asks to be understood as dialectical sequence. Baudelaire writes a work as diverse as it is unitary, its dissonances reaching towards a consonance, its mathematics towards an overarching criticism of life. The part supposes the whole; evil implies the good; the satanic poet, ever the naysayer of himself, is God's workman. Such an art of composition, pursued in its large design, is a responsible act, and the poet could not fail to appreciate the bitter irony of this most compellingly moral of books being accused of public outrage.

We are tempted to refer to the interpretations of *Les Fleurs du mal* proposed by two of the most influential French writers of the last fifty years. It is difficult to forget the impact of Jean-Paul Sartre's *Baudelaire,* which was the existentialist study of a man guilty of choosing his own unhappiness. Sartre held that life was not unjust to Baudelaire but that Baudelaire himself opted for a somber destiny: "Et s'il avait mérité sa vie?" Again: "[C]ette vie misérable qui nous paraissait aller à vau-l'eau, nous comprenons à présent qu'il l'a tissée avec soin . . . nous chercherions en vain une circonstance dont il ne soit pleinement et lucidement responsable."[39] He could not but come up short in all he undertook, be it life, love, work; he deliberately gave a demonstration of what he claimed to be his predestined ill luck. Sartre's essay was answered by Georges Bataille in *La Littérature et le Mal.* Bataille did not question Baudelaire's "failure" but considered it to be inherent in a project that expresses the fascination of evil. The poetry of Baudelaire, like the line of French poetry that was his heritage from symbolism to surrealism, was marked by spiritual dispersion and final dissolution. Bataille concluded: "La poésie de Baudelaire, elle-même, est dépassée: la contradiction d'un refus du Bien (d'une valeur ordonnée par le souci de la durée) et d'une œuvre durable engagea la poésie sur une voie de décomposition rapide, où elle se conçut, de plus en plus négativement, comme un parfait silence de la volonté."[40] Both Sartre and Bataille found that Baudelaire's life and work bore witness to a failure of the will—chosen in Sartre, accepted in Bataille—though the poet wrested an aesthetic trophy from the ashes. But *Les Fleurs du mal,* as I would hope to have shown, is the attempt to exhaust the question of evil by an engagement of the will, which pits knowledge against desire in order to write a "negative morality." I see Baudelaire then, not only as the poet of the most piercing cry of suffering humanity, nor as the master of a new sensibility and a new critical intelligence in poetry, nor as the wonderful virtuoso of a multitude of literary styles, but as the creator of a unique, superbly exigent dialectic. The struggle subsumes his matter from end to end. He gauges his destiny to achieve the whole truth of his book, which is its terrible beauty.

Notes

1. Baudelaire, *Correspondance,* 2:114: "For the first time in my life I am almost happy. The book is *almost right.*"

2. Georges Poulet, *La Poésie éclatée* (Paris: Presses Universitaires de France, 1980), p. 41: "De tous les poètes français, Baudelaire est peut-être celui qui au plus haut degré a l'intuition du dynamisme numéral qui ne cesse de se manifester dans le moindre mouvement" [Of all French poets Baudelaire is perhaps the one who, in the highest degree, has the intuition of the numerical dynamism that ceaselessly manifests itself in the slightest movement]. Number is Baudelaire's means of living with the vertigo of thought, just as Being, affirmed in voice, image, form, enables him to live with the void. As he writes in a late sonnet: "Ah! ne jamais sortir des Nombres et des Etres!" [Ah! never to leave Numbers and Beings!] ("Le Gouffre"). Thus would he achieve ontological sense by his book.

3. Baudelaire, "Le poème du hachisch," 1:431: "each rhythmic movement beating a movement of your soul, each note changing into a word."

4. Baudelaire, "Le *Confiteor* de l'artiste," in *Œuvres complètes,* 1:278: "my irremediable life."

5. "All the new poems were written to fit a curious frame I had chosen."

6. Baudelaire, "Mon cœur mis a nu," 1:703: "As a small child, I felt in my heart two contradictory feelings, the horror of life and the ecstasy of life."

7. Ibid., p. 683: "In every man, at every moment, there are two simultaneous postulates, one in favor of God, the other, Satan."

8. Baudelaire, "Fusées," 1:667: "For there are in man some things that strengthen and prosper while others languish and waste away."

9. Baudelaire, "Mon cœur mis a nu," 1:702: "The more man cultivates the arts, the less he gets the big stick."

10. Ibid.: "Cruelty and enjoyment, identical sensations like extreme heat and extreme cold."

11. Ibid., p. 683: "It would perhaps be pleasant to be alternately victim and hangman."

12. Baudelaire, "Aphorismes," in *Œuvres complètes,* 1:710: "To learn is to contradict oneself."

13. Baudelaire, "Mon cœur mis a nu," 1:676: "I understand a man who gives up one cause to know what he will feel by serving another."

14. Baudelaire, "Aphorismes," 1:710: "There is a degree of consequence that can be attained only by a lie."

15. Baudelaire, "Fusées," 1:659: "Two fundamental literary qualities: supernaturalism and irony."

16. Baudelaire, "Mon cœur mis a nu," 1:676: "Concerning the vaporization and centralization of the *Self.* That is everything."

17. Baudelaire, *Correspondance*, 1:473: "the result of great mental concentration."

18. Ibid.: "I hope that I shall succeed in producing a curious work, more curious, at least more willed, than *Les Fleurs du mal.*"

19. Ibid.: "I shall combine terror with buffoonery, and even tenderness with hatred." Baudelaire uses the word "disagreeable" to describe the morality of *Le Spleen de Paris* ("une morale désagréable," *Correspondance*, 2:583) in contrast to the "terrible" morality of *Les Fleurs du mal.*

20. Baudelaire, *Correspondance*, 1:615: "It is once again *Les Fleurs du mal*, but with much more freedom both of details and of raillery."

21. Robert Kopp, *Petits Poèmes en prose* (Paris: José Corti, 1969), p. lxiii. I do not wish to hide the fact that my approach to *Le Spleen de Paris* will appear to some critics no less contentious than my reading of *Les Fleurs du mal.* I advance it nonetheless as my response to Baudelaire's letter to Houssaye but, above all, as my considered interpretation of the series of prose poems. For further recent discussion, see A. W. Raitt, "On *Le Spleen de Paris*," *Nineteenth Century French Studies* 18, nos. 1-2 (fall-winter): 1989-90, pp. 151-64; James Hiddleston, "'Chacun son spleen': Some Observations on Baudelaire's Prose Poems," *Modern Language Review* 86, pt. 1 (January 1991): 66-69 ("as late as February 1866 Baudelaire . . . intended its order to be random . . ."); and, in particular, the book-length study by Edward K. Kaplan, *Baudelaire's Prose Poems: The Esthetic, the Ethical, and the Religious* (Athens: University of Georgia Press, 1990).

22. Baudelaire, "A Arsène Houssaye," in *Œuvres complètes*, 1:275: "Take away a vertebra and the two pieces of this tortuous fantasy will easily join up again. Chop it into numerous fragments and you will see that each can exist separately."

23. Ibid.: "My friend, I am sending you a small book, which could not be said to have neither head nor tail since everything in it is, on the contrary, tail and head at one and the same time, alternately and reciprocally."

24. "I love the clouds . . . the passing clouds . . . yonder . . . yonder . . . the marvelous clouds."

25. "[W]e horrify the little children we want to love."

26. "The study of the Beautiful is a duel in which the artist shrieks with fright before being vanquished."

27. "[A] fine gentleman gloved, varnished, cruelly cravated and imprisoned in brand-new clothes," "this gorgeous jester," "this magnificent fool."

28. "That supreme life," "Life, unbearable, implacable Life."

29. "There are purely contemplative natures quite unfit for action that nonetheless . . ."

30. "But what does eternity matter to the man who has found infinite delight in a moment?"

31. Barbara Johnson, *Défigurations du langage poétique* (Paris: Flammarion, 1979); also idem, *The Critical Difference* (Baltimore: Johns Hopkins University Press, 1980).

32. "Let me breathe at leisure, at leisure . . ."

33. "If you could know all I see! all I feel! all I hear in your hair! . . ."

34. "A true land of plenty, I tell you, where everything is rich, clean and shining like a clear conscience, splendid gold plate, multicolored jewelry."

35. "Shall we ever live, shall we ever enter . . ."

36. "[I]t is you," "it is again you," "these are my thoughts," "these are again my thoughts enriched."

37. "Your hair contains an entire dream," "Dreams! always dreams!"

38. Baudelaire does not "resolve" contradictory impulses so much as posit them; tensions deepen rather than disappear. I think of Valéry: "La conscience sort des ténèbres, en vit, s'en alimente, et enfin les régénère, et plus épaisses, par les questions mêmes qu'elle se pose, en vertu et en raison directe de sa lucidité" [Consciousness emerges from the shadows, lives on them, feeds on them and finally regenerates them still denser than before through the very questions it puts to itself by virtue of its lucidity and as a direct consequence of that lucidity] ("Choses tues," in *Œuvres complètes*, 2:497). Let me illustrate, one last brief time, the fruitfulness of this process in *Le Spleen de Paris.* In *Donner le temps* Jacques Derrida has recently dissected the subtleties of truth and falseness as he finds them in the twenty-eighth poem, "La Fausse Monnaie." Yet cannot we say that this prose poem becomes still more luminously subversive when read with its accompanying text, the twenty-seventh in the series, "Une Mort héroïque"? In the latter the Prince causes the death of his page Fancioulle out of satanic rancor: feeling himself overwhelmed by Fancioulle's success, or humiliated, or frustrated, or rebuffed—the alternatives are set before us—he avenges himself knowingly, purposely. "La Fausse Monnaie," on the other hand, recounts what may be termed a crime of counterfeit morality. The poet's friend gives a bad coin to a beggar while naively think-

ing that he will be considered charitable sub specie aeternitatis—in the eyes of God—by reason of this gift. Where the Prince carries out murder, the friend commits his petty moral crime self-deceptively, from blind silliness. Nothing could be more characteristic of Baudelaire than that his narrator should find more moral merit in the Prince than in the friend. He sums up the meaning of his two poems when taken together: "On n'est jamais excusable d'être méchant, mais il y a quelque mérite à savoir qu'on l'est; et le plus irréparable des vices est de faire le mal par bêtise" [One can never be excused for being wicked, but there is some merit in knowing that one is; and the most irreparable of vices is to do evil out of stupidity]. "Une Mort héroïque" and "La Fausse Monnaie," by their joint resources, open limitless fields for reflection on the nature of evil.

39. Jean-Paul Sartre, *Baudelaire* (Paris: Gallimard, 1947), p. 18: "And what if he had deserved the life he led?"; pp. 223-24: "We now understand that this miserable life, which seemed to us to be a failure, was carefully woven by him . . . We would vainly seek any circumstance for which he was not fully and lucidly responsible."

40. Georges Bataille, *La Littérature et le Mal* (Paris: Gallimard, 1957), p. 68: "Baudelaire's poetry itself is outmoded: the contradiction between a refusal of the Good (the refusal of a value commanded by care for duration) and a durable artwork steered poetry into a path of swift decomposition where it conceived itself, ever more negatively, as a perfect silence of the will." The remark would need to be contested not only with respect to Baudelaire but also many more recent poets. Not, however, as regards the surrealists. Bataille was of the generation of René Char who, when he came of age, could not but reject surrealism in a similar way to Bataille: "Onze hivers tu auras renoncé au quantième de l'espérance, à la respiration de ton fer rouge, en d'atroces performances psychiques" [For eleven winters you will have forsworn your daily share of hope, the respiration of your red-hot iron, in frightful psychic exploits] (*Œuvres complètes*, p. 145). Char and Yves Bonnefoy, the two greatest French poets of the second half of the twentieth century, have both reached back beyond the surrealism of their youths to Baudelaire. For Char Baudelaire was a vital Aquarius, for Bonnefoy the exemplary poet of incarnation. Must we not feel, at the end of our reading of *Les Fleurs du mal*, that Bonnefoy's words go to the heart and soul of the book? "La vérité de parole," he writes, "est au-delà de toute formule. Elle est la vie de l'esprit, et non plus décrite mais en acte" [The truth of the word is beyond any formula. It is the life of the spirit, no longer described but enacted] (*L'Improbable et autres essais,* p. 31).

Select Bibliography

Bataille, Georges. *La Littérature et le Mal.* Paris: Gallimard, 1957.

Baudelaire, Charles. *Correspondance.* Edited by Claude Pichois and Jean Ziegler. Bibliothèque de la Pléiade. 2 vols. Paris: Corti, 1949.

———. *Journmaux intimes: Fusées, Mon cœur mis á nu, Carnet.* Edited by Jacques Crépet and Georges Blin. Paris: Corti, 1949.

———. *Les Fluers du mal.* Edited by Jacques Crépet and Georges Blin. Paris: Corti, 1942.

———. *Les Fluers du mal.* Edited by Max Milner. Paris: Imprimerie Nationale, 1976.

———. *Œuvres complétes.* Edited by Claude Pichois. Bibliothèque de la Pléiade. 2 vols. Paris: Gallimard, 1975-76.

———. *Œuvres complétes.* Edited by Jacques Crépet. 15 vols. Paris: Conrad, 1922-48.

———. *Petits Poèmes en prose.* Edited by Robert Kopp. Paris: Corti, 1969.

Derrida, Jacques. *Donner le temps.* Paris: Galilée, 1991.

Johnson, Barbara. *The Critical Difference: Essays in the Contemporary Rhetoric of Reading.* Baltimore: Johns Hopkins University Press, 1980.

———. *Défigurations du langage poétique: La seconde révolution baudelairienne.* Paris: Flammarion, 1979.

Poulet, Georges. *La Poésie éclatée.* Paris: Press Universitaires de France, 1980.

Sartre, Jean-Paul. *Baudelaire.* Paris: Gallimard, 1947.

Timothy Raser (essay date spring-summer 1998)

SOURCE: Raser, Timothy. "The Politics of Art Criticism: Baudelaire's *Exposition universelle*." *Nineteenth-Century French Studies* 26, nos. 3-4 (spring-summer 1998): 336-45.

[*In the following essay, Raser asserts that Baudelaire's art criticism should be regarded as a political endeavor as well as critical commentary.*]

It would be hard to imagine a discourse more removed from politics than art criticism: the contemplation of works of art, the impartial consideration of disinterested representations of beauty, the disinterested evaluation of such representations, everything that makes æsthetic discourse æsthetic also brings it away from politics. Except one thing: æsthetic judgments, at least according to Kant, make a claim to universal validity, but are also unable to advance reasons or concepts in support of this claim. The result, as Kant so delicately put it, is that judges, and with them art critics, must sometimes "put up with a rude dismissal of [their] claim to universal validity" (54). Within art criticism's very aim lies thus the distinct possibility of conflict, and rude conflict at that. Further, because æsthetic judgments cannot be argued, they cannot be verified, and thus art criticism looks a bit more like politics than it did at first glance.

A case in point is Baudelaire's art criticism. On the personal level, this writing represented a refuge from the attacks the poet felt he was enduring, and a freedom from the constraints that, beginning with the nomination of Narcisse Ancelle as his *conseil judiciaire,* he had to accept (Raser, "Traumatic Origins" 192). This does not preclude the possibility that art criticism might be political: indeed, the political dimension of art criticism would have been attractive to someone who had effectively become a minor in the eyes of the law, and in art criticism Baudelaire could engage in politics even if he couldn't do so in other arenas.

But from 1846 on, Baudelaire made a point of antagonizing his readers, addressing them directly and mocking the things they believed in. Such attacks are a characteristic feature of his art criticism, but are not limited to that form: his introductory **"Au Lecteur"** from *Les Fleurs du mal* is a case in point. In his art criticism, of course, these attacks are sustained, reasoned, and supported with argument and example. More often than not, an example of bourgeois belief—progress, free trade, high art—is held up to ridicule, while the readers, who in all probability firmly hold that belief, writhe uncomfortably in their seats. This tendency was first noted by Walter Benjamin regarding *Les Fleurs du mal,* who asked why a poet would deliberately set out to conquer an un-poetic audience (155). Its presence in art criticism, especially the *Salon de 1846* has also been noted, by David Carrier (3-5) among others (e.g., Kelley 331), but in each case, the question asked is ethical: was it prudent of Baudelaire to address such remarks to such people? I'd like to suggest that these remarks might not have been deliberate at all, but a necessary by-product of the art-critical essay, whose ideological component has not undergone systematic analysis.

Let me take the example of the three articles written in May of 1855, and collected in the 1868 edition of Baudelaire's works under the title *Exposition universelle.* From the outset, this essay was political and controversial. Its blunt and sustained opposition of Delacroix and Ingres, praising the former and mocking the latter is already quite polemical, but when one consid-

ers that Ingres, Commander of the Legion of Honor, ex-vice president of the École des Beaux-Arts (1849), ex-president of the École des Beaux-Arts (1850), was to be named Grand Officer of the Legion of Honor on the occasion of the Exposition, Baudelaire seems to be courting disaster. Such, at least, was the judgment of the editors of *Le Pays* in the Spring of 1855, who, having accepted to publish the chapter entitled "Méthode de critique" and the one on Delacroix, declined to publish the chapter on Ingres, fearing perhaps some kind of backlash. Even the editors of *Le Portefeuille,* where the rejected chapter was finally published, thought it best to preface the article with a disingenuous disavowal qualifying Baudelaire's harsh judgments as "une appréciation si ingénieuse et si modérée des œuvres de M. Ingres" (Baudelaire 2: 1372). This polemic could be dismissed as an Œdipal antagonism of a very particular father-figure, and thus not political, but other features of the essay support the claim that politics is at its heart. The pairing of Ingres and Delacroix is just one of several such oppositions. Victor Hugo is discredited while Edgar Allan Poe is praised; a nameless *professeur-juré* (who doubtless designates Victor Cousin)[1] is cast aside as the model of criticism, while an anecdote about the "naïve" Honoré de Balzac is put forward as "une excellente leçon de critique" (2: 579). If the "Exposition" was nominally intended to celebrate the "progress" of the nineteenth century, what Baudelaire finds to admire is not progress, but art. If Ingres, Hugo, Cousin, and "progress" represent something that could be called the French "ideology," Baudelaire is all-too-clearly rejecting that ideology by a sustained series of oppositions where each champion of French culture is compared unfavorably to a contender. As literature is added to painting, and æsthetics to literature, as progress too comes under fire, it becomes evident that Baudelaire's target is not an individual, however august he might be, but a more general state of affairs, and with that, his essay becomes political.

The politics of the essay were implied by the exposition itself: a response to the 1851 exposition in London, its organizers claimed that Paris could rival and surpass London, France could match or exceed England in the fields important to such national rivalries.[2] At the same time, it was a "universal" exposition, nominally inviting for impartial consideration all the nations of the world to show off their cultures and products (Trapp 300). Baudelaire takes up this dual ambition and makes it his: on the one hand, the essay is oppositional and polemical, while on the other, the theme of harmony, derived from the "universal" ambition of the exposition, comes back repeatedly.

The exposition was initiated in a decree of March 8, 1853, in which Napoleon III called for a universal exposition of industrial products (*Rapport* 170). Three months later, the Emperor attached to the industrial exposition an exposition of the fine arts, and did so by delaying the Salon of 1854 until the following year; he justified this course by invoking French industry's special debt to the arts: ". . . il appartient spécialement à la France, dont l'industrie doit tant aux beaux-arts, de leur assigner, dans la prochaine Exposition universelle, la place qu'ils méritent" (*Rapport* 171).

As the May 1st (then 15th) opening day approached, the exposition grew larger, occupying several buildings and outdoor areas at the foot of the Champs-Élysées. Accommodation appeared to be the *leitmotif*: visitors were not required to leave their canes or umbrellas at the entry; there were wheelchairs for those unable to walk; there were reading rooms, tobacanists, telegraph offices, and post offices. Within the Palais de l'Industrie, there was a primitive air-conditioning system (disliked by Prince Napoleon [*Rapport* 64]) as well as fire hydrants. Nurses were stationed on hand in case of need, and the police were instructed to be pleasant, informed, and forbidden to take tips (*Rapport* 66-74). Prices could be displayed, provided they were displayed openly, and provided they were the true price (*Rapport* 185). And prohibited products (*marchandises prohibées*) could be displayed and even sold, just this once, provided a 20% duty was paid (*Rapport* 187). An entry fee structure was devised in order to promote maximum attendance by all strata of society: 1 Fr. on Monday, Tuesday, Wednesday, Thursday, and Saturday; 5 Frs. on Friday, and 0 Fr. 20 on Sunday. The much-criticized Friday fee was reduced to 2 Frs. on August 1. Further, special arrangements with the railways combined the price of rail travel and exposition tickets. 5 million people visited the Exposition over its six-month existence: 4 million went to the Palais de l'Industrie; 1 million went to the Palais des Beaux-arts (*Rapport* 87). According to Prince Napoleon, three-quarters of a million of these visitors came from outside of Paris just to see the exposition. Universality was the goal: people from all countries, of all classes, of all kinds came to the show to see all the products of civilization.

Within the Palais des Beaux-Arts, universality was also the order of the day: artists from all countries were invited to show their works; certain (living) artists were invited to show works of theirs from their entire careers, thus inaugurating retrospective shows. Here, I point out that the very conception of retrospective shows was ideological, arising from the desire to impose a certain interpretation on the career of an artist (Jensen 113-7). Further, awards were based on the works shown, without regard to nationality or to prior success or failure: "Toute considération d'origine ou de nationalité, *tout souvenir de récompenses antérieures,* doivent être écartés par les juges du *concours universel* ouvert en ce moment" (*Catalogue* LVII).

These decrees and decisions, made at the highest level of government, amount to an ideology of the 1855 Ex-

position. All will be invited; all will be welcome; efforts will be made to facilitate exposition and viewing by all; all will coexist, for the duration of the exposition, in an atmosphere of peace, tolerance, and mutual respect. Foreign and French, artists and manufacturers, the high and the low will live together in harmony in the summer of 1855.

This ideology finds an echo in the *Figaro,* which two years later was to lead the government to bring charges against Baudelaire for the offence given by his *Fleurs du mal* to public morality. In the Spring and Summer of 1855, Louis Énault wrote a series of articles on the exposition, largely dedicated to its most famous French painters: Ingres, Decamps, and Vernet. Énault admires the construction of the Exposition even more than Prince Napoleon, and insists at length on the numbers of countries, artists, and types of objects present. He depicts the Palais des Beaux-Arts as a refuge from the more crowded Palais de l'Industrie, one where the productions of different nations co-exist in peace and harmony.

Like the official account of the exposition, Énault's articles compare the *Exposition universelle* to its precursor. His comparison is largely quantitative: the buildings' dimensions, the number of their windows, their columns, the square footage of the entire exposition are all listed and compared to those of the Crystal Palace. The result: the Crystal Palace was indeed bigger (74,318 square meters vs. 50,011), but only for the main building. When annexes are taken into account, the Paris exposition (117,000 square meters) surpassed its predecessor. Interestingly, the French surpassed the English by eschewing a proposal to cover the Champs Élysées with a glass roof, and instead to develop multiple buildings, one of which was dedicated to the fine arts: the *Palais des Beaux-Arts.* ". . . on voulait, par-dessus les arbres des Champs-Élysées, jeter un dôme de verre et de fer qui se serait arrondi en absides immenses d'un côté, près de l'avenue d'Autin, et de l'autre sur la place de la Concorde, non loin des piliers où se cabrent les chevaux de Coustou. On a reculé devant cette grandeur sublime . . ." (Énault, 4/15/55, p. 1). In other words, and according to a man fascinated by numbers, the French exposition achieved universality not by size ("grandeur sublime"), but by other principles: inclusiveness (of all nations, more equitably represented; of all visitors[3]), variety (of products exposed), durability (the French exposition is made of "monuments durables", not "les tentes d'un jour"). Religious metaphors permeate the descriptions of the buildings' architecture (*transcept, abside, chapelle,* etc.) (Énault, 6/3/55, p. 6). It surpassed the English exposition because it represented time, not just space (a historical perspective of works of arts), more human accomplishments (art, not just industry),[4] and more countries (not just France and England). While the creature comforts of the exposition are mentioned (air-conditioning, fire protection, and so forth), its most considerable novelty is its postal service, allowing visitors to be contacted and to contact their countries. According to Énault, the "universality" of the show permitted it to go beyond the materialism of its predecessor, and to become spiritual, religious, or just more human. And this ideology was lasting: even eighty years later, Raymond Isnay used the same language to qualify the exposition: "L'ensemble formait un salon, tel qu'on n'en avait vu jamais encore: un salon sans frontières historiques ni limites géographiques; un salon qui, par sa vaste envergure, par le succès qu'il obtint, par le bruit qu'il suscita, contribua à rehausser, dans une société matérialiste, le prestige des valeurs esthétiques" (63).

In the *Journal des Débats,* the response to the Exposition was still more ingratiating: "Non, l'industrie, quoiqu'elle s'exerce sur la matière, n'est point d'essence matérielle. Elle relève de la noble partie de l'esprit humain." (Chevalier, 5/15/55 p. 3). But five months later, the *Journal* published an article by Ernest Renan criticizing the exposition for its lack of "poetry": "Comment une réunion d'hommes qui autrefois, et même à des époques très rapprochées de nous, eût été couronnée d'une auréole de poésie a-t-elle passé sans rien dire à l'imagination et sans produire une strophe digne de mémoire?" (Renan, 11/27/55, p. 3) Renan argues that industrialized society has produced greater comfort for the greatest number, but the price of that progress has been a feminization of society and an acceptance of mediocrity in the arts. In this strange article, Renan claims that the privations of ancient Athens and the Italy of the Renaissance were compensated by the artistic excellence of the periods; in China, by contrast, he asserts, conspicuous technological advancement was always accompanied by artistic mediocrity. So doing, Renan proves the existence of an ideology of the exposition, one that he thought it necessary to combat.

The tenets of this ideology can be summed up thus: 1) all can live at peace and in harmony; 2) art is as necessary as industry to that harmony; 3) the arts thus require a special attention; 4) the display of all such works, industrial or artistic is beneficial to the spectators and the producers, for 5) rivalry brings out the best in man; 6) tolerance of cultural differences is more beneficial than condemnation.

It was in this context of near-universal admiration for the Universal exposition that Baudelaire published his three articles, and, characteristically, Baudelaire sought to differentiate his offering from those of the exposition's admiring journalists and self-congratulating officials. After a cursory appreciation of cultural differences, Baudelaire launches into an attack of one of the very premises of the exposition: the value of progress. The more salient features of the discussion have been

treated elsewhere; I only point out that Baudelaire is criticizing the notion of progress as such, as well as its embodiment in the culture of the Second Empire. On the one hand, the steam power, electricity, and gaslight that are used to document progress fail to demonstrate that society has "progressed" since earlier times, while on the other, the very notion of progress is, Baudelaire claims in a line anticipating Renan, a celebration of decadence and decline: ". . . les races amoindries . . . s'endormiront sur l'oreiller da la fatalité dans le sommeil radoteur de la décrépitude" (2: 580). Against progress, Baudelaire proposes the notion of art, where each creator begins with a clean slate, not benefitting from earlier works, owning no debt to a precursor.

What is surprising here is that Baudelaire's account of the Exposition, deliberately provocative as it is, still shares the main lines of its argument with Second-Empire ideology. Baudelaire's condemnation of doctrinal beauty, his opposition of art and progress, his elevation of tradition at the expense of novelty, are all fundamental theses in his argument, and are also at home in the government's *Catalogue* and *Rapport* or such journalistic accounts as Énault's.

To take the notion of doctrinal beauty: Baudelaire opposes the professor of æsthetics to the explorer, asking who is better suited to perceive "beauty." Presumably, the former judges by references to rules and models, inherited, learned, memorized; the latter doesn't even judge, but explores, discovers, and is agreeably surprised by unexpected beauty. Such an argment fits perfectly within the discourse of universality avanced by Énault: the opening of the exposition to the products of more nations, the lessening of English and French domination of the exposition, both presuppose the potential value of unacknowledged forms of art and industry and the need for an alternative to a doctrinal approach. While Prince Napoleon and Énault didn't by any means condemn academic juries or praise the explorer as Baudelaire did, nor did they extend their appreciation to the countries of the Orient, they nevertheless articulated a principle of openness that is also found in Baudelaire.[5]

Or to take the question of progress: certainly Baudelaire's denunciation of progress is one of the most celebrated passages of the article, famous both for its argument (that "progress" is merely another name for age) and for its hyperbole ("ce fanal obscur," etc.). Baudelaire also denounces a culture that celebrates its superiority while neglecting all changes but those in the standard of living, praising electricity, gaslight, sewers, and so forth while forgetting moral stagnation. Here too, Énault, and with him, official France, went before Baudelaire in the very conception of the exposition, which deliberately included art where the Crystal Palace did not, which deliberately provided a retrospective view, while the 1851 exposition insisted on the most modern manifestations of progress. Implicit in the conception of the 1855 exposition was an appreciation of art and tradition which lacked in London.

The notion of rivalry was also strongly apparent: comparisons with the Crystal Palace exposition abound, making it clear that the Second Empire wanted to outdo the earlier show. But within the exposition, rivalries also were cultivated, the most notable being the extensive space given to retrospective exhibitions of the works of Ingres and Delacroix, inviting the usual comparisons of classical and romantic art, of linear and colorist painting. Both painters were awarded medals of honor, but Ingres was promoted to the rank of *Grand Officier* in the *Légion d'Honneur.*

Baudelaire is thus developing and amplifying a position articulated by the Second Empire, while disavowing its origin. Further, he attributes to the Second Empire positions that were not in fact its own, far simpler than those voiced in *Le Figaro.* He is expressing an ideology, that ideology is borrowed, and all the while he claims that the lender's ideology is not his. The phenomenon is something like projection in psychoanalysis, where an unrecognized, repressed impulse is attributed to another, in whom it is seen as a grotesque caricature.

This relation of unacknowedged debt to official ideology is nowhere more apparent than in the poem **"Les Phares,"** published in 1857, and a stanza of which was added by Baudelaire to his article on the *Exposition universelle.* I point out that one of the items on display at the *Exposition* was a full-sized lighthouse (Énault, **Le Figaro,** 4/30/55)[6] and that the ideology of progress so vehemently denounced by Baudelaire in his article is qualified there as a "fanal obscur, invention du philosophisme actuel, . . . cette lanterne moderne jette des ténèbres sur tous les objets de la connaissance" (2: 580). The poem postulates a relay structure in its account of artistic genius, where each great artist owes a debt to a precursor, and sends a message that will be retransmitted by a successor, in an infinite series. Each artist builds on the work of another, and others still will build on his, transmitting a message that will arrive, eventually, at eternity or God. Art is thus incremental, small steps taken after other small steps, in a metaphor identical to that of progress. And yet, in 1855, in the very article where a stanza of **"Les Phares"** was later placed, Baudelaire argued the exact opposite: the great artist owes nothing to anyone: "Transportée dans l'ordre de l'imagination, l'idée du progrès . . . se dresse avec une absurdité gigantesque, une grotesquerie qui monte jusqu'à l'épouvantable. . . . Dans l'ordre poétique et artistique, tout révélateur a rarement un précurseur. Toute floraison est spontanée, individuelle . . . L'artiste

ne relève que de lui-même. Il ne promet aux siècles à venir que ses propres œuvres. Il ne cautionne que lui-même. Il meurt sans enfants" (2: 581). In other words, in order to write the admiring poem **"Les Phares,"** Baudelaire uses an argument he rejected elsewhere, and not simply rejected, but rejected in the most explicit terms, and not simply does he use it later, but he uses it in the most complimentary terms. Further, having done so, he inserts a fragment of his poem in the article, as if the two expressed the same idea. It would be hard to imagine a clearer sharing of a denied, yet common property, or a more explicit repudiation of a shared trait.

The choice of artists for inclusion in **"Les Phares"** is also at odds with the principles evoked in the *Exposition universelle* article: if the critic was an explorer of the American prairies, or a traveller to China, the poet of **"Les Phares"** does nothing more venturesome than to go to the Louvre: the names of the artists evoked are strictly canonical, recognized artists, hardly exemplary of the aphorism "le beau est toujours *bizarre.*"

The very movement of the poem is illustrative of what has happened in the æsthetic experience: comprised of thirteen stanzas, the poem moves from visual imagery (its first eight stanzas are "medallions" (Prévost) evoking images of individual artists's works) to verbal imagery (in its last stanzas, the artists direct a message towards God or eternity). In the ninth stanza, the preceding eight stanzas are reduced to epithets, as if ten pictures were worth one or two words: introduced by plural demonstratives, the artists' works are labelled "ces blasphèmes, ces *Te deum*," etc. The list of eight epithets is in turn assimilated to single words: "sont un cri" or "un ordre." It's as if in order to carry further, the message had to be made louder or stronger, and this could only be done at the expense of simplification (Raser, *Poetics* 129-31). This simplification is exactly what happens when an ideology is promulgated: complex states of affairs (e.g., æsthetic experiences) become simple slogans; descriptions become orders; differences become similarities, and æsthetic appreciation becomes political ideology.

I'd like to summarize my argument by repeating that Baudelaire's art criticism (and by extension, art criticism more generally), is political, not a-political. It becomes political because æsthetic judgments, which cannot be justified, nonetheless demand justification, and before this double-bind, critics must choose when they have no choice. What they choose is ideology. This is dramatically the case for Baudelaire, who, in his article denouncing the ideology of the *Exposition universelle,* unconsciously avails himself of the Exposition's ideology, and, failing to recognize the beliefs he shares with the authorities he attacks, simultaneously ascribes beliefs to them that they nowhere state. This misprision continues within Baudelaire's own poetry, where in **"Les Phares,"** itself a by-product of the Exposition, he avails himself of the ideology he attacked so vehemently two years earlier. Art criticism needs ideology to support its æsthetic judgments, but needs only to state that ideology in order to feel compelled to disavow it.

Notes

1. The facts that the judge is a professor, that he professes æsthetics, that he possesses a doctrine of the "beautiful" all point to Victor Cousin, Professor at the Sorbonne, and author of *Du Vrai, du beau et du bien.*

2. Prince Napoleon, *Président de la Commission,* stated at the inauguration of the Exposition that he had followed the model of the 1851 exposition (*Rapport* 400). Raymond Isnay goes even further, saying that the *Exposition Universelle* was above all else an expression of ideology: "L'Exposition de 1855 reflète . . . toute l'*idéologie* du temps" (12).

3. Isnay points out that beyond the democratic price structure of admission tickets, the official desire of inviting all possible visitors to the Exposition went so far as to impress soldiers of the Paris garrisons to attend (23).

4. As if to illustrate the theme of universality, Énault published an article on April 22 on Courbet, whose one-man show was located next to the Palais des Beaux-Arts: even those not invited are included.

5. One should not apply late twentieth-century standards of multi-culturalism to the *Exposition universelle* of 1855: its "universality" was confined resolutely to the countries of the first world. The spaces that Énault enumerates, for example, were allocated to France, England, the German states, Austria, Belgium, Spain, Portugal, Switzerland, Sardinia, Italy and the United States. The official catalogue lists 10,691 exhibits from France, Algeria, and French colonies; the rest of the world contributed 10,148. The European countries contributed the bulk of this number, but there were, for example, 6 exhibits from Argentina, 4 from Brazil, 6 from Egypt, 7 from Guatemala, 5 from Hawaii, and 107 from Mexico. With the publication of the Supplement, these numbers increased significantly, many entries, from France as well as from other continents, arriving after the March 15th deadline set by the Commission Impériale (*Rapport* 52).

6. Class IX, Section 8 of the exposition was devoted to "phares, signaux et télégraphes aériens," (*Rapport* 283); this class was dominated by the French (325 expositions) and the British (57 expositions) (445).

Works Cited

Baudelaire, Charles. *Œuvres complètes.* 2 vols. Ed. Claude Pichois. Bibliothèque de la Pléiade. Paris: Gallimard, 1975-6.

Benjamin, Walter. *Illuminations.* Harry Zohn, trans. New York: Schoken Books, 1969.

Carrier, David. "The Style of the Argument in Baudelaire's 'Salon de 1846.'" *Romance Quarterly* 41.1 (Winter, 1994): 3-14.

Chevalier, Michel. "Exposition universelle." *Le Journal des Débats* May 15, 1855.

Énault, Louis. "Exposition universelle." *Le Figaro* April 14, April 22, May 6, May 27, June 3, June 10, and June 17, 1855.

Isnay, Raymond. *Panorama des Expositions universelles.* Paris: Gallimard, 1937.

Jensen, Robert. *Marketing Modernism* in fin-de-siècle *Europe.* Princeton: Princeton UP, 1994.

Kant, Immanuel. *The Critique of Judgement.* Trans. James Creed Meredith. New York: Oxford UP, 1952.

Kelley, David. "Deux Aspects du *Salon de 1846* de Baudelaire: La dédicace et la couleur." *Forum for Modern Language Studies* 5.4 (October 1969): 331-46.

Littré, Émile. *Dictionnaire de la langue française.* 7 vols. Paris: Gallimard/Hachette, 1967.

Paris, Ville de. *Exposition des produits de l'industrie de toutes nations. 1855, Catalogue officiel publié par ordre de la Commission Impériale.* Paris: Imprimerie Impériale, 1855.

Prévost, Jean. Baudelaire: *Essai sur l'inspiration et la création poétiques.* Paris: Mercure de France, 1953.

Raser, Timothy. *A Poetics of Art Criticism: The Case of Baudelaire.* Chapel Hill: North Carolina Studies in the Romance Languages and Literatures, 1989.

———. "The Traumatic Origins of Baudelaire's Poetics: Criticism out of Crisis." *Nineteenth-Century French Studies* 20.1-2 (Fall-Winter, 1992): 187-95.

Renan, Ernest. "La Poésie de l'exposition." *Le Journal des Débats* November 27, 1855, 3.

S. A. I. le Prince Napoléon, Président de la Commission Impériale. *Rapport sur l'Exposition universelle de 1855.* Paris: Imprimerie Impériale, 1857.

Trapp, Frank Anderson. "The Universal Exposition of 1855." *The Burlington Magazine* No. 107 (1965): 300-5.

Debarati Sanyal (essay date spring-summer 1999)

SOURCE: Sanyal, Debarati. "Conspiratorial Poetics: Baudelaire's 'Une Mort héroïque.'" *Nineteenth-Century French Studies* 27, nos. 3-4 (spring-summer 1999): 305-22.

[*In the following essay, Sanyal examines the confluence of the poetic and political in Baudelaire's response to the republicanism that followed the 1848 Revolution.*]

In *Pauvre Belgique*! (1864-65), Baudelaire portrays the republican spirit of 1848 as a disease circulating in the veins of the social body with the tenacity of a venereal affliction: "Nous avons tous l'esprit Républicain dans les veines comme la vérole dans les os. Nous sommes démocratisés et syphilisés" (1: 961). The recognition of a collective political pathology that fully contaminates the poet himself marks a dramatic departure from Baudelaire's claim, made in the aftermath of Napoleon III's coup over a decade earlier, that "Le 2 décembre m'a physiquement dépolitiqué" (*Corr.* 1: 188). Both statements record the poet's contrasting responses to politics through bodily images of contamination and immunity. His earlier declaration of disenchantment suggests a virtually physical evisceration of the political, as if it were possible to excise oneself—or to be excised—from the body politic. The later passage seems to renounce this possibility, and even perversely embraces the inevitable contagion of history's virulent legacy. How are we to situate this shift in terms of Baudelaire's own *poetic* corpus and in terms of mutations in the political body over this period? The notion of physical depoliticization conjures up Baudelaire's celebration, elsewhere, of poetry's immunity to considerations beyond itself, an immunity that seems inscribed in the very expression *art pur*. Yet the powerful imagery of disease in *Pauvre Belgique*! beckons us to examine symptoms of the political in Baudelaire's poetic works and to reflect on how contamination itself may be seen as a compelling figure for the relationship between poetry and politics.

Indeed, even after the rupture with politics declared in 1852, symptoms of the political continue to haunt Baudelaire's later poetic works with the enigmatic persistence of scars that refuse erasure. The depiction of the republican legacy as an incurable disease infusing the social body with its venom is particularly suggestive when we consider, for example, Baudelaire's collection of prose poems, in which the political and the poetic realms repeatedly bleed into each other. Indeed, this contamination is inscribed in the very genre of the prose poem, described in the preface to *Le Spleen de Paris* as an *impure* discursive space, as the contaminated site of a "croisement de rapports" not only between the lyric and prosaic, but also between the self and the city, the subjective and the intersubjective: "C'est surtout de la fréquentation des grandes villes, c'est du croisement de leurs innombrables rapports que naît cet idéal obsédant" (1: 276). The emergence of poetry from the crossroads of urban experience, from the multiple bodies and voices that jostle within the public sphere, inevitably topples poetic sovereignty from its hieratic throne, from its immunity to the collective pathology. Nowhere is this contamination more vividly illustrated than in the prose poem **"Perte d'Auréole,"** where the poet's fall is literally one into the 'commonplace,' into the "mauvais lieu" of the "lieu commun".

The following analysis of **"Une Mort héroïque"** examines one particular "croisement," or transgression, that recurs in various poems such as **"La Corde," "Les Foules," "Assommons les pauvres!,"** and **"L'Invitation au voyage,"** where the poetic and political spheres, so often divorced in Baudelaire's theoretical writings, gradually contaminate and mirror one another.[1] These works self-consciously weave the poetic text into the social and political fabric and subtly disclose underlying zones of contagion between aesthetic and political bodies. By challenging poetry's immunity to politics and ultimately unveiling art's potential complicity with political power, such texts contest the absolute claims of both aesthetic and ideological sovereignty. In **"Une Mort héroïque,"** the trope of contamination, paradoxically enough, enables the emergence of a poetics of opposition, one based on complicity rather than denunciation. The refusal of an aesthetic that would remain autonomous from the collective pathology, the disavowal of a *poetically* depoliticized work, is precisely what enables this poem to illuminate historical shifts in the representation of political sovereignty and to probe the paths that remain for a contestatory poetics.

"Une Mort héroïque" stages what appears to be at first sight an antagonistic struggle between the aesthetic and the political realms, embodied, respectively, by a jester and a Prince. Yet the boundaries between these two spheres are blurred, if not collapsed, throughout the poem. Fancioulle, the Prince's favorite jester and almost his friend, conspires against his sovereign and is denounced. He is commanded to perform in a pantomime that may purchase clemency. Yet, at the moment the histrion reveals himself to be a consummate artist whose power exceeds that of his sovereign, the Prince orders one of his pages to blow a whistle so shrill that it interrupts the performance and causes the artist to drop dead on stage. Despite the apparent antithesis between despot and artist—or executioner and victim—that could be inferred from the poetic plot, the opposition between the Prince and Fancioulle systematically inverts the exigencies of the political and aesthetic domains. Fancioulle, the court's jester, is "voué par état au comique," a condition that "despotically" impresses political ideas of liberty and nation upon his brain and lead him into the conspiracy. The Prince, himself an accomplished dreamer and aesthete, reverses the exigencies between the comic and the serious (a dichotomy that also opposes the aesthetic to the political) by imposing a rule of "nonseriousness," of 'plaisir et étonnement' in his own state. The very conception of an "état", then, is defined entirely by its transgression: Fancioulle transgresses into the political domain just as the Prince transgresses into the aesthetic realm. These transgressions define their identities and positions *vis à vis* both the stage and the state, presenting from the outset the stage and the state as parallel sites for the performance of power.

The key to these reversals between the aesthetic and political states is the disjunction repeatedly underlined between one's "facultés" and one's "état." The emphasis on this recurrent disjunction is crucial, for it reveals the common goal of both artistic and political projects: the fusion of one's inner possibilities (or imagination) and one's outer circumstance. The artist's embattled relationship to a given empirical predicament strives towards the imaginary fusion of "faculties" and "estates" in the work of art. This coincidence between self and estates has its political analogues, for example, in republican idealism. Indeed, the infinitely renewed reconciliation of one's faculties with one's social conditions in a mobile, democratic community whose sovereignty fully reflects the collective will is the very premise of the incurable political utopianism both repudiated and perversely celebrated in the closing passage of ***Pauvre Belgique!***. Several poems in the ***Spleen de Paris*** are satirical deflations of this idealism and foreground the irreconcilable gap between one's "facultés" and one's "états." In **"Assommons les pauvres!,"** for instance, the beggar's impotent gaze, "un de ces regards inoubliables qui culbuteraient les trônes, *si l'esprit remuait la matière*," is likened to both the poet's idealizing imagination *and* to the socialist theories of 1848 (1: 358).[2] The poet's beating of the beggar is thus an assault upon a utopian mystification that is both aesthetic and political and which holds that the faculty of imagination may in any way *materialize* itself in the empirical world. I will return to this point but wish to note for now that this transformative desire, attributed in other texts to bankrupt revolutionary and aesthetic idealism, in **"Une Mort héroïque"** characterizes both the authoritarian Prince and the conspiring artist. Both figures are defined by the discrepancy between their imagination and their empirical circumstance. The emergence of their identities through the vacillating tension between "faculté" and "état," rather than through identifiable roles and positions (subject and sovereign, victim and executioner, artist and despot, actor and spectator), dramatically complicates the distribution of power in the poem.

The parallel treatment of the Prince and the artist-conspirator, as I shall suggest, indicates a startling convergence of aesthetic and political forms of absolute sovereignty.

Indeed, the Prince initially occupies both the position of the artist who strives to transfigure his empirical predicament into a stage for the play of his aesthetic faculties and, paradoxically, that of the disempowered political subject thwarted by the discrepancy between his inner possibilities and his outer, unfavorable circumstances: "Le grand malheur de ce Prince fut qu'il n'eut jamais un théâtre assez vaste pour son génie . . . L'imprévoyante Providence avait donné à celui-ci des facultés plus grandes que ses Etats." A similar discrepancy defines Fancioulle, whose faculties lead him astray into an *état* which is not his own: "Mais pour les personnes vouées par état au comique, les choses sérieuses ont de fatales attractions." Moreover, when the jester moves from the wings of conspiracy to the center of the stage—his proper domain—it is so as to demonstrate how his imaginative, *artistic* faculties will relate to his state as the Prince's doomed *political* subject: "Il [le Prince] voulait profiter de l'occasion pour faire une expérience physiologique d'un intérêt *capital,* et vérifier jusqu'à quel point les *facultés* habituelles d'un artiste pouvaient être *altérées* ou *modifiées* par les circonstances où il se trouvait." The dis*location* of art and politics in the poem foregrounds their equal status as competitors for agency and ascendancy over the givenness of empirical conditions, thus calling into question the very distinction between artistic and political sovereignty.

If Fancioulle as conspirator is reminiscent of Baudelaire during the active phase of his republicanism in 1848, the Prince incarnates the sovereign indifference and aestheticism of the poet as dandy.[3] He is "Assez indifférent relativement aux hommes et à la morale" and *therefore* a "véritable artiste lui-même." In striking contrast to the alienated and impotent figurations of the artist in poems such as **"Le Vieux Saltimbanque"** or **"Le Mauvais vitrier,"** the Prince's domain is a powerful, albeit incomplete, attempt at realizing the aesthetic ideal of "surnaturalisme" and of "art pur." Here, however, the vehicle for an ideal transcendence of empirical conditions is the *political* state. Baudelaire's definition of pure art as a self-reflexive "magie suggestive contenant à la fois le sujet et l'objet, le monde extérieur à l'artiste et l'artiste lui-même" (2: 598) is radicalized in **"Une Mort héroïque"** as the inscription of the Prince's desires ("facultés") upon his domain ("états"). The aestheticization of the political sphere, implicit in the portrait of a state as a theatre "governed" by the sovereign's imagination, is a powerful echo of Baudelaire's celebratory representation, in the Salon of 1859, of the aesthetic process through the rhetoric of political sovereignty. Imagination, "cette reine des facultés," is an absolute sovereign that "creates and governs the world" (2: 623). The political incarnation of imagination's power in **"Une Mort héroïque,"** however, is a critical moment that starkly illuminates the despotism common to both absolute political and aesthetic constructions of sovereignty. The seamlessness of the Prince's tyranny is explicitly established by the narrator's comment that "les efforts qu'il faisait pour fuir ou vaincre ce tyran du monde [l'Ennui] lui aurait attiré de la part de l'historien sévère l'épithète de *monstre* s'il était permis dans ses domaines, d'écrire quoi que ce fut qui ne ne tendit pas uniquement au plaisir et a l'étonnement." Writing that does not conform to the royal text of pleasure and surprise and that may testify to the sovereign's monstrosity is occulted or erased just as Fancioulle's fellow-conspirators are erased from life itself—"effacés de la vie."

Yet a conspiracy has formed within the fissures of the royal domain, and while Fancioulle's political opposition has failed, his symbolic opposition when he appears on stage challenges the sovereign's political authority precisely because the artist's own faculties (unlike the Prince's) do momentarily transcend his state. The locus of opposition thus shifts from the wings of conspiracy to the centre of the spectacle. The Prince may not have been unstaged by the conspiracy, but he is symbolically upstaged by Fancioulle during the performance.[4] If aesthetic and political performances mirror each other in their common pursuit of the fusion between one's "facultés" and one's "états," Fancioulle's pantomime, a "chef d'œuvre d'art vivant" is a triumph that eclipses the despot. The authority of his performance is even more powerful over his subjects than that of the Prince's over his subjects, who, after all, conspired against him. The narrator points out the structural similarity between political and aesthetic performances when he speculates that the Prince is envious of the histrion's despotic grip on his audience: "Se sentait-il vaincu dans son pouvoir de despote? humilié dans son art de terrifier les cœurs et les esprits?" Despotism, the absolute mastery over one's circumstances and subjects, is thus disclosed as common to both aesthetic and political constructions.

Fancioulle's consummate spectacle, however, temporarily pits aesthetic mastery against political subjugation, and despite the contamination effected between these two realms, we now have a configuration of power that briefly ruptures the sadistic hierarchy underlying the spectacle as a royal "experience physiologique" enacted upon and by a subject performing under the threat of capital punishment. The jester momentarily embodies the victory of the symbolic over the political, or, rather, the victory of one's "facultés" over one's "état." It is important to note that the pantomime, "une parfaite

idéalisation," is emblematic of an idealist Romantic aesthetic. The absolute fusion between self and ideal turns the spectacle into a transcendental buffoonery in which the histrion soars above the conditions of his performance. Portrayed by the narrator in metaphysical terms as a defiant consciousness who infinitely recreates the world according to his own edicts, Fancioulle embodies a pure, untrammeled and unrepresentable self-invention: "Fancioulle introduisait . . . le divin et le surnaturel jusque dans les plus extravagantes bouffoneries."[5] Yet this spectacular idealization is also a powerful gesture of political defiance. Fancioulle's bodily translation of a "paradis excluant toute idée de mort ou de destruction" creates an autonomous, imaginary state over which the Prince's power has no bearing. Performing a transfiguration of temporality into infinity, of mortality into the divine and the immutable, the jester's flawless mimesis of life becomes a contestatory fiction that masters death itself through irony ("celui qui bouffonait si bien la mort"). This aesthetic fiction challenges the basis of the Prince's "expérience physiologique" by disregarding its very conditions (the sovereign's power over a subject's life or death). Fancioulle performs his own "expérience physiologique": the sublime incarnation of a utopian metaphysical and political *état* beyond the Prince's law.

The pantomine thus raises the central question of whether art can provide a lasting symbolic contestation of the ruling order—does Fancioulle's utopic fiction allegorize art's transcendence of official hegemony, or does it instead suggest that art's resistance to power is a mystification? Perhaps we should reframe the question and ask if Fancioulle's idealist recreation of imaginative sovereignty matches the Prince's real political power. The narrator, significantly, punctures the perfection of the pantomime's metaphoricity (in which being fuses with fiction) by displacing the *symbolic* representation of Fancioulle's body (as a seamless and absolute incarnation of freedom and aesthetic sovereignty) with an *allegorical* one. This subtle shift occurs in the allusion to the artist's halo, visible to the narrator alone, "où se mélaient, dans un étrange amalgame, les rayons de l'Art et la gloire du Martyre." The amalgamation of art and martyrdom in what was until now a victory of metaphoricity over empirical conditions marks a shift from symbolic to allegorical representation and interrogates the status of Fancioulle's symbolic transcendence; however victorious the histrion's transfiguration of life into fiction may be, its price is martyrdom.[6] The doubleness of the halo prefigures the doubleness of Fancioulle's position prior to the fatal whistle. The subject of his imaginary state on stage, he nevertheless is the sacrificial object of the Prince's own experimental stage *and* state. The fragility of the fictional world, its inextricable link to a broader frame of reference including its reception, even if the process of self-creation seems autonomous from any empirical exigencies, is such that a whistle of disapproval ruptures the act and executes the actor. The poem thus offers a shimmering vision of aesthetic transcendence only to revoke it.

The disempowerment of the artist by political authority suggested by the outcome of Fancioulle's performance is nevertheless complicated by the specular relationship established between artist and sovereign, one that unravels the initial opposition between "victime" and "bourreau." Baudelaire's reticence towards such an oppositional structure becomes particularly significant in light of an important intertext, if not pre-text, for **"Une Mort héroïque"**: Edgar Allan Poe's "Hop -Frog," published in 1849 and translated by the French poet in 1855, eight years before **"Une Mort héroïque"** was published in *La Revue nationale et étrangère*. One could argue that a more significant intertextual translation occurs in the prose poem, which rewrites Poe's scenario in terms that irrevocably dislocate the opposition between despot and conspirator. "Hop Frog" narrates the conspiratorial revenge of a dwarf and court jester upon a tyrannical king, who has struck his companion. Compelled by the King to devise an ingenious and novel costume for his courtiers and himself for a masquerade, Hop-Frog disguises them as eight chained orangutans. During the festivities, amidst the general panic caused by the appearance of the orangutans, a contraption lifts the king and his men up and Hop-Frog sets them on fire before escaping, presumably to his native land.

Hop-Frog's origins and character are as enigmatic as Fancioulle's, yet unlike Baudelaire's histrion, Poe's protagonist—a disfigured dwarf—is portrayed as absolutely alien to the court's norms. Whereas Fancioulle, as "presqu'un ami du Prince," has an ambiguous proximity to power, Hop-Frog, the king's property, is only a commodity whose monstrosity enhances his market value: "Sa valeur était triplée aux yeux du roi par le fait qu'il était à la fois nain et boiteux" (Poe 171).[7] This position of radical reification and disempowerment ironically sets the stage for a systematic reversal of hierarchies. In Poe's tale, the opposition between "victime" and "bourreau" is initally absolute and then reversed according to a carnivalesque logic that is sustained to the last spectacular *dévoilement,* when the jester lights the king and his courtiers on fire as expiation for their cruelty. Thus, although initially Hop-Frog is closer to beast than man, man and beast are reversed, for while the king promises the dwarf humanity in exchange for his ingenious plot—"Hop Frog! nous ferons de toi un homme!" (177)—it is the dwarf who uses the bestial mask to unmask the bestiality of the king, thereby reclaiming his humanity for himself. Baudelaire's translation of the text indicates his awareness of its ironies, for whereas Poe merely writes that the buffoon tied the king and his men together, the translation reads "On se procura une longue chaine. D'abord on la passa autour de la taille du roi et on l'y *assujetit*" (178) Baudelaire

italicizes the verb "assujetir" in a brilliant swerve that illuminates the king's unsuspecting subjugation before the dwarf and suggests that his apish disguise indicates his authentic status as subject. Not only does Hop-Frog engineer the script of this performance, but it is he who whistles and then vociferously asserts his status as conspirator, demystifier and executioner before the stunned court:

> Maintenant, dit-il, je vois *distinctement* de quelle espèce sont ces masques. Je vois un grand roi et ses sept conseillers privés, un roi qui ne se fait pas scrupule de frapper une fille sans défense, et ses sept conseillers, qui l'encouragent dans son atrocité. Quant à moi, je suis simplement Hop-Frog le bouffon, et *ceci est ma dernière bouffonnerie!*
>
> (181)

Hop-Frog's denunciation is as vocal as Fancioulle's pantomime is silent. The repeated assertion of his privileged vision and of his identity finds no echo in Baudelaire's text, where instead, opposition—both covert in the form of the conspiracy and spectacular in the form of the dumb show—has literally been silenced. The central distinction between these two parables is symbolized by Hop-Frog's flight and conjectured return to the native land from which he was abducted. The histrion's flight indicates a separation of spheres between his own "state" and the sovereign's. Fancioulle, however, is part of the Prince's nation and conspires for its sake, his powers as artist structurally mirror the sovereign's political power. Moreover, his very identity emerges only as a fluctuating tension between his "facultés" and his "états" within the Prince's domain. It is hardly surprising, given Fancioulle's existence *as* his role, that the rupture of mimesis should lead to death.[8] Much like the shock of laughter described in Baudelaire's **"De l'essence du rire,"** the page's whistle shatters the mime's fictional, mystified self-representation and hurls him back into an empirical, intersubjective and censored realm. The disjunction between "facultés" and "états," between the imaginary contestation and its historical frame, is absolute.

Baudelaire's significant swerves from Poe's carnivalesque logic, his contamination of the aesthetic by the political, stage the loss of a prophetic mode of denunciation and suggest the absence of an autonomous or even a distinct sphere from which social reality can be rearticulated. The utopic state for which Fancioulle conspires and which he then embodies is so fragile, so inextricably bound to the context of the performance, that the whistle of a mere page suffices to destroy it. Representation cannot sever itself from the conditions of its articulation and of its reception. The mystification of a contestation that strives to be autonomous is punished by death.

Fancioulle's fleeting metaphoric freedom is a vivid illustration of Baudelaire's idealist conception of "art pur" and of imagination's absolute, transcendent sovereignty over the empirical world. The whistle, in sabotaging the triumph of an autonomous poetics seems to figure Baudelaire's own "dédoublement" into the executioner and victim of an aesthetics of *surnaturalisme.* One could even say that Fancioulle's convulsive death figures a kind of poetic suicide, transforming the prose poem into a "gibet symbolique où pendait mon image," to quote from Baudelaire's **"Voyage à Cythère"** (1: 119). In what follows, I will examine the alternative poetic voice that emerges from this self-decapitation and argue that the whistle interrupting Fancioulle's spectacle, like the Stendhalian "coup de pistolet," ushers in the politics occluded by the Prince's *régime.* I hope to show that the narrator refigures the oppositional politics so spectacularly—and suicidally—embodied by the mime into a conspiratorial poetics.

The narrator's contestatory testimony eludes immediate legibility and reflects, *en abyme,* a general crisis of reading in the kingdom itself, where 'truth' is the unreadable product of a performance of power. Indeed, the court's "esprits superficiels" are explicitly indicted for their naïve reading of the Prince's plot, as a "signe évident" of his clemency. Even more striking is the audience's response to Fancioulle's performance. The mime's sublime and disarticulated convulsions are in turn mimetically duplicated by the audience: "Les explosions de joie et d'admiration ébranlèrent à plusieurs reprises les voûtes de l'édifice avec l'énergie d'un tonnerre continu." The spectators' response is an immediate, visceral surrender to the performance's seduction. Their unquestioning, collective prostitution is underlined by the erotic vocabulary of *volupté, abandon, enivrement, convulsion*: "chacun s'abandonna, sans inquiétude, aux voluptés multipliées que donne la vue d'un chef d'œuvre d'art vivant."

The narrator himself participates momentarily in the court's submissive and deluded reception, for the mime's sublime incarnation of Art precludes a detached and analytical reading. Significantly, the pantomime remains an irreducible mystery at the core of the text, and the narrator can only allude to the resistance of such an ineffable "physiological" experience to linguistic figuration: "Ma plume tremble, et des larmes d'une émotion toujours présente me montent aux yeux pendant que je cherche à vous décrire cette inoubliable soirée." It is an experience before which writing, and language itself, falters and is silenced, leaving the body's convulsive response (the infinitely renewed tears) as testimonies to its power.

Fancioulle's hyperbolic, unrepresentable performance and the narrator's own untranslateable witnessing exemplify Baudelaire's conception of the "comique absolu," a category that elucidates the competing oppositional positions in **"Une Mort héroïque."** Fancioulle's

dumb show is a virtual re-enactment of the English pantomime evoked in **"De l'Essence du Rire"** as the culmination of "le comique absolu." Just as the narrator's pen trembles before Fancioulle's ineffable performance, the analyst of the essay mourns his pen's inability to transcribe the spectacle's hyperbolic vertigo: "Avec la plume, tout cela paraît pâle et glacé. Comment la plume pourrait-elle rivaliser avec la pantomime?" (2: 540).

In the essay on laughter, Baudelaire's distinction between the "comique absolu" and the "comique significatif'" hinges precisely upon the question of legibility and translation. The absolute comic, denoting man's superiority over nature, is akin to "l'art pur," for it marks imagination's transcendence of empirical conditions. The "ivresse terrible et irrésistible" performed both by the English Pierrot and Fancioulle engenders a rapturous vertigo in which the spectator is lost in the performance. Whereas the absolute comic "se présente sous une espèce une" and thus incarnates a symbolic fusion of signifier and signified that is intuitively and instantly grasped, the "comique significatif," addressing man's superiority over man, is a hieroglyphic, analytical and temporal expression requiring reflection and judgement from the viewer.

Baudelaire's distinct articulations of the "comique absolu" and the humbler "comique significatif," when mapped onto the oppositional strategies of **"Une Mort héroïque,"** illuminate the historical significance of the narrator's conspiratorial voice. Baudelaire characterizes the absolute comic as "Les créations fabuleuses, les êtres dont la raison, la légitimation ne peuvent pas être tirés du code commun" (2: 535).[9] Fancioulle's living masterpiece ("un chef d'œuvre d'art *vivant*") opens a vision of absolute otherness. In bringing to life an aesthetic and political experience that defies "le code commun," he voids the Prince's reign of its legitimacy and imposes his own self-legitimating sovereignty. Yet, the visionary "ivresse" is precariously situated within a historical, political and collective reality that shatters its contestatory power. If Fancioulle's performance incarnates Baudelaire's celebrated "comique absolu," the narrator, instead, offers a different, more vigilant oppositional discursive strategy modelled on the "comique significatif," one attentive both to the conditions of its articulation and its reception. The "comique significatif" is characterized by doubleness—"l'art et l'idée morale"—and by deferral, "le rire après coup." Not only a more analytical form of communication, the "comique significatif'" also addresses a common frame of reference, "le code commun." Whereas the absolute comic personified by Fancioulle indicates man's superiority over nature—the mime's ability to veil the abyss of death through art—the "comique significatif" is contextual, occurring in an intersubjective realm of power relations and hence more suited to negotiation. It is precisely through intertextuality and irony, both of which share the structure of doubleness and deferral characteristic of the "comique significatif," that the narrator inscribes his contestatory testimony.[10]

In contrast to the symbolic fusion of Fancioulle's pantomime, the narrator articulates the gap between an act and its possible significances, as we saw in his allegorical presentation of Fancioulle's halo. His translation of the Prince's physionomical shifts, juxtaposes yet another frame upon the Prince's "expérience physiologique": the sovereign subject observing the jester's body becomes the object of the narrator's gaze. The narrator's privileged insights, both into the recesses of the sovereign's mind and into the doubleness of Fancioulle's spectacle (as sovereign of his imaginary state and subject of the Prince's) turn him into an ambiguous accomplice for both figures. An impotent witness to the scenario that unfolds, he nevertheless is its sole agent of transmission, since neither historian nor histrion may record or denounce the Prince's tyranny. Yet his pen falters at every turn, trembling before the spectacle and erasing its testimony in a repeated gesture of self-censorship. Indeed the narrator's conjectures on the Prince's motives are parodically voided by remarks such as "C'est un point qui n'a jamais pu être éclairci"; "Le Prince avait-il lui-même deviné l'homicide efficacité de sa ruse? Il est permis d'en douter"; "De telles suppositions non exactement justifiées mais non exactement injustifiables . . .". These self-erasing speculations suggest the complex negotiations of an oppositional voice striving to be heard in a censored domain.

The final conjecture is crucial in this regard, for, through the double voice of intertextuality, it performs a complicitous subversion of the Prince's discursive terror. Amidst a tyrannical reign of "plaisir et étonnement" that either coopts serious contestation or erases it, the narrator's cautious rhetoric evokes yet another critical intertext: "[Le Prince] regretta-t-il son cher et inimitable Fancioulle? Il est doux et légitime de le croire." The citation from Horace—*Dulce et decorum est pro patria mori* is all the more powerful for its truncation. The gaping absence of both nation and death in this formulation ("il est doux et légitime de . . . croire" that the Prince regretted his jester) denounce the travesty that the capricious sovereign's stage makes of the state. The translation of *decorum* into the politically loaded term "légitime" underscores what Virginia Swain has called the "legitimation crisis" performed by the poem, a crisis that ripples out to encompass the post-revolutionary body politic.[11] The fragmented Horatian intertext resurrects the 'serious' national ideal for which the jester and his fellow conspirators die at the same time that the decapitation of politics is textually performed by the narrator's fragmented testimony.[12] Such a double gesture restores the political opposition erased by the official discourse, just as the final italicized word

of the poem, *faveur,* beckons an allusion to the *droits* denied to the Prince's subjects.[13] The "expérience physiologique" conducted in the poem is indeed "un intérêt capital," for it fully implicates the head of the political body.

In his correspondence, Baudelaire makes two intriguing references to possible versions of **"Une Mort héroïque."** The first is in a letter to Gustave Rouland, where he alludes to a project entitled "Un aperçu historique du conspirateur et du favori" (**Corr.** 1: 405); the second, two years later to Poulet-Malassis, announces: "Enfin j'ai fait une nouvelle basée sur l'hypothèse: découverte d'une conspiration par un oisif, qui la suit jusqu'à la veille de son explosion, et qui alors tire pile ou face pour savoir s'il la déclarera à la police" (1: 584). The prose poem retains the terms of these *ébauches,* yet departs from them at several points. The conspirator is *favoured* by the Prince, and the historical parameters of the tale seem erased. Moreover, the oscillation between complicity and denunciation described in the letter to Poulet-Malassis is presented from the stance of an absolutely disengaged *flaneur* who bears no allegiances to the state or to a contestatory counterculture and yet can determine the destinies of both. The narrator of the prose poem however is denied any direct intervention. His speculative faltering seems to mimic Fancioulle's own dying convulsions. Yet as I have argued, the narrator inscribes his own oppositional stance through the tactics of the "comique significatif," through complicity, irony and intertextuality. In tracing the failure of absolute aesthetic sovereignty, personified by the mime, the political state as the incarnation of an individual's despotic consciousness, one structurally akin to artistic transcendence, is also shown in all its frailty and illegitimacy.

"Une Mort héroïque" may be closer to the "aperçu *historique* du conspirateur et du favori" described to Rouland than it appears at first glance. The portrait of the Prince's carefully crafted reign of censorship resonates with the Empire's tight system of surveillance (the discretionary measures of the *Sureté Générale)* and censorship to counter the threat of republican conspiracies.[14] It also puts on trial the republican ideological legacy. The utopic homology between "facultés" and "états" upheld by the revolutions as the cornerstone of a nascent democracy is systematically evoked only to be ironically suppressed in the poem. Moreover, by tracing the displacement of individual and collective "droits" to the arbitrariness of "faveur" (the poem's last italicized word), the revolutionary promise of a collective sovereignty is parodically replaced by a return to an *ancien régime* form of despotism. Opposition in this *régime* literally costs the conspirators their heads, yet it is precisely through a textual self-decapitation, through the sabotage of aesthetic sovereignty and autonomy, that the narrator, with the deftness of a textual conspirator, resuscitates in fragments the utopian politics embodied by Fancioulle.

While **"Une Mort héroïque"** subtly indicts the Second Empire's masked despotism and conspiratorially gestures towards the republican ideals it coopted or censored, the very definitions of despotism and resistance are considerably complicated. The unveiling of structural complicities between aesthetic and political sovereignty collapses the very possibility of an oppositional stance towards the state's englobing power. The fissure pried open by Fancioulle's contestatory spectacle seems definitively sealed off by his execution, leaving the task of conspiratorial witnessing to the narrator. Yet, in an even more disturbing turn, the poem ultimately discloses a gaping absence at the heart of the mechanism of state power. Authority is cut loose from a governing agency, for both Fancioulle and the Prince are ultimately subject to the vagaries of an indeterminate authority, an "imprévoyante providence." The Prince is haunted by a law greater than his own, *Ennui*: "il ne connaissait d'ennemi dangereux que l'Ennui . . . ce tyran du monde." Similarly, Fancioulle is daemonically possessed by politics "bien qu'il puisse paraître bizarre que les idées de patrie et de liberté s'empare despotiquement du cerveau d'un histrion." *Ennui* intercedes between the royal "facultés" and its "états," just as the page's whistle shatters the jester's embodiment of a politicized fiction.

It is crucial, in light of this repeated diffusion of intention and agency, to remember that the free state beyond censorship and capital punishment performed by Fancioulle is "executed" (if indeed the whistle was of homicidal intent) not by the Prince but by an unsuspecting young proxy.[15] This dislocation of agency precludes the translation of the text's configuration of power as one between "victime et bourreau," between artist and political sovereign. Just as Fancioulle's political commitment is the result of floating ideological principles (of freedom and of nation) despotically' capturing the histrion's brain, the Prince's act of punishment is carried out without a clearly intending agent and executioner. The narrator's question, "Le sifflet, rapide comme un glaive, avait-il réellement frustré le bourreau?," suggests that the shrill whistle preempts the hiss of the guillotine's blade, that censorship is akin to capital punishment. Yet the source of this capital punishment is displaced onto the lips of a blind executionary agent.

This startling dislocation of agency and its replacement with an unpredictable and mindless form of collective complicity can in fact be traced from the beginning of the poem. The state's resistance to social upheaval is implicit in the denunciation of the conspiracy. The bewitched and credulous public's thunderous applause before Fancioulle's absolute sovereignty on stage echoes their absorption into the Prince's state; their unreflec-

tive faith in the power of signs makes them unwitting accomplices to the perpetuation of absolute power, aesthetic or political.[16] The pervasive complicity staged in the poem between the tyrant and his subjects is a compelling echo of the collective legitimation of Napoleon III's reign through a plebiscite that cloaked the Empire with the mystique of popular sovereignty. Baudelaire's rage at his compatriots' blind consent to the Empire's despotism is recorded in a passage that testifies to the eclipse of direct modes of opposition in the paradoxical context of an authoritarian democracy:

> En somme, devant l'histoire et devant le peuple francais, la grande gloire de Napoléon III aura été de prouver que le premier venu peut, en s'emparant du télégraphe et de l'imprimerie nationale, gouverner une grande nation.
>
> Imbéciles sont ceux qui croient que de pareils choses peuvent s'accomplir sans la permission du peuple,—et ceux qui croient que la gloire ne peut être appuyée que sur la vertu.
>
> Les dictateurs sont les domestiques du peuple,—rien de plus—, un foutu rôle d'ailleurs, et la gloire est le résultat de l'adaptation d'un esprit avec la sottise nationale.
>
> (1: 692)

For the poet, the dislocation, or quite literally, *decapitation* of power, its dissemination into the social field, dooms the possibility of a reflective and consensual democracy. Instead, politics, like the syphilitic contagion of republicanism, has been voided of all contestatory force and has mutated into an impersonal, venomous plague whose circulation collapses any possible distinction between despot and subject, or "dictateur" and "domestique." Neither dictator nor subject is an agent in this social organism. They are blind participants in the construction of a mass delusion—"la sottise nationale"—in the fiction of a democratic nation. Baudelaire's paradoxical vision of this authoritarian democracy, where dictator and crowds converge through new systems of representation and communication, ominously foreshadows emerging forms of power, forms that may no longer be identified and contested from a vantage point of separation and knowledge.

In the excerpt from **Pauvre Belgique!** which opens my reading, the representation of politics as a virulent contamination is significantly preceded by the declaration that "Non seulement je serais heureux d'être victime, mais je ne haïrais pas d'être bourreau—pour sentir la révolution de deux manières! Nous avons tous l'esprit Républicain dans les veines comme la vérole dans les os." The juxtaposition of revolutionary, sacrificial terror and the pathology of republicanism serves as a reminder of democracy's violent origins, its debt to revolutionary terror. In the context of the Second Empire's camouflaged perpetuation of violence in the form of an authoritarian democracy, such a declaration explodes the mystified assumption that terror has ceded to collective legislation. Instead, terror has taken an altered, and perhaps even more virulent face. The final image of contagion corrodes the antithesis between victim and executioner in spite of the poet's attempt to resuscitate the revolutionary experience from oppositing stances, "de *deux* manières." The decentering of power and the intricate web of complicity woven into **"Une Mort héroïque"** traces this collapse as one that leaves the dissenting voice with no room for resistance or opposition, confronted with the alternative of suidical defiance or conspiratorial complicity. The diagnosis of the political disease, conducted in poems such as **"Une Mort héroïque"** under the mask of irony, ultimately points to the erasure of politics as an arena for contestation.

Indeed, the catastrophic vision of history and progress recorded elsewhere in Baudelare's notebooks are testimonies to the poet's prescience. In his account of historical progress, Baudelaire describes the teeming urban crowds as blind accomplices to unforeseen strains of ideological tyranny breeding in the ruins of an oppositional political culture:

> Ai-je besoin de dire le *peu qu'il restera de politique* se débattra péniblement dans l'étreinte de l'animalité générale, et . . . les gouvernements seront forcés, pour se maintenir et pour créer un fantôme d'ordre, de *recourir à des moyens qui feraient frissoner l'humanité actuelle* . . . —Ces temps sont peut-être bien proches; qui sait même s'ils ne sont pas venus, et si l'épaississement de notre nature n'est pas le seul obstacle qui nous empêche d'apprécier le milieu dans lequel nous respirons!
>
> Quant à moi, qui sens quelquefois en moi le ridicule d'un prophète . . . Perdu dans ce vilain monde, coudoyé par les foules, je suis comme un homme lassé dont l'œil ne voit en arrière, dans les années profondes, que désabusement et amertume, et devant lui, qu'un orage où rien de neuf n'est contenu, ni enseignement, ni douleur.

(1: 667)

Walter Benjamin's commentary on this passage elucidates its prophetic insight into the modern face of political tyranny: "Est-il trop audacieux de prétendre que ce sont ces mêmes foules qui, de nos jours, sont pétries par les mains des dictateurs?" (15). The convergence of archaic despotism in **"Une Mort héroïque"** and a disseminated circulation of power that nevertheless *conserves* the Prince's absolute sovereignty suggests that it would not in turn be too audacious to trace a similar foreshadowing in Baudelaire's prose poem.

The "expérience physiologique d'un intérêt capital" conducted in **"Une Mort héroïque"** probes the pathologies of power at multiple levels, implicating the political and poetic bodies while also tracing the convergences between old and new forms of authoritarianism.

Perhaps the most lucid, and most poignant, demystification performed in this poem is the decapitation of aesthetic idealism. The *mise en spectacle* of symbolic authority, both held and lost by Fancioulle and the Prince, is a powerful interrogation of the mythic autonomy of political and aesthetic constructions. The narrator's wily rhetorical shifts, in conspicuously pressing to the margins the subversive political content of the tale, suggest that if no separate symbolic sphere may exist for contesting such forms of power, the voice of conspiracy, relying on the contamination of the political and the aesthetic as well as of text and intertext, can craftily inscribe its opposition. This is indeed a 'capital' experience, for that which is of utmost importance may only be uttered at the cost of one's head. If both symbolic opposition and covert conspiracy are doomed to failure, textual conspiracy, by intertwining the political and the poetic and, in a suicidal gesture, sacrificing thus the dream of aesthetic autonomy, points the way towards a new poetics of opposition, one that vigilantly traces the complicity between aesthetic and political performances.

Notes

1. The most famous formulation of this emancipation of poetry from any exigencies beyond itself is: "La poésie ne peut pas, sous peine de mort ou de défaillance, s'assimiler à la science ou à la morale; elle n'a pas la Vérité pour objet, elle n'a qu'Elle-même" (1: 333) and re-cited in the essay on Théophile Gautier (1: 113).

2. My italics. See also "Le Don des Fées," where the utopian homology between self and state inherited from 1789 is parodied as the fairies' incongruous gift of "l'amour du Beau et de la Puissance poétique au fils d'un sombre gueux, carrier de son *état,* qui ne pouvait, en aucune façon, aider les *facultés,* ni soulager les besoins de sa déplorable progéniture" (1: 306). Italics mine.

3. The significance of Baudelaire's participation in the revolutionary republicanism of 1848 remains a contested terrain in criticism. Two distinct views are found in Claude Pichois's and Jean Ziegler's biography of the poet, which considers Baudelaire's Republican fervour at the barricades as a primarily personal rebellion against his stepfather, Général Aupick, and in Richard Burton, which offers a detailed account of the political influences leading to Baudelaire's early radical republicanism.

4. See Nathaniel Wing, whose compelling reading of this poem argues that the explosive novelty of Fancioulle's performance constitutes a subversive interruption of the sovereign's power and hence opens the possibility for a shift in the implicit consent upon which hegemonic power is based. My reading concurs with this analysis at several

points: the partial complicity suggested between art and power, the spectacular originality of Fancioulle's oppositional stance and its disruptive implications for the discursive contract upon which both artistic and political power is based. However, I believe the poem to offer two distinct modes of opposition—the defiance provided by idealist art, embodied by Fancioulle, and the conspiratorial, complicitous poetics modelled on Baudelaire's "comique significatif." The development of this contextual and ironic mode of contestation (as *self*-contestation) is the central point of my reading of "Une Mort héroique" and of other texts that similarly contaminate poetic idealism and political rhetoric ("Le Gateau," "Le Joujou du pauvre," "La Corde" among others).

5. Friedrich Schlegel's treatment of irony as transcendental buffonery is vividly embodied by Fancioulle's performance: "There are ancient and modern poems that breathe, in their entirety and in every detail, the divine breath of irony. In such poems there lives a transcendental buffoonery. Their interior is permeated by mood, which surveys everything and rises above everything limited, even above the poet's own art, virtue and genius; and their exterior form by the histrionic style of an ordinary good Italian *buffo*" (Willson:115).

6. Once more, Baudelaire's poem uncannily repeats Schlegel's portrait of the English 'wit' in "Lyceum 67" an aphorism that tersely associates wit to madness, absolute freedom and martyrdom and suggests the irrevocable gap between idealism and reality. The absolute freedom claimed by the ironist/wit will lead him to commit suicide rather than to surrender to the empirical conditions his stance negates: "In England, wit is at least a profession, if not an art . . . They [the wits] introduce into reality absolute freedom, the reflection of which lends a romantic and piquant air to wit, and thus they live wittily, hence their talent for madness. They die for their principles" (Willson: 116).

7. Edgar Allan Poe, *Contes, Essais, Poèmes,* trans. Charles Baudelaire and Stéphane Mallarmé, (929). Subsequent citations from Poe will refer to this edition.

8. Poe's tale sustains the distinction between the authentic emotion and its masks. Hop-Frog audibly grinds his teeth in rage before the King's brutality and then conceals this rage with laughter. Both Fancioulle and the Prince however remain opaque throughout Baudelaire's tale—Fancioulle's specific motives for the conspiracy remain as enigmatic as the Prince's own intentions in commanding the performance.

9. The response to Fancioulle's performance closely follows Baudelaire's analysis of the convulsive shattering of all frames of reference in "le comique absolu," one inducing in the viewer "une hilarité folle, excessive, et qui se traduit en des déchirements et des pâmoisons interminables" (2: 535). Baudelaire will insist on the Englishness of this phenomenon in his national taxonomy of comic forms. His essay on English caricature addresses the hyperbolic violence of, for instance, Seymour's caricatures as such an example of "l'explosion dans l'expression" (2: 566).

10. According to Baudelaire, "le comique significatif" is also a specifically French phenomenon reflecting a national predilection for analysis. On several occasions, Baudelaire alludes to the French sacrifice of beauty on the altar of politics and philosophy. Philosophical art appeals to the nation's interpretive, analytical bent, as he states in "L'Art Philosophique": "La France aime le mythe, la morale, le rébus; ou pour mieux dire, pays de raisonnement, elle aime l'effort de l'esprit" (2: 601). This passion for analytical and decipherable art forms also indicates an obsession with politics. In his essay on Gautier, for instance, Baudelaire views the French thirst for legible allegories as the sacrilegious demand for a politicized aesthetic: ". . . pour la France, le beau [n'est] facilement digestible que relevé par le condiment politique . . . le caractère utopique, communiste, alchimique, de tous ses cerveaux, ne permet qu'une passion exclusive: celle des formules sociales" (2: 125). In light of the repeated connection between rational analysis and political reading, the "comique significatif," translated as a poetic mode of opposition, acquires complex political significances. The strategies of the 'comique significatif' found in "Une Mort héroique" mark an ironic concession towards the poet's readership, since the "comique significatif" promises the intellectual satisfaction of hermeneutic disclosure and political legibility. Yet the narrator's elliptical and ironic statements both point towards an unrealized political content in the tale and thwart its legibility. Instead, we are presented with a wavering between the absolute, or symbolic (embodied by Fancioulle and untranslated by the narrator), and the significant, or allegorical, a contamination of poetic and political modes which is performed by the very narration of the poem.

11. Virginia Swain's analysis addresses the truncated Horatian intertext as the symptom of a "legimation crisis," an undoing of cognition which occurs at all levels of the poem and to which the narrator's own self-censorship contributes. The article concludes that the undecideability of the poem's closure is characteristic of radical irony (as de

Man defines it in his "The Rhetoric of Temporality"). I propose a distinction between irony as a mode of (self) representation doomed to its own cognitive unravelling, and irony as a performance that preserves the contestatory force traditionally attributed to this trope.

12. Baudelaire intertwines suicide and conspiracy in a curious note: "Qui donc niera le droit au suicide? J'ai cependant voulu lire, tant j'ai l'esprit critique et modeste, tout ce qui a été écrit sur le suicide. . . . Si les conspirateurs lachent pied, plus d'intérêt dans ma vie. Je suis donc intéressé à ranimer la conspiration" (1: 593).

13. Depuis lors, plusieurs mimes, justement appréciés dans différents pays, sont venus jouer devant la cour de ***; mais aucun d'eux n'a pu . . . s'élever jusqu'à la même *faveur.*

14. It is interesting to note that a large portion of the issue of *La Revue nationale et étrangère* publishing "Une Mort Héroïque" (Oct. 1863) hotly denounces the excesses of the "pouvoir indépendant et irresponsable de la sûreté générale," specifically the censorship of the press through the taxing of political journals (*Revue* 10). Baudelaire himself suffered from this censorship as he was publishing "Une Mort héroique." As Steve Murphy notes, two poems had already been refused by the journal for their subversive political content. For an excellent reading of the political context of "Une Mort héroïque," see Steve Murphy. There are many affinities between our readings, particularly regarding Baudelaire's understanding of political intervention as a series of tactical positions that are always susceptible to mutate into their opposite, and of the poet's ambivalence towards the collective—one which, according to Murphy, dooms the poet's oppositional stance to a "révolte individuelle larvée" (57).

15. Once again, the distinction between victim and executioner is blurred—not only is the page a blind executionary agent, but his very youth mirrors the curious youthfulness inscribed in Fancioulle's name: Fancioulle, *fanciullo.*

16. The portrait of the court's delighted passivity before both aesthetic and by implication political performances of power suggestively recalls the consent of 7 million Frenchmen to the legitimation of a régime whose "extraordinary measures," implemented by the discretionary powers of the "Sureté Générale," led to 20,000 arrests and deportations.

Works Cited

Baudelaire, Charles. *Œuvres complètes.* 2 vols. Ed. Claude Pichois. Bibliothèque de la Pléiade. Paris: Gallimard, 1975-76.

———. *Correspondance.* 2 vols. Ed. Claude Pichois et Jean Ziegler. Bibliothèque de la Pléiade. Paris: Gallimard, 1966.

Benjamin, Walter. *Charles Baudelaire: Un poète lyrique à l'apogée du capitalisme.* Paris: Payot, 1979.

Burton, Richard. *Baudelaire and the Second Republic: Writing and Revolution.* London: Oxford UP, 1991.

Laboulaye, Edouard. "Le Parti Libéral." *Revue Nationale et Etrangère.* (13/10/1863): 54.

Murphy, Steve. "Scène parisienne: lecture d'Une Mort héroïque' de Baudelaire." *Le Champ Littéraire 1860-1900: Etudes offertes à Michael Pakenham.* Ed. Keith Cameron et James Kearns. Amsterdam: Faux Titre (1996): 50-61.

Pichois, Claude and Ziegler, Jean. *Charles Baudelaire.* Paris: Julliard, 1987.

Poe, Edgar Allan. *Nouvelles Histoires extraordinaires.* Trans. C. Baudelaire. Paris: GF Flammarion, 1965.

———. *Contes, Essais, Poèmes.* Trans. C. Baudelaire and S. Mallarmé. Paris: Laffont, 1989.

Schlegel, Friedrich. "Dialogue on Poetry." Tr. Ernst Behler and Roman Struc. *German Romantic Criticism.* Ed. A. Leslie Willson. NY: Continuum, 1982.

Swain, Virginia "The Legitimation Crisis: Event and Meaning in Baudelaire's 'Le Vieux saltimbanque' and 'Une Mort héroïque.'" *Romantic Review* 73:4 (1982): 452-462.

Wing, Nathaniel. "Poets, Mimes and Counterfeit Coins: On Power and Discourse in Baudelaire's Prose Poetry." *Paragraph* 13.1 (1990): 1-18.

Peter Broome (essay date 1999)

SOURCE: Broome, Peter. Introduction to *Baudelaire's Poetic Patterns: The Secret Language of* Les Fleurs du Mal, pp. 7-19. Amsterdam, The Netherlands: Rodopi, 1999.

[*In the following essay, Broome explores the formal and thematic features of* The Flowers of Evil *and asserts that the collection stands as a crossroads of modern French poetry.*]

It would be almost superfluous, in the wake of so many searching critical studies, to attempt a survey of Baudelaire's enormous contribution to the realization of new directions in modern poetry, and to try to define the incomparable stimulus which he has given to a more problematical view of the possibilities of 'modernism.' What is clear is that **Les Fleurs du Mal** stands not at, but *as,* the busiest crossroads, multi-directional and endlessly complex, of the history of French poetry. Within its pages, Baudelaire has locked and interlocked all the re-percussions of a major crisis of values, producing a po-etry which is snared in contradictions, pulled this way and that by conflicting attractions and imperatives, ani-mated, tormented and shaped by tensions running through the body of the verse.

To use the phrase the 'body of the verse' could hardly be more appropriate: not only in that Baudelaire is the most *physical* of poets, savouring the luxury of the senses to the full and venturing to the very brink of tol-erance and beyond, but in that he turns the text itself into a pliable sensual medium which, beyond the hedo-nistic profusion of actual references to sight, scent, sound, taste and touch, moves and vibrates, resounds and reverberates, twists and wavers, fattens and thins as if of its own accord, manipulating and moulding, per-meating and penetrating the intimate, perhaps uncon-scious, sensual instincts of the reader at the very instant of verbal contact and exposure. But to emphasize the indulgent physicality of *Les Fleurs du Mal* is not to suggest that this is a poetry which is only skin-deep. On the contrary, no poet has delved in greater depth into the extremism of the human passions: to uncover the obsessions, the treacherous undercurrents, the destruc-tive deviations, the sophisticated compromises. No poet has refined more courageously the study of the psyche: partly through the fluctuating moods of drugs in a kind of *connaissance par les gouffres,* but essentially through the more versatile self-exploration of poetry, probing the ambiguities, confronting the censored and the half-confessed, bringing to light the hidden layers, the threat-ened frontiers and the points of conflict. And if the life of the senses is so acute, so overwhelming, in Baude-laire, this is not to the exclusion, but to the further en-largement, of more abstract dimensions, ontological is-sues and spiritual preoccupations. For the senses are a *translation.* They do not move without awakening and dislodging farreaching implications. Their intensity, their very extravagance, their journeying to the edge, becomes the doorway of significance. They are meshed inseparably with what exceeds them: the great unfurling domain of analogies and equivalences, links and corre-spondences. The senses, then, for Baudelaire, are the touch-paper of the imagination: stimulating simile and metaphor in almost unprecedented abundance, creating a poetry which goes leaping far beyond, not only simple physicality, but the more insipid and self-contented *poésie du cœur* of the Romantics, so justifying his per-suasive *caveat* that 'il ne faut pas confondre la sensibil-ité de l'imagination avec celle du cœur' (*OC* [*Œuvres complétes*] II, p.604).

And if the imagination is sensitized to an extraordinary degree and, with it, what one might call the intuitive vi-sionary sense endowing all aspects of the material world with a 'double life', with the facility to unveil their own

'otherness', then so is the moral sense. The poetry of *Les Fleurs du Mal* is not an escapist poetry, despite symptomatic titles like *L'Invitation au voyage* (*OC* I, pp.53-54) and *Any where out of the world* (*OC* I, pp.356-57). It is no more a poetry given to distraction and distant dreams than it is to sentimentality. It comes home to roost uncomfortably close to the festering breeding-ground of hypocrisies, guilty consciences and evasive feints. It injects into modern verse a new acute-ness of moral urgency and perplexity, a probing aware-ness of the issues at stake in questions of truth and fal-sity, self-awareness and self-deception, love and hatred, commitment and alienation, creative and destructive impulses, responsibility and recklessness, discipline and *laisser aller,* self-betterment and whirling dissolution: to say nothing of liberty and enslavement.

It is a poetry also which opens up the most searching and perturbing spiritual dimensions, questioning from the very roots the tremors of faith and non-faith, the tormented relationships of spirit and matter, the inter-mittent glimpses of transcendence, the wayward possi-bilities for salvation or perdition. Nor are these simply *themes.* No-one, more than Baudelaire, has made of the poetic act, of the verbal mediation, of the transforming potentialities of art, a *sacred* or quasi-religious act: not just a prayer, a confession, an attempted exorcism, a sublimation, a yearning for the ideal (though it may be simultaneously all of these things), but a passage from intransitive to transitive and from one plane to another, a transmutation of one's own base matter, a self-purification and self-conquest through the mysterious alchemy of language, and a tentative communication between the inadequacies of the word as known to all poets and the unimaginable model to which it aspires which is the Word, reigning supreme like a mirage above the signs and symptoms of one's linguistic 'fall from grace' and suggesting a redemption. More than this, his poetry is one which enlists and puts to the test, if not on trial, all the opposites of one's deepest nature and of the human definition. It is a polarized poetry, racked between extremes (the divine and the satanical, ecstasy and horror, self-acceptance and self-refusal, the ethereal and the carnal, volatility and inertia, idolatry and universal indifference), which throws up the most restless and, one might say, the most ruthless self-awareness.

This is, then, a poetry of 'irresolutions': not of solved equations, secure values and safely closed doors, but of fractures, antitheses, clash and internecine warfare (registered as much in the form, style, tones and verbal textures as in the more patent emotional substance). It is a poetry shaped and deriving its rhythms from duali-ties of voice. Before the more systematic analyses of the twentieth century, Baudelaire has uncovered and ex-plored the plurality of self: the voices at different lev-els, their ambivalent or ambiguous dialogues, their incompatibilities and compromises, those coming from undetermined sources and invisible horizons, their repressed shadows and refracted patterns, their ingenious proxies and *alter ego*s. What this means, among other things, is that this is not an example of 'emotion recollected in tranquillity', however nostalgic or dreamy certain moods may be. It is the poem *as* struggle, the text *as* arena, the stanzas *as* debate. The drama, whichever of its many faces it may assume, is enacted 'live' in the pressure-chamber of the poem, which becomes the very crucible of self-confrontation, self-interrogation and the painful processes of potential self-transmutation. Hence the multifarious force of disturbance in Baudelaire's texts: stemming not simply from emotions which are disconcertingly two-faced and suspiciously ambivalent, from attitudes and implications which challenge moral stability, from probes into human psychology which hunt out demons, strip hypocrisy and show the subconscious as a sea of counter-currents, from a metaphysical or spiritual obstinacy which spirals between *ciel* and *gouffre* with howls of blindness and blasphemy, but, more importantly perhaps, from a verbal matter which is pulled between composition and decomposition, *forme* and *informe,* harmony and dissonance, to be characterized by its unpredictabilities, its sudden influxes of homeless energy, its *volte-faces,* its pockets of vertigo, its hollowing suction, its almost unmanageable changes of direction. It is Baudelaire's achievement to have grappled magnificently and, from the poetic point of view, triumphantly with a muse of Beauty who is not benign but embattled: whose resistant and perverse proximity has forced poetry away from the pallid, the tame, the platitudinous, and into new zones of vitality, energy and shock where language and expression have been obliged to invent new responses at the risk of their own *naufrage.*

* * *

So much is well known. What has not been so fully appreciated, however, is the extent to which Baudelaire has opened up for modern poetry, and immeasurably enlarged, the awareness of new dimensions of *active* form. It might be thought, glibly, that his 'modernism' lies essentially in his consciousness—the virulence of his passion, his revolutionary sensitivity to internal conflicts, the discomforting ambivalence of feelings, his incisive self-analysis and unearthing of multiple selves, the aggravated inner dialogues, the prickling confessions, the corrosive encounter with hypocrisy and its inventive disguises, the subversive challenge thrown out to simplistic notions of moral decency, the notes of blasphemy and wails of anguish which radically undermine facility of faith and sanguine reassurances of salvation—rather than in his poetic form which might be seen (with its predilection for the disciplines of the sonnet, its classic Alexandrines, its stout stanza-forms and fully fashioned rhyming patterns) to belong firmly to

another century. This would be to overlook, however, what we have already stressed: that poetry, for Baudelaire, is a total commitment. It is a complete and uncompromising investment of the self—its intensities, its dilemmas, its perplexities and frustrations, its irreconcilables, its 'unacceptables'—in the living act of language. Thus form is not a mould, but an intimate correspondent; not an inheritance, but a willed invasion, an irruption/eruption of the moment. It fluctuates with each flicker of feeling. It advances and retreats, clenches and relents, with each wavelet of doubt or assertion, purpose or hesitation. It is the instantaneous and inseparable *translation* of every reverberation of the active self, never more problematical than in that moment of linguistic inflammation. So, if one sees 'modernism' as representing something more subversive, more fragmentary, more inquisitorial, split between selves and moving in a more complex play of mirrors, then this is not just a state of mind but a state of form and language—perhaps the essential realization of twentieth century criticism being that they are one and the same, virtually interchangeable, twin parts of that 'throw of the dice which will never abolish chance'[1]. Form, then, in the case of the poetry of Baudelaire, *is* its modernism. It is not simply a question of an increased responsiveness to the expressive potential of verse-form or the intuitive discovery of new possibilities for pattern, though the artist of **Les Fleurs du Mal** has enlarged the poetic medium in this respect, awakened it to its latent 'selves', almost beyond recognition. It is more that he has created a fabric, an inventive infinity of fabrics, in which self and style are consubstantial, in which the depth of the fluctuation or impulse within goes hand in hand with the visible reverberations, jolts, adjustments, contortions, unpredictabilities and palpitations of the expressive entity on the page, in which they mesh, multiply and define each other: in which every unfurling or blockage of syntax, every tentative affinity of rhyme, every irony or complicity of juxtaposition, every shimmering or occluded analogy, every variable pulse of rhythm, every gear-change or shift in tempo, every sensual ripple of sonority or deliberate clash of sound, every caressed syllable or lingering mute <u>e</u>, *are* the man, *are* the theme, *are* the battleground of spirit.

Much has been made of Baudelaire as a *lover*. Perhaps not enough has been made of Baudelaire as a *lover of form*. He admires in Poe

> des symptômes curieux de ce goût immodéré pour les belles formes, surtout pour les belles formes singulières
>
> (*OC* II, p. 335)

by which he means forms strangely moulded to the restless and eccentric imagination, creating their shapes in concordance with the (often discordant) play of initiatives and impulses. And he attributes Théophile Gautier's artistic distinction to 'ce goût inné de la forme et de la perfection dans la forme', adding

Nul n'a mieux su que lui exprimer le bonheur que
donne à l'imagination la vue d'un bel objet d'art, fût-il
le plus désolé et le plus terrible qu'on puisse supposer

(*OC* II, pp. 122-23)

a testimony to Baudelaire's own belief in the efficacy of
form, regardless of the leanings of the subject-matter,
creating a beauty in bleakness, tension and ugliness
which is almost a redemption by form, a conversion
into its second self. Of Poe, he also says: 'Sa poésie,
profonde et plaintive, est néanmoins ouvragée . . .'
(*OC* II, p.274). And of an anonymous bard, no doubt
referring, if only by reflection, to himself, he writes:

Je connais un poète, d'une nature toujours orageuse et
vibrante, qu'un vers de Malherbe, symétrique et carré
de mélodie, jette dans de longues extases.

(*OC* II, p. 754)

Clearly, turbulence of poetic nature and a heaving, unruly inner inspiration are not incompatible with the delights of literary order, which, on the contrary, may be
their necessary or ideal corollary; and æsthetic euphoria
can be as powerful and overwhelming as, if not more
complete than, its physical and emotional counterparts.
Imagination, for Baudelaire, is not merely a free-
wheeling adventurer. It is a structured sensitivity. It is
meshed with *métier.* It discovers its own range through
the disciplines and subtleties, the strategies and symmetries, of accomplishment of technique. Imagination demands its own versatile linguist, its travelling translator.
So, he can state:

Plus on possède d'imagination, mieux il faut posséder
le métier pour accompagner celle-ci dans ses aventures
et surmonter les difficultés qu'elle recherche avide-
ment. Et mieux on possède son métier, moins il faut
s'en prévaloir et le montrer, pour laisser l'imagination
briller de tout son éclat.

(*OC* II, p. 612)

And speaking of Poe again he says admiringly:

Non seulement il a dépensé des efforts considérables
pour soumettre à sa volonté le démon fugitif des minutes heureuses, pour rappeler à son gré ces sensations
exquises, ces appétitions spirituelles, ces états de santé
poétique, si rares et si précieux qu'on pourrait vraiment
les considérer comme des grâces extérieures à l'homme
et comme des visitations; mais aussi il a soumis
l'inspiration à la méthode, à l'analyse la plus sévère.
Le choix des moyens! il y revient sans cesse, il insiste
avec une éloquence savante sur l'appropriation du
moyen à l'effet, sur l'usage de la rime, sur le perfec-
tionnement du refrain, sur l'adaptation du rythme au
sentiment.

(*OC* II, p. 331)

If, then, the poet of **Les Fleurs du Mal** can emphasize
as the underlying intent of his collection the desire, the
compulsion, to 'exercer mon goût passionné de

l'obstacle' (*OC* I, p.181), then that 'obstacle', setting its
strictures and resistance against the imagination (the exercise of will, the application of technical means, the
complex engineering of prosody), is not an imposition
but a partnership, not an impediment but a facilitator:
an obstacle enabling the flood to break into an infinity
of *passages* and to define itself multifariously as pattern. Technique, indeed, makes the imagination speak
more articulately, refine and crystallize the most far-
reaching of its intuitions, explore itself as a moving network of correspondences, expand and enhance its own
complexity. 'Toutes les ruses du style' (*OC* II, p.3) are
put at the service of a *formal* imagination: such as that,
perhaps, which prompts Baudelaire to promote the distinction between the 'imagination poétique' and the
'imagination de l'art' or 'imagination du dessin'; or,
quoting Mrs Crowe, between mere *fancy* and

'the *constructive* imagination, which is a much higher
function, and which, in as much as man is made in the
likeness of God, bears a distant relation to that sublime
power by which the Creator projects, creates and up-
holds his universe.'

(*OC* II, p. 624)

Might one therefore argue that the very *essence* of a
text by Baudelaire may lie, not only in the manipulation
of a chosen stanza-scheme or the broader symmetry of
parallels and oppositions, but, within that framework, in
the merest twist of a rhyme, in a curl of syntax, in the
hesitation of a mute e or the momentary giddiness of an
enjambement? For few poets have stressed with such
conviction, with such pressing personal commitment,
the *virtues* of prosody. One of his earliest exercises in
literary criticism laments the laxity and vagueness of
form of M. de Senneville, saying:

il ignore les rimes puissamment colorées, ces lanternes
qui éclairent la route de l'idée; il ignore aussi les effets
qu'on peut tirer d'un certain nombre de mots, diverse-
ment combinés.

(*OC* II, p. 11)

Gautier, by contrast, is seen as the perfect model of
'knowingness' in the apposite use of metre and finely
focused rhyme:

et il l'a parfaitement prouvé en introduisant systéma-
tiquement et continuellement la majesté de l'alexandrin
dans le vers octosyllabique (*Émaux et Camées*). Là
surtout apparaît tout le résultat qu'on peut obtenir par
la fusion du double élément, peinture et musique, par
la carrure de la mélodie, et par la pourpre régulière et
symétrique d'une rime plus qu'exacte.

(*OC* II, p. 126)

Rhymes as lanterns, illuminating and furthering the progression of ideas; rhymes as part of a structured grandeur and solidity, as a regal colouring: to these he adds

more sophisticated contributions, subtly attuned to twin or divergent strains of the human mind, as sensed, for instance, in the poetry of Leconte de Lisle whose rhymes

> répondent régulièrement à cet amour contradictoire et mystérieux de l'esprit humain pour la surprise et la symétrie.
>
> (*OC* II, p. 179)

or, in the case of Poe, the analytical awareness of the 'plaisir mathématique et musical que l'esprit tire de la rime' and the fact that, anticipating more disconcerting and ambivalent possibilities behind the customary chiming relationships,

> il a aussi cherché à rajeunir, à redoubler le plaisir de la rime en y ajoutant cet élément inattendu, l'*étrangeté,* qui est comme le condiment indispensable de toute beauté.
>
> (*OC* II, p. 336)

Rhythm is no less alive, for Baudelaire, with renewable expressive potential: 'Rhythme, parfum, lueur, ô mon unique reine!' (*OC* I, p.25). Perhaps even more than rhyme, this is the soul of verse, its moving spirit, its animating force. He expresses his liking for a 'poésie profondément rythmée' (*OC* II, p.131)—by which is meant one in which rhythm is not one of the range of cosmetics, but a power which transfuses, sets currents in motion, breeds highs and lows, surges and relapses, and wraps itself dynamically round the alternations and contrasts of thought and mood. In Banville, for example, he admires the facility with which 'la pensée se coule d'elle-même dans un rythme' (*OC* II, p.162): the foretaste of a spontaneous fusion in which the self *becomes* the medium. And, as with the *étrangeté* of some of Poe's rhymes, he is open to the *dépaysement* and disturbance of texts, one might say,

> dont les muscles ne vibrent pas suivant l'allure classique de son pays, dont la démarche n'est pas cadencée selon le rythme accoutumé . . .
>
> (*OC* II, pp. 576-77)

open to the influence of 'new rhythms' which take tradition beyond its familiar boundaries. More than this, Baudelaire the rhythmic artist sees rhythm, not simply as an intimate correspondent, a kind of spiritual *alter ego,* but as an agent of transformation, working on and through the emotions in the course of the poetic act to turn them into a superior equivalent, intervening to effect an actual exorcism, transmuting pain, for instance, into an æsthetic serenity, phonetically and rhythmically induced, and absorbing and resolving what was a series of tensions:

> C'est un des privilèges prodigieux de l'Art que l'horrible, artistement exprimé, devienne beauté, et que la *douleur* rythmée et cadencée remplisse l'esprit d'une *joie* calme.
>
> (*OC* II, p. 123)

Rhythm and rhyme, as exercised in verse, are part of the almost 'sacred' science of numbers. Hence Baudelaire's respect for Gautier in these terms:

> Il y a dans le style de Théophile Gautier une justesse qui ravit, qui étonne, et qui fait songer à ces miracles produits dans le jeu par une profonde science mathématique.
>
> (*OC* II, p. 118)

In more general terms he adds, indicating how such mysterious permutations can conjure up and bring things to life on the page, give them relief, multiply their language, and turn sensations into a hub of analogical perceptions:

> Il y a dans le mot, dans le *verbe,* quelque chose de *sacré* qui nous défend d'en faire un jeu de hasard. Manier savamment une langue, c'est pratiquer une espèce de sorcellerie évocatoire. C'est alors que la couleur parle, comme une voix profonde et vibrante; que les monuments se dressent et font saillie sur l'espace profond; que les animaux et les plantes, représentants du laid et du mal, articulent leur grimace non équivoque; que le parfum provoque la pensée et le souvenir correspondants . . .
>
> (*OC* II, p. 118).

It is in this way that the word *jongleur* (*OC* II, p.321), in its superior sense (that of ritual intermediary, transformer of appearances, magician or manipulator of occult signs, and not as mere juggler of words), can be applied to the poet as a supreme term of praise. In the pithy language of his *Journaux intimes,* Baudelaire homes in on the same hypnotic centre of thinking:

> De la langue et de l'écriture, prises comme opérations magiques, sorcellerie évocatoire.
>
> (*OC* I, p. 658)

Rhythm and rhyme, then, not seen as casual or occasional literary devices, but as ministers of a demanding 'spiritual prosody':

> Car il est évident que les rhétoriques et les prosodies ne sont pas des tyrannies inventées arbitrairement, mais une collection de règles réclamées par l'organisation même de l'être spirituel,
>
> (*OC* II, pp. 626-27)

he writes. The same point is made in numerous guises and with various shades of colouring. The author's *Projets de préfaces* for **Les Fleurs du Mal** emphasize

> comment la poésie touche à la musique par une prosodie dont les racines plongent plus avant dans l'âme humaine que ne l'indique aucune théorie classique;

while the special 'porousness' of music as a language which can, with a minimum of resistance, espouse and express every movement of the inner being, enabling the transfusion between inner and outer worlds with an uncanny reflectiveness and a clinging precision, is doubly appreciated through the 'second state' of hashish-inspired perception:

> La musique [. . .] vous parle de vous-même et vous raconte le poème de votre vie; elle s'incorpore à vous, et vous vous fondez en elle. Elle parle votre passion, non pas d'une manière vague et indéfinie, comme elle fait dans vos soirées nonchalantes, un jour d'opéra, mais d'une manière circonstanciée, positive, chaque mouvement du rythme marquant un mouvement connu de votre âme, chaque note se transformant en mot, et le poème entier entrant dans votre cerveau comme un dictionnaire doué de vie.

> (*OC* I, p. 431)

Such is this intuition of all notes (each sonority, each pulse of rhythm, each cadenced contour, each melodic thread or reverberation) contributing to a supreme harmonic entity—and a structure of the spirit—that the perfection of the text (its form, its proportions, its 'consonance') is almost, for Baudelaire, a moral re-integration, a redemption through harmony. It is in this way that he can write:

> Aussi, ce qui exaspère surtout l'homme de goût dans le spectacle du vice, c'est sa difformité, sa disproportion. Le vice porte atteinte au juste et au vrai, révolte l'intellect et la conscience; mais, comme outrage à l'harmonie, comme dissonance, il blessera plus particulièrement certains esprits poétiques; et je ne crois pas qu'il soit scandalisant de considérer toute infraction à la morale, au beau moral, comme une espèce de faute contre le rythme et la prosodie universels.

> (*OC* II, p. 334)

If Baudelaire the poet is supremely sensitive (as a *duty*) to 'l'harmonie, le balancement des lignes, l'eurythmie dans les mouvements' (*OC* I, p.432), and if, in venturing into the unversified form of the prose-poems of *Le Spleen de Paris,* he continues to seek through a new medium

> le miracle d'une prose poétique, musicale sans rythme et sans rime, assez souple et assez heurtée pour s'adapter aux mouvements lyriques de l'âme, aux ondulations de la rêverie, aux soubresauts de la conscience,

> (*OC* I, pp. 275-76)

then rhythm and rhyme are not his only agents. The 'sorcellerie évocatoire', the 'spiritualization' of the word, enlist all the resources of style, form and expression: all the potentialities of *significant form*. It may be the shape of a phrase and its pattern of evolution, an intensification or a thinning out of syntax, a clausal concatenation or contraction, a thrust of development or a holding back, a crest or trough of intonational energy. It is in this sense that he can state so confidently, as if nothing is beyond the evocative (and therefore correspondent) flexibilities of form,

que la phrase poétique peut imiter (et par là elle touche à l'art musical et à la science mathématique) la ligne horizontale, la ligne droite ascendante, la ligne droite descendante; qu'elle peut monter à pic vers le ciel, sans essoufflement, ou descendre perpendiculairement vers l'enfer avec la vélocité de toute pesanteur; qu'elle peut suivre la spirale, décrire la parabole, ou le zigzag figurant une série d'angles superposés.

> (*OC* I, p. 183)

Within such shapes and designs, no element of language is inactive. The poet, through the optic of the art critic, speaks of 'la science infinie des combinaisons de tons' (*OC* II, p.753): a thought amplified when he writes, of the inexhaustible 'mix' of ingredients and interplay of savours available to his expressive art, that

> la poésie se rattache aux arts de la peinture, de la cuisine et du cosmétique par la possibilité d'exprimer toute sensation de suavité ou d'amertume, de béatitude ou d'horreur par l'accouplement de tel substantif avec tel adjectif, analogue ou contraire.

> (*OC* I, p. 183)

Even grammar (the art of conjunctions and disjunctions, tenses and tempos, dominances and subordinations, action and description, movements and fine shadings, line and colour)—as the dynamics of hashish bring out to the 'visionary' with even greater impact and splendour—is a kind of resurrection, language leaving the limbo of its cocoon and taking flight, the abstraction of signs and functions turned into a host of living, creative energies on the page:

> La grammaire, l'aride grammaire elle-même, devient quelque chose comme une sorcellerie évocatoire; les mots ressuscitent revêtus de chair et d'os, le substantif, dans sa majesté substantielle, l'adjectif, vêtement transparent qui l'habille et le colore comme un glacis, et le verbe, ange du mouvement, qui donne le branle à la phrase.

> (*OC* I, p. 431)

Similar notes elsewhere in Baudelaire's artistic jottings, such as

> La danse grammaticale
> La voix de l'adjectif me pénétra jusqu'à l'os,

> (*OC* I, p. 594)

serve to convince one that one cannot approach his work with anything less than the assumption that each and every word, each and every part of speech, each intimation of movement (from whatever source) in the body of a text, is *necessary* and must *necessarily* form part of any appreciation. As he says in his earliest 'advice to young writers', 'Il faut donc que tous les coups portent, et que pas une touche ne soit inutile' (*OC* II, p.17). The message is still there, visible in a pressing letter, at the time of the composition of the prose-poems, indicating that the presence and positioning of a mere comma can be crucial to the balance, emphasis and significance of a whole section, part of an inviolable interdependence, and that one cannot play fast and loose with it:

> Je vous avais dit: supprimez tout un morceau, si une virgule vous déplaît dans le morceau, mais ne supprimez pas la virgule; elle a sa raison d'être.
>
> (***Corr.*** [*Correspondence*] II, p. 307)

A most interesting observation by Baudelaire the 'theatre critic' acts perhaps as a guide to any act of criticism of his own poetry. He writes:

> Ce que j'ai toujours trouvé de plus beau dans un théâtre, dans mon enfance et encore maintenant, c'est *le lustre*—un bel objet lumineux, cristallin, compliqué, circulaire et symétrique [. . .]
>
> Après tout, le lustre m'a toujours paru l'acteur principal, vu à travers le gros bout ou le petit bout de la lorgnette.
>
> (*OC* I, p. 682)

Should one approach *Les Fleurs du Mal* in the same way: imbued with the sense that it is the *lustre* which is the chief actor, that 'bel objet lumineux, cristallin, compliqué . . .' constituted by each and every individual text, almost regardless of its subject-matter, intricately fashioned, endlessly facetted, glimmering and inter-reflecting whichever way one looks at it, a unified centre of artistic activity surviving all opposites and available to an infinity of perspectives, somehow gathering to itself all elements of persons, places and plots and taking them into a superior realm which is both their sublimation and its own justification?

* * *

The approach represented by the present study respects above all the integrity of the individual poem. Each 'chapter' is a closely focused analysis of a single text from *Les Fleurs du Mal.* The aim in this way is to see all aspects of Baudelaire's poetic art working in concert towards a single end, under the influence of one surge or poetic moment of inspiration: rhymes, rhythms, cadences, sonorities, intonations, verbal textures, run-on effects, hiatuses, juxtapositions, structures of sentences, verse-forms, parallels and pairings, moulding the words, creating links, accentuating implications, shaping patterns and so on, as they conspire towards the same artistic unity. It is an approach which demands a certain 'comprehensiveness' of reading, in that the tiniest comma has its part to play, or the unobtrusive slippage of an *enjambement,* or the momentary slackness of an alleviated rhythm, or the intensified note of an exclamation, adjusting at each turn the space of the mind and imagination, modifying its trajectories, changing the

tempos of the journey. For the flesh of the verse (the 'thickness' of its rhetoric, the mobility of its prosody, its verbal muscularity, the fitfulness of its textual moodiness, its expressive impulses and interventions) is inseparable from the aspirations and agitations of the 'âme intérieure.' The *âme is* the form, and vice versa. And if Baudelaire can say of Poe:

> le style est serré, *concaténé;* la mauvaise volonté du lecteur ou sa paresse ne pourront pas passer à travers les mailles de ce réseau tressé par la logique,
>
> (*OC* II, p. 283)

then his own is all the more close-knit. It is a network which, if it is to be studied, traversed in all directions and brought together finally as a meaningful entity—as the full living expression of the poet at any given compositional moment—leaves little room for the convenience or casualness of mind of the reader more concerned for gobbets of theme of broader selective patterns skimmed from various points of the compass (a reader more given to the contents of the play than to the attractions of the *lustre*). Lamenting his inability to do justice, as translator, to Edgar Poe the poet, Baudelaire speaks of the impossibility of compensating for the 'voluptés absentes du rythme et de la rime' (*OC* II, p.347). Perhaps it is just such a loss, as if one were slipping into a more distant language where certain correspondences are no longer possible, that one risks in any *critical* translation. But it is hoped that the technique of individual analysis, clinging through the most minute aspects of expression to the intimate movements and evolutionary stirrings of the single text, will best do justice to the *living* Baudelaire and to the very process of poetry, turning *volupté* into *connaissance* but without relinquishing the *volupté,* and enabling the reader to feel immersed in the whole of a text as it lives and breathes, finds patterns, and asserts itself finally as an indissociable unity.

But such a study would be soon expedited were it nothing but one amplified *explication de texte.* Nor, perhaps, would its interest be very far-reaching. For, of all poetic collections, *Les Fleurs du Mal* is bewilderingly varied, self-contradictory, multivocal and chameleon-like. No one poem, no matter how many lines of attack it can be made to reveal, could be thought to be representative. It is also a collection with an architecture: a structural entity, with groupings and evolutionary traces, mutually illuminating clusters, and parts which support and counterbalance each other. The present study is therefore a carefully chosen juxtaposition of fourteen poems: a kind of poetic 'constellation', made up of textual bodies of different shapes and sizes, with different degrees and tones of luminosity, in different phases of activity and emissions of energy. The texts are drawn from various quarters of the work as interreflective partners: to illustrate complementary and contrasting facets, disruptions and continuities, family-likenesses and disfigurements, coincidences and contradictions; but, above all, to give some idea, across the gaps and despite the inevitable *lacunes,* of the 'ténébreuse et profonde unité' (*OC* I, p.11) of that cohesive universe which is **Les Fleurs du Mal,** to show in a new way and in new combinations that

> tout, forme, mouvement, nombre, couleur, parfum [. . .] est significatif, réciproque, converse, *correspondant,*
>
> (*OC* II, p. 133)

or that, both *within* the individual poem and *between* poems, all things are 'bien unies, conjointes, réciproquement adaptées [. . .] prudemment concaténées' (*OC* II, p.803). So, by favouring the present approach, one is striving to keep in a delicate balance two overriding interests, always in harness: the unity of the single poem and the unity of the whole. While focusing on the *lustre,* one hopes never to lose sight of the whole play.

To have stretched the number of poems studied here would have been impossible or self-defeating, such is the detail of the analysis and the multiplication of comparative perspectives opened with the addition of each new text. Fourteen is, perhaps, an arbitrary limit. But it does have, obliquely, something of the authority of the author's own observations when he writes:

> Pourquoi le spectacle de la mer est-il si infiniment et si éternellement agréable?
>
> Parce que la mer offre à la fois l'idée de l'immensité et du mouvement. Six ou sept lieues représentent pour l'homme le rayon de l'infini. Voilà un infini diminutif. Qu'importe s'il suffit à suggérer l'idée de l'infini total? Douze ou quatorze lieues (sur le diamètre), douze ou quatorze de liquide en mouvement suffisent pour donner la plus haute idée de beauté qui soit offerte à l'homme sur son habitacle transitoire.
>
> (*OC* I, p. 696)

To choose the individual poem as the first 'frame' of study is to give the poetry (and all about it which is nebulous and uncontainable) a finite context: a limited contour designed to counter excessive dispersion or the vagueness of the undifferentiated, and within which to appreciate 'l'infini dans le fini' (*OC* II, p.636), including all that conspires to make poetry 'tick.' Then to multiply that one example (say to twelve or fourteen) is to extend human attention—or in this case critical capaciousness—almost as far as it will go without its being overwhelmed and swallowed by sheer vastness: an 'infini diminutif' at another level, a structured and delimited sample, adequate and ideally proportioned enough to suggest the 'total' infinity of the collection as a whole and of Baudelaire's immeasurable genius. Adequate, too, one hopes, by its very restriction and the intensification which comes from it, and in its creation of a form conducive to innumerable other *dessins,* to give

'la plus haute idée de beauté qui soit offerte à l'homme' or something closely resembling it: the beauty of **Les Fleurs du Mal,** as one text and as a configuration of texts, almost without argument the greatest work of poetry in the history of French literature.

Note

1. See Stéphane Mallarmé, *Œuvres complètes,* Bibliothèque de la Pléiade, Gallimard, 1965, pp. 453-77.

Abbreviations

Quotations from Baudelaire's work appearing in this study are identified by the following abbreviations:

OC I: *Œuvres complètes,* Vol. I, Bibliothèque de la Pléiade, Gallimard, 1975

OC II: *Œuvres complètes,* Vol. II, Bibliothèque de la Pléiade, Gallimard, 1976

Corr. I: *Correspondance,* Vol. I, Bibliothèque de la Pléiade, Gallimard, 1973

Corr. II: *Correspondance,* Vol. II, Bibliothèque de la Pléiade, Gallimard, 1973

For all other quotations used, details are given in footnotes.

Sonya Stephens (essay date 1999)

SOURCE: Stephens, Sonya. "Thresholds." In *Baudelaire's Prose Poems: The Practice and Politics of Irony,* pp. 1-29. Oxford: Oxford University Press, 1999.

[*In the following essay, Stephens focuses on Baudelaire's handling of the boundaries of genre in* Le Spleen de Paris.]

> Il n'est de seuil qu'à franchir.
>
> Genette

Baudelaire's **Spleen de Paris** (**Petits Poèmes en prose**) invites an exploration of genre, not just because its title signals genre (the only genre with an oxymoron for a name) but because Baudelaire here offers a text with no real generic precedents. The way in which these prose poems present Baudelaire's consciousness of boundaries and of the contours of different literary landscapes figured in the hybrid requires further exploration since, in operating on the boundary between genres, and between different modes of discourse, Baudelaire makes choices which deliberately uphold or subvert existing literary models.

The lack of any significant precursory models lends an indeterminacy to the text, especially as, despite earlier pioneering attempts at something approaching the prose poem, it was only with the posthumous publication of *Le Spleen de Paris* (*Petits Poèmes en prose*) in 1869 that any sort of generic blueprint can be said to have been established.[1] But if it is generally agreed that Baudelaire's prose poems constitute the model which was to determine the parameters of the genre and validate all such literary enterprises in the future, establishing expectations and conditioning the reader's response to such texts, the nature of that model remains sketchy, little more elaborate on the subject than Baudelaire's *lettre-dédicace* to Houssaye.

This letter is, of course, significant, for not only does it make reference to the need for an authenticating precursory text, it is very much a part of the paratext, what Gérard Genette refers to as the 'contrat (ou pacte) générique',[2] or elsewhere as the threshold of the text, the *seuil,* that indeterminate zone between the outside of the text and the inside, 'une zone non seulement de transition mais de *transaction*: lieu privilégié d'une pragmatique et d'une stratégie, d'une action sur le public au service, bien ou mal compris et accompli, d'un meilleur accueil du texte et d'une lecture plus pertinente.'[3] The questions of titling and precedents, both of which constitute elements forming a part of the threshold, or paratext, of Baudelaire's prose poems are an appropriate place to start in a study which sets out to uncover the textual strategies of a new genre and to show these to be predicated on duality, and sometimes even duplicity.

The title of the work, Baudelaire's other major poetic collection, is itself highly problematic. We know that *Les Fleurs du mal* was the title Baudelaire settled on for his first collection only after several alternatives and much hesitation,[4] and there is similar evidence of long reflection and measured alternatives in relation to the collected prose poems. The very first prose poems were published in 1855 alongside verse poems and under no specific collective title.[5] From 1857 to 1861, Baudelaire used the collective title of *Poèmes nocturnes,* which recurs several times in his correspondence, but as a title accompanying the publication of prose poems only once.[6] From 1861 to 1866 the publications in various newspapers and reviews consistently give the titles *Poëmes en prose* or *Petits Poëmes en prose,* with *Le Spleen de Paris, Poèmes en prose* occurring twice in 1864.[7] There is only one other title used, *Petits poèmes lycanthropes,* which appears suddenly in June 1866,[8] only a matter of days before another newspaper prints a poem under the heading of *Le Spleen de Paris.*[9] The first collection of the prose poems in volume form is posthumous and appears in 1869 as the fourth volume of Baudelaire's *Œuvres complètes: Petits Poèmes en prose. Les Paradis artificiels.*[10]

A certain critical reflection is behind these titles, all of which have the status of *official* titles, that is to say titles agreed or used by Baudelaire (and/or his editors),

in his lifetime and in the context of a publication of one or more prose poems.[11] Other titles exist, *La Lueur et la fumée, Le Promeneur solitaire,* or *Le Rôdeur parisien,* for example, but these cannot be considered official,[12] since they never accompanied a publication of the prose poems and occur only in private correspondence which, despite a growing awareness of the private document as destined for public consumption,[13] can only be considered part of the 'epitext' and as *officieux.*[14] The hesitation and reflection that these changes and the correspondence suggest lead us to attach significance to them, although they are, independently of all hesitation, textual items which invite analysis and speculation.

The role of the title of any work is to identify it, to designate its contents, and to seduce the public into reading the work in question. The title might also indicate the form of the text. It can be considered significant, then, that Baudelaire chose variations on a similar theme and also that he selected titles offering the complete range of possibilities (title, subtitle, and generic indicator). Most of Baudelaire's titles for the publication of the prose poems belong to the class of *titres rhématiques,* titles which designate the text itself, or which designate the text as object. Genette takes the title of the prose poems, at one point, as illustrative of the very distinction he is elaborating:

> Si le thème du *Spleen de Paris* est bien (admettons-le par hypothèse) ce que désigne ce titre, le rhème en est [. . .] ce que Baudelaire en dit (en écrit), et donc ce qu'il en fait, c'est-à-dire un recueil de petits poèmes en prose. Si Baudelaire, au lieu de l'intituler par son thème, l'avait intitulé par son rhème, il l'aurait nommé par exemple *Petits poèmes en prose.*[15]

This recognizes that Baudelaire did indeed do this and sees the poet's hesitation as resolved only after his death, with the decision of Banville and Asselineau in favour of the *rhème.*[16] This distinction, however, indicates a central problem facing critics of the prose poems: how to designate the work? A glance at the critical editions published since 1869 suggests a clear preference for the *rhématique,*[17] but it is a position opposed by Claude Pichois in his edition for the Bibliothèque de la Pléiade, who insists that *Le Spleen de Paris* is 'le seul titre attesté avec certitude durant les dernières années de la vie de Baudelaire' and that '*Petits poèmes en prose* est trop peu attesté pour qu'on puisse retenir cette expression comme un titre qui correspondrait à l'intention de Baudelaire.'[18]

The solution to this thorny problem is not to be found in Genette's discussion of titles, although some elements can usefully be pressed into service. There is, for example, the question of timing. Pichois refers mainly to the later years, justifiably, since it is probably at this point that clear plans for presenting the prose poems as a collected volume are forming in Baudelaire's mind.

Genette, on the other hand, suggests that the title is born with the first publication, although he admits that hesitations may persist and titles may change after that point. The official status of the title is, however, restricted to those appearing (the last appearing?) 'du vivant de l'auteur et avec son aveu.'[19] Both of these positions raise further problems. Since the titles appearing in Baudelaire's lifetime are in newspapers and accompany a variable number of poems, they might be said to constitute a very different publication from a collection in volume form. In this context, there are also questions to be raised about authorial and editorial choice, for although the same can be true of other editions, it is unquestionably the case that Baudelaire was largely at the mercy of newspaper editors at the time of publication of these prose poems. The problem with the title of *Le Spleen de Paris* is that it occurs less frequently in the peritext (though more frequently in the epitext) and, most importantly, it does not appear in isolation, with one exception (and accompanying only one poem), in Baudelaire's lifetime. Pichois offers what seems like a way out of this impasse of official and unofficial titles when he says that 'deux publications seulement reflètent la volonté de l'auteur' (*OC* [*Œuvres complétes*] i. 1305), those of *La Presse* and the posthumous *Œuvres complètes,* both of which paradoxically offer *Petits poèmes en prose* as the title.

The purpose of this discussion is less to open a debate about which is the correct title than to demonstrate the prevalence of what is often seen to be only a descriptive superscription, a generic indicator appended to the title. *Petits Poèmes en prose* often stood alone as a title and accompanied an overwhelming majority of the publications in the press, and indeed is the title given to most editions since (where it is *Le Spleen de Paris* which has appeared as subtitle). It seems perfectly reasonable to speculate, however, that Baudelaire might well have changed the title for publication in volume form, particularly given his predilection for 'les titres mystérieux ou les titres pétards',[20] and the correspondence very much points in that direction.[21]

There is, moreover, an article accompanying the first publication of three prose poems in the *Figaro,* which, in the view of Robert Kopp, although it may not have been written by Baudelaire, was almost certainly heavily influenced by his view of the work (not to mention by his vocabulary) and is worth, therefore, quoting in full:

> *Le Spleen de Paris* est le titre adopté par M. C. Baudelaire pour un livre qu'il prépare, et dont il veut faire un digne pendant aux *Fleurs du mal.* Tout ce qui se trouve naturellement exclu de l'œuvre rythmée et rimée, ou plus difficile à y exprimer, tous les détails matériels, et, en un mot, toutes les minutes de la vie prosaïque, trouvent leur place dans l'œuvre en prose, où l'idéal et le trivial se fondent dans un amalgame inséparable. D'ailleurs, l'âme sombre et malade que l'auteur a dû

> supposer pour écrire *Les Fleurs du mal* est, à peu de choses près, la même qui compose *Le Spleen de Paris.* Dans l'ouvrage en prose, comme dans l'œuvre en vers, toutes les suggestions de la rue, de la circonstance et du ciel parisiens, tous les soubresauts de la conscience, toutes les langueurs de la rêverie, la philosophie, le songe et même l'anecdote peuvent prendre leur rang à tour de role. Il s'agit seulement de trouver une prose qui s'adapte aux différents états de l'âme du flâneur morose. Nos lecteurs jugeront si M. Charles Baudelaire y a réussi.

> Certaines gens croient que Londres seul a le privilège aristocratique du spleen, et que Paris, le joyeux Paris, n'a jamais connu cette noire maladie. Il y a peut-être bien, comme le prétend l'auteur, une sorte de spleen parisien; et il affirme que le nombre est grand de ceux qui l'ont connu et le reconnaîtront.[22]

Here the generic indicator is missing, but the first paragraph elaborates not only the relationship with the earlier poetic volume,[23] it also offers an explanation of the way in which Baudelaire's prose poetry form will embrace a range of other genres. Having rehearsed the formal qualities and innovative shape of this new prose collection, the author—the article is signed Gustave Bourdin—proceeds to justify the title as it is given, linking the poetry of the street with the 'noire maladie' of Paris.

From this we can infer two things. If this article is the fruit of Baudelaire's mind in any way at all, we can read it as an explanation of his choice of titles and a conscious elaboration of the way in which he would hope the careful reader would apprehend the text. If it is solely the product of Bourdin's mind and pen, it is a perfect example of such apprehension of the text (or a gloss on the *lettre-dédicace* published in *La Presse* in 1862). In either case, we are compelled to see the titling of the work as a significant part of the peritext and as a threshold not to be crossed without some reflection. The same can be said to be true both of this Bourdin article and the letter to Houssaye, since at the time of publication (and, in the case of Houssaye, ever since) these form part of the peritext, or the *perigraphie* as Compagnon terms it,[24] and exercise a powerful influence over the way in which the text is both approached and appreciated.

We must, however, remain with titles for the moment, for these are the most public face of the text, that part of the work which will reach a wider audience than its readers, like headlines, and which may or may not seduce into further participation. Baudelaire's love of 'les titres mystérieux ou les titres pétards' is an avowed desire to seduce, or at very least to enter into some form of ludic relationship with the reader. There is, indeed, a paradox here, in that the mystery of a title (its refusal to yield concrete meaning and its suggestiveness) would seem to run counter to the descriptive function elaborated above.[25] The paradox is further compounded by the apparent reassurance of a generic description, for we are told we are dealing with prose poems, and the shock of the new, for prose poems have no precedent for the average reader.[26] What actually seduces is the epithet *petits* which, in its familiarity and unthreatening diminutive, appeals to the reader's indulgence. This is, of course, misleading, since there is nothing slight about the prose poems as a collection, although the lack of any authenticating precursory text might well have led Baudelaire to anticipate such a reaction. It is misleading, too, because it plays with the convention of the generic superscription which, by the mid-1850s was falling into disuse,[27] and suggests an ironic appropriation of an archaic tradition in the service of an innovative and experimental enterprise. In this respect, Baudelaire could be seen to be participating in a tradition to come where generic descriptions would suggest innovation with genre, and where there would be a blending of different literary forms and traditions, or at least their appellations, to create new hybrids of which the *poème en prose* would be but the first of many more elusive generic indicators.[28]

The past tradition, such as it is, is clearly invoked in the *lettre-dédicace* to Arsène Houssaye and in this dedicatory letter there is further evidence of the pre-eminence of the *rhématique* which serves, in some ways, to explicate, or at very least to amplify, the generic debate already present in the titling of the work. Indeed, the explicit function of the letter to Houssaye is precisely to set these prose poems in a generic context. In the case of earlier attempts at prose poetry (or what have been called 'poèmes en prose avant la lettre')[29] writers of prose poetry had linked their work to established verse models. This included both foreign-language originals, which prose poetry could translate, and literary transpositions of works from the plastic arts, so that the ends were seen to justify the means and distracted attention from form to content. This is, of course, the case with the secondary (or concealed primary) debt acknowledged in Baudelaire's letter to Houssaye where he refers to **Gaspard de la Nuit,** a work subtitled **Fantaisies à la manière de Rembrandt et de Callot.** Though known only to a few cognoscenti (only forty copies were sold), the text was, in fact, becoming increasingly renowned. The renown of the work is also explicitly, indeed rather heavy-handedly, referred to in Baudelaire's letter:

> J'ai une petite confession à vous faire. C'est en feuilletant, pour la vingtième fois au moins, le fameux *Gaspard de la Nuit* d'Aloysius Bertrand (un livre connu de vous, de moi et de quelques-uns de nos amis, n'a-t-il pas tous les droits à être appelé *fameux*?) que l'idée m'est venue de tenter quelque chose d'analogue, et d'appliquer à la description de la vie moderne, ou plutôt d'*une* vie moderne et plus abstraite, le procédé qu'il avait appliqué à la peinture de la vie ancienne si étrangement pittoresque.

> (*OC* i. 275)

Gaspard de la Nuit's poetic and artistic focus was to be the alibi for much of what succeeded as the prose poem continued to search for generic identity and the new prose poets' enlistment of Bertrand in their cause is a manifestation of the conventions of all dedicatory practice.[30] In other words, dedications of this public kind imply an acknowledgement of power, if not of influence. What is significant about the passage quoted above is that the dedication mimics an exchange of views, an aesthetic triangle in which Baudelaire seems to enlist Houssaye in a shared enterprise (prose poetry and aesthetic interest), a shared circle (*nos amis*) and a shared cultural inheritance in this domaine (Bertrand). The exchange is suggested through the interrogative parenthesis, which plays upon the celebrity of the work—with irony emblazoned in the italics. With a circulation of just forty copies, the work could hardly merit an epithet suggesting great celebrity or reputation, but it could justifiably be argued that, within a given literary circle, it might merit being held in esteem. But *fameux* precisely means something of great or poor reputation (even without italics) and there is subterfuge here in Baudelaire's feigned artistic association with Houssaye, who is, himself, treated to a helping of the same ambiguous recognition in a subsequent paragraph.

Indeed, when Baudelaire completes this aesthetic exchange, he refers to Houssaye's similar aspirations and efforts, in relation particularly to *La Chanson du vitrier*: 'Vous-même, mon cher ami, n'avez-vous pas tenté de traduire en une *chanson* le cri strident du *Vitrier,* et d'exprimer dans une prose lyrique toutes les désolantes suggestions que ce cri envoie jusqu'aux mansardes, à travers les plus hautes brumes de la rue?' (*OC* i. 276). The italics masquerade as integrated title, but what this mask barely conceals is Baudelaire's own 'désolante suggestion' that this *attempt* fell far short of poetry and what must surely be a deliberate intertext in his own titling of a prose poem treating a similar theme then begs the question: which of the two is truly the 'mauvais vitrier'?

It is in no way surprising that Baudelaire should seek to flatter Houssaye, who was, after all, *directeur littéraire* at *La Presse* in 1862 and the reference to **La Chanson du vitrier** as a precursory text, and indeed the dedication as a whole, is clearly ironic.[31] The acknowledgement of Bertrand must, then, also be ironic since, no sooner has Baudelaire referred to this than he insists upon the difference of his own enterprise.[32] It is a difference, moreover, to which the poet returns in relation to his own model as well as to Bertrand's:

> Mais, pour dire le vrai, je crains que ma jalousie ne m'ait pas porté bonheur. Sitôt que j'eus commencé le travail, je m'aperçus que non seulement je restais bien loin de mon mystérieux et brillant modèle, mais encore que je faisais quelque chose (si cela peut s'appeler *quelque chose*) de singulièrement différent, accident

dont tout autre que moi s'enorgueillirait sans doute, mais qui ne peut qu'humilier profondément un esprit qui regarde comme le plus grand honneur d'accomplir *juste* ce qu'il a projeté de faire.

(*OC* i: 276)

This apparently self-deprecating conclusion is already to be found in a more private letter to Houssaye (dating from Christmas 1861) in which Baudelaire expresses the view that Bertrand's work is *inimitable* and says: 'J'ai bien vite senti que je ne pouvais pas persévérer dans ce pastiche' (*C* [*Correspondence*] ii. 208). Here again, Baudelaire's apparent self-deprecation creates a sense of unease and the reservations seem to attach themselves to the object of imitation rather than to himself as imitator. This 'malaise' appears justified by the questioning of form, by the experimentalism of any precursory texts, by all the suggestions of this new poetry as a 'low' art form. Bertrand himself describes his texts as 'bambochades romantiques' and 'fantaisies', while other 'precursors' use similarly unpretentious terms to designate their works, including 'ballades', 'chants', 'rhythmes primitifs', and 'fusains.'[33] Baudelaire's statement about models in the *lettre-dédicace* reinforces a sense of poets in search of a form, thereby providing an interface between the textual production of prose poems and the social and literary situation (between text and context). Just as it situates itself, however, it draws away, so that the ironic acknowledgement to precursors and the insincere self-deprecation of the concluding paragraph and of the ***Petits Poèmes en prose*** all become suspect. And just as pastiche seems to apply to Bertrand rather than to Baudelaire, so the 'mystérieux et brillant modèle' appears to remain the true outcome rather than the expression of failure it purports to be.

Readers of Baudelaire have every reason to be cautious since, as Ross Chambers has shown, his dedications 'have inspired suspicion and raised questions concerning their sincerity and the degree of opportunism, or possibly irony, they reveal.'[34] The ***Salon de 1846*** (**"Aux Bourgeois"**), Baudelaire's public dedication of ***Les Fleurs du mal*** (to Théophile Gautier), this double (and doubly suspicious) acknowledgement of Bertrand and Houssaye, not to mention the dedications of individual poems all create a sense in which one would not wish to trust the hand that dedicates. There is no doubt that Baudelaire, in these dedications, is recruiting established power in order to secure a better reception for his work than his own reputation might otherwise enable, and for this reason he settles on respectable figures of the period. He exploits, in other words, their social prestige for his own ends and, at the same time, generates an aesthetic context in which he is able to set his own work apart from that of others. In so doing, he recruits through intertextuality these favoured literary figures of the regime, but with covert and self-interested

oppositional ends. The dedicatee is simultaneously both a presence and an absence, since his name is his reputation (a cultural item) and his work is brought into relation with Baudelaire's text *in absentia*. Where that absence is also figured as difference, as it is in this case, and indeed as it might be said to be in any intertext, what the dedication and the acknowledgement of Houssaye foreground is contrast and a deliberately duplicitous invocation and acknowledgement of influence.

This assertion of difference through such duplicitous discourse suggests also that both public and private discursive systems are simultaneously in operation. The public act of dedication moves here, in other words, towards the more private act of communication. This is an evolution which can be traced through the act of dedication itself, as Chambers has noted in respect of the increasingly common practice of the public dedication to a private person: 'Here the publicity given to the dedicatory gesture combines with the anonymity of the dedicatee so as to confuse the functions both of public dedication (whose dedicatee [. . .] is necessarily a public figure) and of the private *envoi* (an interpersonal gesture).'[35] This point is amplified by tracing the evolution of the dedication through four main periods—the classical or 'pious' dedication, the neo-classical or 'political' dedication, the 'esthetic' dedication (the category into which we can place Baudelaire), and the 'privatized' dedication—and by seeing the recruitment of established literary figures as a direct development of the 'political' (patronage) period. The 'privatized', Chambers argues, breaks with the tradition 'in that it seeks less to place the text under the protection of some source of power than to acknowledge a new type of social situation in which messages are by definition privatized, that is alienated.' He also elaborates two further categories in his classification of dedications: whether or not the dedication is *plain* or *motivated* and the extent to which it is integrated into the text it accompanies.[36]

Baudelaire's letter to Houssaye is clearly a *motivated* dedication, and one which displays all the rhetoric of ironic obsequiousness. His duplicity in presenting this as a dedication, or his insincerity, makes available a private message which, one can only assume, Houssaye did not receive, since it was undoubtedly his decision to preface the first publication of the prose poems in *La Presse* with this letter. This emphasizes the extent to which the covert implications of Baudelaire's writing were more difficult to perceive in their own age than they are now, so that even implausible dedicatees can function effectively in this process as 'screen-mechanisms' and even obvious 'noise' in the message can appear to go unheard.[37] The function of this, then, goes well beyond the attempt to place the new text under the 'protection' of respectable figures; it goes further, even, than recruiting these respectable figures for oppositional ends. Like the dedication of the *Salon de 1846,* which has been described as a 'self-contradictory motivating text',[38] this implies cultural isolation more than it implies any sort of debt or influence. It is, in short, a parody of influence performed by a further parody of the prose poetry genre's referential practice.

Baudelaire uses the letter to Houssaye to launch the concerns of the prose poetry experiment (in the broadest sense) as well as the concerns of the text. As Chambers argues, 'if the prime function of a dedication is to tie the text as a structure to an address that situates it in a system of exchange, a corollary function is to make this system available in its historical specificity, as an indicator of the circumstances of production in light of which the text assumes it is most appropriately read.'[39] The insincerity of the dedication to Houssaye, particularly in the context of a literary debate, emphasizes Baudelaire's aesthetic isolation, and provides further evidence of a 'privatizing' effect of this dedicatory discourse, since the irony alienates him from it. Indeed, it is Baudelaire's truly 'private' dedication (that of the *Paradis artificiels* to J.G.F.) which suggests absolute isolation from any readership:

> Il importe d'ailleurs fort peu que la raison de cette dédicace soit comprise. Est-il même bien nécessaire, pour le contentement de l'auteur, qu'un livre quelconque soit compris, excepté de celui ou de celle pour qui il a été composé? Pour tout dire, enfin, indispensable qu'il ait été écrit pour *quelqu'un*? J'ai, quant à moi, si peu de goût pour le monde vivant que, pareil à ces femmes sensibles et désœuvrées qui envoient, dit-on, par la poste leurs confidences à des amis imaginaires, volontiers je n'écrirais que pour les morts.
>
> (*OC* i. 399-400)

To this extent, one might argue that, apart from a desire to set his prose-poetry experiment apart from any precursor, the dedicatory act is spurious, a mere pretext for an elaboration of the concerns of the text and, as such, less a dedication than a preface, less a contextual-textual act than a purely textual one and, in the case of the prose poems, more akin to a liminary poem, such as **"Au Lecteur"**, than to a dedicatory letter. Like **"Au Lecteur"**, too, the dedications to Houssaye and to J.G.F. (both of which are letters) are written in an apostrophic mode. This textual strategy implies an economy of exchange (of ideas, of favours, of language), but an exchange which is dysfunctional, because of the poet's cultural isolation in his historical moment.

Despite all this, the letter to Houssaye does address a reader, and significantly a reader who is other than the dedicatee, despite the apostrophe:

> Mon cher ami, je vous envoie un petit ouvrage dont on ne pourrait pas dire, sans injustice, qu'il n'a ni queue ni tête, puisque tout, au contraire, y est à la fois tête et queue, alternativement et réciproquement. Considérez,

je vous prie, quelles admirables commodités cette combinaison nous offre à tous, *à vous, à moi et au lecteur. Nous pouvons couper où nous voulons, moi ma rêverie, vous le manuscript, le lecteur sa lecture; car je ne suspends pas la volonté de celui-ci au fil interminable d'une intrigue superflue.*

(*OC* i. 275, my italics)

Here Houssaye is addressed as editor, rather than reader and this can clearly be seen as further evidence of a *motivated* dedication. The reader, on the other hand, is a third party in the system of exchange, but one who is precisely significant in that it is he who is the true *destinataire*. So, although Chambers could be said to be right in suggesting that it is an error 'to read the dedicatee as a figure for the reader and to see the text-dedicatee relation as a model of the text-reader relation',[40] we can say that in this case the text-reader relation is *also* figured and independently of the dedicatee. In this respect, we might argue that the role of the reader in the dedication to Houssaye is to receive the text and that the role of Houssaye is merely to make the text, the generic context, and the reading strategy available. The dedication is, in other words, both a social and textual vehicle which ensures safe delivery of the *envoi*. It is a preface.

In this respect, too, we might say that the *lettre-dédicace* develops the generic superscription or the *titre rhématique* and that it amplifies the literary context of that superscription, so that the threshold of the text is an account of the text's objectives, and functions in a series of reciprocal relations. The act of dedication is, then, an amplification and explanation of the title, in its thematic focus—*Le Spleen de Paris* becomes 'c'est surtout de la fréquentation des villes énormes que naît cet idéal obsédant'—but more significantly, in its generic invitation to (or confrontation with) the reader. Indeed the relationships are most carefully sustained by the way in which the *lettre-dédicace* seems to cross its own generic threshold in mimicking, through its very form, the text which it purports to describe. It is, in other words, a prose poem on the prose poem which provides a commentary on the title and the dedicatory act and, in form and function, speaks of genre.

If Houssaye is merely the intermediary in an indirect act of communication, with the reader, the *lettre-dédicace* is also properly a preface in that it postulates an imminent reading of the text it introduces. What is more, it suggests the kind of non-linear reading that the text requires. This indirect mode of communication with the reader not only reinforces the ironic distance between the named circle of readers (Houssaye and 'nos amis'), but also suggests, in fact, that it is only to an unknown reader (as in the J.G.F. preface), or a future reader that this *text* can be addressed whatever the letter might *appear* to say. Houssaye is a *destinataire-relais*[41] who has a role to play, but who is not, as is often the case in such instances, the reader's representative. And because the reading process figured in the prefatory *dédicace* is accomplished by another, Houssaye's role is limited to that of editor ('Nous pouvons couper où nous voulons [. . .] vous le manuscrit').

As a form of preface, then, this *lettre-dédicace* does all that it should. It situates the work in a context and offers some sort of genesis of it; it offers a commentary on the title of the work (although not explicitly); it offers a way, an order, of reading and raises questions of genre. All of these are, according to Genette's typology of the *préface originale,* functions of this kind of paratext.[42] The danger of such a preface is, of course, that it runs the risk of not being attached to the work, of not forming a part of the 'perigraphie' and, therefore, of not *completing* the text. But this is a danger most likely to occur in early, rather than later, editions of the work, since epitextual information moves increasingly into the peritext as editions become more complete. It is not, in any case, a situation which poses problems in this instance.

The dedicatory act, and the choice of dedicatee, enables Baudelaire to compose a preface which, while it does not specify the kind of reader it would like, contains an oppositional discourse which tells us the kind of reader to whom it is not addressed. In its *mimed* act of communication, it constitutes a structural entity which has meaning and it indissolubly associates specific historic conditions of textual production and questions of genre, which amount to ways of securing *une bonne lecture.* As a poetic text in its own right (a prose poem on the prose poem), indissolubility of poetic enterprise and generic debate, of literary and social context and textual reception, the *lettre-dédicace* is, as much as the text itself, an object of reading. The discursive function of the paratext would, then, appear to be the bringing into sharper focus of the lack of connection between dedicatee and intended reader and between text and precursor. By emphasizing this disconnection, this dysfunction, the *lettre-dédicace* foregrounds communicational failure (alienation) and prefigures the conflicting discursive, ideological, and generic modes of interaction of the prose poems themselves.

"L'Étranger" reflects just such a communicational failure. Despite the fact that we are told that we can begin where we like and read in any order, the convention of reading is such that any reader would be unlikely to 'skip' the first poem, and it is this text which is placed at the conventional head of the work.[43] The title of this prose poem is, of course, significant, too, and compounds the sense of alienation already present in the paratext, and indeed amplifies it by the disturbing intangibility of the exchange and, indeed, of the speakers, neither of whom are identified.

The questions asked in the poem would seem to represent the position of the socialized individual, the man who, by association with his suggestions of what might be important to his interlocutor, values family, friends, patriotism, faith, wealth, and beauty. All of these values are socially inscribed in an ideological, and by extension, a discursive system in which the stranger does not share, and would not want to share:

> 'Qui aimes-tu le mieux, homme énigmatique, dis? ton père, ta mère, ta sœur ou ton frère?
>
> —Je n'ai ni père, ni mère, ni sœur, ni frère.
>
> —Tes amis?
>
> —Vous vous servez là d'une parole dont le sens m'est resté jusqu'à ce jour inconnu.
>
> —Ta patrie?
>
> —J'ignore sous quelle latitude elle est située.
>
> —La beauté?
>
> —Je l'aimerais volontiers déesse et immortelle.
>
> —L'or?
>
> —Je le hais comme vous haïssez Dieu.
>
> —Eh! qu'aimes-tu donc, extraordinaire étranger?
>
> —J'aime les nuages . . . les nuages qui passent . . . là-bas . . . là-bas . . . les merveilleux nuages!'
>
> (*OC* i. 277)

The act of communication fails because the interlocutors do not recognize each other's cultural referents, they do not speak the same language. Even at points of contact, such as beauty, ambiguity is introduced by a response which defines a (no doubt very different) form of beauty and which specifies an inability to embrace this as a value because of the doubt over its existence introduced by the conditional form of *aimer* here. The response to the suggestion of gold is also significant for it elicits a more negative response, but one which is ultimately left ambiguous because of a lack of information regarding the faith of the questioner. This, too, then is an exchange characterized by indirectness which in its dysfunction signifies social and cultural alienation. It is, moreover, an alienation reinforced by the implied social disrespect for artistic values of the *tu* form used by the questioner, and an alterity which the artist desires since this is the mark of his benediction in a hostile environment. He, then, uses the *vous* form and dominates the exchange by his expression of incomprehension, his manipulation of the discourse of the other, and by the rejection of the interlocutor's code.

It has been shown that a similar, but inverted dynamic, is in operation in another of the poems which also occurs in proximity to this text, 'Chacun sa chimère', and which also expresses the displacement or desertion of meaning in the particular cultural and historical context.[44] Here, however, the exchange is reported, and only summarily: 'Je questionnai l'un de ces hommes, et je lui demandai où ils allaient ainsi. Il me répondit qu'il n'en savait rien, ni lui, ni les autres; mais qu'évidemment ils allaient quelque part, puisqu'ils étaient poussés par un invincible besoin de marcher' (*OC* i. 282). The exchange, as reported, does function. Communication occurs even if the experience of the force which motivates all parties is different (each having his own *chimère*).

In **"Le Miroir"**, on the other hand, there is an equivalent dialogue and one which expresses an equivalent opposition of discursive and ideological positions.

> Un homme épouvantable entre et se regarde dans la glace.
>
> 'Pourquoi vous regardez-vous au miroir, puisque vous ne pouvez vous voir qu'avec déplaisir?'
>
> L'homme épouvantable me répond: '—Monsieur, d'après les immortels principes de 89, tous les hommes sont égaux en droits; donc, je possède le droit de me mirer; avec plaisir ou déplaisir, cela ne regarde que ma conscience.'
>
> Au nom du bon sens, j'avais sans doute raison; mais, au point de vue de la loi, il n'avait pas tort.

Even before the exchange occurs, the position is fixed, since the narrative discourse unequivocally asserts a position which finds the interlocutor 'épouvantable.' The narrator challenges the man he considers ugly and receives a reasoned answer (that no self-justification is required). The exchange appears to function unproblematically, despite different ideological positions, but the delay in the articulation of the response (*I can look at myself if I like*) and the justification of the response, which is apparently at odds with the thrust of the challenge, allows a form of communicational dysfunction to occur anyway.

The narrator, a reasonable man, concedes the point and appears to accept the position as being no less valid than his own initial challenge. One man's response is considered from the point of view of authority—'la loi'—the other from the perspective of common sense—'le bon sens.' In a functional system—both communicational and political—one might reasonably expect these to be synonymous or, at very least, to be operative together. The poem uses a certain rhetoric to suggest the same kind of acknowledgement as the *lettre-dédicace* mimes. The more positive formulation couples common sense with reason (and an affirmation that the narrator *is right*); on the other hand, the *homme épouvantable* receives narrative treatment which negatively counterbalances the positive affirmation and gives him only ambiguous credence: from the point of view of the law, the man has done no wrong (which does not necessarily mean that he was not misguided in his belief). This text

can be read, then, as a claim that equality is not a feature of existence and that justice and reason are not always compatible. And as an allegory of the kind of exchange economies that interest us here, it can be seen as a conflict of personal taste (or prejudice) and aesthetics, as well as a statement about public reception. By incorporating the rather facile statement of his interlocutor about the rights of all citizens, the accepted currency of speech act is called into question and consequently devalued.

The reader approaches the text with certain codes in mind and a willingness to respond to variants of those codes. Reception, or reader expectation of genre, implies recognition of certain modes of discourse, both literary and extraliterary, employed by the writer. The writer operates subtle shifts or modifications to codes to elicit different reader responses and in so doing to break out of generic and often ideological constraints. The complex narrative and linguistic strategies used to manipulate reader response also imply a rhetoric which could be seen to be the intersection of register and reception. All of these have their thresholds, because all have distinct identities.

Uncertainty about the generic identity of the prose poem means that a reader cannot be programmed by any historical conception of genre in its case, but rather proceeds to conceptualize the form based on the guidance of the paratext and on individual experience of the texts. It could be argued that the author's most important communicational act is his choice of type or genre which determines the text's meaning and that by reconstructing this genre the critic can make possible the representation of that meaning.[45] There is no doubt that choice of genre *means*. The choice of prose poetry is subversive, strictly formally, in literary-political and in socio-ideological terms. It transgresses an established boundary, by permitting the prosaic into the world of poetry and this is compounded by adding the generically descriptive subtitle to a generically non-descriptive, thematic title. Since these prose poems are often short narratives, and narratives for the most part which themselves transgress boundaries, the labelling seems deliberately misleading (or as arbitrary and cynical as Baudelaire's dedicatory practice).

Baudelaire's aesthetic doctrine of surprise, 'après le plaisir d'être étonné, il n'en est pas de plus grand que de causer une surprise' (*OC* i. 323) might thus translate into unexpected discursive and paradigmatic shifts. Baudelaire patterns the identity of the ***Petits Poèmes en prose*** by moving in and out of conventional structures which trigger reader response to genres, just as he moves in and out of the conventions of the dedication. What programmes reader response to these texts is precisely the peritext (the dedicatory letter, the title of the work), as well as the title of each piece (the *intertitres*) and the mode of discourse chosen to open each autonomous part. The register not only defines the identity of the piece, it tends to define the relationship with the audience and, therefore, to establish the rhetoric. To transgress the boundaries by introducing a different sort of discourse, literary or extraliterary, not only offends, or, at very least, unsettles the audience, it also challenges the literary because it introduces extra-generic possibilities into the confines of a specific generic space. By playing upon the conventions of any form or practice, and such conventions translate into reader expectation, limits can be both abolished and respected, bringing into question the boundaries of different forms, the way in which these can identify a content, and the seriousness of the intent.[46]

By launching the concerns of the text with duplicitous rhetorical strategies allowing different value systems to coexist, Baudelaire signals what he will do with the prose poem as genre. **"L'Étranger"** and **"Le Miroir"**, in staging exchanges which are 'sans queue ni tête' offer no resolution and sustain this discursive strategy. The texts are a continuum of different views, of conflicting perspectives, as mobile and as unstable as the clouds. The social interaction figured here is not properly identified (as it must at least appear to be in the *dédicace*), but is constituted only in the differential discursive positions which, because communication is dysfunctional, leave the poems as moments of enunciation, brief encounters of the unintelligible kind.

By contrast, certain poems which figure similar exchange mechanisms and which express similar confrontations and paradoxes seem almost too clear in their meaning. **"Le Chien et le flacon"**, for example, is a closed form, *lisible,* as opposed to *scriptible,* and can, like the *dédicace* and **"Le Miroir"** be read as an allegory of reception. Henri Lemaître sees this poem as characteristic of the 'poème-boutade': 'une sorte de genre littéraire auquel il semble, d'après certains passages des *Journaux intimes,* Baudelaire ait aimé s'exercer [. . .] où tout un monde de désillusion et de rancœur se ramasse dans une incisive brièveté.'[47] There is indeed a fragment from *Mon cœur mis à nu* in the context of which this closed prosaic allegory might best be read:

> Le Français est un animal de basse-cour, si bien domestiqué qu'il n'ose franchir aucune palissade. Voir ses goûts en art et en littérature. C'est un animal de race latine; l'ordre ne lui déplaît pas dans son domicile et en littérature, il est scatophage. Il raffole des excréments.
>
> (*OC* i. 698)

This diary entry might be said to function in a similar way to the *lettre-dédicace* in that it provides an interface between text and reading tactic, with self-

referential resonances which emphasize the nature of the creative (and generic) limits, as well as the limitations of reader response. **"Le Chien et le flacon"** is a laboured allegory, an overdetermined text which, given its point, might be seen as a parody of just what the implied reader might achieve. This poem can, however, be read as more than a mere allegory of a certain kind of reader's limited reception, and, as the diary entry suggests, as an attempt to go beyond defined limits, beyond the *palissades* of the literary *basse-cour* (with all the limits implied by *cour* and limitations of *basse*). There is, furthermore, a playful Rabelaisian intertext which activates such a reading:

> Mais vesites vous oncques chien rencontrant quelque os medulare? C'est, comme dict Platon [. . .] la beste du monde plus philosophe [. . .]. A l'exemple d'icelluy vous convient d'être saiges, pour fleurer, sentir et estimer ces beaulx livres de haulte gresse, légiers au prochaz et hardiz à la rencontre; puis par curieuse leçon et meditation frequente, rompre l'os et sugcer la sustantificque mouelle [. . .] avecques espoir certain d'être faictz escors et preux à ladicte lecture; car en icelle bien aultre goust trouverez et doctrine plus absconce, laquelle vous revelera de très haultz sacremens.[48]

The generic playfulness embedded in the text is here the substantial marrow in the bone. Baudelaire's poem plays upon Rabelais's own intertextual game in a complex system of allegorical signification in which the dog and bone, though not a stock allegory, can be activated to suggest the same topos of textual surface and depth and, by being juxtaposed with other stock allegories, appears to belong in the same way. The intertextual reference brings to the surface the allegorized substance of the relationship of reader to text but, whereas Plato's dog responds to the master he knows, Baudelaire's is an *indigne compagnon* who does not like what he does not know, who barks and wags his tail en *manière de reproche.*

"Le Chien et le flacon" constitutes a different kind of threshold in the text in that it appears to represent the lowest limit of poetry, no longer suggestive but heavy-handedly explicated, while all the time emphasizing the implied reader's threshold of understanding and consciously straining the limits of genre to explode textual stability and the categorization within which it simultaneously and self-consciously remains.

In making available different meanings and in staging oppositional discursive relationships in a genre which is itself dependent on contrasting formal modes, the *Petits Poèmes en prose* constitutes a textual encounter representative of the dysfunctional social and linguistic encounters it stages. The *lettre-dédicace* constitutes a tactic which enables the social release of these figural instabilities and discursive incompatibilities. And one prose poem in particular exemplifies how the discursive system of the *Petits Poèmes en prose* replicates the relations between the formal, the social, and the ideological.[49]

"La Fausse Monnaie" consists of various modes of dissimulation embedded in the structure of the narrative text. If we effect the same *triage* of these as the donor does of his coins, it is clear that each irony in the text is presented as a unity with its own mechanisms. In the first instance, the text presents a dramatized irony. The narrator introduces a situation to the reader which he explicitly encourages us to interpret as ironic. The explicitness of this encouragement to read in a particular way is directly related to the act of narration, for although the narrator recounts the events with the conventions of retrospect, his discourse moulds a dramatic present in the past. This is helped along by some incorporation of direct speech and includes suspense dependent upon the misinterpretation of gesture, the gradual rise to awareness and the double dupe of the narrator and (possibly) the beggar.

The complicating action, and the ironic situation, is that a beggar is given an apparently generous donation of a two-franc coin. This is established as an ironic sequence only by the structure of the narrative which begins with a description of a careful sorting of coins, one of which is *particulièrement examinée* before being placed in the right-hand pocket. There is no certainty that the coin is counterfeit, but the title and the insistence upon the details of separation activate our suspicions. The narrator's apparent unawareness of the motives for this sorting of coins is itself set apart from the text of the poem in flagrant isolation: *'Singulière et minutieuse répartition!' me dis-je en moi-même* (*OC* i. 323). This, one might insist, is a sentence ironic only when invested with the powers of retrospect. Indeed, it is a structural mechanism which comes into play only when the coin is confirmed as false, but which, nevertheless, contributes subconsciously to the reader's suspicions.

This contribution can be assigned to its position within the narrative (raising questions which are not yet to be resolved) or to linguistic elements which trigger negative responses in the receiver, indicating how discursive 'noise' interferes with the structure of narrative. The division of coins is *singulière,* suggesting, on a straightforward level, something which, *de bonne ou mauvaise part,* elicits a reaction of surprise, but it has the additional meanings of separateness, of something which is different (from the Latin 'singularis' meaning unique), and, more familiarly, it carries the meaning of *peu convenable.* The ambiguities of the word reflect, therefore, the central debate of the poem which questions conventional morality. *Minutieuse* should also not go unnoticed since, while it suggests an attention to detail, these details—or 'minuties'—are normally 'choses de peu de conséquence.'

Both the structure of the tale and the terms of its telling suggest that what is morally at stake is not potentially endangering an unsuspecting beggar, or taking advantage of someone when the appearance is that of charity, but rather the motives for behaving in a conventionally immoral manner. The impact of the initial irony—a beggar receiving a counterfeit coin in good faith from an apparently generous benefactor—points to the beggar as the ironic victim, whereas the suspended focus of evaluation in this poem highlights the ironic victim as the conceited and foolish donor, since 'le plus irréparable des vices est de faire le mal par bêtise' (*OC* i. 324). Between the two, however, is situated the feigned gullibility of the narrator, who credits the donor with the generosity of the socially sensitive man and compounds that by bestowing upon him the faculties of great philosophy, soon tainted by the light of his blatant dishonesty and cheap morality.

The narrative of beggar duped by false coin reveals itself as something of a decoy (and one, moreover, which is left unresolved since we never learn the outcome of the coin or the beggar), yielding ironic supremacy to the fatuous bourgeois who, unlike the man who can *read* a situation in the eyes of a beggar, is not only blind to the *reproaches,* but is also insensitive to the narrator's interpretation of his gesture.

This can be seen by comparing the direct speech of the narrator with the echoed version of the donor which comes later in the poem:

> 'Vous avez raison; après le plaisir d'être étonné, il n'en est pas de plus grand que celui de causer une surprise.'

> 'Oui, vous avez raison; il n'est pas de plaisir plus doux que de surprendre un homme en lui donnant plus qu'il n'espère.'

> (*OC* i. 323-4)

The subtle shift in sentence pattern lays bare the transposition of perspective, the monistic outlook of the donor, compared with the pluralistic vision of the narrator. The friend's purblindness to what the narrator is suggesting is, therefore, emphasized by his linguistic patterning of the sentence and by the structural echo it establishes. In the self-satisfied donation of a valueless coin, the friend in **"La Fausse Monnaie"** is confident that he is doing the beggar a favour and getting charity on the cheap. On every level, his gesture is counterfeit, but he himself is blind to the hypocrisy, if not to the fake coin.

What is established in **"La Fausse Monnaie"** is a complex structure of moral incongruities in which a narrator offers not just a narrative but a range of interpretations of that narrative:

> Mais dans mon misérable cerveau, toujours occupé à chercher midi à quatorze heures (de quelle fatigante faculté la nature m'a fait cadeau!), entra soudainement

cette idée qu'une pareille conduite, de la part de mon ami, n'était excusable que par le désir de créer un événement dans la vie de ce pauvre diable, peut-être même de connaître les conséquences diverses, funestes ou autres, que peut engendrer une pièce fausse dans la main d'un mendiant. Ne pouvait-elle pas se multiplier en pièces vraies? Ne pouvait-elle pas aussi le conduire en prison? Un cabaretier, un boulanger, par exemple, allait peut-être le faire arrêter comme faux-monnayeur. Tout aussi bien la pièce fausse serait peut-être, pour un pauvre petit spéculateur, le germe d'une richesse de quelques jours. Et ainsi ma fantaisie allait son train, prêtant des ailes à l'esprit de mon ami et tirant toutes les déductions possibles de toutes les hypothèses possibles.

(*OC* i. 324)

The coin, like the fictions spun by this narrator, will have an unpredictable future and the donation releases a wealth of possibilities. All of these possibilities are conceived of within a given social and ideological structure, a structure which binds the outcomes of the fiction. If the counterfeit coin operates as genuine within that system, it is an uncontrollable and potentially subversive force. As Nathaniel Wing has shown in relation to this passage, the coin is a figure for writing, for all writing which does not simply accept and repeat the language and figures of ideology:

> this poem problematizes the opposition between 'serious' symbolization, here figured by gold and silver coins, and the 'non-serious', or counterfeit. The issue concerns less the 'inherent' value of one discourse or token than the precarious relativity of value in any discursive system and the capacity of fictions to lay bare the conventional relations which maintain equilibrium in discursive systems.[50]

In exactly the same way, the counterfeit gesture/discourse of the *lettre-dédicace* launches the prose poetry into a context where circulation of meanings is uncontrolled and unpredictable, or where encounters with the other might not be propitious. The economy of exchange elaborated is, in fact, also that of **"A une heure du matin"** where the list of the day's activities is centred upon contact and contacts. On the one hand, the poet-narrator takes to the streets with the intention of placing his writing (for some return); on the other, he expends time and energy on meaningless encounters where others beg him for favours. A close analysis of the 'recapitulation' of the day's events is revealing.

He starts out in what we might think good company, that of *plusieurs hommes de lettres,* but these men (and their collective worth) are summarily dismissed by the rejection of one man's question. The pretension of the implied question is equalled only by its idiocy and ignorance; its heavy irony is determined by the poet-narrator's association of educated interlocutor and the asking of a stupid question (Russia as island). This distances the narrator from his interlocutor and establishes

a contract with the reader through the veiled apostrophe (the parenthesis and the 'sans doute' insisting upon the joke, but excluding the butt of it). He then goes to kill time (suggesting at least some entertainment) and ends up wasting it with an illiterate *sauteuse* whose mispronunciation comes to characterize her (as *rustre*).

These encounters are compounded by an argument with another (more powerful) figure from the literary world whose retort to each and every objection, '*C'est ici le partie des honnêtes gens*', brings into question not only the honesty of his colleagues, but also his own candour and intelligence. The inclusion of direct speech here, as with the mispronunciation of *Vénus,* introduces another voice and also a different idiom, and here it expresses a view in a way which is patently at odds with that of our narrator. This dispute draws upon the same techniques of opposition as the earlier exchange, with *honnêtes gens—coquins* introducing a hierarchy of superiorities. This episode of rejection has been attributed to a biographical detail from Asselineau's *Baudelairiana* which recounts that, upon returning a rejected manuscript, a certain M. Amail (described as a *saint-simonien* and *ré-publicain vertueux*) said to Baudelaire: '*Nous n'imprimons pas de ces fantaisies-là, nous autres.*'[51] By drawing out through opposition and linguistic implication the attitudes inherent in such a statement, the poet-narrator can play upon this notion of *honnêtes gens* (as equivalent to *nous autres*) as heavily ironic.[52] His superiority is revealed by a dismissive attitude disclosed by the choice and position of the adverb *généreusement,* which draws attention to itself by breaking the rhythm of the sentence, slowing it down to insist upon the quality of the narrator's contribution and upon the derisive mocking of his interlocutor. The range of potential meanings calls into question the narrator's stance. Does *généreusement* here mean nobly, or at length, or does it mean without sympathy or prejudice for the interlocutor's position?[53] Retrospectively, the generosity of the narrator's spirit attracts all subsequent magnanimous acts (handshakes, letters of recommendation) and shows each such act to be counterfeit.

This same dynamic can also be seen to operate in the exchange with the theatre director, to whom the poet-narrator pays court in the hope that such an investment will pay off. The return is less than he bargains for, as he is dismissed ('congédier' having the somewhat ambiguous undertones both of the courteous 'to be given leave' and the rather more discourteous 'to be sent packing') with advice which amounts to selling his soul (to Z . . . —the initial indicating greater universality than a name—a man who is living proof that merit has no currency). There is no situation more prosaic than the need to keep body and soul together, and this list of the day's activities becomes a balance sheet on which all transactions are recorded and where outlay and profit are examined. The rejection (by *directeurs—de revue et de théâtre*) harnesses the stupidity of the successful to that of the press (for it is here that reputations are made),[54] and emphasizes how little purchasing power the true artist really has.

What is worse, however, is that the exchange mechanisms of the poet-narrator do not succeed in maintaining face value either, for he brags of actions not accomplished and denies successes; he refuses simple favours to friends and writes recommendations for those for whom he has no respect or time. In other words, he is as corrupted by the transactional system as the next man. He waves to people he does not know and exchanges handshakes hypocritically (the gloves are the vestimentary equivalent of the locked door which is the threshold separating him from these exchanges),[55] ever fearful of contracting some form of contagion which is as much spiritual as physical. Each and every exchange into which he enters is, in other words, as meaningless and dishonest as the next, whether it is a question of giving or receiving. The currency is counterfeit, the power-holders corrupt, and all exchange dysfunctional. There is a progressive devaluation of mood and language, as the clamour of the day overwhelms the space reserved for poetic expansion and as it becomes apparent that the darkness of this particular night will not bring the *repos* required to compose the *beaux vers* so badly needed. The devaluation of art and of self which occurs in the day's transactions, the question of artistic merit, and the attendant frustrations and disappointments all come together in the climactic prayer. Even here, there is question of a return on earlier investment, almost as if the poet-narrator in addressing the intercessors ('Âmes de ceux que j'ai aimés, âmes de ceux que j'ai chantés') is recalling a debt. The capital once regained can be put back to work with the purpose of redemption (significantly *bought* in the French *se racheter*).

The ending of the poem is highly significant, for it returns to the desires of the opening paragraphs to frame the central vicissitudes which militate against the fulfilment of these desires. The prayer of the final paragraph is itself framed by a statement of the poet's discontent ('mécontent de tous et mécontent de moi' balancing with 'que je ne suis pas le dernier des hommes, que je ne suis pas inférieur à ceux que je méprise!'), a formulation which echoes the apparently self-deprecating conclusion of the *dédicace* and the poet's situation of his own work in relation to others, as well as the *motivation* of the gesture.

The threshold of the text, that 'zone non seulement de transition mais de *transaction*', figures the exchange economy into which the prose poems are launched. Through an analysis of the paratext, we are able to better understand not only the context of the text's production, but also the way in which the 'discours d'escorte'

strives to define the project it accompanies. Moreover, in its duplicitous discursive strategies, it sets up a dysfunctional circuit of communication which prefigures the conflicting discursive and ideological discourses of the poems themselves. The text's threshold, which elaborates the problem of boundaries between the genres, suggests ways in which we might read the generic thresholds within texts. In order fully to understand the way in which this functions, we need to look more closely at the way in which prose and poetry are conjoined.

Notes

1. See Suzanne Bernard *Le Poème en prose de Baudelaire jusqu'à nos jours* (Paris: Nizet, 1994 [1959]), 19-93 and more especially Nichola Ann Haxell, 'The Name of the Prose: A Semiotic Study of Titling in the Pre-Baudelairian Prose Poem', *French Studies* 44 (1990), 156-69.

2. G. Genette, *Palimpsestes: La Littérature au second degré* (Paris: Seuil, 1982), 9.

3. Genette, *Seuils* (Paris: Seuil, 1987), 8.

4. See Pichois's 'Notice' for further details, esp. *OC* i. 796ff.

5. 'Le Crépuscule du soir' and 'La Solitude' appeared together without any other title in *Hommage à C. F. Denecourt, Fontainebleau. Paysages, légendes, souvenirs, fantaisies* (Paris: Hachette, 1855).

6. In *Le Présent* (24 Aug. 1857) as a collective title for 'L'Horloge', 'La Chevelure', 'L'Invitation au voyage', 'Le Crépuscule du soir', and 'Les Projets.'

7. For *Petits Poëmes en prose/Poëmes en prose,* see, in chronological order: *Revue fantaisiste* (1 Nov. 1861); *La Presse* (26 Aug., 27 Aug., and 24 Sept. 1862); *Revue nationale et étrangère* (10 June 1863); *Le Boulevard* (14 June 1863); *Revue nationale et étrangère* (10 Oct. and 10 Dec. 1863); and *L'Artiste* (1 Nov. 1864). For *Le Spleen de Paris. Petits Poèmes en prose* or [*Petits Poèmes en prose*], see: *Figaro* (7 and 14 Feb. 1864); *La Revue de Paris* (25 Dec. 1864); and *Œuvres,* iv (Paris: Michel Lévy frères, 1869).

8. *Revue du XIXe siècle,* 1 June 1866 ('La Fausse Monnaie' and 'Le Joueur généreux').

9. 'La Corde' in *L'Événement* (12 June 1866).

10. Published by Michel Lévy frères. This first edition in volume form was established by Asselineau and Banville, although they are not named, and is considered by Claude Pichois to be one of two publications which reflect Baudelaire's intentions. The title-page preceding the prose poems bears an in-

version of the volume's title: LE SPLEEN DE PARIS [*Petits Poèmes en prose*].

11. Genette clarifies: 'Est officiel tout message para-textual ouvertement assumé par l'auteur et/ou l'éditeur, et dont il ne peut esquiver la respons-abilité. Officiel, ainsi, tout ce qui, de source aucto-riale ou éditoriale, figure au péritexte anthume, comme le titre ou la préface originale', *Seuils,* 14-15.

12. These are considered part of the 'épitexte' and are unofficial inasmuch as they are private, may never have been intended for public consumption, and only form part of the 'paratext' as a result of recent scholarly editions; ibid. 15.

13. As indeed Baudelaire's title *Mon cœur mis à nu* suggests.

14. 'Est officieuse la plus grande part de l'épitexte auctorial [. . .] dont il peut toujours dégager plus ou moins sa responsabilité par des dénégations du genre: "Ce n'est pas exactement ce que j'ai dit", C'étaient des propos improvisés", ou: "Ce n'était pas destiné à la publication."' Genette, *Seuils,* 15.

15. Genette, *Seuils,* 75-6.

16. Ibid. 76, n. 1.

17. Examples include *Poëmes en prose* (*Revue fantai-siste,* 1 Nov. 1861, and *Le Boulevard,* 14 June 1863) and *Poèmes en prose* (*Le Boulevard,* 14 June 1863); *Petits Poëmes en prose* (*La Presse,* 26 Aug., 27 Aug., and 24 Sept. 1862, *Revue natio-nale et étrangère,* 10 June 1863, and *L'Artiste,* 1 Nov. 1864); and *Le Spleen de Paris. Petits Poèmes en prose* (*Figaro,* 14 Feb. 1864, and *La Revue de Paris,* 25 Dec. 1864).

18. See 'Notice' to *Le Spleen de Paris* (*OC* i. 1299).

19. Genette, *Seuils,* 66.

20. Letter to Poulet-Malassis, 7 Mar. 1857 (*C* i. 378).

21. See letters to Ancelle (*C* ii. 566, 581, and 615); and the letter to his mother (*C* ii. 625).

22. Quoted by Robert Kopp in *Petits Poëmes en prose* (Paris: Corti, 1969) and by Claude Pichois (*OC* i. 1297).

23. Baudelaire elsewhere refers to the prose poems as complementing *Les Fleurs du mal.* See, for example, *C* ii. 615.

24. Antoine Compagnon, *La Seconde Main ou le tra-vail de la citation* (Paris: Seuil, 1979), 328-56.

25. Genette also highlights this as a problem. Quoting Lessing, he writes: '"Un titre ne doit pas être comme un menu (*Küchenzettel*); moins il en dit sur le contenu, mieux il vaut". Pris à la lettre, ce conseil mettrait en totale opposition la fonction séductrice et la fonction déscriptive. La vulgate entend plutôt ici un éloge des vertus apéritives d'une certaine dose d'obscurité, ou d'ambiguïté: un bon titre en dirait assez pour exciter la curi-osité et assez peu pour ne pas la saturer.' *Seuils,* 87.

26. For more on the significance of precursory texts, see Nichola Ann Haxell, 'The Name of the Prose', 160-2.

27. 'Sauf', as Genette puts it, 'recherche archaïsante.' *Seuils,* 91.

28. Genette cites a range of such generic superscrip-tions and concludes, rather appropriately in the context of our discussion, that: 'Innover, c'est souvent marier deux vieilleries', ibid. 93-4.

29. H. Fluchère, review of Maurice Chapelan, *An-thologie du poème en prose* (1946) in *French Stud-ies,* 2 (1948), 188. Cited by Haxell in 'The Name of the Prose', 156.

30. Haxell asserts that this group of poets, 'by emulat-ing the thematic and stylistic focus of this increas-ingly renowned work, hoped to gain prestige and kudos and to reinforce the poetic import of their own prose texts by indirect association with "un des saints de notre calendrier poétique", as Asse-lineau called Bertrand. This notion of a talisman of poeticity, of an authenticating precursory text, recurs throughout the evolution of the prose-poetry genre.'

31. See Pichois's notes to this dedication where he describes the comparison as 'accablante pour Houssaye' (*OC* i. 1311) and also Chambers, 'Baudelaire's Dedicatory Practice', *Sub Stance,* 56 (1988), 5 and 16-17 n. 2.

32. Chambers sees this as the acknowledgement of a genuine debt, art. cit. 14, while Haxell notes Baudelaire's reference to Bertrand (and his subse-quent denial of his influence); she does not, how-ever, develop this point further to explain what sort of relationship to the precursory text this might imply, 'The Name of the Prose', 160.

33. See respectively Aloysius Bertrand, 'Bambochades romantiques', *Le Provincial* (May-Oct. 1828) and *Gaspard de la Nuit: Fantaisies à la manière de Rembrandt et de Callot* (Paris: Renduel, 1842); Jules Champfleury, 'Fantaisies et ballades', in *Chien-Caillou, Fantaisies d'hiver* (Paris: Marti-non, 1847), Henry Mürger, 'Ballades', *L'Artiste* (12 July 1846), and Charles Monselet, 'Ballades parisiennes', *Le Figaro* (25 July 1857); Jules Clar-etie, 'Chants du Limousin', *L'École du peuple*

(1861), Louis de Lyvron, 'Chants du désert', *Revue française,* 5 (1 July 1863), Paul-Ernest de Rattier *Chants prosaïques* (Paris: Dentu, 1861); Arsène Houssaye, reprint of 'Poèmes antiques' as 'Rhythmes primitifs' in 'Fresques et basreliefs. Tableaux et pastels', *Poésies complètes* (Paris: Charpentier, 1850); and Louis de Lyvron 'Fusains', *Revue des lettres et des arts,* I (27 Oct. 1857). For a much fuller list of examples, see Haxell, 'The Name of the Prose', table II, 168-9.

34. Chambers, 'Baudelaire's Dedicatory Practice', 5.

35. Ross Chambers, 'Baudelaire's Dedicatory Practice', 6-7.

36. Ibid. 15.

37. Ibid. 12.

38. Ibid. 16.

39. Ibid. 13.

40. Ross Chambers, 'Baudelaire's Dedicatory Practice', 13.

41. The term is Genette's, *Seuils,* 180.

42. See 'Les fonctions de la préface originale', ibid. 182-218.

43. It was, in fact, also one of the first group of poems to be published alongside the preface on 26 Aug. 1862 in *La Presse.*

44. This is number VI in the 1869 (and subsequent) editions and was also in the first ten to be published in *La Presse.* Jérôme Thélot sees this poem in a close relationship with 'L'Étranger': '[ils] s'expliquent l'un par l'autre: dans le même espace vacant, poète et communauté y intervertissent leur position respective, l'interrogé de "L'Étranger" devenant l'interrogateur de "Chacun sa chimère", pour un semblable dialogue de sourds.' For a full account of Thélot's argument, see 'Langage et autrui', in *Baudelaire: Violence et Poésie* (Paris: Gallimard, 1993), 71-111. The above quotation is on p. 75 n. 4.

45. This is a view of a number of critics in the fields both of generic theory and Baudelaire studies. See, for example, E. D. Hirsch, *Validity in Interpretation* (New Haven: Yale University Press, 1967), esp. ch. 3. Richard Terdiman in *Discourse/Counter-Discourse: The Theory and Practice of Symbolic Resistance in Nineteenth-Century France* (Ithaca and London: Cornell University Press, 1985) and Jonathan Monroe in *A Poverty of Objects: The Prose Poem and the Politics of Genre* (Ithaca and London: Cornell University Press, 1987) have explored the prose poem's significance as a socio-political genre, as a formal construction

representing absolute counter-discourse; and Marie Maclean in *Narrative as Performance: The Baudelairean Experiment* (London: Routledge, 1988) has considered the prose poem as narrative, in perfect but minimal form, as deterritorialized and, therefore, newly empowered.

46. The *dédicace* is quite explicit in this regard, referring to Baudelaire's hope (and, therefore, stated intention) that these prose poems might please and amuse. The earlier letter to Houssaye of 25 Dec. 1861, parts of which have already been cited, make this point, too: 'Je me suis résigné à être moi-même. Pourvu que je sois amusant, vous serez content, n'est-ce pas?' (*C* ii. 208).

47. See his edition of the *Petits Poèmes en prose* (Paris: Garnier, 1962), 185.

48. *Gargantua* (Paris: Gallimard, 1969), 58-9. This passage comes, significantly, from the prologue.

49. Although his focus is not the same as mine, Jacques Derrida has considered these two poems in conjunction in *Donner le temps, 1: La Fausse Monnaie* (Paris: Galilée, 1991), chs. 3 and 4.

50. 'Poets, Mimes and Counterfeit Coins: On Power and Discourse in Baudelaire's Prose Poetry', *Paragraph,* 13 (1990), 14.

51. See *Petits Poèmes en prose,* ed. Lemaître.

52. This is a commonplace which Baudelaire enjoys exploiting; cf. *Fusées,* XI: 'Ceux qui m'ont aimé étaient des gens méprisés, je dirais même méprisables, si je tenais à flatter *les honnêtes gens*' (*OC* i. 660).

53. The Dictionnaire E. Littré defines *généreusement* in the following terms: 'D'une manière généreuse, avec un grand cœur; d'une main libérale; courageusement; se montrer magnanime; d'un naturel noble' (Paris, 1885).

54. This is reminiscent of 'Les Tentations' where the third temptress, Fame, represents some kind of gain for favours. Here the courtesan which is the Press arrives blowing the trumpet of worldly renown, and is resisted by the poet only because the seductive virago is recognized as a woman who keeps the company of men with whom he would not wish to be associated. The poet overcomes the temptation here, but with the same form of twisted morality and worship as is present in the litany of 'A une heure du matin.'

55. This is a reprise of a locution in Baudelaire's own *Journaux intimes* in a section where there is a high concentration of ideas occurring in the prose poems in note form: 'Beaucoup d'amis, beaucoup de gants,—de peur de la gale' (*Fusées,* XI, *OC* i. 660).

Abbreviations

For references to all Baudelaire's texts (unless otherwise stated), I have used Baudelaire, *Œuvres complètes,* edited by Claude Pichois, Bibliothèque de la Pléiade, 2 vols. (Paris: Gallimard, 1975-6), henceforth designated by *OC,* followed by the volume and page number. For his correspondence, references are made to Baudelaire, *Correspondance,* edited by Claude Pichois, Bibliothèque de la Pléiade, 2 vols. (Paris: Gallimard, 1973), henceforth designated as *C,* followed by the volume and page number.

Maria Scott (essay date July 2001)

SOURCE: Scott, Maria. "Superfluous Intrigues in Baudelaire's Prose Poems." *French Studies* 55, no. 3 (July 2001): 351-62.

[*In the following essay, Scott analyzes* Paris Spleen, *arguing that the apparent simplicity of the texts obscures their more complex meaning.*]

In recent years, Baudelaire's *Petits poèmes en prose* have been enjoying a high level of scrutiny by literary critics of all persuasions. The ironic layering of the prose poems has proven to be of particular interest to many.[1] However, despite the well-documented duplicity of almost every aspect of the prose poems, there is a widespread tendency to assume that the narrator's somersaults between irony and good faith occur in synchrony with those of the poet. Even where criticism avoids referring to the speaker or main character in a text as 'the poet', it usually guards the assumption that this figure expresses Baudelaire's own views in a more or less direct fashion. Thus, for example, **"La Femme sauvage et la petite maîtresse"** is often cited as an illustration of the poet's misogyny, **"Le *Confiteor* de l'artiste"** as a snapshot of his aesthetic, **"L'Invitation au voyage"** as evidence of his wish to undermine or parody his own poetic project, and so on. This article proposes that there may be another angle from which Baudelaire's prose poems can be read.

The assumption of authorial sincerity would indicate that we generally approach these 'poèmes en prose' as poetic self-expressions rather than as prose fictions. Marcel Ruff, for example, writes of 'la communication directe que le poème en prose s'efforce d'établir entre l'âme de l'auteur et celle du lecteur.'[2] However, as Winifred Nowottny points out, it is when poems seem most transparent, least artificial, that critics should be most alert to their authors' linguistic deviousness.[3] If we are to read Baudelaire's texts as poetic communications, it is logical to give their internal analogies and correspondences as much attention as their overt message. Baudelaire himself placed correspondences at the centre of his

aesthetic. To read the prose poems for the places where they reflect back on themselves, though, is to be led to suspect that the kind of communication that takes place between poet and reader in these texts is quite different from the sort described by Ruff.

This article will argue that certain texts of *Le Spleen de Paris* hinge on a critical disjunction between their teleological logic and their analogical logic. It will contend that the explicit message of these texts is writ so large that it conceals their oblique message. The very simplicity of the device might be responsible for its success, just as Poe's purloined letter was never better hidden than when it was most obviously displayed. Indeed, Poe's ironized first-person narrators could be viewed as the older brothers of the various authorial semblances that feature in the prose poetry of his French translator.

In many texts in the collection, half-hidden internal echoes and symmetries seem ironically to undermine the explicitly advertised irony. In **"Les Yeux des pauvres"** and **"La Belle Dorothée,"** for example, the first-person narrator's prestige as a Baudelairean ironist may be contested by an uncanny analogy between what the text says and how it says it.

"Les Yeux des pauvres" retrospectively recounts the shattering of the narrator's illusion of unity with his mistress after she fails to echo his own thoughts in relation to a poor family that stands staring into a café outside which the two are sitting. The stated moral of the story is that, even between people who love each other, communication is impossible. The vehement tone of this conclusion is established by the text's opening address to the mistress:

> Ah! vous voulez savoir pourquoi je vous hais aujourd'hui. Il vous sera sans doute moins facile de le comprendre qu'à moi de vous l'expliquer; car vous êtes, je crois, le plus bel exemple d'imperméabilité féminine qui se puisse rencontrer.[4]

In view of the fact that the mistress is addressed here as 'vous', and thus stands alongside the reader in the position of narratee, it seems advisable to reread the text to see if there is any aspect of its communication to which we too might need to be more sensitive.

The text's title refers not to the insensible gaze of the mistress, upon which it eventually concentrates, but to 'les yeux des pauvres.' Indeed, the text dwells at some length on the eyes gazing into the new café:

> Ces trois visages étaient extraordinairement sérieux, et ces six yeux contemplaient fixement le café nouveau avec une admiration égale, mais nuancée diversement par l'âge.
>
> Les yeux du père disaient: 'Que c'est beau! que c'est beau! on dirait que tout l'or du pauvre monde est venu se porter sur ces murs.'—Les yeux du petit garçon:

'Que c'est beau! que c'est beau! mais c'est une maison où peuvent seuls entrer les gens qui ne sont pas comme nous.'—Quant aux yeux du plus petit, ils étaient trop fascinés pour exprimer autre chose qu'une joie stupide et profonde.

(*O.c.* [*Œuvres complétes*], I, 318)

After reflecting on how he was moved by this vision of the poor family's admiration for the café's splendour, and on how he was slightly shamed by the size of the glasses and carafes in front of him, 'plus grands que notre soif', the narrator states that he turned to his mistress:

> Je tournais mes regards vers les vôtres, cher amour, pour y lire *ma* pensée; je plongeais dans vos yeux si beaux et si bizarrement doux, dans vos yeux verts, habités par le Caprice et inspirés par la Lune, quand vous me dites: 'Ces gens-là me sont insupportables avec leurs yeux ouverts comme des portes cochères! Ne pourriez-vous pas prier le maître du café de les éloigner d'ici?'
>
> Tant il est difficile de s'entendre, mon cher ange, et tant la pensée est incommunicable, même entre gens qui s'aiment!

(*O.c.*, I, 319)

It seems to be the mistress's failure to read both his own eyes and the eyes of the poor family that is responsible for the narrator's ire. As Geraldine Friedman points out, 'the man's condemnation of the woman's callousness ultimately charges her with being a bad reader' because she fails to give a sensitive reading to 'the texts of his and the family's faces.'[5]

The temptation here is to assume that the narrator is justified in his attack on the woman. However, what undermines the legitimacy of this attack is, firstly, that he is as guilty of misreading her thoughts as she is guilty of failing to intercept his. Indeed, the narrator's guilt is aggravated by the fact that he is interested only in reading his own thoughts ('*ma* pensée') in his partner's eyes. Secondly, the narrator's superior sensitivity to the suffering of the poor family is belied by several details in the text. After his initial description of the family's obvious penury and physical frailty, the narrator remarks ignorantly that the father 'remplissait l'office de bonne et faisait prendre à ses enfants l'air du soir' (*O.c.*, I, 318). In addition, the narrator accounts for his slight sense of shame at the sight of the poor family's gazes by reference to a songster's cliché, thus placing the sentiment firmly in the realm of programmed, superficial response: 'Les chansonniers disent que le plaisir rend l'âme bonne et amollit le cœur' (*O.c.*, I, 318). Furthermore, the narrator averts his gaze from the poor family as soon as they begin to make him feel even a little uncomfortable, and seems easily to forget their eyes as soon as he loses himself in those of his mistress.

All of the above points have been made before. However, the narrator's obtuseness tends to be underlined even while the perspicacity of his judgement against the

mistress is accepted. For example, Maurice Delcroix's excellent study of the text insists on the narrator's egotism while also crediting him with self-irony.[6] This attributes a moral superiority to the narrator that is nowhere warranted by the text and seems dependent instead on the assumption that the narrator speaks for the author. If, as Stephens points out, 'there is, at the very least, an ironizing of the narrator of **"Les Yeux des pauvres,"**'[7] there is nothing to suggest that this irony is self-directed.

Despite the often-noted fallibility of the narrator's reading strategy, the accuracy of his optical reading of the poor family seems rarely to be questioned.[8] Nevertheless, all the signs point to the possibility that the speaker is mistaken in his assumption that the eyes of the poor express admiration for the café's aesthetics. After all, what the three outside the café are staring at is described earlier in the text as 'toute l'histoire et toute la mythologie mises au service de la goinfrerie' (*O.c.*, I, 318). What the physically weak family is seeing is an apotheosis of food.

The speaker's shame at the size of his drinking vessels recalls the text of Arsène Houssaye's "La Chanson du vitrier," heavily ironized by Baudelaire in **"Le Mauvais Vitrier."**[9] In Houssaye's painfully unironic text, a ridiculous first-person narrator offers a drink to a hungry man. Obviously unused to feeling hungry, the narrator seems unaware of the potentially disastrous effects of pouring alcohol into an empty stomach (particularly when valuable glass assets are in close proximity to that stomach). Similarly, the narrator of Baudelaire's prose poem seems to have no sense that food is a need more primary than wine. It may be that the mistress, not as successful as the narrator in putting the poor family out of her mind, reads their eyes more accurately than he: 'leurs yeux ouverts comme des portes cochères' is far more descriptive of physical hunger than the narrator's pretty 'Que c'est beau!' speech bubbles.

In his (mis)readings of the poor family and of his mistress, the narrator projects his own aestheticizing vision on to the eyes he regards. The crucial difference between his two egotistical projections is that the second is more explicitly exposed as an illusion by the text than the first. Unlike the mistress, the three members of the poor family are not in a position to make their real thoughts directly heard by the narrator. However, that the poet 'hears' those thoughts is suggested by way of correspondences that seem too artful to be accidental. Firstly, there is the correspondence between the two scenes of (mis)reading within the text. Secondly, there is the symmetry between the thematic meaning of the title and its self-referential import: the narrator's aesthetic reading of 'les yeux des pauvres' might be seen to reflect the kind of reading that 'Les Yeux des pauvres' invites.

The new café might be interpreted as a model of the workings of the text itself. Firstly, the artificial brightness of the new café would mirror the fake transparency of the prose. Secondly, the café's mirrors would reflect the text's own intricate reflexivity. Thirdly, the *trompe-l'œil* mural would present an image of the textual trickery in play.[10] Fourthly, the bourgeois tastelessness of the café's decoration, with its picturesque pages dragged by dogs on leashes, might be understood to echo the simultaneous sentimentality and brutality of Baudelaire's text, as well as the strange reversals of reading-direction that it organizes.

However, this unfolding of the text against 'naïve' readings does not measure the full extent of its irony. The 'sceptical' reader might also be targeted by the prose poem. Recalling the first-person narrator of Houssaye's 'Chanson du vitrier,' the suspicious reader might be lured into making the inane presumption that s/he alone, 'seul au milieu de tous ces passants' (*O.c.,* I, 1309), is sensitive to the other's hunger. Furthermore, to the extent that his or her reading of irony in the poet's textual gaze relies on an analogical deduction rather than on anything that is explicitly stated in the text, there can be no certainty that s/he is not merely repeating the narrator's egotistical gesture of self-projection on to the eyes of those he regards.

"Les Yeux des pauvres" both thematizes and dramatizes the problem of interpretation. It makes a mockery of distinctions between naïvety and scepticism in reading. To a reading that treats the text as a more or less transparent communication on the part of a poet-narrator, it states that misreading is inevitable, 'même entre gens qui s'aiment' (*O.c.,* I, 319). To a reading that assumes the impossibility of correct readings and that consequently distrusts the narrator's undisassembled first optical reading, the text offers what seems like a 'correct,' if ironic, reading. Both naïve and sceptical readings arrive, therefore, at conclusions that undo their own premises.

The irreducible poverty of the reader's eyes may be at the centre of a text that demonstrates that all readings, even the most apparently impartial, necessarily make possibly mistaken assumptions about authorial intentions. The prose poem does not suggest, however, that attempts at deciphering the other should be avoided: indeed, it overtly attacks the mistress precisely for her apparent evasion. It may be that what the text suggests is that the only 'correct' reading of the other is one which admits that there can be no definitive reading of the other, including the other that is Baudelaire's text.

If there is a hidden attack on the reader beneath the explicit attack on the mistress in **"Les Yeux des pauvres,"** **"La Belle Dorothée"** might be seen to turn on a similar device. In this text, an oblique reading is invited by the implied parallel between the poetically inclined narrator and the object of his scorn.

The text begins with an evocation of the voluptuous and deathly slothfulness induced by the terrible heat of the midday sun. Only Dorothée is out walking on the deserted road. The text describes in languorous detail the physical appearance of this beautiful black woman. She is wearing a clinging pink silk dress and heavy earrings and is carrying a red parasol. The narrator explains Dorothée's inappropriate attire and the fact that she is out walking at midday by repeated reference to her prodigious vanity. For example, he claims that she is 'heureuse de vivre et souriant d'un blanc sourire, comme si elle apercevait au loin dans l'espace un miroir reflétant sa démarche et sa beauté' (*O.c.,* I, 316). The narrator goes on to propose that the reason Dorothée is out in the cruel heat is because she has a meeting with 'quelque jeune officier qui, sur des plages lointaines, a entendu parler par ses camarades de la célèbre Dorothée' (*O.c.,* I, 317). At the end of the text, we learn that the woman is saving her 'piastres' desperately so that she can buy her eleven-year old sister back from slavery. In conclusion, the narrator exclaims virulently that the master will, no doubt, release the sister, because 'le maître de l'enfant est si avare, trop avare, pour comprendre une autre beauté que celle des écus!' (*O.c.,* I, 317). There is an oblique suggestion here that the narrator would know better than to release the young girl whom he describes, possibly lasciviously, as 'déjà mûre, et si belle!' (*O.c.,* I, 317).

Although recent commentators have deduced, from the evidence of the text, that Dorothée is a prostitute, the narrator never says this. Instead, he accounts for her (presumably excruciating) midday walk in all her finery by reference to her immense vanity, thereby managing temporarily to exclude a corruptive reality from his picturesque notion of a happy, innocent woman.[11] As if her indolence were necessary to his fantasy, the narrator represents Dorothée as lazy rather than industrious: she is 'la paresseuse Dorothée, belle et froide comme le bronze' (*O.c.,* I, 317). If the sister's master is blind to beauty, seeing only commerce, the narrator is blind to industry, seeing only beauty. Each type of vision might be understood to be as cruelly reductive as the other.

The analogy between the narrator and the slave-master is most clearly established in the paragraph that stands in the exact middle of the text (just as the excessively glaring sun seems to be situated, by the text, in the middle of the sky):

> De temps en temps la brise de mer soulève par le coin
> sa jupe flottante et montre sa jambe luisante et superbe;
> et son pied, pareil aux pieds des déesses de marbre que
> l'Europe enferme dans ses musées, imprime fidèlement
> sa forme sur le sable fin. Car Dorothée est si prod-

igieusement coquette, que le plaisir d'être admirée l'emporte chez elle sur l'orgueil de l'affranchie, et, bien qu'elle soit libre, elle marche sans souliers.

(O.c., I, 316)

The appropriation of exotic works of art by European museums is placed here in direct relation with the appropriation of 'exotic' human beings by European individuals. By reducing Dorothée to an object of visual pleasure, the narrator's description of her combines both forms of appropriation. Instead of evoking the pain of walking on hot ground in bare feet, the narrator insists on the beauty of those feet. In claiming that Dorothée foregoes shoes because her vanity is greater than the pride she feels in her liberation, other possibilities are effectively hidden from the reader's view: penury, defiance, market demand, for example. Finally, the narrator's twofold assertion, in the above passage, of the woman's current state of freedom betrays no perceptible nuance of irony, despite the fact that it is difficult to see how Dorothée the prostitute intent on buying her sister out of slavery is more free than Dorothée the slave.

The high sun is described in the first paragraph as inducing a deathly sleep. Similarly, the very centrality of the analogy between enslavement and aestheticism in the text might dull our sensitivity to it. Like the feather fan in the woman's boudoir, the text may play a dual role: as a static mirror, it offers Dorothée's beautiful reflection for our delectation; as something that the reader must unsettle a little, by contrast, it suggests the extent to which the woman must suffer in the terrible heat:

> Pourquoi a-t-elle quitté sa petite case si coquettement arrangée, dont les fleurs et les nattes font à si peu de frais un parfait boudoir; où elle prend tant de plaisir à se peigner, à fumer, à se faire éventer ou à se regarder dans le miroir de ses grands éventails de plumes, pendant que la mer, qui bat la plage à cent pas de là, fait à ses rêveries indécises un puissant et monotone accompagnement, et que la marmite de fer, où cuit un ragoût de crabes au riz et au safran, lui envoie, du fond de la cour, ses parfums excitants?

(O.c., I, 317)

The discreet placement of 'à si peu de frais' suggests a suppression of Dorothée's hardship, while the syntactic sidelining of 'à se faire éventer' by the subsequent clause suggests the narrator's occlusion of the functional by the artistic. This eclipsing of the prosaic is also figured stylistically in so far as 'se faire éventer' is a far more pedestrian construction than the bizarrely elliptical 'se regarder dans le miroir de ses grands éventails de plume.'

All the signs in the text suggest that the narrator is a pleasure-seeking aesthete. In **"L'École païenne,"** published ten years before **"La Belle Dorothée,"** Baudelaire wrote scathingly about the artist who values physical beauty too highly, neglecting virtue and usefulness:

> L'utile, le vrai, le bon, le vraiment aimable, toutes ces choses lui seront inconnues. Infatué de son rêve fatigant, il voudra en infatuer et en fatiguer les autres. Il ne pensera pas à sa mère, à sa nourrice; il déchirera ses amis, ou ne les aimera *que pour leur forme;* sa femme, s'il en a une, il la méprisera et l'avilira.

(O.c., II, 48)

Eileen Souffrin-Le Breton points to possible intertextual references in **"La Belle Dorothée"** to the work of Théophile Gautier, noting the fact that a fixed feathered fan containing a mirror also features in *Mademoiselle de Maupin.*[12] It may be that Baudelaire's text, which brings aesthetic, sexual and commercial appropriation into direct correspondence, parodies the ambitions of the first-person narrator-aesthete of *Mademoiselle de Maupin.* The latter longs to find 'une maîtresse tout à fait à moi' and wonders if 'un sac ou deux de piastres' could not help him fulfil this 'idéal presque bourgeois.'[13] It may also be that Baudelaire's prose poem parodies Gautier's view that 'Il n'y a de vraiment beau que ce qui ne peut servir à rien.'[14] For Baudelaire's narrator, it seems that Dorothée is beautiful only to the extent that she can be distanced from the logic of exchange which, at the end of the text, is shown to rule her.

The narrator does not acknowledge, until the moment when this acknowledgement can be framed as a defence of aesthetics, that Dorothée must save every penny and endure the heat of the streets so as to free her young sister. Both the overt nature of the text's concluding attack on materialism and the sensuousness of the poem's subject and style function to blind us to the narrator's suppression of the reality of Dorothée's pain, 'faisant sur la lumière une tache éclatante et noire' (**<i>O.c.,</i>** I, 318). It may be that Baudelaire's text plays upon our blind spot to Dorothée's suffering. Like her fan, the prose poem may contain a mirror in which the poet could be suspected of watching us reading from behind our backs.[15]

As in **"Les Yeux des pauvres,"** the text also catches the sceptical reading in its artful folds and mirrors. By insisting on the text's suppression of Dorothée's misery, the reader who suspects a ruse is implicitly aligned with the anti-aesthetic slave-owner, the object of the narrator's scorn. Baudelaire's text allows for no absolute certainty, therefore, as to the direction of its irony.

What our analysis of two prose poems has insisted on is the irremediable partiality of our knowledge about Baudelaire's intention. In each instance, the act of narrative *énonciation* undermines the narrative *énoncé* so artfully that the reader may be led to suspect that a clandestine critical disjunction is at work. This suspicion would be ungrounded, however, if it could not be extended to the entirety of *Le Spleen de Paris,* Baudelaire having always insisted on the unity of his collection.[16]

If Baudelaire made the reading habits of his nineteenth-century public the target of his venom, his decision was undoubtedly influenced by the hostile reception accorded by that public to *Les Fleurs du mal.* Although two prose poems by Baudelaire were published in 1855, the first ones to appear as part of a projected collection were published in *Le Présent* only four days after the trial of the verse poems in 1857. It is very possible that the prose poems were motivated as much by a desire for vengeance as by a wish to experiment with new textual forms. Scott Carpenter claims that the anecdotal aspect of Baudelaire's prose poems masks their subversive, allegorical attacks on a repressive dominant culture: 'Silenced by the law, Baudelaire finds a way to speak, but "mutely", as it were.'[17] In a similarly sceptical vein, Jacques Derrida writes of one of the prose poems, **"La Fausse Monnaie,"** that the structure of the text seems to mirror its content, such that the transparent naturalism of the text might be as counterfeit as the coin that the narrator's friend offers to the beggar.[18] As Derrida's careful analysis seems obliquely to suggest, Baudelaire's texts might very well deconstruct deconstruction. Instead of revealing themselves, upon deconstruction, to say something other than what they mean to say, the prose poems may catch the sceptical reader off guard precisely by seeming to intend to say something other than what they appear to say.

In a letter of 1866 to Sainte-Beuve, Baudelaire describes the narrator of *Le Spleen de Paris* as 'un nouveau Joseph Delorme accrochant sa pensée rapsodique à chaque accident de sa flânerie et tirant de chaque objet une morale désagréable.'[19] What our reading of two texts from the collection suggests is that the situational readings carried out by Baudelaire's narrators, complete with rhapsodic aestheticism and disagreeable morality, may function as an ironic *mise en abyme* of the very acts of reading that the texts invite. Every reader might be seen to become, from one angle or another, and whether s/he knows it or not, the butt of a grotesque joke. The best response to the caricatural assault of the prose poems may thus be the 'philosophical' laughter associated with Baudelaire's 'comique absolu.' This is the kind of laughter we might give forth when we suddenly see ourselves as ridiculous.

Stephens has discussed certain parallels between Daumier's caricatures of the Parisian bourgeoisie and the texts of *Le Spleen de Paris.*[20] It is interesting to note, in this connection, that Daumier produced a series of visual caricatures entitled *Cent et un Robert Macaire,* in which a swindler, adopting different disguises, moves invisibly among the crowd.[21] Although there are only fifty poems in *Le Spleen de Paris,* the fact that the poet had intended to produce one hundred prose poems, which along with the sardonic 'dédicace' would have made one hundred and one, suggests that his collection may owe a certain debt to Daumier's conception.[22] It

may be that, like Macaire, Baudelaire aimed to deceive the readers he was to encounter along the road. If so, the otherwise radically heterogeneous collection of prose poems would be unified by its cruel but discreet parodying of the reader who feels sure of the ground s/he walks on.[23]

Caricature was, in Baudelaire's time, a popular strategy of retaliation for artistic rejection: 'The *Salon caricatural* at midcentury, anticipating the *Salon des Refusés,* provided a means by which artists whose work had not been accepted for display in the prestigious Parisian salons could express their disdain for the conventions governing those salons.'[24] Indeed, Baudelaire penned the following possibly far-seeing lines in his prologue to the *Salon caricatural* of 1846:

> J'ai l'orgueil, tant je suis innocent et naïf,
> D'amuser ceux-là même à qui mon crayon vif
> Infligea le tourment de la caricature
>
> (*O.c.,* II, 500)

If the public had failed to recognize the beauty of Baudelaire's poetry of correspondences, what better way to attack this blindness than subtly to mobilize an artillery of veiled correspondences in prose? The public's incomprehension of analogies could be turned invisibly against it.

To the extent that Baudelaire feigned acceptance of the moral and aesthetic principles of the nineteenth-century bourgeoisie, he might be understood to resemble the artist of 'le comique absolu,' whom he conceived as encouraging a sense of personal superiority ('le comique significatif') in his audience precisely by seeming less self-aware than he really was (*O.c.,* II, 543). However, if the poet were simultaneously and secretly to mock the very audience he pleases, he too could indulge in 'le comique significatif,' seeing his audience figuratively decapitated at the same time as he decapitates himself figuratively for their benefit.[25] For Baudelaire, as for Flaubert and other nineteenth-century writers, and as for innumerable satirical writers before and since, 'Le *ridicule* est plus tranchant / Que le fer de la guillotine' (*O.c.,* II, 116).

The first collective title that Baudelaire gave to his prose poems was *Poëmes nocturnes.* Ruff comments on the thematic inappropriateness of the title.[26] However, it may be that the nocturnal epithet refers to the shrouded workings of the texts rather than to their themes. Another of Baudelaire's titles for the prose poetry collection was *Petits poèmes lycanthropes,* the reference to lycanthropy suggesting a ferocious transformation of form as well as alluding to Pétrus Borel's love of violating 'les habitudes morales du lecteur' (*O.c.,* II, 154). Yet another provisional title was equally suggestive of malicious intent and of a potential for transformation:

J'ai cherché des titres. Les 66. Quoique cependant cet ouvrage tenant de la vis et du kaléidoscope [. . .] pût bien être poussé jusqu'au cabalistique 666 et même 6666 . . .

(O.c., II, 365)

One formula, 'La Lueur et la Fumée: Poème, en prose,' was referred to by Baudelaire as 'un titre qui rend bien mon idée.'[27] This title might be understood to evoke the kind of spectral (transparent/opaque, multi-faceted, malevolent, intangible) intrigue that this essay is arguing for.

That Baudelaire was interested in deceptive transformations is suggested by his interest in Ernest Christophe's anamorphic sculpture, *Le Masque,* which hides a sorrowful face behind a smiling one. A similarly unsettling kind of twist might be at play in the collection that Baudelaire described as a snake in dedicating it to a newspaper editor. It may be that **Le Spleen de Paris** directs its poison at the Parisian newspaper-reading public which gave Baudelaire his spleen (the prose poems were published in newspapers and reviews before being published posthumously as a collection). As Derrida asks: 'Que fait-on quand on dédie un serpent—tout entier ou en morceaux?'[28]

If the content of certain texts is reflected back upon the way in which that content is framed, what is revealed is the possible existence of 'une intrigue superflue' *(O.c.,* I, 275). Symmetries between *énoncé* and *énonciation* remain invisible to the kind of teleological reading that is often accorded to prose, but offer themselves quite readily to the kind of analogical reading conventionally associated with poetry. Emmanuel Adatte associates Baudelaire's particular interest in analogy with an assertion of his freedom from mortality and 'les turpitudes du spleen.'[29] It may be that the title 'Le Spleen de Paris' refers to the workings of the collection at least as much as to its content. In other words, the prose poems may have permitted Baudelaire's self-liberating but strangely tactful venting of spleen against the very audience that gave him his spleen. Similarly, 'le galant tireur' in the prose poem of the same name decapitates his muse in effigy, before graciously thanking her for his success.

Notes

1. See, in particular, Sonya Stephens, *Baudelaire's Prose Poems: The Practice and Politics of Irony* (Oxford University Press, 1999) and J. A. Hiddleston, *Baudelaire and 'Le Spleen de Paris'* (Oxford, Clarendon Press, 1987).

2. *Baudelaire: l'homme et l'œuvre* (Paris, Hatier-Boivin, 1955), p. 180.

3. *The Language Poets Use* (London, Athlone Press, 1962), p. 11.

4. *Œuvres complètes,* ed. by Claude Pichois, Bibliothèque de la Pléiade, 2 vols (Paris, Gallimard, 1975-76), I, 317. Future page references to this collection will appear in the text alongside the abbreviations *O.c.,* I or *O.c.,* II.

5. 'Baudelaire's Theory of Practice: Ideology and Difference in "Les Yeux des pauvres",' *PMLA,* 104, no. 3 (1989), 317-28 (p. 320).

6. 'Un poème en prose de Charles Baudelaire: *Les Yeux des pauvres,' Cahiers d'analyse textuelle,* 19 (1977), 47-65.

7. *Baudelaire's Prose Poems,* p.96.

8. Delcroix remarks on 'la présomption de cette lecture du regard d'autrui' ('Un poème en prose de Charles Baudelaire,' p. 60) but goes no further than this in challenging the narrator's reading of the eyes of the poor family. Friedman does go further by suggesting that the family may 'crave food more urgently than they do beauty' ('Baudelaire's Theory of Practice,' p. 320) but makes this point marginal to her analysis of the text and avoids the questions that it raises with regard to the poet's ironic intention. Margery A. Evans remarks on the reader's 'ironic awareness that the poet's interpretation of "les yeux des pauvres" may have been as unfounded as his analysis of his mistress' but, as her wording here suggests, does not give Baudelaire himself the benefit of the doubt (*Baudelaire and Intertextuality: Poetry at the Crossroads,* (Cambridge University Press, 1993), p. 52).

9. See Stephens's incisive analysis of the ironic treatment of 'La Chanson du vitrier' in Baudelaire's dedicatory letter to Houssaye and in 'Le Mauvais Vitrier' (*Baudelaire's Prose Poems,* pp. 9-10, pp. 75-78).

10. Without proposing the existence of a possible *mise en abyme,* Delcroix observes that the text's description of the café's mural might initially mislead the reader into thinking that its nymphs and goddesses are moving around the café itself ('Un poème en prose,' p. 54).

11. Ainslie Armstrong McLees remarks on the narrator's self-protection from reality, but nevertheless reads the text as a caricatural attack on (the master's) materialism and a defence of (the narrator's) aesthetic sensibility (*Baudelaire's 'Argot Plastique': Poetic Caricature and Modernism* (Athens, University of Georgia Press, 1989), p. 77). Rosemary Lloyd, by contrast, noting that the poetic style of narration suggests 'a nostalgic reluctance to move into the hard-nosed world of quotidian reality,' identifies the poet with Dorothée ('Some Reflections on "La Belle Dorothée",' *French Studies Bulletin,* 41 (1991-92), 8-10).

12. 'More on the Mirror of "La Belle Dorothée",' *French Studies Bulletin,* 50 (1994), 16-18.

13. *Mademoiselle de Maupin* (Paris, Gallimard, 1932), pp. 50, 61.

14. *Mademoiselle de Maupin,* p. 29.

15. Souffrin-Le Breton remarks that the purpose of the fixed fan with mirror was 'to enable the lady holding this fixed fan both to contemplate her own image and to check on what was happening behind her' ('More on the Mirror,' p. 17).

16. For a study of this oblique irony as it might apply to other texts by Baudelaire (and others), see my doctoral thesis, 'Anamorphic Texts: Stendhal, Baudelaire, Lacan, Derrida' (October 1999). This thesis was supervised by David Scott, whose help, then and now, was indispensable.

17. 'The Esthetic Mask: Irony and Allegory in Baudelaire's *Spleen de Paris,*' in *Acts of Fiction: Resistance and Revolution from Sade to Baudelaire* (Pennsylvania State University Press, 1996), pp. 125-48.

18. *Donner le temps: 1. La Fausse Monnaie* (Paris, Galilée, 1991), p. 214. Derrida also states that 'ce qu'on dit du titre de ce bref récit peut aussi se dire du titre du livre bien qu'il n'en intitule qu'une part, une petite pièce' (p. 112).

19. *Correspondance,* ed. by Claude Pichois, 2 vols (Paris, Gallimard, 1973), ii, p. 583.

20. See Stephens's chapter on 'The Prose Poem and the Dualities of Comic Art,' in *Baudelaire's Prose Poems,* pp. 108-59.

21. On Baudelaire's admiration for Daumier's *Robert Macaire,* see *O.c.,* ii, 555.

22. See Baudelaire's letter to Sainte-Beuve of May 1865, *Correspondance,* ii, 493. *Les Fleurs du mal,* to which *Le Spleen de Paris* was conceived as a 'pendant,' originally contained one hundred poems; however, this number changed after the edition of 1857.

23. In *Baudelaire and Caricature: From the Comic to an Art of Modernity* (University Park, Pennsylvania State University Press, 1992), Michèle Hannoosh insists on a caricatural dimension to *Le Spleen de Paris* but does not continue or develop that intuition of a motivated deception that inflects her analysis of the prose poem 'Une mort héroïque.' In *Baudelaire's 'Argot Plastique,'* McLees also writes about the centrality of caricature to Baudelaire's literary production, including his prose poems, but does not suggest that the latter parody the strategies of reading they invite.

David Scott's study of *Le Spleen de Paris* (London, Grant and Cutler, 1984) gives particular attention to the category of the 'poème-boutade,' and even states that poems outside this category too contain 'more than a smack of the *boutade*' (p. 88), but does not construct an argument for hidden irony. Hiddleston's *Baudelaire and 'Le Spleen de Paris'* observes caricatural elements in the prose poems, noting that 'interpretations of these poems which do not take sufficient account of the poet's irony and his desire to mystify run the risk of being naïvely literal' (p. 40). However, Hiddleston continues to assume an identity between an albeit self-ironizing narrator and the poet (see for example pp. 29, 36, 51). Hiddleston's identification may be no more 'naïve' than our separation of narrator and poet, but it necessarily excludes consideration of the possibility that the reader who is sensitive to the narrator's irony is himself or herself targeted by the poet's irony. While Stephens overtly defends the conventional association of the author of the prose poems with his apparent spokesperson (*Baudelaire's Prose Poems,* p. 61), her argument that the texts parody genre reveals a degree of scepticism with regard to the good faith of the narrator or main speaker.

24. McLees, *Baudelaire's 'Argot Plastique,'* p. 59.

25. On the distinction between 'le comique absolu' and 'le comique ordinaire' or 'significatif,' see Baudelaire's 'De l'essence du rire,' *O.c.,* ii, 525-43. On the comic value of mimed decapitation, see *O.c.,* ii, 539-40.

26. *Baudelaire: l'homme et l'œuvre,* p. 170.

27. Letter to Houssaye, *Correspondance,* ii, 197.

28. *Donner le temps,* p. 116.

29. *'Les Fleurs du mal' et 'Le Spleen de Paris': essai sur le dépassement du réel* (Paris, Corti, 1986), p. 135.

Jean-Christophe Bailly (essay date 2001)

SOURCE: Bailly, Jean-Christophe. "Prose and Prosody: Baudelaire and the Handling of Genres." In *Baudelaire and the Poetics of Modernity,* edited by Patricia A. Ward, translated by Jan Plug, pp. 124-33. Nashville, Tenn.: Vanderbilt University Press, 2001.

[*In the following essay, Bailly asserts that Baudelaire's "little poems" constitute an attempt to transcend the limits of genre.*]

The "book" that is absent but surrounded by all the pages that prepare, sound, pursue, or deny it: one will find nothing of the like with respect to Baudelaire's prose poems. They appear and are gathered together quietly, so to speak, and what perhaps surprises us most about their invention is that it is neither preceded nor followed by any effect of announcement. Such discretion does not mean that with this new form Baudelaire revolutionized literature on the quiet or in a roundabout way: the dedicatory letter to Arsène Houssaye proves sufficiently that he was conscious of the singularity of his enterprise; but it is surely not out of false modesty that he there describes his endeavor as in part aborted or deviated. However, we who can unravel right up to ourselves the entangled texture of the modern he gave birth to know that with the prose poem he deposits the question of genre in its center, and that he bequeaths it to us.

The prose poem reveals this question of genre raised by the escape of the poem outside its prosodic rule and lexical customs; it is the most obvious emergence of it. But, like a cloud of milk one adds to a cup of tea and that colors it completely, Baudelaire's entire oeuvre is invested in it. Neither the verse poems, which rear up against and become distended within what Mallarmé will later call the "hereditary instrument," nor his critical prose, nor, of course, the fragmentary form of the *Fusées* can be thought outside of what the intrusion of prose in prosody comes to turn upside down. And the question is so crucial and generic that even the genres Baudelaire did not practice, such as the novel, are dragged for us to figure at the heart of the problematic it institutes.

Yet, one will find nothing in Baudelaire that could be compared to the theoretical fever that circulated, concerning genre, in the circle of the Jena romantics, a half century earlier. Baudelaire neither knew nor shared Friedrich von Schlegel's or Novalis's paradoxical formulas crossing the recognized separations in order to transcend them in formally permeable *ideas* of genre, or their intuition of a kind of genre of genres that ends up by sublating all these ideas in a superior unity to come, and there is nothing in him that recalls them, not even the atmosphere of such a speculation. But in him everything takes place as though he had tried, on a strictly practical level, to put into play that emancipation of the poem or that other prose at which the "little poems" are the attempts. It will be Walter Benjamin's historical role to propose to us to make the connection ourselves beginning with his oeuvre—to such a point that between his early essay on *The Concept of Aesthetic Criticism in German Romanticism* and his later writings on Baudelaire, it is, via genre, a true genealogy of modernity that his oeuvre confronts us with. Let us say that on the side of the romantics of the *Athenaeum* we have the theoretical slant (the slant on which the fragment itself functions as a state of form),[1] and that on Baudelaire's side we would have the effectuation of it. A mountain without a summit that on one side is still

lit by the last morning fires of German Idealism and that on the other is already lit by the gas lighting of the big city. From the one to the other, in fact, the absolute had to agree to roll in the mud of the suburbs and measure itself against the registers of objects of the industrial age. This fall, the Baudelairean version of what Novalis (in a letter to Friedrich von Schlegel dated 12 January 1798 and cited by Benjamin) called "enlarged poetry" *(erweitere Dichtung),* fulfills it.

The dedicatory letter to Arsène Houssaye might very well not have wanted to assert itself as the discovery of a theoretical continent and true new world of phrasing; after so many other commentators, it is dense enough in its concision for me to stop there—by illustrating that this density and speed are obviously not unrelated to those of the prose poems themselves. As we know, Baudelaire invokes a model at the threshold of his book, and it is *Gaspard de la Nuit,* Aloysius Bertrand's only book, published in 1842, a year after the untimely death of the young poet from Dijon. Perhaps it is advisable to look at it more closely than is usual or, at least, listening to Baudelaire, to take it seriously as an origin. The poems composing the six books of the collection are in prose, indubitably, a prose, moreover, that is extremely supple and sober, with a slightly magical lightness. But, as is often the case with an origin, the rupture is only half consummated with the form from which the new work has disengaged. The difference that jumps out between these prose poems and Baudelaire's (other than that capital one of the era and the urban type that are evoked—but I will of course come back to that) is the abandonment of strophic structure. Internally organized like songs of equal length and interconnected according to the riskless order of a strictly composed collection, each poem being a bit like a plate in a volume of engravings, Aloysius Bertrand's poems do not, like Baudelaire's, constitute a fantasy—the word is his—in which each fragment can exist by itself. The Baudelairean broadening is thus carried by the internal form—a prose completely gone out of verse—and by composition—a composite collection of diverse formats and even tones. The medieval connotation of Aloysius Bertrand's book allows us this image—every poem in *Gaspard de la Nuit* is like the square of a medieval garden, while with Baudelaire we must leave this *hortus conclusus* to penetrate into a land lying fallow, into a sort of vague literary ground. But beyond the almost complete abandonment of all cadence and according to the very slope that its escape toward the prosaic opens, the Baudelairean prose poem comes to verge on another brief form, that of the story. Baudelaire himself must have thought about this proximity, since in the outline in which the list of the prose poems, still in the state of a plan, figures, one finds twice, between brackets after the title, the indication "perhaps a story." It would no doubt be fruitless or scholastic to want to separate the prose poem and the story normatively, but what we must remember is this encounter, in the bed of the prosaic, this proximity that, however, does not and should not go all the way to fusion: whatever the hold over it by the fictional pulsion, there must be something in the prose poem that holds it back and acts in such a way that it does not purely and simply go about abolishing itself, something that does not abolish what comes to it from the poem. Thus, much more than a fixed genre disposing of its laws, codes, and standing, the prose poem appears as a form in the process of becoming, as a displacement that leaves the text unstable, as though wandering between an origin that it must at once leave and not entirely lose and a destination at once to be glimpsed and not united with. This all the more so since the story is not the only pole toward which the prose poem is led. In fact, everything that stems from descriptive and critical prose, everything that can be related to the essay provides another, perhaps still closer, encounter. With such discontinuous and superimposed movements ("La Chambre double," from this point of view, being at least triple: short story, short essay on art and time, and prose poem), it is a question of rebounds, ricochets, billiard balls. Is it a certain passage of the aesthetic writings that transforms itself into a "prose poem" or, conversely, a certain passage of **Le Spleen de Paris** that converts itself into a fragment of aesthetic theory? And can't we consider that in many respects **Le Peintre de la vie moderne** itself also approaches, and very truthfully, that is, on the level of its very writing, that "musical prose without rhythm and rhyme" that the dedication to Arsène Houssaye defines as a dream and a tension, as an active element that we know in fact disrupts the totality of the Baudelairean text?

Just after having defined this dreamed-of prose as "supple and uneven enough to adapt to the lyrical movements of the soul, to the undulations of reverie, to the jolts of conscience," a virtual prose in which we can recognize, precisely foretold and as though recognized, the Proustian sentence, for example (everything taking place as though Baudelaire discreetly confided to the future a task to be accomplished or a breakaway to be caught up with), just after this, which is the nucleus of the dedication, Baudelaire moves without transition, with an astonishing and almost technical calm, onto what will be the point of impact of his aim: "It is most of all from the frequenting of enormous cities, it is from the crossing of their innumerable relations that this obsessive ideal is born." To attempt, as he put it above, to do with the modern city, with Paris, what Aloysius Bertrand had "applied to the painting of ancient life, so strangely picturesque," to attempt a *description,* such is the program of the prose poems, a program that establishes Baudelaire (need it be said?) in an incredible lucidity, since he makes of himself the connection between the formal innovation he proposes

and the epochal form that rules it, the effect of which is to suggest to us that his endeavor is neither more nor less than that of the institution of a symbolic form.

The formal movement of this endeavor is double: it implies that voyage between the genres that we have spoken of, but it equally implies that what was latent in the regular poem finds in the new form the surface of its fulfillment. Here I am thinking above all of that lexical rupture for which Baudelaire's poetry is the experimental ground or the trial laboratory, a rupture that is already a rift caused by the prosaic in the resistant matter of the alexandrine. This is what Benjamin writes: "*Les Fleurs du Mal* is the first book to have used words not only of prosaic but of urban origin in lyric poetry,"[2] and he cites in passing a few of those words that disturb the tone and hierarchical position of the genre: *quinquet* (oil lamp), *wagon* (truck, wagon), *omnibus* (train, omnibus), *bilan* (balance sheet, assessment), *réverbère* (street light), *voirie* (road maintenance). The occurrences of these terms or of similar words are obviously even more numerous in the prose poems, but, most of all, they are at home there: their introduction into poetic material no longer stems from what Benjamin, speaking of *Les Fleurs du Mal,* defines as being a *putsch* (143). From such a point of view, the prose poem becomes the place in which the tension proper to Baudelaire's poetry—that is, this telescoping of the lyric by the trivial and of correspondences by the urban theme—is assuaged. This does not mean—far from it—that the prose poems fall over entirely and unanimously to one side, but at least indicates that they have, on this side, more range and freedom, and, also, on the level of their production, less tension. Into the very definition of the "obsessive ideal" in fact passes a certain gentleness, passes the phantom of a pure malleability. And thus the passages closest to the collection give the impression of having been written "off the cuff" or in that neglected sublime Baudelaire liked to identify in painters, as though their very matter had been diluted in the water of Constantin Guys's watercolors.

Such a relative relaxation does not mean that there is anything at all in these prose poems that could be likened to distraction or that borrows from the genre of physiology, so in vogue in their time (and let it be said in passing, Claudel's famous formula talking about "a mixture of Racine's style and of the journalistic style of his time" is scarcely appropriate to save us from such an error). Simply, this dreamed-of prose that Baudelaire finally says he did not achieve opposes to a fixed or at least scanned time a fluidity and a possibility of dilation that the regulation and even the prosodic deregulation of the poem forbids it from reaching; it constitutes another aim.

The violence of what he achieves by jumping outside of the tension proper to the poem, in which the intrusion of the prosaic does not manage to stop being a transgression, Baudelaire condenses into an allegory. It is that of the loss of the halo in the prose poem that carries that very name. We know its motif, and it is clear and radical. In the phrase by which the fallen poet tells about the accident that brought him down to earth, the entire contradiction of *Les Fleurs du Mal* relaxes in laughter: "my halo, in an abrupt movement, slipped from my head into the mire of the road *(macadam)*." And in such a way that we can imagine that this dialogue is really, despite its caricatural aspect, an interview between two faces of Baudelaire himself: on the one hand, the lucid narrator who is only the witness and confidant of the affair, on the other, the poet he has stopped or wanted to stop being, but who, in a much more pregnant way than his cheap double, continues to lurk in him. In the course of this dialogue, we remember, the loss of the halo is immediately converted into a gain, and the immediate form, immediately accessible, of this gain is the joy of the incognito. Having climbed down from his imaginary pedestal, the poet is literally depos(it)ed in the crowd in which he will be able to lose himself, and we, we have witnessed in a few lines a true metamorphosis: the chrysalis having fallen like the halo, there springs up a new poet already ready to laugh at his old colleagues, but ready most of all, instead of believing that he flies or glides, ready to walk like anyone at all on the tarmac *(macadam)*—the modern and trivial English word here having almost the value of a password.

Certain aspects of the prose poems respond to the radicality of this allegory, and these aspects are those in which derision is brushed up against. Thus, the brief hyperfocalized poem that is **"La Soupe et les nuages,"** a title—and a narrative—that, all the same, one would be at pains to imagine in the table of contents of *Les Fleurs du Mal*; thus again **"Les Bons Chiens,"** where, to sing "the calamitous dogs" with a fervor that, moreover, is not feigned, Baudelaire revokes the high style with almost coarse accents, letting one think that the voyage of genre includes a detour through bad genre: "Stand back, academic muse! I have nothing to do with that old prude. I invoke the familiar, the city-dwelling, the living muse."

However, everything is not so simple or smooth (we suspected as much), and the conversion of which **"Perte d'auréole"** tells retains, beyond the sarcasm, something theoretical about it. The rhetorical brake that is continually at work in *Les Fleurs du Mal* in fact remains active in the prose poems, even if it acts differently there. No doubt, it can no longer exert itself as a continuous pressure on the verbal flood, no longer having at its disposition the regular and fatal brake of verse, but one senses its presence no less, and this presence, although unequally divided among the different poems and facets of the collection, contributes to giving the form for which they try that hybrid character that has so often

been noticed. I am thinking less here of a given involuntary rising up of the alexandrine or of a given effect of tonal handling than of a sort of exclamatory unction that appears as a weakening of the design, and I will take as an example **"Le Thyrse,"** that poem that begins so well by supposing that the ancient and sacred object is only a simple stick, but that ends so poorly, with a very pompous dedicatory eulogy to Franz Liszt. It would be ridiculous, however, to probe the whole of *Le Spleen de Paris* in this way, by distributing good and bad points. What is at stake here, beyond all criteria, is the work of a form, the work of the adventure of a form: how it comes, what it comes to, how it yields itself to, or, on the contrary, resists, what it gives rise to. To understand the nature of these resistances is not to judge Baudelaire; it is to accompany him in his movement, to the extent that it is effectively deployed.

At bottom, the poet crowned with a halo of **"La Perte,"** "drinker of quintessence" and "eater of ambrosia," is but the inferior and comic version or the terrible parody of the tragic figure of the poet as it appears from the edge of *Les Fleurs du Mal* in **"L'Albatros"**: for this giant who can no longer glide above the waves, the ship's deck is the equivalent of the tarmac, the surface, of a fall into the real, but this time disastrous and no longer salvatory. No doubt, the "vast birds of the sea" have nothing of the ridiculousness of the pretentious poet, who, for his part, is only a kind of crested crane. But in the crossing of these two figures and at the speed of a hurried passerby cutting across the crowd a new Baudelairean dream takes shape: that of a poet who would be entirely the poet of prose, who would still know how to be, on bare ground and among humans, the "winged traveler," one who, without halo and having lost the azure, would however still, and perhaps even finally, have access to the aura. Baudelaire wanted to be this poet frankly and with bravado, but to get there he had to defy himself. Baudelaire could only see or foresee the ultimate movement of the fall and the farthest reach of the prose, but one can guess that he sensed there equally an abandonment and perhaps even, as he indicated to Manet about his art, a decrepitude. It seems that Baudelaire could not resign himself to what Mallarmé later would call "the illocutionary disappearance of the poet"[3] and that he suddenly rowed violently against the flood that carried him toward this disappearance.

We do not have the clear sign of such a mistrust, and if Baudelaire shifts in relation to the prose poems, it is with respect to their success, which he seems to judge imperfect, not to their ideal, which continues to be for him a "mysterious and brilliant model." But it is the very substance of the prose poems that conveys this sign to us, to the extent that a glimmer of the sublime that it does not manage to depose still flickers within it. Baudelaire quite often, and more often in turn than any other poet, is also the "painter of modern life," but there is, despite everything, something forced in his gesture that puts him in a bad position, and the strongest thing about his genius, what places him right in the middle of the nineteenth century as a hearth that irradiates it completely, is no doubt this open contradiction between what he senses and what holds him back from yielding to it.

To what point this "Baudelairean problem" (which one would find identical in his relation to painting, in what tears him between the last fires of the great genre revisited by the genius and "prose" of modern painting, between Delacroix and Guys),[4] does not concern him alone is testified to by his entire lineage, beginning with Rimbaud, Verlaine, and Mallarmé, even if it is strange or at least significant that in "Crise de vers" no mention is made of the prose poem, prosaic tension intervening, according to this fundamental text that does not cite Baudelaire a single time, except by the bursting open of verse itself, under the form of free verse. It is not my intention here to explore this lineage—that would be the subject of a book up to Apollinaire, who revives it with a force much too underestimated, a book that would analyze the entire tension between the prosaic and what some thinkers (Agamben or Berman) have called musaic. Nor is it my aim to enter very far into this highly complex text that is "Crise de vers," since it would only be a question of retaining an echo of it that applies to the understanding of Baudelaire.

In the way that Mallarmé saves verse from its ruin or fatigue, especially in the reasons he invokes for restoring it, despite everything, as a vibratory model that is at bottom unsurpassable but not turned toward the past from which it comes, something perceptibly makes a sign toward the impeccable handling of Baudelairean verse, but still more seems to trace from a distance, even if it is in other terms, Baudelaire's contradiction, and also to foresee ours.

For Mallarmé, it is to the degree that it "pays for the defect of languages" ("imperfect in that there are a number of them"[5] that verse, unpredictably, saves itself and becomes, by this defect, the "superior complement." Verse owes this position not to some authority, to a legitimacy of genre, and of a national genre, but to its law, which is simple: "this prosody, such brief rules, all the more uncompromising." In other words, as absolutely specific and sonorous form, verse strains from the paper toward its notion, because it is the memory of itself, the elimination of chance. This tension proper to verse and to it alone does not qualify it as "genre," but as oeuvre—not in the greedy sense of Hugo, of the Hugo machine, but in the sense of an absolute that bypasses the defect of languages like the chance of individuality. Not to throw verse out, but to throw it differently—this is how one could understand Mallarmé's

endeavor, as respects the poems as well as **"Un coup de dés,"** where chance is incurred. But as soon as it is thrown, the die falls again, and Mallarmé was the first to know this. We can see that the throw that does not return, coming under the book like a shadow or phantom, the angel of literature itself, resembles that "obsessive ideal" Baudelaire defined as out of reach of his prose. There is, in the one case as in the other, a taking aim at a target that conceals itself, but also the movement of engendered form that becomes frantic.

It is here, facing this chance, this returned chance, that verse straightens up, old this time, and that rhetorical prestige plays anew, with nostalgia in Baudelaire, with irony in Mallarmé, only Rimbaud perhaps managing to eliminate nostalgia. But what is sure, as far as we may have been able to go in the freeing up of genres and in the direction of that "enlarged poetry" that Novalis conceived two centuries ago, is that we have not got out of this tension, not because the charm, in the Greek and strong sense of *charis,* not because the *charis,* then, of prosody (or of "musaic") would take hold of us (which it does at any rate), but because that of which prosody is the delayed echo belongs to language itself. What a called-for genre of genres covets is not a simple mixture or an ultimate sublation, it is a language—that is to say, the purest acting of language, without veil. And the prosodic belongs to this unknown language like an integrated shadow: by accepting and accentuating the "defect of languages," that which, verse or not, recalls prosody, recalls also the most secret layer of language, that layer in which it is still the *phoné* that listens and speaks, that layer in which, in the most intimate connection to this voice, language stands beyond signification, in a disclosing of the world of which it is the echo. Now, this "lost paradise" of language accompanies the human being in time, not as a memory, but as an indication on the watch beneath language, preserving it. Rather than as a song, we should think of it as a sort of continuous bass; it is this bass that the prosodic lets be heard, not at all as a sonorous or musical value, but as the sign of the truth of naming. And from this moment we can understand the "gentle native tongue" spoken to the soul in secret, not as something evanescent, but as what has made this sign vibrate from the beginning of things.

Still in "Crise de vers," Mallarmé opposes, without our knowing exactly which way he is leaning, two manners of speaking. The one, which includes "in the subtle paper . . . for example the horror of the forest or the mute thunder scattered to the leaves," the other, which would go looking for "the intrinsic and deep wood of the trees." It seems to me that between these two manners resides the gap I have wanted to talk about and that the modern endeavor might be defined as the one that moves away from the side of this "intrinsic wood," effacing itself before it, having deposed everything: the poet, myth, the oracle, hymn, song, verse, and even prose no doubt—everything except what would still remain of language in which everything abandoned would be included. It appears to me, and this is my conclusion, that Baudelaire's oeuvre, in its historical position, opens the path that goes toward this wood, but that it does so by keeping "the mute thunder scattered to the leaves" from which, however, it distances itself, giving it, although it opens and is opened to modernity, the characteristic of a farewell: a morning, accordingly, but an autumn morning.

Notes

1. And this slant is an *invention*. What has to be examined with Jena romanticism is, as Philippe Lacoue-Labarthe and Jean-Luc Nancy write in *L'Absolu littéraire,* "the inauguration of the *theoretical* project in literature" (1978, 9).

2. Walter Benjamin, *Charles Baudelaire, un poète lyrique à l'apogée du capitalisme,* 143. Retranslated from the French.

3. This citation, like all those of Mallarmé in this text, is taken from "Crise de vers," in *OC,* 360-68.

4. On the form this distancing takes in Baudelaire's attitude toward painting, see my "Harmony in Red and Green," in number 3 of *L'Année Baudelaire.*

5. It is at the heart of the "defect of languages" that translation works. Far from having to be thought of as the passive heir of this defect, translation, like poetry, pays for it, and very substantially. It is even the fact of confronting this defect (that is, also the mass of all the qualities that make every language distinct and inimitable) that constitutes the essence of the translating act. On this organic connection between the translating act and poetic writing, I refer to the works of Antoine Berman, and notably to *Pour une critique des traductions: John Donne.* It must be emphasized that the question of genre—that is, the flux and flow between prose and poetry—belongs directly to what is at stake in translation; and one could even suggest that there is a connection between the invention of the prose poem and the register of choice that his translation of Poe could have imposed upon Baudelaire. Poe is completely at the center here since it is still he who comes back with the impeccable French prose writings that his poems translated by Mallarmé become.

A Note on Abbreviations and Translations

References to the editions by Claude Pichois of the complete works and correspondence of Charles Baudelaire, published in the Bibliothèque de la Pléiade and cited in the bibliography at the end of this volume, are abbreviated as *OC* and *COR,* respectively.

This book is directed toward an English-speaking readership with a knowledge of French. Titles to Baudelaire's poetry and prose writings have been given in French because these are generally well known. Poetry in verse has been cited in French, followed by a prose translation. All prose poetry or critical writing has been translated into English. Unless otherwise indicated, the translations are those of the individual essayists.

Works Cited

Bailly, Jean-Christophe. 1997. "'Harmony in Red and Green': Un tableau de Baudelaire." *L'Année Baudelaire* 3:123-31.

Baudelaire, Charles. 1961. *Les Fleurs du Mal.* Ed. Antoine Adam. Paris: Garnier.

———. 1964. *The Painter of Modern Life and Other Essays.* Trans. Jonathan Mayne. London: Phaidon. Distributed by New York Graphic Society, Greenwich, Conn.

———. 1965. *Art in Paris, 1845-1862: Salons and Other Exhibitions.* Trans. Jonathan Mayne. London: Phaidon. Distributed by New York Graphic Society, Greenwich, Conn.

———. 1970. *Paris Spleen.* Trans. Louise Varése. New York: New Directions.

———. 1973. *Correspondance.* 2 vols. Ed. Claude Pichois. Paris: Gallimard (Bibliothéque de la Pléiade).

———. 1975-76. *Œuvres complètes.* 2 vols. Ed. Claude Pichois. Paris: Gallimard (Bibliothéque de la Pléiade).

Benjamin, Walter. 1982. *Charles Baudelaire, un poète lyrique à l'apogée du capitalisme.* Trans. Jean Lacoste. Paris: Payot.

Lacoue-Labarthe, Philippe, and Jean-Luc Nancy (in collaboration with Anne-Marie Lang). 1978. *L'Absolu littéraire: Théorie de la littérature du romantisme allemand.* Paris: Seuil.

Mallarmé, Stéphane. 1945. *Œuvres complétes.* Ed. Henri Mondor and G. Jean-Aubry. Paris: Gallimard (Bibliothéque de la Pléiade).

Kalliopi Nikolopoulou (essay date April-December 2002)

SOURCE: Nikolopoulou, Kalliopi. "Baudelaire's Province." *Bulletin Baudelairien* 37, nos. 1-2 (April-December 2002): 44-59.

[*In the following essay, Nikolopoulou traces Baudelaire's relationship to the city and the country respectively and how this is reflected in his poetry.*]

That Baudelaire claims simultaneously the origin and summit of modern poetry is more than a mere truism in the history of literature. From T. S. Eliot's declaration that "Baudelaire is indeed the greatest exemplar in *modern* poetry in any language" (377) to Benjamin's "Motifs," Baudelaire is thought of as the poet of the city, the rhapsode of the crowd and alienation, and the subtle recorder of all things urbane. The implicit and uncontested equation between modernity and the city has come to be exemplified in Baudelaire.

At the same time, as Jonathan Culler maintains, "The Devil [. . .] is one thing that makes Baudelaire seem scarcely modern" (Introduction to *The Flowers of Evil,* xxxiii). The devil—and, I would argue, a number of other mythological creatures and places—is a theological trace, a medievalism that wanders uncomfortably through the bustling streets of the modern city. It is as if Baudelaire were the inspiration for the vampire who leaves his isolated castle in the Carpathians for the center of the town. As Eugène Crépet begins his biographical study of Baudelaire, "Le poète, qui a donné dans son œuvre une si large place à la vie des grandes villes était le petit-fils d'un paysan champenois" (1). Add to this that Baudelaire was the grandson of a certain Marie-Charlotte Dieu, and we arrive at an overdetermined ancestry for a poet who identified two attitudes within himself and humankind: "l'un vers Dieu, l'autre vers Satan" (*OC* [*Œuvres Complétes*], 682). Therefore, to sustain the claim of an unambiguous and undisturbed urbanity, Baudelaire criticism must settle such unsettling theological archaisms in the secularized scene of modernity, either by translating them into modern symbols, or by explaining them away as ironic instantiations of a past now extinct.

Although I, too, am convinced of Baudelaire's "modernity," I am also interested here in pushing the limits of the modern to see precisely what is the modality, the "mode," which is also the *measure,* of the modern. How and against what does the measure (modernity) measure itself? To do so, I am led to disclose another scene in Baudelaire's *œuvre:* a scene that is prior to and necessary for the construction of the modern city, and that presents itself, even if displaced, in much of Baudelaire's poetry and other writings. This other scene, which privileges vicinity instead of alienation, takes the name of the province. Sociologically speaking, the modern city begins with the displacement and influx of peasants, but—more importantly for this essay's concerns—philosophically, the city marks the passage from a world of proximity to one of distance as well as from *poiesis* to industry.

Although the common associations with nature, peasantry, parochialism, and superstitious belief could readily disqualify the term "province" from serious consideration, I use this word in a twofold manner to

effect a displacement: ironically, to distance Baudelaire from his typical urban dwellings, and metaphorically, to evoke an experience of nearness that is fundamental to the aesthetic act. If, as Heidegger notes, poetry has to do with beginnings, with the *polemos* that splits two intimate entities—gods and men—thus bringing them forth into being, then at the origin of poetry also lies an intimacy and a conflict that both binds and tears apart. Heidegger writes: "We do not learn who man is by learned definitions; we learn it only when man contends with the essent, striving to bring it into its being, i.e. into limit and form, that is to say when he projects something new (not yet present), when he creates original poetry, when he builds poetically" (144). Later on he identifies the origin of language *qua* poetry with the mysterious and the terrible: "The origin of language is in essence mysterious. And this means that language can only have arisen from the overpowering, the strange and terrible, through man's departure into being. In this departure language was being, embodied in the word: poetry" (171).

"Hymne à la Beauté" thematizes this abysmal experience of proximity and rupture as the very condition of poetic writing (*OC* I, 24-25). Whether from the sky or the abyss, the visit of the Muse—here personified as Beauty—is a foundational encounter, a presence that exalts or shatters the poet. True, Beauty arrives arbitrarily (**"Tu sèmes au hasard la joie et les désastres"**), but the poet's capacity to respond to this arbitrariness and to undergo the bliss and the blows are not to be diminished. In other words, the capacity to write in front of the abyss ("le gouffre"), whether sociological or existential in kind, is predicated on this mysterious scene of visitation, which is lost to the noise and indifference of Haussmann's Paris. Poetry is based on this type of close encounter with the otherworldly. This is also the reason why Baudelaire sees the poet as the modern refuse, an anachronism that offends bourgeois sensibility, a ghost that the city tolerates not because of its democratic inclusion, but because of its oblivion.

But what would it mean to argue for a Baudelaire of the province? What does such a claim do to the venerated figure of the *poète maudit,* and even more, what does it do to the understanding of modern poetry? Such a statement could be construed of course as a claim of a "devil's advocate," and that is why it should not be dismissed, since when it comes to Baudelaire, the devil stands very near. A profound, if unorthodox Catholic, Baudelaire may, in turn, ironize the gullibility of his urbane readers: "La plus grande malice du diable est de faire croire qu'il n'existe pas," he answers (Baudelaire qtd. by Docteur H. Fiessinger). André Gide, who appreciated Baudelaire's conversations with Lucifer,[1] was right to note that the devil is affirmed in our negation (*OC* I, 1338, n. I). After all, only a certain pedantry would insist on separating irony from mystery. For

Baudelaire, supernaturalism and irony are hailed as the two most essential literary qualities: "Deux qualités littéraires fondamentales: surnaturalisme et ironie" (*OC* I, 658). But in arguing so, I do not mean only to assume the position of the *agent provocateur*. What I hope to do is address the interval between his irrevocable modernity and his poetics of mystery, his poetry of blasphemy which is also a sacramental poetry.

With Baudelaire then we have a double mystery: not only the poetic mystery which is exemplified in his thematics of religiosity (his passion for allegory, his rewriting of myth), but also the critical mystery (the mystification, blindness, and falsification—all of which derive from *muein*²), that insists on an untenable dichotomy between the secularized city as a sociological space, and a poetics of mystery as an ontotheological and philosophical space. We are also confronted with the paradox of a poet whose classical obsession with form betrays our obsession with his modernity. The suggestion that Baudelaire exploits the irony of the disjunction between immaculate form and profane content does not exhaust this problematic. I argue that Baudelaire's anachrony points also to an anatopy—the disclosure of another space that haunts the city as its sacrificed foundation and its repressed menace. While I intersperse my remarks with illustrative moments from his poems, I take my cues from several entries in *Mon cœur mis à nu* (1864-1866), a collection of journal writings which, as the title connotes, lays bare the poet's heart.

> *Mon Cœur mis à nu* [. . .], although it cannot rank amongst his greatest works, bears witness to his ultimate development as a spiritual being, and this final vision explains much in retrospect which, otherwise, would not have been made clear from the purely literary works, whilst these literary works themselves take on a new significance and a deeper meaning, when seen in the light of this last phase. [. . .] *Mon Cœur mis à nu* is the "examen de conscience" of an upright man who never deluded himself into thinking that he was better than he was. Never perhaps was the poet so worthy of admiration and pity as now, in defeat. A new Baudelaire is here seen who was not apparent in his greatest works, a man broken and defeated in a worldly sense, striving against great odds, yet keeping in his suffering nobility and pride.
>
> (Starkie 501)

This is how Enid Starkie, Baudelaire's noted biographer, comments on this work. While recognizing the limitations of a personal memoir, Starkie also applauds its sincerity and draws attention to the fact that in light of these final thoughts, another Baudelaire may be constructed. A reading backwards may reveal beginnings lying elsewhere than once imagined.

Speaking of his beginnings, the poet reminisces: "Dès mon enfance, tendance à la mysticité. Mes conversations avec Dieu" (*OC* I, 706). Mystery is placed at the beginning as tendency and inclination. Baudelaire, the child, inclines toward the mystical. Inclination could be thought of as a gift, a talent, but also as bending and vulnerability. Baudelaire tends or extends toward the world of mystery, a world proximate to him, yet not exactly conterminous with him. Tendency, while fostering proximity, safeguards and separates through a necessary distance. Childhood for Baudelaire is not only the source of his mysticism, but of his solitude as well: "Sentiment de *solitude,* dès mon enfance. Malgré la famille,—et au milieu des camarades, surtout,—sentiment de destinée éternellement solitaire" (*OC* I, 680). "Dès mon enfance" is the chronological marker that appears twice in these two returns to an origin, where the poet finds mysticism and solitude—two postures that resemble and foster each other. Perhaps retroactively, we can discern the hermit as the earliest blueprint of the dandy and the *flâneur*. Alone in the crowd, slow-paced in his cynicism, the *flâneur* strolls eternally lonely and profoundly ascetic amidst decadence and debauchery. Hermit or *flâneur,* the poet is destined to solitude. Destiny, like tendency, traverses a distance whose endpoint, however, bespeaks of innateness, inherence, and proximity.

In yet another repetition, Baudelaire reflects on poetry in terms of destiny and proximity in a scene that seems torn out of a painting of a medieval province: "Il n'existe que trois êtres respectables: Le prêtre, le guerrier, le poète. Savoir, tuer et créer"³ (*OC* I, 684). Imagine the tableau: the soldier back from the Crusades receives the priest's blessings in the town square while the poet composes the saga of victory and sacrifice. The very category of respect reeks of obsolescence in an era where value was deflated to transaction and in a poet who lived out the depths of ill repute. To speak of respectable beings summons an earlier world of hierarchical order—let alone the hieratic order of a trinity of the most sacrosanct male occupations. The poet is the last of the trinity, as if synthesizing the abilities of the previous two: to create, one is endowed with the power of knowledge and the right to destroy. All-knowing God and destructive Beelzebub are here united in the figure of the poet. The later variation inverts the order, putting the poet first: "Il n'y a de grand parmi les hommes que le poète, le prêtre et le soldat, l'homme qui chante, l'homme qui bénit, l'homme qui sacrifie et se sacrifie" (*OC* I, 693). The poet, the priest, the soldier, this time: still a provincial trinity that would offend any urban sensibility both in its conservative and progressive colors; still a medieval trinity that exudes moral traditionalism in the proximity it draws amongst language, God, and nation. Whereas the modern city distanced these three types (the poet may be considered the ultimate dissenter from institutional concerns—religious or military—and the soldier of the bourgeois nation-state lacks the fervor of the Crusader), Baudelaire re-imagines them in their previous proximity to one another. After all, what he finds in each and all of them is an exemplar of proximity through passion: they are all creatures of passion, intimacy, blood, and destiny. Singing, consecrating, and dying are gestures of offering one's body first as language and voice, then as silence. Being not professions but vocations, all three cancel distance and accentuate election. One is chosen to be a poet, a martyr, or a hero; one cannot simply will it or profess it. Over and against the elected ones, Baudelaire sets the professional man: "Les autres hommes sont taillables et corvéables, faits pour l'écurie, c'est à dire pour exercer ce qu'on appelle des *professions*" (*OC* I, 684). Baudelaire's exemplary beings are both sacred and damned lovers, whose kin reside in Dante's *Inferno*. It is therefore no wonder that Dante was Baudelaire's companion in Eliot's canon.

Following Starkie's suggestion of reading retrospectively, we could read the poem **"L'Héautontimorouménos"** as an allegory that condenses these three figures into a self-portrait of self-punishment (*OC* I, 78-79). The outward aggression of the opening stanza ("Je te frapperai sans colère / Et sans haine, comme un boucher, / Comme Moïse le rocher!") turns inward by the middle of the poem: "Ne suis-je pas un faux accord / Dans la divine symphonie, / Grâce à la vorace Ironie / Qui me secoue et qui me mord?" Irony reverses the transitive into the self-reflexive, sadism into masochism. Put differently, irony—the poet's weapon—transforms the warrior's attack into a rite of self-mortification, an auto-vampirism the poet describes in his final stanza: "Je suis de mon cœur le vampire, / —Un de ces grands abandonnés / Au rire éternel condamnés, / Et qui ne peuvent plus sourire!" Instead of producing a distancing effect, irony turns somewhat ironically in this poem to produce a condensation of soldier and priest into the tormented figure of the poet feasting on his own heart. It should certainly be noted that the most notorious of vampires, Count Dracula, was also a Crusader, who—betrayed by his Church—signed the poetic contract *par excellence*: he sold his soul to the devil, punishing himself eternally in revenge for his lost love.[4] Poet, warrior, and priest are thus consolidated in one as the lyric I identifies repeatedly with the warlike and theological metaphors of this passion: "Je suis la plaie et le couteau! / Je suis le soufflet et la joue! / Je suis les membres et la roue, / Et la victime et le bourreau!" Wound and knife, limbs and rack, victim and tormentor are borrowed from the language of war, while cheek and slap echo the Christian morality of self-infliction. **"L'Héautontimorouménos"** then unites in adult fantasy the alternatives of a childhood memory the poet revisits in *Mon cœur mis à nu*: "Étant enfant, je voulais être tantôt pape, mais pape militaire, tantôt comédien" (*OC* I, 702).

Such premodern theological motifs afford the poet the sense of passion and suffering that the work requires in order to be written in the first place. Suffering and self-annihilation, the predicament of the mystic and the soldier, is also that of the poet. To alleviate suffering, the human being is called upon to make a work of art, but the work's demands overcome its maker to the point of annihilation.[5] This is the truth behind the *cliché* of the self-destructive artist. Urban modernity belittles this suffering and scorns the poet, transforming art from the placeholder of truth to yet another profession, and a not so respectable one at that. Giorgio Agamben locates this modern shift in the role of art as early as in Kant's replacement of artistic interest with spectatorial disinterest, and proceeds to return to the artist some of his or her forgotten dues: "For the one who creates it, art becomes an increasingly uncanny experience, with respect to which speaking of interest is at the very least a euphemism, because what is at stake seems to be not in any way the production of a beautiful work but instead the life and death of the author, or at least his or her spiritual death" (5). Soon after this statement, Agamben cites the example of Baudelaire, who thought that the experience of writing is like a duel unto death, with the poet always the defeated party (5). Paradoxically, affirming this pathos that the poet undergoes to the death marks also the last sign of life in a world where passion yields to indifference and even art is deprived of the privilege of exception.

This may have given us a cursory insight into the reasons why Baudelaire, the most Parisian of Parisians, also hated Paris. Crépet tells us how much the poet was repulsed by the capital especially toward the end of his life, when he also became nostalgic for Honfleur, his mother's residence: "Ce poète qui avait tout aimé de Paris, non seulement ses verrues, comme Montaigne, mais ses plaies, finit par le prendre en dégoût. Il voulut s'expatrier" (155). In a letter to his mother the year before he died, Baudelaire expressed his dream to live at Honfleur: "Mon installation à Honfleur a toujours été le plus cher de mes rêves" (*Correspondance* II, 626). Yet his dislike of Paris and his nostalgia for Honfleur are not to be limited to this time of illness and final despair. Although it was expressly stated only toward the end of his life, the dream of Honfleur had been inherent in Baudelaire's poetic project all along, as Jérôme Thélot astutely points out: "le projet de s'installer à Honfleur n'est pas anodin ni seulement un fait de la biographie: c'est un projet intérieur à la poésie baudelairienne, et c'est même *le plus cher de ses rêves* parce que c'est celui, donc, d'en finir avec la poésie" (133, emphasis in the original). The move from Paris to Honfleur is a literalized metaphor for the more general significance of the space I call the "province" in Baudelaire's overall poetic project, since this space marks for him both the beginning and the end of poetry.

While Baudelaire's visits to Honfleur were productive, Honfleur is also identified with the abandonment of poetry. Over and against Paris, the actual residence of the poet, Honfleur is the idealized place of inspiration and at the same time of complete liberation from the burden of the work. Honfleur thus is imagined as the pure space of interruption: it interrupts the poet's urban inertia with interludes of fruitful work, but it also promises its opposite—the interruption of writing once and for all. It is precisely this idealized aspect of Honfleur that Thélot evokes when he remarks that Honfleur remains a "project" for Baudelaire, "[p]ure possibilité, dont la jouissance serait perdue si de possible elle devenait actuelle, pure jouissance d'éviter la satisfaction qui serait la fin de la jouissance" (135). To go to Honfleur means to produce and to complete producing work, but also to keep producing and completing—an endless accumulation of ends. To not go to Honfleur, but to imagine going there, means to keep one final end in sight—an unrealizable yet singular end. Pure possibility, the province emerges as the condition of the desire for a work to come, which is also the desire to postpone it indefinitely, to never write it, thus obeying completely the law of the imagination. Central in its withdrawal, Honfleur is not simply the faded background of Baudelaire's cityscapes, but a space "rigoureusement tragique" in Thélot's words (137), the Orphic space of promise and non-retrieval, of beginnings and ends.

The poetological significance of the dream of moving to Honfleur illustrates concretely that Baudelaire's modernity cannot be defined solely in terms of his urbanity. In fact, that his love for Paris was always at least ambivalent proves to be the very point of Baudelaire's poetry: the immortalization of the city in his verses depends largely on his simultaneous recognition of its sordidity and oblivion. The question then concerning Baudelaire's modernity and urbanity is one of degrees, of measure. It has to do with how seriously we weigh Baudelaire's objections to the city and his nostalgia for a time prior to modernity. Is the Baudelairean "before" simply a construct determined from the present of his modern consciousness, or is this "before" external to and constitutive of his experience of the modern? In other words, it all depends on whether we read this nostalgia dialectically as a symptomatic effect of the city itself, or whether we allow for an excess of longing that invades from outside the city borders.

"Le Cygne" is probably the most programmatic of these poems in which Baudelaire explicitly addresses urban oblivion (*OC* I, 85-87). Like the awkward and comical albatross that was once a beautiful bird,[6] the swan is also now pitifully and spasmodically flapping its wings into the dust, looking for the dried-up lake it had inhabited. Once sublime and now ridiculous, these birds allegorize the shift of the poet's position in the world. Equally ridiculous now, the once venerated poet turns to the single posture that keeps poetry constant by saying the other of the world: *allegorein.* As everything be-comes allegory to the melancholy poet ("tout pour moi devient allegorie"), he ends up allegorizing poetic allegory itself: the swan, an allegory of the poet, is further allegorized in a "mythe étrange et fatal," the myth of enslaved Andromache, whom the poem apostrophizes in the first verse. First allegory: the swan flaps nervously its wings on dry land just as the poet is mocked by the bourgeoisie. Second allegory: Andromache captured by Pyrrhus allegorizes the trapped swan, while the fall of Troy stands for the destruction of old Paris. Double allegorization leads to mythopoetic plots, establishing another pre-modern triad, that of poetry, nature, and myth. Yet even this allegorical recourse to myth could be mobilized to maintain an urban and modern Baudelaire. Myth, in this "modern" reading, would serve demythologization and the undoing of the past. The poet could be saying that the "once upon a time" of the beautiful swan and the beloved poet is as real as the mythical Troy. In short, we lost something that never was: we lost nothing. This is the dialectical outmaneuvering of the non-identical: reduce externality to self-sufficiency, resolve inexplicable beginnings into dialectical returns of the same, console either by concealing the loss or exposing it as non-loss. Over and against this reading, which neutralizes nature and myth as dialectical byproducts of the present, I would like to advance another reading: not only is myth not a nothing, but myth is all that unfolds in the beginning. Myth is the poetry of beginnings and the beginning of poetry. As modern poetry allegorizes itself in ancient poetic figures, it does not simply fold upon itself as its own measure, but it literally articulates the other of itself—myth as the interruption of literature.[7] We have come full circle with Homer and Virgil haunting the *Tableaux parisiens.*

In order not to reduce Baudelaire to a facile nostalgia and an unproblematic embrace of nature and myth, critical interpretations insist on hypostatizing his urbanity, thus risking to render his poetry somewhat into a Lukácsian reflection of a specific historical experience. Baudelaire's poetry is unquestionably modern, but with the following modest qualification: the modern exceeds the city walls, and likewise, remnants prior and external to the modern constitute the modern as such. Consequently, mystery, evil, myth, nostalgia, and nature—all persistent themes in Baudelaire's writings—can be thought in conjunction with, but also apart from, the specificities of the present; not only as symptoms, but also as determinants of the present.

Baudelaire opens up this latter possibility, but backs away from it in his sonnet **"Obsession"** (*OC* I, 75-76), a poem that struggles to delineate the language of nature *vis à vis* that of humanity and culture. Nature's classical temple, which already spoke a confusing speech in **"Correspondances"** (*OC* I, 11), is transformed in **"Obsession"** into a frightening cathedral echoing deathly *De Profundis*. The synaesthesia of sounds and perfumes, and the mysterious unity of the senses described in the former sonnet, is interrupted in the latter by the inarticulate language of cries, bitter laughter, and roaring—now the sole medium of correspondence between nature and humanity.

In the first two stanzas the poet describes vehemently his dislike of two natural landscapes: the woods and the ocean. But in both cases it turns out that what he hates of these landscapes is, in fact, the human: "Grands bois, vous m'effrayez comme des cathédrales; / Vous hurlez comme l'orgue; et dans nos cœurs maudits, / Chambres d'éternel deuil où vibrent de vieux râles, / Répondent les échos de vos *De profundis*." The poet disavows his own anthropomorphization of the forest at the very same time that he refuses to accept a landscape without a human trace in it.[8] The forests terrify him because they remind him of human culture: architecture and music, the cathedrals with their organ. But even more terrifying is the fact that this music turns out to be a mortal cry equally shared by the human heart. This shared language of howling and mourning is the language of the inarticulate, the paradox of a language struck dumb. In a rewriting of Dante's wood of suicide, Baudelaire effects a metamorphosis in which, rather than personifying nature, he renders humanity dumb and mute.

The poem continues: "Je te hais, Océan! tes bonds et tes tumultes, / Mon esprit les retrouve en lui; ce rire amer / De l'homme vaincu, plein de sanglots et d'insultes, / Je l'entends dans le rire énorme de la mer." Again, the poet hates the ocean because his own human spirit is patterned after its crests and troughs. The sea rhymes with bitterness ("la mer," "amer," and perhaps even implicilty with "la mère" in the port of Honfleur— the figures of extreme pain and ambivalence in Baudelaire's imagination), the sobs contain spills of blood (the "sang" in "sanglots"), and the vast ocean cannot purge the suffering and defeat of a single human.

Tormented by the presence of trees and water, the poet turns to the absence of the starless night: "Comme tu me plairais, ô nuit! sans ces étoiles / Dont la lumière parle un langage connu! / Car je cherche le vide, et le noir, et le nu!" The starless night signifies the search for a new language. Tired of the familiar language of light, the poet wishes for the empty, the black, and the bare. Is this not the mute expression, or the inexpression of an utterly inhuman landscape, of sheer nothingness? The poet offers here the glimpse of a possibility to read otherwise or, better yet, not to read at all, for there is nothing to read. *Noli me legere.*[9] The confusing symbols of **"Correspondances"** have been driven to inscrutable silence, to the neutrality of the blank page and the interruption of writing. Mute nature promises metaphorically the leap beyond metaphor, a place that the poem

finds it impossible to dwell in for more than a breath. Hence, the poem returns quickly to the safe notion of filling the void with the image of the dark night ("les ténèbres"). Just as Honfleur symbolizes the impossible possibility—the project to stop writing by continuing to write—so this poem cannot finish with the desire for silence. One step further in the last tercet and we are back to the melancholy but also profoundly comfortable realization that even darkness is humanized as it displays the poet's ghosts: "Mais les ténèbres sont elles-mêmes des toiles / Où vivent, jaillissant de mon œil par milliers, / Des êtres disparus aux regards familiers." After the brief excursion into the vacuum, this gesture reinstates familiar humanity and presses to be read as inevitably modern: man is the measure of all things, including of the impenetrable night.

However, despite the poem's return to the familiar, the question of the possibility of complete emptiness remains suspended. Is there a void, an outside, that dares be kept out of reach? This may be the singular but unavowable truth that we would rather exchange for the *ennui* of repetition. Here then also lies the key to the rather cryptic meaning of the title of this sonnet which, on the surface, does not seem to describe anything particularly obsessive: the sonnet performs the quintessentially modern obsession of mastering the emptiness, reducing exteriority to self-reflection, and replacing being with its representation. This is nothing less than an understanding *avant la lettre* of Freud's dramatization of the obsessive-compulsive repetition in the *fort/da* game—the game of mastering the other's absence through symbolization.[10]

Through the suggestive triangles of poet—priest—soldier, then poet—swan—Andromache, or poet—nature—myth, and several other related themes, I hoped to question the unproblematized equivalence between urbanity and modernity in Baudelaire's work, and to suggest that despite its cultural specificity his work relies on a provocative metaphor, a spatio-temporal transport alluded to in the very title of his poetic collection ***Les Fleurs du mal***: evil—a word offensive to the ears of the modern sophisticate—resonates with anachronism, just as the flowers evoke a space outside the city limits. Benjamin astutely remarked that the crowd, the central motif of Baudelaire's poetry, does not appear explicitly anywhere in his work (167). I would add to this motif the province as its supplement, as the other structuring principle that appears only by being even more concealed. Thanks to this supplement the poet can rest amidst the city's restlessness. He survives precisely via this transposition, this carrying over of a province, or rather a vicinity—a space both proximate and solitary that makes writing (if not life) possible amidst the crowd. This solitude is precisely the posture of the *flâneur*. Alone, not simply because of social alienation, but inherently solitary and slow-paced in a certain vicinity, the vicinity of art which, according to Heidegger, requires also distance. The Black Forest in Paris.

Hence, this province is not about a sentimental return to unspoiled nature, whose presence is otherwise ample in Baudelaire's images and motifs, as much as the city. What I mean by the province has to do with that which stands before (*pro-*) the processes of seeing and conquering (*-vince*), thus making poetic vision and mastery possible in the first place. Province also as vicinity, the closeness—both hermeticism and proximity—of poetry with respect to the human. In a sense, one cannot but only have a poetry of the province. And if Baudelaire is a modern poet, he is in the sense of disclosing the secrets of modernity, as a "hierophant," or a "mystes" of the city.

Notes

1. Gide was struck by Baudelaire's prose poem "Le Joueur généreux" from *Le Spleen de Paris* (*OC*, I, 325-328).

2. The etymology of mystery is traced to the Greek verb *muein* which meant to shut one's eyes or mouth. This double usage implies that either one is still blinded to the truth, or alternately, that the initiate to the mystery is prohibited from divulging it.

3. On note 22 on this fragment in his facsimile edition of *Mon cœur mis à nu*, Claude Pichois cites a similar trinity from Balzac's *Colonel Chabert*: the Priest, the Doctor, and the Judge, whose black robes symbolize the suffering of humankind in its most essential aspects—the plight of the soul, the pain of the body, and the fear of the law: "Savez-vous, mon cher, [. . .], qu'il existe dans notre société trois hommes, le Prêtre, le Médecin et l'Homme de justice, qui ne peuvent pas estimer le monde? Ils ont des robes noires, peut-être parce qu'ils portent le deuil de toutes les vertus, de toutes les illusions."

4. The historical Dracula was a famed warrior of Christendom against the Ottoman Turks. His name links him both to the religious order of the Knights of the Dragon, established by the Holy Roman Emperor Sigismund to fight the Turks, and to the devil, since Dracul in Romanian stands for dragon and for the devil (Florescu and McNally 40-41). Francis Ford Coppola's rendition of Bram Stoker's novel begins with Dracula's vow of revenge against the Church that refused proper funeral to his beloved because she committed suicide upon hearing wrong news that he was killed in battle.

5. This latter part constitutes the central thesis in Blanchot's *The Space of Literature*.

6. I am referring to another poem, "L'Albatros" (*OC* I, 9-10) which, like "Le Cygne," serves as an allegory of the poet's inability to live in the human city. In the last stanza of "L'Albatros," the poet is portrayed as an idealistic figure, dwelling in the clouds, whose giant and clumsy wings obstruct his earthly walk.

7. I am playing on Jean-Luc Nancy's statement that literature is the interruption of myth (63-64).

8. Baudelaire made this tendency very clear in his critical writings on landscape painting in the Salon of 1859: "Si tel assemblage d'arbres, de montagnes, d'eaux et de maisons, que nous appelons un paysage, est beau, ce n'est pas par lui-même, mais par moi, par ma grâce propre, par l'idée ou le sentiment que j'y attache" (*OC* II, 660).

9. Blanchot uses this trope in *The Space of Literature* to describe the inability of the author to read his or her own work (23). I borrow it here to suggest the inscrutability of writing, which is initially predicated on the metaphor of an inscrutable landscape.

10. See Freud's *Beyond the Pleasure Principle*.

Works Cited

Agamben, Giorgio. *The Man Without Content*. Trans. Georgia Albert. Stanford: Stanford UP, 1999.

Baudelaire, Charles. *Mon cœur mis à nu*. Facsimile edition by Claude Pichois. Textes littéraires français. Geneva: DROZ, 2001.

Benjamin, Walter. "On Some Motifs in Baudelaire." *Illuminations*. Ed. Hannah Arendt. Trans. Harry Zohn. New York: Schocken, 1969. 155-194.

Blanchot, Maurice. *The Space of Literature*. Trans. Ann Smock. Lincoln: U of Nebraska P, 1982.

Coppola, Francis Ford, dir. *Dracula*. Columbia/Tristar Studios, 1992.

Crépet, Eugène. *Charles Baudelaire: étude biographique*. Paris: A. Messein, 1906.

Culler, Jonathan. "Introduction." Charles Baudelaire's *Flowers of Evil*. Trans. James McGowan. Oxford World's Classics. Oxford: Oxford UP, 1993. xiii-xxxvii.

Eliot, T. S. "Baudelaire." *Selected Essays*. New York: Harcourt, Brace & World, 1960. 371-381.

Fiessinger, H. "La peur du diable." *Le Monde* 23 May 1956.

Florescu, Radu R. and McNally, Raymond T. *Dracula: Prince of Many Faces*. Boston: Little, Brown & Co., 1989.

Freud, Sigmund. *Beyond the Pleasure Principle*. Trans. and ed. James Strachey. The Standard Edition. New York: Norton, 1961.

Heidegger, Martin. *An Introduction to Metaphysics.* Trans. Ralph Manheim. New Haven: Yale UP, 1959.

Nancy, Jean-Luc. "Myth Interrupted." Trans. Peter Connor. *The Inoperative Community.* Ed. Peter Connor. Theory and History of Literature 76. Minneapolis: U of Minnesota Press, 1991. 43-70.

Starkie, Enid. *Baudelaire.* New York: New Directions, 1958.

Thélot, Jerôme. "Paris/Honfleur ou l'impossibilité d'œuvrer." *L'Année Baudelaire* 1, 1995. 133-146.

Cheryl Krueger (essay date fall 2002)

SOURCE: Krueger, Cheryl. "Surgical Imprecision and the Baudelairean *poéme en prose.*" *French Forum* 27, no. 3 (fall 2002): 55-72.

[*In the following essay, Krueger points out Baudelaire's use of the surgical metaphor in his prose poems to illuminate the poet's shaping of these texts.*]

Though Baudelaire's **"Dédicace à Arsène Houssaye"** provides a dubious manifesto of the prose poem genre,[1] it more importantly builds a network of repeated images and allusions from which, along with the other prose poems in the collection (**Le Spleen de Paris** or **Petits Poèmes en prose,** 1869) the reader may piece together the prose poems' poetics. Of these, the presence of the snake, and the invitation to perform multiple surgeries on it, are among the most intriguing. Now exceedingly familiar to readers of **Le Spleen de Paris,** Baudelaire's serpent might be considered, in literary circles at least, a dead metaphor. Yet by reading beyond the anticipated symbolic power of the snake (the power of evil, the power of the phallus), and of surgery (a masculine vocation, an act of precision), one begins to understand the serpent as not just an ambiguous simulacrum of the prose poems, but a simulacrum of the prose poems' ambiguity. In **Le Spleen de Paris,** modulations of recognizable and ostensibly masculine acts and images not only erode articulations of *gender* throughout the prose poems' narrative, thematic and metaphorical systems, but in so doing, accentuate the *genre* ambiguity implicit in the *poème en prose.*

Baudelaire's serpent has become a well-known figure in the French literary menagerie, playing a crucial, metaphorical role in the characterization of would-be textual operations in **Le Spleen de Paris**:

> Mon cher ami, je vous envoie un petit ouvrage dont on ne pourrait pas dire, sans injustice, qu'il n'a ni queue ni tête, puisque tout, au contraire, y est à la fois tête et queue, alternativement et réciproquement. Considérez, je vous prie, quelles admirables commodités cette com-

> binaison nous offre à tous, à vous, à moi et au lecteur. Nous pouvons couper où nous voulons, moi ma rêverie, vous le manuscrit, le lecteur sa lecture; car je ne suspens pas la volonté rétive de celui-ci au fil interminable d'une intrigue superflue. Enlevez une vertèbre, et les deux morceaux de cette tortueuse fantaisie se rejoindront sans peine. Hachez-la en nombreux fragments, et vous verrez que chacun peut exister à part. Dans l'espérance que quelques-uns de ces tronçons seront assez vivants pour vous plaire et vous amuser, j'ose vous dédier le serpent tout entier.

> (*OCI* [*Œuvres Complétes.*], 275)[2]

The versed reader has already encountered sundry endangered species in Baudelaire's metaphorical bestiary, among them the tortured albatross, the displaced swan, the mentally imprisoned cat (Miner 1997, 105) and the disoriented bat. It is tempting at first to rely upon this serpent, passively waiting to be clinically segmented and reattached by the reader *cum* surgeon, as a viable if vulnerable analog of the prose poem collection. Baudelaire's serpent *appears* to embody vital signs for reading the genre and the text. In fact, the characterization of the serpent and reader is at first so convincing, one easily forgives a zoological inaccuracy: while some small *worms* (planaria) will regenerate if cut lengthwise, no snake could survive the sort of vivisection Baudelaire prescribes.

Poetic license justifies such biological imprecision, yet the figure of the serpent still conceals the anatomy of the prose poems. For the reader who approaches **Le Spleen de Paris** as a group of poems, the metaphor of the serpent seems in itself superfluous, more a decoy than a model for reading the collection. While Baudelaire did specify in a letter to Vigny that the second edition of **Les Fleurs du mal** had a beginning, an end, and a lexical order,[3] readers do not necessarily feel bound to follow poetry collections methodically from the first poem to the last. Baudelaire's references to the serpent and to the "interminable thread of a superfluous plot" represent a rejection of the boundaries normally imposed upon *prose,* not poetry, specifically the narrative prose of the novel and the short story.

Even if we consider each element in the collection to be a short *prose* piece, the suggested dynamics of surgeon and snake, reader and text, are not obvious. The prose poems most certainly may be read in any order, but reconsidering the question of plot, what control has the reader over further cutting up a collection already divided into fifty narrative segments? Baudelaire (and this is shorthand for "Baudelaire's narrative persona," for the "dedication" to Houssaye is as much a prose poem as the fifty other pieces), describes the snake with confidence and control, offering Houssaye, and presumably any reader amenable to the narrative arrangement proposed in the letter, the same sort of invasive power over his text. However, the final, punning reference to the severed serpent—"In the hope that some of these segments will be *lively enough*" (emphasis my own)—casts doubt upon whether or not cutting into the serpent is as benign an act as initially presented. Both the innocence of the surgeon and the malleability of the snake become still more suspect in the intertextual shadow of *Les Fleurs du mal,* where the reader is not invited to tamper with this reptilian manifestation of evil, sensuality, or a fusion of the two.[4]

While the prose poems' serpent seems both more protected and more harmless than the creatures of *Les Fleurs du mal,* its thematic appearance in **"Les Tentations, ou Éros, Plutos et la Gloire"** reinforces its duality as a metaphor and as a beast. As we will see, the snake in **"Les Tentations,"** and allusions to surgical scalpels and stitches in **"Mademoiselle Bistouri,"** revive the preface's "serpent" and "fil," and may be read as representations of plot itself, their literal depiction mirroring the evasiveness of the *dédicace.* An examination of the literal incorporation of these previously figurative serpents and threads provides further evidence of the constant presence and denial of plot throughout the prose poems. This narrative equivocation parallels a penetrability of genre reflected throughout the text in images of alterable gender and identity.

The snake appears, head and tail intact, in **"Les Tentations"** (*OCI,* 307-10), when the narrator is visited in a dream by three devils proposing another kind of literary pact, enveloped, like that of the **Dédicace,** in the polyvalent figure of the serpent. The first visitor, an androgynous Eros with parted lips, "la mollesse des anciens Bacchus," and whose "visage était d'un sexe ambigu" wears "en manière de ceinture, un serpent chatoyant qui, la tête relevée, tournait langoureusement vers lui ses yeux de braise" (*OCI,* 308). The rich sexual implications of this seductive Bacchus, a fiery-eyed snake coiled around his hips, cannot be denied.[5] Textually speaking, the demon, with its taunting androgyny, suggests the ambivalently defined literary "genre" *poème en prose.* At the same time, by confronting the narrator with a shimmering snake, it provides a *mise en scène* and *mise en abyme* of the dynamics of reader and text projected earlier in Baudelaire's letter to Houssaye. The docile yet resilient metaphorical snake introduced in the preface establishes the reader's superiority over a text s/he may chop up and rearrange at will. The poised snake in **"Les Tentations,"** however, does not necessarily invite such intervention. A closer look at Eros shows this serpentine belt to be weighed down with dangerous potions and cutlery:

> A cette ceinture vivante étaient suspendus, alternant avec des fioles pleines de liqueurs sinistres, de brillants couteaux et des instruments de chirurgie. Dans sa main droite il tenait une autre fiole dont le contenu était d'un rouge lumineux, et qui portait pour étiquette ces mots bizarres: "Buvez, ceci est mon sang, un parfait cor-

dial;" dans la gauche, un violon qui lui servait sans doute à chanter ses plaisirs et ses douleurs, et à répandre la contagion de sa folie dans des nuits de sabbat.

(*OCI,* 308)

Does the proximity of the blood and blades to the living snake indicate that it is impervious to their danger, that they are medicinal? Are they meant for the serpent's own use? For Eros himself? Or do the surgical tools represent a constant threat to "cette ceinture vivante," an invitation to cut the snake? Just as the figure of Eros casts doubt upon the safety of the metaphorical surgery at first enthusiastically prescribed in the preface, the malleability of the serpentine belt remains questionable in **"Les Tentations."**

Along with the equivocal snake, Eros wears chains which impede his mobility: "A ses chevilles délicates traînaient quelques anneaux d'une chaîne d'or rompue" (*OCI,* 308). The narrator eventually cites all that is suspended from Eros' body as reason for spurning his offer: "[. . .] ta mystérieuse coutellerie, tes fioles équivoques, les chaînes dont tes pieds sont empêtrés, sont des symboles qui expliquent assez clairement les inconvénients de ton amitié" (*OCI,* 309).

This rejection is rendered all the more poignant by the phrasing of Eros' pact, tailored to echo the poetic ideal expressed throughout Baudelaire's writings: "'et tu connaîtras le plaisir, sans cesse renaissant, de sortir de toi-même pour t'oublier dans autrui, et d'attirer les autres âmes jusqu'à les confondre avec la tienne'" (*OCI,* 308). Eros offers the dreamer not only a chance to always *be,* but perhaps more importantly, a chance always *to be a poet,* to experience reality outside himself. The rejection of his gift signifies in part a rejection of poetry itself under Satan's conditions, that is, with strings attached.

Most importantly, Eros promises an endless source of the poet's singular power to penetrate others, as described in the earlier prose poem **"Les Foules,"** published first in 1861, then again in 1862 along with a series including **"Les Tentations"** and the dedication to Houssaye:

> Le poète jouit de cet incomparable privilège, qu'il peut à sa guise être lui-même et autrui. Comme ces âmes errantes qui cherchent un corps, il entre, quand il veut, dans le personnage de chacun. Pour lui seul, tout est vacant; et si de certaines places paraissent lui être fermées, c'est qu'à ses yeux elles ne valent pas la peine d'être visitées.

(*OCI,* 291)

Eros' promise reads as a paraphrase of this excerpt from **"Les Foules,"** which is not the only text expressing the poet's uncanny powers of penetration. In **"Les Fenêtres"** (*OCI,* 339), the narrator invents "histoires" and "légendes" for the strangers he glimpses through windows. He then goes to bed, "fier d'avoir vécu et souffert dans d'autres que [lui]-même." Anticipating the reader's concern that his stories may not be true, he replies, "Qu'importe ce que peut être la réalité placée hors de moi, si elle m'a aidé à vivre, à sentir que je suis et ce que je suis?" To reject Eros' offer, then, clearly implies rejection of an insured, constant access to an ideal and much desired poetic privilege.

As he gives up the power to enter others so often associated with Baudelaire's poetic ideal, the dreamer in **"Les Tentations"** also rejects the surgical tools necessary to cut the serpent, metaphor of the collected prose poems. Pieces of a whole are not viewed as desirable in **"Les Tentations,"** where broken chains—perhaps the halos of other fallen poets[6]—only entangle the feet of the demon and contribute to his apparent inconsolability. Leaving the snake intact may be read then as leaving the narration vulnerable yet intact, as allowing some form of plot to unfold, at least within the collection's individual poems.

The narrator's unwillingness to use the shiny knives and surgical instruments, or his willingness to leave narrative unbroken within the prose poems, is revealed in the treatment of the dream itself in **"Les Tentations."** By telling the story of a dream rather than representing a dream state, **"Les Tentations"** remains separated from the other "dream poems" in the collection. In a list of "poèmes à faire" (*OCI,* 366-68), Baudelaire classified prospective prose poem titles under the headings, "Choses parisiennes," "Onéirocritie," and "Symboles et moralités." While none of these titles reappeared with the finished prose poems, readers tend to classify the fifty prose poems in the definitive collection under the same often overlapping headings. Brief, more lyric pieces from the "Poèmes nocturnes" series published in *Le Présent* (August 1857)[7] have been seen as the most "dream-like" and, not surprisingly, prior to deconstructive readings, the most "poetic" works in the collection.[8] These include the prose poems written alongside *Les Fleurs du mal* and considered a counterpart or companion piece (le "pendant") to the poems in verse.[9]

The longer, later, narrative poems tend to vacillate between the Parisian and Moral headings. As Marie Maclean notes:

> The fifty poems we have divide more or less evenly between these classes though there are overlaps. Do we class "Counterfeit Coinage" as a Parisian story or a moral story? "Which is the true one" as a dream or symbol? In fact, as will become apparent, these classes are more an indication of possible alternative readings, since we have seen, any division of *The Little Prose Poems* into generic types is subverted by the kaleidoscopic nature of the collection.
>
> (55)

"Les Tentations" further muddies these taxonomical distinctions by allowing a reinterpretation of the category, "Onéirocrite." The dream, formerly associated in Baudelaire's verse and prose poetry with elevation, transcendence, the ideal, the poet's vertical, sublime aspirations, now functions on a horizontal axis as narration. **"Les Tentations"** never evokes a dream-state or poetic reverie. Instead, the narrator *recounts* the rich dream story, which includes descriptions of the second and third demons, a pot-bellied, eyeless personification of human misery offering wealth, and a throaty-voiced "fausse déesse" whose fame-blowing horn brought to the dreamer's ears "je ne sais quel souvenir d'une trompette prostituée" (*OCI,* 310). Once awake, the narrator regrets his moralistic refusal of the devils' gifts. Closing the narrative with wry self-chastisement: "'Ah! s'ils pouvaient revenir pendant que je suis éveillé, je ne ferais pas tant le délicat!" He then pleads aloud, hoping the demons will give him a second chance to accept their offer, but "ils ne sont jamais revenus" (*OCI,* 310).

The narrator has refused to trade his soul for the demons' favors, all of which pertain to poetic success: it is *textual* desire, *literary* fortune and fame that Plutos, Éros and **"La Gloire"** offer the dreamer. And while he refuses the commercial and poetic paradise that comes with compromise, he allows the metaphorical serpent, the dream tale, to remain neatly enclosed in a brief introduction and conclusion. The dream becomes a whole, framed story. This constant presence and denial of stories and storytelling suggests that plot must first exist if it is to be subverted. It is fortuitous then that Baudelaire chose the metaphor of the serpent to represent his collection: had he used the more zoologically appropriate term, "worm" or "vers," *Le Spleen de Paris* may have appeared to be all the more firmly anchored in a purely poetical mutation.

The sort of cutting tools suspended from the serpent-belt and rejected by the narrator in **"Les Tentations"** reappear in a second framed story featuring *genre* ambiguity and, this time, literal allusions to medicine, prostitution and madness. Here the *flâneur,* strolling near the outskirts of Paris, is picked up by a tall, young, streetwalker whose name (itself a merging of feminine title and masculine noun) is disclosed only in the prose poem's revealing title, **"Mademoiselle Bistouri,"** or **"Miss Scalpel."**[10] In this nearly complete reversal of the poet's role in **"Les Fenêtres,"** the narrator allows himself to become a character in Mademoiselle Bistouri's story: the woman invents the narrator's "legend" in this piece, where the roles of surgeon, storyteller and prostitute are perpetually interchanged.

Compelled by strictly *prosaic* interests, the *flâneur* allows Mademoiselle Bistouri to lead him home: "J'aime passionnément le mystère, parce que j'ai toujours l'espoir de le débrouiller. Je me laissai donc entraîner par cette compagne, ou plutôt par cette énigme in-espérée" (*OCI*, 353). Relinquishing the narrative power to describe ("J'omets la description du taudis"), the narrator/*flâneur* instead allows Mademoiselle Bistouri to tell what she considers to be his story, thus allowing her to penetrate him in the style of the Baudelairian poet/prostitute. While her identity is never explicitly revealed, the profession of this made-up woman referred to as a "fille," is obvious.

In **"Mademoiselle Bistouri"** the roles of prostitute and client, doctor and patient, storyteller and protagonist perpetually overlap. Like the real-life public hygienist Alexandre Parent-Duchâtelet,[11] the author of *Le Spleen de Paris* and *Hygiène* deals in sex and cadavers, prostitution and dissection, simultaneously and with equal fascination. Baudelaire attributed the desire to "penetrate" others to poets in several prose poems (**"Les Tentations," "Les Fenêtres," "Les Foules," "Le Joueur Généreux"**), and to lovers and writers in his *Journaux intimes,* where love, poetry, and God share the common denominator of representing a sort of prostitution that Baudelaire defines as a capacity to enter and be entered by others: "L'amour, c'est le goût de la prostitution" (*OCI,* 649); "Qu'est-ce que l'amour? / Le besoin de sortir de soi" (*OCI,* 692); "Qu'est-ce que l'art? Prostitution" (*OCI,* 649); "L'amour veut sortir de soi, se confondre avec sa victime, comme le vainqueur avec le vaincu, et cependant conserver des privilèges de conquérant" (*OCI,* 650); "L'être le plus prostitué, c'est l'être par excellence, c'est Dieu, puisqu'il est l'ami suprême pour chaque individu, puisqu'il est le réservoir commun, inépuisable de l'amour" (*OCI,* 692).[12]

The interaction between Mademoiselle Bistouri and the narrator underscores the related roles of poet and prostitute specified in the *Journaux intimes.* It is normally the *flâneur* who tells stories in *Le Spleen de Paris,* and the men who smoke cigars (**"Portraits des maîtresses"**). But like her phonetically linked, literary precursor Madame Bovary,[13] Mademoiselle Bistouri lights up her own. She then proceeds to deliver a series of portraits (visual and verbal) of *men.* And like the *maîtresse* who "voulait toujours faire l'homme" (**"Portraits des maîtresses,"** *OCI,* 346), she dominates the conversation. The *flâneur,* who earlier had Mademoiselle Bistouri "suspendue à [s]on bras," finds himself suspended from his companion's thread of plot, not only as a listener, but as a main character in her story:

> Faites comme chez vous, mon ami, mettez-vous à l'aise. Ça vous rappellera l'hôpital et le bon temps de la jeunesse.—Ah ça! où donc avez-vous gagné ces cheveux blancs? Vous n'étiez pas ainsi, il n'y a pas encore bien longtemps, quand vous étiez interne de L . . . Je me souviens que c'était vous qui m'assistiez dans les opérations graves. En voilà un homme qui aime couper, tailler et rogner! C'était vous qui lui tendiez les instruments, les fils et les éponges.—Et comme,

l'opération faite, il disait fièrement, en regardant sa montre: "Cinq minutes, messieurs!"—Oh! Moi, je vais partout. Je connais bien ces Messieurs.

(*OCI,* 353-54)

Throughout the poem, the symbolically castrating Mademoiselle Bistouri reduces the identity of doctors to synecdochic, capital letters (L., Z., X., K., W.), then to portraits. Both the portraits and the letters, conventional symbols and elliptic forms in the novel (and in prose poems such as **"Portraits des maîtresses," "Perte d'auréole,"** and **"A Une Heure du matin"**),[14] figure prominently in Mademoiselle Bistouri's story-telling repertoire, demonstrating her control of the novelist's tools, and suggesting a mastery of the surgical tool for which she is named: capital letters amputate whole names, portraits depict bodiless heads. At the same time, the constant displacement and condensation of identity adds to the dream-like quality of her story. Playing the analysand who recounts her dreams and fantasies to the *flâneur,* Mademoiselle Bistouri succeeds, temporarily at least, in creating the narrator's identity as a doctor.[15]

It is worth noting, too, that portraits discovered in a house of prostitution figure in the nightmare that Baudelaire reported to Asselineau in a letter that would later become the subject of Butor's mesmerizing *Histoire Extraordinaire: Essai sur un rêve de Baudelaire.*[16] By allowing elements of his own reported dream to penetrate his art, (the fictional narration of a woman who is most likely a prostitute) and vice versa, Baudelaire quite literally illustrates his definition of art: "Qu'est-ce que c'est que l'art? Prostitution."

Perhaps realizing that his power (masculine and narrative, alternatively and reciprocally) has been subjugated to this seductive *Doppelgänger,* the *flâneur* eventually protests. He denies having held the sutures ("fils") and says he has never been a surgeon "à moins que ce ne soit pour te couper la tête!" As if in response, Mademoiselle Bistouri presents a bundle of portraits—disembodied heads—from her cupboard to see if the narrator recognizes them. Indeed he does, and while his hand touches "un paquet ficelé," he does not pull the strings. Instead, Mademoiselle Bistouri opens it—"Et elle déploya en éventail une masse d'images photographiques, représentant des physionomies beaucoup plus jeunes" (*OCI,* 354)—and asks the narrator to return next time with a portrait of himself for her collection—one more head to narrate, and one more story to unfold.

The *flâneur* maintains a position of passive uncertainty, neither literally playing out his verbal threat by decapitating his hostess (an image further elaborated, however, in **"Le Galant Tireur"**), nor offering to add his own symbolic head to her collection. And while *she* has penetrated *him* by creating his story, we are never told whether he exercised the anticipated client/prostitute contract by physically "penetrating" her. It is, like the description of the *taudis,* extracted from his own narration. A sudden shift from "vous" to "tu" suggests that either during or after Mademoiselle Bistouri's initial monologue, she and the *flâneur* have reached a new level of intimacy: "Quelques instants plus tard, me tutoyant, elle reprenait son antienne, et me disait: 'Tu es médecin, n'est-ce pas? [. . .]—Chirurgien, alors?'" (*OCI,* 354). It is possible (though unlikely, I think) that the act of physical prostitution has taken place in ellipses. Considering the *flâneur's* chronic hesitation and relative immobility, along with the *Fusée,* "Il y a dans l'acte de l'amour une grande ressemblance avec la torture, ou avec une opération chirurgicale" (*OCI,* 659), one might conclude that the rejection of surgical tools indicates a rejection of the sexual act in this text as well: the *flâneur* physically rejects "*la* Bistouri" along with "*le* bistouri." More obviously, though, the *flâneur* has performed a sort of narrative prostitution, temporarily conforming to Mademoiselle Bistouri's narrative desire, and relinquishing his (masculine) dominance to this storyteller.

The rest of the poem is devoted to Mademoiselle Bistouri's explanation of her strange attraction to doctors, surgeons especially, and of one young doctor whom she invited to visit free of charge. By way of conclusion she adds, almost off-handedly, that she wishes said doctor would come to see her in his surgeon's smock with a little blood splashed on it. At first one could imagine this to be the blood of a surgical patient. Less literally, though, and in light of the poem's gender role-reversals, we might "read" this blood as that of the surgeon himself, deflowered (and hence, symbolically castrated) by the narrating Scalpel. Mademoiselle Bistouri's narrative "penetration" of the original storyteller (our *flâneur*) was not just poetic: by casting him as a doctor in her story, she has included him, with the young surgeon and the others, as a character in her sexual fantasy. Yet in this game of role-reversals, the *flâneur* has the last word, closing this story with his own assessment of the young woman, whose tastes he deems bizarre. Peter Brooks' observation on Balzac's Esther Gobseck (*Splendeurs et misères des courtisanes*) resonates in the narrative power struggle between Baudelaire's *flâneur* and streetwalker, who concurrently narrate one another: "In her transformational role, in her capacity to provoke metamorphoses, the prostitute is not only herself narratable, she provokes the stuff of story in others" (157).

In both **"Les Tentations"** and **"Mademoiselle Bistouri"** the narrator denies proprietorship, past or future, of knives and surgical tools, the preface's metaphorical plot-killers. At the same time, he does not altogether give in to straightforward story telling. As **"Les Tentations"** represents a framed dream, the narrator is in a sense relieved of responsibility for this unsolicited, su-perfluous plot that visited him in the night. In **"Mademoiselle Bistouri"** the narrator changes roles with a character, prostituting himself to her storytelling, and presenting himself innocently again, as the reporter of a strange meeting. At the very end of each poem, though, the narrator complicates matters by revealing a certain attachment to the story, as he fuses the picture (the dream tale and Mademoiselle Bistouri's fantasy) with the frame (the narrator's introduction and conclusion to each). After completing the narration of the dream in **"Les Tentations,"** the narrator pleads with the dream visitors as if they were a part of waking reality, in hope that he may have another chance to accept their offer. And by asserting his narrative dominance at the end of **"Mademoiselle Bistouri,"** the *flâneur* inadvertently (we might say "unconsciously") assumes the doctor's role he had vehemently denied throughout the piece: he tries to solicit the streetwalker's medical history ("Peux-tu te souvenir de l'époque et de l'occasion où est né en toi cette passion si particulière?") then "diagnoses" her as mad.[17]

The fascination with and rejection of surgical tools in **"Les Tentations,"** and the reluctance to assume the role of doctor in **"Mademoiselle Bistouri,"** recall references to surgery as an alternatively constructive and destructive act elsewhere in Baudelaire's writing. In *Choix de Maximes consolantes sur l'amour,* Baudelaire alludes to surgery as a morbid spectacle:

> Pour certains esprits plus curieux et plus blasés, la jouissance de la laideur provient d'un sentiment encore plus mystérieux, qui est la soif de l'inconnu, et le goût de l'horrible. C'est le sentiment dont chacun porte en soi le germe plus ou moins développé, qui précipite certains poètes dans es amphithéâtres et les cliniques, et les femmes aux exécutions publiques.
>
> (*OCI,* 548-49).

In the clinical amphitheater, as in Mademoiselle Bistouri's fantasy, surgery (like poetry in prose) represents a dangerous and seductive performance. Baudelaire's well-known discussion of "fantaisie" (in his *Salon de 1859, OCII,* 608-80) clearly identifies openness and ubiquity as prose-poetical qualities rendering the genre vulnerable, and therefore dangerous, because easily contaminated by the interpreter: "Elle [. . .] est la première venue souillée par le premier venu" (*OCI,* 645). As Donald Aynesworth observes, the narrator and Mademoiselle Bistouri ("le premier venu" and "la première venue," who interpret one-another) dramatize Baudelaire's conception of poetry as a dangerous form of prostitution (213).[18]

If surgery is understood as multifarious in nature, then the act of surgery fittingly dramatizes Baudelaire's articulation of the irresistibly dangerous character of both prose poetry. Like Baudelaire's versions of these literary and physical phenomena, surgery comprises simultaneous contradictions: opening and closing; destruction and reconstruction; disjunction and augmentation; healing the living body, and dissecting the cadaver. "Precision" (from the Latin for "cutting off") refers to only one aspect of surgical intervention. In his 1749 *Traité des opérations de chirurgie,*[19] surgeon Henri François Le Dran delineates four general surgical methods: synthesis ("an operation of surgery by which those parts that are divided are brought together and retained in that situation"[3]); diëresis ("dividing those parts that are naturally united" [4]); exëresis ("removing extraneous substances out of the body" [5]); and prothesis [sic] ("putting on, and adapting an artificial member where the natural one is wanting" [5]). These four procedures correlate to the multi-directional textual and thematic operations demonstrated in the letter to Houssaye, **"Les Tentations"** and **"Mademoiselle Bistouri,"** and apparent throughout the collection: the penetration and fusion of images, narrative voices and stories; a fragmentation of the narrative persona; the overt denouncing of the superfluous, and more subtle denial and cutting short of both poetry and prose; and, above all, the doubly prosthetic procedure of narrating the poetic, and poeticizing prose. By pursuing a fusion of poetry and prose through the paradoxical denial and invasion of each, the Baudelairean prose poet indeed plays doctor, performing multiple and concurrent operations on the doubly prostituted textual body.

An episode reported by Nadar reinforces the iconic appeal of both doctors and prostitutes in Baudelaire's time, and in his immediate circle. It also illustrates that Baudelaire's storyteller figures as doctor not only in fiction. In his intimate biography of the poet, Nadar describes the surgical precision with which Baudelaire described every inch of Jeanne Duval's body to his audience of friends:

> Passant aux détails, notre émérite praticien, sa vie entière étant là, se complaisait à consigner et développer chaque spécification avec précision de procès-verbal en un état de lieux: tel le chirurgien professeur didactiquement stipule les divers états d'un cas. Et comme chez nous dès lors le terme parlé devançait net et ferme la littérature dit naturaliste, je fus crûment mis au courant de tout le reste, comme à une exhibition anatomique, d'autant que le physiologiste ayant d'abord passé par quelques mois d'études à l'École de Médecine, sa clinique entendait ne nous faire grâce de rien.

> (18-19)

Unlike Bistouri's casting of the *flâneur* in the role of doctor, Nadar's depiction of Baudelaire as a willing "chirurgien professeur" features the surgeon as uninterrupted storyteller. Is it coincidence that the "robuste" Mademoiselle Bistouri resembles Jeanne Duval, described by Nadar as "une grande, trop grande fille qui dépasse d'une bonne tête les proportions ordinaires,"

remarkable for "l'exubérant, invraisemblable développement des pectoraux" (6-7), and whose status as prostitute has been rumored, though not confirmed? This retouched portrait of Duval, embedded in the highly fictionalized rewriting of a story Baudelaire must have heard about or read in *L'Événement* or *L'Époque,*[20] adds to the layers of narrative ("archeological deposits," as Maclean calls them), in the final prose poem. Reality penetrates fiction, and one story permeates the other in this *mise en abyme* of competing fictions.

Nadar's colorful portrait of Baudelaire playing doctor exemplifies the nineteenth-century trend for depicting the naturalist writer as anatomist. As Bernheimer notes:

> Now, probably no image for the literary stance of the realist or naturalist writer was more widespread in France than that of the anatomist dissecting a cadaver. In a famous cartoon by Lemot [. . .], Flaubert was pictured extracting organs from Emma Bovary's corpse [. . .]. Zola himself liked to flout the public's taste for sentimental idealism, declaring that a good writer should "put on the white apron of the anatomist and dissect, fiber by fiber, the human beast laid out completely naked on the marble slab of the amphitheater."

> (214)

Oddly perhaps, since he never shied away from the depiction of cadavers and their abject emissions, Baudelaire's metaphorical surgery (the cutting up of the snake and a detailed verbal unveiling of Jeanne Duval's most intimate anatomy)[21] entails verbal vivisection—not dissection—a reminder that in Baudelaire's textual universe, pain accompanies seductive pleasures.

In fact, Baudelaire invokes the medical *Zeitgeist* to characterize painful and erotic episodes in his own life. When six of Baudelaire's **Fleurs du mal** were suppressed shortly after publication in 1857, Baudelaire wrote to publisher Auguste Poulet-Malassis: *"—Si vous pouviez comprendre quel tort vous vous êtes fait avec votre ridicule opération chirurgicale!"* (*CI,* 429). As Poulet-Malassis later explains, surgery here represents the amputation of poems from his collection: *"L'opération chirurgicale* c'est le retranchement des pièces condamnées dans quelques ex[emplaires] pour donner une satisfaction apparente au tribunal" (*CI,* 949). Just one month later Baudelaire uses the medical figure positively, assigning Madame Sabatier the role of doctor (though not surgeon) in his own fantasy: "Très chère Amie, je me proposais de vous demander aujourd'hui la permission de vous faire une de ces bonnes visites, où vous jouez, sans le savoir, le rôle divin du médecin" (*CI,* 433).

The prose poem's allusions to medicine, and particularly the surgical intervention, serve as forceful reminders of a textual cosmology governed by simultaneous penetration and rejection, fusion and fragmentation, opening and closing: operations that are literally and literarily surgical in their imprecise and varied nature. Through perpetual synthesis, division, excision and prosthesis, Baudelaire's much dissected textual serpent indeed endures, ever mutable and "assez vivant." Storytelling and narrative desire remain constantly present yet altered in poems throughout the collection, where embedded narrative voices, stories within stories, half-thwarted efforts to frame stories, and innumerable echoes of one prose poem in another, forestall plot's anticipated progression and closure. In **"Les Tentations"** and **"Mademoiselle Bistouri,"** layers of suspended reality, fantasy and dreams obstruct both linearity and poetic transcendence, and reinforce instead the hesitation and indecision through which the "tortueuse fantaisie" of *Le Spleen de Paris* is projected in the preface. This sense of ambiguity, bolstered by representations of permeable gender and identity within the prose poems, illuminates the larger question of literary genre and textual identity raised by the very notion of poetry in prose. What is at stake in the persistent yet indeterminate figure of the serpent as enduring surgical patient is the precision of *genre* identity, not only that of poetry, but more remarkably perhaps, that of narrative prose.

Notes

1. For insightful discussions of Baudelaire's dubious tribute to Houssaye, I refer the reader to Chambers 1988, Evans 1993, Hiddleston 1987, Kaplan 1990, and Stephens 1999.

2. Charles Baudelaire, *Œuvres complètes,* ed. Claude Pichois, 2 vols., Bibliothèque de la Pléiade. Paris: Gallimard, 1975-76. All further references to page numbers in this two-volume edition will appear parenthetically in the text, abbreviated *OCI* and *OCII.*

3. "Le seul éloge que je sollicite pour ce livre est qu'on reconnaisse qu'il n'est pas un pur album et qu'il a un commencement et une fin. Tous les poèmes nouveaux ont été faits pour être adoptés au cadre singulier que j'avais choisi." From a letter to Vigny dated December, 1861 (*CII,* 196). In Charles Baudelaire, *Correspondance,* ed. Claude Pichois, 2 vols. Bibliothèque de la Pléiade. Paris: Gallimard, 1973. All further references to page numbers in this two-volume editions will appear parenthetically in the text, abbreviated *CI* and *CII.*

4. In the merging of gender imagery that marks so much of Baudelaire's poetry, the woman's body in "Le Serpent qui danse"(*OCI,* 26) is compared at once to a fine vessel and to a dancing snake. In "Au Lecteur"(*OCI,* 6) serpents figure among the "monstres glapissants, hurlants, grognants, rampants" that make up the "ménagerie infâme de nos vices." And just after describing his shuddering, undulating, mounting and descending desire in "A

une Madone (*OCI,* 58)," the poet declares: "Je mettrai le Serpent qui me mord les entrailles / Sous tes talons, afin que tu foules et railles, / Reine victorieuse et féconde en rachats, / Ce monstre tout gonflé de haine et de crachats."

5. See Michel Butor's *Histoire extraordinaire* for a thorough discussion of the phallic interpretation of the serpent in this poem.

6. In "Perte d'Auréole," the prose-poem dialogue opens with an unidentified interlocutor's expression of surprise at finding the poet (*sans auréole*) in a "mauvais lieu" (*OCI,* 352).

7. The "Poèmes nocturnes" included six poems: "Le Crépuscule du soir," "La Solitude," "Les Projets," "L'Horloge," "La Chevelure," and "L'Invitation au voyage."

8. See Barbara Johnson's *Défigurations du langage poétique.*

9. This reference is made in a letter to Victor Hugo dated 1863, years after the first publication of the early prose poems. Disenchanted with Parisian publishers, Baudelaire hopes Hugo will put in a good word for him with Albert Lacroix, who published *Les Misérables* in Belgium. In closing, Baudelaire promises to send Hugo more of his works: "Je me propose de vous envoyer prochainement *Les Fleurs du mal* (encore argumentées) avec *Le Spleen de Paris,* destiné à leur servir de pendant" (*CII,* 339).

10. Though etymologically unrelated, *bistouri* phonetically recalls *bistourner* (from *bestourner* or *mal tourner*) or *bistournage,* a castration procedure performed on animals. The name "La Mère Bistouri" appeared in an article published first in *L'Epoque* (30 January, 1866, see note 20), and the next day in *L'Evénement,* 31 January 1866. A spinster, probably of American origin it is reported, dressed in black and performed adroit surgery, with great pleasure: "After ten years of pathological involvement, she became as skilful at cutting off an arm or a leg as M. de Lambelle himself." The entire article appears in translation in Maclean's *Narrative as Performance,* 158-59.

11. Parent, a medical doctor and public hygienist, published the two-volume *De la Prostitution dans la ville de Paris* in 1836. Bernheimer notes that Parent's writings contain "the personal element of compelling fascination that links his reports on sewers, cadavers, and the like to the rest of his report on prostitution" (15). Likewise, fascination, repulsion, prostitution and surgery go hand in hand in the work of poet and author of *Hygiène,* Baudelaire.

12. Charles Bernheimer's *Figures of Ill Repute: Representing Prostitution in the Nineteenth-Century*

provides a thorough and intriguing analysis of the relationship between male artists and prostitution: "Their relationship to the figure of the prostitute was compelling, involving both identification and repulsion" (1). Bernheimer treats Baudelaire's references to prostitution on pages 71-74.

13. As these details reveal, Mademoiselle Bistouri uncannily embodies features of a more scandalous and canonical literary figure, likewise the product of an embellished news story: Emma Bovary. The phonetic echoes of the eponymous "Madame Bovary" and "Mademoiselle Bistouri" represent just one example of our scandalous heroines' many shared idiosyncrasies: both exhibit a taste for playing the man's role in their erotic scenarios (both smoke, and Emma cross-dresses); both temporarily succeed in casting men in their own stories (see Nathaniel Wing's chapter on Emma's stories, pages 41-77 in *The Limits of Narrative*). Even Bistouri's attraction to men who perform surgery recalls Emma's desire to make a man (and a surgeon) of Charles by getting him to operate on Hippolyte. Real-life doctor Charles Richet diagnosed the fictional Emma Bovary as hysterical (see Beizer 132-66), while Baudelaire's poet-practitioner considers the fictionalized Miss Scalpel as one of "des fous et des folles" whom God should pity.

Baudelaire's review of *Madame Bovary* appeared in *L'Artiste* 18 October, 1857. In this essay, Baudelaire makes much of Emma's masculine characteristics: "Je disais tout à l'heure qu'elle était presque mâle, et que l'auteur l'avait ornée (inconsciencieusement peut-être) de toutes les qualités viriles" (*OCII,* 82). Having thus "diagnosed" Flaubert's intentions as unconscious, Baudelaire goes on to enumerate Emma Bovary's virile traits, which include her "goût immodéré de la séduction, de la domination [. . .] en deux mots: dandyisme, amour exclusif de la domination." (Compare Mademoiselle Bistouri, who like the dandy, roams the streets of Paris dressed in black). Baudelaire finally diagnoses Emma Bovary as "le poète hystérique" (*OCII,* 83).

14. In "A une heure du matin" as in "Mademoiselle Bistouri" and "Portraits de maîtresses," the narrator quotes another character using elliptical capital letters: "avoir fait ma cour à un directeur de théâtre, qui m'a dit en me congédiant: '—Vous feriez peut-être bien de vous adresser à Z . . . ; c'est le plus lourd, le plus sot et le plus célèbre de tous mes auteurs, avec qui vous pourriez peut-être aboutir à quelque chose. Voyez-le, et puis nous verrons." In both "A une heure du matin" and "Portraits" the capital letters undermine the authenticity of the anecdote, marking too clearly the

editorial power of the narrator, who could be misquoting, or quoting fictive sources. The use of the unlikely first letter "Z," along with the ironic and exaggerated tone of the theater director's reported discourse, suggests that the conversation is the narrator's own invention. However Mademoiselle Bistouri has so effectively assumed the role of storyteller, that it is not at all clear that the use of elliptical letters represents editing on the part of the narrator.

15. For a close reading of Mademoiselle Bistouri's performance as analysand, see Maclean 145-60.

16. Michel Butor, *Histoire extraordinaire* (Paris: Gallimard 1961). The dream itself is described in a letter dated 18 March 1856 in *CI,* 338-41.

17. Eliane DalMolin concludes that Baudelaire's *flâneur* "creates a fantasy in which he appears simultaneously as a lover and a slasher, a poet-surgeon simultaneously loving and dissecting the female body. 'Miss Scalpel' transfigures the poet into a surgeon whose love for cutting bodies is transmuted into poetic operations of dissection" (21).

18. Aynesworth continues: "If fantasy resembles the love inspired by a prostitute, Bistouri impersonates Baudelaire's definition of the poetic act: 'cette sainte prostitution de l'âme qui se donne, tout entière, poésie et charité, à l'imprévu qui se montre, à l'inconnu qui passe'" (216).

19. I am using the 1749 English translation, *The Operations of Surgery of Monsieur Le Dran*.

20. In his critical edition of *Petits Poèmes en prose,* Robert Kopp prints an excerpt from the story reported in L'Époque (30 janvier 1866), entitled "La Mère Bistouri." The woman in the original story is not identified as a prostitute, and she lacks the erotic appeal of Mademoiselle Bistouri: "C'était une vieille fille sèche, au teint jaune, toujours vêtue de noir. Elle longeait dans l'hôpital, attendait le docteur [Lamballe] dans les salles, où elle était arrivée bien avant les internes, et ne quittait pas le chef de service d'une semelle.

Le grand chirurgien en faisait grand cas et ne dédaignait pas de lui confier certaines fonctions dont elle s'aquittait à ravir. Elle avait notamment une légèreté de main impossible à rendre et fendait une plaie avec une vitesse (j'allais dire une grâce) que j'ai rarement rencontrée"(347).

21. "Pour édification plus que complète, il me découvrit, comme si je les voyais, les deux fameuses *'médailles de bronze'* dans leur frisson comme figées à la coulée et flottant sur les masses molles, profondes, soyeuses à filtrer entre les doigts: '—une mer en foulard,'—insistaitil. Et n'en arriva-

t-il pas jusqu'à me colorier au vif les plus secrètes intimités du pigment, l'intensité sanglante des carmins poussant au violacé pour se crêter au noir-bleu . . ." (19).

Works Cited

Aynesworth, Donald. "Humanity and Monstrosity in *Le Spleen de Paris.*" *Romanic Review* 73, no. 2 (1982): 209-21.

Baudelaire, Charles. *Correspondance.* Ed. Claude Pichois. Bibliothèque de la Pléiade. 2 vols. Paris: Gallimard, 1973.

————. *Œuvres complètes.* Ed. Calude Pichois. Bibliothèque de la Pléiade. 2 vols. Paris: Gallimard, 1975-76.

————. *Petits Poèmes en prose.* Ed. Robert Kopp. Paris: Corti, 1969.

Beizer, Janet. *Ventriloquized Bodies: Narratives of Hysteria in Nineteenth-Century France.* Ithaca: Cornell University Press, 1993.

Bernheimer, Charles. *Figures of Ill Repute: Representing Prostitution in Nineteenth-Century France.* Durham: Duke University Press, 1997.

Brooks, Peter. *Reading for the Plot.* New York: Knopf, 1984.

Butor, Michel. *Histoire extraordinaire: Essai sur un rêve de Baudelaire.* Paris: Gallimard, 1961.

Chambers, Ross. "Baudelaire's Dedicatory Preface." *Substance* 56 (1988): 5-17.

DalMolin, Eliane. *Cutting the Body: Representing Women in Baudelaire's Poetry, Truffaut's Cinema, and Freud's Psychoanalysis.* Ann Arbor: University of Michigan Press, 2000.

Evans, Margery. *Baudelaire and Intertextuality: Poetry at the Crossroads.* Cambridge: Cambridge University Press, 1993.

Hiddleston, J. A. *Baudelaire and* Le Spleen de Paris. Oxford: Clarendon, 1987.

Johnson, Barbara. *Défigurations du langage poétique: La Seconde Révolution baudelairienne.* Paris: Flammarion 1979.

Kaplan, Edward. *Baudelaire's Prose Poems: The Esthetic, the Ethical, and the Religious in the Parisian Prowler.* Athens: University of Georgia Press, 1990.

Le Dran, Henri François. *The Operations in Surgery of Mons. Le Dran.* Trans. Thomas Gatker. London: Hitch and Dodsley, 1749.

Maclean, Marie. *Narrative as Performance: The Baudelairean Experiment.* London: Routledge, 1988.

Miner, Margaret. "Fur in my Brain: 'Le Chat.'" *Understanding Baudelaire's* Les Fleurs du mal. Ed. William J. Thompson. Nashville: Vanderbilt University Press, 1997.

Nadar. *Charles Baudelaire intime.* Neuchâtel: La Bibliothèque des Arts, 1994.

Stephens, Sonya. *Baudelaire's Prose Poems: The Practice and Politics of Irony.* Oxford: Oxford University Press, 1999.

Wing, Nathaniel. *The Limits of Narrative: Essays on Baudelaire, Flaubert, Rimbaud, and Mallarmé.* Cambridge: Cambridge University Press, 1986.

Rosemary Lloyd (essay date 2002)

SOURCE: Lloyd, Rosemary. "To the Reader." In *Baudelaire's World,* pp. 1-9. Ithaca, N.Y.: Cornell University Press, 2002.

[*In the following essay, Lloyd discusses the relationship between Baudelaire and the narrative voice of his poems.*]

> A book about poetry ought to be a book about life.
> —Richard Jenkyns, *Virgil's Experience*

> Trim dualistic Baudelaire,
> Poet of cities, harbours, whores,
> Acedia, gaslight and remorse.
> —W. H. Auden, "New Year Letter"

A temperament half nervous, half bilious. A cultivated mind, sharpened by the study of shape and color; a tender heart, wearied by sorrow, but still ready for rejuvenation. We could even, if you like, go so far as to admit former faults, and, as the inevitable result of a nature that is easily excited, if not real remorse, at least a sense of regret for time profaned and ill-spent. A taste for metaphysics, a knowledge of the various hypotheses philosophy has made about human destiny— these are certainly not useless additions. Neither is that love of virtue, an abstract, stoic or mystical virtue that can be found in all those books in which the modern child seeks nourishment, virtue seen as the highest summit to which a distinguished soul can climb. If we add to all that a great delicacy of feeling, which I omitted as something superfluous, I think I've assembled the most common elements generally to be found in the sensitive modern man, in what might be called the banal form of originality.

(**I** 429-30)

This is Baudelaire giving a portrait of what the eighteenth century might have called the sensitive individual or of what Romanticism might have dubbed the misunderstood, but that his own bourgeois age burdened with the epithet "original." It is also of course, and above all, a self-portrait of the writer who is for many not just the greatest of France's nineteenth-century poets, but one of modernism's founding voices. Remarkable for the variety and intensity of his vision, the breadth of his linguistic register, and the relationship he establishes between his themes and his poetic forms, Baudelaire remains both profoundly challenging and deeply satisfying. Reading him demands an intellectual and imaginative endeavor that is different from the effort needed to respond, say, to Victor Hugo or William Wordsworth, Rainer Maria Rilke or Eugenio Montale, Les Murray or Elizabeth Bishop. Attempting to enter through imagination the poet's physical and affective world is one way of preparing a more satisfactory reading of his poetry. But how do we enter anyone's world, and especially the world of writers who not only lived in very different circumstances from our own, but also spoke a language that is not ours? How do we pick our way through the palimpsest of their memories and the spider's web of their reading? And if our task is not only to read but also to translate their writing, how best do we respond to that very considerable challenge?

In the opening paragraphs of his biography of Baudelaire, the poet's close friend Charles Asselineau justifies his task by saying that Baudelaire's "work, as has often been said, is the man himself; but the work is not all the man. Behind the written and published work there is another complete work which was spoken and acted and lived, and that needs to be known, because it explains the other and contains, as he himself would have said, its genesis."[1] My book is in part about the relationship between those two works—the public and the private—in his verse poetry, in the poems in prose, and in his criticism. By building an image of Baudelaire's world around major themes of his writing (childhood, women, reading, the city, dream, art, nature, death), I set the poems themselves in a richer context, made up of Baudelaire's other writings, the writers and artists who preceded him or were his contemporaries, and some of the historical and physical realities of life in mid-nineteenth-century Paris.

Baudelaire's collection of verse, *Les Fleurs du mal* (*The Flowers of Evil*), explores the development of a poet from childhood to death and thereby reveals the shaping of his character through a range of different experiences—love, art, city life, dreams, intoxication, revolt, perversion. The work opens with an unnumbered poem, **"Au lecteur"** (**"To the Reader"**), which precedes six books: *Spleen et Idéal* (*Spleen and Ideal*), *Tableaux parisiens* (*Parisian Paintings*), *Le Vin* (*Wine*), *Fleurs du mal*, *Révolte* (*Revolt*) *La Mort* (*Death*).

As Baudelaire remarked in a letter to the poet Alfred de Vigny, *Les Fleurs du mal* is not a mere album of randomly grouped poems, but one built according to what

he termed a "secret architecture."[2] Each poem gains further resonance by its position in the work, by poems that precede and follow it. In some cases, poems of joy have counterparts of pain or rage, inviting us to read the collection not just as a progression but also as a series of cycles. The protagonist whose life *Les Fleurs du mal* charts in this manner is not identical with the Baudelaire who fought on the barricades in 1848 or walked across the New Carrousel in the 1850s, but the two figures exist in a close symbiotic relationship.

That relationship is even closer in Baudelaire's criticism, as he suggests in the opening paragraph of his study of Wagner. Justifying the use of "I" he affirms:

> This *I,* justly accused of impertinence in many cases, nevertheless implies a great modesty. It locks the writer into the strictest limits of sincerity. By reducing the task, the use of *I* facilitates it. Finally, there is no need to be a truly consummate probabilist to feel certain that this sincerity will find friends among impartial readers. Obviously there is the odd chance that the ingenuous critic, merely by recounting his own impressions, also recounts those of some unknown enthusiasts.
>
> (**II** 779)

Which did not, of course, prevent him from skating around the truth when it was expedient to do so. In a letter to his mother, for instance, he refers to Victor Hugo's *Les Misérables* which he had reviewed quite favorably, while still revealing the fundamental conflict between Hugo's belief in progress and his own conviction that evil is ineradicable. To his mother, however, he confesses: "The book is disgusting and clumsy. On this score I've shown that I possess the art of lying" (*L* [*Selected Letters of Charles Baudelaire*] 190: CII 254). For the reader, charting a course through the sincerity and the lies of the critical writing demands an awareness both of the rhetorical and of the biographical elements at play.

A more complex relationship between narrative "I" and author is at work in the prose poems, *Petits poèmes en Prose* (*Short Prose Poems*), which appeared in volume form only after the poet's death. This is poetry inspired above all, Baudelaire insists, by the city and its crowds. As a result, the narrative persona changes from poem to poem, and the poetic voice is sometimes split between two characters, as it is in **"Le Vieux Saltimbanque"** (**"The Old Mountebank"**) or in **"Le Mauvais Vitrierx"** (**"The Bad Glazier"**). And for the prose poems, Baudelaire no longer claimed a pre-established architecture, but instead insisted that they could be read in any order. He uses the image of a kaleidoscope: the poet has provided the fragments that the reader then assembles and reassembles to form multiple and ever-changing patterns.

Baudelaire's poems and criticism reveal a sharply observant eye and an analytical mind that drew its sustenance from everyday events but transformed them into something more powerful and more universal. This book is not a traditional biography, but it does draw on biographical funds and techniques, and like biographies it has been forced to schematize the haphazard nature of life. We live sequentially—what other choice do we have? But when we remember and particularly when we attempt to make some kind of sense and narrative of those memories, we work in a different time-frame, one that groups together disparate events, doubles back, and leaps forward. We experience time in terms of thickness rather than linear progression. That thickness I have attempted to represent here. Readers who would like to follow Baudelaire's development chronologically will find a concise chronology on pages xi-xii. Thinking about those events, however, we need to remember that, as Baudelaire himself argues in his study of the poet Théophile Gautier, this is the life of a man whose most dramatic adventures take place in silence under the dome of his brain (**II** 104).

In Baudelaire's case, moreover, the biographical record is often fragmentary or distorted. Letters are missing. He kept no diaries (the collection of jottings known as the *journaux intimes,* the intimate diaries, are disparate notes on his thinking and reading, preparations for possible future works, rather than any regularly kept exploration of his activities). He rarely comments in either letters or notebooks on his own works, or on their reception, except in the most general of terms. Gustave Courbet, who painted his portrait and knew him as a friend, is reported as lamenting, "I don't know how to bring off a portrait of Baudelaire. His face changes every day."[3] Contemporary memoirs depict him as shifting allegiances almost as often. The philosopher Emmanuel Swedenborg would be his idol one day, the next it would be the mathematician Hoëné Wronski. Bronzino, the Italian mannerist, would arouse his ardent enthusiasm for a brief period, then he would be abandoned in favor of the Flemish painter Jan Van Eyck. Baudelaire's notebooks include the cavalier aphorism, "I understand how someone could desert one cause in order to find out what it would be like to serve another" (1676). Part of this is a mask, an aspect of his determination to forge his own personality. But masks have a habit of changing the features of those who wear them.

Yet, however much Baudelaire may have changed his allegiances and his masks, certain questions, preoccupations, and convictions run through all his writings. It is not that the answers are fixed, or that his esthetic positions remain constant. It is more that he did not erect barriers between the genres he used. You can follow debates and see him working out solutions across a range of different kinds of writing, from letters and criticism to poetry. My study of Baudelaire's writings sets out to investigate different aspects of the experience of reading him in order to trace a personal path toward a sympathetic response. Above all, I want to set the poems in the context of Baudelaire's other writings—his art and literary criticism, his translations of Edgar Allan Poe (see figure 5) and Thomas De Quincey, the studies of wine, hashish and opium, and his letters.

But I want also to explore translations of certain verse and prose poems, and to offer some of my own, in an attempt to indicate what elements (textual, thematic, rhetorical, rhythmic, and stylistic) demand particularly close attention, elements not always easily seized by non-French readers and frequently weakened or lost in translation.

Many people have tried their hand at translating or adapting Baudelaire. Nicholas Moore, in his thirty-one versions of one of the poems entitled **"Spleen,"** the one beginning "Je suis comme le roi (I am like the king)," gives an indication of how much variation there can be in a translation. One of his versions boils the essence of the sonnet down into four lines:

> Not riches, power, advisers, pets, sport, gold
> Nor even naked women cheer the old
> In heart. Bones will be bones. All that remains
> Instead of blood, green water, clotted veins.[4]

Is the best translation one that aims for accuracy or for imagination? Robert Fitzgerald includes a poem called "Baudelaire's Music" in his 1971 collection, *Spring Shade.* Here is Baudelaire's sonnet **"La Musique"**:

> La musique souvent me prend comme une mer!
> Vers ma pâle étoile,
> Sous un plafond de brume ou dans un vaste éther,
> Je mets à la voile;
>
> La poitrine en avant et les poumons gonflés
> Comme de la toile,
> J'escalade le dos des flots amoncelés
> Que la nuit me voile;
>
> Je sens vibrer en moi toutes les passions
> D'un vaisseau qui souffre;
> Le bon vent, la tempête et ses convulsions
>
> Sur l'immense gouffre
> Me bercent. D'autres fois, calme plat, grand miroir
> De mon désespoir!

> (*FM* [*Les Fleurs du Mal*] LXIX)

A straightforward translation might read something like this: "Music often seizes me like a sea! Towards my pale star, under a ceiling of mist or beneath the vast ether, I set sail. Chest out and lungs filled, like canvas, I climb on the back of the mountains of waves that night hides from me. I feel vibrating within me all the passions of a storm-tossed vessel. Favoring winds, storms and their convulsions rock me. At other times, dead calm, great mirror of my despair!" Fitzgerald's poem uses Baudelaire's as a springboard to give:

On music drawn away, a sea-borne mariner,
   Star over bowsprit pale,
Beneath a roof of mist or depths of lucid air
   I put out under sail:

Breastbone my steady bow and lungs full, running
free
      Before a following gale,
   I ride the rolling back and mass of every sea
      By Night wrapt in her veil;

All passions and all joys that vessels undergo
      Tremble alike in me;
Fair winds or waves in havoc when the tempests blow

      On the enormous sea
Rock me, and level calms come silvering sea and air,
      A glass for my despair.

Which both is, and is not, Baudelaire.

Should a translator seek to write for a particular Anglophone group (Scottish or Welsh, Irish or Cornish, English or American, South African or Australian, New Zealand or Indian)? Keep the rhymes at all cost? Favor rhythm over rhyme? Choose a particular idiom over another—prefer the archaic or the colloquial? Let's say I translate the tercets of the sonnet "Brumes et pluies (Mists and Rain)" in the following way:

Rien n'est plus doux au cœur plein de choses funèbres,
Et sur qui dès longtemps descendent les frimas,
Ô blafardes saisons, reines de nos climats,

Que l'aspect permanent de vos pâles ténèbres,
—Si ce n'est, par un soir sans lune, deux à deux,
D'endormir la douleur sur un lit hasardeux.

(*FM* CI)

as:

To a heart that's full of grief nothing's so sweet,
A heart long covered with the winter's sleet,
O pallid seasons, you who rule our airs,

Than knowing we'll always see your pale shade,
—Unless it is on a moonless night, in pairs,
To send our grief to sleep by getting laid.

With this translation, I convey part of the meaning, but the vulgarity of the final expression distorts the original, adds a veneer to what Baudelaire had made neutral, and through the clash between its vulgarity and the tone of the rest of the poem, suggests a sudden outburst of anger that is not only not present in the French, but that also indicates a move away from the lethargy that dominates the narrative voice throughout the sonnet.

Of course, translators can also impose a personal reading. Ciaran Carson, for instance, translates the title "Duellum" as "Warriors," which changes the emphasis from the struggle to the protagonists and uses a highly individual idiom that also gives it an unequivocally homoerotic focus. Here is the original:

Deux guerriers ont couru l'un sur l'autre; leurs armes
Ont éclaboussé l'air de lueurs et de sang.
Ces jeux, ces cliquetis du fer sont les vacarmes
D'une jeunesse en proie à l'amour vagissant.

(XXXV)

A literal translation would go something like this: "Two fighters rushed against each other. Their weapons spattered the air with sparks and blood. These games, this clattering of iron, are the uproar created by a youth preyed on by wailing love." In Carson's version this becomes:

Two boys got stuck into each other, pushed and shoved
Their flick and shiv in bloody glimmers, fists on hafts
In blue-veined steel-struck sparks of adolescent love,
Like knights riding to joust with tumultuous shafts.

Baudelaire's sonnet makes that reading possible, but it does not force us to interpret the *guerriers* as both male, as Carson's does, or confront us with that brash phallic image of the shafts. Neither does the slang of "flick and shiv" represent the register of Baudelaire's language, which remains mainstream even when his subject matter is not.

Translators determined to preserve the rhyme can also distort meaning. Of course, it is true that Baudelaire delighted in rhyme and used it, as we'll see, to convey truths or suggestions not stated in other ways within the poem; for this reason he claimed that he had decided against translating the poetry of Edgar Allan Poe because to do so meant abandoning the pleasure of rhyme. But it is also the case that English has a long tradition of blank verse, as French does not, and that rhyme is less essential to our pleasure of English poetry than it is to traditional French poetry. Forcing a rhyme at the cost of restricting, distorting or changing the meaning throws a veil between us and the poem. Take for instance the poem **"Spleen"** beginning "J'ai plus de souvenirs que si j'avais mille ans (I have more memories than if I were a thousand years old)." Four lines here summon up boredom through analogies with slow, snowy winter days:

Rien n'égale en longueur les boiteuses journées,
Quand sous les lourds flocons des neigeuses années
L'ennui, fruit de la morne incuriosité
Prend les proportions de l'immortalité.

(*FM* LXXVI)

Dorothy Martin translates this as:

Naught could there be longer than these maimed days
When, 'neath the snowy years' thick-falling maze,
Spleen, of indifference the mournful flower,
Grows more immortal through each lingering hour

which not only inflicts on Baudelaire an archaic idiom (naught, 'neath) that runs counter to his modernism, but in the search for a rhyme, turns into a flower the fruit of indifference, an image Baudelaire mentions to his publisher as being of particular importance to him (*L* 94, *CI* 395). Walter Martin, writing some 70 years later, gives us a fairly free version:

> Limping days as far as the eye can see,
> And snowblind years for all eternity;
> Indifference expands into ennui,
> With overtones of Immortality.

Martin has caught the intentional boredom of the repeated rhymes here (the rhyme of *journées* and *années* recurring phonetically in *incuriosité* and *immortalité*) and his idiom is much more analogous to Baudelaire's than that of Dorothy Martin. Yet to squeeze out those last two rhymes, he has sacrificed the image that links indifference to ennui, and reduced "the proportions of immortality" to the weaker "overtones of immortality."

Norman Shapiro's version is markedly different again:

> Nothing can match those endless, crippled days
> When, blizzard-blown, chill winter overlays
> Ennui with heavy snows: drear apathy,
> Taking the shape of immortality.

However much you might admire "the shape of immortality," the sense of snow falling over long years is lost in Shapiro's second line, and that "drear apathy" demonstrates the triumph of rhyme over the image connecting apathy and the lack of curiosity. You win and you lose in reading a translation. The solution, it would seem, is to read stereoscopically, drawing on several different versions, and keeping the original to hand.[5]

Whether we read him in French or in translation, Baudelaire's writing is often unnerving, as likely to get under our skin like a form of poison ivy as it is to delight us. How does a modern reader, particularly a modern female reader, deal with Baudelaire? How does one put up with his misogyny, his bouts of self-destructive selfishness, and his flashes of acidic bad temper? One cannot simply separate out the man and his work in this case, somehow distilling a calm quintessence in verse. It does not happen, or if it does, something vital is lost. Personal experience is of course transformed, metamorphosed into something quite different, but it is still something that retains the strongest features of his personality. I think you have to recognize that the destructive streak is what enabled him to be so wonderfully creative and so original at a time when a throng of powerful figures dominated poetry. By tearing apart the comfortable universe that could have been his, by consistently gazing at rather than glossing over the sources of evil not just in society but also in himself, he did succeed in hacking out a domain that was his alone. No other writer of his time saw so keenly the conflicts that make up modern life. His destruction is also a creation, his misogyny and his misanthropy are as much hatred

of himself as of others; his mud, as he would put it, is also gold. But reading him has to be as much a question of resisting him as of allowing him to take over. And unlike the image of the world that Baudelaire gives us in **"Le Voyage,"** experience does not shrink his achievement: as a reader of the maps and prints that his writing offers, I'm still the child who finds a universe as vast as my appetites.

Notes

1. Jacques Crépet and Claude Pichois, *Baudelaire et Asselineau* (Paris: Nizet, 1953), 61.

2. For an outstanding recent exploration as well as historical survey of this concept see James R. Lawler, *Poetry and Moral Dialectic: Baudelaire's "Secret Architecture"* (Madison, N.J.: Fairleigh Dickinson University Press, 1997).

3. Quoted in Champfleury, *Souvenirs et portraits de jeunesse* (Paris: Dentu, 1872), 135.

4. For details of translations, consult the bibliography of translations, pp. 237-39.

5. Clive Scott's *Translating Baudelaire* (Exeter: Exeter University Press, 2000) reached my library only after I had sent my manuscript to Cornell. As with all Professor Scott's books, it is an erudite and eloquent exploration of poetry, drawing on his vast knowledge of French prosody. Its exploration of translation theory, its clarification of methodologies and possibilities, and its contributions to translating Baudelaire all make it a striking addition to studies of both the discipline and the poet. My own purposes have been rather different, driven above all by the desire to see "Baudelaire" as more than just the poet of *Les Fleurs du mal*.

Note and Abbreviations

Except where otherwise indicated, all translations are my own. For details of translations by others quoted in the text see the bibliography of translations, pp. 237-239. In the text, poems from *Les Fleurs du mal* are referred to by *FM* followed by the Roman numeral Baudelaire assigned to the particular poem. Verse poems not included in *Les Fleurs du mal* are located by volume and page number of Baudelaire's complete works. The prose poems are referred to as PPP followed by the Roman numeral Baudelaire assigned.

I, II = Baudelaire, *Œuvres complètes*. Ed. Claude Pichois. 2 vols. Paris: Gallimard, 1975-1976.

CI, CII = Baudelaire, *Correspondance*. Ed. Claude Pichois and Jean Ziegler. 2 vols. Paris: Gallimard, 1973.

LAB = *Lettres à Baudelaire*. Ed. Claude Pichois. Neuchâtel: A la Baconnière, 1973.

L = Selected Letters of Charles Baudelaire. Trans. and ed. Rosemary Lloyd. Chicago: University of Chicago Press, 1986. (Some translations revised for this study.)

MO = Un Mangeur d'Opium. Ed. Michèle Stäuble. Neuchâtel: A la Baconnière, 1976. (Parallel texts of Thomas De Quincey's *Confessions of an English Opium-Eater,* his *Suspiria de profundis,* and Baudelaire's adaptation.)

NL = Baudelaire, *Nouvelles Lettres.* Ed. Claude Pichois. Paris: Fayard, 2000.

Pichois = Claude Pichois, *Baudelaire.* Trans. Graham Robb. London: Hamish Hamilton, 1989.

Geraldine Friedman (essay date 2002)

SOURCE: Friedman, Geraldine. "Baudelaire's Re-Reading of Romanticism: Theorizing Commodities/The Commodification of Theory." In *Romantic Poetry,* edited by Angela Esterhammer, pp. 419-42. Amsterdam, The Netherlands/Philadelphia, Pa.: John Benjamins Publishing Company, 2002.

[*In the following essay, Friedman explores Baudelaire's poem "Assomons les pauvres!" in the context of the revolution of 1848 in France.*]

Perhaps no imperative so dominates literary studies today as the turn to history (Culler [1988], Eagleton [1983]). But can this imperative always be completely fulfilled by the act of historicizing? To pose this question is not to deny the invaluable contribution of historicist work, which has transformed and reinvigorated literary scholarship, but rather to suggest that in some limit cases history resists recovery as context, referent, signifier, narrative, or discursive system and thus cannot be comfortably accommodated within historicism. What if, for instance, history under certain conditions functions as a trauma, an event that the mind cannot take in because it can assign it no meaning? Precisely because it is not wholly accessible on its first occurrence, the traumatic experience returns, and with a disturbing literality (Caruth [1991]). Since it involves a failure to produce meaning, trauma poses an epistemological problem that forces a rethinking of history. When the returns cause the past to break into the present, the temporal continuity that underlies conventional forms of historical understanding and the intelligibility of narrative structure is disrupted.

Or, alternatively, what if history acts as the Derridean trace, a difference prior to the opposition between presence and absence on which classical metaphysics depends? "The trace," Derrida writes, "is not only the disappearance of origin . . . it means that the origin did not even disappear, that it was never constituted except

reciprocally by a nonorigin, the trace, which thus becomes the origin of the origin" (Derrida [1976], 61). On the basis of passages like this one, recent commentators have taken the early Derrida's theory of a text's internal difference from and deferral of itself to suggest a theory of history based on differance (Bennington and Young [1987], 1-2; cf. Hobson [1987], 101-2, 109): "If the word 'history' did not carry with it the theme of a final repression of differance, we could say that differences alone could be 'historical' through and through and from the start" (Derrida [1973], 141). Since the trace "is not a being-present" (Derrida [1973], 153), historical and narrative temporality is once again disrupted, but this time on the level of metaphysics, in which presence is modeled on the present tense. The trace undoes the usual logical sequence in which appearance is followed by disappearance, for the trace is already effaced at the moment of its first appearing: "Effacement constitutes it as a trace . . . and makes it disappear in its appearing" (Derrida [1973], 156). Barred from entering the entire tense-inflected network of being, the trace is an absence not in view of presence. Strictly speaking, then, history as differance does not exist, not because it is an airy fiction but because it is outside the metaphysical system in which existence has its place and meaning. More accurately, history can be said to insist; it returns because it never existed in the metaphysical sense but from the very beginning was a trace.

I contend that in numerous canonical texts of European Romanticism, the French Revolution acts as a trauma or trace. Although, to be sure, not all of European Romantic poetry works in this way, there is nonetheless something valuable to be learned from these anomalous instances. In attempting to record the history of a crisis, they also mark "a crisis within history," but, as Shoshana Felman and Dori Laub have written in another context, it is one "which precisely cannot be articulated, witnessed in the given categories of history itself" (Felman and Laub [1992], xviii). Not simply a failure, this incapacity plays a critical role. Arising from within the normative frames and concepts of historical understanding, both empirical and speculative, it reveals their presuppositions and limitations and thus transforms them in incalculable ways. As a test case, I would like to explore these issues in reference to a narrative mode of historical understanding in which history is often understood to return but not to insist: the dialectic. On this interpretation, the dialectic, at least in its idealist version, is taken to be a metaphysical system, however complex. Thus one would expect it, in contrast to the missed experience of trauma or the Derridean trace structure, to be constituted by presence and characterized by epistemological accessibility. But, if, against expectation, this nonetheless turns out not to be the case, a thoroughgoing re-reading and reconceptualization of the dialectic is needed.

Underlying Harold Bloom's understanding of Romanticism as crisis-literature (Bloom [1970]) and Geoffrey Hartman's mapping of Wordsworth's poetry according to the shifting relations of nature, consciousness, and imagination (Hartman [1971]), the dialectical reading of Romanticism finds its fullest and most explicit version in M. H. Abrams's *Natural Supernaturalism,* 1971. Abrams traces the emergence of dialectical thinking in German and English Romantic literature and philosophy themselves, with their emphasis on the necessity of human pain, loss, and suffering (Abrams [1971], 77, 124, 201, 217, 219, 220). This philosophical tradition begins with Schiller, Fichte, and Schelling and culminates in Hegel, whose *Phenomenology of Spirit* is most relevant to the present argument. In the *Phenomenology,* consciousness is educated through its own negation and destruction; negation drives the entire process. But it is a particular kind of negation, a *"determinate* negation," which differs crucially from the "pure nothingness" of scepticism. "The scepticism that ends with the bare abstraction of nothingness or emptiness cannot get any further from there. . . . But when, on the other hand, the result is conceived in its truth, namely as a determinate negation, a new form has thereby immediately arisen" (Hegel [1977], 51). The mind involved in this process experiences the path it must travel as "the way of despair" (Hegel [1977], 49; qtd. in Abrams [1971], 229), but viewed from the endpoint of the process, this despair is converted into a positive, precisely because determinate negation is not wholesale destruction. For by "los[ing] its truth on this path," consciousness acquires the ability to "purify itself for the life of the spirit, and achieve finally, through a completed experience of itself, the awareness of what it really is in itself" (Hegel [1977], 49). Thus, on this first approach, consciousness gains by its losses. Through them it accedes to a higher standpoint: "The series of configurations which consciousness goes through along this road is, in reality, the detailed history of the *education [Bildung]* of consciousness itself to the standpoint of science [*Wissenschaft*]" (Hegel [1977], 50; qtd. in a slightly different translation in Abrams [1971], 229). Understood in this way, the dialectic is a sacrificial, recuperative model of narrative and reading, because, in it, consciousness gives something up in order to receive something greater in return.

On the thematic level, this pattern is evident in English and German Romantic writing that inscribes the Revolution in narratives of the fall and redemption or of the loss and restoration of a golden age. One of Hölderlin's early hymns addressed to revolutionary ideology, the 1792 "Hymne an die Freiheit" (Hymn to freedom), provides an especially clear example. Synthesizing Christian and classical images and themes, the poem traces a trajectory from a prelapsarian, pastoral "paradise" (*Paradieß*) (Hölderlin [1946-1985], 1: 139; line 24) of love and innocence, to a harsh world ruled by "the rod of law" (*des Gesezes Ruthe*) (line 49), and finally to a new kingdom of love, articulated in revolutionary discourse (the millenarian language of brotherhood and calls for the end of tyranny: "Wenn verödet die Tirannenstühle, / Die Tirannenknechte Moder sind" [When the tyrants' seats are deserted, / The tyrants' slaves decayed]) (99-100). Each stage in this tripartite sequence is defined by the presence or absence of the goddess of freedom on earth. The "curse" (*Fluch*) (42) she pronounces before she deserts earth to return to the heavens corresponds to the moment of dialectical negation. Indeed, under the rule of law following the curse, love is reversed into "the tribunal's vengeance sword" (*Racheschwerdt[] des Gerichts*) (52); the goddess of freedom, the "smiling . . . Olympian" (*lächenld[e] . . . Olympier*) (30) is reversed into a "spirit in black thunderstorms" (*Geist in schwarzen Ungewittern*) (53); and the unfallen "son of earth" (19) is negated into a "slave" who is also a "nothing": "Lernte so der blinde Sklave zittern, / Fröhnt' und starb im Schrecken seines Nichts (So the blind slave learned to tremble, / toiled and died in terror of his nothingness) (55-6). Similarly, the goddess's return marks the dialectical recuperation of love, and it occurs, just as Hegel says it does, through the education of consciousness to self-consciousness. Virtue in the prelapsarian realm was unconscious: "Unverkennbar in der schönen Hülle / Wußte Tugend nicht, wie schön sie war" (Unmistakable in the beautiful garment / Virtue did not know how beautiful she was) (35-6), but in the renovated world, the entire race gains self-recognition: "Staunend kennt der große Stamm sich wieder" (Astonished, the great race recognizes itself) (73). The movement from one state to the other can be seen in a play on words between "unmistakable," the adjective that modifies unconscious "virtue," and "recognized itself," the verb governed by the subject "the great race." In the German text, "unmistakable" is *unverkennbar,* which could be translated more literally as "unmisrecognizable." "Recognizes itself" is *kennt sich wieder,* or "knows itself again." Thus both phrases have the same root: *kenn,* "know." The sense is that virtue was recognized by others but did not recognize herself, whereas the race acquires the very self-reflexivity she lacked. In short, two positive states are mediated by a negative one to produce a net gain; the advance comes about through negation, because otherwise there would be no "re-moment" for re-cognition to take place.

One could ask whether recuperative readings like these, attractive as they are in yielding coherent and intelligible narratives even under less than promising circumstances, can stand up under closer textual scrutiny. However, a prior and more fundamental question is whether the Hegelian dialectic itself adheres to this optimistic account. Hegel's critique of the Reign of Terror in the *Phenomenology* is a good place to consider this issue because the negative gets freer rein there than anywhere else in the text. In this historical stage, where "spirit

. . . comes before us as absolute freedom," "there is left for it only negative action; it is merely the fury of destruction" (Hegel [1977], 356, 359; qtd. in Abrams [1971], 353). Since negation here works as "unmediated pure negation" (Hegel [1977], 360), the dialectical machinery would seem to come grinding to a halt. Even when in a further development, it turns out that "pure negativity" contains "the element of subsistence, or . . . Substance" and thus "the matter which it can utilize in accordance with its own determinateness" (Hegel [1977], 361), the dialectic is still not restored: "Out of this tumult, Spirit would be thrown back to its starting-point, to the ethical and real world of culture . . . Spirit would have to traverse anew and continually repeat this cycle of necessity if the result were only the complete interpenetration of self-consciousness and Substance" (Hegel [1977], 361-2). Under these conditions, although something positive does emerge for the purely negative universal will to work on, Spirit would oscillate forever between the same two poles, passing over immediately into its antithesis and back again, without advancing towards its telos. It takes a further development for mediation and the complicated forward motion of the dialectic to resume. This new development occurs when "for consciousness, the immediate unity of itself with the universal will, its demand to know itself as this specific point in the universal will, is changed round into the absolutely opposite experience" (Hegel [1977], 362-3). For what vanishes from the perspective of consciousness is "abstract being or the immediacy of that insubstantial point": "this vanished immediacy is the universal will which it now knows itself to be in so far as it is pure knowing or pure will. Consequently, it knows that will to be itself, and knows itself to be essential being" (Hegel [1977], 363). In short, when consciousness seeks to recognize itself in the individual will, it negates the individual will, and that negation is the universal will. Consciousness now forms a mediated unity with the universal will, in which it recognizes itself. With this essential being, something new arises, and the dialectic begins again: "There has arisen the new shape of Spirit, that of the moral spirit" (Hegel [1977], 363). At this point, since the dialectic has recovered from pure negation, it seems theoretically impossible that it could ever be interrupted. For this reason, it is the most powerful model of totalization we have.

Yet some of the most interesting recent work on Hegel finds that, when his text is rigorously read, dialectical negation is not so easily contained and subordinated to the positive (Kristeva [1984]; Lacoue-Labarthe [1978, 1979]; Derrida [1982], 69-108; de Man [1982, 1983]; Warminski [1987], xxxi-xxxv). Derrida, de Man, and Warminski all suggest in various ways that what specifically interrupts the dialectic is something not of the order of consciousness or its negation but something of a completely different order: language or the textual. An example Warminski gives in an altogether different context, where he analyzes metaphor and the abusive figure called catachresis, is particularly revealing because it also occurs in the section of the *Phenomenology* on the Terror: the figure of cutting off a head of cabbage (Warminski [1987], lv, lx). Hegel writes: "the sole work and deed of universal freedom is therefore death, a death too which has no inner significance or filling, for what is negated is the empty point of the absolute free self. It is thus the coldest and meanest of all deaths, with no more significance than cutting off the head of a cabbage" (Hegel [1977], 360). Warminski shows how catachresis, a borrowed name for something that has no proper name of its own, differs from traditional metaphor, which is modeled on a four-term analogy: A is to B as C is to D. Traditional metaphorical transport occurs when the terms are exchanged chiastically, or cross-wise. The key point is that this exchange is a dialectical reversal: the determinate negation of the literal by the figural (Warminski [1987], xl). However, catachresis disrupts this symmetrical movement from literal to figurative. As a borrowed name, it is not literal, but since it does not substitute for a proper name, it is also not figurative. At once both and neither literal and figurative (Warminski [1987], liii-lv), catachresis is the place where the difference between them and consequently any simple transport from one to the other are put into question.

This account of catachresis rejoins the issue of the dialectic and the possibility of its interruption. Since in catachresis one of the four terms of the analogy is missing, it is the product of an asymmetrical exchange in which something is given for nothing (Warminski [1987], xxxv-lxi). Thus catachresis is also the place where the sacrificial narrative of the dialectic, which depends on symmetrical exchange, breaks down. Here, what Hegel says of the universal will in absolute freedom obtains but in a way that cannot be superseded: with its missing fourth term, catachresis "can give nothing in return for the sacrifice" (Hegel [1977], 362). When he speaks catachrestically of a death "with no more significance than cutting off a head of cabbage," he thus introduces a negative that is outside of and in excess of determinate negation because it is not the negative of something. This excessive negative is not really a negative at all but a nothing: a sheer blank or absence of name upon which a name is abusively imposed, the imposition of sense on non-sense (Warminski [1987], lv). Thus it is truly "the meaningless death" of the Terror, for, being of a different order from all dialectical categories, it cannot be recuperated by the work of the negative. Catachresis interrupts the dialectic precisely because it is outside it; it introduces a linguistic death that is the real terror of the text and the limit of its totalizing power. Terror is in fact the catachrestic name that the *Phenomenology* imposes on this linguistic death. Thus the story of language and its radical nothing doubles the story of recuperable negations in the dialectic and interferes with it. Yet catachresis is also the condition of possibility of that story, because, as the imposition of a name on non-sense, it is the condition of possibility of sense itself. Since the dialectic is a narrative about knowledge and especially self-knowledge, it depends on this imposition of sense and cannot get beyond it. Consequently, the dialectic is constituted by its own radical impossibility.

A similar double narrative, based on a problematic figural exchange, structures Wordsworth's account of Revolutionary violence in book 10 of *The Prelude,* a text that Abrams sees "in general content and overall design" as "notably parallel" to the almost exactly contemporary *Phenomenology* (Abrams [1971], 236). Wordsworth writes not of the 1793 Terror but two 1792 events often called the pre-Terror: the August storming of the Tuileries Palace and the September Massacres, which he witnessed only in their aftermath. Resident in France since late 1791, he spent most of his time in Blois and Orléans, passing through Paris only on his return trip to England in October 1792. As in Hegel, the challenge is to incorporate the negativity of these events into a narrative that, according to Wordsworth, is "in the end / All gratulant if rightly understood" (*Prelude* 13: 384-5). Wordsworth's strategy is to overlay the dialectical model with one deriving from the Christian, Pauline hermeneutics of biblical typology. In this paradigm, the movement of the dialectic is posited as a testamentary shift from an Old Dispensation, characterized by vengeful interpretation according to the letter of the law, to a New Dispensation, characterized by merciful interpretation according to the figure or spirit of love. This pattern is also called figural or prefigurative, since the letter is a literal meaning that anticipates its transformation into a spiritual one and mirrors itself in it.

According to this typology, Revolutionary violence in book 10 corresponds to the letter. Although earlier Wordsworth had seen the Revolution as a regenerative force (10: 244), it now appears to him a vengeful one. This can be seen in the fact that the storming of the Tuileries Palace took the form of an attack and counterattack between the Swiss palace guard and the Parisian crowd, resulting in heavy losses on both sides. The dead were burned on Carrousel Square, which was made "a black and empty area then" (10: 46). The September Massacres, for their part, sought revenge for the counterrevolutionary coalition's victory at Verdun by summarily executing in Parisian jails so-called royalist prisoners, many of whom were in fact common criminals. Thus the Revolution has come to function like the retributive letter of the law it was supposed to abrogate:

> I crossed—a black and empty area then—
> The square of the Carousel [*sic*], few weeks back
> Heaped up with dead and dying, upon these

> And other sights looking as doth a man
> Upon a volume whose contents he knows
> Are memorable but from him locked up,
> Being written in a tongue he cannot read,
> So that he questions the mute leaves with pain,
> And half upbraids their silence. . . .

(10: 46-54)

In these lines Wordsworth tries to imagine the past, which means to read it by the spirit, but since that past appears as an illegible foreign text, he has no possibility of getting at its meaning. He is forced into a *reductio ad absurdum* of reading by the dead letter, inscribed in the passage as the conspicuously absent, literal bodies of "the dead and dying." It is this negative situation that the passage has the burden of transcending.

When the second part of the passage systematically reverses the pattern of the earlier section, an implicit textual logic indeed promises the arrival of a new dispensation:

> But that night
> When on my bed I lay, I was most moved
> And felt most deeply in what world I was;
> My room was high and lonely, near the roof
> Of a large mansion or hotel, a spot
> That would have pleased me in more quiet times—
> Nor was it wholly without pleasure then.
> With unextinguished taper I kept watch,
> Reading at intervals. The fear gone by
> Pressed on me almost like a fear to come.
> I thought of those September massacres,
> Divided from me by a little month,
> And felt and touched them, a substantial dread
> (The rest was conjured up from tragic fictions,
> And mournful calendars of true history,
> Remembrances and dim admonishments):
> 'The horse is taught his manage, and the wind
> Of heaven wheels round and treads in his own steps;
> Year follows year, the tide returns again,
> Day follows day, all things have second birth;
> The earthquake is not satisfied at once'—
> And in such way I wrought upon myself,
> Until I seemed to hear a voice that cried
> To the whole city, 'Sleep no more!'

(10: 54-77)

The earlier part of the passage gets rewritten point for point here. The *figure* of reading Carrousel Square becomes *actually* "reading at intervals," an activity that by evoking a "substantial," tangible ("felt and touched") dread metaphorically supplies the bodies missing from the scene of violence. With the words from *Macbeth,* "Sleep no more," the disembodied, mute foreign text is incarnated as a speaking English one, and Wordsworth gains an abrupt accession to the spirit. In contrast to his earlier distance from recent events, he is now "most moved / And fe[els] most deeply in what world" he is. Acting out on the rhetorical level the physical "crossing" of the square named in line 46, the move from letter to spirit presides over a chiastic turn that reverses the figural structure of the passage's first part. With the accomplishment of this formal symmetry, the hermeneutic shift seems to have occurred. Wordsworth's non-understanding has now become comprehension: the reading material that conjures dread in bodily form provides a displaced version of the "regular chronicle" "giving . . . unto events / A form and body" (9: 101, 105-6) that Wordsworth earlier said he lacked.

Yet accession to the spirit results not in the advent of love but the return of violence, which presages the Great Terror of 1793: "The fear gone by / Pressed on me almost like a fear to come." Thematized by cyclical patterns of the horse's rounds ("manage"), the wind, the years, the tide, the days, and the earthquake, this return is an insistence by repetition rather than a punctual dialectical turn. The difference between the two emerges most clearly in an earlier description of the self-same events as "crimes" that "were past, / Earth free from them forever (as was thought), / Ephemeral monsters, to be seen but once, / Things that could only show themselves and die" (10: 31, 34-7). When the violence of August and September 1792 is no longer a one-time occurrence, the already precarious interval of time, "a little month," that "divide[s]" Wordsworth from "those September Massacres" disappears (10: 64-5). The past then erupts into the future, so that temporality and narrative structure, which is constituted by time, collapse, with enormous consequences for reading. Since it occurs "at intervals" (10: 62), it, too, depends on temporal measure, but with those articulations gone, both temporality and language become inarticulate. Thus instead of achieving the understanding promised by the hermeneutical paradigm, Wordsworth experiences a kind of hallucinatory madness, in which he hears voices. At this point the dialectic of knowledge has clearly gone off track.

How has the apparent fulfilment of the hermeneutic paradigm led to such a catastrophe? The problem seems to lie in the identification of the foreign script of the Revolution with simple literality, because interpretation by the letter of the law actually occurs in a *figure* of reading, a simile: "upon these / And other sights looking *as* doth a man / Upon a volume" (10: 48-50; emphasis added). Thus the shift in the passage from letter to figure is doubled by a countermovement where reading itself is the figure that gets literalized, as when Wordsworth stays up all night "reading at intervals." Furthermore, what gets figured in the original scene of reading is the materiality of marks on a page, which is all one can see when looking at a book in an unknown language. Since for Wordsworth they carry no meaning, they fall short of the literal. In sum, he comes up against something that is both and neither letter and figure, at the same time prior to the literal and already beyond it. Disrupting the reflexive time of prefiguration where the beginning of a story mirrors itself in its end, this "something" reveals a different, aberrant letter and figure irreducible to but produced by figural logic. With the uncanny doubling of the hermeneutic paradigm, *The Prelude*'s figuration and the dialectic that depends on it are forced to confront their linguistic conditions of possibility, as the arrival of the new dispensation is thwarted not by some external contingency but by its own internal workings.

If these texts deal with the linguistic complication of the dialectic in the French Revolution, Baudelaire's prose poem **"Assommons les pauvres!"** (**"Let's beat up the poor!"**) confronts similar issues in the historical relation between the French Revolution and the Revolution of 1848. The brief readings I have offered of Hölderlin, Hegel, and Wordsworth will serve as a prelude to a more prolonged consideration of Baudelaire's text.

A commentary on the Revolution of 1848 as an uncontrolled repetition of the French Revolution and thus an instance where history insists, **"Assommons"** provides a belated critical reading of Romanticism and its idealist revolutionary heritage. The text registers, with its own surprising twists, the cumulative reinflections that 1848 and the subsequent Second Empire imposed on 1789's speculative discourse of rights and, indeed, the poetic tradition that invoked them. Written in 1865, during that empire, the text begins with the speaker's reading of "books in style from that time (sixteen or seventeen years ago)" (Baudelaire [1975-1976], 1: 357).[1] Thus by simple arithmetic, the text situates itself with reference to 1848, not just the revolution but also the prodigious explosion of social theory that characterized that moment. From his retrospective position, Baudelaire considers that theory a recycled idealism that on its second appearance has become a parody of itself, and he searches for a materialist alternative to it. Yet we shall see that the brand of materialism he offers is at least as problematic as the idealism he rejects. It seems that putting the idealist dialectic into question inevitably also subverts its materialist counterpart.

Yet, to begin with, **"Assommons"** raises the question of theory not in general but regarding one particular theoretical kind. Since the speaker's reading material treats "the art of making the masses happy, wise, and rich in twenty-four hours" (Baudelaire [1975-1976], 1: 357),[2] the text targets what we might specify as "mere" theory. Its fault is not the usual one of ignoring social reality; rather, it elides the moment of dialectical mediation and particularly the negation from which a new positive would spring. Skipping over the work of practice—the difficulties of materially transforming any historical society—this kind of theory simply assumes its own instant realization, to become the most vacuous kind of utopianism. In this vulgarized, cartoon version of itself, theory relinquishes the magisterial authority the term usually claims, to be put into play in a highly ironic text.

Telling a double story, **"Assommons"** displays the speaker's fascinated contempt for his theoretical reading material (if he finds it "bad" [*mauvaise*], he nonetheless has a "passionate taste" [*goût passioné*] for it) and traces his ensuing search for a materialist alternative that takes practice into account—as the process that would transform the condition of "the masses." What comes to him is the idea that the poor must earn social welfare for themselves rather than receive it from those who would paternalistically make them happy. Actualizing his notion in the most perverse way, the speaker goes out and beats up a beggar, purportedly to allow the man to prove his worth. At work in this parodic literalization of the idea is a switch not simply from theory to practice but from "mere" theory to theory as itself a kind of practice. For the speaker receives his original idea as and on the occasion of its verification: "Only he who *proves* it is equal to another, and only he who knows how to *conquer* liberty is worthy of it" (Baudelaire [1975-1976], 1: 358; emphasis added).[3] Since such a proof is internal to the concept itself, the speaker in his mad way out-materializes any materialist philosophy of practice by offering philosophy as practice: the hands-on labor of a fist fight. My reading of **"Assommons"** will attempt to follow out the complications of the shift from the utopian, idealist version of theory to this one, and especially the implication in the text that the shift necessarily occurs with the violence of a dialectical, revolutionary reversal.

In what follows, I shall argue that **"Assommons"** questions the constitution of both the idealist and materialist moments of dialectical theory and (theoretical) practice in Baudelaire, bringing to light the difficulties of positioning them, both philosophically and politically. From this perspective, the speaker's recourse to the ardors of bodily combat effects a rewriting of the entire Baudelairean corpus and of Romanticism itself, for by rejecting theory as magically self-actualizing, the text also rejects the poet's own Romantic spiritualism, most prominent in his salvific discourse of the imagination, the mystical language of the correspondences, and his location of reality in the creations of mind rather than in "matter" (Baudelaire [1975-1976], 1: 649). Yet the rewriting does not occur simply as the difference between the early and late Baudelaire because his spiritualism, in the guise of utopianism, has from the beginning a complicated relation to what he calls action.

The manuscript version of **"Assommons"** gives this difficult relation a proper name, for the text ends with an apostrophe: "What do you say about that, Citizen Proudhon?" (Baudelaire [1975-1976], 1: 1350).[4] A so-

cial theorist and man of the people, Proudhon embodies the shifting position of spiritualism, and thus of Romanticism, vis-à-vis action in Baudelaire. Writing in 1851 that poetry "always carries in itself the divine utopian character" (*porte toujours en soi le divin caractère utopique*) because "it ceaselessly contradicts fact" (*Elle contredit sans cesse le fait*) and "transforms itself into revolt" (*elle se fait révolte*), Baudelaire associates Proudhon's utopianism with "the genius of action" (*le génie de l'action*) (Baudelaire [1975-1976], 2: 34-5). But in 1864, the poet repudiates as dupery the connection between revolution and utopianism, as if he had never affirmed it: "When I agree to be a republican, *I commit evil, knowingly. Yes! Long live the Revolution!* always! anyhow! But I am not a dupe! I was never a dupe! I say *Long live the Revolution!* as I would say: *Long live Destruction! Long live Expiation! Long live Punishment! Long live Death!*" (Baudelaire [1975-1976], 2: 961).[5]

In contrast to Baudelaire's intoxication with violence, Proudhon holds that social transformation can occur peacefully because he exempts certain categories from the material forces and relations of a given social formation: "Justice" and "labor," which have in fact been the stakes of specific historical struggles. Proudhon sees the salvation of "the masses," the objects of the literature of "that time," not in revolution but in a non-violent movement called mutualism, whose institutions—mutual-aid societies, workers' associations, and exchange banks—refused the exploitative financial and economic practices of society at large. Baudelaire's complicated attitude toward Proudhon's non-violence is perhaps best caught in a late letter, where the poet writes: "Pen in hand, he [Proudhon] was a *good fellow* [*bon bougre*]; but he was not and never would have been *a Dandy,* even on paper!" (Baudelaire [1973], 2: 563).[6] While *bon bougre* in French is usually a condescending dismissal of an ineffectual, limited person, Baudelaire presents it here partially as a defence, implying a degree of appreciation for Proudhon's writings. We can say, then, that **"Assommons"** recasts around utopianism the unresolved theory-contest that runs throughout the Baudelairean corpus.

More specifically, the text formulates its dissatisfaction with utopian theory as a critique of mutualism, a critique that was also made by "that time"'s best known materialist: Karl Marx. In one of his own texts on 1848, Marx dismisses the mutualist movement because of its self-defeating refusal to wage a real struggle with society: "In part it [the proletariat] throws itself into doctrinaire experiments, exchange banks and workers' associations, hence into a movement in which it renounces the revolutionising of the old world by means of the latter's own great, combined resources, and seeks, rather, to achieve its salvation behind society's back, in private fashion, within its limited conditions of existence, and hence necessarily suffers shipwreck" (Marx and Engels [1975-1991], 11: 110-11).

Yet it will become clear that, if **"Assommons"** inscribes a materialist position, it is not a rigorously Marxist one, for the poem's materialism is as parodic as its idealism. Since the parody occurs in repeated scenes of reading, we shall trace the ways in which they function not as passive registerings of written signs but as an activity, a series of slippages that results in new theory at each point of contact. The reading of theory is drawn by this productive aspect into the debate among nineteenth-century social theorists about programs and their effectivity. Thus, for Baudelaire, the dispute between utopianism and materialism that emerged in 1848 revolves around the relation between word and deed, a relation at the heart of what J. L. Austin calls performative utterances. If in **"Assommons"**'s work of production the performative demands a theory of reading, it also asks an additional question: what does reading do, especially when it is the reading of theory? The literalism with which the speaker takes the advice given in the title **"Assommons les pauvres!"** suggests that the question is not just academic but bears directly on practice. For practice is what the speaker's violence restores—however, less as mediation than as a troubling third term in the dialectic between social theory and social reality. As its own practice, **"Assommons"** is caught up in the problem it poses, and this self-implication is what catches up a smooth reading. Far from recovering the perfect functioning of a dialectical theory machine, this ironic text can perform itself only by differing from itself: the condition of possibility for its normal operation is an unavoidable slippage.

This internal distance, which constitutes a certain textual opacity, is, according to Michel Serres ([1980], 22), history. Since the Revolution of 1848, the moment that literally gets read in **"Assommons,"** has been seen as deviating from "normal" historical development, it can be considered a deviation of a deviation. As part of the conversation in and about 1848 that is encrypted in the prose poem, I here offer Marx's classic analysis from *The Eighteenth Brumaire.* Coming after the bourgeois revolution of 1789-1814 that had abolished feudalism, the Revolution of 1848 was a proletarian revolution, which, according to the dialectical laws of history, should have smashed the bourgeois order. But, despite some apparent early victories for the masses, the expected result was not achieved: "The February revolution was a surprise attack, a taking of the old society unawares, and the people proclaimed this unexpected *coup de main* as a deed of historical importance, ushering in the new epoch. On December 2 the February revolution is conjured away by a cardsharper's trick, and what seems overthrown is no longer the monarchy but the liberal concessions that were wrung from it by centuries of struggle. Instead of society having con-

quered a new content for itself, it seems that the state only returned to its oldest form, to the shamelessly simple domination of the sabre and the cowl. This is the answer to the *coup de main* of February 1848, given by the *coup de tête* of December 1851. Easy come, easy go" (Marx and Engels [1975-1991], 11: 106).

From the perspective of dialectical materialism, the Revolution of 1848 represents a series of backward steps: instead of replacing the bourgeois monarchy of Louis-Philippe with the social republic, all efforts to extend political and economic rights ended in a restoration of empire by way of a constitutional bourgeois dictatorship. Ironically, this backwardness results from the easy success of the February uprising: "When it came to the actual conflict, however, when the people mounted the barricades, the National Guard maintained a passive attitude, the army offered no serious resistance and the monarchy ran away, the republic appeared to be a matter of course" (Marx and Engels [1975-1991], 11: 109). As events would soon show, however, the February uprising did not work precisely because it worked so well, occurring with hardly a struggle. Louis-Napoleon's success in "conjur[ing] away" "a deed of historic importance" indicates that that deed must always have been incompletely realized, or, according to a frequent image in *The Eighteenth Brumaire,* ghostly, more empty spirit than substantial material reality.

In his *Journaux intimes* (Intimate journals), Baudelaire notes both the repetitive and utopian aspects of 1848. Writing of his "fury at the coup d'État," he exclaims: "Another Bonaparte! What a shame!" (Baudelaire [1975-1976], 1: 679).[7] But in a lighter vein, he quips: "Eighteen forty-eight was amusing only because each one built utopias there, like castles in the air" (Baudelaire [1975-1976], 1: 680).[8] Both strands converge in **"Assommons"**'s reading of 1848 through a re-reading of the slogan of the French Revolution, *Liberté, Égalité, Fraternité*: the repeated element here is the speculative rights of man, where "man" is conceived as an abstract, universal, ahistorical construct. The first two words of the slogan of 1789 are spoken by the inner voice in the poem that says equality must be proved and liberty conquered. The speaker himself pronounces the third one, "fraternity," after the fight, when he commands the old man to apply the theory that has been tried out on him (the beggar) to all his "fellows," or *confrères,* a word whose French root means "brothers." As we have seen, these are the very values that are celebrated and problematized in Hölderlin's "Hymne an die Freiheit," Hegel's *Phenomenology,* Wordsworth's *Prelude,* and, indeed, many other Romantic poems. Thus although **"Assommons"** does not specifically target these texts, they are nonetheless subject to its critical operations by virtue of participating in French Revolutionary discourse.

The shockingly violent pronouncements in **"Assommons"** are demands to put speculative rights into action, and they express the speaker's dissatisfaction with the theories in his reading material, which divide into two equally absurd groups: "those who advise the poor to become slaves, and . . . those who persuade them that they are all dethroned kings" (Baudelaire [1975-1976], 1: 357-8).[9] The speaker qualifies both extremes as examples of "all the old wives' tales of which I had recently run through the dictionary" (Baudelaire [1975-1976], 1: 358),[10] and the counter-theory suggested by his inner voice implies that these received ideas include first and foremost *Liberté, Égalité, Fraternité,* which another prose poem calls *les immortels principes de 89* (the immortal principles of 89) (Baudelaire [1975-1976], 1: 344). The thoroughly conventionalized and hackneyed character that these words had taken on for Baudelaire by 1865 is suggested by the treatment one of them receives at the end of the prose poem **"La solitude,"** where the speaker writes of "a prostitution that I could call *fraternitaire,* if I wanted to speak the beautiful language of my century" (Baudelaire [1975-1976], 1: 314).[11] The dismemberment of the slogan *Liberté, Égalité, Fraternité* in **"Assommons"** suggests that the French Revolution is itself a split text that resists interpretation and simple repetition.

Here emerges a striking convergence between Baudelaire and Marx, because the latter also classifies as a received idea one of these principles: equality, which came to the fore of political discussions after the Bourbon Restoration limited universal suffrage (Wüstemeyer [1986], 42-3). For Marx, the development of economic theory depends on the belief in equality between men becoming entrenched as a *Volksvorurteil,* or popular prejudice. What is particularly suggestive for **"Assommons"** is that, in the Marxian account, this belief is not eternal but occurs at a specific moment, which happens to be Baudelaire's: the peak of the first wave of capitalism in France, when commodities began to circulate with unprecedented speed. The key statement comes in a discussion of Aristotle's economic analyses, where Marx credits Aristotle with seeing that two commodities that are directly exchangeable against each other must be both qualitatively and quantitatively equal. In Marxian theory, these insights eventuate in the concept of abstract, social labor as the equal something represented in two such commodities. As crystallizations of human labor, they are qualitatively equal, or commensurable; as crystallizations of the same labor-time, they are quantitatively equal. Yet, despite his insights into the money form and the simple form of value, Aristotle cannot admit commensurability between unlike things. He finds, according to Marx, that "Such an equalisation can only be something foreign to their real nature, consequently only 'a makeshift for practical purposes'" (Marx [1967], 1: 59). In Marx's analysis, Aristotle stops at this point because he could not develop a concept of

value, more specifically, a labor-theory of value, which, in foregrounding human practice, would be the opposite of the vacuous idealism of 1848: "Aristotle therefore, himself, tells us, what barred the way to his further analysis; it was the absence of any concept of value. What is that equal something, that common substance, which admits of the value of the beds being expressed by a house? Such a thing, in truth, cannot exist, says Aristotle. And why not? Compared with the beds, the house does represent something equal to them, in so far as it represents what is really equal, both in the beds and the house. And that is—human labour. There was, however, an important fact which prevented Aristotle from seeing that, to attribute value to commodities, is merely a mode of expressing all labour as equal human labour, and consequently as labour of equal quality. Greek society was founded upon slavery, and had, therefore, for its natural basis, the inequality of men and of their labour-powers. The secret of the expression of value, namely, that all kinds of labour are equal and equivalent, because, and so far as they are human labour in general, cannot be deciphered, until the notion of human equality has already acquired the fixity of a popular prejudice. This, however, is only possible in a society in which the great mass of the produce of labour takes the form of commodities, in which, consequently, the dominant relation between man and man, is that of the owners of commodities. The brilliancy of Aristotle's genius is shown by this alone, that he discovered, in the expression of the value of commodities, a relation of equality. The peculiar conditions of the society in which he lived, alone prevented him from discovering what, 'in truth,' was at the bottom of this equality" (Marx [1967], 1: 59-60).

The historical convergence between the belief in human equality and the dominance of commodity production that Marx discusses occurs with the French Revolution, in its liberal, bourgeois character. However, it is only later, according to **"Assommons"** in 1848, that this belief acquires "the fixity of a popular prejudice." But the prose poem suggests another link, one between the entrenched belief in equality and the spread of commodity production into a new area. For the text begins from the discovery that 1848 marks the commodification of social theory, which is now sold for profit by "all those entrepreneurs of public happiness" (Baudelaire [1975-1976], 1: 357).[12] Consequently, political economy itself enters the realm of popular prejudice: Marx's effort to develop a rigorous economic analysis and a radical critique of political economy finds itself doubled by the "old wives' tales" of charlatans and of utopians, like Proudhon's doctrine of mutualism.

Mutualism was a response to the poverty caused by growing unemployment among French workers in the 1830s and 1840s. The program aimed to replace the older private, individual practices of charity and alms with the general establishment of equality between and justice for all men: "We want neither to be clients nor to be given assistance; we want to become EQUALS. We reject begging, we want justice" (Proudhon [1865], 88). For Proudhon, the principles of mutualism are linked to the French Revolution, since he finds them expressed in *The Declaration of the Rights and the Duties of Man and the Citizen* as the golden rule: "The principle of mutuality was expressed for the first time with a certain philosophical hauteur and a reforming intention in that famous maxim that all the sages have repeated, and that our Constitutions of the years II and III, by their example, put in the *Declaration of the rights and the duties of man and the citizen*: 'Do not unto others as you would not have them do unto you. Always do unto others as you would they should do unto you'" (Proudhon [1865], 85). Proudhon holds that the democratic gains of 1789, which guarantee equality before the civil, economic, and political law, were a first step toward a mutualist constitution of society, because a revolution based on an ethical reciprocity between persons would aim to eliminate the privilege of the few and the exploitation and poverty of the many (Proudhon [1865], 90, 103-4). Since Proudhon correctly sees that that exploitation lies in the extraction of surplus value from labor-power (and thus ultimately from workers), he makes mutualism turn on payment in kind. As a form of barter based on use-value, mutualism gives "service for service, product for product, loan for loan, insurance for insurance, credit for credit, security for security, guarantee for guarantee, etc." (Proudhon [1865], 92; [1969], 59-60). This restricted, because equal, type of exchange would suppress the more ramified circuit of exchange that transforms money into capital: profit is to be allowed only inside an established margin (Proudhon [1865], 155), while rent, bonuses, tithes, interest, bribery, and dividends are to be abolished altogether (Proudhon [1969], 68; [1871], 21-3). The goal of this measure is to extend the limited economic equality that Proudhon thought the French Revolution yielded into a complete restructuring of society. Hence mutualism's claim to a kind of non-violent revolutionary force.

Yet the mutualist revolution is far from Marxist because, in establishing financial institutions whose desired function is to insulate against capitalist society, mutualism refuses to acknowledge that social change depends on transforming existing material conditions. According to Marx, such a transformation can be only "the spontaneous product of a long and painful process of development" (Marx [1967], 1: 80). Thus, in attempting to eliminate surplus-value and the exploitation it entails, Proudhon, like all "entrepreneurs of public happiness," ignores that practice consists of historical struggle, and, in so doing, he provides the model for the utopian theory read by the narrator at the beginning of **"Assommons."**

Distinguished by its commodified character, this theory implies an instrumentalized use of language. Since the literary entrepreneurs of 1848 "advise" and "persuade" in order to move their audience to certain determinate actions (to become slaves and submit or take themselves for dethroned kings and revolt), their language has a rhetorical function; in Marxian terms, the entrepreneurial conception of language as persuasion is that of a use-value. Such a made-for-consumption discourse can putatively be converted without remainder into social reality because, as a set of clichés ("old wives' tales") with one sole and very familiar meaning, it can be easily assimilated. According to a metaphor in the first paragraph, it gets "digested, swallowed, I mean" (Baudelaire [1975-1976], 1: 357),[13] and one way the digestive process occurs is through a transformation of the digestive figure itself. The ingestion of food for thought becomes the desire for actual food and drink, as metaphorical taste becomes literal: "And I went out very thirsty. For the passionate taste for bad reading material engenders a proportional need for open air and refreshments" (Baudelaire [1975-1976], 1: 358).[14] Thus this narrative of 1848 moves initially from figure to letter.

But Baudelaire's textual strategy encounters resistance, for at this point, **"Assommons"** takes a curious turn. The literalization of the figure of taste, which is precisely the kind of complete transformation at the heart of utopian, mutualist theory, is interrupted, and, what is worse, by a character in whose name that theory speaks: a beggar the speaker encounters outside a cabaret. The narrator is brought up short by the man's seeing gaze, which seems endowed with magical powers: "As I was about to go into a cabaret, a beggar held out his hat to me, with one of those unforgettable looks that would overturn thrones, if spirit moved matter, and if a mesmerist's eye made grapes ripen" (Baudelaire [1975-1976], 1: 358).[15] Previously in the poem, reading the kind of theory that sees everything happening in the mind, through the agency of spirit, led to an unseating of mind and spirit; the speaker's mental state was overturned into "a state of mind [*un état d'esprit*] bordering on vertigo or stupidity" (Baudelaire [1975-1976], 1: 358),[16] to reveal a moment of unconsciousness or missed experience in an idealist system based on the presence of consciousness to itself. With the encounter of the beggar, this *coup d'état d'esprit* becomes a *coup d'état* in the more usual sense, for his gaze is conditionally credited with the power to "[overturn] thrones" (*[culbuter] les trônes, si . . .*). The beggar's look thus possesses the revolutionary potential that the utopian literature of 1848 ascribes to the immaterial. Put in terms of spirit moving matter, this power takes the form of the idealist dialectic, which in the context of revolution becomes the question of the motor of history, one of *the* questions of the nineteenth century. What is at issue here is the possibility of a smooth historical passage, such as the one that at first seemed to obtain between the French Revolution and the February Revolution. Since spirit, the moving force of the idealist dialectic, is the key category of utopian theory, this passage itself depends on the seamless transformation of theory into material reality. We have, then, two related continuities: between spirit and matter and between two historical moments.

But these continuities are also breaks, for, in interrupting the plot of **"Assommons,"** they interrupt its idealist trajectory as well. As tenets of idealism, they are in fact absorbed into the parodic rewriting of the entire idealist tradition, so that its most elite forms are juxtaposed with their cartoon versions. Thus, in the conditions qualifying the revolutionary power of the beggar's gaze, the dignified philosophical language of spirit and matter, later identified with Socrates and the prestige of Platonism, appears in a common figure of speech: "if spirit moved matter." This figure is in turn yoked to the widespread nineteenth-century belief in the dubious spiritualism of mesmerism: "if a mesmerist's eye made grapes ripen."

It is against these parodic idealisms, examples of the theoretical writings of 1848, that the speaker poses his counter-theory of a more materialist dialectic. Yet it is not only a question of opposing theories, for, in a kind of leaky transfer that governs the entire text, the speaker's new idea is produced by his reading, but as a deviation from it. Thus the beggar's request for alms, or unearned money, inspires the speaker to create a new theory of the speculative rights of 1789, not exactly by rejecting them but by demanding that they be earned in action. What he produces is a labor theory of value with a twist, where only the worthy are deemed to merit liberty and equality: "At the same time, I heard a voice that whispered in my ear, a voice that I knew well; it was that of a good Angel, or of a good Demon, who goes everywhere with me. Since Socrates had his good Demon, why wouldn't I have my good Angel . . . ? There exists this difference between Socrates's Demon and mine, that Socrates's only showed itself to him to prohibit, warn, and prevent, and that mine deigns to advise, suggest, and persuade. That poor Socrates had only a prohibiting Demon; mine is a big affirmer, mine is a Demon of action, a Demon of combat. Now, its voice whispered this to me: 'Only he who proves it is equal to another, and only he who can conquer liberty deserves it.' Immediately, I jumped on my beggar" (Baudelaire [1975-1976], 1: 358).[17]

Here, philosophy takes on two opposing political thrusts. Against a Socratic idealism that entails quietism, the speaker discovers a philosophy of action as combat, in a hilarious and vicious parody of the long and painful struggle that Marx sees as the work of history. The speaker's attack on the beggar literalizes class struggle, but in a perverse way, because, as bohemian idler and beggar, the two combatants are members of the non-class: the unproductive lumpen-proletariat. Their encounter thus cannot be subsumed under any classical Marxist narrative. Even if in the face of this oddity we take the fist fight to restore practice, the speaker's interventionist philosophy nonetheless becomes the double of the utopianism it opposes; for both of them "advise" and "persuade" (the speaker's "suggests" in addition), and both of them take instantaneous effect (one "in twenty-four hours" and the other "immediately"). The difference that emerges from this parallel is that, where one rhetorically bludgeons the poor with advice, the other physically bludgeons them with blows, so that the interrupted literalization of the figure of taste is replaced with the literalization of rhetorical violence.

As the move from the realm of words to the realm of action, the dialectic that the text sets up between 1789 and its improved version of 1848 functions, like all dialectics, by reversing things into their antitheses. Thus the translation of linguistic production into physical confrontation is accompanied by a series of related reversals. The abstract, inalienable rights of 1789 become concrete, pre-eminently alienable ones, which must be won in battle. Now belonging only to those who earn them, liberty and equality are limited rather than extended. The progressive, liberatory stance of the French Revolution preludes not the left-wing victory of the proletariat predicted by historical materialism but rather a right-wing thuggism of all classes against the poor. The emphasis moves from political equality to economic equality (in addition to the principle of equal exchange discussed above, the speaker at the end of the poem gives the beggar half his money). Finally, the feminized, theoretical language of "all the old wives' tales of which I had just run through the dictionary" becomes transformed into practical struggle between men (*confrères*).

To the extent that these reversals are posed as complete, their model is what **"Assommons"** implicitly identifies as one of the "old wives' tales" it means to dismantle: Proudhon's utopian mutualism. The poem turns on the connection (itself a reversal) that Proudhon makes between the benevolent principle of exchange in kind and the ancient law of vengeance. Of the equal rendering of goods for goods and services for services, he writes: "Such is the law. It is the ancient law of retribution [talion, or claw], an eye for an eye, a tooth for a tooth, a life for a life, as it were, turned upside down and transferred from criminal law and the atrocious practices of the vendetta into economic law, to the tasks of labor, and to the good offices of free fraternity. On it depend all the mutualist institutions: mutual insurance, mutual credit, mutual aid, mutual education; reciprocal guarantees of openings, exchanges, and labor for good quality and fairly priced goods, etc. This is what the principle of mutualism claims to use, with the aid of certain institutions, as the foundation of the State, the law of the State . . . which will be just as easy for citizens as it is advantageous to them. It demands no police force, no repression or restrictions" (Proudhon [1969], 59-60; translation modified according to Proudhon [1865], 92).

"Assommons" seems to dramatize what Proudhon here describes discursively. If mutualism establishes a State that needs no police, the fist fight between the speaker and the beggar occurs in a setting "out of the reach of any police officer" (Baudelaire [1975-1976], 1: 359).[18] If the mutualist principle revises the ancient retributive justice of "an eye for an eye, a tooth for a tooth, a life for a life," the fist fight also specifically involves eyes, teeth, and lives. And if mutualism claims to eliminate alms and begging with a more productive solution to poverty, the beating of the beggar in **"Assommons"** is meant to be in service of precisely this reform. To pick up the text where we left off: "Immediately, I jumped on my beggar. With one single punch [blow with the fist, *coup de poing*], I blackened his eye, which in one second became as big as a ball. I broke one of my nails in breaking two of his teeth, and as I didn't feel strong enough, having been born delicate and being unskilled in boxing, to finish off [*assommer*] this old man quickly, I grasped him with one hand by the collar of his clothes, with the other, I gripped him by the neck, and I began to shake his head vigorously against a wall. Having afterwards downed this weakened sexagenarian, with a kick [blow with the foot, *coup de pied*] launched at his back, energetic enough to break the shoulder blades, I seized a big tree branch that was lying on the ground, and I beat him with the stubborn energy of a cook who wants to tenderize a beefsteak. All of a sudden [in one stroke, *tout à coup*],—o miracle! o joy of the philosopher who verifies the excellence of his theory!—I saw this antique carcass turn around, get up with an energy I would never have suspected in a machine so singularly out of order, and, with a look of hatred that seemed to me *a good omen,* the decrepit thief threw himself on me, blackened my two eyes, broke four of my teeth, and with the same tree branch beat me to a pulp [beat me into plaster dust, *me battit dru comme plâtre*].—By my energetic medication, I had thus restored his life and pride" (Baudelaire [1975-1976], 1: 358-9).[19]

With this trading of beatings between the speaker and beggar, the notion of use-value as something to be consumed seems smoothly continuous with a parodic version of exchange-value. By literally turning around ("I saw this antique carcass turn around"), the beggar would seem to balance the books and make this instance one of restricted, equal exchange, without surplus-value, that Proudhonian root of all evil. The result is a declaration of human equality—"Sir, *you are my equal*" (Baudelaire [1975-1976], 1: 359),[20] where the sharing of

the speaker's purse also brings about economic equality. The speaker now judges his mission a success. As a philosopher who has the "pleasure" (*jouissance*) of verifying the excellence of his theory, he seems to have outdone the utopian entrepreneurs of public happiness, because his theory has proven itself in the rigors of empirical combat.

At this point, the speaker is satisfied that his theory works in practice, and his satisfaction closes the circuit of writing and reading, also shutting down the social question of what to do about the poor. Yet the exchange between the fighters is decidedly not equal, and its inequality opens a space in which the reader must intervene, for the text continues to pose questions about the politics and economy of reading, even if the speaker is no longer interested in them. Thus we must note that the speaker inflicts one black eye but receives two, he breaks two of the beggar's teeth but has four of his own broken, and he restores the old man's life without either having to give up his own or being similarly renewed. And if he reduces his victim to a raw steak, that victim reduces him even further, to dust. The passage works not on the principle of an eye for an eye, a tooth for a tooth, and a life for a life, but of an eye for two eyes, two teeth for four teeth, and no life for one life. Instead of vengeance reversed into its opposite, that is, into the founding principle of a benevolent economics and State, we get vengeance redoubled, vengeance with a vengeance, so to speak. These results show that the machine that would translate theory into fact has somehow produced an excess from a supposedly remainderless exchange. From value, the concept that depended on a firm belief in human equality, surplus-value has emerged: the speaker gets back double the "investment" he puts in the beggar.

These developments put into question not only the utopian notion of a smooth passage from social theory to social reality; they also cast doubt on the possibility of finding a clear alternative to utopianism. Consequently, **"Assommons"** cannot be seen as simply rejecting Proudhon's utopianism for materialism, for the text's revolution uses a discourse of rights, perversely, to beat the poor up and down, an end dialectical materialism would strenuously reject. In the move that the text attempts to negotiate, the theory that promises to be transferred intact to the realm of practice is reversed by the transfer, and this can happen only if theory is not some ideal, self-identical entity that predates practice. The unsettling implication is that the speaker's theory can never exist in the present but is either projected forward, as "the idea of an idea, something infinitely vague" (Baudelaire [1975-1976], 1: 358),[21] or backward, as the origin of the practical encounter in which it is first formed. In light of the non-presence of theory, we can see why the speaker's "Demon of action" (*Démon d'action*) is a "Demon of combat" (*Démon de combat*)

(Baudelaire [1975-1976], 1: 358). The assimilation of action to combat might seem at first glance to suggest the violence inevitably done to abstract, speculative ideas, like equality and liberty, by their realization, but the case is more complicated. For the real violence lies in the combat that generates ideas as a material force to be earned and fought for. We can say, then, that the speaker's materialist theory, even more than its idealist counterpart, governs practice only by not governing it, and this is because the temporal sequence where ideas arise first and practice comes after no longer obtains. Thus **"Assommons"**'s materialist theory is, like the decrepit beggar, *une machine . . . singulièrement détraquée* (a machine . . . singularly out of order), but in the opposite sense. If being put out of commission makes the beggar fight better, the speaker's theory machine malfunctions due to its excellent functioning. Indeed, the "enjoyment" (*jouissance*) that attaches to the verification of theory is also a pain: "the theory that I had the *pain* of trying out on your back" (Baudelaire [1975-1976], 1: 359),[22] and this "pain" is as close as the participants in the fist fight get to practice, the "long and *painful* history of development" described by Marx ([1967], 1: 80; translation modified and emphasis added). As lumpen-proletarians, they are both equally removed from social production until their violent encounter makes something happen.

Ironically, the materialist moment in the combat of ideas emerges most forcefully when the speaker represents the fight as occurring wholly within the realm of verbal, theoretical production. He speaks of the request for alms and his physical response to it as a purely linguistic circuit of dialogue, with no possibility of painful collision between bodies: "So, I made many a sign to make him understand that I considered the discussion finished" (Baudelaire [1975-1976], 1: 359).[23] Cast in terms of signs and their understanding, this transaction between the speaker and the beggar is represented as cognitive. Hence it forms the elementary unit in a broader circuit of exchange, which extends from the speaker to the beggar and from the beggar to his *confrères;* for the beggar is to "apply" to them the speaker's theory, which they will presumably understand and reapply to others. The primacy of comprehension in all these transactions lies in its power to govern further action: "He swore to me that he had understood my theory and that he would obey my advice" (Baudelaire [1975-1976], 1: 359).[24] As an idea to be used, the fist fight is thus brought back to the realm of theory as rhetorical instrument, where the assumption is not, let us emphasize, that words have no real effects but rather that they produce only the intended effect and with an automatism and immediacy that pre-empt all the hard work of practice. In other words, just where the poem tells the beggar to "remember" (*souvenez-vous*), it seems to forget the monkey wrench in the theory machine that its violence has just demonstrated.

But if the move from physical blows to linguistic comprehension obviously suppresses violence, that suppression nonetheless occurs through a kind of epistemic force. For the speaker not only inscribes the beggar in a theoretical experiment of which the beggar cannot be aware, he also prevents the old man from addressing the reader directly in the text. Instead, the beggar's words are reported in an already interpreted indirect discourse: "He swore to me that. . . ." This appropriation of the language of the other suggests an unexpected way of reading the *force signes,* the many a sign, by which the speaker makes the beggar "understand" that the "discussion" is over. If the text insinuates that these *force signes* are euphemisms for a very physical struggle, they also refer to the force of signs: the violence that words perform, for example, in the speaker's representation of the beggar as nothing more than a sounding board (and pounding board) for someone else's theory. **"Assommons"** identifies this verbal force as rhetoric, the aim of theoretical discourse to persuade, and for this activity, the text itself contains "many a sign." Obvious instances include the verbs "advise" (*conseiller*), "persuade" (*persuader*), and "suggest" (*suggérer*), all of which denote the rhetorical force of theory. But we must also add *assommons* (beat up), the title word, and *entreprendre* (undertake), the verbal form of "entrepreneurs," because, according to the *Dictionnaire Robert,* both can mean to overpower, confuse, or attack by words or arguments.

As names for the force of signs, these *force signes* are, however, also signs of force: another acceptation of *entreprendre,* "to seize, attack, or surprise," is a synonym for the usual sense of *assommer,* which is illustrated by the many *coups,* whether of the fist, foot, or branch, the beggar and speaker inflict on each other. If language at first glance seems to act in **"Assommons"** as currency, the exchange medium of figurative and literal that allows the move from utopian theory to theory as practice, here it exhibits a verbal excess, where words repeat each other and divide within themselves. Language thus obtains a kind of materiality that prevents its full assimilation or subservience to the idea and its simple opposition to the material. By virtue of this complication, **"Assommons"** cannot simply shift, by some mutualist model of equal exchange, from the order of words to the order of interacting bodies, because the two orders are already inserted in each other. Rather, the path from words to actions is complicated by language's performance of itself. Thus instead of tracing a smooth trajectory, **"Assommons"** enacts a perverse economic circulation, doomed to encounter its own internal blockages.

"Assommons"'s attempt to break with the received ideas of nineteenth-century idealism by dialectically reversing the speculative rights of man cannot, therefore, be thought outside another reversal it performs: that of the received language or idioms of which the text is the veritable dictionary (even received ideas are named in the idiom of idiom, as *formules de bonne femme,* old wives' tales). For example, the speaker's *bon Ange* (good Angel) is also his *bon Démon* (good Demon); the beggar's look of hatred appears to be *de bon augure* (a good omen) instead of the expected bad one; and the speaker has *la douleur* (the pain) instead of the usual *plaisir* (pleasure) of making the beggar's acquaintance. But these switches hit a snag with *coup* (blow), the word that names physical, historical, and linguistic violence. *Coups* in the sense of "blows" block the dialectic of history in **"Assommons"** because they are not reversed into their opposite but redoubled in vengeance, a vengeance associated with the letter. For *coup* also appears in the text in two idioms. With *un coup d'oeil,* "a glance" or, more literally, "an eye-shot," the speaker makes sure there are no police around before he lands the first blow, or *coup.* And *tout à coup,* "suddenly" or, more literally, "all at one blow," describes the speed with which the beggar turns around and returns the beating. Since such linguistically pre-coded expressions have just one meaning, and that meaning depends on an absolute fixity of the signifier, idioms qualify along with the clichés of an age as commodified language. Hence, unlike the language of excess, we would expect them to be thoroughly consumable. Yet it is precisely one aspect of their commodification, their linguistic configuration, that resists total consumption because it constitutes an inert materiality that cannot be turned around. The *coup*-expressions thus force us to reread the reversal of idiom and the literalization of the figure (of eating and of the fight for rights) in **"Assommons."** To the extent that it is a structure of exchange, the figure can be literalized and dialecticized. But in contrast, *coup,* the very thing that passes between the speaker and the beggar, is what cannot pass; it is the inevitable remnant that resists the subsuming reversals of any dialectic, including a materialist one. For, as anyone who has tried to teach Baudelaire in a non-French-speaking context knows, the idioms of the text do not survive the dialectical operations of translation. Simultaneously the essence and limit of commodity, the word *coup,* in the violence of its idiomatic, material letter, poses a radical challenge to the theory machine.

The best the text can do with its idioms is what the speaker does with the literature of 1848: "I had thus digested—I mean swallowed—all the lucubrations" (Baudelaire [1975-1976], 1: 357).[25] The correction of "digest" by "swallow" suggests an ingestion that falls short of assimilation, a kind of textual heartburn that makes **"Assommons"** regurgitate its idioms at every turn. Consequently, this absolutely static language is just as linguistically irreducible as the self-disseminating language of excess. Since the materialism of both modes gums up the dialectical works, we might say, on the one hand, that **"Assommons"** stages the status of history as text, where *coups,* like indigestible language, are doomed to repeat themselves. But since, on the

other hand, the repetitions can be no more complete than the transformations, these glitches are also what keeps history going, preserving it from stasis or utopian apocalypse. It is in this sense that we should understand Baudelaire's suggestion that the demon inhabiting this machine is an affirmative one, *un grand affirmateur,* for its malfunctions have a positive side. If they are breakdowns, in the end they are also breakthroughs. As an event that does not work because it works so well, the Revolution of 1848 finds its correlative in this system that works only by not working. This is to say that the anomalousness of the Revolution has been not domesticated but resituated. Precisely as an anomaly, it provides the paradigm for the normal functioning of machines, be they of history, theory, or language, because 1848 reveals the irreducible strangeness within normalcy. Under these conditions, it is no wonder that the success and failure of the text have become difficult to tell apart.

Notes

1. des livres à la mode dans ce temps-là (il y a seize ou dix-sept ans) (Baudelaire [1975-1976], 1: 357).

2. l'art de rendre les peuples heureux, sages et riches, en vingt-quatre heures (Baudelaire [1975-1976], 1: 357).

3. Celui-là seul est l'égal d'un autre, qui le *prouve,* et celui-là seul est digne de la liberté, qui sait la *conquérir* (Baudelaire [1975-1976], 1: 358; emphasis added).

4. Qu'en dis-tu, Citoyen Proudhon? (Baudelaire [1975-1976], 1: 1350).

5. MOI, quand je consens à être républicain, *je fais le mal, le sachant.* Oui,! *Vive la Révolution!* toujours! quand même! Mais moi, je ne suis pas dupe! Je n'ai jamais été dupe! Je dis *Vive la Révolution!* comme je dirais: *Vive la Destruction! Vive l'Expiation! Vive le Châtiment! Vive la Mort!* (Baudelaire [1975-1976], 2: 961).

6. La plume à la main, c'était un *bon bougre;* mais il n'a pas été et n'eût jamais été, même sur le papier, *un Dandy!* (Baudelaire [1973], 2: 563).

7. Ma fureur au coup d'État. . . . Encore un Bonaparte! quelle honte! (Baudelaire [1975-1976], 1: 679).

8. 1848 ne fut amusant que parce que chacun y faisait des utopies comme des châteaux en Espagne (Baudelaire [1975-1976], 1: 680).

9. ceux qui conseillent à tous les pauvres de se faire esclaves, et . . . ceux qui leur persuadent qu'ils sont tous des rois détrônés (Baudelaire [1975-1976], 1: 357-8).

10. toutes les formules de bonne femme dont j'avais récemment parcouru le dictionnaire (Baudelaire [1975-1976], 1: 358).

11. une prostitution que je pourrais appeler *fraterni- taire,* si je voulais parler la belle langue de mon siècle (Baudelaire [1975-1976], 1: 314).

12. tous ces entrepreneurs de bonheur public (Baudelaire [1975-1976], 1: 357).

13. digéré,—avalé, veux-je dire (Baudelaire [1975- 1976], 1: 357).

14. Et je sortis avec une grande soif. Car le goût pas- sionné des mauvaises lectures engendre un besoin proportionnel du grand air et des rafraîchissants (Baudelaire [1975-1976], 1: 358).

15. Comme j'allais entrer dans un cabaret, un mendi- ant me tendit son chapeau, avec un de ces regards inoubliables qui culbuteraient les trônes, si l'esprit remuait la matière, et si l'oeil d'un magnétiseur faisait mûrir les raisins (Baudelaire [1975-1976], 1: 358).

16. un état d'esprit avoisinant le vertige ou la stupid- ité (Baudelaire [1975-1976], 1: 358).

17. En même temps, j'entendis une voix qui chu- chotait à mon oreille, une voix que je reconnus bien; c'était celle d'un bon Ange, ou d'un bon Dé- mon, qui m'accompagne partout. Puisque Socrate avait son bon Démon, pourquoi n'aurais-je pas mon bon Ange . . . ? Il existe cette différence en- tre le Démon de Socrate et le mien, que celui de Socrate ne se manifestait à lui que pour défendre, avertir, empêcher, et que le mien daigne conseiller, suggérer, persuader. Ce pauvre Socrate n'avait qu'un Démon prohibiteur; le mien est un grand affirmateur, le mien est un Démon d'action, un Démon de combat. Or, sa voix me chuchotait ceci: "Celui-là seul est l'égal d'un autre, qui le prouve, et celui-là seul est digne de la liberté, qui sait la conquérir." Immédiatement, je sautai sur mon mendiant (Baudelaire [1975-1976], 1: 358).

18. hors de la portée de tout agent de police (Baudelaire [1975-1976], 1: 359).

19. Immédiatement, je sautai sur mon mendiant. D'un seul coup de poing, je lui bouchai un oeil, qui devint, en une seconde, gros comme une balle. Je cassai un de mes ongles à lui briser deux dents, et comme je ne me sentais pas assez fort, étant né délicat et m'étant peu exercé à la boxe, pour as- sommer rapidement ce vieillard, je le saisis d'une main par le collet de son habit, de l'autre, je l'empoignai à la gorge, et je me mis à lui secouer vigoureusement la tête contre un mur.

Ayant ensuite, par un coup de pied lancé dans le dos, assez énergique pour briser les omoplates, terrassé ce sexagénaire affaibli, je me saisis d'une grosse branche d'arbre qui traînait à terre, et je le battis avec l'énergie obstinée des cuisiniers qui veulent attendrir un beefteack.

Tout à coup,—ô miracle! ô jouissance du philos- ophe qui vérifie l'excellence de sa théorie!—je vis cette antique carcasse se retourner, se redresser avec une énergie que je n'aurais jamais soupçon- née dans une machine si singulièrement détraquée, et, avec un regard de haine qui me parut de *bon augure,* le malandrin décrépit se jeta sur moi, me pocha les deux yeux, me cassa quatre dents, et avec la même branche d'arbre me battit dru comme plâtre.—Par mon énergique médication, je lui avais donc rendu l'orgueil et la vie (Baudelaire [1975-1976], 1: 358-9).

20. Monsieur, *vous êtes mon égal!* (Baudelaire [1975- 1976], 1: 359).

21. l'idée d'une idée, quelque chose d'infiniment vague (Baudelaire [1975-1976], 1: 358).

22. la théorie que j'ai eu la *douleur* d'essayer sur votre dos (Baudelaire [1975-1976], 1: 359).

23. Alors, je lui fis force signes pour lui faire com- prendre que je considérais la discussion comme finie (Baudelaire [1975-1976], 1: 359).

24. il m'a bien juré qu'il avait compris ma théorie, et qu'il obéirait à mes conseils (Baudelaire [1975- 1976], 1: 359).

25. J'avais donc digéré,—avalé, veux-je dire,—toutes les élucubrations (Baudelaire [1975-1976], 1: 357).

Bibliography

Abrams, M. H. 1971. *Natural Supernaturalism: Tradi- tion and Revolution in Romantic Literature.* New York: Norton.

Baudelaire, Charles. 1973. *Correspondance.* Ed. by Claude Pichois with Jean Ziegler. 2 vols. Paris: Galli- mard.

———. 1975-1976. *Oeuvres complètes.* Ed. by Claude Pichois. 2 vols. Paris: Gallimard.

Bennington, Geoff, and Robert Young. 1987. Introduc- tion: Posing the Question. *Post-structuralism and the Question of History.* Ed. by Derek Attridge, Geoff Ben- nington, and Robert Young, 1-11. Cambridge: Cam- bridge University Press.

Bloom, Harold. 1970. The Internalization of Quest- Romance. *Romanticism and Consciousness: Essays in Criticism.* Ed. by Harold Bloom, 3-24. New York: Norton.

Caruth, Cathy. 1991. Unclaimed Experience: Trauma and the Possibility of History. *Yale French Studies.* 79: 181-92.

Culler, Jonathan. 1988. The Call to History. *Framing the Sign: Criticism and its Institutions.* Oklahoma Project for Discourse and Theory. Norman: University of Oklahoma Press.

De Man, Paul. 1982. Sign and Symbol in Hegel's *Aesthetics. Critical Inquiry.* 8.4: 761-75.

————. 1983. Hegel on the Sublime. *Displacement: Derrida and After.* Ed. by Mark Krupnik, 139-53. Bloomington: Indiana University Press.

Derrida, Jacques. 1973. Differance. *Speech and Phenomena and Other Essays on Husserl's Theory of Signs.* Trans. by David B. Allison, 129-60. Studies in Phenomenology and Existential Philosophy. Evanston, IL: Northwestern University Press.

————. 1976. *Of Grammatology.* Trans. by Gayatri Chakravorty Spivak. Baltimore: Johns Hopkins University Press.

————. 1982. *Margins of Philosophy.* Trans. by Alan Bass. Chicago: University of Chicago Press.

Eagleton, Terry. 1983. *Literary Theory: An Introduction.* Oxford: Basil Blackwell.

Felman, Shoshana, and Dori Laub. 1992. *Testimony: Crises of Witnessing in Literature, Psychoanalysis, and History.* New York: Routledge.

Hartman, Geoffrey H. 1971. *Wordsworth's Poetry 1787-1814.* New Haven: Yale University Press.

Hegel, Georg Wilhelm Friedrich. [1807]. 1977. *Phenomenology of Spirit.* Trans. by A. V. Miller. Oxford: Oxford University Press.

Hobson, Marian. 1987. History Traces. *Poststructuralism and the Question of History.* Ed. by Derek Attridge, Geoff Bennington, and Robert Young, 101-15. Cambridge: Cambridge University Press.

Hölderlin, Friedrich. 1946-1985. *Sämtliche Werke.* Ed. by Friedrich Beissner. Stuttgart: Cotta.

Kristeva, Julia. 1984. *Revolution in Poetic Language.* Trans. by Margaret Waller. New York: Columbia University Press.

Lacoue-Labarthe, Phillipe. 1978. The Cesura of the Speculative. Trans. by Robert Eisenhauer. *Glyph.* 4: 57-84.

————. 1979. Hölderlin et les Grecs. *Poétique.* 40 (November): 465-74.

Marx, Karl. 1967. *Capital: A Critique of Political Economy.* Ed. by Friedrich Engels. Trans. by Samuel Moore and Edward Aveling. 3 vols. New York: International Publishers.

Proudhon, Pierre-Joseph. 1865. *De la capacité politique des classes ouvrières.* Ed. by E. Dentu. Paris: Dentu.

————. 1871; new ed. *Théorie de la propriété.* Vol. 33 of *Ouvrages de Pierre-Joseph Proudhon.* Ed. by J. A. Langlois, G. Duchêne, F. G. Bergmann, and F. Delhasse. 35 vols. Paris: Librairie Internationale.

————. 1969. *Selected Writings of Pierre-Joseph Proudhon.* Ed. by Stewart Edwards. Trans. by Elizabeth Fraser. Garden City, NY: Doubleday.

Serres, Michel. 1980. *Le Parasite.* Paris: Grasset.

Warminski, Andrzej. 1987. *Readings in Interpretation.* Theory and History of Literature. Minneapolis: University of Minnesota Press.

Wordsworth, William. 1979. *The Prelude, 1799, 1805, 1850: Authoritative Texts, Context and Reception, Recent Critical Essays.* Ed. by Jonathan Wordsworth, M. H. Abrams, and Stephen Gill. New York: Norton.

Wüstemeyer, Manfred. 1986. *Demokratische Diktatur. Zum politischen System des Bonapartismus im zweiten Empire.* Dissertationen zur neueren Geschichte 18. Cologne: Böhlau.

FURTHER READING

Bibliography

Cargo, Robert T. *Baudelaire Criticism 1950-1967: A Bibliography with Critical Commentary.* Tuscaloosa: University of Alabama Press, 1968, 171 p.
    A bibliography of works by and about Baudelaire.

Biographies

Hemmings, F. W. J. *Baudelaire the Damned: A Biography.* New York: Charles Scribner's Sons, 1982, 251 p.
    Detailed examination of Baudelaire's life.

Hyslop, Lois Boe. *Baudelaire: Man of His Time.* New Haven, Conn.: Yale University Press, 1980, 207 p.
    Discusses Baudelaire's personal and professional relationship with artists, musicians, writers, and politicians of his era.

Richardson, Joanna. *Baudelaire.* London: John Murray, 1994, 602 p.
    Offers a modern perspective on the life of the poet.

Starkie, Enid. *Baudelaire.* New York: New Directions, 1958, 622 p.
    Considered the definitive biography in English.

Criticism

Benjamin, Walter. *Charles Baudelaire: A Lyric Poet in the Era of High Capitalism,* translated by Harry Zohn. London: NLB, 1973, 179 p.
    Examines the structure and content of *The Flowers of Evil,* focusing on Baudelaire's poetic vocabulary.

Bowles, Brett. "Poetic Practice and Historical Paradigm: Charles Baudelaire's Anti-Semitism." *PMLA* 115, no. 2 (March 2000): 195-208.
    Examines Baudelaire's treatment of Jewish stereotypes.

Burt, E. S. "Materiality and Autobiography in Baudelaire's 'La Pipe.'" *MLN* 116, no. 5 (December 2001): 941-63.
    Discusses the usefulness of applying the concepts of materiality and materialism in the study of Baudelaire's poem.

Chesters, Graham. *Baudelaire and the Poetics of Craft.* Cambridge: Cambridge University Press, 1988, 184 p.
    Detailed study of Baudelaire's poetics.

Efstratiou, Dimitrios. "From Flesh to Matter: Anti-Essentialist Circumscriptions of Sexuality in Charles Baudelaire's Poetry." *Parallax* 8, no. 4 (October-December 2002): 8-20.
    Judges Baudelaire's poetry from a materialist point of view.

Gouldbourne, Russel. "The Sound of Silence . . . *Points de suspension* in Baudelaire's *Les Fleurs du Mal.*" *Australian Journal of French Studies* 36, no. 2 (May-August 1999): 200-13.
    Explores Baudelaire's use of punctuation as an enhancement of his poetic style.

Jamison, Anne. "Any Where out of This Verse: Baudelaire's Prose Poetics and the Aesthetics of Transgression." *Nineteenth-Century French Studies* 29, nos. 3-4 (spring-summer 2001): 256-86.
    Analyzes Baudelaire's prose poems with an emphasis on questions of aesthetics.

Leakey, F. W. *Baudelaire: Collected Essays, 1953-1988.* Edited by Eva Jacobs. Cambridge: Cambridge University Press, 1990, 320 p.
    Collection of essays, mostly on *The Flowers of Evil,* by an important Baudelaire critic.

————. "*Les Fleurs du Mal*: A Chronological View." *The Modern Language Review* 91, part 3 (July 1996): 578-81.

Discusses the order in which the poems of *The Flowers of Evil* were written and published in order to draw conclusions about Baudelaire's intentions in these works.

Lloyd, Rosemary. *Baudelaire's Literary Criticism.* Cambridge: Cambridge University Press, 1981, 338 p.
    Argues that Baudelaire's critical writings on art served as the inspiration for his creative writings.

Nicolay, Claire. "The 'Fatal Attractions' of 'Serious Things': Regency Politics and Performance in Baudelaire's *Le Spleen de Paris.*" *European Romantic Review* 11, no. 3 (summer 2000): 322-47.
    Explores the subjects of dandyism and social class in *Paris Spleen.*

Peyre, Henri, ed. *Baudelaire: A Collection of Critical Essays.* Englewood Cliffs, N.J.: Prentice-Hall, 1962, 184 p.
    Collection of essays by prominent commentators on Baudelaire.

Porter, Laurence M. In *Approaches to Teaching Baudelaire's* Flowers of Evil. New York: Modern Language Association of America, 2000, 206 p.
    Discusses the difficulties of teaching *The Flowers of Evil* to college students and ways that Baudelaire's poems might be made more accessible to student readers.

Sanyal, Debarati. "The Tie That Binds: Violent Commerce in Baudelaire's 'Le Corde.'" *Yale French Studies* 101 (2001): 132-49.
    Examines the treatment of suicide in a one of Baudelaire's poems.

Scott, Clive. *Translating Baudelaire.* Exeter, U.K.: University of Exeter Press, 2000, 287 p.
    Discusses the various methods of and difficulties posed by translating the poetry of Baudelaire.

Simek, Nicolas. "Baudelaire and the Problematic of the Reader in *Les Fleurs du Mal.*" *Pacific Coast Philology* 37 (2002): 43-57.
    Treats the notion of the "authorial self" in *The Flowers of Evil.*

Jane Eyre

Charlotte Brontë

(Also wrote under pseudonym of Currer Bell) English novelist and poet.

The following entry presents criticism of Brontë's novel *Jane Eyre: An Autobiography* (1847); for further discussion of the novel, see Volume 8. For a complete discussion of Brontë's career, see *NCLC,* Volume 3. For discussion of the novel *Vilette,* see Volume 33; for discussion of the novel *Shirley,* see Volume 58; for discussion of the novel *The Professor,* see Volume 105.

INTRODUCTION

Published in 1847, *Jane Eyre: An Autobiography* is considered Brontë's literary masterpiece and remains one of the most widely read novels from the nineteenth century. The novel brought fame and recognition to Brontë upon publication, especially for her portrayal of Jane, her first-person narrator/protagonist, whose confident demeanor was a major departure from the typically submissive heroines of most nineteenth-century literature. Brontë uses conventions of the Gothic genre as well as plot and setting to discuss issues such as gender relationships, education, religion, and self-realization. These issues, along with the development of Jane's character, continue to generate interest among both critics and readers.

PLOT AND MAJOR CHARACTERS

Jane Eyre is narrated in the first person by an adult Jane, who begins the book by recalling events from her childhood as an orphan living with her hard-hearted aunt, Mrs. Reed. At the age of eight, Jane is sent off to Lowood, a boarding school for orphans. Life continues to be difficult for Jane, but she perseveres, making friends with another girl at the school, as well as a beloved teacher, Miss Temple. Jane stays at the school until she is eighteen, first as a student and later as a teacher herself. However, after Miss Temple leaves Lowood to get married, Jane longs for new experiences and finds a position at Thornfield Hall as a teacher for young Adéle Varens, the French ward of the owner, Mr. Rochester. Hired by Mrs. Fairfax, the housekeeper at Thornfield, Jane quickly settles into a routine, but does not feel content. She is unnerved by the sound of a strange laugh and muttering that is explained by Mrs. Fairfax as belonging to one of the servants, and she has an innate longing for something more than the life she is leading. When Jane meets Mr. Rochester she is drawn to the strange and morose man, and a relationship begins between the two. Their burgeoning relationship is interrupted, however, when Jane is awakened one night by a scream. After traversing a smoky hallway, she eventually traces the fire to Mr. Rochester, whom she awakens and saves just in time. The next morning, Mr. Rochester departs, returning a week later with a party of several houseguests, including the charming and beautiful Miss Blanche Ingram; Jane finds herself retreating from the clamor of the party and from her employer. At this point in the novel, she is summoned to the death bed of her aunt. Jane leaves Thornfield, and when she returns after a nearly month-long absence, the estate has returned to normal, with all of Mr. Rochester's houseguests departed. In an intense conversation with Mr. Rochester, during which he reveals his engagement to Miss Ingram, Jane professes her own love for him. The story now takes a dramatic turn, with Mr. Rochester admitting that his engagement to Miss Ingram is a farce, and to his own feelings for Jane. He offers her a proposal of marriage, which Jane accepts. Four weeks later, Jane and Mr. Rochester set out alone for the church to be married. The ceremony, however, is interrupted with the revelation that Mr. Rochester is already married, and that the strange murmurs and laugh that Jane has heard through her months at Thornfield belong to his insane wife, Bertha, who has been locked in the attic. Faced with an awful choice between her love for Mr. Rochester and her loyalty to her own principles, Jane leaves Thornfield that very night. She finds shelter with the Rivers family and eventually learns that she has inherited a small fortune from her Uncle John. In the meantime, St. John Rivers, her clergyman cousin, tries to convince Jane to marry him. During the course of his proposal, Jane suddenly becomes aware of Mr. Rochester's voice calling out to her. Stunned, she returns to Thornfield, only to find the estate in ruins; the house was set afire by Bertha, who herself has perished in the fire. In his attempt to save Bertha, Mr. Rochester has lost his sight. To her shock, Jane also finds out that it was, indeed, Mr. Rochester who was calling out to her in desperation. Now that he is free of his marital obligations, she agrees to marry him.

Since *Jane Eyre* is narrated in the form of an autobiography, the reader's perception of the other characters in the book is always filtered through Jane's viewpoint. In addition to her, the most significant character in the book is Mr. Rochester. Presented as a strange and enigmatic man, many critics regard him as almost peripheral to the development of Jane's own character and judgment, which form the crux of novel. Other characters in the book, including Jane's aunt, Miss Temple, Mrs. Fairfax, and Blanche Ingram, are also similar to Mr. Rochester, providing smaller, but nonetheless significant foils and contrasts to Jane, helping her shape and mold her own character through the course of the book.

MAJOR THEMES

Brontë uses the canvas of Thornfield and its inhabitants to comment on many aspects of Victorian society, including gender relationships, social structure, education, religion, and spirituality. The heart of the novel, however, revolves around the development of Jane's character, and Brontë uses numerous situations in the young governess's life to highlight these defining moments. Perhaps the most significant of these is the incident when Jane rejects Rochester based on her own personal principles. Her relationship with Mr. Rochester is the strongest bond Jane has formed in her life, and it is also the strongest test of her own convictions. Her strength and self-confidence at a moment of great anguish is, according to many critics, the climax of her personal development. Brontë herself commented on her heroine, noting that despite her plainness, Jane is a figure who is "as interesting as any" other, more typical Victorian heroine. According to several scholars, Jane's refusal to give in to temptation by staying with Mr. Rochester is an almost feminist response to Mr. Rochester's lack of trust. Similarly, although Jane adheres to her own personal code of ethics, Brontë is clear in her rejection of evangelical religion, represented through the figure of St. John Rivers, who is depicted as heartless and mechanical. Jane's ultimate rejection of his offer of marriage and her response to Rochester's call are a triumph of both her personal ethics and the emotional commitment she has to her self.

CRITICAL RECEPTION

During her lifetime, Brontë was considered the most outstanding literary figure of her family, receiving praise from such notable figures as Queen Victoria and George Eliot. Her works, especially *Jane Eyre,* were lauded for their powerful prose style and strong characterizations. In the early twentieth century, however, an influential essay by critic David Cecil compared the works of

Charlotte and Emily Brontë, declaring that Emily was the better of the two writers. For many years afterward, Charlotte's works were studied mostly in comparison to Emily's, with attention focused more on details of her private life rather than the qualities of her writing. Since then, *Jane Eyre* has been reappraised by critics and is now generally acknowledged as one of the most significant novels of the late-nineteenth century. In his essay discussing the novel, W. A. Craik declares that *Jane Eyre* still "bursts upon the reader" just as powerfully as it did when it was first published. Characterizing it as a "rare masterpiece," the critic attributes the novel's enduring power to its vivid descriptions of contemporary life as well as its masterfully drawn characters. In addition to discussions of characterization, many of which focus on either Jane or Mr. Rochester, much critical attention has been focused on the thematic elements of the novel. In a study of Brontë's works, Lawrence Jay Dessner (see Further Reading) writes that the most interesting contrast presented in the novel is the one between the power of orthodox morality versus the passion evidenced in the character of its heroine. According to Dessner, this tension is what gives the novel its power. In her appraisal of Jane's character, Maria Yuen notes that the conflict Jane faces at the climax of *Jane Eyre* is central to Brontë's vision of the self as it is presented in the novel. Yuen contends that Jane's decision to leave Rochester when she finds out about his marriage, although it has given rise to much critical debate, is in complete harmony with Brontë's perception of a personal ideal where the principles of honor and conscience override the desire for comfort and personal happiness. Several other studies of *Jane Eyre* have focused their attention on its imagery, symbolism, and literary style. For example, Cynthia A. Linder (see Further Reading) views the first-person narrative technique of the novel as proof of its author's romantic philosophy. Linder contends that the subjective viewpoint of the narrator is completely in line with the romantic theory that attempts to "make the external internal, to make nature thought and thought nature." In his book-length study of the imagery of death as it is used in Brontë's works, Robert Keefe proposes that *Jane Eyre* represents Brontë's culminating effort in dealing with the "presence of death in the midst of life." According to Keefe, there are strong parallels between events in the novel and the author's own life, such as Brontë's rendering of Lowood. Keefe regards Lowood as Brontë's imaginary recreation of Cowal Bridge, the boarding school where two of Brontë's sisters died. The critic theorizes that the complex reaction Brontë had to the death of her sister Maria was the impetus behind the creation of *Jane Eyre*. Other interpretations of the novel have focused on how Jane's character relates to and reveals contemporary English society. For example, John G. Peters explains that Jane is an outsider, both in the novel's social context and in the view of Brontë's contemporaries, and that both of these groups feared her because she served to undermine established norms. Other readings of the novel include several discussions of the gothic imagery in the work, as well as numerous studies focusing on its feminist themes.

PRINCIPAL WORKS

Poems by Currer, Ellis, and Acton Bell (poetry) 1846
Jane Eyre: An Autobiography. 3 vols. [as Currer Bell] (novel) 1847
Shirley: A Tale. 3 vols. [as Currer Bell] (novel) 1849
Vilette. 3 vols. [as Currer Bell] (novel) 1853
The Professor: A Tale. 2 vols. [as Currer Bell] (novel) 1857
The Twelve Adventurers and Other Stories (juvenilia) 1925
Legends of Angria: Compiled from the Early Writings of Charlotte Brontë (juvenilia) 1933
Five Novelettes (novelettes) 1971

*Poems published collectively by Charlotte, Emily, and Anne Brontë

CRITICISM

Quarterly Review (review date December 1848)

SOURCE: "*Vanity Fair—and Jane Eyre*." *Quarterly Review* 84, no. 167 (December 1848): 153-85.

[*In the following excerpted review, the critic offers an appraisal of* Jane Eyre.]

Jane Eyre, as a work, and one of equal popularity, is, in almost every respect, a total contrast to [William Makepeace Thackery's] *Vanity Fair.* The characters and events, though some of them masterly in conception, are coined expressly for the purpose of bringing out great effects. The hero and heroine are beings both so singularly unattractive that the reader feels they can have no vocation in the novel but to be brought together; and they do things which, though not impossible, lie utterly beyond the bounds of probability. On this account a short sketch of the plan seems requisite; not but what it is a plan familiar enough to all readers of novels—especially those of the old school and those of the lowest school of our own day. For Jane Eyre is merely another Pamela, who, by the force of her character and the strength of her principles, is carried victoriously through great trials and temptations from the

man she loves. Nor is she even a Pamela adapted and refined to modern notions; for though the story is conducted without those derelictions of decorum which we are to believe had their excuse in the manners of Richardson's time, yet it is stamped with a coarseness of language and laxity of tone which have certainly no excuse in ours. It is a very remarkable book: we have no remembrance of another combining such genuine power with such horrid taste. Both together have equally assisted to gain the great popularity it has enjoyed; for in these days of extravagant adoration of all that bears the stamp of novelty and originality, sheer rudeness and vulgarity have come in for a most mistaken worship.

The story is written in the first person. Jane begins with her earliest recollections, and at once takes possession of the reader's intensest interest by the masterly picture of a strange and oppressed child she raises up in a few strokes before him. She is an orphan, and a dependant in the house of a selfish, hard-hearted aunt, against whom the disposition of the little Jane chafes itself in natural antipathy, till she contrives to make the unequal struggle as intolerable to her oppressor as it is to herself. She is therefore, at eight years of age, got rid of to a sort of Dothegirls Hall, where she continues to enlist our sympathies for a time with her little pinched fingers, cropped hair, and empty stomach. But things improve: the abuses of the institution are looked into. The Puritan patron, who holds that young orphan girls are only safely brought up upon the rules of La Trappe, is superseded by an enlightened committee—the school assumes a sound English character—Jane progresses duly from scholar to teacher, and passes ten profitable and not unhappy years at Lowood. Then she advertises for a situation as governess, and obtains one immediately in one of the midland counties. We see her, therefore, as she leaves Lowood, to enter upon a new life—a small, plain, odd creature, who has been brought up dry upon school learning, and somewhat stunted accordingly in mind and body, and who is now thrown upon the world as ignorant of its ways, and as destitute of its friendships, as a shipwrecked mariner upon a strange coast.

Thornfield Hall is the property of Mr. Rochester—a bachelor addicted to travelling. She finds it at first in all the peaceful prestige of an English gentleman's seat when 'nobody is at the hall.' The companions are an old decayed gentlewoman housekeeper—a far away cousin of the squire's—and a young French child, Jane's pupil, Mr. Rochester's ward and reputed daughter. There is a pleasing monotony in the summer solitude of the old country house, with its comfort, respectability, and dulness, which Jane paints to the life; but there is one circumstance which varies the sameness and casts a mysterious feeling over the scene. A strange laugh is heard from time to time in a distant part of the house—a laugh which grates discordantly upon Jane's ear. She listens, watches, and inquires, but can discover nothing but a plain matter of fact woman, who sits sewing somewhere in the attics, and goes up and down stairs peaceably to and from her dinner with the servants. But a mystery there is, though nothing betrays it, and it comes in with marvellous effect from the monotonous reality of all around. After awhile Mr. Rochester comes to Thornfield, and sends for the child and her governess occasionally to bear him company. He is a dark, strange-looking man—strong and large—of the brigand stamp, with fine eyes and lowering brows—blunt and sarcastic in his manners, with a kind of misanthropical frankness, which seems based upon utter contempt for his fellow-creatures, and a surly truthfulness which is more rudeness than honesty. With his arrival disappears all the prestige of country innocence that had invested Thornfield Hall. He brings the taint of the world upon him, and none of its illusions. The queer little governess is something new to him. He talks to her at one time imperiously as to a servant, and at another recklessly as to a man. He pours into her ears disgraceful tales of his past life, connected with the birth of little Adèle, which any man with common respect for a woman, and that a mere girl of eighteen, would have spared her; but which eighteen in this case listens to as if it were nothing new, and certainly nothing distasteful. He is captious and Turk-like—she is one day his confidant, and another his unnoticed dependant. In short, by her account, Mr. Rochester is a strange brute, somewhat in the Squire Western style of absolute and capricious eccentricity, though redeemed in him by signs of a cultivated intellect, and gleams of a certain fierce justice of heart. He has a *mind*, and when he opens it at all, he opens it freely to her. Jane becomes attached to her 'master,' as Pamela-like she calls him, and it is not difficult to see that solitude and propinquity are taking effect upon him also. An odd circumstance heightens the dawning romance. Jane is awoke one night by that strange discordant laugh close to her ear—then a noise as if hands feeling along the wall. She rises—opens her door, finds the passage full of smoke, is guided by it to her master's room, whose bed she discovers enveloped in flames, and by her timely aid saves his life. After this they meet no more for ten days, when Mr. Rochester returns from a visit to a neighbouring family, bringing with him a housefull of distinguished guests; at the head of whom is Miss Blanche Ingram, a haughty beauty of high birth, and evidently the especial object of the Squire's attentions—upon which tumultuous irruption Miss Eyre slips back into her naturally humble position.

Our little governess is now summoned away to attend her aunt's death-bed, who is visited by some compunctions towards her, and she is absent a month. When she returns Thornfield Hall is quit of all its guests, and Mr. Rochester and she resume their former life of captious cordiality on the one side, and diplomatic humility on

the other. At the same time the bugbear of Miss Ingram and of Mr. Rochester's engagement with her is kept up, though it is easy to see that this and all concerning that lady is only a stratagem to try Jane's character and affection upon the most approved Griselda precedent. Accordingly an opportunity for explanation ere long offers itself, where Mr. Rochester has only to take it. Miss Eyre is desired to walk with him in shady alleys, and to sit with him on the roots of an old chesnut-tree towards the close of evening, and of course she cannot disobey her 'master'—whereupon there ensues a scene which, as far as we remember, is new equally in art or nature; in which Miss Eyre confesses her love—whereupon Mr. Rochester drops not only his cigar (which she seems to be in the habit of lighting for him) but his mask, and finally offers not only heart, but hand. The wedding-day is soon fixed, but strange misgivings and presentiments haunt the young lady's mind. The night but one before, her bed-room is entered by a horrid phantom, who tries on the wedding veil, sends Jane into a swoon of terror, and defeats all the favourite refuge of a bad dream by leaving the veil in two pieces. But all is ready. The bride has no friends to assist—the couple walk to church—only the clergyman and the clerk are there—but Jane's quick eye has seen two figures lingering among the tombstones, and these two follow them into church. The ceremony commences, when at the due charge which summons any man to come forward and show just cause why they should not be joined together, a voice interposes to forbid the marriage. There is an impediment, and a serious one. The bridegroom has a wife not only living, but living under the very roof of Thornfield Hall. Hers was that discordant laugh which had so often caught Jane's ear; she it was who in her malice had tried to burn Mr. Rochester in his bed—who had visited Jane by night and torn her veil, and whose attendant was that same pretended sew-woman who had so strongly excited Jane's curiosity. For Mr. Rochester's wife is a creature, half fiend, half maniac, whom he had married in a distant part of the world, and whom now, in his self-constituted code of morality, he had thought it his right, and even his duty, to supersede by a more agreeable companion. Now follow scenes of a truly tragic power. This is the grand crisis in Jane's life. Her whole soul is wrapt up in Mr. Rochester. He has broken her trust, but not diminished her love. He entreats her to accept all that he still can give, his heart and his home; he pleads with the agony not only of a man who has never known what it was to conquer a passion, but of one who, by that same self-constituted code, now burns to atone for a disappointed crime. There is no one to help her against him or against herself. Jane had no friends to stand by her at the altar, and she has none to support her now she is plucked away from it. There is no one to be offended or disgraced at her following him to the sunny land of Italy, as he proposes, till the maniac should die. There is no duty to any one but to herself, and this feeble reed quivers and trembles beneath the overwhelming weight of love and sophistry opposed to it. But Jane triumphs; in the middle of the night she rises—glides out of her room—takes off her shoes as she passes Mr. Rochester's chamber;—leaves the house, and casts herself upon a world more desert than ever to her—

'Without a shilling and without a friend.'

Thus the great deed of self-conquest is accomplished; Jane has passed through the fire of temptation from without and from within; her character is stamped from that day; we need therefore follow her no further into wanderings and sufferings which, though not unmixed with plunder from Minerva-lane, occupy some of, on the whole, the most striking chapters in the book. Virtue of course finds her reward. The maniac wife sets fire to Thornfield Hall, and perishes herself in the flames. Mr. Rochester, in endeavouring to save her, loses the sight of his eyes. Jane rejoins her blind master; they are married, after which of course the happy man recovers his sight.

Such is the outline of a tale in which, combined with great materials for power and feeling, the reader may trace gross inconsistencies and improbabilities, and chief and foremost that highest moral offence a novel writer can commit, that of making an unworthy character interesting in the eyes of the reader. Mr. Rochester is a man who deliberately and secretly seeks to violate the laws both of God and man, and yet we will be bound half our lady readers are enchanted with him for a model of generosity and honour. We would have thought that such a hero had had no chance, in the purer taste of the present day; but the popularity of **Jane Eyre** is a proof how deeply the love for illegitimate romance is implanted in our nature. Not that the author is strictly responsible for this. Mr. Rochester's character is tolerably consistent. He is made as coarse and as brutal as can in all conscience be required to keep our sympathies at a distance. In point of literary consistency the hero is at all events impugnable, though we cannot say as much for the heroine.

As to Jane's character—there is none of that harmonious unity about it which made little Becky so grateful a subject of analysis—nor are the discrepancies of that kind which have their excuse and their response in our nature. The inconsistencies of Jane's character lie mainly not in her own imperfections, though of course she has her share, but in the author's. There is that confusion in the relations between cause and effect, which is not so much untrue to human nature as to human art. The error in Jane Eyre is, not that her character is this or that, but that she is made one thing in the eyes of her imaginary companions, and another in that of the actual reader. There is a perpetual disparity between the account she herself gives of the effect she produces, and the means shown us by which she brings that effect about. We hear nothing but self-eulogiums on the perfect tact and wondrous penetration with which she is gifted, and yet almost every word she utters offends us, not only with the absence of these qualities, but with the positive contrasts of them, in either her pedantry, stupidity, or gross vulgarity. She is one of those ladies who put us in the unpleasant predicament of undervaluing their very virtues for dislike of the person in whom they are represented. One feels provoked as Jane Eyre stands before us—for in the wonderful reality of her thoughts and descriptions, she seems accountable for all done in her name—with principles you must approve in the main, and yet with language and manners that offend you in every particular. Even in that *chef-d'œuvre* of brilliant retrospective sketching, the description of her early life, it is the childhood and not the child that interests you. The little Jane, with her sharp eyes and dogmatic speeches, is a being you neither could fondle nor love. There is a hardness in her infantine earnestness, and a spiteful precocity in her reasoning, which repulses all our sympathy. One sees that she is of a nature to dwell upon and treasure up every slight and unkindness, real or fancied, and such natures we know are surer than any others to meet with plenty of this sort of thing. As the child, so also the woman—an uninteresting, sententious, pedantic thing; with no experience of the world, and yet with no simplicity or freshness in its stead. What are her first answers to Mr. Rochester but such as would have quenched all interest, even for a prettier woman, in any man of common knowledge of what was nature—and especially in a *blasé* monster like him? A more affected governessy effusion we never read. The question is à propos of *cadeaux*.

"Who talks of cadeaux?" said he gruffly: "did you expect a present, Miss Eyre? Are you fond of presents?" and he searched my face with eyes that I saw were dark, irate, and piercing.

"I hardly know, Sir; I have little experience of them; they are generally thought pleasant things."

"Generally thought! But what do *you* think?"

"I should be obliged to take time, Sir, before I could give you an answer worthy of your acceptance: a present has many faces to it, has it not? and one should consider all before pronouncing an opinion as to its nature."

"Miss Eyre, you are not so unsophisticated as Adèle: she demands a cadeau clamorously the moment she sees me; you beat about the bush."

"Because I have less confidence in my deserts than Adèle has; she can prefer the right of old acquaintance and the right too of custom; for she says you have always been in the habit of giving her playthings; but if I had to make out a case I should be puzzled, since I am a stranger, and have done nothing to entitle me to an acknowledgment."

"Oh! don't fall back on over modesty! I have examined Adèle, and find you have taken great pains with her: she is not bright—she has no talent, yet in a short time she has made much improvement."

"Sir, you have now given me my cadeau; I am obliged to you: it is the meed teachers most covet; praise of their pupil's progress."

"Humph!" said Mr. Rochester.

—vol. i., p. 234.

Let us take a specimen of her again when Mr. Rochester brings home his guests to Thornfield. The fine ladies of this world are a new study to Jane, and capitally she describes her first impression of them as they leave the dinner table and return to the drawing-room—nothing can be more gracefully graphic than this.

'There were but eight of them, yet somehow as they flocked in, they gave the impression of a much larger number. Some of them were very tall, and all had a sweeping amplitude of array that seemed to magnify their persons as a mist magnifies the moon. I rose and curtseyed to them: one or two bent their heads in return; the others only stared at me.'

'They dispersed about the room, reminding me, by the lightness and buoyancy of their movements, of a flock of white plumy birds. Some of them threw themselves in half-reclining positions on the sofas and ottomans; some bent over the tables and examined the flowers and books; the rest gathered in a group round the fire: all talked in a low but clear tone which seemed habitual to them.'

—vol. ii. p. 38.

But now for the reverse. The moment Jane Eyre sets these graceful creatures conversing, she falls into mistakes which display not so much a total ignorance of the habits of society, as a vulgarity of mind inherent in herself. They talked together by her account like *parvenues* trying to show off. They discuss the subject of governesses before her very face, in what Jane affects to consider the exact tone of fashionable contempt. They bully the servants in language no lady would dream of using to her own—far less to those of her host and entertainer—though certainly the 'Sam' of Jane Eyre's is not precisely the head servant one is accustomed to meet with in houses of the Thornfield class.

For instance, this is a conversation which occurs in her hearing. An old gypsy has come to the Hall, and the servants can't get rid of her—

"What does she want?" asked Mrs. Eshton.

"To tell the gentry their fortunes, she says, Ma'am: and she swears she must and will do it."

"What is she like?" inquired the Misses Eshton in a breath.

"A shocking ugly old creature, Miss; almost as black as a crock."

"Why she's a real sorceress," cried Frederick Lynn. "Let us have her in of course."

"My dear boys, what are you thinking about?" exclaimed Lady Lynn.

"I cannot possibly countenance any such inconsistent proceedings," chimed in the Dowager Ingram.

"Indeed, Mama, but you can—and will," pronounced the haughty voice of Blanche, as she turned round on the piano-stool, where till now she had sat silent, apparently examining sundry sheets of music. "I have a curiosity to hear my fortune told: therefore, Sam, order the beldame forward."

"My darling Blanche! recollect—"

"I do—I recollect all you can suggest; and I must have my will—quick, Sam!"

"Yes—yes—yes," cried all the juveniles, both ladies and gentlemen. "Let her come, it will be excellent sport."

The footman still lingered. "She looks such a rough one," said he.

"Go!" ejaculated Miss Ingram, and the man went.

Excitement instantly seized the whole party; a running fire of raillery and jests was proceeding when Sam returned.

"She won't come now," said he. "She says it is not her mission to appear before the 'vulgar herd' (them's her words). I must show her into a room by herself, and them who wish to consult her must go to her one by one."

"You see now, my queenly Blanche," began Lady Ingram, "she encroaches. Be advised, my angel girl—and—"

"Show her into the library of course," cut in the "angel girl." "It is not my mission to listen to her before the vulgar herd either; I mean to have her all to myself. Is there a fire in the library?"

"Yes, Ma'am; but she looks such a tinkler."

"Cease that chatter, blockhead! and do my bidding!"

—vol. ii., p. 82.

The old gypsy woman, by the way, turns out to be Mr. Rochester—whom Jane of course alone recognizes—as silly an incident as can well be contrived. But the crowning scene is the offer—governesses are said to be sly on such occasions, but Jane out-governesses them all—little Becky would have blushed for her. They are sitting together at the foot of the old chestnut tree, as we have already mentioned, towards the close of evening, and Mr. Rochester is informing her, with his usual delicacy of language, that he is engaged to Miss Ingram—'a strapper! Jane, a real strapper!'—and that as soon as he brings home his bride to Thornfield, she, the governess, must 'trot forthwith'—but that he shall make it his duty to look out for employment and an asylum for her—indeed, that he has already heard of a charming situation in the depths of Ireland—all with a brutal jocoseness which most women of spirit, unless grievously despairing of any other lover, would have resented, and any woman of sense would have seen through. But Jane, that profound reader of the human heart, and especially of Mr. Rochester's, does neither. She meekly hopes she may be allowed to stay where she is till she has found another shelter to betake herself to—she does not fancy going to Ireland—Why?

> 'It is a long way off, Sir.' 'No matter—a girl of your sense will not object to the voyage or the distance.' 'Not the voyage, but the distance, Sir; and then the sea is a barrier—' 'From what, Jane?' 'From England, and from Thornfield; and—' 'Well?' 'From *you*, Sir.'
>
> —vol. ii., p. 205.

and then the lady bursts into tears in the most approved fashion.

Although so clever in giving hints, how wonderfully slow she is in taking them! Even when, tired of his cat's play, Mr. Rochester proceeds to rather indubitable demonstrations of affection—'enclosing me in his arms, gathering me to his breast, pressing his lips on my lips'—Jane has no idea what he can mean. Some ladies would have thought it high time to leave the Squire alone with his chestnut tree; or, at all events, unnecessary to keep up that tone of high-souled feminine obtusity which they are quite justified in adopting if gentlemen will not speak out—but Jane again does neither. Not that we say she was wrong, but quite the reverse, considering the circumstances of the case—Mr. Rochester was her master, and 'Duchess or nothing' was her first duty—only she was not quite so artless as the author would have us suppose.

But if the manner in which she secures the prize be not inadmissible according to the rules of the art, that in which she manages it when caught, is quite without authority or precedent, except perhaps in the servants' hall. Most lover's play is wearisome and nonsensical to the lookers on—but the part Jane assumes is one which could only be efficiently sustained by the substitution of Sam for her master. Coarse as Mr. Rochester is, one winces for him under the infliction of this housemaid *beau idéal* of the arts of coquetry. A little more, and we should have flung the book aside to lie for ever among the trumpery with which such scenes ally it; but it were a pity to have halted here, for wonderful things lie beyond—scenes of suppressed feeling, more fearful to witness than the most violent tornados of passion—struggles with such intense sorrow and suffering as it is sufficient misery to know that any one should have conceived, far less passed through; and yet with that stamp of truth which takes precedence in the human heart before actual experience. The flippant, fifth-rate, plebeian actress has vanished, and only a noble, high-souled woman, bound to us by the reality of her sorrow, and yet raised above us by the strength of her will, stands in actual life before us. If this be Jane Eyre, the author has done her injustice hitherto, not we. Let us look at her in the first recognition of her sorrow after the discomfiture of the marriage. True, it is not the attitude of a Christian, who knows that all things work together for good to those who love God, but it is a splendidly drawn picture of a natural heart, of high power, intense feeling, and fine religious instinct, falling prostrate, but not grovelling, before the tremendous blast of sudden affliction. The house is cleared of those who had come between her and a disgraceful happiness.

> 'Only the clergyman stayed to exchange a few sentences of admonition or reproof with his haughty parishioner; this duty done, he too departed.'

> 'I heard him go as I stood at the half-open door of my own room, to which I had now withdrawn. The house cleared, I shut myself in, fastened the bolt, that none might intrude, and proceeded—not to weep, not to mourn, I was yet too calm for that, but—mechanically to take off the wedding dress, and replace it by the stuff gown I had worn yesterday, as I thought for the last time. I then sat down: I felt weak and tired. I leaned my arms on a table, and my head dropped on them, and now I thought: till now I had only heard, seen, moved, followed up and down where I was led or dragged, watched event rush on event, disclosure open beyond disclosure: but *now, I thought*.'

> 'The morning had been a quiet morning enough—all except the brief scene with the lunatic. The transaction in the church had not been noisy: there was no explosion of passion, no loud altercation, no dispute, no defiance or challenge, no tears, no sobs; a few words had been spoken, a calmly pronounced objection to the marriage made, some stern, short questions put by Mr. Rochester; answers, explanations given, evidence adduced; an open admission of the truth had been made by my master, then the living proof had been seen, the intruders were gone, and all was over.'

> 'I was in my own room as usual—just myself, without obvious change: nothing had smitten me, or scathed me, or maimed me; and yet where was the Jane Eyre of yesterday? where was her life? where were her prospects?'

> 'Jane Eyre, who had been an ardent, expectant woman—almost a bride—was a cold, solitary girl again: her life was pale, her prospects were desolate. A Christmas frost had come at Midsummer; a white December storm had whirled over June; ice glazed the ripe apples, drifts crushed the blowing roses; on hayfield and corn-field lay a frozen shroud; lanes, which last night blushed full of flowers, to-day were pathless with untrodden snow; and the woods which, twelve hours since, waved leafy and fragrant as groves between the tropics, now spread waste, wild and white as pine forests in wintry Norway. My hopes were all dead—struck with a sudden doom, such as in one night fell on all the firstborn in the land of Egypt; I looked on my cherished wishes, yesterday so blooming and glowing—they lay stark, chill, living corpses, that could

never revive. I looked at my love; that feeling which was my master's—which he had created; it shivered in my heart, like a suffering child in a cold cradle; sickness and anguish had seized it: it could not seek Mr. Rochester's arms—it could not derive warmth from his breast. Oh! never more could it turn to him, for faith was blighted! confidence destroyed! Mr. Rochester was not to me what he had been, for he was not what I thought him. I would not ascribe vice to him; I would not say he had betrayed me: but the attribute of stainless truth was gone from his idea; and from his presence I must go: *that* I perceived well. When—how— whither? I could not yet discern; but he himself I doubted not would hurry me from Thornfield. Real affection, it seemed, he could not have for me; it had been only fitful passion: that was baulked—he would want me no more. I should fear even to cross his path now; my view must be hateful to him. Oh, how blind had been my eyes! how weak my conduct!'

'My eyes were covered and closed; eddying darkness seemed to swim round me, and reflection came in as dark and confused a flow. Self-abandoned, relaxed, and effortless, I seemed to have laid me down in the dried-up bed of a great river; I heard a flood loosened in remote mountains, and felt the torrent come; to rise I had no will, to flee I had no strength. I lay faint, longing to be dead; one idea only throbbed life-like within me—a remembrance of God. It begot an unuttered prayer: these words went wandering up and down in my rayless mind, as something that should be whispered; but no energy was found to express them:—"Be not far from me, for trouble is near: there is none to help."'

'It was near; and as I had lifted no petition to heaven to avert it—as I had neither joined my hands, nor bent my knees, nor moved my lips—it came: in full heavy swing the torrent passed over me. The whole consciousness of my life lorn, my love lost, my hope quenched, my faith dead-struck, swayed full and mighty above me in one sullen mass. That bitter hour cannot be described: in truth "the waters came into my soul; I sank in deep mire; I felt no standing; I came into deep waters; the floods overflowed me."'

—vol. ii., p. 300.

We have said that this was the picture of a natural heart. This, to our view, is the great and crying mischief of the book. Jane Eyre is throughout the personification of an unregenerate and undisciplined spirit, the more dangerous to exhibit from that prestige of principle and self-control which is liable to dazzle the eye too much for it to observe the inefficient and unsound foundation on which it rests. It is true Jane does right, and exerts great moral strength, but it is the strength of a mere heathen mind which is a law unto itself. No Christian grace is perceptible upon her. She has inherited in fullest measure the worst sin of our fallen nature—the sin of pride. Jane Eyre is proud, and therefore she is ungrateful too. It pleased God to make her an orphan, friendless, and penniless—yet she thanks nobody, and least of all Him, for the food and raiment, the friends, companions, and instructors of her helpless youth—for

the care and education vouchsafed to her till she was capable in mind as fitted in years to provide for herself. On the contrary, she looks upon all that has been done for her not only as her undoubted right, but as falling far short of it. The doctrine of humility is not more foreign to her mind than it is repudiated by her heart. It is by her own talents, virtues, and courage that she is made to attain the summit of human happiness, and, as far as Jane Eyre's own statement is concerned, no one would think that she owed anything either to God above or to man below. She flees from Mr. Rochester, and has not a being to turn to. Why was this? The excellence of the present institution at Casterton, which succeeded that of Cowan Bridge near Kirkby Lonsdale—these being distinctly, as we hear, the original and the reformed Lowoods of the book—is pretty generally known. Jane had lived there for eight years with 110 girls and fifteen teachers. Why had she formed no friendships among them? Other orphans have left the same and similar institutions, furnished with friends for life, and puzzled with homes to choose from. How comes it that Jane had acquired neither? Among that number of associates there were surely some exceptions to what she so presumptuously stigmatises as 'the society of inferior minds.' Of course it suited the author's end to represent the heroine as utterly destitute of the common means of assistance, in order to exhibit both her trials and her powers of self-support—the whole book rests on this assumption—but it is one which, under the circumstances, is very unnatural and very unjust.

Altogether the auto-biography of Jane Eyre is preeminently an anti-Christian composition. There is throughout it a murmuring against the comforts of the rich and against the privations of the poor, which, as far as each individual is concerned, is a murmuring against God's appointment—there is a proud and perpetual assertion of the rights of man, for which we find no authority either in God's word or in God's providence— there is that pervading tone of ungodly discontent which is at once the most prominent and the most subtle evil which the law and the pulpit, which all civilized society in fact has at the present day to contend with. We do not hesitate to say that the tone of mind and thought which has overthrown authority and violated every code human and divine abroad, and fostered Chartism and rebellion at home, is the same which has also written *Jane Eyre*.

Still we say again this is a very remarkable book. We are painfully alive to the moral, religious, and literary deficiencies of the picture, and such passages of beauty and power as we have quoted cannot redeem it, but it is impossible not to be spell-bound with the freedom of the touch. It would be mere hackneyed courtesy to call it 'fine writing.' It bears no impress of being written at all, but is poured out rather in the heat and hurry of an instinct, which flows ungovernably on to its object, indifferent by what means it reaches it, and unconscious too. As regards the author's chief object, however, it is a failure—that, namely, of making a plain, odd woman, destitute of all the conventional features of feminine attraction, interesting in our sight. We deny that he has succeeded in this. Jane Eyre, in spite of some grand things about her, is a being totally uncongenial to our feelings from beginning to end. We acknowledge her firmness—we respect her determination—we feel for her struggles; but, for all that, and setting aside higher considerations, the impression she leaves on our mind is that of a decidedly vulgar-minded woman—one whom we should not care for as an acquaintance, whom we should not seek as a friend, whom we should not desire for a relation, and whom we should scrupulously avoid for a governess.

There seem to have arisen in the novel-reading world some doubts as to who really wrote this book; and various rumours, more or less romantic, have been current in Mayfair, the metropolis of gossip, as to the authorship. For example, *Jane Eyre* is sentimentally assumed to have proceeded from the pen of Mr. Thackeray's governess, whom he had himself chosen as his model of Becky, and who, in mingled love and revenge, personified him in return as Mr. Rochester. In this case, it is evident that the author of *Vanity Fair,* whose own pencil makes him grey-haired, has had the best of it, though his children may have had the worst, having, at all events, succeeded in hitting that vulnerable point in the Becky bosom, which it is our firm belief no man born of woman, from her Soho to her Ostend days, had ever so much as grazed. To this ingenious rumour the coincidence of the second edition of *Jane Eyre* being dedicated to Mr. Thackeray has probably given rise. For our parts, we see no great interest in the question at all. The first edition of *Jane Eyre* purports to be edited by Currer Bell, one of a trio of brothers, or sisters, or cousins, by names Currer, Acton, and Ellis Bell, already known as the joint-authors of a volume of poems. The second edition the same—dedicated, however, 'by the author,' to Mr. Thackeray; and the dedication (itself an indubitable *chip* of Jane Eyre) signed Currer Bell. Author and editor therefore are one, and we are as much satisfied to accept this double individual under the name of 'Currer Bell,' as under any other, more or less euphonious. Whoever it be, it is a person who, with great mental powers, combines a total ignorance of the habits of society, a great coarseness of taste, and a heathenish doctrine of religion. And as these characteristics appear more or less in the writings of all three, Currer, Acton, and Ellis alike, for their poems differ less in degree of power than in kind, we are ready to accept the fact of their identity or of their relationship with equal satisfaction. At all events there can be no interest attached to the writer of *Wuthering Heights*—a novel succeeding *Jane Eyre,* and purporting to be written by Ellis Bell— unless it were for the sake of more individual reproba-

tion. For though there is a decided family likeness between the two, yet the aspect of the Jane and Rochester animals in their native state, as Catherine and Heathfield, is too odiously and abominably pagan to be palatable even to the most vitiated class of English readers. With all the unscrupulousness of the French school of novels it combines that repulsive vulgarity in the choice of its vice which supplies its own antidote. The question of authorship, therefore, can deserve a moment's curiosity only as far as *Jane Eyre* is concerned, and though we cannot pronounce that it appertains to a real Mr. Currer Bell and to no other, yet that it appertains to a man, and not, as many assert, to a woman, we are strongly inclined to affirm. Without entering into the question whether the power of the writing be above her, or the vulgarity below her, there are, we believe, minutiæ of circumstantial evidence which at once acquit the feminine hand. No woman—a lady friend, whom we are always happy to consult, assures us— makes mistakes in her own *métier*—no woman *trusses game* and garnishes dessert-dishes with the same hands, or talks of so doing in the same breath. Above all, no woman attires another in such fancy dresses as Jane's ladies assume—Miss Ingram coming down, irresistible, 'in a *morning* robe of sky-blue crape, a gauze azure scarf twisted in her hair!!' No lady, we understand, when suddenly roused in the night, would think of hurrying on '*a frock.*' They have garments more convenient for such occasions, and more becoming too. This evidence seems incontrovertible. Even granting that these incongruities were purposely assumed, for the sake of disguising the female pen, there is nothing gained; for if we ascribe the book to a woman at all, we have no alternative but to ascribe it to one who has, for some sufficient reason, long forfeited the society of her own sex.

And if by no woman, it is certainly also by no artist. The Thackeray eye has had no part there. There is not more disparity between the art of drawing Jane assumes and her evident total ignorance of its first principles, than between the report she gives of her own character and the conclusions we form for ourselves. Not but what, in another sense, the author may be classed as an artist of very high grade. Let him describe the simplest things in nature—a rainy landscape, a cloudy sky, or a bare moorside, and he shows the hand of a master; but the moment he talks of the art itself, it is obvious that he is a complete ignoramus.

We cannot help feeling that this work must be far from beneficial to that class of ladies whose cause it affects to advocate. Jane Eyre is not precisely the mouthpiece one would select to plead the cause of governesses, and it is therefore the greater pity that she has chosen it: for there is none we are convinced which, at the present time, more deserves and demands an earnest and judicious befriending. If these times puzzle us how to meet

the claims and wants of the lower classes of our depen-
dants, they puzzle and shame us too in the case of that
highest dependant of all, the governess—who is not
only entitled to our gratitude and respect by her position, but, in nine cases out of ten, by the circumstances
which reduced her to it. For the case of the governess is
so much the harder than that of any other class of the
community, in that they are not only quite as liable to
all the vicissitudes of life, but are absolutely supplied
by them. There may be, and are, exceptions to this rule,
but the real definition of a governess, in the English
sense, is a being who is our equal in birth, manners,
and education, but our inferior in worldly wealth. Take
a lady, in every meaning of the word, born and bred,
and let her father pass through the gazette, and she
wants nothing more to suit our highest *beau idéal* of a
guide and instructress to our children. We need the im-
prudencies, extravagancies, mistakes, or crimes of a
certain number of fathers, to sow that seed from which
we reap the harvest of governesses. There is no other
class of labourers for hire who are thus systematically
supplied by the misfortunes of our fellow-creatures.
There is no other class which so cruelly requires its
members to be, in birth, mind, and manners, above their
station, in order to fit them for their station. From this
peculiarity in their very qualifications for office result
all the peculiar and most painful anomalies of their professional existence. The line which severs the governess
from her employers is not one which will take care of
itself, as in the case of a servant. If she sits at table she
does not shock you—if she opens her mouth she does
not distress you—her appearance and manners are likely
to be as good as your own—her education rather better;
there is nothing upon the face of the thing to stamp her
as having been called to a different state of life from
that in which it has pleased God to place you; and therefore the distinction has to be kept up by a fictitious barrier which presses with cruel weight upon the mental
strength or constitutional vanity of a woman. People
talk of the prevailing vanity of governesses, and we
grant it in one sense fully—but how should it not be
so? If a governess have a grain of vanity in her composition, it is sought and probed for by every species of
slight and mortification, intentional or not, till it starts
into unnatural life beneath the irritation. She must be a
saint, or no woman at all, who can rise above those perpetual little dropping-water trials to which the self-love
of an averagely-placed governess is exposed. That fearful fact that the lunatic asylums of this country are supplied with a larger proportion of their inmates from the
ranks of young governesses than from any other class
of life, is a sufficient proof how seldom she can. But it
is not her vanity which sends her there, but her *wounded*
vanity—the distinction is great—and wounded vanity,
as all medical men will tell us, is the rock on which
most minds go to pieces.

Man cannot live by the head alone, far less woman. A
governess has no equals, and therefore can have no
sympathy. She is a burden and restraint in society, as all
must be who are placed ostensibly at the same table
and yet are forbidden to help themselves or to be helped
to the same viands. She is a bore to almost any gentleman, as a tabooed woman, to whom he is interdicted
from granting the usual privileges of the sex, and yet
who is perpetually crossing his path. She is a bore to
most ladies by the same rule, and a reproach too—for
her dull, fagging, bread-and-water life is perpetually
putting their pampered listlessness to shame. The servants invariably detest her, for she is a dependant like
themselves, and yet, for all that, as much their superior
in other respects as the family they both serve. Her pupils may love her, and she may take the deepest interest
in them, but they cannot be her friends. She must, to all
intents and purposes, live alone, or she transgresses that
invisible but rigid line which alone establishes the distance between herself and her employers.

We do not deny that there are exceptions to this statement—that there are many governesses who are treated
with an almost undue equality and kindness—that there
are many who suffer from slights which they entirely
make for themselves, and affect a humility which is
never needed—and also that there is no class in which
there are women so encroaching, so *exigeantes,* and so
disagreeable. But still these are exceptions, let them be
ever so numerous. The broad and real characteristics of
the governess's qualifications, position, and trials are
such as we have described, and must be such. Nor have
we brought them forward with any view, or hope, or
even with any wish to see them remedied, for in the inherent constitution of English habits, feelings, and
prejudices, there is no possibility that they should be.
We say English, for foreign life is far more favourable
to a governess's happiness. In its less stringent domestic habits, the company of a *teacher,* for she is nothing
more abroad, is no interruption—often an acquisition;
she herself, again, is pleased with that mere surface of
politeness and attention which would not satisfy an En-
glishwoman's heart or pride; the difference of birth,
too, is more obvious, from the non-existence in any
other country of an untitled aristocracy like our own.
But all this cannot be altered with us. We shall ever
prefer to place those immediately about our children
who have been born and bred with somewhat of the
same refinement as ourselves. We must ever keep them
in a sort of isolation, for it is the only means for maintaining that distance which the reserve of English manners and the decorum of English families exact. That
true justice and delicacy in the employer which would
make a sunshine even in a barren schoolroom must ever
be too rare to be depended upon. That familiarity which
should level all distinction a right-thinking governess
would scorn to accept;—all this must be continued as it
is. But there *is* one thing, the absence of which need

not be added to the other drawbacks of her lot; which would go far to compensate to her for the misfortunes which reduced her to this mode of life, and for the trials attendant upon it—for the years of chilly solitude through which the heart is kept shivering upon a diet that can never sufficiently warm it, and that in the longing season of youth—for the nothing less than maternal cares and solicitudes for which she reaps no maternal reward—for a life spent in harness from morning till night, and from one year's end to another—for the old age and incapacity creeping on and threatening to deprive her even of that mode of existence which habit has made endurable—there is something that would compensate for all this, and that is *better pay*. We quite agree with Mr. Rochester, in answer to one of Jane's sententious speeches, that 'most freeborn things will submit to anything for a salary;' in other words, that most men and women of average sense will put up with much that is fatiguing to do, or irksome to bear, if you make it worth their while; and we know of no process of reasoning by which it can be proved that governesses, as is too often required from them, can dispense with this potent stimulus.

There is something positively usurious in the manner with which the misfortunes of the individual or the general difficulty of the times is now-a-days constantly taken advantage of to cut the stipend of the governess down to the lowest ratio that she will accept. The Jew raises his rate of interest because the heedless spendthrift will pay anything to get that loan he needs; and by the same rule the Christian parent lowers the salary because the friendless orphan will take anything rather than be without a situation. Each traffics with the necessities, and not with the merits of the case; but the one proceeding is so much the harder than the other, because it presses not upon a selfish, thoughtless, extravagant man, but upon a poor, patient, and industrious woman. 'And they are very glad to get that, I can tell you,' is the cold-hearted rejoinder, if you expostulate on the injustice of throwing all the labour of the teacher and many of the chief duties of a parent upon the shoulders of a young woman, for the remuneration of thirty or even twenty pounds a-year. It may be quite true that she is glad to get even this; and if so, it is very deplorable: but this has no relation to the services exacted and the assistance given; and these should be more especially the standard where the plaintiff, as in the case of the governess, possesses no means of resistance. Workmen may rebel, and tradesmen may combine, not to let you have their labour or their wares under a certain rate; but the governess has no refuge—no escape; she is a needy *lady,* whose services are of far too precious a kind to have any stated market value, and is therefore left to the mercy, or what they call the *means,* of the family that engages her.

But is not this an all-sufficient plea? it may be urged. If parents have not the means to give higher salaries, what can they do? We admit the argument, though it might be easily proved how often the cheap governess and the expensive servant are to be found in the same establishment; but the question is in truth whether they have the means or the excuse to keep a governess at all? Whether it be conscientiously honest to engage the best years of a hard-working, penniless woman, without the power of making her an adequate return? The fine-ladyism of the day has, we regret to observe, crept into a lower class than that one was wont to associate it with, and where, from its greater sacrifice of the comforts and rights of others, it is still more objectionable. Women, whose husbands leave them in peace from morning till night, for counting-houses or lawyers' offices—certainly leave them with nothing better to do than to educate and attend to their children—must now, forsooth, be keeping ill-paid governesses for those duties which one would hope a peeress only unwillingly relinquishes. Women, from whom society requires nothing but that they should quietly and unremittingly do that for which their station offers them the happy leisure, must now treat themselves to one of those *pro-mammas* who, owing to various causes, more or less distressing, have become so plentiful that they may be had *cheap!* If more governesses find a penurious maintenance by these means, more mothers are encouraged to neglect those duties, which, one would have thought, they would have been as jealous of as of that first duty of all that infancy requires from them. It is evident, too, that by this unfair demand the supply has been suddenly increased. Farmers and tradespeople are now educating their daughters for governesses as a mode of advancing them a step in life, and thus a number of underbred young women have crept into the profession who have brought down the value of salaries and interfered with the rights of those whose birth and misfortunes leave them no other refuge.

Even in the highest rate of salary—in the hundred, and hundred and twenty guineas, which so few now enjoy—so very few get beyond—the advantage is too much on the one side not to be, in some respects, an injustice to the other. There has been no luxury invented in social life equal to that which gives a mother all the pleasure of her children's society, and the reward of their improvement, and at the same time relieves her of the trouble of either. At the highest salary, it is the cheapest luxury that can be had; and yet a mother satisfies her conscience when she gives the patient drudge who not only retails to her children every accomplishment and science of the day, but also performs the part of maternal factotum in every other department, the notable sum of 40*l.* or 50*l.* a-year; and then, when she has lived in the family for perhaps fifteen years, and finished the sixth daughter, dismisses her with every recommendation as 'a treasure,' but without a fragment of help in the shape of a pension or provision to ease her further labours or approaching incapacity. In nine cases out of ten, the old servant is far more cared for than the old governess.

Some amiable Mrs. Armytage will be ready to say— 'We have nothing to do with the governess's most frequent cause of need for a larger salary: we are not required to maintain her family as well as herself.' True enough. At the same time women with women's hearts might be expected to bear in mind that the same reasons that have placed her in this position will, with rare exceptions, be the drain upon her the whole time she is in it; and that though she may squeeze something out of the smallest salary to help disabled parents or orphan sisters, she is deprived of all possibility of laying up a provision for herself.

While we therefore applaud heartily the efforts for their comfort and relief which have been made within the last few years, in the establishment of the Governesses' Benevolent Institution, we look with sorrow, and almost with horror, at the disclosures which those efforts have brought to light. There is no document which more painfully exposes the peculiar tyranny of our present state of civilization than those pages in the Report of this Society containing the list of candidates for the few and small annuities which the Institution is as yet in the condition to give. We know of nothing, in truth or fiction, more affecting than the sad and simple annals of these afflicted and destitute ladies, many of them with their aristocratic names, who, having passed through that course of servitude which, as we have shown, is peculiarly and inevitably deprived of most of those endearing sympathies which gladden this life, are now left in their old age or sickness without even the absolute necessaries for existence. With minds also which, from their original refinement and constant cultivation, have the keener sense of the misery and injustice of their lot; for the delicate and well-bred lady we at first congratulated ourselves on having engaged in our family is equally the same when we cast her off to shift for herself. What a mockery must all this thankless acquisition of knowledge, which has been the object of her study and the puff in her credentials, appear to her now! Conversant with several languages—skilled in many accomplishments—crammed with every possible fact in history, geography, and the use of the globes—and scarcely the daily bread to put into her mouth! If there be any of our female readers so spoiled by prosperity as to magnify small annoyances into real evils—if there be one who, forgetting

> 'What she is, and where—
> A sinner in a life of care'—

is unmindful of the blessings of a *home,* because it contains some trial which it is difficult to bear—let her look through this list now before us of her hard-working

and ill-requited fellow-gentlewomen, and be thankful to God that her name does not stand *there.* We give a few specimens—omitting the surnames, as not required here:—

'Miss Juliana———, aged sixty-seven. Became a governess at the age of sixteen, being left, by her father's death, without any provision. Has received too low salaries to save, and has now no prospect but the hope of being enabled to support herself by needlework while she has health and can obtain employment, and an occasional present from some of her few friends. Reference: Mrs. T. Babington, 14, Blessington Street, Dublin.'

'Miss Amelia———, aged sixty-one. Father, a naval officer, died when she was an infant, and her mother when she was sixteen—compelling her to become a governess. Unable to save on account of small salaries, ill health, and the want of a home. No income whatever, having only occasional assistance from an old friend who will have nothing to leave her at her death. Reference: Miss Anderson, 32, Cadogan Street, Chelsea.'

'Miss Catherine———, aged sixty-three. Became a governess on the insolvency of her father. The support of an aged father and afflicted mother prevented her laying by for herself. Her mother, dependent upon her for twenty-six years, died of cancer. Present income less than 5*s.* a-week. Reference: Miss Boycatt, Great Ormesby, Yarmouth.'

'Miss Margaret———, aged seventy-one. Fifty years a governess, having been left an orphan at three years old, and the uncle who meant to provide for her being lost at sea. Assisted her relations as far as possible from her salaries. She is now very feeble, and her health failing fast. Her entire support is an annuity of fourteen guineas.'

'Miss Dorothea———, aged fifty-four. Father a surgeon in the army; governess, chiefly in Scotch families, for thirty years; was the chief support of her mother and the younger members of her family from 1811 to 1838, when her mother died, leaving her with failing health through over exertion, and only 5*l.* a-year from the Government Compassionate Fund. Reference: R. W. Saunders, Esq., Nunwick Hall, near Penrith.'

'Miss Mary———, aged sixty-five. Her parents having lost all their property, she never had a home, and has devoted her whole life to her profession, supporting herself and her father, who attained his eightieth year. But she has been unable to provide for herself; and with failing health and sight, her income (an uncertain one) never exceeds 10*l.* a-year. Reference: Mrs. Campbell, Bickfield, Ipswich.'

'Miss Mary———, aged sixty-four. Her father formerly possessed very large property; but having many children, and having suffered heavy losses, he was unable to make any provision for his family. She has devoted her whole life to tuition, but has unhappily been unable to make any fund for old age; and now, in the decline of life, and with failing health, has no income whatsoever. Reference: the Countess Poulett, 5, Tilney Street, Park Lane.'

'Miss Ann————, aged sixty-two. Has been a governess all her life. Supported and educated two orphan nieces and a nephew, and apprenticed the latter. He is since dead; as is her eldest niece, after five years' illness, which at last destroyed her intellects. The consequent expenses were ruinous; and she is now companion to a lady for her board—an engagement which ceases with the present year. Reference: Mrs. Bradley, Hark Hill, Clapham.'

We need add no more from this touching list of ninety ladies, all more or less reduced to indigence by the edifying fulfilment of their natural duties, and who, after a life of labour and struggle, presented themselves, in November, 1847, as candidates for four annuities of 15*l.* each. Of the ninety it seems seven only had incomes exceeding 20*l.*, two of those derived from public institutions; sixteen had incomes varying from 36*s.* to 14*l.*, and the rest had no certain means of livelihood at all. These facts are serious lessons to all, but especially to two classes of society—to those parents who are living in ease and affluence without a thought of their children's future provision, and to those who allow themselves the luxury of a governess without either the means of remunerating her adequately, or the right conscientious desire to do it.

But if, as a people, we are, from love of habit or hatred of change, prone to submit too long to abuses, and careless how they press upon the weaker classes of the community, we are, it is to be hoped, active in assistance and redress, when once roused to a sense of its necessity. This Governesses' Benevolent Institution, though still comparatively in its infancy, is an important step towards the atonement for past neglect. If it be, in the nature of the thing, impossible to shed more social sunshine upon a governess's life, and almost equally so to secure to her a full compensation for her labours, the public have at all events now been shown the way how to assist in protecting her interests, increasing her comforts and advantages, and solacing her old age. The distinct objects of the society are these—1st, to bestow temporary assistance on governesses in distress; 2nd, to found elective annuities for aged governesses; 3rd, to assist governesses in purchasing annuities upon government security; 4th, to provide a home for governesses at a low expense during their intervals of engagement; and, 5th, to carry on for them a system of registration free of expense. The two first objects—that of temporary assistance, and the annuity for the aged governesses—call for a considerable increase of resources—but not more, we hope, than it is reasonable to look for from the liberality and right feeling of a British public. How justly the temporary-assistance fund has been bestowed may be seen by a glance into the First Report, where cases, of which we give a few samples, occur in painful reiteration:—

'Obliged to maintain an aged sister, who has no one else to depend upon.'—'Entirely impoverished by endeavouring to uphold her father's efforts in business.'—'Supported both her aged parents, and three orphans of a widowed sister.'—'Has helped to bring up seven younger brothers and sisters.'—'Incapable of taking another situation from extreme nervous excitement, brought on by over exertion and anxiety.'—'Had the entire support of both parents for nearly twenty years.'

As to the annuities, the number already founded, including the five ladies elected on the 16th of this last November, amounts to thirty-two, consisting of one of 30*l.*, four of 20*l.*, and the remainder of 15*l.* each; but it is hoped that this branch of the society may be so supported and endowed as to secure the foundation of several fresh annuities, at each succeeding May and November, for some years to come.

To these several departments of charitable purpose has been added one, within the last year, which, as being more consonant with the habits and usages of the olden time, is more especially attractive to our feelings—we mean the commencement of that fund for the building and endowment of an asylum for aged governesses, which was made known to the votaries of *Vanity Fair* last June by the great fancy sale at Chelsea. This is not precisely the way our forefathers would have adopted to start a scheme of this character, but this is also not the occasion to discuss so much-involving a subject. The sale, at all events, realised a considerable sum of money, and Becky's stall, we have no doubt, more than any other there.

The 'Queen's College for Female Education, and for granting Certificates of Qualification to Governesses' is another new establishment which promises very essentially to promote the interests of this class of ladies. We have not space to enter into its many merits: we would only observe, that, as the real and highest responsibility and recommendation of an *English* governess must ever rest more upon her moral than her literary qualifications, the plan of subjecting her to an examination upon the latter appears to us neither wise nor fair. This plan, it is true, has been pursued with tolerable success abroad, but it must be kept in mind that the foreign governess is a mere teacher, whose duties cease with the school-room hours, who has her three-months' holiday in the year, and who has, in short, little or nothing to do with the moral guidance of her pupils. What we, on the contrary, require and seek for our children is not a learned machine stamped and ticketed with credentials like a piece of patent goods, but rather a woman endowed with that sound principle, refinement, and sense, which no committee of education in the world could ascertain or certify. At the best, all parents of sense must be aware that no governess can teach an art or accomplishment like a regular professor, and that her vocation is rather the encouraging and directing her pupils in such pursuits, than the positive imparting of them. We perceive that the submission to this examination is, for the present, nominally optional; but it is easy to foresee that if some ladies, in order to obtain the promised certificate, go through it, it will soon be made a necessary condition with all. This we consider unfair. As it is, the advantage is already sufficiently on the English mother's side in the balance. If she wishes for the same system as that pursued on the continent in one respect, she should adopt it in all, and she would soon discover how greatly she was the loser.

North British Review (review date May-August 1849)

SOURCE: "Noteworthy Novels: *Emilia Wyndham, Jane Eyre,* and *Fanny Hervey.*" *North British Review* 11 (May-August 1849): 475-93.

[*In the following excerpt, the critic offers a somewhat negative evaluation of* Jane Eyre, *viewing Jane's character as "hard" and "angular" and thus inappropriate for a woman.*]

But it is now full time we were looking after Miss Eyre, for we can see her little lip beginning to pout at the thought of being so long neglected; and the first favour we shall do her, by way of restoring her equanimity, will be to acquit her of the charge of conventional vulgarity, which has been brought against her by a contemporary. There is an old proverb which prohibits the throwing of stones to those who dwell in palaces of glass; and we think there is enough that comes to light, in the pages of our contemporary, to show that a bandying of conventionalities was a sport in which he could not very safely indulge. There is a continual anxiety to display his acquaintance with the little social peculiarities of civilized life, which we never find in those to whom they are habitual; and there are observations on blue-crape dresses, and other pieces of female gear, which would lead us to suppose that the article (if written by a man at all) was the production of a man-milliner; and if Mr. Mantalini had not long since become "a body," we should infallibly have suspected him. Notwithstanding, then, this authority, we venture to assert that, neither conventionally nor absolutely, is Jane vulgar; and we go so far as to say that, with her organization, mental and physical, (unless the book had been a blunder from beginning to end, which is not alleged,) it was scarcely possible that she should be so. Where great intellectual power and activity, accompanied, as it usually is, by the gift of entering into the feelings of others, is united to a nervous temperament of the most sensitive texture, the result must be a person to whom conventional refinements, which others must painfully learn, (and of which they are sometimes painfully vain,) will be intuitive. We have then present in the individual the causes which have slowly given

rise to such habits in the mass; and from the source from which they sprang originally, it will require little tutoring to make them spring again. The process of their first production will be re-enacted *en petit;* and if Jane Eyre had been the daughter of Robinson Crusoe, and brought up in the island of Juan Fernandez, she would not have been without them. But we are by no means clear that graver faults might not have been assigned to Jane. Though there is nothing that is coarse as a human being, there is much about her that is hard, and angular, and indelicate as a woman. Notwithstanding her love for Rochester, we feel that she is a creature more of the intellect than of the affections; and the matter-of-course way in which she, a girl of nineteen, who had seen nothing of the world, receives his revelations of his former life, is both revolting and improbable. To a pure woman they would surely have soiled, for the time at least, the image of him who related them; and for the probability of the story, if for no better reason, we think that different feelings ought to have been assigned to her on this occasion. One of Mrs. Marsh's little homilies would here have been a natural and seemly tribute to virtue. We cannot blame her for ultimately falling in love with Rochester, for in doing so she did nothing more than every woman who has read the book has done since. Proud, tyrannical, violent, and selfish though he was, he had the element of power, which, involuntarily and almost unconsciously, in a woman's eyes, supplies the deficiency of every other good quality; and his system of wooing, apparently indifferent almost to rudeness, was consistent with the theory of the greatest masters in the art. Hear the opinion of Goethe, by the mouth of the "Erfahrene:"

> "Geh den Weibern zart entgegen,
> Du gewinnst sie, auf mein Wort;
> Und wer rasch ist, und verwegen,
> Kommt vielleicht noch besser fort;
> Doch wem wenig dran gelegen
> Scheinet, ob er reizt und rührt,
> Der beleidigt, der verführt."[1]

To the same effect Sir John Suckling's exquisite little poem—"Why so pale?"—will at once suggest itself to our readers; and though the witty knight died young, there is little question that, in this matter at least, he was entitled to the character of an "Erfahrener."

The stratagem thus practised, and thus recommended, is a tolerably obvious one when we consider it. As Goethe very justly remarks, the secret consists in calling forth the "amour propre" of the party attacked, and enlisting it on our side. It is the male counterplot to female coquetterie, and the *modus operandi* consists in throwing upon the party to be gained the *onus* of attacking, and affecting the defensive, in order that we may get the conduct of the siege into our own hands. If the party on whom the duty of besieging has thus been imposed, does not suddenly lose heart, an accident which it is part of the *ruse* to prevent, the game is with the original besieger, for though it may not be always possible to gain a victory, it is always possible to lose one. Such was precisely the game which Rochester played with Jane Eyre. By an affectation of indifference he contrived, in the midst of his passion, to retain the air of superiority, which was one of the principal charms which belonged to him, and to bring matters at last to such a pass that her pride consisted, not in resisting, but in being vanquished. But the weapon which Rochester used, happily for the tone of general society, will be effective, for the most part, only in the hands of a thoroughly well-bred man—skilful though he was, his conduct seems often to tread very hard on the borders of rudeness—almost of brutality; and even to such a character as Jane, it must have been revolting, but for other most attractive qualities which he possessed. He had one of the most enviable attributes of genius, that of sympathizing and of calling forth sympathy. There was no want of compass in his spiritual scale; and whatever note you struck he could speedily supply you with a chord. Jane says, that he "suited her to the finest fibre of her nature." He who reads Swift's "Journal to Stella," will see this quality exhibited in its highest perfection, in a character in some respects resembling that of Rochester, and it is equally conspicuous in Goethe at every turn, and we all know how fatally they both were beloved. This power of entering into the nature of another, is indeed one of the most indispensable qualities of the poet—it is the feeler which he stretches out into the waters of life, and in the possession of it, as in many other respects, Mr. Rochester comes nearer to the man of genius than any hero of romance that we know. He is, besides, a thoroughly manly character, which we do not find to be always the case, even in those whose will is strong. He has no littlenesses at all, he neither frets himself nor others about trifles, he never quarrels with servants, or indeed with anybody lightly, he has no crotchets, no avarice, and above all, no vanity, though abundance of pride. Nobody "toadies" or can "toady" him—he has neither foes nor favourites, though he might well have had friends, and the absence of them is perhaps the greatest blemish in the book. Male companionship could not have been wanting to a character so masculine. It is in consequence of these qualities that even his selfishness, like his rudeness, becomes less revolting. It is rather an assertion of a right over, than the infliction of a wrong upon, his fellow-creatures. There was a sort of instinctive giving way by those around him, from the feeling that his requirements were the more urgent. Jane's feeling at all events seems to have been precisely that expressed by the poet, where he says—

> "Woman is the lesser man, and all her passions
>   match'd with mine,
> Are as moonlight is to sunlight, are as water is to
>   wine."

The mutual relation of the two characters is, indeed, most admirable. In contemplating the one, we feel its truth from recognising its adaptation to the other. Mankind is said to be manufactured in pairs, and every one of us is supposed to have his counterpart in petticoats—if he could but find her. Rochester had been so long engaged in the search, that he had begun to doubt of the truth of the maxim; he was long past the admiring and the wondering age; women, like most things in life, had become a bore to him, and if any one had told him that he yet was destined to love, he would have said that nothing could be less likely. But the moment that he encountered Jane, he felt that his hour was come—the complement of his own nature stood before him; she was not what he anticipated, what his imagination had pictured, he was disappointed rather with himself than with her, but she filled up the measure of his being such as it was, and since he could not be indifferent, he must e'en be contented. It was no longer a matter of choice, but of necessity, and the complete self-consciousness which he at once exhibited is very characteristic of the manner of man he was. The difference between the male and female character is well preserved in this respect. Jane is long doubtful—she suspects that she is in love, but she is not quite certain; whereas Rochester never doubts for a moment, and the whole of the affair with the vain and stupid Miss Ingram was intended, not to test himself, but Jane. Now Jane from the very first was more in love than he was, but she had not courage to examine the mystery of her own heart, and the consequence was that she deceived herself about her feelings, as women usually do.

The great defect in the otherwise most successful character of Rochester, consists in representing his life as utterly objectless. This we look upon as a positive artistical blunder. No such man could have been contented, during his whole life, to sit tamely and silently by, and see the affairs of mankind, his own included, managed by others. Duty being altogether out of the question, a sort of internal necessity would have prompted him, sooner or later, to make his voice heard. Ambition, in some form, is seldom wanting to the powerful, and Rochester's love of enjoyment, which seems never to have gained the mastery over his reason, so far from indicating an inaptitude for affairs, went rather to prove the completeness of his nature. Literature may not have been consistent with his early training, and he was too wealthy for a profession; but politics, and social economy, in all their departments, were open to him. He might have been an enthusiastic aspirant after a glorious future, or a pious conservator of the blessings of the past, and in one character or other it is probable he would have sought the arena, if for no other purpose than to flee from the misery of his domestic hearth.

Of the crime which Rochester committed in attempting to marry Jane whilst his wife was alive, we do not think

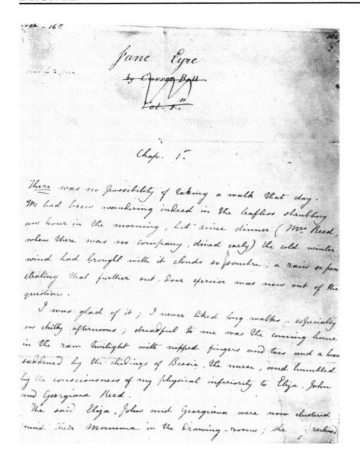

First manuscript page from Jane Eyre, *1847.*

it necessary to say much. A transgression of so heinous a nature, as to come within the reach even of human laws, is not likely to become attractive in the eyes of many. But there are more latent objections to the tendency of this powerful book, which we are apt to overlook on a first perusal, and of the perniciousness of which we can only judge properly, when we have seen them developed in other works, professedly proceeding from the same source. In Jane herself there is a recklessness about right and wrong which is very alarming, and although in the great action of her life, that of leaving Rochester, she valiantly resists a very powerful temptation, and her general conduct is not very reprehensible, the motive by which she is actuated is seldom a higher one than worldly prudence; and there is often a kind of regretful looking-back, which makes us fear that the fate of Lot's wife may overtake her. In the other novels, *Wuthering Heights,* and *The Tenant of Wildfellhall,* these, like all the other faults of **Jane Eyre,** are magnified a thousand-fold; and the only consolation which we have in reflecting upon them, arises from the conviction that they will never be very generally read. With *Wuthering Heights* we found it totally impossible to get along. It commences by introducing the reader to

a perfect pandemonium of low and brutal creatures, who wrangle with each other in language too disgusting for the eye or the ear to tolerate, and unredeemed, so far as we could see, by one single particle either of wit or humour, or even psychological truth, for the characters are as false as they are loathsome. How it terminates we know not, for the society which we encountered on our first introduction was so little to our taste, that we took the liberty of declining the honour of a farther acquaintance. *The Tenant of Wildfellhall* has a better beginning, and the conclusion is an unimpeachable instance of poetical justice; but in the body of the tale there are scenes in which the author seems to pride himself in bringing his reader into the closest possible proximity with naked vice, and there are conversations such as we had hoped never to see printed in English. There is a coarseness and brutality in the manner of speaking of almost all the characters, never to be met with among gentlefolks, however depraved; and there is a continual use of "slang" throughout the book, even where the author speaks in his own person, which might well have justified our contemporary, if he had pronounced over it, instead of Jane Eyre, the social anathema of vulgarity. There is even a frequent inaccuracy of style, and an apparently involuntary slipping into provincialisms, which would lead us to think that, if Currer Bell be the editor of Acton Bell's books, as would seem from their title-pages, he must have been napping on the occasion of this publication.

But with all their faults, there is no denying the family resemblance between these unpleasing productions, and their more happily constituted elder sister. They are vigorous dwarfs, in whose mis-shapen limbs the idea of the same powerful nature is still to be traced; of whom we can say, that if they had not been dwarfs, they would have been strong and beautiful beings. Their fault is deformity, not weakness. Nor is this resemblance perceptible in the characterization only. In the scenery it is even more striking. There is always a wild upland district, with the wind howling through a few gnarled and weather-beaten Scotch firs, or an old untenanted manor-house, buried in trees, and haunted by horrors—not supernatural. In the colouring, so to speak, there is an unity of tone throughout. It is *grey,* and there is an evident partiality for rough and boisterous weather. The artist has a contempt for "the pretty," which might have satisfied our poor friend David Scott himself; but the sketches show an acquaintance with nature in her rougher moods not often to be met with. In two or three words we have the scene so vividly before us, that we seem to experience with our bodily senses the phenomena described. The following picture of a "drear November day" makes us cold and comfortless. "Afar it offered a pale blank of mist and cloud; near, a scene of wet lawn and storm-beat shrub, with ceaseless rain sweeping away wildly before a long and lamentable blast."

We shall not attempt to resolve the much agitated question of the sex of the author of these remarkable works. All that we shall say on the subject is, that if they are the productions of a woman, she must be a woman pretty nearly unsexed; and Jane Eyre strikes us as a personage much more likely to have sprung ready armed from the head of a man, and that head a pretty hard one, than to have experienced, in any shape, the softening influence of female creation.

We would gladly have indulged ourselves in farther speculations on the ever-suggestive subject of *Jane Eyre,* and illustrated what we formerly hinted at as the true secret of her importance, by dwelling at some length on the peculiarities of that class of young ladies, of which she has been recognised as the type, and which consequently is now beginning to be known by the epithet of "Jane Eyrish;" but our limits forbid us to linger much longer in such fair companionship; and there is a new divinity who has lately made so great an impression on our imagination that we cannot resist the temptation of filling up the number of the graces by still adding her to our group.

Notes

1. Which may be rendered or approximated thus:—

> He who meek and mildly sues
> Shall win her—if the maiden choose;
> He who woos with better pluck
> Will have, believe me, better luck;
> But he who still the matter views
> As a piece of careless sport,
> Will surprise and storm the fort.

Donald H. Ericksen (essay date fall 1966)

SOURCE: Ericksen, Donald H. "Imagery as Structure in *Jane Eyre*." *The Victorian Newsletter* 30 (fall 1966): 18-22.

[In the following essay, Ericksen discerns in Jane Eyre *a "substructure of imagery that intensifies our involvement with the main character."]*

It is easily demonstrated that *Jane Eyre* contains a number of implausible circumstances that in the hands of a lesser author would be fatal to the credibility of the narrative. We tend, however, to overlook or forgive these weaknesses for we are moved in this novel by a substructure of imagery that intensifies our involvement with the main character, an involvement that one critic[1] considers a characteristic unique in its time. Because Jane Eyre stands in the place of the author, it is through Jane's consciousness that we see the other characters. She is intensely aware of everything that surrounds her

and colors, or is colored by, her moods. Thus, the imagery of the novel, imagery primarily involving the moon and arboreal nature, reflects her own emotional state and that of the other characters and underlies the melodramatic surface of the novel, giving it a poetic depth and intensity that few critics have recognized.[2] This imagery, in addition to reflecting the loneliness and isolation of the protagonist, possesses a pronounced romantic and, at times, even erotic character that parallels the main narrative movement of the novel. Although this amatory element has been identified, never, to my knowledge, has its function in the nature imagery been examined at any length.[3] This nature imagery, along with its intense amatory elements, as it parallels the main events of the story of Jane Eyre clearly serves as the main source of the novel's power.

The story of Jane Eyre is the search of a neglected and lonely young girl for love and kindness. Even the earliest pages of the book show the wintry nature of Jane's youth, for they are filled with somber references to rain, sleet, and penetrating winter winds that howl sorrowfully about the eaves of Gateshead. It is always January in the heart of little Jane Eyre, especially under the unfriendly care of Mrs. Reed at Gateshead, as the following typical passage shows:

> . . . the shrubbery was quite still: the black frost reigned, unbroken by sun or breeze, through the grounds. I covered my head and arms with the skirt of my frock, and went out to walk in a part of the plantation which was quite sequestered: but I found no pleasure in the silent trees, the falling fir-cones, the congealed relics of autumn, russet leaves, swept by past winds in heaps, and now stiffened together. I leaned against a gate, and looked into an empty field where no sheep were feeding, where the short grass was nipped and blanched. It was a very gray day; a most opaque sky, "onding on snaw," canopied all; thence flakes fell at intervals, which settled on the hard path and on the hoary lea without melting. I stood, a wretched child enough, whispering to myself over and over again, "What shall I do?—what shall I do?"[4]

The barrenness, coldness, and essential hostility of this world, and Jane's subjective response to it, is shown repeatedly by such nature imagery early in the narrative. It is one of the unique characteristics of this novel that most of the significant imagery involves trees, forests, shrubbery, and like objects. The palette used to describe this wintry world is appropriately limited to whites, greys, and blacks as befits the emotional barrenness of Jane's early life and her subsequent perceptions of it. Only at Thornfield, later, is there a shift to the vivid and intense colors of summer and of love.

Jane is eventually sent away to Lowood, but there the drizzly January in her soul is still unrelieved:

> . . . at the latter end of January, all was wintry blight and brown decay. I shuddered as I stood and looked round me: it was an inclement day for outdoor exer-

cise; not positively rainy, but darkened by drizzling yellow fog; all underfoot was still soaking wet with the floods of yesterday.

(I, 57)

And even after May comes with days of "blue sky" and "placid sunshine" and Lowood becomes "all green, all flowery," the area where Lowood lies becomes "the cradle of fog and fogbred pestilence; which, quickening with the quickening spring . . . breathed typhus . . ." (I, 94, *et passim*). These descriptions of a nature so sterile and lonely occur repeatedly in the early chapters of the book and clearly parallel the emotional state of Jane Eyre, thus becoming, in fact, impressionistic images.

While at Lowood, however, Jane's description of her drawings reveals the first glimmerings of a new kind of imagery that is to be associated with Thornfield in general and Mr. Rochester in particular:

> . . . I feasted instead on the spectacle of ideal drawings, which I saw in the dark; all the work of my own hands: freely pencilled houses and trees, picturesque rocks and ruins, Cuyp-like groups of cattle, sweet paintings of butterflies hovering over unblown roses, of birds picking at ripe cherries, of wrens' nests enclosing pearl-like eggs, wreathed about with young ivy sprays.
>
> (I, 92)

Here is a conceptualization of nature, quite romantic and idealized but filled with references to lushness and fruition, representing a pale but significant anticipation of the erotic nature imagery that will surround Thornfield.

After surviving eight years at Lowood, Jane journeys to Thornfield and her new position as governess. Her first impression of Thornfield mansion is that it is surrounded by an array of mighty old thorn trees ". . . strong, knotty, and broad as oaks . . ." (I, 125). This imagery is often applied to Mr. Rochester whose corresponding strength and will comprise his foremost characteristics. But the moon, in this instance particularly, becomes the dominant image. When it arises in association with Rochester, as it does with other romantic characters in *Villette*,[5] it functions as a dual symbol of sexual fulfillment and chastity. For example, as Jane nears Thornfield, just before her first encounter with Rochester, and looks down at its woods and dark rookery rising against the west, she sees the moon and feels its strange effect on her:

> On the hill-top above me sat the rising moon; pale yet as a cloud, but brightening momently: she looked over Hay, which half lost in trees, sent up a blue smoke from its few chimneys; it was yet a mile distant, but in the absolute hush I could hear plainly its thin murmurs of life. My ear too felt the flow of currents; in what dales and depths I could not tell. . . .
>
> (I, 141)

On the appearance of the moon she hears the sound of hoofbeats, and her first meeting with her master takes place. Afterward, as she lingers on the lawn, the moon becomes as mystically compelling as her future love for the mysterious, dark Mr. Rochester:

> . . . both my eyes and spirit seemed drawn from the gloomy house—from the gray hollow filled with rayless cells, as it appeared to me—to that sky expanded before me,—a blue sea absolved from taint of cloud; the moon ascending it in solemn march; her orb seeming to look up as she left the hill tops, from behind which she had come, far and farther below her, and aspired to the zenith, midnight-dark in its fathomless depth and measureless distance: and for those trembling stars that followed her course, they made my heart tremble, my veins glow when I viewed them.
>
> (I, 148)

After the fortune-telling incident and the arrival of Mr. Mason from the West Indies, the moon appears not only as a romantic symbol of Jane's aspiring love but as a premonitory image:

> I had forgotten to draw my curtain . . . the moon, which was full and bright (for the night was fine), came in her course to that space in the sky opposite my casement, and looked in at me through the unveiled panes, her glorious gaze roused me. Awaking in the dead of night, I opened my eyes on her disk—silver-white and crystal-clear. It was beautiful, but too solemn: I half rose, and stretched my arm to draw the curtain.
>
> Good God! What a cry!
>
> (I, 266)

Later, after her return to Thornfield from attending the dying Mrs. Reed at Gateshead, the moon once again functions as an image of love, here described in terms suggestive of the mysterious and romantic East:

> It was now the sweetest hour of the twenty-four. . . . Where the sun had gone down . . . with the light of red jewel and furnace flame. . . . The east had its own charm . . . its own modest gem, a rising and solitary star: soon it would boast the moon; but she was yet beneath the horizon.
>
> (II, 10)

But the most striking employment of this imagery takes place after she discovers that Rochester is married and realizes that Rochester wishes her to overcome this barrier by entering into an illicit relationship. On this occasion the moon serves as an image of chastity:

> . . . the gleam was such as the moon imparts to vapours, she is about to sever. I watched her come—watched with the strangest anticipation; as though some word of doom were to be written on her disk. She broke forth as never moon yet burst from cloud: a hand first penetrated the sable folds and waved them away; then, not a moon, but a white human form shone in the azure,

inclining a glorious brow earthward. It gazed and gazed on me. It spoke to my spirit: immeasurably distant was the tone, yet so near, it whispered in my heart—

"My daughter, flee temptation!"

(II, 105)

When Jane accepts Rochester's proposal of marriage before she learns of his insane wife, the moon, she notes, is strangely absent. When Jane receives Rochester's telepathic call for help, she is in a room flooded with moonlight.[6] Thus, the moon serves as one powerful strand of the nature imagery that forms such an important part of the substructure of this novel.

But a more important part of the substructure seems to be the arboreal imagery, particularly in its erotic aspects when associated with the love scenes involving Rochester. For example, Jane's most important meetings with Rochester seem to take place almost always in the outdoors or in a garden. As in the following passage, Rochester is typically seen in a garden setting among roses:

> He strayed down a walk edged with box; with apple trees, pear trees, and cherry trees on one side, and a border on the other, full of all sorts of old-fashioned flowers, stocks, sweet-williams, primroses, pansies, mingled with southern wood, sweet-briar, and various fragrant herbs. They were fresh now as a succession of April showers and gleams, followed by a lovely spring morning, could make them: the sun was just entering the dappled east, and his light illumined the wreathed and dewey orchard trees and shone down the quiet walks under them.
>
> "Jane, will you have a flower?"
>
> He gathered a half-blown rose, the first on the bush, and offered it to me.

(I, 279)

Similarly, any imagery preceding Jane's view of Rochester usually contains references to roses, trees, foliage, and so forth. For example, when Jane returns from Gateshead she crosses various fields and remarks how full the hedges are of roses and regrets she cannot gather any. She passes a tall briar, a sure sign of Rochester, which is shooting "leafy and flowery branches across the path," and then she sees Mr. Rochester.

Perhaps the most striking example of this kind of erotic nature imagery is associated with the ensuing meeting that just precedes the climax of the book. The midsummer evenings are described as "a band of Italian days," trees are "in their dark prime," even hedges are "full-leaved." The moon, as described earlier, is about to rise opposite a western sky where a sun "had gone down . . . with the light of red jewel and furnace flame" (II, 10). And as Jane enters the garden, she notes as follows:

> . . . a subtle, well-known scent—that of a cigar—stole from some window . . . I went into the orchard. No nook in the grounds more sheltered and more Eden-like; it was full of trees, it bloomed with flowers . . . a winding walk, bordered with laurels and terminating in a giant horse-chestnut, circled at the base by a seat, led down to the fence. Here one could wander unseen. While such honey-dew fell, such silence reigned, such gloaming gathered, I felt as if I could haunt such shade for ever: but in threading the flower and fruit-parterres . . . my step is stayed— . . . once more by a warning fragrance.

(II, 10-11)

It is important to note the shift from past to present tense—a common device used by the author to convey a sense of emotional intensity and produce correspondingly greater reader involvement. Not only does the description of the garden become increasingly erotic in its reference to fruit-bearing branches, ripeness, and manifold other signs of a procreant nature, but the actions of the two main characters in this little Eden resemble a romantic game of hide-and-seek.

> Sweet briar and southernwood, jasmine, pink, and rose have long been yielding their evening sacrifice of incense: this new scent is neither of shrub nor flower; it is—I know it well—it is Mr. Rochester's cigar. I look round and I listen. I see trees laden with ripening fruit. I hear a nightingale warbling in a wood half a mile off; no moving form is visible, no coming step audible; but that perfume increases: I must flee. . . . I step into the ivy recess. . . .

From the ivy recess the quarry watches the hunter:

> . . . he strolls on, now lifting the gooseberry-tree branches to look at the fruit, large as plums, with which they are laden; now taking a ripe cherry from the wall; now stooping towards a knot of flowers, either to inhale their fragrance or to admire the dew-beads on their petals. A great moth goes humming by me; it alights on a plant at Mr. Rochester's foot. . . .

(II, 11)

These substantial quotations are given because they precede the grand climax of the novel, Jane's near-wedding to Rochester when she learns the awful truth of the secret of Thornfield Hall. We would expect any elements of imagery that contribute to the structure of the novel to intensify at this point and they do. The passages are the most romantically charged of the book, possessing the most intense erotic suggestiveness, producing the concentration,[7] in spite of the improbabilities of the plot, that we find in the novel. On the occasion of Jane's acceptance of Rochester's proposal, when Rochester states in a kind of tormented soliloquy that he defies man's opinion, the face of this burgeoning nature ominously changes and the moon, that symbol of love, disappears:

> But what had befallen the night? The moon was not yet set, and we were all in shadow: I could scarcely see

my master's face, near as I was. And what ailed the chestnut tree? it writhed and groaned; while wind roared in the laurel walk, and came sweeping over us.

(II, 21)

The same night after this omen, a storm breaks over Thornfield. The next morning, on the way to the [sic] Jane surveys the chestnut tree, arboreal symbol of Rochester and her love:

. . . I faced the wreck of the chestnut-tree [sic]; it stood up, black and riven: the trunk, split down the centre, gasped ghastly. The cloven halves were not broken from each other, for the firm base and strong roots kept them unsundered below; though community of vitality was destroyed—the sap could flow no more: their great boughs on each side were dead, and next winter's tempests would be sure to fell one or both to earth: as yet, however, they might be said to form one tree—a ruin; but an entire ruin.

(II, 47-48)

It was mentioned in the opening paragraph that Jane's intense personal involvement colors her awareness of things. The above passage and the one quoted earlier in which the moon, accompanied by a strange form in the sky, warns her to flee temptation—in fact, most of the emotionally charged passages involving the moon and arboreal imagery—contain strong elements of impressionism, that is, the shaping of the environment by the mental states of the characters. One critic calls this "a flair for the surreal," and notes that in this involvement in feeling Charlotte Brontë discovers a new dimension of Gothic.[8] Thus, after the revelation of Rochester's secret and the subsequent dashing of all Jane's hopes, the intense imagery, with its erotic suggestions remains, but it is strangely modified by her mental state: "A Christmas frost had come to midsummer; a white December storm had whirled over June; ice glazed the ripe apples, drifts crushed the blowing roses; on hay-field and cornfield lay a frozen shroud. . . ." (II, 74)

Jane, of course, leaves Thornfield, and as she travels across England the nature of the descriptive imagery changes. Not only is there much less description of landscape, it is now relatively devoid of the heavy sensuality of the descriptions of Thornfield; nor is it possessed of the dreary barrenness of the nature imagery of Gateshead or Lowood. It is, on the other hand, primarily pictorial or descriptive. Even when Jane is trudging through the rain, hungry and exhausted, the impressionistic element is much reduced. Of course, Jane has changed as a person, she has been emotionally tempered by her experience and although only nineteen, is a creature of judgment and maturity now, or so she seems when at Moor House.

Nature, though pushed into the background, is still an essential part of the structure, for in Charlotte Brontë's characterization of St. John Rivers, she defines his character by showing his reactions to it:

. . . Nature was not to him that treasury of delight it was to his sisters. He expressed once, and but once in my hearing, a strong sense of the rugged charm of the hills, and an inborn affection for the dark roof and hoary walls he called his home: but there was more of gloom than pleasure in the tone and words in which the sentiment was manifested; and never did he seem to roam the moors for the sake of their soothing silence—never seek out or dwell upon the thousand peaceful delights they could yield.

(II, 149)

The mental attitude of St. John Rivers—"Reason, and not feeling, is my guide" (II, 180)—represents, therefore, the polar opposite of the feelings associated with Mr. Rochester, and the imagery linked with each character varies accordingly. Although she feels "the consecration of its loneliness" (II, 146), Jane's descriptions of Moor House, typically quaint and romantic, are still not possessed with the emotional coloration characteristic of those of Thornfield.

When Jane receives the telepathic cry for help from Rochester while sitting in the moonlight flooded room, she hurries to Thornfield only to see the mansion as she had once seen it in a dream: "a shell-like wall . . . perforated by paneless windows: no roof, no battlements, no chimneys—all had crashed in" (II, 247). But although winter had sent its snows and rain "amidst the drenched piles of rubbish, spring had cherished vegetation: grass and weed grew here and there between the stones and fallen rafters" (II, 248). The sensuality of description is gone, but when she approaches Ferndean the arboreal imagery of before recurs, reminding the reader of Jane's lament while at Gateshead, where she regrets her inability to find the elves among foxglove leaves, mushrooms, and ground ivy: ". . . they were all gone out of England to some savage country, where the woods were wilder and thicker. . . ." (I, 20) Thus, as she approaches Ferndean, she notes that:

Even when within a very short distance of the manor-house, you could see nothing of it; so thick and dark grew the timber of the gloomy wood about it. Iron gates between granite pillars showed me where to enter, and passing through them, I found myself at once in the twilight of close-ranked trees. There was a grass-grown track descending the forest aisle, between hoar and knotty shafts and under branched arches.

(II, 254)

She sees Rochester outside the house: "His form was of the same strong and stalwart contour as ever: his port was still erect, his hair was still raven-black . . . nor . . . his vigorous prime blighted" (II, 255-56). Significantly enough, he is blindly reaching for the trees around him. Later, when they are reunited, he is reluctant to burden her with himself now; and he returns to the image of the blasted chestnut tree to express his condition: "I am no better than the old lightning-struck chestnut tree in Thornfield orchard. . . . And what right would that ruin have to bid a budding woodbine cover its decay with freshness?" Jane replies, continuing the nature metaphor:

> You are no ruin, sir—no lightning-struck tree: you are green and vigorous. Plants will grow about your roots, whether you ask them or not, because they take delight in your bountiful shadow; and as they grow they will lean towards you, and wind round you, because your strength offers them so safe a prop.
>
> (II, 273)

Then she leads him home through the woods for "that will be the shadiest way" (II, 275).

Thus from that first dreary November at Gateshead to the last mile of Jane's walk through the shade of Ferndean Woods, the passionate intensity of Jane's quest is defined and illuminated by the poetic substructure. But the secret of the book's power over us is perhaps best expressed by Virginia Woolf: "It is the red and fitful glow of the heart's fire which illumines her page. . . . We read Charlotte Brontë not for exquisite observation of character—her characters are vigorous and elementary; not for comedy—hers is grim and crude; not for a philosophic view of life—hers is that of a parson's daughter, but for her poetry."[9]

Notes

1. Bruce McCulloch, *Representative English Novelists: Defoe to Conrad* (New York, 1946), p. 170.

2. Mark Schorer, ed., *Jane Eyre* (Boston, 1959), pp. v-xvii. Schorer identifies and traces some of the principal nature imagery but with no attention to its amatory content.

3. Cf. Wayne Burns, "Critical Relevance of Freudianism," *Western Review,* XX (1956); Joseph Prescott, "Jane Eyre: A Romantic Exemplum with a Difference," *Twelve Original Essays on Great English Novels,* ed. Charles Shapiro (Detroit, 1960).

4. Charlotte Brontë, *Jane Eyre,* ed. T. J. Wise and J. A. Symington, I (London, 1931), 43-44. All citations will be from this, the Shakespeare Head edition, with page and volume numbers placed in parentheses following the quotations.

5. Charles Burckhardt, "Brontë's *Villette,*" *Explicator,* XXI (1962), Item 8.

6. In Burns's "The Critical Relevance of Freudianism," this scene is revealed, more or less convincingly, as the most erotic in the novel. ". . . it becomes clear that Jane is experiencing a form of orgasm." Burns suggests that "this passage, far from being an excrescence, is of a piece with the sexuality, or if one wishes, the passionate physicality, that permeates every aspect of the novel" (p. 312).

7. Melvin R. Watson, "Form and Substance in the Brontë Novels," *From Jane Austen to Joseph Conrad,* ed. Robert C. Rathburn and Martin Steinmann (Minneapolis, 1958), p. 112.

8. Robert B. Heilman, "Charlotte Brontë's New Gothic," in *From Jane Austen to Joseph Conrad,* p. 121.

9. Virginia Woolf, *The Common Reader* (New York, 1925), p. 223.

Dale Kramer (essay date summer 1968)

SOURCE: Kramer, Dale. "Thematic Structure in *Jane Eyre.*" *Papers on Language & Literature* 4, no. 3 (summer 1968): 288-98.

[*In the following essay, Kramer analyses the structure and major themes of* Jane Eyre.]

An attempt, such as the present paper's, to comment on structure and theme in **Jane Eyre** recognizes, first of all, that over the past three decades the former topic has attracted more critical discussion than any other aspect of the novel's artistry. Most commentators remark upon Charlotte Brontë's use of a rigid, mechanical organization. For example, William Peden scores her division of the novel into "three loosely connected sequences" as "artificial." Arthur Zeiger suggests that "the third large division of the novel, dealing with Jane's residence at Moor House," comes very close to being "an intolerable deviation from the main line of plot." It is not, says Zeiger, because Brontë's stress upon "the divergent aspects of her characters" allows the contrast in the last division "to point up the human quality that led Jane to prefer the passionate, self-willed Rochester to the frozen, disciplined St. John." One of the earliest critics of the novel's arrangement, David Cecil, says that the novel lacks unity of action, and is thus incoherent, because it has not a single drama, but three: Jane's life as a child, her relationship with Rochester, and her relationship to St. John Rivers.[1]

Several critics have offered rationales for the schematized structure, following principles that subdivide the novel in differing ways. Melvin Watson, in pointing out that **Jane Eyre** has what all of Charlotte's other novels lack (concentration), asserts that "the first and the third sections contrast not only with each other but with the much longer and more dramatic second part." Eric Solomon divides the novel into four sections (and a brief conclusion), calls them "acts," and says that "in each act the same scenes are played out: Jane comes into conflict with authority, defeats it by her inner strength, and departs into exile." Q. D. Leavis also divides the novel into four "sharply distinct phases" which take

Jane from childhood to maturity. "Each move leaves behind the phase and therefore the setting and characters which supplied that step in the demonstration" of "how a woman comes to maturity." Joe Lee Davis isolates seven plot sequences and the features that provide the novel's unity: Jane Eyre appears in each sequence, each is chronologically straightforward, the suspense in each is cumulative and affects the overall suspense of the novel, and "considerable use is made of such unifying devices as prospective or foreshadowing incident, character balancing or counterpoint, and recurrent settings and images." Another critic, Mark Schorer, says the novel's action "falls into four large blocks," but in adding that the structure is based on strands of poetic imagery, he implicitly denies the relevance of evaluation in terms of traditional views of structure. Leavis, although stressing the structure of maturation, agrees with Schorer that "the parts are not linked by a plot as in most previous fictions but organically united (as in Shakespeare) by imagery and symbolism which pervades the novel."

Each of these critics has assessed the novel with the aid of a respectable critical dictum, even though one may not agree with one or more of the dicta even in principle, let alone in its application to *Jane Eyre.* Cecil's antipathy to the "Ages of Man" approach, for example, seems peculiarly insular and short-sighted, especially in view of Cecil's usually urbane eclecticism. But what is surprising is the failure of these critics to employ their structural readings in a more encompassing manner than they do. They tend to discuss plot (Cecil, Watson), character (Zeiger, Davis), and theme, but in isolated arguments. Those who argue that the novel does possess unity, then, seem to contradict themselves by their own rhetoric. Only Solomon discusses structure and theme in the same paragraph; and even he does not treat the relationship clearly. In talking about structure he emphasizes that "authority" opposes Jane; whereas in briefly mentioning theme he refers to a "series of temptations" that she overcomes.[2]

My own structural reading of *Jane Eyre* follows a different procedure from those used by these critics. Their work is valuable, but there is little point in again delimiting the "sections" of this novel. It is clear that Charlotte Brontë herself did, as a simple technical expedient, plan an organization that took Jane through a variety of consecutive experiences. In that Jane begins as an orphan, is misunderstood or misappreciated by the adults around her, passes through a number of events that mature her, and gains material wealth and personal happiness, the pattern of her story approximates that of a *Bildungsroman*. To the contrary of Cecil's strictures, the novel has an inherent unity sanctioned by age-old narrative expectations. As these critics have demonstrated, it is possible to arbitrarily subdivide the structure with equal plausibility into three, four, or seven parts. But to so subdivide the novel tends to obscure the novelist's exploitation of structure as a device of communication as distinct from a simple quality of plot.

Nor is it necessary to trace laboriously through the structure the maturation of Jane, from her experience in the Red Room to her extrasensory "hearing" of Rochester's cry. (It is worth noting as an aside that the mental telepathy occurs at the precise moment when both Jane and Rochester subject their wills as to their fates entirely to God [cf. pp. 398, 424].)[3] A close examination of Jane's progress is not rewarding in a study of functional structure. In most respects, Jane's growth is both obvious and straightforward.

Another method of structural criticism—the one employed here—offers a clearer perspective of the structure of *Jane Eyre* than does either dividing the story line into segments or tracing the personality of the main character. In many novels, statements by the narrator (i.e., in *Jane Eyre* by Jane herself) indicate elements of structure that are more organic and functional than are sections of plot. For example, the statements by Nellie Dean and Lockwood in *Wuthering Heights* regularly apprise the reader that the structure of that novel exemplifies a tension between mystic and mundane interpretations of human relationships. Such statements in novels interact with other aspects of the narrative; the ultimate results of the interaction constitute the thematic resolution of the issues raised by the statements.

The interaction of materials in *Jane Eyre* makes it quite clear that much of the tension of the structure is resolved by the marriage of Jane and Rochester. There is nothing arcane, then, about the novel's structure; but critical explanations of the nature of this resolution are, paradoxically, frequently both overintellectualized and over-simplified. The most widely accepted view at the present seems to be that Jane will accept only an emasculated Rochester, that until he has been punished and chastened for his presumption in asserting directiveness over her, she is psychologically unable to marry him. Indeed, one version of this idea has it that Mrs. Rochester is an impediment to marriage created in a kind of psychological fantasy by Jane herself in order to avoid a marriage with an overpowering master.[4] This opinion seems to be a development from Robert Heilman's more defensible reading, that Charlotte's novels give rise to nonrational and nonsocial reactions by "giving dramatic form to impulses and feelings which, because of their depth of mysteriousness or intensity or ambiguity, or of their ignoring or transcending everyday norms of propriety or reason, increase wonderfully the sense of reality in the novel." Heilman emphasizes Jane's direct response to Rochester's maleness and physicality. Jane's sleeplessness following Rochester's obvious desire to seduce her after she douses the fire in his room makes it clear that Heilman is right on this point. Heilman also attributes Jane's nearly succumbing to St. John's proposal to the same sort of sexual attraction.[5]

While their readings of *Jane Eyre* are variously interesting, some of the psychological critics' occasional free use of the text calls for modification of their views.[6] Martin Day's opinion that Jane can marry only an emasculated Rochester is supported in the text only by the mild and inconclusive passage in which she briefly "half lost the sense of power over him" after accepting his first proposal (p. 252). Again, Heilman's view that Jane is sexually drawn to St. John does not take into account all of the relevant material; a broader reading suggests that Jane is repelled by St. John precisely because their sexual natures are so utterly different. St. John relaxes his stern self-discipline to devote fifteen minutes to thoughts of Rosamond Oliver; Jane rushes from Thornfield Hall rather than risk an extended trial of her feelings toward Mr. Rochester. A subconscious or suppressed sexual drive may account for the dogged urgency and command of St. John's manner of proposal to Jane, but St. John's motives are not at issue. Jane's are; and she is repelled by the idea of sexual relations with such a cold and selfish being as St. John. She explicitly rejects him because she cannot bear the thought of fulfilling the "forms of love" with the spirit of love absent (p. 384; cf. also pp. 387-88). When Jane says she can go to India with St. John, unmarried, and live with him as a sister, no one in the novel doubts her meaning or sincerity, not even St. John (pp. 387, 392).

There is, of course, considerable truth in the psychological critics' judgment of the nature of the resolution of *Jane Eyre.* The relative status of Jane and Rochester does change in the course of the novel. But the present critical interest in sexual motivations of both characters and authors diverts attention from more germane features of an individual fiction, especially a piece of fiction whose author's inner life is as mysterious as Charlotte Brontë's. To overcome the effect of that critical bias, one needs only to examine the fiction itself. Rather than possessing inchoate and inexpressible psychosexual motivations, Jane Eyre in general evinces an honest, self-aware acceptance of the physical side of life—expressed not as clearly as it could be in the 1840's, which was before the age of extreme Victorian prudery, but as clearly as it need be.[7]

The fact is that the motivating forces of Jane Eyre's personality are not sexual concepts at all but personal concepts. She reacts as she does to erotic situations not because of repressions or of desires to emasculate or castrate her menfolk but because she fully understands her own motivations.[8] She also comprehends the significance of alternatives she is presented with, and the states of life that her choice of action can lead her to. Unlike the actions of modern protagonists, whose lives are a continual process of self-frustration and self-

discovery, Jane's conform to her principles and her understanding of her moral and physical needs.

Jane herself controls the point of view and provides the standards by which she herself and all the other characters are evaluated; thus she herself is not only the principal integrating force in the novel but is also the most complex character in the story, with instincts and standards at odds with each other. The psychological action will therefore be the interplay of divergent impulses within her, and the final reconciling or proper ordering of these impulses will be the principal part of the final resolution of the novel as a whole. She demonstrates her self-confessed impulsiveness (p. 15), her vehemence, curiosity, and rebellious nature (pp. 27, 35-36); she admits that she cannot live without love (p. 28) but is independent enough to castigate Mrs. Reed, the person whom in other circumstances it would be the most natural for her to love. Again, by the time she becomes involved with Rochester, she communicates clearly the various conflicting impulses that impel her to thought and action. She consciously allows her attraction to Rochester to have temporary sway (p. 145), enjoys a sublimated coquetry with him in argument (p. 150), uses both common sense and impassioned self-chastisement to rid her mind of fancies that Rochester might return her love (pp. 152-54), and then recognizes that however Rochester may feel toward her, they are of the same nature and that Rochester has little in common with his social acquaintances (pp. 166, 178). Toward Blanche Ingram, Jane first feels inferiority, accepting as likely that Rochester would prefer beauty (pp. 152-54), but she shortly realizes the barrenness of Blanche's heart, the emptiness of her mind, and the unnaturalness of her "spontaneity." In short, Jane sees that Blanche is not "genuine," and she accepts the loss of Rochester with sorrow for his sake rather than with self-pity (pp. 176-77). The material in this paragraph, and the often-quoted arguments Jane offers in refusing to become Rochester's mistress (pp. 282-305), indicate that Brontë exhibits in the characterization of her heroine a battle between passion and common sense, between conscience and unformulated desire. Jane is a character of conflicting motivations, all of which she herself recognizes and enunciates. Logically, then—to return to specific features of structure—the novel's reconcilement-by-marriage should provide either a balance of the conflicting elements or a judgment upon their dichotomy, or both. The marriage of Jane and Rochester furnishes both: passion and reason complement each other in their final relationship, and Jane's reliance upon conscience is justified not only by her final happiness but by Rochester's coming to believe that she had been correct to refuse his unsanctioned love.

The movement toward this reconcilement is structurally amplified by a kind of "doubling" technique. Jane's simultaneous but contradictory propensities for passion and reason are paralleled, on a different level of personality, by a belief in equality of persons and compulsion either to submit to or to rebel against individuals.

Throughout her history, Jane has declared her "equalness." She has presumed, as a child, to criticize her protectress, Mrs. Reed; she asserts, with Rochester's acquiescence, that she is his equal (p. 240); with the acquisition of wealth, she becomes the literal equal of her family, the Riverses, through her division of her inheritance. One reason she refuses St. John's proposals is that he discounts her value as a person when she raises objections to his scheme of taking her to India as his unloved and unloving wife; upon seeing his "hardness and despotism," Jane realizes that he is no better than she (p. 386). Jane's obsession with equality is kept from being narrow egotism by the feminist core of the novel, as when Jane muses that "women feel just as men feel; they need exercise for their faculties, and a field for their efforts as much as their brothers do" (p. 106), and by the mystical undertones that make *Jane Eyre* a corollary to *Wuthering Heights,* as when Jane sits with the dying Mrs. Reed and recalls Helen Burns' "doctrine of the equality of disembodied souls" (p. 225). The climax of Jane's interest in equality comes when Jane and Rochester become nearly co-identical: "I am my husband's life as fully as he is mine" (p. 428). This final absolute equality has not been adequately considered by the critics who believe that Jane accepts Rochester at the last because he is helpless.

Jane's conflict between revolt and submission subtilizes her concern for equality. Jane explicitly and publicly asserts her equality; she also, and contradictorily, tends to classify individuals as either stronger (superior) or weaker (inferior) than she is.[9] In other words, while insisting she is the equal of everyone she meets, regardless of social rank, Jane in her actual personal relationships weighs and evaluates her own qualities against those of her associates. Her dilemma is, of course, the dilemma of every democrat, all the sharper and more compelling when the democrat in question is in the lower social position and perforce relies upon nature for acceptance rather than upon artificial distinctions of class and wealth.[10] Jane's inclination to evaluate becomes manifest especially when people try to exert their wills upon her in a masculine manner. She herself recognizes fully her reactions to such people: "I know no medium: I never in my life have known any medium in my dealings with positive, hard characters, antagonistic to my own, between absolute submission and determined revolt" (p. 380).

She makes that statement about St. John's dominance over her before he proposes; but it obviously applies as well to other characters in the novel. St. John and Rochester are a great deal alike in their behavior toward Jane; as she points out (pp. 397-421), their manners of proposing equally beset her. Both are, in their individual ways, personifications of masculinity, Rochester by his roughness and his indifference to flaccid conventions, St. John by his moral rigor and power and intellect. More significantly, neither feels any compunction about forcing his will upon another human being. Both are determined to have Jane, against her desire if need be, since each man is so confident about his own way of life as to feel certain that any reluctance to share in it is a manifestation of childish whim. Both see people as objects to be fitted to their own purposes; Rochester wants Jane to ensure his own peace of mind and St. John believes that Jane's powers of self-discipline will be useful implements in his missionary duties. The case should not be overstated; they are not entirely indifferent to Jane as a person. Rochester worries about Jane's comfort and St. John may even concede a separate missionary goal for Jane after she refuses adamantly to marry him. Nevertheless, where Jane is concerned, dominating their words and thoughts and actions is the possibility of her usefulness to them. In masculine authority, the parallels to these two "lovers" are Mr. Brocklehurst, the third major male character, and Mrs. Reed, Jane's major female antagonist, who is in the masculine position of the head of a household. Since all these figures are stronger than Jane, since she cannot alter the balance of strength, and since she knows no medium between submission and rebellion, she has to escape from them. (To submit would destroy not only her individuality but her cherished equality.) She flees physically from Rochester and St. John, at a point when each is attempting to make her submit totally and irrevocably. She flees Brocklehurst's oppression with the aid of the investigating committee which reduces Brocklehurst's role in Lowood School to that of a mere financial officer; and she escapes from Mrs. Reed's sternness because in this case the antipathy is mutual.

Jane's tendency to categorize her relationships reveals itself further in her attitude toward other women who—unlike Mrs. Reed—are in feminine roles. On almost every remotely appropriate occasion, she classifies her female associates as servants, pupils, or teachers. Miss Temple and Helen Burns serve as teachers, of kindness and of submission respectively (pp. 67-79). When Jane stumbles exhausted and starving to Moor House, she comes as a supplicant, and the servant Hannah chastizes her. Jane determinedly asserts her superiority over Hannah before "becoming friends" with her (pp. 323-24) but bends readily to an "active will" she can respect, that of Diane Rivers (p. 326). Jane's attitudes toward her pupil Adèle and toward Rosamond Oliver, the beautiful girl who vainly loves St. John, are similar: "Still I liked her," she says of Rosamond, "almost as I liked my pupil Adèle" (p. 349). Her attitudes toward the adult Georgiana and Eliza Reed are less explicitly developed—partly because she refuses to become involved in the egoistic plans of either, submitting to their orders only because of the temporary nature of their association after the death of Mrs. Reed. But she is censorious toward Georgiana's social frivolousness and vanity and Eliza's barren religious fanaticism: "Feeling without judgment is a washy drought indeed; but judgment untempered by feeling is too bitter and husky a morsel for human deglutition" (pp. 224-25).

With men, then, Jane establishes relationships based on force and power, and that approximate unsatisfactory parent-child relationships. Jane frequently refers to Rochester as "father"-like; Mrs. Reed is a surrogate father; St. John is Jane's closest male relative. With women, on the other hand, Jane establishes a governess-pupil relationship consistent with her profession, a relationship that is, significantly, generally congenial for all involved. She may not be in control, as in her relations with Miss Temple and Diana Rivers, but these women exercise their authority over Jane with consideration for Jane's rational acceptance. They do not force her to accept their superiority or their correctness on certain points; they persuade her, albeit partially by her own willingness to concede their superiority. To put the matter differently, female dominance combines emotional predisposition and rational sway, whereas male appeals are either emotional (Rochester's) or rational (St. John's) but are not both simultaneously.

The argument here would seem to be converging upon the conclusion of the psychologists, i.e., Rochester must be emasculated before he is acceptable to Jane. But that is not quite the case. For one thing, Rochester is not feminized, even in the arguments of those critics who think he is emasculated by the fire that destroys Thornfield Hall. To repeat, there is much truth in the psychological critics' analysis of Jane's personality. But the novel does not suggest that a sexual neurosis impels Jane to eventually marry a man she can dominate sexually. It is true that as soon as the crippled Rochester's "old impetuosity was rising," Jane starts to talk about the weather; but it is also true that she evidently *does* marry him in three days, as he had insisted (p. 426, where she writes to St. John, who is still at Cambridge for his brief visit).

It may be recalled that Jane is of course deeply concerned with her absolute equality; the relationships in which she is dominated by a masculine figure or is either exerting her superiority over or accepting her inferiority to a woman are all in a final sense recognizably incomplete, and unacceptable to her. Only with the chastened and blinded but still virile Rochester, who has suffered remorse for his guilty intentions toward Jane, does she establish a position of equality and of co-identity, in which relative powers are irrelevant. Rochester, who previously had accepted the equality of her spirit (p. 240), now accepts her as a necessary helpmate; and her wealth removes the onus she herself had

felt (p. 255) of coming to Rochester without a suitable worldly portion. At the end of the novel, Jane says she loves Rochester even better now than before, because now she can be useful to him (p. 423). On all the levels of their relationship, Brontë emphasizes balance rather than forced adjustment.

As far as Rochester himself is concerned, during Jane's absence from Thornfield Hall he goes through an educative process that enables him finally to make the same discriminations between rational and emotional arguments that she had made after the revelation of the existence of a living Mrs. Rochester. Rochester's reformation justifies Jane's solution of the moral dilemma between reason and desire that she evinces after the disclosure that the first Mrs. Rochester is still alive. Similarly, erasing distinctions, the marriage of Rochester and Jane harmonizes the two concerns that provide a structural scaffolding for the moral dilemma—Jane's belief in the equal worth of persons and her inner conflict between acquiescence and rebellion, the conflict that causes her to react to her associates in terms of inequality.

The foregoing analysis of the structure and characterization of *Jane Eyre* is not especially revolutionary. Indeed, it enhances previous interpretations by approaching the central issues of the novel from new directions without either invalidating other readings or distorting the text. Identifying the dual aspect of Jane's movement toward self-realization provides a fresh indication of Charlotte Brontë's command of her materials and her clarity of vision.

Notes

1. William Peden, "Introduction" to *Jane Eyre,* Modern Library College Edition (New York, 1944), p. x; Arthur Zeiger, "Afterword" to *Jane Eyre,* Signet Books edn. (New York, 1965), p. 460; David Cecil, "Charlotte Brontë," *Early Victorian Novelists: Essays in Revaluation* (London, 1934), pp. 114-15. References in the next paragraph are to Melvin Watson, "Form and Substance in the Brontë Novels," *From Jane Austen to Joseph Conrad: Essays Collected in Memory of James T. Hillhouse,* eds. Robert C. Rathburn and Martin Steinmann, Jr. (Minneapolis, Minn., 1958), pp. 110-11; Eric Solomon, "*Jane Eyre:* Fire and Water," *College English,* XXV (1963), 215; Q. D. Leavis, "Introduction" to *Jane Eyre,* Penguin Books edn. (Baltimore, Md., 1966), pp. 11-13; Joe Lee Davis, "Introduction" to *Jane Eyre,* Rinehart Edition (New York, 1950), pp. xii-xiii; Mark Schorer, "Introduction" to *Jane Eyre,* Riverside Edition (Boston, Mass., 1959), pp. xi-xii, xiv-xvii.

2. Solomon, pp. 215-16. Despite the vagueness of this particular logical connection, Solomon's is a

fine germinal essay. My own reading of *Jane Eyre* is a development upon Solomon's noticing Jane's "two opposing methods of fighting injustice—by aggression and by submission," *idem.* Leavis, too, uses the term "theme," but the process of maturation seems more of a motif than a theme. This may be only a quibble over terms.

3. Parenthetical page references throughout the text are to the Riverside Edition of *Jane Eyre.*

4. Martin S. Day, "Central Concepts of *Jane Eyre,*" *The Personalist,* XLI (1960), 503.

5. Robert B. Heilman, "Charlotte Brontë's 'New' Gothic," *From Jane Austen to Joseph Conrad* (cf. n. 1), pp. 131-32, 123.

6. An interesting example of interpreting what may or may not have been conscious sexual imagery and diction on Brontë's part is Joseph Prescott's "*Jane Eyre:* A Romantic Exemplum with a Difference," *Twelve Original Essays on Great English Novels,* ed. Charles Shapiro (Detroit, Mich., 1960), pp. 87-102. The "difference" is an "erotic strain which grows more and more pronounced as the narrative unfolds."

7. Kathleen Tillotson, *Novels of the Eighteen-Forties* (London, 1956), p. 258.

8. Cf. Earl A. Knies, "The 'I' of *Jane Eyre,*" *College English,* XXVII (1966), 546-55, for an analysis of the plausibility of Jane's self-projection on the basis of narrative stance—that is, on what is logically posited of the first-person point of view in the novel.

9. These two aspects of Jane's character are complementary as well as contradictory; they even show themselves in the same scenes.

10. This is the case even though, as Q. D. Leavis points out, Jane considers herself a lady—at Lowood and at Morton school explicitly: "Notes" to *Jane Eyre* (Baltimore, Md., 1966), p. 481.

W. A. Craik (essay date 1968)

SOURCE: Craik, W. A. "*Jane Eyre.*" In *The Brontë Novels,* pp. 70-122. London: Methuen and Company, 1968.

[In the following essay, Craik studies the narrative techniques employed by Brontë in Jane Eyre *as well as the autobiographical elements in the novel.]*

Jane Eyre still bursts upon the reader as it burst upon its first readers in 1847. Even though most people are now conscious of works by two sisters accompanying it, and now know that it is one of four novels by its author, and that it was preceded by *The Professor* and a huge quantity of writing never intended for publication, it still seems to spring into the world as an achieved masterpiece: an Athena from the head of Jove, or a Venus from the sea. There are very few signs of the writer still learning his trade, a rare state for any first book to enjoy. *Jane Eyre* has many idiosyncrasies, and its structure and method are highly unconventional, so inevitably praise has been accompanied and qualified by condemnation of a whole range of 'faults', which vary according to the climate of criticism when they are discovered. But these faults are never those of an apprentice, and are never attributed to immaturity; as indeed they should not be, since the same qualities are to be seen again in both *Shirley* and *Villette.* One must examine *Jane Eyre* with a candid judgement, as free as possible from preconceived notions both of what a novel should contain and how it should achieve its ends. This is generally agreed to be the case with *Wuthering Heights,* but not so much with *Jane Eyre,* mainly because Charlotte Brontë seems to be working with the common stuff of the novel, the adventures of a central character which end with a marriage. Consequently *Jane Eyre* has suffered with time, since the two main kinds of novel which give the modern reader these preconceived notions are the great Victorian and nineteenth-century novels which are almost all written later than *Jane Eyre,* and the large number of second-rate Brontë-imitations, which take over some of the situations and character types from Charlotte and Emily Brontë's works, without any real understanding of their model.[1] This recognizable novel form—adventure ending in marriage—was one of the qualities which made *Jane Eyre* acceptable to the novel-reader of the 1840s when *Wuthering Heights* was not; it is also the quality which has swung critical opinion over the last forty years the other way, so that while *Wuthering Heights* is an accepted masterpiece *Jane Eyre* has sunk in esteem. *Wuthering Heights* compels us to examine its purpose, that of its characters, its structure, and the style and expression used. *Jane Eyre* does not. Yet those features are equally the demonstration of its kind, and the proof of its excellence, are equally original and independent, and in fact have more in common with *Wuthering Heights* than with any other writer or work.

Any study of a work begins with the essential and the obvious, since these are by definition likely to be more enlightening than the abstruse. The most obvious things in *Jane Eyre* are the simple single story and the personality of its narrator Jane herself, with Mr Rochester coming a very close third. Everything that is done bears directly on these three. This is partly the result of having a narrator who is also the hero, but the concentration shows it is more than a natural consequence. There are no sections of this novel like the story of Steerforth in *David Copperfield* (another 'autobiography') which has a life and artistic significance beyond what the career and character of the narrator require. This perfectly proper and legitimate use of a narrator, which Charlotte Brontë employs in *Villette,* is not present in *Jane Eyre.* Like *Wuthering Heights, Jane Eyre* might be called a love story. This would be true in one way, since it shows that the marriage at the end is the moral and artistic culmination of the whole—not merely a convenient rounding-off of a whole collection of different kinds of material, like Amelia Sedley's marrying Dobbin at the end of *Vanity Fair,* or even Dorothea Brooke's marrying Ladislaw in *Middlemarch.* In another way it is considerably less than the truth, since by the time this marriage is reached it has come to represent the resolution of moral and emotional conflicts, and the growth of moral and emotional grasp of life as a whole; for all of which the word 'love-story' is a very inadequate counter. The story really examines that period of life in which its heroine (and in secondary place its hero also) makes the most influential decisions of her life; the period which arouses the most extreme emotions of which her nature is capable, and brings out and tests the strength of the moral principles which rule her.

Such complete concentration on the moral and emotional growth of an individual, done wholly by self-revelation, had not been attempted before.[2] Charlotte Brontë, therefore, doing something new, had to work out her own way of doing it. Her way is the fictional autobiography. It is her great claim to genius, proved by the claims to greatness of *Villette* and *Jane Eyre,* and demonstrated conversely by *Shirley,* which, trying the more customary author's narrative, is far less successful. The autobiography not only allows Charlotte Brontë to reveal the main character, it imposes a form on the material available—we can perceive only what it is possible for the narrator to perceive—and it forces the reader to share in that character's growth and self-knowledge. The reader's emotional and moral sympathy with Jane Eyre is vital, and no one questions Charlotte Brontë's power of obtaining and keeping it. But complete emotional sympathy generally suggests complete identification, the reader feeling that he actually becomes the character throughout, or for long portions of the action. *Jane Eyre* obviously approaches this state at points, but this is not really the whole truth, and Charlotte Brontë never meant the story to produce so total an immersion. It would come much too near the emotional state Jane Eyre herself rejects during Mr Rochester's courtship:

> 'I'll not sink into a bathos of sentiment: and with this needle of repartee I'll keep you from the edge of the gulph too; and, moreover, maintain by its pungent aid that distance between you and myself most conducive to our real mutual advantage.'
>
> (Chapter 24)

Jane, who cares passionately for Mr Rochester, preserves her detachment from him; and Charlotte Brontë takes care that the reader, who comes rapidly to care passionately about Jane, shall preserve his degree of detachment as well. The reader is quite often addressed, and so forced to think of himself and his own personality as very much a thing apart from the narrator's, and the demands that he shall do so grow more frequent as the story goes on. They increase in direct proportion to the emotional and moral complexity of the material. The first exhortation is unobtrusive:

> Have I not described a pleasant site for a dwelling, when I speak of [Lowood] as bosomed in hill and wood, and rising from the verge of a stream? Assuredly, pleasant enough: but whether healthy or not is another question.
>
> (Chapter 9)

and it is followed soon by a short discourse to the reader on Helen Burns. It is an indication of two things: first, that we are to watch, as well as feel, at Helen's death, since the incident's artistic purpose is to increase Jane's emotional and moral understanding; and second, that we are now drawing away from Lowood, for the next chapter (10) is the one in which Jane resigns her post as teacher and prepares to move to Thornfield. Apostrophes to the reader continue to be used in the same way: to mark the opening of a new scene (Chapter 11) or to mark a stage in the emotional development (Chapter 18), and also, originally and remarkably, at moments of extreme emotional tension, when it would seem like artistic sacrilege to destroy the willing suspension of disbelief. This is the most remarkable and original use of the device, and the one that jars the reader's sensibility the most if he is reading in a spirit of mere emotional indulgence. They occur equally at joyful and painful moments:

> 'Jane, you look blooming, and smiling, and pretty,' said he: 'truly pretty this morning. Is this my pale, little elf? Is this my mustard-seed? This little sunny-faced girl with the dimpled cheek and rosy lips; the satin-smooth hazel hair, and the radiant hazel eyes?' (I had green eyes, reader; but you must excuse the mistake: for him they were new-dyed, I suppose.)
>
> (Chapter 24)

> Gentle reader, may you never feel what I then felt! May your eyes never shed such stormy, scalding, heart-wrung tears as poured from mine. May you never appeal to Heaven in prayers so hopeless and so agonized as in that hour left my lips: for never may you, like me, dread to be the instrument of evil to what you wholly love.
>
> (Chapter 27)

> The caged eagle, whose gold-ringed eyes cruelty has extinguished, might look as looked that sightless Samson.

And, reader, do you think I feared him in his blind fe-
rocity?—if you do, you little know me.

(Chapter 37)

These apostrophes occur so consistently that they must
be there for a purpose. They are clearly a call to attention from author to reader,[3] but not to draw closer, to
share in the experience, but to detach oneself momentarily from something that may lull one's rational or
moral awareness.[4]

This detachment in varying degrees is consistently
maintained, and the tension between it and emotional
involvement is one of the work's great achievements.
Detachment of the usual kind—that resulting from an
observing author and a reader who observes the author
in his turn—is largely done away with. Autobiography
involves an apparently simplified narrative viewpoint:
that solely of the teller of the story; and Charlotte
Brontë preserves the impression of simplicity. She never
disagrees with Jane, and neither does the reader. Even
so, there are many fine distinctions in the degrees of detachment of writer from material. They are not immediately obvious or obtrusive on reading, but the effects
they have on how the reader perceives what is happening are very considerable, and are a vital part of the intellectual and emotional control which, despite the more
obvious passions, one feels throughout the story.

There are two obvious narrative stances available: the
story can either be seen and revealed by Jane at the age
at which she experiences it, or it can be interpreted by
the Jane who is supposedly looking back at her youth
from the age of about thirty—the age she claims to be
in the last chapter, where she says she has been married
ten years. Charlotte Brontë uses both stances frequently.
But as the action develops, other points of view are
taken up within this main framework. The eighteen-
year-old Jane at Thornfield has the opportunity to revisit the scene of her first sufferings and her first defiance, Gateshead, and to reassess both herself and those
who hurt her; and there are many other equally vital but
even smaller time-lapses and retrospects: Jane at
Lowood looks back and tells her sufferings at Gateshead to Miss Temple; at Morton, she contrasts herself
as schoolteacher with what she would have been as Mr
Rochester's mistress; and the whole of the section at
Thornfield is punctuated by pauses for Jane to review,
analyse or assess what has gone before. These degrees
of involvement make it easy to suppose that when we
have reached the most detached narrator, we have
reached the author. It is easy to feel that Jane Eyre at
her wisest and most omniscient is Charlotte Brontë herself, and probably the majority of readers do so, consciously or not, at some time during their acquaintance
with the work. It is the measure of Charlotte Brontë's
triumph. It is natural to like Jane, and when we know
that many of the things that happen to her, and many of

the places she goes to, belong equally to Charlotte
Brontë, it is both natural and inviting to think that Jane
and Charlotte may be equated. It is a temptation that
must be resisted if one intends to get the most possible
out of the novel.[5]

These degrees of detachment are never automatic or
systematized; they are always determined by the emotion and the attitude to it that is necessary both in Jane
and in the reader. At the beginning of the story the
method is created and established. It would be all too
easy here to assume complete identification with the
ten-year-old Jane, see all through her eyes, and make
her sufferings quite unnaturally painful, and her adult
tormentors monstrous or merely ridiculous. Charlotte
Brontë never permits it. From the magnificently simple
and dramatic opening paragraphs, describing John,
Georgiana and Eliza Reed in the comfort of the
drawing-room, and Jane in disgrace reading Bewick in
the window of the cold breakfast-room, she moves to
Jane's opinions on her book—a book which sets the
sinister tone for Jane's future superstitious agonies in
the red room:

> Of these death-white realms I formed an idea of my
> own: shadowy, like all the half-comprehended notions
> that float dim through children's brains, but strangely
> impressive. The words in these introductory pages con-
> nected themselves with the succeeding vignettes, and
> gave significance to the rock standing up alone in a sea
> of billow and spray; to the broken boat stranded on a
> desolate coast; to the cold and ghastly moon glancing
> through bars of cloud at a wreck just sinking.
>
> I cannot tell what sentiment haunted the quite solitary
> churchyard, with its inscribed headstone; its gate, its
> two trees, its low horizon, girdled by a broken wall,
> and its newly-risen crescent, attesting the hour of even-
> tide.
>
> The two ships becalmed on a torpid sea, I believed to
> be marine phantoms.
>
> The fiend pinning down the thief's pack behind him, I
> passed over quickly: it was an object of terror.
>
> So was the black, horned thing seated aloof on a rock,
> surveying a distant crowd surrounding a gallows.
>
> Each picture told a story; mysterious often to my unde-
> veloped understanding and imperfect feelings, yet ever
> profoundly interesting.

(Chapter 1)

Here we see clearly that what Jane thinks is not fact,
but an imaginative heightening and distortion—'half-
comprehended notions that float dim through children's
brains', 'mysterious often to my undeveloped understanding and imperfect feelings'—and this prepares the
way for her dealings with people to show equally 'undeveloped understanding and imperfect feelings'. There
is no emotional indulgence in Jane's childish sufferings

and the reader is not allowed to indulge either: in the red room Jane wonders pitifully whether she is indeed as wicked as everyone declares:

> I grew by degrees cold as a stone, and then my courage sank. My habitual mood of humiliation, self-doubt, for-lorn depression, fell damp on the embers of my decay-ing ire. All said I was wicked, and perhaps I might be so: what thought had I been but just conceiving of starving myself to death? That certainly was a crime: and was I fit to die? Or was the vault under the chancel of Gateshead Church an inviting bourne? In such vault I had been told did Mr Reed lie buried; and led by this thought to recall his idea, I dwelt on it with gathering dread.
>
> (Chapter 2)

and from this grows her 'singular notion':

> I doubted not—never doubted—that if Mr Reed had been alive he would have treated me kindly; and now, as I sat looking at the white bed and overshadowed walls—occasionally also turning a fascinated eye to-wards the dimly gleaming mirror—I began to recall what I had heard of dead men, troubled in their graves by the violation of their last wishes, revisiting the earth to punish the perjured and avenge the oppressed; and I thought Mr Reed's spirit, harassed by the wrongs of his sister's child, might quit its abode—whether in the church vault or in the unknown world of the departed—and rise before me in this chamber. I wiped my tears and hushed my sobs; fearful lest any sign of violent grief might waken a preternatural voice to comfort me, or elicit from the gloom some haloed face, bending over me with strange pity. This idea, consolatory in theory, I felt would be terrible if realized: with all my might I endeavoured to stifle it—I endeavoured to be firm.
>
> (ibid.)

But in between these two passages which brilliantly re-produce Jane's feelings is an interpolation:

> I could not remember him; but I knew that he was my own uncle—my mother's brother—that he had taken me when a parentless infant to his house; and that in his last moments he had required a promise of Mrs Reed that she would rear and maintain me as one of her own children. Mrs Reed probably considered she had kept this promise; and so she had, I dare say, as well as her nature would permit her; but how could she really like an interloper not of her race, and uncon-nected with her, after her husband's death, by any tie? It must have been most irksome to find herself bound by a hard-wrung pledge to stand in the stead of a par-ent to a strange child she could not love, and to see an uncongenial alien permanently intruded on her own family group.
>
> (ibid.)

This is clearly a mature mind looking back, and, while it breaks the emotional continuity, serves in the long run to make Jane's sufferings even more dreadful (since we are not allowed the emotional relief of thoroughly loathing her tormentors), and they are even more potent for having a recognizable relation with common life. This scene establishes a moral attitude, and a sense of claims other than merely those of the child's sufferings, a state which is continued throughout the novel. This moral poise is unusual in any writer concerned with children, as a comparison with any other would show. In Charlotte Brontë's closest contemporary, Dickens, the Murdstones are as terrible to the young David Cop-perfield as the Reeds to Jane, while the pathos is prob-ably even more painful to the reader, since David can-not rise against them as Jane does, and since he has to watch them torture his mother too; yet to the reader the Murdstones are mere grotesques, on whom he is never asked to spend a serious thought. The superiority of Charlotte Brontë's method is proved in the novel as a whole, since the Reeds return eight years later, and while they impress Jane the independent young woman very differently, they are still—especially Mrs Reed—very recognizably themselves. Later in *David Copper-field* Miss Murdstone appears as Dora's chaperone, and David meets Mr Murdstone buying his marriage licence to another unfortunate victim. But there is no life in them now their place in the child David's mind is no more: they have no function and no personality.

When the Gateshead experience appears again, and Jane tells her story to Miss Temple, we can measure Jane's emotional and moral development by the combined ef-fects of the two levels of narrative comment in the first chapter:

> Exhausted by emotion, my language was more subdued than it generally was when it developed that sad theme; and mindful of Helen's warnings against the indul-gence of resentment, I infused into the narrative far less of gall and wormwood than ordinary. Thus re-strained and simplified, it sounded more credible: I felt as I went on that Miss Temple fully believed me.
>
> In the course of the tale I had mentioned Mr Lloyd as having come to see me after the fit: for I never forgot the, to me, frightful episode of the red room; in detail-ing which, my excitement was sure, in some degree, to break bounds; for nothing could soften in my recollec-tion the spasm of agony which clutched my heart when Mrs Reed spurned my wild supplication for pardon, and locked me a second time in the dark and haunted chamber.
>
> (Chapter 8)

Again there are two narrative levels: the first paragraph is all ten-year-old (though already a wiser one than she was at Gateshead); the latter half of the second one suggests the eye of an ever maturer self, looking back on both Lowood and Gateshead.

When Jane again meets Mrs Reed, she has been proved to be still structurally and emotionally important, and we recognize her by the insight the earlier detached comments have given us:

The well-known face was there: stern, relentless as ever—there was that peculiar eye which nothing could melt; and the somewhat raised, imperious, despotic eyebrow. How often had it lowered on me menace and hate! and how the recollection of childhood's terrors and sorrows revived as I traced its harsh line now! And yet I stooped down and kissed her: she looked at me.

(Chapter 21)

This is the largest and longest single retrospect in time, and involves us in two levels: Jane at eighteen seeing Jane at ten and measuring her development, and Jane at thirty seeing both.

When Jane is grown up—at Thornfield and at Morton—there are of course the obvious retrospects, like this, at Morton:

. . . to have been now living in France, Mr Rochester's mistress; delirious with his love half my time—for he would—oh, yes, he would have loved me well for a while. He *did* love me—no one will ever love me so again. I shall never more know the sweet homage given to beauty, youth, and grace—for never to any one else shall I seem to possess these charms. He was fond and proud of me—it is what no man besides will ever be.— But where am I wandering, and what am I saying; and, above all, feeling? Whether is it better, I ask, to be a slave in a fool's paradise at Marseilles—fevered with delusive bliss one hour—suffocating with the bitterest tears of remorse and shame the next—or to be a village-schoolmistress, free and honest, in a breezy mountain nook in the healthy heart of England?

(Chapter 31)

Passages such as this show Jane's attempts to subdue and control her own grief, as she has subdued and controlled her sense of anger and injustice at Mrs Reed, to see life steadily and see it whole; at the same time it reminds the reader of the passion and suffering that the action at this point cannot disclose. Yet it would seem natural on the whole for the narrative detachment to decrease and simplify, as it does in *David Copperfield.* In fact the tendency is the opposite, and the more the emotional pressure increases, the more Jane's understanding of herself and ours of her is clarified by the way the narrator reveals them. The closest-knit section of the book in all ways is that at Thornfield, from Mr Rochester's first appearance on the icy causeway to his last in despair when Jane leaves him. This section consists of a series of emotional surges forward, with pauses or even withdrawals between them, like the waves of a rising tide. At every pause the reader is made to stand away from the emotional experience, and assess it in relation to others, to moral standards, or simply to ordinary common life. This is achieved by a shift in the narrator's view, and Jane herself stands away from events. After she has rescued Mr Rochester from the fire, Jane thinks of Grace Poole, and rejects the idea that she may have some romantic hold over Mr Rochester:

. . . Mrs Poole's square, flat figure, and uncomely, dry, even coarse face, recurred so distinctly to my mind's eye, that I thought, 'No; impossible! my supposition cannot be correct. Yet,' suggested the secret voice which talks to us in our own hearts, '*you* are not beautiful either, and perhaps Mr Rochester approves you: at any rate you have often felt as if he did; and last night—remember his words; remember his look; remember his voice!'

I well remembered all: language, glance, and tone seemed at the moment vividly renewed. I was now in the school-room; Adèle was drawing; I bent over her and directed her pencil. She looked up with a sort of start.

'Qu'avez-vous, mademoiselle?' said she; 'Vos doigts tremblent comme la feuille, et vos joues sont rouges: mais, rouges comme des cerises!'

'I am hot, Adèle, with stooping!' She went on sketching, I went on thinking.

I hastened to drive from my mind the hateful notion I had been conceiving respecting Grace Poole: it disgusted me. I compared myself with her, and found we were different. Bessie Leaven had said I was quite a lady; and she spoke truth: I was a lady. And now I looked much better than I did when Bessie saw me: I had more colour and more flesh; more life, more vivacity; because I had brighter hopes and keener enjoyments.

(Chapter 16)

Though love is not yet mentioned, we now see the force of the feeling Jane is refusing to admit to herself, we see the sound sense on which she bases her belief in Mr Rochester's favour, and the feeling that it is not preposterous or improper, as his association with the commonplace Grace undoubtedly would be. Jane's assessments are usually—when Blanche Ingram has appeared—repressions, but they show the same uncompromising and rational fairness, and the following extract is an example of the use of the multiple narrative stance revealing the number of levels at which we are asked to view a single situation: Jane has now admitted to herself that she loves Mr Rochester, that there is no longer any question of, as she says 'extirpating from her soul the germs of love there detected' (Chapter 17), but she now tries to come to terms with the situation when it seems very plain that he is going to marry Blanche Ingram. Though the reader is certain he will not (even on a first reading), this must not seem a preposterous situation, nor Jane a fool for being deluded.

I have not yet said anything condemnatory of Mr Rochester's project of marrying for interest and connexions. It surprised me when I first discovered that such was his intention: I had thought him a man unlikely to be influenced by motives so common-place in his choice of a wife; but the longer I considered the position, education, etc., of the parties, the less I felt justified in judging and blaming either him or Miss Ingram, for acting in conformity to ideas and principles instilled into them, doubtless, from their childhood. All their class held these principles: I supposed, then, they had reasons for holding them such as I could not fathom. It seemed to me that, were I a gentleman like him, I would take to my bosom only such a wife as I could love; but the very obviousness of the advantages to the husband's own happiness, offered by this plan, convinced me that there must be arguments against its general adoption of which I was quite ignorant: otherwise I felt sure all the world would act as I wished to act.

But in other points, as well as this, I was growing very lenient to my master: I was forgetting all his faults, for which I had once kept a sharp look-out. It had formerly been my endeavour to study all sides of his character: to take the bad with the good; and from the just weighing of both, to form an equitable judgment. Now I saw no bad.

(Chapter 18)

This is an important review, taking place just after the charade in which Mr Rochester has 'married' Blanche Ingram, an incident which leads naturally to such a train of thought. Charlotte Brontë guides us wonderfully through Jane's situation. The first paragraph reveals a very young Jane, who does not know enough of the world to be sure of her own opinion that it is best to marry for affection ('there must be arguments against its general adoption of which I was quite ignorant'), and who accepts, without understanding, the 'ideas and principles instilled into them, doubtless, from their childhood'. Such a view shows us the difficulties which beset Jane, and which she triumphantly surmounts. However, the second paragraph involves a shift, for the Jane who objects to sliding over Mr Rochester's faults is at a further remove, both wiser and older, and the reader is being led towards the belief that the first attempt at marriage is morally wrong for more subtle reasons than that it is bigamous, a belief that is expressed most fully much later: 'I could not, in those days, see God for his creature: of whom I had made an idol' (Chapter 24). The comments are not restricted to the ends of scenes, nor do they all reduce the emotion: the effect of distance can produce nostalgia and turn simple statements into pathos:

What charade Colonel Dent and his party played, what word they chose, how they acquitted themselves, I no longer remember; but I still see the consultation which followed each scene: I see Mr Rochester turn to Miss Ingram, and Miss Ingram to him; I see her incline her head towards him, till the jetty curls almost touch his shoulder and wave against his cheek; I hear their mutual whisperings; I recall their interchanged glances; and something even of the feeling roused by the spectacle returns in memory at this moment.

(Chapter 18)

Finally, there are the comments which seem to come from some personality even further from the protagonist then her mature self is, and to speak with a more general authority. An example is the outburst on modern poetry occasioned when St John brings *Marmion,*

one of those genuine productions so often vouchsafed to the fortunate public of those days—the golden age of modern literature. Alas! the readers of our era are less favoured. But, courage! I will not pause either to accuse or repine. I know poetry is not dead, nor genius lost; nor has Mammon gained power over either, to bind or slay: they will both assert their existence, their presence, their liberty, and strength again one day.

(Chapter 32)

And another example, a less obtrusive one, is the comment:

Miss Ingram was a mark beneath jealousy: she was too inferior to excite the feeling. *Pardon the seeming paradox: I mean what I say.* She was very showy, but she was not genuine: she had a fine person, many brilliant attainments; but her mind was poor, her heart barren by nature: nothing bloomed spontaneously on that soil; no un-forced natural fruit delighted by its freshness. She was not good; she was not original: she used to repeat sounding phrases from books: she never offered, nor had, an opinion of her own.

(Chapter 18, my italics)

The rarity of such comments shows how thoroughly Charlotte Brontë has subdued herself to her purpose, as we can see by recalling **Shirley,** where, there being no artistic impropriety, they appear very much more often.

It is clear that on the question of attitude to material alone, the first-person narrator is being used with great subtlety and with a sure hand. Jane is a great advance on Crimsworth in this respect. Even though *Wuthering Heights* and *Agnes Grey* both precede **Jane Eyre,** Charlotte Brontë has not borrowed from them, since neither uses its narrator in this way. But the use does show that Charlotte Brontë shared with Emily this desire to make her novel a complete vision of life, where one event does more than merely follow another, and events are constantly seen in the light of the significant events which precede and come after them, even though Charlotte's methods are on the surface less revolutionary than Emily's. This constant reference of past to present action may account for another resemblance between **Jane Eyre** and *Wuthering Heights:* there is no real attempt at anything approaching a sub-plot. Charlotte Brontë's publishers protested to her about the 'want of *varied* interest' (my italics) in **The Professor,** but it does not apparently occur to her to remedy the deficiency by adding variety, but by adding, as she says, 'a more *vivid* interest', that is, intensity.[6] It is not until she has succeeded—and indeed attained something like perfection—that, in **Shirley,** she tries her hand at the multiple plot. The resolve to chronicle the moral and spiritual growth of a single character determines her choice of material and her shaping of it.

As a mere love story, the Thornfield and Ferndean sections seem to be the only vital ones, and the others— the two Gateshead ones, Lowood and Moor House—

become extraneous padding or biographical self-indulgence. This very elementary carping is easily done away with. No reader denies the power of Jane's story of her childhood, and few would fail to see that the qualities of the adult Jane are present or developed or foreshadowed in the ten-year-old cousin at Gateshead, and the passionate friend of Helen Burns. But Charlotte Brontë has undoubtedly taken great risks with her plot; no writer could use it as a model and expect coherence in his own work; the Gateshead section is a complete plot in itself, the story of an oppressed child who rises against her tyrants and succeeds in escaping them; so is the Lowood story, that of a lonely girl, who, through Helen Burns, experiences suffering and death and the value of friendship; even more striking is the apparently completely separate Moor House story, where Jane begins a new life as a village schoolmistress, acquires three new cousins, comes into a fortune, and is sought in marriage by St John Rivers. What is more, all these plots are more realistic, more obviously likely, than the central one—of a man of property, with an insane wife concealed in the house he actually uses, who courts the governess of his illegitimate daughter, attempts to commit bigamy, and when that has failed, loses his sight and his hand in attempting to save the life of his wife, before being reunited (through a supranormal event) with the woman he has injured. But their common purpose unifies them: and great care is taken on the practical level to make sure that no detail is inaccurate. A sound structural basis is provided, and while the effect is frequently an emotional one, there are no practical inconsistencies. The amount of knowledge various characters have about Bertha Mason provides a useful demonstration of apparent anomalies and shows the author's complete control. Jane knows nothing, and, as Mr Rochester says,

> 'I charged them to conceal from you, before I ever saw you, all knowledge of the curse of the place; merely because I feared Adèle never would have a governess to stay if she knew with what inmate she was housed'
>
> (Chapter 27)

but from time to time she hears hints from servants and from Mrs Fairfax: when we first hear the sinister laugh we have Mrs Fairfax's cryptic remark, 'Too much noise, Grace. Remember directions' (Chapter 11), and later Jane overhears Leah and the charwoman discussing Grace Poole:

> 'Ah!—she understands what she has to do,—nobody better,' rejoined Leah, significantly; 'and it is not every one could fill her shoes; not for all the money she gets.'
>
> 'That it is not!' was the reply. 'I wonder whether master—'
>
> The charwoman was going on; but here Leah turned and perceived me, and she instantly gave her companion a nudge.
>
> 'Doesn't she know?' I heard the woman whisper.
>
> (Chapter 17)

We wonder what they know, and how much, and Charlotte Brontë satisfies our curiosity, when all is known:

> 'At last I hired Grace Poole, from the Grimsby Retreat. She and the surgeon, Carter (who dressed Mason's wounds that night he was stabbed and worried), are the only two I have ever admitted to my confidence. Mrs Fairfax may indeed have suspected something; but she could have gained no precise knowledge as to facts.'
>
> (Chapter 27)

I doubt whether it occurs to one reader in a thousand to wonder why Grace or Carter did not tell what they knew; and Grace at least has been employed to be secret and it will pay her to continue. The rest of the intrigue also concerns the West Indies, and it is much more artistically fitting for the revelation to come from the same place. Mason stops the wedding because he has heard from Jane's uncle, whom Jane herself informed (Chapter 24). This same information is the reason why he leaves his fortune to Jane instead of to his other nieces and nephew the Riverses, so the plot is entirely and economically coherent, and entirely centred on Jane. Although Charlotte Brontë does not shirk the coincidence involved in Jane's meeting her cousins—

> The two girls, on whom, kneeling down on the wet ground, and looking through the low, latticed window of Moor House kitchen, I had gazed with so bitter a mixture of interest and despair, were my near kinswomen; and the young and stately gentleman who had found me almost dying at his threshold, was my blood relation.
>
> (Chapter 33)

—yet she has used coincidence as little as her given plot permits, and really very little by comparison with other novelists—Dickens and Hardy for instance—who make it a prerequisite.

The characters other than Jane and Rochester are of widely different types, and are presented in very different styles. While there have been many to disparage the presentation of the gentry, at the house-party, there have been few to praise the many successes who are necessarily less obtrusive: Mrs Fairfax, or Bessie, or St John Rivers. Again the problem is one of recognizing the novel's purpose. None of these characters can exist and stand alone as characters can when the narrator is the author. They exist as Jane sees them, not as Charlotte Brontë might have done. Again *Shirley* provides a useful comparison. Nothing so elementary as the house-party appears in *Shirley,* and there are many full-length portraits of forceful and original characters for which there is no parallel in *Jane Eyre*. It was not incapacity which prevented their appearing in *Jane Eyre* (as *The Professor* proved); it is a difference in function: in *Jane Eyre* Charlotte Brontë allows characters to reveal themselves only when what they do and are reveals Jane, or creates or illuminates her predicament. The range from which characters are drawn corresponds to the society in which Jane moves. The degree to which they are congenial indicates their worth, and by implication the moral worth of their kind and class. This moral worth is always an element in their presentation, a matter on which the reader is never left in any doubt, the only possible exceptions to the generalization being Mr Rochester and St John Rivers, who will be dealt with in due course. At the highest end of the social scale are the titled personages of the house-party, country gentry who descend in rank from young Lord Ingram[7] by way of Sir George and Lady Lynn, Colonel and Mrs Dent, to the magistrate Mr Eshton; and at the lowest are the family servants Bessie and Robert Leaven at Gateshead, Hannah at Moor House, Leah and Grace Poole at Thornfield, John and Mary at Ferndean. At intervals between these range the Reed family, the Rivers family, Mrs Fairfax, Adèle, Bertha Mason and her brother, the Lowood characters Miss Temple, Helen Burns and Mr Brocklehurst, and a few vividly-realized incidental persons such as the few people Jane meets at Morton, and the proprietor of the inn, who tells her where to find Mr Rochester. The characters group themselves obviously according to the place and episode in which they appear, but there are resemblances and parallels between them and their relation to Jane, which appear as the story progresses. Generally speaking, characters are simple in the opening sections, and grow more subtle the further the story progresses, as Jane's capacity for subtle appreciation increases, and as the moral growth requires elaborate personalities to reveal it.

The first people we meet besides Jane herself are representatives of Gateshead life: her cousins Eliza, John and Georgiana, her aunt Mrs Reed, the nurse Bessie and the apothecary Mr Lloyd. The Reed family are a demonstration of Jane's power to overcome her circumstances, and link with and balance the Riverses—another family of two sisters and a brother, whose relations with Jane are another, more searching, test of her powers of resistance. Eliza and Georgiana Reed have only the personality necessary to show in contrasting forms the absence of human sympathy Jane suffers: Eliza 'would have sold the hair off her head if she could have made a handsome profit thereby' (Chapter 4), while Georgiana's curls are essential to her; they are her virtues, and claims to affection.[8] The simplicity of the representations make them forceful, and emphasize the pain they cause the child Jane, yet the simple attributes can be taken and made to work morally when they reappear as grown-up young women. Both are credible recreations, since the basis of character is the same. We believe easily in the plump and fashionable Georgiana and in the less predictable evolution of Eliza into the rigorous recluse. Their soullessness contributes to the grimness of their mother's death, and the fact that they can no longer hurt Jane and that she can be

useful to both is a measure of her development. They are deliberately balanced and opposed:

> True, generous feeling is made small account of by some: but here were two natures rendered, the one intolerably acrid, the other despicably savourless for the want of it.
>
> (Chapter 21)

John Reed is a spoilt brute: his sisters' physique represents their mentality; he is wholly physical and lives, tortures Jane, and dies in physical terms: we never find out what kind of despair led to suicide, or even how he died. 'I dream sometime that I see him laid out with a great wound in his throat, or with a swollen and blackened face,' says his mother (Chapter 21); and so artistically he dies by two ways, both brutal; an end in keeping with the boy with 'a dim and bleared eye and flabby cheeks', who, in the one incident when we see him, is 'thrusting out his tongue at me as far as he could without damaging its roots' (Chapter 1). He has a borrowed power from being the physical expression of his mother's repressed impulses. Mrs Reed is a more developed person, adult and dangerous. She is no mere childhood monster, and Jane is painfully fair in speaking of her:

> I know that had I been a sanguine, brilliant, careless, exacting, handsome, romping child—though equally dependent and friendless—Mrs Reed would have endured my presence more complacently; . . . Mrs Reed probably considered she had kept the promise [to rear and maintain Jane as one of her own children]; and so she had, I dare say, as well as her own nature would permit her.
>
> (Chapter 2)

> She was an exact, clever manager, her household and tenantry were thoroughly under her control; . . . she dressed well, and had a presence and port calculated to set off handsome attire.
>
> (Chapter 4)

These comments feel absolutely just, having no tinge of Jane's hatred in them; they render Mrs Reed both more interesting and more terrible, and they prove that the child Jane is not at all sentimentalized, a fact which is proved again when Jane sees recognizably the same Mrs Reed through adult eyes and perceptions. We can see Mrs Reed has feelings of her own that can be troubled—she is distressed by Jane's passionate defiance in Chapter 4—and so we are prepared for her deathbed to be troubled by remorse (though not repentance), while her desire to put herself in the right does not, ironically, prevent her from still hating Jane: 'My last hour is racked by the recollection of a deed, which, but for you, I should never have been tempted to commit' (Chapter 21). Her death is a conscious and structural partner to Helen Burns's, a measurement of Jane's spiritual independence and understanding:

nothing soft, nothing sweet, nothing pitying, or hopeful, or subdued, did it inspire; only a grating anguish for *her* woes—not *my* loss—and a sombre tearless dismay at the fearfulness of death in such a form.

(Chapter 21)

Bessie has as much structural importance as the Reeds, though less thematic relevance, and is in many ways more interesting. She attracts our attention by being the only person to show any affection for Jane, though again there is no concession to sentimentality:

I remember her as a slim young woman, with black hair, dark eyes, very nice features, and good clear complexion; but she had a capricious and hasty temper, and indifferent ideas of principle or justice.

(Chapter 4)

By visiting Jane just before she leaves Lowood, and by being the subject of odd allusions and recollections when quite other matters are the first concern, she keeps Gateshead in the reader's mind when it would otherwise be forgotten. She connects with all that large part of Jane's perception which expresses itself by means of folklore: her stories of the Gytrash introduce Mr Rochester to us; her belief that 'to dream of children was a sure sign of trouble, either to one's self or one's kin' (Chapter 21) prepares us, when Jane dreams too, first for Jane's return to Gateshead and Mrs Reed's death, and second for Jane's dreams of a child just before her wedding (Chapter 24) to be seen as a serious omen of disaster.

Mr Brocklehurst is one of the links between Gateshead and Lowood. He is unlike the Reeds in the attitude we adopt towards him, and an example of one of the attributes Charlotte Brontë is often denied—humour. He is a comic grotesque.[9] The Rev. Carus Wilson may or may not be the original of the portrait, but we have no doubt of its truth to the type.

I looked up at—a black pillar!—such, at least, appeared to me, at first sight, the straight, narrow, sable-clad shape standing erect on the rug: the grim face at the top was like a carved mask, placed above the shaft by way of capital.

(Chapter 4)

He reveals himself ironically and unconsciously (to us) in his own words and behaviour, and Jane, the overliteral child, registers, though not consciously analysing, his absurdity:

'I buried a little child of five years old only a day or two since,—a good little child, whose soul is now in heaven. It is to be feared the same could not be said of you, were you *to be called hence.*'

Not being in a condition to remove his doubt, I only cast my eyes down at the two large feet planted on the rug, and sighed; wishing myself *far enough away.*

(Chapter 4, my italics)

Jane is capable of seeing him in a ridiculous light, and so he is a measure of her resilience—he contrasts with Mrs Reed who is not seen until her power and presence are proven—and he continues to be so at Lowood: in spite of being terrified of public disgrace, Jane can still observe him as 'longer, narrower and more rigid than ever', and the irony of the portrait of his wife and children 'splendidly attired in velvet, silk, and furs' (Chapter 8) needs no demonstration. His idiom is excellent:

'This girl, this child, the native of a Christian land, worse than many a little heathen who says its prayers to Brahma and kneels before Juggernaut—this girl is—a liar!'

(Chapter 8)

The conclusion is both an anticlimax (not so dreadful a failing, after all) and a surprise: this is almost the last sin to apply to Jane, whose frankness is perhaps the only genuine virtue we have seen in her so far.

The teachers Miss Miller, Miss Scatcherd, and Mlle Pierrot are of the stock types that she used in *The Professor,* and uses again in *Villette*; they serve their purpose and are unobtrusive, allowing us to concentrate on the more vital Miss Temple and Helen Burns. These two both have the literary virtue of being interesting though noble characters. There is tact in stressing Helen's slovenliness before revealing her fortitude, and in deliberately underplaying her learning: she is first seen reading *Rasselas,* which daunts Jane, and probably the reader as well; and tact also in keeping Miss Temple at a distance: we never see her relations with Jane as she grows older and more intimate with her. If Jane learns 'patience under apparent injustice, and the wholesome distrust of too much reliance on human affections' from Helen (as Robert Martin thinks),[10] we also learn a great deal about Jane. Both Helen and Miss Temple demonstrate Jane's need simply for human affection, and her power to inspire it, before she meets Mr Rochester and the force of love is added. They prove also that Jane chooses the highest when she sees it.[11] From Miss Temple we learn also Jane's characteristic willingness to acknowledge her superior, which in its turn prepares her and us for the way she submits happily to her cousins Diana and Mary, both for the energy of their characters and for their learning.

At Thornfield there is another change in the type and the presentation of characters. As governess, Jane now has a social as well as a personal position, and the people she meets are consequently seen in their place in society as well as in their individual selves. Social position is to be at odds with personal worth and personal relationships at Thornfield: it is the essence of these society characters that their rank is wholly disproportionate to their personal worth; and the culmination is Mr

Rochester's social contract to his mad wife. Startling and sensational as the burlesques of the house-party and the final revelation are, the way is prepared for them from even before Jane arrives at Thornfield, when she receives Mrs Fairfax's answer to her advertisement:

> Mrs Fairfax! I saw her in a black gown and widow's cap; frigid, perhaps, but not uncivil: a model of elderly English respectability.
>
> (Chapter 10)

It is position, not personality, which is being suggested by 'widow' and 'respectability', and it is significant of the way things are to go that Jane is mistaken: Mrs Fairfax is not the mother of Adèle, nor the lady of the house, but only the housekeeper.

Mrs Fairfax, 'a placid-tempered, kind-natured woman, of competent education and average intelligence' (Chapter 12), 'kindly as usual—and, as usual, rather trite' (Chapter 13)—the perfect foil for Jane and Mr Rochester in their first interviews—is something new, and creates, assisted by Sophie and Adèle, the atmosphere of positive, if placid, goodwill that is a necessary feature of Thornfield, and a strong contrast to what has gone before. Charlotte Brontë will abandon verisimilitude if occasion demands,[12] yet Mrs Fairfax's personality and idiom are as accurate as Bessie's, and recognizably of a generation or more before Jane's:

> 'I'm sure last winter (it was a very severe one, if you recollect, and when it did not snow, it rained and blew), not a creature but the butcher and postman came to the house, from November till February; and I really got quite melancholy with sitting night after night alone; I had Leah in to read to me sometimes; but I don't think the poor girl liked the task much: she felt it confining.'
>
> (Chapter 11)

The only other adult resident of the house of any significance is Grace Poole, faintly comic with her unexpectedly commonplace appearance, homely speech, and her prosaic 'pint of porter and bit of pudding on a tray' (Chapter 16). She is in her way a modest triumph, since she is the antithesis of the sinister servant of Gothic romance, whose sinister machinations come to naught in the light of common day. When the light is let in on Grace's function, it is in fact something much worse than Jane or the reader could suspect, and knowing that she is commonplace makes us more ready to accept anything so sensational as a secretly kept insane wife. At the same time she helps us to see Jane as a person of sound sense, who, while preceiving a mystery, never lets her imagination get the better of her:

> 'What if a former caprice (a freak very possible to a nature so sudden and headstrong as his) has delivered him into her power, and she now exercises over his actions a secret influence, the result of his own indiscretion, which he cannot shake off and dare not disregard?'

But, having reached this point of conjecture, Mrs Poole's square, flat figure, and uncomely, dry, even coarse face, recurred so distinctly to my mind's eye, that I thought, 'No; impossible! my supposition cannot be correct.'

> (Chapter 16)

She is right when she thinks Grace has some power over Mr Rochester, equally right in rejecting a romantic connection: and the incident is structural in that it ironically directs and prepares us for Bertha: it is indeed 'a former caprice' that has delivered him into her power.

The house-party displays a different type of minor character, with less relevance outside the incidents where they actually appear and a great deal less realism—or, as Charlotte Brontë might have said, 'more real than true'. They resemble Mr Brocklehurst in distressing Jane and being comic and grotesque at the same time. Once one recognizes the comedy, the obvious improbabilities become much less offensive, and one reads Blanche and her corsair-song, and the resplendent dowagers Lady Lynn and Lady Ingram, not so much as one reads Thackeray's satiric portraits, but Fielding's.[13]

There is a gusto in Charlotte Brontë's language which prevents any suspicion that Jane is envious of these people, and suggests that she may know very well that she is exaggerating details of dress and modes of speech.[14] We are prepared for distortion when they first appear:

> There were but eight; yet somehow as they flocked in, they gave the appearance of a much larger number. Some of them were very tall; many were dressed in white; all had a sweeping amplitude of array that seemed to magnify their persons as the mist magnifies the moon.
>
> (Chapter 17)

The elevated diction here is a symptom of coming burlesque, which is promptly developed in the case of the dowagers:

> Her dark hair shone glossily under the shade of an azure plume, and within the circlet of a band of gems.
>
> She had Roman features and a double chin, disappearing into a throat like a pillar: these features appeared to me not only inflated and darkened, but even furrowed with pride; and the chin was sustained by the same principle, in a position of almost preternatural erectness. She had, likewise, a fierce and a hard eye: it reminded me of Mrs Reed's; she mouthed her words in speaking; her voice was deep, its inflections very pompous, very dogmatical,—very intolerable, in short. A crimson velvet robe, and a shawl turban of some gold-wrought Indian fabric, invested her (I suppose she thought) with a truly imperial dignity.
>
> (ibid.)

It is a brave writer and a superbly confident one who can use the same means for comic inflation as for serious writing: this passage recalls in turn Mr Brocklehurst (the pillar) and Mrs Reed (a direct allusion), anticipates Bertha Mason ('inflated and darkened'), and, best of all, epitomizes the whole supranormal intensity of the story in the very characteristic word 'preternatural'. The chief functions of this house-party group are to provide a setting for Blanche Ingram, to be the instruments performing the highly significant charade, to show us Jane's passive fortitude (since the earlier episodes have all shown her ability to act), and to force Jane and the reader to assess and acknowledge the relationship between Jane and Mr Rochester. It is not until the society of his social equals separates him, apparently, from Jane, that she admits what she feels, and names it—'I had not intended to *love* him' (Chapter 17) is the first use of the word—and goes on,

> 'He is not of their kind. I believe he is of mine;—I am sure he is,—I feel akin to him,—I understand the language of his countenance and movements: though rank and wealth sever us widely, I have something in my brain and heart, in my blood and nerves, that assimilates me mentally to him.'
>
> (ibid.)

The presence of Blanche has forced into utterance something never before expressed in the novel, something which is essentially the same as Edgar Linton's proposal precipitates in Catherine's declaration of her feelings for Heathcliff:

> 'Nelly, I *am* Heathcliff! He's always, always, in my mind: not as a pleasure, any more than I am always a pleasure to myself, but as my own being.'
>
> (*Wuthering Heights,* Chapter 9)

Charlotte's expression is less poetic than Emily's, but her achievement is to make so revolutionary a relationship a part of something much closer to recognizable everyday existence than *Wuthering Heights* can ever be. Blanche herself may be unrealistic—even if at this late date we must take Miss Rigby's word that ladies did not dress as Charlotte Brontë describes Blanche,[15] there can be little doubt that no young lady talked like her—but she is superbly and comically convincing in her way, with her elementary Italian and French, and her outdated sentimental romantic enthusiasm for bandit heroes and highwaymen, contrasting with the painfully genuine and repressed feelings of Jane and Mr Rochester. Jane does not waste much narrative on her, and we do not care twopence for her feelings at being jilted by Mr Rochester, and this again shows the sound tact of Charlotte Brontë's portrait, which completely precludes pity for her, and consequent disapproval of Mr Rochester for deceiving her. However, she has taken up time in the courtship of Mr Rochester and Jane; we know and feel that Mr Rochester has had plenty of time in which

to decide his course of action: he has committed bigamy out of calculation as well as passion, and so merits the moral judgement which he suffers.

Bertha Mason (whom it is offensive even to think of as Bertha Rochester) is the incubus of Thornfield, who has no 'character' until Mr Rochester reveals her history in Chapter 27, and whose character when it is finally exposed is no real surprise, though her existence is a shock. She is the embodiment of ungoverned passion, contrasting with Blanche, who has none (but who yet looks like her: 'I found her a fine woman in the style of Blanche Ingram; tall, dark and majestic,' Chapter 27), and demonstrates both the power and the failing of Mr Rochester, who will not send her to Ferndean because it is unhealthy, but insists on his right to act as if she does not exist. She develops from the vague to the explicit, from the unseen possessor of the laugh, who starts a mysterious fire in the night, to the violent attacker of Mason which seems the climax to her activities but is not so, since her worst offence is simply to exist as Mr Rochester's wife. She is the purveyor of horror, but is not herself revolting until it is most necessary for her to be so, when her full story is heard, and we must be made to pity Mr Rochester.

A character more important to the novel as a whole than her part in the action would suggest is Adèle Varens. Seemingly only the pretext for Jane's presence at Thornfield, Adèle is structurally invaluable. She is clearly a touchstone of character: Amy and Louisa Eshton call her 'a love of a child' (Chapter 17) and convict themselves of sentimentality; Blanche calls her a 'puppet' (ibid.) and demonstrates her own deficiency. Adèle herself is fond of her 'chère Mlle Jeannot' and so proves that Jane can attract more than merely her superiors, while Jane is cool but just about Adèle:

> She had no great talents, no marked traits of character, no peculiar development of feeling or taste which raised her one inch above the ordinary level of childhood; but neither had she any deficiency or vice which sunk her below it.
>
> (Chapter 12)

And this very coolness helps her to be useful. Mr Rochester is no monster for not loving her, and he is clearly philanthropic in bringing her up, when she may not even be his daughter. The way he treats her, providing a governess and keeping her at Thornfield (when he might have got her out of the way at a boarding school) predisposes us to accept his keeping a mad wife at home instead of having her shut up. Adèle is living evidence of Mr Rochester's past, which, literary and conventional as his expression of it is, gains solidity by her recollections of life 'chez maman'.[16] She has numerous incidental structural uses: commentary on the house-party, the pretext for Jane to appear in the drawing-room with the guests (not normally a governess's privilege); the recipient of Mr Rochester's whimsical badinage about Jane; another temptation not to leave Thornfield and Mr Rochester; and one of the few things to survive the fire.

In sharp contrast to anyone at Thornfield are the characters at Morton: St John, Diana and Mary Rivers, Hannah, Rosamond Oliver and the few villagers and farmers. Charlotte Brontë's touch with the rustics is sure: when Jane is starving, their equally unsentimental and unmalevolent treatment gives vivid conviction to her sufferings:

> At the door of a cottage I saw a little girl about to throw a mess of cold porridge into a pig trough. 'Will you give me that?' I asked.
>
> She stared at me. 'Mother!' she exclaimed; 'there is a woman wants me to give her these porridge.'
>
> 'Well, lass,' replied a voice within, 'give it her if she's a beggar. T' pig doesn't want it.'
>
> (Chapter 28)

The servant Hannah is another 'Bessie' character, helping Jane to return to contact with society, and re-establish her own place in it, clearly not as a beggar nor even a servant, and Hannah's verdict, 'You look a raight down dacent little crater' (Chapter 29), is entertaining in its inadequacy.

Mary never appears without Diana, and is really a shadow of her, and both are overshadowed by their brother. They are the first women friends Jane has had since she left Lowood and Miss Temple, and represent the pleasures of the intellect, which Jane has not had, or missed. Despite their beauty, they are not at all young-lady-like and nor are their conversations with Jane. St John is a finely-observed study of a man who turns egotism and ambition to the service of religion. He is the most important single character in the book after Mr Rochester, and is obviously his antithesis, religious, idealistic, handsome, cold-blooded, seeing in Jane 'nothing attractive . . . not even youth—only a few useful mental points' (Chapter 37). He is indeed not attractive himself, and all his speeches are about, or soon turn to, himself. The following exchange, a discussion of Jane's post as schoolmistress, is characteristic:

> 'You will not stay at Morton long: no, no!'
>
> 'Why! What is your reason for saying so?'
>
> 'I read it in your eye; it is not of that description which promises the maintenance of an even tenor in life.'
>
> 'I am not ambitious.'
>
> He started at the word 'ambitious'. He repeated, 'No. What made you think of ambition? Who is ambitious? I know I am: but how did you find it out?'
>
> (Chapter 30)

He implicitly condemns himself and his aspirations: his sermon is symptomatic:

> Throughout there was a strange bitterness; an absence of consolatory gentleness: stern allusions to Calvinistic doctrines—election, pre-destination, reprobation—were frequent; and each reference to these points sounded like a sentence pronounced for doom. When he had done, instead of feeling better, calmer, more enlightened by his discourse, I experienced an inexpressible sadness.
>
> (ibid.)

His decision to become a missionary saddens his sisters, and is against his dead father's wishes. Even his passion for the elementary Miss Oliver indicates his deficiency, in caring in such a way for a woman so clearly inferior to what he has been accustomed to in his sisters, apart from Jane herself. His treatment, solemn, using Biblical allusion, and constantly described in terms of marble, and even as a pillar, all recalls that other columnar clergyman, Mr Brocklehurst. It is surprising that he can generate enough power to become the danger he is to Jane at the end of the episode, and that the reader shares her unwilling admiration for one who tempts her to do violence to her own nature, in antithesis to Mr Rochester, who tempted her to violate her moral standards. The impression of his influence builds up gradually: Rosamond links them:

> She said I was like Mr Rivers (only, certainly, she allowed, 'not one-tenth so handsome; though I was a nice neat little soul enough, but he was an angel'). I was, however, good, clever, composed, and firm, like him.
>
> (Chapter 32)

He understands Jane up to a point:

> 'Well, if you are not ambitious, you are—' He paused.
>
> 'What?'
>
> 'I was going to say, impassioned; but perhaps you would have misunderstood the word, and been displeased. I mean, that human affections and sympathies have a most powerful hold on you.'
>
> (Chapter 30)

And Jane herself increases their intimacy and consequently his power over her by invading his feelings for Rosamond. Impersonal though he may be, Charlotte Brontë yet makes us and Jane very conscious of him physically: his handsomeness makes him interesting at the same time as it separates him from Jane:

> The thing was as impossible as to mould my irregular features to his correct and classic pattern, to give to my changeable green eyes the sea-blue tint and solemn lustre of his own.
>
> (Chapter 34)

It can even make him moving:

> I waited, expecting he would say something I could at least comprehend; but his hand was now at his chin, his finger on his lip: he was thinking. It struck me that his hand looked wasted like his face. A perhaps uncalled-for gush of pity came over my heart.

(Chapter 33)

There remain only the two people at the heart of the book—Mr Rochester and Jane. Mr Rochester has been seen by many as the idealized, even the impossible, hero: 'No flesh and blood man could be so exclusively composed of violence and virility and masculine vanity as Mr Rochester,' says David Cecil.[17] But he does not completely fill the romantic bill, and we are pulled up smartly if we try to make him; he is no nineteenth-century Sir Charles Grandison, nor even a Victorian re-working of the Byronic outcast. As usual, the attempt to identify the character with an actual person does not get us very far. M. Héger lurks at the back of every critic's mind, as with every hero in Charlotte Brontë's work, as though it were impossible for her either to depend on her imagination, or to adapt the material of life to her purpose. The other more respectable impulse, to explain historically, and analyse Mr Rochester's undoubted debt to Byronism, does not go far either, since the great interest of Mr Rochester is in what Charlotte Brontë creates out of her materials, rather than the nature of the materials themselves. Proof of this is that although in his place in the novel he convinces us completely, he cannot be taken out of his context: he exists as part of Jane's consciousness, and for his relation to her. But within this context we have no reservations about him other than those Charlotte Brontë specifically intends, and the impulse to think of him as isolable, as if 'real', is a measure of the success she has achieved by her autobiographical method. To describe a hero only by what the heroine sees, when the former must reveal more of himself to the reader than the other can observe, and when that other must be hampered by youth, inexperience, and passion, is a great achievement.

Mr Rochester is both the remote hero and the man whom Jane understands because she is 'akin' to him; he is a man whose moral nature is like Jane's, who is yet the one who tempts her to evil; he is a good man who suffers a dreadful punishment for his sin. Here for the first (and perhaps the only) time we have the romantic hero who becomes not less but more exciting as he becomes familiar, for whom marriage is the triumph, not merely the convenient and correct end to the adventures of courtship, who does not 'dwindle into a husband' as Millamant deplored dwindling into a wife.

The essence of Mr Rochester is to be unpredictable, to shock with the unconventional and the unexpected; but it is essential that the reasons for his behaviour shall be clearly and unambiguously discernible, in retrospect if not at the time. A useful example is the conversation after Jane has rescued him from the fire (Chapter 15), and the events which immediately follow.[18] This is all sensational enough, but the receptive reader is able to understand Mr Rochester's behaviour in the light of what follows. Like Jane we believe Mr Rochester:

> 'I knew,' he continued, 'you would do me good in some way, at some time;—I saw it in your eyes when I first beheld you: their expression and smile did not—(again he stopped)—did not (he proceeded hastily) strike delight to my very inmost heart so for nothing.'

(Chapter 15)

But unlike her, we understand his precipitate departure and return with Blanche Ingram. One reason he gives himself:

> 'I wished to render you as madly in love with me as I was with you; and I knew jealousy would be the best ally I could call in for the furtherance of that end.'

(Chapter 24)

This is obvious and elementary. Another is suggested in another scene, when in his gipsy disguise Mr Rochester muses to himself with Jane kneeling before him in the firelight:

> 'I should wish to protract this moment *ad infinitum;* but I dare not. So far I have governed myself thoroughly. I have acted as I inwardly swore I would act; but farther might try me beyond my strength.'

(Chapter 19)

After the fire the emotional situation has clearly got very nearly out of hand, as Mr Rochester's hesitant words indicate.[19] We realize also that Mr Rochester must make up his mind about his moral position; he does so between the fire and the house-party, and returns having resolved on his right to commit legal bigamy. This is the reason why we hear of his mistress Céline Varens so very early in his acquaintance; it is indeed almost the first thing we find out about him other than what the immediate present reveals. Mr Rochester must be attractive (as Céline Varens's attachment proves indeed), but all the associations of illicit union must be kept in mind as repellent, since we must never for a moment think that Jane is wrong in refusing to live unmarried with Mr Rochester; we must see and feel, as well as know, that Mr Rochester himself abhors the idea, and that by his own lights he is no mere self-indulgent seducer of yet another mistress.

While he does a good deal of the explaining himself (being a man of vigour in words as well as actions, and being 'self-conscious' in the same way as Jane is self-conscious), we are constantly being called upon as the action progresses to try to judge Mr Rochester at the same time as we come with Jane under his spell, by standards which he himself is not aware of and will not admit. In almost every one of his conversations with Jane we are prepared for the moral impasse of Chapter 27: in their second conversation Mr Rochester declares 'unheard-of combinations of circumstances demand unheard-of rules' (Chapter 14); by his own admission later,

> 'If I bid you do what you thought wrong, there would be no light-footed running, no neat-handed alacrity, no lively glance and animated complexion.'
>
> (Chapter 20)

while he recognizes the danger that Jane will refuse him, he does not yet realize as we do the violence he is doing to her personality in deceiving her, and that Jane's moral sense just as much as her passion is what distinguishes her: it is not until Ferndean that he realizes the part of her that declared:

> '*I* care for myself. The more solitary, the more friendless, the more unsustained I am, the more I will respect myself. I will keep the law given by God; sanctioned by man. I will hold to the principles received by me when I was sane, and not mad—as I am now.'
>
> (Chapter 27)

We have learned to respond to Mr Rochester's moral predicament, and sympathize, while not condoning his behaviour.

The whole of his association with Jane is a series of surprises, of shocks to which Jane responds and draws back for periods of assessment, before the next shock impinges. By this means, he, like St John Rivers, develops a kind and degree of power we should not suspect from his beginnings, natural though it seems when we reach the end. These delays Mr Rochester introduces into the courtship have many uses, besides the obvious ones of producing suspense and excitement. They allow Jane to classify and come to terms with her experience; they show Mr Rochester's self-control and consciousness of his feelings and so make him worthy of Jane, since he is not acting merely on passion and impulse; at the same time there can be no doubt that he is morally at fault in committing a calculated legal crime, and violating Jane's known nature. He clearly enjoys the invidious relationships of this long courtship (as in a way Jane clearly does also), deliberately building up the excitement: almost all his speeches to Jane after Blanche arrives are ambiguous declarations or invitations.[20] He is rightly the mover of the romance and these many half-declarations are emotional attacks, and make Jane's position an artistically and emotionally satisfying one: she has had ample opportunity to see that he loves her when in Chapter 23 she does not receive the conventional proposal and conventionally submit, but attacks in her turn and so asserts her equality—as Mr Rochester says, 'it was you who made me the offer'.

Information about him is given as Jane acquires it, where it is most appropriate. The various ways in which we are invited to perceive him blend into a whole, and gain richer meaning as others accumulate. At first he is a figure of folklore; his dog is perhaps the Gytrash, and he himself is described in terms which are both physical and violent, and remote from the commonplace:

> Still, he looked preciously grim, cushioning his massive head against the swelling back of his chair, and receiving the light of the fire on his granite-hewn features, and in his great, dark eyes—for he had great, dark eyes, and very fine eyes, too: not without a certain change in their depths sometimes, which, if it was not softness, reminded you, at least, of that feeling.
>
> (Chapter 14)

There is physical vigour even in 'the *swelling* back of the chair', the 'massive head' recalls Pilot's 'lion-like' one (Chapter 18), and the passage is reinforced by the mention earlier of 'purple curtains', the imperial colour. The suggestion of something superhuman remainse and the amoral and physical is taken up and shifted, by way of the, oriental charade, so that during the month's engagement Mr Rochester as the imperial sultan is deliberately rejected and even ridiculed (Chapter 24): it stands for that side of him which distresses Jane and causes his downfall, since if he had not patronized Jane so that she feels like 'a second Danaë with the golden shower falling daily round [her]' (Chapter 24) she would not have written to her uncle, and he would not have told Mason of the wedding. Similarly the feeling of his violence is taken up and used. Mrs Fairfax says, 'the Rochesters have been rather a violent than a quiet race in their time' (Chapter 11), yet by Chapter 27 the physically violent, like that in *Wuthering Heights,* is merely a reflection of much greater spiritual turmoil.[21]

Mr Rochester at Thornfield is coherent enough, but many readers have wondered whether he is the same man whom Jane meets and marries at Ferndean. Charlotte Brontë is careful to provide many links, perhaps the most notable of them being the Samson image; this was first expressed in Chapter 24 ('I was thinking of Hercules and Samson with their charmers'), reappears when Mr Rochester exclaims 'I long to exert a fraction of Samson's strength' (Chapter 27), and finds its true application at Ferndean where he is indeed 'a sightless Samson' (Chapter 37). He is certainly changed, just as Mrs Reed changed between Chapters 1 and 21; but Charlotte Brontë has no doubts about him: what is emphasized is that he is still essentially the man he was, vigorous and in the prime of life. He is reintroduced by his full name, his relationship with Jane is instantly re-established, he speaks with the same voice in the same terms, using the pet-name Janet, and seeing her as 'a fairy', making the same brisk leaps from the impassioned to the practical:

'And you do not lie dead in some ditch under some stream? And you are not a pining outcast amongst strangers?'

'No, sir; I am an independent woman now.'

'Independent! What do you mean, Jane?'

'My uncle in Madeira is dead, and he left me five thousand pounds.'

'Ah, this is practical—this is real!' he cried: 'I should never dream that.'

(Chapter 37)

The main differences are that he is blind and maimed, and that he hesitates to ask her to marry him. Again it is over-sentimental to over-estimate the disaster, and Charlotte Brontë never does so. Mr Rochester blind is still a romantic figure, to be seen as a falcon or as Vulcan (as he could not be with one leg for instance). Jane's attitude is the robust one she showed in happiness: she discounts his injuries:

'I thought you would be revolted, Jane, when you saw my arm, and my cicatrized visage.'

'Did you? Don't tell me so—lest I should say something disparaging to your judgment.'

(ibid.)

and rejects emphatically any suggestion of 'sacrifice' in marrying him.[22] He is realistically allowed to recover a good deal of his sight. Mr Rochester and Jane are now felt to be more equal and better suited than they were at Thornfield; we feel that Jane is right when she says:

'I love you better now, when I can really be useful to you, than I did in your state of proud independence, when you disdained every part but that of the giver and protector.'

(ibid.)

At last it is impossible for Jane to seem 'an English Céline Varens' (Chapter 23) to be showered with favours, even though a marriage ceremony has taken place. The danger has always been lurking, all the more because Céline has managed to bear Mr Rochester's child, and so assume one of the chief functions of a wife. These considerations annihilate the other question that besets most readers: whether there is not an emotional indulgence, whether Charlotte Brontë is making Mr Rochester more of a Samson and Jane more a Delilah than she consciously intends, in letting Mr Rochester be so dreadfully maimed. It is right, too, that Mr Rochester's injuries are not his moral punishment for the suffering he caused Jane (his mental tortures are that). He is injured as a paradoxical reward for virtue: if he had not tried to save Bertha he would not have been hurt. This is not at all poetic justice, but there is a real psychological rightness about it, just as there was when he would not shut Bertha away at Ferndean because it was too unhealthy (Chapter 27) and she might die.

There remains very little to be said about Jane Eyre herself, because more than most eponymous heroines she is the whole of the novel in which she appears. Sympathy with her is essential, and there can be few characters in fiction to whom it has been so readily given. She calls up emotions every reader must recognize and probably have experienced, and at the times and ages that most people felt them, though in the novel they are intensified: Jane in terror of a bullying boy cousin, hating a powerful aunt, cringing from public exposure at school, giving her heart to a school-friend and a kind teacher, all readily find echoes in the reader's past; and when Jane's circumstances become stranger, we continue to respond as she does, and feel the truth of the response. With her passions Jane combines qualities more rational, equally sympathetic, which every reader's vanity flatters him he possesses too: sound common sense, the power to see herself as others see her, a robust sense of humour, the power to act right under the most powerful of temptations, and survive the most testing physical conditions. Charlotte Brontë is quite safe, with such a basis, in making her heroine small and plain and 'Quakerish' in matters of dress, and in making her not incidentally but genuinely so, as the occasional pointed comments of others prove:

'You are genteel enough; you look like a lady, and it is as much as ever I expected of you.'

(Chapter 10)

'Il m'a demandé le nom de ma gouvernante, et si elle n'était pas une petite personne, assez mince et un peu pâle.'

(Chapter 13)

Bessie's faint praise and Adèle's candid summary are utterly convincing.[23] We even accept the excessive independence which makes her declare that when married

'I shall continue to act as Adèle's governess: by that I shall earn my board and lodging, and thirty pounds a year besides. I'll furnish my own wardrobe out of that money, and you shall give me nothing but [your regard].'

(Chapter 24)

When Mr Rochester calls this 'cool native impudence, and pure innate pride' we feel he is understanding the case; but we are still on Jane's side. This is the obvious strength of the book, this power to involve the reader so intensely in Jane's fortunes.[24] Although a narrating heroine in one sense reveals herself, in another Charlotte Brontë avoids doing so as much as possible. There is proportionately very little retail of thought and states of mind in *Jane Eyre*. Wherever possible Charlotte Brontë uses action and dialogue. Thought or state of mind, when it must be done, is done by various objectifying devices: the interior dialogue, the address to the reader, the use of imagery to reveal by parallels, or a simple flat statement using almost eighteenth-century abstract concepts. The result is that we never approach the sentimental or the mawkish.

The shape of the novel is very much represented by the places where the action occurs, which Charlotte Brontë makes an essential part of the structure, as well as the atmosphere, of her stories. Places have indeed as much character as people, and serve many of the same purposes, a use which *Jane Eyre* shares with *Wuthering Heights,* or, to name a later novelist, Hardy. They operate by accurately and vividly selected detail, and often on more than one level. Just as a single person is felt and judged in different ways at the same time, so places may arouse a variety of conflicting feelings, and the tensions, beginning fairly simply with the child's view of Gateshead, increase in complexity through Lowood, Thornfield, Morton, and Ferndean. Gateshead is plainly a place of torment, the house of the Reeds, where all the rooms are places of cold and dread, whether in company or isolation; even in the nursery Jane cannot touch the dolls' house furniture 'for the tiny chairs and mirrors, the fairy plates and cups were [Georgiana's] property' (Chapter 4), and the windows are fretted with 'frost-flowers'. Jane's only pleasures there are melancholy, uncertain, fleeting, and solitary: the vignettes in Bewick,

> The rock standing up alone in a sea of billow and spray; the broken boat stranded on a desolate coast; the cold and ghastly moon glancing through bars of cloud at a wreck just sinking.
>
> (Chapter 1)

are a brilliant choice: Bewick's vignettes do arouse such feelings, so Jane's reactions seem authenti. Bessie's kindness, represented by 'a tart on a certain brightly painted china plate, whose bird of paradise, nestling in a wreath of convolvuli and rosebuds, had been wont to stir in me a most enthusiastic sense of admiration' (Chapter 3), is, when she obtains it, 'like most other favours long deferred and often wished for, too late! I could not eat the tart: and the plumage of the bird, the tints of the flowers, seemed strangely faded' (ibid.). Yet these pleasures remain with Jane: Bewick can be clearly seen as an influence on the visionary paintings Jane does at Lowood and shows Mr Rochester at Thornfield: the pleasure in brilliant artefacts inspires her admiration for

> a very pretty drawing-room, and within it a boudoir, both spread with white carpets, on which seemed laid brilliant garlands of flowers; both ceiled with snowy mouldings of white grapes and vine-leaves, beneath which glowed in rich contrast crimson couches and ottomans; while the ornaments on the pale Parian mantelpiece were of sparkling Bohemian glass, ruby red; and between the windows large mirrors repeated the general blending of snow and fire.
>
> (Chapter 11)

—which Mr Rochester later dismisses (with reason):

> 'The glamour of inexperience is over your eyes,' he answered; 'and you see (Thornfield) through a charmed medium: you cannot discern that the gilding is slime and the silk draperies cobwebs; that the marble is sordid slate, and the polished woods mere refuse chips and scaly bark.'
>
> (Chapter 20)

reproducing thus the movement of the earlier passage about the plate.

Lowood is physically hard and aesthetically repulsive. A reader's immediate recollections of it are of burnt porridge, 'a strong steam redolent of rancid fat', 'a keen north-east wind, whistling through crevices of our bedroom windows all night long, [that] had made us shiver in our beds, and turned the contents of the ewers to ice' (Chapter 6), girls 'in brown stuff frocks of quaint fashion, and long holland pinafores' (Chapter 5), whose hair is not allowed to curl, even naturally. But the pleasures are more mature and more extensive. Sensuous pleasure remains; in food for the famished such as Miss Temple's supper ('How fragrant was the steam of the beverage, and the scent of the toast', and that ever memorable 'good-sized seed-cake' (Chapter 8)); and in the scenery ('prospects of noble summits girdling a great hill-hollow, rich in verdure and shadow; a bright beck, full of dark stones and sparkling eddies' (Chapter 9)). It is also the place of congenial companionship—Miss Temple, Helen Burns, and even Mary Ann Wilson; and intellectual pleasures are added—of drawing, learning French and conversing with Miss Temple.

Such simple combinations of good and bad prepare for the much more subtle use of Thornfield. The place has several aspects: freedom and happiness are embodied in some parts of the house, in its gardens, and in the surrounding landscape; while the sinister and evil are embodied in the upper storeys (especially at night); the grand world of society, heartless and tasteless, belongs in the drawing-room. These are all directly related to Jane's association with Mr Rochester, and help us to feel the moral weight of what happens. Jane first meets Mr Rochester outside, in Hay Lane; he tells her about Céline in the cold wintry garden, standing outside the house as he is standing, mentally, outside his own experiences and coldly assessing them; after Mason has been attacked and departed, Mr Rochester sits in the garden in summer sunrise with Jane, reviewing in the dawn of his new emotions the painful and violent ones of his youth, which link so closely with what has just happened inside the house; he proposes to Jane in the garden, in the orchard on Midsummer-eve, where all is 'Eden-like' and as he said before 'all is real, sweet and pure' (Chapter 20). The proposal is unlawful, but its spirit is not, and the setting of it cannot fail to make us feel so. By contrast what happens indoors is ambiguou or evil. When she has just met Mr Rochester, Jane, returning from Hay in the evening and loitering outside, sees the house as a 'grey hollow filled with rayless cells' (Chapter 12); the suggestion of prison and place of the dead continues: Bertha Mason is shut up on the third floor, and when she escapes, setting fire to Mr Rochester's bed, visiting Jane and tearing her veil, and setting fire finally to Jane's room, all she does is done indoors and upstairs. Downstairs the Gothic terror is replaced by vapid society and the pressure it exerts on Jane and Mr Rochester: he can only half-communicate with her, 'in mortal dread of some prating prig of a servant passing' (Chapter 17), or disguised as a gipsy, and as soon as they enter the hall after the proposal, Mrs Fairfax, 'pale, grave, and amazed' (Chapter 23), recalls us to the standards of society, Thornfield is precious because Jane has 'lived in it a full and delightful life' (ibid.); but it is insubstantial and doomed to perish, representing the falsity that must be burned away by suffering before Jane and Mr Rochester can come together, and that Jane's dreams of it as a crumbling ruin foreshadow (Chapter 25).

Moor House is in many ways its antithesis: the building is a symbol of security and family unity, a place Jane can 'care for' in the most practical sense, as the 'cleaning down' process with Hannah proves (Chapter 34). It provides Jane with a family and a function, but subjects her to more anxiety than Thornfield ever did, when St John's calls her to submit to a soulless and self-destroying marriage of duty. To read about Moor House reproduces Jane's experiences there: it is both less absorbing than Thornfield, and a great deal more trying. On the other hand, Moor House and Jane's life there gain dignity, power and health from the surrounding hill-country. Moorland comforts her in her flight:

> Beside the crag, the heath was very deep: when I lay down my feet were buried in it; rising high on each side, it left only a narrow space for the night-air to invade. I folded my shawl double, and spread it over me for a coverlet; a low, mossy swell was my pillow.
>
> (Chapter 28)

It is also a fitting background for St John, a stern setting for his stern proposals, which are made high in the hills where

> 'the mountain shook off turf and flower, had only heath for raiment, and crag for gem—where it exaggerated the wild to the savage, and exchanged the fresh for the frowning—where it guarded the forlorn hope of solitude, and a last refuge for silence'[25]
>
> (Chapter 34)

Jane's schoolteacher's cottage—one-up, one-down— offers a contrast to Thornfield (the bare necessities of life, physical, mental and emotional), just as the moorland landscape offers a noble but barren contrast to the fertile country round Thornfield:

> A little room with white-washed walls, and a sanded floor; containing four painted chairs and a table, a clock, a cupboard, with two or three plates and dishes, and a set of tea-things in delf.
>
> (Chapter 31)

Here are merely the essentials for physical life, to correspond with the meagre mental life offered by teaching ignorant farmgirls; the setting makes one understand how Jane can say, 'I felt desolate to a degree. I felt . . . degraded', and then, in the next paragraph, be thankful to be 'a village schoolmistress, free and honest, in a breezy mountain nook in the healthy heart of England' (Chapter 31).

The story ends at Ferndean Manor, about thirty miles from Thornfield, 'quite a desolate spot', 'deep buried in a wood' in an 'ineligible and unsalubrious site', with 'dank and green decaying walls' (Chapters 36 and 37). Though the house and its milieu obviously provide a new setting for what is to be a new relationship, a setting in harmony with a meeting where 'rapture is kept well in check by pain' (Chapter 37), they are not relevant in the same way as the others have been, since they contrast with the present action, rather than reveal it. Although Jane does not tell us, we can safely assume that once married, she and Mr Rochester leave so unhealthy and gloomy a place, where it is difficult to accommodate even one guest. The house and its setting as seen at the beginning of Chapter 37 present the epitome of what Mr Rochester has suffered and become in the last year; and as soon as possible, on the morning after her arrival, Jane leads Mr Rochester 'out of the wet and wild wood into some cheerful fields' (ibid.) where 'the flowers and hedges looked refreshed' by the 'sad sky, cold gale, and small penetrating rain' of the night before, just as his sufferings have at last brought new life to Mr Rochester.

Thus the various sections of the story have a moral and artistic relevance to the main action and to each other which helps to prevent any feeling that the book has a broken back. The story is unified also in ways more obviously structural. Innumerable threads of association and construction link section to section and incident to incident; and Charlotte Brontë creates proportioned emphasis, subtle parallels, and a sense of layers of simultaneous action to her basically linear story. The mere proportion of space occupied plays a large part in suggesting relative importance to the reader: four chapters for Gateshead, six for Lowood, fifteen for Thornfield (interrupted by a single very long chapter when Jane returns to Gateshead); one long chapter for her suffering and starvation, seven for Morton, and three for Ferndean. Within the Thornfield period there is only one chapter before Mr Rochester appears, twelve chapters for the courtship (more than is spent on anything else in the novel), but also two very long ones which cover the span between the wedding and Jane's flight. It can clearly be seen that the narrative movement runs against the natural passage of time, but nevertheless time and the hour run through the roughest day. References to season and weather, and even dates and days of the week, are frequent and exact as well as atmospheric: the intervals of time between Jane's arrival at Thornfield in October and Mr Rochester's proposal on Midsummer Eve are carefully noted, and equally accurate are those between her midsummer agony on the moors, St John's news of her fortune brought on a snowy November the fifth, and her return to Ferndean on a wet Thursday summer evening (the third of June). Jane does not live wholly in the present (as fictional characters so often do) but is always aware of her own past and possible future—she imagines with frightening truth what marriage to St John would entail—and she recognizes death as an accepted fact for others and herself:

> I laughed at him as he said this. 'I am not an angel,' I asserted; 'and I will not be one till I die: I will be myself.'

> (Chapter 24)

The single long chapter in the middle of the Thornfield episode, when Jane revisits Gateshead and Mrs Reed dies, is probably the finest example of Charlotte Brontë's sure sense of shape. This chapter (21) covers the space of a month (May), the month immediately after the dreadful night when Mason is attacked, and the summer dawn when Mr Rochester almost tells Jane about his marriage and almost proposes to her. The next main event, two weeks after her return, is his real proposal. No one can fail to feel that the emotional effect of the interruption and return is right, but the reasons why Charlotte Brontë takes such a risk as to break off here, when things between Jane and Mr Rochester are clearly reaching a culmination, are not immediately clear.

The most obvious and mechanical reason why Jane returns is to hear Mrs Reed's deathbed confession telling her of the uncle to whom she will owe both the breaking off of her wedding and also her fortune. It is much more organically a culmination of what has gone before, and an anticipation of what is to come. The culmination is necessary because Jane is to return to Thornfield to face the two greatest emotional experiences of her life: Mr Rochester's and her own mutual declarations, and her renunciation of him. For these to have their full power we must see Jane as a whole being, a part of all that she has met, moulded to this experience by all that has happened to her hitherto. The return to Gateshead recreates her childhood and its sufferings, and charts her moral and emotional growth. Georgiana and Eliza can no longer oppress her, and of Mrs Reed she can say, and we can believe:

> I had left this woman in bitterness and hate, and I came back to her now with no other emotion than a sort of ruth for her great sufferings, and a strong yearning to forget and forgive all injuries.

> (Chapter 21)

The episode is equally vital as anticipation and preparation in perhaps more separate ways. It separates Mr Rochester's proposal from the scenes which have led up to it, and sets it apart from them. Jane, away from Mr Rochester and Thornfield for the first time, shows no weakly conventional or self-indulgent pain at the temporary separation; we are therefore the more ready to credit her extreme agony when she is forced to leave for good. So utterly unsentimental a handling of death prepares for the equally unsentimental love and agony to come:

> A strange and solemn object was that corpse to me. I gazed on it with gloom and pain: nothing soft, nothing sweet, nothing pitying, or hopeful, or subduing, did it inspire; only a grating anguish for *her* woes—not *my* loss—and a sombre tearless dismay at the fearfulness of death in such a form.

> (ibid.)

Gateshead and its affairs have reached a climax, which prepares for the even greater climax to come. As a climax, it is the antithesis of Mr Rochester's proposal; dreadful and unfeeling, it moves us and Jane, so that we are moved even more by the intense happiness which follows. Jane's power to hate intensely and to express it, recalled here, presupposes that her love and its expression will be equally intense. The episode puts before us distinctions we shall have to make at Morton, where 'judgement untempered by feeling' (ibid.) will again be offered, but in a more subtle guise, as religious renunciation. A view of life is created in which death takes a realistic place, so that when Bertha Mason dies, this convenient event seems not improbable, since four (Helen Burns, John Reed, his mother, and the West Indian uncle) have died before her.

Within the larger individual sections of the action, the movement varies, but Charlotte Brontë tends always to work in terms of the big scene, completely realized and dramatically presented. She likes to use the effect of shock on her reader, but she never loses her emotional continuity; she therefore moves from one big scene to the next, by a variety of methods: the smaller (but significant) intermediate scene, the pause for Jane's reflection and analysis of what has passed, and, very rarely, the juxtaposition of sharply contrasting important scenes. She is also careful to provide proper preparation where shock is unsuitable; and the prefatory material, though of various kinds, is always concerned with building up the right associations, or recalling the necessary personalities. The result is a wave-like movement, with a drawing-back between each surge of an incoming tide. Attention to continuity descends even to the nice placing of chapter divisions. The most interesting place to examine her structural methods is where they are at their finest and most sustained, that is, during the fifteen chapters chronicling the events at Thornfield. These move by a series of exciting, even sensational, events, seen in entirety. The sense of shock is as much in the material as the presentation, and Charlotte Brontë never cheats by cutting a scene off short to get her excitement. The first of these big scenes is the one where Mr Rochester falls off his horse in Hay Lane (Chapter 12), but this is unmistakably being underplayed, partly to gain power in retrospect, and partly so as to keep plenty of power in reserve. Mr Rochester is at this point, as Jane says, 'only a traveller taking the short cut to Millcote'. There must, after all, be no suggestion of falling in love at first sight—though this is what Mr Rochester almost does: 'It was well that I had learnt that this elf must return to me—that it belonged to my house down below—or I could not have felt it pass away from under my hand, and seen it vanish behind the dim hedge, without singular regret' (Chapter 12). Thereafter Charlotte Brontë has a good deal to do in the way of establishing relationships, and filling in past history, which all prevents action. But immediately this is done, the movement begins in Chapter 15, with the fire, the very night after Mr Rochester has told Jane about Céline Varens. The next is the first evening Jane and Adèle meet the house-party (Chapter 18), where Jane suffers her social inferiority, Mr Rochester's flirtation with Blanche, and finally Mr Rochester's all too perceptive questions; the charade comes next (18), then the fortune-telling gipsy (19), then the dreadful night when Mason is attacked, and the tête-à-tête in the orchard at dawn which follows (20); then at last (after Mrs Reed's death) and the very brief scene where Jane meets Mr Rochester in Hay Lane again, the proposal at midsummer (23). These chapters form an entity. The scenes are splendidly varied: there is the passionate tête-à-tête after the fire, and the disguised one of the fortune-telling; there are scenes when Mr Rochester makes the advances (the fire, his few words in the hall, his confession in the orchard when Mason has left), and scenes where Jane does (the proposal itself, and the little scene in Hay Lane preceding it); there are scenes where others are the real actors, and the relevance is in the emotions Jane feels (the 'polite' conversations about governesses, and the charade), scenes where the action is shared (Mason's terrible night). They take place at night, and by day, indoors and out (and not arbitrarily, for the setting is always significant); but however they occur, whoever is concerned, and wherever and whenever they happen, they each sweep things a little nearer to that Midsummer Eve in the orchard. After them comes another movement, whose motive is foreboding, which works in terms of fantasy and illusion, where dreams seem more real than life, where an ecstatic day-

light reality runs alongside frightening omens at night, which coalesce after the abortive wedding, and culminate when Jane tears herself away from Thornfield. Similarly the chapters at Morton move by way of various excitements and pressures until Jane hears Mr Rochester's voice and breaks free from St John.

The transitions between these scenes are as varied as the scenes themselves, and equally superb. We never feel that Charlotte Brontë is having to summon her resources, or rest between engagements. The action has all the continuity of real life, and the interest never slackens. What goes on in between the events absorbs us just as much as the events themselves, since our eye never leaves what absorbs us most—Jane herself—though *her* eye of course may wander very considerably. Hence the variety in the interludes. These are generally a pause for breath, and for reassessment. The day after the fire is a fine example of Charlotte Brontë's method, involving in a short space a number of the devices she employs. After the fire Jane cannot sleep, and admits to us and herself for the first time how she feels about Mr Rochester—not yet explicitly but in images:

> Till morning dawned I was tossed on a buoyant but unquiet sea, where billows of trouble rolled under surges of joy . . . [but] a counteracting breeze blew off land, and continually drove me back. Sense would resist delirium: judgment would warn passion.
>
> (Chapter 15)

The following day (Chapter 16) bears out what she says. The first incident is the servants Leah and Grace Poole putting the bedroom to rights, sense and the light of common day taking over the scene of delirium. Grace in person de-romances herself, with her 'pint of porter and bit of pudding' (Chapter 16). Having left her, Jane tries to explain Mrs Poole's position to herself: Mr Rochester may once have put himself in her power; they are the same age: 'she may possess originality and strength of character to compensate for the want of personal advantages. Mr Rochester is an amateur of the decided and eccentric.' Jane's reasoning is quite sensible, and even more sensible is the way she rejects the hypothesis when she considers Mrs Poole in person. The passage has an extra layer of significance, since all the points which make her reasoning sound here point to herself, not Mrs Poole, as the partner for Mr Rochester, as Jane herself recognizes. At this point Jane's thoughts again impinge upon action:

> I was now in the schoolroom; Adèle was drawing; I bent over her and directed her pencil. She looked up with a sort of start.
>
> 'Qu'avez-vous donc, mademoiselle?' said she; 'Vos doigts tremblent comme la feuille, et vos joues sont rouges: mais, rouges comme des cerises!'
>
> 'I am hot, Adèle, with stooping!' She went on sketching, I went on thinking.
>
> (ibid.)

The day ends with conversation between Jane and Mrs Fairfax at tea, with the same kind of external manifestation of feeling:

> 'You must want your tea,' said the good lady, as I joined her; 'you ate so little at dinner. I am afraid,' she continued, 'you are not well today: you look flushed and feverish.'
>
> (ibid.)

and the conversation reveals that Mr Rochester has left, and that the events are about to take a new course, with the arrival of the house-party and Blanche. Jane accepts this check to her feelings, and supplements it by contrasting herself with Blanche and drawing the two portraits. The whole interlude is 'sense' resisting 'delirium':

> When once more alone, I reviewed the information I had got; looked into my heart, examined its thoughts and feelings, and endeavoured to bring back with a strict hand such as had been straying through imagination's boundless and trackless waste, into the safe fold of common sense.
>
> (ibid.)

The use of incident as well as thought demonstrates at the same time that her conduct is always ruled by this sense, and that her feelings are so powerful as to break through the restraint she imposes on herself; the conclusion to the chapter drives home its point and directs us forward to what is to happen next:

> Ere long, I had reason to congratulate myself on the course of wholesome discipline to which I had thus forced my feelings to submit: thanks to it, I was able to meet subsequent occurrences with a decent calm; which, had they found me unprepared, I should probably have been unequal to maintain, even externally.
>
> (ibid.)

As the action at Thornfield sweeps itself forward speed gathers, the intervals between scenes get shorter and less obtrusive. After Jane's dreadful night with Mason, her talk with Mr Rochester in the orchard immediately follows. The events of the month of courtship rush on upon another without pause, and make their own comment on themselves, so Jane need interpose no more than

> My future husband was becoming to me my whole world; and more than the world: almost my hope of heaven. He stood between me and every thought of religion, as an eclipse intervenes between man and the broad sun. I could not, in those days, see God for his creature: of whom I had made an idol.
>
> (Chapter 24)

We are swept forward to the disaster at the altar, on past Mr Rochester's public admission, into his confession and persuasion of Jane; their agonizing battle of wills, from one startling revelation to the next, and have no pause to breathe until Jane gets into the coach which leaves her at Whitcross;

> Gentle reader, may you never feel what I then felt! May your eyes never shed such stormy, scalding, heart-wrung tears as poured from mine. May you never appeal to Heaven in prayers so hopeless and so agonized as in that hour left my lips: for never may you, like me, dread to be the instrument of evil to what you wholly love.
>
> (Chapter 27)

Since Charlotte Brontë's method is in many ways a dramatic one, she uses a good deal of dialogue. *Jane Eyre* has the advantage over *Villette* and *The Professor* that its characters (all except Adèle and Sophie) are English-speaking. Charlotte Brontë has a fine ear for characteristic idioms of class and age, which the deliberate and obvious artificiality of the house-party dialogues tends to obscure. She moves in a narrow compass, making little use of dialect, having no character to compare with Emily Brontë's Joseph; Hannah, the only really broad speaker, is generally reported, and her direct speech gets its flavour from idiom rather than pronunciation:

> 'Are you book-learned?' she inquired presently.
>
> 'Yes, very.'
>
> 'But you've never been to a boarding-school.'
>
> 'I was at a boarding-school eight years.'
>
> She opened her eyes wide. 'Whatever cannot ye keep yourself for, then?'
>
> (Chapter 29)

The idiom of the respectable servant is precisely caught, whether in Leah, Grace Poole, Bessie or Robert Leaven here:

> 'And how is Bessie? You are married to Bessie?'
>
> 'Yes, Miss: my wife is very hearty, thank you; she brought me another little one about two months since—we have three now—and both mother and child are thriving.'
>
> 'And are the family well at the House, Robert?'
>
> 'I am sorry I can't give you better news of them, Miss: they are very badly at present—in great trouble . . . Mr John died yesterday was a week, at his chambers in London.'
>
> (Chapter 21)

Mrs Fairfax (whatever the actual or ostensible date of the book) goes back a generation or more, and her idiom recalls Jane Austen. Dialogue between Jane and others, expecially Mr Rochester, performs many functions besides verisimilitude: it is often not naturalistic, yet it almost always convinces, and always has a flavour of its own. Like the speech in *Wuthering Heights* it is often quite literally unspeakable, and is, despite its dramatic method, quite unlike that of a play or of life.

Charlotte Brontë's style is like no one else's. This is generally agreed and immediately obvious. Being odd, it has often been called bad, by those who have preconceived notions of what a novelist's style should be, and in particular a Victorian lady novelist's. But as Mr Rochester says in another context, 'unheard-of combinations of circumstances demand unheard-of rules' (Chapter 14). Both Charlotte Brontë and Emily found this to be so in their writing; both solved their own problem in their own way, and while Charlotte occasionally allows herself to copy other novelists (the voice heard most frequently besides her own is that of Thackeray, whom she greatly admired), her best effects are always her most individual ones. Again the distinction must be made between Charlotte Brontë and her creation Jane Eyre. While Jane has many of Charlotte Brontë's characteristics, it is clear that what she says is almost always 'in character', and Charlotte Brontë's success is so complete that it is only noticeable in her occasional failures, where an idiom is heard that we recognize from *Shirley* or *Villette*:

> Women are supposed to be very calm generally: but women feel just as men feel; they need exercise for their faculties, and a field for their efforts as much as their brothers do; they suffer from too rigid a restraint, too absolute a stagnation, precisely as men would suffer; and it is narrow-minded in their more privileged fellow-creatures to say that they ought to confine themselves to making puddings and knitting stockings, to playing on the piano and embroidering bags. It is thoughtless to condemn them, or laugh at them, if they seek to do more or learn more than custom has pronounced necessary for their sex.
>
> (Chapter 12)

> I know poetry is not dead, nor genius lost; nor has Mammon gained power over either, to bind or slay: they will both assert their existence, their presence, their liberty and strength again one day. Powerful angels, safe in heaven! They smile when sordid souls triumph, and feeble ones weep over their destruction. Poetry destroyed? Genius banished? No! Mediocrity, no; do not let envy prompt you to the thought. No; they not only live, but reign, and redeem: and without their divine influence spread everywhere, you would be in hell—the hell of your own meanness.
>
> (Chapter 32)

Both these jar by being generalizations, and being divorced from the topic, though the one is meditative and the other rhetorical. Generally, however, Charlotte Brontë's expression is determined by the speaker, by the occasion, by the emotional content of what is being said, or by the atmosphere of the episode, always bearing in mind that everything that is not spoken by one of the other characters is, whatever else it is doing, being used to express Jane.

With *Jane Eyre* Charlotte Brontë establishes what the novel is to be and do in her hands, and has found her course between what she herself summarized as the 'real' and the 'true', between which she was confused in *The Professor*.

Notes

1. Most of these latter books are not literature at all, and so, while they are part of most readers' consciousness, they are not recognized as having any bearing on their habits of criticism. Examples one might mention are the novels of Ethel M. Dell, of Daphne du Maurier, and of countless contributors to women's magazines.

2. Earlier novelists who spring to mind are Defoe, Richardson and Jane Austen. Defoe, while using the first-person narrative, does not concern himself primarily, if at all, with either moral or emotional development; Richardson's heroines (even Clarissa) do not grow, change, and learn from what they suffer to anything like the extent Jane Eyre does (they do not begin as children), and a good deal of the revealing of them is done by others—to achieve what Charlotte Brontë achieves Richardson would have to write letters from his heroine exclusively. Jane Austen does not use the first-person narrative, and when in *Emma* she comes close to seeing life through the perceptions of a single personality, she is still concerned with a whole society and the heroine's moral obligations towards it.

3. As Robert Martin observes (*The Accents of Persuasion*).

4. In the first example, the remark about green eyes, it would be easy to fall into a number of false attitudes here; one might not notice the false note, might accept it as an example of the power of 'the loving eye' which has already given Mr Rochester himself 'a power beyond beauty' (Chapter 22), or might think Charlotte Brontë is romantically indulging her heroine at last with a small share of good looks. But the word 'reader' jolts us, we are forced to notice that Mr Rochester is being ridiculous, because his attitude to Jane is a wrong one—contrast his proposal, where he frankly calls her 'small and plain' (Chapter 23); and, though Jane's humorous comment keeps the tone light, this incident combines with others to make us see that Mr Rochester is morally wrong, in the way he treats Jane, in small details just as much as in attempting bigamy.

5. The obvious case against this identification theory—that the novelist's mind contains his whole work whereas the mind of any one character within it manifestly does not—is not easy to

maintain here, since the mind of Jane Eyre comes very near to containing the whole work. However, it is pretty clear that if Jane Eyre were Charlotte Brontë, there would have been no *Shirley* and no *Villette.* And the case for identification of author and character can, if one wishes, be made out equally effectively with Lucy Snowe, and Lucy is patently not like Jane in many fundamental ways. Likewise the evidence of biography and letters will corroborate one's critical opinion that Charlotte Brontë's personality—irrespective of her experiences—is not Jane Eyre's. There are, in particular, occasional remarks which suggest that the 'I' speaking is further from the events than even a thirty-year-old Jane can be, and that we are very close to hearing the voice of Charlotte Brontë herself, and this suspicion receives support from *Shirley,* where the same astringent note occurs very frequently.

6. Letter to Messrs Smith and Elder, 6 August 1847.

7. What kind of Lord is not made clear—he has inherited the title from his father, since his mother is the Dowager, which is itself odd since he is not married.

8. 'Yes, I doat on Miss Georgiana!' cried the fervent Abbot. 'Little darling!—with her long curls and her blue eyes, and such a sweet colour as she has; just as if she were painted!' (Chapter 3)

9. And one of the few figures to suggest that Charlotte Brontë learned anything from the writer she so much admired—Thackeray. He has much of the gusto and the comic horror of old Sir Pitt Crawley.

10. *The Accents of Persuasion.*

11. This is the only reason for the appearance of Mary Ann Wilson, who enhances Helen Burns by the contrast she provides, which also has an important relevance to Mr Rochester. Having seen Jane's choice of friends here, we accept without hesitation Mr Rochester's worth too, which might otherwise be a matter for serious doubt. We have, after all, only his care for Adèle as proof of any kind of virtue.

12. Mrs Fairfax is unable to analyse Mr Rochester in Chapter 11 (where mystery is requisite), but can do very well with Blanche Ingram in Chapter 16 when there is need of someone to be explicit.

13. The mixture of tones is like Fielding—unemotional approval of the two Eshton girls, who demonstrate a degree of worth by playing with Adèle, sudden gentleness for Mrs Colonel Dent and her liking for flowers, 'especially wild ones', flat disregard of the 'apathetic and listless' Lord Ingram

and his sister Mary, limited and humorous approval of Colonel Dent (a 'père noble de théâtre'), and the hyberbolical ridicule of the Dowagers; all these range round Blanche.

14. Robert Martin claims that the unreality of the portraits may deliberately suggest how young and inexperienced Jane is. It may well be that Charlotte Brontë is not capable of a psychologically realized full-length portrait of a frivolous character—Ginevra Fanshawe at least suggests it—but the failure to do one here rises from a different intention, and not from incompetence.

15. Review of *Vanity Fair* and *Jane Eyre, The Quarterly Review,* December 1848.

16. That Adèle can say her La Fontaine fable with 'a flexibility of voice and appropriateness of gesture unusual at her age' (Chapter 11) suggests that Céline could act, a fact not indicated by her performance of outraged virtue as retailed by Mr Rochester in Chapter 15.

17. *Early Victorian Novelists.*

18. It comes immediately after he has recounted his affair with Céline Varens, and is his first profession of affection, and the first time he uses Jane's Christian name. The next morning he leaves for the Leas for an indefinite period, leaving Jane with feelings stirred by his words and actions, which she attempts to crush with the idea of Blanche Ingram.

19. It is far too soon to make love to Jane, when he has no reason to believe she is fond of him; and it is in any case a considerable risk for a man near middle age, with a fortune, to put himself in the power of a penniless girl of eighteen with no background or family. And these are the objections we see as soon as the house-party arrives.

20. Note for instance how he says good-bye when Jane leaves for Gateshead, Chapter 21; both of them know that a kiss is the form of farewell in both their minds.

21. We never fear that Jane is in danger of physical rape and Jane's reaction to the threat is a most robust one: 'I still possessed my soul, and with it the certainty of ultimate safety' (Chapter 27); indeed we feel as she says that 'the crisis was perilous, but not without its charm: such as the Indian, perhaps, feels when he slips over the rapid in his canoe' (ibid). This is the *Clarissa* situation utterly transmuted, and rendered both more realistic and more wholesome, leading now to life instead of death.

22. We believe her the more because St John has offered her sacrifice already, to a religious ideal, and been rejected as repulsive.

23. We must bear in mind what beauty was in 1847, not what it is today: 'I sometimes wished to have rosy cheeks, a straight nose, and small cherry mouth; I desired to be tall, stately, and finely developed in figure.' (Chapter 11)

24. It is worth while by way of contrast to consider *David Copperfield* again, which, though based on its author's own experiences, does not exact the same emotional commitment of its reader: David the narrator regards the young David's love of Dora, and the whole of their marriage, with a detachment and a sense of 'knowing better' quite different from the way the mature Jane ever regards her young self. Jane is much more like Ann Elliot in *Persuasion* (who is incidentally the same age):

> 'I have been thinking over the past, and trying to judge impartially of the right and wrong, I mean with regard to myself; and I must believe that I was right, much as I suffered from it.'
>
> (*Persuasion,* Chapter XI of *Northanger Abbey and Persuasion,* Vol. IV, ed. R. W. Chapman, Oxford 1923.)

25. The reader's mind recalls the hills round Lowood, the 'noble summits' which also provided a setting both for suffering, when 'mists chill as death wandered to the impulse of east winds along those purple peaks' (Chapter 9), and for a new companionship and intellectual growth.

Bibliography

So much has been written about the Brontës and their works that any bibliography must necessarily be selective. I have here included, besides the writings cited in the foregoing chapters, only those others which I have found particularly important, whether for their intrinsic value, or for the profitable disagreement which they provoke.

I WORKS BY THE BRONTËS

The Shakespeare Head Brontë, ed, T. J. Wise and J. A. Symington, 19 vols., Oxford, 1931-8.

II OTHER WORKS

BENTLEY, PHYLLIS, *The Brontës,* Home and Van Thal, 1947.

———.*The Brontë Sisters,* Longmans, Green & Co., 1950.

BRADBY, G. F., 'Emily Brontë', *The Nineteenth Century,* CVIII, 1930.

BRONTË SOCIETY TRANSACTIONS, Shipley, Yorks, 1895-.

CECIL, LORD DAVID, *Early Victorian Novelists,* Constable, 1934.

CHRISTIAN REMEMBERANCER, XV, Review of *Jane Eyre.*

COOPER-WILLIS, I., *The Authorship of 'Wuthering Heights',* Hogarth, 1936.

DELAFIELD, E. M., *The Brontës: their Lives Recorded by their Contemporaries,* Hogarth, 1935.

DIMNET, E., *Les Soeurs Brontë,* Paris, 1910.

DOBELL, S., 'Emily Brontë', *Life and Letters,* I, 1878.

DRY, FLORENCE S., *The Sources of 'Jane Eyre'* and *The Sources of 'Wuthering Heights',* Heffers, 1940.

ELTON, O., *A Survey of English Literature,* 1830-1888, II, 1924.

EWBANK, INGA-STINA, *Their Proper Sphere,* Arnold, 1966.

FORÇADE, E., Reviews of *Jane Eyre* and *Shirley, Revue de Deux Mondes,* XXIV and XL, 1849.

GASKELL, E. C., *Life of Charlotte Brontë,* Smith, Elder & Co., 1857 (first and third editions).

GÉRIN, W., *Anne Brontë,* Nelson, 1959.

———.*Branwell Brontë,* Nelson, 1961.

GOODRIDGE, F. G., *Emily Brontë: 'Wuthering Heights',* Arnold, 1964.

HARDY, BARBARA, *'Wuthering Heights',* Blackwell, Oxford, 1963.

———.*'Jane Eyre',* Blackwell, Oxford.

LEAVIS, F. R., *The Great Tradition,* Chatto & Windus, 1948.

LEAVIS, Q. D., *Fiction and the Reading Public,* Chatto & Windus, 1932.

LEWES, G. H., 'Recent Novels; French and English', *Fraser's Magazine* XXXVI, 1847.

———.Review of *Jane Eyre* and *Shirley, Edinburgh Review,* January 1850.

MILLER, J. H., *The Disappearance of God,* Harvard, 1963.

MARTIN, R. B., *The Accents of Persuasion,* Faber & Faber, 1966.

MOORE, GEORGE, *Conversations in Ebury Street,* Heinemann, 1936.

OLIPHANT, M., *Women Novelists of Queen Victoria's Reign,* Hurst and Blackett, 1897.

Oxford and Cambridge Magazine, I, 1856. 'Charlotte Brontë and Thackeray.'

RALLI, A., 'Emily Brontë: the problem of personality', *Critiques,* Longmans, 1927.

RATCHFORD, F. E., *The Brontës' Web of Childhood,* Columbia, 1941.

————.*Gondal's Queen,* Texas, 1955.

RIGBY, E., '*Jane Eyre* and *Vanity Fair*' in *Famous Reviews,* ed. R. B. Johnson Pitman, 1914.

ROBINSON, A. M. F. (Mme Duclaux), *Emily Brontë,* W. H. Allen, 1883.

SAINTSBURY, G., *A History of Nineteenth Century Literature,* Macmillan, 1896.

S(ANGER), C. P., *The Structure of 'Wuthering Heights',* Hogarth, 1926.

SCHORER, 'Fiction and the Matrix of Analogy', *Kenyon Review* XI, 1949.

SHORTER, C. K., *The Brontës and their Circle,* Hodder and Stoughton, 1896.

————.*The Brontës: Life and Letters,* Hodder and Stoughton, 1908.

SINCLAIR, MAY, *The Three Brontës,* Hutchinson, 1912.

SPARK, M. and STANFORD, D., *Emily Brontë,* Peter Owen, 1953.

TILLOTSON, KATHLEEN, *Novels of the Eighteen-forties,* Oxford, 1954.

The Times, Review of *Shirley,* 7 December 1849.

TURNELL, MARTIN, 'Wuthering Heights', *Dublin Review,* CCVI, 1940.

VAN GHENT, DOROTHY, *The English Novel: Form and Function,* Harper, 1961.

VISICK, MARY, *The Genesis of 'Wuthering Heights',* Hong Kong, 1958, Oxford, 1959.

WARING, S. M., 'Charlotte Brontë and Lucy Snowe', *Harper's Magazine,* XXXII, 1865.

WOOLF, VIRGINIA, *The Common Reader,* First Series, Hogarth Press, 1925.

Maria Yuen (essay date June 1976)

SOURCE: Yuen, Maria. "Two Crises of Decision in *Jane Eyre*." *English Studies* 57, no. 3 (June 1976): 215-26.

[*In the following essay, Yuen examines elements of Jane's character that form the basis for significant conflicts in the novel.*]

Jane Eyre's decision to leave Rochester on discovering that he is a married man has often been misunderstood or misinterpreted, simply dismissed as a matter of principle, or applauded for the wrong reason. Critics generally feel a certain uneasiness, a certain wariness when they come to this part of the novel, which, all agree, is the emotional climax, the crux of the Jane-Rochester relationship, the key to an understanding of Jane's character. It oversimplifies the issue to say, as Joan Bennett does, that 'it is wrong to live with a man who is legally and religiously bound to another woman. It is right to refuse to do so whatever the consequences may be'.[1] It shows a lack of understanding of the heroine and her problem to suggest, as Q. D. Leavis does, that 'her artificially trained "conscience" forces her to go'.[2] And it leaves too many questions unanswered to relegate Jane's decision to the world of God or religion or whatever name one chooses to call it, as Kathleen Tillotson does, when she offers the explanation that Jane's 'resistance belongs to the world beyond that of human love'.[3] Even George Eliot's famous condemnation of *Jane Eyre*— 'All self-sacrifice is good—but one would like it to be in a somewhat nobler cause than that of a diabolical law which chains a man soul and body to a putrefying carcase' (Letters, I.268)—is notable more as a prediction of her own later moral decision to live with George Henry Lewes than as an indication of her powers of judgement and criticism. 'All self-sacrifice is good'— George Eliot is here acquiescing in a popular Victorian assumption, but I think the basic motivation underlying Jane's decision is not so much sacrifice, as the self, and this central issue of the self is intimately connected with Jane's emotional, moral, and intellectual development, culminating in her discovery of her individual identity. It is interesting to note, by way of comparison, that Maggie Tulliver in *The Mill on the Floss* also experiences a comparable emotional and moral crisis in her renunciation of Stephen Guest, her decision similarly motivated by her concept of self, and in particular, of self and others.

The climax of *Jane Eyre* (as with *The Mill on the Floss*) is a 'crisis of event, character, and spirit'[4] in which the heroine has to make a painful decision on which her whole future life hinges. In *Jane Eyre* as in *The Mill on the Floss,* it is not a decision of the moment—it involves the whole personality; and the experience, background, and past life of the heroine are all behind the making of the decision. Therefore I propose to begin by reviewing the early life of Jane Eyre because the early chapters of the novel largely account for the character of the heroine, and it is the pressures of childhood experience on the full-grown character which crucially determine the crisis of decision.

Like all the other Charlotte Brontë heroines, Jane Eyre is presented as a solitary individual in isolated circumstances, unlike Maggie, whose tragedy is solidly set in the narrow provincial society of St. Ogg's, with its materialism, its banal realism, its lack of any true idealism. If her family is the strongest tie in Maggie's life, Jane's life has absolutely no strings attached since she has no family and no status. Jane's lack of family differs most significantly from her creator's real-life situation. Whereas Charlotte Brontë's whole life was conditioned by her duties as daughter and sister, Jane is free of all ties, living only for herself. The loneliness of Jane's existence may come from Charlotte Brontë's own feelings, but the outward facts of her life come mostly from the author's imagination. Maggie is an individual deeply embedded in society; Jane is 'an individual . . . enmeshed in, yet independent of . . . circumstances'.[5] The early chapters of Gateshead portray dramatically Jane's struggle for survival in a hostile atmosphere. Jane is 'a discord' at Gateshead Hall, leading the mean existence of a dependent among relatives who are not really her 'kin', with whom she has no sense of shared identity. In contrast to the first two books on normal, innocent childhood in *The Mill on the Floss,* here we find the terrifyingly lonely child in an alien household, full of 'rebellion and rage', defying the world about her on the strength of her own feelings of right and wrong, and defeating moral oppression with moral courage. Maggie is a 'free spirit' caught in a web of society, but Jane not only transcends her limiting environment, she even emerges as victor in a clash of personalities with her aunt, Mrs. Reed. But living in a household of selfish, inconsiderate, egocentric people, the growing child naturally turns in on herself. By force of circumstances, she learns self-interest, self-protection, self-survival. She is the centre of her own universe; she cannot relate spontaneously to other people, except when they strike a chord of harmony in her soul. It is not that she is devoid of natural affection or human sympathy, but these fundamental feelings are buried deep in her heart, until they are aroused when they will burst forth with overwhelming force.

When Jane is emancipated from the thraldom of her aunt's family, she moves on to a larger social unit, the community of Lowood, exchanging moral oppression for the religious oppression of Mr. Brocklehurst. But Jane has by now built up her defenses: 'I stood lonely enough, but to that feeling of isolation I was accustomed: it did not oppress me much' (V.81). By nature antipathic to Brocklehurst's hypocritical Evangelicalism, Jane is nevertheless drawn towards two other representatives of religion at Lowood. Helen Burns represents a Christian ideal that Jane admires but does not aspire to. Jane, with her intense awareness of self and her fierce sense of justice, could never adopt Helen's attitude of resignation and forgiveness. Again, with her passionate longing for life, Jane could not subscribe to Helen's calm acceptance of death. Miss Temple, on a more human level, embodies the religion of love, goodness and kindness which provides the inspiration and

motivation for Jane through her eight years at Lowood. But with the departure of Miss Temple, all Jane's old hunger for life, for experience returns in force: 'I tired of the routine of eight years in one afternoon. I desired liberty; for liberty I gasped . . . For change, stimulus' (X.117). 'I longed to go where there was life and movement' (X.120). Jane is formed not for religion, but for love. Her repressed nature now reasserts itself as she prepares to embark on a new adventure in life.

Jane's world is an even smaller one than Maggie's—she progresses from a barely tolerated dependent in a household of unloving relatives, through a charity child in a charity institution among similarly deprived children, to a governess of a foreign born child of questionable birth in a strange environment, Thornfield. The first two main phases of Jane's life are spent almost exclusively in the two houses or establishments—Gateshead Hall and Lowood—which form the background for her early development. Through these experiences and vicissitudes Jane's personality becomes more and more withdrawn, so that from the solitary child she grows into the 'quaint, quiet, grave' (XIV.162) young woman whose cool exterior nevertheless conceals 'a heart hungering for affection'.[6] It is 'this need of love, this hunger of the heart'[7] that precipitates the emotional and moral crisis in the novel.

Jane Eyre's dilemma is very much like George Eliot's own—whether to live with Rochester as his unmarried wife or sever all relations with him—and George Eliot's strong condemnation of Jane's renunciation is understandable. Perhaps a quotation from George Eliot's own novel will throw light on her reaction to Jane's decision. Near the end of *The Mill on the Floss,* in a passage that comes nearest to George Eliot's own conception of the moral problem at the heart of the novel, we find this authorial comment: 'Moral judgements must remain false and hollow unless they are checked and enlightened by a perpetual reference to the special circumstances that mark the individual lot' (VII.ii). This is central to George Eliot's notion of morality and explains in large measure her censure of *Jane Eyre,* George Eliot obviously thinks that Jane's 'special circumstances' justify a defiance of conventional morality and social laws. Her dissatisfaction arises from what she interprets as Jane's misplaced good faith and good intentions. What George Eliot fails to see is that Jane's renunciation of Rochester is made not in the interests of a law, diabolical or not, but in self-interest. And the motivation of Jane's action is not self-sacrifice, but rather self-protection.

Rochester tries to appeal to Jane's judgement of the balance of consequences:

> Is it better to drive a fellow-creature to despair than to
> transgress a mere human law, no man being injured by

the breach?—for you have neither relatives nor acquaintances whom you need fear to offend by living
with me.

(XXVII. 343)

Jane is almost convinced as she tries to reason within
herself:

> Think of his misery; think of his danger; look at his
> state when left alone; remember his headlong nature:
> consider the recklessness following on despair—soothe
> him; save him; love him; tell him you love him and
> will be his. Who in the world cares for *you*? or who
> will be injured by what you do?

(344)

And then comes the reply from the depths of Jane's
soul:

> *I* care for myself. The more solitary, the more friend-
> less, the more unsustained I am, the more I will respect
> myself.

(344)

In the crisis, she can only fall back on herself, on her
sense of self-protection, on her instinct for self-survival.
Maggie has to think of Lucy and Philip in her distress,
but Jane's only duty is to herself. For Maggie, a moral
sense is a sense of the rights of others; for Jane, it is a
sense of her own rights. Maggie's feelings for the past
help to sustain her in her resistance against excessive
self-indulgence, but Jane's whole past life has conditioned her to fend for herself in adverse circumstances.
Small and frail as she is, she has a fierce tenacity for
life—she survives Gateshead Hall and Lowood (even
the epidemic that killed so many of her schoolmates)
largely unscathed. And now, in the greatest crisis of her
life, her instinctive reaction is to withdraw into herself,
in contrast to Maggie who reaches out to others when
she realizes she cannot just live and choose for herself.
Maggie's decision is a suppression of self, in recognition of the needs of others, and an extension of self—an
advance from egoism to intelligent sympathy, an
outward-looking development of character. Jane's decision is an assertion of self—a step towards self-
discovery and the establishment of an identity—and it
is inwardlooking. Although Jane's problem is defined in
terms of Christian morality, her final decision is reached
not through any sense of social convention or traditional morality, but rather 'a heroic assertion of the
sanctity of the individual soul',[8] in obedience to a higher
personal morality. I agree with Ruth Bernard Yeazell
that the essential nature of Jane's conflict is a struggle
'to preserve the integrity and independence of the self'.[9]
Q. D. Leavis is of the opinion that Jane is violating her
own nature in conforming to principles and ideas instilled in her from childhood.[10] I think what motivated
Jane in her decision is not the Lowood training of self-
sacrifice and obedience to convention, but rather the

spirit of independence and individuality that the
Lowood environment fostered in her, as expressed in
Helen Burns's inspired speech, that when everything is
taken from us, 'only the spark of the spirit will remain—the impalpable principle of life and thought'
(VI.91), in other words, the essence of one's soul. If
Jane is adhering to a principle, it is the principle of
self-respecting personal integrity. As she said: 'I still
possessed my soul' (XXVII.344). Rochester in his saner
moments would have understood the motivation of her
decision, as is shown by his penetrating analysis of
Jane's character in the guise of a gypsy woman on an
earlier occasion:

> That brow professes to say—'I can live alone, if self-
> respect and circumstances require me so to do. I need
> not sell my soul to buy bliss. . . . Reason sits firm and
> holds the reins, . . . judgement shall have the casting
> vote in every decision. . . . I shall follow the guiding
> of that still small voice which interprets the dictates of
> conscience'.

(XIX. 230)

This is of course ironic in the light of later events, for it
is precisely these same self-respect, reason, judgement,
and conscience that combine to frustrate Rochester.

Jane Eyre's painful decision to leave Rochester is in
line with her magnificent outburst in the moonlit garden
on Midsummer's eve:

> Do you think, because I am poor, obscure, plain, and
> little, I am soulless and heartless? You think wrong!—I
> have as much soul as you—and full as much heart!
> And if God had gifted me with some beauty and much
> wealth, I should have made it as hard for you to leave
> me, as it is now for me to leave you. I am not talking
> to you now through the medium of custom, conven-
> tionalities, nor even of mortal flesh: it is my spirit that
> addresses your spirit; just as if both had passed through
> the grave, and we stood at God's feet, equal—as we
> are!

(XXIII. 281)

In a further demonstration of spirit before she understands Rochester's intentions, she declares proudly: 'I
am a free human being with an independent will, which
I now exert to leave you' (282). She might have said
the same at the later crisis of emotion and event in
which she actually leaves him. In this outburst of
pent-up emotions, Jane is assuming for herself and her
sex a position and an attitude never before granted to
heroines in English fiction—equality in love. Charlotte
Brontë believes that love between man and woman is
an all-consuming passion shared not only physically,
but mentally and spiritually—'to the finest fibre of my
nature', as Jane says. What Charlotte Brontë is asking
for is a recognition of the emotional needs of a
woman—the right to feel, to love unreservedly. In a
way, Jane is a more liberated woman than Maggie, and

certainly a more unconventional heroine. She claims independence and rejects subservience. She will consent only to a marriage which is the union of equals in independence. Charlotte Brontë sees the relationship between man and woman as one of mutual need, a kind of equal partnership in which the woman is not just the object of pursuit or desire, but is recognized as an active contributor—unafraid to love with all-consuming passion, willing to devote herself to the man, and yet exacting respect and a recognition of her rights as an individual. Charlotte Brontë does not advocate an absolute union, a complete merging of man and woman—this would mean the dissolution of the self. Unlike Catherine Earnshaw who declares: 'I *am* Heathcliff', Jane asserts: '*I* care for myself'. Instead of losing herself in some 'otherness', Jane fights to preserve her own identity. The relationship between Catherine and Heathcliff involves a fusion of personalities and leads towards mutual annihilation. The relationship between Jane and Rochester is grounded on the equality and integrity of two independent selves and leads towards life.[11] In the 'Eden-like' garden of Thornfield, Jane appears to have secured both love and independence (of spirit, at least); but when it turns out to be a Paradise Lost, Jane must flee temptation and her lover, in order to preserve the integrity of her self against an overwhelming passion.

In a curious passage earlier on, Charlotte Brontë expresses what could well be taken as the manifesto of the Women's Liberation Movement:

> Women are supposed to be very calm generally: but women feel just as men feel; they need exercise for their faculties, and a field for their efforts as much as their brothers do; they suffer from too rigid a restraint, too absolute a stagnation, precisely as men would suffer; and it is narrow-minded in their more privileged fellow-creatures to say that they ought to confine themselves to making puddings and knitting stockings, to playing on the piano and embroidering bags. It is thoughtless to condemn them, or laugh at them, if they seek to do more or learn more than custom has pronounced necessary for their sex.
>
> (XII. 141)

Charlotte Brontë's concern with the 'condition of women' question in her day is revealed here. She herself has struggled for independence and equality not as an exhilaration dreamed of but as a necessity, and the feminist attitude expressed here is assumed by her heroine. George Eliot is a 'liberated' woman in her day and associates with the foremost thinkers of her society, but her heroine Maggie learns the hard way that the only thing a girl can do is to submit to fate and to practise self-denial. Charlotte Brontë really prepares the way for Maggie Tulliver and other 'rebel' heroines by showing her heroine overcoming social and sexual inferiority with moral, emotional, and intellectual superiority. Jane first encounters Rochester not as his equal but as his subordinate. She escapes the confines of Lowood to enter into a 'new servitude' (X.117), a servitude not just in terms of work but also in terms of love. The relationship between Rochester and Jane is that of master and servant, just as the relationship between hero and heroine in all the other Charlotte Brontë novels is that of teacher and pupil. But the master-servant relationship between Rochester and Jane is essentially one of mutual admiration and respect. Rochester loves Jane for her superiority of mind and heart, and Jane feels 'akin' to Rochester and has, in her own words, 'something in my brain and heart, in my blood and nerves, that assimilate me mentally to him' (XVII.204). F. A. C. Wilson suggests that for Charlotte Brontë, the ideal relationship between man and woman is an extremely flexible one 'by which both partners freely alternate between "masculine", or controlling, and "feminine", or responsive roles' and that 'Jane, for her part, enjoys her sexual status as a subordinate, but this is only insofar as it is a role in a game'.[12] Jane has no feeling of inferiority at all: she is only conforming outwardly to the Victorian concept of the prescribed roles for men and women, while in reality she believes in equality between the sexes, as evidenced in her vehement assertion of equality in the garden of Thornfield, and Rochester's response 'My bride is here, . . . because my equal is here, and my likeness' (XXIII.282) testifies to his agreement. Her sexual status as a subordinate may be more apparent than real, but her social status as an employee makes her dependent on her master for her livelihood. Jane's sensitive feelings about her position and her strong sense of individuality and independence make her resent any attempt to encroach on her personality. Just before their marriage, when Rochester wants to shower her with fineries and to deck her out in jewels and satin and lace, Jane feels 'a sense of annoyance and degradation' (XXIV.297), partly because her aesthetic sense tells her she looks better as 'plain Jane', partly because her moral taste finds such extravagance abhorrent, but mainly because she feels this is a violation of her sense of self and a reflection on her essential dependence. Refusing to play the pampered slave to Rochester's benevolent despot of a sultan, she tells him: 'I will be myself' (XXIV.288) and 'I only want an easy mind, sir; not crushed by crowded obligations' (XXIV.298). She prefers to be herself and to be loved for what she is. It is in a state of reaction against what she construes as Rochester's attempted violation of her sense of self that immediately after this Jane writes to inform her wealthy Uncle John in Madeira of her impending marriage with the underlying motive of perhaps obtaining what she terms an 'independency', thereby bringing about the chain of events that leads to the interrupted wedding. So Jane unwittingly incurs her own unhappiness through her desire for independence, which means more than just economic and social status—independence means personal identity and self-esteem.

Jane Eyre is as much a novel of conflict as *The Mill on the Floss*. Just as Maggie is torn between love and duty, Jane is torn between the desire to succumb to her passions and the determination to be true to herself. The emotional struggle is as difficult and as painful for her as for Maggie, perhaps more difficult and more painful, because no sooner has this lonely heart's hunger for affection been nearly satisfied than the life-giving morsel is snatched from her. 'Jane Eyre, who had been an ardent expectant woman—almost a bride—was a cold, solitary girl again: her life was pale; her prospects were desolate' (XXVI.323). She has to give up a love on which she has come to depend, on which her whole life is centred, on which all her future is based. Although Jane claims equality and independence, she is actually emotionally dependent on Rochester whom she calls her 'love and idol' (XXVII.342). She says: 'My future husband was becoming to me my whole world; and more than the world; almost my hope of heaven' (XXIV.302). It is when her hopes are shattered that she once more turns to God for strength to resist temptation. The temptation is no less real although, unlike Maggie, Jane is a victim of circumstances. Whereas Maggie's mental and physical inertia at the critical moment is partially responsible for landing her in a compromising situation, Jane is entirely at the mercy of external circumstances, and the outcome of events is totally beyond her control or expectation. She could not have imagined the existence of the mad wife or foreseen the interrupted wedding. In a way, too, she is manipulated by Rochester who tries to take fate into his own hands, believing that an immoral action would be justified by a moral objective. It is interesting to compare the process by which Maggie and Jane arrive at their decisions. Maggie's decision is felt—a kind of instinctive reaction inspired by inherent moral feeling. George Eliot recognizes that feeling, not thought, is the major source of action, and her heroine acts not as a result of her analysis of the situation, but out of her instinct for goodness, and her feelings for others and for the past. Jane's decision, on the other hand, is thought out—she is in the habit of analysing her feelings and her situation, and her description of what goes on in her mind actually constitutes the core of the book. On an earlier occasion, when she first learned of Rochester's supposed intention to marry Miss Ingram, she 'reviewed the information [she] had got; looked into [her] heart, examined its thoughts and feelings' (XVI.190), suppressing her emotions, 'raptures, agonies' (192), and obeying the dictates of 'reason', 'discipline', and 'principles' (190-2). And now in a state of bewilder-

ment after the interrupted wedding, Jane shut herself up in her room and began to think, to receive into her consciousness the full impact of the blow:

> And now I thought: till now I had only heard, seen, moved—followed up and down where I was led or dragged—watched event rush on event, disclosure open beyond disclosure: but *now, I thought.*
>
> (XXVI. 323)

One clear-cut conclusion of her analysis of her feelings and the situation is that she must hold on to the 'laws and principles . . . given by God, sanctioned by man' (XXVII.344) in order to retain her sanity against a madness that threatens to destroy her. Jane stands by what she has 'always believed', to guard against that 'chaotic distintegration of the self' exemplified by Bertha Rochester's madness. Ruth Bernard Yeazell has pointed out that 'the laws and principles to which Jane clings keep her sane, for they provide that continuity by which the self is defined'.[13] The final resistance to temptation has not been easy, although Jane knows exactly what to do. What George Eliot said in *Felix Holt* could be said of Jane here: 'It is not true that love makes all things easy: it makes us choose what is difficult' (Chapter 49). And this is exactly what Jane has done. Charlotte Brontë expects us to understand the motivation of Jane's decision because, at this point at least, she has completely identified herself with her heroine in her crisis and expects the reader to share the identification, unlike George Eliot who is able to view the situation independently in the person of the impartial Dr. Kenn. Perhaps this is why, as an artist, Thackeray found fault with Charlotte Brontë for 'writing in a passion about her characters'.

As Jane was leaving Thornfield, she thought with dread of what the future had in store for her, 'and oh! with agony I thought of what I left. I could not help it' (XXVII.348). She could not help being herself—she could not consent to a total surrender of her self in becoming Rochester's mistress, she would not consent to anything less than a complete relationship between two independent individuals. In the conflict between love and independence, she chooses the latter. At this point she is overwhelmed by self-reproach. 'In the midst of my pain of heart and frantic effort of principle, I abhorred myself. I had no solace from self-approbation: none even from self-respect. I had injured—wounded—left my master. I was hateful in my own eyes. Still I could not turn, nor retrace one step' (348). Like Maggie, who feels like an automaton on leaving Stephen, Jane does not feel moral victory on leaving Rochester—instead she suffers a collapse of will and hopes to die. But her instinct for survival makes her hang on to the precarious thread of life. It should be noticed that when Jane leaves Rochester, she goes away to start a new life—she is free to be herself, to realize her own independent identity. But Maggie has to return to St. Ogg's in disgrace; she goes back to society to bear the consequences of her deed—to demonstrate George Eliot's central belief that the individual and society are inextricably interrelated. Their respective actions are in the nature of their different circumstances and characters. They also illustrate their authors' different concepts of the existence of the individual—solitary survival in Charlotte Brontë, and in a context of society in George Eliot.

The next section of the novel—the Moor House section—is the least powerful, least poignant part of the narrative. Charlotte Brontë devotes one-fifth of her novel to portraying the completion of the moral and emotional growth of her heroine. But before the final resolution of moral and emotional conflicts, Jane has to go through another crisis of decision, to survive another temptation. I think in this section of the novel Charlotte Brontë also means Jane, and the reader along with her, to review her decision of leaving Rochester. Is the decision wrong after all? Has Jane, in her concern to be true to herself, denied one side of her nature—the need for love? Why does she keep having 'strange dreams at night', dreams of 'passing a lifetime' with Rochester (XXXII.393)? Why is she not happy 'in the midst of this calm, this useful existence' (393) as village schoolmistress, although knowing she is doing something good and meaningful? Daylight gives her the courage to assert that it is better to be 'free and honest' than 'to be a slave in fool's paradise at Marseilles' as Rochester's mistress (XXXI.386), but 'dark night witness[es] the convulsion of despair, and hear[s] the burst of passion' (XXXII.393). Why is she suffering such anguish and torment of heart and soul even in the midst of her new-found independence and relations? Surely it is because she feels that her life is unfulfilled, that her nature is unsatisfied. The St. John Rivers relationship, the antithesis of Jane's relations with Rochester, serves to bring out this point. St. John, who is consistently characterized in terms of marble and ice, sees Jane only as 'a diligent, orderly, energetic woman' (XXXII.401), who would make a good missionary wife, little suspecting the fire that rages beneath her cool exterior. Although he is the agent of Jane's change of fortune, he represents the gravest threat to her independence and freedom of mind. He is the kind of religious fanatic who perverts his own will and the will of others, all in the name of religion. He commits the cardinal sin, according to D. H. Lawrence, of destroying the selfhood, the 'otherness' of other people, and his moral and spiritual domination (described in images of 'fetters' and 'iron shroud') is stifling and inhibiting to Jane. Jane says: to please St. John, 'I felt daily more and more that I must disown half my nature, stifle half my faculties, wrest my tastes from their original bent, force myself to the adoption of pursuits for which I had no natural

vocation' (XXXIV.424). She tells him: 'If I were to marry you, you would kill me. You are killing me now' (XXXV.438). She means St. John is destroying her true self in attempting to violate her nature. Rochester, on the other hand, helps her to fulfil her nature and to realize herself. Jane's relationship with St. John is one fierce psychological battle of wills, with St. John demanding a complete submission of the self, and Jane fighting to preserve her own individuality and identity. It is only after Jane becomes gradually aware of St. John's 'imperfection' of self and the 'fallibilities' of his arguments that she realizes she is with 'an equal', which gives her courage to resist his assault on her nature and to defend the integrity of her self. St. John's offer of marriage without love (the antithesis of Rochester's offer of love without marriage) arouses from Jane defiant self-assertion: 'I scorn your idea of love, . . . I scorn the counterfeit sentiment you offer: yes, St. John, and I scorn you when you offer it' (XXXIV.433). But when St. John adopts the tactic of gentle persuasion and attacks the most vulnerable chink in her armour—her hunger for affection—Jane feels her defenses giving way. Jane feels physically paralysed by St. John's mental power; her will and spirit are about to surrender: 'I was tempted to cease struggling with him—to rush down the torrent of his will into the gulf of his existence, and there lose my own' (XXXV.443). Inga-Stina Ewbank has pointed out that the imagery of floods and torrents here recalls 'George Eliot's later use of the river-image to express the suspension and abandonment of will in Maggie at the moment of crisis in *The Mill on the Floss*'.[14] Just as Maggie's second temptation by Stephen is the greater temptation because it comes to her in a time of deprivation and despair, Jane's temptation by St. John is the more difficult to resist because his appeal is based on those very principles and laws which have previously sustained her. 'Religion called—Angels beckoned—God commanded' (XXXV.444). It takes a call from Heaven or a cry from the depths of Jane's soul or whatever one chooses to interpret the mysterious summons to break the spell that St. John has cast over her. It gives her courage to resist, and therefore subdue, St. John. The physical act of breaking away from St. John symbolizes Jane's final assertion of independence and her ultimate achievement of an identity. 'It was *my* time to assume ascendancy. My powers were in play and in force' (XXXV.445). The call, quite apart from its external source, is really an externalization of Jane's innermost desires and needs. Jane could not have married St. John—it would mean a denial of self, a suppression of personality, and it would make meaningless her earlier struggle for self-assertion. For George Eliot, the motive for self-sacrifice should be the happiness of other people, but Jane's self-sacrifice would be of certain injury to herself and uncertain benefit to the Indian masses she is supposed to help.

Jane's rejection of St. John in a way reinforces her earlier renunciation of Rochester, although the two proposals are vastly different in circumstances and emotional intensity. Jane is deliberately made to draw a parallel between her temptation by St. John and her earlier temptation by Rochester, when she says: 'I was almost as hard beset by him now as I had been once before, in a different way, by another' (XXXV.443). And Jane the mature narrator concludes that 'to have yielded then would have been an error of principle; to have yielded now would have been an error of judgement' (443). W. A. Craik has succinctly differentiated the two temptations. St. John 'tempts her to do violence to her own nature, in antithesis to Mr. Rochester, who tempted her to violate her moral standards'.[15] Jane's renunciation of Rochester is necessary in order to preserve her integrity of self and to establish a separate identity for herself; her rejection of St. John is imperative if she were to retain her individuality and independence. On both occasions Jane succeeds in resisting the pressure brought on her by choosing to be true to herself, by insisting on her own rights as an individual. Ironically, it is St. John who sends Jane back to Rochester in spite of himself. Jane's escape from St. John is the reverse of her flight from Thornfield. She leaves Moor House with alacrity, with a sense of purpose and direction, with none of the doubts and heartsickness she felt on leaving Rochester. She returns to Rochester now as a free individual and a passionate woman. It is true that her return journey is expressly undertaken to secure news of her master, but as she is hastening towards Thornfield and Rochester, Jane's thoughts run as follows:

> Could I but see him! Surely, in that case, I should not be so mad as to run to him? I cannot tell—I am not certain. And if I did—what then? God bless him! What then! Who would be hurt by my once more tasting the life his glance can give me?
>
> (XXXVI. 448-9)

She is using the same argument that Rochester used before—she has come round to his way of thinking by a tortuous process and a different rationale. She can respond to Rochester's passion now because she has finally discovered herself. She can become Rochester's mistress now that she has become, in her own words, 'my own mistress' (XXXVII.459). And now in gratifying her need for love, she chooses once more to assert herself, knowing full well what she is doing. Jane, with her greater maturity, experience, and confidence, with her new awareness of life and love, with her new-found independence, is a more equal match for Rochester who is now blind and maimed. They revert to the position of their first meeting, when Rochester has to lean on Jane for support. This appears to be Charlotte Brontë's ideal of a relationship—a kind of comradeship with each partner as the other's prop and stay, since Jane leans on Rochester's wisdom and strength as much as he on her.

What Jane said to Rochester earlier on her return from Gateshead Hall could be said here as well: 'I am strangely glad to be back again to you; and wherever you are is my home—my only home' (XXII.274). She has finally discovered herself and has come home. And the beautifully subdued reunion and marriage at the end represent the resolution of all moral and emotional conflicts, when both the heroine and the hero have reached a new moral and emotional understanding of life as a whole.

Given Charlotte Brontë's concept of the individual self, given her conception of her heroine's character and environment, the decisions made by Jane Eyre in the two greatest crises of her life are inevitable. At the moment of choice, Jane feels bound to behave according to her deepest ideas of herself, according to her notion of honour and conscience and self-respect, regardless of comfort or personal happiness. She is genuinely motivated by ideals that are really her author's own.

Notes

1. Joan Bennett, *George Eliot: Her Mind and Her Art* (Cambridge, 1948; Paperback edition, 1962), p. 122.

2. Q. D. Leavis in the introduction to the Penguin edition (1971) of *Jane Eyre,* p. 21. All quotations from the novel are from this edition; for convenience I cite chapter and page number.

3. Kathleen Tillotson, *Novels of the Eighteen-Forties* (London, 1956; Corrected edition, 1962), p. 307.

4. K. Tillotson, *op. cit.,* p. 306.

5. K. Tillotson, *op. cit.,* p. 299.

6. K. Tillotson, *op. cit.,* p. 304.

7. George Eliot, *The Mill on the Floss,* I.v.

8. R. B. Martin, *The Accents of Persuasion: Charlotte Brontë's Novels* (London, 1966), p. 83.

9. R. B. Yeazell, 'More True than Real: Jane Eyre's "Mysterious Summons"', *Nineteenth-Century Fiction,* XXIX.ii (1974), p. 137.

10. Q. D. Leavis, Introduction to *Jane Eyre,* p. 21.

11. Yeazell, *op. cit.,* p. 133.

12. F. A. C. Wilson, 'The Primrose Wreath: the Heroes of the Brontë Novels', *Nineteenth-Century Fiction,* XXIX.i (1974), pp. 41, 44.

13. Yeazell, *op.cit.,* p. 136.

14. Inga-Stina Ewbank, *Their Proper Sphere* (London, 1966), p. 196.

15. W. A. Craik, *The Brontë Novels* (London, 1968), p. 100.

Jerome Beaty (essay date winter 1977)

SOURCE: Beaty, Jerome. "*Jane Eyre* and Genre." *Genre* 10, no. 4 (winter 1977): 619-54.

[*In the following essay, Beaty disputes critical appraisals of* Jane Eyre *that classify it as a Gothic novel, contending instead that the literary conventions of Gothicism are subordinate to the structure and world view of the novel.*]

Discussions of **Jane Eyre** and genre usually center on the Gothic. Although many of the memorable episodes of the novel do indeed play on Gothic expectations, only the middle third of the novel is predominantly Gothic and the form or structure of the novel as a whole is not Gothic at all.[1] This essay seeks to define a more appropriate generic context which will inform and enrich our reading of the novel, and in the process it necessarily touches on issues of methodology and critical theory involving influence, convention, genre and the phenomenology of reading.

It is possible, of course, to ignore genre entirely yet still see **Jane Eyre** in a literary context of one sort or another. It can be read against another novel, its "source," for example, perhaps to show how Brontë the epigone misread a major predecessor in order to free herself from his influence and to realize her own vision, a vision that we can thus more accurately define by comparing **Jane Eyre** to its source. That the source of **Jane Eyre** was in fact a major novel—*Pamela*—Janet Spens suggested almost fifty years ago in a detailed and persuasive essay.[2] She summarizes the most important parallels as follows:

> Jane is a nursery governess and her social position as such is nearly indistinguishable from that of Pamela as waiting-woman to Mr. B.'s mother. Both habitually talk of the hero as "my Master" and are sent for to his presence. There is no doubt that part of the success of *Jane Eyre,* as of *Pamela*, was due to the romance of the rise of the heroine in social position. Mrs. Fairfax corresponds closely to Mrs. Jervis—the housekeeper who befriends Pamela. The house party with the egregious Miss Ingram has a parallel in the party which comes to dine and inspect Pamela, and in Mr. B.'s sister who objects to the marriage. Rochester plans and nearly carries through a sham marriage with Jane, and Mr. B. plots a sham marriage. Many of the scenes correspond exactly, and it is amazing how many little points are reproduced.
>
> (Spens, p. 56)

Some of the points of comparison are not "little": for example, a key element in suspense and expectation, the "alternative lover," is, in both novels, a clergyman. Some of the "little" parallels are quite striking:

> One of the servants who wishes Pamela well and cannot get access to her, disguises himself as a gipsy, and, pretending to tell fortunes, brings her a letter warning her about the mock-marriage. In **Jane Eyre** Rochester disguises himself as a gipsy and, pretending to tell Jane's fortune, hints at the truth of his position. One tiny point is significant of the method. In *Pamela* the gipsy wishes to draw Pamela's attention to the fact that she is going to hide the letter in the grass, since she dare not give it to her then. She does it thus: 'O! said she, I cannot tell your fortune: your hand is so white and fine, I cannot see the lines: but said she, and stooping, pulled up a little tuft of grass, I have a way for that: and so rubbed my hand with the mould part of the tuft: Now, said she, I can see the lines.'
>
> In **Jane Eyre** Rochester disguised as a gipsy asks for Jane's hand, and then says, 'It is too fine . . . I can make nothing of such a hand as that; almost without lines; besides what is in a palm? Destiny is not written there.'
>
> (Spens, pp. 56-57)

Many of the similarities in the two novels which may be borrowings may just as easily be explained as commonplace fictional conventions. Here, however, though both gypsies and disguises are conventions,[3] the verbal echo would seem to be too explicit and too exact to be anything but conscious or, more probably, unconscious borrowing—unless we can believe it to be mere coincidence. Spens's case for Brontë's borrowing of the structural pattern of *Pamela* is forced, however, and this forcing weakens her argument.[4]

Even if the Pamela-Mr. B./Jane-Rochester plots were precisely parallel, the structures of the novels would remain significantly different, for that plot in *Pamela* is, of course, the entire novel, whereas in **Jane Eyre** it is, though central and significant, only a portion of the novel: Rochester does not appear in the first quarter of the novel and is at least physically absent from most of the final quarter.

Still, to place these novels side by side may well suggest *Pamela* as the source of **Jane Eyre,** and as the frame of reference within which we read the Brontë novel. It is thus somewhat disconcerting to find another novel offered as a source of **Jane Eyre.** Inga-Stina Ewbank, pointing out that Barbara Hofland's popular works were available to the Brontës through the Keighley Mechanic's Institute library, suggests that Hofland's frequently reprinted novel of 1814, *Ellen the Teacher,* might have served as one of the sources of **Jane Eyre**: "Without wishing to press the point I even think it possible that a story like *Ellen, the Teacher,* about a poor orphan girl who suffers miserably in a boarding school, eventually makes good as a governess and ultimately marries her cousin, Sir Charles Sedley, might have been one of the germs from which **Jane Eyre** grew."[5] Ewbank may not have pressed the point far enough. There are common uses of conventions and particular resemblances large and small that may seem more than coincidence.

Young Ellen Delville, like young Jane, is a fiery little girl who must learn self-control. Ellen's friend Betsy Burns is, in marked contrast to Jane's friend Helen Burns, even more fiery than she: indeed, Ellen protests that she is "not passionate—I mean not *very* passionate; I never go into a rage, like Betsy Burns."[6] Her mother suggests that she does nonetheless get excessively angry with too little cause, and warns her that shame always follows passion. Jane, even with considerable cause for anger, discovers, when she turns on her aunt, that the aftermath of losing control of her emotions is unpleasant:

> A child cannot quarrel with its elders, as I had done: cannot give its furious feelings uncontrolled play, as I had given mine; without experiencing afterwards the pang of remorse and the chill of reaction. . . . [A] half an hour's silence and reflection had shewn me the madness of my conduct, and the dreariness of my hated and hating position.
>
> (*JE*, [*Jane Eyre*] pp. 40-41)

Ellen is not punished for losing her temper, as Jane is. Her mother dies; her father places her in school, goes abroad and is inexplicably not heard from for two years. Her fees not having been paid, Ellen is treated like a pauper. On one occasion she is, like Jane, falsely accused of lying, and it is for this that she is, like Jane for her temper, locked in a room. Like Jane, she passes out there, and like Jane she is ill afterwards. Ellen's badly infected finger requires medical attention, and Dr. Carr, like Dr. Lloyd in *Jane Eyre,* befriends the mistreated orphan. Both heroines serve as teachers and governesses. Both heroines have their prayers answered. On one occasion Ellen prays for help and her brother Tom shows up almost immediately; on another occasion Ellen runs away from school as Jane runs from Rochester, prays, throws herself on God and is saved by Dr. Carr, just as Jane, threatened with death by exposure and starvation on the moors prays that Providence aid her and almost immediately sees a light which proves to be the candle in the window of Moor House, the abode of cousins she does not know she has. Jane, however, refuses to marry her cousin, St. John Rivers, while Ellen does marry hers, Sir Charles Sedley, though both orphans marry gentlemen. Indeed, a contemporary reader's awareness of the outcome of *Ellen* may have heightened suspense about Jane's response to Rivers' proposal of marriage in *Jane Eyre.*

Clearly, however, if the Hofland tale is a source for *Jane Eyre* it is a source primarily for the opening chapters, Jane's childhood and schooling, just as *Pamela* is a source, perhaps, of the middle portion of the Brontë novel, the Rochester-Jane love affair and marriage. It is conceivable then that if neither is *the* source each is *a* source, the "Pamela" section of *Jane Eyre* (conflated with the Gothic) being grafted on to the "Ellen" sec-tion. The hybrid seems to have flourished. For the reader, however, *Ellen* complicates matters: he can no longer read *Jane Eyre* with only *Pamela* as context; and if he shifts from *Ellen* to *Pamela* when Rochester appears, he must shift back again for Rivers.

A third novel complicates matters still further. The eponymous heroine of Mrs. Sherwood's *Caroline Mordaunt* [*CM*] (1835), it has been pointed out, "is brought back into religion by a pious little pupil who, like Jane Eyre's Helen Burns, dies in her arms."[7] Like Helen *Burns* (and like Maria Brontë) Emily Sel*burn* dies of consumption. Like Helen too she seems preternaturally informed on religious matters, knowledge that Sherwood claims is attained only "in cases resembling that of this most lovely one, where the time is short, and that which is to be done must be done quickly."[8] Helen's and Emily's Protestantism are, however, quite different. Helen believes in an invisible world of spirits which oversees and guards each of us and believes in universal salvation or Arminianism. "'Why . . . should we ever sink overwhelmed with distress, when life is so soon over,'" she asks Jane, "'and death is so certain an entrance to happiness: to glory?'" (*JE*, p. 81). She dies certain of heaven, for herself and for Jane:

> "God is my father; God is my friend: I love him; I believe he loves me."
>
> "And shall I see you again, Helen, when I die?"
>
> "You will come to the same region of happiness: be received by the same mighty, universal Parent, no doubt, dear Jane."
>
> (*JE*, p. 96)

Emily Selburn is equally sure of salvation, for herself and for some others, but not, apparently for all; she believes in faith, not works, and in predestination:

> "Dear Miss Mordaunt," she said, "my kind Miss Mordaunt, do not think me conceited when I presume to say that mamma is wrong in her opinions of my religion; she acknowledges the corruption of our nature; she sometimes says that we can do no good thing; and yet she adds that our entering into happiness in the world to come must depend on ourselves."
>
> "And does it not?" I answered.
>
> "Thank God," replied the lovely girl, clasping her hands and looking first upwards, and then down on me (for I was sitting and she standing), "or what would become of Emily? No, no, Miss Mordaunt, my heavenly Father predestined me, with thousands, and tens of thousands, and thousands of thousands of lost and undone creatures like myself, to glory, before the world began; and provided justification and sanctification for me in the death and merits of his Son, who is at once both God and man, before I entered into life; and, being entered, he revealed his Son to my soul, and made me to be assured not only that I am justified, but also that I am

sanctified: therefore I know that I am redeemed, and that I possess a life eternal, and that nothing can snatch me from my heavenly Father's arms."

(*CM,* p. 278)

Despite these differences, both novels are fully informed by one central religious tenet, providentialism. Critics have become increasingly aware of the structural and thematic centrality of Providence in *Jane Eyre,*[9] so there is no need fully to rehearse the arguments for such a reading here. Suffice it to say that *Jane Eyre* is essentially the story of Jane's increasing awareness of the role of Providence in her life. She gradually comes to recognize that, as Helen had told her, we do have resources outside ourselves, that a spirit or spirits watch over us, warn and lead us. At eighteen or nineteen Jane could not read and so could not heed such signs as that of the writhing chestnut tree which was split by lightning on the night of Rochester's proposal. A few months later, her dreams of a life with Rochester turned into a nightmare, having fled the temptations of Thornfield, she faces death alone on the moors; she prays that Providence sustain, aid, and direct her (*JE,* p. 421), and almost immediately, she sees the light in a window of the Rivers' house. Less than a year later, sorely beset by her missionary cousin, St. John Rivers, she is about to agree to a loveless marriage out of a sense of duty, when she beseeches heaven to show her whether such a decision is right. Whereupon she hears a voice that seems to be Rochester's calling her across the intervening spaces (*JE,* pp. 535-36). At the time she says it is not a miracle but nature doing her best. Later, when she learns that Rochester was at that very time praying and calling to her and that he thought he heard her answer, she sees in the event the possibility of the supernatural (*JE,* p. 572).

One of the reasons, perhaps, that critics have been rather slow in apprehending the providential nature of *Jane Eyre* lies in the way Brontë uses the first-person narrator. Jane, the voice or narrator, telling her story some ten years after the last of the action in the novel and twenty years after the opening scenes, seldom intervenes to explain the "truth" behind the thoughts and perceptions of Jane the focus,[10] so that we, like Jane, must learn to see and interpret events for ourselves. This responsibility of the individual for participating in his or her own salvation is consonant with Brontë's unpredestinarian religious views. Jane Eyre must herself read the providential signs and read them aright, must stand on her principles, use her reason, hearken to her conscience. Since her fate is uncertain, the reader, to participate experientially in her story (and to understand his or her own life in a providential contingent cosmos), must be kept in the dark just as Jane is. The reader, like Jane, must gradually dismiss the superstition of Gothic terror and the scepticism of mere natural knowledge to *dis-cover* Divine Providence. Sherwood's predestinari-

anism dictates a different strategic use of the first-person narrator. Though Caroline Mordaunt may be ignorant of God's will and her own fate in her early years, it has been written. The reader, too, was saved or damned, "before the world began." No need, then, for interpretation, doubt, even judgment; no need for suspense about the outcome; no need to keep the focus on the ignorant Caroline and to deny the voice of the wiser Caroline its all but certain knowledge. The very first words of *Caroline Mordaunt* do away with all uncertainty about how the heroine will fare and even with most questions of the means by which she will be brought, or has been brought, to a safe harbor:

I am now arrived at that period of life, and, I thank God, to that state of mind, in which I can look back at the various adventures of my past years with no other feelings than those of gratitude to that Divine Providence which has rendered every apparent accident, and every difficulty which I have encountered in my passage down the stream of time, more or less subservient to my everlasting welfare: for I cannot doubt but that the peace I have enjoyed during some of the latter years of my life is no other than an earnest of that perfect rest in which I hope to enter, through the merits and death of my Divine Redeemer.

(*CM,* p. 203)[11]

Even with that explicit opening she fears being misunderstood or leaving the reader in doubt. So not many pages later she feels obligated to explain why in writing her autobiography she is not recording her earlier religious thoughts:

I beg my reader to understand that I had no idea of whatever of religion at that period of my life of which I am speaking. She therefore (for I am chiefly addressing my own sex) must not expect to find from my conduct then, or from any of such of my private thoughts as I may think it expedient to make known to her, any traces of those divine influences—the effects of which I trust to be able to make more manifest in the latter portions of my narrative.

(*CM,* p. 219)

And half-way through the novel she once more expresses concern lest her "serious" (not "gentle") reader should misapprehend:

I almost fear that my serious reader may be tired of me, and may begin to have some apprehensions lest, as I have already stated myself to have been in six families in the situation of governess, without having evidenced the smallest regard for religion, I should have nothing better to say of myself to the end of my history; neither have I any thing whatever as yet to mention, nor do I ever hope to have any good to say of myself; but I have much, very much to say of the various providences by which I was gradually brought to know myself, to esteem myself as the chief of sinners, and to comprehend in some degree what the Almighty has done and is still doing for me.

(*CM,* p. 252)

She is instructed, as we have seen, by the dying child, Emily Selburn, has a couple more trials to go through, and is instructed in the ways of Providence in her own life by her cousin:

> My good cousin loved to enumerate these sundry per-ambulations, and to trace the hand of God in all that had befallen me, showing how my various misadventures had been calculated to humble me, and bring me to a knowledge of myself . . . ; ". . . blessed, therefore, are those who have been stripped of all self dependance [sic], even although the process may not have been over agreeable to flesh and blood."
>
> (*CM*, p. 298)

The novel closes with still more reassurance: she counts her blessings—peace, happiness, "the best of husbands," children, friends—and, she adds,

> I have reason to think, nay I am assured that there is a divine hand leading on all I love to that land which is very far off, where we shall see the King in his beauty, and shall be better able to understand the consolatory truth which our spiritual enemy would willingly hide from us, namely, that God is love.
>
> (*CM*, p. 305)

Both *Caroline Mordaunt* and *Jane Eyre,* then, are "autobiographies" written from a vantage point years after the events narrated, and both testify to the beneficient role of Providence in their narrators' lives.[12] Alerted by the major similarities, an attentive reader may see "little" parallel details as well, which, individually insignificant, may nonetheless juxtapose the novels in the reader's mind. Chapter 11 of *Jane Eyre,* for example, serves as a transition from Lowood to Millcote (the town near which Thornfield is located):

> A new chapter in a novel is something like a new scene in a play; and when I draw up the curtain this time, reader, you must fancy you see a room in the George Inn at Millcote, with such large-figured papering on the walls as inn rooms have. . . . [T]he Millcote town clock is now just striking eight.

It is an awkward but not unusual scene-shifting passage for an eighteenth- or nineteenth-century novel, so it is probably not enough in itself to trigger a reader's memory of a similar passage in Sherwood:

> And now, my readers, if they please, must follow me again to the stage [coach], hear my cousin's parting advice, and accompany me till I am set down at the White Hart, in the beautiful city of Bath, where I arrived about six in the evening. . . .
>
> (*CM*, p. 227)

The coach and inn, the address to the reader, the specification of the time and place seem notably parallel, and the similarity is heightened by the contrast in the young travelers' reception: Caroline is met by a sedan chair and carried off to her new place of employment in "the beautiful city of Bath"; there seems to be no one to meet Jane, and when, a half hour later, she finds there is transportation, it is in "a one-horse conveyance . . . a sort of car" driven by a plain and rather abrupt-speaking servant.

Later in the Sherwood novel, when Caroline has still another employer, that universal bane of Victorian children—porridge—may, under the pressure of other similarities, forge still another link between the two novels. On Jane's first morning at Lowood, remember, the breakfast porridge was "'Disgusting! . . . burnt again!'" (*JE,* p. 50). Caroline finds even unburnt porridge bad enough: Mrs. Fenton's four girls get for breakfast, "four basins of porridge, . . . a sort of mess which is generally loathed by English palates, and which I presently perceived that nothing but excessive hunger would have compelled the young people to swallow." (*CM,* p. 285). The unsatisfactory breakfast is part of a strict regimen that includes other unpleasantness, such as a fanatical insistence on walking. Mrs. Fenton believes her children should walk in all weathers, twice daily in winter, thrice in summer.

> Such was the walking mania, that it rarely happened that we had got into the spirit of a lesson . . . but Mrs. Fenton would come in, saying, "Miss Mordaunt, you will not forget your exercise"; and then she would generally advance to the window, and examine the sky from thence, looking up to the heavens, and down again upon the earth, never failing to find some very particular reason for putting up the books, and setting out to walk at that precise moment. "You certainly will lose your walk to-day, Miss Mordaunt," she would say, "if you do not take the present moment—it rains now, to be sure . . . but it will be fine before you have your things on, and then you will be able to take the very first advantage of the sunshine;" or, "it is now moderately cool; it will be excessively hot by-and-by; you had better avail yourself of the present hour; you will never be able to endure the heat at noon"; and then again at twelve o'clock, "we shall have rain, or thunder, or mist, or snow, or wind, in the evening; you had better get your second walk before dinner"; and again before tea, or after tea, in summer, it was the same thing; and we were to be out so long, and to walk so far.
>
> (*CM*, pp. 286-87)

Our notions of the Victorians may be such, and our usual images of the Brontë sisters striding across the moors may be such, that we would expect Charlotte, if not Caroline Mordaunt herself, to approve such a healthful addiction. The Sherwood passage might thus be useful in heightening our awareness of what soon follows that memorable opening sentence of Jane Eyre—"There was no possibility of taking a walk that day"—namely, "I was glad of it; I never liked long walks, especially on chilly afternoons: dreadful to me was the coming home in the raw twilight, with nipped fingers and toes. . . ."

Even leaving these somewhat trivial (or, some would say, illusory) echoes aside, of the three works so far cited *Caroline Mordaunt* seems to have the best claim to be considered the major "source" of ***Jane Eyre***; the autobiographical mode and the providential theme span the entire novel and not just the childhood sections, as in the case of *Ellen,* or the Thornfield half, as in the case of *Pamela.* Whether *Caroline Mordaunt* was, in fact, Brontë's source is critically less important, perhaps, than whether contemporary readers would, to any significant extent, consciously or unconsciously read ***Jane Eyre*** against or in terms of the Sherwood novel. We have already seen how Brontë's views of salvation play off against Sherwood's, despite the common providentialism. Did Caroline's marrying a clergyman, initially without love, in order to serve as his helpmate, throw into doubt the outcome of St. John's insistent proposal of a similar marriage to Jane for the informed contemporary reader? did it heighten the suspense? did it by contrast sharpen the definition of the proper role of love in Brontë's vision of moral realities? Ewbank says of the Sherwood novel,

> Caroline's course, through one governess's position after another, is not a picaresque satire but a domesticated Pilgrim's Progress; her various humiliations do not lead to the arms of a lord [as in Blessington's *The Governess*], but to those of The Lord. True, she marries at the end, but the bridegroom is a clergyman (who wants, not romance but "a housekeeper") of humble means. Mrs. Sherwood's intention is to show how Caroline, who starts as an irreligious and self-opinionated young woman, is brought by degrees to mortification and the Church. . . . [T]he heroine becomes a good Christian by realising "how my various misadventures had been calculated to humble me, and bring me to a knowledge of myself. . . ."
>
> (p. 63)

The Brontë governess who moves from position to position is Agnes Grey not Jane Eyre, but the names, especially the place names—Gateshead, Lowood, Thornfield, Moor House—the frequent references to Bunyan, and the pattern of the heroine's moral progress make "domesticated Pilgrim's Progress" as appropriate a description of ***Jane Eyre*** as of *Caroline Mordaunt.* The Brontë novel, if equally religious, is less pious and less narrow in its definition of human possibilities, not entirely limiting self to soul; Jane does not marry a clergyman and does not marry without love, nor does the novel suggest we should think less of her for that.[13] How do we read the last portion of Ewbank's description of Sherwood's novel in terms of ***Jane Eyre***? To what extent are Jane's misadventures a way of humbling her and bringing her to knowledge of herself? To what extent is the religiously uninformed, if not irreligious, rebellious and passionate Jane of the early chapters brought, if not to mortification and the Church, at least to reason, self-control, and the awareness that she needs and has divine love and guidance? To a greater

extent, I would argue, than most twentieth-century readers would admit, (or wish), and the context of contemporary fiction, including Mrs. Sherwood's *Caroline Mordaunt,* helps to bring into relief this somewhat anti-romantic reading. Not, again, that such a reading is necessarily "right," but that it is a possible reading, and one whose potential presence enriches the novel. ***Jane Eyre,*** read now, but read in its contemporary context, is a more ambivalent or indeterminate novel than it is usually held to be.

That a novel may seem to have three or more sources (we've not even touched on the Gothic "borrowings" here, remember) might appear embarrassing to the literary historian, and the number of possible contextual referents may well complicate or confuse any simple notion we may have of the response of the contemporary reader. Nonetheless, such is the complexity of historical circumstance and literary context within which a new literary work must almost invariably create its place and meaning, regardless of what our theories of genesis or influence might prefer. The almost irreducible complexity of the reality of literary history—if this be the reality—whatever the effect on theorist or critic, offers more than compensatory advantages to the reader and the work. The very multiplicity of referents, while it more or less precludes definitiveness, means that most novel-readers of any experience will be familiar with one or more of the works which go to make up the context and will respond accordingly. And any work that is not wholly derivative will be all the richer for innumerable expectations and possibilities engendered by the context.

While innumerable, such expectations and readings cannot be both effective and infinite however. That is, a fictional situation where anything and everything (or nothing) might happen, where precedent or convention or structure of some sort does not define or limit expectation cannot create for the reader any expectation at all. It can create neither narrative nor epistemological expectation. Narrative strategies and literary vision must then operate between the extremes of absolute predictability and originality so lacking in precedent as to preclude recognition and entirely discourage prediction.

It is possible, then, that one of the functions of genre is to "package" individual works and even discrete conventions for the reader in such a way as to reduce the infinite variety of contextual possibilities while not offering so rigid a structure and set of expectations as to reduce substantially the richness or individuality of the work itself.

It is here that *Caroline Mordaunt* is even more important to the reading of ***Jane Eyre*** than as a source or self-contained context, for it is probably the first paradigmatic governess novel, a short-lived but significant early Victorian fictional kind which *Jane Eyre* ultimately crowned and transcended. The governess novel as a "concrete historical genre" is, as Alistair Fowler says of all such genres, "closely linked to specific social forms. . . ."[14] With the burgeoning middle class entering the "governess market," by mid-century there were some 24,770 governesses in England, and their plight even by 1841 was serious and widespread enough to occasion the founding of the Governesses' Benevolent Institution. Appeals to the new Institution revealed such misery that the Christian Socialists set about to improve the status of the governess by improving her education. In the year in which *Jane Eyre* was published, a series of Lectures to Ladies began in London, their popularity leading immediately to the founding of Queen's College for Women in 1848 and Bedford College in 1849. "It is easy," then, "to understand the popularity of the governess with the Victorian novelist. . . . An allusion to a governess in a novel was . . . sure to arouse a stock emotional response in the minds of the readers."[15]

Though the "concrete historical genre" of the governess novel thus had an appropriate, perhaps determining social context, the fictional kind has a history of its own.[16] It is rarely possible, of course, to say precisely when and where any genre began with any certainty, but we might reasonably begin to trace the history of the form with a popular and influential work published almost a century before *Jane Eyre*. Not very long after the publication of *Pamela,* Sarah Fielding, an admirer and correspondent of Richardson's and sister of his great rival, published *The Governess; or, Little Female Academy* (1749). This is not in any sense a governess *novel*. It is, rather, a series of secular sermons and illustrative fairy tales strung together on the rather thin structural device of a girls' school. Miss Teachum, the governess, does surprisingly little of the moralizing or tale-telling, leaving that to her nine pupils, who also give brief autobiographical sketches centering on how their moral education cured them of one vice or another. Self-righteous and sentimental to modern taste, no doubt, *The Governess* was nonetheless immediately and enduringly successful: seven London editions appeared by 1789; some twenty-four appearances by 1804, including American and Irish editions and a German and a Swedish translation.[17] The Oxford edition lists some fifty "progeny" in the first seventy years or so after publication and eleven in its eighth decade, the decade in which Charlotte Brontë was born. Many of these are books for children, courtesy books or manuals, even fictionalized educational theory such as Maria Edgeworth's *The Good French Governess* (1801). *Ellen the Teacher* (1814), though closer to a novel than most works listed, suggests by its subtitle (*A Tale for Youth*) that it too is not an "adult" novel, intended primarily for an adult audience.

In 1820 the history and influence of Sarah Fielding's *Governess* takes a sharp and significant turn. Mrs. Sherwood puts her hand to Fielding's work and executes "the fiercest example of editorial recension in the whole of literature."[18] She shifts the emphasis from the behaviorally moral to the piously religious; according to Jill Grey, "Mrs. Sherwood not only re-wrote the story, changing many details, but substituted dull, moral tales for Sarah's fairy stories and also inserted the gloomiest quotations from the Bible on practically every page" (Fielding, p. 74). Early nineteenth-century readers apparently did not agree: by the 1840s Mrs. Sherwood's version had gone into six editions (Fielding, p. 74).

Before those two decades had elapsed, however, Mrs. Sherwood herself wrote a work that, no matter how Evangelical, how religious and didactic, is clearly a novel and a novel aimed at an adult female audience: *Caroline Mordaunt.* Several factors had contributed to the formation of the genre. Besides the movement within the genre from children's literature and the moral tale toward the novel in such works as *Ellen,* the character-type of the governess as she would appear in early Victorian fiction had been becoming increasingly familiar during the early decades of the century, in fiction as well as in British life. There are, for example, a number of governesses in Jane Austen. Those who are presently governesses—like Miss Lee in *Mansfield Park*—are minor and shadowy, and those who have important supporting roles—like "poor Miss Taylor" and Jane Fairfax in *Emma*—are either no longer or not yet governesses, but the vulnerability of the genteel, educated, unmarried woman, neither a servant nor an equal, living in a household as a dependent is a situation with great potential for narrative exploitation. *Caroline Mordaunt* was apparently the first novel[19] to exploit the possibilities in a full-length work, and it seems clearly to have established the pattern. Thomson (p. 39) indicates the fictional governess's "conventional attributes. She was bound to be a lady—preferably the daughter of a clergyman; she was always impoverished, unprotected, and, by virtue of her circumstances, reasonably intelligent and submissive." Ewbank (pp. 59-63) adds that she is usually orphaned, that she is subjected to some form of social humiliation, and that where she is the heroine she marries either a gentleman (if not a lord) or a clergyman. Ewbank's taxonomy, it will be noticed, in fact identifies three varieties of the governess novel: those in which the governess is not the heroine and so does not marry; those in which she is the heroine and marries, the latter category breaking down into those in which she marries a gentleman and those in which she marries a clergyman. Though Ewbank (p. 211) thinks it, too, a tale for youth, *Caroline Mordaunt* seems to have leaped at once from governess tale to governess novel; it is a perfect representative of the last of Ewbank's categories.

The heroine of Lady Blessington's *The Governess* is named Clara Mordaunt,[20] and the subtitle of Mrs. Sherwood's *Caroline Mordaunt* is *The Governess*. Clara is an orphan—her father was a bankrupt and suicide—and like Caroline she moves from one governess position to another. As a governess-heroine she marries, not a clergyman but Lord Seymourville whom, as Clarence Seymour, she had long loved. If Sherwood's *Caroline Mordaunt* is "as much a Low Church religious novel as a governess tale" (Ewbank, p. 63), Blessington's is even more a Silverfork novel in which the well-educated genteel heroine is beleaguered by newly-rich employers:

> The real interest in Lady Blessington's novel does not lie in the governess *per se;* it lies in the various social milieus that Clara passes through by virtue of being a governess. Clara is a convenient vehicle in a picaresque tour of various strata of English society. . . . Clara's own high breeding seems to have fitted her not so much for teaching their children as for ridiculing the bourgeois manner of . . . parvenus, their conversations . . . , their taste in clothes . . . , and so on. . . .
>
> . . . Rich heiress becomes poor governess, but the poor governess even tually (thanks to the timely death of a rich uncle) becomes rich heiress again and marries lord. This pattern of success story is common enough in the "fashionable" novels of Lady Blessington; and the fact that Clara spends her time of ill-fortune as a governess has nothing to do with her ultimate good fortune.
>
> (Ewbank, pp. 62-63)

If neither of these works is a governess novel, perhaps there is no such kind. In any case, we ought to distinguish two subtypes, not just based on whether the heroine marries a gentleman or clergyman but on the essentially religious or secular nature of the work, for in these two governess novels at least the distinction runs far deeper than the status of the heroine's mate. Moreover, those governess novels in which the governess is not a heroine and does not marry may also be classified as either "religious" or "secular." Ewbank (p. 62) says of *Deerbrook* (1839) and *Amy Herbert* (1844), for example, "Both these novels . . . insert studies of the ideal governess—not so much *qua* governess as *qua* Christian stoic. . . ."

Clara Mordaunt, who like Jane is recipient of a legacy from her uncle and marries a gentleman, is, also like Jane, *not* a Christian stoic; feeling herself superior to those she serves, she is neither meek nor submissive. This independence combined with her gentility make those scenes of humiliation which she must undergo in her role of governess almost unbearable. Though such scenes are more frequent and more intense in *The Governess,* perhaps, than in other representatives of the genre, they are an almost constitutive element in the governess novel. Indeed, they predate the governess novel as such, going back at least as far as *Pamela:* "The house-party with the egregious Miss Ingram" in *Jane Eyre,* Spens says, "has a parallel in the party which comes to inspect Pamela, and in Mr. B.'s sister who objects to the marriage." (p. 56). It may be well to remind ourselves of the scene in *Jane Eyre* before glancing at its varieties in the other governess novels.

Blanche, who apparently will soon be Mrs. Rochester, is visiting Thornfield with an entourage that includes her mother and brother. Though she sees that Jane is present behind the window-curtain, she nonetheless chides Rochester about the inconvenience and expense of keeping a governess; he dismisses her objections, but she goes on:

> "No—you men never do consider economy and common sense. You should hear mama on the subject of governesses; Mary and I have had, I should think, a dozen at least in our day; half of them detestable and the rest ridiculous, and all incubi—were they not, mama?"
>
> "My dearest, don't mention governesses: the word makes me nervous. I have suffered a martyrdom from their incompetency and caprice: I thank Heaven I have now done with them!"
>
> Mrs. Dent here bent over the pious lady, and whispered something in her ear: I suppose from the answer elicited, it was a reminder that one of the anathematized race was present.
>
> "Tant pis!" said her ladyship. "I hope it may do her good!"
>
> (*JE,* p. 221)

Blanche, joined by her brother, recalls how they used to torment their governesses, spilling tea, throwing books, even "blackmailing" Miss Wilson, who seemed to have had the audacity to fall in love with the tutor. Amy Ashton also recalls how she and her sister used to "quiz" their governess, "but she was such a good creature, she would bear anything. . . ." "I suppose now," said Miss Ingram, curling her lip sarcastically, "we shall have an abstract of all the memoirs of all governesses extant . . ." (*JE,* p. 233).

In *Amy Herbert* (1844), Emily Morton, the governess, though "remarkably" lady-like, is at first taken for a lady's maid. When the pious and naive Amy tells her young friends, the Harringtons, that it is only their mother and not themselves who can discharge the governess, she's told, "'What a simpleton you are! . . . There are a hundred ways of getting rid of a person you don't like. . . .'"[21] Later the Harrington children have a visitor, a Miss Cunningham, even ruder than they:

> She [Emily Morton] was not introduced to Miss Cunningham; but the young lady cast many curious glances at her as she came into the room, and then a whispered conversation followed between her and Margaret, quite

loud enough to be heard. She was described as "the person who teaches us music and drawing," and her birth, parentage, and education were given. And when Miss Cunningham's curiosity was satisfied, she condescended to look at her attentively for nearly a minute, and then appeared entirely to forget that such a being was in existence. Miss Morton bore this gaze without shrinking. There was not a flush on her delicate cheek, or the slightest curl of anger about her gentle mouth; and all that showed she was aware of what was said was the momentary glistening of her eye as she caught the words—"Oh! she is an orphan, is she?" and then Margaret's reply—"Yes; she lost her father and mother both in one month."

(AH, pp. 103-04)[22]

Such scenes are not developed to any great length in Sherwood, though Caroline Mordaunt does undergo humiliation (meekly, of course): she is treated as an inferior by Lady Euphrasia, abused by other employers, and, after having become a lady's companion, by two spinsters who visit every evening to play cards and "to abuse domestics and companions of every description—which they did with little reference to the only person present of these denominations . . ." (CM, p. 296).

Clara, on the other hand, is insulted on at least three occasions in scenes that are presented dramatically in *The Governess*. In one scene, like Jane and Emily Morton and Caroline Mordaunt, she is spoken about in her presence. As in *Jane Eyre,* here the crassness is not that of upstarts but of titled ladies. In Clara's presence the Ladies Meredith gossip unreservedly and insensitively. Lady Elizabeth rattles on from one tidbit to another: "'. . . Have you not heard about Lady Fanny Elton's *femme-de-chambre*? O! it is a horrid affair, I assure you; but, if people *will* take beauties into their families, they must take the consequences; it is not every woman who has the good fortune to possess such a husband as Lord Axminster [Clara's employer]. . . .'"[23] Her sister speaks of the governess directly as if she were not present:

> "And who is this young person?" enquired Lady Arabella; "who are her friends and connexions, and among whom has she been living? One can never be sufficiently careful on such points, for there is no knowing to what vulgar associations one may be exposed."

(G, II, 156)

Of course here, as elsewhere in the novel, it is the governess who is being exposed to vulgar associations.

One such exposure is reminiscent of Mrs. Elton in Jane Austen's *Emma,* who, having known that Emma's friend had been her governess, upon meeting her is "astonished to find her so lady-like! But she is really quite a gentlewoman."[24] When Clara Mordaunt's eldest pupil discovers that Clara is in fact an heiress, she insensitively remarks, "'And so, Miss Mordaunt, you are a

lady after all?' said Miss Williamson, looking at Clara, 'Well who'd have thought it; for though I told Betsey [the maid] that you were, it was only to vex her; I did not believe it. . . . This proves that mama is *not* always right, for she said that governesses were never ladies . . .'" (G, II, 69-70).

Blessington, like Richardson, makes explicit the vulnerability of the governess/employee to humiliating sexual exploitation—the capitalist version of the medieval *droit de seigneur*—that is very near the surface in *Jane Eyre* and implicit even if in some instances unthinkable in the governess novel as a kind. The Marsdens, West Indian friends of Clara Mordaunt's parvenu mistress, Mrs. Williamson, are, in their "half-caste" way even crasser than their hostess. Given the conventional hotness of West Indian blood (Bertha Mason, of course, is from the West Indies), Hercules Marsden, the son, makes vulgar advances:

> "How much do you pay miss for looking after your piccaninies?" asked Mrs. Marsden. . . .
>
> "I pay her twenty-five guineas a year," replied Mrs. Williamson.
>
> "Just what I pay my maid," remarked the creole.
>
> "And what I have agreed to pay my tiger," said her hopeful son. "Faith! I think I shall take a governess for myself . . . but I shall bargain for her being as young and pretty as miss," looking impudently at Clara, who felt indignant at being made the object of his indelicate remarks.
>
> "Single gentlemen do not keep governesses," said Mrs. Williamson.
>
> "O! that, I suppose, is a privilege reserved for the married men, and a devilish agreeable privilege it is, eh,—my old boy!" turning to his host, "do you not find it so?"

(G, I, 93-94)

Hercules makes further, more forthright and more physical advances, but, just as Clara is in this scene indignant rather than humiliated and meek, she does not suffer in silence or leave him in doubt that she will not put up with such conduct.

Just as the "scene of humiliation" is most fully exploited in the most secular of the governess novels and least fully exploited in the most religious, *Caroline Mordaunt,* so the child-death scene present in all the more religious governess novels is absent from *The Governess*. We have already seen how fully Sherwood exploits the convention for her religious purposes in depicting the death of Emily Selburn and how Brontë exploits the convention which had such personal meaning to her just as fully and functionally but more quietly in the death of Helen Burns. While in Harriet Martineau's *Deerbrook* young Matilda Rowland dies of the plague off-stage, though her decline is reported from time to time, the death of little Rose Harrington as the result of an accident which is caused by the neglect of the older children but is blamed on the governess (Emily Morton), is the central incident in Elizabeth Sewell's *Amy Herbert.* Helen Burns is sickly, so it is no wonder we see her doom in her face, but Rose, who will not die of natural causes, seems equally doomed. Well before the fatal accident a cottager had observed that Rose, "had an angel's face, and that it was fitter for heaven than for earth" (*AH,* p. 299). As in Helen's case, Rose's death seems an escape from the trials and pains of life, though we learn this from the governess, not the dying child: Emily is resigned to the death of her charge, for she recognizes that death "for Rose . . . would be an escape from all the dangers of the world to the enjoyment of rest and peace for ever . . ." (*AH,* p. 307). So, too, it is not the dying child who apprehends the spirit world. The night before little Rose dies, Emily sits by her bed praying, and when Rose awakens assures her that "'God is near, and the angels, though you cannot see them'" (*AH,* p. 309). Mrs. Harrington, after the death of her daughter, seeks consolation in a belief somewhat like Helen Burns', a belief in an ambient world of invisible spirits, and she finds "inexpressible comfort" in the possibility, neither confirmed nor denied by the Bible, she says, "'that those whom I have loved might still be near, though I could not see them . . .'" (*AH,* pp. 321-22). Though it is mediated through the experience of the dying child, at the moment of her death Rose's vision, like Paul Dombey's, seems to confirm in the world of the novel, the immortality of the soul and the prevalence of angels or spirits:

> A momentary strength had been granted her, and with a clear though feeble voice, she followed the [Lord's] prayer to the end; and then, stretching out her little hand, she said, "Mamma, it is bright now. They are come to take me." And with a faint smile, as she half repeated Emily's name, her head once more sank upon the pillow, and the innocent spirit was at rest.
>
> (*AH,* p. 309)

There is no such revelation in *Jane Eyre.* Just as earlier young Jane, the focus of the narration, questions Helen's assurances of personal immortality and of heaven— "Again I questioned; but this time only in thought. 'Where is that region? Does it exist?'" (*JE,* p. 96)— with no interruption from the older Jane who narrates, so here there is no confirmation of Helen's salvation *in the scene.* Helen says good-night, the children kiss and fall asleep. Jane awakens while she is being carried back to her own bed. She learns that she was found, "my face against Helen Burns' shoulder, my arms round her neck. I was asleep, and Helen was—dead" (*JE,* p. 97).

The "Janian" understatement in Helen's death-bed scene is perhaps best appreciated in the context of the early Victorian novel, and modern readers no doubt appreci-

ate the relative indeterminacy of the religious element in the novel filtered as it is through the uncertainty of young Jane. The indeterminacy is only experiential and evanescent, however, functioning as a kind of heuristic suspense, during the course of our reading. When we come to the end of the novel there is, or should be, no doubt about the nature of reality, the existence of God, the immortality of the soul, the intercession of Providence. Indeed, at this very point in the novel Jane the narrator takes one of her rare leaps forward from the time-frame of the narrative to confirm, in no matter how restrained and mediated a manner, the essentially Christian world-view of the novel: "Her grave is in Brocklebridge churchyard: for fifteen years after her death it was only covered by a grassy mound: but now a grey marble tablet marks the spot, inscribed with her name, and the word 'Resurgam'" (*JE,* p. 97).

Jane Eyre shares with all the other governess novels except Blessington's a central religious concern. The taxonomy of the governess novel as a fictional kind can thus be expanded from Ewbank's description: the governess novel has as its heroine or as a major character, a poor but respectable orphan who is forced by circumstances to take a position as governess, who undergoes some sort of humiliation because of her dependent status, who attends the deathbed of a pious child, who has or comes to have a deep religious, providentialist conviction, and who, when she is the heroine, marries a gentleman or clergyman. Obviously all or most of the governess novels lack one or another of these constituents: *Agnes Grey* is not an orphan; Caroline Mordaunt's humiliation is scarcely mentioned and never dramatized; Maria Young in *Deerbrook* does not attend the dying child; in Blessington's *The Governess* there is neither a dying child scene nor a central religious concern, and the religion in neither *Deerbrook* nor *Amy Herbert* is primarily providentialist. And, of course, some of these novels employ other conventions, modes, or genres so extensively as to call into question their genuine identity: Blessington's *The Governess* is sometimes considered a fashionable novel, *Jane Eyre* a Gothic novel. Yet each is nonetheless rather clearly a member of the same fictional kind. By the late 1840s readers would have had their expectations conditioned by one or more of the earlier novels in the genre; recent critics like Thomson, Ewbank, and Robert Colby, though often with qualifications, have treated all of these novels as members of the governess genre.

In the years between Blessington and Brontë contemporaries may have noticed at least two other novels which by their titles at least belong in the genre but which have so far eluded the attention of twentieth-century critics: Mrs. Ross's *The Governess; Or, Politics in Private Life* (London: Smith, Elder, 1836) and Rachel Mac-Crindell's *The English Governess* (1844),[25] both of which, with the usual deviations, rather closely follow the taxonomy. Ross's heroine, Gertrude Walcot, was born a lady, but, orphaned, is reduced to seeking a position as governess. She has rare luck in her employers who treat her with respect and regularly introduce her to society, a practice that results in a number of "humiliation scenes," since the employers' acquaintances do not share their liberal values. Though there is frequent mention of religion, the novel stresses the moral rather than intellectual role of governess; though Gertrude is a paragon, and though there is even a pious deathbed scene (adult, however), the tone is that of a fashionable novel, somewhat like Blessington's. Gertrude, after all, was born a lady; and she does mary *Sir* Herbert Lyster, brother of one of her pupils. Ross vehemently supports the cause of the poor governess (lest her readers be fearful, she points out that Gertrude first met her husband socially, through a mutual [and titled] friend, not as a single and attractive young woman dependent living in his family's home). She makes the didactic nature of her fiction quite clear—in this respect it resembles the pre-novel governess tales—especially in authorial asides to the reader: "I will resume this point of my argument in a future chapter,—I must now return for one moment to the little, smart, ill-educated being . . ." (*PPL,* pp. 68-69); "I shall treat more largely of this subject by-and-bye, when I hope, after pointing out the errors of parents, with regard to those to whose care they commit their children, I may be enabled to suggest at least a better order of things" (*PPL,* p. 103).

MacCrindell's novel is more to our purpose in that it fits my expanded definition of the genre more snugly than Ross's, and it so resembles *Jane Eyre* in certain particulars not inherent in the genre it could claim a place beside *Pamela, Ellen, the Teacher* and *Caroline Mordaunt* as a "source" or referent. It is a providentialist governess novel in which the orphaned heroine attends the death of a confidently religious child and marries a gentleman who resigns his army commission to become a clergyman. As in *Jane Eyre,* in *The English Governess* the religion is broad and the set pieces of religious discussion or didacticism few. Like *Jane Eyre* also, it is not primarily concerned with the trials and tribulations of the governess in contemporary society. And, just as Brontë imports the Gothic and Blessington the fashionable modes, MacCrindell exploits both contemporary melodrama and the contemporary mode or motif of "the English(wo)man abroad."[26] Because of its relevance to *Jane Eyre* and to the governess genre, then, and because it has, to my knowledge, received no recent critical attention, it may be worth looking more closely at *The English Governess.*

Clara (as in Blessington's Mordaunt) Neville (rhymes more or less with Hofland's Ellen Deville) did not seem destined to become the English governess, but after the death of Clara's father, her mother married an evil, hypocritically pious drunkard named Ashton, who per-

Charlotte Brontë, 1816-1855.

secutes his stepdaughters, Clara and Maria, and abuses their mother. In a fit of drunkenness he finally strikes and kills his wife and is sentenced to a year in prison. Clara's sister, who first goes to live with atheistical relatives, has married Lieutenant Lionel Sydenham, the younger son of a baronet, over the objections of his family, in a ceremony performed, sad to relate, by a Roman Catholic priest. Clara herself in her pious way is in love with and seems committed to marry one Edward Seymour: she believes "that he, the brother of her heart, the future partner of her life, was not only bound to her by ties of earthly affection; that he was one to whom she might look for advice, direction and assistance, in running her heavenward race, and with whom she might hope to spend, not only a life of holiness and usefulness on earth, but an eternity of bliss in the regions of never-ending joy and praise" (*EG,* p. 30). At Cambridge Edward stumbles in his heavenward race, is somehow corrupted, becomes dissipated and irreligious. Clara, of course, breaks the engagement.

Pursued once more by the newly released Ashton, she accepts a position as governess in the family of Lt. Col. Wentworth at Gibraltar. We learn lots about North Africa and Jews, about Spanish customs and Roman Catholics and apes in Gibraltar, and we learn that everyone we know seems to be in the area. Seymour turns up, still debauched, and once more Clara rejects him. Maria is there with her husband who is living loosely and squandering money. Ashton arrives in hot pursuit of Clara. Seymour is reported killed in a reckless steeple-chase; Ashton seizes Clara at last on a Gibraltar cliff but she survives and it is he who falls to his death.

Back in London, her term of employment near an end, her London friends dead, her sister dying and then her sister's child, all seems lost. But there appears at her nephew's deathbed Edward Seymour, minister, reports of his death having been exaggerated. Unlike Blessington's more worldly hero, Clarence Seymour, Edward Seymour has found God, resigned his commission in the army, and become a minister.

Despite its echoes of Blessington's fashionable novel, *The Governess,* despite its melodrama and its travel-ogue elements, this is clearly a governess novel, and, like most of the others, is dominated by its religious world-view. This is nowhere more evident than in its deathbed scenes. Clara first attends the deathbed of her sister Maria who comes to Christ during her lingering illness and consoles her children with the thought that death is the "bright herald of everlasting blessedness" (*EG,* p. 256). Not long thereafter Clara has the sad duty of attending her four-year-old nephew Charles who is seriously ill with measles.

> "Dear, darling aunt," said the infant sufferer, "do not grieve so much for Charles; you know I am going to the Lord Jesus Christ, and to live with Him and dear mamma. God will take care of you and dear Emma [his sister], and you will soon come to live with us in heaven."
>
> (*EG,* p. 258)

He has all the confidence in salvation and heaven that Emily Selburn, Rose Harrington, and Helen Burns have. Clara, like Caroline Mordaunt and Emily Morton, seems as certain as the dying child she attends, with none of young Jane Eyre's doubts and questions, and the novel hammers the assurance home. Before Charles dies a minister appears to read over him the latter part of I Corinthians and Hebrews 12:5-6, promising resurrection and finding in suffering a sign of God's favor. The minister himself seems to have been resurrected, for it is, of course, none other than Edward Seymour.

The English Governess, like *Caroline Mordaunt* and **Jane Eyre** in particular, is providentialist in its narrative strategy as well as in its world-view. MacCrindell's heroine, like Sherwood's but unlike Brontë's, early in her career recognizes the hand of Providence in her affairs. Clara and Jane, for example, set out on their journey through life with similar views of its perils but varying degrees of confidence in their direction. Jane

"remembered that the real world was wide, and that a varied field of hopes and fears, of sensations and excitements, awaited those who had courage to go forth into its expanse, to seek real knowledge of life amidst its perils" (*JE,* p. 100). Clara saw her path "strewed with dangers, difficulties, and trials; but the hand of Providence pointed towards it, and she had no right to hesitate. The only resource open to her, indeed the only one which the present state of society leaves to an educated young person, was the instruction of youth" (*EG,* pp. 43-44). No need for a fairy to drop suggestions on Clara's pillow.

As we have seen, Brontë, in distinct contrast to Sherwood, by keeping the focus of the narrative on and through the younger and ignorant Jane and permitting the voice of the older Jane who is narrating the story to interrupt very seldom, leaves for the reader as he reads vast areas of indeterminacy in interpreting the more extraordinary events of the novel. Even toward the end of the novel, when the implication of providential intercession is clear—when Jane hears that Rochester was in fact calling her at the very time she heard his voice, for example (*JE,* p. 573)—the novel does not state categorically as "fact" that there was intercession. Nor are the earlier episodes of Jane's life recalled and re-evaluated: the chestnut tree remains writhing without apparent cause fixed in its place in the novel forever. Some part of us knows the reason on our second reading (but only a part of us) but even on repeated readings, even when we understand rather fully the providential nature of the Brontë world, we cannot be sure about the nature or cause of certain events: the "ghost" in the Red Room is explained away as merely the effect of light from a passing lantern—in all probability—but can we be sure? is the fairy who suggests advertising for a position a joke or a metaphor? are Jane's dreams that tell her to flee temptation merely dreams? is the timing of Bertha's escape from the third story in order to tear the wedding veil coincidence? Such indeterminacy is not a virtue merely on aesthetic grounds or in terms of the more secular and sceptical reading public of the twentieth century, but is inherent in the providentialist vision. We know we are being watched over by Divine Providence, but we are not always sure what events are signs or whether our will or desire is imposing meaning on neutral nature. The individual is always in the position of having to interpret experience and patterns of experience. Leadings and warnings must be both perceived and interpreted and one's own wishes and will must be dissociated from God's will. Indeterminacy in such a world is not ornamental or rhetorical but fundamental and functional.

In *The English Governess* the hand of Providence is apparent. Its appearance and meaning at times seem scarcely mediated even to the degree that the first-person narration in *Caroline Mordaunt* mediates the equally determinate Providence there. Clara Neville sees the hand of Providence and follows where it leads her. She is therefore specially protected. At times the workings of Providence come to her only secondhand, like the story of a providential rescue occasioned by one man's dreaming of a spot where another man had fallen (*EG*, pp. 150ff.), but they are made apparent to her. Worse, there are moments of trial when she must struggle "to keep in mind that 'not a sparrow can fall to the ground' without the permission of our heavenly father" (*EG*, p. 216). But that Providence does intervene in her own life is ultimately made quite clear: Her villainous stepfather catches up with our heroine on a ledge fifteen hundred feet above the Mediterranean and throws her over—but not to her death.

> It was evident that her fall had been providentially arrested, first by some thorny shrubs which had entangled in her muslin dress, and then by a very large American aloe. . . .
>
> (*EG*, p. 234)

Eagles fly by, apes peer down from crags. She hangs on until rescued. Ashton is less protected. He stumbles on loose stones and falls to his death. There seems to be no reason to doubt Colonel Wentworth's judgment that the villain's fatal fall was providential. Clara early knows the ways of Providence and though she must endure hardship and struggle with occasional doubt, she does not seem to have to earn providential intercession by fervent prayers at extreme moments of physical or moral peril, as Jane does, who only gradually learns of the role of Divine Providence in her life.

Edward Seymour and Edward Rochester are both good men who go through periods of debauchery and temptation, suffer traumatic experiences, benefit from near miracles, and each reforms in time to marry the woman he loves. Rochester, after his wife goes mad, enters a round of conventional dissipation which had ended before he meets Jane, but his acquired amorality and the pressure of great love and great need lead him to attempt to deceive Jane into a marriage he knows to be a sham, and, after his former marriage is revealed, to propose she become his mistress. She refuses, flees temptation, and he can find no trace of her. His insane wife sets fire to Thornfield, and he, despite the burden her living presence puts upon him, attempts to rescue her. She dies in the flames, he is blinded and maimed. The physical darkness brings spiritual light, and he now sees the beneficent acts of Providence in his life. As he later tells Jane,

> "Jane! you think me, I daresay, an irreligious dog: but my heart swells with gratitude to the beneficent God of this earth just now. . . . I did wrong: I would have sullied my innocent flower . . . : the Omnipotent snatched it from me. . . . Of late, Jane—only of late—I began to see and acknowledge the hand of God

in my doom. I began to experience remorse, repentance; the wish for reconcilement to my Maker. . . ."

> (*JE*, p. 571)

He had longed for her, he tells Jane, prayed, and believing her dead, had wished himself to die so that he might join her—"if it seemed good to Him." The cry "Jane! Jane! Jane!" had burst from his lips. This is the cry that Jane heard at that very moment across so many miles and which she had at the time deemed not a miracle but nature at her best.

Seymour, living a dissipated life, also an "irreligious dog" for a time, is refused by Clara as unworthy but pursues his debauchery. He, like Rochester, benefits from a near miracle, but in his case it is pure grace, free and unmerited: though his accident in the reckless steeplechase should have been fatal, he is spared. He tells Clara later that he considers that his "preservation from death was almost a miracle" (*EG*, p. 262). Like Rochester, he is recovering from his wounds when he sees that the events of his life have been controlled by Divine Providence. He seems to slough off all responsibility for his dissipation and recklessness, however, as part of God's plan for his salvation, and seems to claim responsibility only for the resolution to change his course of life:

> [R]eflections on the awful risk to which I had so thoughtlessly exposed myself, and the life of guilty dissipation which had led to it, were, I trust, sanctified by the divine Spirit, to the renovation and salvation of my soul. I now saw everything in a new light, and resolved, in the strength of divine grace, to enter on an entirely new course of life.
>
> (*EG*, p. 262)

Like Rochester, he sees that he had been wrong in his immoral period to press his love and jeopardize the innocence of his beloved, and he sees that Clara was right therefore to refuse him: "I felt that you had done quite right, in refusing to unite yourself to me; indeed, I had always felt so, even when I made the most strenuous efforts to overcome your resolution. I now resolved, however, never more to obtrude myself on your notice, till I had given ample proof that my present change was both a radical and a permanent one" (*EG*, p. 263).

Rochester and Seymour, as immoralists, had too a common strategy in putting responsibility for their own reformation and salvation on to the shoulders of the young women they love. Rochester tells Jane that if she will not become his mistress she will condemn him "'to live wretched, and to die accursed. . . . You fling me back on lust for a passion—vice for an occupation . . . ,'" and he asks her, "'Is it better to drive a fellow-creature to despair than to transgress a mere human law . . . ?'" (*JE*, pp. 403-04). Jane's advice is to "'. . . trust in God and yourself. Believe in heaven. Hope to meet again there'" (*JE,* p. 403). Early in *The English Governess,* when Seymour first becomes irreligious and begins to live loosely, and Clara breaks the engagement, he urges her not to treat him so, arguing that even if he were worse, "'. . . she might very easily have reclaimed him . . . ; her influence over him was unbounded . . .'" (*EG,* p. 42). Much later, in Gibraltar, he says she still has the power to change him and make him reform if she will marry him. "'Ah, Edward!'" she says, "'you speak against your own convictions. I have no such power. How can I hope to sway a heart which continually resists the stirrings of the Spirit of grace?'" (*EG,* p. 125). He warns her again that she is driving him to desperation.

Despite her rejection of Seymour—which may merely be submission to a higher authority than man—and despite her many adventures, Clara is, on the whole, the conventionally submissive Victorian female. She resembles Helen Burns more than she does Jane, even to an apparent sickliness that at the beginning of the novel seems to promise an early death. Indeed in the opening chapter, though she seems spiritually sound, she seems physically doomed:

> a complexion, delicate almost to transparency, [which] announced a weak and precarious state of health, while the idea of early death . . . [was confirmed by the sun's rays which] might have been fancifully said to surround her with a kind of celestial radiance, prophetic of angelic glory.
>
> (*EG,* p. 9)

In this first chapter too her sister Maria is cast in the Jane role and Clara in that of Helen as it concerns the proper response to mistreatment. Helen, remember, urges Jane to love her enemies, as the New Testament would have her do, to eschew violence and vengeance which are ineffective as well as wrong, but Jane's position is that,

> ". . . If people were always kind and obedient to those who are cruel and unjust, the wicked people would have it all their own way: they would never feel afraid, and so they would never alter, but would grow worse and worse. When we are struck at without a reason, we should strike back again very hard; I am sure we should—so hard as to teach the person who struck us never to do it again."
>
> (*JE,* p. 65)

Maria insists that she will not, like Clara, patiently endure mistreatment from the man their widowed mother wants to marry:

> "You may have a great deal of scripture, and even reason on your side; but I cannot believe that it is my duty to sacrifice my feelings, my interest, my happiness, and every thing that is dear to me, merely because my mother [wants to remarry]. Your principles of passive obedience and non-resistance may lead you to bear it patiently; [but I will not]"
>
> (*EG,* pp. 10-11).

At this early point in *The English Governess* the reader is not sure which sister will be the heroine—indeed, he may fully expect that Clara will not survive—and so he may not be too sure which moral position will be supported by the novel. Christian forebearance, in the context of the Victorian religious novel, we would no doubt expect to triumph, as here it does. When it is the heroine who preaches resistance and even violence, however, as in *Jane Eyre,* and when she does so in convincing moral terms, we cannot be too sure; our interest, expectation and values are challenged and engaged.

Jane is only a child during the exchange with Helen in which she takes a dubious, pagan position. Eight years later, however, having been a teacher for two years, her conduct may seem even more morally questionable in the contemporary context. The episode, which may largely escape the attention of the modern reader, is the mirror-image of an episode in *The English Governess.* Whether Brontë is deliberately playing off of the MacCrindell passage or MacCrindell is presenting a moral norm within which or against which Brontë is working, contemporary readers may have responded to the passage in *Jane Eyre* in ways we do not. Knowledge of the earlier work may inform and enrich our reading of *Jane Eyre.*

After eight years at Lowood, with Miss Temple and her calming influence recently gone, Jane is restless. She wants to go out into the world "to seek real knowledge of life amidst its perils" (*JE,* p. 100). She prays for liberty, but her prayer "seemed scattered on the wind then faintly blowing. . . . 'Then,' I cried, half desperate, 'Grant me at least a new servitude!'" (*JE,* p. 101). That new, more modest request will be granted, but not before she wrestles with means:

> "What do I want? A new place, in a new house, amongst new faces, under new circumstances: I want this because it is of no use wanting anything better. How do people do to get a new place? They apply to friends, I suppose: I have no friends. There are many others who have no friends, who must look about for themselves and be their own helpers; and what is their resource?"
>
> (*JE,* p. 102)

She racks her brain, gets out of bed and looks out the window, but sees no solution. She shivers and returns to bed.

> A kind fairy, in my absence, had surely dropped the required suggestion on my pillow; for as I lay down it came quietly and naturally to my mind:—"Those who want situations advertise: you must advertise in the———shire Herald."
>
> (*JE,* p. 102)

All this would seem logical and innocent enough. She prays, seems sensitive to the response or non-response of heaven, lowers her expectations, defines her problem but without reaching a solution, and finally receives real or metaphorical supernatural help—an answer to her prayers or a non-rational "inspiration" as she relaxes her overwrought brain.

It surely does not occur to a modern reader to believe that Jane's action in advertising may be morally suspect. Jane herself, however, is a little less certain. She is relieved to find that the handwriting of the "Mrs. Fairfax" who answers her advertisement is

> old fashioned and rather uncertain, like that of an elderly lady. The circumstance was satisfactory: a private fear had haunted me, that in thus acting for myself and by my own guidance, I ran the risk of getting into some scrape; and above all things, I wished the result of my endeavours to be respectable, proper, en regle.
>
> (*JE,* p. 105)

The twentieth-century reader is as ready as Jane to dismiss this private fear, and there is no more than the usual suspense or anticipation in Jane's journey to her new position.

Most fictional governesses get positions through friends, or, failing that, answer those advertisements by prospective employers that seem respectable and safe. When Clara Neville decides to become a governess and "began seriously to consider what would be the best means of accomplishing her purpose," she, like Jane, proposes to act for herself, and, as in Jane's case, the suggestion seems to come from outside herself: "the idea of advertising in a newspaper *presents itself*" (*EG,* p. 48, emphasis added). This seems the only reasonable way that she can, unaided, find a position, but the rector's wife "entertained a decided objection to this method, and she [Clara] therefore, for the present, relinquished it. She did not see, however, much probability of her obtaining a situation in any other way . . ." (*EG,* p. 48). In a providential world this is mere lack of faith, for, no doubt providentially, a lady requiring a governess does indeed soon appear.

A reader aware of the MacCrindell episode—or of the social or fictional convention which it implies—would be more open to expectations of dire consequences from Jane's indecorous act and less ready to be reassured than Jane herself by Mrs. Fairfax's old-fashioned hand or, later, by her old-fashioned and unprepossessing appearance. When it is revealed that Mrs. Fairfax is not indeed Jane's employer, that there is a Mr. Rochester, such a reader will have had already part of a pattern of expectation in mind into which this new fact could be placed to form a new configuration, and that reader is less likely than others to be certain for some time whether Rochester is Byronic hero or Gothic villain. Rochester's professions of love, his proposal of marriage, and the preparations for the wedding will only

partially allay suspicions that seem to have had so many conventional and generic signals go into their formation. When Bertha's existence is revealed the configuration will take its all but final shape. For the informed reader Jane's accepting a life of Christian self-sacrifice by marrying that soldier of Christ, St. John Rivers, denying her mere fleshy desire for Rochester, long remains a real and strong possibility. After all, in governess novels governesses usually marry clergymen. From the morally questionable decision to advertise to the intense moment of St. John's importunate proposal, the novel-reader will form and keep in mind an entire alternative plot-line and a wholly different tentative interpretation of *Jane Eyre.*

Rachel MacCrindell's *The English Governess,* a novel not used to derive our definition of the governess novel, substantiates gratifyingly the definition we did derive by its extensive use of identical conventions and its conformation to the basic pattern of the genre. The generic form acts here, as it does in *Caroline Mordaunt* and other of the novels, to attract other contemporary fictional conventions into its magnetic field which have no inherent connection to the genre; we find, therefore, in *The English Governess* character types, patterns of behavior, dramatic scenes and thematic motifs that remarkably resemble their counterparts in *Jane Eyre,* but, having seen such "coincidences" before, we do not find it necessary to assume that MacCrindell's novel was the source of or the major influence upon Brontë's novel.

Understanding how conventions cluster into kinds, how works in the genre attract other conventions, and how works can thus strikingly resemble each other even where there is no borrowing, may be of great historical and theoretical interest; it may be useful in defining genre, its relation to conventions, and its pattern of development; it may prevent our speaking of source or influence too glibly. But what does it mean where it counts? what does it mean to us as serious readers of fiction? What, after all, is the advantage of being alert to possible plot developments or configurations in a novel when all that means is that we are more likely to be wrong?

One advantage is that the reader is more affectively involved in the novel through that much-maligned narrative element, suspense.[27] Suspense is, after all, only a manifestation of temporary uncertainty or indeterminacy in the action of the work, the plot taking its full shape and each event its place in the pattern only when the action concludes (or fails to conclude). That certain consequences follow certain actions is, moreover, more than a matter of plot; it defines the vision of reality, the cosmology of the whole work. We now seem to value most ultimate or epistemological indeterminacy that leaves the nature of reality undetermined even at the end of the novel, where the line between fiction and reality or between fiction and the fiction we sometimes call reality does not exist. There is no such indeterminacy in *Jane Eyre*: there Divine Providence is the ultimate reality of human life. For the reader, however, the fictional conventions and generic signals load each event in the novel with multiple possibilities which can accommodate for the time many possible world-views; as we read we are constantly creating, uncreating, adjusting the "future" and meaning of the work. We are thereby engaged affectively and intellectually in the Brontëan world. Each reader helps create the parameters and complexity of that world by the richness of reading and other experience brought to that reading, and though readers of course cannot, and know they cannot, create or change the outcome, they do help create the quality of the reading experience, even as a student can change the quality of discussion in a class.

The extensive and intensive enrichment of the reader's response and expectations with regard to virtually each episode in *Jane Eyre* by heightened awareness of the narrative traditions and the conventions of the contemporary fictional context, of minor as well as major novels, suggests the limitations of reading *Jane Eyre* as Brontë's anxious misreading of a "source," such as *Pamela*. (If one had to read *Jane Eyre* as an escape from dominant influence it would probably be both historically and critically more accurate and rewarding to use Mrs. Sherwood's popular but eminently forgettable *Caroline Mordaunt*, rather than *Pamela*.)

There is no reason to be so exclusive, however. Even if only one of the novels we have discussed was for Brontë *the* conscious source of *Jane Eyre,* there is nothing in the text to insist that the reader use that work specifically as the matrix and context for reading *Jane Eyre,* as *Pamela* must be used for reading *Shamela,* for example. The way *Jane Eyre* defines itself, in other words, is not in terms of a single work, one which the reader is presumed to have read and to be able consciously or unconsciously to juxtapose to the Brontë novel, but in terms of a group of works, a genre or fictional kind, all of the members of which have a good deal in common—some one or several of which the reader can be expected to bring to the reading of *Jane Eyre.* But the elements or conventions of the fictional kind are not invariable. The conception of genre implied here is not that of a rigid carapace of structure within which or against which a new work defines itself, but that of a cluster of elements from a large but limited pool of contemporary conventions, many or all of which appear in novels outside the genre. I have already mentioned that gypsies and disguise are subjects of entire chapters in Reed's *Victorian Conventions;* so are deathbeds (with a whole section devoted to child deaths), so are orphans; Reed also gives whole divisions of chapters, with their own titles, to "illness in the moral design" and Providence. Yet these discrete conventions, together with a governess, would make a typical governess novel.

If this is the case, why bother with genre at all? Since no two governess novels have precisely the same cluster of conventions, why not explore one by the scenic or situational conventions or character types and ignore genre? As has been suggested earlier, the answer seems to lie in the phenomenology of reading: the reading process is accretive, involving perception and identification of what is being read, recapitulation and configuration of what has gone before and projection or anticipation on that basis of what is to come. Though on the one hand, awareness of the conventions increases the potentialities of a character type or scenic topos, a series of disconnected conventional signals offers too many possibilities and so cannot readily imply a pattern or configuration—it is *too* indeterminate. If at any moment anything might happen, then there is no point in recapitulation or expectation, and reading is episodically fragmented, the reader distanced from rather than engaged in the cooperative creation of the work.

Such is not the case in *Jane Eyre*. Brontë uses not only the discrete conventions of the time but generic and modal clusters of conventions that were familiar to the contemporary reader: the conventions of the governess novel are not only present but are clustered in the usual way. That *Jane Eyre* was to be a governess novel, however, was not predictable from the first nine chapters or so where there is no hint of her future profession; these chapters are made up of conventional scenes and motifs, but they are generically indeterminate and so perhaps retard too quick a configuration even after Jane becomes a governess. And very soon after the governess theme is announced retroactively linking past elements—Jane as orphan, the dying child scene—the mystery of Thornfield begins to take shape, complicating our expectation, forcing us to keep governess and Gothic patterns in our minds at the same time and thus more deeply engaging us in the experience of the novel. The Gothic conventions which for a time push the generic expectations of the governess novel into the background are also familiar individually and in their clusters—the deserted-wing motif, for example—and they also attract into their orbit elements from the first nine chapters—the Red Room episode, for example. When Bertha's existence is revealed and Jane flees, we are at a loss once again for a generic configuration, though neither of the earlier ones leaves our mind entirely. The governess expectations push their way to the fore again, in all probability, when Jane, teaching school at Morton, is offered marriage to a cousin and clergyman and a life of self-sacrifice. The richness of competing configurations makes a novel composed of conventional elements and familiar generic clusters ultimately surprising. We are uncertain not only of the outcome, we are uncertain as we read on of the very nature of the world in which the actions of the novel are taking place. Even when we know how it all comes out—who's upstairs and whom Jane will marry—the configuration of the Brontëan world does not seem rigid or even certain. The ending enforces a conservative, conformist, providential reading but it cannot erase the *experience* of the reading which has involved the projection of alternative configurations over large stretches of the novel and subsumed innumerable details. *Jane Eyre,* through its very wealth of conventions and generic signals exists affectively in the moral territory somewhere between rebellion and obedience, self-indulgence and self-sacrifice, scepticism and superstition that conventions and genres can describe but not confine. Alternative readings stressing one side of the territory or another persist beyond the conclusion, however; indeed, I do not believe they are true alternatives but necessary constituents—like the Gothic mode and governess genre—existing in symbiotic relationship in the world of *Jane Eyre.* Charlotte Brontë might well say, in fact, "Reader, I married them."

Notes

1. This essay is adapted from a work in progress entitled "Charlotte Brontë's Hippogryph: *Jane Eyre* in the Context of Contemporary Fiction," where it is preceded by a detailed examination of the Gothic conventions and strategies in *Jane Eyre* and of their significant but subordinate function in the structure and in defining the world-view of the novel.

2. "Charlotte Brontë," *Essays and Studies by Members of the English Association,* 14 (1929), 53-70. In *Novels of the Eighteen-Forties* (Oxford: The Clarendon Press, 1954), p. 149n., Kathleen Tillotson, a rigorous scholar and keen-eyed critic, finds Spens's argument convincing. She points out that others had noted the similarity between the two novels: the *Quarterly Review* for 1848 briefly, and Helen Shipton in the *Monthly Packet* for November 1896 more lengthily, but not in such depth and detail as Spens. *Pamela* is mentioned in *Jane Eyre* as one source of the stories of love and adventure that Bessie tells young Jane (Charlotte Brontë, *Jane Eyre,* ed. Jane Jack and Margaret Smith [Oxford: The Clarendon Press, 1969], p. 5; all subsequent references are to this edition).

3. John Reed, *Victorian Conventions* (Athens, Ohio: Ohio University Press, 1975), has lengthy sections on gypsies (pp. 363-400)—briefly mentioning the scene in *Jane Eyre* on p. 373—and disguises (pp. 289-361)—treating *Jane Eyre* and this scene in a little more detail on pp. 314-15. He says little of the gypsy as messenger. There is one in Mrs. Sherwood's *The History of John Marten* (London: J. Hatchard and Son, 1844), however; a gypsy girl carries messages from the "insidious" Roman Catholic priest to the servant Maurice whom he's attempting to "pervert." A verbal echo in *Jane Eyre* of a sentence in Anne Marsh-Caldwell's *The Deformed* so embarrassed Brontë when she read that novel after having published her own that she feared charges of plagiarism (Elizabeth Gaskell, *The Life of Charlotte Brontë* [New York: Dutton, 1971], p. 387).

4. She finds in each novel precisely five matched hero-heroine interviews. There are parallels: interviews in gardens, for example, and the motif of a sham marriage, but the latter is a good example of forcing—Pamela suspects Mr. B. of planning such a marriage with someone else, while Jane is herself nearly a victim of such a scheme (if a bigamous marriage is, indeed, a "sham" marriage). Moreover, bigamous or sham marriages are Victorian fictional conventions. Rochester proposes that Jane be his mistress in "an interview," but Mr. B. *sends* his proposal in writing, not precisely an interview. Nor are riding and walking precisely the same: "Pamela's marriage is decided on during a long drive she takes with her master, just as Rochester's successful proposal is made during a walk" (Spens, p. 58). A case might be made for muffled echoes here, but not for precise structural parallelism.

5. Inga-Stina Ewbank, *Their Proper Sphere* (Cambridge, Mass.: Harvard University Press, 1966), p. 21.

6. Barbara Hofland, *Ellen the Teacher. A Tale for Youth* (London: J. Harris and Son, 1819), p. 4; hereafter *ET.*

7. Vineta Colby, *Yesterday's Woman: Domestic Realism in the English Novel* (Princeton: Princeton University Press, 1974), p. 165.

8. Mrs. Sherwood, *Caroline Mordaunt; or, The Governess,* in *The Works of Mrs. Sherwood,* 13 (Boston: Harpers, 1834-58), 280; hereafter *CM.*

9. See, for example, the chapter on "dogmatic form" in Barbara Hardy, *The Appropriate Form* (London: The Athlone Press, 1964), and the detailed treatment of providentialism in Charlotte Brontë in Lawrence Jay Dessner, *The Homely Web of Truth* (The Hague: Mouton, 1975).

10. I am here following the structuralist distinction between two aspects of point of view often lumped together; "focus" and "voice" are cogently defined and illustrated by Gérard Genette. See Shlomith Rimmon, "A Comprehensive Theory of Narrative: Genette's *Figures III* and the Structuralist Study of Fiction," *PTL,* 1 (1976), 33-62. The chronology of *Jane Eyre* is traced in Appendix I, Clarendon edition, pp. 610-14.

11. These are the first words of the novel which begins on p. 203 of volume 13 of *Works*.

12. J. Paul Hunter, *The Reluctant Pilgrim* (Baltimore: The Johns Hopkins University Press, 1966), p. 71, points out that in the providentialist view the beneficiaries of such intercession are obligated to write down their experiences: "Because man's memory was not wholly to be trusted and because one man's deliverance could benefit others, recipients of God's mercy ought not only to *recall* but to *record* their experiences" (emphasis Hunter's).

13. I do not mean to imply that St. John Rivers is a Brocklehurst or is morally inferior to Jane herself; his way (to salvation) is merely different from hers, Agape as opposed to Eros. I expand this reading in "Hippogryph."

14. "The Life and Death of Literary Forms," in *New Directions in Literary History*, ed. Ralph Cohen (Baltimore: The Johns Hopkins University Press, 1974), p. 92.

15. Patricia Thomson, *The Victorian Heroine, A Changing Ideal, 1837-1873* (London: Oxford University Press, 1956), p. 39.

16. See Hans Jauss, "Literary History as a Challenge to Literary Theory," in *New Directions*. Jauss, admitting that diachronic analysis of a genre must not ignore the synchronic moment of the appearance of a work—works in other genres and histories and events in other disciplines at that moment—nonetheless insists (p. 32) that "the variety of events of one historical moment are *de facto* moments of completely different time curves, determined by the laws of their special history . . . ," so that synchronic history distorts if it does not take into account the diachronic dimension of the genre, the history of the form.

17. Sarah Fielding, *The Governess*, ed. Jill E. Grey (London: Oxford University Press, 1968), pp. 353-59; a facsimile edition of the first edition, but I here use the Oxford edition's, not the first edition's, page numbers.

18. F. J. H. Darton, quoted in Fielding, p. 73.

19. There seems no reason to doubt the *English Catalogue* dating—1835—though Block and *CBEL*, followed by Thomson and R. Colby, suggest 1845.

20. Mordaunt is a common name in the fiction of the time. Scott's Mordaunt Merton appeared in 1822 in *The Pirate*, Bulwer-Lytton's Algernon Mordaunt Mordaunt in *The Disowned* (1829), the 1852 advertisement identifying him "as a type of the Heroism of Christian Philosophy,—a union of love and knowledge placed in the midst of sorrow, and labouring on through the pilgrimage of life, strong in the fortitude that comes from belief in Heaven" (not a bad type for the religious governess-heroine); Lizzie Mordaunt, later Lady Rawbone, is the heroine of Mrs. Gore's *Memoirs of a Peeress* (1837), and Mordaunts continue to appear later in the century. There may be a special reason for the name to appear in the governess novel, however: the maiden name of Mrs. Poyntz, to whom Sarah Fielding's *The Governess* is dedicated, was Anna Maria Mordaunt.

21. Elizabeth Missing Sewell, *Amy Herbert* (London: Longmans, Green & Co. 1886), p. 62; hereafter *AH*.

22. Cf. *Jane Eyre* where Jane reports learning "that my father had been a poor clergyman; that my mother had married him against the wishes of her friends, who considered the match beneath her; that my grandfather Reed was so irritated at her disobedience, he cut her off without a shilling; that after my mother and father had been married a year, the latter caught typhus fever . . . ; that my mother took the infection from him, and both died within a month of each other" (p. 26).

23. Marguerite, The Countess of Blessington, *The Governess*, 2 vols. (London: Longmans, Orme, Brown, Green and Longmans, 1839), II, 155; hereafter, *G*.

24. Jane Austen, *Emma* (London: Oxford University Press, 1971), p. 250.

25. I here refer to the American edition of the same year published in Philadelphia by Herman Hooker; henceforth *EG*. Ross's work, published you will notice, by Charlotte Brontë's publisher, will be *PPL*. Anne Brontë's *Agnes Grey*, though written before *Jane Eyre*, was not published until 1848. It could have been a source but not a referent for the very first readers of *Jane Eyre*, and I have therefore not treated it here. I discuss its complex relationship to *Jane Eyre* in "Hippogryph."

26. Cf. the Pumpernickel sections of *Vanity Fair*, and the American scenes in *Martin Chuzzelwit*. I am indebted to Karen R. Johnson for pointing out the prevalence of this motif in her unpublished paper "English Fashionables Abroad: The Pumpernickel Section of *Vanity Fair* in Relation to the Travel Sections of Six Fashionable Novels." The novels span the 1820s, 1830s, and early 1840s and include works by Ladies Bury and Blessington, Mrs. Gore, Bulwer-Lytton, Disraeli. One, by Mrs. C. D. Burdett, is entitled *English Fashionables Abroad* (1827).

27. The issue of second-reading is too complex to engage here, but it is my contention that a plot that offers numerous other possible configurations or

expectations and adjusts possibilities frequently remains more gripping than one that does not, even when we have read the work before, perhaps many times before, and know how it will all come out. Aren't films of a 23-21 game played yesterday more exciting than films of yesterday's 45-3 game?

Robert James Merrett (essay date 1984)

SOURCE: Merrett, Robert James. "The Conduct of Spiritual Autobiography in *Jane Eyre*." *Renascence* 37 (1984): 2-15.

[*In the following essay, Merrett argues that, contrary to the contention of some critics, Brontë adequately depicts the title character's spiritual development in* Jane Eyre.]

A significant objection to ***Jane Eyre*** is that Charlotte Brontë does not detail her heroine's spiritual development. In raising this objection, Barbara Hardy alleges that there is a radical incongruity between Jane's motives and actions.[1] Hardy attributes this incongruity to the author's failure to understand spiritual autobiography. She futher contends that, whereas Brontë develops Jane's psychological and social awareness, she simply takes for granted the growth of religious sense which underlies this awareness. Hardy suggests that no clear relation exists between young Jane's religious views and the narrator's spiritual condition, and similarly, that Jane's personal and spiritual progress is far less integral than the novel pretends it to be.[2] Hardy's provocative views oblige the critic to grapple with three questions. First, is Jane's religious perspective less a matter of dramatized conscience than of unrealized assumptions? Second, does Brontë merely ignore Jane's religious development except when depicting moments of crisis which require reliance upon divine law? Third, is the characterization of Jane based upon a vague concept of grace rather than upon precise spiritual self-examination because Brontë is unable to regard faith as a human problem?[3]

An answer to the first question must recognize that Brontë does detail and dramatize Jane's religious education. This is evidenced by the large number of religious allusions which Jane either articulates or meditates upon. As character and narrator, Jane employs expressions and ideas which derive more from the Bible and the liturgy than from secular literature. An answer to the second question must admit that not only does Brontë insist upon the orthodoxy of Jane's formal religious training but she also frequently implies the development of Jane's religious sensibility through emphasizing her character's knowledge of religious facts and principles. Jane's religious allusions are often related to dramatic irony and narrative perspective in order to betoken her increasing awareness of biblical truth and theological values. Certainly, Brontë exhibits authorial responsibility when she endeavors to generate thematic implications from the tension between the religious feelings and ideas her character's allusions embody. If, however, the first two questions can be answered in Brontë's favor, this in not the case with the third. While Brontë's authorial responsibility may be greater than estimated by Hardy, her religious sense is dubious. Paradoxical though it may seem, the novel's flaws are more attributable to Brontë's desire to establish a religious dialectic in Jane's character than they are to an unawareness of its fictional necessity. It is the faultiness of her attempts to derive themes from religious allusions which suggests that Brontë's problem is the nature of faith.

Brontë does, however, consistently detail the formal religious ideas to which Jane is exposed. Although she is first presented as seeking to escape oppression and injustice by cultivating fancy and by seeing the world in literary and pictorial terms, Jane is obliged to confront religious ideas which inform the rest of her life. Preached at by the Reed's servants, she develops an awareness of original sin and her "corruption".[4] This awareness manifests itself when Jane confesses that she is "a defective being, with many faults and few redeeming points" (p. 79). When interviewed at Gateshead by Mr. Brocklehurst, she gives "ready and orthodox" replies which reveal a clear understanding of catechism (p. 32). Moreover, her private reaction to the theological problem of converting an evil heart indicates shrewd criticism of Mr. Brocklehurst's religious complacency. Since the rhythm of the children's days is founded on the Bible and the Book of Common Prayer at Lowood, Jane's religious ideas are reinforced. Meals are preceded by a "long grace" and by a hymn and followed by thanksgiving and by another hymn (p. 46); Sunday evenings are taken up with learning by heart the catechism and the Sermon on the Mount (p. 61). Although Jane quite naturally resists the length of the religious forms, and although she is aggravated by Mr. Brocklehurst's facile ideas about depravity, grace, and primitive Christianity, she still looks at herself and the world from the perspective of her religious training. When she reacts against the 'Babel clamour' of her classmates (p. 47) and when she compares the pasteboard that is stuck on Helen to a 'phylactery' (p. 74), she confidently applies her biblical perspective. That she is content with the way in which her religious training has informed her habits is evidenced upon her arrival at Thornfield. Hoping it to be a "safe haven," she naturally offers up "thanks where thanks were due" and implores aid on her "further path" (p. 99).

Jane's predisposition to self-mortification is further evidence of her religious training. She often depreciates her plain appearance calling it "Quaker-like" (p. 99). At Thornfield she usually dresses in a "Quaker trim" (p. 130). She demonstrates that she gains moral self-respect from her ascetic habits when she refuses Mr. Rochester's jewelery and insists that she must remain his "plain, Quakerish governess" (p. 261). Such Quaker references might be thought to convey discontent with traditional Christianity, but since they reflect Jane's concern with moral self-respect rather than an unorthodox concern with spirituality, they do not convey a sectarian viewpoint. In fact, Jane does not appreciate Quaker principles as is evident when she is moved by unjustifiable indignation to regard Grace Poole as a fiendish hypocrite who possesses "the demureness of a Quakeress" (p. 157). Ironically, Jane's prejudice against Grace Poole leads her to call Mrs. Poole a Quaker precisely when Mrs. Poole utters views about providence acting through second causes, views a Quaker would not present. Jane overlooks this for she is too concerned with seeing Quaker demureness as a type of hypocrisy, a concern which casts doubt upon the times she refers to herself as a Quaker. Despite this particular irony, Jane's Quaker references, taken as a group, exemplify asceticism and an acceptance of her religious training. In her own eyes, as shown when she disapproves of Eliza Reed's belief that the rubric is the most valuable part of the Book of Common Prayer (p. 237), Jane is an orthodox Anglican confident of seeing the spirit in the letter of church law.

Jane's orthodox commitment to the church is evident in her reactions to setting. Her responsiveness to the symbolic possibilities of her environs often implies that the physical structure of churches has been important to her. To her eyes Lowood presents a "church-like aspect" and its garden strikes her as "convent-like" (p. 49). Having been excluded from the house party at Thornfield, she finds the schoolroom a "sanctum," and using the words of Psalm 46, she intensifies the religious reference by describing it as "a very pleasant refuge in time of trouble" (p. 168). The spiritual reflexiveness of Jane's symbolic reaction to setting is questionable at times. At issue are not her formal religious education or biblical knowledge but the value of her religious analogies and the seriousness with which the church has informed her imagination. Consider the instance when, on returning to Thornfield after Mrs. Reed's death, she is moved to regard the western sky "as if there was a fire lit, an altar burning behind its screen of marbled vapour" (p. 246). Here her feelings about returning home to Rochester prompt her to superimpose an image of a sanctuary upon the sunset; she obviously wishes to associate him with natural and ritual splendour. But Jane checks herself from symbolizing the environs of the house and from regarding it as her home. However, there is no connection between the

symbolic enthusiasm and restraint, nor is there narrative commentary on the "golden redness" of the sunset imagery and its ironic forestall of the fire that destroys Thornfield. The problem in this episode is that Jane is made to seem creative in her application of symbolism, responsible in her restraint of it, and somehow intuitive by its very occurrence although there is no autobiographical structure for dealing lucidly with the abrupt change in the character from the narrator's perspective. It is clear that Brontë presents as a characteristic feature Jane's impulse to associate her emotional needs with religious imagery even when such imagery appears susceptible to dramatic irony. Another example occurs just before Jane provokes Rochester into acknowledging his love when she describes the garden at Thornfield as "Eden-like" and the scents of its flowers as the "sacrifice of incense" (p. 250). Despite the irony of the name "Thornfield" and of Jane's later recognition that the house could only have been "a temporary heaven" (p. 324), no narrative commentary criticizes the attempt to endow the house and grounds with edenic and ceremonial associations. Again, although the lightning strike upon the horse-chestnut is a providential sign against Rochester's complacent appropriation of divine sanction (p. 259), it is not made to reflect upon Jane's habitual symbolizing. That Jane sometimes gives meaning to experience by seeing it in ecclesiastical symbols is substantiated by her comparison of the stillness of Ferndean to that of "a church on a week-day" (p. 436). Since Jane habitually relates her emotional needs to the church, how does Brontë incorporate into the autobiographical form an estimation of the value of Jane's religious symbols?

One answer could be that Brontë gives Jane an emblematic sense, an awareness of biblical typology. To a degree, Jane does possess an emblematic sense, yet she seems inconsistent in her figurative thinking. For example in her reaction to the old-fashioned pieces furnishing the third story of Thornfield, she displays an alertness to emblems. Jane regards the discarded pieces of furniture as "effigies" and "relics." The old pieces render the third-story a "shrine of memory." She looks upon the ancient chests as "types of the Hebrew ark" (pp. 106-7). But this emblematic perspective cannot prevent her from being simply afraid of the third-story. That the monstrous Bertha Mason with her unholy past lives here displaces the notion of divine covenant conveyed by the emblem of the ark. From this example it is not hard to see that Brontë's gothic interests work against Jane's emblematic sense.

Another example of Jane's emblematic sense being undermined by Brontë's gothic interests is found when, after Jane enthusiastically declares she would give her life to save Rochester, she is called upon by him to tend the injured Mr. Mason. Locked into one of the "mystic cells" of the third-story and fearing for her own safety in a way that ironically qualifies her declaration concerning Rochester, she cares for Mason in a manner which seems to re-enact the Crucifixion. She has to dip her hand "again and again in the basin of blood and water, and wipe away the trickling gore" (p. 212). As she does so, she has a heightened experience of the great cabinet the panels on which figure the carved heads of the twelve apostles with an "ebon crucifix and a dying Christ" above. But her emblematic sense is not clear: she develops an overwhelming awareness of Judas as the agent of Satan which, while appropriate to the horrific situation, displaces the emblem of Christ's dying for man and prevents her from examining her spiritual condition.

Of course, Jane's emblematic sense is laudable in contrast to that of Grace Ingram. Grace announces that she has suffered "martyrdom" at the hands of governesses and thanks God that she has finished with them (p. 179), her false piety and merely social understanding of anathema make Jane's refusal to suffer the "martyrdom" of a loveless marriage to St. John Rivers more praiseworthy (p. 410). There is, however, no steady relation between Jane's sensibility and her application of religious emblems. Neither as character nor as narrator is she led to spiritual meditation or fortified against superstition by emblems. When she sees nothing symbolic about the rending of the veil in two and is too easily soothed by Rochester's prevaricating explanation of her dream (pp. 286-7), the reader is justified in asking why her emblematic sense did not lead her to think about the Temple at Jerusalem and to challenge Rochester's explanation. Again it is surprising that when she saves him from the fire in his bed by baptizing him with water and calling on "God's aid" and he gives her "anathemas," calling her "witch" and "sorceress" and summoning the "elves in Christendom" to enlighten him (p. 150), she does not comment on the extreme differences of their spiritual perspectives. Her emblematic sense does not prompt her to judge him as she should. Instead, as exemplified when she views Adele as an "emblem" of her past and Rochester as the "type" of her future (p. 289), her typological thinking is often vague and self-dramatizing and so prevents her from defining spiritual reality.[5]

Since biblical typology is not an organizing principle of Jane's autobiography, what it contributes to her sensibility is doubtful. Certainly, Brontë intends biblical typology to reflect well on Jane. For instance, she interprets very quickly the charade which Grace Ingram and Rochester perform because with her strong appreciation for the history of Israel she can relate it easily to the biblical account of Eliezer and Rebecca (p. 186). This typological awareness can even control her fantasies about Rochester. When imaginatively she tries to reach "the hills of Beulah," her judgment prevents her from personalizing the emblem; she realizes that delirium

alone would equate the promised land with marriage (p. 153). Her typological awareness also leads to narrative wit. Recalling that the pupils at Lowood fell asleep during tiresome sermons, she relates this phenomenon as an ironical re-enactment of "the part of Eutychus" (p. 61). The girls fell not from the third loft but from the fourth form; as Paul raised Eutychus from the dead, so they were picked up half dead from exhaustion. But typological awareness is not handled in a way that consistently reveals Jane's sensibility. In recounting her battle with Mrs. Reed, Jane employs the twofold "emblem" of the "lighted" and "black and blasted" heath to depict the fierceness of revenge and the wretchedness of remorse (p. 38). This non-biblical emblem is clearly more related to dramatic forestall than to sensibility. Again, when she refers to her love for her doll as dotage upon "a faded graven image" (p. 28), the biblical reference to idolatry says little about narrative sensibility, given the propaganda about the inherently sound instincts of children and the far less critical attitude toward her more sinful idolization of Rochester.

Jane's unsteady emblematic sense is matched by her attitude towards people. In particular, her reactions to Helen Burns, Rochester, and Rivers reveal weaknesses in her religious sensibility. Given her knowledge of the catechism and the Sermon on the Mount, it is odd that Jane is surprised by what she calls Helen's "doctrine of endurance" (p. 56). To return good for evil and to love one's enemies are not Helen's doctrines but tenets of Christ's Sermon. Jane resists these tenets because she attends more to Helen's person than to the superior light in which Helen regards doctrinal matters. Considering that Jane later warns Rochester that he attends too much to people and too little to divine truth, it is interesting to note that there is no evidence that Jane internalizes this same warning which is made to her by Helen. It is also revealing, considering how much original sin and damnation have been preached to her, that Jane does not question Helen's unorthodox view that God will permit no soul to be damned (p. 59).

Although she regards Helen as exemplary, her reaction to Helen does not seem to affect Jane's religious sensibility. When Jane has to stand on the "pedestal of infamy" before Mr. Brocklehurst, Helen implicitly urges her to endure the humiliation. But in what way the "extraordinary sensation" and "new feeling" which Helen's encouraging smile prompts in Jane extends her sensibility is uncertain. For, although Jane compares the smile to "a reflection from the aspect of an angel," she abandons herself to despair as soon as Helen leaves the schoolroom (p. 68). In later scenes Jane seems alert to Helen's spiritual intensity, but this alertness does not result in new spiritual strength. Jane may apply Solomon's proverb that love with poverty is better than hatred with riches to her admiration for Helen and Miss Temple (p. 75), but she does not model herself on them. When

Miss Temple leaves Lowood, Jane's restlessness shows how undeveloped her spiritual sensibility is. That fifteen years after Helen's death Jane places a stone carved with "Resurgam" upon Helen's grave implies love for Helen and conviction about resurrection. But the narrative shows a gap between Jane's love for Helen and Jane's faith; it does not evidence a reconciliation of personal and doctrinal tensions.

In her relationship with Rochester, Jane often represents religious orthodoxy, but she does not do so consistently. While Rochester habitually appropriates religious terms to himself, sometimes Jane fails to upbraid him and sometimes she is guilty of the same fault. For example, Jane does not criticize Rochester when he arrogantly feigns superiority to conventional expression by drawing a parallel between himself and the faithful centurion who believed that Christ's power to perform miracles had to be greater than his own military authority (p. 125). Her failure to criticize this reduction of parabolic truth is perhaps not surprising since she uses the same parable to describe the servitude imposed upon her by Rivers, for she similarly ignores its spiritual import (p. 402). Although she tells Rochester that repentance is the cure for remorse, that aggressive pretensions to religious inspiration are usually self-deceiving, and that the "human and fallible should not arrogate a power with which the divine and perfect alone can be safely entrusted" (pp. 137-9), these orthodox tenets do not protect her against the dangers of spiritual rationalization. Rather they expose her to the irony that she possesses the faults which she warns Rochester against.

In this ironic context, Rochester's testimony that Jane trusts her "inward treasure" and obeys "that still small voice which interprets the dictates of conscience" (p. 203) is unreliable not only because he intends to persuade Jane to accept his unorthodox notion that the repentant man can ignore social convention but also because it misrepresents her spiritual capacity. She may properly resist his spiritual flattery by maintaining that "a wanderer's repose or a sinner's reformation should never depend on a fellow creature" and by urging that he look for help from "higher than his equals" (p. 221), but her authority to instruct him is questionable. By her own admission, she is "a wanderer on the face of the earth" (p. 230). This admission reflects her own spiritual alienation, especially since it appropriates biblical terms for emotional as distinct from spiritual concerns. She is responsible for the same sort of appropriation when she likens herself to a bird that wishes "to taste but of the crumbs" which Rochester scatters and views him as the "master" whose "feast" conveys happiness and whose words are "balm" (p. 247). Here she employs terms from the Eucharist not out of sacramental respect but out of a desire to dramatize her emotional dependence. When she admits that Thornfield has given her "communion" with everything that is "bright and

energetic and high," that she reverences Rochester's mind, and that leaving him is like confronting death (p. 255), she provides more evidence that she appropriates sacramental and religious principles in the interest of her sentiments. Her comparison of not being able to love Rochester with having her "morsel of bread snatched" from her lips and her "drop of living water dashed" from her cup is stronger evidence that she subordinates biblical and sacramental to romantic expression. Her claim to be speaking not in conventional language but spiritually as if before God's throne after death cannot conceal her actual debasement of religious inspiration. This groundless claim to transcendence devalues the spiritual reality of death and the Eucharist. The claim is histrionic because it establishes a false dichotomy between secular and religious ideas. Soon after this histrionic claim about spiritual language, Jane states she is better than Rochester and the hollowness of her pretension becomes clear: she accuses him of temporizing since he is as good as married to Grace Ingram and rejects being endearingly called a bird. Her charge against his temporizing, which is true from the viewpoint of dramatic irony, does not redound to her moral superiority and her initial image of herself as a bird ironically brings her to Rochester's level.

Jane's reaction to Rochester's secret marriage proves her religious sensibility to be precarious. Feeling that her only recourse is to call on God, she experiences despair. Her mind is "rayless"; she remembers God rather than prays to Him (p. 299). The Psalms help her to express her despair, but they do not provide her with meditative strength. That she cites the Psalms, which she told Mr. Brocklehurst she did not read, implies that she has studied them, although there is no direct evidence for this. That her conscience speaks in the terms of the Sermon on the Mount when it reminds her to "pluck out [her] own right eye" and to "cut off [her] own right hand" (p. 301) also implies the enduring effects of her religious education. But this allusiveness does not clarify the relation between Jane's conscience and her despair. Similarly, it is hard to understand why Jane suddenly becomes fearless because of an "inward power" and "sense of influence" when she almost succumbs twice to Rochester when he offers himself as the shepherd intent on caring for a lost lamb (p. 306).

This fearlessness is related neither to a critical awareness of Rochester's misappropriation of a pastoral role nor to a meditative containment of despair. It is not presented as the effect of grace. It is surprising, then, that Jane should offer herself to Rochester as a model of trust in God and in the self because the relation of spiritual power and self-reliance is so remote. Certainly, Jane does not spiritually resolve to leave Rochester. She wards off the temptation to stay by means of "preconceived opinions" and "foregone determinations" (p. 322). In this case, her religious sensibility amounts to no more than an easy acceptance that her emotional disturbance inhibits spiritual deliberation. Consequently, her claim that she can strive and endure and that she accepts the law of God as sanctioned by man is unimpressive because her religious sensibility is much more dissociated than she knows.

Ironical aspects to Jane's reaction to Rivers also make her religious sensibility questionable. Hostile to his doctrines, she condemns the inconsistency between the man and the priest. She also finds fault with the bitterness of style and creed in his sermons, criticizing them for lacking "consolatory gentleness" (p. 356). Yet the tone with which she blames Rivers's "insatiate yearnings" and "disquieting aspirations" does not reflect that she suffers from similar enthusiasms. She may acknowledge that they are both unable to possess the peace that passeth understanding. But her readiness to condemn him overrules concern about her own religious condition. That she can lament her "broken idol and lost elysium" while expressing confidence in Rochester's salvation indicates how incoherent her religious perspective is (p. 329). The fact that Jane pretends to venerate Rivers's talent and principles while recognizing the gap between his corruption and Christianity (p. 416) precisely reveals how unconsidered her perspective on him is. At the end of the novel when Jane unconditionally views Rivers as an apostle possessing a primitive religious intensity, Brontë suggests that her heroine is capable of reconciling "human tears" with "divine joy" (p. 458), but there is no evidence that she has learned to really balance her criticism and praise of Rivers in a self-conscious way.

The problem with *Jane Eyre* as a spiritual autobiography is that it assumes rather than validates Jane's religious sensibility. In other words, Brontë does not concentrate upon her character's spiritual life. Indeed, her account of Jane's religious feelings and ideas is confusing as well as inadequate. Jane is given no steady perspective on her former emotions and thoughts. At one moment she says of her half-comprehended childish notions that they were "strangely impressive" and "profoundly interesting" (pp. 8-9), at another she indignantly dissociates herself from cant and "solemn doctrines about the angelic nature of children" (p. 109). That is, she both emphasizes the imaginative sensitivity of her former self from a doctrinaire romantic view about children and harshly condemns the "dense ignorance" and "morbid suffering" of her childhood. The aggressive tone which she often adopts when describing her former self is inconsistent with the allusive implications about her religious education. When she insists that fear made her a "miserable little poltroon" (p. 31), that her "trifling taste" rendered her unfit to comprehend serious things (p. 50), and that her juvenile mind was stored with the "rubbish" of folk literature (p. 113), the severity of the commentary exposes the pretensions

of her moral and spiritual growth; such harsh judgments suggest that as narrator Jane has no balanced perspective upon how she has developed.

The motif of time illustrates *Jane Eyre*'s insufficiency as a spiritual autobiography. Despite the fact that Brontë employs considerable dramatic irony about time, neither as character nor as narrator does Jane learn to deal with time successfully. As she grows up, Jane often looks ahead to the future because she wishes to escape the past, but Brontë makes Jane's past inescapable. For example, in anticipating Lowood Jane hopes to enter "a new life" (p. 25), however she has to recognize that the future is robbed of its newness when Mrs. Reed confides in Mr. Brocklehurst. Another example of Jane's inability to shut out the past is found when she visits Mrs. Reed although she had vowed she never would (p. 37). Again, it is ironic that, just as she is about to set off for Thornfield and a desired new phase of life, Bessie arrives at Lowood to tell Jane about the Reeds (p. 90). Clearly, Brontë's irony questions how well Jane relates the past, present, and future. Just before the abortive wedding Jane experiences a "hypochondriac foreboding" which makes her wish the present will never end (p. 282). This wish, while dramatically appropriate, shows up her continual desire to escape time. Following Rochester's disclosure of Bertha, Jane loses all sense of her past life and future prospects (p. 298). This episode is reminiscent of the overwhelming sense of the present which she feels when she first apprehends her mortality (p. 80). On both occasions, however, the present has vague associations rather than a rational meaning. Similarly, when leaving Rochester, Jane thinks of the past as heavenly and the future as life after the flood (p. 325), but this emblematic distinction is not realized in the way she regards the present. Far from showing that Jane has achieved a religious sense of time, the distinction merely represents an emotive attempt to deal with frustration. That she is not educated by the ironical treatment of time is evident in her ineffectual temporal perspective as narrator. At times she is coy and reticent in her narrator's stance towards temporality while on occasion she speaks of the "quiet medium" of time as a source of moral consciousness (p. 15 and p. 423). But there is no resolution of such diverse attitudes in terms of religious sensibility.

Jane's lack of a religious sense of time affects her interpretation of the Bible. Although Brontë gives her narrator biblical allusions which suggest that Jane relates herself to Christian history, the occasions when Jane directly applies biblical typology to herself are often problematic. Sometimes such application is precise and self-consciously critical as when she emphasizes her avoidance of Helen's religious ideas, saying that she did "not ponder the matter deeply" but "like Felix, put it off to a more convenient time" (p. 56). This allusion to Acts 24:25 suggests that Jane is a type of Felix, the spiritual coward who temporized rather than judged Paul; it implies that the narrator has a firm Christian perspective on her earlier self. But other of the narrator's biblical allusions are less straightforward; they reveal that the narrator distorts typology for selfish purposes and ignores the ironic impact which the allusions have upon one another. For example, when she describes her decision not to acknowledge that she has heard Rochester's invocation of her, Jane says that she "kept these things" and "pondered them in her heart" (p. 453). There is a problem with this allusion to Luke 2:19, for Mary's meditation about the shepherds' report of the angelic visitaiton is an ineffable experience which is not comparable to Jane's wariness about Rochester and her belief that hearing him was merely a supernatural coincidence. To the extent that Jane discounts Rochester's "mute devotion," she compares herself to the Virgin Mary to prove to herself her spiritual superiority to Rochester. Another ironic allusion occurs after Rochester's disclosure of Bertha when Jane says that all her hopes were killed and "struck with a subtle doom, such as, in one night, fell on all the first born in the land of Egypt" (p. 298). This reference to Exodus 12:29 reveals Jane's awareness of divine punishment. But she seems not to notice that this allusion identifies her as an enemy of the children of Israel whom God destroyed in the Passover. The allusion is inappropriate not only because the death of hope and the deaths of Egyptians are not equivalent, but also because it clashes with Jane's claim that providence led her from captivity at Thornfield (p. 364). As in this and the previous example, Jane's narrative allusions to the Bible are too freely adapted and they do not contribute to emblematic patterns. For further evidence consider two references to Paul. While breaking away from Rivers, Jane prays to understand the voice which has called to her and, as a result, she seems "to penetrate very near a Mighty Spirit" (p. 425). Recalling the unspeakable strangeness of the inward sensation, she compares it to the earthquake which set Paul and Silas free from prison. As an emblem of grace, however, the allusion is ineffective for Jane applies the miracle of Acts 16:25-26 to an imprecise awareness of the separateness of soul and body. Whereas the grace of the miracle emphasizes the equivalence of physical and spiritual freedom, Jane's application of it is limited by selfish doctrinaire intentions. That Paul is not a type for her is made plain when, recalling Rivers's proposal, she likens his suit to the appeal of the man of Macedonia to Paul (p. 407). Jane confesses that she refused Rivers because she is no apostle. Clearly, this dismissive attitude towards typology explains why Jane's references to Paul do not form an emblematic pattern by which she might steadily examine her religious identity.

Occasionally, Jane's narrative exploitation of biblical allusions is so extreme that it implies serious spiritual faults. For example, in recounting the relationship of Rochester and Grace Ingram, Jane says of Grace that she "scorned to touch me with the hem of her robes as she passed" (p. 187). In this allusion to Matthew 9:20 and 14:36, Jane parallels herself to those who, needing to be healed, faithfully approached Christ whereas she makes Grace an unwilling saviour. In this allusion, then, Jane tries to give a biblical sanction to her own self-pity and to her contempt for Grace. As narrator she is more concerned with private myth than with emblematic truth. The same can be said of her narrative reaction to Mrs. Reed. Although as character Jane freely forgives Mrs. Reed on the latter's death-bed (p. 242), as narrator she cannot forget Mrs. Reed's cruelty although she reminds herself that she ought to forgive Mrs. Reed "for [she] knew not what [she] did" (p. 20). Even though the discrepancy between the reported action and the narrative stance prompts the reader to wonder whether Jane forgives Mrs. Reed, this technical problem is not as significant as the misuse of the allusion. For, not only does Jane appropriate the words in Luke 24:34 where Christ asks the Father to forgive His crucifiers, but the logic behind this appropriation requires the reader to recognize that Jane affects the divine response. Only God can respond to the Son's prayer and pronounce forgiveness. When Jane chattily reminds herself to forgive Mrs. Reed, whom she has already forgiven, her vanity and pride are apparent in her abuse of the ultimate divine sanction.

While she intends through biblical and liturgical allusions to depict Jane's orthodox education and religious sensibility, Brontë does not employ them carefully enough to establish Jane's spiritual development. Brontë seems not to respect the traditional meaning of emblems consistently. She certainly does not recognize their structural value in autobiography. The presence of uncontrolled ironies and of unsteady narrative perspective indicates that, despite her intent, Brontë could not treat faith as a human problem in a concentrated way. Her numerous religious allusions hint at rather than establish spiritual themes; they provide not a significant autobiographical structure but aesthetic difficulties.

Notes

1. Barbara Hardy, *The Appropriate Form: An Essay on the Novel* (London, 1964), pp. 51-70. See also Robert Keefe, *Charlotte Brontë's World of Death* (Austin and London, 1979), pp. 96-129. For Keefe, the novel is a "quasi-religious odyssey," although its structure is a reflection of *The Pilgrim's Progress*. Keefe regards Jane's ultimate triumph as an irreligious emanation of Brontë's fantasy life. The view that the religion of the novel is orthodox is found in Robert Bernard Martin, *The Accents of Persuasion: Charlotte Brontë's Novels* (New York, 1966), pp. 81-100. A very fine ac-

count of Brontë's religious views is found in Elisabeth Jay, *The Religion of The Heart: Anglican Evangelicalism and the Nineteenth Century Novel* (Oxford, 1979), pp. 244-60.

2. Praise of Brontë's narrative integrity is found in Kathleen Tillotson, *Novels of the Eighteen Forties* (Oxford, 1961) and W. A. Craik, *The Brontë Novels* (London, 1968). Tillotson maintains that the reader watches a "personality discovering itself not by long introspection but by a habit of keeping pace with her own experience" (pp. 294-5), while Craik, who regards Brontë as the pioneer of fictional autobiography, insists that neither Brontë nor the reader ever disagrees with Jane (p. 75). Both views misrepresent the dynamics of first-person narration as established by Defoe and Sterne; both views overlook the intended and accidental ironies of the double narrative perspective. Cynthia A. Linder, *Romantic Imagery In The Novels Of Charlotte Brontë* (London, 1978), is forced to throw over notions of autobiographical structure in her attempt to find narrative integrity in the novel. She describes two separate narrative points of view, claiming that they do not come together until the end of the novel (pp. 66-7).

3. Critics commonly describe Brontë as unconcerned with the problem of faith. For example, Helene Moglen, *Charlotte Brontë: The Self Conceived* (New York, 1976), says that Brontë possessed "a religious aspiration that transcended traditional belief" (p. 107), and Margot Peters, *Charlotte Brontë: Style In The Novel* (Madison, 1973), insists that the legal language disqualifies the novel as a Christian parable and makes self-judgment rather than faith the controlling theme (p. 147).

4. Charlotte Brontë, *Jane Eyre,* ed. Margaret Smith (London, 1973), p. 27. All references to the novel are to this Oxford English Novels editon, and are cited parenthetically in the text.

5. Margaret Howard Blom, *Charlotte Brontë* (Boston, 1977), after calling Jane a solitary pilgrim, maintains that Jane is so "self-involved" that she "sees others only as adjuncts or impediments to her own fulfilment" (pp. 89 and 104). Ironically, Jane's concern with self overrides her spirituality.

Carol Bock (essay date 1992)

SOURCE: Bock, Carol. "The Political Arts of Reading and Storytelling in *Jane Eyre*." In *Charlotte Brontë and the Storyteller's Audience,* pp. 69-108. Iowa City: University of Iowa Press, 1992.

[*In the following essay, Bock asserts that reading and storytelling are central motifs in* Jane Eyre *and serve to indicate Jane's growth toward self realization.*]

One critic has described the story line of *Jane Eyre* as a "plot against the reader" because it appears to deliberately baffle our interpretive maneuvers through its "dogged and mysterious indeterminacy" (Hennelly 1984, 709), and studies of *Villette* during the last decade have persuasively shown that Brontë was, indeed, capable of writing a highly indeterminate novel. In this context we might also remember that, aside from early criticisms of its "coarseness," the most frequent objections to *Jane Eyre* have focused on its supposed violations of the storytelling situation: narrative moments that suddenly disturb or disregard the established relationship between the reader and the narrator. For some readers, such moments occur when the writer intrudes to express an idea or emotion that is apparently her own rather than Jane's, thus drawing attention to the author behind the narrating protagonist instead of maintaining a focus on the character who is supposed to be central not only to the events of the story but also to the event of storytelling itself.[1] Others feel discomfited by passages that invoke the reader and thus call attention to the audience's role in responding to the narrative.[2] In either case, the effect of these moments is to expand our focus beyond a limited but intense preoccupation with the narrator-protagonist and to enforce a broader perspective on the narrating-receiving instance itself.

This emphasis on the creation and reception of Jane's narrative may seem less peripheral to her story when one realizes, as critics are beginning to do, that reading and telling tales form a central motif in the novel, one that marks the stages of Jane's growth and delineates the nature of her struggles toward selfhood.[3] But though proving the thematic centrality of reading and storytelling in *Jane Eyre* is a relatively straightforward task, arguing against the view that the passages that evoke the narrating instance in this novel are distracting rather than intriguingly self-reflexive is, in fact, quite difficult. That is, while the motif of reading and storytelling as it is used *within* Jane's narrative seems to emphasize the importance of those activities, Brontë's narrative method itself seems to obscure this very point quite effectively, so much so that the passages that remind us of our reading experience are usually thought intrusive or otherwise digressive. Thus, if one asks the question, "What does *Jane Eyre* tell us about reading and telling stories?" we may well find that we arrive at two different answers, depending on how we focus our investigation. Having traced the motif of reading and storytelling as it is used in Jane's story, I will conclude by considering the narrative method employed in *Jane Eyre* itself. This two-part analysis will help determine whether these apparently incompatible messages about the literary experience are reconcilable.

Teller, Text, Audience: The Struggle toward Selfhood

As more than one critic has noticed, in *Jane Eyre* the way one reads is a clue to one's personality.[4] Blanche Ingram appears fashionably to "beguile, by the spell of fiction, the tedious hours" of her day but, in fact, does not actually read the book that she holds before her (*Jane Eyre,* 236). In contrast to her social glitter and personal vacuity, the emotional and mental depth of the Rivers sisters is signaled by their warm response to Schiller, while their brother's rigorous self-discipline is suggested by his daily studies of a Hindustani grammar book. The calm resignation of Helen Burns is underlined, of course, by her reading of *Rasselas,* just as Jane's rebellious nature is suggested by her inability to comprehend the same volume. Eliza Reed studies *The Book of Common Prayer* three times a day for "the Rubric" only (294), thus revealing her obsession with the external forms of conduct and her obliviousness to the moral roots of behavior in emotion and value. Finally, and perhaps most obviously, little Jane's vehement description of John Reed as "wicked and cruel . . . like a murderer . . . like a slave-driver," seems at least partially justified by his simultaneous abuse of both books and people: taking Bewick's *History of British Birds* away from Jane, he first declares exclusive ownership and then violently flings the large volume at her head (8). *Jane Eyre* thus begins with an impressive demonstration of the power of books and immediately suggests a parallel between one's character and one's literary habits.[5]

The motif also seems to suggest a correlation between one's reading practices and one's proficiency as a storyteller. Like Blanche Ingram, Georgiana Reed uses books to fill up any hiatus in her social existence, but unlike Blanche she is not even capable of keeping up the pretense and falls asleep over her novel. Not surprisingly, Jane contemptuously dismisses Georgiana as a purveyor of self-indulgent pulp fiction and compares her conversation to a "volume of a novel of fashionable life" that "always ran on the same theme—herself, her loves, and woes" (293). Ironically, this theme applies equally well to Jane's own narrative, and the differences between Georgiana and Jane as storytellers may have less to do with their subject matter than with their respective abilities as readers of the world they live in. Jane, we learn from Miss Abbot, "always look[s] as if she were watching everybody, and scheming plots underhand" (25-26), much like Charlotte's favorite early storyteller, Charles Wellesley/Townshend. Georgiana, on the other hand, is simply too selfish and unimaginative to expend energy on interpreting other people, and her stories about her own experience are consequently shallow and vapid. Mrs. Fairfax, though far from selfish, suffers from a

similar lack of interpretive expertise; a poor reader of other people, she is also a poor storyteller who has "no notion of sketching a character" (127).

In contrast, Rochester is apparently able to read much of Jane's nature not only in her face and conduct but in her paintings as well; his wondering questions about her work—"What meaning is that in their solemn depth? . . . Who taught you to paint wind?"—suggest that he is a warmly appreciative interpreter of her character (154). Clearly a good reader, particularly of Jane, Rochester is also a fluent storyteller. At one point he is shown writing his own life history, which at other times he tells Jane in two sequential narratives, the longest embedded tales in Jane's own story. He also spontaneously concocts the fiction about Jane's supposed new employer, Mrs. Dionysius O'Gall of Bitternutt Lodge, and perplexes Adèle with a highly fanciful account of his relationship with her governess. Perhaps most importantly, in posing as a fortune teller, Rochester becomes reader and storyteller at the same time, just as Jane becomes, simultaneously, both his audience and the text he interprets.

Indeed, next to Jane, Rochester is the most proficient reader-storyteller in the novel, a fact that makes his loss of both hand and sight at the end all the more significant. Unable to write or read, Rochester loses his status as a skilled interpreter at the end of Jane's story when she assumes full responsibility for "gazing for his behalf, and of putting into words . . . the landscape before us" (577). Jane, that is, has complete authority as reader and narrator of the life that she and Rochester share at the end of the novel. His loss of interpretive control over their experience and her concomitant empowerment in this respect mark the triumphant conclusion of Jane's growth toward selfhood, a progress articulated in terms of both sexual politics and literary proficiency. Her story begins when she is literally knocked off her feet by the book that her male cousin throws at her, an efficient way of suggesting Jane's powerlessness as both a female and a reader, and it concludes as she compares herself to Scheherazade (561), the woman who preserves her own life and liberates her sex through her skill as a teller of tales.[6] A captivating storyteller in the end (perhaps almost literally so), Jane struggles toward literary proficiency from most unpromising beginnings.

At Gateshead, reading is a purely consolatory pursuit for young Jane, not simply because it is a refuge from the unhappiness of her actual environment, but also because it allows her to "[draw] parallels," to see analogies in books that help her accept her own experience. Having read Goldsmith's history of Rome, she can compare her cousin to "Nero, Caligula, &c." and describe him in a way that affirms her understanding of his character: "You are like the Roman emperors!" (8). Jane uses books, that is, to confirm her own sense of reality.[7]

But the most puzzling of life's mysteries for Jane is her own self, the alternately searing and chilling moods of passion and despair that characterize her inner experience, and it is especially in an attempt to understand herself that she pursues reading as a little girl. She finds the barren landscapes in Bewick's *British Birds* "profoundly interesting" because they pictorially express her own feelings of isolation and affective deprivation. She is happy in reading Bewick, "happy at least in [her] way" (5), because the book validates her sense of self, morbid and pathetic though it may be. It allows her, in Norman Holland's terms, to pursue her "identity theme," interpreting books so that they confirm her understanding of experience and thereby strengthen her sense of self-identity (1980, 124-26). In the descriptive passages in *British Birds,* Jane initially finds an objective correlative for her inner feelings, and reading those passages prepares her to interpret the following illustrations in a satisfying (though, to us, sad) manner: "The words in these introductory pages connected themselves with the succeeding vignettes, and gave significance to the rock standing up alone in a sea of billow and spray; to the broken boat stranded on a desolate coast; to the cold and ghastly moon glancing through bars of cloud at a wreck just sinking" (5). The verbal description of these images of death and isolation prepares Jane to interpret the pictures as personally meaningful to her.

Though Jane can be "happy" in thus confirming her sense of reality through Bewick's, the novel clearly shows that such subjective criticism is dangerous as well as appealing. Jane goes to books, as to life, predisposed to find reflections of her internal reality. The "parallels" she draws are thus often no more than mirror images of her own mind, and reading becomes a solipsistic pursuit in which meaning is imposed rather than discovered or created. This becomes particularly clear in the red room episode, when Jane misinterprets a glimmer of light ("in all likelihood, a gleam from a lantern, carried by some one across the lawn," the older narrator explains) for "a herald of some coming vision from another world" (15). We learn that she has been "prepared . . . for horror," and we suspect not only the ghoulish stories she has heard about "dead men . . . revisiting the earth" but also her recent imaginative wanderings in the "deathwhite realms" of Bewick's (5). Predisposed to discover images of death and sterility in her reading, Jane responds subjectively to books and stories, which further disposes her to find such terrifying images in the phenomenal world as well.

Her hysterical breakdown in the red room and the aftermath of that incident reveal precisely how destructive Jane's interpretive habits have become. Once delighted by the world depicted in *Gulliver's Travels,* Jane now sees Gulliver as "a most desolate wanderer in most dread and dangerous regions," that is, as a figure who parallels her own psychic bewilderment (20). Bessie's songs, also once a source of "lively delight," now convey "an indescribable sadness" because Jane's doleful state of mind accentuates certain refrains "like the saddest cadence of a funeral hymn" (21). Initially attracted to a reading method that seemed to validate her own experience, Jane now discovers that she is incapable of employing any other kind of interpretive strategy, so that all signs yield the same, sad meaning.

After the Bewick/red room episode, Jane is never able to enjoy reading again at Gateshead; in a novel that equates character with the quality of one's literary experience, this surely reflects her dangerously eviscerated sense of self. As compelling and justified as Jane's rebellions at Gateshead appear, they arise, as even little Jane seems to see, not from a sane command of herself in relation to others but from the "madness of [her] conduct, and the dreariness of [her] hated and hating position" (41). Having unleashed her fury at Mrs. Reed after Mr. Brocklehurst's visit, Jane soon regrets her "fierce speaking" and tries to "exercise some better faculty," that is, reading. But she can "make no sense of the subject [of the *Arabian Nights*]; my own thoughts swam always between me and the page" (41), an apt description of a reading experience in which subjectivity is so excessively amplified that it no longer interferes creatively with the text but actually drowns out the storytelling voice. Ironically, the storyteller Jane cannot hear because of her troubled self-absorption is Scheherazade: because she is unable to read in a way that allows her to perceive anything beyond the limited scope of her own experience, Jane cannot recognize, much less imitate, a role model who provides a clear example of how to assert oneself through effective storytelling.

Jane's struggles and quick defeat as a reader at Gateshead are accordingly paralleled by her frustrated attempts as a young storyteller. Prior to her encounter with John Reed over *British Birds,* Jane has apparently been habitually taciturn in her aunt's household. She seems to have been an avid reader of books and a close observer of those around her (much to Abbot's annoyance), but she has "drawn parallels in silence" and "never thought . . . to have declared aloud" her particular reading of people and events at Gateshead (8). When Jane finally does break silence and offers her cousin a succinct analysis of his character, we may agree with her assessment; but, like Jane, we must concede that her manner of speaking has in fact been counterproductive since it leads directly to her incarceration in the red room. Repeatedly, the young Jane misjudges her task as an explicator of things as she sees them, and though we may admire her honesty and courage, we should perhaps also pity her ineptitude at calculating the effect she will produce when she addresses her listeners.

Jane understandably wishes to create a compelling narrative about Mrs. Reed's cruel treatment of her (as ultimately she does, of course, in writing her autobiography); but instead of persuasively telling her tale to a potentially sympathetic audience like Mr. Lloyd, she unwisely announces her intention to the very person she hopes to discredit: "I shall remember how you . . . thrust me back into the red-room, and locked me up there. . . . *I will tell* anybody who asks me questions *this exact tale*" (39, emphasis added). When the apothecary does ask questions about her life at Gateshead, however, she discovers that she can neither examine her experience critically nor articulate it in a rational yet expressive manner. She therefore stumbles through an account of her feelings that is sadly deficient when contrasted against the powerful story the adult narrator has told, and the productive result of her conversation with Mr. Lloyd—Jane's being sent away to school—is largely attributable to his skill as an auditor rather than to her proficiency as a speaker. The fact that, despite Jane's bumbling speech, her interchange with the apothecary produces truth suggests how imperative it is that an audience be responsive to the teller's tale, that readers be actively engaged in interpreting the text before them. Mr. Lloyd does not simply affirm Jane's story—indeed, he repeatedly opposes her interpretation of events and accuses her of being "a baby" and "silly" (22-24); but he does engage her in a vigorous discussion of the reality she must face and thus helps Jane create a verbal arena in which truth can emerge and solutions to her predicament be considered.

But Jane rarely enjoys the luxury of such a skilled and disinterested audience. Mrs. Reed repeatedly orders her to be quiet, and others often either speak for her—as Bessie does when she answers the first questions Mr. Lloyd puts to Jane—or tell her how to speak—as when John instructs her to "Say, 'What do you want, Master Reed?'" (6). And while Mr. Brocklehurst does not apply the brutal methods of silencing and censoring Jane's speech that the Gateshead inhabitants do, his interlocutory style is one that just as effectively transforms the potential storyteller into a mute and helpless object of his own interpretive maneuvers.

While ostensibly trying to draw Jane out, Mr. Brocklehurst asks questions that neatly play into the Gateshead reading of her character and make it difficult for the child to assert her own interpretation of herself. Asked if she is a good girl, Jane finds it "impossible to reply to this in the affirmative" since her "little world held a contrary opinion." Her silence allows Mrs. Reed to supply a negative response to this first, crucial question in their conversation (33). Predisposed to see people—especially children placed under his authority—as fallen creatures, Mr. Brocklehurst finds gratifying confirmation of his views in Mrs. Reed's assessment and proceeds to investigate Jane's character according to the assumption that she is, in fact, "a naughty child" (34). When questioned about her reading habits, Jane responds promptly and decisively only to be told that her literary tastes are "shocking" (35) proof of her wickedness. Clearly, the intent of this conversation is to confirm Mr. Brocklehurst's narrow, preformed interpretation of Jane's character rather than to give her the opportunity to express herself.

As Jane is preparing to respond to his recommendation that she exchange her wicked heart for a good one, Mrs. Reed characteristically preempts the child's part in the discussion, which, nevertheless, continues to focus on Jane's unsatisfactory "character and disposition." The combined forces of Mr. Brocklehurst's coercive questioning and Aunt Reed's interdiction completely silence Jane, preventing her from even trying to tell her own story. Instead, she becomes the subject of the interpretive biases of her two unfavorably disposed critics. Looking on helplessly, Jane knows that she can do "nothing, indeed" (36), to correct their misreadings of her character since she has been deprived of all interpretive authority in this storytelling situation. As she recognizes, Mrs. Reed and Mr. Brocklehurst have "transformed" her not only into a maliciously misinterpreted story—a victimized text, if you will—but also into a mute, secondary audience to a libelous account of herself. Appropriating Jane's rightful role as storyteller of her own experience, Mrs. Reed tells her primary audience, Mr. Brocklehurst, that the child is a liar and explains to Jane that "I mention this in your hearing . . . that you may not attempt to impose on Mr. Brocklehurst" (35). Since Aunt Reed and Mr. Brocklehurst have imposed their view of reality on Jane rather than the other way around, this latter statement is, of course, bitingly ironic. In the triadic configuration of teller-text-audience that makes up the literary experience, this scene portrays Jane both as an abused text subject to the hermeneutic impositions of hostile readers and as a disempowered audience incapable of correcting the false narrative that two ill-motivated storytellers tell each other in her presence.

In contrast to Mr. Lloyd's conversation with Jane, the verbal arena that Mr. Brocklehurst and Mrs. Reed create is one that sacrifices truth to power. Jane's description of the retaliation following Mr. Brocklehurst's visit underscores the political nature of their discussion about Jane: having forced Mrs. Reed from the breakfast room by an explosion of "fierce speaking," Jane is left "winner of the field," free to muse in "conqueror's solitude" on the "battle . . . fought" and the "victory . . . gained" (40). A characteristically chilling reaction of remorse soon follows the pleasures of vengeance, however, and the delicious sensation of speaking hateful words is replaced by the "metallic and corroding" aftertaste of poisoned speech. Having driven the enemy from the field, the storyteller regretfully finds that she has no audience with whom to interact; she must learn to tell her view of the truth in a manner that will captivate rather than assault.

Not coincidently, just when Jane realizes how dramatically she has failed in this way, she also discovers that she is no longer capable of reading. Sadly putting down the *Arabian Nights,* she walks out of the house and attempts to read the face of nature instead. But there in the frozen landscape she encounters the same images, symbolically reflecting the same theme that has persistently interfered with her appreciation of other symbolic texts: "I found no pleasure in the silent trees, the fallen fir-cones, the congealed relics of autumn, russet leaves, swept by past winds in heaps, and now stiffened together. I leaned against a gate, and looked into an empty field where no sheep were feeding, where the short grass was nipped and blanched. . . . I stood, a wretched child enough, whispering to myself over and over again, 'What shall I do?—what shall I do?'" (41).

The answer to that question is revealed, of course, in the next section of Jane's narrative, which tells of her experience at Lowood. There she begins to learn a new way of reading, one that will assist in the reformation of her identity theme and prepare her to become a more authoritative narrator of her own life. In contrast to the private and consolatory nature of Jane's reading at Gateshead, reading at Lowood is a communal activity in which everyone is expected to participate. Jane's first view of her schoolmates is that of eighty female readers uniformly dressed and simultaneously engaged in conning their lesson books. The next morning, she sees them "all drawn up in four semicircles . . . all [holding] books in their hands" and waiting for the school bell to ring so they may start the "business" of reading together, a scene that suggests a radically different reading environment for the child accustomed to smuggling books into a "hiding-place" like the window seat at Gateshead (49).

Reading at Lowood usually entails a collective effort in which the group as a whole or a recognized authority such as a teacher or senior student reads an authoritative text or recites it out loud. The act of reading aloud in the presence of others transforms each reader into a kind of storyteller whose audience is, like herself, both reading and narrating at the same time. The situation has parallels, of course, in Brontë's own school experience as well as in the storytelling situation she shared with Branwell, Emily, and Anne. Charlotte's siblings were a creatively refractory audience, however, whose noisy interpretive responses ensured the protean growth of their tales. At Lowood, a deadening concern with factual trivia and matters of form silence such interpretive noise, as Helen Burns discovers when she is asked "questions about tonnage and poundage, and ship-money" and sent to the bottom of the class for "some error of pronunciation or some inattention to stops" (60).

Indeed, while each reader must become engaged in the transmission of texts to her audience of fellow readers and thereby adopts an active role like that of a storyteller, in fact, the simultaneous reading and narrating of works at Lowood comprise an essentially passive act designed to confirm the values of the community through mechanical repetition of canonical texts. Immediately upon rising each morning the girls "[form] in a file, two and two" to hear prayers read aloud and then are ordered to "form classes!" for more exercise in reading (49). Appropriately, lessons begin each day with the repetition of the Collect, a brief prayer whose original purpose was to facilitate the gathering of worshippers so that they might proceed to church en masse. After this, "certain texts of scripture were *said,* and to these succeeded a protracted reading of . . . the Bible" (50, emphasis added). The emphasis on the repetition, recitation, and "saying" of authoritative texts suggests that reading is not a creative, interpretive pursuit at Lowood but one that relies on memorization and rote practice to maintain an orderly, conventional consensus about the nature of reality.

Despite the negative features of the reading methods prescribed at Lowood, they appear to have some salutary effect on Jane, for they serve as a check against her previous, dangerous interpretive habits. An insistence upon group work discourages the morbidly introspective reading Jane has grown familiar with and forces her to participate in a communal literary experience. Reading at Lowood is thus a social act that helps define Jane's relationship to others rather than a solipsistic experience that destructively confirms her separateness. But like her life in general at Lowood, this new way of reading is only a partial help to Jane, and her need to be creatively engaged in the literary endeavor must also be fulfilled.

Because of this need, Jane is immediately attracted to Helen Burns, who, like herself at Gateshead, reads in quiet isolation from the rest of the group. "Her occupation," Jane remarks, "touched a chord of sympathy somewhere; for I too liked reading" (55). Indeed, the first event of their relationship is an act of joint textual interpretation. In contrast to John Reed, who grabs a book away from Jane and then hits her with it, Helen gently hands her friend the volume of *Rasselas* she has shown interest in with no more interpretive commentary than the unassuming remark, "I like it." When Jane demonstrates an apparent lack of appreciation for the text, Helen merely takes it back "quietly, and without saying anything" resumes reading. Here, a text is a means for bringing together two readers in a situation that allows for diversity of response. Each girl apparently holds to her own reading of the work, but neither claims authority over the text as John Reed does in declaring exclusive ownership; nor does one reader attempt to impose her interpretation upon the other as John Reed also dramatically does when he hurls the book at his cousin's head.

Though their interchange about *Rasselas* appears egalitarian, Helen is really something more than Jane's peer in reading, however. Being older, she has more literary experience and consequently greater skill as an interpreter of texts, a fact the younger child implicitly acknowledges through her eager questions about the inscription over the Lowood door. Helen demonstrates her proficiency as a reader most convincingly when she analyzes Jane herself. She rejects Brocklehurst's characterization of her friend as a liar, "for I read a sincere nature in your ardent eyes and . . . clear front," and also sees that Jane is "too impulsive, too vehement," and too needy of the "love of [other] human beings" (81). Having listened to Jane's account of Mrs. Reed, Helen wisely explains that "she has been unkind to you . . . because . . . she dislikes your cast of character" (66), an analysis that the mature narrator has already presented: "I thus suffered [because] . . . I was a discord in Gateshead-hall: I was like nobody there. . . . They were not bound to regard with affection a thing . . . opposed to them in temperament, in capacity, in propensities" (13-14).

Helen also notes that Jane is "but a little untaught girl" who will probably change her mind as she grows older (65), a comment less remarkable for its perceptiveness than for its power to confirm Helen's authority in judging Jane. Growth from immaturity and ignorance to a changed, mature perspective is precisely what readers of the genre to which *Jane Eyre* belongs expect, and, besides, such growth has already been signaled by the knowing interventions of the older narrator. Helen's skill as an interpreter of Jane's personality is thus validated both by the generic conventions that readers expect to find in the text and by a narrative perspective that reinforces those expectations.[8]

Given the correlation between reading and storytelling in *Jane Eyre,* it is almost predictable that Helen should also turn out to be Jane's first guide in the art of telling tales. Emboldened by Helen's kindness, Jane recounts her experience at Gateshead with characteristic vehemence: "I proceeded . . . to pour out in my own way, the tale of my sufferings and resentments . . . [speaking] as I felt, without reserve or softening" (66). Unable to respond favorably to Jane's "bitter and truculent" manner of telling her tale, Helen at first makes no reply, just as she had made no comment on Jane's apparent lack of appreciation for *Rasselas.* When confronted with Jane's impatient demand for audience response,

however, she remarks that, from her perspective, certain parts of the narrative seem excessive. Warned by Helen's response, Jane is later able to revise her narrative so that it seems more credible and hence produces the desired effect on Miss Temple:

> I resolved in the depth of my heart that I would be most moderate: most correct; and, having reflected a few minutes in order to arrange coherently what I had to say, I told her all the story of my sad childhood. . . . My language was more subdued than it generally was when it developed that sad theme; and mindful of Helen's warnings . . . , I infused into the narrative far less of gall and wormwood than ordinary. Thus restrained and simplified, it sounded more credible: I felt as I went on that Miss Temple fully believed me.
>
> (82-83)

For the first time, Jane has not been blindly preoccupied with her need to validate herself and her experience but has considered the perceptions of those whom she has invited to participate in the unfolding of her story. She has learned to anticipate audience response somewhat and to "arrange" her narrative so that the truth as she sees it will also be apparent to her listener.

Jane is immediately rewarded for her first success at storytelling by being given those things she most desperately needs: a reassuring kiss from a loving, respected mother figure; nourishing and delicious food to eat; and a place by a warm fireside. But even more important to Jane's development is her presence during the following "conversation . . . between [Miss Temple] and Helen, which it was indeed a privilege to be admitted to hear" (85). Once again, Jane is cast in the role of silent, secondary audience, but this time the subject of discussion is not herself but "books: how many they had read!"—and not only those of English authors, but also French and, to Jane's unbound astonishment, Latin writers as well. Having followed Helen and the appropriately named Miss Temple through dark and "intricate passages" (82), Jane has entered the sanctum of the head teacher's private apartment, has passed the first test of telling her tale, has "feasted . . . on nectar and ambrosia" (84), and now becomes initiated into the full mystery of the arts she is apparently appointed to perform. Listening to Helen translate Virgil, Jane's amazement turns to "veneration" as she hears a reader creatively transform an ostensibly indecipherable text into an articulate, meaningful tale.

Jane's silent participation in the conversation between Helen Burns and Miss Temple thus allows her to see the literary experience in a new way. In contrast to her Gateshead habits, books here bring people together, and interpretation becomes a creative act performed for the mutual delight of all participants. That these activities are conducted by a highly exclusive group in a private, almost sacred place suggests that those involved are, indeed, privileged individuals with unusual powers, reminiscent perhaps of the little Brontë children themselves. This quality, in addition to the pleasurable intimacy of the environment—the nourishing presence of food, warmth, and physical affection—sharply contrasts with the reading and storytelling methods practiced in the Lowood classroom. Neither dangerously solipsistic nor oppressive due to an insistence on conformity, the acts of reading and storytelling Jane witnesses in Miss Temple's room counter the extremist paradigms represented at Gateshead and Lowood respectively and provide a model for Jane's newly aroused aspirations.[9]

The episode in Miss Temple's apartment thus marks an important turn in Jane's development and underscores the centrality of storytelling and reading to the heroine's struggle for self-actualization. Appropriately, one of her first scholastic efforts at Lowood is to learn how to translate French, an activity that fuses the interpretive skills of reading with the expressive craft of storytelling. No longer hampered by a purely solipsistic method of interpretation or silenced by an ineffectual rhetorical stance, Jane simultaneously becomes a successful reader and storyteller when she learns to translate "the first two tenses of the verb *Etre*" (87). She learns to interpret and articulate the meaning of the phrases "I am" and "I was"—that is, to understand and tell the story of what she is and has been—rather than remain the object of other people's interpretations. Interpretive and expressive talents thus emerge as the essential elements of Jane's character, the core of her self, which she must preserve at all costs. Her further experiences, first at Thornfield and then at Marsh End, demonstrate how difficult such self-preservation can be.

The Thornfield section of *Jane Eyre* concludes its introductory chapter with a scene that parallels the red room episode and suggests that, despite Jane's increasing abilities as a reader and a storyteller, her interpretive skills are still not adequate to the complicated task of explicating reality. Hearing for the first time the solemn laughter that emanates from Thornfield's third floor, Jane misunderstands the significance of what she hears just as she had earlier misinterpreted the gleam of light she had seen moving across the red room wall. Even though she recognizes that "the laugh was as tragic, as preternatural a laugh as any I ever heard," she is not suspicious because "it was high noon, and . . . neither scene nor season favoured fear" (130). As in the red room, where she had been "prepared . . . for horror" (15) and accordingly finds supernatural and terrifying significance in a mere streak of light, so here she is predisposed to miss the truly threatening implications of Bertha's laughter since the circumstances in which the interpreting takes place do not favor a fearful reading. The predispositions that cause these two interpretive mistakes are the obverse of each other, of course—as an adult Jane too hastily dismisses the su-

perstitious fear that she had embraced too thoroughly as a child—but in both cases the process is the same. Warning against the dangers of the solipsistic imagination on the one hand and against the equal danger of discounting our imaginative instincts on the other, these scenes show Jane interpreting reality in light of presuppositions that obscure the meaning of her experience and that consequently weaken her authority as an interpreter of her own life.

Appropriately, this scene in which Jane first hears and misinterprets Bertha's laughter immediately precedes the now-famous depiction of Jane pacing the corridor of Thornfield's third story, telling and listening to "a tale that was never ended—a tale my imagination created, and narrated continuously" (132). Rosemarie Bodenheimer correctly notes that this is a critical image of the "fiction maker" whose only audience is herself and that Jane's progress in the novel is in "finding a fit audience" for her story (1980, 157). But Jane succeeds in gaining that audience only after she has also proved her proficiency as a *reader* of the reality her tale interprets. Successful storytelling in *Jane Eyre* depends, that is, on successful reading; and the juxtaposition of Jane's misreading of Bertha's laughter against her directionless storytelling on Thornfield's roof implies that at this stage in her development, she is still struggling for expertise in both areas. Through her relationship with Rochester, Jane has the opportunity to strengthen the interpretive skills necessary to the art of storytelling, though, as we shall see, that opportunity also paradoxically puts her at risk as an authoritative teller of her own tale.

In getting to know Edward Fairfax Rochester, Jane enjoys the most stimulating and challenging pleasures she has yet experienced. Central to that pleasure are their "piquant" conversations, those emotionally charged discussions in which their frankness borders on rudeness and both delightedly take up arms in a war of words that adds zest to their growing infatuation with each other. Their affectionately adversarial stance in such dialogue reminds us of the hostile yet oddly loving conversations between William Crimsworth and Yorke Hunsden in *The Professor* and is equally reminiscent of the manner in which William Percy and Charles Townshend characteristically speak to each other. In this aspect of their relationship, Jane and Rochester are like the narrators and narratees in Brontë's earlier fiction, and their mutual joy in provocative verbal interchange should be understood within the context of Brontë's view of the storytelling situation itself. Janet Freeman has called Rochester a "slippery ironist," a description that rightly connects him to the storytellers in Brontë's juvenile tales, but her claim that Jane is merely the victim of his irony, which she does not understand and which is the opposite of her own "straightforward speech" (1984, 693), does not do justice to the complexity of Jane's character. Happily poking Rochester with the sharpened "needle of repartee" (344), Jane, too, enjoys the verbal parry and thrust that are at the core of their mutual admiration.

Indeed, life for Jane becomes so "piquant" upon Rochester's arrival at Thornfield that she has little need to read actual books, an activity which had previously absorbed much of her time. She declares herself quite content with the few volumes allotted to her for Adèle's instruction because a new and more appealing type of text now presents itself for her scrutiny. That new text is, of course, Rochester himself. Like many skilled readers, Jane is especially fascinated by those passages in the text that seem resistant to conclusive interpretation, those mysterious and seemingly indecipherable parts of his character that she associates with an abyss: "As for the vague something . . . that opened upon a careful observer, now and then, . . . I longed only to dare—to divine it; and I thought Miss Ingram happy, because one day she might look into the abyss at her leisure, explore its secrets and analyze their nature" (234-35). Jane's ability to analyze the text that is Rochester's self is limited, of course, by her ignorance of Bertha; knowledge of that part of his experience would help to fill in the gaps—the abyss—and resolve the indeterminacy of his character. Yet, in spite of this limitation, Jane is largely successful in her interpretation of Rochester, as he himself admits. In recounting her plan to insist on wearing a simple bridal veil of her own making rather than the costly one he provided, Jane explains how she has imagined he would respond: "I saw plainly how you would look," she tells him, "and heard your . . . answers" (354). Through his uneasy remark, "How well you read me, you witch!" Rochester corroborates her depiction of him in regard to the bridal veil issue and thus testifies to her skill both as a reader of his character and as a storyteller who can re-create that character in a dramatized, hypothetical situation. Jane is competent, that is, not only to analyze Rochester but also to narrate him into fictional scenes of her own imagining.

Though by his own admission Jane has accurately portrayed Rochester in this little story about the veil, he experiences her interpretive and re-creative powers as an unwelcome appropriation of his self to the needs of another—a process we have already seen enacted maliciously through the fictions Mrs. Reed and Mr. Brocklehurst tell each other about Jane in chapter 4. Appropriately, Rochester acknowledges the threat that Jane thus poses to his self-integrity by calling her a witch for her ability to "read" and depict him so well. Similarly, Jane expresses a degree of unease at Rochester's ability to understand her: he "sometimes read my unspoken thoughts with an acumen to me incomprehensible" (308), she comments, and one suspects that this mystery is especially unnerving to Jane precisely because it attributes to Rochester an interpretive authority that she

might do well to restrict to herself. As Jane's experience at Gateshead has taught her, when she allows herself to be silenced—when she allows others to tell her story for her—then she loses the power to create, explain, and thus preserve herself against those who would narrate her into fictions that damage and falsify her character. Indeed, her admission that she "feared to meet [Rochester's] eye" (191) reveals that Jane, too, is threatened by the prospect of being turned into an object for analysis; the lover-become-reader is a legitimate source of fear for one who has been subject in the past to the interpretive manipulations of biased, ill-motivated critics.

In this politically charged relationship, the safest roles for Jane to adopt with respect to Rochester are those of reader and storyteller, observing, analyzing, and re-creating his character in tales of her own making. These are roles that Rochester, however, does not often allow her to play. Instead, he repeatedly asks her to serve as the audience for the tales *he* chooses to tell. When these stories are about Rochester himself, they do not pose a threat to Jane's right to self-interpretation, and she accordingly derives great pleasure from hearing them, particularly since they describe an external reality that her sheltered life has precluded her from seeing. "I . . . talked comparatively little; but I heard him talk with relish," she recounts, for his stories provide her with "glimpses of [the world's] scenes and ways . . . and I had a keen delight in receiving the new ideas he offered, in imaging the new pictures he portrayed, and following him in thought through the new regions he disclosed" (180). Just as Jane is clearly a fine listener who receives, imagines, and thus "follows" the story she hears with accuracy and creative insight, so we gather Rochester is also a talented teller of tales. Indeed, Jane wants to "hear his voice again" just as much as she "[fears] to meet his eye" (191).

Despite the pleasure Jane takes in hearing Rochester, one still senses that being reduced to a mere audience places her once again in a position of vulnerability, just as being silenced at Gateshead had disempowered her. It is significant, for example, that Rochester literally commands Jane to believe that she is *not* a storyteller: "Know . . . that it is not your forte to talk of yourself, but to listen while others talk of themselves" (166). "Made," in his view, "to be the recipient of [other people's] secrets" (176), Jane is debarred from exercising the interpretive and expressive talents that we have seen are essential to her sense of self.

Rochester's capacity for rendering Jane powerless in this way is acknowledged most fully, perhaps, when he presents himself to her in the guise of a fortune-telling gypsy. In wearing a costume, Rochester conceals his own features from Jane's observant eye at the same time that he requires her to show her palm and, more importantly, her face for his unobstructed view. Jane later complains justly that this "is scarcely fair" (253) since it completely destroys the tenuous balance of interpretive power that protects her and makes their relationship potentially egalitarian. In the political activity of mutual interpretation, Rochester gains an unfair advantage by placing Jane, kneeling with her face uplifted, before the fire's glare, a position that "only threw [his] face into deeper shadow." "Mine," Jane remarks significantly, "it illumined" (247).

The gypsy's proposal is, of course, to "read" or "tell" Jane's fortune, and, given the novel's insistent linking of reading, narrating, and the self, we should not feel surprised that such fortune-telling turns out to be an act of character analysis rather than a prediction of Jane's future. Leaning back in his chair, Rochester studies her features at his leisure, just as in Jane's earlier expressed desire to "look into the abyss" of Rochester's character at her leisure. From this highly privileged perspective, he is able to read her self quite accurately—so accurately, in fact, that even he is able to see momentarily that her mouth "was never intended to be compressed in . . . silence . . . : it is a mouth which should speak much . . . and have human affection for its interlocutor" (251). Ironically, it is his arrogation of her right to explicate her own character and tell her own story that is, at that very moment, compressing her lips in silence. Listening to his "strange talk," she becomes "wrapped . . . in a kind of a dream" and "involved in a web of mystification" (250). She has the uneasy feeling that some unidentified "other" understands her at least as well as, perhaps better than, she understands herself. In listening to Rochester's assessment of her personality, Jane begins to lose all sense of interpretive authority over herself.

Our sense that Rochester can be unfair or even underhanded in appropriating Jane's story for his own needs becomes quite strong in chapter 25 when he attempts to explain away Bertha's frightening appearance in Jane's bedroom. The night before their planned wedding, Jane tells him several short tales, one about her activities the preceding day, two about her nightmares, and one about her encounter with Bertha. Haunting and prophetic, these stories are most un-welcome to Rochester, who wants only to think that all will be well with their impending marriage. He consequently makes a most unsatisfactory audience for these tales, dismissing them in a patronizing tone and repeatedly expressing surprise that Jane is not yet done talking. Most importantly, he announces at the outset that he "will not believe [her stories] to be anything important" (356), a predisposition that prevents him from adopting an interpretive perspective that Jane—and we, the readers—sense is most appropriate.

Rochester *does* see the sinister significance of Jane's last tale, of course, but he refuses to acknowledge what he sees. Having dismissed her dreams as meaningless, he then provides an interpretation that obscures the meaning of the fourth story about her confrontation with a ghoulish woman in the dead of the night. Knowing, like Brontë, that the appearance of truth in storytelling is achieved through a blending of actuality and imagination, Rochester cleverly explains to Jane that what happened to her was "half dream, half reality" (360). His interpretation thus acknowledges at least some of the facts of Jane's experience and forces her to accept a reading that is essentially false. His promise to explain himself more fully "when [they] have been married a year and a day" implies that he is manipulating the conventions of the fairy tale rather than telling a story that conveys the true significance of Bertha's prophetic appearance.

Though Jane has willingly, even eagerly, provided Rochester with the opportunity to interpret and retell her story about the encounter with Bertha, her relationship with him in this scene is somewhat similar to the one she experienced with Mrs. Reed and Mr. Brocklehurst in chapter 4. Like them, he silences Jane through a misreading of her own experience; like them, he refuses to serve as an affectionate interlocutor who, by responding to her gift for narration and interpretation, could help create a verbal space in which truth might emerge. Instead, the significance of her experience is denied and truth is once again sacrificed to power. Indeed, Rochester's appropriation of Jane's experience in this scene may be understood as even more malicious than Mrs. Reed's and Mr. Brocklehurst's behavior: they at least seem to be genuinely convinced that they are telling the truth, whereas Rochester deliberately lies in order to keep his hold over her. Furthermore, Jane's very willingness to have Rochester explain her experience is a sign of her vulnerability. Helpless to stop Mrs. Reed and Mr. Brocklehurst from appropriating her character for their own false accounts of her, Jane had at least felt silent outrage at their misinterpretations and mistellings of her story. With Rochester, Jane is dangerously willing to resign her authority as explicator of her own experience even though she is not "satisfied," as she puts it, with the account he offers her.

Mason's intervention at the wedding and the subsequent revelation of Rochester's past allow Jane to see more clearly how threatened she has been by his interpretive control. Her first response is to revert to the reading of her life and self that had obsessed her in early childhood: "Jane Eyre," she tells herself, is a "cold, solitary girl" wandering in a psychic landscape that is "desolate," "ice glazed," "waste, wild," and "wintry" (373-74). Overwhelmed by this "consciousness of my life lorn" (375), she becomes "self-abandoned, relaxed and effortless" (374); she gives up, that is, all responsibility for asserting the significance of her own existence. Fortunately, this mood of self-annihilation is short-lived and is followed by Jane's famous validation of self, "*I* care for myself" (404), an assertion that gives her the courage to leave Thornfield and continue her attempts to read life and tell her story.

Just as the Thornfield section of *Jane Eyre* opens with two juxtaposed scenes that respectively demonstrate Jane's deficiencies as a reader and a storyteller, so the Moor-House section begins with a scene that reveals her growing competence in these activities. In almost blinding darkness, Jane is able to find her way to her new home by following a brilliant point of light that suddenly shines out across the wild marsh landscape. As mysterious at first in its sudden appearance as the glimmer of light on the red room wall, this light immediately catches Jane's eye and awakens her interpretive curiosity. Observing it carefully, she rejects her first two hypotheses—that it is an *ignis fatuus* or a newly kindled bonfire—and rightly determines that it is a candle in a house window. As she follows it, the light becomes "my star" and, as she approaches the house itself, a "friendly gleam" (423)—metaphorical readings that turn out to be valid: at Moor-House Jane discovers friends, a new home, and, literally, a family she did not know she had.

Jane's ability to interpret this first given sign in the Moor-House section is crucial, of course, to her survival. Starved and bereft, Jane lives only because she has been able to find her way to the Riverses' door. Quite literally, her life depends here on her ability to interpret signs correctly. Her success in doing so contrasts with her earlier misinterpretations of key signs—first the light on the red room wall and then the mysterious laughter at Thornfield—and thus suggests that she is becoming increasingly competent at preserving herself through an accurate reading of the world she inhabits. This is not to say that life has become an open book to Jane, for much remains mysterious, even incomprehensible, to her. But by the time she reaches Marsh End, she seems to have learned how to identify the incomprehensible as such and not to fall into misreadings of signs she cannot understand. This point becomes clear as Jane gazes through the narrow kitchen window at Moor-House and attempts to understand the scene she observes.

The Moor-House kitchen is initially presented *ut pictura poesis,* as a static image framed by the window casement, while Jane stands outside that frame "reading" this picture. The vividness and detail with which Jane describes the kitchen suggest her acute powers of visual observation, and references to the ticking of the clock and the clicking of Hannah's knitting needles similarly suggest her alertness to minute audible signs as well. As Mary and Diana begin to speak, the presentation shifts from the pictorial to the dramatic mode; but Jane's role is essentially unchanged, for she now stands in the place of an audience to a play enacted in a kind of shadowbox before her,[10] and her task is still to interpret what she observes.

Yet, for all her reportorial skills, evidenced in the detail and apparent accuracy of description, Jane repeatedly—and self-confessedly—fails at interpreting this scene. She cannot, for example, understand why the genteel-looking Rivers sisters are consorting with a rustic like Hannah, nor can she make sense of the Schiller they read aloud since she does not know German: "It was only like a stroke on sounding brass to me—conveying no meaning" (425). Likewise, Hannah's remark that Mary resembles her mother while Diana looks more like her father leaves Jane perplexed. She is able to observe fine distinctions in their appearance ("one . . . had hair a shade darker than the other," she notes [427]), but because she does not know their characters as Hannah does, she is blind to the differences the long-time servant sees.

What is so striking about this scene is that Jane, while clearly intrigued by what she observes, seems willing nevertheless to remain in uncertainty about its significance. Alert to signification, she yet refrains from leaping to interpretive conclusions as she had earlier mistakenly done at both Gateshead and Thornfield. Just as Jane on the roof at Thornfield is a critical image of the fiction maker whose only audience is herself, so Jane at the window of Moor-House is a positive image of the mature, experienced reader: alert to the potential meaning of the signs before her, she curbs her enthusiasm for interpretation and recognizes when a particular text—in this case, a picture or dramatic scene—is, for the present, largely incomprehensible. Jane thus acknowledges the mystery that the text of life frequently presents for our incomprehension—the mystery that she had denied, for example, in her false reading of Bertha's laughter; and at the same time she contains that mystery by naming it and distinguishing it from known, observable facts—a disarming of the incomprehensible which she was incapable of as a little child in the red room. Demonstrating Jane's increased maturity as a reader of the world around her, the scene is appropriately followed by a parallel scene that reflects her growth as a teller of her own tale.

Faint, wet, and famished, Jane is brought into Moor-House and then requested to give her name and an account of herself; in effect, she is asked to tell her story. As we have seen, Jane has rarely had the opportunity to tell her tale to an eager audience, and we might expect that the Riverses' solicitude would move her to expressivity if not eloquence. Instead, she asks to be "excuse[d] . . . from much discourse" and claims that she "can give . . . no details" about herself. Pressed for her name, she offers an alias. She pleads that her wasted physical condition prevents her from telling her story:

"my breath is short—I feel a spasm when I speak" (431). Indeed, to the Riverses she appears a "bloodless," eviscerated being who has been "worn to nothing" (430). Her adopting a false name, her apparent incapacity to speak of herself, and her nearly total physical debilitation might suggest Jane's severely, even dangerously, diminished ability to define and express herself.

Yet what is most telling about Jane's behavior in this scene is not her incapacity in these respects but rather her self-pride and stubborn insistence on *not* telling the story she has been asked to tell. Despite the Riverses' perfectly reasonable request for a little information about the vagrant stranger they have taken into their home, Jane manages to preserve complete silence about her identity, her character, her past, and her present circumstances. Once given the storyteller's traditional place by the fire and "brought face to face" with her audience, she clearly feels quite sure of herself in spite of her weakened physical state. Refusing to play any longer the part of "the mendicant," she looks inward for the means of self-preservation, resumes her "natural manner and character," and "[begins] once more to know [her]self" (431). Jane's silence is thus not a consequence of an eviscerated sense of identity but the very opposite. It is a strategy deliberately employed for self-preservation. Just as she is capable of restraining her impulse to impose a reading on truly indecipherable signs, thereby saving herself from making false interpretations of reality, so she is also competent to maintain silence when eloquence would be her undoing.

Very quickly, Jane has sized up the politics of the potential storytelling situation in which she finds herself and has realized how vulnerable she is with respect to her listeners. Although she has been given the storyteller's privileged place by the fire, and although her audience is solicitously eager to hear her tale, she knows that, ultimately, they have the upper hand: they may choose to cast her back out again. In these circumstances, Jane must at all costs avoid any storytelling situation that might further weaken her position. She will not, therefore, engage in the vehement expressivity that had been so damaging to her at Gateshead, nor will she attempt to make her tale "credible" to her listeners as she learned to do at Lowood (an excellent judgment call, when one considers how *incredible* and morally problematic her experience with Rochester and Bertha has been). Instead, her pressing need is to buy time so that she may read her audience more clearly than has hitherto been possible. Her goal, therefore, is "to avoid discovery" (430): to make sure that she maintains absolute control over her story by refusing to open the text of her self to others' perusal. At this critical juncture in Jane's experience, when her life literally depends on

her skill in the political art of storytelling, Jane learns to employ the Scheherazadean strategy of gaining power by withholding the tale.

Jane would have less need of such power, of course, if all of her listeners were like Mary, whose "remarkable countenance" immediately wins Jane's trust. But St. John's "demand" for an account of herself warns her of his intent to exert his authority over her and accordingly provokes her defensive claim to remain silent. Indeed, from the moment she first becomes aware of St. John's presence, Jane has good reason to fear him. Denied admission to Moor-House by Hannah and thinking herself alone, she utters aloud a confession of her complete powerlessness, which St. John overhears. Potentially eloquent and self-expressive, the defeated storyteller resigns herself to death and *silence:* "I can but die . . . and I believe in God. Let me try to wait His will in silence" (429). At that moment, Jane hears "a voice quite close at hand" and realizes that she has just enacted her powerlessness before an audience standing behind her in the dark, an observer who has seen her clearly in the light of the kitchen window and door and has heard her clearly from a vantage point of obscure proximity. St. John's positioning with respect to Jane— she in the light, he in concealing darkness—parallels and intensifies the dynamics of the fortune-telling scene and suggests that he may be even more dangerous than Rochester as a usurper of Jane's authority to interpret her own self and experience. She is "terrified at the unexpected sound" of his voice, for she now knows that while she was attempting to read the scene framed by the kitchen window, she herself was the text for another reader's silent perusal; and as she formulated aloud her assessment of her present, sad experience, that interpretation was being received and reformulated by a hidden audience who corrects her reading in a tone of confident authority.

The circumstances of Jane's first meeting with St. John comment effectively on his personality with respect to the question of hermeneutic power and accurately forecast the dynamics of their relationship as it will develop in this section of the novel. He exercises his power to exert interpretive control over Jane when he studies her "unusual physiognomy" (433) as she lies "motionless as a stone" in her sickbed. Assessing her character with an accuracy that rivals Rochester's, St. John reads Jane in a situation that renders her powerless. "I could understand what was said . . . ," she relates, "but I could not answer: to open my lips or move my limbs was equally impossible" (432). Even after she is well, St. John continues to treat Jane as a text open for his interpretive perusal while at the same time jealously guarding himself from such observation. He is able "leisurely to read [her] face, as if its features and lines were characters on a page" (452). St. John's eyes, on the other hand, "were difficult to fathom. He seemed to use them rather as instruments to search other people's thoughts, than as agents to reveal his own" (441). St. John's furtive observations of Jane seem especially sinister when he uses the literal act of reading as a subterfuge for such behavior: ostensibly engaged in studying his Hindustani textbook, he "appeared . . . quiet and absorbed . . . but that blue eye of his had a habit of leaving the outlandish-looking grammar, and wandering over, and sometimes fixing upon us [Jane and his sisters] with a curious intensity of observation" (506). Using an actual book as a cover for arguably reprehensible conduct, St. John is like other characters in *Jane Eyre* who abuse reading material—his second cousin, John Reed, for example. St. John's fundamentally inappreciative view of literature is further emphasized by his apparent indifference to the "glorious" Schiller that engrosses Jane and his sisters. Given his apparently pragmatic approach to reading—he learns Hindustani because it is "necessary to his plans" (506)—one finds it somewhat chilling to learn that "it was his unsocial custom to read at meals" (504).[11] In one sense a highly astute reader of people and words, St. John can also be a frigidly unresponsive interpreter of signs both human and verbal.

As Jane had feared to meet Rochester's eye, so now she is doubly justified in feeling discomfited when St. John uses his metallic blue "instruments" to "search" and "fix" her character in his own reading of her. Jane tries to baffle such interpretive maneuvers by maintaining silence with regard to her experience at Thornfield, thus presenting for St. John's observation a text that is incomplete and therefore, she hopes, incomprehensible. Her attempt to make herself mysterious, even unknowable, by withholding her story fails, however, when St. John hears that story from other sources. Indeed, he learns important facts that even Jane herself does not possess and so gains the power to assume "the narrator's part, . . . converting [Jane] into a listener" (484).

While St. John's arrogation of Jane's right to tell her own story is reminiscent of her past experience with presumptuous storytellers, the very accuracy and purely factual nature of his tale pose a more significant threat to her integrity. Mrs. Reed and Mr. Brocklehurst had exploited their authority as adults to impose a blatantly false reading on Jane's character, and Rochester had manipulated his insightful reading of Jane for his own selfish ends; but St. John, in his telling of her tale, is apparently an objective narrator of verifiable facts that Jane can have no need or desire to dispute. In this sense, he appears to have gained legitimate authority as the storyteller of Jane's life, an authority he displays by "converting [Jane] into a listener" and by producing the fragment of paper on which she had abstractedly scribbled her real name. As his possession of her true signature implies, in telling her story St. John has come dangerously close to possessing her self.

Indeed, from this point on, St. John's power over Jane seems to increase despite the fact that he must now recognize her as a financially independent relative rather than as a dependent object of his charity. Appropriately, Jane's reluctant submission to his control is described through situations that involve the reading, interpretation, and transmission of texts. Her first "sacrifice" is to give up learning German in order to help St. John study Hindustani. Enamored of German poetry and indifferent, at best, to "Oriental" languages, Jane becomes St. John's pupil not because learning Hindustani will contribute to her own growth, as, for example, learning French did at Lowood, but purely because it will be of service to him. St. John's selfish motives for making such a request are all the more disturbing when one realizes (as Jane at the time does not) that he is getting her to learn Hindustani under false pretenses, so that she can be of even greater service to him as his missionary wife. Teaching Jane to speak and read another language, then, is the first step in preparing her to interpret and write her life differently; having gained possession of her history, St. John seems bent on possessing her future as well.

St. John's tutelage is notably effective in training Jane for such self-sacrifice. Responding to a pedagogical style that is "very patient, very forbearing, and yet . . . exacting," Jane finds that "he acquired a certain influence over me that took away my liberty of mind" (508). The fact that St. John gains this command over Jane in his capacity of language teacher suggests a correlation in this text between self-possession and the way one acquires verbal skills. Jane's earlier experience in learning foreign languages had not included such tutelage. Madame Pierrot presumably taught French to Jane at Lowood, but those lessons are not depicted in the narrative, which emphasizes Jane's increased self-possession in learning to say "I am" and "I was" instead. At Marsh End, the women study German either collaboratively, as we see in the first scene Jane observes through the kitchen window, or independently, as Jane is doing when St. John requests that she give up that pursuit. But when St. John assumes the responsibility for teaching Jane how to read and to speak, then learning a language means relinquishing all self-authority.[12] St. John's nearly absolute control of Jane in his role as language teacher is clearly illustrated by the scene in which memories of her past life with Rochester interrupt her daily lesson:

> St. John called me to his side to read; in attempting to do this my voice failed me: words were lost in sobs. . . . My companion expressed no surprise at this emotion, nor did he question me as to its cause; he only said:—
>
> "We will wait a few minutes, Jane, till you are more composed." And while I smothered the paroxysm with all haste, he sat calm and patient, leaning on his desk

and looking like a physician watching with the eye of science an expected and fully-understood crisis in a patient's malady.

(511)

What follows, of course, is his proposal of marriage, which Jane anticipates as a "fatal word" and which St. John presents as that which her heart cannot speak. This time he refuses to respect her desire for silence and tells her what she must, in his opinion, truly feel:

"And what does *your* heart say?" demanded St. John.

"My heart is mute,—my heart is mute," I answered, struck and thrilled.

"Then I must speak for it," continued the deep, relentless voice. "Jane, come with me to India: come as my help-meet and fellow-labourer."

The glen and sky spun round: the hills heaved! It was as if I had heard a summons from Heaven—as if a visionary messenger, like him of Macedonia, had enounced, "Come over and help us!"

(513-14)

Here St. John clearly exceeds his legitimate authority as a teacher of language, attempting to put words not merely in his pupil's mouth but in her very heart. Powerfully attracted by the call that she has been told is from her inner being, Jane nevertheless manages to recognize her inability to be a recipient of its message: "I was no apostle,—I could not *behold* the herald,—I could not *receive his call*" (emphasis added). Unable to read the text that St. John has attempted to inscribe on her heart, and unable to understand the voice he has projected there, Jane recognizes her incomprehension and refuses to be tutored in a language that belies her own sense of self-identity.

A patient yet coercive and despotic man, St. John later tries again to force Jane's acquiescence, this time by exerting his rhetorical and hermeneutic skills to get her to understand her own character and behavior differently. Reading the Bible in a voice "at once so sweet and full," he turns his eyes on Jane as he reads Revelation 21:8: "'The fearful, the unbelieving . . . shall have their part in the lake which burneth with fire and brimstone, which is the second death'" (532). Jane is clearly aware of St. John's intent to make her see rejecting him as rejecting God's will, and we as readers can hardly fail to note the similarity between the "fate St. John feared for [her]" and Mr. Brocklehurst's earlier prognostication that, as a "naughty little girl," she is bound for "a pit full of fire . . . to be burning there for ever" (34). In neither case is Jane seriously dismayed by the threat of hell, but, as she was earlier silenced by Brocklehurst's speech, so is she now moved to silent awe by St. John's eloquence. At this moment he renews his marriage offer in words "spoken earnestly, mildly" and in a "sublime" manner calculated to "subdue and rule" (534).

Jane is "tempted to cease struggling with him—to rush down the torrent of his will into the gulf of his existence, and there lose [her] own." She stands "motionless under [her] hierophant's touch," almost prepared to accept him as her interpreter and expounder of life's sacred mysteries, including the most important of all, that of her identity. "Contend[ing] with . . . inward dimness of vision" (535), Jane silently pleads for a sign she may read for herself and physically anticipates the most important interpretive experience in her life: supernaturally alert to signification, her "senses . . . [are] summoned, and forced to wake. They rose expectant: eye and ear waited" (536). The sign she receives, of course, is her own name, which she instantly and correctly interprets as a call back to the life she must create, live, and tell independent of St. John's tutelage.

Reading the world perceptively in this most crucial moment, Jane is suddenly able to reverse the political dynamics of her conversation with St. John. "It was *my* turn to assume ascendancy," she tells us. "*My* powers were in play, and in force." Having the "energy to command," she forbids even "question or remark" from her perplexed interlocutor, thus silencing the importunities that had nearly engulfed her in a compelling tide of rhetoric. Threatened with annihilation, Jane has willed into expression an audible sign of her own existence; in responding to that sign she frees herself from St. John's eloquence and reclaims the storyteller's right to narrate her own story.

Like the preceding sections, the final section of *Jane Eyre* opens with juxtaposed scenes of reading and storytelling that comment on the protagonist's growth as an interpreter and narrator of her own life. Returning to Thornfield in a mood of ardent hopefulness, Jane takes "strange delight" in imagining the anticipated experience of seeing Rochester's home again. She decides that her "first view of it shall be in front . . . where its bold battlements will strike the eye nobly at once, and where I can single out my master's very window: perhaps he will be standing at it" (541). Through this fantasy, she formulates a particularly satisfying reading of the scene she expects to see and prepares herself for an interpretive experience that will gratify the expectations of the narrative she has started to tell herself. Relishing in advance the moment of viewing Thornfield again, she cautiously hides behind a pillar to "peep . . . at the full front of the mansion" (542). Her behavior is suggestively voyeuristic, of course, as her hope of seeing Rochester in his bedroom window implies and as the narrator's extended analogy of the lover spying on his sleeping mistress further confirms.

But the text that opens itself for her observation is, in Barthes' terms, no text of pleasure satisfying the reader's desire (1975, 14). Seeing the charred ruins of Thornfield forces Jane out of voyeuristic peeping for her own pleasure into "a protracted, hardy gaze" that seeks to understand the significance of an apparently incomprehensible text. The more obvious meaning of the scene is immediately evident: "The grim blackness of the stones told by what fate the Hall had fallen—by conflagration." But the question of larger significance remains: "What story belonged to this disaster?" Jane asks. At this point, for Jane there is no answer to that "dreadful question . . . not even dumb sign, mute token" (543).

Jane's inability to discover a "sign" or "token" by which to interpret this scene and thus formulate the "story [that] belonged" to it is reminiscent of the incomprehension she had earlier experienced in gazing through the kitchen window at Moor-House. In both cases, Jane confronts a text that is observable but not readable, one that presents phenomena that can be noted and reported but not interpreted. For Jane at least, there are no "signs" in this text of the ruined Thornfield, only a mystery that invites and simultaneously defies interpretation. As in the Moor-House scene, Jane refrains from drawing a reading from her view of Thornfield and instead admits her incomprehension, thereby demonstrating her maturity as a reader who can abandon those false expectations one sometimes brings to an interpretive experience. Conscientiously noting the "spectacle of desolation" that reality has substituted for her fantasized spectacle of delight, she is "prepared . . . in a measure for a tale of misery" (544) that she must now hear from another person. Recognizing that she cannot fully comprehend this text, she also acknowledges that she cannot tell its story—or place it within the text of her own story—until she has heard the tale from a legitimately authoritative narrator.

She turns, therefore, to the innkeeper of the Rochester Arms, converting herself into an audience and skillfully eliciting from him the story she needs to know. Such conversion has its risks, of course, since in becoming an audience, Jane has in the past often lost interpretive control over her own identity. Indeed, as she listens to the host's account, she "fear[s] . . . to hear [her] own story" (545) distorted from the point of view of local gossip, and she repeatedly urges him to focus instead on the most recent episode in Rochester's history: "You shall tell me this part of the story [Rochester's engagement to Jane] another time, . . . but now I have a particular reason for wishing to hear all about the fire" (546). The innkeeper's portrayal of Jane is, in fact, quite different from the sympathetic view she has created in her own narrative; he contemptuously describes her as "that midge of a governess' and wishes she "had been sunk in the sea before she came to Thornfield Hall" (547). But in this storytelling situation Jane is not threatened, and only mildly discomfited, by the unflattering account of herself she is forced to hear.

Despite the fact that she has relinquished her privileged position as storyteller and assumed the normally less powerful role of listener, Jane is clearly in control of the narrative, which is only ostensibly the innkeeper's to tell. *She* asks the questions that prompt his story and "recall him to the main fact[s]" she needs to know (545). *She* provides the answer to at least one of the tale's mysteries when she suggests that Bertha may have set Thornfield on fire, and the host is quick to acknowledge her interpretive authority: "You've hit it, ma'am: it's quite certain that it was her" (546). Jane is not, in this case, the mute and helpless listener she has often been in the past but rather a vocal audience whose responses evoke, shape, and give significance to the story the landlord tells. While she initially does not possess the facts of the tale—these the innkeeper must provide—she establishes the plot by making specific inquiries and by choosing the topics he is to cover. (For example, he describes the fire in great detail because that is what she demands to hear, and she forces him to give a truncated account of her relationship with Rochester even though he is clearly interested in that topic.)

Jane also determines his story's closure, abruptly cutting it short when she learns that Rochester is still alive and in England. In full command of "the story that belonged to . . . the spectacle of desolation" (543-44) she had earlier viewed with incomprehension, Jane now knows how the burning of Thornfield fits into her own life story. She therefore departs for Ferndean with full confidence in her skill to incorporate Rochester's tragic "tale of misery" into the larger comic history of her own experience.

These final scenes of reading and storytelling thus show Jane as a skilled explicator of her own experience. Secure in her powers, she returns to Rochester knowing that *she* will now have the authority to interpret and compose the life they will share. His loss of power in this respect, metaphorically signaled by the loss of eye and hand, is further emphasized by the scenes in which she closely observes him without his knowledge of her presence and by his repeated references to the power her voice has over him. Three times in chapter 37, she takes advantage of his sightlessness to study leisurely his appearance and read his mood. By not signaling her presence on such occasions (and especially by withholding her identity when they meet again for the first time), she reverses the dynamics of the fortune-telling scene and of the scene with St. John by the Moor-House window, now being the surreptitious observer as she had earlier been the object of surreptitious observation.

Rochester now reverses his opinion that listening is Jane's "forte" and repeatedly asks her to "speak again." In the last scenes of the novel he has little to tell her of his own experience and instead requests to hear her story, acknowledging that "all the melody on earth is concentrated in my Jane's tongue to my ear" (562). Engaged to a man who is blind to the reality around him and who is spellbound by his lover's voice, Jane is rewarded at the end of the narrative with a dependent and ardently grateful audience. She has, indeed, finally managed to captivate a listener by her power to read and to re-create expressively the world she inhabits.[13]

Jane's success in these final scenes is, as some critics have previously noted in other contexts, triumphant almost with a vengeance. Although she later claims that she is "bone of [Rochester's] bone, and flesh of his flesh" and that "to talk to each other is but a more animated and an audible thinking" (576), this depiction of egalitarian mutuality is not borne out by the final chapters, which clearly show Jane in control of their conversations much as she had been in control of the landlord's narrative. She apparently uses her power beneficently (for example, she provokes Rochester's jealousy by giving a teasing account of St. John in order "to make [her lover] less sad" [568]), and Bodenheimer may be partly correct when she says that Jane employs the art of storytelling for the "amusement, relief, and animation of her audience" (1980, 161).

But like most of the other characters in this novel, Jane seems more than willing to sacrifice truth in order to maintain power in the storytelling situation. She withholds, for example, the story that she might tell Rochester to corroborate his own account of their telepathic communication ostensibly because her "tale would be such as must necessarily make a profound impression on the mind of [her] hearer," who is already "too prone to gloom" (573). Her comment that this part of their experience "struck [her] as too awful and inexplicable to be communicated or discussed" suggests another, less selfless explanation for her reticence, however. Because she cannot decipher these "inexplicable" episodes in their life stories, she "[keeps] these things [to herself], . . . and ponder[s] them in [her] heart," since to share them with Rochester would be to admit her inability to exert interpretive control over a part of her experience and thus invite him to reclaim the hermeneutic command he once held over her.

In a world where the storytelling situation is usually political, it is safer, apparently, to keep secret possession of incomprehensible texts than to encourage readings that might appropriate such mystery to a story of someone else's creation. Jane will employ her art to soothe Rochester as David had comforted Saul, and she will tell stories to amuse him as Scheherazade had entertained Schahriah (561), but she will never allow him to participate fully in the interpretive and expressive acts by which she creates her life and identity. Like David, she uses her voice to wrest power from her brooding Saul, ultimately gaining the kingdom that had formerly been at his command. And like Scheherazade, she lives by her power to enthrall her audience in stories of her own creation.

DISARMING THE WILLING READER

The motif of reading and storytelling as it is used within Jane's narrative thus implies that the interpretive and expressive faculties requisite to reading and storytelling are skills by which one creates and preserves one's self. These skills allow one to respond to experience in a way that constructively validates and actualizes the self. Furthermore, Jane's narrative presents this process of self-actualization through reading and storytelling as political in nature: nearly all of Jane's attempts to interpret her experience and tell her story involve a struggle for the power to assert her own reading against those fictions that others would narrate about her. As an analogue for the process of self-definition and self-preservation, the relationship of storyteller-text-audience is one fraught with both risk and potential for the self.

That Brontë should see the storytelling situation as a metaphor for the process of self-definition is natural: throughout her childhood and adolescence, no experience was more central to her sense of self than the storytelling that engaged her and her siblings. That she should see storytelling as intensely political is also understandable, given the rivalry among the Brontë children and the contentiousness of the literary scene they saw depicted in *Blackwood's* and elsewhere. What is surprising about *Jane Eyre* is that while Brontë seems very serious about the dangers and rewards of storytelling as she explores that issue within Jane's narrative, she seems to undermine that concern through narrative strategies that draw attention away from the storytelling situation in which she has engaged us. Unlike *The Professor,* which obtrusively establishes a fictional storytelling situation in the first chapter, and unlike *Shirley,* which begins with the narrator's chastising her hapless narratees, *Jane Eyre* opens quietly, with a remark that effectively closes the distance between the storyteller and her audience: "There was no possibility of taking a walk that day" (3). The reference to "that day" suggests our prior familiarity with Jane and establishes a relationship of sympathy that makes it difficult to remember that, as an intradiegetic narrator, Jane cannot really address us or even assume our existence. Looking back over the novel, one thus has the sense that by effacing the situation of reception in *Jane Eyre,* Brontë has not meant us well. From the outset, we are assigned a role that prevents us from adopting the kind of self-preserving caution that Jane herself learns to employ.[14]

In her discussion of *Jane Eyre*'s narrative method, Janet Freeman notes that critics have been "nearly unanimous" (1984, 683) in their opinion that the vision in the novel is exclusively single, that we are carried away by the power of Jane's story and do not, in Martin's words, "[peer] over [the narrator's] shoulder in order to form our own opinions" (1966, 59). The critical consensus is that we do not attempt to assert our own reading in opposition to, or correction of, that of the storytelling narrator. In support of this claim, Freeman cites Margaret Blom, Virginia Woolf, Lord David Cecil, G. Armour Craig, Margot Peters, and Helene Moglen; she might have added to her list the names of Charles Burkhart, Robert Bernard Martin, and the numerous contemporary reviewers who, like Margaret Oliphant, felt "swept on in the current" of a narrative that gives one "not a moment's pause to be critical" (1855, 559).

While I believe that this account of Brontë's narrative method is not entirely accurate, the responses of such readers are, in fact, at least partially warranted by narrative strategies that blunt our consciousness of ourselves as readers and make us forgetful of the storyteller as an individual quite other than ourselves. For example, directly addressing the reader normally compels us to acknowledge our role as narrative recipient; but these addresses are minimal in the early chapters of *Jane Eyre,* though they increase dramatically near the end of the novel, as if Brontë were attempting to remind us of a situation that she had earlier encouraged us to ignore. The first of these direct addresses (19) turns out to have the reverse effect that invocations of the audience usually have: it strengthens our alliance with Jane because the audience invoked is one that we cannot possibly join. In speaking directly to Mrs. Reed, the narrator forces our disaffiliation from this fictive audience and increases our tendency to identify with the narrator instead. Casting Mrs. Reed in the double role of antagonist and reader certainly corroborates the view of storytelling given within Jane's narrative; but while it serves to underline the adversarial relationship between the narrator and one of her narratees, it also has the effect of apparently exempting us, the implied readers, from such antagonism. Since in speaking to Mrs. Reed, Jane is clearly addressing an audience other than, and obviously unlike, ourselves, we necessarily define our own relationship with the storyteller quite differently. It is possible, however, that in identifying with the storyteller we have also injudiciously given up our separate identity as the storyteller's audience.

This mode of reading is further encouraged in the early chapters of *Jane Eyre* by narrative strategies that focus our attention so exclusively on the experience of the developing protagonist that we are prevented from thinking about the storytelling situation in which that experience is being recounted.[15] Rhetorical questions, which in *Shirley* are repeatedly posed *by the narrator* to invite the reader's interpretive participation in the unfolding narrative, are here given as questions that pass through the mind of the acting *protagonist.* Called suddenly to

the breakfast room upon Mr. Brocklehurst's arrival at Gateshead, little Jane ponders the meaning of this unexpected summons: "Who could want me? . . . What should I see besides Aunt Reed in the apartment?" (32-33). Such questions clearly prompt us to share the *protagonist's* hermeneutic struggles and heighten the narrative's suspense since we must see things from little Jane's limited perspective. But by engrossing us in the experience of the younger Jane, they prevent us from concentrating on the storyteller herself. Admittedly, the mature narrator does occasionally appear in these early chapters, as when she breaks her narrative to comment that "now, at the distance of—I will not say how many years, I see it [the cause of her suffering] clearly" (13). But as Jerome Beaty has pointed out, the presence of this adult narrator in the Gateshead section is so inobtrusive that most readers do not even take notice of her (1984, 185); we become so thoroughly absorbed in the narrator's past that we fail to pay attention to the narrative present in which we listen to the storyteller's tale.

Brontë further ensures our emotional engagement in young Jane's experience and prevents us from focusing on the narrating instance by withholding information about Jane's past until the moment in her narrative at which the heroine herself gained such information. Thus we know almost nothing about Jane's family, other than the Reeds, until St. John recounts that part of her history to her late in the novel. What little we do know early on, we learn not directly from the narrator but from little Jane's musings in the red room about her dead uncle and from the account of her parents that she overhears in the Gateshead nursery.

Though this manner of reporting past events strikes Earl Knies as "thoroughly natural" (1969, 105-6), I would submit that a good deal of artistry is actually being employed when a storyteller withholds such information from her audience. Such restraint not only heightens the reader's pleasure by creating suspense and increasing the opportunity for vicarious experience, it also restricts our ability to decipher the phenomenal world that the protagonist herself is struggling to interpret. When Jane dismisses Bertha's ominous laughter as inconsequential, for example, we remain confined to the younger woman's misreading because the older narrator offers no commentary that would warrant a different interpretation of this event in spite of the fact that she has the knowledge to correct our misunderstanding. We thus experience Jane's recounted life in much the same way that she herself experienced it; we are forced to participate in her misreadings as she struggles toward the literary competence that will constitute her mature identity. By limiting our knowledge about the protagonist's past to what she herself knows at that point in the story, and by largely confining us to her sometimes faulty understanding of her environment, the storyteller remains in full command of the narrative and interpretive functions that make up the storytelling experience. It is not simply that "the writer . . . makes us see what she sees," as Virginia Woolf claimed (1925, 156), but that the storyteller prevents us from seeing anything except what she wants us to see.

Because Brontë is so successful in focusing our attention on her protagonist rather than on her narrator in these early chapters, we experience the later evocations of the narrating situation as problematic and disruptive. Accustomed to being immersed in the action of Jane's past, we feel discomfited when she makes comments that refer to the narrative present and to our respective roles as reader and storyteller. Such references highlight the differences between the mature, narrating Jane and her younger self and also somewhat rudely check our by now habitual tendency to identify with her. When Jane suggests that "perhaps you think I had forgotten Mr. Rochester, reader" (509), we feel somewhat perplexed because, in obediently playing the role that the narrative has assigned to us, we have not been in the habit of thinking about Jane critically; we have been more than content simply to participate in her past experience. Similarly, when Jane breaks the action of her narrative to give a two-page description of the guests at Thornfield and then tells us that we "are not to suppose . . . that Adèle has all this time been sitting motionless" at her feet (216), we may well feel bemused since the suggestion implies a tendency on our part to take a more active role in creating the narrative than we have elsewhere been encouraged to do.

Yet given Brontë's practice in the preceding tales, including *The Professor,* of emphasizing the narrating-receiving situation, we might question whether she wholly intended that our absorption in the protagonist's experience be so complete. Clearly this was not her intent in *Shirley,* where the storytelling situation is aggressively obtruded upon our notice, nor does it seem to be the case in *Villette,* which returns to the juvenile practice of employing a fallible and not entirely likable first-person narrator. Perhaps the narrative elements that appear intrusive in *Jane Eyre* are actually more characteristic of Brontë's method than are those strategies by which she gains our uncritical affiliation with the heroine of that novel. If this is so, then we must reverse the question as it has usually been posed and ask not why she intrudes upon our vicarious experience of Jane's life with allusions to a present, and apparently somewhat problematic, narrating instance, but why she so effectively keeps that problematic storytelling situation under cover.

Expressing a minority view, Craik, Maynard, and Beaty have all seen the tendency to conflate the novel's narrative levels as "a temptation that must be resisted" because to do so brings us "much too near the emotional state Jane Eyre herself [eventually] rejects" (Craik 1968,

76, 73). It not only prevents us from hearing "the cautionary voice of the older Jane . . . alerting us to the fallacy of young Jane's perceptions of the nature of reality" (Beaty 1984, 169), it also keeps us unaware of the "process of art that makes the central subject [of *Jane Eyre*] Jane, not, as in an actual first-person memoir, Jane's life and opinions as seen by herself" (Maynard 1984, 99). It keeps us from seeing Jane, the storyteller, as a conscious artist in control of *her* audience and from recognizing the presence of the implied author, that persona Brontë identified as Currer Bell, as the creative force manipulating her narrator from behind the scenes.

If readers wholeheartedly identify with a heroine whom they do not adequately distinguish from either her older narrating self or from the implied author of the novel (and both current and past responses to *Jane Eyre* suggest that they often do), then such readers also lose sight of their own place as the narrative's recipients. Absorbed in the protagonist's experience, we forget that our role is to respond creatively, perhaps even critically, to the story we are hearing and to take an active part in the interpretive experience that the storytelling situation affords.

And yet, perhaps this is precisely the effect that the two storytellers of *Jane Eyre* intend. Given the narrator's struggles to wrest from others the authority to exert interpretive and expressive control over her own identity, we should expect her to employ narrative strategies, both draconian and shrewd, to guard that authority from her potentially meddlesome readers. By creating the appearance of solidarity between herself and her audience, Jane effectively disarms them and stays in full command of the storytelling that constitutes her actualized self. Similarly, the narrative methods adopted in *Jane Eyre* allow the implied author, Currer Bell, to take command of the implied audience Brontë had envisioned for this novel by pandering (as she saw it) to their taste for "passion, stimulus, and melodrama" (*Shirley,* 7). Envisioning an image of herself as a storyteller who could gratify the audience who had looked so coldly on *The Professor,* Brontë was finally able to captivate the reading public. Like Jane, she had learned to exert power over others in the storytelling situation.

Author, narrator, and protagonist of *Jane Eyre* all know that the literary experience is political and that, to retain interpretive and expressive control over one's world, one must sometimes sacrifice truth for power. When one considers the odds against which Charlotte Brontë struggled from obscurity into literary fame with the publication of *Jane Eyre,* then this view of storytelling as an intensely political struggle for self-identity seems perfectly apt. When one reads her derisive remarks about her first published novel, both in the preface to *The Professor* and in the opening pages of the original manuscript of *Shirley,* one senses Brontë's unease about having gratified her readers' "preference for the . . . wonderful" and having thus compromised her own commitment to a storytelling situation in which truth might emerge from a more creative interaction among its participants. Invocations of the audience in *Jane Eyre,* which disrupt its more pervasive mode of reader passivity, are surely expressions of Brontë's repressed desire to engage her audience rather than merely hold us in thrall. Having made her way into the literary marketplace by means she did not entirely approve of, Brontë devoted herself in her next two novels to a more honest consideration of the issue she largely evades in *Jane Eyre.* Having gained power, she was prepared to write about truth.

Notes

1. See, for example, Craik (1968, 122) and Virginia Woolf's more famous complaint in *A Room of One's Own* (1929, 72-73).

2. See, for example, Monod (1971).

3. Considering the reading motif in *Jane Eyre* in relation to the religious and secular texts available to Brontë, Peterson (1986) provides a detailed discussion of Jane as a reading protagonist and offers more limited commentary on Jane as a narrator. Her argument includes a number of points I make in the first part of this chapter but differs significantly in its assessment of Brontë's narrative method. Peterson's claim that Jane's relationship with the reader is one of implicit trust and sympathetic engagement seems based on an uncritical assumption of equivalence between implied author and narrator and between implied reader and narratee. Furthermore, it does not sufficiently account for the metadiegetic depictions of reading and storytelling as political and potentially threatening activities. For additional discussions of this motif, see Hennelly (1984) on reading and Bodenheimer (1980) on storytelling in *Jane Eyre.*

4. See, for example, Martin (1966, 70, 86) and Hennelly (1984, 696).

5. Pauline Nestor also notes that *Jane Eyre* demonstrates "in its opening pages the dangerous power of reading" but locates the source of that power with Jane herself, who has committed the "crime" (in John's view) of taking "his" books and thus gaining access to "knowledge [which] gives power" (1987, 51-52).

6. For a full discussion of Jane as a Scheherazade figure, see Workman, who persuasively demonstrates that Brontë's heroine, like her literary predecessor, "is empowered . . . through her role as narrator. By being a storyteller, she overcomes all the limitations of her personhood . . . [and] in-

verts power relationships by her ability to speak" (1988, 183-85).

7. Nestor claims that reading Goldsmith allows Jane to place "her suffering in an historical context" and thus gain the control over her experience that understanding affords (51-52), but a child of Jane's age would hardly have the grasp of historical, gender, and socioeconomic issues that such a claim implies. Instead, I believe she uses the "parallels" between her case and that of "any other rebel slave" (*Jane Eyre,* 9) simply as an effective means of reinforcing her not inaccurate view of herself as oppressed and isolated in the Reed household.

8. This brief reference to "the genre to which *Jane Eyre* belongs" admittedly oversimplifies a complex issue, which Jerome Beaty addresses more thoroughly in his article "*Jane Eyre* and Genre" (1977). In allying *Jane Eyre* with the popular governess stories of the day, Beaty essentially supports the point I am making here since this cautionary genre emphasizes the central protagonist's development from a limited and faulty perspective to that of a wiser maturity.

9. The mutuality of the literary experience as depicted in this scene is rare in *Jane Eyre* and only possible, apparently, among women. A similar situation is depicted in chapter 28, when Jane overhears Mary and Diana translating German together. In both cases, Jane is temporarily allowed to be a part of the experience such literate women share (when Miss Temple invites her to tell her story and for the brief period during which Jane studies German with the Rivers sisters), but in both cases her peripheral position in the group is clearly emphasized: as little Jane listens in awed silence to Helen and Miss Temple, so she uncomprehendingly listens to Mary and Diana from *outside* the Moor-House window. The fact that Brontë does not allow Jane to remain part of a harmoniously collaborative literary experience among women—even removing her in the latter case from Mary and Diana's company to put her under the harsh tutelage of St. John—suggests her desire to explore the political contentiousness of the storytelling situation, particularly as it serves to comment analogically on sexual politics.

10. Hennelly also uses the term *shadowbox* in reference to this scene and points out that when the reader suddenly becomes aware of St. John's presence (at the same moment that Jane does), then the reader also becomes, like Jane, "entrapped . . . in the . . . shadowbox" of her narrative (1984, 698). His reading is similar to mine but emphasizes at this point in his argument an identi-

fication of reader and protagonist that I discuss as problematic in the final section of this chapter.

11. Martin makes a similar point in a brief note (1966, 86).

12. Jane's relationship to St. John Rivers points to a need for modifying Sadoff's otherwise persuasive claim that "language acquisition and female self-mastery . . . appear linked in Brontë's narrative project with the presence of a punishing and approving master" (1982, 164). In the case of St. John, this "punishing and approving" language master does not facilitate female self-mastery but rather attempts to master the female self.

13. My reading of the conclusion of *Jane Eyre* is somewhat similar to those given by the two other critics centrally concerned with Jane as a storyteller (Bodenheimer 1980) or speaker (Freeman 1984). However, viewing *Jane Eyre* within the broader context of Brontë's entire canon, including the juvenilia, I see Jane's captivity of her audience as more problematic than they do.

14. Chambers has persuasively argued that allusions to storytelling, reading, interpreting, and so on embedded within a narrative serve as either models or antimodels of the text in question, thus providing a "clue to the situational model the text is producing" (1984, 34). If such is the case, then Jane's experience as a reader/storyteller should make us wary of being "seduced" (the term is Chambers') by a narrative that effaces the political nature of the storytelling experience, a nature that embedded details have emphatically highlighted.

15. Lanser observes that this is true of many narratives in which the narrator is a character within the described fictional realm: "In many homodiegetic texts the discourse is dominated not so much by the I-as-narrator as by the younger I-character, and nothing may be said about the narratee. In fact, homodiegetic narration may present an I-character who, while ostensibly doubling as a narrator, inhabits a context that does not provide for the acknowledgment of narrative activity" (1981, 176).

References

PRIMARY TEXTS

"*Ashworth:* An Unfinished Novel by Charlotte Brontë." Edited by Melodie Monahan. *Studies in Philology* 80 (1983): 1-133.

The Brontës: Their Lives, Friendships, and Correspondence. 4 vols. Edited by Thomas James Wise and John Alexander Symington. The Shakespeare Head Brontë. Oxford: Basil Blackwell, 1932.

An Edition of the Early Writings of Charlotte Brontë. Vol. 1: *The Glass Town Saga, 1826-1832.* Edited by Christine Alexander. Oxford: Basil Blackwell, 1987.

Five Novelettes: Passing Events, Julia, Mina Laury, Captain Henry Hastings, Caroline Vernon. Edited by Winifred Gérin. London: Folio Press, 1971.

Jane Eyre. Edited by Jane Jack and Margaret Smith. Oxford: Clarendon, 1969.

The Miscellaneous and Unpublished Writings of Charlotte and Patrick Branwell Brontë. 2 vols. Edited by Thomas James Wise and John Alexander Symington. The Shakespeare Head Brontë. Oxford: Basil Blackwell, 1936 and 1938.

The Professor. Edited by Margaret Smith and Herbert Rosengarten. Oxford: Clarendon, 1987.

Shirley. Edited by Herbert Rosengarten and Margaret Smith. Oxford: Clarendon, 1979.

The Spell, An Extravaganza: An Unpublished Novel by Charlotte Brontë. Edited by George Edwin MacLean. Oxford: Oxford University Press, 1931.

Villette. Edited by Herbert Rosengarten and Margaret Smith. Oxford: Clarendon, 1984.

SECONDARY TEXTS

Barthes, Roland. *The Pleasure of the Text.* Tranlsated by Richard Miller. New York: Hill and Wang, 1975.

Beaty, Jerome. "*Jane Eyre* and Genre." *Genre* 10 (1977): 619-54.

———. "Jane Eyre at Gateshead: Mixed Signals in the Text and Context." In *Victorian Literature and Society: Essays Presented to Richard D. Altick,* edited by James R. Kincaid and Albert J. Kuhn. Columbus: Ohio State University Press, 1984.

Bodenheimer, Rosemarte. "Jane Eyre in Search of Her Story." *Papers on Language and Literature* 16 (1980): 155-68.

Chambers, Ross. *Story and Situation: Narrative Seduction and the Power of Fiction.* Theory and History of Literature 12. Minneapolis: University of Minnesota Press, 1984.

Craik, W. A. *The Brontë Novels.* London: Methuen, 1968.

Freeman, Janet. "Speech and Silence in *Jane Eyre.*" *SEL* 24 (1984): 683-700.

Hennelly, Mark M., Jr. "*Jane Eyre*'s Reading Lesson." *ELH* 51 (1984): 693-717.

Lanser, Susan Sniader. *The Narrative Act: Point of View in Prose Fiction.* Princeton: Princeton University Press, 1981.

Martin, Robert Bernard. *Charlotte Brontë's Novels: The Accents of Persuasion.* New York: Norton, 1966.

Monod, Sylvère. "Charlotte Brontë and the Thirty 'Readers' of *Jane Eyre.*" In *Jane Eyre: An Authoritative Text, Backgrounds, Criticism,* edited by Richard J. Dunn. New York: Norton, 1971.

Nestor, Pauline. *Charlotte Brontë.* Women Writers. Totowa, N.J.: Barnes and Noble, 1987.

Peterson, Carla L. "*Jane Eyre* and *David Copperfield*: Nature and Providence." In *The Determined Reader: Gender and Culture in the Novel from Napoleon to Victoria.* New Brunswick, N.J.: Rutgers University Press, 1986.

Workman, Nancy V. "Scheherazade at Thornfield: Mythic Elements in *Jane Eyre.*" *Essays in Literature* 15 (1988): 177-92.

Jerome Beaty (essay date January 1996)

SOURCE: Beaty, Jerome. "*Jane Eyre* Cubed: The Three Dimensions of the Text." *Narrative* 4, no. 1 (January 1996): 74-92.

[*In the following essay, Beaty examines the narrative structure, rhetoric, and ontology of the novel.*]

When we finish reading *Jane Eyre,* looking back, what do we (what should we) see? The novel that begins with ten year-old Jane Eyre on a cold, rainy November afternoon glad that she will not have to take a walk that day, ends with St. John Rivers, "chosen and faithful," writing from India, near death and praying for the quick approach of "Lord Jesus." The novel that began with rebellion ends with martyrdom. The story of the proud, saucy, self-reliant orphan Jane Eyre ends with the chastened, religious, privileged and satisfied wife and mother Jane Rochester.

Reading backward from the certainty of Rochester's conversion, the supernatural nature of Jane's having heard across a vast distance Rochester calling her when she asked for a sign, back to the leading light in the Rivers' window when Jane asked Providence for guidance, farther back to the twisting chestnut tree on the hitherto calm night of Rochester's proposal, through the still ambiguous instances of fairies dropping advice on Jane's pillow and the ambiguously discounted ghostly light in the red-room, we can at last see clearly the nature of the universe according to the narrator, Jane Rochester, and wonder how we, like the younger Jane, could have missed the signs for so long.

The strategy of serial disclosure is superbly and significantly appropriate for the narrative, rhetoric, and ontology of *Jane Eyre.* It greatly enhances the suspense and justifies the very gradual release of the secrets of the plot and outcome as fitting and natural. The reader is surprised by sin, led to recognize that identifying with the proudly self-reliant young Jane has been not only a misperception but a moral lapse. The providentialist ontology is insinuated into the narrative and through the narrative cumulatively and precisely defines its own nature and further justifies the strategic reticence.

Jane's Providence is not fate and her deliverance not predetermined. Mrs. Sherwood's *Caroline Mordaunt, or The Governess* (1835), an earlier providentialist, first-person governess novel[1], using an entirely different but appropriate narrative strategy begins with the narrator's announcement that she has been providentially guided, and, through no deeds of her own but "through the merits and death of my Divine Redeemer" (203 [this is first page of the novel]), has been chosen to enter heaven. Since Caroline, and readers who had been similarly chosen, have been saved from the beginning of time, there is no rhetorical or ontological reason for withholding the "truth." In Brontë's providentialism, however, the individual has free will, is responsible for seeking and perceiving providential leadings and warnings, for choosing to follow such signs, and is thus responsible for his or her own salvation. Jane must acknowledge God's Providence, but she must learn to see and interpret events for herself, stand on her principles, use her reason, hearken to her conscience and must herself choose to follow the leadings and heed the warnings. Since her fate is undetermined, the narrative pattern is thus appropriately one of a journey toward enlightenment and deliverance punctuated with crises and consequent choices. The reader, to participate experientially in her story (and to understand his or her own life in a providential, contingent cosmos), must therefore be kept in the dark just as Jane is.

Read as a self-consuming artifact, the world of *Jane Eyre* is revealed as patently providential to authorial readers[2] at the end of the novel now in the position of author, or at least mature narrator, looking back over the novel as a spatial, closed and permanent structure, the narrative and ontological misleadings and misunderstandings dismissed. Even the cause and occasion of the narrating follow from the providential vision: beneficiaries of providential deliverance are obligated to record their experiences to secure their memory and to instruct and inspire others (Hunter 71).

After the twists and shifts of the plot, the confusing multiplicity of generic signals, the uncertainty of the moral and ontological grounding of the fictional world, there is at last a sense of narrative and thematic unity and of significant and comforting closure. As a finalized, spatial and monologic construct re-viewed from the vantage point of the end, then, the authorial intention seems incontrovertible: *Jane Eyre* is a Providential novel and its structure and strategies are designed to that end.

The strategy of serial disclosure, no matter how appropriate, especially when it is shrewd and subtle, has its own risks, however: it is liable to underestimate the continuous experiential engagement of the reader with the text and the obliterative power of "primacy." In defining the signifying power of the early portions of novels, Meier Sternberg cites a psychological experiment in which blocks of character description of identical length but opposite meaning were offered subjects in their entirety but in different order: "Due to the successive order of presentation, the first block was read with an open mind, while the interpretation of the second—in itself as weighty—was decisively conditioned and colored by the anterior, homogeneous primacy effect; the leading block established a perceptual set, serving as a frame of reference to which the subsequent information was subordinated as far as possible" (94). More surprisingly, the experiment revealed that as a rule not only did that which was presented first determine the interpretation but despite explicit instructions to respond in terms of the passage as a whole, "the overwhelming majority of subjects did not even notice the glaring incompatibility of the information contained in the two successive segments" (94).

Brontë's strategy of serial disclosure and the power of primacy, then, enable readers not only to fail to anticipate (much less desire) the ultimately disclosed providentialism and its socializing, subduing consequences but to be "blind" to it. For a good many readers then and now Jane Eyre is first and foremost the unloved, abused but independent, self-assertive and rebellious child at Gateshead and Lowood. Her restless adventurousness, her thirst for experience at eighteen when she chooses to leave Lowood; her passion and self-reliance at Thornfield, where she falls in love, is loved and betrayed; her refusal to sacrifice herself even to God's work in the East, and her defiant return to the man she loved and loves, readily reinforce, elaborate, and deepen that image and the consequent interpretation of the novel as valorizing rebellion, independence, self-assertiveness.

Brontë does provide from fairly early on in the novel numerous though brief and occasional "anticipatory cautions" (Sternberg 129ff.)[3] about Jane's views and behavior, chiefly in the monologic and "intrusive" voice of the mature narrator, but not numerous or weighty enough to balance, much less counteract the "deep emotional commitment" into which many readers have been "lured" (Sternberg 129), by the power of the opening. There are two somewhat more extensive descriptions of a quite different Jane, one closer to the mature narrator.

She first appears in the eight glossed over years at Lowood when, under the influence of Miss Temple, we are told, she had "more harmonious thoughts," "better regulated feelings" and "believed [she] was content" (99). That period is covered summarily in two or three pages, chiefly as an introduction to her restless desire to seek "real knowledge" of life outside the schoolroom, and the "other" Jane is scarcely realized. A comparable passage also fails to realize or dramatize this Jane sufficiently and comes, in any case, too late. Though we are told that in the time between the end of the narrative and the narrating, Jane has had ten years of happy marriage, these few pages are also expositional, undramatized summary narrative. The reader hardly knows the Jane Rochester who has narrated her life-story.

Though the stubborn commitment of so many readers to the values of the younger Jane may be explained by what Sternberg has identified as the power of primacy, the undramatized "other" Jane, the "inadequate" cautions or "excessive" subtlety of the serial disclosure (at least for readers not already committed to and anticipating a providential, or at least conventionally religious ending and ontology), regardless of these explanations, to overlook, ignore or dismiss the providential ontology of *Jane Eyre* is a misreading of what seem demonstrable authorial intentions.

Though modern critical discussion when it deigns to speak of authors or intentions almost invariably refers to the implied or virtual rather than the historical author, "[n]onetheless, the initial question most commonly asked of a literary text in our culture is, What is the author saying?" (Rabinowitz 30). That Charlotte Brontë, as well as "Currer Bell," thought valorizing young Jane a misreading can be inferred from her complaints in her proper person, outside the novel, about how she thought her novel was misread. Though most critical discussion of her "intentions" focus on the morality of the text attacked in the conservative press by a few (and only a few) early reviewers, this "timorous or carping few" were disposed of in Brontë's much applauded preface to the second edition of her novel. Those misreaders who most troubled Charlotte Brontë, however, were not the carping critics but those she called the "injudicious admirers" of her heroine, Jane's many friends, the well-intentioned readers. When Brontë came to write *Villette,* she was determined that her new heroine-narrator, Lucy Snowe, "should not occupy the pedestal to which 'Jane Eyre' was raised by some injudicious admirers" (*LL,* 4: 52-53).

The Jane the "injudicious readers" too much admired is clearly the younger Jane, the Jane first experienced in the temporal reading, buttressed by the primacy effect—and blinded by it. That Brontë's image of Jane, is not the rebellious child or defiantly independent and wholly self-reliant young lady, but the mature Jane

Rochester who writes the story of how she found God's plan and her place we can infer from Mrs. Gaskell. Gaskell reports that Charlotte Brontë "when she read the *Neighbours*, . . . thought every one would fancy that she must have taken her conception of Jane Eyre's character from that of 'Francesca,' the narrator of Miss Bremer's story" (387). Gaskell is puzzled: "For my own part," she says, "I cannot see the slightest resemblance between the two characters, and so I told her; but she persisted in saying that Francesca was Jane Eyre married to a good-natured 'Bear' of a Swedish surgeon" (387).

Gaskell's response is understandable. Bremer does *tell* us things about her heroine that resemble what we know of Jane Eyre: Francesca "is little, very little" (Bremer 9); poor; "had no beauty" (13); when sixteen, thought she "must have adventures, let it cost what it would" (43), and she says she thought herself in youth "unquiet and unreasonable" (51). But just as we see little of Jane Eyre when she is settled and mature, so we see little if anything of Francesca when she was young and adventurous. The young Francesca and the mature Jane are not dramatically present; they are characters the reader has only more or less heard "about." The characters the readers know ("realize") from their sequential reading experience do not substantially resemble each other, though they may be similar in the eyes or mind of the authors who see them sub specie aeternitatis, spatially. The grown up but still rebellious and self-assertive Jane Eyre that Brontë does not see, the Jane who is injudiciously admired by many readers from 1847 to the present day, and the matronly Jane Brontë does see, but who is only insubstantially there in the text suggests that Brontë herself may be "misreading" Jane Eyre and *Jane Eyre*,[4] the text presented to the reader but which must be performed by the reader into the work.[5]

Like Charlotte Brontë herself, the author implied by the text misreads the text, as paradoxical as that may seem. For the experience of the novel being read and the shape of the novel after having been read are two different textual objects. The Author looks at the novel as a spatial configuration seen from the end with full disclosure, and sees one novel; the engaged Reader looks at the novel from the beginning and projects configurations sequentially and continuously and experiences a quite different novel. Both are good readings and both are misreadings. *Jane Eyre* the novel as read and being read exists both as an *experience* of rebellion and as a meaningful *statement* of reconciliation to God and society. These two voices and ideologies are in dialogue; not in a dialogue with a reconcilable thesis and antithesis nor as an antinomy, but interactively, as if the whole novel were a single utterance hybridized.

Such dialogic "misreadings"—the readers' or the implied (and actual) author's—are virtually constitutive of long narratives, for they have both the experiential or

horizontal dimension of the point to point reading, and the global, spatial, or final configuration of the ending. While such dialogue is characteristic of the novel as a form, in *Jane Eyre* it is intensified, more dramatically constitutive perhaps because of the historical and cultural occasion of its utterance, that is, on the cusp of the Romantic and the Victorian; because of its psychological negotiation between passions and reason, and because of its intense realization of the powerful tension between individual desire and social restraint, the first term in each of these pairs incarnated in the sequential, experiential progress through the text and the second in the spatial, finalized statement of the completed text. A significant share of its effect and significance lies in its dramatically and archetypically incarnating the tension of that dialogue of languages, of social forces.

The heterogeneity and contradictoriness of the dialogue suggests why all readings must be misreadings. A "reading" suggests a translation of the text into a different language, one with its own—and different—frame of reference, and into a monologic "meaning." That "reading" or "meaning" seems convincing only when the frame of reference into which the text is translated fits "collectively recognized values." The varying interpretations over time and even within the contemporary reception show clearly that these interpretations are not objective or definitive but "sophisticated subjectivity," culture- or group-specific (Iser 23). Our reading "the text as it cannot see itself" (Eagleton 43) from a modern site in a way that seems "natural" or "self-evident" depends on the "sophisticated subjectivity" and "collectively recognized values" of the modern reader's culture or group and is once more a "misreading." Yet com-prehending the text means taking it somehow into our own frame of reference, for we cannot continuously "experience" the text without inwardly or outwardly articulating our responses, rendering it into our own language. Even the affective, experiential, aesthetic "meaning" for the reader reading the text "constantly threatens to transmute itself into discursive determinacy— . . . it is amphibolic: at one moment aesthetic and at the next discursive. . . . [I]t is impossible for such a meaning to remain indefinitely as an aesthetic effect" (Iser 22). We cannot, then, avoid mis/readings.

Common sense tells us that because we read a novel from word-one to word-the-last, the form of the novel is linear or temporal. Our reading experience tells us, however, that when we come to the end, we will look back upon the whole work as a shape or structure, and the form of the finished novel will appear "spatial." Indeed, we know that even in the experiential temporal reading we are constantly making shapes or configurations—projections of what will happen, of what the fictional world of this novel is like, of what we infer of the author's intention—for we have been not only taking in what we are reading as we read it, but are also recalling what has already "happened" or been said and anticipating what will be coming and what it will all amount to. The temporal reading emphasizes the on-going, the affective, or what Iser calls the "aesthetic," and the spatial construction—especially at the end but also during the reading process—the interpretive or "discursive." There is almost always a tension between these two dimensions of reading. For certain kinds of novels—the detective story may epitomize these—the ending is the final cause, what went before erased. Traditional interpretive criticism is similarly, but not identically monologic: earlier traces in the text matter insofar as they contribute to realizing the figure in the carpet and the more traces woven into the pattern the better (to the point of "total relevance"). Even dialogic novels, Bakhtin admits, often have monologic endings, "compositional and thematic completedness" (Bakhtin *PDP* 39). However, this finalization often, as in *Jane Eyre,* has the air of falsifying the reading experience, just as the experiential overriding of gradually disclosed authorial intention has the air of falsifying the "meaning" of the novel, the authorial intent. As we have seen, both the aesthetic and the discursive are, if not distortive, at least incomplete readings. In dialogic novels—and I am implicitly arguing that *Jane Eyre* is such a novel—the temporal and spatial dimensions are, to use Bakhtin's metaphor, "polyphonic"[6], involving two voices, "an encounter, within the arena of an utterance, between two different linguistic consciousnesses" (Bakhtin, *DI* 358) which are neither reconciled, synthesized, nor antinomic but are "fused into a concrete unity that is contradictory, multi-speeched and heterogeneous" (365).

There is, however, still another dimension in the reading of a novel text which is both aesthetic and discursive, formalist and historical, contextual and dialogic, emphasizing, even celebrating, the multiple possibilities of misreadings and the unfinalizable nature of the text. That dimension or echo-chamber is the intertextual. If the temporal is imagined as unilinear and the spatial as a two-dimensional shape on a plane surface, the intertextual may be thought of as a third dimension, a morass of "systems of intelligibility" (Fish 335), social and literary conventions by which text and reader are to some degree constrained. Though grammar, syntax, mores, and ideologies may be seen as "texts," I focus here on the contemporary literary, indeed the novel context within which *Jane Eyre* makes its meaning and effect (though it is impossible to totally ignore the ideological implications of these literary conventions). This area of the third dimension, the literary context, is present from the very first words of the text—indeed earlier. Before the reading of the first sentence of *Jane Eyre* can begin, for example, on the title page the subtitle, "An Autobiography," signals one of the generic patterns which will provide a "strateg[y] for reading" (Rabinowitz 177).[7]

Given the intertextual third dimension," *Jane Eyre* is even more "multi-speeched" than suggested by the "misreadings" of implied author or primacy-primed reader. Each of the novel species incorporated into *Jane Eyre* generates batteries of conventional narrative and ideological expectations, and even as it operates within the fictive context of *Jane Eyre* it retains its own ethical, epistemological, and ideological "voice." Fictional autobiography, for example, valorizes the individual's rights and freedoms—his *and hers*—and the mind's interiority, not as a source of subjective distortion but as the source of truth; it is ideologically radical (which in the nineteenth century includes the radicalism of capitalism and laissez faire). The orphan or foundling novel is often radical as well in its assumption of human innocence and innate virtue, and society's corrupting influence. The Gothic novel, while valorizing the imagination and both the role and limitations of rationalism, tends to support traditional, aristocratic, and patriarchal values; the governess novel valorizes the feminine and the genteel; domestic realism the feminine, the traditional and the bourgeois, and so on. These are oversimplifications, but they suggest the value-laden nature of the generic voices incorporated by the intertextuality of *Jane Eyre* and the novel's intuitive apprehension of the undifferentiated ideologemes that were transforming the rebellious Romantic and aristocratic Regency world into the bourgeois Victorian world:

> Literature does not ordinarily take its ethical and epistemological content from ethical and epistemological systems, or from outmoded ideological systems . . . , but immediately from the very process of generation of ethics, epistemology, and other ideologies. . . . Literature is capable of penetrating into the social laboratory where these ideologemes are shaped and formed. The artist . . . sees [ideological problems] in *statu nascendi,* sometimes better than the more cautious "man of science," the philosopher, or the technician. The generation of ideas, the generation of esthetic desires and feelings, their wandering, their as yet unformed groping for reality, their restless seething in the depths of the so-called "social psyche"—the whole as yet undifferentiated flood of generating ideology—is reflected and refracted in the content of the literary work.
>
> (Medvedev/Bakhtin 17)

Though *Jane Eyre* is implicated in the ideological furor at the moment of its occasion-specific utterance, it is also specifically *novelistic* utterance at a specific time in the history of the proleptically Darwinian genre called the novel. Though it appears at a particular moment of social and political history, its position as a novel is on a different time curve: "the variety of events of one historical moment . . . are *de facto* moments of completely different time curves, determined by the laws of their special history, as becomes obvious in the different 'histories'—of art, of law, of economics, political history, etc." (Jauss 32), and it is on *Jane Eyre*'s place along the time curve of the novel that I shall concentrate. Charlotte Brontë was involved in the same early Victorian literary project as her revered Thackeray, parody, the kind of parody necessary for the birth of a new kind of novel: "Literary parody of dominant novel-types plays a large role in the history of the European novel. One could even say that the most important novelistic models and novel-types arose precisely during this parodic destruction of preceding novelistic worlds" (Bakhtin, *DI* 309). Thackeray, by deliberate parody of contemporary authors and conventional narrative types, was trying to forge a new novel for the new, Victorian, bourgeois era; consciously or not,[8] Brontë was doing so by a different kind of parody. Rather than aiming at specific novels or authors as satiric targets, she was fusing different generic ways of telling a story in transgeneric scenic topoi.

The transgeneric scene or topos is a conventional scene that appears in contemporary or precedent novels of different genres, so that the scene is "occupied" by different, often conflicting, ideological and narrative voices. The "occupation" refracts the new novelistic utterance, as Bakhtin would put it, rendering it polyphonic, "multi-speeched," or, as Iser would suggest, by putting the familiar in an "unfamiliar light," the intertextual topos interrogates the conventional, holding it up to revaluation (Iser 78). The use of this transgeneric scenic topos thus functions at the narrative level as heteroglossia does at the verbal. It could even be thought of as "heterogeneric": the novel species, types, or genres bringing their context and ideological implications to the topical scene serving as the rough equivalent of the "languages" brought to the word or utterance via hybridization or heteroglossia. Indeed, since it operates on larger units and on narrative units it may generally be a more appropriate and useful concept than is heteroglossia for analysis of dialogic forms like the novel.

There are points in or portions of *Jane Eyre* where heterogeneric scenic topoi are most dramatically foregrounded—the child-punished-by-confinement, for example, at the beginning, many scenes or incidents involving the "deserted wing motif" (the madwoman in the attic) in the Thornfield chapters—but to demonstrate the more pervasive interaction of the contextual with the other two dimensions of the text let us look at a passage in which the intertextual dimension is significant but not dominant.

If at the beginning of a novel there is no novel-past to recapitulate, one would expect the early chapters to be unilinear. But, especially in a novel by an unknown writer who has no canon to serve as context for reading the new work, the early chapters must establish kinship claims by directly or indirectly, loudly or quietly, precisely or vaguely echoing earlier novels and novel genres. At the end of a novel there is no future, the forward progress is halted and the direction of the refer-

ences and of the reader's attention are chiefly to the novel's own past, so that the ending of the novel is the most spatialized of its loci, and because it has established its own finalized world, there is less need at the end to define itself intertextually. Where the text is most textured, the three dimensions of the text are most interactive, then, is between its two termini.

In *Jane Eyre* there is an unusually explicit narrative midpoint in which the forward movement of Jane's narrative seems brought to a dead end, turns back on itself to the beginning, spatializing the moment, and proceeds only after some of the detritus of her recent past and hopes for the future have been cleared away. So dramatic and traumatic is the revelation of the existence of Rochester's mad wife Bertha, the solution of the mystery of Thornfield, so disruptive of the reader's expectations and Jane's, of her life and her life-story, it is difficult for Jane or the reader to see clearly how to go on. Jane has remained calm, almost numb, throughout the scene and the disclosures. Now she retires to her room.

> I was in my own room as usual—just myself, without obvious change: nothing had smitten me, or scathed me, or maimed me. And yet, where was the Jane Eyre of yesterday?—where was her life?—where were her prospects?
>
> Jane Eyre, who had been an ardent, expectant woman— almost a bride—was a cold, solitary girl again: her life was pale; her prospects were desolate.
>
> (373)

She is devastated, her life since Gateshead emptied of significance. Her memories of her recent past and the prospects then before her seem to mock her present state, nor can she wholly exonerate herself from blame—"Oh, how blind had been my eyes! How weak my conduct" (374).

The novel too is laid waste. The love story as well as the Gothic mystery seems to disappear. The reader too is bereft of recent prospects, expectations, generic indicators, and perhaps a bit ashamed of his or her "blindness" or conventional expectations. We are invited to retreat to the Jane of page one: to concern ourselves with that "cold, solitary girl again."

Neither Jane nor the reader can (or would want to) literally retreat to Gateshead. Jane may have found "real knowledge" (100) amidst life's perils, as she set out to do, but the perils were greater than anticipated and the knowledge now more bitter:

> . . . I seemed to have laid me down in the dried-up bed of a great river; I heard a flood loosened in remote mountains, and felt the torrent come: to rise I had no will, to flee I had no strength. I lay faint; longing to be dead. One idea only still throbbed life-like within me—a remembrance of God: it begot an unuttered

prayer: these words went wandering up and down in my rayless mind, as something that should be whispered; but no energy was found to express them:—"Be not far from me, for trouble is near: there is none to help."

It was near: and as I had lifted no petition to heaven to avert it—as I had neither joined my hands, nor bent my knees, nor moved my lips—it came: in full, heavy swing the torrent poured over me. The whole consciousness of my life lorn, my love lost, my hope quenched, my faith death-struck, swayed full and mighty above me in one sullen mass. That bitter hour cannot be described: in truth, "the waters came into my soul; I sank in deep mire: I felt no standing; I came into deep waters; the floods overflowed me."

(374)

It is at this point that the second volume ends, producing a powerful pause that invites the reader to recapitulate and reconfigure. The hectic forward movement of the love story and the mystery checked, the narrative comes to a close and curls back on itself. Thornfield, even Lowood, and the intervening years are as if erased. Her situation is now as it was—Jane is a cold solitary girl again—but she has changed, as the reader's perspective of her must. She is not the girl who saucily told the Reverend Mr. Brocklehurst she did not like Psalms. She is a bereft young woman-child who, in her pain, finds in her "rayless mind," though she cannot utter them, the words of the eleventh verse of Psalm 22: "'Be not far from me, for trouble is near: there is none to help.'" And the elder Jane, the narrator, can only describe that painful time in words adapted from another Psalm, 69 (1-2): "That bitter hour cannot be described: in truth, 'the waters came into my soul; I sank in deep mire: I felt no standing; I came into deep waters; the floods overflowed me'" (375).[9]

"'Psalms are not interesting,'" the child Jane had told Brocklehurst, we remember. He replied that, "'That proves you have a wicked heart; and you must pray to God to change it: to give you a new and lean one: to take away your heart of stone and give you a heart of flesh'" (35). Her saucy answer in retrospect seems ironic indeed: her heart is all too much vulnerable "flesh." It is ironic, too, that the Philistine Brocklehurst seems in retrospect right—if no less repulsive—and spunky, lovable Jane wrong. We are meant to be driven at this point, it seems, to review that past and dramatically adjust our judgment of Jane the rebellious child and therefore our moral configuration of the world of the novel, and to box again our intertextual, generic compass.

The passage at the end of volume two in its water imagery recalls similar imagery in the passage that ends volume one, when, ironically, the possibility of being loved by Rochester first thrilled Jane, though even then the prospective joy surged on an undercurrent of trouble. At that point, Jane, having rescued Rochester from fire,

sees "strange fire in his look." Her eyes, he said, had from the first struck "delight" to his "inmost heart" (187); his meaning seems clear. He has to be tricked into letting go of her hand, but she does "escape": "I regained my couch, but never thought of sleep. Till morning dawned I was tossed on a buoyant but unquiet sea, where billows of trouble rolled under surges of joy" (187). The two passages of water imagery, marking the ends of the first and second volumes significantly bracket the Thornfield love story.

All Jane has left at the end of the second volume is "a remembrance of God." If we can believe the experiencing-I—the mature narrator is strategically silent—Jane and Rochester are parted forever, even though some love may remain. If there will be passion ahead, it will be religious; if there is religion ahead, it will be religious passion, agony. This dark shadow over the future cannot wholly obliterate our hope that it will be otherwise, but the shadow can (should) put that hope in doubt. Modern readers may confidently expect *Jane Eyre* to end happily because that, after all, is what Victorian novels almost invariably do, and that was what Victorian readers expected and demanded, we have been told over and over. It may come as a surprise, then, to discover that in October 1847—the very month in which *Jane Eyre* was published—a critic in the *Westminster Review,* reviewing Anne Marsh's *Norman's Bridge,* could complain that "It has of late been the fashion among novelists to avoid what is called 'poetical justice,' and to disappoint the reader with a catastrophe made as unhappy as possible, to harmonize with what is assumed to be the natural order of events" (*WR* 48:132). Many of the domestic novels of the day, including governess novels, and others that claimed in subtitles or text to be "stories of everyday life," distanced themselves from what they thought of as the romantic popular fashion, the happy ending. Thus Mrs. Hall, in "The Governess," published in *Chamber's* in 1842, says,

And now, if my tale were to end, as made up stories do, with a report that the old man found his grandchild [Emily, a governess, suffering from consumption] much better than he had anticipated; that they lived for a short time happily together, and then the governess was married to a great lord, to the discomfiture of all gossip, I should substitute fiction for fact—which I cannot do.

(Hall 92)

Cold, solitary Jane no longer seems the heroine of a romance but of a novel of domestic realism, of a governess novel, especially a religious one. There may be no happy ending, and if there is to be one, its means and nature now seem obscure.

The final volume of *Jane Eyre* does not, despite the terminal nature of the ending of volume two, open on a new scene, nor does it promise relief from the despair at the end of the second volume or even hint at a happy ending. When the newly cold and solitary Jane asks herself what she is to do, "the answer my mind gave—'Leave Thornfield at once'"—comes immediately and insistently. She tries to squirm out of it, but "conscience, turned tyrant, held passion by the throat," and tells her that if she were to stay he would "thrust her down to un-sounded depths of agony" (379). One more Thornfield chapter, one long, wrenching farewell scene, one more devastating stripping away of a layer of selfhood remains. Before it is over, just as Jane must choose what path to follow, readers must project the configuration of the rest of the novel, basing their expectations on familiar social and literary norms, conventions, genres.

That crucial final Thornfield chapter opens with Jane's coming to the surface of the flood, still questioning what she must do. It is then that the awful and relentless voice within tells her, "you shall tear yourself away; none shall help you: you shall, yourself, pluck out your right eye; yourself cut off your right hand: your heart shall be the victim" (379). This "preventive measure" for resisting adultery comes from the fifth chapter of Matthew (27-32), a chapter learned by heart at Lowood (69); Jane and the reader are again driven back to the religious aura of Lowood, though now, perhaps, with less contempt for its harsh restrictions on the celebration of the autonomous self. When she emerges from her room, Rochester is waiting, full of love and violence, almost like Lovelace. The Richardsonian note is struck first by the mention of *Pamela* in the first chapter (5) and echoes, at times faintly, at other times more resonantly, throughout the Thornfield section, where there is always the potential threat of signeur and "servant." He urges her passionately to enter a bigamous marriage, to fly with him to France. Jane confesses that she loves him, but must leave him. To resist, she realizes, is cruel, "to yield was out of the question. I did what human beings do instinctively when they are driven to utter extremity—looked for aid to one higher than man: the words 'God help me!' burst involuntarily from my lips" (388). Again we revisit Lowood. Helen Burns had warned Jane that she cared too much for the love of human beings—as she cares for the love of Rochester now—and relied too much on her self and not on God and the world of spirits. Jane's agonized echoing of the Psalms, her recollection of the passage from Matthew, and now her involuntary prayer suggest a cataclysmic change in the moral world of the secular self-reliant and independent Jane. This is not the voice or world of the first, the rebellious and sceptical Jane, but a second, more knowledgeable and humble Jane.

She will need all her new resources, for Rochester, telling her the story of his marriage and misery, pleads with her to come live with him and be his love. There are more vague echoes of *Clarissa*—Lovelace argues as does Rochester (403-04) that he can be saved from returning to dissipation, perhaps debauchery, only through true, pure, self-sacrificial love; Rochester even conjectures about taking Jane by force (385, 405-06). Lovelace has had in the intervening years, numerous progeny in the English novel, however, and these sites the reader may revisit as well. Colonel Hargrave, in Mary Brunton's *Self-Control* (a novel of 1811 but in a new edition in 1832), tells Laura that "'bound by your charms, allured by your example, my reformation would be certain, my virtue secure'" (18), but when she resists, he turns ugly: "'cold, pitiless, insensible woman—yes, I renounce you. In the haunts of riot, in the roar of intemperance, . . . when I am lost to fame, to health, to usefulness—my ruin be on your soul'" (39). He finally asks for, and receives, two years' "probation" to prove his resolve, but fails again. In Bremer's *The Neighbors,* whose Francesca resembled Jane in Brontë's eyes, the Byronic Bruno, whose past sins are greater than those of Rochester, proposes to his childhood sweetheart Serena and says he would change if he had a pure wife: "'She must become mine,' he says, 'if I am to find peace on earth'" (Bremer 193). Later, when they are to be married, he says he sought her in order "'to acquire an angel for my distempered soul . . .'" (Bremer 373). Jane, Rochester says, is his "'better self—my good angel . . .'" (402). Like Jane, Serena, refuses to yield while there is a moral impediment. When Clara Neville, the heroine of Rachel McCrindell's *The English Governess* (1844) discovers her fiancé is living loosely and has lost his religion, she breaks the engagement, but he urges her not to treat him so; even if he were worse, he insists, "'she might very easily have reclaimed him . . .'" (McCrindell 42). Later, he says she still has the power to reform him if she would agree to marry him. "'Ah, Edward,'" she says, "'you speak against your own convictions. I have no such power. How can I hope to sway a heart which continually resists the stirrings of the Spirit of grace?'" (McCrindell 125). To those familiar with the fictional context, Rochester's threats and protestations sound hollow, and Jane's response expected and applauded. Saving your lover's soul by sacrificing your own moral values is not, in nineteenth-century fiction, a laudatory, moral, or religious act.

Nor is this morality or definition of what is properly an act of love limited to governess or domestic fiction. Such scenes do appear in the more modest and religious of eighteenth-century and contemporary novels but also in Gothic novels. Radcliffe's Valancourt, in his gentler way, tells Emily, who, he thinks, is casting him off at another's behest, "'Would you not otherwise be willing to hope for my reformation—and could you bear, by estranging me from you, to abandon me to misery—to myself! . . . if you still loved me, you would find your happiness in saving mine'" (*Udolpho* 515). There are, as well, comparable scenes in a very recent melodramatic, heated, notorious "feminist" novel, Jewsbury's *Zoe* (1845), which **Jane Eyre** has evoked before, for just as the fire in Rochester's bed has brought Jane to him in the middle of the night, and first brought the possibilities of their love and their physical union to the fore, so a fire had thrown Zoe, deliciously disheveled, into the arms of a priest, Everhard (sic!). They, especially Everhard, resist temptation with great difficulty. He and Zoe part. Despite her attempt to live up to Everhard's image of her, Zoe is later tempted to "live the life of passion" by her strong feelings for the Byronic Comte de Mirabeau. Only the existence of a wife prevents her from doing so. Mirabeau must return to France, to a high post, and asks Zoe to accompany him, "to be my angel, my support, my councillor" (Jewsbury 120). "'If it is to become your wife, Gabriel, that you are asking me, I am willing to do so,'" she responds. Even though he is divorced he confesses that his religion prevents him from marrying again. When she refuses him he accuses her of being capable only of shallow love, of loving position and wealth like all ordinary women, just as Rochester asks bitterly, "'. . . you don't love me, then? It was only my station, and the rank of my wife, that you valued?'" (386). Mirabeau warns Zoe that her "selfish" refusal will save her reputation but damn him:

> ". . . When I am gone, what comfort will you find in the consciousness that you have saved yourself and lost me? for if you fail me now, all hope of good is over for me. You have the power to do with me what you will, make of me what you will . . ."
>
> (Jewsbury 121)

Like Jane, she refuses, like Jane (398) and Clarissa, she believes once she becomes his mistress, she will lose her power over him, will be like the others.

Zoe is as staunch and moral in her refusal as Jane, and indeed rededicates her life in "Platonic constancy" to Everhard and is ennobled thereby—which may cast some shadow over what is to come in **Jane Eyre**. But Zoe is not your typical Victorian heroine. She is illegitimate, half Greek, attains a "masculine" education and hates domesticity. She is passionate (permissibly so because half Greek, no doubt) and unconventional. Jewsbury says, "Women gifted like Zoe often present instances of aberration from the standard of female rectitude" (Jewsbury 41). They have too much energy and not enough channels for activity (Jewsbury 42). Even when they have children, as Zoe does, they realize "the maternal instinct is only one passion amongst the many with which a woman is endowed" (104). Their feelings are so strong that maxims do not always guide them: "A strong, vivid sensation, a vehement temptation, has, when it comes, a vitality and reality that make the most firmly believed and most emphatic maxims seem very vague and ineffectual" (Jewsbury 104).

So Richardson and his progeny do not have the stage to themselves, and the "generic static" makes the ultimate shape of Jane's story problematic. If Zoe is the prototype, the projected configuration of the last volume of **Jane Eyre** will assume the shape of the novel of Godwinian and feminist rebellion prefigured in the first volume—"women feel just as men feel; they need exercise for their faculties, and a field for their efforts as much as their brothers do . . ." (133): "vivid sensation" and "vehement temptation" may still deflect Jane from her "emphatic maxims"—and many readers have wished this to be the case.

Though Jane resists, and advises Rochester to "'. . . trust in God and yourself. Believe in heaven. Hope to meet again there'"—a moral growth in Jane since Lowood where she wondered if heaven existed—her struggle with her sense of right, with her "most firmly believed and most emphatic maxims," is terrible. When he pledges fidelity and asks her to pledge the same, she must play iconoclast. She experiences "an ordeal: a hand of fiery iron grasped my vitals. Terrible moment: full of struggle, blackness, burning! Not a human being that ever lived could wish to be loved better than I was loved; and him who thus loved me I absolutely worshipped: and I must renounce love and idol" (402-03). When he pits humanity, compassion against mere law, argues that if she says no, he will be injured, but that if she says yes, since she has no family, no one will be hurt, Jane's "very Conscience and Reason turned traitors against me" (404). There is, however, a Self beyond feeling, conscience, and reason. "'*I* care for myself. The more solitary, the more friendless, the more unsustained I am, the more I will respect myself.'"

But now, as important as respect for the autonomous self, are those "most firmly believed and most emphatic maxims" that Jewsbury finds weak in time of crisis but Jane finds the only safe stars to steer by:

> "I will keep the law given by God; sanctioned by man. I will hold to the principles received by me when I was sane, and not mad—as I am now. Laws and principles are not for the times when there is no temptation: they are for such moments as this, when body and soul rise in mutiny against their rigour: stringent are they; inviolate they shall be. If at my individual convenience I might break them, what would be their worth? They have a worth—so I have always believed; and if I cannot believe it now, it is because I am insane—quite insane: with my veins running fire, and my heart beating faster than I can count its throbs. Preconceived opinions, foregone determinations, are all I have at this hour to stand by: there I plant my foot."
>
> (404-05)

Even after this outburst, even when Rochester knows himself defeated, she cannot leave the room without turning back, kissing his cheek, smoothing his hair.

"'Farewell!' was the cry of my heart, as I left him. Despair added,—'Farewell for ever!'" (407). The temptation would not be so great, the struggle so titanic, if her love were not so powerful. Nor would other possible outcomes to the fictional events still be possible were it not for the din of generic voices, the heterogeneric overdetermination of the farewell scene occupied and refracted by the Richardsonain and the Godwinian. The rebellious Jane is kept alive for the reader by more than the opening chapters and power of primacy.

The discordant voices of Richardson and the Godwins, the domestic, feminist, religious, problematizing the ontology as well as the plot of the novel, are once more joined by the ghostly whisper of the Gothic, complicating matters still further, and spatializing the narrative form once more. That night, having decided to leave Thornfield but uncertain she has the strength to do so, Jane dreams that she is in

> the red-room at Gateshead; that the night was dark, and my mind impressed with strange fears. The light that long ago had struck me into syncope, recalled in this vision, seemed glidingly to mount the wall, and tremblingly to pause at the centre of the obscured ceiling. I lifted up my head to look: the roof resolved to clouds, high and dim; the gleam was such as the moon imparts to vapours she is about to sever. I watched her come— watched with the strangest anticipation; as though some word of doom were to be written on her disk. She broke forth as never moon yet burst from cloud: a hand first penetrated the sable folds and waved them away; then, not a moon, but a white human form shone in the azure, inclining a glorious brow earthward. It gazed and gazed on me. It spoke, to my spirit: immeasurably distant was the tone, yet so near, it whispered in my heart—
>
> "My daughter, flee temptation!"
>
> "Mother, I will."
>
> So I answered after I had waked from the trance like dream.
>
> (407)

This is an extraordinarily powerful though extraordinarily qualified episode. To start within the experience: is the vision that of Jane's mother, Mrs. Eyre, emerging from the image of the moon, or is it the moon it-/herself that speaks to Jane and she to it/her? This may be rendered moot, since the experience takes place within a dream and indeed communicates the montage-like experience of many dreams. But dreams have been authorized by the narrator for the accuracy of their predictive value earlier in the text (prior to the summons to her aunt's deathbed, prior to the invasion of her room by Bertha on the night before the wedding), and perhaps by their ontological relationship to presentiments, signs, and sympathies which were explicitly endorsed by the narrator (276). This experience, too, may gain some credence in being described as a "trance-like dream."

That the vision may be, indeed, that of Jane's mother whose spirit is guarding her daughter, might be reinforced by the firm belief of Helen Burns that alongside this world is "an invisible world and a kingdom of spirits: that world is round us, for it is everywhere; and those spirits watch us, for they are commissioned to guard us . . ." (81).

The substance of Jane's dream may seem qualified by its taking place "in the red-room at Gateshead," and by the fact that the vision of the moon/mother is preceded by a repetition of the experience of a gliding light there. That earlier experience, we recall, had been explained away, with the apparent, if qualified, authority of the narrator: "I can now *conjecture* readily that this streak of light was, *in all likelihood,* a gleam from a lantern, carried by some one across the lawn; but then . . . I thought the swift-darting beam was a herald of some coming vision from another world" (15, emphasis added). Should this episode like the earlier, be "conjectured away," or should the red-room as "herald of some coming vision" be retrospectively authenticated?

Awake, Jane feels enabled to leave Thornfield, and at dawn she does so. Even now she thinks of turning back, sickened by the thought of what her disappearance will do to Rochester. The dissolution of her former self, of her only self as she knows it, is all but complete. A few hours earlier, though Conscience and Reason and Feeling aligned themselves with Rochester, she could and would resist, she told him, because "'*I* care for myself. . . . I will respect myself'" (404), but that passage cannot be extracted from the context and be used to represent Jane's ultimate moral position or to define conclusively the reality of the world of the fiction. It is, in effect, one of Jane's voices, the voice of Jane at one stage of her moral growth, one of the many world-visions that speak through Jane. Like all other passages in this novel it must be treated *in sequence* and as occasion-specific, a tentative if momentarily convincing stage in the gradually evolving history of Jane's moral life, as if, that is, in quotation marks. For within a half-dozen pages her present moral solution or resolution will be itself devastated, her self no longer autonomous or in control, even her "frantic effort of principle" offering no sure guidance or goal:

> What was I? In the midst of my pain of heart, and frantic effort of principle, I abhorred myself. I had no solace from self-approbation: none even from self respect. I had injured—wounded—left my master. I was hateful in my own eyes. Still I could not turn, nor retrace one step. God must have led me on. As to my own will or conscience, impassioned grief had trampled one and stifled the other.
>
> (410)

Jane boards a coach, the Thornfield center of the novel is left behind. She is not even the cold and solitary girl of Gateshead and Lowood, for now even her vaunted sense of "self" has been left behind. Nor has she placed herself in God's hands: it is not her voice but that of the Jane who is narrating from the future who says (and even then conjecturally), "God *must have* led me on."

There is a disruption at this point in the linear, forward thrust of the narrative, suspense without expectation. There is little help from the textual past to give shape to the future. The reader no more than young Jane knows what lies ahead. The future, though vague, is not entirely void, however. There are in the third, intertextual dimension of the text persistent if muffled voices of multiple generic possibilities. Though in the end, Charlotte Brontë will opt for "a *conventionally literary, conventionally monologic* ending" (Bakhtin *PDP* 39), these voices that occupy so many heterogeneric scenes, refracting the narrative utterance by their presence will refuse to be reduced to finalized monologic unity and meaning. By their "encounter within the arena of an utterance" (Bakhtin *DI* 358) they will dialogize *Jane Eyre,* fusing it "into a concrete unity that is contradictory, multi-speeched and heterogeneous" (365).

Notes

1. Vineta Colby indicates that Caroline "is brought back into religion by a pious little pupil who, like Jane Eyre's inspiration Helen Burns, dies in her arms" (165).

2. I am generally following Peter J. Rabinowitz's conception of the authorial audience and authorial reader or reading. See, e.g., "the initial question most commonly asked of a literary text in our culture is, What is the author saying?. . . . [E]ven among the most jaded readers—academics—the majority still attempts to read as authorial audience" (30); "[Authors] design their books rhetorically for some more or less specific *hypothetical* audience, which I call the *authorial audience.* Artistic choices are based upon these assumptions—conscious or unconscious—about readers, and to a certain extent, artistic success depends on their shrewdness, on the degree to which actual and authorial audience overlap" (21); "The notion of the authorial audience . . . allows us to treat the reader's attempt to read as the author intended, not as a search for the author's private psyche, but rather as the joining of a particular social/interpretive community; that is, the acceptance of the author's invitation to read in a particular socially constituted way that is shared by the author or his or her expected readers" (22); "authorial reading has a special status against which other readings can be measured (although not necessarily negatively); it is a kind of norm (although not necessarily a positive value), in that it serves as a point of orientation (although not necessarily as an ultimate destination)" (36). I will argue, however, that the success of *Jane Eyre* is due in part to Brontë's choice of a rhetorical strategy based on a miscalculation of her actual audience; briefly, she assumed that her audience was providentialist or at least religious, but in actuality, even in 1847 and increasingly since, it was more secular.

3. I am taking a little liberty with Sternberg's usage of the term. In the "rhetoric of anticipatory caution," dramatically illustrated in the novels of Jane Austen, "our attitude to the protagonist, whose information or view largely gives rise to it—is perceptibly qualified from the beginning" (129), whereas in other narratives "only in retrospect does the reader come to spot the discordant anticipatory hints that have been smuggled into the preliminary account right from the start though temporarily submerged by its overall import or dissimulated by specific means" (129). His formalistic attribution of all power to the text makes a distinction in texts here that may in some cases be differences among readers—when is a qualification "perceptible," or, rather, perceptible to whom? There were, perhaps are, significant ideological differences among even the authorial readers of *Jane Eyre,* as will be evident below.

4. Brontë's Rochester, too, seems milder than the hero most readers see. Though Gaskell's report does not categorically say that Brontë sees him as good-natured and grumpy, like Francesca's husband, it is clear elsewhere—in her 14 August 1848 letter to her publisher's man W. W. Williams—that she believes Rochester's "nature is like wine of good vintage, time cannot sour but only mellow him," and she seems to realize that not all readers see him so: "Such at least was the character I meant to portray" (*LL* 2:245). She understands that he has been misread but still resents comparisons with Anne Brontë's Huntingdon in *The Tenant of Wildfell Hall,* who, she says, "is naturally selfish, sensual, and superficial" (2:244) and perhaps even more those who compare Rochester to Heathcliff, who is, she says "naturally perverse, vindictive, inexorable," and made worse by hard usage (2:245). Though Rochester "grows on us," our first impressions of him are not of a man of unqualifiedly "good nature."

5. In Wolfgang's Iser's sense, the "work," is "virtual," it "cannot be reduced to the reality of the text or to the subjectivity of the reader" (Iser 21).

6. "It must be noted that the comparison we draw between Dostoevsky's novel and polyphony is meant as a graphic analogy, nothing more" (Bakhtin *PDP* 22).

7. See my "Jane Eyre at Gateshead: Mixed Signals in the Text and Context," and *Misreading "Jane*

Eyre": A Post-Formalist Paradigm, forthcoming, Ohio State University Press.

8. She was hurt when she heard that her idol Thackeray thought the plot of *Jane Eyre* unoriginal: "The plot of 'Jane Eyre' may be a hackneyed one. Mr. Thackeray remarks that it is familiar to him. But having read comparatively few novels I never chanced to meet with it, and I thought it original" (*LL* 2:150). *Misreading "Jane Eyre"* (see previous note) affirms Thackeray's "charge" and Brontë's denial, exploring the parameters of influence and intertextuality.

9. "Save me, O God; for the waters are come into my soul. / I sink in deep mire, where there is no standing; I am come into deep waters, where the floods overflow me." The prayerful opening phrase is suppressed, young Jane still apparently unable to pray. When another governess of the 1840s, Rachel McCrindell's *The English Governess* (1844), is somewhat similarly bereft and overwhelmed, the epigraph to the chapter in which she learns that her fiancé has become dissipated and irreligious has similar imagery and is from the same source: "Deep calleth unto deep at the noise of thy waterspouts: all thy waves and thy billows are gone over me" (Psalms 43:7).

Works Cited

"Anne Marsh, *Norman's Bridge,*" *Westminster Review* 48 (October 1847), 132.

Bakhtin, M. M. *The Dialogic Imagination.* Austin: Univ. of Texas Press, 1981. (*DI* in text.)

——. (P. N. Medvedev). *The Formal Method in Literary Scholarship.* Baltimore: The Johns Hopkins Univ. Press, 1978.

——. *Problems of Dostoevsky's Poetics.* Minneapolis: Univ. of Minnesota Press, 1984. (*PDP* in text.)

——. *Speech Genres and Other Late Essays.* Austin: Univ. of Texas Press, 1986.

Beaty, Jerome. "Afterword." In Charlotte Brontë, *Villette,* 476-85. New York: New American Library, 1987.

——. "Jane Eyre at Gateshead: Mixed Signals in the Text and Context." In *Victorian Literature and Society.* Essays Presented to Richard D. Altick, edited by James R. Kincaid and Albert J. Kuhn, 168-96. Columbus: Ohio State Univ. Press, 1984.

——. *Misreading Jane Eyre: A Postformalist Paradigm.* Columbus: Ohio State Univ. Press (forthcoming).

Bremer, Frederika. *The Neighbors. A Story of Everyday Life.* tr. Mary Howitt. London: C. Bell & Sons, 1910. (first Eng. tr. 1842)

Brontë, Charlotte. *Jane Eyre.* Edited by Jane Jack and Margaret Smith. Oxford: Clarendon Press, 1969. (1847)

Brunton, Mary. *Self-Control.* London: Colburn and Bentley, 1832. (1811)

Colby, Vineta. *Yesterday's Woman: Domestic Realism in the English Novel.* Princeton: Princeton University Press, 1974.

Eagleton, Terry. *Criticism and Ideology: A Study in Marxist Literary Theory.* London: New Left Books, 1976.

Fish, Stanley. *Is There a Text in This Class?* Cambridge, Mass.: Harvard Univ. Press, 1980.

Gaskell, Elizabeth. *The Life of Charlotte Brontë.* London, Dent, 1971. (1857)

Gilbert, Sandra M. and Susan Gubar. *The Madwoman in the Attic. The Woman Writer and the Nineteenth-Century Literary Imagination.* New Haven: Yale Univ. Press, 1979.

Hall, Anna Maria [Mrs. Samuel Carter]. *Stories of the Governess.* Printed for the Benefit of the Governess' Benevolent Institution. London: J. Nisbet and Co., 1852. (1842 in *Chamber's Edinburgh Journal.* Includes "The Old Governess," "The Governess, a Tale," "The Daily Governess," and, in 23 March 1844, "Our Governess," a first-person story by "Mr. Johnson."

Hunter, J. Paul. *The Reluctant Pilgrim.* Baltimore: The Johns Hopkins Univ. Press, 1966.

Iser, Wolfgang. *The Act of Reading: A Theory of Aesthetic Response.* Baltimore: The Johns Hopkins Univ. Press, 1980.

Jauss, Hans Robert. "Literary History as a Challenge to Literary Theory." In *New Directions in Literary History,* edited by Ralph Cohen, 11-41. Baltimore: The Johns Hopkins Univ. Press, 1974.

Jewsbury, Geraldine Endsor. *Zoe: The History of Two Lives.* New York: Harper and Brothers, 1845. (1845, Chapman and Hall)

McCrindell, Rachel. *The English Governess. A Tale of Real Life.* Philadelphia: Herman Hooker, 1844. (London 1844)

Rabinowitz, Peter J. *Before Reading: Narrative Conventions and the Politics of Interpretation.* Ithaca, N.Y.: Cornell Univ. Press, 1987.

Sherwood, Mrs. Mary Martha. *Caroline Mordaunt; or, The Governess.* In *The Works of Mrs. Sherwood,* 13. Boston: Harpers, 1834-58. (1835)

Sternberg, Meir. *Expositional Modes and Temporal Ordering in Fiction.* Baltimore: The Johns Hopkins Univ. Press, 1978.

Wise, T. J. and J. A. Symington eds. *The Brontës: Their Lives, Friendships and Correspondence.* 4v. The Shakespeare Head Brontë. Oxford: Basil Blackwell, 1932. (*LL* in text.)

John G. Peters (essay date spring 1996)

SOURCE: Peters, John G. "Inside and Outside: *Jane Eyre* and Marginalization through Labeling." *Studies in the Novel* 28, no. 1 (spring 1996): 57-75.

[*In the following essay, Peters looks at the ways in which Jane is marginalized by other characters in the novel.*]

Commentators have universally recognized that many of Brontë's contemporaries were uncomfortable with *Jane Eyre.* Many have also noted that Jane is a social outsider in the novel. However, none has argued that these phenomena are simply different manifestations of the same problem. The novel's characters systematically marginalize Jane and her ideas, as do many of Brontë's contemporaries. In addition, the reason the characters and the contemporary negative reviewers marginalize Jane has yet to be discussed. Both groups fear Jane subverts established cultural norms, and so, in order to minimize her influence on society, they attempt to transform Jane into the other by excluding her from society and by labeling her as something other than human.

I

Throughout the novel, Jane appears as a threat to the other characters. Either because she is an intruder from outside the community, because she is an enigma, or because her ideas are threatening, the other characters marginalize Jane in order to dismiss her or her ideas and thereby transform her into something nonthreatening. From the very outset, the characters exclude Jane; even as a child she is isolated from the social group:

> Eliza, John, and Georgiana were now clustered round their mama in the drawing-room . . . Me, she had dispensed from joining the group; saying, "She regretted to be under the necessity of keeping me at a distance; but that until she heard from Bessie, and could discover by her own observation that I was endeavouring in good earnest to acquire a more sociable and child-like disposition, a more attractive and sprightly manner,—something lighter, franker, more natural as it were—she really must exclude me from privileges intended only for contented, happy little children."[1]

This scene is indicative of Jane's situation at Gateshead, and her otherness in relation to the Reeds remains unchanged throughout the novel. Even later at her aunt's deathbed, Jane says of Mrs. Reed, "Poor, suffering woman! it was too late for her to make now the effort to change her habitual frame of mind: living, she had ever hated me—dying, she must hate me still" (p. 242). Gateshead becomes representative of Jane's position outside the social order as a whole.

Except for those at Lowood and Marsh End (who are also social outsiders in part), the other characters in *Jane Eyre* generally exclude Jane from their social spheres, and they do so in various ways. For example, John Reed says to Jane, "You have no business to take our books: you are a dependant, mama says; . . . you ought to beg, and not live here with gentlemen's children like us, and eat the same meals we do, and wear clothes at our mama's expense" (p. 11). He wants to separate Jane from himself by removing from her some of the outward signs of their similarity. Similarly, Mrs. Reed also marginalizes Jane; Jane recalls, "[S]ince my illness she [Mrs. Reed] had drawn a more marked line of separation than ever between me and her own children; appointing me to a small closet to sleep in by myself, condemning me to take my meals alone, and pass all my time in the nursery while my cousins were constantly in the drawing-room" (pp. 26-27). By separating Jane from her own children, Mrs. Reed removes her from the Reeds' social group, placing Jane instead among the servants. And when Jane falls ill during the red-room incident, Mrs. Reed sends for Mr. Lloyd, an apothecary, who was "sometimes called in by Mrs. Reed when the servants were ailing: for herself and the children she employed a physician" (p. 19). In this way, Mrs. Reed marks a clear distinction between her own children and Jane by lumping Jane with the servants. But the servants will not have Jane either; Miss Abbot says, "No; you are less than a servant, for you do nothing for your keep" (p. 12). So Jane is not allowed inside either community.

Even outside Gateshead, Jane continues to exist as the other. Soon after she arrives at Lowood, Brocklehurst attempts to exclude Jane from the society of the school; he places her on a stool and tells the inhabitants that Jane "is a little castaway: not a member of the true flock, but evidently an interloper and an alien" (p. 67). He then advises: "You must be on your guard against her; you must shun her example: if necessary, avoid her company, exclude her from your sports, and shut her out from your converse" (p. 67). By his choice of "interloper" and "alien" (words Jane also used to describe Mrs. Reed's view of her), Brocklehurst tries to transform her into the other and then urges those of the school to reject Jane if they wish to remain members of the larger social group.

Jane is shunned in a like manner when she arrives in Morton. Not only do the inhabitants treat her as an outsider because she is one but also because she does not fit into any recognizable category. She begs food but is not a beggar. She looks like a lady but has no money. When she offers to trade belongings for food, they rebuff her. When she seeks employment, they answer her evasively. When she seeks out the clergyman, he is unavailable. When she attempts to gain entrance to the Rivers' home, Hannah, both literally and symbolically, shuts the door on her. As a result, the isolation she experiences when she first arrives there is more than simply a spiritual isolation; she is literally shut out from all aspects of life until St. John finally takes her into the Rivers' home.

Even at Thornfield, by the very nature of her being a governess, she does not easily fit into the established roles of either gentry or servants. As a governess, she is a dependent; yet she is better born and better bred than the other servants. Only Mrs. Fairfax is of the same social group, but their differences of age and interests make them merely superficial companions. As far as her relationship to the gentry is concerned, the way the Ingram party relegates Jane to the category of governesses (whom they considered to be completely outside their social group) also emphasizes Jane's place outside the social sphere at Thornfield. Blanche Ingram says of governesses, "I have just one word to say of the whole tribe: they are a nuisance" (p. 179). She then goes on to describe the Ingrams' vicious treatment of them when they were children. And Blanche's mother says, "[D]on't mention governesses: the word makes me nervous. I have suffered a martyrdom from their incompetency and caprice: I thank Heaven I have now done with them!" (p. 179). Then specifically aiming her remark at Jane, she says, "I see all the faults of her class" (p. 179). So, as at Gateshead, Jane fits neither among the gentry nor among the servants.

In order for Jane to appear outside the community, the characters must actively exclude her, and among the various ways the characters transform Jane into the other, the labels and imagery with which they describe her are the most subtle, poignant, and effective.[2] These labels consistently depict Jane as non-human. Others call her "angel," "cat," "sprite," "imp," "thing," "rat," and "fairy"—to name just a few. In fact, such terms appear nearly a hundred times in the novel, and given their sheer frequency alone, they are more than merely incidental.

Early in the novel, characters describe Jane almost exclusively with derogatory labels. And by so doing, they marginalize Jane. When the Reeds call her an "imp" or a "rat," they both punish her by the insult and psychologically isolate her from their family. These terms also reinforce for the Reeds the goodness of their family by excluding an "imp" or "rat" from their community. Jane's otherness at Gateshead culminates in the red-room incident. Immediately after they call her "rat" and

"mad cat," they thrust Jane into the red-room, a tomb-like room they had left undisturbed since Mr. Reed's death. This symbolic interment, and the labels they use on Jane represent the physical and spiritual solitary confinement to which the Reeds relegate her. Jane's transformation into the other is important for the Reeds, because if they can think of Jane as an animal or creature, then they can treat her as non-family (in opposition to Mr. Reed's deathbed request [p. 240]). A retrospective Jane understands her position; she says she was "an interloper not of her [Mrs. Reed's] race, and unconnected with her" (p. 16). During her feverish, death-bed ravings, Mrs. Reed reveals her motivation in excluding Jane from their community:

> Such a burden to be left on my hands—and so much annoyance as she caused me, daily and hourly, with her incomprehensible disposition, and her sudden fits of temper, and her continual, unnatural watchings of one's movements! I declare she talked to me once like something mad, or like a fiend—no child ever spoke or looked as she did: I was glad to get her away from the house . . . I hated it [Jane] the first time I set eyes on it—a sickly, whining, pining thing! It would wail in its cradle all night long—not screaming heartily like any other child, but whimpering and moaning. Reed pitied it; and he used to nurse it and notice it as if it had been his own: more, indeed, than he ever noticed his own at that age.
>
> (Pp. 233-34)

Here, Mrs. Reed excludes Jane not only from her own family, but also from the human family as well. In this brief passage, she calls Jane "unnatural," "fiend," "thing," "beggar," "creature," and finally "it," thus emphasizing her relationship to Jane. Equally clear is the reason for Mrs. Reed's attitude: Jane represents a threat to her aunt's family. When Mrs. Reed says her husband used to "notice it [Jane] as if it had been his own: more indeed, than he ever noticed his own at that age," she expresses the unspoken concern that Jane is usurping the place of her own children. Mrs. Reed's natural protective instinct toward her children takes over, and she attempts to rid the family of Jane's ties to it. Her attitude toward Jane also sheds light on Mrs. Reed's withholding of John Eyre's letter. She suggests she acts out of vengeance (which is true), but she also keeps Jane from joining her class through Jane's becoming a financial equal; as long as Jane remains financially dependent she remains both outside the Reed's family and outside their social circle.

Separating the other from society is perhaps the oldest and most basic of acts against those we regard as enemies. By transforming the enemy into something other than human in our minds, we can treat them other than humanely—thereby avoiding guilt and possible retribution. René Girard, in speaking of scapegoats, says:

> All our sacrificial victims, whether chosen from one of the human categories . . . or, *a fortiori*, from the animal realm, are invariably distinguishable from the non-

sacrificeable beings by one essential characteristic: between these victims and the community a crucial social link is missing, so they can be exposed to violence without fear of reprisal. Their death does not automatically entail an act of vengeance.[3]

Of course, Jane functions less as a scapegoat at Gateshead than she does as the other (although she does refer to herself as "the scape-goat of the nursery" [p. 16]), but the underlying principle is the same. By transforming Jane into the other—an animal, creature, or nonentity—her aunt avoids the guilt of crimes against her family and social group. Mrs. Reed divests Jane of human, family, or social ties that could claim retribution.[4] Consequently, Mrs. Reed has no fear of reprisal from conscience or from other people and in fact can view herself and her behavior positively, in that she removes a threat to her family and society.

Besides the possibility of Jane's usurping her own children's place, Jane's fiery temper and strength also threaten Mrs. Reed. These characteristics challenge Mrs. Reed's authority as head of the family and as a member of the ruling class; they also threaten to influence the Reed children. In addition, Jane exposes the Reeds' selfishness and uncharitability. This becomes particularly important, because the Reeds represent the ruling class as a whole. As a result, although Jane's threat as a child is primarily limited to the Reeds, on a larger scale, her challenge to their authority also implies a challenge to the society and class they represent. This becomes clear as Jane grows and continues to challenge cultural norms concerning the role of women and class in society. Brocklehurst recognizes this threat to the Reeds and to society and says to those at Lowood, "[A]t last her excellent patroness [Mrs. Reed] was obliged to separate her [Jane] from her own young ones, fearful lest her vicious example should contaminate their purity" (p. 67). With Jane marginalized, Mrs. Reed can ship her off to Lowood and then relinquish "all interference in [Jane's] affairs" (p. 90).

Transforming a person into the other through labeling also occurs elsewhere in the novel. For example, Blanche Ingram calls Jane a "creeping creature" (p. 225). Whether Blanche does this because she senses Rochester's interest in Jane, because of her opinion of governesses in general, or because of class snobbery, the result is the same: she relegates Jane to a position outside at least the social community if not outside the human community entirely. Similarly, Blanche refers to Adèle as a "tiresome monkey" (p. 191), and Rochester calls Adèle a "French floweret" (p. 141). In both cases, they dismiss Adèle by using an epithet. And even though Rochester appears to have some affection for the child, he often dismisses her as superficial and insignificant. Jane herself also uses this tactic; when John Reed attacks her, she turns him into a "murderer,"

"slave-driver," and "Roman emperor" (p. 11). He seems to understand the implications of this transformation when he replies, "What! what! Did she say that to me? Did you hear her, Eliza and Georgiana?" (p. 11). And this in part accounts for Jane's assertion to Helen that she could never love or bless him (p. 58), since in Jane's mind he is the other. As she does with John Reed, Jane also wishes to sever ties with Mrs. Reed when she says, "I am glad you are no relation of mine: I will never call you aunt again as long as I live" (pp. 36-37). In this case, the *withholding* of the label then transforms her aunt into a non-relation. And of course Rochester consistently uses this method to rid himself of his ties to Bertha. By calling her a "maniac" (p. 304), a "demon" (p. 296), a "monster" (p. 313), and a "fiend" (p. 304), by referring to her "wolfish cries" (p. 312) and "demon-hate" (p. 312), by designating her attic room as "the mouth of Hell" (p. 296), and by otherwise describing Bertha using animalistic or non-human terms, Rochester tries to divest her of humanity in order to free himself from her. His marginalizing of Bertha through labeling culminates when he says, "For a wife I have but the maniac up-stairs: as well might you refer me to some corpse in yonder churchyard" (p. 320). The transformation now complete, Rochester then feels free to "form what new tie" (p. 313) he chooses.

Besides others marginalizing Jane through labeling, she sometimes does this to herself as well. She labels herself playfully with Rochester at times, but early on her self-marginalization is potentially tragic. The most poignant example is when she looks into the mirror in the red-room and thinks:

> [T]he strange little figure there gazing at me, with a white face and arms specking the gloom, and glittering eyes of fear moving where all else was still, had the effect of a real spirit: I thought it like one of the tiny phantoms, half fairy, half imp, Bessie's evening stories represented as coming out of lone, ferny dells in moors.
>
> (P. 14)

This passage couples the loneliness and isolation of Jane with the otherworldly, non-human description of her image (appropriate for the red-room). Her visualization is representative of her spiritual situation. For Jane, because of her age and child-like impressionability along with the constant labeling by the Reeds, she becomes in her own mind as well a "phantom" or "imp." She sees herself moving through Gateshead either ignored or attacked and at all points an outsider—ultimately even to herself.

Although as Jane grows older, she rejects more and more the labels assigned her, even as an adult she occasionally marginalizes herself through labeling. When Jane chastises herself for thinking Rochester could possibly favor her, she calls herself, "Blind puppy!" (p.

163). Jane aligns herself with the non-human world, both as punishment and as explanation for her unusual belief that one of Rochester's class could consider Jane worthy of notice. And soon after arriving in Morton, Jane refers to her broken heart as being "impotent as a bird with both wings broken" (p. 328). At this time when Jane feels most isolated from those around her, most outside every social community, she again labels herself with terminology from the non-human world.

The role then of negative labels is plain enough in their transforming Jane into a social outsider, but there are just as many positive terms describing Jane. For example, among other things, she is called "angel," "fairy," "dove," and "genii." But regardless of whether the labels are positive or negative, their function is the same: that is, they marginalize Jane from the community, because in the minds of those who label her, she must be transformed into something other than human.

Rochester uses the majority of these eulogistic terms, and he also, like so many others, wishes to marginalize Jane. Even though he loves Jane, he clearly believes in the traditional role of women in the nineteenth-century social order, and part of this view is the idea of woman as idol.[5] In order to worship Jane, however, he must first make her other than mere mortal. By calling her "angel" and "fairy," he separates her from other people and lifts her onto a pedestal. Jane fully understands the implications of this position and consistently rejects Rochester's attempts to turn her into what she is not. For example, when Rochester calls Jane an angel, she says, "I am not an angel" (p. 262); elsewhere she says, "Don't address me as if I were a beauty: I am your plain, Quakerish governess" (p. 261). And after Rochester threatens to dress Jane in fine clothes and jewels, she says, "And then you won't know me, sir; and I shall not be your Jane Eyre any longer, but an ape in a harlequin's jacket,—a jay in borrowed plumes" (pp. 261-62). Jane's use here of "ape," "harlequin," and "jay" shows she recognizes that to change her as Rochester wishes would transform her into something she is not. And Jane wishes to be neither sub-human nor super-human.

Similarly, Rochester uses non-human terms for Jane (even his eulogisms) because she is an enigma to him, as she is for St. John later and for society in general. Some are threatened by this; others are merely puzzled. Those at Gateshead (except Bessie) consistently find Jane different from most children. Abbot says, "I never saw a girl of her age with so much cover" (p. 12), and Mrs. Reed says, "[T]here is something truly forbidding in a child taking up her elders in that manner" (pp. 7-8). At Gateshead, Jane's difference is threatening. However, others merely see Jane as unusual. Bessie says to Jane, "You are a strange child . . . a little roving, solitary thing . . . [Y]ou're such a queer, fright-ened, shy little thing" (p. 39). St. John says to her, "You *are* original" (p. 379). And Rochester implies the same, when he says to her, "[A]ny other woman would have been melted to marrow at hearing such stanzas crooned in her praise" (p. 276). Rochester often cannot understand Jane's ideas or actions, and if she becomes for him (even if unconsciously) other than mortal, then he need not consider the implications of her views. Yet Jane simply wants to be thought of as a normal human being. And this attitude is precisely the problem, in that her assertion of equality threatens to take her out of the nineteenth-century feminine role of subservience in a male-dominated world.[6]

To twentieth-century readers, the threatening character of the novel is less apparent. But clearly such was not true for many of Brontë's time. For example, when Jane claims equal status with the Ingrams, based not on birth or wealth but rather on character, she rejects the usual criteria for evaluating class. In fact, at one point, she even claims a superiority to Blanche: "Miss Ingram was a mark beneath jealousy: she was too inferior to excite the feeling" (p. 187). And when Jane thinks Rochester "is not of their [the Ingram's] kind. I believe he is of mine;—I am sure he is . . . though rank and wealth sever us widely, I have something in my brain and heart, in my blood and nerves, that assimilates me mentally to him" (p. 177), she again asserts her equality based on character, not birth, and rejects the usual criteria for determining a mate. Similarly, when Jane says, "[W]omen feel just as men feel; they need exercise for their faculties, and a field for their efforts as much as their brothers do; they suffer from too rigid a restraint, too absolute a stagnation, precisely as men would suffer" (p. 110), she questions the traditional roles of women, again asserting an equality based on character, not birth. In each instance, she threatens established social norms. And despite the fact that Jane's views ostensibly only affect her own life, she carries the seeds of change, and the implied changes represented by Jane's actions are unusually troubling to those of her time—both inside the novel and outside it.[7] As evidenced by the virulence of some of the negative contemporary reviewers of *Jane Eyre,* many perceived Jane and the novel to be subverting social, political, and religious norms. For example, Jane's strength of character and will along with her refusal to be forced into a submissive position seem very masculine. Rochester says, "Jane, be still; don't struggle so, like a wild, frantic bird that is rending its own plumage in its desperation." Jane replies, "I am no bird; and no net ensnares me: I am a free human being with an independent will; which I now exert to leave you" (p. 256). Rochester tries to type Jane as a bird, but she rejects this label and insists on human status. He likes Jane's fiery strength, but for him Jane is a "bird" or a "fairy" at those times. If he were to think of her as a woman asserting her independence, then his position as sole master would be threatened. Consequently, even though Rochester's motives in marginalizing Jane are not malicious (as are the Reeds' and the Ingrams'), as is true for many of the characters in the novel, Rochester can deal more easily with Jane if he can view her as other than normal.

Despite the fact that Rochester accepts the traditional role of nineteenth-century women, he does not fit the stereotypical mold of the nineteenth-century male. His openness concerning his continental affairs, his willingness to engage in bigamy, and his desire to marry a woman so far below his social standing all show that Rochester rejects many of the social conventions of his day, and his willingness to move outside the social mores explains why his relationship with Jane becomes possible. One of the effects of Rochester's flouting social customs and Jane's marginalization is the curious influence it has on the rapport between them. As Rochester becomes more and more interested in developing a romance with Jane, he begins more and more to use terms of animal and supernatural imagery to describe himself. He calls himself "devil" (p. 263), "ogre" (p. 273), "ghoul" (p. 273), "dog" (p. 451), "toad" (p. 307), and "ape" (p. 307), among other things. And since Rochester has already come to view Jane as a "bird" and "fairy" (and so on), his self-labeling moves him into the non-human world inhabited by Jane and thus allows in his mind (and perhaps in hers as well) for the progression of their relationship, because Jane too picks up this labeling; she says Rochester's hair is "raven-black" (p. 436) and that he is a "fierce falcon" (p. 192), a "wild-beast or bird" (p. 436), a "caged eagle" (p. 436), a "demon" (p. 284), and "phantom-like" (p. 281), so that finally, as a consequence of this labeling, they begin to inhabit the same world. Once their engagement occurs, Rochester says, "[W]herever I stamped my hoof, your sylph's foot shall step also" (p. 262). And when Jane returns to him (in a sense sealing their engagement), she says, "[Y]ou talk of my being a fairy; but, I am sure, you are more like a brownie" (p. 443). Later, she continues this idea when she says that Rochester is like "a royal eagle, chained to a perch, . . . forced to entreat a sparrow to become its purveyor" (p. 444). At this point in the novel, they realize they are different, and they both become inhabitants of the non-human world, a world where their relationship finally comes to fruition.

Ultimately, this labeling becomes more than merely metaphoric and affects the conclusion of the novel. Certainly, Rochester's injuries from the fire are necessary to humble him, bring him to religious susceptibility, reduce his power, and make Jane more his equal; however, his physical disabilities also move him visibly away from his position as a "normal" member of society. In fact, at Ferndean, he actively seeks isolation from other people. Mary says to Jane late in the novel, "I don't think he will see you. He refuses everybody"

(p. 437). And this isolation then qualifies him to engage in a relationship with Jane. He, like Jane, becomes, in part at least, the other—because of his mutilation, his reclusive behavior, and the non-human labels used on him. Consequently, he moves more literally into Jane's sphere outside social boundaries.

As a result of all this, the rather out-of-the-ordinary relationship between Jane and Rochester becomes both possible and non-threatening to society. Of course, they are not social lepers, but they are unusual, and they seem to fit each other—and perhaps no one else. John says of the match, "She'll happen do better for him nor ony o' t' grand ladies" (p. 455). And earlier in the novel, after leaving Rochester, Jane herself feels she could marry no one but him. Also amply implied is that had Jane not returned Rochester never would have married. Consequently, their relationship at the close of the novel is much better than it would have been had they married earlier as originally planned.

Although outside the social norm, their marriage is based on mutual respect and spiritual equality, and these qualities differ sharply with the questions of wealth and class that usually determined the suitability of a match. And just as the basis for Blanche Ingram's courtship with Rochester (money) contrasts with that of Jane's courtship with Rochester (love), so also does the Rivers' kindness toward Jane contrast with the response of so many of the other characters toward her. And Jane fully recognizes her exclusion from society in the past and present. Throughout the novel, she continues to retain her solitary nature, and her isolation is both a blessing and a curse. Because others marginalize her, she learns self-reliance and strength. She also learns to trust her values and beliefs. This is in opposition to others in the novel who act in accordance with social norms rather than truths. Jane's self-reliance also carries her through her two most difficult temptations to exchange individuality and truth for acceptance. Jane spurns Rochester's offer to live with him as his mistress not because she does not love him but because she will not give up her values and her self in order to belong. Similarly, Jane rejects St. John's proposal not because she rejects the value of missionary work but because she would have to surrender her self in so doing. On the other hand, Jane also bears the loneliness of the other and often refers to herself as a social outsider. She says at Gateshead she is "an uncongenial alien permanently intruded on her [Mrs. Reed's] own family group" (p. 16). Even at Lowood, initially, she feels like an outsider: "I stood lonely enough: but to that feeling of isolation I was accustomed" (p. 49). And the scenes she painted during the holidays she passed alone at school are both solitary and otherworldly (pp. 126-27). Nor does this feeling of isolation end there. After her discovery of Bertha, Jane thinks, "Jane Eyre, who had been an ardent, expectant woman—almost a bride—

was a cold, solitary girl again: her life was pale; her prospects were desolate" (p. 298). And the night she arrives at Whitcross, she reflects, "Not a tie holds me to human society at this moment—not a charm or hope calls me where my fellow-creatures are—none that saw me would have a kind thought or a good wish for me" (p. 327); continuing on, she refers to herself as an "outcast" (p. 328) and thinks that from other humans she "could anticipate only mistrust, rejection, insult" (p. 328). This feeling of isolation from all human community culminates in her cry when turned away by Hannah: "Alas, this isolation—this banishment from my kind!" (p. 340).

In the end, this marginalization of Jane becomes a criticism of the society of that time. This becomes particularly clear in St. John's response to Jane. Throughout the novel, the characters have excluded Jane, but St. John's acceptance of her is the turning point of the novel. Brontë seems to suggest it is a terrible crime to marginalize other human beings merely because they are different from us. Where so much of the novel is spent in showing Jane (and a few others) placed outside social groups, in the Rivers' home Jane is accepted *despite* her differences. And this acceptance is precisely what Jane spends her existence trying to find. Jane's quest in the novel is always, if possible, to avoid exclusion and to move from outside to inside whatever social group in which she finds herself. For example, she says to Helen:

> [I]f others don't love me, I would rather die than live—I cannot bear to be solitary and hated, Helen. Look here; to gain some real affection from you, or Miss Temple, or any other whom I truly love, I would willingly submit to have the bone of my arm broken, or to let a bull toss me, or to stand behind a kicking horse, an let it dash its hoof at my chest.
>
> (P. 70)

Nor does this feeling change as she grows older, because when Jane discovers she is related to the Rivers, she says:

> Glorious discovery to a lone wretch! This was wealth indeed!—wealth for the heart!—a mine of pure, genial affections. This was a blessing, bright, vivid, and exhilarating!—not like the ponderous gift of gold: rich and welcome enough in its way, but sobering from its weight. I now clapped my hands in sudden joy—my pulse bounded, my veins thrilled.
>
> (Pp. 389-90)

Jane wished for such a situation. With her marriage to Rochester at the end of the novel she finally finds fulfillment by moving inside her small social group. Brontë seems to have felt it extremely important for human beings to belong somewhere, and when the Rivers take in an unknown and alien creature they are breaking away from what is otherwise the tendency of society in the novel.

One could perhaps read *Jane Eyre* as a novel that begins with a character isolated from those around her and ends with that same character accepted by her peers, because she finds her place in a family that includes the Rivers, Rochester, and her children. This certainly seems to be the intent of Jane the narrator, who wishes to see herself as moving from outside the group to inside the group. She recognizes her marginalization and tries to use her narrative to move from outside to inside. But she is only partially successful. At the close of the novel, Jane is a member of her immediate family, but she and Rochester come together because they are both outsiders; despite Rochester's religious conversion and the softening of their earlier flouting of custom, they remain both physically and spiritually outside society and its norms. As a result, Jane's relationship to society in general has not changed significantly from what it was at the opening of the novel. She is still, as St. John called her, "original" (p. 379); she still carries the seeds of change, as is seen by (in what would have been unusual for the time) her equal marriage, which if imitated would alter familial, social, and perhaps even religious forms of order. As long as Jane appears threatening to those around her, she must remain marginalized.

II

The marginalization that occurs with respect to *Jane Eyre* is not limited to the characters in the novel in their response to Jane. The contemporary negative reviewers of the novel also responded to Jane as did the novel's characters. They sought to marginalize her in order to minimize her influence on society, because, whereas Jane was simply a single insignificant person in the world inside the novel, outside the novel she carried a great deal more weight. As a character in a novel, her ideas, though threatening, have little opportunity to affect those around her, and so the other characters can comfortably transform Jane into the other and then dismiss her. As the main character in an enormously popular novel, though, her subversiveness becomes much more problematic for the reviewers because of the possible wide-reaching influence of her ideas. Consequently, although the contemporary negative reviewers respond to the same ideas as do the characters in the novel, their response is much more aggressive; they not only marginalize Jane but also Brontë herself and, through labeling, try to portray Jane, Brontë, and the novel as unnatural and something to be shunned.

Soon after the publication of the first edition of *Jane Eyre*, a virulent review appeared in *The Mirror.* The reviewer begins by suggesting, "It would be no credit to any one to be the author of 'Jane Eyre.'"[8] The reviewer then elaborates by saying that the novel "trample[s] upon customs respected by our forefathers, and long destined to shed glory upon our domestic circles" (p.

376) and that *Jane Eyre* is an example of the "many blows" that were being "aimed at our institutions, political and social" (p. 377). The reviewer continues:

> The question to be decided is, whether we shall continue to cherish respect for the faith, the customs, and religion of our ancestors, and go on in a steady course of improvement until we reach the perfection of human civilisation, or shall we pause in our career, and instead of the dictates of virtue, follow those alone which a debased nature awakens within us?
>
> (P. 377)

The reviewer further suggests, "People were once ashamed to stand forth as the advocates of vice—as the encouragers of immorality—as the promoters of every degrading vice; but such barriers are unhappily broken through" (p. 377). This reviewer sees *Jane Eyre* as one such example. The article concludes that the novel's "opinions are bad—the notions absurd. Religion is stabbed in the dark—our social distinctions attempted to be levelled, and all absurdly moral notions done away with" (p. 380). Throughout, the reviewer labels the novel and its author as subversive.

To twentieth-century readers of the novel, *The Mirror*'s accusation of such wide-sweeping subversion in *Jane Eyre* may be somewhat surprising. However, although *The Mirror* published perhaps the most virulent of the early reviews, it was not alone in its accusation that *Jane Eyre* subverted social, political, and religious institutions. For example, *The Guardian,* in disputing a theological point, says, "Neither the writer nor the editor of the book can have considered how much mischief may be done by publishing such a *creed* as this."[9] The "mischief" the reviewer implies is one that would alter (subvert) the norms of religious practice. Similarly, *The Church of England Quarterly Review* complains that Jane "is a merely *moral* person" who "might have been a Mahomedan or a Hindoo for any bias of Christianity we discover in her actions or sentiments."[10] The reviewer's fear is that others will take Jane's example and not make Christianity the basis for their moral actions.

Others complain of what they perceive as the novel's overturning proper social behavior. For example, *The Spectator* refers to "hardly 'proper' conduct between a single man and a maiden in her teens" and of "a low tone of behaviour" in the novel.[11] And the reviewer for *Graham's Magazine* writes, "We accordingly think that if the innocent young ladies of our land lay a premium on profligacy, by marrying dissolute rakes for the honor of reforming them, *à la* Jane Eyre, their benevolence will be of questionable utility to the world."[12] Again, as was true of the complaints in *The Guardian* and *The Church of England Quarterly Review* concerning the overturning of religious conventions, the reviewers here are concerned with the novel's overturning social conventions.

Brontë attempted to respond to these and other early criticisms in her "Preface" to the second edition of the novel, in which she referred to "the timorous or carping few . . . in whose eyes whatever is unusual is wrong" (p. 3). She went on to argue:

> Conventionality is not morality. Self-righteousness is not religion. To attack the first is not to assail the last. To pluck the mask from the face of the Pharisee, is not to lift an impious hand to the Crown of Thorns. These things and deeds are diametrically opposed: they are as distinct as is vice from virtue. Men too often confound them: they should not be confounded: appearance should not be mistaken for truth; narrow human doctrines, that only tend to elate and magnify a few, should not be substituted for the world-redeeming creed of Christ.
>
> (Pp. 3-4)

In this preface and in a number of letters to W. S. Williams,[13] Brontë both defends and apologizes for the otherness of the characters and events in *Jane Eyre.* In this Brontë herself sometimes shows signs of uncertainty concerning the otherness of her characters and how they may be perceived (or misperceived) by a large reading public. In part, this is because the arguments Brontë marshalled in the "Preface" to the second edition of the novel did little to change the views of the hostile reviewers. In fact, the most famous and vicious of these appeared in *The Quarterly Review* a full year after Brontë wrote the "Preface" to the second edition of *Jane Eyre.* In *The Quarterly Review*'s response to the novel, Elizabeth Rigby (later Lady Eastlake) reasserts the earlier reviewers' complaints against the novel. Among the numerous accusations leveled at both the novel and the author is the following:

> Altogether the auto-biography of Jane Eyre is preeminently an anti-Christian composition. There is throughout it a murmuring against the comforts of the rich and against the privations of the poor, which, as far as each individual is concerned, is a murmuring against God's appointment—there is a proud and perpetual assertion of the rights of man, for which we find no authority either in God's word or in God's providence—there is that pervading tone of ungodly discontent which is at once the most prominent and the most subtle evil which the law and the pulpit, which all civilized society in fact has at the present day to contend with. We do not hesitate to say that the tone of mind and thought which has overthrown authority and violated every code human and divine abroad, and fostered Chartism and rebellion at home, is the same which has also written Jane Eyre.[14]

Consequently, notwithstanding Brontë's earlier attempt to refute such accusations, Rigby re-asserts the accusations of *The Mirror,* suggesting that the novel undermines established religious, social, and political institutions of the day.[15] In fact, Rigby's may be a more considered opinion than that of *The Mirror,* since it comes well after the initial publication of the novel and is not just a reaction against the novel itself, as was that of *The Mirror* (which appeared soon after the publication of the first edition of *Jane Eyre*), but is also a reaction against the influence of the novel. By December 1848, in addition to the negative reviews, there were many positive reviews of the novel, and excerpts of a number of these were included in the third edition of *Jane Eyre* (which also appeared well before Rigby's review). Rigby was responding as much to the positive reviews of the novel as she was to Brontë and the novel itself.

Despite Brontë's assertions otherwise, then, the negative reviewers continued to view the novel as dangerous, and in order to circumvent what they saw as subversive, they used various means to marginalize the author, characters, and events of the novel. For example, they often tried to portray both Jane and Rochester (the most unconventional characters) as unnatural or abnormal and by so doing place them outside the social norm. The reviewer for the *North British Review* remarks:

> [T]here is much about her [Jane] that is hard, and angular, and indelicate as a woman . . . [T]he matter-of-course way in which she, a girl of nineteen, who had seen nothing of the world, receives his revelations of his former life, is both revolting and improbable. To a pure woman they would surely have soiled, for the time at least, the image of him who related them.[16]

The reviewer questions Jane's womanliness, suggesting that a normal "girl of nineteen" would have been revolted rather than attracted by Rochester's revelations; in others words, Jane responds contrary to what society expected of a normal young woman, and so she must be unnatural.

Rigby, commenting on the same incident, also accuses both Rochester and Jane of acting unnaturally: "He [Rochester] pours into her [Jane's] ears disgraceful tales of his past life . . . which any man with common respect for a woman, and that of a mere girl of eighteen, would have spared her; but which eighteen in this case listens to as if it were nothing new, and certainly nothing distasteful" (p. 164). As in the *North British Review,* so also does Rigby point to the unnaturalness of Rochester's and Jane's behavior in this incident and implies that any right thinking and acting person would reject such behavior.

Similarly, although most of the negative reviews of *Jane Eyre* rarely complain about the novel's aesthetics—questioning instead its ethics and propriety—they do occasionally accuse the novel's plot of being unrealistic or unbelievable. For example, Rigby writes that "the reader may trace gross inconsistencies and improbabilities" (p. 166). *The Christian Remembrancer* re-

marks, "The plot is most extravagantly improbable."[17] And *The Spectator*'s reviewer writes that the novel "is not probable in the principal incidents" and that "the whole is unnatural" (p. 1074). However, this criticism is less one of aesthetics than of ethics. The intention again appears to be an attempt to portray the novel's plot, like Jane and Rochester, as unnatural and, therefore, unsatisfactory as a model for imitation. This concern is partly perhaps because the novel is subtitled "An Autobiography" and since any claim to the reality of the actual events in *Jane Eyre* could imply their imitation in real life. And that is precisely what the negative reviewers did not want to happen.

Such accusations rarely appear, however, in the positive reviews, since they did not view the novel as threatening. In fact, they often lauded *Jane Eyre*'s realism. For example, *The Westminster Review* remarks: "[N]or can there be any question as to the *reality* of many of the scenes and personages."[18] The reviewer for *Fraser's Magazine* writes, "Reality—deep, significant reality—is the great characteristic of the book."[19] The reviewer for *Douglas Jerrold's Shilling Magazine* comments, "[W]e are inclined to think much of it veritable biography."[20] And the reviewer for *The Dublin Review* emphasizes throughout the reality of the novel, concluding by saying, "[E]very incident is exciting, unexpected; not one can be taxed with being forced, unnatural, or even improbable."[21] These reviewers did not see the novel as subversive, so they are unconcerned with whether society imitates its characters or events.

In addition to the accusations that Rochester, Jane, and the events in the novel are unnatural, many of the reviewers questioned Brontë's gender and femininity (since the novel appeared under the pen name "Currer Bell"); in these reviews, this questioning is an attempt not only to marginalize the characters and events but also to marginalize the author herself. For example, the reviewer for *The Christian Remembrancer* writes:

> Yet we cannot wonder that the hypothesis of a male author should have been started, or that ladies especially should still be rather determined to uphold it. For a book more unfeminine . . . it would be hard to find in the annals of female authorship . . . There is an intimate acquaintance with the worst parts of human nature, a practised sagacity in discovering the worst parts of human nature, a practised sagacity in discovering the latent ulcer, and a ruthless rigour in exposing it, which must command our admiration, but are almost startling in one of the softer sex.
>
> (Pp. 396-97)

Rigby concurs with *The Christian Remembrancer* concerning the authorship of the rovel: "[I]t appertains to a man, and not, as many assert, to a woman, we are strongly inclined to affirm" (p. 175). She then goes on to say, "[I]f we ascribe the book to a woman at all, we have no alternative but to ascribe it to one who has, for some sufficient reason, long forfeited the society of her own sex" (p. 176). And the reviewer for the *North British Review* writes: "All that we shall say on the subject is, that if [it is] the [production] of a woman, she must be a woman pretty nearly unsexed" (p. 487). In each instance, they portray Brontë as unnatural, and so her ideas also become unnatural.

Although there was confusion concerning the author's sex even among some of the positive reviewers, this unsexing of Brontë is not evident. For example, the reviewer for *The Westminster Review* writes: "Whoever may be the author, we hope to see more such books from *her* pen; for that these volumes are from the pen of a lady, and a clever one too, we have not the shadow of a doubt" (p. 581). *Fraser's Magazine* records: "The writer is evidently a woman" (p. 690). And the reviewer for *The Dublin University Magazine* writes, "[W]e take it for granted that this book is the work of a female pen."²² Since the favorable reviewers did not find the novel threatening, they did not need to question the possibility that a woman could have written it.

As a result, whether the characters inside the novel isolate Jane and label her as something other than human or the contemporary negative reviewers outside the novel label *Jane Eyre*'s characters, events, and author as unnatural, both the result and the motivation are the same. The community rejects Jane and her ideas because they perceive them to be threatening. Although the characters in the novel find Jane's ideas threatening, unlike the reviewers of the time who attacked *Jane Eyre,* those inside the novel can take a different tack. With the exception of the Reeds (to whom Jane represents a more immediate threat), the characters merely transform Jane into the other and then dismiss her as an enigma outside the social group. Once she is transformed, they can ignore Jane as a tiny foreign particle in the social fabric. However, this is not possible for those outside the novel; the hostile reviewers cannot merely marginalize Jane and then ignore her, because, whereas inside the novel she is only a single individual (and one with no power), outside the novel, as a popular character in a widely-read work of fiction and as a popular autobiographer/author, Jane is far more influential. Inside the novel, Jane has only limited exposure; outside the novel, she has unlimited exposure. And this influence upon society is what the reviewers so feared. Therefore, they can only defuse *Jane Eyre*'s subversiveness by attacking the novel: the characters, the events, and even the author herself. If the reviewers can show these to be unnatural and marginal, they can hinder the novel's ability to affect society. So although their methods and purposes differ, both the hostile reviewers outside the novel and the characters inside the novel attempt to minimize the subversiveness of the novel's ideas. Whether from those inside or outside the

novel, then, the response is the same: *Jane Eyre*'s ideas are a significant threat to the foundations of social, political, and religious institutions of the time, and the degree to which they can marginalize Jane and the novel itself is the degree to which they can maintain the status quo.

Notes

1. Charlotte Brontë, *Jane Eyre,* ed. Margaret Smith (Oxford: Oxford Univ. Press, 1980), p. 7. Hereafter, all quotations from *Jane Eyre* will be taken from this edition and will be followed by their page numbers in parenthesis.

2. Lynn Hamilton ("Nicknames, Forms of Address, and Alias in *Jane Eyre,*" *Literary Onomastics Studies* 14 [1987]: 69-80) suggests, "Nicknames in *Jane Eyre* function not only to indicate relation but also to reflect the protagonist's initial isolation and her transition out of isolation into relation and community" (p. 76). However, I disagree with Hamilton and will argue that the labeling used on Jane always serves to transform her into the other and that there is no real "transition out of isolation into relation and community." At the close of the novel, Jane is still isolated from all those except her family.

3. René Girard, *Violence and the Sacred,* trans. Patrick Gregory (Baltimore: The Johns Hopkins Univ. Press, 1977), p. 13.

4. Jane recognizes this when she remarks that Mrs. Reed "was resolved to consider me bad to the last; because to believe me good, would give her no generous pleasure: only a sense of mortification" (p. 233).

5. See, for example, John Ruskin's popular essay "Of Queen's Gardens."

6. In recent years, many critics have noted aspects of gender and gender equality in *Jane Eyre*. See, for example, Eva Figes, *Patriarchal Attitudes* (New York: Stein and Day, 1970), pp. 157-63; Adrienne Rich, "Jane Eyre: The Temptations of a Motherless Woman," *Ms.* 2 (October 1973): 69-72+; Carolyn Heilbrun, *Toward a Recognition of Androgyny* (New York: Alfred A. Knopf, 1973), pp. 58-59; Ellen Moers, *Literary Women* (Garden City, NY: Doubleday & Company, 1976), pp. 15-20; Nancy Pell, "Resistance, Rebellion, and Marriage: The Economics of *Jane Eyre,*" *Nineteenth-Century Fiction* 31 (March 1977): pp. 397-420; Sandra M. Gilbert and Susan Gubar, *The Madwoman in the Attic* (New Haven: Yale Univ. Press, 1979), pp. 336-71; Margaret Miller, "Happily Ever After: Marriage in Charlotte Brontë's Novels," *Massachusetts Studies in English* 8.2 (1982): 21-38; Elaine Showalter, *A Literature of Their Own: Brit-*

ish Women Novelists from Brontë to Lessing (London: Virago Press, 1982), pp. 100-32; and Cynthia Carlton-Ford, "Intimacy without Immolation: Fire in *Jane Eyre*," *Women's Studies* 15 (1988): 375-86.

7. There has been some debate as to whether *Jane Eyre* suggests any real changes in social, political, or gender issues. See, for example, Robert Bernard Martin, *The Accents of Persuasion: Charlotte Brontë's Novels* (New York: W. W. Norton & Company, 1966), p. 93; Jina Politi, "*Jane Eyre* Class-ified," *Literature and History,* 8 (Spring 1982): 56-66; Gayatri Chakravorty Spivak, "Three Women's Texts and a Critique of Imperialism," *Critical Inquiry,* 12 (Autumn 1985): 243-61; Valerie Grosvenor Myer, *Charlotte Brontë: Truculent Spirit* (London: Vision Press, 1987), p. 113; and Parama Roy, "Unaccommodated Women and the Poetics of Property in *Jane Eyre*," *Studies in English Literature 1500-1900,* 29 (Autumn 1989): 713-27. To one degree or another, these critics all suggest that Jane does not actually subvert traditional norms but rather reinforces those norms. However, whether this is true or not is irrelevant to the fact that the characters in the novel and the contemporary negative reviewers of the novel perceive Jane to be subversive.

8. Anonymous, "The Last New Novel," *The Mirror* 2 (December 1847): 376. Hereafter, quotations from this review will be followed by their page numbers in parenthesis.

9. Anonymous Review of *Jane Eyre, The Guardian,* no. 98 (December 1, 1847): 717. I should mention, however, that this was not a wholly negative review.

10. Anonymous Review of *Jane Eyre, The Church of England Quarterly Review* 23 (April 1848): 492.

11. Anonymous Review of *Jane Eyre, The Spectator,* no. 1010 (November 6, 1847): 1074. Hereafter, quotations from this review will be followed by their page numbers in parenthesis.

12. Anonymous Review of *Jane Eyre, Graham's Magazine* 32.5 (May 1848): 299. Similarly, even some of the fairly positive reviews had qualms about the novel's propriety: Mrs. [Sarah Strickney] Ellis, Review of *Shirley, The Morning Call: A Table Book of Literature and Art,* 4 vols. (London: John Tallis and Co., 1850-52), 1:35; Anonymous, "A Few Words about Novels—A Dialogue, in a Letter to Eusebius," *Blackwood's Magazine* 64 (October 1848): 474; and Anonymous Review of *Shirley, Sartain's Union Magazine of Literature and Art* 6 (February 1850): 172.

13. See, for example, December 13, 1847, December 15, 1847, February 4, 1849, March 2, 1849, April 2, 1849, August 16, 1849, August 29, 1849, August 31, 1849, September 13, 1849, and September 21, 1849.

14. [Elizabeth Rigby], "*Vanity Fair*—and *Jane Eyre*," *The Quarterly Review* 84 (December 1848): 173-74. Hereafter, quotations from this review will be followed by their page numbers in parenthesis.

15. A number of modern critics have come to agree with Rigby (and others) that *Jane Eyre* is essentially "anti-Christian," or at least that it does not profess an orthodox Christianity as the basis for individual action; among these critics are Margot Peters, *Charlotte Brontë: Style in the Novel* (Madison: The Univ. of Wisconsin Press, 1973), pp. 131-54; M. A. Blom, "Charlotte Brontë, Feminist *Manquée*," *Bucknell Review* 21 (1973): 87-102; M. A. Blom, "'Jane Eyre': Mind as Law Unto Itself," *Criticism* 15.4 (1973): 350-64; Robert Keefe, *Charlotte Brontë's World of Death* (Austin: Univ. of Texas Press, 1979), pp. 96-129; Robert James Merrett, "The Conduct of Spiritual Autobiography in *Jane Eyre*," *Renascence* 37.1 (1984): 2-15; and Carolyn Williams, "Closing the Book: The Intertextual End of *Jane Eyre*," *Victorian Connections,* ed. Jerome J. McGann (Charlottesville: Univ. Press of Virginia, 1989), pp. 60-87. Others, however, disagree and argue that Christianity forms a very important part of the makeup of the characters in the novel; see, for example, Barbara Hardy, *The Appropriate Form: An Essay on the Novel* (London: The Athlone Press, 1964), pp. 61-72; Robert Bernard Martin, *The Accents of Persuasion: Charlotte Brontë's Novels* (New York: W. W. Norton & Company, 1966), pp. 57-108; and Earl A. Knies, *The Art of Charlotte Brontë* (Athens: Ohio Univ. Press, 1969), pp. 102-43.

16. Anonymous, "Noteworthy Novels," *North British Review* 11 (August 1849): 483. Hereafter, quotations from this review will be followed by their page numbers in parenthesis.

17. Anonymous Review of *Jane Eyre, The Christian Remembrancer* n.s. 15 (April 1848): 399. Hereafter, quotations from this review will be followed by their page numbers in parenthesis.

18. Anonymous Review of *Jane Eyre, The Westminster Review* 48 (January 1848): 581. Hereafter, quotations from this review will be followed by their page numbers in parenthesis.

19. Anonymous, "Recent Novels: French and English," *Fraser's Magazine* 36 (December 1847): 691. Hereafter, quotations from this review will be followed by their page numbers in parenthesis.

20. Anonymous Review of *Jane Eyre, Douglas Jerrold's Shilling Magazine* 6 (November 1847): 473.

21. Anonymous, "*Jane Eyre—Shirley*," *Dublin Review* 28 (March 1850): 223.

22. Anonymous, "An Evening's Gossip on New Novels," *The Dublin University Magazine* 31 (May 1848): 608.

Valerie Beattie (essay date winter 1996)

SOURCE: Beattie, Valerie. "The Mystery at Thornfield: Representations of Madness in *Jane Eyre*." *Studies in the Novel* 28, no. 4 (winter 1996): 493-505.

[*In the following essay, Beattie examines the relationship between insanity and femininity in* Jane Eyre, *theorizing that Brontë's use of Bertha throws into relief the political and theoretical inconsistencies of feminist interpretations of the novel.*]

> Leah shook her head, and the conversation was of course dropped. All I had gathered from it amounted to this—that there was a mystery at Thornfield; and that from participation in that mystery I was purposely excluded.
>
> (***Jane Eyre**, [p. 161])[1]*

Whether she is construed as the champion of female rebellion, or as the image of monstrosity that Jane Eyre must reject in the course of her *Bildung*, Bertha Mason, Charlotte Brontë's paradigmatic madwoman, continues to compel feminist criticism to address the highly problematic yet omnipresent conjunction of madness and femininity. This interaction between feminist literary criticism and the text of madness in *Jane Eyre* continues to yield uneasy conclusions, and madness remains one of feminism's central contradictions. In "The Madwoman and Her Languages," Nina Baym deplores "the work Brontë has put into defining Bertha out of humanity" (p. 48), and proceeds to take feminist literary theory (ranging from French-affiliated feminisms to deconstruction) to task for its valorization of madness which, for her, "seems a guarantee of continued oppression" (p. 49).[2] Hence the conceptual impasse implied in the statement that follows the colon in her title: "Why I Don't Do Feminist Literary Theory." On the opposite side the most obvious approach is Sandra Gilbert and Susan Gubar's influential *The Madwoman in the Attic*, called after Bertha herself.[3] Although providing these critics with an inspiring title, an equally inspirational analysis of Bertha is, however, effectively blocked by their ideological alignment with the views of Rochester and Jane on madness (incidentally, Baym similarly errs in assuming the coincidence of the viewpoints of author and fictional heroine). While in their chapter on female creativity they argue that, "Specifically, a woman writer must examine, assimilate and transcend the extreme images of 'angel' and 'monster' which male authors have generated for her" (p. 17), in the chapter on *Jane Eyre* they reproduce the same repressive logic by examining Jane and Bertha in these very terms, referring to Jane as a "sane version of Bertha" (p. 366) and viewing "the loathsome Bertha" (p. 369) solely as a negative example from which Jane must be freed. In this, Gilbert and Gubar's analysis is representative of a considerable body of feminist criticism which, setting out to explicate the role of madness in *Jane Eyre* does little more than replicate ideologically problematic nineteenth-century attitudes to it.[4] Above all, what becomes apparent in the divergent positions of Baym (madness blocks feminist interpretation) and Gilbert and Gubar (madness provides feminists with an essential metaphor in a theory of female subversion of patriarchy) is not only that Bertha enacts a split within feminist literary theory regarding interpretations of female madness, but more tellingly, she throws into relief the theoretical and political inconsistencies upon which readings of her are based, betraying materialist/socialist and psychoanalytic feminism's recurring anxiety with the relation of madness to femininity. Feminist literary criticism has yet to come to terms with this madwoman in the attic.

Well over a decade following critiques of Gilbert and Gubar's ideological blindspots (their hermeneutical approach, their concept of patriarchy as all-encompassing, their race and class blindness), the thesis of madness as positive subversion in *Jane Eyre* continues either to be contradicted by feminist critical approaches, or redeemed only by reading it on a figurative level, hence divorcing it from its realist context.[5] As Shoshana Felman has remarked elsewhere, "Madness and women turn out to be the two outcasts of the establishment of readability" (p. 6).[6] In feminist interpretations of *Jane Eyre* this manifests itself as the incompatibility of realist rebellion and gothic revolt, of Jane and Bertha. However, it is my claim that Brontë does not confine Bertha within a Romantic narrative mode. Her role within the realist *Bildungsroman* is as significant as Jane's: that she overspills its boundaries adds to her importance rather than detracts from it. Eugenia DeLamotte's approach is typical of interpretations that focus on the gothic elements of the novel, posing Bertha as a foil to its realist/materialist feminism.[7] This interpretive framework necessitates that she view Bertha as the evil Other (in this case to both Jane and Rochester). Of course there is evidence in the novel to support such a reading, particularly if we as readers allow ourselves to be situated imaginatively in relation to Jane, a positionality actively encouraged by the first-person narration of the text plus, as Penny Boumelha has noted, by the plot of *Bildung,* romance, fairy-tale, folk-tale, and spiritual autobiography, to mention but a few of the narrative strands that comprise *Jane Eyre* and which encourage identification with the heroine's viewpoint.[8] But, as Boumelha goes on to argue in her analysis of class and race in the novel, feminist criticism "must not, surely, reproduce the silences and occlusions of nineteenth-century English culture in allowing the white, middle-class woman to stand as its own 'paradigmatic woman'" (p. 63).

The frequent reproduction by feminist critics of the problematic ideologies of the nineteenth century with regard to Bertha is the result, in my view, of four inter-related factors: first, of seeing her as the sole representative of madness in the novel, thereby assuming a univocal representation of Victorian insanity; second, of denying her any agency as an active subject within the narrative by interpreting her wholly metaphorically; third, by adopting an uncritical identification with the heroine/narrator, and by extension, with Rochester, given Jane's feeling that she has "something in my brain and heart, in my blood and nerves, that assimilates me mentally to him" (p. 171); and fourth, of collapsing the views of author and heroine. The second reason mentioned above, that is, Bertha's downgrading to metaphor, hinges on concepts of relations of power. It is all too often assumed that Bertha is materially powerless because of her consignment to the attic (and for some, to the always already problematic madness) whereas in fact, she spends more narrative time out of the attic, verbally and physically, than in it. In this, Brontë appears to be exploring a complexity of power relations to which critics, who are constrained by a pre-constructed categorization of madness that does not allow for the development of counter-thought, are blind. In contrast, Michel Foucault has pointed out that relations of power rely upon a certain form of liberty:

> One must observe that there cannot be relations of power unless the subjects are free. If one or the other were completely at the disposition of the other and became his thing, an object on which he can exercise an infinite and unlimited violence, there would not be relations of power. In order to exercise relations of power, there must be on both sides at least a certain form of liberty.
>
> (P. 12)[9]

The double downfall (of Rochester and Thornfield) that Bertha single-handedly brings about is inexplicable without an informed concept of agency/power relations. Brontë's overlapping of madness and power indicates a deliberate undermining of the disciplinary force of confinement. On her visits to prisons and insane asylums Brontë clearly obtained more than visions of repression. Indicatively, in her letters she associates the reality of life with repression and oppression: "I selected rather the *real* than the *decorative* side of Life—I have been over two prisons ancient and modern—Newgate and Pentonville—also the Bank, the Exchange, the Founding Hospital,—and to-day if all be well—I go . . . to see Bethlehem Hospital."[10] Furthermore, the parallel between these subjected states and, collectively, Brontë's solitary confinement in the parsonage, her fictional

metaphors of release, and her own physical release through enforced self-starvation, are striking. It would appear that madness and confinement generally presented Brontë with a powerful analogy for patriarchy's reception of female rebellion; at once active and passive, dangerous and containable, meaningful and meaningless.

There have been notable exceptions to interpretations that "shut up" Bertha in the "attic" of pathological feminine sexuality. Deborah Kloepfer's analysis, drawing on Julia Kristeva's concept of the semiotic, sees Bertha as an aspect of the repressed maternal force in language, thus extending the discussion to incorporate nineteenth-century women's problematic relationship to language in a way that moves beyond the popular psychoanalytic concept of the dark double.[11] This approach also avoids the impasse of madness as monstrosity. But while her analysis does attribute a certain power to Bertha, Kloepfer concentrates on Jane's relation to the maternal, so that Bertha's power in not linked to her madness, and the connection between it and Kristeva's semiotic is never explored, with the result that a comprehensive discussion of madness is omitted. Penny Boumelha's account is remarkable for its sensitivity to Bertha's status in the novel as "the maddening burden of imperialism" whose "'moral madness' serves to exculpate Rochester, and with him the English gentry class, from so much as complicity in her plight" (p. 61).[12] For Pauline Nestor, Bertha's madness takes second place to her importance as a sexual force.[13] Quoting the passage in chapter 27 where Rochester attempts to excuse his treatment of his mad wife by reference to her "'pigmy intellect'," and "'nature most gross, impure, depraved'" (*Jane Eyre*, p. 304), Nestor argues that it is Bertha's licentiousness not her madness *per se* that is cause for revulsion. I do not think it is useful or possible to separate the two: madness, feminine sexuality, and the female body are directly bound up with each other in both nineteenth-century and present day discourses on insanity, so that arguing for their mutual independence ultimately misrepresents both.

What is persistently lacking in interpretations of *Jane Eyre* is a concentrated focus on the text of madness. In attending to the representations of madness in the novel, my reading, like Kloepfer's, uses Julia Kristeva's theory of the semiotic as it helps to focus the significance of Bertha, designating "the contribution of sexual drives to signification."[14] However, as both novel and theory hinge on the coupling of madness and social/linguistic subversion, I will interpret them in relation to each other. That is to say, the semiotic is not viewed solely as a maternal language as in Kloepfer, but as further having an intrinsic relationship to both feminine sexuality and madness, a relationship Brontë exploits to the full. By way of the insights into linguistic and physical rebellion that Kristeva's theory offers, I hope to demonstrate that Brontë's deployment of madness does not entail social paralysis, given that she neither makes female protest unintelligible nor limits it to mental rebellion. Instead, by relating insanity to supposedly "sane" characters like Jane, Rochester and St. John Rivers, Brontë refuses to subjugate it to reason, destabilizes the relationship of signifier to signified, highlights the roles that language and the unconscious play in the constitution of subjectivity, and challenges the ideological conjunction of madness/femininity/the female body. In this, Brontë prefigures Michel Foucault's important insights into the constitution of madness in the eighteenth century as a behavioral and linguistic dis-order, a divergence from the values and practices of hegemonic society, that demonstrates how the triumph of sanity is ensured by the social nature of insanity.[15] Within the terms of the novel she enacts a "violent hierarchy" (to borrow Derrida's term) between sanity and insanity, realism and gothic revolution, so that each constantly fights for supremacy. Finally, the metaphorical echoes of madness in the last chapters of *Jane Eyre* register Brontë's refusal to surrender the thematic and linguistic disruptions afforded by her deployment of insanity for a safe, familial enclosure at Ferndean.

Julia Kristeva's theory of the semiotic is essentially non-linguistic. She locates the semiotic in literature/ "poetic language" at the level of the "genotext," denoting its relationship to genesis, hence to notions of generation, creation, production, and the maternal body. She calls the expression of symbolic language (Lacan's Name/No-of-the-Father) the "phenotext," a term that has its roots in phenomenology. While all texts are "phenotexts," that is, all texts refer to observable phenomena, they also include within them that which is outside or other to empirical reality. In this way phenotext and genotext are dependent on each other for their existence. The force of the maternal semiotic is such that it is in constant conflict with the symbolic/paternal force: while the symbolic is established by means of the repression of the semiotic, the repression is not complete, allowing the constant re-emergence of the latter into the symbolic. Its articulation in the phenotext is negative, destablizing meaning. As Kristeva argues:

> The presence of the *genotext* within the *phenotext* is indicated by what I have called a *semiotic disposition*. In the case, for example, of a signifying practice such as "poetic language," the *semiotic disposition* will be the various deviations from the grammatical rules of the language: articulatory effects which shift the phonemative system back towards its articulatory, phonetic base and consequently towards the drive-governed basis of sound production; the over-determination of a lexeme by multiples which it doesn't carry in ordinary usage but which accrues to it as a result of its occurrence in other texts; syntactic irregularities such as ellipses, non-recoverable deletions, indefinite embeddings, etc.
>
> (P. 28)[16]

The deployment of madness generally in *Jane Eyre* can be called semiotic in so far as it enacts an overdetermination of the signifier "madness." As Kloepfer has remarked, "there is an unsettling sense of something *working beneath the surface*" (emphasis mine; p. 28) in Brontë's novel. However, because of the centrality and power of "mad" behavior in the narrative of *Jane Eyre,* I interpret this "something" as the disruptive force of madness generally, rather than the threat of incest, or engulfment by the mother. As I have stressed, Bertha is not the sole representative of subversion in the novel. But what makes her pivotal is that her character embodies the fusion of a continuous literal *and* figurative challenge to social norms, a challenge that other characters enact in a perfunctory way. And because of her figurative ascendancy over other characters, her threatening presence is not expelled from the novel with her immolation.

The ways in which Brontë applies the word "madness" and its cognate terms, "maniac," "lunatic," and "insanity," to several of the characters in *Jane Eyre* is a rejection of semantic certainty, and could be viewed in Kristeva's terms as an oscillation between semiotic and symbolic. All in all there are approximately forty occurrences of the word itself, or of its related terms. It is used most often to describe Bertha, but occurs also in descending order of frequency in descriptions of Jane, Rochester, Bertha's mother and brother, and St. John Rivers. Its function as a descriptive and prescriptive mode of application varies from character to character and from situation to situation. Genotextually, it is most obvious when Rochester speaks indirectly to Jane of Bertha, and Jane perceives his language as "all darkness to me," "enigmatical" and bewildering (pp. 134-35). A similar effect occurs when he is telling Jane of his first inkling of Bertha's power to destroy:

> "kindly conversation could not be sustained between us, because whatever topic I started immediately received from her *a turn at once coarse and trite, perverse and imbecile.*"
>
> (Emphasis mine; p. 304)

She overturns Jane's thoughts in a similar and equally potent way. In relation to the novel's structure and its theme of feminist rebellion, I think it is no coincidence that the reader's and Jane's first encounter with Bertha is aural, and that the sound we hear is her laughter, "jolt[ing]" both reader and Jane out of the symbolic realm.[17] While, as Linda Kauffman asserts, "the master has the supreme authority to impose silence on all the women of Thornfield" (p. 170), Bertha is not relegated to silence.[18] In effect, she occupies the forbidden place within symbolic language. Additionally, given the general schematic contexts in which her laughter takes place, we, like Jane, are clearly meant to take notice of it. Note also that when it is first presented in the narrative Jane describes it as "distinct, formal, mirthless" (p. 102), not hysterical, or blubbering. And it is surely ironic that Brontë reintroduces Bertha's laugh at the moment in Jane's narrative when she is most overtly political in her aspirations regarding women's status. The juxtaposition of Jane's liberal rhetoric with "the same low, slow ha! ha!," and "eccentric murmurs" (p. 105) would appear to be a subtle prevision to the reader of the ideological prejudices that will accompany Jane's impending transition from penniless orphan and "revolted slave" to family heiress. As such, Bertha's semiotic intrusion into the text becomes an implicit but crucial disparagement on the class and race bias of Jane's imperatives, particularly her passionate admonition that it is "thoughtless to condemn [women], or laugh at them, if they seek to do more or learn more than custom has pronounced necessary for their sex" (p. 105). For as we later discover, Jane's approach to women's liberation is exclusive. She may desire a power of vision surpassing the limits assigned to her gender and class for herself, yet she deems the norm appropriate for Adèle who is forced to forget "her little freaks, and bec[o]me obedient and teachable" (p. 104).

Given Rochester's fury at the verbal perversion Bertha imposes on him, it is clear that it is in the realm of ideas that she is most oppositional. According to Kristeva, the phenotext is a "structure" that "obeys the rules of communication and presupposes a subject of enunciation and an addressee" (*Kristeva Reader*, p. 122). Although Rochester presents his Rousseauian expectations of women and his language as eminently rational, Bertha undermines them. This is because her voice, which Jane likens to a "mocking demon" (p. 206), does not presuppose a subject of enunciation and an addressee. Rather, it drives through the phenotext articulating the re-emergence of repressed feminine rebellion, thereby "evading the censorship of realism."[19] In this way her presence, whether visible or invisible, is repeatedly mobilized by Brontë to undercut Rochester's (and to a lesser degree, Jane's) expectations of femininity. Materially, she contrives to overthrow his corrupt plans by revealing her social presence as his wife, and succeeds, despite Rochester's displacement of her existence onto Jane's "'over-stimulated brain'" (p. 281). It is, after all, primarily around the fact of Bertha's existence that the novel constructs its implicit critique of the problematic conventions of Victorian romantic courtship and the misogynist prison-like conditions of patriarchal marriage. Viewed through a theory that allows feminists to intervene on behalf of the madwoman from a standpoint that grants her validity, the body and mind of Bertha Mason come to provide incontrovertible proof of the veracity of Jane's blithe statement to Rochester that the tales she hears "'generally run on the same theme—courtship; and promise to end in the same catastrophe—marriage'" (p. 194). It is by virtue of her deformation of traditional meanings associated with middle-class femininity ("'I had marked neither modesty nor benevolence, nor candour nor refinement in her mind or manners'"); feminine sexuality (Rochester tells Jane that Bertha is debauched [p. 309]); and marriage (Rochester's inability to lead his wife's thoughts along his lines: "her cast of mind common, low, narrow, and singularly incapable of being led to anything higher" [p. 303]), that the novel unites a concept of linguistic rebellion with a redefinition of femininity. The agency that Brontë bestows on Bertha—her calculated attack on Rochester in his bed; her timely rending of the wedding veil, her laugh—runs counter to interpretations of her offered by Rochester and by critics who collude with his viewpoint as simply mad and beyond reach. In addition, the personal, sexual and social benefits her rebelliousness has for Jane places her in a powerful position in the narrative, one that belies disempowering discussions of her as materially ineffective, or merely Jane's double, or not worthy of examination.

I now want to turn to chapters 25 and 26 of *Jane Eyre* as it is here that some feminists have found the most objectionable descriptions of Bertha, while at the same time she is at her most powerful physically. It is clear that the two are interconnected, and I would like to explore why.

It has been noted that the Victorian preoccupation with physiognomy and phrenology links natural status and natural character.[20] Physically, Bertha is described as "a big woman, in stature almost equalling her husband, and corpulent besides" (p. 391). Such is the unfeminine excess she unleashes that finally, she can no longer be delineated in human terms: "it grovelled, seemingly, on all fours; it snatched and growled like some strange animal" (p. 290). Yet the implication of imbecility this implies is contradicted by Grace Poole's announcement that "'One never knows what she has, sir: she is so cunning: it is not in mortal discretion to fathom her craft'" (p. 291). Sexually, she is "unchaste," "depraved" (p. 304), and the imperialist Rochester views her Creole origins as a reflection of her sexual difference, making her antithetical to Jane's English Protestant purity. Patricia White has noted that in classic horror films a potentially empowering affinity exists between the woman and the monster, enabling the articulation of deviant femininity.[21] In *Jane Eyre* this effectively applies to both Jane and Bertha: Jane becomes like a "mad cat"; Bertha is "like some strange wild animal" who springs at Rochester and "grapple[s] his throat viciously" (p. 291). Through the variable verbal and physical release afforded by madness, both women contest the subjected positions into which they have been forced through the restrictions of gender, class, and race norms. Furthermore, it clearly demonstrates Brontë's refusal, contrary to nineteenth-century masculine philosophical thought, to divorce emotion and reason in her delineation of a revolutionary character. And, it is through the resistance offered by madness that Jane achieves integrity of self. Her narrative makes it manifest that however distastefully her subversion is viewed, it is through "madness" that principal and virtue find a voice:

> *Speak* I must: I had been trodden on severely, and must turn: but how? What strength had I to dart retaliation at my antagonist? I gathered my energies and launched them in this blunt sentence—[. . .]
>
> "Deceit is not my fault!" I cried out in a savage, high voice. [. . .]
>
> I was left there alone—winner of the field. It was the hardest battle I had fought, and the first victory I had gained.
>
> (Brontë's emphasis; pp. 30-31)

Although she later regrets the "madness of my conduct" (p. 32), it is a fleeting regret, recognizably bound up in the economic impotence associated with childhood. This is borne out later when the same anarchic force fails to prevent Jane from announcing to Helen how she would treat the loathsome Miss Scatcherd if she struck her with a rod (p. 50), despite the threat of expulsion. And so, while Jane is acutely aware of the implicit and explicit mechanisms of control that the label "madness" activates and justifies, at this stage in the narrative she refuses discipline and submission when they knowingly conflict with what she believes to be right and humanitarian, albeit within the confines of her class and race prejudices. By thus rendering "madness" as a primary motivating force in her heroine, Brontë defies the negative meanings historically associated with it, and bestows on it a power that extends beyond mere disruption, a power that recognizes wrongs and will act to right them. And this power is nowhere more tangible than with the representation of Bertha Mason. With Bertha, Brontë seems to exploit the verbal and physical release afforded by madness to its (logical?) conclusion: her rebellion oversteps "natural" bounds and becomes atavistic. This would seem to be the inevitable result of situating a sexually voracious, independent-minded and wealthy woman within the confines of a white, Protestant, nineteenth-century *Bildungsroman*. My central point, however, is that examined closely, Bertha frustrates a "normal" or unproblematic reading of Jane-as-heroine and dramatizes the oppression on which her final success is based. In this way the threat she poses is never contained. In line with this, Julia Kristeva has elsewhere characterized the conflict in literature between the semiotic and the symbolic as literature's "speaking schizo" because it enacts conceptual splits or contradictions. Literature causes a "new rationality" to be "unceasingly reconstituted . . . in the tension, the battle between the symbolic and the semiotic" (p. 33).[22]

Linda Kauffman has argued that the similarities in the positions of Jane and Bertha in relation to Rochester signify an empathy between them and that Jane's retrospective narration enacts a vocalization of Bertha's mute suffering, "speak[ing] the silence that is woman" (p. 193). However, this ignores the divergent subject positions that the two have taken up in the course of the narrative. Jane's rebellion against social codes is fleeting and with maturity is repudiated. Thus, she denounces as "madness" the temptation to stay with Rochester, preferring instead to "keep to the law given by God; sanctioned by man" (p. 314). At Moor House she pronounces "household joys" "'The best thing the world has!'" (p. 388). Thereafter, as many critics have noted, Jane providentially inherits the earth.

I noted earlier that Bertha's power extends to the figurative level of *Jane Eyre*. Her sexuality and "mad" rebellion is linked with fire throughout, and she operates most forcibly at night when others are asleep and conscious control is at its minimum. The fire she sets in Rochester's chamber becomes her voice: the "tongues of flame" (p. 145) announce her presence as much as her laughter. Her figurative position sustains her literal one: her primary symbolic color is black, connoting the unconscious, the unknown, the repressed; and her attacks coincide with the lunar cycles.[23] Because of the subversive significance this imagery has throughout the novel, it is noteworthy that its illustrative potential recurs in the final chapters. As such, it operates in a like manner to the metaphorical level of *Villette*: Rosemary Clark-Beattie comments that the realist narrative in *Villette* "never achieves the ontological priority over figurative language" (p. 832), so that the ending remains ambiguous.[24] The density of images of darkness in the final chapters of *Jane Eyre* is striking, especially given that the last two see Jane in Ferndean, a place ordinarily conceptualized as the sanctuary of the happy couple. Instead of images of benevolent happiness, however, we find Jane married to a blind Rochester, living in a house that is "buried deep in a wood" which grew "so thick and dark . . . about it" that it is invisible even from "a very short distance" (p. 429). The almost overwhelming gloom produced by this claustrophic environment clearly complicates the 'happy ending'. Essentially, it signals the omnipresence of the dark forces that have been at the heart of the narrative, and which will not be banished. Even when Rochester regains his sight signalling a respite from darkness, a son is born whose eyes are "large, brilliant and black" (p. 451). The last words in the novel come from St. John who is saving "dark" souls in "darkest" India: and he is dying. Thus, the imagery of the Ferndean chapters exceeds the novel's closed ending. Dark forces refuse to be expelled despite Bertha's exit, implying that the threat of the semiotic remains after her death. Given this, the homeliness of Ferndean is, finally, as precarious as that of Thornfield.

The displacement of rebellion onto the figurative level of the text is inscribed on and follows Bertha's suicide.

The way feminist critics interpret her death depends largely on the way Bertha herself has been construed. Elisabeth Bronfen disallows this transposition of Bertha's usurping power, claiming that "death puts closure on [her] liminality and the disruption [her] presence caused" (p. 222). Given the power allocated to her from the moment she enters the narrative I feel that it is essential to recuperate the symbolism of the last chapters and relate it to Bertha and to her exit from the novel. In effect, her exit is no more spectacular than her presence throughout. Her glorious conflagration relies heavily on myth and signifies her final condemnation of Rochester and her refusal to face life on his terms. Instead she chooses death on her own terms. The description of the actual moment of her death is horrific, emphasizing the way her body overspills its boundaries even at the moment of her exit from the novel: "'Dead! Ay, as dead as the stones on which her brains and blood were scattered'" (p. 427). This is by no means an unproblematic end for Bertha, or for a feminist reading that seeks to incorporate her. But what it does highlight is the irreconcilable dualities of femininity within Victorian culture: to be deviant, whether as Jane or Bertha, is to partake of "insanity" and run the risk of being locked up in the Red Room or in the attic at Thornfield. The heroine's punishment for childish rebellion was confinement in the Red Room for a few hours: Bertha's confinement lasted years, so it is only fitting that her escape should be dramatic and, unlike Jane's, on her own terms. This polarity also enacts a split on the level of narrative mode exemplified in Bertha's oscillating realist and metaphoric roles. The way in which she is allocated a figurative presence in the end signifies Brontë's unwillingness to banish the power she has represented, thus enacting a lasting evasion of the closure and disappointment Gillian Beer sees as endemic to the *Bildungsroman* (p. 110). As such, the semiotic continues to enact a split, weakening Jane's surface recuperation of socially approved femininity and exceeding a closed ending. Literal madness has been expelled, final freedom attained, and Bertha's power legitimated in its figurative omnipresence. Thus, the novel is open-ended. Rachel Bowlby comments that Jensen's *Gradiva* positions archaeology as both theme and metaphor in the narrative articulating psychoanalytic methods, scientific and general knowledge, and the status and role of Gradiva, the heroine.[25] It has been my argument that Bertha specifically, and madness broadly, operate similarly to vocalize and denounce the philosophy of "suffer and be still" applied to women in the nineteenth century. An acknowledgement of the danger of choosing the path of madness need not and should not foreclose explorations into its specific literary and sociohistorical usage. It is only if we choose to downgrade the role of madness that we blind ourselves to the painful "new rationality" that Brontë has "unceasingly reconstituted

. . . in the tension, the battle between the symbolic and the semiotic," between "normal" confinement and an always already dangerous female revolution.

Notes

My thanks to Trudi Tate for her invaluable advice and encouragement.

1. *Jane Eyre* (1847; rpt., London: Chatto & Windus, 1972). All subsequent references to this work are to this edition and are cited parenthetically in the text by page number.

2. Nina Baym, "The Madwoman and Her Languages: Why I Don't Do Feminist Literary Theory," *Tulsa Studies in Women's Literature* 3.1-2 (Spring/Fall 1984): 45-59.

3. Sandra Gilbert and Susan Gubar, *The Madwoman in the Attic: The Woman Writer and the Nineteenth-Century Literary Imagination* (New Haven: Yale Univ. Press, 1979). All subsequent references to this work are cited parenthetically in the text by page number.

4. Karen Chase interprets Bertha as reflecting Jane "at certain angles and at certain times" (p. 73), and is a "false alternative" (p. 79) for her, *Eros and Psyche: The Representation of Personality in Charlotte Brontë, Charles Dickens and George Eliot* (New York: Methuen, 1984); Barbara Hill Rigney discusses Bertha as the insane doppelgänger "who must be done away with physically and as a shadow in the mind" (p. 32), *Madness and Sexual Politics in the Feminist Novel* (Wisconsin: Univ. of Wisconsin Press, 1987); Elisabeth Bronfen interprets her as "an agency of Freud's murderous Id," Jane's "darkest double" (p. 221), *Over Her Dead Body: Death, Femininity and the Aesthetic* (Manchester: Manchester Univ. Press, 1992), pp. 219-24. Recent accounts that tend to marginalize Bertha's role in the novel include, Nancy Jane Tyson, "Altars to Attics: The State of Matrimony in Brontë's *Jane Eyre*," in *The Aching Hearth: Family Violence in Life and Literature*, ed. Sara Munson Deats (New York: Plenum, 1991); Alison Milbank, *Daughters of the House: Modes of the Gothic in Victorian Fiction* (New York: St. Martins, 1992); Craig Randall, "Logophobia in *Jane Eyre*," *Journal of Narrative Technique* 23.2 (Spring 1993): 94-113.

5. In their reading of Charlotte Perkins Gilman's "The Yellow Wallpaper," Lynne Pearce and Sara Mills take issue with critics who divorce madness from its materialist basis in the text, arguing that madness "cannot be regarded as revolutionary if, for the subject concerned, it is co-terminous with their material oppression" (p. 194), Sara Mills et

al., *Feminist Readings/Feminists Reading* (London: Harvester Wheatsheaf, 1989). The same problem arises with attempts to construe Bertha's situation as purely revolutionary as, by implication, they must override her real oppression in the novel. However, I want to argue that Brontë's text privileges neither a reading that denies Bertha power on the basis of her incarceration, nor one that attributes unequivocal power to her, but rather, by way of the varied linguistic and material representations of madness, complicates both these readings. For similar objections to the trope of madness by feminist critics see Janet Todd, *Feminist Literary Theory* (Cambridge: Polity Press, 1988).

6. Shoshana Felman, "Women and Madness: The Critical Phallacy," *Diacritics* 5 (1975): 2-10.

7. Eugenia C. DeLamotte, *Perils of the Night: A Feminist Study of Nineteenth-Century Gothic* (New York: Oxford Univ. Press, 1990), pp. 193-228.

8. Penny Boumelha, *Charlotte Brontë* (London: Harvester Wheatsheaf, 1990), p. 63. All subsequent references to this work are cited parenthetically in the text by page number.

9. Michel Foucault, "The ethic of care for the self as a practice of freedom," *The Final Foucault,* ed. J. Bernauer and D. Rasmussen (Cambridge, MA: MIT Press, 1988).

10. Ellipses and emphasis in original. Qtd. in Robert Keefe, *Charlotte Brontë's World of Death* (Austin: Univ. of Texas Press, 1979), p. 36.

11. Deborah Kloepfer, *The Unspeakable Mother: Forbidden Discourse in Jean Rhys and H.D.* (Ithaca, NY: Cornell Univ. Press, 1989). All subsequent references to this work are cited parenthetically in the text by page number. In her discussion of language in *Jane Eyre,* Margaret Homans focuses on Jane only. See chapter 4 in *Bearing the Word: Language and Female Experience in Nineteenth-Century Women's Writing* (Chicago: Univ. of Chicago Press, 1986).

12. See also Gayatri Spivak, "Three women's texts and a critique of imperialism," *Critical Inquiry* 1 (1985): 243-61; and Jean Rhys's fictional exposition of Bertha in *Wide Sargasso Sea* (Harmondsworth: Penguin, 1988).

13. See Pauline Nestor, *Jane Eyre* (London: Harvester Wheatsheaf, 1992), p. 59.

14. Elizabeth Grosz, *Sexual Subversions* (Sydney: Allen & Unwin, 1989), p. 42. Other critical commentaries include, John Lechte, *Julia Kristeva* (New York: Routledge, 1990); *Abjection, Melancholia, and Love: The Work of Julia Kristeva,* ed. J. Fletcher and A. Benjamin (New York: Routledge, 1990); Kelly Oliver, *Reading Kristeva: Unraveling the Double-bind* (Bloomington: Indiana Univ. Press, 1993), and *Ethics, Politics and Difference in Julia Kristeva's Writing,* ed. Kelly Oliver (New York: Routledge, 1993). For Kristeva's own detailed account of the semiotic see *Desire in Language: A Semiotic Approach to Literature and Art,* ed. Leon S. Roudiez, trans. Thomas Gara et al. (New York: Columbia Univ. Press, 1980) and *The Revolution in Poetic Language,* trans. Margaret Waller (New York: Columbia Univ. Press, 1984).

15. Michel Foucault: "the constitution of madness as mental illness, at the end of the eighteenth century, affords the evidence of a broken dialogue, posits the separation as already effected, and thrusts into oblivion all those stammered, imperfect words without fixed syntax in which the exchange between madness and reason was made" (p. 67), *Madness and Civilisation: A History of Insanity in the Age of Reason,* trans. Richard Howard (New York and London: Tavistock, 1967).

16. "The System and the Speaking Subject," in *The Kristeva Reader,* ed. Toril Moi (Oxford: Basil Blackwell, 1987). All subsequent references to this work are cited parenthetically in the text by page number.

17. Kristeva characterizes laughter as a semiotic impulse in *Desire in Language,* p. 284.

18. Linda Kauffman, *Discourses of Desire: Gender, Genre and Epistolary Fictions* (Ithaca: Cornell Univ. Press, 1986). All subsequent references to this work are cited parenthetically in the text by page number.

19. This phrase is taken from Mary Jacobus's reading of *Villette* to which I am indebted for clarifying some of my thoughts regarding Bertha's role, *Reading Woman: Essays on Feminist Criticism* (London: Methuen, 1986), p. 48.

20. Gillian Beer, *Darwin's Plots: Evolutionary Narrative in Darwin, George Eliot and Nineteenth-Century Fiction* (New York: Routledge and Kegan Paul, 1983). All subsequent references to this work are cited parenthetically in the text by page number.

21. Patricia White, "Female Spectator, Lesbian Spectre: *The Haunting,*" in *Inside/Out: Lesbian Theories, Gay Theories,* ed. Diana Fuss (New York: Routledge, 1991), p. 44.

22. "The Subject in Signifying Practice," *Semiotexte* 1.3 (1975): 55-87.

23. Elaine Showalter ties this in with the tenets of psychiatric Darwinism which holds the female body, particularly the reproductive organs, accountable for madness, *The Female Malady: Women, Madness and English Culture, 1830-1980* (London: Virago, 1987).

24. Rosemary Clark-Beattie, "Fables of Rebellion: Anti-Catholicism and the Structure of *Villette*," *ELH* 5 (1986): 821-47.

25. Rachel Bowlby, *Still Crazy After All These Years: Women, Writing and Psychoanalysis* (New York: Routledge, 1992), p. 163.

Nels C. Pearson (essay date fall 1996)

SOURCE: Pearson, Nels C. "Voice of My Voice: Mutual Submission and Transcendental Potentiality in *Jane Eyre*." *Victorian Newsletter* 90 (fall 1996): 28-32.

[*In the following essay, Pearson proposes that the final sentences of* Jane Eyre, *which are a quotation from a letter by St. John Rivers, represent the culmination of a number of religious and spiritual themes explored throughout the novel.*]

In setting out to discuss any novel that falls into the category of "fictions of female development" (as ***Jane Eyre*** certainly does), I am always struck by a vivid recollection of the final sentences of Virginia Woolf's *Mrs Dalloway:* "'It is Clarissa,' he said. For there she was" (194). Unlike the protagonist of a *bildungsroman,* Clarissa Dalloway achieves self-affirmation in terms of being, not becoming; in terms of steadfast spiritual identity amid the whirlwind of society, not in terms of individual development versus society. In short, we read Clarissa Dalloway as a woman who has established herself in spite of the cultural and textual conventions that might otherwise define and inform her identity. I submit that we owe Jane Eyre the same reading, and that Jane's often debated submissiveness to Edward Rochester at the end of the novel is actually a strong example of Christian humility and spiritual identity that serves as a fitting closure for the theme of resurrection that the novel passionately evokes. In terms of narrative voice, I wish to argue that Jane's autobiographical "I," or her passion for and ultimate possession of a narrative voice, results not from her success or failure as a woman exercising her free will as "other," but from the mutual submission to the will of God and subsequent spiritual rebirth that she and Rochester ultimately achieve.

One of the keys, I believe, to how we read, or misread, Jane is in how closely we examine the unexpected and intricately heteroglossic[1] final sentences of the book.

Jane ends her narrative by quoting a letter from the resolute missionary St. John Rivers, to whom she narrowly escapes betrothal in chapter thirty-four. The final words of St. John's letter come directly from the Revelation of St. John the divine, and they comprise the penultimate sentence of the Bible: "'My master,' he says, 'has forewarned me. Daily he announces more distinctly,—Surely I come quickly! and hourly I more eagerly respond,—Amen; even so come, Lord Jesus!'" (398). As Carolyn Williams has pointed out, this ending is more than a final appeal to St. John Rivers and a seeming submission (or entrusting of narrative closure) to a male voice. It is, in fact, a coming together of many voices, and, upon closer reading, we notice that these sentences combine the voices of Jane (who writes the words), St. John Rivers (whose letter they come from), and St. John the Divine, whose biblical prophecy ends with them (Williams 68). Ultimately, however, the words belong to God, who originally "spoke" them to St. John the Divine during his vision of the Revelation. Thus the book closes with a voice that is at once male and female, but also with a voice that is, first and foremost, the voice of God. Most importantly, the final words serve as an allusion to resurrection and rebirth in which the narrative authority subtly slips outward from Jane, to Rivers, to a Christian prophet, and, finally, to God. If ***Jane Eyre*** is about submission, then it is *mutual* submission that the text is ultimately working towards.

Turning from the end of the book to the first page, we notice that Jane begins her narrative not with the "I" that dominates the book, but with "We": "There was no possibility of taking a walk that day. We had been wandering indeed, in the leafless shrubbery an hour in the morning . . ." (5). Curiously enough, the pronoun "we" has no clear antecedent. The penultimate chapter of the book ends with the sentence "We entered the wood and wended homeward" (395), and the "we," in this case, refers to the reunited and soon to be married Jane and Rochester. Thus the narrative of events leading up to Jane's marriage begins and ends with "we," and the novel itself ends with a potential symbol of a mutual submission to a higher authority (God) out of which something entirely new is created. Perhaps ***Jane Eyre*** is not, after all, the story of an individual voice "becoming," but the story of a mutual voice restoring its prodigal halves (male and female) into a resurrected "being," so that it can "speak." But such an assertion requires a re-investigation of how we have read Jane, and ***Jane Eyre*** up until this point.

Reading Jane as a potential heroine of individual development has understandably inspired many feminist critics to express their dissatisfaction concerning the circumstances under which Jane finally returns to Rochester.[2] Celebrating the manner in which Jane has matured, for thirty-seven chapters, by rejecting a series of male authorities, these critics read her eventual marriage to the deformed Rochester as a final act of submission, typical of any Victorian woman, that seriously damages Jane's emergence as a strong and independent heroine. It seems to me, however, that the majority of contemporary debates on *Jane Eyre's* obvious vacillation between submission and self-actualization assume that we are obliged to describe the process by which she inhabits and rejects phallic authorities in terms of how successful she is in scaling the steps of social or political advancement. That is, we judge her on grounds of becoming. But if we champion Jane's role as "woman becoming," then we are not only setting ourselves up to be disappointed by her ultimate submission to Rochester, but, far worse, we also are limiting Jane by attempting to gauge her (and the novel itself) according to traditional patterns of achievement that are both male and secular. Such a reading is no doubt prefigured by our culturally, historically, and textually based expectations concerning plots of ascension, and these expectations are understandably strengthened by the first quarter of the novel in which we hear Jane confidently beginning to exercise her right to self-expression.

I doubt that we ever see a more openly defiant and outspoken Jane than we do in the novel's opening scenes when she confidently lashes out at her guardian, Mrs. Reed: "'How dare I, Mrs Reed? How dare I? Because it is the *truth.* . . . People think you a good woman, but you are bad; hard hearted. *You* are deceitful!'" (33). If we expect Jane to establish a stronger individual voice that this, then we will end up with a jeremiad, and not a *bildungsroman.* This early impression of Jane's emerging voice is one that we do not readily want to part with, but I think that is Brontë's point. Much as she does with Rochester (who eventually loses his hand, his sight, and his agnosticism before marrying Jane), Brontë builds Jane up only to demonstrate the spiritual value of humility by bringing her back "down."

It is during this same scene, and in a reference to it many chapters later, that Brontë gives us several important clues about the sources and components of Jane's narrative voice, and about the problems we ought to encounter in trying to read her narrator into the role of a male protagonist in a *bildungsroman.* Notice, for example, the somber realization that Jane has after she finishes her aforementioned tirade. After her speech to Mrs. Reed, she stands on the same spot where Mr. Brocklehurst (that "black pillar" of male authority) had previously stood. Especially since it follows Jane's strong assertion of voice, this act should function as a symbol of female authority replacing male authority (and of youth replacing adulthood), but Jane tells us that she was already uncomfortable with such a pattern of ascension. As the mature Jane recalls, "I was left there alone—winner of the field. . . . and I enjoyed

my conqueror's solitude. First, I smiled to myself and felt elate; but this fierce pleasure subsided in me as fast as did the accelerated throb of my pulses" (32). She later adds that her outspokenness "gave me a sensation as if I had been poisoned" (32). Clearly, Jane has realized early in life that the triumph of individual voice is not much of a triumph at all.

But what gives Jane the impetus to break out of her silence and to speak with such defiance in the first place (here and elsewhere in the novel) may be more than just her own developing "female" voice. There is at least the suggestion of a male voice in this scene as well, and it is quite possibly that of the late Mr. Reed, whose supernatural presence had earlier caused Jane to scream out in the "red room." In fact, Jane's description of the scene prior to her outburst against Mrs. Reed sounds curiously as if Mr. Reed is more than just in her thoughts as she prepares to speak out against her confinement:

> [Mrs. Reed] dared me in an emphatic voice to rise from that place, or utter one syllable, during the remainer of the day.

> "What would uncle Reed say to you, if he were alive?" was my scarcely voluntary demand. I say scarcely voluntary, for it seemed as if my tongue pronounced words without my consenting to their utterance: something spoke out of me over which I had no control.
>
> (23)

Several times throughout the novel, Jane refers to a "voice within" over which she has no control. On this particular occasion, the "voice within" seems mysteriously connected with a male voice, or a male presence. If there is any doubt as to whether or not a male voice is partly responsible for Jane's outburst, that doubt is cleared up nearly 200 pages later, when Mrs. Reed, on her deathbed, recalls the moment and tells Jane about the frightening sensation she experienced upon hearing Jane's unusual voice:

> "I could not forget your conduct to me, Jane—the fury with which you once turned on me . . . the unchildlike look and voice with which you affirmed that the very thought of me made you sick. . . . I could not forget my own sensations when you thus started up and poured the venom of your mind: I felt fear, as if an animal that I had struck or pushed had looked up at me with human eyes and cursed me in a *man's* voice."
>
> (210, my italics)

The possibility of a muted male voice throughout Jane's narrative, the theme of disembodied voices, and symbols of male and female voices merging are anything but foreign to the text of ***Jane Eyre.*** When Jane recalls how she returned to Rochester's mansion at Thornfield only to find it destroyed by fire, she adopts a third-person male perspective to compose an extended metaphor for her own sensations upon seeing the charred remains of the house:

Hear an illustration reader.

A lover finds his mistress asleep on a mossy bank; he wishes to catch a glimpse of her fair face without waking her. . . . All is still: he again advances: he bends above her; a light veil rests upon her features: he lifts it, bends lower; now his eyes anticipate the vision of beauty. . . . How hurried was their first glance! But how they fix! How he starts!. . . . He thought his love slept sweetly: he finds she is stone dead.

I looked with timorous joy towards a stately house: I saw a blackened ruin.

(373)

Asking us to "hear" her "illustration," Jane is calling attention to her own narrative voice, and the passage that follows is an exercise in constructing an effective metaphor to capture the emotion of the scene in words. But the important thing here is that Jane, in one of her longest intimate addresses to the reader, decides that *male* experience, a man's emotions upon finding his lover dead, best explains her own feelings on seeing Thornfield burned and confronting the possibility that Rochester died in the blaze. The best way, or perhaps the only way, for Jane to describe metaphorically the female's sensation upon finding the male dead is to describe concretely the male's sensation upon finding the female dead. Thus, for Jane, the male and female perspectives are not unique, the loss or separation is *itself* unique, and in recounting the events leading up to the merger of male and female, she can easily slip from a female to a male perspective to describe the sensation of their union, or the anxiety of their separation. In fact, as Jane moves from third person male perspective back to her autobiographical "I," she poetically repeats the sentence structure (and very nearly the meter) to emphasize the fluidity of the transition: "He thought his love slept sweetly: he finds she is stone dead. I looked with timorous joy towards a stately house: I saw a blackened ruin" (373).

In chapter nineteen, Jane encounters Rochester in the disguise of a gypsy woman, and she notices something peculiar about the gypsy's voice: "The old woman's voice had changed: her accent, her gesture, and all were familiar to me as my own face in glass—as the speech of my own tongue" (177). This is actually a multiple figuration of the androgynous voice.[3] Rochester speaks in a woman's voice, while Jane describes the features of Rochester's male voice that slip through his feigned female voice as "the speech of my own tongue." Not unlike her earlier experience with a "voice within," however, Jane is mystified by the sensation of feeling uncontrollably connected with a male voice. It is not until the "call scene," in which she hears the disembodied voice of Rochester crying, "Jane! Jane! Jane!," that she immediately responds to a male voice, follows its commands, and returns, without reservation, to be united with its source. Jane leaves Rochester after dis-

covering that he is already married, but, during their separation, Jane is preparing to marry the "cold, hard, ambitious" St. John Rivers when she hears a voice on the wind calling her:

"What have you heard? What do you see?" asked St. John. I saw nothing but I heard a voice somewhere cry—"Jane! Jane! Jane!" nothing more. . . . it did not come out of the air—nor from under the earth—nor from overhead. . . . And it was the voice of a human being—a known, loved, well remembered voice—that of Edward Fairfax Rochester, and it spoke in pain and woe wildly, eerily, urgently.

"I am coming," I cried. "Wait for me! Oh, I will come!"

(369)

The important thing about the call scene, as we find out in chapter thirty-four when we hear Rochester's version of the event, is that *each* lover hears the *disembodied* voice of the other. St. John's inability to hear the voice proves that Rochester is "speaking" to Jane through some medium altogether removed from the physical world. This is a symbol of the potential for *spiritual* union that was absent during the entire tenure of the couple's relationship at Thornfield.

In the gypsy scene, Rochester's disguise functions as a symbol of how his desire to be spiritually attached to Jane is actually a masquerade of the truth, which is that he is already married. Thus the symbol of the androgynous voice is suggested, but the actual spiritual coalescence of male and female cannot be realized until he confesses that what he is really proposing to Jane is adultery, and until he admits that no true union of spirit and flesh can be achieved under such circumstances. But Jane has her own impediments to admit. Looking back at her desire for Rochester at Thornfield, Jane tells us that she too was incapable of submitting to a full spiritual commitment:

My future husband was becoming my whole world. . . . He stood between me and every thought of religion, as an eclipse intervenes between man and the broad sun. I could not, in those days, see God for his creature: of whom I had made an idol.

(241)

Jane's mature words remind us that, throughout much of the novel, the typically Victorian and myopically secular problems of the flesh—of social status imposing upon and impeding the physical consummation of "true love"—have clouded the minds and souls of *both* Jane and Rochester. Thus we cannot say that either Jane or Rochester is more to "blame" than the other for the couple's inability to achieve love in the spiritual sense, nor, in light of the call scene, can we say that one "gets" or "wins" the love of the other. In short, it ought to be very difficult to politicize their relationship, seeing as each must surrender his or her stubborn individuality, and sacrifice his or her role as man or woman "becoming" in secular society, to gain a higher understanding of a transcendental reality.

The best explanation, I think, for why the disembodied voices achieve chiasmic unity on the wind is that during their separation Jane and Rochester have each come to a more complete understanding of the spiritual nature of their attraction, and of human attraction in general. Once the couple is reunited, Rochester tells Jane that he has recently confessed his sins to God: "'I began to see and acknowledge the hand of God in my doom. I began to experience remorse, repentance; the wish for reconcilement to my maker.'" Most importantly, he tells Jane that after saying his "'brief but sincere'" prayers, he longed for her "'both with soul *and* flesh'" (393, my italics). Jane, on the other hand, overcomes her concern with *individual* physical submission, and longs to embrace the mutual joys of both the spirit and the flesh, when she realizes that a marriage to St. John Rivers on terms of "principle" alone would be a "murderous martyrdom" in which "the spirit is quite absent" (356). In fact, Jane ultimately bases her decision to leave St. John on the impossibility of merging with him in both the spirit and the flesh. "'I can not marry you and become part of you,'" says Jane (359). She rejects him not because she refuses to submit to him, but because she cannot go through with a marriage in which mutual submission is not the rule. Marriage to St. John would be a spiritual death, but marriage to Rochester is ultimately a spiritual resurrection.

Many contemporary readings of *Jane Eyre,* however, tend to disagree strongly with that statement. Critic Bonnie Zare, whose recent essay entitled "*Jane Eyre*'s Excruciating Ending" gave me the initial impetus to do the research for this article, tells us that "to readers with feminist concerns, the ending may make for painful reading" (205). I would argue that it is not what side of the gender coin we call as readers that unveils the potential pitfalls of the text. Instead, it is the fact that we are so inclined to define our existence in terms of binary oppositions in the first place that makes the text seem to resist, or blunt, the ways in which we *want* to read it. Regardless of whether we approach the text with feminist sympathies, the primary reason we read *Jane Eyre* as a blunted exercise in free will is that we come to it with pre-conceived ideas about the relative position of men and women in society, and with ready-made assumptions concerning the "conventions" of marriage. Both culturally and textually, they are plots we know all too well. But our notions about marriage, as well as our awareness of the gender hierarchy, also have some of their deepest roots in our reading of another text—the Bible. But Brontë is out to question the standard interpretation of that text as well, as her 1848 preface to *Jane Eyre* makes abundantly clear: "conventionality is not morality. Self righteousness is not religion. To attack the first is not to assail the last. To pluck the mask from the face of the Pharisee, is not to lift an impious hand to the Crown of Thorns" (1).

Indeed, one of the main conventions that Brontë attacks in *Jane Eyre* is the manner in which Victorian society (specifically the church) interpreted the Bible's approach to marriage. The popular reading was (and, for the most part, still is) that marriage is an act of free will for men, and an act of submission for women. The biblical reading that Brontë bestows on *Jane Eyre,* however, is probably related to the view of marriage as mutual submission that Paul proposes to the Ephesians when he writes that marriage is "submitting yourselves one to another in the fear of God" (Eph. 5:12). But the strongest relationship between Brontë's text and arguably "unconventional" biblical stories of marriage is that between Jane and Rochester's "call scene" and the highly sensual dialogue of bride and groom that comprises the Song of Solomon.[4] The plots of the two stories are curiously similar, as is the manner in which each tale suggests the potentiality of metaphysical discourse between lovers. According to the biblical story, Solomon and his Shulamite bride endure a "lapse and restoration" much as Jane and Rochester do. In fact, almost the entire dialogue of the Song takes place as the two separated lovers search for each other. Drawn by the *disembodied* voice of the bridegroom, the bride passionately pines away for the moment when she can be reunited with him in the flesh: "The voice of my beloved! Behold, he cometh leaping upon the mountains, skipping upon the hills. . . . My beloved spake, and said unto me, Rise up, my love, my fair one, and come away" (Song 2: 8-10). What is true for the biblical lovers is true for Jane and Rochester: the disembodied voices of each "other" can establish presence only by achieving a unity that is at once physical and spiritual.

Throughout the novel, then, Brontë has been battling against convention—in a sense the conventions of her own text—to define the equality of Jane and Rochester on terms that are increasingly spiritual, and decreasingly democratic or political. As Jane says to Rochester moments before he makes his *first* marriage proposal, "'I am not talking to you now through the medium of custom, conventionalities, nor even of mortal flesh—it is my spirit that addresses your spirit; just as if both had passed through the grave, and we stood at God's feet, equal—as we are!'" (222). Although the trial of separation must occur before Jane's pleading becomes prophecy, these words anticipate the spiritual harmony that Jane and Rochester ultimately realize. In order to fully "be," or in order to achieve complete "existence" and, ultimately, presence of voice, Jane Eyre must unite herself with her spiritual equal, Edward Rochester. Thus in terms of autobiographical narrative, it is Rochester's voice (the missing male counterpart to her female voice) that Jane must find before she can achieve" her own voice—before she can truly narrate the story not simply of her life, but of *their* life. As Carolyn Williams writes, "the call scene produces the last turn in the plot, its resolution, and thus—according to the logic of first-person retrospective form—the achieved voice which generates the entire narration" (79). According to this reading, the novel is not about the development or becoming of a single voice (male or female); it is about the coming together into being of two separate voices. Instead of seeking to establish equality by tenuously balancing their relative positions on a social hierarchy that is responsible for the creation of sexual "others," Brontë's hero and heroine combine in mutual submission to God, who, by this analogy, becomes the "transcendental other." Or, to be more precise, Brontë's answer to the problem of earthly "otherness" is that if a woman and a man *mutually* submit to the understanding that all humans, regardless of sex or race, are collectively "other" even to the mere *idea* of God, then something "new" can be created. That something "new," in the unique case of *Jane Eyre,* is the text itself, or the authoritative presence of its narrative voice.

But how can we know that Jane's marriage has had such a powerful effect on her when she explains painfully little about the ten years between her marriage and her decision to begin writing her story? If we re-examine the chronology of events in *Jane Eyre,* we realize that Jane does in fact do something of great importance during these ten years. At the end of the first quarter of the novel, Jane's childhood friend Helen Burns, a mysteriously saint-like and submissive Christian, dies of consumption, and Jane writes that "for fifteen years" Helen's grave "was only covered by a grassy mound; but now a grey marble tablet marks the spot, inscribed with her name, and the word 'Resurgam'" (72). Jane is ten years old when Helen dies, at least eighteen when she is married, and at least twenty-eight when she begins her narrative. Thus, Jane erects the stone after her marriage and before she begins to write. The importance of the inscription, Latin for "I shall rise," is that it symbolizes how Jane has finally come to realize the significance of Helen Burns's steadfast allegiance to the virtues of Christian humility. In her formative years at Lowood, Jane was mystified by Helen's seeming stoicism, especially in the face of death. But Helen's final act of submission, Jane finally understands, was not a submission to her disease, but an acceptance of the will of God—an act of sacrificing one's mundane identity and status that, like Jane's own, leads to resurrection or spiritual rebirth. Jane's choice of Helen's epitaph is actually her first "narration" (since she chooses the words that appear on the stone), and, significantly, the brief narrative on the headstone indicates that Jane has come to a deeper understanding of the connection between submission and resurrection *before* she begins her story. Jane does not mention Helen in the final chapter, but the final words of the book ar-

guably contain the voice of Helen as well as the other voices I mentioned previously. As St. John, anxiously awaiting a reunion with God, closes the book with the words "'hourly I more eagerly respond,—Amen; even so come, Lord Jesus,'" so too had Helen, on her death-bed, told Jane 'I count the hours till that eventful one arrives which shall restore me to him, reveal him to me'" (71).

In this respect, the last chapter of the book ought to read as a thematic coda, and not a note of dissonance or insignificance. Zare, however, contends that the ten-year time lapse between the wedding and the final chapter indicates that Jane feels that her life after marriage is no longer interesting enough to write about, and that she has sacrificed her individuality to Rochester. She states that the final chapter, with its "shrinking time frame, and matter-of-fact tone," suggests:

> a shrinking of fulfillment and creativity. . . . It is telling that Jane does not create a tapestry of words to describe her married life. In the pattern of most eighteenth-century heroines, once she is married her communication stops. The disturbing suggestion is that once women are wives, they do not see their experiences as individuated enough to merit description.
>
> (213)

I couldn't disagree more. It is exactly the influence of the marriage, or the union of two souls and voices, that has sparked Jane's creativity, for it is under these circumstances that she begins to write. Unlike nearly *all* eighteenth-century heroines, Jane ends by returning to write her own story. Once she is married, her communication *starts.* In fact, Jane suggests that her passion for narrative grows out of her passion for Rochester. As she tells us in the last chapter,

> He saw nature—he saw books through me; and never did I weary of gazing for his behalf, and of putting into words the effect of field, tree, town, river, cloud, sunbeam . . . and impressing by sound on his ear what light could no longer stamp on his eye.
>
> (397)

With respect to the assertion that marriage is a "deindividuating" experience that does not "merit" description, Brontë's reply is that marriage, in the ideal spiritual sense, is *about* sacrificing our stubborn individuality and becoming "one flesh." Furthermore, the reason Jane doesn't narrate the important details of her marriage is that mere everyday language can no longer tell the "facts" of her story. Or, in Jane's own words,

> I have been married for ten years. I know what it is to live entirely for and with what I love best on earth. I hold myself supremely blest—blest *beyond what language can express;* because I am my husband's life as fully as he is mine. No woman was ever nearer to her mate than I am; ever more absolutely bone of his bone and flesh of his flesh.
>
> (397, my italics)

In other words, the lovers discourse that they share—the impetus for Jane's narrative voice—is at once androgynous and metaphysical;[5] it is pleasantly "other" to the entire system of language as we know it. "To talk to each other," writes Jane, "is but a more animated and audible thinking" (397). Because common speech is based on binary oppositions, it can neither penetrate nor translate their discourse, nor does their discourse require translation. We might add to Jane's description that Rochester has become "voice of her voice" (and vice versa), for within the mind or soul of each partner forever lies the voice of the other.

Notes

1. For the sake of context, I have made an educated guess at the adjectival form of the term "heteroglossia," which Mikhail Bakhtin coined to describe a text, or parts of a text, in which any number of "voices" are represented in what otherwise seems to be a single layer of narrative.

2. See London. According to London, while the novel is revolutionary in that it insists on portraying feminine psychology and establishing a female voice, the subject of the novel nevertheless remains Jane's (or Brontë's) ultimate submission to both the literary and social conventions of the Victorian era. London contends that while Jane has established her literary voice, she only uses it to "document and produce the docile body approved for Victorian womanhood, a body organized for social use: to serve, to suffer, to sacrifice, to (silently) obey" (199). Also see Zare, in which the author argues that Jane's final submission to Rochester makes for "painful reading" for "readers with feminist concerns" (205).

3. I use the term *androgynous* somewhat reluctantly. Although it does describe a union of male and female, it does not necessarily imply that any new voice or new being has been created from the synthesis of the two, nor does it imply a spiritual, as well as a physical, merger, both of which I mean to describe.

4. Although the "Song" never explicitly mentions Christ or the Church, it is often thought to be an allegory for Christ, the bridegroom, ravishing his bride, the church. However, the Song of Solomon is so overtly sensual that many churches and temples are hesitant to teach it. At one time, the Jewish faith decided that no one should read the song until he or she reaches the age of thirty (Henry 811).

5. In fact, Brontë seems to have answered, by adding the dimension of transcendence, the question of androgynous discourse that would later fascinate Virginia Woolf. As Woolf writes in *A Room of One's Own,* "One has a profound, if irrational, instinct in favour of the theory that the union of a man and a woman makes for the greatest satisfaction, the most complete happiness. But . . . [I] also ask whether there are two sexes in the body, and whether they also require to be united in order to get complete satisfaction and happiness? . . . The normal and comfortable state of being is that when the two live in harmony together, spiritually cooperating. If one is a man, still the woman part of the brain must have effect; and a woman also must have intercourse with the man in her. Coleridge perhaps meant this when he said that a great mind is androgynous. It is when this fusion takes place that the mind is fully fertilized and uses all its faculties" (170-71). Jane's gradual surrender of authority makes us aware that to accomplish this act of unity is also to achieve transcendence, and thus to submit to an idea or design beyond the circumambient world.

Works Cited

Brontë, Charlotte. *Jane Eyre.* 2nd ed. New York: Norton, 1987.

Henry, Matthew. *Commentary on the Whole the Bible.* Ed. Rev. Leslie F. Church. Grand Rapids, MI: Zondervan, 1961.

London, Bette. "The Pleasures of Submission: *Jane Eyre* and the Production of the Text." *ELH* 58 (1991): 195-213.

Williams, Carolyn. "Closing the Book: The Intertextual End of *Jane Eyre.*" *Victorian Conventions.* Ed. Jerome McGann. Charlottesville: U of Virginia P, 1989. *60-89.*

Woolf, Virginia. *A Room of One's Own.* New York: Harcourt, 1929.

———. *Mrs. Dalloway.* New York: Harcourt, 1990.

Zare, Bonnie. "Jane Eyre's Excruciating Ending." *College Language Association Journal* 37 (1993): 204-220.

Chih-Ping Chen (essay date winter 2002)

SOURCE: Chen, Chih-Ping. "'Am I a Monster?': *Jane Eyre* among the Shadows of Freaks." *Studies in the Novel* 34, no. 4 (winter 2002): 367-84.

[*In the following essay, Chen focuses on the attic scene at Thornfield Hall, contending that its power is derived from several contemporary references, including the dramatic intensity and narratives employed by nineteenth-century freak shows.*]

Is it an Animal? Is it Human? Is it an Extraordinary Freak of Nature? Or is it a legitimate member of Nature's Work?

—*The Illustrated London News,* 29 August, 1846

In the deep shade, at the farther end of the room, a figure ran backwards and forwards. What it was, whether beast or human being, one could not, at first sight tell [. . .].

—*Jane Eyre*

For Charlotte Brontë's readers, a generation indulging their appetite for monstrous marvels, the attic scene on the third floor of Thornfield in *Jane Eyre* might have been surprising, but not unfamiliar. When Rochester reveals the existence of his mad wife Bertha Mason, Jane Eyre and her wedding party are led into "a wild beast's den" (336), their eyes drawn toward a dark figure:

> In the deep shade, at the farther end of the room, a figure ran backwards and forwards. What it was, whether beast or human being, one could not, at first sight tell: it grovelled, seemingly, on all fours; it snatched and growled like some strange wild animal: but it was covered with clothing, and a quantity of dark, grizzled hair, wild as a mane, hid its head and face.
>
> (321-22)

Rochester's audience is witnessing a scene that, in image, rhetoric, and form, echoes many nineteenth-century displays of anomalous bodies—giants, dwarfs, Siamese twins, hermaphrodites, fat ladies, living skeletons, wild men, and noble savages—in taverns, on street corners, in upper-class houses or courts, or in metropolitan exhibition places like Leicester Square and Egyptian Hall in London. Bertha's entrance recalls that of the "Hottentot Venus," one of the most notorious figures in London freak shows, who would emerge "like a wild beast, and [was] ordered to move backwards and forwards, and come out and go into her cage, more like a bear in a chain than a human being" (qtd. in Altick 269). The suspense surrounding Bertha's appearance echoes the provocation in advertisements such as that of "the Wild Man of the Prairies" in *The Illustrated London News* cited above. Though the show, the first of the "What Is It?" exhibitions staged by the famous showman Phineas Taylor Barnum, was promoted particularly with the appeal of the "missing link"; Barnum's advertisement, like many nineteenth-century freak show advertisements or handbills, established the attraction by emphasizing how the freak body borders on the boundaries of human and animal.

Yet the astounding power of this scene relies on more than the *images* from nineteenth-century freak shows. Significantly, the scene achieves much of its dramatic effect and intensity by evoking the entwined narrative forms that *produce* freak shows, including, as Rosemarie Garland Thomson notes, the advertisement ac-

count of the freak's "extraordinary" life and identity, the showman's pitch that introduces the exhibited body by emphasizing its "deformity" or "anomaly," the staging that involves performances monitored by the showman, and the display that functions to establish the distance between the "civilized" spectator and the freak (Introduction 7).

With the rhetoric of a freak show host, Rochester introduces Bertha, highlighting her "exotic" background and hybrid inheritance as the "anomalous": "Bertha Mason [. . .] came from a mad family; idiots and maniacs through three generations! Her mother, the Creole, was both a madwoman and a drunkard!" Describing himself as both a "civilized" host and a human victim of deception, Rochester invites his audience to see her as the monstrous: "You shall see what sort of a being I was cheated into espousing, and judge whether or not I had a right to break the compact, and seek sympathy with something at least human" (320). In Bertha's "goblin cell" (336), Rochester enacts the performance of a man and a "clothed hyena," making Bertha a supporting player:

> [T]he clothed hyena rose up, and stood tall on its hind-feet. [. . .] Mr. Rochester flung me behind him: the lunatic sprang and grappled his throat viciously, and laid her teeth to his cheek: they struggled. [. . .] He could have settled her with a well-planted blow; but he would not strike: [. . .] he bound her to a chair. The operation was performed amidst the fiercest yells and the most convulsive plunges.
>
> (321-22)

The audience's gaze ends at center stage, not on the figure but on the host. They are directed to see him as a non-violent, therefore, "civilized" keeper of the bestial body and also a wronged man—"Mr. Rochester turned to the spectators: he looked at them with a smile both acrid and desolate." Rochester further highlights the differences between Bertha and Jane in physical features to dehumanize Bertha—"Compare these clear eyes with the red balls yonder—this face with that mask—this form with that bulk." Jane is given definite human characteristics, she is "this young girl" with a face, a form, and "clear eyes"; while the black-visaged Bertha is called a "mask" and "bulk" with "red balls" of a "demon." Rochester closes the scene in the words of a show keeper and Bertha as his property—"off with you now. I must shut up my prize" (322).

By foregrounding the tensions in the framing structure of freak shows, Brontë reveals her interest in the dynamics of identification and differences surrounding Victorian freak bodies, and in how the meaning of "freakishness," as Robert Bogdan argues, depends heavily on the strategies of presentation; it is "something we created: a perspective, a set of practices—a social construction" of "freakishness" (xi). My discussion of *Jane Eyre* explores Bertha's "enfreakment" as a paradigm for the larger drama of Jane's identity quest. The Rochester-Bertha freak show is but one of the freak show metaphors underlining Jane's struggle toward a desired female selfhood. From Gateshead Hall to Lowood School and to Thornfield, Jane's journey in status from being discriminated against as a "bad animal" (41)—because of her social hybridity (the orphan child of a poor curate and a rich man's daughter)—to becoming a British "lady" reveals the metaphoric connection of the struggles of a woman to assert her "self" and freakery as a cultural discourse.

Feminist readings of Bertha have emphasized her as the colonial body whose presence is inseparable from Brontë's inscription of her Victorian heroine's subjectivity. Gayatri Chakravorty Spivak argues that Jane's progress from the "counter-family marginalization" to "the marital and sexual self-location in the family-in-law set" is conditioned by the "unquestioned ideology of imperialist axiomatics." Jane's struggle for feministic individualism, she notes, excludes the claim for humanity by Bertha, the "native subject" (265). Susan Meyer challenges Spivak's idea of exclusion and sees more ambiguity in the ways in which the ideology of imperialism is questioned and then re-affirmed in Jane's identification with and differentiation from Bertha's body of the dark race (66, 95). While Meyer's argument persuasively brings out more complexities of Bertha's function as supported by Brontë's text, it is clear, in addition, that Brontë intends Bertha to be read as a racial freak body because Jane's most defining "colonial encounter" with Bertha is coined emphatically in the images and form of a freak show. Bertha's oppression and inferiority are configured and fused in images of both the racial other and the exotic display. Bertha's "enfreakment," her deviant womanhood defined by Rochester, and her body mediated and appropriated by him for display embodies the gender hierarchy that also oppresses Jane as the cultural/social "other." Brontë, however, is not merely using the "other" to create or define Jane. Posing Jane's body both in association and dissociation with a woman's subjected body, Brontë uses freak shows to reinforce patriarchal oppression as well as to articulate her awareness of how the perception of the freakish bodies becomes overdetermined culturally and politically in the nineteenth-century, during which the British people witnessed the most intense phenomena of freak shows.

The concept of "freak" finds its root in the etymology of an older term, "monster," the term used in the nineteenth century. "Monster," as defined in Hensleigh Wedgwood's 1878 *Dictionary of English Etymology,* is related to *moneo,* "to warn" and *monstro,* "to show forth." Encoded in this etymology of "freak," freak shows, from their earliest appearances, embody a power that marks the "monstrous" body as a lesson for the

viewers. Until the eighteenth-century, religious justification had dominated the interpretation of the monstrous births in Europe as "ominous signs of God's displeasure with sinful behavior" for the intended viewers (Semonin 71). As Victorian spectacles, Rosemarie Garland Thomson argues, the "monstrous" became important images in the society's self-examination and self-definition in the increasing expansion of scientific knowledge, marketplaces, and England's relations with non-European countries (Introduction 2). Reading monstrosity within the bio-social context of evolution, Charles Darwin in his chapter "Varieties Under Nature" in *Origin of Species* (1859) does not dismiss the importance of monstrosities as "varieties" forming a part of the evolution drama of the human species; but he also acknowledges his society's recognition of the monstrous as defective products of the human species: "By a monstrosity I presume is meant some considerable deviation of structure in one part, either injurious or not useful to the species and not generally propagated" (38). In popular culture, such "deviation" is imbued with political and racial significations. The extraordinary bodies, in Thomson's words—"rare, unique, material, and confounding of cultural categories"—function as "magnets to which culture secures its anxieties, questions, and needs" (Introduction 2). They intrigue because they are perceived as emerging from humans to "traverse the very boundaries that secure the 'normal' subject in its given identity and sexuality"; they destroy the boundaries between self and other because the monstrous "involve all kinds of doubling of the human form" (Grosz 64). The freak spectacles invited the British viewers to speculate on human development and civilization but also helped feed the viewers' sense of secured social/cultural status by inviting the audience to confirm their "normality" and the "superiority" of British nationality. The gratifying affirmation of "normality" broadened to include cultural superiority when bodies of indigenous people—American Indians, Hottentots, "Kaffirs," and unknown racial types—became booked in the same venues as the physiologically monstrous bodies (Kaplan xvii). Racial otherness and deformity became related phenomena and were treated as such. The former was often interpreted by viewers' associating the racialized body with monstrous bestiality. The keeper of "Hottentot Venus" was not considered unjustified in his claim that his exotic creature had "as good a right to exhibit herself as an Irish Giant or a Dwarf etc. etc" (Edwards and Walvin 172). This dehumanizing blurring extended to the indigenous as races. As Paul Jeoffrey Edwards and James Walvin argue in their study of Africans employed as freaks, although white freaks were exhibited as oddities whose attraction was determined by how they were distinguished from the other members of their species, dark freaks were invariably exhibited as representative of their race: "The Black freak could be used to blur this distinction, as [. . .] in the case of the Hottentot Venus, by placing members of an already degraded race in a position of further degradation and by reinforcing the conception of Africa as a place of monsters" (151). Charles Mathews, a visitor of the show, described how "Hottentot Venus" was treated: She was "surrounded by many persons, some females! One pinched her, another walked around her; one gentleman poked her with his cane; and one lady employed her parasol to ascertain that all was, as she called it, 'nattral'" (qtd. in Altick 269). The process of "othering" also functions to justify the colonial relation. The "Hottentot Venus," her keeper, Henrick Caesar, contended, was "a subject well worthy of the attention of the [European] Virtuoso" after "the English last took possession of the colony" (qtd. in Edwards and Walvin 172). The production of the "Hottentot Venus" as an appealing display for the gaze of Europe thus served white supremacy and legitimated colonial exploitation. Likewise, Rochester's display of Bertha Mason as the "clothed hyena" (321) aims to justify his "civilized" status and treatment of his colonial "other."

Brontë's insights into freakery as a cultural discourse do not end here. She also draws attention to the logic of Victorian freak shows as a product of a dynamic relation between the host, the exhibit, and the viewer. In this triangle, the host figures in different roles-an exhibitor, a representative of the imperialist culture, and sometimes, a gazer. She reworks this dynamic to define and destabilize the structure of domination in patriarchal power relations: her heroine confronts the host in a variety of displays to gain a measure of agency and selfhood. In *Discipline and Punish*, Foucault sees in the spectacles of public torture and execution in the seventeenth and eighteenth centuries a power that operates through discriminatory differentiation (32-33). "The body of the condemned" is the emblem of the sovereign's power in establishing the truth of the crime and marking the criminal's body "either by the scar it leaves on the body or by the spectacle that accomplishes it, to brand the victim with infamy; even if its function is to 'purge' the victim" (34). Yet the punishing subject also faces a political danger, as the criminals' gallows speeches or the spectacle of the devastated body may invite sympathetic identification from the spectators who "never felt closer to those who paid the penalty than in those rituals intended to show the horror of the crime and the invincibility of power; never did the people feel more threatened, like them, by a legal violence exercised without moderation or restraint" (63). The boundaries between the spectators and the displayed body are replaced by the tension between the spectators and the sovereign power, since "through the tortured body of the criminal, the power that condemned confronted the people that was the witness, the participant, and the possible and indirect victim of this execution" (68). The crowd, seeing the tortured body or listening to the condemned individual cursing the judges, the

laws, and the government, might regard the punishment as unjust. Protests and revolts were incited, and "rules were inverted, authority mocked and criminals transformed into heroes" (61). The spectators, subverting the sovereign authority, inscribe themselves and the criminal into power.

Shifting the spectacle from political tensions to gender tensions, Brontë's *Jane Eyre* uses a woman's marked and displayed body in a freak show as a "site," a configuration of the effects of power relations played out in the interactions of the host, the spectacle, and the spectator. A woman's body exhibited as freak becomes an insignia of patriarchal authority, which defines women's secondary social positions by connecting women closely to the body and containing them within bodies that are represented, even constructed, as inferior and unruly. Discussing the disturbing cultural images of freaks, Thomson emphasizes the similarities between freaks and women, the connections that Brontë obviously pursues: "the freak is represented much like the woman: both are owned, managed, silenced, and mediated by men; both are socially defined as deviations from the ideal masculine body; both are marginalized in the realm of economic production; both are appropriated for displays as spectacles; both are seen as subjugated by the body" (*Extraordinary Bodies* 71). In *Jane Eyre,* Brontë evokes the images, form, and the ideological significations of freak shows to inform a gendered dynamic of dominance and resistance.

In her encounters with patriarchal authorities—her emotional and physical abuse by "Master" John in her adopted family, her disciplinary exposure by Rev. Brocklehurst at Lowood Institution, and her gender "education" under Rochester at Thornfield—Jane is forced to see herself, whether as the exhibit or the spectator, in the image of an anomalous body. With "exhibition" as the key configuration of his power and practices, the defining gaze of the patriarch in the figure of a show host establishes the truth about the "crime" of a woman. Her disobedience or transgression justifies his power to punish her by marking, through racialization and/or bestialization, a woman's unruly body as a freak body. On the other hand, "exhibition" also becomes a site for a woman's resistance by repositioning and enabling her to re-invent herself. Jane defies male authority by rejecting the imposed image of monstrosity but also by embracing the freak's unruly energy in her artistic imagination, creating her own spaces in which she can be a host to herself in order to express an escape from, a comment on, and finally a defiance of the subjecting power and gaze.

Jane is first associated with the freak image in the Red Room, when she is punished for daring to strike back at John Reed, her "Master." At Gateshead, she is subjected to gazes that judge her as anomalous. She is scolded by Mistress Reed for lacking a "social and childlike disposition" (39) and called a "wild cat" (44) by the servants. In confronting John Reed, she is incriminated as a "bad animal" (41) and locked in the Red Room. In this space where objects of no use to the household are exiled, she is made to "see" her anomalous position inside her stepfamily and outside in the world. The room mirrors her perceived alien-ness in the image of a folklore freak: "the strange little figure there gazing at me with a white face and arms specking the gloom [. . .] like one of the tiny phantoms, half fairy, half imp, Bessie's evening stories represented as coming out of lone, ferny dells in moors, and appearing before the eyes of belated travellers" (46). The supernatural creature intruding on human paths defines for Jane her social heterogeneity in the image of the "other" as seen by her foster family: "I was a discord in Gateshead Hall; I was like nobody there; [. . .] They were not bound to regard with affection a thing that could not sympathize with one amongst them; a heterogeneous thing, opposed to them in temperament, in capacity, in propensities" (47). If the folklore freak image interprets for Jane the impossibility of her being accepted in the world of Gateshead, it also defines the energy she can rely on to assert herself. The fairy-imp combines the elements of benevolent and malevolent, monstrous and angelic; Jane, the orphan who wants to be accepted, both fears and embraces the unruly energy to challenge her closely defined existence and the conventional "order of things."

Such energy manifests itself already at the beginning of the novel, in her window-seat reading. Drawing the curtain "nearly close," she enshrines herself in a space inside Gateshead but outside its society like a barbaric Turk (39) to read her uncle's *History of British Birds,* a book belonging now to "Master" John. As critics such as Carla L. Peterson have noted, her reading encodes a subversive rebellion against male authority in ownership and in interpreting the world. Her creative imagination transforms the male-authored "vignettes" of science into a female psychological landscape. History is made obsolete, and objective knowledge becomes a signifier for self-expression. The "death-white realms" of "solitary rocks and promontories" of "the bleak shores of Lapland, Siberia, Spitzbergen, Nova Zembla, Iceland, Greenland" and of the "vast sweep of the Arctic Zone" are emptied of their referential world of ornithology, geography, and natural history, displaced by a female point of reference to convey her sense of death-like alienation: "I formed an idea of my own: shadowy, like all the half-comprehended notions that float dim through children's brain, but strangely impressive." The sense of marginalization is mixed with an unconscious desire for power, the ability to control or punish, conveyed in the images of a "fiend pinning down the thief's pack behind him" and "the black, horned thing seated aloof on a rock, surveying a distant crowd surrounding

a gallows" (40). For Jane, the possible power lies in the ability to see without being seen. Her private gallery becomes a sheltered space in which she asserts her visual power, assuming the role of a host who displays the re-imagined vignettes for her own viewing, forming her interpretation without being seen and judged.

At Lowood, the structural elements of freak shows—the host's discriminatory and defining gaze, a monitored display, and the problematic boundaries between the spectacle and the spectators—surface more fully to realize patriarchal oppression. Gender discipline, as the collective experience of Lowood girls, takes on institutional dimensions. Foucauldian propositions of the "technologies of discipline" on "docile bodies" can be applied only too well to the Lowood girls' lives under the manager, the Rev. Brocklehurst. The patriarchal authority of Lowood, Brocklehurst appropriates Christian spirituality to justify the physical starvation and regulation of the female body. To serve "a Master" "whose kingdom is not of this world" (96), Brocklehurst proclaims, "my mission is to mortify in these girls the lusts of the flesh" (97). The discipline is imposed on behaviors as well as activities. Female "vile" (96) bodies are regulated in temporal rhythms, physical appearances, space distribution, and gestures, with power dissociated from the body. The body's energy is then reversed and turned into a relation of strict subjection. Jane's "enfreaked" body emerges from this shared oppression of women to image the atrocity of this subjecting power.

When Jane's dropped slate, the tool of Brocklehurst's "educational" system, exposes Jane during his inspection, Brocklehurst denigrates her in front of the Lowood teachers and girls. Using racial impurity as a signifier of Jane's moral impurity, Brocklehurst visualizes for his audience a heathen unruly body whose viciousness is beyond the redeeming power of his Christian "civilizing" mission: Jane is like "the native of a Christian land, worse than many a little heathen who says its prayers to Brahma and kneels before Juggernaut," and then he and the teachers must "punish her body to save her soul—if, indeed, such salvation be possible." Warning his audience against Jane's influence, he imposes a boundary between his exhibit and his spectators: "avoid her company, exclude her from your sports, and shut her out from your converse" (98), "lest her vicious example should contaminate [your] purity" (99). Brocklehurst's images connect Jane's "monstrosity" to an imperialist racial order. Jane's social freakery is suggested by the images of the racial other eroticized and dehumanized, while the Lowood girls' expected moral purity is defined in the images of the civilized Britishness and the superiority of Christianity in contrast to the non-European religious and racial other.

Jane's resistance is articulated by her embracing of the freakish rebellious energy through her rejection of the "docile bodies." The subversion of Brocklehurst's authority is played out in her relations with two female spectators of her display, Helen and Miss Temple. Wearing "the untidy badge" (99), Helen, like Jane, is a "condemned" body, marked by Miss Smith, one of the "female Brocklehursts" (98). The "strange light" in her eyes invites Jane to view both of them as the oppressed heroes rather than the detestable criminals: "What an extraordinary sensation that ray sent through me! How the new feeling bore me up! It was as if a martyr, a hero, had passed a slave or victim, and imparted strength in the transit" (99).

Helen's "docile body" in her Christian submission—"It is far better to endure patiently a smart which nobody feels but yourself, [. . .] it would be your duty to bear it" (88)—invites Jane to see herself as a human victim rather than an inhuman monster. In contrast to Helen, the director Miss Temple's rebellious mind and will facilitate Jane's transformation. As the subversive mediator between the patriarchal Brocklehurst and the oppressed Lowood girls, Miss Temple has been quietly disobeying Brocklehurst's regulations to better provide for the Lowood girls in food and clothes. A sympathetic spectator of Jane's public humiliation, Miss Temple encourages Jane to challenge Brocklehurst's accusation: "You have been charged with falsehood; defend yourself to me as well as you can" (103). Accepting Jane's version of "truth," she hosts an exonerating display of Jane to subvert Brocklehurst's incriminating gaze and narrative: "Miss Temple, having assembled the whole school, announced that inquiry had been made into the charges alleged against Jane Eyre, and that she was most happy to be able to pronounce her completely cleared from every imputation" (106).

Miss Temple initiates Jane's new life at Lowood; Jane's own celebration, however, takes place in her private and imagined gallery of paintings:

> That night, on going to bed, I forgot to prepare in imagination the Barmecide supper, of hot roast potatoes, or white bread and new milk, with which I was wont to amuse my inward cravings. I feasted instead on the spectacle of ideal drawings, which I saw in the dark—all the work of my own hands; freely pencilled houses and trees, picturesque rocks and ruins, Cuy-like groups of cattle, sweet paintings of butterflies hovering over unblown roses, of birds picking at ripe cherries, of wrens' nests enclosing pearl-like eggs, wreathed about with young ivy sprays.
>
> (106)

Her artistic imagination had provided a space of escape, though temporarily, from patriarchal abuse at Gateshead; at Lowood, pictures of delicious food—"hot roast potatoes, white bread, and new milk"—are evoked for comfort in her constant hunger. In her moment of celebrating her exoneration, "sweet paintings" of an Arcadian pastoral paradise define her harvesting of her re-

ward and her embrace of new birth—"birds picking at ripe cherries," "butterflies hovering over unblown roses," and "wrens' nests enclosing pearl-like eggs" are painted, viewed, and consumed with pleasure and content: "I feasted instead on the spectacle of ideal drawings, which I saw in the dark—all the work of my own hands."

Creating, presenting, and interpreting "the spectacle of ideal drawings" becomes an act of empowerment. The gallery of the drawings of her celebrated self emblematizes the authority Jane desires to claim in her autobiography as two-fold, relational and narrative. She won her first victory in narrative authority by being able to present her childhood experience at Gateshead as a sad but "credible" story proving her innocence (103); she celebrates this victory by imagining herself in the figure of an exhibition host who, being also the painter, and the viewer, is in absolute visual control over her display and interpretation of the pictures. In her autobiography, Jane is to define her female authority in the figure of a female host in these two contexts. As a character, she subverts the power of her male hosts over her body and image. As the writer, she seeks to use her narrative to inscribe self-authorization. Her final identity is Mistress Eyre-"I," a thirty or thirty-one year old woman and writer. She looks back at her past experiences and the people who affected her life and incorporates the pictures of other characters to frame her autobiographical portrait, using language as a medium to make her reader "see" the characters, but defends herself against the reader's critical gaze. The host-exhibit-viewer dynamics thus configure Jane's struggles for empowerment in both Jane's fictional relations with her patriarchs and her textual relations with her reader. Her involvement in this dynamic, however, makes her susceptible to adopting an imperial viewing position.

While patriarchal oppression is inextricably tied to gender discipline, in its starkest manifestation, the oppression is underscored by its association with the imperial implications of power and domination. The gendered triangular relations of host, viewer, and viewed at Thornfield are saturated with the Victorian discovery rhetoric and images of imperial museum. When Rochester unfolds for the first time his sexual history to Jane Eyre, specifically the story of his French mistress Céline Varens, Brontë transforms the relationship between the "master" and the governess into one of viewing and being viewed. Jane is enchanted as a listener but also invited as a viewer to see a new world through "new pictures":

> I, indeed, talked comparatively little, but I heard him talk with relish. [. . .] he liked to open to a mind unacquainted with the world, glimpses of its scenes and ways; [. . .] and I had a keen delight in receiving the new ideas he offered, imagining the new pictures he portrayed, and following him in thought through the

new regions he disclosed, never startled or troubled by one noxious allusion.

(177)

Jane follows Rochester's lead to discover "new regions" in which women become objects of conquests and discriminatory gaze—Céline Varens, Giacinta, Clara, Blanche, and Bertha Mason. Rochester is the explorer-writer to Jane, the invited voyeur/reader, of the "scenes" and "ways" of his sexual conquests. Rochester seduces Jane with the visual pleasure of seeing and the desire to be the seeing subject, but he is also, without Jane's awareness, inscribing himself sexually into her. Jane is made his listener and opens her inexperienced self to his glimpses and disclosure. He guides her through the presentations of these women to "educate" Jane into submitting to his pleasure and gaze, to become his object of desire.

With the sights and stories of these women seen as pictures, Rochester is also an exhibitor leading Jane through a house museum that records his history of conquests in displays. Nancy Armstrong, in *Desire and Domestic Fiction,* uses the metaphor of the imperial Victoria and Albert Museum (whose prototype actually is the Crystal Palace) to define Brontë's authorial power in *Jane Eyre. Jane Eyre* predates these exhibits but the image of an "imperial museum" does inform the power relations between Rochester, Jane, and his women. By re-contextualizing "the materials of other writings" to define the reality of writing through containing and re-organizing "the debris of culture," Armstrong contends, "domestic culture as Brontë represents it has all the qualities of a museum".

> I have in mind such a museum as the Victorian and Albert where objects are quite deliberately arranged according to the strangest mix of categories [. . .] not unlike our modern literary histories, which sort out and assemble a canon according to a similar principle. [. . .] The museum effectively conceals the human effects of the Empire within the very structure organized by its acquisitive strategies [. . .].

(208)

The "imperial museum" in Armstrong's metaphoric connection becomes a signifier for a gendered authority in transforming cultural materials into literature, but in the character relations in *Jane Eyre,* "imperial museum" also surfaces as an extended metaphor for Rochester's power. Rochester, who has "battled through a varied experience with many nations, and roamed over half the globe" (165), hides the systematic rules of its formation—the acquisition, possession, and objectification of women as servile bodies—in his representation of women, in his ordering of their displays, and in his manipulation of the relations of the displays to Jane, his targeted female viewer. The third floor of Thornfield Hall, to which "furniture once appropriated to the lower apartments had from time to time been removed [. . .] as fashions changed," gives the hall, Jane reflects, "the aspect of a home of the past-a shrine of memory" (137). The symbolically resonant language describing the third floor where Bertha is "stored" away and the mansion, Susan Meyer argues, suggests that Thornfield stands as "a material embodiment of the history of the English ruling class as represented by the Rochesters," as "the repressed history of crimes" (71). The crimes concealed behind the furniture and the women's stories become encoded in the Thornfield master's acquisitive and display strategies. Rochester's women, like furniture, are subjected to the owner's decisions about their use, replacement, and display. The history of both the furniture and the women is disclosed and interpreted within the structure of power that organizes them and through the displays monitored by the owner/exhibitor. Mrs. Fairfax, acting as Jane's first guide through the rooms at Thornfield, believes that the Rochesters have been "rather a violent race than a quiet race" (137). Rochester explains what qualifies him as the "winner" of Bertha and her West Indian wealth: "because I was of a good race" (332). "Race," of course, means "kinship" and "lineage" in the general nineteenth-century uses of the word, but Rochester's differentiating himself from Bertha and her West Indian society in their marriage relation clearly reveals the fact that his proclamation of his superiority is in part based on race.

Woman as an attractive body but inferior mind is the subtext that Rochester propagates in his presentations, against which he defines his "imperial" superiority. In different degrees, the images of his mistresses and Blanche Ingram become associated with his verbal portrait of his Creole wife Bertha, a female body that seduces but also repulses. Bertha, according to Rochester, "lavishly displayed" for his pleasure all her charms (332), but soon revealed a nature "wholly alien" to his: "her tastes obnoxious to me, her cast of mind common, low, narrow, and singularly incapable of being led to anything higher, expanded to anything larger" (333). Although Rochester compares keeping mistresses to keeping slaves, he interprets these relationships as degrading to him, the buyer/employer, rather than to the servile women dehumanized by him: "[H]iring a mistress is the next worse thing to buying a slave: both are often by nature, and always by position, inferior; and to live familiarly with inferiors is degrading. I now hate the recollection of the time I passed with Céline, Giacinta, and Clara" (339). He criticizes their inferior intellect and moral looseness—"What was their beauty to me in a few weeks? Giacinta was unprincipled and violent [. . .]. Clara was [. . .] heavy, mindless and unimpressible [. . .]" (338). Dismissing the mistresses as attractive bodies with minds that fail to please him, Rochester justifies himself as the master in his sexual relations: "To women who please me only by their faces, I am the very devil when I find out they have neither souls nor hearts [. . .]" (289).

Blanche Ingram, in spite of her British aristocratic status, is manipulated by Rochester as a specially curated exhibit. Rochester's power over Blanche is essentially validated by the patriarchal ideology at work in the particular nature of courtship marketing, in which Blanche voluntarily participates and allows herself to be packaged as a desirable commodity, her body and its attributes in exchange for the money of her suitor/buyer. In this arrangement, Blanche is not unlike Rochester's mistresses or wife Bertha. In one of the charades, Rochester dresses up as an Eastern emir; while Blanche is "attired in oriental fashion," "her cast of form and feature, her complexion and her general air [. . .] suggested the idea of some Israelitish princess of the patriarchal days; and such was doubtless the character she intended to represent" (212, 213). As a courted lady, Blanche is entitled to demand her suitor's performance and withdraw herself from the potential marriage transaction if the prospects prove dissatisfying; nevertheless, in both aspects her power over her suitor's performance depends largely on the suitor's response.

Yet if Blanche sees herself as a princess courted by her rich emir, her emir, Rochester, is interested mainly in hosting a courtship performance to draw out Jane's jealousy. Pretending to be a suitor, he orchestrates the whole courtship only to see it fail. He curates Blanche as an instrumental display. He lets her play out all her tempting acts and induces her rejection by creating a rumor about his fortune. More the host than the player of the courtship, Rochester's real interest is in monitoring Blanche's performance and surveying its impact on Jane, the spectator. Rochester's conscious comparison of Blanche with Bertha also implies a hidden agenda of devaluing Blanche as a white-race Bertha. Blanche is similar to Bertha in "darkness"—she is "big, brown, and buxom" (248). Arguing for the necessity to subdue her—"Her feelings are concentrated in one—pride; and that needs humbling" (291), Rochester interprets Blanche as yet another female body on which he can exert control and claim superiority.

The most important display in Rochester's imperial museum is, of course, Bertha. In the Rochester-Bertha scene, "freak" as a constructed but also a problematic gendered identity underlines Rochester's power over her coined both in his images as host of a racial freak and as imperialist curator of a colonial body. Bertha's freak display both defines and problematizes Rochester's host authority in verbal, physical, and spectacular control at its greatest visibility and intensity. Bertha's status as a freak of nature, presented and interpreted under Rochester's derogatory gaze, is what Susan Stewart terms "a freak of culture": "His or her anomalous status

is articulated by the process of the spectacle as it distances the viewer and thereby it 'normalizes' the viewer as much it marks the freak as an aberration" (109). Imposing overlapping boundaries, the physiological boundary between the "human" and the "monstrous" and the racial boundary between the British and the West Indian, Rochester, the host/patriarch, minimizes Bertha's "humanity" to confirm the "normality" of his British spectators and, more importantly, his own.

Yet the boundaries and authority imposed by Rochester are established only to be called into question. In spite of his claim, his audience recognizes Bertha as his legal wife regardless of her bestial appearance. His "conjugal embrace" (322) of Bertha, who can throttle him, symbolically maps out the entrapment and the limitations of his power in his union with the colonial wealth and colonial body. Her colonial wealth contributes to his British gentry's life of comfort and leisure but also traps him in a marriage that cannot be annulled. She is the most important piece of his collection, but one he cannot show to the outside world, and one whose inherited "colonial" lunacy makes it impossible for him to claim total control over her for collection or display. His narrative reduces her to a colonial body that seduces the British gentleman, but her body also exposes the shameful history of his acquisition of her wealth. Bertha's low groan in the dark has made Jane wonder "[w]hat crime was this that lived incarnate in the sequestered mansion, and could be neither expelled nor subdued by the owner?" (239), and voices the danger and burden of imperialist desire.

If Bertha's presence conveys Brontë's uneasiness about British imperialist ventures in the West Indies and the author's association of the ideology of patriarchal domination with the ideology of imperialist domination, Brontë's anti-imperialist politics, as Susan Meyer suggests, are more self-interested than benevolent. The implicit opposition to imperialism arises, not primarily out of the concern for the well-being of the colonized, but for the British in contact with the dark race and in danger of being contaminated by such contact (Meyer 81). Bertha's display and racial hybridity expose the historical crime of the imperialist practices, but it is the present Rochester's entrapment that destroys Jane's hope for love and marriage at Thornfield. Jane's "colonial encounter" with Bertha serves to centralize the gender tensions in the domestic relations of power; Bertha's image of monstrosity locates Jane's anxiety about her social status and self-image. Such anxiety is made explicit in her cry—"Am I a monster?" (293)—when she senses Mrs. Fairfax's seeming disapproval of her marrying Rochester and becoming the mistress of Thornfield Hall. Bertha's anomalous figure thus becomes a signifier of the tensions between the derogatory gaze of the society that continuously alienates Jane and Jane's struggles toward assertion and acceptance.

Bertha's display as freak, embodying domination and resistance, functions most importantly as the object lesson for Jane about the danger she is exposed to as a viewer. Bertha's display alerts her to how she has followed without questioning her host's gaze in interpreting his portraits of women. Rochester has led Jane to "see" more humanity in him and his mistresses as a stereotype and a category: "As he had said, there was probably nothing at all extraordinary in the substance of the narrative itself: a wealthy English*man*'s passion for a French *dancer*" (italics mine, 177). In spite of her expressed sympathy for Blanche and her criticism of Rochester's "dishonest coquetry" (291), Jane is more than willing to be assured that Blanche does not suffer the bitter pain she feels during his designed courtship. It is only through her own victimization, when Rochester's dishonest marriage proposal proves to be nothing more than a sexual manipulation, that Jane begins to regard the mistresses as "poor girls" (339) and Bertha as "that unfortunate lady" (329), and Rochester as self-righteous and "inexorable": "you speak of her [Bertha] with hate—with vindictive antipathy. It is cruel—she can not help being mad" (328).

Bertha's displayed body also images Jane's increasing vulnerability to being transformed from the viewer to the viewed under Rochester's authoritative gaze in appropriating her as a display and a property. Jane's exhibiting, upon Rochester's request at their first meeting, the "elfish" portraits of herself in the watercolors—the lonely landscape of sea, hill, and iceberg; the relic of sunken ship, the female shape rising into the sky, the blank gaze of a colossus in despair (157)—wins her Rochester's reception into his museum. If she falls in love with Rochester, as Sandra Gilbert and Susan Gubar suggest in *The Madwoman in the Attic,* because he is "the only qualified critic of her art and soul" (352), Rochester soon claims his authority as a host in appropriating her art as exhibit items for the gaze of his male friends (160) at his dinner party. Nor does he hesitate to use the "heirlooms for the ladies of Thornfield" (287) to define and display her as *his*—"I will make the world acknowledge you a beauty [. . .]. I will attire my Jane in satin and lace, and she shall have roses in her hair; and I will cover the head I love best with a priceless veil." Jane is quick to perceive the degrading nature of the display: "I shall not be your Jane Eyre any longer, but an ape in a harlequin's jacket" (288). The freak image imposed on Jane at Gateshead and Lowood and rejected by Jane here emerges, in a more hideous manifestation, in Bertha's body.

Jane faces the danger of becoming not only a dehumanized display, but also a subjugated mind. Her imagination, which she has used to create a space for shelter and self-assertion and to be a host to herself, becomes at Thornfield an expression of powerlessness and self-repression. She transforms Rochester, through painting his face, into a visual object that only confirms her subjection to his charm. His painted eyes look back at her and she "smiled at the speaking likeness [. . .] absorbed and content" (262). For her own image, Jane not only paints her social and sexual unattractiveness—she paints herself into the crayon and chalk "Portrait of a Governess, disconnected, poor, and plain" (190) in contrast to the watercolor of "Blanche, an accomplished lady of rank" (191). Even more self-critical, she sees, in her agony over her undesirability in Rochester's eyes, "a deformed thing" in herself that she fears to "own and rear" and has to strangle (272). Her anxiety, described as a deformed part of her mind she wants to, but finds it difficult to dissociate from, dominates her perception of herself.

Bertha's body, embodying Jane's potential danger and absorbing Jane's anxiety, sets in motion a reversal of roles and an inversion of power relations that structure the remainder of the text, culminating in Jane's reunion with Rochester. The spectacle of the inarticulate Bertha brings out her voice against being objectified—"Mr. Rochester, I will not be yours" (342). She breaks away from Rochester's emotional prison to re-assert herself, while Bertha the "wild" lunatic escapes from her attic prison to bring down Thornfield. The fire caused by Bertha, his "collection," symbolically burns away Rochester's colonial wealth and destroys his power as a male host and gazer, leaving Rochester growing not only "dangerous"—"he never was a mild man, but he got dangerous after he lost her [Jane Eyre]"—but also "savage" (452). The novel finally punishes him by turning him into a deformed body, a tamed freak body but emptied of the rebellious energy, in the eyes of the reader.

In Jane and Rochester's union, Brontë transforms the power relation between them by giving her the superior position of a host. When she brings herself back to Rochester as "an independent woman" and her own mistress (459), his mutilated body and his "cicatrized visage" (461) remind her of "some wronged and fettered wild beast" (456) that she has to "rehumanize" (461), and his faint gaze can no more manipulate her. Rochester does not face the danger of becoming a freak display, but his body is forever a sight of ugly deformity by the side of his "mistress." The domestic "harmony" Jane finds fulfilling is established on her superiority as the seeing "Eyre": "we are precisely suited in character—perfect concord is the result. [. . .] I was then his vision". Jane is more than Rochester's vision. She is the host that controls what can be "seen" by him and how it should be presented. In their marital "perfect concord," she becomes the authoritative Exhibitor—"He saw nature—he saw books through me; and never did I weary of gazing for his behalf" (476).

The novel concludes Jane's female defiance of male domination by according her not only visual but also textual authority as a host. Jane's privileged host position and power extend to her relation with her reader. She follows Rochester as a host at Thornfield when he begins revealing his past. Under his guiding gaze, she views "the new pictures he portrayed" "through the new regions he disclosed," and receives "the new ideas he offered" (177). As a narrator and the writer of a book defiantly entitled *Jane Eyre,* she also discloses to and leads her reader through her "gallery of memory" (147), but she makes explicit her authority in curating and exhibiting: "I am only bound to invoke memory where I know her responses will possess some degree of interest" (115). Her reader is to read a new face like "a new picture introduced to the gallery of memory" (147), a new chapter "like a new scene in a play," and Jane directs, "when I draw up the curtain," "reader— you must fancy you see" (125). Presenting, interpreting, and judging other characters, Jane the host, on the other hand, does not allow her reader to frame her in well-defined pictures. Her "self" is one of discontent, a woman resisting the confined feminine images of "making puddings and knitting stockings." Presenting her tale as "quickened with all of incident, life, fire, feeling" (141), she gives her reader no position to criticize her authority over the verbal pictures of memory she presents in her autobiography: "I am not writing to flatter parental egotism, to echo cant, or prop up humbug; I am merely telling the truth. [. . .] Anybody may blame me who likes [. . .]" (140).

The novel's critique of patriarchal oppression through the metaphoric structure of freak shows finally does not escape the structure it condemns. At the end of the novel, the narrative inscribes Jane's subject position by placing her into the masculine positions of the host and the gazer. The visual authority and pleasure associated with the patriarchal oppressors become justified in Jane's self-authorization, while the reformed patriarch is displaced into a freakish visual object. The subversion of freak show power relations concludes with the reinstatement of power hierarchy. Gender inequality and social marginality faced by a woman are "corrected" only by the reversal of the gendered roles of the host and the exhibit.

Ambiguity also circulates through the narrative's defining both Jane's social unacceptability and her successful integration into the British middle-class society in the images of the freakish other. Edward Said contends that the exorcism of the West Indian Bertha is "Brontë's way of telling us that denizens of the outlying Empire are useful as a source of wealth or as a moral ordeal for English men and women to experience, but never are they people to be accepted into the heart of metropolitan society" (273). The novel's metaphoric linking of Bertha and Jane by the freak body connects Bertha's social exclusion created by the ideology of race to Jane's inferiority and hybridity created by the ideologies of gender and class. The exorcising of Bertha,

therefore, indicates the necessary erasure of the freakish from Jane to authorize her entry into the "normal" British middle-class society. Yet at the end of the novel, Jane's integration into British middle-class society is coined ambiguously in her embracing a physical freak, her marrying the deformed Rochester. Jane's attainment of her own social power and justification of her femininity depends on another freakish body to facilitate her enrollment into normal womanhood as a wife and a mother and secures her status as a social-ethical subject.

Richard Altick concludes his famous chapter on the exhibitions of the exotic bodies in Victorian London with this comment: "We cannot know for sure; but to many a mind and sensibility higher than those of the strange beings on display [. . .] the experience of gazing on such creatures must have induced thoughts too troubling for easy utterance" (287). In Brontë's novel, the experience of a woman's gazing on the freak body is presented as no less troubling; gazing on is also gazing in and being gazed upon. Brontë's subversive but ambiguous criticism of gender dominance in domestic relationships articulated through the freakish as a deviant and anomalous femininity leaves the boundaries between the self and the other forever shifting and the freak image forever reflecting and reflected in a woman's image of her self.

Works Cited

Altick, Richard. *The Shows of London.* Cambridge: The Belknap P of Harvard UP, 1978.

Armstrong, Nancy. *Desire and Domestic Fiction: A Political History of the Novel.* Oxford: Oxford UP, 1987.

Bogdan, Robert. *Freak Show: Presenting Human Oddities for Amusement and Profit.* Chicago: U of Chicago P, 1988.

Brontë, Charlotte. *Jane Eyre.* Ed. Q. D. Leavis. Harmondsworth: Penguin, 1966. Rpt. 1985.

Darwin, Charles. *The Origin of Species.* Ed. Gillian Beer. New York: Oxford UP, 1996.

Edwards, Paul, and James Walvin. *Black Personalities in the Era of the Slave Trade.* Baton Rouge: Louisiana UP, 1983.

Foucault, Michel. *Discipline and Punish: The Birth of the Prison.* Trans. Alan Sheridan. New York: Pantheon Books, 1977.

Gilbert, Sandra M. and Susan Gubar. *The Madwoman in the Attic: The Woman Writer and the Nineteenth-Century Literary Imagination.* New Haven: Yale UP, 1979.

Grosz, Elizabeth. "Intolerable Ambiguity: Freaks as at the Limit." In *Freakery: Cultural Spectacles of the Ex-*

traordinary Body. Ed. Rosemarie Garland Thomson. New York: New York UP, 1996. 55-66.

Kaplan, Cora. Introduction. *Olive.* By Dinah Mulock Craik. New York: Oxford UP, 1996.

Meyer, Susan. *Imperialism at Home: Race and Victorian Women's Fiction.* Ithaca, NY: Cornell UP, 1996.

Peterson, Carla L. *The Determined Reader: Gender and Culture in the Novel from Napoleon to Victoria.* Piscataway, NY: Rutgers UP, 1986.

Said, Edward. *The World, the Text, and the Critic.* Cambridge, MA: Harvard UP, 1983.

Semonin, Paul. "Monsters in the Marketplace: The Exhibition of Human Oddities in Early England." In *Freakery: Cultural Spectacles of the Extraordinary Body.* Ed. Rosemarie Garland Thompson. 69-81.

Spivak, Gayatri Chakravorty. "Three Women's Texts and a Critique of Imperialism." In *"Race," Writing, and Difference.* Ed. Henry Louis Gates, Jr. Chicago: U of Chicago P, 1986, 262-80.

Stewart, Susan. *On Longing: Narratives of the Miniature, the Gigantic, the Souvenir, the Collection.* Baltimore: John Hopkins UP, 1984.

Thomson, Rosemarie Garland. *Extraordinary Bodies: Figuring Physical Disability in American Culture and Literature.* New York: Columbia UP, 1997.

———. Introduction. *Freakery: Cultural Spectacles of the Extraordinary Body.* New York: New York UP, 1996. 1-22.

FURTHER READING

Criticism

Blom, Margaret Howard. "Jane Eyre." In *Charlotte Brontë,* pp. 84-105. Boston: Twayne Publishers, 1977.

Provides a general overview of the novel.

Bronfen, Elisabeth. "Femininity—Missing in Action." In *New Casebooks: Jane Eyre,* edited by Heather Glen, pp. 196-204. New York: St. Martin's Press, 1997.

Studies the manner in which feminine identity is depicted in *Jane Eyre.*

Burkhart, Charles. "Jane Eyre: The Art of the Adolescent." In *Charlotte Brontë: A Psychosexual Study of Her Novels,* pp. 63-77. London: Victor Gollancz, 1973.

Analyses the plot and narrative structure of *Jane Eyre.*

Carlton-Ford, Cynthia. "Intimacy without Immolation: Fire in *Jane Eyre.*" *Women's Studies* 15, no. 4 (1988): 375-86.

Contends that Jane is presented as a character who challenges social and literary norms and that Brontë's descriptions of fire as something both beautiful and destructive correlates with this conflict.

Craig, Randall. "Logophobia in *Jane Eyre.*" *Journal of Narrative Technique* 23, no. 2 (spring 1993): 92-113.

An analysis of the language and speaking voices used by the characters in the novel.

Dessner, Lawrence Jay. "*Jane Eyre.*" In *The Homely Web of Truth: A Study of Charlotte Brontë's Novels,* pp. 64-81. The Hague, The Netherlands: Mouton, 1975.

Examines the juxtaposition of the principles of divine justice and morality versus individual realization in *Jane Eyre.*

Imlay, Elizabeth. *Charlotte Brontë and the Mysteries of Love: Myth and Allegory in* Jane Eyre. New York: Harvester Wheatsheaf, 1989, 211 p.

Anthology of essays discussing various aspects of the novel, including characters, themes, and literary context.

Keefe, Robert. "*Innocence:* Jane Eyre." In *Charlotte Brontë's World of Death,* pp. 96-129. Austin: University of Texas Press, 1979.

View of *Jane Eyre* as an autobiographical novel related to Brontë's triumph over the idea of death.

Knies, Earl A. "The Single Vision: *Jane Eyre.*" In *The Art of Charlotte Brontë,* pp. 102-43. Athens: University of Ohio Press, 1969.

Traces Brontë's progression as a writer from *The Professor* to *Jane Eyre.*

Langford, Thomas A. "Prophetic Imagination and the Unity of *Jane Eyre.*" *Studies in the Novel* 6, no. 2 (summer 1974): 228-35.

Argues that despite its simple structure, the novel achieves a level of imagination and insight that "borders on the visionary and prophetic."

Linder, Cynthia A. "*Jane Eyre.*" In *Romantic Imagery in the Novels of Charlotte Brontë,* pp. 31-67. London: Macmillan Press, 1978.

A general analysis of *Jane Eyre,* arguing that the novel displays a more logical structure than sometimes admitted by critics.

Mason, Michael. Introduction to *Jane Eyre,* edited by Michael Mason, pp. vii-xxxii. London: Penguin Books, 1996.

Discusses the plot, characters, imagery, and symbolism of the novel.

Meyer, Susan. "Colonialism and the Figurative Strategy of *Jane Eyre*." In *Macropolitics of Nineteenth-Century Literature: Nationalism, Exoticism, Imperialism,* edited by Jonathan Arac and Harriet Ritvo, pp. 159-83. Durham, N.C.: Duke University Press, 1995.
> Considers colonialist and racial aspects of the novel.

Nemesvari, Richard. Introduction to *Jane Eyre,* edited by Richard Nemesvari, pp. 9-49. Peterborough, Canada: Broadview Literary Texts, 1999.
> Discussion of *Jane Eyre* in the context of Brontë's life.

Politi, Jina. "*Jane Eyre* Class-ified." *Literature and History* 8, no. 1 (spring 1982): 56-66.
> Examines the characters in the novel from the perspective of their social class.

Simmons, James R. "*Jane Eyre*'s Symbolic Paintings." *Brontë Studies* 27, no. 3 (November 2002): 247-49.
> Argues that three paintings featured in the novel foreshadow later events in the narrative.

Starzyk, Lawrence J. "'The Gallery of Memory': The Pictorial in *Jane Eyre*." *Papers on Language & Literature* 33, no. 3 (summer 1997): 288-309.
> Conceives of a "museum of memory" in which images drive the narrative of *Jane Eyre*.

Sternlieb, Lisa. "*Jane Eyre*: 'Hazarding Confidences.'" In *Charlotte Brontë: Jane Eyre,* edited by Richard J. Dunn, pp. 503-15. New York: W. W. Norton & Company, 2001.
> Postulates that the relationship between Jane and Rochester, as well as that between Jane and her reader, are built on a series of paradigmatic games that occur in various conversations throughout the narrative.

Additional information on Brontë's life and career is contained in the following sources published by Thomson Gale: *Authors and Artists for Young Adults,* **Vol. 17;** *Beacham's Guide to Literature for Young Adults,* **Vol. 2;** *British Writers,* **Vol. 5;** *British Writers: The Classics,* **Vol. 2;** *British Writers Retrospective Supplement,* **Vol. 1;** *Concise Dictionary of Literary Biography, 1832-1890;* *Dictionary of Literary Biography,* **Vols. 21, 159, 199;** *DISCovering Authors;* *DISCovering Authors: British;* *DISCovering Authors: Canadian Edition;* *DISCovering Authors Modules: Most-studied Authors, Novelists;* *DISCovering Authors 3.0;* *Exploring Novels;* *Literature and Its Times,* **Vol. 2;** *Nineteenth-Century Literature Criticism,* **Vols. 3, 8, 33, 58, 105;** *Novels for Students,* **Vol. 4;** *Twayne's English Authors, World Literature and Its Times,* **Ed. 4; and** *World Literature Criticism.*

Juan Francisco Manzano
1797(?)-1854

Cuban poet and autobiographer.

INTRODUCTION

Manzano was a Cuban-born slave who gained recognition during his lifetime for his poetry and his *Autobiografía* (1840). Manzano's memoir of his years as a slave is widely regarded as the most important work documenting life in the Cuban slave period, as well as being one of the earliest Latin American autobiographies. In addition to his autobiography and poems, Manzano wrote a play and several letters during his years in Havana after he received manumission from his owner. Today, both his poetry and his autobiography are studied as representative examples of Cuban literature, especially for what they reveal about slavery and its abuses in nineteenth-century Cuban society.

BIOGRAPHICAL INFORMATION

Manzano was born sometime around 1797, on a vast sugar plantation called El Molino, near the city of Matanzas. His parents, Torbio Castro and María Pilar Manzano, were slaves in the service of Marquesa de Santa Ana, and until the age of twelve Manzano lived in relative comfort and contentment working in the Marquesa's household. Following her death, the family passed on to the Marquesa de Prado Ameno. By all accounts, she was a hard taskmaster, and Manzano's memoir is replete with examples of her cruelty. In his autobiography, Manzano alludes to the harsh life and punishments he endured during this period of his life, attributing both his stunted physical growth and lifelong depression to the treatment he received at Marquesa Prado Ameno's hands. He eventually escaped the Marquesa by fleeing to Havana.

As a slave, Manzano had no access to formal education. He taught himself to read and write by tracing over the writing of one of his masters, don Nicolás de Cárdenos y Manzano, the second son of the Marquesa de Prado Ameno. Don Nicolás also happened to be part of a literary group surrounding Domingo del Monte, a reformist who led Cuban writers and publishers in opposing the most extreme forms of slave abuse. It was don Nicolás who introduced Manzano to del Monte. In 1836, Manzano was invited to recite a poem he had written,

"Mis treinta años," to the literary salon headed by de Monte. The same year, members of del Monte's literary group, including don Nicolás, collected enough money for Manzano to be able to purchase his freedom. Following his manumission, Manzano began living in Havana, gaining permission to work as an artisan. In 1835, del Monte commissioned Manzano to write an autobiography. The work was eventually published in 1840, after several revisions and a translation into English by Irish abolitionist, Robert R. Madden. Following the publication of his autobiography, Manzano continued to live and write in Havana, where he contributed to a number of major literary publications of his time. In 1844, Manzano was imprisoned after being accused of participating in a conspiracy. Found innocent of all charges and released from prison a year later, Manzano wrote and published very little in the years following his incarceration, blaming the ill treatment he received in prison for his state of mind. He died in 1854.

MAJOR WORKS

Manzano lived during the most intense years of Cuban slavery, and it is a testament to his commitment that he became, even while he was a slave, the first black poet in Cuba to publish a book of poetry. Titled *Poesías líricas (Cantos a Lesbia)* (1821), the work was composed and issued just three years after Manzano had taught himself to read and write. A second book of poems followed, *Flores pasajeras* (1830). Unfortunately, there are no extant copies of this manuscript, although many of Manzano's poems were anthologized both during and after his lifetime, including his first presentation to the del Monte literary group, "Mis treinta años."

Although known primarily as a poet during his life and for some years after his death, Manzano's most important work is now acknowledged to be his autobiography. It is studied as a slave narrative, as well as a literary text that is significant in its attempt to bridge a social, historical, and literary gap between the narrator and his audience. Originally written in Spanish, the work was first edited by Cuban writer Suárez y Romero before being handed off to Madden. It was Madden who translated the text into English, publishing it in London for the General Anti-Slavery Convention of 1840. Romero's edition subsequently disappeared, and for nearly a hundred years Madden's translation was the only version of the autobiography available. It was not until 1937, when the original manuscript came into the hands of the Cuban National Archives, that it was eventually reissued in Spanish by José L. Franco. Since then, several other versions of the work have been published, including editions in 1975 and 1996.

CRITICAL RECEPTION

While Manzano was known for his poetic contributions during his lifetime, and his works continue to be anthologized with other Cuban and Latin American poets, modern scholarship has focused most intensively on his autobiography. Commissioned as it was by del Monte for a documentary rather than a literary purpose, and then edited and altered by Romero and Madden, this work has often raised questions among critics about how Manzano really felt about slavery. Although the work contains several graphic descriptions of the brutality Manzano suffered at the hands of his masters, critics such as Robert Richmond Ellis have contended that the autobiography does not completely portray the extent of Manzano's suffering. In contrast, his poetry, which almost never directly mentions slavery, is cited as a more fervent indictment of this practice. Some scholars attribute this disparity to the fact that del Monte, who commissioned Manzano's autobiography, was a proponent of the gradual reform and eventual abolition of slavery rather than its complete and immediate abolition. Richard L. Jackson charges that the autobiography was intended by del Monte to serve more as a means of revealing the existence of progressive and humanitarian individuals inside Cuba rather than as an indictment of slavery. Jackson points to the criteria del Monte imposed on Manzano, including the need for "moderation and restraint" when depicting the state of the black slave. According to Jackson, del Monte was concerned that if the text depicted slaves as rebellious, it would undermine sympathy for them. Ultimately, writes Jackson, Manzano's autobiography was intended by del Monte to be an indictment not of slavery as an institution but merely of the abuses committed by some slave owners. Several critics concur with this viewpoint, pointing to several letters by Manzano that explain his intention to comply with del Monte's restrictions. In contrast, Edward J. Mullen (see Further Reading) explains the importance of the abolitionist literary network in helping writers such as Manzano gain recognition as well as providing them with a forum for expression. He characterizes Manzano's autobiography as a "singular document of Afro-Cuban literature" and one that cannot be dismissed easily. Calling the work "a remarkable expression of human experience," Mullen further contends that the work is a complex text that reflects many aspects of Cuban society. Similarly, Susan Willis also characterizes Manzano's autobiography as a

work that must be studied within its social and literary context, downplaying the role of the del Monte literary circle.

PRINCIPAL WORKS

Poesías líricas (Cantos a Lesbia) (poetry) 1821
Flores pasajeras (poetry) 1830
Autobiografía (autobiography) 1840
Poems by a Slave in the Island of Cuba, Recently Liberated; translated from the Spanish by R. R. Madden, M.D. with the History of the Early Life of the Negro Poet, written by Himself; To which are prefixed Two Pieces Descriptive of Cuban Slavery and the Slave-Traffic (poetry and autobiography) 1840
Zafira (play) 1842
Autobiografía, cartas y versos de Juan Fco. Manzano (autobiography) 1937
Autobiografía de un esclavo (autobiography) 1975
The Life and Poems of a Cuban Slave: Juan Francisco Manzano, 1797-1854 (poetry and autobiography) [edited by Edward J. Mullen] 1981
The Autobiography of a Slave: by Juan Francisco Manzano (autobiography) [*Autobiografía de un esclavo*] 1996

CRITICISM

Richard L. Jackson (essay date 1984)

SOURCE: Jackson, Richard L. "Slavery, Racism and Autobiography in Two Early Black Writers: Juan Francisco Manzano and Martín Morúa Delgado." In *Voices from Under: Black Narrative in Latin America and the Caribbean,* edited by William Luis, pp. 55-64. Westport, Conn.: Greenwood Press, 1984.

[*In the following essay, Jackson traces the history of Manzano's writings, noting the influence of his editors and patrons on these works.*]

Slavery was living hell for Blacks. One can imagine the problems slaves faced, especially the slave man of letters, particularly if he dared to write about his plight. Juan Francisco Manzano (1797?-1854) was the best known of the slave poets; he was also the first Black to publish a book of poetry in Cuba, *Poesías líricas (Cantos a Lesbia)* in 1821. This work was a considerable achievement, whatever its literary value, when we realize that the author had begun to teach himself to read and write just three years before. His second book of poetry, *Flores pasajeras,* of which there are no extant copies, was published in 1830. These two books, some poems such as his much anthologized "Mis treinta años," his letters, his *Autobiografía* (1840) and his play *Zafira* (1842) represent the corpus of Manzano's work that has come down to us.

The year 1836 was perhaps Manzano's best: He gained his freedom as well as a wider forum for his literature. In that year he was allowed to appear before the prestigious Del Monte literary *tertulia* ("group") to read his poem **"Mis treinta años,"** which continues to enjoy success even today. This sonnet, which speaks of his "thirty unhappy years,"[1] does not mention slavery directly nor does it need to, as oblique references leave little doubt what his thirty years spent as a slave have been like. We marvel at Manzano's restraint in suppressing direct reference to external circumstances of which he, a Black and a slave writing in a slave society, had to be acutely aware. Even his *Autobiografía* is underplayed.

Domingo del Monte, the "liberal" responsible for Manzano's freedom, "commissioned" the slave author to write his *Autobiografía.* This Autobiografía[2] is perhaps Manzano's greatest claim to fame: It is the only slave autobiography that we know of that was written during that long period in Cuban history, and perhaps it is Latin America's first and only slave narrative. In the United States and Africa black autobiographies, some of them classics, abound. The slave narrative itself was a prominent literary genre in the United States, and black autobiographies and autobiographical books continued to pour forth following the Civil War. To date, an estimated four hundred of these books have been published in the United States.[3] In Latin America, however, the black autobiography is not a primary form, although autobiographical books by Afro-Latin Americans do exist, including Candelario Obeso's *La lucha de la vida* (1882), Manuel Zapata Olivella's *Pasión vagabunda* (1949) and *He visto la noche* (1959) in Colombia, Martín Morúa Delgado's *La familia Unzúazu* (1901) and Miguel Barnet's *The Autobiography of a Runaway Slave* (1966) in Cuba."[4]

Were it not for Del Monte's insistence, we would not have Manzano's *Autobiografía.* The circumstances of its creation, therefore, are illuminating and warrant some attention if we are to appreciate this slave narrative. The work's view from below offers perspective partly shaped by Del Monte's view from above. Del Monte who has been called "the first great patriarch of Cuban belles-lettres,"[5] was, in a sense, the Carl Van Vechten of his time. Del Monte's relation to black Cubans like Manzano was similar to the position Carl Van Vechten, who published his own *Nigger Heaven* in 1926, had in relation to black Americans like Langston Hughes, and indeed, to the Harlem Renaissance in early twentieth-century America. Both men were wealthy, white critic-patrons who sponsored black art. It must be remembered that in Manzano's time, as in the early days of Langston Hughes, Blacks, and some Whites too when dealing with black themes, wrote what influential Whites wanted and expected them to write, a fact of great significance in the history of antislavery literature in Cuba.

Both Manzano's *Autobiografía* and Anselmo Suárez y Romero's *Francisco,* the Cuban antislavery novel that has the distinction of preceding *Uncle Tom's Cabin* by several years, were written at the request of Del Monte, who had them produced largely for foreign readers. Both works were in fact first published out of the country: *Francisco* in New York in 1880 and Manzano's *Autobiografía* in English in London in 1840. Both works, however, did circulate in Cuba in manuscript form. Although Manzano's text circulated in Spanish, the original version was not published until 1937. Foreign exposure for these two works was to be gained through Richard Madden, the English author and friend of Del Monte who was entrusted with an antislavery portfolio containing them. Madden chose to publish Manzano's *Autobiografía* rather than Suárez y Romero's *Francisco.*

These two works were partly designed to reveal to the world outside Cuba the progressive and humanitarian positions of the concerned citizens within the country or at least those represented by Del Monte's group. The major limitation, though, was that neither book was allowed to go "beyond what are the 'official' criteria of the group."[6] The standard imposed by the Del Monte group, which was more reformist than abolitionist, called for "moderation and restraint"[7] in the depiction of the black slave. For this reason Manzano's own *Autobiografía,* controlled from above by Del Monte and resembling other antislavery works written around the same time, had to play down the threatening image of the rebellious slave while playing up the image of the docile and submissive slave. According to Ivan Schulman, the restraint served "to call forth a sympathetic reaction to slavery's abuses from the more enlightened members of the community, who would probably have been offended by a rebellious protagonist."[8]

Del Monte achieved something of a literary coup by having Manzano, an authentic black slave and an "admirable example of meekness and resignation,"[9] conform to these guidelines. Conforming was the only way Manzano could hope for continued support and protection. Since Del Monte knew he had a showpiece Black with a good image and intellectual capacity, why not display him? His talent made him one of the excellent exceptions: a slave who was not vile, stupid, and immoral, defects that Del Monte felt people born and raised as slaves inevitably had.[10] Further, and perhaps even more important, his display would prove that such exceptions could be produced under slavery, providing, of course, they had good masters.

Francisco Calcagno's phrase, "being a slave owner is no crime, but abusing that privilege is,"[11] is of enormous importance both in understanding the meaning of Manzano's *Autobiografía* and in clarifying Del Monte's reasons for supporting it. Manzano recounts numerous cruelties and punishments suffered for much of his life at the hands of the Marquesa de Prado Ameno, a sadistic, warped owner. Now, if Manzano represented one of the excellent exceptions to the mass of undesirable slaves, so too, it is inferred, was the marquesa an exception to other *amitos,* some of whom Manzano served under, who were paragons of kindness and goodness.

Manzano readers take note of his mistreatment at the hands of that cruel lady, and Calcagno asks the telling question in his *Poetas de color,* "Why could not the fate that made Manzano a slave at least have made him always a slave of Cárdenas? He would not have suffered the horrible treatment of which he often lamented with such humility and good reason; perhaps we would not today be reading this autobiography of his written with such bitterness."[12] It was during the period Manzano served with this *amito,* who was "correct, benevolent and magnanimous,"[13] that he taught himself to read and write, patterning his behavior on the good example set by his master. But the implications of the question Calcagno raises are clear, namely, that slavery, when not poisoned by bad masters or mistresses who abuse the system, is not really evil. This was a message even the censors would take kindly to, especially if the system could produce a man like Manzano.

Del Monte's reasons for wanting the book written and Manzano's concern about his personal safety meant the work essentially misrepresented slavery. Were it not written under control, its publication would have been "the biggest anathema of all"[14] against slavery. But as it turned out, Manzano had very little to fear since his *Autobiografía* is really an indictment not of slavery but only of abuses by some misguided owners. Further, perhaps Manzano had Del Monte's assurances that no harm would come to him in any event, as his book was destined largely for a foreign audience. We should remember that when Manzano dared publish his first book of poems approximately twenty years earlier, it was done "under guarantee," Calcagno tells us, "since slaves were not allowed to publish anything."[15]

Manzano's insistence on assurances or guarantees could perhaps account for his reluctance to get on with the writing of his *Autobiografía.* We know that he made four attempts before getting the manuscript under way. We know too, from his letter to Del Monte dated June 4, 1835, that once Manzano reconciled himself to the undertaking, he practiced the selective censorship required to bring his story in line with his benefactor's guidelines. In the same letter he writes, "I have prepared myself to account to Your Grace for a *part* of the story of my life, *reserving its most interesting events* for some day when, seated in some corner of my homeland, tranquil, *certain of my destiny* and my means of livelihood, I could write a truly Cuban novel."[16]

This letter, I believe, tells us more about Manzano than his entire *Autobiografía,* which, by the way, he labeled part 1. Part 2, as we shall discuss shortly, was mysteriously "lost." This letter suggests more than just intention to comply with the acceptable image, for the italicized parts are the keys to a fuller reading of Manzano's intentions. He is well aware that he is narrating only "a part" of his life story, that he is "reserving its most interesting events" for another time when "certain of [his] destiny" he could write what he calls "a truly Cuban novel." Manzano knew very well, in short, that it would take more assurances than those Del Monte guaranteed to get him to reveal more of his life story. But two questions linger: Did he dare elaborate on other aspects of his life in part 2, and is that why that volume was so quickly "lost"?

The fate of part 2 of Manzano's *Autobiografía* is problematic, and its disappearance "shortly after having been written and copied"[17] has not been satisfactorily explained. Madden suspects foul play. Writing in the prologue to his translation of the first part, he says: "The work was written in two parts; the second one fell in the hands of persons connected with the former master, and I fear it is not likely to be restored to the person to whom I am indebted for the first portion of this manuscript [Del Monte]."[18] Del Monte reports that the second part "was lost in the care of [Ramón de] Palma and was never seen again."[19]

When we recall that Manzano at the end of part 1 of his *Autobiografía* was finally beginning to come out from under the lamblike image he had so carefully constructed in that volume, we can assume that part 2 could well have been franker than part 1. Perhaps Manzano in part 2 forgot the original guidelines and expressed some views that, for all concerned including Manzano, were better left unsaid. Perhaps Manzano had tired of being circumspect and wanted to go faster and farther than his liberal white friends were prepared to go. At any rate it is unfortunate that part 2 was lost, or destroyed, particularly as it could well have come as close as he ever got to writing the book he tells us he was saving up for. Certainly the purge in 1844 seems to have silenced him—and many other Blacks. It is not surprising, therefore, that we have nothing from Manzano during the last ten years of his life. As it turns out, we are left only with part 1. Since it is written by a black slave who could tell us much, his autobiography is, perhaps, the most tragically controlled piece of literature coming out of that period of Cuban and Latin American literary history, certainly more so than Anselmo Suárez y Romero's *Francisco,* even though Suárez y Romero's novel did have the *subversivo* excised from it by the Del Monte group to make it conform to their requirement of presenting Blacks as submissive.[20]

Even tragically controlled, the first part of Manzano's *Autobiografía* does stand as an early example of black writing in Latin America, and as such it does bequeath something to following generations in terms of its faithfulness to themes and traditions relevant to black history in the New World. The theme of liberty, for example, that runs throughout the history of Afro-Latin American literature does exist in a very basic form in the *Autobiografía.* Manzano's search for identity (the development of which was interrupted by the division of his work into two parts) within the confines of his New World environment is also evident. With part 2 missing we can only guess whether his motivation in that second part derived from some radical change in his life that might have led to an "internal transformation of the individual."[21] We can only wonder, in other words, whether Manzano "describes not only what has happened to him at a different time in his life, but above all how he became—out of what he was—what he presently is."[22] Self-formulation or the discovery of the present self that was just beginning to take over at the end of part 1 could well have formed the organizing principle for part 2 of Manzano's *Autobiografía.* "Black autobiographies, including the slave narratives, are unique statements about identity,"[23] and Manzano's, even though he concealed a great deal, is no exception.

This is so even though Manzano presents himself in part 1 not as an *engaged* activist but as a *disengaged* pacifist, a harmless victim of the system and no danger to it. These two categories that Saundra Towns has defined, black autobiographies of the engaged and of the disengaged, help us understand and categorize part 1 of Manzano's *Autobiografía.*[24] In Towns' first group are authors who make a personal commitment to black liberation. But the single-minded pursuit by these men—political activists, social reformers and public men—of their goals is absent in the other category, the autobiography of the disengaged, whose authors show little interest in their ancestry or at best are reluctant to acknowledge it.

Arriving at what I consider a key phrase in her characterization of the second group, Towns writes that black writers in this group find it far better to forget the past and to subsume one's blackness under one's Americanness. I find this phrase crucial because I believe that is

precisely what Manzano did. If we substitute "Cubanness" for "Americanness," we have what is a fairly accurate assessment of Manzano's integrationist concept of the future he desired in his *patria.* Being the artist that he was with a sensitivity to match his inclination, Manzano could not help but hope for some tranquil moments to develop his art and his identity. These quiet moments for Manzano could come only with his emancipation from slavery. But again we must remember that the purge in 1844 epitomized the hostile white environment of his time and put a quick end to whatever peaceful moments he was able to have.

Manzano, then, wanted not only to be free but also to be left to blend quietly into the Cuban landscape, for he felt as Cuban as anyone else. This is the same desire for integration, as we shall see, that will be picked up later by Martín Morúa Delgado with a political zeal matched only by his political clout. But Morúa, writing in the late nineteenth century, when slavery and colonialism were on the wane, was in a much better position to bring to fruition his ideas of belonging for himself and for his people in Cuba. Part 1 of Manzano's *Autobiografía* largely covers his period as a child slave and rightly belongs to the category of the black autobiography of the disengaged. We do not know how Manzano took the loss or the destruction of part 2 of his *Autobiografía,* but we cannot help but wonder whether this part, which probably reflected more consciousness of being a man, would have belonged to the category of the engaged.

With his freedom Manzano joined the other colored segment of colonial society, the free Black. Ironically, Manzano's plight worsened after gaining his freedom, and he even served a prison term. Life for free Blacks, especially writers who were under constant supervision in slave societies, was difficult, as they faced obstacles and persecution, sometimes worse than those faced by slaves. These early second-class citizens "outnumbered their slave counterparts in Spanish America well before the struggles for political independence."[25] Although not slaves, they too had their problems and obstacles to overcome. Occupying "an ambiguous intermediate position between the fully free and the enslaved"[26] free Blacks like "Plácido," Gabriel de la Concepción Valdés (1804-1844), were more of a threat than the slave and as a result were more feared. We repeatedly read such statements as the following: "For the Government, the free black, who was more intelligent, was more dangerous than the slave,"[27] and "the dangers of Cuba come not so much from the slaves as from the multitude of free blacks and mulattoes."[28] Or, "Consciously and unconsciously, free blacks and free mulattoes offered the seeds of revolt or threatened revolt to the unfree blacks. The free colored were usually among the first to raise the issues of personal liberty and class discrimination in the societies."[29] Free Blacks, particularly in Cuba, had no choice but to react, since "by the nineteenth century, racism was a prominent feature of Cuba's white society, and its most hostile manifestation was toward the free colored community."[30] This society, paranoid from suspicion and "blinded by fear and racial prejudice,"[31] came down hardest on the free Black in 1844 and after, when the purge of that year practically decimated the free black community for its involvement in political and racial plotting designed to free the slaves and give independence to Cuba.

These two features, racism and racial prejudice, are the ones the black novelist and politician Martín Morúa Delgado (1856-1910) chose to criticize in post-abolitionist Cuba. Martín Morúa Delgado was also a journalist, but his most substantial and ambitious work was done in the novel genre. Morúa launched a series of novels that he entitled "Cosas de mi tierra," and he completed two in this series, *Sofía* (1891) and *La familia Unzúazu* (1901), before his death. His novels are quite often placed in the tradition of the antislavery novels, because they deal with the evils of slavery. But by striking primarily against the white Cuban's "imponderable pride of caste, of class, of race,"[32] Morúa moves beyond the simple condemnation of slavery as an evil institution to a larger future vision of the role and place of the soon-to-be-liberated black slave in post-abolitionist Cuban society. His novels really address the crippling psychological effects of racism, the holdover from slavery that prevented white Cubans from accepting black people without reference to their past. Franklin W. Knight wrote that "the slave society in the Americas was essentially a coercive and racist society."[33] Morúa, who knew this as well as anyone, hardly ascribed to the preconceived theory of social class and race held by other writers like Villaverde, whose antislavery novel *Cecilia Valdés* (1882) Morúa took to task for its narrow view of black people. Morúa saw Villaverde as a typical example of a White who still harbored prejudices against Blacks; it was precisely Villaverde's racist approach that Morúa opposed in his own antiracist view. Unlike *Cecilia Valdés* and other antislavery novels from the nineteenth century, *Sofía* and *La familia Unzúazu* were written by a Black whose mother had been an African slave.

Morúa's novels, unlike the antislavery works that preceded him, were published after slavery had been abolished. It is not surprising, therefore, that he chose to turn his attention to the pervasive effects of the system that even after abolition continued to shape public opinion toward Blacks. Racism, as an evil inherited from slavery, was much more difficult to regulate, for unlike slavery, "conscious and unconscious feelings of racial superiority"[34] could not simply be abolished. For this reason the challenges facing Morúa as a black writer were greater than those faced by earlier abolitionist writers. The institution of slavery had been a large,

fixed target, easy to attack, but Morúa used that system as a point of departure in his efforts to get the ex-slave to claim his rights under the law, to feel as though he belonged, and to get the ex-slave owner to recognize these rights and to look beyond appearances to see the worth of the individual. These are the points that Morúa emphasizes, first in *Sofía* and later in *La familia Unzúazu*.

Fidelio, perhaps one of Morúa's most significant characters in *La familia Unzúazu,* takes on autobiographical significance. A free Black who has numerous similarities with the author, Fidelio was prepared, like Morúa, to work toward the realization of a new Cuba. He, therefore, made the decision to join the enslaved Black with the "natural revolutionary impulse"[35] that had to become the trademark of the new "Cuban ideal,"[36] an ideal that has no time for ethnic divisions. Morúa's concern, first raised in *Sofía,* was with "the future of his homeland and the destiny of the race" (p. 176). Fidelio decides, as Morúa had done, to be useful to his country "by helping the improvement of a race that has been held back" (p. 305). He would do this by opting for journalism as a career, as Morúa had done at a crucial point in his development. "In the mind of Fidelio that night was born with powerful force the goal to which from then on he subordinated his inclinations: The publication of a newspaper in which he, usually at a loss for words, would expose the world of ideas which had accumulated in his brain" (p. 306).

Fidelio does little in the novel aside from making that decision, but it was for him, as it had been for Morúa, perhaps the most important one in his life. Commitment to all the people, particularly to the underprivileged, which at that time were the enslaved Blacks, was a necessary first step for anyone who genuinely wanted to work for the greater goal of a free Cuba. Martín Morúa Delgado made that commitment, one we should not forget even though it, like the literary blackness expressed in his novels, was overshadowed by subsequent and more controversial events in his political life.

Morúa's *La familia Unzúazu,* though not an autobiography in the true sense, nevertheless like Manzano's *Autobiografía* is a unique statement about his identity. If we accept that Fidelio represents the author, the "internal transformation of the individual" that we spoke of earlier in the case of Manzano is also evident here. If our speculations are correct regarding Manzano's lost autobiography, Morúa, like Manzano, changes from a disengaged pacifist to an engaged activist, thus making a personal commitment to black liberation. His attack will be not on slavery but on racism and racial prejudice, and his weapons will be politics and the black press.

In a sense, then, we may say that Martín Morúa Delgado's desire for integration is reflected in Fidelio's determination to work for the incorporation of the Black into the future plans of his homeland. What we have is an excellent example of an autobiographical statement that uniquely does in one work what we may speculate Manzano tried to do in two, namely, the merging of the goals of the engaged activist and the disengaged pacifist, which are black liberation on the one hand and integration on the other.

Notes

1. Juan Francisco Manzano, *Autobiografía, cartas y versos,* con un estudio preliminar por José L. Franco (Havana: Municipio de La Habana, 1937), p. 92.

2. This autobiography has just received new life in a modernized edition by Ivan Schulman. See Juan Francisco Manzano, *Autobiografía de un esclavo,* Introducción, notas y actualización del texto de Ivan Schulman (Madrid: Ediciones Guadarrama, 1975).

3. See Russell C. Brignano, *Black Americans in Autobiography: An Annotated Bibliography of Autobiographies and Autobiographical Books Written Since the Civil War* (Durham, N.C.: Duke University Press, 1974).

4. Jean Franco calls Miguel Barnet's *The Autobiography of a Runaway Slave,* put together from interviews with his ex-slave subject, "imaginative documentary writing," a documentary type, she says, that has already been given literary respectability by Norman Mailer, William Styron and Truman Capote. See Jean Franco, "Literature in the Revolution," *Twentieth Century,* nos. 1039/40 (1968-69): 64.

5. R. Anthony Castagnaro, *The Early Spanish American Novel* (New York: Las Américas Publishing, 1971), p. 158.

6. César Leante, "Dos obras antiesclavistas cubanas," *Cuadernos Americanos* 207, no. 4 (1976): 177.

7. Ivan Schulman, "The Portrait of the Slave: Ideology and Aesthetics in the Cuban Antislavery Novel," *Comparative Perspectives on Slavery in New World Societies,* ed. Vera Rubin and Arthur Tuden (New York: Academy of Sciences, 1977), p. 36.

8. Ibid.

9. Francisco Calcagno, *Poetas de color,* 4th ed. (Havana: Imprenta Mercantil de los Herederos de Santiago, 1887), p. 71.

10. Domingo del Monte, *Escritos* (Havana: Cultural, 1929), 1:44, reprinted in *Autobiografía de un esclavo,* pp. 37-38.

11. Francisco Calcagno, fragment of the nineteenth-century novel *Romualdo, uno de tantos,* in *Islas* (Cuba), no. 44 (1973), pp. 107-8, reprinted in Manzano, *Autobiografía de un esclavo,* p. 30.

12. Calcagno, *Poetas de color,* p. 60.

13. Ibid., p. 62.

14. Ibid., p. 52.

15. Ibid., p. 62.

16. Reproduced in Ibid., p. 82 (emphasis added).

17. Manzano, *Autobiografía de un esclavo,* p. 47.

18. Reprinted in Calcagno, *Poetas de color,* p. 76.

19. Manzano, *Autobiografía de un esclavo,* p. 47.

20. Leante, "Dos obras," p. 185.

21. Jean Starobinski, "The Style of Autobiography," in *Literary Style: A Symposium,* ed. Seymour Chatman (London: Oxford University Press, 1971), p. 289.

22. Ibid., p. 290.

23. Catharine R. Stimpson, "Black Culture/White Teacher," in *New Perspectives on Black Studies,* ed. John W. Blassingame (Urbana: University of Illinois Press, 1971), p. 181.

24. Saundra Towns, "Black Autobiography and the Dilemma of Western Artistic Tradition," *Black Books Bulletin,* (1975): 17-23.

25. Frederick P. Bowser, "Colonial Spanish America," in *Neither Slave nor Free: The Freedman of African Descent in the Slave Societies of the New World,* ed. David W. Cohen and Jack P. Greene (Baltimore: Johns Hopkins University Press, 1972), p. 19.

26. Franklin W. Knight, "Cuba," in *Neither Slave nor Free,* ed. Cohen and Greene, p. 281.

27. Leonardo Guinán Peralta, "La defensa de los esclavos," in his *Ensayos y conferencias* (Santiago de Cuba: Editora del Consejo Nacional de Universidades, 1964), p. 75.

28. José Antonio Saco, cited in Peralta, "La defensa," p. 78.

29. Cohen and Greene, *Neither Slave nor Free,* p. 16.

30. Knight, "Cuba," p. 282.

31. Ibid., p. 292.

32. Martín Morúa Delgado, *Sofía* (1891; reprint ed., Havana: Instituto Cubano del Libro, 1972), p. 22.

33. Knight, "Cuba," p. 281.

34. Charles Boxer, *Race Relations in the Portuguese Colonial Empire* (Oxford: Clarendon Press, 1963), p. 56.

35. Morúa, *Sofía*, p. 165.

36. Ibid., p. 168. All other references to this novel will be cited parenthetically in the text.

Susan Willis (essay date 1985)

SOURCE: Willis, Susan. "Crushed Geraniums: Juan Francisco Manzano and the Language of Slavery." In *The Slave's Narrative*, edited by Charles T. Davis and Henry Louis Gates, Jr. pp. 199-224. Oxford, U.K.: Oxford University Press, 1985.

[*In the following essay, Willis proposes that the key to understanding a slave narrative lies in comprehending the position of the narrator.*]

> Malo es ser esclavo, pero mil veces peor es ser esclavo despierto; un esclavo que piensa es una protesta viva, es un juez mudo y terrible que esta estudiando el crimen social.
>
> Francisco Calcagno

The scene is a slave compound on the island of Barbados in the eighteenth century. The narrator is seated beside a young girl named Gow and her six year old brother, Thry, who lies curled in her lap. They have been in Barbados about a week; have been fed very little; and, while they await being sold, have been set to work picking oakum. Thry is hungry and begs his sister to get him something to eat, which of course is impossible.

> They both burst into a flood of tears, which continued for some time. After their lamentation ceased, she spoke to me, saying, I should not feel so bad if the white people had not taken from me the bracelet of gold, which was on my right arm, as my grand-father, when my grand-mother died, took it from her arm and gave it to me (on account of my bearing her name) as a token of remembrance and affection, which was always expressed; and now I have nothing in this foreign land to remember her by, it makes me feel as if it would break my heart; but what's worse than all, I fear, if they don't kill me, they will take away my little brother; and if they don't starve him, he will mourn himself to death. . . . At this instant the driver came in with a long whip under his arm, and placed himself in the center of the circle in which we were chained, he stood about four minutes, cast his eyes upon the slaves, a dead silence prevailed through the whole house except the re-echoing of sobs and sighs. He fixed his eyes upon us, stepped up to the bunch of oakum which Gow had been picking, took it up in his hand with some vehemence, threw it down instantly, struck her upon the side of her head with the butt end of the whip, which laid her quivering upon the ground for one or two min-

utes. When she began to recover and to get upon her hands and feet, during which time he continued whipping her. Her little brother began to scream and cry, begging in his artless manner and unintelligible dialect for her relief. She at length regained her former situation, when he again turned the butt of his whip and struck her on the other temple, which levelled her with the ground; she seemed frantic, and instantly rose upon her feet, the driver with a terrible grin and countenance, that bespoke his brutality, struck her with a drawing blow over the left shoulder, which came round under her right arm, near the pit of her stomach, and cut a hole through, out of which the blood gushed every breath. The wretch continued whipping until he had satiated his unprovoked vengeance, then he sat her up and handed her a rope to pick, he composedly walked round to see some of the rest of the slaves. She sat reeling backwards and forwards for about two or three minutes, the blood gushing from her wounds every breath, then fell down and expired. Thry, her little brother, went and laid his head upon her neck and said, Come Gow, don't cry any more, come get up, don't go to sleep and leave me awake, because I am so lonesome I cannot bear it, do wake up.[1]

The plight of the kidnapped children, torn from a loving family; the sorrow of the young girl whose own anguish is heightened by her need to care for her little brother; and finally her merciless beating, from which there is no escape and no one to comfort her dying moments, make this a most profoundly horrible scene of human victimization and suffering. The powerful emotions stirred by this passage are largely due to the narrator's sympathetic understanding of the young girl's situation, expressed in the care with which he describes her background and her tender regard for her younger brother. Because the reader perceives the episode from the narrator's point of view, he cannot help but experience its deep emotional impact.

What I would propose is that understanding the position of the narrator is the key to understanding the slave narrative as a whole. What this passage clearly demonstrates is the narrator's limited comprehension of his new situation as a slave. While he has full access to his own past experience and that of his people, he is unable to grasp the motives behind the overseer's actions. This bestows a deeply human quality to his description of the young girl, whom he identifies with and understands; and at the same time renders the overseer's actions all the more brutal because they are given as raw information.

The striking horror of the scene is largely produced by its apparent spontaneity. It seems the overseer, for no reason at all, has chosen to torture and kill a totally innocent girl, whom he falls upon at random. This, however is not the case; and if we look at the raw information supplied by the narrator, interpreting it with a basic knowledge of Caribbean slavery, which the narrator, himself, lacked, we gain a fuller understanding of the episode, which while it diminishes the brute spontaneity of the overseer's actions by supplying the missing motives, in no way lessens the guilt of his extreme cruelty.

First of all it is important to note that the slaves are recent arrivals. They have not yet been sold and in the meantime have been set to work picking oakum, which, by comparison to the extreme economic importance of their future toil in the cane fields, is a somewhat insignificant task. This, then, is a transitional period; and the slaves, half famished and lamenting their lost homelands, pass the uncertain hours with meaningless toil. So as not to let them experience the moment as one of relaxation or indecision on the part of the overlords, an example must be made. To introduce them to the full meaning of slavery—the absolute and unquestionable authority of the white man over the black—someone must be killed.

The choice of victim is not as spontaneous as the narrator seems to suggest. This is clear even in the way he has described the scene; the overseerer "stood about four minutes, cast his eyes upon the slaves, a dead silence prevailed through the whole house except the re-echoing of sobs and sighs. He fixed his eyes upon us." Obviously surveying the group, the overseer selects his victim. What gives the narration a sense of spontaneity, even though the process of selection takes four minutes, is the narrator's inability to know what is happening and for what purpose.

Then, too, the choice is not random. That the overseer singles out the young girl, as the narrator senses but cannot explain, is directly related to the bunch of oakum she had been working on which the overseer seizes and disdainfully casts aside. This is an important bit of information which the narrator cannot interpret from his limited point of view. Quite possibly the young girl had done the least work on her pile of oakum; most probably, out of the group of slaves, she is the least productive and offers the least potential for future production. What the narrator doesn't know is that Caribbean slavery, based on an intensive, one-crop economy, needed a steady supply of young adult male slaves. Women were less important, for as long as the slave trade continued, there was no need to tolerate less productive field laborers solely for the purpose of reproducing the labor force. A young girl not yet big enough or strong enough to be a fully productive field laborer, and not yet mature enough to function sexually was the least valuable property. Her younger brother escapes murder solely on the promise of his future productivity.

Moreover, the overseer's actions were premeditated, intended for their pedagogical effect. This is evident as he "composedly walked round to see some of the rest of the slaves" while the young girl agonizes in the throws of death. Parading his authority and surveying his de-

fenseless chattels, he has made sure everyone gets the message by placing the oakum once more in the dying girl's hand—for the slave there is only work and death.

To varying degrees all slave narratives are conditioned by the narrator's partial understanding of his situation. While the narrator can report on his condition, giving a full, often tactile, account of physical and emotional experiences, he has no access to the realm of causality. He is a blind receiver whose perspective on the motives behind all the demands and actions which govern his life has been short circuited. This then places the narrator in a very different relationship to the reader than what normally obtains in the tradition of prose literature; for the narrator often cannot supply his reader with meaning.

Perspectival limitations are particularly strong in the slave narratives from the Caribbean, where the influence of abolitionists, either as editors or instigators of the narrative, is not a strong factor. By comparison, the fugitive North American slave, once in the free states and in contact with abolitionists, could, with broadened perspective, look back over the events of his life and understand them in a more meaningful way. Essentially, the first hand experience of the difference in mode of production between the slave-based agricultural South and the wage-labor North, took the fugitive out of the microcosmic master/slave relationship and supplied the logic necessary to write, not raw data, but a meaningful narrative. Then, at a secondary level, the strong influence of Christian religion so often voiced in the American slave narrative, functions as a means to further interpret and evaluate past experience.

In comparison with other slave narratives published in North America, the Boyrereau Brinch text is atypical. After escaping from the Caribbean, he wound up in Vermont where the abolitionist, Benjamin Prentiss, transcribed his memoirs. However, his narration occurred at a time prior to the great interest in slave literature (1810) and so is less influenced by abolition as a cause and the American slave narrative as a genre. The narrator, not fully aware of an audience and the purpose to which his narrative might be put, is not constrained to supply meaning. Brinch, in the process of relating the past, re-experiences the lack of perspective which conditioned his life as a slave and narrates the raw unevaluated material of experience as an assemblage of undigested bits and pieces. Even his appeals to Scripture, which occur unexpectedly throughout the text, are given as data, juxtaposed, rather than integrated in the narration.

A few decades after Brinch's narration, in Havana, Cuba, Juan Francisco Manzano, a recently liberated mulatto, wrote a narrative where the lack of perspective and the distance from an audience produced an extremely disordered narration. To understand Manzano's narrative it is first of all necessary to define his relationship to literature. While he was not writing in a total void, his access to literary texts, tradition and audience was limited by the two-fold influence of slavery and colonialism. The early nineteenth century Cuban reading public was comprised basically of sugarocrats and urban professionals, whose class interests were tied to sugar production—neither of which could have been an audience for Manzano's narrative text. Furthermore, those who could read were often more interested in cards and dice and only a few enlightened individuals actually sought out literary and scientific reading material.[2]

Nevertheless, nineteenth century Cuba did possess a strong center of literary interest, organized and defined by Domingo del Monte and his circle of writers and critics.[3] While its influence was highly localized, it had close contact with European critical debates, sponsored indigenous literary production, and published more than one literary journal. The critique of neo-classicism and the general espousal of romanticism was one of the group's central concerns. The strong interest in Rousseau, Goethe and Chateaubriand provided an atmosphere favorable to autobiography and confessional literature, which suggests a possible generic background for Manzano's narration.

While many of our observations will suggest the confessional[4] nature of Manzano's text (the way in which it becomes a vehicle for self observation through monological discourse and the re-living of past experience in the process of narrating), the direct influence of the del Monte group and its critical concerns ought not to be taken too seriously. While Manzano was a participant in the literary circle, he was not one of its central members. Moreover, the group saw him as a poet rather than a prose essayist and thus would have had only minimal influence on his prose writing.

Another possible area of literary influence is the slave narrative itself and its relationship to abolition as a movement. While Manzano's narrative was probably prompted by his contact with the English abolitionist, Richard R. Madden,[5] the slave narrative as a genre had no real presence in Cuba. Rather, anti-slavery was the literary concern of the novel; notably, Suarez y Romero's *Francisco*.

While the influence of literary models on Manzano's text was at best partial, the lack of tangible audience was perhaps the most significant factor. Just as Manzano was not writing for the reading public of sugarocrats and professionals, so too the small group of anti-slavery writers and critics could not have been his intended audience. To some extent he wrote his fragmented and incoherent remembrances as confessions directed to himself with no real audience in mind. But this is only a partial explanation; for Manzano's text (much like many contemporary texts from the third world) is a text written for export—entrusted with Madden on the eve of his departure from Cuba and destined for the English abolitionist audience. If this was Manzano's ultimate audience, it (being foreign and unknowable) could have had no concrete presence or function for the writer. In this way, all of Manzano's possible audiences—the indigenous, the self, and the foreign—are partialities, which, as the text demonstrates, are incapable of fulfilling the demands of narrative communication.

What one notices first about the Manzano text is its total ignorance of form. Paragraphs begin and end at random, sometimes encompassing only a few sentences, sometimes stretching over pages. Indeed, the Soviet linguist, Volosinov, has observed that the ability to formulate orderly paragraphs representing whole conceptual units is directly related to the narrator's awareness of his audience. A paragraph is "a vitiated dialogue worked into the body of a monologic utterance." And "if we could imagine speech that absolutely ignored the addressee (an impossible kind of speech, of course), we would have a case of speech with organic partition reduced to the minimum."[6] In Manzano's narration the impossible becomes reality. Rather than a "speech" directed to an audience, his is an interiorized monologue entrusted to Madden and sent like a message in a bottle to London and an unknown readership.

Directly related to the text's breakdown at the level of the paragraph is its flagrant disregard for sentence punctuation. As is generally agreed among stylistic critics,[7] the sentence is the basic unit of meaning in prose writing. As such, it functions to "direct" the reader's apprehension of the material in a particular and meaningful way. However, Manzano, recording his own interior voice and writing with only partial awareness of literary models, is not constrained to supply sentence punctuation. Consequently, the reader can follow the text only by suspending learned habits of reading and allowing the text to speak. Only then does the narration become logical. Otherwise, sentences run on and subjects get lost or attached to the wrong verbs. However the experience of reading in the context of speech patterns is not unrewarding, for it suggests a wholly different direction prose literature might have taken had it not been for the invention of punctuation which eliminates textual variety and readerly sport.

Obviously the narration has a strong oral orientation; however it exhibits a very special form of orality. Manzano, whose punishments occasionally included field labor, was primarily a houseslave, a *falderillo,* or personal page, who from the age of ten had to wait upon a cruel and pretentious woman of the provincial landed elite. His was the world of operas, *tertulias* and gambling halls. His language was never that of the field workers; consequently his access to oral culture, in the traditional sense, was certainly limited.

The oral influence on his narration derives instead from poetry and the circumstances under which he learned to write. While his first mistress, something of a benevolent aristocrat, sent him to school as she had his mother before him, Manzano's education was early ended by the death of this mistress. From then on, he received no formal training, was discouraged from learning to read and write on his own, and only sporadically came in contact with people, basically professionals and artists, who gave him assistance. However, with only the rudiments of reading and writing, Manzano was able to become an accomplished poet. This he achieved by cultivating his innate ability to listen, memorize, and, when allowed, recite. As a houseslave, he was exposed to (or could overhear) prodigious sermons (sometimes two hours long) and poetry readings by local artists or devotees—all of which he memorized, mumbling and musing over them through the long hours of his daily and nightly toil. It was not long before his inner voice was able to compose and record for memory his own *décimas*. That his poetry, particularly one unpublished poem which we will examine, transcends the lifeless, second-rate provincial models he had to work with gives all the more credit to his remarkable achievement and poetic insight.

Born in 1797, Manzano divides his life in two phases: a prehistory of childhood plenitude, during which his first mistress gave him every advantage; and his "real history" which began after her death in 1809. While the narrative follows a linear sequentiality and there are no digressions, it is nevertheless disorderly. On close analysis, while the lack of punctuation contributes to the confusion, narrative disorder is more profoundly linked to the fragmentation of the episodes described and the seemingly arbitrary selection of material for narration. Because the overall text is extremely short, it is obvious that some process of selecting certain events out of the flow of life experience has occurred. However, there appears to be no meaningful logic behind the selection.

Here is where the Brinch narrative, with its perspectival limitations and partial access to meaning, supplies the key. Manzano's text is incomprehensible only if we try to make meaning a criterion for narration. By trying to force his narration into conventional categories of prose, we overlook and exclude the possibility of other organizational features.

Once we suspend the need for meaning, a very different narrative framework is revealed. Essentially, the narrative is based on a series of discontinuous events, each of which is a crystalized moment of torture.

For Manzano, the child of twelve, the first of these memorable moments is of dark and dank solitary confinement, where tormented by thirst, hunger and cold, and liable for a whipping if he should cry out, his active mind played host to nightmare visions.

> I suffered for the slightest act of boyish mischief, shut up in a coal pit with not even a plank for a bed nor anything to wrap myself up in for more than twenty four hours I was extremely frightened and wanted to eat my jail as can still be seen needs in the brightest noontime light a strong candle for one to see anything inside it here after suffering a severe whipping I was shut up under orders and the threat of a severe punishment for anyone who might give me even a drop of water, what I suffered there afflicted with hunger, and well I know it, tormented with fear, in such a deep and isolated place separated from the house, in a backyard next to a stable, and a pestilent, foul-smelling trash heap, along side a wet, infested and noxious outhouse which was only separated by a wall full of holes, a den for huge rats that walked over me without even stopping, so afraid was everyone in the house that absolutely no one dared even if they had the opportunity to give me even a bite my head was full of stories about evil things from long ago, of apparitions from beyond the grave and of spells cast by the dead so that when a troop of rats rushed out making a lot of noise I imagined the cave was full of ghosts and cried out asking for pity they then took me out and tormented me with so many lashes that I couldn't take any more and they shut me up again keeping the key in my mistress's own room.[8]

The words tumbling out in a rush, these lines, while written some twenty years later, bear the stamp of fresh experience as if they were spoken by the young Manzano only moments after being removed from the pit and allowed to seek comfort in his mother's waiting arms. The lack of sentence divisions gives the narrative a hurried and unreflected appearance as if the narrator wanted to say everything at once—the rats, the ghosts, the damp, the darkness, the stench, the people who might have helped him, and those who intensified his suffering—all are given in the form of narrative raw material, which another, more literary hand, might have transformed into a coherent narration. It is this disregard for literary convention, the result of the narrator's separation from an audience, which differentiates Manzano's narration from the North American slave narratives.

Although Manzano openly expresses the desire for readerly contact—someone to verify that his cell really was as dark as he claims—his writing shows that he has no sense of a reader or how to direct the reader's apprehension of his story. This is particularly evident in the unintended—and consequently ridiculous—juxtaposition within the phrase, "I was extremely frightened and wanted to eat my jail. . . ."

While the rush of words that the passage evokes is visibly related to its lack of sentence markers, it is a direct consequence of extreme parataxis. Substantive phrase follows upon substantive phrase with no more than a comma, a reiteration of the subject or some new piece of descriptive detail to bind the phrases together. Rendering a strong sense of immediacy, the passage records sensory data but cannot account for causal relationships. It is significant that the only hypotactic construction introduces a troop of rats—of a lower order than the condemned slave and therefore belonging to a system of causality to which he has access. "Paratactic bluntness" is the phrase used by Auerbach to describe Roland's inescapable doom and it equally applies here. In parataxis "everything must happen as it does happen, it could not be otherwise and there is no need for explanatory connectives."[9]

While Manzano informs us that he was often punished in the coal pit (sometimes two or three times a week) he describes the event only once. Significantly, all the episodes of torture described in the narration are given as single, isolated events, each different from the others and therefore all the more horrifying for its novelty. These form the nodal points of the narrative, and at the same time suggest the sadistic nature of his mistress whose agile mind had but one task, and that to conceive ever new ways of torturing her young slave.

While the organization of Manzano's narration is based on a series of isolated anecdotes of torture, other Caribbean slave narratives demonstrate the same importance of the nodal moment, where novelty and singularity are not necessarily related to torture. The most interesting example is the adventure filled narration of Olaudah Equiano,[10] who for very good reasons has been called the Caribbean Robinson Crusoe. Not a field slave, but a ship's steward, who served under a variety of Caribbean traders and Mediterranean military commanders, Equiano's narrative has as its basic structuring unit the moment of discovery. Each nodal moment is marked by the confrontation with some new object, cultural practice, situation, scientific discovery, religious revelation, personality or geographic terrain. His long term achievements, such as learning to read and write, mastering the art of navigation, and earning enough money through petty trade to eventually buy his own freedom, are secondary to the narrative emphasis on the moment of discovery. With each episode the narrative renews itself, and in each discovery creates something of the vivid shock experienced by the Aztecs when they first beheld their mounted Spanish conquerors. In this way, the narrative is a continual expression of the collision between two very different worlds, in which the slave, ignorant of the new situation, is made to feel inferior. Then too, in a deeper sense, Equiano's discoveries express the same uncertainty about the future and inability to attach meaning to the events which mark his life as a slave that inform the more brutal slave narrations.

For Manzano, the second nodal moment occurs when he, accompanying his mistress home late one night, as he had done on many a previous night, is lulled to sleep by the motion of the carriage. He wakes to see, glimmering behind, the lantern which he is supposed to carry. Leaping down from the carriage, he is able to retrieve the lantern but it is impossible to regain the disappearing carriage. Numb with fear, he knows he must return on foot. Once at the hacienda he is seized and taken away to be punished. His mother intercedes but is struck down by the angered *mayoral*. This so maddens the young Manzano that he strikes back at the mayoral, biting and scratching like "a lion." For this impudence, both Manzano and his mother are to be whipped.

> they led us out my mother brought to the place of sacrifice for the first time in her life even though she was a part of the hacienda she was exempt from work being the wife of a respected slave [a carpenter who probably bought the privilege to work his own jobs]; seeing my mother in this state I couldn't cry, move, or flee I was shaking all over the four Negroes took hold of her and threw her on the ground to whip her I asked God to help her I restrained myself but on hearing the first whip lash, transformed into a lion or tiger or the wildest beast I was ready to lose my life [for her] at the hands of don Silvestre [the mayoral] but let's leave to silence the rest of this painful scene.[11]

The novel feature of this episode is the punishment of the mother, who, because she had never been whipped before, had been Manzano's one source of emotional strength. The fact that she too is subject to punishment for the slightest affront to authority demonstrates that she is really nothing more than a slave. The episode has a pedagogical purpose similar to the beating of the young girl in the Brinch narrative. However, while the mother's punishment is intended totally to demoralize her son, and it does have this overall effect, Manzano's immediate response is to fight back. This rebellious outburst is a significant opposition to the narrator's admitted sense of martyrdom which he expresses when he refers to the place of punishment as the place of "sacrifice." It is important to understand that the slave's deep desire for freedom can manifest itself spontaneously and often in apparent contradiction to his overall attitude of excessive passivity and timidity. While Manzano presents himself as long-suffering and totally defenseless, he is nevertheless capable of flying at four powerful adults armed with whips and the tremendous weight of authority. Many years later, the same submerged desire for freedom causes the poet to flee his mistress and undertake a hazardous night-time ride to Havana. As is the case in numerous slave narratives,[12] Manzano's determination to be free comes as a result of some new threat which brings with it a tightening of the bonds of slavery. For Manzano, this occurs on his coming of age, a time when his first mistress had intimated that he would be freed. However, seeing that the new mistress has no such intentions, and instead plans to condemn him to the rural hacienda, Manzano decides his only recourse is to seek his own freedom. This decision radically changes the organization of the narrative for it supplies the sense of a long range goal, which Manzano, living from moment to moment, had previously lacked. However, because the impetus to freedom comes toward the end of the first part of Manzano's narration, and because the second part was never published[13] the narrative effects of this decision cannot be fully known, and manifest themselves only in the persistently stated longing for the metropolis of Havana, which by comparison to the country hacienda, becomes charged with the illusion of freedom.

There is, however, one very false note in the above passage and that is its melodramatic closing. The narrator's veil of silence smacks of literary convention,[14] which seems out of place by comparison with the full, vivid detail and immediate nature of the rest of the narration. Moreover, this sort of artificial lapse in the narration occurs more than once and always at an extreme moment of torture. The following is a good example:

The mistress is strolling in her garden and Manzano, her page, must follow her every footstep. He is rather bored, and in a detached state, passes the time mentally composing poems. While wandering about the garden, he has picked a leaf from a fragrant geranium, which he absent-mindedly crumples between his fingers. Upon leaving the garden and entering the closed atmosphere of the house, the mistress passes very close to her slave, notices the fragrance about his body and is thrown into a horrible rage.

> What do you have in your hands; I was as still as death my body suddenly frozen and without being able to keep my two legs from shaking, I dropped the remaining pieces [of leaf] on the floor she took my hands and smelled them and taking hold of the pieces as if it were a great pile, a whole bush, the most audacious act, my nose was broken and immediately in came the administrator, don Lucas Rodriguez an emigrant from Santo Domingo to whom she turned me over, it must have been six o'clock in the evening and in the depths of winter the carriage was ready to leave for town and I was to have gone but how fragile luck is for the one who is subject to its vicissitudes, I never had a moment of certainty as can be seen in this case and in many others, I was taken to the place of punishment, a former infirmary where fifty beds fit along two walls since the field laborers from the hacienda and those from the San Miguel plantation were taken there but at that time it was empty and not used for anything the stocks were there and only an occasional cadaver was left there until the time to carry it to town for burial left standing there in the freezing cold without a single blanket I was shut up scarsely did I find myself alone in that place when I seemed to see the dead rise up and wander about the room there was a broken window which gave on a river near a steep place which made a waterfall cascading without stopping and with every cascade

> I seemed to see a dead man entering from beyond the tomb imagine how the night passed it had hardly begun to grow light when I heard the door bolt slide a contra mayoral enters followed by the administrator they take out a plank intended for me which was attached to a gibbet from which hung a bunch of hooks, about fifty of them at the foot of the plank I see the administrator wrapped in his cape from under his scarf he tells the others in a rough voice to gag me they bind my hands tie them up like Christ's they pick me up and put my feet in the two openings [of the stocks] and also tie my feet Oh God! let us draw a veil over the rest of this scene my blood has poured out I lost consciousness[15]

What makes this episode of torture so poignant is the way in which novelty is used to re-create well established fears. Knowing that Manzano is terrified by solitary confinement, the administrator (who we must assume acts under the direction of the mistress) shuts him in the cold, empty infirmary rather than the coal pit, where Manzano is again haunted by night-long visions of the dead.

It is not gratuitous that such an extreme form of physical punishment should follow what appears to be so trivial an act. What the slave learns in this, another instance of pedagogical torture, is that damage done to private property is the greatest crime. The reason why property is so highly significant is a direct expression of capitalism. That slavery was a mode of capitalist production has been demonstrated by Eric Williams,[16] whose central thesis is that colonial slavery provided the terrific increase in accumulation needed to transform European capitalism from the commercial to the industrial form. Later, as an extension of this process, the influx of European finance capital and the large scale importation of industrial machinery then made slavery unprofitable and brought an end to this mode of production.

Williams's work is important in its attempt to define a necessary relationship between slavery and capitalism, which according to traditional economics are separate historical modes which come into simultaneous existence only because of unequal development. However, it is not until Immanuel Wallerstein's[17] elaboration of dependency theory that slavery can be understood as a mode of production within capitalism. Whereas Williams sees the relationship between capitalism and slavery solely in terms of accumulation, Wallerstein defines it as one of three forms of labor control in a global capitalist system, where the resulting modes of production define three dialectically related economic areas: the periphery, semiperiphery and core. From this point of view, once capitalism comes into existence it governs all modes of production from the third world periphery, where a single crop economy and slave based production are determined by the demands of a global market; to the Eastern European semiperiphery, where the dominant mode is coerced serf labor; and finally, the European core, which gives birth to the form wage labor.

It is significant that theorists not trained in dependency economics have also sensed the global nature of capitalism.[18] Certainly C. L. R. James's description of slave labor captures the essence of Wallerstein's theory:

> When three centuries ago the slaves came to the West Indies, they entered directly into the large-scale agriculture of the sugar plantation, which was a modern system. It further required that the slaves live together in a social relation far closer than any proletariat of the time. The cane when reaped had to be rapidly transported to what was a factory production. The product was shipped abroad for sale. Even the cloth the slaves wore and the food they ate was imported. The Negroes, therefore, from the very start lived a life that was in its essence a modern life.[19]

Essentially, Manzano's crushed geranium is not a part of nature, nor did it ever belong to the natural order. Nature exists only for tribal economy; as such, it is a part of the slave's cultural past. In the Caribbean periphery all that might be seen as nature—the freshly turned soil, the orderly cane rows, the vast fields of green—belong instead to the order of production. The plantation is a nature factory where the mode of production—the tools and the laborers themselves—are owned by the capitalist, who in this case appears in the guise of an agrarian rather than an industrialist. The geranium growing in the garden is thus not a natural phenomenon to be shared, enjoyed or destroyed, but a piece of capital.

Moreover, slavery and a money economy are not antagonistic. It is not gratuitous that another of Manzano's severest tortures is occasioned by the suspicion that he stole a coin. We are not dealing here with a form of feudalism (an interpretation of plantation economy often raised in Latin American economics which has no real basis in fact but seems to derive purely from the agrarian nature of production). The relationship between master and slave is not based on the feudal exchange of protection for production, governed by mutual loyalty, but on coerced bondage and the extraction of surplus value. Money becomes the universal equivalent of human lives, and the moment of torture represents the renewal and reconfirmation of the terms of the laborer's relationship to the owner of the means of production.

The logic of the system which makes torture its most significant movement confirms its place and organizational function in Manzano's narration. That the moments are so vividly described is largely due to narrative discontinuities which a more practiced writer of prose might have avoided. For example, in the passage which describes the consequences of the crushed geranium, there is a marked rupture in the narration which occurs when Manzano, confined in the infirmary, hears the door bolt slide open. Up to this point he has described everything in the past tense. However, the moment the administrator enters and the instruments of torture are revealed to him, Manzano begins to relive the horrible event, noting each detail as he re-sees it in the present tense. Here, what literary minds might criticize as a lapse in temporal form makes the scene all the more real and demonstrates how deeply these moments of torture are etched in the poet's memory. Later, the shift to the past perfect followed by the simple past ("my blood has poured out" and "I lost consciousness") expresses a total temporal disorientation which coincides with the moment of extreme physical pain. What these shifts suggest is that while Manzano relives the moment up to the commencement of torture, the remembrance of the first sensation of pain drives his narration into an empty phrase "Oh God! let us draw a veil over the rest of this scene," through which he is able to repress the memory of pain. The past perfect initiates the process of distancing the event and finally, Manzano, something of a detached bystander notes that his blood "has poured out." Distancing is fully achieved with the simple past "I lost consciousness," a moment which the author could not have felt, but only realized later upon regaining consciousness.

Here, Manzano's use of the veil of silence, which we previously criticized as lending a false note to the narration, serves an extremely meaningful function. What better means than this hollow sounding phrase to repress severe pain and agony and, at the same time and by the fact that its hollowness contrasts so sharply with the rest of the narration, suggest to the reader the inexpressible magnitude of torture. This interpretation, then, sheds light on Manzano's earlier inability to describe his mother's whipping. Rather than a genteel cover up for his mother's disgrace and pain, the veil of silence here represses Manzano's deep investment in his mother's semi-privileged position, which had become the reservoir of his own hopes and aspirations for the future, and which were then shattered the instant her beating began. By refusing to describe his mother's beating, Manzano avoids having to come to grips with the essential contradictions of slavery which manifest themselves in unlimited, unquestionable and perpetual authority. However, Manzano is not a revolutionary, nor is his moment one of radical polarization, which in the Caribbean was only achieved in Haiti.

Nevertheless, one of the most striking demystifications of Cuba as a third world colony and slavery as its appropriate mode of production is found in one of Manzano's poems. As we shall see, the poem focuses on a number of third worldisms (the mythic supports and rationalizations for peripherality), then demystifies them by demonstrating their ideological nature. Manzano's ability to see through the veil of myth suggests that the Caribbean, as the locus for the convergence of the accumulation of European capital, is the place where the contradictions of the system, expressed in the most inflated myths, are most readily exploded and reduced to their basic contradictory nature. The poem also demonstrates how Manzano, as a slave and therefore the most highly exploited link in the chain of accumulation, while limited in his ability to confront the contradictions of slavery manifested in his personal life (as the narrative voids suggest), is capable of understanding the broad system of contradictions which define the Caribbean as a whole.

Simply titled, **"To Cuba"** the poem was for obvious reasons not published in Cuba at the time it was written. Rather, it was presented to the abolitionist, Madden, at the time of his departure from Cuba and later translated by him and included with Manzano's narration and other of his poems in a book which Madden published in London.[20] The text I will use here is Madden's translation, whose authenticity I accept based on his able translations of other poems by Manzano which I have compared to the original Spanish versions.

"To Cuba"

Cuba, of what avail that thou art fair!
Pearl of the seas, the pride of the Antilles!
If thy poor sons, have still to see thee share
The pangs of bondage, and its thousand ills;
Of what avail the verdure of thy hills?
The purple bloom the coffee plain displays
Thy canes luxuriant growth; whose culture fills
More graves than famine, or the swords find ways
To glut with victims calmly as it slays.

Of what avail that sweet streams abound
With precious ore: if wealth there's none to buy,
Thy children's rights, and not one grain is found
For learning's shrine, or for the altar nigh,
Of poor forsaken, downcast liberty!
Of what avail the riches of thy port,
Forests of masts, and ships from every sea,
If trade alone is free, and man the sport,
The spoil of trade, bears wrongs of ev'ry sort?

Oh, if the name of Cuban! makes my breast
Thrill with a moment's pride, that soon is o'er,
Or throb with joy to dream that thou art blest!
Thy sons were free—thy soil unstained with gore.
Reproach awakes me, to assail once more,
And taint that name, as if the loathsome pest
That spreads from slavery had seized the core,
Polluting both th' oppressor and the oppressed:—
Yet God be thanked, it has not reached my breast.

'Tis not alone the wretched negro's fate
That calls for pity, sad as it may be;
There's more to weep for in that hapless state
Of men who proudly boast that they are free,
Whose moral sense is warped to that degree,

That self-debasement seems to them unknown,
And life's sole object, is for means to play,
To roll a carriage, or to seek renown
In all the futile follies of the town.

Cuba! canst thou, my own beloved land,
Counsel thy children to withhold a curse,
And call to mind the deeds of that fell band
Who's boasted conquests, mark one frightful course
Of spoil and plunder, wrung by fraud or force;
Of human carnage in religious gear,
Of peace destroyed—defenceless people worse
Than rudely outraged, nay, reserved to wear
Their lives away in bondage and despair.

To think unmoved of millions of our race,
Swept from thy soil by cruelties prolonged,
Another clime then ravaged to replace
The wretched Indians; Africa then wronged
To fill the void where myriads lately thronged,
And add new guilt to that long list of crimes,
That cries aloud, in accents trumpet-tongued,
And shakes the cloud that gathers o'er these climes,
Portending evil and disastrous times.

Cuba, oh, Cuba, when they call thee fair!
And rich and beautiful, the Queen of isles!
Star of the West, and ocean's gem most rare!
Oh, say to them who mock thee with such wiles
Take of these flowers, and view these lifeless spoils
That wait the worm; behold the hues beneath
The pale cold cheek, and seek for living smiles,
Where beauty lies not in the arms of death,
And bondage taints not with its poisoned breath.

The poem opens with the myth of exotic third world beauty, conjuring an image of shimmering seas and jewel-like islands. It is not gratuitous that the first important literary movement to emerge from Latin America and find acceptance in the European metropolis is one based on an orgy of *exotismos*. Coming some fifty years after Manzano's poem, the Modernist movement brought to Europe a full cargo of rich clothes, rare jewels, exotic princesses; and in a highly exaggerated manner, made of the third world just what the first world had always imagined it to be; namely, the source of unlimited wealth. However, in the Manzano poem, Cuba's exotic beauty is undermined by its cliché-like formulation, something which the later Modernist poetry, convinced of its own exoticism, never achieves. In this way, the poem recognizes the ideology behind the myth, whose function is to inhibit the possibility for historical change. Essentially, the hard perfection of the pearl defines Cuba as impenetrable and unchanging; its setting in the boundless sea serves to isolate the island making it inaccessible to change.

Here, cliché works two ways. On the one hand, it expresses the durability of the myth, which takes on the well-worn acceptability of a slogan; and on the other, it manifests its own hollow nature. That mythic clichés are exceptionally durable is evident in the contemporary reiteration of the same myth in George Lamming's autobiographical novel, *In the Castle of My Skin*:

> "An where's England?" Boy Blue asked.
>
> Bob smiled and to our utter astonishment spoke with a kind of religious conviction: "Barbados or Little England, an island of coral formation set like a jewel in the Caribbean Sea."
>
> We heard the words, and we know they weren't Bob's. "That ain't in no Michael John hist'ry book," Trumper said. "'Cause 'tis no joke," Bob answered. "'Tis facts. Facts."[21]

While the historical moment is pre-World War II, the island Barbados rather than Cuba, and the colonial heritage English rather than Spanish, the ideology behind the myth has the same function. "Little England" is made the hard and fast bastion of colonial integrity, indoctrinated by rote learning, and endowed with the mystique of "fact," which Lamming's novel, then, confronts and demystifies by examining the social and cultural institutions which support the ideology.

Manzano never allows the reader to believe in the Caribbean pearl, making its beauty problematical even in the opening line, "of what avail that thou art fair." Then, to totally explode the image, he names the real source of Cuba's wealth and beauty: slavery. In like manner, the lush and abundant landscape is removed from the realm of nature (which as we shall see throughout is the common source of many third world exoticisms) and rightly defined as the products of cultivation and human toil.

The second stanza continues the demystification of the natural order by redefining it in terms of the early history of the colonies. The promise of gold, or spontaneous natural wealth, which brought the Spaniards and condemned Cuba's Indian population to slavery and extinction in the mines, is devalued by comparison to the vast sums needed to buy the freedom of Cuba's black slaves. With this notion, wealth too is transformed into a capitalist category, suggesting the profits reaped in the buying and selling of human slaves.

An historical understanding of slavery as it evolved through various stages is evident throughout the poem. Manzano posits a period of prehistorical plenitude when "Thy sons [the Indians] were free—they soil unstained with gore," which was transformed into real history, defined by the wholesale acquisition of a labor force: first Indian, then African,—and finally Chinese. (The latter lies outside the historical scope of Manzano's poem, since the importation of coolies became common practice after the slave trade was abolished and at a time when the heavy use of British machinery increased the demand for production in the field. Nevertheless, the voracious production machine, which the poem describes, defines the need for ever new sources of labor supply.)

Just as the category of wealth is defined in historical terms, so too is economic accumulation. The development of the second stanza is from the early mercantile economics of exploration and conquest to the more advanced form, of commerce. In the colonial periphery, trade or commerce, is a polite term for trafficking in human lives.

The third stanza brings out a theme often encountered in the slave narrative: that slavery corrupts master and slave alike. This is clearly the case in Frederick Douglass's account of his gentle young mistress who became a fierce tiger once aware of her unlimited power over her young slave. In similar fashion, Harriet Jacobs (alias, Linda Brent) sees beyond the cruelty of slave owners and the remorseless jealousy of their wives to condemn slavery as a whole for its degradation of the oppressed and the oppressor.

The importance of Manzano's similar critique is the way in which he understands the debasement of the master class in terms of a uniquely third world phenomenon: the boredom of daily life. The essence of the third world is its distance from the European metropolis, which is the center, not only of economic accumulation, but of recognized cultural production. The colony, dependent on the importation of culture along with manufactured goods, is made to feel incapable of generating a viable indigenous culture. However, this does not imply that the inability to create culture informs all classes of the third world. As Manzano's poem clearly shows, only that class which defines itself in terms of the European center is bereft of culture and wastes itself in futile amusements and gambling.

By comparison, and this is the recurring image of daily life in another Cuban slave narrative—*Autobiografía de un Cimarron* by Esteban Montejo—the cultural life of the deprived class is extremely rich. Montejo, who at the age of 105 was discovered and interviewed by the Cuban anthropologist, Miguel Barnet, gives an account of slavery which focuses, not on work or even the master/slave relationship, but on the slaves' cultural production. He describes in detail the dances, the mode of dress, the hair styles, the types of food and their preparation, the music, religious beliefs, witchcraft and the art of curing. While his reminiscence raises a question common to all slave narratives—that is their dialogical[22] nature, wherein the selection of material and the mode of its narration is influenced by an invisible interlocutor, be it the anthropologist interviewer with a pre-determined list of questions, or the nineteenth century abolitionist who solicits the slave's life story with the tacit understanding that the narrative will be used for a specific purpose—we should not discount Montejo's narration purely on the grounds of its contrived origin. The strength of his memory of daily life, the rich detail of his account, as well as the freely loquacious mode of his narration speak for the prominence and durability of cultural production. Moreover, while Montejo was for many years a solitary cimarron, who of necessity cut himself off from human society, his understanding of culture is strictly communal in nature. The celebrations marking the día de San Juan, the contests and games in the local tavern, the practice of witchcraft—all are defined as group praxis.

From a novelistic point of view, Cuba's great contemporary writer, Alejo Carpentier, depicts a similar contrast between the vitality of slave culture and the degradation of colonial society in his *El Reino de Este Mundo.* Set in Haiti, the novel traces the history of early slave revolt, linking the leaders, Mackandal and Boukman, to a process of political consciousness-raising realized within *vaudou* culture. Political revolt aimed at the extermination of the white overlords is understood in terms of group cultural practice and preached to the rhythm of drum beats and chants. On the other hand, *colono* culture is presented as a festering wasteland of imported European commodities—wigs, engravings and second rate operas performed by third rate artists. What's more, those *colonos* who manage to escape the fire and poison of slave revolution by fleeing to Cuba—a more secure preserve of slavery—find themselves doubly exiled from their European cultural center. To the French colonists, Spanish provincials appear uncouth, their culture barbaric. Carpentier's ultimate condemnation of the *colono* class dooms them to spend the remainder of their days in exile, living off the remnants of their hollow, commodified culture.

While the boredom of the third world is experienced as a breakdown of culture, it has its roots in concrete physical and historical factors. C.L.R. James, writing in *Black Jacobins,* attributes the "monotony" of the third world to the orderly, unchanging landscape, the result of large-scale, single crop cultivation, and to the absence of seasons which had so conditioned the European emigrant that their lack left him in a state of limbo. But the most profound cause of boredom was slavery itself. As James sees it, "The ignorance inherent in rural life prior to the industrial revolution was reinforced by the irascibility and conceit of isolation allied to undisputed dominion over hundreds of human beings."[23] The colonists, surfeited with leisure time, their every wish indulged by a ready slave, wallowed in "food, drink, dice and black women."[24]

The importance of Manzano's poem is its ability to comprehend the degradation of colonial life which defined his own historical period, then to place this colonial present in a larger historical perspective which encompasses both the past and the future. The fifth stanza records the past, which, in the Spanish empire, was defined by the two-pronged intervention of conquistadors ("the fell band Who's boasted conquests, mark one frightful course of spoil and plunder,") and priests ("Of human carnage in religious gear,").

Once more the critical understanding which Manzano brings to bear in his poems transcends his historical moment and finds continued relevancy in contemporary Spanish American texts. One in particular is Mario Vargas Llosa's *La Casa Verde,* where soldier and nun join forces to capture and enslave young Indian girls, condemning them to the contemporary servitude of mission schools and the future of a *criada.* The significance of the union of political and religious power, both during the conquest and throughout the process of acculturation, cannot be over-stated. One has only to remember that Padre Bartolome de las Casas, recognized savior of the Indians, was one of the official spokesmen responsible for the importation of Negro slaves. That the Indian population, particularly on the islands, was at that time already decimated suggests to what extent his priestly concerns were motivated by economic priorities.

However, the end of Manzano's fifth stanza gives rise to a new and gathering presence which by the end of the sixth cannot be denied. Here the cumulative history of outrage, torture and wholesale genocide gives shape and voice to the enslaved masses. Their centuries-long agony swells to produce the poem's only optimistic "trumpet-tongued" outcry, heralding the growing storm of rebellion. The direct historical influence is of course the Haitian revolution, whose image of blood and poison continues to haunt the Cuban slaveowners thirty years later. Then too, the period of the late 1830's, during which Manzano wrote this poem, saw an increase in rural slave rebellion particularly in Matanzas, the poet's home province, and the savage reaction of General O'Donnell, who by the 1840s had single-handedly set out to destroy Cuba's urban black bourgeoisie. The moment was thus one of political ferment countered by heightened repression. Manzano himself was thrown in jail and only narrowly escaped death, while other black poets and professionals were murdered.[25] These grim realities make a mockery of the poem's closing epithets, Cuba "rich and beautiful, the Queen of isles! Star of the West, and ocean's gem most rare!." By coming full circle to the already debunked myth of gem-like Caribbean beauty, the poem strikes a hollow note, which, by contrast, makes all the more meaningful the historical realities it has defined and all the more resonant the voice of the oppressed.

Significantly these epithets don't end the poem, rather they frame an imperative directing the reader to tell those who perpetuate the falsehoods of the third world, those who refuse to see the reality behind its beauty, those who profit by its myths to "Take of these flowers." Here Manzano deflowers the poetic image, showing it to be a worldly beauty, doomed to decay. But the poem goes much further than this, for the closing lines are based on a complicated set of reversals whereby false beauty is transformed into real beauty, and death into life. In the first phrase ("Take of these flowers, and view these lifeless spoils That wait the worm"), the products of cultivation which define false beauty are shown to be a part of death. The second phrase is transitional ("behold the hues beneath The pale cold cheek"). It asks the reader to merge antithetical notions and look for life in death. Here, color, which we associate with beauty and the flower, is still related to death, but beginning to be separate from it. The final phrase ("and seek for living smiles, Where beauty lies not in the arms of death, And bondage taints not with its poisoned breath") accomplishes the separation of beauty and death, which can only come about with the end of slavery.

The flower image is pivotal because it maintains the whole death/beauty transformation. And as we noted it functions in a command, throwing its empty falsehood in the face of those who do pick Cuba's wealth. In a sense, Manzano is throwing the geranium, for which he suffered and bled as a child, back into his mistress's face. With his words, he acknowledges the right of the first world to harvest the wealth of the third world—an activity which he early learned could not be his. However, by his act of appropriating traditional poetic form and making it the vehicle for critical discourse, he has in fact picked and profited by a European flower. This then is the poem's final and most profound transformation—the ode is written not to praise, but to condemn; and the most marginal of poets, separated from the center by his racial and colonial heritage, seizes the hegemonic form and turns it back on the metropolis.

Essentially, the flower image can function in these many ways and be so highly charged with meaning because it partakes of established poetic form. On the other hand, the geranium in Manzano's narration is not much more than an important piece of narrative detail. The fact that in one mode of writing the author can speak with a high degree of comprehension and frames his words with a sophisticated rhetorical style, while in another mode he recounts raw, received information and has very little recourse to literary form suggests something about the influence of slavery on the writer. Essentially, Manzano is incapable of perspectivizing the lived experience of slavery. Those things which touch his life personally and form the basis of his narration escape evaluation. On the other hand, when slavery is understood with a degree of abstraction, as it is in the poem, then everything falls into place and critical discourse is possible.

The fact that Manzano has two very different languages—one immanent and monological, the other abstract and directed to a reader—demonstrates the frag-

mentation of the slave's relationship to language. For Manzano, struggling within the dominant language, one mode is more personally his own voice, but not a very apt means of communication; while the other is more communicative, but an appropriation and therefore less personal. The historical significance of these discontinuities becomes evident only when Manzano's fragmented language is compared to that of later black Caribbean poets, particularly Nicolás Guillen and Aimé Césaire. Manzano's is the lone and frustrated voice of the black slave who will not in his life time see the end of slavery nor experience the tremendous surge of cultural revolution and its implications for black language wrought by the Négritude movement. Within his historical frame, Manzano's narrative truly is a message found in a bottle; his poem, a stolen flower.

Notes

1. Benjamin F. Prentiss, *The Blind African Slave or Memoirs of Boyrereau Brinch* (St. Albans, Vt.: Harry Whitney, 1810), pp. 97-100.

2. One of the most enlightened sugarocrats was Francisco de Arango y Parreno who published a book on sugar production, studied its cultivation on the other sugar islands, and traveled extensively in Europe seeking out industrial innovations applicable to sugar refining. Arango's endeavors as well as those of the small group of progressive sugarocrats are described in Moreno Fraginals, Manuel, *The Sugarmill* (New York: Monthly Review Press, 1976). See the chapter "The Sugarmill as Intellectual Adventure."

3. For a sample of the kind of work done by the del Monte group, see Cintio Vitier, *La Critica Literaria y Estética en el Siglo XIX Cubano* (Havana, 1968).

4. Robert Scholes and Robert Kellogg, *The Nature of Narrative* (New York: Oxford University Press, 1966), p. 179.

5. Madden was in Cuba serving on the Comision Mixta, a committee set up to observe anti-slave trade agreements between England and Spain.

6. V. N. Volosinov, *Marxism and the Philosophy of Language* (New York: Seminar Press, 1973), p. 111.

7. As an example, see Richard Ohmann's article, "Literature as Sentences" in *Essays in Stylistic Analysis,* Howard S. Babb, ed. (New York: Harcourt Brace, 1972).

8. Jose L. Franco, *Autogiografía, Cartas y Versos de Juan Francisco Manzano* (Havana, 1937), p. 38. In this and subsequent translations, I have tried to

render Manzano's incoherencies while at the same time substituting certain English words and phrases for the sake of understanding.

> Sufria p^r. la mas leve maldad propia de muchacho, enserrado en una carbonera sin mas tabla ni con q^e. taparme mas de beinte y cuatro oras yo era en estremo medroso y me gustaba comer mi carsel como se puede ber todavia en lo mas claro de medio dia se necesita una buena bela p^a. distinguir en ella algun objeto aqui despues de sufrir resios azotes era enserrado con orden y pena de gran castigo al q^e. me diese ni una gota de agua, lo q^e. alli sufria aquejado de la ambre, y la se, atormentado del miedo, en un lugar tan soturno como apartado de la casa, en un traspatio junto a una caballeriza, y un apestoso y ebaporante basurero, contigua a un lugar comun infesto umedo y siempre pestifero q^e. solo estaba separado p^r. unas paredes todas agujereadas, guarida de diformes ratas q^e. sin sesar me passaban p^r. en sima tanto se temia en esta casa a tal orden q^e. nadie nadie se atrebia a un q^e. ubiera collontura a darme ni un comino y tenia la cabeza llena de los cuentos de cosa mala de otros tiempos, de las almas aparesidas en este de la otra vida y de los encantamientos de los muertos, q^e. cuando salian un tropel de ratas asiendo ruido me paresia ber aquel sotano lleno de fantasmas y daba tantos gritos pidiendo a boses misericordia entonses se me sacaba me atormentaban con tanto fuete hasta mas no poder y se me enserraba otra vez guardandose la llabe en el curato mismo de la Sra.

9. Erich Auerbach, *Mimesis* (Princeton: Princeton University Press, 1968), p. 101.

10. Olaudah Equiano (alias Gustavas Vassa), *The Life of Olaudah Equiano* (Boston: Isaac Knapp, 1837).

11. Franco, *op. cit.,* pp. 44-45.

> nos codugeron puesta mi madre en el lugar del sacrifisio p^r. primera vez en su vida pues aunq^e. estaba en la asienda estaba esenta del trabajo como muger de un esclavo q^e. se supo condusir y aserse considerar de todos; viendo yo a mi madre en este estado suspenso no podia ni yorar ni discurrir ni huir temblaba inter sin pudor lo cuatro negros se apoderaron de ella la arrojaron en ticrra p^a. azotarla pedia p^r. Dios p. ella todo lo resisti pero al oir estallar el primmer fuetazo, combertido en leon en tigre o en la

fiera mas animosa estube a pique de perder la vida a manos de el sitado Silvestre pero pasemos en silencio el resto de esta exena dolorosa.

12. For Harriet Jacobs (alias Linda Brent), the decision to flee her master came only after she had been transferred from household service to the more exacting and degrading slavery of the plantation. While her life as a household slave was one of daily torment, caught between the leachery of her master and jealousy of her mistress, her yearning for freedom was unfocused until she reached the plantation. Here, her actual flight was triggered by her master's decision to bring her children as well to the plantation, thus condemning them to the grim toil of field labor. See Linda Brent, *Incidents in the Life of a Slave Girl* (New York: Harcourt Brace, 1973).

13. While some accounts hold that Manzano never wrote a second part, Jose L. Franco's explanation that the second half of the narration fell into the hands of various supporters of Manzano's master seems plausible given the political unrest at the time Manzano wrote the first part and entrusted it to Madden.

14. The veil of silence may be attributed to two very different literary modes: the confessional, and the realism of Walter Scott—both of which were available in Cuba at the time.

15. Franco, *op. cit.,* pp. 51-52.

> q^e. traes en las manos; yo me quedé muerto mi cuerpo se eló de improviso y sin poder apenas tenerme del temblor q^e. me dió en ambas piernas, dejé caer la porsión de pedasitos en el suelo tomóseme las manos se me olio y tomandose los pedasitos fue un monton una mata y un atrevimiento de marca mis narises se rompieron y en seguida vino el arministrador Dn. Lucas Rodriguez emigrado de S^to. Domingo aquien se me entregó, serian las seis de tarde y era en el rigor del ivierno la volante estaba puesta p^a. partir al pueblo yo debia seguirlos pero cuan frajil es la suerte del q^e. esta sujeto a continuas visisitudes, yo nunca tenia ora segura y en esta vez se berifico como en otras muchas como beremos, yo fui p^a. el cepo en este lugar antes enfermeria de hombres cabran si esiste sincuenta camas en cada lado pues en ella se resibian los en fermos de la finca y a mas los del ingenio S^n. Miguel pero ya estaba basia y no se le daba ningun empleo alli estaba el cepo y solo se depositaba en el

algun cadaber hasta la ora de llebar al pueblo a darle sepultura alli puesto de dos pies con un frio q^e. elaba sin ninguna cuvierta se me enserro apenas me vi solo en aquel lugar cuando todos los muertos me paresia q^e. se le levantaban y q^e. vagavan p^r. todo lo largo de el salon una bentana media derrumbada q^e. caia al rio o sanja serca de un despenadero ruidoso q^r. asia un torrente de agua golpeaba sin sesar y cada golpe me paresia un muerto q^e. entraba p^r. alli de la otra vida considerar ahora q^e. noche pasaria no bien avia empesado a aclarar cuando senti correr el serrojo entra un contra mayoral seguido del arministrador me sacan una tabla parada a un orcon q^e. sostiene el colgadiso un maso de cujes con sincuenta de ellos beo al pie de la tabla el arministrador embuelto en su capote dise debajo del panuel q^e. le tapaba la boca con una voz ronca amarra mis manos se atan como las de Jesueristo se me carga y meto los pies en las dos aberturas q^e. tiene tambien mis pies se atan Oh Dios! corramos un belo p^r. el resto de esta exena mi sangre se ha derramado yo perdi el sentido.

16. Eric Williams, *Capitalism and Slavery* (New York: Capricorn Books, 1966).

17. Immanuel Wallerstein, *The Modern World System* (New York: Academic Press, 1974).

18. While my own work is strongly influenced by dependency theory and the desire to apply this economic model to literary criticism, it should be noted that Wallerstein's work is highly controversial, particularly among Latin American economists; and a number of alternative explanations for dependency have been formulated. In terms of Cuba and slave labor, the work of the Cuban Marxist, Moreno Fraginals, is the most important. In his book, *The Sugarmill,* Fraginals gives a detailed account of sugar production from cultivation to refinement. However, his central thesis includes a number of contradictions. First of all, Fraginals sees the class of Cuban sugarocrats as an independent bourgeoisie, and therefore, not determined by developments in global capitalism. While it is true that Cuba's sugarocrats, unlike their French and English counterparts in the Caribbean, were basically free of colonial controls and that the influence of Spain had greatly diminished in relation to the rise of European capital, Cuban sugar production was clearly for the global market (even if labelled contraband). The function of the sugarocrats as a class was determined, not by national politics, but by their relationship to the demands of world-wide production. Finally, Fraginals defines slave labor outside of capitalism. This produces a somewhat tragic view of the sugarocrats, who, as capitalists, were essentially bound and limited by their relationship to a non-capitalist mode of production. Here, Fraginal's definition of slavery is based on the impossibility of innovation under slave labor and the fact that changes in production can only be quantitative rather than qualitative. The problem is that Fraginals is looking at the internal dynamic of slavery rather than seeing it as a complete mode of production. It is inconceivable that the owners of the means of production can be defined in terms of capitalism while the labor force is not.

19. C. L. R. James, *The Black Jacobins* (New York: Random House, 1963), p. 392.

20. Richard R. Madden, *Poems by a Slave in the Island of Cuba, Recently Liberated* (London: Thomas Ward and Co., 1840), p. 112.

21. George Lamming, *In the Castle of My Skin* (New York: Macmillan Publishing Co., 1975), p. 172.

22. Bakhtin defines the pure Socratic form of the dialogical discourse as one in which the truth is not known or possessed, but born out of the discussion between two people. This, he sees eroded by monological forms until the dialogue becomes nothing more than an uncovering of pre-existing truths. In this context, the vested interests of the abolitionist or anthropologist define the slave narrative somewhere between the pure dialogical and monological. Mikhail Bakhtin, *La Poetique de Dostoievski* (Paris: de Sevil, 1970), pp. 151-169.

23. James, *op. cit.,* p. 29.

24. *Ibid.*

25. During the early part of the 19th century, Cuba's black bourgeoisie became a strong social factor, concentrated in certain professions: dentistry, teaching, music, writing, the military and dock work. However, in 1844, the class of free black professionals was all but exterminated. As a reaction against violent uprisings throughout the rural plantations, urban blacks were unmercifully persecuted. The culmination was the Escalera Conspiracy during which 98 Negroes were executed, 600 imprisoned, and 400 exiled. For an understanding of the situation of the blacks in 19th century Cuba, see: Pedro Deschamps Chapeaux and Juan Perez de la Riva, *Contribucion a la historia de la Gente sin Historia* (Havana: Editorial de Ciencias Sociales, 1974).

Miriam DeCosta-Willis (essay date July-December 1988)

SOURCE: DeCosta-Willis, Miriam. "Self and Society in the Afro-Cuban Slave Narrative." *Latin American Literary Review* 16, no. 32 (July-December 1988): 6-15.

[*In the following essay, DeCosta-Williams explains that it is difficult to evaluate slave narratives as independent literary offerings due to the changes these texts undergo in the process of being translated and selected by editors who themselves were not slaves. She uses Manzano's narrative as an example, pointing to the thematic and structural similarities of this work with other slave literature of the nineteenth century as evidence that the original text underwent several changes at the hands of its various editors and translators.*]

> As for me, from the moment that I lost my hopes, I ceased to be a faithful slave; from an humble, submissive being, I turned the most discontented of mankind: I wished to have wings to fly from the place, and to go to Havana; and from that day my only thoughts were in planning how to escape and run away.
>
> *Autobiography* by Manzano

> . . . I had the spirit of a runaway watching over me, which never left me. And I kept my plans to myself so that no one could give me away. I thought of nothing else; the idea went round and round my head and would not leave me in peace; nothing could get rid of it, at times it almost tormented me.
>
> *Autobiography of a Runaway Slave* by Montejo

The autobiography in its various forms—slave narrative, journal, diary, personal chronicle, and autobiographical novel—is one of the primary genres of Afro-American literature for a number of reasons: (1) it developed out of a very rich African oral tradition with a strong emphasis on cultural identity, communal experience, and tribal history, (2) its form (a first-person synchronic narrative) was particularly appropriate for expressing the dialectical tension between the subjective consciousness of the individual and the objective history of the society, and (3) its theme (the search for self identity and freedom in a hostile society) expressed the existential and metaphysical ethos of the race.

The most important early form of the Afro-American autobiography was the slave narrative, and it has been estimated that more than 400 works, including the narrative of distinguished writers like Olaudah Equiano, Frederick Douglass, and William Wells Brown, as well as the little-known narratives of Black women writers such as Jarena Lee, Harriet Jacobs, and Amanda Smith, were published between 1705 and 1901. There are actually two modes of narration in Afro-American literature: written narratives, the works of literate, often self-educated, Blacks like Frederick Douglass and Rebecca Jackson; and oral narratives, the works of unlettered former slaves, who told their stories to others. In the 1930s, for example, members of the Federal Writers Project collected more than 2,000 oral narratives, which formed the corpus of the Slave Narrative Collection, an invaluable source of eye-witness accounts of the antebellum period.

Significantly, the slave narrative was not an important genre in early Afro-Latin American literature. In fact, Juan Francisco Manzano's *Autobiografía* is the only slave narrative extant from Cuba's long period of slavery, and, according to Richard Jackson, "it is Latin America's first and only slave narrative."[1] The *Autobiography,* first published in 1840 in an English translation by Richard Madden, was written by a self-educated slave poet at the request of a White abolitionist who became his patron. More than a century later, in 1963, Miguel Barnet transcribed, edited and published *Biografía de un cimarrón,* the oral narrative of a 106-year-old former runaway slave. The *Biografía,* like Manzano's autobiography, is a slave narrative, but the two works represent distinct modes of autobiography: the *Autobiografía* is a written narrative by an autodidact who wrote in a consciously literary style, while the *Biografía* is an oral narrative similar to those collected in the Federal Writers Project.

Although the slave narrative was not a primary literary form in Latin America and the Caribbean (and it might be provocative to speculate why it was not), the two works cited above attest to the interconnectedness of diasporan literature in the Western hemisphere, where Blacks in the United States, the Caribbean, Central and South America shared the experiences of enslavement, oppression and marginality in Euro-centered cultures. Recent scholarship, particularly in history and literary criticism, has examined the cultural links between New World Blacks of diverse linguistic and geographic origins.[2] Such linkage is most apparent, perhaps, in African survivals, particularly in the language, music, dance, folk tales, and symbolic imagery of Surinam, Brazil, Haiti, Cuba, and the Sea Islands of the Southern United States, but it is also evident in the artistic expressions that derived from the assimilated dominant cultures.

The slave narrative is a case in point. Edward J. Mullen maintains that Manzano's "mode of presentation is more clearly imitative of traditional literary models (the picaresque, the romantic, the Costumbrista),[3] two of which—the picaresque and the Costumbrista—were highly developed by Spanish peninsular writers. Research, particularly on the works of nineteenth-century Black women writers, suggests that the Afro-American slave narrative incorporated many of the received conventions and stock devices of Anglo-American literary models such as tales of Indian captivity, Puritan and Quaker autobiographies, and the rhetoric of abolitionism and of evangelical Methodism. The various Euro-American traditions explain, in part, some of the stylistic differences between Cuban and North American slave narratives.

In spite of these differences, however, the narratives of English-and Spanish-speaking slaves bear striking similarities in form and content because the works had a common origin in African oral literature and because the writers shared the same oppressive experiences. In both cultures, the slave narrative has a discernible pattern. It is an episodic first-person narration of traumatic events placed in a chronological or linear framework, beginning with the narrator's genealogy and including a catalog of horrors. The three principle themes are the search for identity, the desire for freedom, and alienation in a hostile society, while secondary themes include education, morality and religion. The narrator often uses stock devices such as the apologia and documents of authenticity, as well as literary motifs like the loss of innocence, physical confrontation, and the daring escape to increase the dramatic tension of the work. The narrator often achieves a sober, unimpassioned tone through irony, satire and understatement, while the gifted writer uses recurrent images—ships, stars, wings, masks, darkness, and dungeons—to evoke emotion, flight, deception of Whites, and the movement toward self-definition.

Manzano's autobiography conforms thematically and structurally to this pattern, although it is unlikely that the young poet was familiar with North American slave narratives when he began his work in 1835. In June of that year, he wrote to Domingo del Monte, the Cuban abolitionist who became his patron:

> . . . the very day that I received your letter I began to retrace the space that fills the course of my life, and when I could, I began to write. . . . I hope to finish soon by limiting myself to only the interesting events. On more than four occasions I decided not to continue writing. A picture of so many calamities seems like nothing more than a ponderous record of lies. From the time that I was very young, cruel whiplashes reminded me of my humble condition. I am ashamed to tell this story and I don't know how to prove what I have been through, since I am leaving the worst part unwritten.[4]

This letter underscores the problems of the slave—physical torture, emotional stress, social ostracism, feelings of shame and humiliation—and the difficulties of the writer—his fear of self projection, of proving the truth, and of filling the horrible lacunae in his life. Indeed, the form, content and style of Manzano's life story was imposed from above, in the same way that American abolitionist editors like William Lloyd Garrison and Lydia Maria Child, however well-intentioned,

shaped the works of Black writers through the selection, rearrangement, omission, and addition of material because, as writers and editors, they had control of the press and of publishing houses. The question of the authenticity of Manzano's work is further complicated by the fact that the translation, which appeared in 1840, varies from the Spanish original, which was not published until 1937; the shorter translation omits names, dates, place names, and descriptions and it reorders details and episodes. Mullen suggests that the British translator might have worked with an earlier first draft or it is possible that the Spanish text was reconstructed "to reflect abolitionist views, which would explain why the text highlights in particular the degradations of slavery."[5] Such intervention produces a literary text which is constantly distanced from the narrator's life through language, translation, and editorial point of view.

Juan Francisco Manzano was known primarily as a lyric poet, one of only two Afro-Cubans to achieve literary prominence during the colonial period.[6] Born about 1797 to two favored mulatto slaves, Manzano led a privileged existence in the homes of various slave owners, including the wealthy Marquesa de Santa Ana, who called him "the child of her old age"; his godparents (important figures in Hispanic society), who took him to the theater and opera but refused him an education; and the lady Joaquina, who combed his hair, dressed him in finery, and treated him like a White child. His owners often served *in loco parentis,* separating him not only from his family but also from other members of his race. His first mistress reprimanded Manzano's father for whipping his own son, while another prevented his praying in church with "*los otros negritos*" (the other Black children). Whatever their intentions, Manzano's owners, like Phillis Wheatley's, created a misfit, an existential outsider, a marginal man, who could never be a part of Cuba's Spanish-Creole society, but who had no roots in Cuba's African community.

Consequently, it was very difficult for the mulatto child to adjust to the traumatic change which befell him at age twelve when he joined the household of the cruel and capricious Marquesa de Prado Ameno. He changed from a sensitive, creative child into a timid and fearful adolescent, whose health was ruined by severe beatings and lengthy confinements in stocks and dungeons. For the first time in his life, he became fully aware of the precariousness of the Cuban slave's existence—the total insecurity, the absolute dependence on others, the unfairness, and the capriciousness of slave owners. He was degraded and humiliated: punished for picking a geranium leaf, accused unjustly of taking a coin and stealing a capon, cheated out of a small inheritance, and thrown into prison. In a single afternoon, he was tied to the front of a galloping horse, savagely bitten by dogs, put into the stocks, and beaten by seven men.

What he calls *"la verdadera isotoria de mi vida"* ("the true history of my life") began with a primal experience—his entombment in a dark coal chute—when he was thirteen years old. He writes:

> . . . I suffered from hunger and thirst, [I was] tormented with fear, in a place so dismal and distant . . . almost suffocated . . . and [was] constantly terrified by the rats . . . My head was filled with frightful fancies, with all the monstrous tales I had ever heard of ghosts and apparitions, and sorcery; and often when a troop of rats would arouse me with their noise, I would imagine I was surrounded by evil spirits, and I would roar aloud and pray for mercy.[7]

The metaphor of his life was a fall—a fall from grace, a precipitous, downward descent into a dark pit where the human self disintegrated into an invisible non-being. At this moment, Manzano understood his status in Cuban society, as he later explained to del Monte: ". . . remember when you read this that I am a slave and that the slave is a dead man (*'un ser muerto'*) in the sight of his master.[8] Manzano was the archetypical tragic mulatto, the miscegenated victim of a slaveowning society. He prefigured the Romantic stereotype depicted in Cuban antislavery novels *Francisco, Sab, El negro Francisco,* and *Cecilia Valdés,* novels written between 1839 and 1882 by Creole writers whose liberal idealism, like that of Thomas Jefferson, often did not prevent their owning slaves. In the case of Manzano, truth was stranger than fiction, for the historical person predated the literary persona, as the archetype at once created and reinforced the stereotype.

In his forty-page autobiography, Manzano, like Richard Wright, traces the early years of his childhood and adolescence, intending to write a second volume, which was either lost or never written. When he was twenty-one years old, Manzano taught himself to read and write, and, just three years later, published his first book of poetry, *Poesías líricas (Cantos a Lesbia)* [*Lyric Poetry (Songs to Lesbia)*]. In 1830, he published his second collection of verse, *Flores pasajeras* [*Transitory Flowers*], of which there is no extant copy; and, in 1835, while still a slave, he married Delia, a free mulatto pianist and poet, who inspired much of his love poetry. The following year, in 1836, he read his most celebrated poems, **"My Thirty Years,"** at a literary gathering at the home of del Monte, who was so moved by the poet's work that he raised $800 to purchase his freedom. Through the influence of intellectuals like del Monte and the abolitionist writers Cirilo Villaverde and Suárez y Romero, Manzano's poetry was published in literary magazines such as *El Aquinaldo Habanero* and *El Album.* His last work, a five-act tragedy entitled *Zafira,* appeared in 1841, but until his death thirteen years later, at age 57, Manzano published nothing. It was likely that he feared for his life in a society where the status of free Blacks was extremely precarious. His

fears were justified, for, in 1844, he was imprisoned after being falsely accused of participating in the slave rebellion known as the *Conspiración de la Escalera.*

The process of selecting, arranging and framing the events of his life helped Manzano to force order and structure upon an existence that was haphazard and chaotic; indeed, the very act of converting his life story to a written text helped him to clarify, to affirm and to authenticate his existence. Henry Louis Gates, in his introduction to the autobiographical novel *Our Nig,* maintains that "[w]riting, for black authors, was a mode of being, of self-creation with words."[9] The self that Manzano created was both historical, for it developed out of a personal history, and literary, for it evolved into the central figure and activating force of a written text. This literary persona is a tragic figure caught in the struggle between two opposing realities: the White plantation society whose cultural values he adopted and the Afro-Cuban slave community to which he belonged.

Scholars such as Francisco Calcagnó and César Leante maintain that Manzano was a Good Negro "who tolerated his harsh enslavement with a few weak tokens of protest,"[10] while Richard Jackson views the slave poet as "a disengaged pacifist, a harmless victim of the system and no danger to it."[11] Manzano certainly does not characterize himself as a rebel, but on two occasions he uses the lamb/lion image to symbolize the traumatic psychological change that he underwent in response to racial oppression. After his mother was beaten by a sadistic overseer, the young man wrote, "I felt this blow deep in my heart. I screamed and suddenly changed from a meek lamb into a fierce lion . . . I attacked him with my teeth and hands, and you can imagine how many slaps, kicks and blows I hit him with." Toward the end of his autobiography, he described an epiphanic experience similar to that of Frederick Douglass, who gained pride, confidence and a passion for freedom after his confrontation with Mr. Covey. The Afro-American affirmed, ". . . however long I might remain a slave in form, the day had passed forever when I could be a slave in fact."[12] In a similar vein, the Afro-Cuban declared, "From the moment when I lost all hopes and illusions I was no longer a faithful slave. I changed from a meek lamb into the most discontented creature."

Douglass, however, moved from the personal to the political, realizing that he was important primarily in terms of his group identity and that his life was significant only in a broad, historical context. One of the major characteristics of the Afro-American slave narrative, according to Stephen Butterfield, is that the "self is conceived as a member of an oppressed social group, with ties and responsibilities to the other members. It is a conscious political identity, drawing sustenance from the past experience of the group. . . ."[13] Indeed, it is often the dialectical tension between self and society, between subjective awareness and objective fact, between individual needs and social responsibilities that gives dramatic force to an autobiographical work. This tension, however, is not present in Manzano's life history, for his narrative is a highly subjective, personal account of his individual struggle to survive in a racist society. The social and historical context in which that struggle takes place is not very clear, although it is apparent from his narrative that there were at least two separate communities in nineteenth-century Cuba: an affluent community of Whites who maintained luxurious homes in Havana and large plantations in the provinces; and a community of slaves, most of whom lived on sugar plantations.

Juan Francisco Manzano was most familiar with the life of the affluent, for he mentions their baptisms, operas, churches, balls, and literary meetings. The son of a tailor and musician, Juan Francisco was a house slave who developed cultural refnements, learning to paint, draw, sew, design elegant clothes, do needlework, and make paper artifacts, as well as to read and write (although he gained his rudimentary education surreptitiously). He alludes only vaguely to the Black plantation community—where slaves lived in huts or barracoons, gave birth in infirmaries, or played cards in a barn from midnight to dawn. Although his work does not describe in detail the social context in which most nineteenth-century Afro-Cubans struggled, it is an important document because it reveals the psychological effect of marginality in an alien society.

There are many similarities between Manzano's ***Autobiografía*** and Esteban Montejo's *Biografía de un cimarrón*. Both are first-person narratives by former slaves who recorded their individual experiences within the context of a collective history—that of Black people living in an oppressive society—and they developed the same themes: (1) the search for self identity and (2) the desire for freedom. Both works were written at the request of White mediators—a patron and translator, in the first case, and an interviewer, in the second—who tampered with the material: Madden and Barnet standardized the language, organized the material, rearranged events, and eliminated repetitive descriptive details, with the result that a third person stands between the author and the narrator of the text.

There are, however, many differences between the two autobiographies. Manzano, who lived between 1797 and 1854, covers the period of his life from age 3 to 20; he was an urban house slave, who was very attached to his family, which included his mother, father, sister and twin brothers; he was concerned with self-identity and emphasized his oppression; he portrayed himself as a victim of Cuban society; he was a gifted, creative person, who taught himself to read and write;

and his writing had a serious, somber tone. Montejo, who was born about 1868 and was still living in 1963, covered the period of his life from age 10 to 35; he was a plantation slave, who lived for long periods of his life in the mountains; he never knew his parents; he described the society in which he lived, and underscored his search for freedom; he portrayed himself as a rebel; he was an independent person and a free thinker; and, although he never acquired an education, he was a gifted story-teller.

Esteban Montejo's autobiography is a valuable eyewitness account of Black life in the Spanish Caribbean during the second half of the nineteenth-century, for he describes in vivid details Cuba's plantation society and the country's long struggle against Spanish colonialism. Contemporary scholars recognize that such a "view from the bottom"—i.e. the personal recollection of an individual, particularly a member of an oppressed minority—is an important perspective of a country's history. In the 1960s, Barnet recognized the significance of Montejo's narrative when he wrote: "This book helps to fill certain gaps in Cuba's history. Not that [it] is primarily a work of history—history merely enters it as the medium in which the man's life is lived."[14] Montejo's life story thus becomes a paradigm of the collective history of nineteenth-century Cuban plantation workers.

His narrative is divided into three parts: I. Slavery (approximately 50 pages), II. Abolition (100 pages), and III. The War of Independence (50 pages). In the first part, he describes life on the sugar plantations, particularly the work, games, dress, food, religion, and witchcraft of the various African tribes. He says:

> The Congolese used the dead and snakes for their religious rites, [and they] worked magic with the sun almost every day. The lucumi liked rising early with the strength of the morning and looking up into the sky and saying prayers and sprinkling water on the ground.
>
> (pp. 34-35)

Montejo destroys the myth that slavery was less virulent in the Spanish colonies than it was in North America, for he describes terrible atrocities. He notes, "They whipped the pregnant women too, but lying face down with a hollow in the ground for their bellies." (p. 40) Living conditions were unbearable. Slaves, after working a twenty-hour day, were locked up in long, windowless barracoons accommodating up to 200 people, where the heat, the fleas, and the stench of the communal toilet (a pot set off in the corner) made sleep impossible.

Social problems were acute. Slave owners used females primarily for breeding; they locked the healthiest women up with males, then sent them back to the fields if they did not become pregnant within a few months.

The sexual imbalance (for men far outnumbered women) led to male homosexuality about where he wants to. The imbalance also led to bestiality, which Esteban also did not engage in, in spite of the fact that he spent ten years alone in the mountains.

> The truth is I lacked for nothing in the mountains. The only thing I could not manage was sex. Since there were no women around I had to keep the appetite in check. It wasn't even possible to fuck a mare because they whinnied like demons, and if the white country-men had heard the noise they would have come rushing out immediately. I was not going to have anyone clap me in irons for a mare.

> (pp. 53-54)

Montejo hated slavery, so one day he attacked his overseer and fled to the mountains, where he lived in a cave inhabited by poisonous snakes and filthy bats. He lived the difficult life of the *cimarrón* or runaway rather than be taken into slavery again. He said, "It was repugnant to me, it was shameful. I have always felt like that about slavery. It was like a plague—it still seems like that today."

When slavery ended, he left the mountains and wandered from plantation to plantation, performing hard work for minimum wages. This part of his narrative, the largest section, describes the Black plantation community after emancipation, while the third section, "The War of Independence," recounts Montejo's activities with the mambises,[15] the Black Cuban soldiers who fought so bravely for independence from Spain. He fought with national heros like Antonio Maceo, Máximo Gómez, and Quintín Banderas, in bloody battles, which he described with vivid action and drama:

> There were men screaming, horses careening about all mutilated, legs dangling from trees, and bits of heads rolling about the place, to appear all dried up a few days later, along with a terrible stench, because unburied bodies give off a dreadful smell after a while.

> (p. 190)

The autobiography ends with Montejo's bitter denunciation of the racist Americans who occupied Cuba following the successful end of the war against Spain in 1898.

The self that emerges from this work is an heroic figure—independent, confident, brave, and assertive. Barnet wrote about Montejo, "He struck me as a lonely, aloof, almost severe character. He received me coldly and with considerable reserve." Esteban did not like or trust White people, explaining, "I never wanted to be on [close] terms with the masters," (p. 21) and, on another occasion, he commented, "I was different in that I disliked having anything to do with the whites. They believed they were the lords of creation." (p. 64) He

kept his distance from other people, referring to himself throughout his narrative as a *separatista,* a separatist, who avoided intimate contact with others. But he adored women, once commenting, "A woman is a wonderful thing. Women, to tell the truth, are what I have got most pleasure from in life." He made many conquests and on occasion stayed with one woman for a year or two until she drove him crazy with her witchcraft, but he avoided long-term relationships. Montejo said that he was born with the independent spirit of the true *cimarrón,* who would rather die than be a slave. Even in the war, when he received an order to serve as the colonel's orderly, he told his commanding officer, "'Look, I didn't join up to be orderly to anyone!' I was damned if I was going to help the colonel on with his leggings and clean his shoes!" (p. 205)

Esteban Montejo knew who he was. He had a clear sense of his own identity as a rebel, and this sense of self derived primarily from the African community. Like many slave children, Esteban was taken from his parents at birth and sold to the owners of another plantation, so he did not know his mother and father. Without a family, he gravitated toward the African elders, the old men and women who sang softly in their native tongues, told him stories about the tortoise and the toad, and shared their visions of spirits and ghosts. Toward the end of his narrative, he says:

> I am coming to the conclusion that the African was a wise man in all matters. [The elders] taught me many things without being able to read or write—customs, which are more important than knowledge: to be polite, not to meddle in other people's affairs, to speak softly, to be respectful and religious, to work hard.

Montejo's self identity was thus forged by the community which nurtured him.

In many ways, Esteban Montejo, an unlettered Black plantation slave, was the antithesis of Juan Francisco Manzano, an educated mulatto house slave, who became a national poet. They were two different individuals—one, an heroic rebel and, the other, a victim of racism—but together they reflect the reality of Black Cuban life in the nineteenth-century, and their autobiographies stand as written testimony to that reality.

Notes

1. Richard L. Jackson, "Slavery, Racism and Autobiography in Two Early Black Writers: Juan Francisco Manzano and Martín Morúa Delgado", *Voices From Under: Black Narrative in Latin America and the Caribbean,* ed. William Luis (Westport, Connecticut: Greenwood Press, 1984), p. 55.

2. See, for example, the collection of essays edited by William Luis and cited above, which examines

the premise that a serious analysis of narratives of and about Blacks can serve as a "basis for a comparative approach to Western literary studies."

3. Edward J. Mullen, ed., *The Life and Poem of a Cuban Slave: Juan Francisco Manzano, 1797-1854* (Hamden, Connecticut: Archon Books, 1981), p. 24.

4. Juan Francisco Manzano, *Autobiografía, cartas y versos de Juan Fco. Manzano,* ed. José L. Franco (Habana: Municipio de la Habana, 1937), p. 83-84.

5. Mullen, p. 13.

6. The other well known Afro-Cuban poet was Plácido (Gabriel de la Concepción Valdés, 1809-44) who wrote sentimental verse in imitation of European Romantic poets.

7. Mullen, p. 84. All other references to this work will be cited parenthetically in the text.

8. Manzano, p. 84.

9. Harriet E. Wilson, *Our Nig,* ed. Henry Louis Gates Jr. (New York: Vintage Books, 1983), p. lii.

10. Francisco Calcagnó, *Poetas de color* (Habana: Imp. Militar de la Soler y Companía, 1878) and César Leante, "Dos Obras antiesclavistas cubanas," *Cuadernos Americano* 4 (July-August 1976): 176. Another important study of Manzano's work is Roberto Friol's *Suite para Juan Francisco Manzano* (Habana: Editorial Arte y Literatura, 1977).

11. Richard L. Jackson, *Black Writers in Latin America* Albuquerque: University of New Mexico Press, 1979), p. 33.

12. Frederick Douglass, *Narrative of the Life of Frederick Douglass an American Slave Written by Himself* (Boston, 1845, rpt. Garden City, N.Y.: Dolphin Books, 1963), p. 74.

13. Stephen Butterfield, *Black Autobiography in America* (Amherst: University of Massachusetts Press, 1974), p. 3.

14. Esteban Montejo, *The Autobiography of a Runaway Slave,* ed. Miguel Barnet (New York: Pantheon Books, 1968), p. 8. Unless otherwise indicated, all subsequent references to Montejo's work are from this translation by Jocasta Innes with page numbers cited parenthetically in the text.

15. The term *mambí* is an African word which means the child of an ape and a vulture, according to Montejo (p. 179). The Spanish used the term because they considered the soldiers to be savages.

Alma Dizon (essay date 1994)

SOURCE: Dizon, Alma. "Mothers, Morals, and Power in the Autobiography of Juan Francisco Manzano." *Revista de Estudios Hispánicos* 21 (1994): 109-17.

[*In the following essay, Dizon remarks on the abundance of mother figures in Manzano's autobiography, proposing that he uses this image to convey the "perversion of the maternal image in the discourse of slavery."*]

In recent years, the mother figure's absence in Golden Age Spanish drama has been a strong catalyst for discussions of order in a patriarchal society. It is certainly striking that when the mother does appear, as in *La Celestina,* she fails to protect her daughter and the home. Even in an enlightenment period work of social criticism such as *El sí de las niñas,* the mother serves as a negative, traditional element through her attempts to match the girl with an aged beau. Between these two works lies the Golden Age of Spanish drama with its dearth of maternal characters. One might well ask where they went since they had to have gone somewhere. After all, the notion of motherhood has positive qualities everywhere, and if these attributes were too good to fit into oft violent drama, they had to serve other areas of discourse. Marianism offers one such possibility where the cult of the Virgin relies heavily on maternal imagery. The thought of the Virgin pleading with her son on the sinner's behalf presents a scene of maternal love and mercy. Despite its political and economic manipulation, it retains a benevolent core as an image. Other discourses, notably the closely interwoven ones of colonialism and slavery, also depend on Maternal imagery to cast a positive light. Yet an inspection of this rhetoric reveals an odd notion of motherhood. Instead of an interceding spiritual mother, we see one who claims complete authority over an adopted child. This tenuous double-talk, in which the devoted mother is at the same time omnipotent and abusive, flounders in the autobiography of Juan Francisco Manzano, a Cuban slave. Unlike in the genre mentioned above, mother figures abound in this early nineteenth-century autobiography. And it is through this abundance of mothers that Manzano demonstrates the perversion of the maternal image in the dicourse of slavery.

Much discussion has arisen of late concerning the strange relationships that can develop between abusers and victims. Kidnapping victims may become emotionally dependent upon their kidnappers as may prostitute upon pimps. Similarly, in Manzano's situation, an odd confusion of emotional ties binds him to his owners despite their open exploitation of him. As Ivan A. Schulman notes (p. 24,) the author was probably born in the latter years of the eighteenth century on the estate of Matanzas. There, in the household of the Marchioness

Justiz, he became her favorite when still a baby. Upon the death of this woman, her title as well as her ownership of Manzano passed on to the Marchioness Joaquina who continued to treat him as a child. Yet strikingly, as he matured, the nature of this treatment changed even while the terminology did not.

The oft used image of the master as parent and the slave as child, mirroring the relationship of God and man, takes on emotional significance in Manzano's situation. Notably, the relationship of master/parent and slave/child adopts the moral overtones of its model. The slave is always expected to falter and must receive punishment for his own good. Thus even while this morality turns into an instrument for oppression, the reader cannot help observe how both marchionesses appear to sincerely believe in their moral right as mother figures. In order to find his own voice, Manzano must not only cast off the legal bond between his owner and himself, he must cut himself off from someone who claims to be his mother and permanent moral superior. To achieve his intellectual freedom, he has to subvert the moral structuring built up around the definitions of master/parent and slave/child.

Naturally, Manzano does accept and follow to some degree certain assumptions of inferiority that his owners have impressed upon him. He appears trapped in a sort of eternal childhood in which everyone of consequence is an elder and superior despite actual ages. Even though he is María del Pilar Manzano and Toribio de Castro's first child, he does not give the impression of having younger siblings who look up to him as the eldest. His description of situations involving his siblings only serve to show their horror at his suffering and to emphasize his inability to alter their fates. For example, after their mother's death, he fails to obtain for his freed sister her share of the inheritance that the marchioness has promised to hold for them (p. 63)[1]. His complete failure in the task underlines his inability to help his younger siblings. Since he cannot be responsible for them, he cannot guide them and cannot practice the role of father or authority figure. In a sense, he demonstrates his incapacity as an author of actions and his unchanging role as a malleable character whom his owner shapes. A natural association thus develops between his interminable childhood—he may never grow up completely—and his lack of power vis-à-vis the elders who own him. His description of his physical state also adds to this picture of himself as a child among adult owners when he notes his small stature, writing ". . . *yo he atribuido mis pequeñez de estatura y la debilidad de mi naturaleza a la amargosa vida qe. desde trese a catorse años he traido siempre flaco debil y estenuado . . .*" (p. 39).[2]

The need to establish the marchionesses as multiple mothers figures to Manzano's eternal child requires some displacement of his father. For in order to expand the role of the marchionesses who, through the tradition of slavery, have the right to form the child in every way once it is born, the father's role must undergo simplification. Toribio de Castro gives neither surname nor intellectual formation to his son though he does try to give him a sense of morality. Manzano describes his father during a stay with his family after a period of upheaval with the Marchioness Joaquina. He writes that ". . . *el cararte seco y las horades de mi padre como estaba siempre a la vista me asian pasar una vida algo mas llevadera . . .*" (p. 39). When his father disapproves of a drawing that Manzano has done of a witch, he writes, ". . . *mi padre con la austeridad de su cararter me proibió no tomase inter el viviese los pinseles . . .*" (p. 42). The two marchionesses do, however, compete with his natural parents. In this manner, he writes that people remind him of how ". . . *mas estaba en sus brasos qe. en los de mi madre . . .*" and that the old woman called him "*el niño de su bejez*" (p. 34). Moreover, the relationship with the first marchioness supersedes the one between the young Manzano and his father. Thus when his father punishes him at one point, the marchioness becomes so angry that she refuses to see the man. Only her confessor can dissuade her. Manzano then writes that she only spoke to him again after establishing ". . . *los derechos de mi padre qe. a mi le correspondian como a tal y lo que a ella como a . . . los de ama, ocupando el lugar de madre . . .*" (p. 35). In a sense, this is a verbal act of castration that deprives the man of any role in the moral upbringing of his son. She effectively posits herself as mother figure and owner above the father, reducing his role in order to make the child socially into a product of the mother/owner's will alone.

So from an early age, Manzano enters upon a confusion of owner and maternal figure, and he realizes that her wishes bear more weight than the opinion of a father who hopes to form him morally. The Marchioness Justiz, however, is not the only one who believes in this image of the owner as parent with rights above and beyond the rights of the natural parent. The slave himself falls back on this familial terminology to describe how Don Nicolás, raised by Manzano's natural mother, María del Pilar, and thus about the age of the narrator, ". . . *me queria no como a un esclavo sino como a hijo apesar de su corta edad.*" (p. 56) Thus even when trying to show how a master was kind to him, he ends by using a simile that reinforces the owner's appearance of superiority. Both Manzano and Don Nicolás subscribe to the notion that the emotional link between a master and a slave follows the model of a parent and a child. This way of looking at their relationship necessarily shapes that relationship. The situation makes sense when one realizes that in order to work as a social definition, the parental role of slavery as supposedly benevolent must gain some acceptance among both parties. One should note, however, that Manzano does not quite go as far as Don Nicolás in his acceptance of this idea. After all, he does not say that he loved the man as a father. So as we shall discuss later, in spite of the unconscious depths these parental definitions have reached in him, he can and does portray their actual lack of benevolence.

After establishing these social definitions found in slavery, one may observe how character judgments found therein help to form a sense of morality. For if these definitions remain fixed, so do the identifications that the slave tradition has foisted upon the individuals. And if the master/parent must teach the slave/child various rules so that the latter may act responsibly in his milieu, what happens when the child can never grow up? In this way, the Marchioness Joaquina's punishments and moral lessons do not follow any sort of development since Manzano could not possibly improve according to his set identification as a moral inferior. The eye she keeps on her slaves becomes a morally vigilant one that seeks to force them to follow rules of behavior that she believes they would never find on their own. When she hears that some of her slaves are gambling, she has Manzano searched. Caught unfortunately at the wrong moment, the narrator has money that he has earned while working for a painter. The marchioness proceeds to take the money away and punish him even though he tells her how he got it since, as she explains, he should have told her about it before (p. 62). No one asks a slave for explanations. Everyone presupposes the inferiority of his intentions.

Interestingly enough, most of the Marchioness Joaquina's punishments have to do with an apparent obsession with what belongs to her and her control of it. During days of torturing Manzano for absent-mindedly shredding some leaves in her garden, she does not offer him any complex morals. The writer remembers that "*. . . me preguntó si queria otra vez tomar unas ojas de su geranio como no quise responder pr. poco me susede otro tanto y tuve abien desir qe. no . . .*" (p. 52). She only emphasizes how the geranium plant belongs to her, and that the slave may not touch it. Likewise, other episodes consist of accusations of stealing money or food forms his owner. For instance, when Manzano exchanges a peseta he has for a shinier one that he is to offer at the church, everyone believes that he has the second one. Notably, he runs to the marquess whom he has previously nursed back to health, but the man exclaims, "*. . . gran perrazo y pr. qe. le fuistes a robar la peseta a tu ama.*" (p. 46). One would think that the peseta, intended as an offering, should belong to the Church, a saint, or even God but not to the marchioness. After all, an accusation of stealing from the divine would constitute a heinous crime. One could take this situation further and argue that in seeking to please the divine, Manzano was seeking to place himself on the side of a higher power. Undoubtedly, he suceeds in portraying the pettiness of his owners since the most heinous crime that Manzano can commit is stealing from them. In fact, it is striking how accusations of stealing abound. The reader can see how the accusations reaffirm the institution of slavery by underlining the moral weakness of the slave. Within this system, one never pays attention to what has actually happened as much as one does to what the marchioness thinks has taken place. The social definitions of master and slave provided blinkers so that everyone ignores the unimaginable—the moral and thus self-monitoring slave.

The inconsistency of the Marchioness Joaquina's unpredictable nature, in contrast to the supposed benevolence of her chosen role, begins to reveal the weaknesses inherent in the definitions that slavery offers. Although Manzano openly uses familial terms to describe his relationship with his owner, the image of the owner as mother cannot remain intact. This comparison gradually falls apart, and with it, the slave owner's claims to a moral superiority. As already mentioned, after the death of her mother, Justiz, the Marchioness Joaquina follows in the footsteps of the old woman as mother/owner to the young Manzano. Too young to serve his new mistress as a page, he takes the place of a beloved pet for the woman. He describes how she would make him sit at her feet to eat as the Marchioness Justiz had done earlier and "*. . . me bestia peinaba y cuidaba de qe. no me rosase con los otros negritos . . .*" (p. 37). For this reason, after she has begun to punish him terribly, he can still return her love when she treats him well again. He sees her as a mother and thus writes:

> *. . . cuando mi ama dulsificó conmigo su genio yo dejé insensiblemente sierta dureza de corazon qe. abia adquirido desde la ultima vez qe. me condenó a la cadena y el trabajo perserverando en no ponerme ni mandarme poner la mano abia olvidad todo lo pasado y la amaba como a madre . . .*
>
> (p. 66).

Nonetheless, even when using the social definitions of master/parent and slave/child, Manzano shows the use of the mother figure to command respect and freeze social relations. The psychologically enslaving purpose of the parent and child metaphor stands revealed when the marchioness takes him back from Don Nicolás, saying "*. . . si yo no conosia mi bien y qe. si ella me llebaba era pr. qe. lo debia de aser pues no debia de estar sino a su lado hasta qe. determinara de mi . . .*" (p. 59). Later on in the same episode, he writes that she "*. . . me preguntó si me acordaba de mama mia [Marchoness Justiz] y le dije qe. si, pues yo he quedado en su lugar ¿me olles? me dijo . . .*" (p. 59). In other words, he must always remain dependent upon her better sense of judgment since, forever childlike, he cannot possess the necessary discernment for independent action. Moreover, the supply of dominating mother figures can never run out. A new one simply inherits the position of the old along with all the other possessions. So the supposed comparison of slavery with parenting only works if one supposes that a child remains stuck at age six or seven without further development.

Despite its overlaying of benevolence, this mother and child relationship between the Marchioness Joaquina and Manzano does not at all resemble María del Pilar's interaction with her son. And so it is through the juxtaposition of the unpredictable marchioness and María del Pilar that the reader can best see how slavery's use of the benevolent parental image falls apart. Whenever the marchioness has Manzano punished, his real mother desperately tries to help him, mourns his pain and at times even throws herself physically in the way to protect him. Manzano describes how on one occasion:

> . . . la culpa de mi madre fue qe. biendo qe. me tiraba a matar se le tiró en sima y asiendose atender pude ponderme en pie cuando llegando los guardieros del tendal nos condujeron puesta mi madre en el lugar del sacrisifisio pr. primera vez en su vida pues aunqe. estaba en la asienda estaba esenta del trabajo como muger de una esclava qe. se supo condusir y aserse considerar de todos . . .
>
> (p. 44).

Notably, at this moment, he adds that his mother has never undergone this kind of punishment before as everyone respects her for her husband's conduct. She usually finds herself high up within the slaves' section of the social hierarchy. In this manner, the injustice of punishing her so harshly for her self-less act serves to show the unnaturalness of the situation. Furthermore, it undermines the position of the marchioness who calls herself "mother" but simply does not follow María del Pilar's model motherhood.

In addition to María del Pilar's protective instincts, another interesting aspect of motherhood becomes apparent in her attempts to buy her son's freedom. After his punishment for tearing the genarium leaves, his mother comes to him and says, ". . . aqui llebo el dinero de tu libertad, ya tu vez qe. tu padre se ha muerto y tu vas a ser ahora el padre de tus hermanos ya no te bolberan a castigar mas . . ." (p. 53). One observes here how María del Pilar not only wishes to defend her son from future suffering, she also recognizes the inevitable obsolescence of her part in her son's life. For as her son matures and assumes responsibilities—here the role of his siblings—she expects to lose her position of dominance. In other words, she plans for him to take the parent's position himself even before her own death. Unlike the marchionesses, she does not represent a continuous line of owners as mothers. In this way, the reader notes how the marchionesses have had to denaturalize the definition of motherhood in order to call themselves Manzano's mother. Speaking in terms of so-

cial definition, the narration of events leaves the marchioness Joaquina redefined not as both mother and owner but merely as owner.

Along with the questioning of the marchioness' claims to the role of mother, one begins to doubt her claim of morality. The episode in which his mother tries to buy his freedom ends with the statement ". . . mas el resultado de eso fue qe. mi madre salió sin dinero y yo quedé a esperar qe. se yo qe. tiempo qe. no he visto llegar." (p. 53). Manzano chooses not to elaborate, and so the reader wonders whether or not the Marchioness Joaquina simply took the money away from his mother as her right as owner. The narrator does hint that he has been waiting for his eventual freedom, and so it is also possible that the marchioness did promise his mother that she would later free him but then broke that promise. The latter seems completely plausible given the situation further on with the inheritance that María del Pilar left in the care of the marchioness. In the case of the inheritance, others knew that the marchioness had made a promise to his mother. It is intriguing to observe how when Manzano first asks her if she has yet revised his mother's papers, he describes that she ". . . contestome en tono agradable qe. todabia [no] . . ." (p. 62). When he asks her again, however, trying to obtain his sister's share for her, he expresses at how ". . . incomoda me respondió mi señora qe. si estaba muy apurada pr. la erensia qe. si yo no sabia qe. ella era eredera forsosa de sus esclavos encuanto me buelbas a ablar de la erensia te pongo donde no beas el sol ni la luna . . ." (p. 63). In using her position as owner to claim his inheritance, she tries to sidestep a scrutinizing of her morality. Whether or not she inherits from her slaves within a system in which slaves can own nothing does not hide the fact that she lied to and even misled María del Pilar. In addition, she does not appear comfortably settled in her stance as it takes her some time and some irritation with Manzano to help her decide to keep the money. The observation of her discomfort reveals the instability of the moral superstructure that she forces down upon the situation. She has just made up a rule that fits in with her notions of property but with little else. Perhaps Manzano does not openly call her a thief and liar due to his protector's urging, but in any case, he does not have to do so. The description of events as he offers them are enough to demonstrate the marchioness' immoral behavior in contradiction with the self-definitions that she has put forth.

Naturally, one does not see a gradual development of Manzano's sense of independence or an inversion of his owner's self-definitions and moral structure in stages. Like the arbitrary behavior of the Marchioness Joaquina, all of the evidence as to her questionable values and the hints of Manzano's separate sense of identity do not grow into a crescendo. They occur irregularly throughout the work, and thus the reader realizes that even though the writer has adapted to such options as the problematic parent/owner one, he nonetheless has a sense of self-worth and separateness from his owners. For instance, when he hears a man say rather ironically *"mire v. qe. este va a ser mas malo qe. Rusó y Vortel . . . ,"* (p. 50), he writes that upon finding out *". . . qe. eran unos enemigos de Dios me tranquilise pr. qe. desde mi infansia mis directores me enseñaron a amar y temer a Dios . . ."* (p. 50). He trusts in the religiosity of those who have raised him, and beyond this simple acceptance, he trusts in his own faith and morality. The moral structure built up around the presumed goodness of the master and the likewise presumed badness of the slaves has not affected either his view of himself or, as we shall see, of the marchioness.

In fact, Manzano ultimately remains quite apart from the Marchioness Joaquina's attempts to correct him. The marchioness might accuse him of all sort of wrong-doings and have him punished terribly, but she fails to introduce a sense of guilt in him. It is possible that she does not bother to do so, thinking that he cannot act responsibly. No matter what her reasons, her failure to involve him at a level such as guilt means that he remains purely a victim of circumstance. In other words, he never deserves her anger, and he knows it. In this way, when he tells of how he explained to his father and another servant about a lost peseta that he was accused of stealing, he notes: *". . . pero mi ama nunca crelló sino qe. era algun ardid de qe. me valia; pero yo creo qe. el tratamiento qe. alli tenia fue disposision sulla . . ."* (p. 49). It is intriguing here how Manzano uses the verb *creer,* to believe, in both clauses to show the difference between his and the marchioness' ability to discern. After explaining the truth about the coin, he says that she believes, wrongly, that he would steal and lie about it. At the same time, he believes, correctly, that any treatment he receives depends upon her mood. In other words, he not only thinks independently of his owner, he observes the irrationality of events and believes himself able to understand things better than she can. He can demonstrate a logical superiority.

Manzano's continued creativity with words first orally and later on paper, despite repeated efforts to stop him, best reveals the extent of his intellectual independence from his masters. As a child, the Marchioness Joaquina has other slaves punish him whenever he recites verses he has invented, and she even spies upon him herself (p. 41). Her need to watch over his creative speech and have him constantly punished belies the fact the she cannot control him. Even when still quite young, he does not readily give in to the simplistic notion that he may not converse with others because his words derive from his creative abilities. His artistic drive leads him to talk whether or not he has an audience. As he puts it,

> *. . . era tal el flujo de ablar qe. tenia qe. pr. ablar ablaba con la mesa con el cuadro con la pared & yo a*

> *nadien desia lo qe. traia comigo y solo cuando me podia juntar con los niños les desia muchos versos y le cantaba cuentos de encantamientos qe. yo componia de memorias . . .*
>
> (p 41).

Some years later, during a stay with Don Nicolás and his wife in Havanna, Manzano begins to teach himself to write, using his master's handwriting as his model. This young man who, as we have already noted, loves Manzano as a son, catches him writing various times and orders him to stop *". . . aquel entretenimiento como nada correspondiente a mi clase . . ."* (p. 57). The narrator does not say whether or not Don Nicolás threatened him with any physical harm, and given the description of his kind nature, he probably did not. Yet even though Manzano respects him, he refuses to stop writing. Although a slave, he nevertheless controls his own intellect. Sylvia Molloy notes that he *". . . does not identify with the master himself: he identifies with reading, with his writing, with the means through which he, Manzano, will ultimately achieve his own identity."* (p. 414).

In examining the autobiography, the reader notes the hesitance of Manzano's memories and how he corrects his doubtful chronology. He seems unable to control his own sense of past and even his sense of self as he frequently writes *"qe. se yo pr. qe."* when speaking not only of what has happened to him but also of his own actions. The use of this phrase does indicate some defensiveness akin to temporary insanity, particularly when he tells of something he did to anger his owners. At the same time, however, he uses this phrase when speaking of others when they torture him. Ultimately, this inability to understand why the others do certain things as well as his failure to present events in historical order function positively to convince the reader. For as Sylvia Molloy notes, the actual seesaw progression of events in the original manuscript is much more overwhelming than the steady increase in torture portrayed in the much revised 1840 translation into English. (p. 407). The overall effect is frightening and gives a strong sense of psychological honesty. It is in the account of his lonely suffering that Manzano's voice finds strength. Yes, he adopts some of the metaphors that slavery uses to defend itself, but his description of his relationship with his owners subverts their definitions of master and slave as parent and child. His autobiography redefines himself as well as them. Their unpredictable cruelty is incomprehensible while he is merely helpless to placate them. Thus the supposedly maternal relationship between mistress and slave finally appears quite unlike what its language initially implies.

As a mulatto and slave of special status within his owner's household, Manzano defies easy classifications. In addition, his unusual ability to write, tied so closely to his experiences and identity, keeps the reader from extending this autobiography to the individual lives of other nineteenth-century Cuban slaves. He hardly appears to have a milieu, a community of peers. Yet it was this remarkable differentiation that led at last to his freedom and the publication of the autobiography by British abolitionists. Even while he was cut off from those who also suffered under slavery, it is telling that his voice remains undeniably human and readily understandable to the present-day reader. As a commentary on the nature of slavery and the control of another's body, his work continues to demonstrate the institution's essential irrationality. In Manzano's case, we have the unusual opportunity to hear the maternal image of slavery in the mouth of a woman who had a certain affection for him. And thus it is through the extremeness of her behavior that the contradictions within this discourse find a sharp portrayal. Manzano takes the mother/child metaphor away from the slave owner, emptying it of its apparent benevolence and revealing it as child abuse.

Notes

1. All quotes are from: Juan Francisco Manzano. Autobiografía, cartas y versos de Juan Francisco Manzano, *Autobiografía, cartas y versos de Juan Fco. Manzano con un estudio preliminar por José L. Franco*, Havana: Municipio de la Habana, 1937.

2. The quotes from Manzano's text includes original misspellings and grammatical idiosyncrasies.

Works Cited

Manzano, Juan Francisco, *Autobiograía, cartas y versos de Juan Fco. Manzano con un estudio preliminar por José L. Franco*, Havanna: Municipio de la Habana, 1937.

Molloy, Sylvia, "From Serf to Self: the Autobiography of Juan Francisco Manzano," *MLN*, Volume 104, No, 2, March 1989, pp. 393-417.

Schulman, Ivan A., "Introducción" in *Juan Francisco Manzano: Autobiografía de un esclavo,* Ed. Ivan A. Schulman, Madrid: Ediciones Guadarrama, 1975.

William Luis (essay date October 1994)

SOURCE: Luis, William. "Nicolás Azcárate's Antislavery Notebook and the Unpublished Poems of the Slave Juan Francisco Manzano." *Revista de Estudios Hispánicos* 28, no. 3 (October 1994): 331-46.

[*In the following essay, Luis examines Manzano's poems, comparing different versions of these works. Luis writes that the disparities evident between the original* versions of Manzano's poems versus their revisions by editors such as Roberto Friol are evidence of the poet's struggle to express and gain recognition for his own poetic voice.]

Para mi madre Petra Santos, amante de la cultura cubana, in memoriam.

El poeta nace: el talento poético es un don gratuito del cielo, que se puede pulir, perfeccionar, mas no formar; muchas veces permanece adormecido por falta de ocasión que lo despierte . . . Mas cuando se manifiesta este don, como es espontáneo, hace cantar al poeta, bien sea en verso o en prosa, en asunto serio o ridículo, con palabras vivificantes y armoniosas, tales que nos cautivan muchas veces a nuestro pesar y de una manera tan fácil como quien hace cosa que le es ingénita por naturaleza, como murmura el río en las quebradas, como nace el pez en el agua, como trina el ruiseñor en las selvas. Los portentos y horrores del mundo físico, las pasiones de buena o mala ley que agitan al hombre, los acontecimientos prósperos o adversos de la humana especie, entran en la fecundante y ardiente fragua de la imaginación del poeta, como otros tantos elementos de inspiración, que luego los devuelve al mundo, transformados en peregrinas creaciones, en figuras palpables, en realidades cuasi, tan animadas como los objetos mismos que vemos y tocamos diariamente, y aun más gratas y apacibles para nosotros, porque sentimos cierto noble orgullo en pertenecer a la misma raza del ente semidivino que ha sido capaz de producir semejantes maravillas.

Domingo del Monte, "La poesía en el siglo XIX"

Juan Francisco Manzano's well-known slave autobiography (written in 1835) is a work of foundation; it is the first Cuban narrative to describe life on an island in which blacks played important social, economic, cultural, and religious roles. In this unprecedented work in Cuban and Spanish-American literature Manzano underscores the evils of the slavery system and the unjust punishments to which he was subjected, often for no apparent reason.[1] But even before writing his autobiography, Manzano was an established poet. While a slave, he published two books of poetry, ***Poesías líricas*** in 1821 and ***Flores pasageras*** [sic] in 1830. His poems were also reproduced in newspapers and magazines of the period, first in the *Diario de la Habana, La Moda o Recreo Semanal del Bello Sexo,* and *El Pasatiempo* and later in *El Aguinaldo Habanero, El Album, Faro Industrial de la Habana,* and *La Prensa.* Manzano had obtained literary success in a historic period when it was inconceivable for slaves to publish in Cuba.

Domingo del Monte (1804-1853), Cuba's most influential critic of the nineteenth century, is responsible for many of Manzano's successes, including the writing of the slave's autobiography. One year after Manzano completed this unparalleled story of his slave life, Del Monte invited him to his literary salon to read his autobiographical poem, **"Treinta años."** That same year members of the group collected more than 800 pesos and purchased the slave's freedom. Del Monte was interested in promoting a Cuban-type education and literature and an end to slavery and the slave trade. To further this cause, he encouraged Manzano and other writers under his tutelage to write about slavery. Manzano's autobiography provided a vision of Cuban life which was critical of the slavery system. Del Monte was a friend of the British Abolitionist David Turnbull (1811-1863) and wanted to implement on the island the slave reforms already in place in countries such as Britain and France. Richard Madden (1798-1886) translated into English Manzano's autobiography along with some of his poems and published them under the title **Poems by a Slave in the Island of Cuba** in London in 1840.[2]

Del Monte recognized Manzano's difficult but unique condition and valued the slave's valiant effort to write poetry. In an essay comparing two non-white poets of the time, Del Monte praised Manzano's talents over those of the better-known Plácido, Gabriel de la Concepción Valdés (1809-1844). Unlike Manzano, Plácido was born free and did not have to overcome the obstacles imposed by slavery. Del Monte writes:

> Plácido nunca fue esclavo, nació libre: era hijo de blanco y de mulata, y por supuesto, su color era casi blanco. No tuvo por lo mismo que luchar en su vida, como Manzano, que era casi negro y esclavo de nacimiento, con los obstáculos insuperables de su condición, para desarrollar las dotes naturales de su imaginación, que era realmente poética. Logró más instrucción literaria que Manzano; y en sus versos, por lo común rotundos y armoniosos, no se encuentran las incorrecciones gramaticales y las faltas de prosodia que en los muy sentidos y melancólicos del pobre esclavo. Plácido se complacía en cantar las pompas y los triunfos de los grandes de la tierra, con una magnilocuencia digna de los poetas clásicos de España. Manzano no sabe repetir en su *encadenada* lira, otro tema que el de las angustias de una vida azarosa y llena de peripecias terribles. Pero yo prefería los cantos tristes del esclavo, a las *nugs canors* (versos simples, aunque armoniosos) del mulato libre, porque notaba más profundo sentimiento de humanidad nativa; porque los principios de mi estética y de mi filosofía, se avienen más con el lamento arrancado del corazón del oprimido, que con el concierto estrepitoso del oficial laureado, del poeta envilecido, de Plácido . . .
>
> (149-50)

Del Monte's judgement may have been based on aesthetic value or personal considerations for Manzano. It is also possible that his opinion was political and pertained to events of the Ladder Conspiracy of 1844.[3] Plácido, who was charged with being the leader of the conspiracy, falsely accused both Del Monte and Manzano of participating in it. The charges were serious and the consequences devastating. Del Monte, whose friendship with Turnbull forced him to abandon the island in 1842, was asked to present himself before the Military Tribunal but decided to remain an exile in Paris and later died in Spain; Manzano received a one-year prison sentence and, after his release in 1845 the ex-slave never wrote again. Del Monte's article was dated Paris, 1845, one year after Plácido's accusation.

The grammatical mistakes in Manzano's poems to which Del Monte alludes in his essay are confirmed by Roberto Friol's findings. In his *Suite para Juan Francisco Manzano* Friol uncovered two versions of some of Manzano's poems, one containing grammatical mistakes and the other written in standard Spanish. In comparing the versions provided by Friol and additional ones contained in other publications, I have observed that many of the changes are cosmetic, in which punctuation marks are inserted, but others are more substantive, in which words, lines, and even stanzas have been altered and rewritten.[4] The two versions speak to Manzano's struggle to give prominence to his voice and gain recognition, and to the interest Del Monte and members of his literary circle had in promoting Manzano, the slave poet.

Like Friol, I have been able to compare the different versions of Manzano's poems and to uncover compositions heretofore unknown to the general public. These new compositions are contained in an unpublished manuscript entitled **Obras completas de Juan Francisco Manzano esclavo de la Isla de Cuba,** copied by Nicolás Azcárate (1828-1894) in 1852, one year before Manzano and Del Monte's deaths. The manuscript is housed in the Latin American collection of Yale University's Sterling Memorial Library.[5] I have had the opportunity to consult the manuscript and would like to report some of the findings of my investigation.

An overview of the Azcárate notebook reveals that just as there is more than one version of Manzano's poems, there are two manuscripts written in Spanish of his autobiography. One, the original written by the slave in 1835 and containing numerous grammatical mistakes, was published with some of his poems and letters by José Luciano Franco under the title **Autobiografía, cartas y versos de Juan Francisco Manzano** in Havana in 1937. The other is an unpublished version corrected by a member of the Del Monte salon, Anselmo Suárez y Romero, in 1839. He not only made grammatical corrections but also altered the structure and order of events and even suppressed positive references to slavery. As I have shown elsewhere, the Suárez y Romero version turns Manzano's autobiography into a stronger denunciation of slavery than the slave's own portrayal of his life suggests and is a more negative account than he intended to communicate to his audience.[6] It was not Manzano's original but Suárez y Romero's rewriting of the slave's autobiography which circulated among the members of the Del Monte literary circle, and it was this version which was translated by Madden as "Life of the Negro Poet."

Azcárate duplicated in his own handwriting the Manzano manuscript which Del Monte possessed. After Del Monte, Azcárate was the next most important promoter of Cuban culture. Although Azcárate was too young to have attended Del Monte's literary circle in Havana, the Cuban critic had a profound impact on his younger disciple, and the life of one appears to follow that of the other. Like Del Monte, Azcárate studied law, and it was in Madrid that he met Del Monte, where the celebrated critic lived his exile years and died in 1853, one year before Azcárate completed his law degree. While in Madrid, Azcárate attended meetings sponsored by Del Monte, and we suspect that it was there that he copied Manzano's works. Like his mentor, Azcárate opposed slavery, and as a lawyer, he was a staunch defender of slaves. He also had a great interest in promoting antislavery literature. In his *Nicolás Azcárate: El reformista,* Rafael Azcárate Rosell mentions that his grandfather copied Cuban and foreign abolitionist literature.[7] The Manzano manuscript represented one of these antislavery texts.

Let us review the content of the Azcárate notebook. It contains the following items: 1) Manzano's autobiography, as corrected by Anselmo Suárez y Romero. 2) Seven letters written to Domingo del Monte, between April 13, 1834 and October 16, 1835, that is, while the slave was writing his autobiography. These letters, with minor changes, have been reproduced in Franco's edition. 3) Twenty poems. Five of these appear among the eight gathered by Franco and others which were published in magazines of the period and in Madden's book. 4) The play *Zafira,* originally published in 1842. 5) A list of the sixty-one names and the amount each contributed to purchasing Manzano's freedom. As with Manzano's autobiography, all of the items copied by Azcárate have been corrected.

For the purpose of this study, I would like to explore further the poems contained in the Azcárate notebook. Of the twenty poems seven or approximately one third of them have not been published, though four of them are included in a notebook entitled *Poesías de J. F. Manzano, esclavo en la isla de Cuba,* housed in the Biblioteca Nacional de Madrid and mentioned in the *Catálogo de manuscritos de América existentes en la Biblioteca Nacional,* edited by Julián Paz (350). The seven unpublished poems and their related themes, in the order in which they appear, are as follows: 1) **"El hortelano"** portrays a gardener who is a slave to love; 2) **"Al besar una flor de maravilla"** equates a flower with the poetic voice's lover; 3) **"Desesperación"** condemns a world in which there is no hope; 4) **"A la muerte"** refers to the poet's confrontation with death; 5) **"La esclava ausente"** alludes to a female slave who thinks of herself as her master's equal; 6) "Memorias del bien pasado" depicts Ortelio's current misfortune and pain; and 7) **"La visión del poeta compuesta en**

un Ingenio de fabricar azucar" [sic] describes the harsh reality of working in a sugar mill and the need to dream in order to escape from it.

As is to be expected, Manzano's poems contain many images conveying anguish and pain. But the slave also labored over their form. Without exception they conform to the aesthetic demands of the period and are written with a rigorous syllabic structure and rhyme scheme. **"El hortelano"** and **"Al besar una flor de maravilla"** are romances with an *abba* consonant rhyme scheme. **"Desesperación," "La esclava ausente,"** and **"La visión del poeta compuesta en un Ingenio de fabricar azúcar"** have eleven-syllable lines; the first two have a consonant rhyme in the even lines, and the last one has an *ababacc* assonant rhyme. "Memorias del bien pasado" is a sonnet, also written in hendecasyllables in *abba.* And **"A la muerte"** has seven-syllable lines with an assonant rhyme in the even ones.

Given Del Monte's desire to publicize a slave who taught himself to read and write and recited poems from memory, I am tempted to speculate why the seven mentioned poems were not published. I am ready to admit that through some oversight on my part, one or more of the poems indeed appeared in one of the publications of the period. However, if this is not the case, there may be other reasons why the poet or an editor may have excluded them from reaching a broader audience. When reading the poems together, the seven compositions appear to be representative of Manzano's corpus. We know that Del Monte asked Manzano to write his autobiography to document the evils of slavery, and that the slave-poet also wrote **"Treinta años"** to highlight his unhappy and cruel life. This poem was well received among the members of the Del Monte salon and published in the *Aguinaldo Habanero* in 1837. But **"Treinta años"** is unusual since the vast majority of Manzano's poems do not make a direct reference to slavery. Manzano was successful in drawing on his unfortunate condition as a slave and transferred those feelings to other themes of intense emotion and sadness. Manzano refers to themes such as death and love to convey the unbearable affliction caused by the slavery system. Nevertheless, his poems about slavery offer an insight into and suggest an origin for the feelings of distress which are present in many of the other compositions. Of the twenty poems included in the Azcárate notebook, only three allude to slavery and the slavery system: **"Treinta años," "La esclava ausente,"** and **"La visión del poeta compuesta en un Ingenio de fabricar azúcar,"** and of these the latter two had not been published. The censors were quick to suppress any literature which questioned slavery or portrayed blacks as innocent victims of the slavery system. The antislavery narratives which emerged out of Del Monte's literary salon circulated in a clandestine manner and were only published in Cuba many decades after slavery ceased to exist.

I would like to study more closely Manzano's unpublished poems which contain direct references to slavery: **"La esclava ausente"** and **"La visión del poeta compuesta en un Ingenio de fabricar azúcar." "La esclava ausente"** describes a master who exercises complete control over his slave, including her uncontrollable desire to love. The composition recalls the principles of the French Revolution and the "Declaration of the Rights of Man and the Citizen," as the poetic voice affirms her freedom and liberty as natural rights which, as a slave, also belong to her. She accuses her master of being inhuman and demands to know the reason for her oppressed slave condition.

> ¡Dueño duro inhumano, hombre terrible!
> ¿Por qué á tan triste suerte me condenas?
> ¿Tanto te valen los lamentos vanos
> De esta debil muger, que sólo peca
> En amar tiernamente?—Y si es delito
> Un verdadero amor ¿como pudiera
> Unirse a la virtud la fé que inspira?
>
> (163)[8]

For the poetic voice love is a God-given right which everyone, including animals, from the lion to the dove, has the right to enjoy. This right is superior to that of the master, whose power is not based on any racial or natural superiority but on chance. The poetic voice questions the basis of the master's dominion over her.

In the poem the master attempts to control the slave and uses his power to put an end to her desire to love, which has caused her unjust suffering and pain. But the slave undermines her master's authority, reduces him to a mere mortal, and accuses him of being directly responsible for her misery and pain.

> ¿Quién estinguir querrá tan noble llama?
> Un hombre con su ley; la mano acerba
> Que á beber me dió tal amargura,
> Con alma dura y condicion severa.
> El agravio que sufro, la injusticia
> La *opresion,* el dolor, cierto son males
> Que al noble corazon jamás arredran.
>
> (165-66)

The poetic voice identifies herself not with her slave condition, but with a woman who is her master's equal; someone who is also human: "Y *como humana,* es justo me resienta." She has been kept in isolation for one year, but this action intending to break her will and spirit has only strengthened her resolve to continue to love. At the end of the poem, she appeals to a higher authority. Like Plácido's "Plegaria a Dios," she prays to God and places all her hope in him. And like Plácido's

destiny, the voice from above conspires against her and orders her to live out her double punishment, represented by love and slavery.

In **"La esclava ausente"** Manzano assumes the voice of a slave woman and uses her subordinate position to describe the cruel conditions of slavery, thus portraying antislavery sentiments. As a black, a woman, and a slave, she is at the bottom of the social, economic, racial, and sexual ladder. But in the poem she is a symbol of defiance of her master and the slavery system; her master can control her body but not her soul. In this poem the master is not privileged by his social or economic position or by his race, but is portrayed as inhumane, especially when taking out his aggression on an indefenseless female slave. The disparity between the master and the slave may have led Manzano to appropriate the female perspective. Perhaps Manzano was experimenting with a different poetic voice, perhaps he wanted to depersonalize slavery and attribute the injustices of the system to other individuals, or perhaps he assumed that women more than men are prone to describing intense feelings of love. However, it is also possible that with a slave woman Manzano is able to refer more clearly to the inequalities of slavery. This was certainly the case with writers belonging to Del Monte's literary circle such as Anselmo Suárez y Romero and his Dorotea, Félix Tanco y Bosmeniel and his Petrona and Rosalía, and Cirilo Villaverde and his Cecilia Valdés and later in the nineteenth century writers such as Antonio Zambrana and his Carlota and Martín Morúa Delgado and his Sofía. Manzano's poetic voice is more vulnerable and physically weaker than her white master who inflicts great pain upon her, but her determination is unyielding. By exposing a woman to her master's rage, the reader is forced to identify with the slave and her condition against her white oppressor. The black woman is also a metaphorical representation of the origin of African culture and tradition, or even of Cuba, the country in which all people, in one form or another, have been affected by the condition of slavery.

Slavery is also present in **"La visión del poeta compuesta en un Ingenio de fabricar azúcar,"** a fifty-two stanza poem about the inhumane treatment of slaves and the need to escape, at least in dreams, from the unbearable circumstances in which they live. The poem begins with the imminent death of the master, thus reminding the slavepoet of his own ever present death. By situating the poem in the sugar mill, the poetic voice is obliged to describe an environment in which work is not only cruel but continuous from morning to night. Death is all around him, from the means of production to the ruthless overseer, to the barren countryside. Time does not advance, it is all the same, there is only work, and no happiness. The poet inserts himself into the poem and associates the sugar mill with Hell:

Tal me figuro estar en lo profundo
Dó está Satán en su destierro eterno,
Cuyas cavernas son en aquel mundo
Recinto infausto del horrendo infierno
Igual en todo este lugar inmundo
A las soturnas cuevas del averno . . .

(175)

The poet cannot understand how he is able to continue living under such onerous circumstances and why he does not die. He even fears a greater tragedy:

No sé como conservo el alma unida
A los choques que estoy aquí sufriendo,
ó por qué desta, tan penosa vida
A la mísera tumba no desciendo,
Tal vez quizas la parca tan temida,
Me estará en sus decretos reservando
Para que un tiempo alcance de ventura,
Y derribarme de mayor altura.

(176)

Almost half way through the poem, in stanza twenty-three, the poetic voice escapes the harsh reality of the sugar mill. A dream transports him to a different setting, not barren and with many references to slavery and death, but of life, of trees, flowers, and birds singing delectable songs, that is, to a paradise in which he is free. As the poetic voice enjoys his new found pleasure, he hears voices celebrating the mother of love, Venus. A deity approaches him, aware of his condition, advises him on love and to seek the person with whom he is in love. In a garden lushly covered with different types of flowers he sees the mother of love, whom he is unable to describe because of his fear of not doing her justice.

No le es dado á mi pluma descifrarte
Cuanto ví de sus pies á la cabeza
La singular postura, que con arte
Demostraba *Diosaica* gentileza
Sus amorosos ojos retratarte
Sería disminuirles su viveza
Pues reina el fuego de un ardiente hechizo
En la gloria y placer de un paraiso.

(184-85)

As the poetic voice hides from her, he listens to the complaints those lost in love bring to mother love about their own situation and her condemnation of one of them to love without any reciprocity. Much to his surprise the poetic voice's beloved Lesbia, a reference to his first wife Marcelina Campos, also appears before the goddess and confesses her burning and uncontrollable love.[9] Like the above-mentioned **"La esclava ausente,"** suffering is further augmented by the hatred she feels her master has towards her which has condemned her to a life without hope. And like the absent slave, the poetic voice realizes his double jeopardy, his slave condition and his unrewarded love. As the poet composes his poem, he relives the insufferable past.

In the poem the harsh reality and the agony caused by slavery and work in the sugar mill is juxtaposed to the dream which recalls paradise; one represents heaven and the other hell. As the poem unfolds, the master, a devil figure, is replaced by the goddess, and the poet's afflictions are replaced by his feelings of love. The poem underscores a relationship between the suffering brought about by slavery and that which results from love. Although one can argue that Manzano may have used the theme of slavery to develop the one about love, or incorporates love to deemphasize slavery, the mere description of the workings of the sugar mill alone condemns the slavery system. After all, it is the poetic voice, a slave, who must endure the pain.

As I have mentioned before, there are similarities between **"La esclava ausente"** and **"La visión del poeta compuesta en un Ingenio de fabricar azúcar,"** insofar as the two poems contain female slaves, but they and the poetic voice of the second poem are denied the basic rights to live their lives and love whom they please. They are refused even a basic emotion, that of the heart, susceptible to other factors beyond their immediate control. Even if the reader or the listener of the poem did not agree with the poetic voice's interpretation of slavery, she/he would understand this spontaneous feeling, the overwhelming emotional need to love, and the anguish experienced when this basic right is forbidden.

There are a few important distinctions between **"Treinta años"** and **"La esclava ausente"** and **"La visión del poeta compuesta en un Ingenio de fabricar azúcar,"** which may explain why the first was published and the other two were not. López Prieto reminds us that Manzano was a free man when Ramón Palma and José Antonio Echeverría helped the ex-slave publish some of his poems, including **"Treinta años"** (252). And if **"Treinta años"** is a confessional composition about the anguish the poet has experienced from birth to the time of writing and that which he must endure for the rest of his life, at no time does it point to the cause of his pain, whereas in the two unpublished poems, the instruments of slavery, as represented by the master and the sugar mill, are revealed as the source of Manzano's affliction. This antislavery discourse may explain why the two poems about slavery were not published at the time of writing. Let us remember that Manzano's autobiography only circulated among members of the Del Monte circle, and because of its stand against slavery, it was only made available in Spanish in the third decade of the twentieth century.

Manzano's poems about slavery are a political statement against the slavery system and appear to respond to Del Monte's ideas of how poetry should be written, ideas he imparted to his followers. In "La poesía en el siglo XIX" Del Monte outlines the function of poetry in creating a better society. He ends the essay with the following assertion:

Antes que *poeta* se considerará *hombre,* y en calidad de tal empleará todas las fuerzas de su ingenio en cooperar con los demás artistas y filósofos del siglo, que sean dignos de llamarse *hombres,* es decir, que se sientan con bríos de tal, y encierren en sus pechos corazones enteros y varoniles, a la mejora de la condición de sus semejantes, generalizando entre ellos ideas exactas y sanas de moralidad y de religión; para conseguirlo, se revestirá de un espíritu militante y denodado, y en vez de renegar cobardemente de la humanidad, y abandonarla con villanía, al verla degradada, o de encerrarse en un prosaico egoísmo, que sólo le inspire anacreónticas sensuales, elegías empalagosas o poemas delirantes y estrafalarios, en que él mismo sea su musa y su héroe, con voz sonora y persuasiva elocuencia enseñará la virtud al ignorante, confundirá al malvado, dará enérgica y poderosa confrontación al desvalido y empeñará, en fin, recia y perenne lucha en favor de esa misma humanidad tan calumniada y tan digna de la sublime lástima de poeta.

He aquí su verdadera misión en el siglo XIX; siglo de ideas graves, y predestinado a resolver en su cuerpo grandes y terribles problemas, pues debe tomar un carácter profundo y trascendental, y la poesía, más que todo, de lo contrario habrá que rebajarla a la triste opinión que de ella tuvo el sensualista Bentham, y mirarla como un juguete pueril, perjudicial a veces, cuando no sea indiferente e *inútil.*

(94)

It is possible that Del Monte may have had Plácido and Manzano's works in mind when writing his essay. Manzano's **"Treinta años," "La esclava ausente,"** and **"Visión del poeta compuesta en un Ingenio de fabricar azúcar"** speak to Del Monte's concern for the themes which a poet should stress in his poems. The poet has a social and moral responsibility to improve his society. The three poems highlight the evils of the nineteenth-century slavery system and express the sad moments inflicted upon the slave. Manzano was a slave, and he, more than anyone else, was best equipped to write about slavery. Unlike other poets or narrators writing about the conditions of blacks, as a victim of the slavery system Manzano only needed to look inward for both inspiration and pain. In so doing, he provided an authentic voice to his ever-present agony, as he lived and relived it through the writing and reciting of his poems.

Manzano wrote about slavery from a "privileged" perspective. However, it is not impossible to understand how difficult it must have been for Manzano to revisit the past. He complied with Del Monte when writing about slavery, but like the poetic voice of **"La visión del poeta escrita en un Ingenio de fabricar azúcar,"** he also needed to escape from it and find refuge in other types of themes which a slave society would publish.

Notes

1. For an analysis of Manzano's autobiography, see my *Literary Bondage: Slavery in Cuban Narrative.*

2. Edward Mullen has edited a modern version of Madden's book. See *The Life and Poems of a Cuban Slave.*

3. The Ladder Conspiracy refers to a plot the Colonial government accused Afro-Cubans of organizing and in which the alleged participants were tied to a ladder, whipped, and made to confess their guilt. The conspiracy also served to eliminate a growing middle class of free Afro-Cubans.

4. For example, Friol cites the following two versions of "Treinta años":

"Treinta Años"

Soneto

Cuando miro al espacio que he corrido
desde la cuna hasta el presente día,
tiemblo, y saludo a la fortuna mía,
mas de terror que de atención movido.

Sorpéndeme la lucha que he podido
sostener contra suerte tan impía,
si tal puede llamarse la porfía
de mi infelice ser, al mal nacido.

Treinta años ha que conocí la tierra;
Treinta años ha que en gemido estado
triste infortunio por do quier me asalta.

Mas nada es para mí la cruda guerra
que en vano suspirar he soportado,
si la calculo ¡oh Dios! con la que falta.

Soneto

Cuando miro al espacio qe he corrido
Desde la cuna hasta el presente día
Tiemblo y saludo a la fortuna mía
Mas de terror qe de atención movido.

Sorpréndeme la lucha qe he podido
Sostener contra suerte tan impia,
Si así puede llamarse la porfía
De mi infelice ser al mal asido;

Treinta años háy, qe conosí la tierra:
treinta años háy, que en gemidor estado,
Triste infortunio pr do quier me asalta.

Mas nada es pa mí la dura guerra
Qe en vano suspirar he soportado,
Si la carculo, oh Dios! con lo que falta.

Friol provides a note after the word "carculo" which appears on the last line of the last version in which he states: "Primero escribió *comparo,* lo tachó y sustituyó por este vocablo de forma imperfecta" (12). In addition, he provides the following observations regarding the two mentioned versions of Manzano's poem: "Dejando aparte las diferencias de puntuación entre las dos versiones, o el empleo de versales en una y no en la otra, llama la

atención la cacografía ostensible en algunas palabras del manuscrito y hasta la imperfecta articulación de algún vocablo que se trasluce en la escritura (carculo), frente a la corrección de escritura de la versión más conocida. Hay cambios de términos de una a otra versión: el *asido* del último verso del segundo cuarteto, se convierte en *nacido;* al *ha* de la epímone de los dos versos iniciales del primer terceto se le ha agregado en el manuscrito, y al parecer por ajena mano, una *y* que desaparece en la versión posterior; el *dura* del primer verso del segundo terceto pasa a ser *cruda;* el artículo *lo* del último verso se vuelve *la.* Cambios mayores o menores, pero todos parecen obedecer a alguna fundamentada razón" (12-13).

In his 1937 edition Franco only reproduces the corrected version of the poem, and he entitles it "Mis treinta años" (92). The same poem is also cited in *Cuba poética* under the title "Soneto" (153). The English translation is published by Friol (34) and Mullen (115). Francisco Calcagno mentions that the poem "Mis treinta años" [sic] was translated into four languages and adds in a note: "La idea de este soneto se asemeja a una del poeta italiano Riciardi, pero no es imitación; el pobre esclavo no había leído hasta entonces más que rezos. Era ya conocido en manuscrito cuando se publicó, 1837, en *El Aguinaldo* con una nota laudatoria de J. A. Echevarría, y en *El Album.* Tanto este soneto como sus poesías Al cerro de Quintana [sic] y 'A la ciudad de Matanzas' fueron traducidas al francés por Mr. V. Schoelcher en su obra 'Abolition de l'esclavage' &. Paris 1840" (*Poetas de color* 79). Except for upper case letters at the beginning of the lines and accent marks, the same poem and parts of the note are reproduced by López Prieto in his *Parnaso cubano* (253).

But "Treinta años" copied by Azcárate is slightly different from the original and corrected versions copied by Friol and the corrected one reproduced by López Prieto. Whereas both Friol and López Prieto show that the last line of the first stanza reads "mas de terror que de atención movido," Azcárate writes the same line as "Mas de atencion que de terror movido."

5. In the early 1980s Roberto González Echevarría informed me of the existence of a Manzano manuscript at Yale University, and Lee Williams, the university's Latin American bibliographer, showed and provided me with a copy of a notebook purchased by his institution entitled "Obras completas de Juan Francisco Manzano esclavo de la Isla de Cuba." Nicolás Azcárate copied the notebook in 1852. I am thankful to the administrators of Yale's Sterling Memorial Library for giving me permission to study and publish the Azcárate notebook and am pleased to announce that a critical edition of it will be made public under the title "Autobiografía del esclavo Juan Francisco Manzano y otros escritos" by Anaya and Mario Muchnick next year in Madrid.

6. For a comparison between the two Manzano manuscripts, see my "Autobiografía del esclavo Juan Francisco Manzano: Versión de Suárez y Romero" in *La historia en la literatura iberoamericana.*

7. Azcárate Rosell writes: "Antes de su matrimonio, cuando Nicolás cortejaba a María Luisa, la cual también era abolicionista, le regaló un álbum, escrito todo, contra la esclavitud. Azcárate, además de pensamientos, redactados por sus amigos y la dedicatoria, que él mismo hizo, copió en él párrafos de la literatura más popular entonces entre los abolicionistas, toda del fondo democrático que en aquel tiempo, en Cuba, igual que fuera de ella, pugnaba con los intereses creados, y de la forma romántica en boga durante esa época" (24).

8. I have decided to reproduce Manzano's poems exactly as they appear in the Azcárate manuscript. All matters pertaining to grammar and punctuation are contained in the original.

9. Roberto Friol suspects that Marcelina Campos was Lesbia in some poems. See Friol p. 17, note 3.

Works Cited

Azcárate Rosell, Rafael. *Nicolás Azcárate: El reformista.* Havana: Editorial Trópico, 1939.

Calcago, Francisco. *Poetas de color: Plácido, Manzano, Rodríguez, Echemendía, Silveira, Medina.* Havana: Imprenta Mercantil, 1887.

Friol, Roberto. *Suite para Juan Francisco Manzano.* Havana: Editorial Arte y Literatura, 1977.

López Prieto, Antonio, ed. *Parnaso cubano: Colección de poesías selectas de autores cubanos desde Zequeira a nuestros días.* Havana: Miguel de Villa, 1881.

Luis, William. *Literary Bondage: Slavery in Cuban Narrative.* Austin: U of Texas P, 1990.

———. "Autobiografía del esclavo Juan Francisco Manzano: Versión de Suárez y Romero." *La historia en la literatura iberoamericana.* Eds. Raquel Chang-Rodríguez and Gabriella de Beer. Hanover, NH: Ediciones del Norte, 1989.

Manzano, Juan Francisco. *The Life and Poems of a Cuban Slave.* Ed. Edward Mullen. Hamden, CT: Archon Books, 1981.

———. *Autobiografía, cartas y versos de Juan Francisco Manzano.* Ed. José Luciano Franco. Havana: Municipio de La Habana, 1937.

———. "Obras completas de Juan Francisco Manzano esclavo de la Isla de Cuba," copied by Nicolás M. de Azcárate in 1852.

Monte, Domingo del. *Escritos de Domingo del Monte.* Vol. 2. Havana: Cultura S.A., 1929.

Paz, Julián. *Catálogo de manuscritos de América existentes en la Biblioteca Nacional.* Madrid: Tipografía de los Hermanos Olozaga, n.d.

Luis A. Jiménez (essay date fall 1995)

SOURCE: Jiménez, Luis A. "Nineteenth Century Autobiography in the Afro-Americas: Frederick Douglass and Juan Francisco Manzano." *Afro-Hispanic Review* 14, no. 2 (fall 1995): 47-52.

[*In the following essay, Jiménez studies similarities between the autobiographies of Frederick Douglass and Manzano, noting that there is an underlying unity in their works despite the differences in language and culture.*]

Jean Jacques Rousseau's *Confessions* opens the door to an archetypal canon associated with the modern autobiography. Throughout the nineteenth century, the genre finds eager adepts from the persecuted, the criminal, the homosexual, and the oppressed who attempt to distance themselves from dominant colonialist societies (Lejeune 172, 175). Social scientists and literary critics attest to the fact that self-expression in the literature of this period was a social and cultural phenomenon. Two cases in the Afro-Americas are the *Narrative of the Life of Frederick Douglass: An American Slave* (1845) and the **Autobiography** written by the Afro-Cuban ex-slave Juan Francisco Manzano and published in London by the British writer and abolitionist Richard Robert Madden in 1840 (Mullen 4-12).

My intention in this paper is to find in the lives of two ordinary people, Douglass and Manzano, a hidden unity that exists in spite of their linguistic and cultural differences. Based on this notion, the analysis tends to be synchronic and centers on the relationship among language, meaning, and the reading and writing of a text. What I am suggesting is that the importance of these autobiographies lies not only in what the text says, but particularly in what it does not say. Paradoxical as it may seem, the voices and silences in the literature of the ex-slave, a new and liberated self, allow the reader's (and critic's) involvement in the author's consciousness and intention to narrate his own past.

The word "autobiography" was first used by Robert Southey in a review of Portuguese literature in 1809. Prior to this time, the term was frequently employed with the meaning of "confessions" and "memoirs" as in the case of Rousseau and Benjamin Franklin (Cox 147-48). Scholars of the genre find a correlation between the concept of the self and the rise of the bourgeoisie as the ruling class in Western cultures, especially in England and France (Howarth, Lejeune, Weintraub). Historical truth has been a popular approach to the confessional mode. Critics share the idea that history humanizes the life story of the self, thus becoming a more marketable product to the public. We may add that the reading of autobiographies written by dark-skinned people in the Americas became a literary fashion in prevalent white aesthetics before the abolition of slavery in the United States and Cuba in the nineteenth century.

Within the presence of a ruling white class in nineteenth century America, Douglass's and Manzano's stories take the form of the individual written account addressed to the slaves, abolitionists and to their oppressive masters (Butterfield 9-89, Towns 17-23). Black ex-slaves become subjects of their writing to demonstrate their language-using capabilities before social and economic mobility could be attained. This critical perspective brings up the issue of language and culture in authors of African descent, a minority rooted in, and molded by, the official discourse of colonialist societies. According to Moreno Fraginals, colonialism in Cuba was the synonym of a new and dominant creole class linked to sugarocracy (1978, 107). The corpus of knowledge held by Douglass and Manzano engenders writing in a language that some contemporary critics call the "counterdiscourse" of the oppressed (González Echevarría 21, Terdiman 15-16).

In his recent book, *Figures in Black: Words, Signs and the "Racial" Self,* Henry Louis Gates, Jr. directs the researcher's attention to language and the nature of black narrative forms (105). He suggests the reading of this literature through the paradigm of vernacular culture as a way of finding African American confrontations with voice and authority. His opinion is a useful tool to examine the degree and the manner in which language and history interact in Douglass and Manzano, leaving aside the ethical and thematic contents that critics see in these autobiographies (Blassingame, Luis, Molloy, Starling). By understanding those voices dominated, displaced or silenced in the autobiography of the ex-slave, we can explore these literary texts as linguistic events.

Douglass' opening statement of his narrative stresses the fact that he has no accurate knowledge of his birth. The autobiographer has never seen an authentic record or document of his birth, although he admits having been born in Talbot County, Maryland. The author's discourse emphatically blames the omission on the desire of the white masters to keep the slaves in ignorance and anonymity, a typical occurrence in plantation culture. The subjugated slaves are dehumanized and animalized by comparison to horses:

> By far the larger part of the slaves know little of their age as horses know of theirs, and this is the wish of most masters to keep slaves ignorant. I do not remember to have ever met a slave who could tell of his birthday. I could not tell why I ought to be deprived of the same privilege.
>
> (23)

As linguistic signs, the horses in this passage are closely connected to illiteracy within the institution of slavery. Douglass has apparently decided to attack and criticize, through the double image of working slaves reduced to animals, the ruling of the dominant class. Indeed, the accuracy in the age of the master and the ignorance of the slave who does not know his, creates a socio-racial barrier within plantation space. And Douglass himself attests to this barrier with his response to a simple public record as a birthdate: "The white children could tell their ages. I could not" (23).

Manzano, like Douglass, verifies his personal identity, but he also informs the reader about the deprivation of his birthdate (34). While discussing the question of origin, the autobiographer opts to use ellipsis points at the end of the sentence, a figure of speech which denotes omission and suppression, a mode of Lacanian repression in the Afro-Cuban self. Manzano's rhetorical strategy assumes the presence of a reader whose task is to decode the absence of language, implied in a missing birthdate. Perhaps it can be stated that he is silenced by the cultural forces that offer him no alternative but submission to a recently formed ruling oligarchy that Moreno Fraginals links to sugarocracy (1978, 106).

Why does an autobiographer silence part of his past? The *Oxford English Dictionary* defines silence as the "voluntary or involuntary omission of an account or a statement." Consciously or not, culture and history rely heavily on memory to record information, and memory is an art rooted in, and transmitted by, the spoken language (González Echevarría 13). The black self, in his

quest for truth, wants to write from what he recalls and eventually produce meaning by recreating the past at the present moment of writing.

If the writer is sincere, he can only say what he remembers from his past life, limiting documentation to what he really knows. Douglass, for example, simply recounts by the use of memory: "My first master's [name] was Anthony. I do not remember his first name" (27). Once again, the enunciation suggests that his own distant "past" exists only in the "present" which is not completely fresh in his memory (Stepto 26-34). Rousseau's experience is not essentially different. The French author connects self-writing and memory with the art of reading: "I can only remember the first books I read and what effect they had on me. This is the period from which I date the uninterrupted awareness of myself" (8).

Memory also plays a crucial role in Manzano's *Autobiography.* If memory fails, the autobiographer cannot be consistent with historical facts as Roberto Friol has already noted (47-49). In the reconstruction of the self, the Cuban ex-slave recreates in his imagination episodes of his childhood and youth, even though he is aware of the difficult task of remembering past events at the age of ten when he narrates the death of his first master, Doña Beatriz, the Marquise of Jústiz: ". . . this epoch for being so remote, is not well fixed in my memory, I only recall . . ." (36) [my translation]. Other times, Manzano chronicles his early days by hearsay. He relies on eyewitnesses still alive within and outside the literary space (34). Especially noteworthy in the text is how the voices of the "others" corroborate the authenticity of the autobiographical "I," testifying to the accuracy of the inner life narration: "there are still *some witnesses* who can attest to the *truth*" (24) [emphasis added]. In point of fact, with the presence of witnesses, Manzano removes himself temporarily from the discourse, avoiding the full responsibility of self's truthfulness. In this interplay of voices and silences, the rupture between the self and other, subject and object, master and slave is linguistically re-enacted.

As autobiographers, Douglass and Manzano conceal or reveal information they consider necessary for the reader's participation in reconstructing past lives. At times, these authors become fugitives of the speech-act, a rhetorical device by which they opt not to speak. Douglass, for instance, deems it appropriate to be apologetic to his audience: "I deeply regret the necessity that impels me to suppress anything of importance connected with my experience in slavery" (135). Black narratives of the nineteenth century demonstrate an understanding of self and circumstances that leads to the conviction that silence is the only means for the black to survive. Consciously or not, by hiding something, they involve the reader in decoding what the text may imply. In semiotic terminology, the autobiographical "I," as a sender of a verbal communication in the discourse makes the "you," his audience, to receive a partial message in order to capture what has not been fully said (Jakobson 66).

For the slave, the command of the written and oral languages represented an entitlement for socio-economic mobility. What is important to note, however, is that in slave culture, learning to read and write was a political act considered to be an irreversible step towards liberation. Literacy was a violation of the law imposed by the master who aimed to manipulate the knowledge of his slaves. For Douglass, "education and slavery were incompatible with each other" since knowledge was the "voice of truth" over the conscience of the slaveholder (64, 66). "Voice" and "truth," echoed by Derrida in *Le voix et le phénomène,* are inseparable components in Western culture and applicable to the nineteenth century writings of the African American self.

In Douglass's own voice, his move from plantation space to Baltimore becomes a crucial step towards literacy and prosperity which eventually leads to freedom. As Moreno Fraginals has persuasively argued, the urban setting required large numbers of slaves for domestic and nondomestic services compared to the plantation setting in which owners would not permit slaves to interact freely for fear of social cohesion and a sense of identity (1977, 20). The city slave, therefore, had a higher standard of living, and could communicate more openly with his peers. In fact, all these factors encouraged learning among the slaves in urban communities.

In 1845, when Douglass makes his private life a public act, he retrospectively recalls the antieducational stand of his new Baltimorean master, Mr. Auld. At first, the author's intention to say something is overshadowed by allowing his master's voice to be fleetingly heard in the text: "Learning would *spoil* the best nigger in the world" (59) [the writer's emphasis].

Why does Douglass allow his master's voice to be part of the autobiographical discourse? I would venture to suggest that the ex-slave opts to be momentarily silent because he wishes to see in the written word, and hear in the short speech, what exactly Mr. Auld's point of view is. Thus, he chooses to become the listener to his own writing and interpreter of the discourse of the "other." It is no surprise that the master's choice of the word "nigger" not only connects illiteracy to slavery, but it also conveys socio-historical connotations whereby the language of the white dominant class deprives the Afro-American slave of his cultural identity. From a sociolinguistic standpoint, the despotic character, a member of the white ruling group, shows his hierarchical superiority by his use of the speech of an empowered class that controls, intimidates, and degrades his subordinate.

As time goes by, Douglass is determined to learn how to read, a goal which he finally accomplishes at the age of twelve. In chapter seven he briefly narrates the secret plan he adopted in his self-learning process. In the confession, the autobiographer is tempted to talk in detail about those little neighborhood boys who taught him to read in what he calls a "testimonial [of] gratitude and affection" (65). However, he does not make their names identifiable to the reader. Instead, he limits himself to mentioning the street where they live in Baltimore. What can be safely stated here is that, after this omission the hidden words generate a religious meaning in the next lines of the story. For Douglass, the Church, like culture, furnishes us with systems of authority. These imposed systems, admits the author, cause racial discrimination: "It is almost an unpardonable offence to teach slaves in this Christian country" (65). Culturally, the nexus between self and religion, self and education, self and society is a distinguishing feature of his narrative.

In addition to reading, writing also becomes Douglass's next priority in his self-learning process. It was in a Baltimore shipyard where the Afro-American slave first watched carpenters write on pieces of timber the letters of parts of the ships (70). He discovered that by naming, renaming and repeating these letters they could be used to write (or spell) ordinary words with which he was already familiar, and so he began copying the italics in *Webster*'s *Spelling* books. The learner completed the remarkable strategem by imitating copy-books left aside by one of his master's sons. Though projecting a simplistic approach to self-instruction through decoding phonemes and mimicking texts, the autobiographer made a good acquisition of the written word. "I finally succeeded in learning how to write" (71), explains Douglass as an affirmation of identity and culture, language and self, knowledge and freedom. In a similar way, Manzano also uses his master's son's discarded notes and scraps of writing. Before a month was over, the Cuban slave was recognizing the letters of the alphabet, "writing lines" and imitating the handwriting of the Marquise's son, Don Nicolás de Cárdenas (57). As in the case of Douglass's master in Baltimore, Don Nicolás did not allow Manzano to learn to write, falsely assuming that writing was an inappropriate skill for slaves even though Nicolás was president of the Patriotic Society's Education Committee (Friol 52).

The correlation between Douglass and Manzano is more direct when it comes to the prohibition of learning, a thematic linkage in the antislavery narrative canon of the nineteenth century. The Cuban author repeatedly admits to the reader that during his life as an urban slave he was denied basic skills such as writing and reading. Even the written word, as in the composition of verses, was forbidden by his godparents (38). Yet Manzano manages to become partially educated before his manumission and writes the *Autobiography* after being a liberated self. For Manzano and the literary community with which he allies himself, the act of writing becomes increasingly important for the denouncing of the voice of the masters in their opposition to the education of the slaves. Larry Jensen informs us that during this period education was a monopoly linked to the sugar elite on the island (22-24). Sugarocracy created a literary atmosphere, thus reinforcing and intensifying the connection between social status and learning.

Learning for Manzano was a more obtainable and less painful goal. Being a domestic urban slave in provincial Matanzas gave Manzano access to classes imparted by Mister Godfría to the master's children. Often related to the act of learning is a mentor. In the nineteenth century, the figure is generally a male for learning, whether teaching, reading or writing, is associated with aristocracy and power (Molloy 49). Despite the limited degree of instruction, the meaning produced by writing is first experienced by Manzano within the oral word through recitative, auditory and retentive mechanisms. Already at an early age, the former slave employed all these channels of oral communication to memorize verses, improvise poetic visions and sketch plastic imageries. Hence, in his autobiographical act he gracefully links the "art of memory" to rhetoric, painting and poetry (41). His ambition leads Manzano to capture the visual and oral word. Consequently, the Cuban author's discourse reflects the writing of an autobiographical text and the possibility of writing and rewriting of poems as subtexts within his autobiography. As Lorna Williams points out, with these accomplishments Manzano not only reverses the traditional role of the slave as a person estranged from his labor, but also lists the skillful abilities that would enable him to earn a living once he becomes a freedman (17).

Manzano also informs the reader that he was a fable teller. Surrounded by children and servants, he repeated sorcerer's tales by the use of memory and oral traditions. The slave composed Cuban country songs called *décimas* by means of which he maintained a love relationship with a young mulatto named Josefina. In the narration of these anecdotes, we can clearly observe the symbiotic relationship between the limited written discourse of the slave and his oral creativity exemplified in the telling of stories and the self's singing. The voice of the slave over the master's authority starts to be heard. Following Gates Jr.'s proposition, this is an instance of "speakerly" discourse, that is, an act which imitates forms of the oral traditions to be found in African (American and Latin American) literature.

In Douglass's views knowledge leads to freedom and equality which in the text is ironically priced in monetary terms. Money, then, is seen by Douglass as being instrumental in his integration within the economic structure of the white dominant class. As in the picaresque tradition, the slave disguises himself in the trickster figure and ends up paying his wealthy master, Mr. Hugh, in exchange for more free time to plan the way of escaping slavery through marronage. The power of Mr. Hugh compels the Afro-American to give up his earnings and, restless and discontented with this discriminatory situation, the slave escapes on September 3, 1838, without giving an explanation of how he succeeded in reaching New York (133).

Manzano, in contrast, is more explicit about his escape in 1817. In the last page of his book, he explains that a servant in the master's house gives him a horse for that purpose (49). If in Douglass's narrative the horse is a linguistic metaphor of the slave's illiteracy, in Manzano's *Autobiography* the animal can be associated with the open space that represents freedom. In fact, the horse acts as a moving force, a textual symbol whose presence is to lead Manzano towards his liberation at the end of the narration. Manzano promises to be the subject in the writing of a second part, but the manuscript is considered lost. His text is, nevertheless, the first slave narrative published in nineteenth century Spanish America.

By juxtaposing Douglass's life story with Manzano's own testimony, I have delimited some of the ways that language and culture are mutually constitutive and reciprocally revealing. From geographically opposite poles in the American continent, the reader senses the relationship between texts and the various linguistic tools or historical contexts that give meaning to these texts. In *The Postmodern Condition,* Jean-François Lyotard has suggested that cross-cultural narratives traditionally cement racial and social bonds (21). Douglass and Manzano make this cross-cultural encounter possible by recurring to writing to express the complex connections between self and other. In doing so, they place the voiceless at the core of their autobiographical space in nineteenth century America.

Works Cited

Blassingame, John W. "Black Autobiography as History and Literature." *Black Scholar* 5 (December 1973): 2-9.

Butterfield, Stephen. *Black Autobiography in America.* Amherst: U of Massachusetts P, 1974. 9-89.

Cox, James M. "Autobiography and America." *Aspects of Narrative.* J. Hillis Miller, ed. New York: Columbia UP, 1971.

Douglass, Frederick. *Narrative of the Life of Frederick Douglass: An American Slave Written by Himself.* Cambridge: Harvard UP, 1960.

Friol, Roberto. *Suite para Juan Francisco Manzano.* La Habana: Editorial Arte y Literatura, 1977.

Gates Jr., Henry Louis. *Figures in Black: Words, Signs and the "Racial" Self.* New York: Oxford UP, 1987.

González Echevarría, Roberto. *The Voice of the Masters: Writing and Authority in Modern Latin American Literature.* Austin: U of Texas P, 1985.

Howarth, William L. "Some Principles of Autobiography." *New Literary History* 5 (1974): 363-81.

Jackson, Richard L. "Slavery, Racism and Autobiography in Two Early Black Writers: Juan Francisco Manzano and Martín Morua Delgado." *Voices from Under: Black Narrative in Latin America and the Caribbean.* Ed. William Luis. Westport, CT: Greenwood P, 1984. 55-94.

Jakobson, Roman. *Language in Literature.* Cambridge: Harvard UP, 1987.

Jensen, Larry R. *Children of Colonial Despotism.* Tampa: U of South Florida P, 1988.

Jiménez, Luis A. "Voces y silencios y su vínculo con el poder en la *Autobiografía* de Juan Francisco Manzano." *Critical Essays in Honor of María Salgado.* Newark, DE: Juan de la Cuesta Hispanic Monographs, Series No. 10, 1995. 45-59.

Kubayanda, Josephat Bekunuru. "Minority Discourse and the African Collective: Some Examples from Latin American and Caribbean Literature." *Cultural Critique* 6 (1987): 113-90.

Lejeune, Philippe. *On Autobiography.* Trans. Katherine Leary. Minneapolis: U of Minnesota P, 1982.

Luis, William. *Literary Bondage: Slavery in Cuban Narrative.* Austin: U of Texas P, 1990.

Lyotard, Jean-François. *The Postmodern Condition.* Trans. Geoff Bennington and Brian Massumi. Minneapolis: U of Minnesota P, 1984.

Manzano, Juan Francisco. *Autobiografía.* Ed. José Luciano Franco. La Habana: Municipio de La Habana, 1937.

Molloy, Sylvia. *At Face Value: Autobiographical Writing in Spanish America.* Cambridge: Cambridge UP, 1991.

Moreno Fraginals, Manuel, ed. "Cultural Contributions and Deculturation." *Africa in Latin America.* New York: Holmes & Meier, 1977. 5-22.

———. *El ingenio.* La Habana: Editorial de Ciencias Sociales, 1978.

Mullen, Edward J., ed. *The Life and Poems of a Cuban Slave: Juan Francisco Manzano, 1797-1854.* Hamden, CT: Archon Books, 1981.

Rousseau, Jean Jacques. *Les Confessions.* Paris: La Pléiade, 1951.

Starling, Marion Wilson. *The Slave Narrative.* Boston: G.K. Hall, 1981.

Stepto, Robert B. "Narration, Authentication and Authorial Control in Frederick Douglass' *Narrative* of 1845." *African American Autobiography.* William L. Andrew, ed. Englewood Cliffs: Prentice Hall, 1993. 26-34.

Terdiman, Richard. *Discourse/Counter-Discourse: The Theory and Practice of Symbolic Resistance in Nineteenth Century France.* Ithaca: Cornell UP, 1985.

Towns, Saundra. "Black Autobiography and the Dilemma of Western Artistic Tradition." *Black Books Bulletin* (1974): 17-23.

Weintraub, Karl J. "Autobiography and Historical Consciousness." *Critical Inquiry* 1 (1975): 821-48.

Williams, Lorna Valerie. *The Representation of Slavery in Cuban Fiction.* Columbia: U of Missouri P, 1994.

Jerome Branche (essay date January 2001)

SOURCE: Branche, Jerome. "*'Mulato entre negros' (y blancos)*: Writing, Race, the Antislavery Question, and Juan Francisco Manzano's *Autobiographía*." *Bulletin of Latin American Research* 20, no. 1 (January 2001): 63-87.

[*In the following essay, Branche reflects on the struggle faced by Manzano in trying to reach a balance between the expectations of his benefactor del Monte and being able to represent his own personal and cultural history in his memoir.*]

> For 'quo ad' morals, nothing can be worse,
> But 'quo ad' sugar, tis the sole resource.
>
> Richard Madden.

Situated as it is between the powerful and the powerless, between literacy and illiteracy, slavers and the enslaved, the life story of Juan Francisco Manzano occupies a unique place in Cuban and Latin American literary history. The fact that it is the only extant autobiography of a person of African descent written during the period of Latin American slavery enhances the particularity of the document. The *Autobiografía* is also noteworthy because it is the historical point of departure for what has been canonized as early Cuban 'antislavery' writing. It has also been regarded as having provided a narrative model for this genre.[1] Cuban man of letters, Domingo del Monte and the corps of literati (the *círculo delmontino*) who were instrumental in the production of these early texts have been remembered accordingly as exemplars of New World enlightenment and humanitarianism. Paradoxically, Manzano, the only member of the *círculo* who could describe slavery from a non-fictional perspective, and who was central to the mostly derivative and fictional slave narrative, has had a somewhat limiting critical harvest in comparison with the historical protagonism accorded the other writers of the group. With few exceptions, the critical gaze, due almost certainly to his condition as a slave, has tended to see him through the prism of pathos and less in terms of his intellectuality or as a literary originator.[2] The intellectual lionization has generally been reserved for the White writers of the group.

From the standpoint that literature is an institution of power and privilege, this essay proposes a look at the Latin American colonial cartography as a backdrop to the prestige of this group of Cuban writers and their writings. It first of all takes into account the occlusion of the unlettered underclass inherent to the canonizing process, and the implications for the latter as historical agents. The second section considers the enhanced critical legacy of the Delmontine group and their prominence in the Cuban discourse of national literary foundation. This section highlights the extent to which the antislavery premise within this discourse has sought purchase and legitimacy in the larger moral and philosophical issue of the day; emancipation and the Rights of Man. Manzano's autobiographical construction of self in a textual and extratextual universe overdetermined by race and the subjugation of enslavement is also relevant to the broader context of this foundational moment in Cuban writing, and will be seen in this regard. This discussion comprises the final section.

In his 1944 study, *Capitalism and Slavery,* Eric Williams referred to the historical inevitability of the ending of the latter institution, whether as a result of metropolitan lobbying 'from above' or of slave insurgency 'from below' (1994, 208). Williams's observation points not only to the essentially heterogeneous nature of transatlantic abolitionism. It highlights what other revisionist historians since then have seen as a major problem in Western antislavery studies, that is, the 'projection of a hierarchical order' in the discussion of the antislavery question (Beckles, 1988, 8). According to colonialist history of emancipation, it was enlightened European humanitarians and intellectuals who brought freedom to the Blacks.[3] When this discourse recognizes a protagonistic role for the enslaved, their action is regarded as marginal to the broad sweep of history; as mostly instinctive, material outbursts against oppression, in effect, 'a lower species of political behavior, lacking in ideological cohesion, intellectual qualities, and a philosophical direction' (Beckles, 1988, 3).

It is interesting to find a not entirely dissimilar tendency to polarize and racially hierarchize the antislavery question in the approach of many scholars of Cuban literature. César Leante, for example, in 'Dos obras antiesclavistas cubanas' ('Two Cuban Antislavery Works'), extols the high moral and philanthropic impulse behind Anselmo Suárez y Romero's novel *Francisco*. He stresses the point that it was to the planter class that the White writer turned in his concern for social justice, and not to the class of the enslaved. Asserting that 'es difícil que pudiera haber sido de otra manera' (it is difficult for it to have been any other way), Leante adds rhetorically, 'pues . . . ¿qué efecto podía ocasionar libro alguno en un conglomerado totalmente analfabeto? (What effect could a book possibly have in a totally illiterate conglomerate?)[4] (1976, 181). Leante's statement would of course be quite logical if indeed all enslaved Blacks were illiterate or incapable of literary or intellectual expression. The same might be said if it were only the enslaved who took up arms for freedom. The historical record indicates otherwise. Another critic, William Luis, while lauding the Delmontine literary project aimed ostensibly at changing slave society, seems to proceed in similar essentialist vein when he states; 'it stands to reason that antislavery, as a concept or as a literary, political, or economic movement in Cuba, could only exist as a white movement' (1990, 65).[5] Whereas both writers do recognize a role for unfree Blacks in casting off the chains of bondage, one wonders if in their analyses of the antislavery question, they are not privileging writing, writers, and the Cartesian premise, along restrictive racial lines.

Contrary to the notion that antislavery protest operated along a racialized axis determined by literacy or literariness, empirical evidence suggests a much more complex and nuanced relationship between the enslaved and the dominant culture of writing not only in Cuba, but across the Black Atlantic.[6] Far from the exclusivism of the Eurocentric premise, or the plantocracy's blanket prohibitions to literacy for its slaves, writing as an intellectual tool was an effective and intrinsic element of the Afrocreole project of liberation. Afrocreole agency through writing is evident if one considers, for example, its role in the Bahia rebellion of 1835, led by literate Muslim slaves. The role of writing is also clear when one considers the different ways in which some Afrocreoles appropriatiated colonial languages to communicate their sociopolitical concerns to the crown and the slaveocracy, or simply by way of their accession to and use of writing in terms of standard literary practice.

The celebration of the Delmontine circle in the discourse of early nineteenth-century Cuban literary beginnings is better understood if we see its members as legatees of what Angel Rama referred to as the *ciudad letrada,* and in terms of the diglossia which characterized the social relations of production in colonial Latin America. Rama reminds us that in the urban/rural dichotomy of the colonial economy, it was in the *ciudad letrada,* or 'lettered city,' where political and administrative power was centered. In an overwhelmingly unlettered population, literacy and erudition among lawyers, royal functionaries, professors, priests, and creative writers, played a crucial role in constituting a hegemonic apparatus located in the urban space. It was an apparatus that kept colonial subalterns—slaves, Blacks, Amerindians, mestizos—at an appropriate distance from the exercise of socio-political and economic influence. In the context of an economy based on forced labor, however, with a documented antislavery praxis of individual and collective acts of rebellion, it is impossible to deny the agents of this rebellion a corresponding antislavery consciousness, or discursivity.[7]

A full account of antislavery voicing from the fringes of the dominant scribal tradition is beyond the scope of this discussion. The challenges to the power of the crown and the colonial oligarchy that include the use of the written medium, however, were a constant in several areas of colonial Latin America. Perhaps the most significant threat to the status quo in Cuba within living memory of the Delmontine group, was the Aponte conspiracy of 1812, which planned an uprising against the plantocracy and Cuba's colonial status. José Antonio Aponte was an *Oni-Shangó,* that is, a leader in the Nigeria originated *lucumí* religious order. His coconspirators included other co-religionists, free Afro-Cubans, slaves, and poor Whites. Aponte's inspiration lay both in the successes of the recently concluded Haitian revolution, and in the progressive initiatives taken by Spanish American deputies to the liberal Spanish Cortes at Cádiz, Spain, to end the slave trade and slavery.

Historian José Luis Franco's account of Aponte's arrest, trial, and execution, provides additional information pertinent to this discussion. It refers to the presence of secret *abakuá* drawings among the conspirators,[8] as well as a proclamation in Spanish that the insurgents had posted up on the wall of the principal government building (the *Palacio de Gobierno*) in Havana. The latter called upon the public at large to be 'alertas para derribar la tiranía' (1974, 175) (on the alert to overthrow tyranny). Another more extended document was directed to the White business sector inviting them to join with the rebels in the liberatory enterprise.[9] Aponte, a talented wood-carver, painter, and owner of a small library had also produced a large book of highly suggestive paintings and illustrations that were used against him at his trial. Among the paintings considered seditious, was one that depicted Black and White soldiers in battle, in which the Black general emerged triumphant. Yet another detailed the city of Havana with its forts, castles, walls, storehouses, military installations, sugar mills, etc. Other portraits depicting Haitian revolutionary leaders, Toussaint L'Ouverture and Henri Christophe enhanced the incendiary symbolism of these illustrations.

What is important about Aponte as an antislavery protagonist, is that on the one hand the materials seized by the authorities point to the variety of texts he used to communicate with his different groups of interlocutors. That is to say that that whereas the *abakuá* illustrations would have been decipherable only by religious initiates, the proclamations in Spanish would have communicated to his literate followers and to the public at large as well. Finally, it is easy to see how the graphic nature and content of the paintings could have been aimed primarily at those of his comrades who could not read. On the other hand, the detailed interrogation to which Aponte and his followers were subjected by the colonial authorities indicates the seriousness with which these texts were regarded. For the authorities they all constituted subversive acts of signifying.

Equally subversive of the slavocratic and colonial status quo, was the role of Arabic in the 1835 *Malê* rebellion in Bahia, Brazil, described by João José Reis as 'the most effective urban slave rebellion ever to occur on the American continent' (1993, xiii).[10] It was an event imbued with a sense of Islamic millennialism in which many of the bodies of the insurgents were later found with amulets containing prayers and Koranic passages that spoke of hope amidst oppression. The rebels had entered the war with these amulets as mystical guarantees of invulnerability. The persistence of a West African Islamic intellectual tradition in these enslaved Muslims is manifest in the documentation that the authorities found that revealed their plans for the execution of the rebellion, and in the Koranic schools they attempted to continue in Brazil. Researchers have also stressed the significance of *Malê* literacy in a context in which a large percentage of the Portuguese and White creole community could neither read nor write (Goody, 1986, 324) (Reis, 1993, 106). Significantly two of the seven leaders, Manoel Calafate and Elesbão do Carmo, were freedmen.

Much earlier, in Colombia, in the 1680s, maroon leader Domingo Criollo, with the help of Spanish clerics, had negotiated for a decade in writing with the local governor and the Council of the Indies, before his village was finally destroyed in 1693.[11] Also in the Guyanese county of Berbice, then a Dutch colony, rebel leader Kofi engaged in a protracted correspondence with governor van Hoogenheim in 1763. Kofi's extended letter writing, according to one commentator, was a delaying ploy by which it was hoped that an eventual peace treaty might ensue.[12] Similarly, in Barbados, Bussa's rebellion of 1816, recalls that of Aponte, in the sense that its leadership was aware of the wider antislavery struggle. In this case the uprising reflected the slaves' understanding of the effect of abolitionist agitation in England and the crisis facing the planter class, in many instances by way of information acquired from local and British newspapers (Beckles, 1985, 94). The awareness of political developments in the local or metropolitan government circles, in the free and enslaved Black communities, through print media, often influenced the nature and timing of their rebellions.

Complementing the texts that were directly related to armed insurgency, were other kinds of Afrocreole antislavery protests that used writing. These challenges to oppression may have been direct or mediated, and may have taken the form of letters, complaints, or even lawsuits. They might have been aimed at obtaining autonomy for maroon sites, as indicated, at securing liberty for already freed individuals under threat of re-enslavement, or at acquiring any number of the perceived rights denied by racially exclusionary colonial laws. Together they constituted a discourse aimed at nullifying the status of object to which Africans and Afrocreoles had been subjected.[13]

The appropriation of written discourse demonstrates the awareness among free and enslaved Africans and Afrocreoles of the relationship between writing and the politico-legal superstructure, as well as their determination to use whatever means were available to achieve their liberation. While learning to read and write may have been illegal in all of the Americas, there can be no question that there is a Black antislavery archive in writing that is available for recovery, whether this consisted of letters, testimony at trials, treaties, or else. The contents of this archive would dramatically enhance our understanding of the nature of the relationship between the dominant and the subordinate groups in colonial Latin America. They would also allow for a more balanced view of who did what in antislavery history, while dispelling notions of unqualified illiteracy and unsophistication among the enslaved. The fact that these texts were part of a crucial existential necessity for those engaged in their writing underscores their importance as a discourse against slavery. Antislavery writing as an abstract fictional endeavour is an entirely different matter.

In the final analysis, action spoke louder than words as far as the antislavery question was concerned. In the foundational moment of Cuban literature in the 1830s, to the extent that fear of antislavery upheaval stalked the minds of the plantocracy and the colonial bureaucrats, it is to be recognized that it was the slaves themselves who were the agents of this unease and not the literati. Their potential for turning Cuban colonial society upside down is recorded in their increased rebelliousness over the preceding four decades.[14] One finds in fact that it was the threat, real or imagined, that they represented, that often hindered otherwise progressive thinking among the Cuban intelligentsia of the period. While on the one hand it is undeniable that this intelligentsia expressed antislavery ideas as they established a national discourse, it is crucial to specify the motivations underlying their antislavery proclamations, and the implications of their ideas for the future nation. On the other hand, conferring epistemological paramountcy on them as the founding fathers of Cuba's national literature on the basis of their presumed liberationist discourse seems to respond to an overvaluing of the role of literature and literati. It suggests a hierarchizing of the antislavery concept that correspondingly devalues the voices, consciousness, and the agency of the slaves who protagonized their own liberation. As indicated, the latter was achieved by means of an essentially heterogeneous praxis that, when necessary, combined the pen with the sword.[15]

The figure of Domingo del Monte (1804-1853) is pivotal to any discussion of Cuban literary beginnings. Litterateur par excellence, Del Monte was widely traveled, knew Latin and five modern languages, and is regarded as having been the most important bibliographer in the Caribbean in the nineteenth century (García, 1993). His passion for literature is seen in his reputation as a voracious reader and through his active promotion and discussion of literary works and theories among his friends. Recognized by scholars as Cuba's first professional literary critic, Del Monte used his discussion groups or *tertulias,* and the journals with which he was associated, to introduce Neoclassicism, Romanticism and Realism to Cuba, and to promote an aesthetic in which New World and Cuban motifs would be central. As Antonio Benítez-Rojo points out, it was from his literary circle that a definably Cuban body of works emerged in the latter 1830s (1994, 106). Among the writers with whom he worked and who he mentored were Ramón de Palma, José Zacarías González del Valle, José Antonio Saco, José Jacinto Milanés, Anselmo Suárez y Romero, and Félix Tanco y Bosmeniel. Occasional participants in his group were mulatto poet Plácido de la Concepción Valdés, and Juan Francisco Manzano. The writing coming out of his athenaeum included articles on customs, drama, travel writing, poetry, novels, literary criticism, and of course, Manzano's slave autobiography.

Del Monte's contribution to Cuban literary beginnings is also seen in his co-founding and co-editing of such periodicals as *La Moda ó Recreo Semanal del Bello Sexo* (1829-1831), *El puntero literario* (January-May 1830), and the *Revista Bimestre Cubana* (1831-1834). These vehicles not only provided an outlet for local writing, they also entertained and educated an ever-widening readership as to the latest scientific and literary trends in Europe and the United States. Through them authors and poets such as Scott, Byron, Zorilla, Hugo, and Balzac, were introduced to the Cuban public, just as their merits were assessed among the new generation of would-be writers. Literary historians regard Del Monte as having achieved a major coup in winning the approval of the Regent Maria Cristina, for the establishment of a Cuban Academy of Literature in

1834. The proposed Academy had grown out of his work since 1830 as President of the Commission on Literature of the influential and prestigious *Sociedad Económica de Amigos del País.* Due, however, to a climate of severe repression of freedom of expression, and the highhanded action of powerful enemies of the Academy, the project never came into being.[16]

The subsequent defense of the right of the Academy to exist, by Del Monte and his colleague José Antonio Saco, constitutes an event of the highest significance. In the current atmosphere of colonial suppression, it signaled liberal Eurocreole determination to have independent opinions about art, politics, and a wide range of subjects, and to express these opinions. Saco pointed out in an erudite and forceful article,[17] that the arguments against official ratification of the Academy in Cuba were specious, and that official ire had been aroused because the literati had shaken off 'el imperio que ellos quería ejercer sobre ellos' (the domination that they [the Patriotic Society] wanted to exercise over them).'[18] Saco's bold and public statement came only two years after he had used the *Revista Bimestre Cubana* to call for abolition of the slave trade because it was bringing too many potentially hostile Blacks into the country. Impugning the pretentions to patriotism of the powerful slavetraders, he called them instead 'parricidas' (parricides), lambasting their lust for profits in an illegal trade, and attacking, in passing, the colonial officials who collaborated with them in the traffic.[19] Spain had signed an agreement in 1817 with Britain to bring an end to its trade in Africans in 1820, and it was established custom that Captains General accepted handsome bribes to look the other way. With slave imports about to peak in 1835, the fact that Captain General Miguel Tacón subsequently sent Saco into exile was not surprising.[20]

Del Monte added to this alienation of the powerful alliance of wealthy landowners, slavetraders, and upper-echelon administrators with his own angry vindication of the Academy in the *Aurora de Matanzas* newspaper on April 2, 1834. Five years later he followed up with a call for freedom of the press, and for equal provincial representation and constitutional rights for Cuba in Spain.[21] Equally damning from the standpoint of the sugar interests, was that he was known to have associated with British abolitionist Richard Madden, resident magistrate on the mixed commission that had been established for liberating Africans rescued from captured slave ships. At Madden's request, Del Monte had some of his group members prepare works on the topic of slavery in Cuba, and in 1839 these were these were handed to him for publication in England.[22] According to Zacarías González del Valle, *tertulia* member, these works were to allow Madden to form 'una idea exacta del estado de la opinión acerca de la trata de los siervos entre los jóvenes que piensan en el país,'[23] (an exact idea of the opinion of the thinking youth of the country as to the treatment of slaves).

It is the profile of Del Monte as defiant, autonomist, and at the same time cosmopolitan man of letters, that has made him an object of pride for many literary historiographers. Along with Saco, he has been seen as central to a 'discourse of resistance' against the powerful sugar interests, and promoter of a 'literary antislavery campaign' (Benítez-Rojo, 1980, 22). It is an assessment premised primarily on economist Francisco de Arango y Parreño's 1792 pro-slavery initiative to the crown, the *Discurso sobre la Agricultura de la Habana y medios de fomentarla,* which had advocated making Cuba a sugar-producing replacement for then insurgent Saint Domingue.[24] William Luis's, *Literary Bondage: Slavery in Cuban Narrative* also vindicates the Delmontine project from the standpoint of its supposed counterdiscursivity.[25]

The Del Monte group has even been promoted in terms of the revolutionary paradigm of the Enlightenment, and its discourse of emancipation. For Francisco González del Valle, he and his companions were young men 'imbuídos de los princípios de libertad, igualdad, y fraternidad' (imbued with the principles of liberty, equality, and fraternity), who exchanged books and ideas in a clandestine manner, and who dedicated their 'nobles y generosos corazones' (noble and generous hearts) to ending the slave trade and slavery (1938, 6). As local versions of the great European humanitarians and encyclopaedists, according to González del Valle, they paved the way for the epic moment in 1868, when Cuban national hero Manuel de Céspedes launched the war for independence, and declared his slaves free (1938, 7). For these reasons, he suggests: 'merecen ser conocidos por las generaciones presentes, porque nos hablan de una época de esplendor de nuestra historia literaria, reveledora de los sentimientos generosos e ideas avanzadas de aquellos jóvenes escritores.'[26]

The oppositional stance of the Cuban literati of the 1830s vis-à-vis the sugar barons and the colonial bureaucracy is undeniable. The abolitionist question is also a key point of difference between them. But here it is important to note that there is a difference between the idea of abolition as an end to the slave trade, and the idea of abolition as an end to slavery, and that neither of the two necessarily implies altruism. In the celebration of Del Monte's humanitarianism and his supposed antislavery dissidence, these distinctions have too often been glossed over. Further, in the particular context of Cuba at the time, the blurring of the difference, ie, describing him in unqualified fashion as 'abolitionist,' can obscure the important implications of the two kinds of abolition for intellectuals like Del Monte. As it turns out Delmontine opposition to slavery as an altruistic vindication of the rights of the enslaved, an idea advanced in the studies previously cited, is a highly questionable proposition. So too is the suggestion that he and his literary group *in toto* espoused the vision of a democratic inclusion of Black ex-slaves in a future Cuban polity.[27] On the contrary, the writings of both Saco and Del Monte repeatedly reveal a sense of paranoia over racial coexistence at the time, as well as the supremacist desire for a White and hence 'civilized' future Cuba.

In the early nineteenth century, Cuban nationalist discourse was intimately tied to the question of political independence from Spain. Independence, in turn, was tied to the island's racial composition and to the possibility of union with the United States. It all resulted in an ideological bottleneck that would not be resolved for decades. Proslavery advocate Arango y Parreño may have expressed confidence in Spain's ability to control Cuba's growing slave population due to increased imports at the turn of the century.[28] But by the 1830s Saco was expressing panic at the rising number of Blacks and slaves in Cuba, and their demographic preponderance in neighbouring countries. Considering it his duty as writer, intellectual, and patriot, to warn his fellow countrymen of impending racial conflagration and financial ruin should the importation of Africans continue, he proposed several reforms aimed at modernizing Cuba's sugar industry in a subsequent essay (*Análisis* 204-205). The key element in these reforms lay in the importation of White labour and the elimination of the Blacks.[29]

Free White workers he maintained were more intelligent, dedicated, and motivated. The Black slaves were lazy, saboteurs, and prone to rebellion (*La supresión* 228-229). Arguing that beet sugar was being produced quite successfully by free labour in the East Indies (*La supresión* 218), Saco exhorted his compatriots to save the Cuban fatherland, describing its current population as 'gravemente enfermo(s)' (gravely ill) as a result of the Black presence (*Análisis* 196). The solution, he asserted in *La Supresión,* lay in closing 'para siempre, las puertas a todos los negros' (forever, the doors to all Blacks) while opening them 'libremente a todos los blancos' (226) (freely to all Whites).

The self-interest and monetary gain of the entrenched power groups, however, militated strongly against Saco's admonitions. It was as situation in which a successful slaving expedition could net a profit of $100,000 dollars in 1835 (Thomas, 1998, 96), Captain General Miguel Tacón had amassed $450.000 in bribes during his four-year tenure,[30] and sugar was showing unprecedented profitability for the saccharocracy. While Saco can certainly be described as having an antislavery ideology, he can hardly be described as a Negrophile. His essay 'Contra la anexión,' in fact, actually made a call for the 'extinción, si fuera posible, de la raza negra' (the extinction, if this were possible, of the Black race).[31]

Antonio Saco's monochrome nationalism was endorsed in all its important points by Domingo del Monte, in spite of the *tertulia's* general endorsement of a racially inclusive Cuban literary landscape.[32] Del Monte was as alarmed as his colleague was on the matter of Cuba's racial imbalance, and supported the idea of importing European labourers to redress the issue. For this reason also, he felt that British-style abolition would be ruinous since it would make free men of the enslaved. As a plantation owner, Del Monte had more of a stake in the preservation of his personal property. In the early decades of the nineteenth century, Cuban sugar barons as a group deployed their political muscle as generators of revenue for a debilitated Spain, to delay *de facto* prohibition of the slave trade, notwithstanding the wave of liberalism in Europe, or the 1817 treaty. With the Saint Domingue antecedent in mind, however, they were acutely aware that their prosperity was precarious, and saw the powerful United States, a slaveholding nation, as a potential source of security. Significant overtures in this regard took place in 1810, 1822, and as late as 1868 when rebel leader Carlos Manuel de Céspedes, on behalf of the sugar interests, wrote Secretary of State, W. H. Seward, to this effect.[33]

Del Monte's correspondence with his American colleague and diplomat Alexander Everett shows how much in line he was with the thinking that defined his class. Everett had been United States minister to Spain in 1825, and had supported those members of the U.S political elite desirous of annexing Cuba.[34] When Del Monte visited the United States in 1829, Alexander Everett, along with his brother Edward, president of Harvard University, was among a group of North American scholars and writers with whom Del Monte established a friendship.[35] A close correspondence covering personal, political, and cultural matters ensued thereafter between the two. In Cuba, writing for a public audience at the time might raise the question of censorship or self-censorship. In Del Monte's private correspondence to Everett, there is no reason to believe that such considerations obtained.

In a series of letters to the powerful diplomat covering a wide range of topics, Del Monte showed remarkable candour as he courted U.S annexation of Cuba, all the while expressing a position on race in Cuba that was unambiguous. The slave-owners, he asserted in August of 1843, are united in their intention to seek 'apoyo y protección y amparo' (help and protection and support) from the great Northern Confederation, should Madrid declare slavery abolished.[36] Earlier in November of 1842, in an unsubtle appeal to the assumed racism of Everett, he described Cuba as 'la hermana menor de la gran Confederación Occidental de los pueblos caucásicos de América' (the youngest sister in the Great Western Confederation of Caucasian peoples of America). In this letter Del Monte tried to persuade Everett that Cuba was a political pawn of the British, who were bent, curiously enough, on freeing the slaves and setting up a Black military republic in Cuba. With this in mind he asked rhetorically, 'Verá impasible el pueblo Americano (sic), como quien contempla la progresión de un drama en el teatro, como se va elaborando curiosa y hábilmente por la astuta Albion, la pérdida de la mayor de las Antillas . . . No lo creo.'[37]

In the same letter he asserted Cuba's destiny as 'la estrella más brillante del pabellón de América' (the most brillant star in the American flag), clarifying on a later occasion that his conversations about emancipation with British abolitionist agent David Turnbull, and with other liberals, were purely theoretical speculations (García, 1989,133). Supporting freedom for Black slaves, he reiterated in June of 1844, would be madness, since it would 'sacrificar la tranquilidad de mi país y la existencia de mi raza' (sacrifice the tranquility of my country and the existence of my race) (García, 1989, 131). Del Monte, after all, had married into a family of 'capitalistas laboriosos y honrados' (hardworking and honourable capitalists), and wished ardently to be cleared of all suspicions of being a 'conspirador . . . abolicionista o revolucionario' (conspirator . . . abolitionist or revolutionary) (García, 1989, 133).[38]

Apologists for Delmontine humanitarianism allude invariably to his role in rescuing Manzano from slavery, and his support of his literary endeavours, as concrete proof of his abolitionist commitment and benevolence.[39] Salvador Bueno, for example, in several articles supportive of the notion of Del Monte's altruism and enlightenment, quotes Cuban national hero José Martí on one occasion in describing him as 'el cubano más real y útil de su tiempo' (the most real and useful Cuban of his time).[40] It is certainly to his credit that we have Manzano's invaluable writings. It bears pointing out though, that in the context of the wider Atlantic, elite White sponsorship of enslaved Blacks with literary ambitions was no novelty. It had been the case several decades before of Ignatius Sancho, Ottobah Cuguano, and Gustavus Vassa in England, Francis Williams of Jamaica, and Phyllis Wheatley of Boston, Massachusetts, among others.[41] Besides, as owner of a hundred slaves and a 900-acre estate, and as member of the slave-trading, slave-owning Alfonso-Aldama-Madam clan, one of the most opulent family groups in Cuba, Del Monte's description of his family's creation of wealth as 'honest capitalism' does little to enhance his humanitarian image.[42]

The spirit of emancipation that characterized the Enlightenment and is exemplified in the American (1776) and French Revolutions (1789), also saw the emergence of abolitionist societies in England, France, and the United States. The ideological radicalism of men like England's Thomas Paine and France's Henri Grégoire,

are examples of the democratic spirit of the age, and of its abolitionism. Paine, noted for his political activism in both the American and French revolutions, also authored the anticlerical and anti-aristocratic *The Rights of Man* (1791), and *The Age of Reason* (1794). As Clerk of the Pennsylvania Assembly, he drafted legislation providing for the gradual emancipation of the state's slaves, and, nearly a hundred years before Lincoln, attempted to write a clause against slavery into the American constitution.[43] Grégoire, a Jacobin and member of the French *Societé des amis des Noirs,* also wrote *De la littérature des nègres* (1808), a vindication of the intellectual achievements of Africans of the diaspora. Grégoire's essay was aimed at combating the burgeoning supremacist discourse that would culminate with Positivism and the pseudo-scientific racism of the nineteenth century.[44]

Eric Williams has called metropolitan abolitionism 'one of the greatest propaganda movements of all time' (1994, 178). The famous seal of the Anti-Slavery Society, for example, depicting an African with one knee on the ground and in a pose of supplication, was reproduced by Josiah Wedgewood by the thousands. It bore the Society's motto 'Am I not a man and a brother?' Supporters of the cause wore it to show their solidarity. Antislavery tracts, numbering as many as 2,802,773 in the period between 1823 and 1831,[45] were complemented in formal literature by a plethora of poems, plays and fiction. Seymour Drescher notes also the influence of the British masses as generalized mobilization through lecture and petition campaigns made candidates in British parliamentary elections of 1832 take careful note of the power of the antislavery constituency.[46]

French *philosophes* of the latter eighteenth century on pondering the oppression of colonial slavery asked the rhetorical question 'Ou est-il çe nouveau Spartacus?' (Where is this new Spartacus?) The reluctant revolutionary in Victor Hugo's novel *Bug Jargal,* however, and the defeatist and suicidal protagonists of Anselmo Suárez y Romero *Francisco* and José Tanco y Bosmeniel's '*Petrona y Rosalía*' (all 'antislavery' works), bear little resemblance to the reality of the Saint Domingue rebels described by C. L. R. James as *The Black Jacobins.* As suggested previously, the image of a Toussaint L'Ouverture and like insurgents did not appeal to the literary imagination of the Delmontine circle. Wedgewood-like supplication, rather, is what is going to characterize the *persona* of Juan Francisco Manzano as he fashions the personal and racial self most likely to promote sympathy from his colleagues, and eventual liberation.

Manzano's first editor, Richard Madden, expressed the opinion in 1840, that the autobiography conveyed 'the most perfect picture of Cuban slavery,' because it was 'so full and faithful in its details.'[47] Madden's observation alludes, presumably, to the verisimilitude of the document as it relates to Manzano's lived experiences. It also alerts us to the metatextual management by the writer, of his persona as he develops it. Much critical discussion of the *Autobiografía,* in its appreciation of Manzano as a representative or generic Black/slave, has bypassed an engagement with the subtleties attendant to the racial self with which he presents us. This section of the essay proposes that colonial determinants surrounding caste, class, and writing, complicate a final appreciation of Manzano's text, and that the subject's representation of himself as a 'mulato entre negros' (mulatto among blacks), and among Whites, one might add, are important to the fullest understanding of the *Autobiografía.*

When Manzano the poet confronts the occasion of the public and unerasable inscription of the self that is implied by Del Monte's request for the autobiography, an inevitable tension becomes evident. This tension derives from the fact that the relative autonomy and distancing afforded by the lyric voice in his previously published work,[48] would be lost due to the heightened self-referentiality of the autobiographic mode. More importantly, as an enslaved person, the multiple dimensions of Manzano's victimization would necessarily claim precedence in an autobiographical relation. As a writer 'testifying' to the grave injustices and brutality of the colonial regimen of slavery (and one in the hope of being rescued from its clutches), extreme care would therefore be required in the fashioning of his story. On the one hand, the manner of its telling should not alienate his benefactor and literary ally the White patrician Del Monte.[49] On the other, its 'accusatory' contents could arouse the anger of real and potential enemies in the planter class and among the colonial authorities.

The question of literary censorship in Cuba and particularly Manzano's self-censorship as it pertains to the autobiography, has been addressed in many studies. The fact that Manzano's primary victimizer, Marchioness of Prado Ameno, was still alive and influential; the repressive policy of the colonial authorities; and the slave's dependence upon his benefactor for his freedom, have all been pointed out. What has not received comparable attention, perhaps, is the way in which all these factors in combination impact upon the narrative strategy of Manzano as autobiographical writer in a very specific socio-racial dynamic of power.

In addressing Del Monte, as well as an implied audience consisting of the other White upper class members of Del Monte's literary circle, and a potential European readership,[50] Manzano takes discursive recourse in a simple binary structure. His life story is divided into a happy period of childhood innocence, and a dramatically sad period beginning with the loss of this innocence; into good and caring masters on the one hand, and an obsessive and tyrannical mistress on the other. Underlying the narrative of the unhappy enslaved speaker also, is the premise that there are 'good' slaves. That is to say, model individuals who, like himself, deserve a better lot in life (i.e. emancipation). By implication, there is another category that does not.

In accordance with the latter, it is those virtues and values important to Manzano's imagined readership, which are stressed. We thus learn of the natural literary talents of his persona, and of his love of, and devotion to letters. He exemplifies this by stressing that at the age of ten, he could already recite Fray Luis de Granada's sermons by heart, imitate passages from French operas for his mistress's guests, and knew 'relasiones, loas, y entremeses, y teoría regular' (relations, short plays, interludes, and some [dramatic] theory) (*Obras,* 1972, 5).[51] When, under the Marchioness Del Prado's ownership, his creative impulse leads him to produce his own *décimas,* and he gives rein to his penchant for performance in front of the other servants and the children of the house, we are told that he is forced to withstand punishment (blows, isolation, a gagging, 13). Beyond this early composition and memorization of his own poems, devotion to the literary vocation is further underscored by the fact that he eventually painstakingly teaches himself to write, and perseveres in this endeavour in the face of his master's injunctions to the contrary.

His talents are not limited to the literary, as is pointed out repeatedly. Just as the rich and powerful applaud his childish flair for the theatrical and his orality while he lived at the Marchioness of Santa Ana's home, so do they his potential as a portrait painter. He is again congratulated and rewarded for his subsequent accomplishments as manservant, sicknurse, fishing companion, confectioner, and seamster of tunics, chemises, draperies, mattresses, trimmings, etc. when he grows older. It turns out to be entirely consistent with the self-centering and self-promotional rhetoric of the autobiography, that he should declare that he was a model slave at nineteen. At that time, he says, he was responsible and 'tenía cierto orgullito en saber cumplir mi obligasion, y no me gustaba que me mandasen las cosas dos veces ni q^(e.) me abochornaran p^(r.) trivialidades;' (34) (I was proud of knowing how to fulfill my duties, not liking to be told twice to do something or to be shamed for trivialities). This assiduousness, he stresses, is what allowed him to ascend in the slave hierarchy. It also gained him the envy of other house slaves, even of ones much older than he was.

To the extent that Manzano's narration foregrounds a deserving and multitalented self, the other Black slaves, with the exception of his family, are anonymous. They are a part of the background; a plurality to which he refers with the generic marker of the *negrada* (29). These slaves are generally identified only in association with a significant event, such as the accident in which Andrés (a *negro criollo*) dies (29), or when a stone thrown by a *moreno* accidentally wounds the protagonist (13). Their anonymity is hardly a rhetorical coincidence, however, since it is what allows his intelligence and his talent to stand out. Neither is it a coincidence that the speaker adheres closely to the colonial nomenclature of caste in describing them. His consistent reference to himself as a *mulato* or a *chinito* or a *mulatico* (eg. 36), with all the associations of 'pedigree' and upward socio-racial mobility inherent to the term, is quite conscious. It allows us to appreciate a distinction between the speaker and the aforementioned subjects, and especially the category referred to as *negros,* that is, the ones occupying the lowest rung of the socio-racial ladder. Manzano's projection of a self that is *different* from the rest of the slave body comes into sharpest focus, perhaps, in these references.

As putative member of a group of writers whose racial ideology associated intellectuality or *razón* (reason) with Whiteness, his own interests could be served in pointing to the distance between himself and the purported baseness of the *negros.* To the degree that his autobiography is a rhetorical construction designed to highlight his suffering to an imaginary White readership, and garner sympathy from them, it could be confrontational and counterproductive to associate that readership with the source of the cruelties that he details. Primary agency in his degradation (and that of his delicate, 'poetic' persona) is therefore often associated with the brutality of the Black males incorporated in the system of oppression. Hence he reminds us of the regularity with which they were the ones who administered the beatings: 'No pocas veses he sufrido p.ʳ la mano de un negro rigorosos asotes' (10) (More than a few times I have suffered vigorous floggings at the hands of a Black man).

When on the occasion of another of his unjust punishments his mother comes to his defense, and she is herself rebuffed and punished, attention is drawn to the four *negros* who manhandle her and hurl her to the ground prior to a whipping (16). And after the capon incident, his innocence and constantly evoked frailness make a sharp contrast with the cruelty of his punishment and his punishers. On that occasion it is the overseer, his assistant, and 'sinco negros' (five Black men, 28) who deliver the heartless thrashing. The role of the latter as 'executioners' is invoked in his relation of yet another incident of excessive punishment when he remarks; 'ya me esperaba un negro, aquien se me entregó' (20) (a Black man was already waiting for me, I was handed over to him). To the extent that the Black men, together with the overseers and the Marchioness are specified as the source of his misery, slavery as an institution recedes as the *raison d'être* of his unhappy con-

dition. Slavery's subjugation of a collective, of which the speaker forms a part, is also attenuated in the process of the relation. Indeed, one might even speak of a rhetorical tactic of scapegoating of the whip-wielding *negros,* as the victim seeks a place to locate blame, while highlighting the wretchedness of his own condition.[52]

Following the binary structure of his story, the early years of his childhood in which he was the object of affection and the center of attention in the home of an apparently doting Marchioness of Santa Ana, are evoked in glowing terms. He refers to them poetically as a 'jardin de bellísimas flores, *una serie de felisidades*' (6) (garden of very beautiful flowers, a series of joys). However, his eventual transferal to the power of the tyrannical Marchioness of Del Prado, and to the rural plantation of El Molino where he says 'la verdadera istoria de mi vida' (9) (the real story of my life) began, does not only signal a radical change in fortune. Reference to the rupture that begins with Santa Ana's death as the period in which his 'real story' begins, also serves the metatextual function of enhancing the degree to which his destiny has changed. It functions as a rhetorical platform upon which to a stress the regularity with which he is now beaten and imprisoned in the dark and forbidding coal shed (two to three times a week, 9), and the tears and nosebleeds which have become his daily lot (22).

The more scandalous of these events relating to his cruel and unjust punishments include the infamous *peseta* incident for which he is condemned to a nine-day period of fifty lashes daily (they are eventually not delivered, 20). They also include the incident of the crushed geranium for which he is placed in the stocks and eventually sodomized,[53] and the incident of the misplaced capon for which he is almost eaten alive by dogs and does receive the *novenario* or nine days of punishment. All contribute to the image of powerlessness and abjection in the speaker. If we can regard this autobiographical enunciation of the pathetic subject as a kind of 'open letter' to a more or less unknown public, it is only in his private letters to his benefactor Del Monte that we find a comparable quality of pathos.

In this regard Sylvia Molloy has characterized as 'excessive' Manzano's expressions of gratitude to Del Monte as literary mentor (1991, 39). She highlights, as do Friol and Mullen, the personal and socio-racial chasm between them expressed in Manzano's likening of himself to a leaf exposed to the inclemency of nature, which finally finds asylum under the 'robusto tronco' (robust trunk) that is represented by Del Monte.[54] Friol even speaks of Manzano's infantilization as he prostrates himself in his letters to Del Monte, as if the latter, a younger man, had become a surrogate father (1977, 57).

Undoubtedly there is a mix of the 'strategic' and the 'temperamental' in Manzano's posture. But it is important to point out that Manzano's abjection is not total, and that the system may not have beaten the rebelliousness out of him, as Molloy's rebuttal of Jackson's argument suggests (1991, 40).[55] There is more than enough evidence of a continuing rebellious strain beneath Manzano's meek exterior in his two escape attempts. It is also there in his confrontation of the terrible *marquesa* with a demand for a letter of *coartación,* and in the times when he drops the mask of submissiveness and pounces like a lion in defense of his mother's honour (eg.16). Like the very act of learning to write, in defiance of orders to the contrary, his management of his persona in the ***Autobiografía*** offers evidence of a dogged determination to fight back.[56] If we juxtapose his hesitation and apprehension at the thought of writing his autobiography, with his decision to write a fictional account that would tell all once he achieved his freedom and felt safe enough to do so, the meekness of the persona in the autobiography becomes clearer.[57] So does the writer's manipulation of his reader(s) through this persona. As Sonia Labrador-Rodríguez observes, the writing in Manzano's ***Autobiografía,*** is neither spontaneous nor naïve (1996, 15).

If my analysis of Manzano's assumption and portrayal of a racial selfhood which sees the *negro* as Other is correct, it follows that he is not as ambivalent about his racial identity as some critics have been wont to assume (eg. Molloy 1991, 45). His avoidance of Blackness in the relation, and his espousal of the cultural markers of Whiteness discussed above, point to a conscious constitution of self as a racial subject; one that is in strict accordance with the dictates of the dominant ideology of Whitening. It is important to remember that the ethic of *pureza de sangre* that evolved in tandem with national consolidation in Renaissance Spain, produced a Manicheistic taxonomy of race that grew ever more complex in the colonies to the degree that racial pedigree could be associated with social, political, and economic privilege. The gradual evolution of seventy-one different categories of certificates of Whiteness by 1795 (cédulas de gracias al sacar), to 'legitimize' access of the mestizo castes to such privilege is but one example of the crown's role in the reification of race in the colonies.[58]

Regarding the ideological aspect of the race question, Althusser's proposal that people work unconsciously or 'by themselves' (1986, 248), in the way they assume subjectivity in a given social order, may explain Manzano's sense of difference in relation to an unlettered collective of *negros.* The writer's insistence on his own specificity as *mulato* in the autobiography, however, is quite conscious. Manzano, in other words, is clear about what he is not, racially speaking.[59] His access to and use of, the medium of writing, therefore, can hardly be seen

as an abandonment of his 'own,' that is 'African' frame of reference, as William Luis suggests (65). He could not abandon an ethnic identity that he had never assumed. His emphasis on his inbetweenness, i.e., what he 'is' within the racial order, is what is important. This recognition may also be taken as an awareness of the relative fluidity of colonial racial barriers, and an indication of his intention to negotiate racial identity vis-à-vis an overarching White Subjectivity.

Key to his self-definition would be his emphasis on the elevated status of his parents as household slaves. (His mother is a *criada de razón* and his father is the *primer criado* of the house 46).[60] Noteworthy in this regard also, is the fact that the Marchioness of Justiz Santa Ana claimed him as the 'el niño de su bejez' (4) (child of her old age), often displacing his biological parents as a source both of parental affection and authority. He, in turn, recognized her in these terms calling her 'mama mia' (5) (my mother), thereby closing the Althusserian circle of mutual inter-subjectual recognition. As surrogate 'son' of the marchioness, he reminds us, he spent more time in her arms than in those of his own mother (4), and would often throw a tantrum if he was brought back home from school too late for his daily visits with her. Even his father's attempts at disciplining such unruly behavior met with Santa Ana's disfavour, and it was the older man who required an intermediary to return to the marchioness's favour (5).

The uncommon process of socialization and the formation of a socio-racial consciousness in Manzano the slave, is further detailed in the fact that his godparents are White aristocrats, and that he attends school and plays with the marchioness's grandchildren. He also notes that he is forbidden from playing with little Black children by his father, and by doña Joaquina, a member of the extended White family to which he belonged (44). His juxtaposition of Joaquina's personal attention to his hair and dress and her vigilance that he avoid contact with other *negritos,* while she herself treated him 'como a un niño' (8) (like a niño), further confirms a de facto treatment beyond his socio-racial condition of which he makes us aware. One might recall here, that *niño* in plantation terminology, referred to White children of the planter class.

Whether or not Manzano really meant to insinuate by the latter statement that he was a treated as a White child by Joaquina, what is evident is his sense of the availability of White privilege, and his insertion of self into that world of power. His recurrent use of the metaphor of the family (i.e., he 'belongs to' or is 'part of' a White family), is therefore revealing both in the sense of this strategic subjective identification with Whiteness, and a skilful manipulation of the system of *padrinazgo* that characterized the patrician universe of the colonial plantation. As the text indicates, his appeals to influential intermediaries or *padrinos* (godfathers) are many, given the frequency with which he gets into trouble. Such occasions all too often derive from the contradictions inherent to his being a slave who is aware that social and racial privilege is negotiable, and that the ideological imperatives concomitant to his identity as slave, are subject to rupture.[61]

Bearing in mind Manzano's insight into the relation between power and racial definition, and his own assumed subject position in this regard, it comes as little surprise in the end, that it is the renewed threat of being reduced to the lowest common denominator of enslavement, which fuels his resolve to escape. The final pages that describe his punishment at taking an unauthorized bath, his accidental breakage of the water barrel, and the impending banishment to the El Molino plantation all illustrate this question. Having already been shorn and stripped of the outer vestiges of his privilege—shoes, clothing—it is the observation by a free servant that he was being treated worse than any *negro bozal* that deals the final blow to his dignity. The prospect of returning alone and unsupported among the field slaves (i.e. of being a 'mulato entre negros' 44, mulatto among Blacks), along with the dangers posed by the Don Saturnino the sadistic overseer, wreaked havoc on his vivid imagination.

If Manzano's negotiation of race serves to reveal the lack of fixity to the concept, paradoxically, it is his success in securing freedom that confirms racism's rigidity in structuring social power. As a theoretically free person or *liberto,* his vulnerability as a Black male outside of the protection and patronage of the plantation 'family' structure becomes tragically evident when he is accused of being involved in the alleged Escalera conspiracy of 1844. Months of imprisonment, torture, and interrogation between 1844 and 1845 must have impressed upon him that literary passing was not enough to place him beyond the clutches of a racialized system of oppression that saw every Black person as a possible conspirator in the supposed uprising. I propose that this is a major factor in his silence after Escalera. Manzano may have read the code on race and written according to its dictates, but as Ivan Schulman his most recent editor observes, he failed to 'grasp the limitations colonial society placed on members of his class and race' (1996, 12). To the extent that his autobiographical persona, as intellectual, ambitious, artistic, and culturally 'assimilated,' represented a vehicle for ideological crossover, therefore, its success was limited. His benefactor Domingo del Monte writing from Paris, expressed dominant racial ideology most succinctly in 1845 when he dismissed both Manzano and Plácido, another *mestizo* poet, as 'dos poetas negros.'[62]

The analysis of Juan Francisco Manzano's autobiography affords us a unique example of the politics of race in a Latin American colonial setting. The place of the document in the Latin American scribal tradition is undoubtedly important. While writing may have been one of his tools for assimilation and upward socio-racial mobility, it is clear that for Manzano, citizenship in the republic of letters required more than being a gifted creative writer or having friends in high places. It is perhaps ironic that more than two decades after responding to the suggestion that as a 'mulatico fino' he had no place among 'negros bozales,' this is precisely what his destiny was. The unified and unmitigated reaction of the plantocracy to the supposed Escalera threat reduced him firstly to the status of *bozal* (in the sense of 'he who does not signify'[63]), and secondly to the status of *negro* (in the sense of 'he who has no political significance'). Unlike thousands of slaves and Black Cubans who lost their lives as a result of the Escalera persecution, Manzano did have a White lawyer (another *padrino*) to defend him.[64] His subsequent invisibility and silence as a writer after Escalera suggest, however, that what he now occupied was a zone of existential liminality in which he was neither slave nor free.

Notes

1. See Bueno (1986: 173), Luis (1990: 39), and Leante (1976: 186).

2. Luis (1990), for example, recognizes his status as an originator in Cuban foundational literature and Labrador-Rodríguez (1996) recognizes his assertiveness and intellect.

3. Beckles illustrates this point by citing Robin Blackburn's *The Overthrow of Colonial Slavery,* which evokes Thomas Clarkson's seminal anti-trade essay of 1808 and asserts that, 'it has been common to identify the origins of anti-slavery within the works of the learned men who first published critiques of slavery or of the slave trade' (1988, 8).

4. This and subsequent translations are the responsibility of the writer.

5. See also Luis's 'La novela antiesclavista: Texto, contexto y escritura,' (1981: 114).

6. The term is taken from Paul Gilroy's *The Black Atlantic: Modernity and Double Consciousness* (1993). I am using the term 'Black' in its contemporary sense as a generic referent to people of African descent. My use of terms like *mulato* and *pardo* later in the essay will recognize the connotations of the Latin American colonial racial taxonomy.

7. See Gordon Lewis's remarks on antislavery ideology in this regard (1983: 172-73).

8. See *La conspiración de Aponte,* (1963: 37).

9. One recipient of this document, a businessman by the name of Pablo Serra, promptly turned it over

to the Captain General of the island, the Marquis of Someruelos (Franco, 1974: 175).

10. 'Malé' is a generic term referring to enslaved Muslims in Brazil. They were primarily of Nagô ethnic origin, but included Jejes, Hausas, Tapas, and Bornus, Reis (1993: 97). I am indebted to Matt Childs of the University of Austin, Texas, for pointing out to me the role of writing in the Bahia rebellion and the Aponte conspiracy.

11. See Olsen (1998: 57) in this regard.

12. See Thompson, 'The Berbice Revolt, 1763-64.' Thompson indicated that the letters were written by Prins, an African ex-slave, and various Whites and captives of mixed ancestry.

13. Castañeda (1995) documents the appeals of Black women in nineteenth century Cuba against sexual predation by their masters, or their refusal to honour the agreed price for the women's freedom.

14. This is the period that began in 1792 when colonial statesman Francisco de Arango y Pareño, in his *Discurso sobre la Agricultura de la Habana y medios de fomentarla,* issued his call for the sugar industry in Cuba to be developed to take the place of Saint Domingue in the world market. See Benítez-Rojo (1980: 10), and Luis (1990: 2). It was an initiative that brought an unprecedented number of African captives to the Caribbean colony. Franco details the link between the 1792 initiative and the spate of rebellions in the latter part of the decade (1974: 133-34).

15. John Beverly in *Against Literature* (1993) argues for a de-emphasizing of the perceived value of the literary text as an artifact of high culture. His premises would permit us to appreciate the historical specificity of subaltern modes of resistance.

16. Jensen (1988) discusses the severity of press censorship in nineteenth-century Cuba, especially in the 1820s.

17. The full title of Saco's paper is 'Justa Defensa de la Academia cubana de la Literatura contra los ataques que se le han dado en el Diario de La Habana, desde el 12 hasta el 23 de abril del presente año, escrito por Don José Saco e impresa en Nueva Orleans por Mr. St.-Romes, oficina de El Courier año de 1834.' The paper was actually published in Matanzas, notwithstanding the reference to New Orleans in the title. See Saco (1963: 25).

18. Saco (1963: 52).

19. Saco, 'Análisis por don José Antonio Saco de una obra sobre el Brasil, intitulada, Notices of Brazil in 1828 and 1829 by Rev. Walsh author of a Journey from Constantinople, etc.' hereinafter cited as 'Análisis,' 202.

20. Thomas reports that '63 slavers [left Havana] in 1828, 45 in 1829, and 80 in 1835' (1998, 200). The decade of the 1830s recorded the highest imports in the history of Cuban slavery (181,600), Schmidt-Nowara (1999: 4).

21. See his 'Estado de la población blanca y de color de la isla de Cuba en 1839' (1929, 1: 158-159).

22. The list, currently regarded by critics as the core of Cuban antislavery writing, includes Manzano's *Autobiografía* and some of his poems and *Francisco: El ingenio, o las delicias del campo,* by Anselmo Suárez y Romero, among other items. *Francisco* was finally published in 1880. Félix Tanco y Bosmeniel's story 'Petrona y Rosalía' (1839) was also a product of the *tertulia.* Antonio Zambrana's *El negro Francisco* (1875) was inspired by Suárez's novel. See Adriana Lewis Galanes, 'El Album de Domingo del Monte (Cuba, 1838/39).'

23. Letter from José Zacaraías González del Valle to Anselmo Suárez y Romero, September 5, 1838. Reproduced in *La vida literaria en Cuba (1836-1840),* 57.

24. The Saint Domingue rebellion started in 1791. At the time it was France's richest colony and the leading producer of cane sugar in the world. Independence was declared in 1804 when the country's name was changed to Haiti.

25. See Luis 1990: 3-81.

26. González del Valle (1938: 5). 'They deserve to be known by present generations, because they speak to us of a splendid era in our literary history, which reveals the generous sentiments and advanced ideas of those young writers'.

27. See Luis's *Literary Bondage,* 28-30 for example.

28. Franco details the frequency of uprisings in the 1790s and their bloody suffocation (1974: 133-34).

29. The essay in question is 'La supresión del tráfico de esclavos africanos en la isla de Cuba, examinada con relación a su agricultura y a su seguridad, por don José Antonio Saco.' It is a reworking of a previous essay, published in 1837, titled: 'Mi primera pregunta. ¿ La abolición del comercio de esclavos africanos arruinará o atrasará la agricultura cubana? Dedícala a los hacendados de la isla de Cuba su compatriota José Antonio Saco. See Saco (1982).

30. Revealed to Madden in an interview with Del Monte. See Mullen (1981: 135).

31. Cited in Cepero Bonilla (1976: 53).

32. Tanco seemed to be the most radical of the group in this regard. He argued for a realist approach a la Balzac to writing by the *tertulia,* and for stories that would include Black characters. Even so, in his exposure of the cynicism and cruelty of the master class in the successive father and son violation of a slave mother and daughter, his implied protest in 'Petrona y Rosalía' doesn't allow for more than a defeatist portrayal of the main Black characters.

33. 'No será dudoso, que después de habernos constituido en nación independiente, formaremos, más tarde o temprano, una parte integrante en tan poderosos estados.' (There will be no doubt, that after constituting ourselves as an independent nation, that we, sooner or later, will form a part of such powerful States). Cited in Cepero Bonilla (1976: 193). See also Murray (1999: 111, 117) Thomas (1998: 100).

34. Murray cites Everett in a letter to President Adams asserting that it was 'the policy and duty of the United States to endeavor to obtain possession of Cuba' (1999: 118).

35. Enildo García identifies Henry Longfellow, George Ticknor, William Prescott, and Washington Irving among these, and refers to them as Del Monte's 'Harvard Connection' (1993: 69).

36. 'Cartas de Domingo del Monte a Alexander H. Everett,' Enildo A. García, (1989: 117).

37. Will the American people watch impassively, as one who contemplates the development of a play in the theatre, while the astute Albion curiously and ably elaborates the loss of the largest of the Antilles? I think not. García (1989: 113).

38. Del Monte had been under suspicion of involvement in the Escalera conspiracy of 1844, a never proven event used by Captain General O'Donnell as an opportunity to purge Cuba of foreign abolitionist agitators like David Turnbull, as well as those he considered potential troublemakers in Cuba. The poet Plácido was tried and executed, Manzano was imprisoned, and hundreds of others died under torture or were exiled. See Murray (1980: 159-180).

39. See, for example, Bueno (1986: 50), González del Valle (1938: 11), Luis (1990: 36).

40. See *Domingo del Monte ¿Quién fue? (1986:* 9), also 'La lucha contra la esclavitud y su expresión literaria' (1986), and 'Las ideas literarias de Domingo Del Monte,' (1954).

41. See Henri Grégoire's *De la littérature des nègres, ou Recherches sur leurs facultés intellectuelles, leurs qualités morales et leur littérature; suives de Notices sur la vie et les ouvrages des Nègres qui sont distingués dans les Sciences, les Lettres et les Arts* (1808).

42. Lisandro Otero observes that by the decade of the 1860s, this clan owned 40 sugar mills, 15,000 slaves, railways, houses of credit, banks and shipping lines, as well as 10 titles of nobility (1990: 724). Del Monte's estate, the 'Ceres,' was located at Cárdenas Thomas (1998: 207).

43. See Michael Foot and Isaac Kramnic, eds, The *Thomas Paine Reader* (1987: 12, 34).

44. Among the Negrophobe writings Grégoire critiques are Jamaican planter-historian Edward Long's *A History of Jamaica,* David Hume's 'Of National Characters,' and Thomas Jefferson's *Notes on the State of Virginia.*

45. James Walvin (1982: 60).

46. Seymour Drescher (1982: 31).

47. Mullen (1998: 79). The document has had many editions and corresponding modifications. See Luis (1990: 83-100) for a fuller discussion of these.

48. *Cantos a Lesbia* 1821, and *Flores pasageras* (sic 1830).

49. Manzano's freedom was purchased with a collection raised by the Delmontine *tertulia* between 1835 and July of 1836. His correspondence with Del Monte of June 25 and September 29, 1835 suggests that the first part of the autobiography was completed in the course of the year preceding his freedom. A further letter dated 16 October 1834 reveals Manzano's frustration and despair over his deferred liberation and the lack of control over his intellectual property. In the letter reproduced by Franco, he confides to Del Monte: 'Si algun dia quisiere Dios que pueda ablar a smd: de serca, berá smd: que no he perdido el juisio tal vez por que no ha llegado mi ora, mucho he sufrido en mi interior' (If one day God willing I had a chance to speak with you: in private, your Grace would see: that I have not lost my mind perhaps because my time has not come yet, I have suffered greatly within' (78).

50. Manzano already knew that Del Monte was sending his poetry to Europe as is apparent in his letter dated 11th December 1834. He had no reason to believe that this other document would be any different, as happened eventually.

51. Quotations from Manzano's autobiography will be taken from José Luciano Franco's 1972 edition of his *Obras.* The translations from the autobiography are my responsibility.

52. In similar fashion, not wanting to name his real victimizers, he often places blame on himself and

sees his punishment as a result of his lack of religious devotion (86).

53. Robert Richmond Ellis makes an entirely plausible argument regarding the homoerotic abuse that Manzano may have suffered at the hands of the sadistic don Saturnino and the veil he draws over such events in his relation. Ellis's reading of Manzano's uninhibited affection for his younger brother Florencio (in the poem 'Un sueño'), as an expression of 'reciprocal homoeroticism' and 'racial solidarity' (433), is not quite as persuasive. An expression of love and empathy for parents and siblings, as in Manzano's case, is hardly to be confused with an intention to vindicate all of the enslaved.

54. See his poem 'A D. Domingo Del Monte,' in Friol (1977: 96-97).

55. Jackson has argued that Manzano was playing up the image of the 'docile slave' and that Del Monte was stage-managing his autobiography from above (1979: 28-30).

56. In this regard it is interesting that he consistently rationalizes and or justifies his misdemeanors to his readers.

57. See Jackson (1979: 29), Williams (1994: 27).

58. See Frederick P. Bowser, 'Colonial Spanish America' (1972: 46).

59. Post revolutionary Cuban critic Roberto Friol takes care to remind us that Manzano was not a 'negro puro' (pure Black) stressing that he was recorded as a 'pardo' (brown) in his publications, on his marriage licence, and in the official documents of the Escalera trial in which he became involved (1977: 153).

60. I.e. she was endowed with 'reason' and he was the 'head servant'. Schulman indicates in a footnote that Manzano had underlined the reference to 'razón' in his manuscript, in relation to his mother (1996: 44). Friol intimates also that Manzano had clarified for Madden, that his maternal grandparents were 'mulato' and 'negro' (49). Manzano's concern for registering socio-racial distinction (value) is further evident in the way he speaks of his second wife to Del Monte in his letter of 11th December 1834. Delia 'es parda libre, hija de blanco, linda como un grano de oro de pies a cabeza' (*Obras,* 82) (is free, her father is White, and from head to feet she is as pretty as a grain of gold).

61. Manzano's insight here might be related to Althusser's observation that; 'all ideology represents in its necessarily imaginary distortion not of the existing relations of production (and of the other relations that derive from them), but above all the (imaginary) relationship of individuals to the relations of production and the relations that derive from them' (242).

62. Not only does ideology involve the 'subjection to the Subject [by the subject],' it also involves the 'mutual recognition of subjects and Subject,' according to Althusser (1986: 248).

63. One of the Peninsular Spanish meanings for 'bozal' is 'muzzle.' I'm indebted to Ed Stanton of the University of Kentucky for pointing this out.

64. The lawyer appointed to him was Julián María Infanzón. His letter dated 5th October 1844, written to Del Monte's mother-in-law, Doña Rosa Alfonso, from the prison at Belén, shows the stark reality of being under the political gun. Besides the hunger and material deprivation arising out of months of imprisonment, Manzano registers his anguish at his inability to find a godfather (*compadre*) for his baby daughter. His complaint raises the interesting question as to whether his erstwhile associates of the Delmontine circle would have accepted this role had the immediate political situation been less volatile; especially since it would have meant recognizing him as a part of the paternal order, and free.

References

Althusser, L. (1986) 'Ideology and Ideological State Apparatuses.' In *Critical Theory Since 1965,* eds. H. Adams and L. Searle, pp. 239-251. University Presses of Florida, Tallahassee.

Beckles, H. (1988) 'Caribbean Anti-Slavery: The Self-Liberation Ethos of Enslaved Blacks.' *The Journal of Caribbean History,* 22, 1&2, 1-19.

Beckles, H. (1985) 'Emancipation by War or Law? Wilberforce and the 1816 Barbados Slave Rebellion.' In *Abolition and its Aftermath: The Historical Context, 1790—1916,* ed. D. Richardson, pp. 80-104, Frank Cass and Company, London.

Benítez-Rojo, A. (1980) 'Power/Sugar/Literature: Toward a Reinterpretation of Cubanness.' *Cuban Studies,* 16, 1-13.

Benítez-Rojo, A. (1994) ¿Cómo narrar la nación? El círculo de Domingo Delmonte y el surgimiento de la novela cubana.' *Cuadernos Americanos,* 45, 3, 103-128.

Beverley, J. (1993) *Against Literature.* University of Minnesota Press, Minneapolis.

Bowser, F. (1972) 'Colonial Spanish America.' In *Neither Slave nor Free: The Freedmen of African Descent in the Slave Societies of the New World,* eds. D. W. Cohen and J. P. Greene, pp. 19-58, The Johns Hopkins University Press, Maryland.

Bueno, S. (1954) *Las ideas literarias de Domingo Delmonte.* Editorial Hercules, Havana.

Bueno, S. (1986) 'La lucha contra la esclavitud y su expresión literaria,' *Unión,* 1, 48-56.

Bueno, S. (1986) *¿Quién fue? Domingo del Monte.* Ediciones Unión, Havana.

Castañeda, D. (1995) 'The Female Slave in Cuba during the first half of the Nineteenth Century.' In *Engendering History: Caribbean Women in Historical Perspective.* Eds. V. Shepherd, B. Brereton, B. Bailey, pp 141-154. St. Martin's Press, New York.

Cepero Bonilla, R. (1976) *Azúcar y abolición.* Editorial crítica, Barcelona.

Del Monte, D. 'Estado de la población blanca y de color de la isla de Cuba en 1839,' in *Escritos,* 2 vols., ed. J. A. Castro, pp. 144-159, vol.1, Cultural, Havana.

Drescher, S. (1982) 'Public Opinion and the Destruction of British Colonial Slavery,' in *Slavery and British Society, 1776-1846,* ed. Walvin, J, pp. 22-48. Louisiana State University Press, Baton Rouge.

Ellis, R. R. (1998) 'Reading through the Veil of Juan Francisco Manzano: From Homoerotic Violence to the Dream of a Homoracial Bond.' *PMLA,* 113, 422-435.

Franco, J. L. (1963) *La conspiración de Aponte.* Publicaciones del archivo nacional, Havana.

Franco, J. L. (1974) 'La conspiración de Aponte, 1812,' pp. 125-190, in *Ensayos históricos,* Editorial de Ciencias Sociales, Havana.

Friol, R. *Suite para Juan Francisco Manzano.* Havana: Editorial arte y literatura, 1977.

García, E. A. (1989) 'Cartas de Domingo del Monte a Alexander H. Everett.' *Revista de Literatura Cubana,* 7, 13, 105-148.

García, E. A. (1993) 'Romanticismo antillano: Domingo del Monte y The Harvard Connection.' *Círculo: Revista de Cultura,* 22, 68-78.

Gilroy, P. (1993) *The Black Atlantic: Modernity and Double Consciousness,* Harvard University Press, Cambridge.

González del Valle, G. (1938) *La vida literaria en Cuba.* Publicaciones de la Secretaría de Educación, Havana.

Goody, J. (1986) 'Writing, Religion, and Revolt in Bahia.' *Visible Language,* 20, 3, 319-345.

Grégoire, H. (1996) *On the Cultural Achievements of Negroes,* Translated with notes and an introduction by T. Cassirer & Jean-François Brière. University of Massachusetts Press, Amherst.

Jackson, R. (1979) *Black Writers in Latin America.* University of New Mexico Press, Albuquerque.

James, C. L. R. (1963) *The Black Jacobins: Toussaint L'Ouverture and the Saint Domingue Revolution.* Vintage Books, New York.

Jensen, L. R. (1988) *Children of Colonial Despotism: Press, Politics, and Culture in Cuba, 1790-1840,* University of South Florida Press, Tampa.

Labrador-Rodríguez, S. (1996) 'La intelectualidad negra en Cuba en el siglo xix: El caso de Manzano.' *Revista Iberoamericana* 62, 74, 13-25.

Leante, C. (1976) 'Dos obras antiesclavistas cubanas.' *Cuadernos Americanos* 4, 175-188.

Lewis, G. (1983) *Main Currents in Caribbean Thought.* Johns Hopkins University Press, Baltimore.

Lewis Galanes, A. (1988) 'El álbum de Domingo del Monte,' *Cuadernos Americanos,* 451-52, 255-265.

Luis, W. (1990) *Literary Bondage: Slavery in Cuban Narrative.* University of Texas Press, Austin.

Luis, W. (1981) 'La novela antiesclavista: Texto, contexto y escritura,' *Cuadernos Americanos,* 234, 3, 103-116.

Manzano, J. F. (1972) *Obras,* ed. J.L.Franco. Instituto cubano del libro, Havana.

Manzano, J. F. (1996) *The Autobiography of a Slave/ Autobiografía de un esclavo,* ed. I. A. Schulman. Wayne State University Press, Detroit.

Molloy, S. (1991) *At Face Value: Autobiographical Writing in Spanish America.* Cambridge: Cambridge University Press.

Mullen, E. (1981) ed. *The Life and Poems of a Cuban Slave: Juan Francisco Manzano 1797-1854.* Archon Books, Connecticut.

Mullen, E. (1988) *Afro-Cuban Literature: Critical Junctures.* Greenwood Press, Westport CT.

Murray, D. (1980) *Odious Commerce: Britain, Spain and the Abolition of the Cuban Slave Trade.* Cambridge University Press, Cambridge.

Murray, D. (1999) 'The Slave Trade, Slavery and Cuban Independence,' *Slavery and Abolition,* 20, 3, 106-126.

Olsen, M. M. (1998) '*Negros horros* and *Cimarrones* on the Legal Frontiers of the Caribbean: Accessing the African Voice in Colonial Spanish American Texts.' *Research in African Literatures,* 29, 4, 52-72.

Otero, L. (1990) 'Delmonte y la cultura de la sacarocracia,' *Revista Iberoamericana,* 152-53, 56, 723-731.

Paine, T. (1987) *The Thomas Paine Reader,* eds. Foot, M, and Kramnic, I. Penguin Books, New York.

Rama, A. (1984) *La ciudad letrada.* Ediciones del norte, Hanover.

Reis, J. J. (1993) *Slave Rebellion in Brazil: The Muslim Uprising of 1835 in Bahia.* Trans. A Brakel. The Johns Hopkins University Press, Baltimore.

Saco, J. A. (1963) 'Justa defensa de la Academia Cubana de Literatura, contra los ataques que se le han dado en el Diario de La Habana, desde el 12 hasta el 23 de abril del presente año, escrita por Don José Antonio Saco e impresa en Nueva Orleans por Mr. St.-Romes, oficina de El Courier año de 1834,' pp 25-67, in *Colección de papeles científicos, históricos, políticos y de otros ramos sobre la isla de Cuba ya publicados, ya ineditados.* Editorial nacional de Cuba, Havana.

Saco, J. A. (1982) 'Análisis por don José Antonio Saco de una obra sobre el Brasil, intitulada, Notices of Brazil in 1828 and 1829 by Rev. Walsh author of a Journey from Constantinople, etc. (Noticias del Brasil en 1828 y 1829 por el presbítero R. Walsh, autor de un viaje a Constantinopla, etc.) in *José Antonio Saco: Acerca de la esclavitud y su historia,* ed. E. Torres-Cuevas, and A. Sorhegui, 173-205, Editorial de ciencias sociales, Havana.

Saco, J. A. (1982) 'La supresión del tráfico de esclavos africanos en la isla de Cuba, examinada con relación a su agricultura y a su seguridad, por don José Antonio Saco,' in *José Antonio Saco: Acerca de la esclavitud y su historia,* ed. E. Torres-Cuevas, and A. Sorhegui, pp. 208-256, Editorial de ciencias sociales, Havana.

Schmidt-Nowara, C. (1999) *Empire and Antislavery: Spain, Cuba, and Puerto Rico, 1833-1874.* University of Pittsburgh Press, Pittsburgh.

Suarez y Romero, A. (1974) *Francisco: El ingenio o las delicias del campo.* Editorial de arte y literatura, Havana.

Tanco y Bosmeniel, F. (1975) 'Petrona y Rosalía,' in *Cuentos cubanos del siglo XIX,* ed. S. Bueno, pp. 103-131, Editorial Arte y Literatura, Havana.

Thomas, H. (1998) *Cuba: Or the Pursuit of Freedom.* Da Capo Press, New York (first. published 1971).

Thompson, A. (1998) 'The Berbice Revolt, 1763-64.' In *Themes in African-Guyanese History,* eds. W. McGowan, J. Rose, D. Granger, pp. 77-106. Free Press, Georgetown.

Walvin, J. Ed. (1982) 'The Propaganda of Anti-Slavery,' in *Slavery and British Society, 1776-1846,* pp. 49-68. Louisiana State University Press, Baton Rouge.

Williams, E. (1994) *Capitalism and Slavery.* University of North Carolina Press, Chapel Hill.

Williams, Lorna Valerie. (1994) *The Representation of Slavery in Cuban Fiction.* University of Missouri Press, Missouri.

Zambrana, A. (1979) *El negro Francisco.* Editorial letras cubanas, Havana.

Jerome Branche (essay date 2005)

SOURCE: Branche, Jerome. "Sub-*poena:* Slavery, Subjection, and Sufferation in Juan Francisco Manzano." In *Nineteenth-Century Literature Criticism,* Vol. 155, pp. 331-40. Farmington Hills, Mich.: Thomson Gale, 2005.

[*In the following essay, Branche discusses the conditions under which Manzano suffered as a slave and how his memoir is a particularly revealing commentary on the master-slave relationship.*]

Spare me, & I will confess anything you say.

Escalera prisoner.

Alsopp's *Dictionary of Caribbean English Usage* defines "sufferation" as "prolonged, intense suffering" (538). The neologism refers to a life-state, and its denotative and connotative charge in everyday use highlights the difference between its cognates in standard English, "suffering" and "long-suffering," even as it reminds us of the process of Caribbean linguistic creolization.[1] Describing the life of nineteenth century Cuban slave Juan Francisco Manzano as a life of sufferation thus seems to the point and appropriate. This is especially so given the fact that the psychological imprint of slavery has shown itself capable of assuming, as African-American critic Hortense Spillers suggests, a transgenerational valency. It is what makes slavery's legacy still palpable in the contemporary specter of despair and poverty as much in America's neglected black communities, as in the Caribbean region or other areas of the slave diaspora.[2]

Similarly, I would like to draw attention to the fact that the term "subpoena," as it will be used in this paper, has little effective bearing on its everyday usage by which a legal writ summons someone to appear in court or face the consequences. Ironically the compulsory invocation of a hypothetical defendant in a hypothetical case in which a slave like Manzano might act as accuser and his abusive slavemasters as defendants remits us to a situation that was highly improbable, in spite of the inherent flexibility of the slave regimen. Notwithstanding the historical and present day apologists of Latin American slave law, slave masters as a whole never felt themselves beholden to legal restrictions on their conduct.[3] My interest, rather, is in stressing the primordial content of the term *poena,* in its etymological reference to punishment, and the condition that one might imagine for a subject, who, like Manzano, lived under its thrall; that is, sub-*poena*.

Juan Francisco Manzano (1797-1853),[4] gained his freedom in 1836 as a result of a collection organized by his principal benefactor Domingo Del Monte, Cuban patriot and man of letters. A neo-classicist by orientation, Del Monte was also his literary mentor, as he was for a generation of aspiring young writers in 1830s Cuba. Manzano published two collections of poems *Cantos a Lesbia* in 1821, and *Flores pasageras* (sic 1830), and with the moral, aesthetic, and material support of Del Monte who he met in 1830, placed several poems in Cuban literary magazines over the next decade.[5] Effectively it was the upper class liberal, Del Monte, who commissioned Manzano, in 1835, to write his autobiography, which the latter concluded, in two parts, four years later.[6] The first part of the autobiography was included in an anti-slavery album prepared by Del Monte for Irish abolitionist Richard Madden in 1839.[7] Madden, who was in Cuba at the time in his capacity as magistrate on the Joint (British-Spanish) Commission for Liberated Africans, took the Autobiography back to England with him, for translation and presentation at the General Anti-Slavery Convention in 1840.[8] Manzano's *Autobiografía* then, curiously enough, first saw light in English, and its manuscript, which remained in Del Monte's power, passed from the hands of his son, Leonardo, to those of one Vidal Morales, and finally to Cuba's José Martí National Library. In other words, it lay practically buried in archival oblivion for close to a hundred years, save for a contemporary translation of some excerpts into French by Martinican abolitionist Victor Schoelcher, and an inclusion of some of its passages in Francisco Calcagno's 1879 *Poetas de color*. It was not until 1934, at the height of the Afro-Cuban literary and cultural vogue, with Ramon Guirao's research into black and *mestizo* poets during slavery in Cuba, that his name resurfaced.[9] Historians José Luciano Franco and Emilio de Leuschsenring subsequently published the first complete original Spanish version of the manuscript in 1937.[10] Part two was lost while in the care of its proofreader and corrector, Ramón de Palma, a fellow member of the Delmontine group.

Since Manzano criticism in recent decades has shed valuable light on a variety of aspects concerning his autobiography, his poetry and drama, his role as a marginal intellectual, and his place in Cuban antislavery writing and in Cuban abolitionism as a whole, I am more interested here in the dynamic of subjection and long-suffering in which he was involved as an enslaved person. The tensions attendant on the recognition by individuals of their subordination to a power greater than themselves, and their paradoxical attachment to the source of their distress, even as they resist their condition of subjection, make Manzano's memoir a particu-

larly revealing commentary on the master/slave dialectic, both in the immediate context of modern slavery, and in the wider context of slavery historically. On the other hand, the reduction of the enslaved individual to the condition of "thinghood" in Hegelian terminology, and the means by which physical violence is deployed in the suppression of their inner volition, allow us to appreciate the imposed, one-dimensional corporeality of enslavement. That Manzano's artistic, creative consciousness is continually forced to confront the fragility and susceptibility of his corporeality, underscores the bodily essentialization of the slave owner's will to power vis-à-vis his human "property." These contradictions compel us to reconsider the dichotomy of mind and body and to appreciate the emphasis on the subjectivity of the body that has been the object of recent feminist theory. As Elaine Scarry has argued, the primordiality of the bodily housing of the subject, especially when the body is in pain or under the effects of infirmity, re-asserts the centrality of our physical selves. Revisiting the subjection of Manzano from this perspective, then, requires little advocacy. Manzano, besides, illuminates the dynamic of domestic slavery in a particularly fruitful manner, uncovering nuances that are nonexistent in the relationship between field slaves and the master class. These aspects of his life story are eminently deserving of a closer look than they have hitherto been given.

To begin with, Manzano's reflections on his family situation as a pre-adolescent show him to be part of an intriguing complex of "kinship," in which consanguinity and property relations intersect in such a way that they would condition his confusion as to who he was in a racialized world divided between the free and the unfree, the powerful and the disempowered. The mysterious workings of a system in which three of his younger siblings were born free, while he and another brother were not, certainly had the potential to produce a sense of intra-familial difference, if not rift. It could also exacerbate the all-consuming lifelong desire for liberation that he so often expressed. More importantly, the mentioned freedom of his siblings was a function of the property determinant, since, as he noted, his benevolent mistress, the Marchioness Jústiz de Santa Ana had exercised the prerogative of granting free birth to his expectant mother.

But if he was at the same time part of a sibling unit that was part free and part slave, one might note that the doubling (or fracturing) of his sense of identification was also produced at the filial level, in that Santa Ana also supplanted his biological mother, having adopted him as, in his words, "the child of her old age" (47). If we subscribe to the belief that kinship is not "natural," and may be spatio-temporally cultivated through contact and affect (Spillers 76), Manzano's declaration of belonging to the Marchioness, and by extension to her own extended family, should not be viewed as a mere trope on his part. It was grounded in their mutual recognition of each other in terms of mother and son. As a young child he called her "my mama" (49), never left her side except at sleep time, and reports that she regularly took him with her when she went to the countryside, or to church or to the theater. What was produced, thereby, notwithstanding the obvious hierarchical juxtaposition of his two "mothers," was an important originary scene of simultaneity and contrast, as regards the son/mother dynamic of identification.[11] Indeed we are led to believe that his bereavement on her death (he cried "buckets" 63), was no less intense than at the loss of his own mother.

Since the extended white captor family lived in adjoining houses, his childish identification with Santa Ana's grandchildren on more or less equal terms completes the picture of his double familial belonging, especially considering his own mother's role as wet nurse for some of the latter. He points out that they played and got into mischief together, that he was baptized in the suit of Beatriz, one of Santa Ana's grandchildren, and that he was sent to school at six as they too presumably were. Schooling for a slave, we recall, would have been extremely rare, since it was, in principle, illegal. Importantly also, when somewhat older he got into trouble, as in the *peseta* incident, his grief evoked as much an outpouring of tears from Santa Ana's grandchildren as from his blood brothers (75-77). Further, the kindness and generosity he received subsequently when in Nicolas's service as a young adult was no doubt attributable to their bonds of affection developed during childhood. By then, of course, he would re-inscribe himself as the "son" of the former, to indicate his subordinate station in the adult world of Cuban slave society. Since Nicolás was but a few years his senior, "son" in this instance would be a strained euphemism for the property relations that had been established as the end product of his subordination as slave.[12]

Manzano's letter to Del Monte on July 25, 1835 spoke of the "cruel blows that from a tender age made me take cognizance of my humble condition." As readers we may take these blows as constitutive of the event that brought the halcyon days of his childhood to an end.[13] They catapulted him into the world of real slavery, and initiated him into the multi-faceted and paradoxical world of subjection as the Marchioness del Prado Ameno took control of his life. According to Judith Butler, power subordinates the subject, who, in recognizing him/herself as subordinated, completes the process of subordination. The violence that Manzano consistently suffers under Del Prado's charge, thus emerges as the definitive marker and maker of his new self. Over time it would serve to reinforce his subjec-

tion, producing a sense of permanent melancholy and even a complex of doom, as he pessimistically contemplated his future.[14]

Manzano's induction into slavery also exemplifies both the curious and contradictory attachment of victims to their abusers, and the struggle for alterity that is produced by slavery's presumption of ownership. Nowhere is the former idea more clearly expressed than in his declaration regarding Del Prado that "I loved her in spite of the harshness with which she treated me" (123), and "I loved her like my mother" (127), which he repeats scant pages later. These assertions of affection are significant, notwithstanding an understandable need on his part to dissimulate any latent hostility he might have felt at the time of writing, towards his sadistic ex-mistress. If Manzano's memoir may be seen as an indictment of slavery and a disavowal of those that enslaved him, his declared attachment to them has to be taken as a signal of the paradox of his subjection, as Butler, following Foucault, might assert. That he himself seems incapable of recognizing his lived contradictions only confirms their paradoxical nature. His labor turns out to be an equally dramatic site of his subordination, especially to the extent that it also involves his struggle for selfhood and alterity.

Butler elaborates on Hegel's description of the slave-master as a consciousness "existent-for-itself," in relation to which the slave is reduced to a status of dependent Thinghood (Hegel, 51). By means of his labor the slave provides for the material conditions of the lord's or slavemaster's existence, and in the process also reflects and reproduces his own subordination and the domination of the latter (Butler, 35). The slave's labor is the object that simultaneously binds the two, even as it distinguishes the one from the other. Butler's emphasis on the fact of the alienation of the bondsman from the objects of his labor, and on the recognition of his own signature on these objects even as this recognition reinforces and reifies his subjection, is of key significance to an appreciation of Manzano's dilemma. The master as "disembodied desire for self-reflection" (Butler 35) in Del Prado, is graphically seen as Manzano is made to become, as it were, an extension of her physical self when he is made to stand at her back during card games and drawing classes, when he is made to literally follow her every step, and when he sleeps at her bedroom door so that he can be available whenever she should wake.[15] Her obsessive possessiveness and self-projection even includes a declaration to the adolescent at one point, that he should regard her as he would his deceased mother, since she had taken her place (115).

Del Prado is no less subtle regarding her slaves' earnings, as she viciously expropriates the money Manzano makes by helping Aparacio the painter and set designer, and has him brutally punished for independently using part of his inheritance to buy masses to the memory of his mother. As she pointedly asserted, she, as their (collective) mistress, was the "automatic heir" of her slaves' belongings (119). If the erasure of the slave's signature from the object of his labor, however, and its expropriation signifies the slave's subjection, and reiterates it, it is important to remember that this object is also a contested site, as is evinced in Manzano's act of autonomy in arranging masses for his mother. It is this being for the Other that becomes a being for the self, which lays the foundations of alterity, as Butler observes in *The Psychic Life of Power.*

Manzano's passage from his childhood days of entertaining Santa Ana's guests on Sundays after church marks an important trajectory in the development of his many personal talents. He progresses from reciting memorized sermons and bits of operatic script, to the eventual mastery of writing and to making himself a professional poet. The phase also represents his growing awareness and embrace of the possibility of autonomy. He doggedly pursues in the cultivation of letters, as he does in the development of his other marketable skills, in spite of the fact that, as we recall, Del Prado had him beaten and gagged for entertaining the house slaves with verse and story telling, and the Marquis forbade him from writing. Although his slave's signature on any of his products in painting, confectionery, or sewing, would remain susceptible to expropriation, his poetry and his creative capacity would continue, in a sense, to be beyond the reach of the slavemistress. This is so despite Del Prado's taking him back to the El Molino plantation when she learned of his success as a poet and artisan in Havana. Notwithstanding its vulnerability as remunerable labor, then, his poetry might well be considered an inviolable expression of his interiority. Manzano's letter to Domingo Del Monte on December 11th 1834, thanking him for arranging to publish his work in Europe, demonstrates the degree to which his poetry had become a contested domain, as well as the extent to which he had won this particular battle in the primordial confrontation of master and slave. If they could not be converted into money, as his books were locally, his poems in Europe would represent the kind of cultural capital that was beyond the purview of his presumptive owner.

> ". . . [W]hen I think of them (the poems) sailing to such distant climates to see public light in the emporium of European illustration where so many poets rightfully dispute primacy, it all seems to me to be a dream: born in the torrid zone under obscurity, they fly from the bosom of my misfortune bearing with them the name of their hapless author farther than it deserves to go; truly sir: I had hoped for much good, but not this much."
>
> (*Obras,* 80)

It would be difficult to overstate the sense of accomplishment experienced by a self-taught black slave in Cuba, who was about to join the hallowed community of writers, not merely at home in the colonial margins, but in the metropolitan center itself.

Considering that his manumission price had been paid years before, however, the elusive prize of freedom remained the bane of his existence, and misfortune and the cumulative years of bodily mortification intensified his sense of insecurity and anxiety. As he confessed to Del Monte in October of 1834, "If I haven't lost my sanity it is perhaps because the time has not yet come" (*Obras,* 78). Del Prado's threat to kill him on an earlier occasion must have seemed to be a possibility that could become reality at any time, given her irascibility and the punishments she continued to mete out over the years. It is what was most likely behind his assertion to Del Monte that a slave is a "dead being" in the hands of his master.[16] Considering that the Marchioness was still alive and still capable of wielding much influence when he wrote his memoir, one can understand his marked hesitancy about telling his whole story.[17]

Critics have noted the generally fragmentary nature of Manzano's narrative, his run-on sentences and breathless disregard for punctuation, and his tendency to bypass certain events that are presumably too disturbing to discuss. "Let us pass over the rest of this painful scene in silence," he says once as he recalls his mother being whipped for the first time, face down, and in the presence of other slaves (73). "Let us draw a curtain over this scene," he repeats on another occasion, as if to shield his psyche from the remembered trauma of buggery (93). The difficulty in Manzano's re-living painful events or dwelling on their unhappy images brings us back to the question of the body in pain, and to slavery as a life-state of sufferation. It confronts us once more with the centrality of the role of violence in the slave regimen, and the exaggerated corporeality of the enslaved subject. Here is bears pointing out that the scope and applicability of violence in colonial production is by no means limited to agricultural fields or mines or other primary sites of economic activity. It relates just as readily to the more benign sphere of domestic work. Jean Casimir points to this foundational feature of violence when he writes: "Torture is the slaves' midwife, the materialization of their relations with their master. Thanks to it—and although it were simply the threat of torture or the right to torture—this relationship is maintained" (77). "It is not only a demonstration of sadism," he continues, "[but] a normal practice in the system, a necessity" (76).[18]

Under Del Prado, Manzano's existence is a dramatic exemplar of this principle, as he cites the series of overseers and their assistants, whose task it was to maintain the slave enclave appropriately terrorized through violence. It is significant that when these are the aggressors, they are named, whether it is Don Silvestre or Don Saturnino, or their black or mulatto helpers. When the Marchioness herself is responsible for his pain, for example, he is clearly more hesitant, and relates the incident in the passive voice. "My nose was shattered," he reports in describing her reaction upon finding the crushed geraniums in his hands, and we only know how directly she is involved in his imprisonment in the coal shed when we are told that the key is kept in her room (59). More important, however, are the overwork and the weekly whippings and nosebleeds which over the long run begin to show in his sad demeanor, in the rings around his eyes, and in his wasted frame. It is as if his scars and slight physiognomy became a bodily inscription of his sufferation.

That Manzano's punishment is consistently disproportionate to his perceived misdeeds, points to its underlying political objective of inspiring fear and submission in slaves, rather than it's being a spur to production, or some sort of "corrective" for them. He relates how for the "least childish mischief," he was whipped and left hungry and thirsty, in a cold and dark coal cellar, exposed to the rats and foul smells from an outhouse, and prey to his overactive imagination (57). The punishment over the *peseta* came about because he switched a new coin that the mistress gave him to give a beggar who came by the house, for an old one already in his possession. Upon discovering that he had the same new coin that she had given him for the beggar, Del Prado assumed he had stolen it and sentenced him to four days and nights in his jail, without food. She banished him as well to the plantation with instruction for a *novenario,* or nine-day period of flogging, consisting of twenty-five lashes each day, and at night two consecutive six-hour shifts of hard labor (81). Del Prado overreacts to the geranium that he absent-mindedly picks and destroys in an equally ugly manner. She again has him locked up. This time he was immobilized in the stocks, with his body exposed to the winter's cold, and in an infirmary where the thought of the ghosts of the unfortunate slaves who had died there wreaked havoc on his mind.[19] It was on this occasion that the overseer sodomized him, from all appearances.[20]

Apart from maintaining slave subjection and hierarchy through fear, what Del Prado's excesses point to also, is the distance that necessarily exists between the torturer and his victim in any regime that is based on brute force. Her sadism takes us inside the structure of violence that ran colonial slavery, and affords us a look at the microcosmic, intersubjectual level, at which victimizer and victim interface. Pain, as Elaine Scarry reminds us, is an unsharable reality between one individual and another. Its self-contained nature makes it possible for someone to be consumed by it, and another to be totally unbothered by its effect. It is also resistant to language, since the sufferer only has a limited vocabulary available to describe its intensity, or its sensory, cognitive and affective content. Ultimately it is the unsharability of pain, empathy apart, that allows the torturer to be impassive in the presence of the suffering that he is inflicting, even as he is aware that his victim is unmistakably reading his agony as a manifestation of power on the part of the torturer. The magnification of sentience in the victim, as a result, becomes proportional to the magnification of agency in the torturer, and in the gulf of feeling between victim and victimizer, lies a guage of the latter's sadism. As it is with prisoners of war, or political prisoners, so it is also in slavery, and pain and bodily injury become the "insignia" that all such regimes have in common.[21] Del Prado's election to unfeelingly discipline and punish, like that of all other slaveholders, concretizes her hold over Manzano, conditioning not only his obedience, but his fear of her. It is also a measure of her malice.

Not only is pain resistant to language, Scarry suggests, it destroys it by making us revert to pre-linguistic forms of weeping and moaning and open-mouthed vociferation when under its thrall. In addressing the practice of interrogation, she stresses that all too often the questioner is less interested in the content of the responses, than in its structural function in triggering and prolonging torture, and in reiterating the power principle: "It is crucial to see that the interrogation does not stand outside an episode of torture as its motive or justification: it is internal to the structure of torture, exists there because of its intimate connections to and interactions with the physical pain" (29). Scarry adds importantly that even though the questions in an interrogation are posed as if the torture accompanying them were a guarantor of truth, it is a fallacy of which the questioner is quite often aware, because at the moment that intense pain is inflicted, bodily sentience displaces and overrides all other considerations in the victim. Torture in this sense then represents and emptying of consciousness, and an end of ideology.[22] This is the conundrum that Manzano faces when punished for a capon that went missing and for which he was held responsible. En route to their final destination, one fewer of these fowl than appeared on the receipt had been delivered to the kitchen where he received them, and he was subsequently called upon to give account for the missing one.

Manzano's predicament in the capon episode, in which there was nothing that he could say to clear himself of the charges, is that while it was an integral part of slaver ideology to discredit his words as a slave and to invalidate his explanations, it was just as important to his oppressors to use the interrogation as justification for his punishment. His own verbal incoherence in response to the lash, the primordiality of bodily sentience, his frenzied creation of impossible "truths," and the fickle premises of torture are all evinced as he recounts the event.

> They mercilessly threw me on the ground, as one throws a sack that has no feelings, one holding down each hand and foot and another seated on my back. They asked me about the chicken or capon. I did not know what to say because I knew nothing about it. I suffered twenty-five lashes. I said a thousand different things because they were demanding I tell the truth and I did not know which truth they wanted. I thought that saying I had taken it would suffice and the whipping would stop, but then I would have to say what became of the money, so I found myself in another dilemma. I said that I had bought a hat. "Where is the hat?" It was a lie. I said I had bought shoes; there were none. I said so many things, over and over again, trying to see how to free myself from so much torture.
>
> I suffered these torments for nine nights; I said nine thousand different things as they shouted at me. I no longer had anything left to say, anything that it seemed might end their punishing me. But not because I knew such things.
>
> (97)

It is easy to see where Juan Francisco Manzano was "writing for his life" in responding to Domingo del Monte's request that he put together his autobiography, in indirect exchange for support to get his freedom. Sadly for Manzano, however, freedom from slavery did not mean liberation. The autonomy that he had achieved as a bondsman by his use of the literary word did not translate into the ability to express himself freely once his shackles had been removed. His ability to hire out his labor did not provide the existence of material satisfaction for which he had hoped and dreamed. On the contrary, his exercise of the word made him a target for the logophobia of Spain's colonial representatives in Cuba, who were inordinately apprehensive over the question of writing and its potential for political subversion. While his association with Del Monte was the key that opened the door to freedom from the slavemaster, there was no escaping Cuba's colonial bosses and their political domination over the local controllers of forced labor. His new identity as a writer who had been a slave, over and against the old one of a slave who was a writer, would ultimately cause him to be ensnared in a combination of the most explosive political issues of the day. These were the autonomist agenda of Cuba's creole intellectual elite, the international abolitionist movement and its local expression, and the ongoing tradition of slave insurgency from below.

The coterie of writers that gathered around Domingo del Monte in the 1830s represented a broad array of genres and interests. It all constituted a foundational moment in Cuba's national literature. In this regard, Del Monte's championing of an autonomous Cuban Academy of Literature in 1834, while serving as president of the Commission on Literature of the *Sociedad Económica de Amigos del País,* is viewed as an important, if short lived, political coup given the presence and influence of Peninsular Spanish representatives in the organization. His re-orientation of the *Revista Bimestre Cubana* in the early issues of this journal to give it significant Cuban content while maintaining a cosmopolitan character, is also reflective of Spanish-Cuban struggles on the inside of the organization. The first issue, under the title *Revista y repertorio bimestre de la isla de Cuba,* had been edited by a Catalan, Mariano Cubí y Soler. Del Monte, besides, founded and co-edited important literary outlets like *La moda ó Recreo Semanal del Bello sexo* between 1829 and 1832, *El Puntero Literario* in 1830, and most importantly the journal *El Plantel* in 1838-1839. Even more successful than the others, *El Plantel* provided a forum for the most talented of Cuba's young writers while featuring articles on primary education, economy, and history, as well as poetry. In *El puntero literario's* 1830 Romantic manifesto, he had staked out for himself the honor of being the first to introduce the movement to Latin America since it antedated Argentine Esteban Echeverria's 1832 narrative poem *Elvira, o la novia del plata.*

The power struggles within the influential *Sociedad Económica de Amigos del País* was reflective of a wider political rift among Cuba's elite. Indeed, the pressures brought to bear on the Commission on Literature mirrored broader censorial tendencies on the outside of the *Sociedad.* Since 1825, with the loss of Spain's continental possessions, Cuba had begun to represent the major portion of colonial income for the old empire. The prodigious growth of the sugar industry in response to the vacuum created by the Haitian revolution three decades before, meant that Madrid was hardly inclined to be overly tolerant of anticolonial dissent on the island. Effectively, emergency powers had been granted to the Captains General of both Puerto Rico and Cuba in that year. The vigilance at Cuba's customs over banned books, and the penalties imposed by Captain General Francisco Dionisio Vives in the 1820s, included forfeiture of the entire cargoes of the ships found at fault. Likewise, booksellers were required to prepare lists of their inventory for submission and to turn in books considered unacceptable. Under his successor, Miguel Tacón, even the luggage of incoming passengers to Cuba was searched for banned books, and private correspondence could be scrutinized as well. Royal permission was required for all publications and Tacón was the one empowered to recommend particular items or, conversely, to disallow them.[23]

It was this atmosphere that led to the banishment into exile of José Antonio Saco in 1835 by Tacón. Saco, editor of the *Revista Bimestre Cubana,* had complained energetically against the Patriotic Society's refusal to ratify the Academy of Literature.[24] In addition, he had used the *Revista* as a forum for critiquing the unabated and increasing importation of slave labor, suggesting that it was patricide on the part of the creole planters to flood the country with more blacks, thus further skewing the racial balance and putting the country at risk of another slave uprising à la Saint Domingue. He also exposed the venality of the colonial officials who collaborated with the planters in the illegal trade. Spain had signed an agreement with Britain in 1817 to bring an end to the trade in African captives, but it was common knowledge that the Captains General enjoyed handsome bribes to ignore the contraband trade. Tacón, in fact, during his four-year tenure, accumulated some $450.000 by these means.[25] Del Monte also took issue openly with the censorship machinery, stressing Cuba's lack of rights and of its lack of proportional political representation in Spanish *cortes*.[26]

Given Del Monte's cosmopolitan outlook and his eclectic intellectuality, his sponsorship of Manzano is probably not surprising, though this is by no means to suggest that he even remotely felt that the multitude of enslaved blacks in Cuba deserved freedom, or that Manzano, despite his not being one of the masses of enslaved Africans and creoles who had been brutalized by the system, might be treated as a social "equal."[27] Writing, as a sign of Occidental acculturation, identification and belonging, distinguished him. Indeed, Del Monte was no different from his friend and colleague Saco, in his fear that Cuba's continuing dependence on intensive slave labor, as a guarantee of continuing prosperity, was a highly risky policy, which held disastrous consequences for the future. Importing free white labor seemed to be one solution. Gradual emancipation seemed another. Yet another might be annexation to the powerful slaveholding United States.[28] His decision to collaborate with abolitionist Richard Madden, in 1839, and offer him literary works designed to help him form an "exact idea of the opinion of the thinking youth of the country as to the treatment of slaves,"[29] should be seen in this light. While it clearly attested to his liberalism and autonomist, antiauthoritarian posture, it was far from being a revolutionary one.

Manzano's incarceration and interrogation over several months between 1844 and 1845, exemplifies the Draconian response by Captain General O'Donnell to the perceived threat of anticolonial discourse associated with the Del Monte group, as well as the ongoing efforts at emancipation by the enslaved laborers themselves. Manzano's charge was that he had written a poem at Del Monte's behest in praise of freedom and British abolitionism. Given his long association with Del Monte and the latter's acquaintance with well known British abolitionists Richard Madden and David Turnbull, the authorities must have been responding to a potentially very dangerous individual who incorporated into his person/a, not only elements of slave insurrection, after

all he had been a slave, but also anticolonial discursivity, on account of his exposure to and possible collaboration with Del Monte. Either profile by itself qualified as treasonous for O'Donnell.

Apart from creole autonomism, the local anti-slave trade critique, and an international abolitionist campaign that by then was in full swing (abolition had been decreed a decade before in the Anglophone Caribbean colonies) O'Donnell was also responding to a spate of slave rebellions. These had culminated in a call on the Captain General, in November 1843, by a panicked group of Matanzas planters to intervene and guarantee them protection, and also to stem the inflow of new slaves. When plans for a supposedly major slave revolt were revealed in early 1844 at the Santísima Trinidad plantation, O'Donnell responded by unleashing his troops on an "intense period of search, seizure, torture, confession, trial, and punishment" throughout the sugar belt (Jensen 219-220). In the blood bath that ensued, slaves from 230 plantations across twenty-five districts were taken prisoner and some 7000 died under the whip in an event infamously known as the Escalera process on account of the brutal method of torture employed, ostensibly to extract confessions.[30] Targeted as well, were notable businessmen and artists of color, members of the incipient black middle class, who lost their property to the Military Commission and its agents as the instinct of self-preservation yielded to the extortionist tactics of the latter. Additionally, British subjects, ordinary mechanics and engineers, were assumed to be abolitionist and opportunely harassed and imprisoned. Delmontine associates, Félix Tanco y Bosmeniel, Martínez Serrano, all suffered brief prison spells, while hundreds of other whites were either incarcerated or exiled. Del Monte, at the time, was in Paris.

Mulatto poet Manuel de la Concepción Valdés, also known as Plácido, itinerant poet and probably the most well known individual of color in Cuba at the time, was given short shrift by the Commission. In spite of the occasional nature of much of his work, the tone of anticolonial defiance in a poem like "Habaneros libertad," and the presumptive commitment to be the "eternal enemy of tyranny" in "El juramento" left too little to the imagination of the censors. He was charged with being the lead conspirator, instigator and recruiter of the Escalera conspiracy, and executed on June 28 of 1844. What is important about Plácido in the present context is that, his own verse apart, he was the one who, under interrogation, and most likely in response to a leading question, identified Manzano as a literary supporter of slave rebellion. As turned out in the trial, their mutual acquaintance was undeniable, as was their association with Del Monte, and with the foreign principals identified with the supposed movement.[31]

Like much of the supposed evidence supporting the premise of the conspiracy, upon which so many were condemned, the poem that Manzano was accused of authoring was never presented, and most likely never existed. The event, however, sealed Manzano into a final state of dejection and seemed to douse permanently his creative spark as a writer. One is only left to imagine, and compare, what he might have been put through during his several months of incarceration, of which he had perforce to remain silent, with what he did reveal about his earlier experiences in the Del Prado household. His description of the six-day walk to Havana from Matanzas, for example, some seven months after his initial arrest, and a trajectory in which, according to Paquette "unknown hundreds died" (220), is sufficiently eloquent indication of whatever else could not be said.[32] His final pleas from prison to Del Monte's mother-in-law, to render monetary aid to his wife and infant daughters, must, in the final analysis, have been supremely costly for an individual who had been able to find dignity even in being a slave.[33] For someone who had intuited dread sufferation in the urn of his destiny, they provide a poignant reminder of the life-state of those for whom justice has left the earth.

Notes

1. For "neologistic" language in Caribbean creolization, see, for example, Edouard Glissant's *Caribbean Discourse: Selected Essays,* more specifically the section "*Man gin-yin an zin*" 191-194.

2. Addressing the U.S-American dimension of slavery, and the physical evidence of the violence that drove it, Hortense Spillers proffers: "The[se] undecipherable markings on the captive body render a kind of hieroglyphics of the flesh . . . We might well ask if this phenomenon of marking and branding actually "transfers" from one generation to another, finding its various *symbolic substitutions* in an efficacy of meanings that repeat the initiatory moments." 67. (Emphasis in the original)

3. After over 300 years of slavery in the colonies, the first Spanish slave code noir was drawn up in 1789. With the Haitian revolution as a contemporaneous event, it was not even promulgated in Cuba. Thomas 74.

4. Manzano never gives his date of birth in a precise manner. Friol (49) places him in January, 1797. Citations from the *Autobiography* will be taken from Schulman's bilingual edition of 1996. All other translations from the Spanish are my responsibility. My citations from his letters are taken from Franco's edition of his *Obras.*

5. These included *La moda, El pasatiempo, El aguinaldo habanero* and *El album.*

6. See Branche regarding the aggrandizement of liberal literati in Cuban historiography and the anti-slavery premise ascribed to Del Monte's literary circle.

7. See Adriana Lewis Galanes, "El álbum de Domingo del Monte" for a discussion of the content and context of Madden's packet.

8. The full title of Madden's publication was as follows: *Poems by a slave in the Island of Cuba, recently liberated; translated from the Spanish, by R.. R.. Madden, with the early life of the negro poet written by himself; to which are prefixed two pieces descriptive of the Cuban Slavery and the slave -traffic, by R.. R.. Madden.* London, Thomas Ward and co., 1840.

9. Guirao's wrote an article titled "Poetas negros y mestizos de la época esclavista." Cited in Friol 41. Guirao also compiled the important *negrista* anthology *Orbita de la poesía afrocubana 1928-37 (Antología).*

10. See Friol and Luis for a useful discussion of the politics of publication regarding the autobiography in its various versions, from the Madden 1840 edition, through the Schulman edition of 1975.

11. In "Mama's baby, Papa's maybe," Spillers argues that conditions on the slave ship and in the regime in general militated against the cultivation of maternity. For Patterson, writing in the same vein, slaves are potentially genealogically isolated, cut off as they are from siblings and ascending and descending lines. Manzano the house slave, occupies a curious position in which he has access to not one, but two sources of parental (maternal) "care." His father, of course, represents two important instances of black male displacement under the system. Toribio de Castro's children did not bear his name, but that of the slave master. His authority as father was further limited by the slaveholder's predominance as exemplified in the case in which he incurred Santa Ana's displeasure for scolding Juan Francisco. 49

12. "Don Nicolás," he asserts, "loved me not as a slave, but as a son, notwithstanding his young age." 103

13. He describes this period as "a garden of very beautiful flowers, *a series of joys.*" 51

14. The assumption of power of both a "present and a futural form," for Butler, is poignantly exemplified by Manzano's terror of what in a letter to Del Monte (Dec. 11, 1834) he calls "the urn of destiny" (*Obras* 81) His crude struggle against "fate" is again the topic of his famous sonnet written to mark his thirtieth birthday "Mis treinta años."

15. Molloy has correctly observed on this that the only privacy he is allowed is when he is in the lavatory. 410

16. In his letter to Del Monte of the 25th of June, 1835. *Obras* 86.

17. In his letter to Del Monte, dated 29th September, 1835, he expresses his intention to reserve the "most interesting episodes" of his life for some future moment when "sure of [his] fate and sustenance" he could write a truly Cuban novel. *Obras* 87.

18. Casimir demonstrates the organically structured role of pain and punishment to the colonial contract by pointing to the specialized division of labor as it related to its purveyors, and the prices set for their services: "Hanging; 30 pounds, breaking of the back; 60 pounds; burning alive 60 pounds; hanging and burning, 35 pounds; cutting of the wrist 2 pounds [. . .] cutting out the tongue; 6 pounds; perforating the tongue; 5 pounds; cutting off the ears and emasculation; 5 pounds." 79.

19. The immobility of the body or parts of it in the stocks, disguises a particularly agonizing form of punishment. This is occasioned in that the body, in its inability to shift and seek comfort, is converted into an active agent of its own anguish. See Scarry 47.

20. Benton Rushing in "Surviving Rape: A Morning/ Mourning Ritual," speaks to the wordless annihilation experienced by the rape victim. In the case of male rape, broader *machista* inhibitions would exacerbate the imposed contract of silence. See Ellis's "Reading through the Veil of Juan Francisco Manzano: From Homoerotic Violence to the Dream of a Homoracial Bond."

21. A stark indication of this in the use of the decapitated slave head, the ultimate sign of terminal punishment, as a sign of terror/power by the slaveholders, for the slave enclave in times of insurgency.

22. The notion of political "betrayal" on the part of the captive under interrogation thus becomes pointless in the sense that corporeality is singularly foregrounded in the subjectivity of the individual under torture, as the world as he knows it becomes unmade (Scarry 36). That confessions made under duress are not acceptable in the legal sphere is a recognition of this principle.

23. See Jensen in this regard.

24. In the "Justa Defensa de la Academia cubana de la Literatura contra los ataques que se le han dado en el Diario de La Habana, desde el 12 hasta el 23 de abril del presente año, escrito por Don José

Saco e impresa en Nueva Orleans por Mr. St.-Romes, oficina de El Courier año de 1834." See Saco 25.

25. As revealed to Madden during his interview with Del Monte. Mullen, 135.

26. Jensen 114.

27. Manzano's strict adherence to slave protocol in his rhetoric of humility is noteworthy when addressing Del Monte, as is seen repeatedly in his letters. See also Del Monte's "Estado de la población blanca y de color en la isla de Cuba en 1839."

28. Del Monte pursued this objective through his correspondence with American diplomat, Alexander Everett, and other influential figures. See Enildo García on this relationship and on Del Monte's "Harvard Connection."

29. Taken from a letter from Del Monte's colleague Zacarías González del Valle to another member of the group, Anselmo Suárez y Romero, dated Sept. 5, 1838, and reproduced in *La vida literaria en Cuba 1836-1840.*

30. If bodily immobility is the operative element defining the punitive efficacy of the stocks, the punishment of the ladder (*escalera*), as described below, can only be seen as one of the more raucous refinements of colonial perversity. According to an eyewitness, the Escalera prisoners were: "Stripped and naked & lashed to a ladder on the ground with a rope around each wrist so tight that the blood could scarcely circulate, and the whole arm drawn above the head till the shoulder fairly cracked, while the ropes were secured to the top of the ladder, the feet and legs stretched in the same manner, and fastened to the lower part with a double turn round the loins and back, binding the whole trunk of the body immoveably to the rounds of the ladder, in this position, the poor negro was thought to be ready to commence his declaration! The first question was, "what more do you know than you told us yesterday? . . . The flogging went on until the men stopped to rest their arms which were tired of the blows given . . . ." Paquette 226.

31. A complete account of the supposed Escalera conspiracy is beyond the scope of this discussion. Paquette points to the fact that slave insurgency was a constant and feels that it was more likely to have been a series of smaller plots, rather than a centrally organized phenomenon (233-266). Franco is of the opinion that it was an invention of the Captain-Generalship and the slave trading elite, that was used as a pretext to silence real and imagined sources of disquiet (193-199).

32. Manzano's letter to Doña Rosa Alfonso on October 5 1844 was even more breathless and uncontrolled than the prose of his autobiography. Under the circumstances, one should hardly be surprised. ". . . from one jail to another, from one stocks to another, from one dungeon to another, one mountain range to another, expecting my strength to come to an unhappy end, so much shame on the walk from Matanzas to Havana, so much embarrassment, vituperation, needfulness not eating more than one meal one day in Jaruco . . ."

33. Manzano asserted with some pride on one occasion that he fulfilled his duties in an efficient manner and that this even caused envy among his peers. 111.

Works Cited

Allsopp, Richard (ed.) *Dictionary of Caribbean English Usage.* Oxford: Oxford University Press, 1996.

Benton Rushing, Andrea. "Surviving Rape: A Morning/ Mourning Ritual. " *Feminist Theory and the Body: A Reader.* Eds. Janet Price and Margrit Shildrick. Edinburgh: Edinburgh University Press, 1999.

Branche, Jerome. "Mulato entre negros (y blancos): Writing, Race, the Antislavery Question and Juan Francisco Manzano's *Autobiografía.*" *Bulletin of Latin American Research,* 20.1(2001): 63-87.

Butler, Judith. *The Psychic Life of Power: Theories in Subjection.* Stanford: Stanford University Press, 1997.

Casimir, Jean. *La cultura oprimida.* México: Editorial nueva imagen, 1980.

Ellis, Robert Richmond. "Reading through the Veil of Juan Francisco Manzano: From Homoerotic Violence to the Dream of a Homoracial Bond." *P.M.L.A.* 113 (1998): 422-435.

Franco, José Luciano. *Ensayos históricos.* Havana: Editorial de ciencias sociales, 1974.

Friol, Roberto. *Suite para Juan Francisco Manzano.* Havana: Editorial arte y literatura, 1977.

García, Enildo. "Romanticismo antillano: Domingo del Monte y 'The Harvard Connection.' *Círculo: Revista de cultura.* 22 (1993): 68-78.

Glissant, Edouard. *Caribbean Discourse: Selected Essays.* Trans. J. Michael Dash, Charlottesville: University Press of Virginia, 1996.

González del Valle, José Zacarías. *La vida literaria en Cuba: (1836-1840).* Ed. Francisco González del Valle. Havana: Publicaciones de la secretaría de educación, 1938.

Guirao, Ramón (ed.) *Orbita de la poesía afrocubana: 1928-1937. (Antología).* La Habana: Ucar, García y Cía, 1938.

Hegel, Georg Wilhelm Friedrich. *Hegel's Phenomenology of Spirit.* Trans. and annotated by Howard P. Kainz. University Park, Pennsylvania: Pennsylvania University Press, 1994.

Jensen, Larry. R. *Children of Colonial Despotism: Press, Politics, and Culture in Cuba, 1790-1840.* Tampa: University Presses of Florida, 1988.

Lewis Galanes, Adriana. "El álbum de Domingo del Monte."

Luis, William. *Literary Bondage: Slavery in Cuban Narrative.* Austin: University of Texas Press, 1990.

Manzano, Juan Francisco. *Obras.* Havana: Instituto cubano del libro, 1972.

Molloy, Sylvia. "From Serf to Self: The Autobiography of Juan Francisco Manzano." *Modern Language Notes.* 104 (2): 393-417.

Mullen, Edward. Ed. *The Life and Poems of a Cuban Slave: Juan Francisco Manzano 1797-1854.* Connecticut: Archon Books, 1981.

Paquette, Robert. L. *Sugar Is Made with Blood: The Conspiracy of La Escalera and the Conflict between Empires over Slavery in Cuba.* Middletown, Connecticut: Wesleyan University Press, 1988.

Saco, Juan Antonio. Justa defensa de la Academia Cubana de Literatura, contra los ataques que se le han dado en el Diario de la Habana, desde el 12 hasta el 23 de abril del presente año, escrita por Don José Antonio Saco e impresa en Nueva Orleans por Mr. St.- Romes, Oficina de El Courier año de 1834," in *Colección de papeles científicos, históricos, políticos y de otros ramos sobre la isla de Cuba ya publicados, ya inéditos.* Havana: Editorial nacional de Cuba, 1963. 25-67.

Scarry, Elaine. *The Body in Pain: The Making and Unmaking of the World.* New York: Oxford University Press, 1985.

Schulman, Ivan, A. *Autobiography of a Slave by Juan Francisco Manzano.* Trans. Evelyn Picon Garfield. Detroit: Wayne State University Press, 1995.

Spillers, Hortense. "Mama's Baby, Papa's Maybe: An American Grammar Book." *Diacritics* 17.2 (1987): 65-81.

Thomas, Hugh. *Cuba: Or the Pursuit of Freedom.* New York: Da Capo Press, 1998.

FURTHER READING

Criticism

Cobb, Martha K. "The Slave Narrative and the Black Literary Tradition." In *The Art of Slave Narrative: Original Essays in Criticism and Theory,* pp. 36-44. Moline: Western Illinois University, 1982.

Compares Manzano's life experiences to those of

Frederick Douglass and other writers of slave narratives.

Ellis, Robert Richmond. "Juan Francisco Manzano: From Homoerotic Violence to the Dream of a Homoracial Bond." In *They Dream Not of Angels but of Men: Homoeroticism, Gender, and Race in Latin American Autobiography,* pp. 31-54. Gainesville: University Press of Florida, 2002.

Discusses the homoerotic elements of Manzano's poetry.

Hauser, Rex. "Two New World Dreamers: Manzano and Sor Juana." *Afro-Hispanic Review* 12, no. 2 (fall 1993): 3-11.

Compares and contrasts the poetic works of Manzano and Sor Juana.

Luis, William. "Textual Multiplications: Juan Francisco Manzano's *Autobiographía* and Cirilo Villaverde's *Cecilia Valdés.*" In *Literary Bondage: Slavery in Cuban Narrative,* pp. 82-119. Austin: University of Texas Press, 1990.

Examines the ways in which Manzano's participation in the intellectual and social circles of his contemporaries affected his writing.

Molloy, Sylvia. "From Serf to Self: The Autobiography of Juan Francisco Manzano." *MLN* 104, no. 2 (March 1989): 393-417.

Recounts the history of the composition of Manzano's autobiography and compares it favorably to the style of many nineteenth-century novels.

Mullen, Edward J. Introduction to *The Life and Poems of a Cuban Slave: Juan Francisco Manzano, 1797-1854,* pp. 1-36. Hamden, Conn.: Archon Books, 1981.

Presents the history behind the creation and publication of Manzano's autobiography, as well as an account of Richard Robert Madden's translation of the text, pointing to the significance of that version as a valid work of African-American slave literature.

Schulman, Ivan A. Introduction to *The Autobiography of a Slave,* translated by Evelyn Picon Garfield, pp. 5-38. Detroit, Mich.: Wayne State University Press, 1996.

Offers a thorough overview of Manzano's autobiography.

Additional coverage of Manzano's life and career is contained in the following source published by Thomson Gale: *Literature Resource Center.*

How to Use This Index

The main references

> **Calvino, Italo**
> 1923-1985 .... CLC 5, 8, 11, 22, 33, 39,
> 73; SSC 3, 48

list all author entries in the following Gale Literary Criticism series:

AAL = *Asian American Literature*
BG = *The Beat Generation: A Gale Critical Companion*
BLC = *Black Literature Criticism*
BLCS = *Black Literature Criticism Supplement*
CLC = *Contemporary Literary Criticism*
CLR = *Children's Literature Review*
CMLC = *Classical and Medieval Literature Criticism*
DC = *Drama Criticism*
HLC = *Hispanic Literature Criticism*
HLCS = *Hispanic Literature Criticism Supplement*
HR = *Harlem Renaissance: A Gale Critical Companion*
LC = *Literature Criticism from 1400 to 1800*
NCLC = *Nineteenth-Century Literature Criticism*
NNAL = *Native North American Literature*
PC = *Poetry Criticism*
SSC = *Short Story Criticism*
TCLC = *Twentieth-Century Literary Criticism*
WLC = *World Literature Criticism, 1500 to the Present*
WLCS = *World Literature Criticism Supplement*

The cross-references

> See also CA 85-88, 116; CANR 23, 61;
> DAM NOV; DLB 196; EW 13; MTCW 1, 2;
> RGSF 2; RGWL 2; SFW 4; SSFS 12

list all author entries in the following Gale biographical and literary sources:

AAYA = *Authors & Artists for Young Adults*
AFAW = *African American Writers*
AFW = *African Writers*
AITN = *Authors in the News*
AMW = *American Writers*
AMWR = *American Writers Retrospective Supplement*
AMWS = *American Writers Supplement*
ANW = *American Nature Writers*
AW = *Ancient Writers*
BEST = *Bestsellers*
BPFB = *Beacham's Encyclopedia of Popular Fiction: Biography and Resources*
BRW = *British Writers*
BRWS = *British Writers Supplement*
BW = *Black Writers*
BYA = *Beacham's Guide to Literature for Young Adults*
CA = *Contemporary Authors*
CAAS = *Contemporary Authors Autobiography Series*
CABS = *Contemporary Authors Bibliographical Series*
CAD = *Contemporary American Dramatists*
CANR = *Contemporary Authors New Revision Series*
CAP = *Contemporary Authors Permanent Series*
CBD = *Contemporary British Dramatists*
CCA = *Contemporary Canadian Authors*
CD = *Contemporary Dramatists*
CDALB = *Concise Dictionary of American Literary Biography*
CDALBS = *Concise Dictionary of American Literary Biography Supplement*
CDBLB = *Concise Dictionary of British Literary Biography*

CMW = *St. James Guide to Crime & Mystery Writers*
CN = *Contemporary Novelists*
CP = *Contemporary Poets*
CPW = *Contemporary Popular Writers*
CSW = *Contemporary Southern Writers*
CWD = *Contemporary Women Dramatists*
CWP = *Contemporary Women Poets*
CWRI = *St. James Guide to Children's Writers*
CWW = *Contemporary World Writers*
DA = *DISCovering Authors*
DA3 = *DISCovering Authors 3.0*
DAB = *DISCovering Authors: British Edition*
DAC = *DISCovering Authors: Canadian Edition*
DAM = *DISCovering Authors: Modules*
   DRAM: Dramatists Module; **MST:** *Most-studied Authors Module;*
   MULT: *Multicultural Authors Module;* **NOV:** *Novelists Module;*
   POET: *Poets Module;* **POP:** *Popular Fiction and Genre Authors Module*
DFS = *Drama for Students*
DLB = *Dictionary of Literary Biography*
DLBD = *Dictionary of Literary Biography Documentary Series*
DLBY = *Dictionary of Literary Biography Yearbook*
DNFS = *Literature of Developing Nations for Students*
EFS = *Epics for Students*
EXPN = *Exploring Novels*
EXPP = *Exploring Poetry*
EXPS = *Exploring Short Stories*
EW = *European Writers*
FANT = *St. James Guide to Fantasy Writers*
FW = *Feminist Writers*
GFL = *Guide to French Literature,* Beginnings to 1789, 1798 to the Present
GLL = *Gay and Lesbian Literature*
HGG = *St. James Guide to Horror, Ghost & Gothic Writers*
HW = *Hispanic Writers*
IDFW = *International Dictionary of Films and Filmmakers: Writers and Production Artists*
IDTP = *International Dictionary of Theatre: Playwrights*
LAIT = *Literature and Its Times*
LAW = *Latin American Writers*
JRDA = *Junior DISCovering Authors*
MAICYA = *Major Authors and Illustrators for Children and Young Adults*
MAICYAS = *Major Authors and Illustrators for Children and Young Adults Supplement*
MAWW = *Modern American Women Writers*
MJW = *Modern Japanese Writers*
MTCW = *Major 20th-Century Writers*
NCFS = *Nonfiction Classics for Students*
NFS = *Novels for Students*
PAB = *Poets: American and British*
PFS = *Poetry for Students*
RGAL = *Reference Guide to American Literature*
RGEL = *Reference Guide to English Literature*
RGSF = *Reference Guide to Short Fiction*
RGWL = *Reference Guide to World Literature*
RHW = *Twentieth-Century Romance and Historical Writers*
SAAS = *Something about the Author Autobiography Series*
SATA = *Something about the Author*
SFW = *St. James Guide to Science Fiction Writers*
SSFS = *Short Stories for Students*
TCWW = *Twentieth-Century Western Writers*
WLIT = *World Literature and Its Times*
WP = *World Poets*
YABC = *Yesterday's Authors of Books for Children*
YAW = *St. James Guide to Young Adult Writers*

Literary Criticism Series
Cumulative Author Index

Author Index

Armah, Ayi Kwei 1939- . **BLC 1; CLC 5, 33, 136**
See also AFW; BRWS 10; BW 1; CA 61-64; CANR 21, 64; CDWLB 3; CN 7; DAM MULT, POET; DLB 117; EWL 3; MTCW 1; WLIT 2

Armatrading, Joan 1950- .... **CLC 17**
See also CA 114; 186

Armitage, Frank
See Carpenter, John (Howard)

Armstrong, Jeannette (C.) 1948- .... **NNAL**
See also CA 149; CCA 1; CN 7; DAC; SATA 102

Arnette, Robert
See Silverberg, Robert

Arnim, Achim von (Ludwig Joachim von Arnim) 1781-1831 ..... **NCLC 5; SSC 29**
See also DLB 90

Arnim, Bettina von 1785-1859 ...... **NCLC 38, 123**
See also DLB 90; RGWL 2, 3

Arnold, Matthew 1822-1888 ..... **NCLC 6, 29, 89, 126; PC 5; WLC**
See also BRW 5; CDBLB 1832-1890; DA; DAB; DAC; DAM MST, POET; DLB 32, 57; EXPP; PAB; PFS 2; TEA; WP

Arnold, Thomas 1795-1842 .... **NCLC 18**
See also DLB 55

Arnow, Harriette (Louisa) Simpson 1908-1986 .... **CLC 2, 7, 18**
See also BPFB 1; CA 9-12R; 118; CANR 14; DLB 6; FW; MTCW 1, 2; RHW; SATA 42; SATA-Obit 47

Arouet, Francois-Marie
See Voltaire

Arp, Hans
See Arp, Jean

Arp, Jean 1887-1966 .... **CLC 5; TCLC 115**
See also CA 81-84; 25-28R; CANR 42, 77; EW 10

Arrabal
See Arrabal, Fernando

Arrabal, Fernando 1932- ... **CLC 2, 9, 18, 58**
See Arrabal (Teran), Fernando
See also CA 9-12R; CANR 15; EWL 3; LMFS 2

Arrabal (Teran), Fernando 1932-
See Arrabal, Fernando
See also CWW 2

Arreola, Juan Jose 1918-2001 .... **CLC 147; HLC 1; SSC 38**
See also CA 113; 131; 200; CANR 81; CWW 2; DAM MULT; DLB 113; DNFS 2; EWL 3; HW 1, 2; LAW; RGSF 2

Arrian c. 89(?)-c. 155(?) .... **CMLC 43**
See also DLB 176

Arrick, Fran .... **CLC 30**
See Gaberman, Judie Angell
See also BYA 6

Arrley, Richmond
See Delany, Samuel R(ay), Jr.

Artaud, Antonin (Marie Joseph) 1896-1948 .... **DC 14; TCLC 3, 36**
See also CA 104; 149; DA3; DAM DRAM; DLB 258; EW 11; EWL 3; GFL 1789 to the Present; MTCW 1; RGWL 2, 3

Arthur, Ruth M(abel) 1905-1979 ..... **CLC 12**
See also CA 9-12R; 85-88; CANR 4; CWRI 5; SATA 7, 26

Artsybashev, Mikhail (Petrovich) 1878-1927 .... **TCLC 31**
See also CA 170; DLB 295

Arundel, Honor (Morfydd) 1919-1973 .... **CLC 17**
See also CA 21-22; 41-44R; CAP 2; CLR 35; CWRI 5; SATA 4; SATA-Obit 24

Arzner, Dorothy 1900-1979 .... **CLC 98**

Asch, Sholem 1880-1957 .... **TCLC 3**
See also CA 105; EWL 3; GLL 2

Ascham, Roger 1516(?)-1568 .... **LC 101**
See also DLB 236

Ash, Shalom
See Asch, Sholem

Ashbery, John (Lawrence) 1927- .. **CLC 2, 3, 4, 6, 9, 13, 15, 25, 41, 77, 125; PC 26**
See Berry, Jonas
See also AMWS 3; CA 5-8R; CANR 9, 37, 66, 102, 132; CP 7; DA3; DAM POET; DLB 5, 165; DLBY 1981; EWL 3; INT CANR-9; MTCW 1, 2; PAB; PFS 11; RGAL 4; WP

Ashdown, Clifford
See Freeman, R(ichard) Austin

Ashe, Gordon
See Creasey, John

Ashton-Warner, Sylvia (Constance) 1908-1984 .... **CLC 19**
See also CA 69-72; 112; CANR 29; MTCW 1, 2

Asimov, Isaac 1920-1992 ..... **CLC 1, 3, 9, 19, 26, 76, 92**
See also AAYA 13; BEST 90:2; BPFB 1; BYA 4, 6, 7, 9; CA 1-4R; 137; CANR 2, 19, 36, 60, 125; CLR 12, 79; CMW 4; CPW; DA3; DAM POP; DLB 8; DLBY 1992; INT CANR-19; JRDA; LAIT 5; LMFS 2; MAICYA 1, 2; MTCW 1, 2; RGAL 4; SATA 1, 26, 74; SCFW 2; SFW 4; SSFS 17; TUS; YAW

Askew, Anne 1521(?)-1546 .... **LC 81**
See also DLB 136

Assis, Joaquim Maria Machado de
See Machado de Assis, Joaquim Maria

Astell, Mary 1666-1731 .... **LC 68**
See also DLB 252; FW

Astley, Thea (Beatrice May) 1925-2004 .... **CLC 41**
See also CA 65-68; 229; CANR 11, 43, 78; CN 7; DLB 289; EWL 3

Astley, William 1855-1911
See Warung, Price

Aston, James
See White, T(erence) H(anbury)

Asturias, Miguel Angel 1899-1974 .... **CLC 3, 8, 13; HLC 1**
See also CA 25-28; 49-52; CANR 32; CAP 2; CDWLB 3; DA3; DAM MULT, NOV; DLB 113, 290; EWL 3; HW 1; LAW; LMFS 2; MTCW 1, 2; RGWL 2, 3; WLIT 1

Atares, Carlos Saura
See Saura (Atares), Carlos

Athanasius c. 295-c. 373 .... **CMLC 48**

Atheling, William
See Pound, Ezra (Weston Loomis)

Atheling, William, Jr.
See Blish, James (Benjamin)

Atherton, Gertrude (Franklin Horn) 1857-1948 .... **TCLC 2**
See also CA 104; 155; DLB 9, 78, 186; HGG; RGAL 4; SUFW 1; TCWW 2

Atherton, Lucius
See Masters, Edgar Lee

Atkins, Jack
See Harris, Mark

Atkinson, Kate 1951- .... **CLC 99**
See also CA 166; CANR 101; DLB 267

Attaway, William (Alexander) 1911-1986 .... **BLC 1; CLC 92**
See also BW 2, 3; CA 143; CANR 82; DAM MULT; DLB 76

Atticus
See Fleming, Ian (Lancaster); Wilson, (Thomas) Woodrow

Atwood, Margaret (Eleanor) 1939- ... **CLC 2, 3, 4, 8, 13, 15, 25, 44, 84, 135; PC 8; SSC 2, 46; WLC**
See also AAYA 12, 47; AMWS 13; BEST 89:2; BPFB 1; CA 49-52; CANR 3, 24, 33, 59, 95, 133; CN 7; CP 7; CPW; CWP; DA; DA3; DAB; DAC; DAM MST, NOV, POET; DLB 53, 251; EWL 3; EXPN; FW; INT CANR-24; LAIT 5; MTCW 1, 2; NFS 4, 12, 13, 14, 19; PFS 7; RGSF 2; SATA 50; SSFS 3, 13; TWA; WWE 1; YAW

Aubigny, Pierre d'
See Mencken, H(enry) L(ouis)

Aubin, Penelope 1685-1731(?) .... **LC 9**
See also DLB 39

Auchincloss, Louis (Stanton) 1917- .. **CLC 4, 6, 9, 18, 45; SSC 22**
See also AMWS 4; CA 1-4R; CANR 6, 29, 55, 87, 130; CN 7; DAM NOV; DLB 2, 244; DLBY 1980; EWL 3; INT CANR-29; MTCW 1; RGAL 4

Auden, W(ystan) H(ugh) 1907-1973 . **CLC 1, 2, 3, 4, 6, 9, 11, 14, 43, 123; PC 1; WLC**
See also AAYA 18; AMWS 2; BRW 7; BRWR 1; CA 9-12R; 45-48; CANR 5, 61, 105; CDBLB 1914-1945; DA; DA3; DAB; DAC; DAM DRAM, MST, POET; DLB 10, 20; EWL 3; EXPP; MTCW 1, 2; PAB; PFS 1, 3, 4, 10; TUS; WP

Audiberti, Jacques 1899-1965 .... **CLC 38**
See also CA 25-28R; DAM DRAM; EWL 3

Audubon, John James 1785-1851 . **NCLC 47**
See also ANW; DLB 248

Auel, Jean M(arie) 1936- .... **CLC 31, 107**
See also AAYA 7, 51; BEST 90:4; BPFB 1; CA 103; CANR 21, 64, 115; CPW; DA3; DAM POP; INT CANR-21; NFS 11; RHW; SATA 91

Auerbach, Erich 1892-1957 .... **TCLC 43**
See also CA 118; 155; EWL 3

Augier, Emile 1820-1889 .... **NCLC 31**
See also DLB 192; GFL 1789 to the Present

August, John
See De Voto, Bernard (Augustine)

Augustine, St. 354-430 .... **CMLC 6; WLCS**
See also DA; DA3; DAB; DAC; DAM MST; DLB 115; EW 1; RGWL 2, 3

Aunt Belinda
See Braddon, Mary Elizabeth

Aunt Weedy
See Alcott, Louisa May

Aurelius
See Bourne, Randolph S(illiman)

Aurelius, Marcus 121-180 .... **CMLC 45**
See Marcus Aurelius
See also RGWL 2, 3

Aurobindo, Sri
See Ghose, Aurabinda

Aurobindo Ghose
See Ghose, Aurabinda

Austen, Jane 1775-1817 ...... **NCLC 1, 13, 19, 33, 51, 81, 95, 119, 150; WLC**
See also AAYA 19; BRW 4; BRWC 1; BRWR 2; BYA 3; CDBLB 1789-1832; DA; DA3; DAB; DAC; DAM MST, NOV; DLB 116; EXPN; LAIT 2; LATS 1:1; LMFS 1; NFS 1, 14, 18, 20; TEA; WLIT 3; WYAS 1

Auster, Paul 1947- .... **CLC 47, 131**
See also AMWS 12; CA 69-72; CANR 23, 52, 75, 129; CMW 4; CN 7; DA3; DLB 227; MTCW 1; SUFW 2

Austin, Frank
See Faust, Frederick (Schiller)
See also TCWW 2

Breton, Andre 1896-1966 .. **CLC 2, 9, 15, 54; PC 15**
See also CA 19-20; 25-28R; CANR 40, 60; CAP 2; DLB 65, 258; EW 11; EWL 3; GFL 1789 to the Present; LMFS 2; MTCW 1, 2; RGWL 2, 3; TWA; WP

Breytenbach, Breyten 1939(?)- .. **CLC 23, 37, 126**
See also CA 113; 129; CANR 61, 122; CWW 2; DAM POET; DLB 225; EWL 3

Bridgers, Sue Ellen 1942- .... **CLC 26**
See also AAYA 8, 49; BYA 7, 8; CA 65-68; CANR 11, 36; CLR 18; DLB 52; JRDA; MAICYA 1, 2; SAAS 1; SATA 22, 90; SATA-Essay 109; WYA; YAW

Bridges, Robert (Seymour)
1844-1930 .... **PC 28; TCLC 1**
See also BRW 6; CA 104; 152; CDBLB 1890-1914; DAM POET; DLB 19, 98

Bridie, James .... **TCLC 3**
See Mavor, Osborne Henry
See also DLB 10; EWL 3

Brin, David 1950- .... **CLC 34**
See also AAYA 21; CA 102; CANR 24, 70, 125, 127; INT CANR-24; SATA 65; SCFW 2; SFW 4

Brink, Andre (Philippus) 1935- . **CLC 18, 36, 106**
See also AFW; BRWS 6; CA 104; CANR 39, 62, 109, 133; CN 7; DLB 225; EWL 3; INT CA-103; LATS 1:2; MTCW 1, 2; WLIT 2

Brinsmead, H. F(ay)
See Brinsmead, H(esba) F(ay)

Brinsmead, H. F.
See Brinsmead, H(esba) F(ay)

Brinsmead, H(esba) F(ay) 1922- ...... **CLC 21**
See also CA 21-24R; CANR 10; CLR 47; CWRI 5; MAICYA 1, 2; SAAS 5; SATA 18, 78

Brittain, Vera (Mary) 1893(?)-1970 . **CLC 23**
See also BRWS 10; CA 13-16; 25-28R; CANR 58; CAP 1; DLB 191; FW; MTCW 1, 2

Broch, Hermann 1886-1951 .... **TCLC 20**
See also CA 117; 211; CDWLB 2; DLB 85, 124; EW 10; EWL 3; RGWL 2, 3

Brock, Rose
See Hansen, Joseph
See also GLL 1

Brod, Max 1884-1968 .... **TCLC 115**
See also CA 5-8R; 25-28R; CANR 7; DLB 81; EWL 3

Brodkey, Harold (Roy) 1930-1996 .. **CLC 56; TCLC 123**
See also CA 111; 151; CANR 71; CN 7; DLB 130

Brodsky, Iosif Alexandrovich 1940-1996
See Brodsky, Joseph
See also AITN 1; CA 41-44R; 151; CANR 37, 106; DA3; DAM POET; MTCW 1, 2; RGWL 2, 3

Brodsky, Joseph . **CLC 4, 6, 13, 36, 100; PC 9**
See Brodsky, Iosif Alexandrovich
See also AMWS 8; CWW 2; DLB 285; EWL 3; MTCW 1

Brodsky, Michael (Mark) 1948- .... **CLC 19**
See also CA 102; CANR 18, 41, 58; DLB 244

Brodzki, Bella ed. .... **CLC 65**

Brome, Richard 1590(?)-1652 .... **LC 61**
See also BRWS 10; DLB 58

Bromell, Henry 1947- .... **CLC 5**
See also CA 53-56; CANR 9, 115, 116

Bromfield, Louis (Brucker)
1896-1956 .... **TCLC 11**
See also CA 107; 155; DLB 4, 9, 86; RGAL 4; RHW

Broner, E(sther) M(asserman)
1930- .... **CLC 19**
See also CA 17-20R; CANR 8, 25, 72; CN 7; DLB 28

Bronk, William (M.) 1918-1999 .... **CLC 10**
See also CA 89-92; 177; CANR 23; CP 7; DLB 165

Bronstein, Lev Davidovich
See Trotsky, Leon

Bronte, Anne 1820-1849 ..... **NCLC 4, 71, 102**
See also BRW 5; BRWR 1; DA3; DLB 21, 199; TEA

Bronte, (Patrick) Branwell
1817-1848 .... **NCLC 109**

Bronte, Charlotte 1816-1855 ...... **NCLC 3, 8, 33, 58, 105, 155; WLC**
See also AAYA 17; BRW 5; BRWC 2; BRWR 1; BYA 2; CDBLB 1832-1890; DA; DA3; DAB; DAC; DAM MST, NOV; DLB 21, 159, 199; EXPN; LAIT 2; NFS 4; TEA; WLIT 4

Bronte, Emily (Jane) 1818-1848 ... **NCLC 16, 35; PC 8; WLC**
See also AAYA 17; BPFB 1; BRW 5; BRWC 1; BRWR 1; BYA 3; CDBLB 1832-1890; DA; DA3; DAB; DAC; DAM MST, NOV, POET; DLB 21, 32, 199; EXPN; LAIT 1; TEA; WLIT 3

Brontes
See Bronte, Anne; Bronte, Charlotte; Bronte, Emily (Jane)

Brooke, Frances 1724-1789 .... **LC 6, 48**
See also DLB 39, 99

Brooke, Henry 1703(?)-1783 .... **LC 1**
See also DLB 39

Brooke, Rupert (Chawner)
1887-1915 ..... **PC 24; TCLC 2, 7; WLC**
See also BRWS 3; CA 104; 132; CANR 61; CDBLB 1914-1945; DA; DAB; DAC; DAM MST, POET; DLB 19, 216; EXPP; GLL 2; MTCW 1, 2; PFS 7; TEA

Brooke-Haven, P.
See Wodehouse, P(elham) G(renville)

Brooke-Rose, Christine 1926(?)- ..... **CLC 40, 184**
See also BRWS 4; CA 13-16R; CANR 58, 118; CN 7; DLB 14, 231; EWL 3; SFW 4

Brookner, Anita 1928- .. **CLC 32, 34, 51, 136**
See also BRWS 4; CA 114; 120; CANR 37, 56, 87, 130; CN 7; CPW; DA3; DAB; DAM POP; DLB 194; DLBY 1987; EWL 3; MTCW 1, 2; TEA

Brooks, Cleanth 1906-1994 . **CLC 24, 86, 110**
See also AMWS 14; CA 17-20R; 145; CANR 33, 35; CSW; DLB 63; DLBY 1994; EWL 3; INT CANR-35; MTCW 1, 2

Brooks, George
See Baum, L(yman) Frank

Brooks, Gwendolyn (Elizabeth)
1917-2000 ... **BLC 1; CLC 1, 2, 4, 5, 15, 49, 125; PC 7; WLC**
See also AAYA 20; AFAW 1, 2; AITN 1; AMWS 3; BW 2, 3; CA 1-4R; 190; CANR 1, 27, 52, 75, 132; CDALB 1941-1968; CLR 27; CP 7; CWP; DA; DA3; DAC; DAM MST, MULT, POET; DLB 5, 76, 165; EWL 3; EXPP; MAWW; MTCW 1, 2; PFS 1, 2, 4, 6; RGAL 4; SATA 6; SATA-Obit 123; TUS; WP

Brooks, Mel .... **CLC 12**
See Kaminsky, Melvin
See also AAYA 13, 48; DLB 26

Brooks, Peter (Preston) 1938- .... **CLC 34**
See also CA 45-48; CANR 1, 107

Brooks, Van Wyck 1886-1963 .... **CLC 29**
See also AMW; CA 1-4R; CANR 6; DLB 45, 63, 103; TUS

Brophy, Brigid (Antonia)
1929-1995 .... **CLC 6, 11, 29, 105**
See also CA 5-8R; 149; CAAS 4; CANR 25, 53; CBD; CN 7; CWD; DA3; DLB 14, 271; EWL 3; MTCW 1, 2

Brosman, Catharine Savage 1934- ..... **CLC 9**
See also CA 61-64; CANR 21, 46

Brossard, Nicole 1943- .... **CLC 115, 169**
See also CA 122; CAAS 16; CCA 1; CWP; CWW 2; DLB 53; EWL 3; FW; GLL 2; RGWL 3

Brother Antoninus
See Everson, William (Oliver)

The Brothers Quay
See Quay, Stephen; Quay, Timothy

Broughton, T(homas) Alan 1936- ..... **CLC 19**
See also CA 45-48; CANR 2, 23, 48, 111

Broumas, Olga 1949- .... **CLC 10, 73**
See also CA 85-88; CANR 20, 69, 110; CP 7; CWP; GLL 2

Broun, Heywood 1888-1939 .... **TCLC 104**
See also DLB 29, 171

Brown, Alan 1950- .... **CLC 99**
See also CA 156

Brown, Charles Brockden
1771-1810 .... **NCLC 22, 74, 122**
See also AMWS 1; CDALB 1640-1865; DLB 37, 59, 73; FW; HGG; LMFS 1; RGAL 4; TUS

Brown, Christy 1932-1981 .... **CLC 63**
See also BYA 13; CA 105; 104; CANR 72; DLB 14

Brown, Claude 1937-2002 ... **BLC 1; CLC 30**
See also AAYA 7; BW 1, 3; CA 73-76; 205; CANR 81; DAM MULT

Brown, Dee (Alexander)
1908-2002 .... **CLC 18, 47**
See also AAYA 30; CA 13-16R; 212; CAAS 6; CANR 11, 45, 60; CPW; CSW; DA3; DAM POP; DLBY 1980; LAIT 2; MTCW 1, 2; NCFS 5; SATA 5, 110; SATA-Obit 141; TCWW 2

Brown, George
See Wertmueller, Lina

Brown, George Douglas
1869-1902 .... **TCLC 28**
See Douglas, George
See also CA 162

Brown, George Mackay 1921-1996 ... **CLC 5, 48, 100**
See also BRWS 6; CA 21-24R; 151; CAAS 6; CANR 12, 37, 67; CN 7; CP 7; DLB 14, 27, 139, 271; MTCW 1; RGSF 2; SATA 35

Brown, (William) Larry 1951-2004 . **CLC 73**
See also CA 130; 134; CANR 117; CSW; DLB 234; INT CA-134

Brown, Moses
See Barrett, William (Christopher)

Brown, Rita Mae 1944- .... **CLC 18, 43, 79**
See also BPFB 1; CA 45-48; CANR 2, 11, 35, 62, 95; CN 7; CPW; CSW; DA3; DAM NOV, POP; FW; INT CANR-11; MTCW 1, 2; NFS 9; RGAL 4; TUS

Brown, Roderick (Langmere) Haig-
See Haig-Brown, Roderick (Langmere)

Brown, Rosellen 1939- .... **CLC 32, 170**
See also CA 77-80; CAAS 10; CANR 14, 44, 98; CN 7

Brown, Sterling Allen 1901-1989 ...... **BLC 1; CLC 1, 23, 59; HR 2; PC 55**
See also AFAW 1, 2; BW 1, 3; CA 85-88; 127; CANR 26; DA3; DAM MULT, POET; DLB 48, 51, 63; MTCW 1, 2; RGAL 4; WP

Brown, Will
See Ainsworth, William Harrison

Brown, William Hill 1765-1793 .... **LC 93**
See also DLB 37

Brown, William Wells 1815-1884 ...... **BLC 1; DC 1; NCLC 2, 89**
See also DAM MULT; DLB 3, 50, 183, 248; RGAL 4

Browne, (Clyde) Jackson 1948(?)- ... **CLC 21**
See also CA 120

Browne, Thomas 1605-1682 .... **LC 111**
See also BW 2; DLB 151

Browning, Robert 1812-1889 . **NCLC 19, 79; PC 2, 61; WLCS**
See also BRW 4; BRWC 2; BRWR 2; CD-BLB 1832-1890; CLR 97; DA; DA3; DAB; DAC; DAM MST, POET; DLB 32, 163; EXPP; LATS 1:1; PAB; PFS 1, 15; RGEL 2; TEA; WLIT 4; WP; YABC 1

Browning, Tod 1882-1962 .... **CLC 16**
See also CA 141; 117

Brownmiller, Susan 1935- .... **CLC 159**
See also CA 103; CANR 35, 75; DAM NOV; FW; MTCW 1, 2

Brownson, Orestes Augustus 1803-1876 .... **NCLC 50**
See also DLB 1, 59, 73, 243

Bruccoli, Matthew J(oseph) 1931- ... **CLC 34**
See also CA 9-12R; CANR 7, 87; DLB 103

Bruce, Lenny .... **CLC 21**
See Schneider, Leonard Alfred

Bruchac, Joseph III 1942- .... **NNAL**
See also AAYA 19; CA 33-36R; CANR 13, 47, 75, 94; CLR 46; CWRI 5; DAM MULT; JRDA; MAICYA 2; MAICYAS 1; MTCW 1; SATA 42, 89, 131

Bruin, John
See Brutus, Dennis

Brulard, Henri
See Stendhal

Brulls, Christian
See Simenon, Georges (Jacques Christian)

Brunetto Latini c. 1220-1294 .... **CMLC 73**

Brunner, John (Kilian Houston) 1934-1995 .... **CLC 8, 10**
See also CA 1-4R; 149; CAAS 8; CANR 2, 37; CPW; DAM POP; DLB 261; MTCW 1, 2; SCFW 2; SFW 4

Bruno, Giordano 1548-1600 .... **LC 27**
See also RGWL 2, 3

Brutus, Dennis 1924- ... **BLC 1; CLC 43; PC 24**
See also AFW; BW 2, 3; CA 49-52; CAAS 14; CANR 2, 27, 42, 81; CDWLB 3; CP 7; DAM MULT, POET; DLB 117, 225; EWL 3

Bryan, C(ourtlandt) D(ixon) B(arnes) 1936- .... **CLC 29**
See also CA 73-76; CANR 13, 68; DLB 185; INT CANR-13

Bryan, Michael
See Moore, Brian
See also CCA 1

Bryan, William Jennings 1860-1925 .... **TCLC 99**
See also DLB 303

Bryant, William Cullen 1794-1878 . **NCLC 6, 46; PC 20**
See also AMWS 1; CDALB 1640-1865; DA; DAB; DAC; DAM MST, POET; DLB 3, 43, 59, 189, 250; EXPP; PAB; RGAL 4; TUS

Bryusov, Valery Yakovlevich 1873-1924 .... **TCLC 10**
See also CA 107; 155; EWL 3; SFW 4

Buchan, John 1875-1940 .... **TCLC 41**
See also CA 108; 145; CMW 4; DAB; DAM POP; DLB 34, 70, 156; HGG; MSW; MTCW 1; RGEL 2; RHW; YABC 2

Buchanan, George 1506-1582 .... **LC 4**
See also DLB 132

Buchanan, Robert 1841-1901 .... **TCLC 107**
See also CA 179; DLB 18, 35

Buchheim, Lothar-Guenther 1918- .... **CLC 6**
See also CA 85-88

Buchner, (Karl) Georg 1813-1837 .... **NCLC 26, 146**
See also CDWLB 2; DLB 133; EW 6; RGSF 2; RGWL 2, 3; TWA

Buchwald, Art(hur) 1925- .... **CLC 33**
See also AITN 1; CA 5-8R; CANR 21, 67, 107; MTCW 1, 2; SATA 10

Buck, Pearl S(ydenstricker) 1892-1973 .... **CLC 7, 11, 18, 127**
See also AAYA 42; AITN 1; AMWS 2; BPFB 1; CA 1-4R; 41-44R; CANR 1, 34; CDALBS; DA; DA3; DAB; DAC; DAM MST, NOV; DLB 9, 102; EWL 3; LAIT 3; MTCW 1, 2; RGAL 4; RHW; SATA 1, 25; TUS

Buckler, Ernest 1908-1984 .... **CLC 13**
See also CA 11-12; 114; CAP 1; CCA 1; DAC; DAM MST; DLB 68; SATA 47

Buckley, Christopher (Taylor) 1952- .... **CLC 165**
See also CA 139; CANR 119

Buckley, Vincent (Thomas) 1925-1988 .... **CLC 57**
See also CA 101; DLB 289

Buckley, William F(rank), Jr. 1925- . **CLC 7, 18, 37**
See also AITN 1; BPFB 1; CA 1-4R; CANR 1, 24, 53, 93, 133; CMW 4; CPW; DA3; DAM POP; DLB 137; DLBY 1980; INT CANR-24; MTCW 1, 2; TUS

Buechner, (Carl) Frederick 1926- . **CLC 2, 4, 6, 9**
See also AMWS 12; BPFB 1; CA 13-16R; CANR 11, 39, 64, 114; CN 7; DAM NOV; DLBY 1980; INT CANR-11; MTCW 1, 2

Buell, John (Edward) 1927- .... **CLC 10**
See also CA 1-4R; CANR 71; DLB 53

Buero Vallejo, Antonio 1916-2000 ... **CLC 15, 46, 139; DC 18**
See also CA 106; 189; CANR 24, 49, 75; CWW 2; DFS 11; EWL 3; HW 1; MTCW 1, 2

Bufalino, Gesualdo 1920-1996 .... **CLC 74**
See also CA 209; CWW 2; DLB 196

Bugayev, Boris Nikolayevich 1880-1934 .... **PC 11; TCLC 7**
See Bely, Andrey; Belyi, Andrei
See also CA 104; 165; MTCW 1

Bukowski, Charles 1920-1994 ... **CLC 2, 5, 9, 41, 82, 108; PC 18; SSC 45**
See also CA 17-20R; 144; CANR 40, 62, 105; CPW; DA3; DAM NOV, POET; DLB 5, 130, 169; EWL 3; MTCW 1, 2

Bulgakov, Mikhail (Afanas'evich) 1891-1940 ..... **SSC 18; TCLC 2, 16, 159**
See also BPFB 1; CA 105; 152; DAM DRAM, NOV; DLB 272; EWL 3; NFS 8; RGSF 2; RGWL 2, 3; SFW 4; TWA

Bulgya, Alexander Alexandrovich 1901-1956 .... **TCLC 53**
See Fadeev, Aleksandr Aleksandrovich; Fadeev, Alexandr Alexandrovich; Fadeyev, Alexander
See also CA 117; 181

Bullins, Ed 1935- ... **BLC 1; CLC 1, 5, 7; DC 6**
See also BW 2, 3; CA 49-52; CAAS 16; CAD; CANR 24, 46, 73, 134; CD 5; DAM DRAM, MULT; DLB 7, 38, 249; EWL 3; MTCW 1, 2; RGAL 4

Bulosan, Carlos 1911-1956 .... **AAL**
See also CA 216; RGAL 4

Bulwer-Lytton, Edward (George Earle Lytton) 1803-1873 .... **NCLC 1, 45**
See also DLB 21; RGEL 2; SFW 4; SUFW 1; TEA

Bunin, Ivan Alexeyevich 1870-1953 ... **SSC 5; TCLC 6**
See also CA 104; EWL 3; RGSF 2; RGWL 2, 3; TWA

Bunting, Basil 1900-1985 ...... **CLC 10, 39, 47**
See also BRWS 7; CA 53-56; 115; CANR 7; DAM POET; DLB 20; EWL 3; RGEL 2; TEA; WP

Bunuel, Luis 1900-1983 ... **CLC 16, 80; HLC 1**
See also CA 101; 110; CANR 32, 77; DAM MULT; HW 1

Bunyan, John 1628-1688 ..... **LC 4, 69; WLC**
See also BRW 2; BYA 5; CDBLB 1660-1789; DA; DAB; DAC; DAM MST; DLB 39; RGEL 2; TEA; WCH; WLIT 3

Buravsky, Alexandr .... **CLC 59**

Burckhardt, Jacob (Christoph) 1818-1897 .... **NCLC 49**
See also EW 6

Burford, Eleanor
See Hibbert, Eleanor Alice Burford

Burgess, Anthony . **CLC 1, 2, 4, 5, 8, 10, 13, 15, 22, 40, 62, 81, 94**
See Wilson, John (Anthony) Burgess
See also AAYA 25; AITN 1; BRWS 1; CD-BLB 1960 to Present; DAB; DLB 14, 194, 261; DLBY 1998; EWL 3; MTCW 1; RGEL 2; RHW; SFW 4; YAW

Burke, Edmund 1729(?)-1797 .... **LC 7, 36; WLC**
See also BRW 3; DA; DA3; DAB; DAC; DAM MST; DLB 104, 252; RGEL 2; TEA

Burke, Kenneth (Duva) 1897-1993 ... **CLC 2, 24**
See also AMW; CA 5-8R; 143; CANR 39, 74; DLB 45, 63; EWL 3; MTCW 1, 2; RGAL 4

Burke, Leda
See Garnett, David

Burke, Ralph
See Silverberg, Robert

Burke, Thomas 1886-1945 .... **TCLC 63**
See also CA 113; 155; CMW 4; DLB 197

Burney, Fanny 1752-1840 .... **NCLC 12, 54, 107**
See also BRWS 3; DLB 39; NFS 16; RGEL 2; TEA

Burney, Frances
See Burney, Fanny

Burns, Robert 1759-1796 ... **LC 3, 29, 40; PC 6; WLC**
See also AAYA 51; BRW 3; CDBLB 1789-1832; DA; DA3; DAB; DAC; DAM MST, POET; DLB 109; EXPP; PAB; RGEL 2; TEA; WP

Burns, Tex
See L'Amour, Louis (Dearborn)
See also TCWW 2

Burnshaw, Stanley 1906- .... **CLC 3, 13, 44**
See also CA 9-12R; CP 7; DLB 48; DLBY 1997

Burr, Anne 1937- .... **CLC 6**
See also CA 25-28R

Burroughs, Edgar Rice 1875-1950 . **TCLC 2, 32**
See also AAYA 11; BPFB 1; BYA 4, 9; CA 104; 132; CANR 131; DA3; DAM NOV; DLB 8; FANT; MTCW 1, 2; RGAL 4; SATA 41; SCFW 2; SFW 4; TUS; YAW

Burroughs, William S(eward) 1914-1997 .. **CLC 1, 2, 5, 15, 22, 42, 75, 109; TCLC 121; WLC**
See Lee, William; Lee, Willy
See also AAYA 60; AITN 2; AMWS 3; BG 2; BPFB 1; CA 9-12R; 160; CANR 20, 52, 104; CN 7; CPW; DA; DA3; DAB;

Campbell, (Ignatius) Roy (Dunnachie)
1901-1957 .... **TCLC 5**
See also AFW; CA 104; 155; DLB 20, 225;
EWL 3; MTCW 2; RGEL 2
Campbell, Thomas 1777-1844 .... **NCLC 19**
See also DLB 93, 144; RGEL 2
Campbell, Wilfred .... **TCLC 9**
See Campbell, William
Campbell, William 1858(?)-1918
See Campbell, Wilfred
See also CA 106; DLB 92
Campion, Jane 1954- .... **CLC 95**
See also AAYA 33; CA 138; CANR 87
Campion, Thomas 1567-1620 .... **LC 78**
See also CDBLB Before 1660; DAM POET;
DLB 58, 172; RGEL 2
Camus, Albert 1913-1960 ...... **CLC 1, 2, 4, 9,
11, 14, 32, 63, 69, 124; DC 2; SSC 9,
76; WLC**
See also AAYA 36; AFW; BPFB 1; CA 89-
92; CANR 131; DA; DA3; DAB; DAC;
DAM DRAM, MST, NOV; DLB 72; EW
13; EWL 3; EXPN; EXPS; GFL 1789 to
the Present; LATS 1:2; LMFS 2; MTCW
1, 2; NFS 6, 16; RGSF 2; RGWL 2, 3;
SSFS 4; TWA
Canby, Vincent 1924-2000 .... **CLC 13**
See also CA 81-84; 191
Cancale
See Desnos, Robert
Canetti, Elias 1905-1994 .. **CLC 3, 14, 25, 75,
86; TCLC 157**
See also CA 21-24R; 146; CANR 23, 61,
79; CDWLB 2; CWW 2; DA3; DLB 85,
124; EW 12; EWL 3; MTCW 1, 2; RGWL
2, 3; TWA
Canfield, Dorothea F.
See Fisher, Dorothy (Frances) Canfield
Canfield, Dorothea Frances
See Fisher, Dorothy (Frances) Canfield
Canfield, Dorothy
See Fisher, Dorothy (Frances) Canfield
Canin, Ethan 1960- .... **CLC 55; SSC 70**
See also CA 131; 135
Cankar, Ivan 1876-1918 .... **TCLC 105**
See also CDWLB 4; DLB 147; EWL 3
Cannon, Curt
See Hunter, Evan
Cao, Lan 1961- .... **CLC 109**
See also CA 165
Cape, Judith
See Page, P(atricia) K(athleen)
See also CCA 1
Capek, Karel 1890-1938 .... **DC 1; SSC 36;
TCLC 6, 37; WLC**
See also CA 104; 140; CDWLB 4; DA;
DA3; DAB; DAC; DAM DRAM, MST,
NOV; DFS 7, 11; DLB 215; EW 10; EWL
3; MTCW 1; RGSF 2; RGWL 2, 3; SCFW
2; SFW 4
Capote, Truman 1924-1984 . **CLC 1, 3, 8, 13,
19, 34, 38, 58; SSC 2, 47; TCLC 164;
WLC**
See also AMWS 3; BPFB 1; CA 5-8R; 113;
CANR 18, 62; CDALB 1941-1968; CPW;
DA; DA3; DAB; DAC; DAM MST, NOV,
POP; DLB 2, 185, 227; DLBY 1980,
1984; EWL 3; EXPS; GLL 1; LAIT 3;
MTCW 1, 2; NCFS 2; RGAL 4; RGSF 2;
SATA 91; SSFS 2; TUS
Capra, Frank 1897-1991 .... **CLC 16**
See also AAYA 52; CA 61-64; 135
Caputo, Philip 1941- .... **CLC 32**
See also AAYA 60; CA 73-76; CANR 40,
135; YAW
Caragiale, Ion Luca 1852-1912 ...... **TCLC 76**
See also CA 157

Card, Orson Scott 1951- .... **CLC 44, 47, 50**
See also AAYA 11, 42; BPFB 1; BYA 5, 8;
CA 102; CANR 27, 47, 73, 102, 106, 133;
CPW; DA3; DAM POP; FANT; INT
CANR-27; MTCW 1, 2; NFS 5; SATA
83, 127; SCFW 2; SFW 4; SUFW 2; YAW
Cardenal, Ernesto 1925- .... **CLC 31, 161;
HLC 1; PC 22**
See also CA 49-52; CANR 2, 32, 66; CWW
2; DAM MULT, POET; DLB 290; EWL
3; HW 1, 2; LAWS 1; MTCW 1, 2;
RGWL 2, 3
Cardinal, Marie 1929-2001 .... **CLC 189**
See also CA 177; CWW 2; DLB 83; FW
Cardozo, Benjamin N(athan)
1870-1938 .... **TCLC 65**
See also CA 117; 164
Carducci, Giosue (Alessandro Giuseppe)
1835-1907 .... **PC 46; TCLC 32**
See also CA 163; EW 7; RGWL 2, 3
Carew, Thomas 1595(?)-1640 . **LC 13; PC 29**
See also BRW 2; DLB 126; PAB; RGEL 2
Carey, Ernestine Gilbreth 1908- ...... **CLC 17**
See also CA 5-8R; CANR 71; SATA 2
Carey, Peter 1943- .... **CLC 40, 55, 96, 183**
See also CA 123; 127; CANR 53, 76, 117;
CN 7; DLB 289; EWL 3; INT CA-127;
MTCW 1, 2; RGSF 2; SATA 94
Carleton, William 1794-1869 .... **NCLC 3**
See also DLB 159; RGEL 2; RGSF 2
Carlisle, Henry (Coffin) 1926- .... **CLC 33**
See also CA 13-16R; CANR 15, 85
Carlsen, Chris
See Holdstock, Robert P.
Carlson, Ron(ald F.) 1947- .... **CLC 54**
See also CA 105; 189; CAAE 189; CANR
27; DLB 244
Carlyle, Thomas 1795-1881 ..... **NCLC 22, 70**
See also BRW 4; CDBLB 1789-1832; DA;
DAB; DAC; DAM MST; DLB 55, 144,
254; RGEL 2; TEA
Carman, (William) Bliss 1861-1929 ... **PC 34;
TCLC 7**
See also CA 104; 152; DAC; DLB 92;
RGEL 2
Carnegie, Dale 1888-1955 .... **TCLC 53**
See also CA 218
Carossa, Hans 1878-1956 .... **TCLC 48**
See also CA 170; DLB 66; EWL 3
Carpenter, Don(ald Richard)
1931-1995 .... **CLC 41**
See also CA 45-48; 149; CANR 1, 71
Carpenter, Edward 1844-1929 .... **TCLC 88**
See also CA 163; GLL 1
Carpenter, John (Howard) 1948- ... **CLC 161**
See also AAYA 2; CA 134; SATA 58
Carpenter, Johnny
See Carpenter, John (Howard)
Carpentier (y Valmont), Alejo
1904-1980 . **CLC 8, 11, 38, 110; HLC 1;
SSC 35**
See also CA 65-68; 97-100; CANR 11, 70;
CDWLB 3; DAM MULT; DLB 113; EWL
3; HW 1, 2; LAW; LMFS 2; RGSF 2;
RGWL 2, 3; WLIT 1
Carr, Caleb 1955- .... **CLC 86**
See also CA 147; CANR 73, 134; DA3
Carr, Emily 1871-1945 .... **TCLC 32**
See also CA 159; DLB 68; FW; GLL 2
Carr, John Dickson 1906-1977 .... **CLC 3**
See Fairbairn, Roger
See also CA 49-52; 69-72; CANR 3, 33,
60; CMW 4; DLB 306; MSW; MTCW 1,
2
Carr, Philippa
See Hibbert, Eleanor Alice Burford
Carr, Virginia Spencer 1929- .... **CLC 34**
See also CA 61-64; DLB 111

Carrere, Emmanuel 1957- .... **CLC 89**
See also CA 200
Carrier, Roch 1937- .... **CLC 13, 78**
See also CA 130; CANR 61; CCA 1; DAC;
DAM MST; DLB 53; SATA 105
Carroll, James Dennis
See Carroll, Jim
Carroll, James P. 1943(?)- .... **CLC 38**
See also CA 81-84; CANR 73; MTCW 1
Carroll, Jim 1951- .... **CLC 35, 143**
See also AAYA 17; CA 45-48; CANR 42,
115; NCFS 5
Carroll, Lewis ..... **NCLC 2, 53, 139; PC 18;
WLC**
See Dodgson, Charles L(utwidge)
See also AAYA 39; BRW 5; BYA 5, 13; CD-
BLB 1832-1890; CLR 2, 18; DLB 18,
163, 178; DLBY 1998; EXPN; EXPP;
FANT; JRDA; LAIT 1; NFS 7; PFS 11;
RGEL 2; SUFW 1; TEA; WCH
Carroll, Paul Vincent 1900-1968 ...... **CLC 10**
See also CA 9-12R; 25-28R; DLB 10; EWL
3; RGEL 2
Carruth, Hayden 1921- ..... **CLC 4, 7, 10, 18,
84; PC 10**
See also CA 9-12R; CANR 4, 38, 59, 110;
CP 7; DLB 5, 165; INT CANR-4; MTCW
1, 2; SATA 47
Carson, Anne 1950- .... **CLC 185; PC 64**
See also AMWS 12; CA 203; DLB 193;
PFS 18
Carson, Ciaran 1948- .... **CLC 201**
See also CA 153; CA-Brief 112; CANR
113; CP 7
Carson, Rachel
See Carson, Rachel Louise
See also AAYA 49; DLB 275
Carson, Rachel Louise 1907-1964 .... **CLC 71**
See Carson, Rachel
See also AMWS 9; ANW; CA 77-80; CANR
35; DA3; DAM POP; FW; LAIT 4;
MTCW 1, 2; NCFS 1; SATA 23
Carter, Angela (Olive) 1940-1992 ...... **CLC 5,
41, 76; SSC 13; TCLC 139**
See also BRWS 3; CA 53-56; 136; CANR
12, 36, 61, 106; DA3; DLB 14, 207, 261;
EXPS; FANT; FW; MTCW 1, 2; RGSF 2;
SATA 66; SATA-Obit 70; SFW 4; SSFS
4, 12; SUFW 2; WLIT 4
Carter, Nick
See Smith, Martin Cruz
Carver, Raymond 1938-1988 ..... **CLC 22, 36,
53, 55, 126; PC 54; SSC 8, 51**
See also AAYA 44; AMWS 3; BPFB 1; CA
33-36R; 126; CANR 17, 34, 61, 103;
CPW; DA3; DAM NOV; DLB 130;
DLBY 1984, 1988; EWL 3; MTCW 1, 2;
PFS 17; RGAL 4; RGSF 2; SSFS 3, 6,
12, 13; TCWW 2; TUS
Cary, Elizabeth, Lady Falkland
1585-1639 .... **LC 30**
Cary, (Arthur) Joyce (Lunel)
1888-1957 .... **TCLC 1, 29**
See also BRW 7; CA 104; 164; CDBLB
1914-1945; DLB 15, 100; EWL 3; MTCW
2; RGEL 2; TEA
Casal, Julian del 1863-1893 .... **NCLC 131**
See also DLB 283; LAW
Casanova de Seingalt, Giovanni Jacopo
1725-1798 .... **LC 13**
Casares, Adolfo Bioy
See Bioy Casares, Adolfo
See also RGSF 2
Casas, Bartolome de las 1474-1566
See Las Casas, Bartolome de
See also WLIT 1
Casely-Hayford, J(oseph) E(phraim)
1866-1903 .... **BLC 1; TCLC 24**
See also BW 2; CA 123; 152; DAM MULT

Casey, John (Dudley) 1939- .... **CLC 59**
See also BEST 90:2; CA 69-72; CANR 23, 100
Casey, Michael 1947- .... **CLC 2**
See also CA 65-68; CANR 109; DLB 5
Casey, Patrick
See Thurman, Wallace (Henry)
Casey, Warren (Peter) 1935-1988 .... **CLC 12**
See also CA 101; 127; INT CA-101
Casona, Alejandro .... **CLC 49**
See Alvarez, Alejandro Rodriguez
See also EWL 3
Cassavetes, John 1929-1989 .... **CLC 20**
See also CA 85-88; 127; CANR 82
Cassian, Nina 1924- .... **PC 17**
See also CWP; CWW 2
Cassill, R(onald) V(erlin)
1919-2002 .... **CLC 4, 23**
See also CA 9-12R; 208; CAAS 1; CANR 7, 45; CN 7; DLB 6, 218; DLBY 2002
Cassiodorus, Flavius Magnus c. 490(?)-c. 583(?) .... **CMLC 43**
Cassirer, Ernst 1874-1945 .... **TCLC 61**
See also CA 157
Cassity, (Allen) Turner 1929- ...... **CLC 6, 42**
See also CA 17-20R; 223; CAAE 223; CAAS 8; CANR 11; CSW; DLB 105
Castaneda, Carlos (Cesar Aranha)
1931(?)-1998 .... **CLC 12, 119**
See also CA 25-28R; CANR 32, 66, 105; DNFS 1; HW 1; MTCW 1
Castedo, Elena 1937- .... **CLC 65**
See also CA 132
Castedo-Ellerman, Elena
See Castedo, Elena
Castellanos, Rosario 1925-1974 .... **CLC 66; HLC 1; SSC 39, 68**
See also CA 131; 53-56; CANR 58; CD-WLB 3; DAM MULT; DLB 113, 290; EWL 3; FW; HW 1; LAW; MTCW 1; RGSF 2; RGWL 2, 3
Castelvetro, Lodovico 1505-1571 .... **LC 12**
Castiglione, Baldassare 1478-1529 ...... **LC 12**
See Castiglione, Baldesar
See also LMFS 1; RGWL 2, 3
Castiglione, Baldesar
See Castiglione, Baldassare
See also EW 2
Castillo, Ana (Hernandez Del)
1953- .... **CLC 151**
See also AAYA 42; CA 131; CANR 51, 86, 128; CWP; DLB 122, 227; DNFS 2; FW; HW 1; LLW 1; PFS 21
Castle, Robert
See Hamilton, Edmond
Castro (Ruz), Fidel 1926(?)- .... **HLC 1**
See also CA 110; 129; CANR 81; DAM MULT; HW 2
Castro, Guillen de 1569-1631 .... **LC 19**
Castro, Rosalia de 1837-1885 ... **NCLC 3, 78; PC 41**
See also DAM MULT
Cather, Willa (Sibert) 1873-1947 . **SSC 2, 50; TCLC 1, 11, 31, 99, 132, 152; WLC**
See also AAYA 24; AMW; AMWC 1; AMWR 1; BPFB 1; CA 104; 128; CDALB 1865-1917; CLR 98; DA; DA3; DAB; DAC; DAM MST, NOV; DLB 9, 54, 78, 256; DLBD 1; EWL 3; EXPN; EXPS; LAIT 3; LATS 1:1; MAWW; MTCW 1, 2; NFS 2, 19; RGAL 4; RGSF 2; RHW; SATA 30; SSFS 2, 7, 16; TCWW 2; TUS
Catherine II
See Catherine the Great
See also DLB 150
Catherine the Great 1729-1796 .... **LC 69**
See Catherine II

Cato, Marcus Porcius
234B.C.-149B.C. .... **CMLC 21**
See Cato the Elder
Cato, Marcus Porcius, the Elder
See Cato, Marcus Porcius
Cato the Elder
See Cato, Marcus Porcius
See also DLB 211
Catton, (Charles) Bruce 1899-1978 . **CLC 35**
See also AITN 1; CA 5-8R; 81-84; CANR 7, 74; DLB 17; SATA 2; SATA-Obit 24
Catullus c. 84B.C.-54B.C. .... **CMLC 18**
See also AW 2; CDWLB 1; DLB 211; RGWL 2, 3
Cauldwell, Frank
See King, Francis (Henry)
Caunitz, William J. 1933-1996 .... **CLC 34**
See also BEST 89:3; CA 125; 130; 152; CANR 73; INT CA-130
Causley, Charles (Stanley)
1917-2003 .... **CLC 7**
See also CA 9-12R; 223; CANR 5, 35, 94; CLR 30; CWRI 5; DLB 27; MTCW 1; SATA 3, 66; SATA-Obit 149
Caute, (John) David 1936- .... **CLC 29**
See also CA 1-4R; CAAS 4; CANR 1, 33, 64, 120; CBD; CD 5; CN 7; DAM NOV; DLB 14, 231
Cavafy, C(onstantine) P(eter) .... **PC 36; TCLC 2, 7**
See Kavafis, Konstantinos Petrou
See also CA 148; DA3; DAM POET; EW 8; EWL 3; MTCW 1; PFS 19; RGWL 2, 3; WP
Cavalcanti, Guido c. 1250-c. 1300 .... **CMLC 54**
See also RGWL 2, 3
Cavallo, Evelyn
See Spark, Muriel (Sarah)
Cavanna, Betty .... **CLC 12**
See Harrison, Elizabeth (Allen) Cavanna
See also JRDA; MAICYA 1; SAAS 4; SATA 1, 30
Cavendish, Margaret Lucas
1623-1673 .... **LC 30**
See also DLB 131, 252, 281; RGEL 2
Caxton, William 1421(?)-1491(?) .... **LC 17**
See also DLB 170
Cayer, D. M.
See Duffy, Maureen
Cayrol, Jean 1911- .... **CLC 11**
See also CA 89-92; DLB 83; EWL 3
Cela (y Trulock), Camilo Jose
See Cela, Camilo Jose
See also CWW 2
Cela, Camilo Jose 1916-2002 .... **CLC 4, 13, 59, 122; HLC 1; SSC 71**
See Cela (y Trulock), Camilo Jose
See also BEST 90:2; CA 21-24R; 206; CAAS 10; CANR 21, 32, 76; DAM MULT; DLBY 1989; EW 13; EWL 3; HW 1; MTCW 1, 2; RGSF 2; RGWL 2, 3
Celan, Paul .... **CLC 10, 19, 53, 82; PC 10**
See Antschel, Paul
See also CDWLB 2; DLB 69; EWL 3; RGWL 2, 3
Celine, Louis-Ferdinand .. **CLC 1, 3, 4, 7, 9, 15, 47, 124**
See Destouches, Louis-Ferdinand
See also DLB 72; EW 11; EWL 3; GFL 1789 to the Present; RGWL 2, 3
Cellini, Benvenuto 1500-1571 .... **LC 7**
Cendrars, Blaise .... **CLC 18, 106**
See Sauser-Hall, Frederic
See also DLB 258; EWL 3; GFL 1789 to the Present; RGWL 2, 3; WP
Centlivre, Susanna 1669(?)-1723 .... **DC 25; LC 65**
See also DLB 84; RGEL 2

Cernuda (y Bidon), Luis
1902-1963 .... **CLC 54; PC 62**
See also CA 131; 89-92; DAM POET; DLB 134; EWL 3; GLL 1; HW 1; RGWL 2, 3
Cervantes, Lorna Dee 1954- ..... **HLCS 1; PC 35**
See also CA 131; CANR 80; CWP; DLB 82; EXPP; HW 1; LLW 1
Cervantes (Saavedra), Miguel de
1547-1616 .... **HLCS; LC 6, 23, 93; SSC 12; WLC**
See also AAYA 56; BYA 1, 14; DA; DAB; DAC; DAM MST, NOV; EW 2; LAIT 1; LATS 1:1; LMFS 1; NFS 8; RGSF 2; RGWL 2, 3; TWA
Cesaire, Aime (Fernand) 1913- .... **BLC 1; CLC 19, 32, 112; DC 22; PC 25**
See also BW 2, 3; CA 65-68; CANR 24, 43, 81; CWW 2; DA3; DAM MULT, POET; EWL 3; GFL 1789 to the Present; MTCW 1, 2; WP
Chabon, Michael 1963- ... **CLC 55, 149; SSC 59**
See also AAYA 45; AMWS 11; CA 139; CANR 57, 96, 127; DLB 278; SATA 145
Chabrol, Claude 1930- .... **CLC 16**
See also CA 110
Chairil Anwar
See Anwar, Chairil
See also EWL 3
Challans, Mary 1905-1983
See Renault, Mary
See also CA 81-84; 111; CANR 74; DA3; MTCW 2; SATA 23; SATA-Obit 36; TEA
Challis, George
See Faust, Frederick (Schiller)
See also TCWW 2
Chambers, Aidan 1934- .... **CLC 35**
See also AAYA 27; CA 25-28R; CANR 12, 31, 58, 116; JRDA; MAICYA 1, 2; SAAS 12; SATA 1, 69, 108; WYA; YAW
Chambers, James 1948-
See Cliff, Jimmy
See also CA 124
Chambers, Jessie
See Lawrence, D(avid) H(erbert Richards)
See also GLL 1
Chambers, Robert W(illiam)
1865-1933 .... **TCLC 41**
See also CA 165; DLB 202; HGG; SATA 107; SUFW 1
Chambers, (David) Whittaker
1901-1961 .... **TCLC 129**
See also CA 89-92; DLB 303
Chamisso, Adelbert von
1781-1838 .... **NCLC 82**
See also DLB 90; RGWL 2, 3; SUFW 1
Chance, James T.
See Carpenter, John (Howard)
Chance, John T.
See Carpenter, John (Howard)
Chandler, Raymond (Thornton)
1888-1959 .... **SSC 23; TCLC 1, 7**
See also AAYA 25; AMWC 2; AMWS 4; BPFB 1; CA 104; 129; CANR 60, 107; CDALB 1929-1941; CMW 4; DA3; DLB 226, 253; DLBD 6; EWL 3; MSW; MTCW 1, 2; NFS 17; RGAL 4; TUS
Chang, Diana 1934- .... **AAL**
See also CA 228; CWP; EXPP
Chang, Eileen 1921-1995 .... **AAL; SSC 28**
See Chang Ai-Ling; Zhang Ailing
See also CA 166
Chang, Jung 1952- .... **CLC 71**
See also CA 142
Chang Ai-Ling
See Chang, Eileen
See also EWL 3

Cobb, Irvin S(hrewsbury)
1876-1944 .... **TCLC 77**
See also CA 175; DLB 11, 25, 86

Cobbett, William 1763-1835 .... **NCLC 49**
See also DLB 43, 107, 158; RGEL 2

Coburn, D(onald) L(ee) 1938- .... **CLC 10**
See also CA 89-92

Cocteau, Jean (Maurice Eugene Clement)
1889-1963 ...... **CLC 1, 8, 15, 16, 43; DC
17; TCLC 119; WLC**
See also CA 25-28; CANR 40; CAP 2; DA;
DA3; DAB; DAC; DAM DRAM, MST,
NOV; DLB 65, 258; EW 10; EWL 3; GFL
1789 to the Present; MTCW 1, 2; RGWL
2, 3; TWA

Codrescu, Andrei 1946- .... **CLC 46, 121**
See also CA 33-36R; CAAS 19; CANR 13,
34, 53, 76, 125; DA3; DAM POET;
MTCW 2

Coe, Max
See Bourne, Randolph S(illiman)

Coe, Tucker
See Westlake, Donald E(dwin)

Coen, Ethan 1958- .... **CLC 108**
See also AAYA 54; CA 126; CANR 85

Coen, Joel 1955- .... **CLC 108**
See also AAYA 54; CA 126; CANR 119

The Coen Brothers
See Coen, Ethan; Coen, Joel

Coetzee, J(ohn) M(axwell) 1940- ..... **CLC 23,
33, 66, 117, 161, 162**
See also AAYA 37; AFW; BRWS 6; CA 77-
80; CANR 41, 54, 74, 114, 133; CN 7;
DA3; DAM NOV; DLB 225; EWL 3;
LMFS; MTCW 1, 2; WLIT 2; WWE 1

Coffey, Brian
See Koontz, Dean R(ay)

Coffin, Robert P(eter) Tristram
1892-1955 .... **TCLC 95**
See also CA 123; 169; DLB 45

Cohan, George M(ichael)
1878-1942 .... **TCLC 60**
See also CA 157; DLB 249; RGAL 4

Cohen, Arthur A(llen) 1928-1986 ...... **CLC 7,
31**
See also CA 1-4R; 120; CANR 1, 17, 42;
DLB 28

Cohen, Leonard (Norman) 1934- ...... **CLC 3,
38**
See also CA 21-24R; CANR 14, 69; CN 7;
CP 7; DAC; DAM MST; DLB 53; EWL
3; MTCW 1

Cohen, Matt(hew) 1942-1999 .... **CLC 19**
See also CA 61-64; 187; CAAS 18; CANR
40; CN 7; DAC; DLB 53

Cohen-Solal, Annie 19(?)- .... **CLC 50**

Colegate, Isabel 1931- .... **CLC 36**
See also CA 17-20R; CANR 8, 22, 74; CN
7; DLB 14, 231; INT CANR-22; MTCW
1

Coleman, Emmett
See Reed, Ishmael

Coleridge, Hartley 1796-1849 .... **NCLC 90**
See also DLB 96

Coleridge, M. E.
See Coleridge, Mary E(lizabeth)

Coleridge, Mary E(lizabeth)
1861-1907 .... **TCLC 73**
See also CA 116; 166; DLB 19, 98

Coleridge, Samuel Taylor
1772-1834 ...... **NCLC 9, 54, 99, 111; PC
11, 39; WLC**
See also BRW 4; BRWR 2; BYA 4; CD-
BLB 1789-1832; DA; DA3; DAB; DAC;
DAM MST, POET; DLB 93, 107; EXPP;
LATS 1:1; LMFS 1; PAB; PFS 4, 5;
RGEL 2; TEA; WLIT 3; WP

Coleridge, Sara 1802-1852 .... **NCLC 31**
See also DLB 199

Coles, Don 1928- .... **CLC 46**
See also CA 115; CANR 38; CP 7

Coles, Robert (Martin) 1929- .... **CLC 108**
See also CA 45-48; CANR 3, 32, 66, 70,
135; INT CANR-32; SATA 23

Colette, (Sidonie-Gabrielle)
1873-1954 .... **SSC 10; TCLC 1, 5, 16**
See Willy, Colette
See also CA 104; 131; DA3; DAM NOV;
DLB 65; EW 9; EWL 3; GFL 1789 to the
Present; MTCW 1, 2; RGWL 2, 3; TWA

Collett, (Jacobine) Camilla (Wergeland)
1813-1895 .... **NCLC 22**

Collier, Christopher 1930- .... **CLC 30**
See also AAYA 13; BYA 2; CA 33-36R;
CANR 13, 33, 102; JRDA; MAICYA 1,
2; SATA 16, 70; WYA; YAW 1

Collier, James Lincoln 1928- .... **CLC 30**
See also AAYA 13; BYA 2; CA 9-12R;
CANR 4, 33, 60, 102; CLR 3; DAM POP;
JRDA; MAICYA 1, 2; SAAS 21; SATA 8,
70; WYA; YAW 1

Collier, Jeremy 1650-1726 .... **LC 6**

Collier, John 1901-1980 . **SSC 19; TCLC 127**
See also CA 65-68; 97-100; CANR 10;
DLB 77, 255; FANT; SUFW 1

Collier, Mary 1690-1762 .... **LC 86**
See also DLB 95

Collingwood, R(obin) G(eorge)
1889(?)-1943 .... **TCLC 67**
See also CA 117; 155; DLB 262

Collins, Hunt
See Hunter, Evan

Collins, Linda 1931- .... **CLC 44**
See also CA 125

Collins, Tom
See Furphy, Joseph
See also RGEL 2

Collins, (William) Wilkie
1824-1889 .... **NCLC 1, 18, 93**
See also BRWS 6; CDBLB 1832-1890;
CMW 4; DLB 18, 70, 159; MSW; RGEL
2; RGSF 2; SUFW 1; WLIT 4

Collins, William 1721-1759 .... **LC 4, 40**
See also BRW 3; DAM POET; DLB 109;
RGEL 2

Collodi, Carlo .... **NCLC 54**
See Lorenzini, Carlo
See also CLR 5; WCH

Colman, George
See Glassco, John

Colman, George, the Elder
1732-1794 .... **LC 98**
See also RGEL 2

Colonna, Vittoria 1492-1547 .... **LC 71**
See also RGWL 2, 3

Colt, Winchester Remington
See Hubbard, L(afayette) Ron(ald)

Colter, Cyrus J. 1910-2002 .... **CLC 58**
See also BW 1; CA 65-68; 205; CANR 10,
66; CN 7; DLB 33

Colton, James
See Hansen, Joseph
See also GLL 1

Colum, Padraic 1881-1972 .... **CLC 28**
See also BYA 4; CA 73-76; 33-36R; CANR
35; CLR 36; CWRI 5; DLB 19; MAICYA
1, 2; MTCW 1; RGEL 2; SATA 15; WCH

Colvin, James
See Moorcock, Michael (John)

Colwin, Laurie (E.) 1944-1992 .... **CLC 5, 13,
23, 84**
See also CA 89-92; 139; CANR 20, 46;
DLB 218; DLBY 1980; MTCW 1

Comfort, Alex(ander) 1920-2000 .... **CLC 7**
See also CA 1-4R; 190; CANR 1, 45; CP 7;
DAM POP; MTCW 1

Comfort, Montgomery
See Campbell, (John) Ramsey

Compton-Burnett, I(vy)
1892(?)-1969 .... **CLC 1, 3, 10, 15, 34**
See also BRW 7; CA 1-4R; 25-28R; CANR
4; DAM NOV; DLB 36; EWL 3; MTCW
1; RGEL 2

Comstock, Anthony 1844-1915 ...... **TCLC 13**
See also CA 110; 169

Comte, Auguste 1798-1857 .... **NCLC 54**

Conan Doyle, Arthur
See Doyle, Sir Arthur Conan
See also BPFB 1; BYA 4, 5, 11

Conde (Abellan), Carmen
1901-1996 .... **HLCS 1**
See also CA 177; CWW 2; DLB 108; EWL
3; HW 2

Conde, Maryse 1937- ..... **BLCS; CLC 52, 92**
See also BW 2, 3; CA 110, 190; CAAE 190;
CANR 30, 53, 76; CWW 2; DAM MULT;
EWL 3; MTCW 1

Condillac, Etienne Bonnot de
1714-1780 .... **LC 26**

Condon, Richard (Thomas)
1915-1996 .... **CLC 4, 6, 8, 10, 45, 100**
See also BEST 90:3; BPFB 1; CA 1-4R;
151; CAAS 1; CANR 2, 23; CMW 4; CN
7; DAM NOV; INT CANR-23; MTCW 1,
2

Condorcet 1743-1794 .... **LC 104**
See also GFL Beginnings to 1789

Confucius 551B.C.-479B.C. .... **CMLC 19, 65;
WLCS**
See also DA; DA3; DAB; DAC; DAM
MST

Congreve, William 1670-1729 ... **DC 2; LC 5,
21; WLC**
See also BRW 2; CDBLB 1660-1789; DA;
DAB; DAC; DAM DRAM, MST, POET;
DFS 15; DLB 39, 84; RGEL 2; WLIT 3

Conley, Robert J(ackson) 1940- .... **NNAL**
See also CA 41-44R; CANR 15, 34, 45, 96;
DAM MULT

Connell, Evan S(helby), Jr. 1924- . **CLC 4, 6,
45**
See also AAYA 7; AMWS 14; CA 1-4R;
CAAS 2; CANR 2, 39, 76, 97; CN 7;
DAM NOV; DLB 2; DLBY 1981; MTCW
1, 2

Connelly, Marc(us Cook) 1890-1980 . **CLC 7**
See also CA 85-88; 102; CANR 30; DFS
12; DLB 7; DLBY 1980; RGAL 4; SATA-
Obit 25

Connor, Ralph .... **TCLC 31**
See Gordon, Charles William
See also DLB 92; TCWW 2

Conrad, Joseph 1857-1924 ..... **SSC 9, 67, 69,
71; TCLC 1, 6, 13, 25, 43, 57; WLC**
See also AAYA 26; BPFB 1; BRW 6;
BRWC 1; BRWR 2; BYA 2; CA 104; 131;
CANR 60; CDBLB 1890-1914; DA; DA3;
DAB; DAC; DAM MST, NOV; DLB 10,
34, 98, 156; EWL 3; EXPN; EXPS; LAIT
2; LATS 1:1; LMFS 1; MTCW 1, 2; NFS
2, 16; RGEL 2; RGSF 2; SATA 27; SSFS
1, 12; TEA; WLIT 4

Conrad, Robert Arnold
See Hart, Moss

Conroy, (Donald) Pat(rick) 1945- ... **CLC 30,
74**
See also AAYA 8, 52; AITN 1; BPFB 1;
CA 85-88; CANR 24, 53, 129; CPW;
CSW; DA3; DAM NOV, POP; DLB 6;
LAIT 5; MTCW 1, 2

Constant (de Rebecque), (Henri) Benjamin
1767-1830 .... **NCLC 6**
See also DLB 119; EW 4; GFL 1789 to the
Present

Conway, Jill K(er) 1934- .... **CLC 152**
See also CA 130; CANR 94

Conybeare, Charles Augustus
See Eliot, T(homas) S(tearns)

Cynewulf c. 770- .... **CMLC 23**
See also DLB 146; RGEL 2

Cyrano de Bergerac, Savinien de
1619-1655 .... **LC 65**
See also DLB 268; GFL Beginnings to 1789; RGWL 2, 3

Cyril of Alexandria c. 375-c. 430 . **CMLC 59**

Czaczkes, Shmuel Yosef Halevi
See Agnon, S(hmuel) Y(osef Halevi)

Dabrowska, Maria (Szumska)
1889-1965 .... **CLC 15**
See also CA 106; CDWLB 4; DLB 215; EWL 3

Dabydeen, David 1955- .... **CLC 34**
See also BW 1; CA 125; CANR 56, 92; CN 7; CP 7

Dacey, Philip 1939- .... **CLC 51**
See also CA 37-40R; CAAS 17; CANR 14, 32, 64; CP 7; DLB 105

Dacre, Charlotte c. 1772-1825? ... **NCLC 151**

Dafydd ap Gwilym c. 1320-c. 1380 ..... **PC 56**

Dagerman, Stig (Halvard)
1923-1954 .... **TCLC 17**
See also CA 117; 155; DLB 259; EWL 3

D'Aguiar, Fred 1960- .... **CLC 145**
See also CA 148; CANR 83, 101; CP 7; DLB 157; EWL 3

Dahl, Roald 1916-1990 .... **CLC 1, 6, 18, 79**
See also AAYA 15; BPFB 1; BRWS 4; BYA 5; CA 1-4R; 133; CANR 6, 32, 37, 62; CLR 1, 7, 41; CPW; DA3; DAB; DAC; DAM MST, NOV, POP; DLB 139, 255; HGG; JRDA; MAICYA 1, 2; MTCW 1, 2; RGSF 2; SATA 1, 26, 73; SATA-Obit 65; SSFS 4; TEA; YAW

Dahlberg, Edward 1900-1977 .. **CLC 1, 7, 14**
See also CA 9-12R; 69-72; CANR 31, 62; DLB 48; MTCW 1; RGAL 4

Daitch, Susan 1954- .... **CLC 103**
See also CA 161

Dale, Colin .... **TCLC 18**
See Lawrence, T(homas) E(dward)

Dale, George E.
See Asimov, Isaac

Dalton, Roque 1935-1975(?) ..... **HLCS 1; PC 36**
See also CA 176; DLB 283; HW 2

Daly, Elizabeth 1878-1967 .... **CLC 52**
See also CA 23-24; 25-28R; CANR 60; CAP 2; CMW 4

Daly, Mary 1928- .... **CLC 173**
See also CA 25-28R; CANR 30, 62; FW; GLL 1; MTCW 1

Daly, Maureen 1921- .... **CLC 17**
See also AAYA 5, 58; BYA 6; CANR 37, 83, 108; CLR 96; JRDA; MAICYA 1, 2; SAAS 1; SATA 2, 129; WYA; YAW

Damas, Leon-Gontran 1912-1978 .... **CLC 84**
See also BW 1; CA 125; 73-76; EWL 3

Dana, Richard Henry Sr.
1787-1879 .... **NCLC 53**

Daniel, Samuel 1562(?)-1619 .... **LC 24**
See also DLB 62; RGEL 2

Daniels, Brett
See Adler, Renata

Dannay, Frederic 1905-1982 .... **CLC 11**
See Queen, Ellery
See also CA 1-4R; 107; CANR 1, 39; CMW 4; DAM POP; DLB 137; MTCW 1

D'Annunzio, Gabriele 1863-1938 ... **TCLC 6, 40**
See also CA 104; 155; EW 8; EWL 3; RGWL 2, 3; TWA

Danois, N. le
See Gourmont, Remy(-Marie-Charles) de

Dante 1265-1321 .... **CMLC 3, 18, 39, 70; PC 21; WLCS**
See also DA; DA3; DAB; DAC; DAM MST, POET; EFS 1; EW 1; LAIT 1; RGWL 2, 3; TWA; WP

d'Antibes, Germain
See Simenon, Georges (Jacques Christian)

Danticat, Edwidge 1969- .... **CLC 94, 139**
See also AAYA 29; CA 152, 192; CAAE 192; CANR 73, 129; DNFS 1; EXPS; LATS 1:2; MTCW 1; SSFS 1; YAW

Danvers, Dennis 1947- .... **CLC 70**

Danziger, Paula 1944-2004 .... **CLC 21**
See also AAYA 4, 36; BYA 6, 7, 14; CA 112; 115; 229; CANR 37, 132; CLR 20; JRDA; MAICYA 1, 2; SATA 36, 63, 102, 149; SATA-Brief 30; WYA; YAW

Da Ponte, Lorenzo 1749-1838 .... **NCLC 50**

Dario, Ruben 1867-1916 .... **HLC 1; PC 15; TCLC 4**
See also CA 131; CANR 81; DAM MULT; DLB 290; EWL 3; HW 1, 2; LAW; MTCW 1, 2; RGWL 2, 3

Darley, George 1795-1846 .... **NCLC 2**
See also DLB 96; RGEL 2

Darrow, Clarence (Seward)
1857-1938 .... **TCLC 81**
See also CA 164; DLB 303

Darwin, Charles 1809-1882 .... **NCLC 57**
See also BRWS 7; DLB 57, 166; LATS 1:1; RGEL 2; TEA; WLIT 4

Darwin, Erasmus 1731-1802 .... **NCLC 106**
See also DLB 93; RGEL 2

Daryush, Elizabeth 1887-1977 ...... **CLC 6, 19**
See also CA 49-52; CANR 3, 81; DLB 20

Das, Kamala 1934- .... **CLC 191; PC 43**
See also CA 101; CANR 27, 59; CP 7; CWP; FW

Dasgupta, Surendranath
1887-1952 .... **TCLC 81**
See also CA 157

Dashwood, Edmee Elizabeth Monica de la Pasture 1890-1943
See Delafield, E. M.
See also CA 119; 154

da Silva, Antonio Jose
1705-1739 .... **NCLC 114**

Daudet, (Louis Marie) Alphonse
1840-1897 .... **NCLC 1**
See also DLB 123; GFL 1789 to the Present; RGSF 2

d'Aulnoy, Marie-Catherine c.
1650-1705 .... **LC 100**

Daumal, Rene 1908-1944 .... **TCLC 14**
See also CA 114; EWL 3

Davenant, William 1606-1668 .... **LC 13**
See also DLB 58, 126; RGEL 2

Davenport, Guy (Mattison, Jr.)
1927-2005 .... **CLC 6, 14, 38; SSC 16**
See also CA 33-36R; CANR 23, 73; CN 7; CSW; DLB 130

David, Robert
See Nezval, Vitezslav

Davidson, Avram (James) 1923-1993
See Queen, Ellery
See also CA 101; 171; CANR 26; DLB 8; FANT; SFW 4; SUFW 1, 2

Davidson, Donald (Grady)
1893-1968 .... **CLC 2, 13, 19**
See also CA 5-8R; 25-28R; CANR 4, 84; DLB 45

Davidson, Hugh
See Hamilton, Edmond

Davidson, John 1857-1909 .... **TCLC 24**
See also CA 118; 217; DLB 19; RGEL 2

Davidson, Sara 1943- .... **CLC 9**
See also CA 81-84; CANR 44, 68; DLB 185

Davie, Donald (Alfred) 1922-1995 .... **CLC 5, 8, 10, 31; PC 29**
See also BRWS 6; CA 1-4R; 149; CAAS 3; CANR 1, 44; CP 7; DLB 27; MTCW 1; RGEL 2

Davie, Elspeth 1919-1995 .... **SSC 52**
See also CA 120; 126; 150; DLB 139

Davies, Ray(mond Douglas) 1944- ... **CLC 21**
See also CA 116; 146; CANR 92

Davies, Rhys 1901-1978 .... **CLC 23**
See also CA 9-12R; 81-84; CANR 4; DLB 139, 191

Davies, (William) Robertson
1913-1995 .... **CLC 2, 7, 13, 25, 42, 75, 91; WLC**
See Marchbanks, Samuel
See also BEST 89:2; BPFB 1; CA 33-36R; 150; CANR 17, 42, 103; CN 7; CPW; DA; DA3; DAB; DAC; DAM MST, NOV, POP; DLB 68; EWL 3; HGG; INT CANR-17; MTCW 1, 2; RGEL 2; TWA

Davies, Sir John 1569-1626 .... **LC 85**
See also DLB 172

Davies, Walter C.
See Kornbluth, C(yril) M.

Davies, William Henry 1871-1940 ... **TCLC 5**
See also CA 104; 179; DLB 19, 174; EWL 3; RGEL 2

Da Vinci, Leonardo 1452-1519 ..... **LC 12, 57, 60**
See also AAYA 40

Davis, Angela (Yvonne) 1944- .... **CLC 77**
See also BW 2, 3; CA 57-60; CANR 10, 81; CSW; DA3; DAM MULT; FW

Davis, B. Lynch
See Bioy Casares, Adolfo; Borges, Jorge Luis

Davis, Frank Marshall 1905-1987 ...... **BLC 1**
See also BW 2, 3; CA 125; 123; CANR 42, 80; DAM MULT; DLB 51

Davis, Gordon
See Hunt, E(verette) Howard, (Jr.)

Davis, H(arold) L(enoir) 1896-1960 . **CLC 49**
See also ANW; CA 178; 89-92; DLB 9, 206; SATA 114

Davis, Natalie Z(emon) 1928- .... **CLC 204**
See also CA 53-56; CANR 58, 100

Davis, Rebecca (Blaine) Harding
1831-1910 .... **SSC 38; TCLC 6**
See also CA 104; 179; DLB 74, 239; FW; NFS 14; RGAL 4; TUS

Davis, Richard Harding
1864-1916 .... **TCLC 24**
See also CA 114; 179; DLB 12, 23, 78, 79, 189; DLBD 13; RGAL 4

Davison, Frank Dalby 1893-1970 ..... **CLC 15**
See also CA 217; 116; DLB 260

Davison, Lawrence H.
See Lawrence, D(avid) H(erbert Richards)

Davison, Peter (Hubert) 1928- .... **CLC 28**
See also CA 9-12R; CAAS 4; CANR 3, 43, 84; CP 7; DLB 5

Davys, Mary 1674-1732 .... **LC 1, 46**
See also DLB 39

Dawson, (Guy) Fielding (Lewis)
1930-2002 .... **CLC 6**
See also CA 85-88; 202; CANR 108; DLB 130; DLBY 2002

Dawson, Peter
See Faust, Frederick (Schiller)
See also TCWW 2, 2

Day, Clarence (Shepard, Jr.)
1874-1935 .... **TCLC 25**
See also CA 108; 199; DLB 11

Day, John 1574(?)-1640(?) .... **LC 70**
See also DLB 62, 170; RGEL 2

Day, Thomas 1748-1789 .... **LC 1**
See also DLB 39; YABC 1

Dent, Lester 1904-1959 .... **TCLC 72**
See also CA 112; 161; CMW 4; DLB 306;
SFW 4

De Palma, Brian (Russell) 1940- ...... **CLC 20**
See also CA 109

De Quincey, Thomas 1785-1859 ..... **NCLC 4,
87**
See also BRW 4; CDBLB 1789-1832; DLB
110, 144; RGEL 2

Deren, Eleanora 1908(?)-1961
See Deren, Maya
See also CA 192; 111

Deren, Maya .... **CLC 16, 102**
See Deren, Eleanora

Derleth, August (William)
1909-1971 .... **CLC 31**
See also BPFB 1; BYA 9, 10; CA 1-4R; 29-
32R; CANR 4; CMW 4; DLB 9; DLBD
17; HGG; SATA 5; SUFW 1

Der Nister 1884-1950 .... **TCLC 56**
See Nister, Der

Der Stricker c. 1190-c. 1250 .... **CMLC 75**

de Routisie, Albert
See Aragon, Louis

Derrida, Jacques 1930-2004 .... **CLC 24, 87**
See also CA 124; 127; CANR 76, 98, 133;
DLB 242; EWL 3; LMFS 2; MTCW 1;
TWA

Derry Down Derry
See Lear, Edward

Dersonnes, Jacques
See Simenon, Georges (Jacques Christian)

Desai, Anita 1937- .... **CLC 19, 37, 97, 175**
See also BRWS 5; CA 81-84; CANR 33,
53, 95, 133; CN 7; CWRI 5; DA3; DAB;
DAM NOV; DLB 271; DNFS 2; EWL 3;
FW; MTCW 1, 2; SATA 63, 126

Desai, Kiran 1971- .... **CLC 119**
See also BYA 16; CA 171; CANR 127

de Saint-Luc, Jean
See Glassco, John

de Saint Roman, Arnaud
See Aragon, Louis

Desbordes-Valmore, Marceline
1786-1859 .... **NCLC 97**
See also DLB 217

Descartes, Rene 1596-1650 .... **LC 20, 35**
See also DLB 268; EW 3; GFL Beginnings
to 1789

Deschamps, Eustache 1340(?)-1404 .. **LC 103**
See also DLB 208

De Sica, Vittorio 1901(?)-1974 .... **CLC 20**
See also CA 117

Desnos, Robert 1900-1945 .... **TCLC 22**
See also CA 121; 151; CANR 107; DLB
258; EWL 3; LMFS 2

Destouches, Louis-Ferdinand
1894-1961 .... **CLC 9, 15**
See Celine, Louis-Ferdinand
See also CA 85-88; CANR 28; MTCW 1

de Tolignac, Gaston
See Griffith, D(avid Lewelyn) W(ark)

Deutsch, Babette 1895-1982 .... **CLC 18**
See also BYA 3; CA 1-4R; 108; CANR 4,
79; DLB 45; SATA 1; SATA-Obit 33

Devenant, William 1606-1649 .... **LC 13**

Devkota, Laxmiprasad 1909-1959 . **TCLC 23**
See also CA 123

De Voto, Bernard (Augustine)
1897-1955 .... **TCLC 29**
See also CA 113; 160; DLB 9, 256

De Vries, Peter 1910-1993 ..... **CLC 1, 2, 3, 7,
10, 28, 46**
See also CA 17-20R; 142; CANR 41; DAM
NOV; DLB 6; DLBY 1982; MTCW 1, 2

Dewey, John 1859-1952 .... **TCLC 95**
See also CA 114; 170; DLB 246, 270;
RGAL 4

Dexter, John
See Bradley, Marion Zimmer
See also GLL 1

Dexter, Martin
See Faust, Frederick (Schiller)
See also TCWW 2

Dexter, Pete 1943- .... **CLC 34, 55**
See also BEST 89:2; CA 127; 131; CANR
129; CPW; DAM POP; INT CA-131;
MTCW 1

Diamano, Silmang
See Senghor, Leopold Sedar

Diamond, Neil 1941- .... **CLC 30**
See also CA 108

Diaz del Castillo, Bernal
1496-1584 .... **HLCS 1; LC 31**
See also LAW

di Bassetto, Corno
See Shaw, George Bernard

Dick, Philip K(indred) 1928-1982 ... **CLC 10,
30, 72; SSC 57**
See also AAYA 24; BPFB 1; BYA 11; CA
49-52; 106; CANR 2, 16, 132; CPW;
DA3; DAM NOV, POP; DLB 8; MTCW
1, 2; NFS 5; SCFW; SFW 1

Dickens, Charles (John Huffam)
1812-1870 .... **NCLC 3, 8, 18, 26, 37, 50,
86, 105, 113; SSC 17, 49; WLC**
See also AAYA 23; BRW 5; BRWC 1, 2;
BYA 1, 2, 3, 13, 14; CDBLB 1832-1890;
CLR 95; CMW 4; DA; DA3; DAB; DAC;
DAM MST, NOV; DLB 21, 55, 70, 159,
166; EXPN; HGG; JRDA; LAIT 1, 2;
LATS 1:1; LMFS 1; MAICYA 1, 2; NFS
4, 5, 10, 14, 20; RGEL 2; RGSF 2; SATA
15; SUFW 1; TEA; WCH; WLIT 4; WYA

Dickey, James (Lafayette)
1923-1997 .... **CLC 1, 2, 4, 7, 10, 15, 47,
109; PC 40; TCLC 151**
See also AAYA 50; AITN 1, 2; AMWS 4;
BPFB 1; CA 9-12R; 156; CABS 2; CANR
10, 48, 61, 105; CDALB 1968-1988; CP
7; CPW; CSW; DA3; DAM NOV, POET,
POP; DLB 5, 193; DLBD 7; DLBY 1982,
1993, 1996, 1997, 1998; EWL 3; INT
CANR-10; MTCW 1, 2; NFS 9; PFS 6,
11; RGAL 4; TUS

Dickey, William 1928-1994 .... **CLC 3, 28**
See also CA 9-12R; 145; CANR 24, 79;
DLB 5

Dickinson, Charles 1951- .... **CLC 49**
See also CA 128

Dickinson, Emily (Elizabeth)
1830-1886 .... **NCLC 21, 77; PC 1; WLC**
See also AAYA 22; AMW; AMWR 1;
CDALB 1865-1917; DA; DA3; DAB;
DAC; DAM MST, POET; DLB 1, 243;
EXPP; MAWW; PAB; PFS 1, 2, 3, 4, 5,
6, 8, 10, 11, 13, 16; RGAL 4; SATA 29;
TUS; WP; WYA

Dickinson, Mrs. Herbert Ward
See Phelps, Elizabeth Stuart

Dickinson, Peter (Malcolm de Brissac)
1927- .... **CLC 12, 35**
See also AAYA 9, 49; BYA 5; CA 41-44R;
CANR 31, 58, 88, 134; CLR 29; CMW 4;
DLB 87, 161, 276; JRDA; MAICYA 1, 2;
SATA 5, 62, 95, 150; SFW 4; WYA; YAW

Dickson, Carr
See Carr, John Dickson

Dickson, Carter
See Carr, John Dickson

Diderot, Denis 1713-1784 .... **LC 26**
See also EW 4; GFL Beginnings to 1789;
LMFS 1; RGWL 2, 3

Didion, Joan 1934- . **CLC 1, 3, 8, 14, 32, 129**
See also AITN 1; AMWS 4; CA 5-8R;
CANR 14, 52, 76, 125; CDALB 1968-
1988; CN 7; DA3; DAM NOV; DLB 2,

173, 185; DLBY 1981, 1986; EWL 3;
MAWW; MTCW 1, 2; NFS 3; RGAL 4;
TCWW 2; TUS

di Donato, Pietro 1911-1992 .... **TCLC 159**
See also CA 101; 136; DLB 9

Dietrich, Robert
See Hunt, E(verette) Howard, (Jr.)

Difusa, Pati
See Almodovar, Pedro

Dillard, Annie 1945- .... **CLC 9, 60, 115**
See also AAYA 6, 43; AMWS 6; ANW; CA
49-52; CANR 3, 43, 62, 90, 125; DA3;
DAM NOV; DLB 275, 278; DLBY 1980;
LAIT 4, 5; MTCW 1, 2; NCFS 1; RGAL
4; SATA 10, 140; TUS

Dillard, R(ichard) H(enry) W(ilde)
1937- .... **CLC 5**
See also CA 21-24R; CAAS 7; CANR 10;
CP 7; CSW; DLB 5, 244

Dillon, Eilis 1920-1994 .... **CLC 17**
See also CA 9-12R, 182; 147; CAAE 182;
CAAS 3; CANR 4, 38, 78; CLR 26; MAI-
CYA 1, 2; MAICYAS 1; SATA 2, 74;
SATA-Essay 105; SATA-Obit 83; YAW

Dimont, Penelope
See Mortimer, Penelope (Ruth)

Dinesen, Isak ..... **CLC 10, 29, 95; SSC 7, 75**
See Blixen, Karen (Christentze Dinesen)
See also EW 10; EWL 3; EXPS; FW; HGG;
LAIT 3; MTCW 1; NCFS 2; NFS 9;
RGSF 2; RGWL 2, 3; SSFS 3, 6, 13;
WLIT 2

Ding Ling .... **CLC 68**
See Chiang, Pin-chin
See also RGWL 3

Diphusa, Patty
See Almodovar, Pedro

Disch, Thomas M(ichael) 1940- ... **CLC 7, 36**
See Disch, Tom
See also AAYA 17; BPFB 1; CA 21-24R;
CAAS 4; CANR 17, 36, 54, 89; CLR 18;
CP 7; DA3; DLB 8; HGG; MAICYA 1, 2;
MTCW 1, 2; SAAS 15; SATA 92; SCFW;
SFW 4; SUFW 2

Disch, Tom
See Disch, Thomas M(ichael)
See also DLB 282

d'Isly, Georges
See Simenon, Georges (Jacques Christian)

Disraeli, Benjamin 1804-1881 ... **NCLC 2, 39,
79**
See also BRW 4; DLB 21, 55; RGEL 2

Ditcum, Steve
See Crumb, R(obert)

Dixon, Paige
See Corcoran, Barbara (Asenath)

Dixon, Stephen 1936- .... **CLC 52; SSC 16**
See also AMWS 12; CA 89-92; CANR 17,
40, 54, 91; CN 7; DLB 130

Dixon, Thomas 1864-1946 .... **TCLC 163**
See also RHW

Djebar, Assia 1936- .... **CLC 182**
See also CA 188; EWL 3; RGWL 3; WLIT
2

Doak, Annie
See Dillard, Annie

Dobell, Sydney Thompson
1824-1874 .... **NCLC 43**
See also DLB 32; RGEL 2

Doblin, Alfred .... **TCLC 13**
See Doeblin, Alfred
See also CDWLB 2; EWL 3; RGWL 2, 3

Dobroliubov, Nikolai Aleksandrovich
See Dobrolyubov, Nikolai Alexandrovich
See also DLB 277

Dobrolyubov, Nikolai Alexandrovich
1836-1861 .... **NCLC 5**
See Dobroliubov, Nikolai Aleksandrovich

Dobson, Austin 1840-1921 .... **TCLC 79**
See also DLB 35, 144

Dobyns, Stephen 1941- .... **CLC 37**
See also AMWS 13; CA 45-48; CANR 2, 18, 99; CMW 4; CP 7

Doctorow, E(dgar) L(aurence)
1931- .... **CLC 6, 11, 15, 18, 37, 44, 65, 113**
See also AAYA 22; AITN 2; AMWS 4; BEST 89:3; BPFB 1; CA 45-48; CANR 2, 33, 51, 76, 97, 133; CDALB 1968-1988; CN 7; CPW; DA3; DAM NOV, POP; DLB 2, 28, 173; DLBY 1980; EWL 3; LAIT 3; MTCW 1, 2; NFS 6; RGAL 4; RHW; TUS

Dodgson, Charles L(utwidge) 1832-1898
See Carroll, Lewis
See also CLR 2; DA; DA3; DAB; DAC; DAM MST, NOV, POET; MAICYA 1, 2; SATA 100; YABC 2

Dodsley, Robert 1703-1764 .... **LC 97**
See also DLB 95; RGEL 2

Dodson, Owen (Vincent) 1914-1983 .. **BLC 1; CLC 79**
See also BW 1; CA 65-68; 110; CANR 24; DAM MULT; DLB 76

Doeblin, Alfred 1878-1957 .... **TCLC 13**
See Doblin, Alfred
See also CA 110; 141; DLB 66

Doerr, Harriet 1910-2002 .... **CLC 34**
See also CA 117; 122; 213; CANR 47; INT CA-122; LATS 1:2

Domecq, H(onorio Bustos)
See Bioy Casares, Adolfo

Domecq, H(onorio) Bustos
See Bioy Casares, Adolfo; Borges, Jorge Luis

Domini, Rey
See Lorde, Audre (Geraldine)
See also GLL 1

Dominique
See Proust, (Valentin-Louis-George-Eugene) Marcel

Don, A
See Stephen, Sir Leslie

Donaldson, Stephen R(eeder)
1947- .... **CLC 46, 138**
See also AAYA 36; BPFB 1; CA 89-92; CANR 13, 55, 99; CPW; DAM POP; FANT; INT CANR-13; SATA 121; SFW 4; SUFW 1, 2

Donleavy, J(ames) P(atrick) 1926- .... **CLC 1, 4, 6, 10, 45**
See also AITN 2; BPFB 1; CA 9-12R; CANR 24, 49, 62, 80, 124; CBD; CD 5; CN 7; DLB 6, 173; INT CANR-24; MTCW 1, 2; RGAL 4

Donnadieu, Marguerite
See Duras, Marguerite

Donne, John 1572-1631 ... **LC 10, 24, 91; PC 1, 43; WLC**
See also BRW 1; BRWC 1; BRWR 2; CD-BLB Before 1660; DA; DAB; DAC; DAM MST, POET; DLB 121, 151; EXPP; PAB; PFS 2, 11; RGEL 3; TEA; WLIT 3; WP

Donnell, David 1939(?)- .... **CLC 34**
See also CA 197

Donoghue, P. S.
See Hunt, E(verette) Howard, (Jr.)

Donoso (Yanez), Jose 1924-1996 ... **CLC 4, 8, 11, 32, 99; HLC 1; SSC 34; TCLC 133**
See also CA 81-84; 155; CANR 32, 73; CD-WLB 3; CWW 2; DAM MULT; DLB 113; EWL 3; HW 1, 2; LAW; LAWS 1; MTCW 1, 2; RGSF 2; WLIT 1

Donovan, John 1928-1992 .... **CLC 35**
See also AAYA 20; CA 97-100; 137; CLR 3; MAICYA 1, 2; SATA 72; SATA-Brief 29; YAW

Don Roberto
See Cunninghame Graham, Robert (Gallnigad) Bontine

Doolittle, Hilda 1886-1961 . **CLC 3, 8, 14, 31, 34, 73; PC 5; WLC**
See H. D.
See also AMWS 1; CA 97-100; CANR 35, 131; DA; DAC; DAM MST, POET; DLB 4, 45; EWL 3; FW; GLL 1; LMFS 2; MAWW; MTCW 1, 2; PFS 6; RGAL 4

Doppo, Kunikida .... **TCLC 99**
See Kunikida Doppo

Dorfman, Ariel 1942- .... **CLC 48, 77, 189; HLC 1**
See also CA 124; 130; CANR 67, 70, 135; CWW 2; DAM MULT; DFS 4; EWL 3; HW 1, 2; INT CA-130; WLIT 1

Dorn, Edward (Merton)
1929-1999 .... **CLC 10, 18**
See also CA 93-96; 187; CANR 42, 79; CP 7; DLB 5; INT CA-93-96; WP

Dor-Ner, Zvi .... **CLC 70**

Dorris, Michael (Anthony)
1945-1997 .... **CLC 109; NNAL**
See also AAYA 20; BEST 90:1; BYA 12; CA 102; 157; CANR 19, 46, 75; CLR 58; DA3; DAM MULT, NOV; DLB 175; LAIT 5; MTCW 2; NFS 3; RGAL 4; SATA 75; SATA-Obit 94; TCWW 2; YAW

Dorris, Michael A.
See Dorris, Michael (Anthony)

Dorsan, Luc
See Simenon, Georges (Jacques Christian)

Dorsange, Jean
See Simenon, Georges (Jacques Christian)

Dorset
See Sackville, Thomas

Dos Passos, John (Roderigo)
1896-1970 ... **CLC 1, 4, 8, 11, 15, 25, 34, 82; WLC**
See also AMW; BPFB 1; CA 1-4R; 29-32R; CANR 3; CDALB 1929-1941; DA; DA3; DAB; DAC; DAM MST, NOV; DLB 4, 9, 274; DLBD 1, 15; DLBY 1996; EWL 3; MTCW 1, 2; NFS 14; RGAL 4; TUS

Dossage, Jean
See Simenon, Georges (Jacques Christian)

Dostoevsky, Fedor Mikhailovich
1821-1881 .. **NCLC 2, 7, 21, 33, 43, 119; SSC 2, 33, 44; WLC**
See Dostoevsky, Fyodor
See also AAYA 40; DA; DA3; DAB; DAC; DAM MST, NOV; EW 7; EXPN; NFS 3, 8; RGSF 2; RGWL 2, 3; SSFS 8; TWA

Dostoevsky, Fyodor
See Dostoevsky, Fedor Mikhailovich
See also DLB 238; LATS 1:1; LMFS 1, 2

Doty, M. R.
See Doty, Mark (Alan)

Doty, Mark
See Doty, Mark (Alan)

Doty, Mark (Alan) 1953(?)- .... **CLC 176; PC 53**
See also AMWS 11; CA 161, 183; CAAE 183; CANR 110

Doty, Mark A.
See Doty, Mark (Alan)

Doughty, Charles M(ontagu)
1843-1926 .... **TCLC 27**
See also CA 115; 178; DLB 19, 57, 174

Douglas, Ellen .... **CLC 73**
See Haxton, Josephine Ayres; Williamson, Ellen Douglas
See also CN 7; CSW; DLB 292

Douglas, Gavin 1475(?)-1522 .... **LC 20**
See also DLB 132; RGEL 2

Douglas, George
See Brown, George Douglas
See also RGEL 2

Douglas, Keith (Castellain)
1920-1944 .... **TCLC 40**
See also BRW 7; CA 160; DLB 27; EWL 3; PAB; RGEL 2

Douglas, Leonard
See Bradbury, Ray (Douglas)

Douglas, Michael
See Crichton, (John) Michael

Douglas, (George) Norman
1868-1952 .... **TCLC 68**
See also BRW 6; CA 119; 157; DLB 34, 195; RGEL 2

Douglas, William
See Brown, George Douglas

Douglass, Frederick 1817(?)-1895 ..... **BLC 1; NCLC 7, 55, 141; WLC**
See also AAYA 48; AFAW 1, 2; AMWC 1; AMWS 3; CDALB 1640-1865; DA; DA3; DAC; DAM MST, MULT; DLB 1, 43, 50, 79, 243; FW; LAIT 2; NCFS 2; RGAL 4; SATA 29

Dourado, (Waldomiro Freitas) Autran
1926- .... **CLC 23, 60**
See also CA 25-28R; 179; CANR 34, 81; DLB 145, 307; HW 2

Dourado, Waldomiro Freitas Autran
See Dourado, (Waldomiro Freitas) Autran

Dove, Rita (Frances) 1952- . **BLCS; CLC 50, 81; PC 6**
See also AAYA 46; AMWS 4; BW 2; CA 109; CAAS 19; CANR 27, 42, 68, 76, 97, 132; CDALBS; CP 7; CSW; CWP; DA3; DAM MULT, POET; DLB 120; EWL 3; EXPP; MTCW 1; PFS 1, 15; RGAL 4

Doveglion
See Villa, Jose Garcia

Dowell, Coleman 1925-1985 .... **CLC 60**
See also CA 25-28R; 117; CANR 10; DLB 130; GLL 2

Dowson, Ernest (Christopher)
1867-1900 .... **TCLC 4**
See also CA 105; 150; DLB 19, 135; RGEL 2

Doyle, A. Conan
See Doyle, Sir Arthur Conan

Doyle, Sir Arthur Conan
1859-1930 .... **SSC 12; TCLC 7; WLC**
See Conan Doyle, Arthur
See also AAYA 14; BRWS 2; CA 104; 122; CANR 131; CDBLB 1890-1914; CMW 4; DA; DA3; DAB; DAC; DAM MST, NOV; DLB 18, 70, 156, 178; EXPS; HGG; LAIT 2; MSW; MTCW 1, 2; RGEL 2; RGSF 2; RHW; SATA 24; SCFW 2; SFW 4; SSFS 2; TEA; WCH; WLIT 4; WYA; YAW

Doyle, Conan
See Doyle, Sir Arthur Conan

Doyle, John
See Graves, Robert (von Ranke)

Doyle, Roddy 1958(?)- .... **CLC 81, 178**
See also AAYA 14; BRWS 5; CA 143; CANR 73, 128; CN 7; DA3; DLB 194

Doyle, Sir A. Conan
See Doyle, Sir Arthur Conan

Dr. A
See Asimov, Isaac; Silverstein, Alvin; Silverstein, Virginia B(arbara Opshelor)

Drabble, Margaret 1939- ...... **CLC 2, 3, 5, 8, 10, 22, 53, 129**
See also BRWS 4; CA 13-16R; CANR 18, 35, 63, 112, 131; CDBLB 1960 to Present; CN 7; CPW; DA3; DAB; DAC; DAM MST, NOV, POP; DLB 14, 155, 231; EWL 3; FW; MTCW 1, 2; RGEL 2; SATA 48; TEA

Drakulic, Slavenka 1949- .... **CLC 173**
See also CA 144; CANR 92

Drakulic-Ilic, Slavenka
See Drakulic, Slavenka
Drapier, M. B.
See Swift, Jonathan
Drayham, James
See Mencken, H(enry) L(ouis)
Drayton, Michael 1563-1631 .... **LC 8**
See also DAM POET; DLB 121; RGEL 2
Dreadstone, Carl
See Campbell, (John) Ramsey
Dreiser, Theodore (Herman Albert)
1871-1945 .... **SSC 30; TCLC 10, 18, 35, 83; WLC**
See also AMW; AMWC 2; AMWR 2; BYA 15, 16; CA 106; 132; CDALB 1865-1917; DA; DA3; DAC; DAM MST, NOV; DLB 9, 12, 102, 137; DLBD 1; EWL 3; LAIT 2; LMFS 2; MTCW 1, 2; NFS 8, 17; RGAL 4; TUS
Drexler, Rosalyn 1926- .... **CLC 2, 6**
See also CA 81-84; CAD; CANR 68, 124; CD 5; CWD
Dreyer, Carl Theodor 1889-1968 ...... **CLC 16**
See also CA 116
Drieu la Rochelle, Pierre(-Eugene)
1893-1945 .... **TCLC 21**
See also CA 117; DLB 72; EWL 3; GFL 1789 to the Present
Drinkwater, John 1882-1937 .... **TCLC 57**
See also CA 109; 149; DLB 10, 19, 149; RGEL 2
Drop Shot
See Cable, George Washington
Droste-Hulshoff, Annette Freiin von
1797-1848 .... **NCLC 3, 133**
See also CDWLB 2; DLB 133; RGSF 2; RGWL 2, 3
Drummond, Walter
See Silverberg, Robert
Drummond, William Henry
1854-1907 .... **TCLC 25**
See also CA 160; DLB 92
Drummond de Andrade, Carlos
1902-1987 .... **CLC 18; TCLC 139**
See Andrade, Carlos Drummond de
See also CA 132; 123; DLB 307; LAW
Drummond of Hawthornden, William
1585-1649 .... **LC 83**
See also DLB 121, 213; RGEL 2
Drury, Allen (Stuart) 1918-1998 .... **CLC 37**
See also CA 57-60; 170; CANR 18, 52; CN 7; INT CANR-18
Druse, Eleanor
See King, Stephen (Edwin)
Dryden, John 1631-1700 ..... **DC 3; LC 3, 21, 115; PC 25; WLC**
See also BRW 2; CDBLB 1660-1789; DA; DAB; DAC; DAM DRAM, MST, POET; DLB 80, 101, 131; EXPP; IDTP; LMFS 1; RGEL 2; TEA; WLIT 3
du Bellay, Joachim 1524-1560 .... **LC 92**
See also GFL Beginnings to 1789; RGWL 2, 3
Duberman, Martin (Bauml) 1930- ..... **CLC 8**
See also CA 1-4R; CAD; CANR 2, 63; CD 5
Dubie, Norman (Evans) 1945- .... **CLC 36**
See also CA 69-72; CANR 12, 115; CP 7; DLB 120; PFS 12
Du Bois, W(illiam) E(dward) B(urghardt)
1868-1963 ..... **BLC 1; CLC 1, 2, 13, 64, 96; HR 2; WLC**
See also AAYA 40; AFAW 1, 2; AMWC 1; AMWS 2; BW 1, 3; CA 85-88; CANR 34, 82, 132; CDALB 1865-1917; DA; DA3; DAC; DAM MST, MULT, NOV; DLB 47, 50, 91, 246, 284; EWL 3; EXPP; LAIT 2; LMFS 2; MTCW 1, 2; NCFS 1; PFS 13; RGAL 4; SATA 42

Dubus, Andre 1936-1999 ..... **CLC 13, 36, 97; SSC 15**
See also AMWS 7; CA 21-24R; 177; CANR 17; CN 7; CSW; DLB 130; INT CANR-17; RGAL 4; SSFS 10
Duca Minimo
See D'Annunzio, Gabriele
Ducharme, Rejean 1941- .... **CLC 74**
See also CA 165; DLB 60
du Chatelet, Emilie 1706-1749 .... **LC 96**
Duchen, Claire .... **CLC 65**
Duclos, Charles Pinot- 1704-1772 .... **LC 1**
See also GFL Beginnings to 1789
Dudek, Louis 1918-2001 .... **CLC 11, 19**
See also CA 45-48; 215; CAAS 14; CANR 1; CP 7; DLB 88
Duerrenmatt, Friedrich 1921-1990 ... **CLC 1, 4, 8, 11, 15, 43, 102**
See Durrenmatt, Friedrich
See also CA 17-20R; CANR 33; CMW 4; DAM DRAM; DLB 69, 124; MTCW 1, 2
Duffy, Bruce 1953(?)- .... **CLC 50**
See also CA 172
Duffy, Maureen 1933- .... **CLC 37**
See also CA 25-28R; CANR 33, 68; CBD; CN 7; CP 7; CWD; CWP; DFS 15; DLB 14; FW; MTCW 1
Du Fu
See Tu Fu
See also RGWL 2, 3
Dugan, Alan 1923-2003 .... **CLC 2, 6**
See also CA 81-84; 220; CANR 119; CP 7; DLB 5; PFS 10
du Gard, Roger Martin
See Martin du Gard, Roger
Duhamel, Georges 1884-1966 .... **CLC 8**
See also CA 81-84; 25-28R; CANR 35; DLB 65; EWL 3; GFL 1789 to the Present; MTCW 1
Dujardin, Edouard (Emile Louis)
1861-1949 .... **TCLC 13**
See also CA 109; DLB 123
Duke, Raoul
See Thompson, Hunter S(tockton)
Dulles, John Foster 1888-1959 .... **TCLC 72**
See also CA 115; 149
Dumas, Alexandre (pere)
1802-1870 .... **NCLC 11, 71; WLC**
See also AAYA 22; BYA 3; DA; DA3; DAB; DAC; DAM MST, NOV; DLB 119, 192; EW 6; GFL 1789 to the Present; LAIT 1, 2; NFS 14, 19; RGWL 2, 3; SATA 18; TWA; WCH
Dumas, Alexandre (fils) 1824-1895 ...... **DC 1; NCLC 9**
See also DLB 192; GFL 1789 to the Present; RGWL 2, 3
Dumas, Claudine
See Malzberg, Barry N(athaniel)
Dumas, Henry L. 1934-1968 .... **CLC 6, 62**
See also BW 1; CA 85-88; DLB 41; RGAL 4
du Maurier, Daphne 1907-1989 .. **CLC 6, 11, 59; SSC 18**
See also AAYA 37; BPFB 1; BRWS 3; CA 5-8R; 128; CANR 6, 55; CMW 4; CPW; DA3; DAB; DAC; DAM MST, POP; DLB 191; HGG; LAIT 3; MSW; MTCW 1, 2; NFS 12; RGEL 2; RGSF 2; RHW; SATA 27; SATA-Obit 60; SSFS 14, 16; TEA
Du Maurier, George 1834-1896 ..... **NCLC 86**
See also DLB 153, 178; RGEL 2
Dunbar, Paul Laurence 1872-1906 ... **BLC 1; PC 5; SSC 8; TCLC 2, 12; WLC**
See also AFAW 1, 2; AMWS 2; BW 1, 3; CA 104; 124; CANR 79; CDALB 1865-1917; DA; DA3; DAC; DAM MST, MULT, POET; DLB 50, 54, 78; EXPP; RGAL 4; SATA 34

Dunbar, William 1460(?)-1520(?) .... **LC 20**
See also BRWS 8; DLB 132, 146; RGEL 2
Dunbar-Nelson, Alice .... **HR 2**
See Nelson, Alice Ruth Moore Dunbar
Duncan, Dora Angela
See Duncan, Isadora
Duncan, Isadora 1877(?)-1927 .... **TCLC 68**
See also CA 118; 149
Duncan, Lois 1934- .... **CLC 26**
See also AAYA 4, 34; BYA 6, 8; CA 1-4R; CANR 2, 23, 36, 111; CLR 29; JRDA; MAICYA 1, 2; MAICYAS 1; SAAS 2; SATA 1, 36, 75, 133, 141; SATA-Essay 141; WYA; YAW
Duncan, Robert (Edward)
1919-1988 .... **CLC 1, 2, 4, 7, 15, 41, 55; PC 2**
See also BG 2; CA 9-12R; 124; CANR 28, 62; DAM POET; DLB 5, 16, 193; EWL 3; MTCW 1, 2; PFS 13; RGAL 4; WP
Duncan, Sara Jeannette
1861-1922 .... **TCLC 60**
See also CA 157; DLB 92
Dunlap, William 1766-1839 .... **NCLC 2**
See also DLB 30, 37, 59; RGAL 4
Dunn, Douglas (Eaglesham) 1942- .... **CLC 6, 40**
See also BRWS 10; CA 45-48; CANR 2, 33, 126; CP 7; DLB 40; MTCW 1
Dunn, Katherine (Karen) 1945- .... **CLC 71**
See also CA 33-36R; CANR 72; HGG; MTCW 1
Dunn, Stephen (Elliott) 1939- .. **CLC 36, 206**
See also AMWS 11; CA 33-36R; CANR 12, 48, 53, 105; CP 7; DLB 105; PFS 21
Dunne, Finley Peter 1867-1936 ...... **TCLC 28**
See also CA 108; 178; DLB 11, 23; RGAL 4
Dunne, John Gregory 1932-2003 ..... **CLC 28**
See also CA 25-28R; 222; CANR 14, 50; CN 7; DLBY 1980
Dunsany, Lord .... **TCLC 2, 59**
See Dunsany, Edward John Moreton Drax Plunkett
See also DLB 77, 153, 156, 255; FANT; IDTP; RGEL 2; SFW 4; SUFW 1
Dunsany, Edward John Moreton Drax
Plunkett 1878-1957
See Dunsany, Lord
See also CA 104; 148; DLB 10; MTCW 1
Duns Scotus, John 1266(?)-1308 ... **CMLC 59**
See also DLB 115
du Perry, Jean
See Simenon, Georges (Jacques Christian)
Durang, Christopher (Ferdinand)
1949- .... **CLC 27, 38**
See also CA 105; CAD; CANR 50, 76, 130; CD 5; MTCW 1
Duras, Claire de 1777-1828 .... **NCLC 154**
Duras, Marguerite 1914-1996 . **CLC 3, 6, 11, 20, 34, 40, 68, 100; SSC 40**
See also BPFB 1; CA 25-28R; 151; CANR 50; CWW 2; DLB 83; EWL 3; GFL 1789 to the Present; IDFW 4; MTCW 1, 2; RGWL 2, 3; TWA
Durban, (Rosa) Pam 1947- .... **CLC 39**
See also CA 123; CANR 98; CSW
Durcan, Paul 1944- .... **CLC 43, 70**
See also CA 134; CANR 123; CP 7; DAM POET; EWL 3
Durfey, Thomas 1653-1723 .... **LC 94**
See also DLB 80; RGEL 2
Durkheim, Emile 1858-1917 .... **TCLC 55**
Durrell, Lawrence (George)
1912-1990 ... **CLC 1, 4, 6, 8, 13, 27, 41**
See also BPFB 1; BRWS 1; CA 9-12R; 132; CANR 40, 77; CDBLB 1945-1960; DAM NOV; DLB 15, 27, 204; DLBY 1990; EWL 3; MTCW 1, 2; RGEL 2; SFW 4; TEA

Eliot, Dan
See Silverberg, Robert
Eliot, George 1819-1880 ...... **NCLC 4, 13, 23, 41, 49, 89, 118; PC 20; SSC 72; WLC**
See Evans, Mary Ann
See also BRW 5; BRWC 1, 2; BRWR 2; CDBLB 1832-1890; CN 7; CPW; DA; DA3; DAB; DAC; DAM MST, NOV; DLB 21, 35, 55; LATS 1:1; LMFS 1; NFS 17; RGEL 2; RGSF 2; SSFS 8; TEA; WLIT 3
Eliot, John 1604-1690 .... **LC 5**
See also DLB 24
Eliot, T(homas) S(tearns)
1888-1965 ...... **CLC 1, 2, 3, 6, 9, 10, 13, 15, 24, 34, 41, 55, 57, 113; PC 5, 31; WLC**
See also AAYA 28; AMW; AMWC 1; AMWR 1; BRW 7; BRWR 2; CA 5-8R; 25-28R; CANR 41; CDALB 1929-1941; DA; DA3; DAB; DAC; DAM DRAM, MST, POET; DFS 4, 13; DLB 7, 10, 45, 63, 245; DLBY 1988; EWL 3; EXPP; LAIT 3; LATS 1:1; LMFS 2; MTCW 1, 2; NCFS 5; PAB; PFS 1, 7, 20; RGAL 4; RGEL 2; TUS; WLIT 4; WP
Elizabeth 1866-1941 .... **TCLC 41**
Elkin, Stanley L(awrence)
1930-1995 .. **CLC 4, 6, 9, 14, 27, 51, 91; SSC 12**
See also AMWS 6; BPFB 1; CA 9-12R; 148; CANR 8, 46; CN 7; CPW; DAM NOV, POP; DLB 2, 28, 218, 278; DLBY 1980; EWL 3; INT CANR-8; MTCW 1, 2; RGAL 4
Elledge, Scott .... **CLC 34**
Elliott, Don
See Silverberg, Robert
Elliott, George P(aul) 1918-1980 .... **CLC 2**
See also CA 1-4R; 97-100; CANR 2; DLB 244
Elliott, Janice 1931-1995 .... **CLC 47**
See also CA 13-16R; CANR 8, 29, 84; CN 7; DLB 14; SATA 119
Elliott, Sumner Locke 1917-1991 ..... **CLC 38**
See also CA 5-8R; 134; CANR 2, 21; DLB 289
Elliott, William
See Bradbury, Ray (Douglas)
Ellis, A. E. .... **CLC 7**
Ellis, Alice Thomas .... **CLC 40**
See Haycraft, Anna (Margaret)
See also DLB 194; MTCW 1
Ellis, Bret Easton 1964- ...... **CLC 39, 71, 117**
See also AAYA 2, 43; CA 118; 123; CANR 51, 74, 126; CN 7; CPW; DA3; DAM POP; DLB 292; HGG; INT CA-123; MTCW 1; NFS 11
Ellis, (Henry) Havelock
1859-1939 .... **TCLC 14**
See also CA 109; 169; DLB 190
Ellis, Landon
See Ellison, Harlan (Jay)
Ellis, Trey 1962- .... **CLC 55**
See also CA 146; CANR 92
Ellison, Harlan (Jay) 1934- .. **CLC 1, 13, 42, 139; SSC 14**
See also AAYA 29; BPFB 1; BYA 14; CA 5-8R; CANR 5, 46, 115; CPW; DAM POP; DLB 8; HGG; INT CANR-5; MTCW 1, 2; SCFW 2; SFW 4; SSFS 13, 14, 15; SUFW 1, 2
Ellison, Ralph (Waldo) 1914-1994 .... **BLC 1; CLC 1, 3, 11, 54, 86, 114; SSC 26, 79; WLC**
See also AAYA 19; AFAW 1, 2; AMWC 2; AMWR 2; AMWS 2; BPFB 1; BW 1, 3; BYA 2; CA 9-12R; 145; CANR 24, 53; CDALB 1941-1968; CSW; DA; DA3; DAB; DAC; DAM MST, MULT, NOV;

DLB 2, 76, 227; DLBY 1994; EWL 3; EXPN; EXPS; LAIT 4; MTCW 1, 2; NCFS 3; NFS 2; RGAL 4; RGSF 2; SSFS 1, 11; YAW
Ellmann, Lucy (Elizabeth) 1956- ..... **CLC 61**
See also CA 128
Ellmann, Richard (David)
1918-1987 .... **CLC 50**
See also BEST 89:2; CA 1-4R; 122; CANR 2, 28, 61; DLB 103; DLBY 1987; MTCW 1, 2
Elman, Richard (Martin)
1934-1997 .... **CLC 19**
See also CA 17-20R; 163; CAAS 3; CANR 47
Elron
See Hubbard, L(afayette) Ron(ald)
El Saadawi, Nawal 1931- .... **CLC 196**
See al'Sadaawi, Nawal; Sa'adawi, al-Nawal; Saadawi, Nawal El; Sa'dawi, Nawal al-
See also CA 118; CAAS 11; CANR 44, 92
Eluard, Paul .... **PC 38; TCLC 7, 41**
See Grindel, Eugene
See also EWL 3; GFL 1789 to the Present; RGWL 2, 3
Elyot, Thomas 1490(?)-1546 .... **LC 11**
See also DLB 136; RGEL 2
Elytis, Odysseus 1911-1996 .... **CLC 15, 49, 100; PC 21**
See Alepoudelis, Odysseus
See also CA 102; 151; CANR 94; CWW 2; DAM POET; EW 13; EWL 3; MTCW 1, 2; RGWL 2, 3
Emecheta, (Florence Onye) Buchi
1944- .... **BLC 2; CLC 14, 48, 128**
See also AFW; BW 2, 3; CA 81-84; CANR 27, 81, 126; CDWLB 3; CN 7; CWRI 5; DA3; DAM MULT; DLB 117; EWL 3; FW; MTCW 1, 2; NFS 12, 14; SATA 66; WLIT 2
Emerson, Mary Moody
1774-1863 .... **NCLC 66**
Emerson, Ralph Waldo 1803-1882 . **NCLC 1, 38, 98; PC 18; WLC**
See also AAYA 60; AMW; ANW; CDALB 1640-1865; DA; DA3; DAB; DAC; DAM MST, POET; DLB 1, 59, 73, 183, 223, 270; EXPP; LAIT 2; LMFS 1; NCFS 3; PFS 4, 17; RGAL 4; TUS; WP
Eminescu, Mihail 1850-1889 .. **NCLC 33, 131**
Empedocles 5th cent. B.C.- .... **CMLC 50**
See also DLB 176
Empson, William 1906-1984 ... **CLC 3, 8, 19, 33, 34**
See also BRWS 2; CA 17-20R; 112; CANR 31, 61; DLB 20; EWL 3; MTCW 1, 2; RGEL 2
Enchi, Fumiko (Ueda) 1905-1986 ..... **CLC 31**
See Enchi Fumiko
See also CA 129; 121; FW; MJW
Enchi Fumiko
See Enchi, Fumiko (Ueda)
See also DLB 182; EWL 3
Ende, Michael (Andreas Helmuth)
1929-1995 .... **CLC 31**
See also BYA 5; CA 118; 124; 149; CANR 36, 110; CLR 14; DLB 75; MAICYA 1, 2; MAICYAS 1; SATA 61, 130; SATA-Brief 42; SATA-Obit 86
Endo, Shusaku 1923-1996 ..... **CLC 7, 14, 19, 54, 99; SSC 48; TCLC 152**
See Endo Shusaku
See also CA 29-32R; 153; CANR 21, 54, 131; DA3; DAM NOV; MTCW 1, 2; RGSF 2; RGWL 2, 3
Endo Shusaku
See Endo, Shusaku
See also CWW 2; DLB 182; EWL 3

Engel, Marian 1933-1985 .... **CLC 36; TCLC 137**
See also CA 25-28R; CANR 12; DLB 53; FW; INT CANR-12
Engelhardt, Frederick
See Hubbard, L(afayette) Ron(ald)
Engels, Friedrich 1820-1895 .. **NCLC 85, 114**
See also DLB 129; LATS 1:1
Enright, D(ennis) J(oseph)
1920-2002 .... **CLC 4, 8, 31**
See also CA 1-4R; 211; CANR 1, 42, 83; CP 7; DLB 27; EWL 3; SATA 25; SATA-Obit 140
Enzensberger, Hans Magnus
1929- .... **CLC 43; PC 28**
See also CA 116; 119; CANR 103; CWW 2; EWL 3
Ephron, Nora 1941- .... **CLC 17, 31**
See also AAYA 35; AITN 2; CA 65-68; CANR 12, 39, 83
Epicurus 341B.C.-270B.C. .... **CMLC 21**
See also DLB 176
Epsilon
See Betjeman, John
Epstein, Daniel Mark 1948- .... **CLC 7**
See also CA 49-52; CANR 2, 53, 90
Epstein, Jacob 1956- .... **CLC 19**
See also CA 114
Epstein, Jean 1897-1953 .... **TCLC 92**
Epstein, Joseph 1937- .... **CLC 39, 204**
See also AMWS 14; CA 112; 119; CANR 50, 65, 117
Epstein, Leslie 1938- .... **CLC 27**
See also AMWS 12; CA 73-76, 215; CAAE 215; CAAS 12; CANR 23, 69; DLB 299
Equiano, Olaudah 1745(?)-1797 . **BLC 2; LC 16**
See also AFAW 1, 2; CDWLB 3; DAM MULT; DLB 37, 50; WLIT 2
Erasmus, Desiderius 1469(?)-1536 ..... **LC 16, 93**
See also DLB 136; EW 2; LMFS 1; RGWL 2, 3; TWA
Erdman, Paul E(mil) 1932- .... **CLC 25**
See also AITN 1; CA 61-64; CANR 13, 43, 84
Erdrich, Louise 1954- .... **CLC 39, 54, 120, 176; NNAL; PC 52**
See also AAYA 10, 47; AMWS 4; BEST 89:1; BPFB 1; CA 114; CANR 41, 62, 118; CDALBS; CN 7; CP 7; CPW; CWP; DA3; DAM MULT, NOV, POP; DLB 152, 175, 206; EWL 3; EXPP; LAIT 5; LATS 1:2; MTCW 1; NFS 5; PFS 14; RGAL 4; SATA 94, 141; SSFS 14; TCWW 2
Erenburg, Ilya (Grigoryevich)
See Ehrenburg, Ilya (Grigoryevich)
Erickson, Stephen Michael 1950-
See Erickson, Steve
See also CA 129; SFW 4
Erickson, Steve .... **CLC 64**
See Erickson, Stephen Michael
See also CANR 60, 68; SUFW 2
Erickson, Walter
See Fast, Howard (Melvin)
Ericson, Walter
See Fast, Howard (Melvin)
Eriksson, Buntel
See Bergman, (Ernst) Ingmar
Eriugena, John Scottus c.
810-877 .... **CMLC 65**
See also DLB 115
Ernaux, Annie 1940- .... **CLC 88, 184**
See also CA 147; CANR 93; NCFS 3, 5
Erskine, John 1879-1951 .... **TCLC 84**
See also CA 112; 159; DLB 9, 102; FANT
Eschenbach, Wolfram von
See Wolfram von Eschenbach
See also RGWL 3

Flaubert, Gustave 1821-1880 .... **NCLC 2, 10, 19, 62, 66, 135; SSC 11, 60; WLC**
See also DA; DA3; DAB; DAC; DAM MST, NOV; DLB 119, 301; EW 7; EXPS; GFL 1789 to the Present; LAIT 2; LMFS 1; NFS 14; RGSF 2; RGWL 2, 3; SSFS 6; TWA

Flavius Josephus
See Josephus, Flavius

Flecker, Herman Elroy
See Flecker, (Herman) James Elroy

Flecker, (Herman) James Elroy 1884-1915 .... **TCLC 43**
See also CA 109; 150; DLB 10, 19; RGEL 2

Fleming, Ian (Lancaster) 1908-1964 . **CLC 3, 30**
See also AAYA 26; BPFB 1; CA 5-8R; CANR 59; CDBLB 1945-1960; CMW 4; CPW; DA3; DAM POP; DLB 87, 201; MSW; MTCW 1, 2; RGEL 2; SATA 9; TEA; YAW

Fleming, Thomas (James) 1927- ...... **CLC 37**
See also CA 5-8R; CANR 10, 102; INT CANR-10; SATA 8

Fletcher, John 1579-1625 .... **DC 6; LC 33**
See also BRW 2; CDBLB Before 1660; DLB 58; RGEL 2; TEA

Fletcher, John Gould 1886-1950 .... **TCLC 35**
See also CA 107; 167; DLB 4, 45; LMFS 2; RGAL 4

Fleur, Paul
See Pohl, Frederik

Flieg, Helmut
See Heym, Stefan

Flooglebuckle, Al
See Spiegelman, Art

Flora, Fletcher 1914-1969
See Queen, Ellery
See also CA 1-4R; CANR 3, 85

Flying Officer X
See Bates, H(erbert) E(rnest)

Fo, Dario 1926- .... **CLC 32, 109; DC 10**
See also CA 116; 128; CANR 68, 114, 134; CWW 2; DA3; DAM DRAM; DLBY 1997; EWL 3; MTCW 1, 2

Fogarty, Jonathan Titulescu Esq.
See Farrell, James T(homas)

Follett, Ken(neth Martin) 1949- .... **CLC 18**
See also AAYA 6, 50; BEST 89:4; BPFB 1; CA 81-84; CANR 13, 33, 54, 102; CMW 4; CPW; DA3; DAM NOV, POP; DLB 87; DLBY 1981; INT CANR-33; MTCW 1

Fondane, Benjamin 1898-1944 ..... **TCLC 159**

Fontane, Theodor 1819-1898 .... **NCLC 26**
See also CDWLB 2; DLB 129; EW 6; RGWL 2, 3; TWA

Fontenot, Chester .... **CLC 65**

Fonvizin, Denis Ivanovich 1744(?)-1792 .... **LC 81**
See also DLB 150; RGWL 2, 3

Foote, Horton 1916- .... **CLC 51, 91**
See also CA 73-76; CAD; CANR 34, 51, 110; CD 5; CSW; DA3; DAM DRAM; DFS 20; DLB 26, 266; EWL 3; INT CANR-34

Foote, Mary Hallock 1847-1938 .. **TCLC 108**
See also DLB 186, 188, 202, 221

Foote, Samuel 1721-1777 .... **LC 106**
See also DLB 89; RGEL 2

Foote, Shelby 1916- .... **CLC 75**
See also AAYA 40; CA 5-8R; CANR 3, 45, 74, 131; CN 7; CPW; CSW; DA3; DAM NOV, POP; DLB 2, 17; MTCW 2; RHW

Forbes, Cosmo
See Lewton, Val

Forbes, Esther 1891-1967 .... **CLC 12**
See also AAYA 17; BYA 2; CA 13-14; 25-28R; CAP 1; CLR 27; DLB 22; JRDA; MAICYA 1, 2; RHW; SATA 2, 100; YAW

Forche, Carolyn (Louise) 1950- .... **CLC 25, 83, 86; PC 10**
See also CA 109; 117; CANR 50, 74; CP 7; CWP; DA3; DAM POET; DLB 5, 193; INT CA-117; MTCW 1; PFS 18; RGAL 4

Ford, Elbur
See Hibbert, Eleanor Alice Burford

Ford, Ford Madox 1873-1939 ... **TCLC 1, 15, 39, 57**
See Chaucer, Daniel
See also BRW 6; CA 104; 132; CANR 74; CDBLB 1914-1945; DLB 34, 98, 162; EWL 3; MTCW 1, 2; RGEL 2; TEA

Ford, Henry 1863-1947 .... **TCLC 73**
See also CA 115; 148

Ford, Jack
See Ford, John

Ford, John 1586-1639 .... **DC 8; LC 68**
See also BRW 2; CDBLB Before 1660; DA3; DAM DRAM; DFS 7; DLB 58; IDTP; RGEL 2

Ford, John 1895-1973 .... **CLC 16**
See also CA 187; 45-48

Ford, Richard 1944- .... **CLC 46, 99, 205**
See also AMWS 5; CA 69-72; CANR 11, 47, 86, 128; CN 7; CSW; DLB 227; EWL 3; MTCW 1; RGAL 4; RGSF 2

Ford, Webster
See Masters, Edgar Lee

Foreman, Richard 1937- .... **CLC 50**
See also CA 65-68; CAD; CANR 32, 63; CD 5

Forester, C(ecil) S(cott) 1899-1966 . **CLC 35; TCLC 152**
See also CA 73-76; 25-28R; CANR 83; DLB 191; RGEL 2; RHW; SATA 13

Forez
See Mauriac, Francois (Charles)

Forman, James
See Forman, James D(ouglas)

Forman, James D(ouglas) 1932- .... **CLC 21**
See also AAYA 17; CA 9-12R; CANR 4, 19, 42; JRDA; MAICYA 1, 2; SATA 8, 70; YAW

Forman, Milos 1932- .... **CLC 164**
See also CA 109

Fornes, Maria Irene 1930- .... **CLC 39, 61, 187; DC 10; HLCS 1**
See also CA 25-28R; CAD; CANR 28, 81; CD 5; CWD; DLB 7; HW 1, 2; INT CANR-28; LLW 1; MTCW 1; RGAL 4

Forrest, Leon (Richard) 1937-1997 .... **BLCS; CLC 4**
See also AFAW 2; BW 2; CA 89-92; 162; CAAS 7; CANR 25, 52, 87; CN 7; DLB 33

Forster, E(dward) M(organ) 1879-1970 ...... **CLC 1, 2, 3, 4, 9, 10, 13, 15, 22, 45, 77; SSC 27; TCLC 125; WLC**
See also AAYA 2, 37; BRW 6; BRWR 2; BYA 12; CA 13-14; 25-28R; CANR 45; CAP 1; CDBLB 1914-1945; DA; DA3; DAB; DAC; DAM MST, NOV; DLB 34, 98, 162, 178, 195; DLBD 10; EWL 3; EXPN; LAIT 3; LMFS 1; MTCW 1, 2; NCFS 1; NFS 3, 10, 11; RGEL 2; RGSF 2; SATA 57; SUFW 1; TEA; WLIT 4

Forster, John 1812-1876 .... **NCLC 11**
See also DLB 144, 184

Forster, Margaret 1938- .... **CLC 149**
See also CA 133; CANR 62, 115; CN 7; DLB 155, 271

Forsyth, Frederick 1938- .... **CLC 2, 5, 36**
See also BEST 89:4; CA 85-88; CANR 38, 62, 115; CMW 4; CN 7; CPW; DAM NOV, POP; DLB 87; MTCW 1, 2

Forten, Charlotte L. 1837-1914 .... **BLC 2; TCLC 16**
See Grimke, Charlotte L(ottie) Forten
See also DLB 50, 239

Fortinbras
See Grieg, (Johan) Nordahl (Brun)

Foscolo, Ugo 1778-1827 .... **NCLC 8, 97**
See also EW 5

Fosse, Bob .... **CLC 20**
See Fosse, Robert Louis

Fosse, Robert Louis 1927-1987
See Fosse, Bob
See also CA 110; 123

Foster, Hannah Webster 1758-1840 .... **NCLC 99**
See also DLB 37, 200; RGAL 4

Foster, Stephen Collins 1826-1864 .... **NCLC 26**
See also RGAL 4

Foucault, Michel 1926-1984 . **CLC 31, 34, 69**
See also CA 105; 113; CANR 34; DLB 242; EW 13; EWL 3; GFL 1789 to the Present; GLL 1; LMFS 2; MTCW 1, 2; TWA

Fouque, Friedrich (Heinrich Karl) de la Motte 1777-1843 .... **NCLC 2**
See also DLB 90; RGWL 2, 3; SUFW 1

Fourier, Charles 1772-1837 .... **NCLC 51**

Fournier, Henri-Alban 1886-1914
See Alain-Fournier
See also CA 104; 179

Fournier, Pierre 1916- .... **CLC 11**
See Gascar, Pierre
See also CA 89-92; CANR 16, 40

Fowles, John (Robert) 1926- . **CLC 1, 2, 3, 4, 6, 9, 10, 15, 33, 87; SSC 33**
See also BPFB 1; BRWS 1; CA 5-8R; CANR 25, 71, 103; CDBLB 1960 to Present; CN 7; DA3; DAB; DAC; DAM MST; DLB 14, 139, 207; EWL 3; HGG; MTCW 1, 2; RGEL 2; RHW; SATA 22; TEA; WLIT 4

Fox, Paula 1923- .... **CLC 2, 8, 121**
See also AAYA 3, 37; BYA 3, 8; CA 73-76; CANR 20, 36, 62, 105; CLR 1, 44, 96; DLB 52; JRDA; MAICYA 1, 2; MTCW 1; NFS 12; SATA 17, 60, 120; WYA; YAW

Fox, William Price (Jr.) 1926- .... **CLC 22**
See also CA 17-20R; CAAS 19; CANR 11; CSW; DLB 2; DLBY 1981

Foxe, John 1517(?)-1587 .... **LC 14**
See also DLB 132

Frame, Janet .. **CLC 2, 3, 6, 22, 66, 96; SSC 29**
See Clutha, Janet Paterson Frame
See also CN 7; CWP; EWL 3; RGEL 2; RGSF 2; TWA

France, Anatole .... **TCLC 9**
See Thibault, Jacques Anatole Francois
See also DLB 123; EWL 3; GFL 1789 to the Present; MTCW 1; RGWL 2, 3; SUFW 1

Francis, Claude .... **CLC 50**
See also CA 192

Francis, Richard Stanley 1920- ... **CLC 2, 22, 42, 102**
See also AAYA 5, 21; BEST 89:3; BPFB 1; CA 5-8R; CANR 9, 42, 68, 100; CDBLB 1960 to Present; CMW 4; CN 7; DA3; DAM POP; DLB 87; INT CANR-9; MSW; MTCW 1, 2

Francis, Robert (Churchill) 1901-1987 .... **CLC 15; PC 34**
See also AMWS 9; CA 1-4R; 123; CANR 1; EXPP; PFS 12

Francis, Lord Jeffrey
See Jeffrey, Francis
See also DLB 107

Frank, Anne(lies Marie)
1929-1945 .... **TCLC 17; WLC**
See also AAYA 12; BYA 1; CA 113; 133;
CANR 68; CLR 101; DA; DA3; DAB;
DAC; DAM MST; LAIT 4; MAICYA 2;
MAICYAS 1; MTCW 1, 2; NCFS 2;
SATA 87; SATA-Brief 42; WYA; YAW

Frank, Bruno 1887-1945 .... **TCLC 81**
See also CA 189; DLB 118; EWL 3

Frank, Elizabeth 1945- .... **CLC 39**
See also CA 121; 126; CANR 78; INT CA-126

Frankl, Viktor E(mil) 1905-1997 ...... **CLC 93**
See also CA 65-68; 161

Franklin, Benjamin
See Hasek, Jaroslav (Matej Frantisek)

Franklin, Benjamin 1706-1790 .... **LC 25;
WLCS**
See also AMW; CDALB 1640-1865; DA;
DA3; DAB; DAC; DAM MST; DLB 24,
43, 73, 183; LAIT 1; RGAL 4; TUS

**Franklin, (Stella Maria Sarah) Miles
(Lampe)** 1879-1954 .... **TCLC 7**
See also CA 104; 164; DLB 230; FW;
MTCW 2; RGEL 2; TWA

Franzen, Jonathan 1959- .... **CLC 202**
See also CA 129; CANR 105

Fraser, Antonia (Pakenham) 1932- . **CLC 32,
107**
See also AAYA 57; CA 85-88; CANR 44,
65, 119; CMW; DLB 276; MTCW 1, 2;
SATA-Brief 32

Fraser, George MacDonald 1925- ...... **CLC 7**
See also AAYA 48; CA 45-48, 180; CAAE
180; CANR 2, 48, 74; MTCW 1; RHW

Fraser, Sylvia 1935- .... **CLC 64**
See also CA 45-48; CANR 1, 16, 60; CCA
1

Frayn, Michael 1933- . **CLC 3, 7, 31, 47, 176**
See also BRWC 2; BRWS 7; CA 5-8R;
CANR 30, 69, 114, 133; CBD; CD 5; CN
7; DAM DRAM, NOV; DLB 13, 14, 194,
245; FANT; MTCW 1, 2; SFW 4

Fraze, Candida (Merrill) 1945- .... **CLC 50**
See also CA 126

Frazer, Andrew
See Marlowe, Stephen

Frazer, J(ames) G(eorge)
1854-1941 .... **TCLC 32**
See also BRWS 3; CA 118; NCFS 5

Frazer, Robert Caine
See Creasey, John

Frazer, Sir James George
See Frazer, J(ames) G(eorge)

Frazier, Charles 1950- .... **CLC 109**
See also AAYA 34; CA 161; CANR 126;
CSW; DLB 292

Frazier, Ian 1951- .... **CLC 46**
See also CA 130; CANR 54, 93

Frederic, Harold 1856-1898 .... **NCLC 10**
See also AMW; DLB 12, 23; DLBD 13;
RGAL 4

Frederick, John
See Faust, Frederick (Schiller)
See also TCWW 2

Frederick the Great 1712-1786 .... **LC 14**

Fredro, Aleksander 1793-1876 .... **NCLC 8**

Freeling, Nicolas 1927-2003 .... **CLC 38**
See also CA 49-52; 218; CAAS 12; CANR
1, 17, 50, 84; CMW 4; CN 7; DLB 87

Freeman, Douglas Southall
1886-1953 .... **TCLC 11**
See also CA 109; 195; DLB 17; DLBD 17

Freeman, Judith 1946- .... **CLC 55**
See also CA 148; CANR 120; DLB 256

Freeman, Mary E(leanor) Wilkins
1852-1930 .... **SSC 1, 47; TCLC 9**
See also CA 106; 177; DLB 12, 78, 221;
EXPS; FW; HGG; MAWW; RGAL 4;
RGSF 2; SSFS 4, 8; SUFW 1; TUS

Freeman, R(ichard) Austin
1862-1943 .... **TCLC 21**
See also CA 113; CANR 84; CMW 4; DLB
70

French, Albert 1943- .... **CLC 86**
See also BW 3; CA 167

French, Antonia
See Kureishi, Hanif

French, Marilyn 1929- .. **CLC 10, 18, 60, 177**
See also BPFB 1; CA 69-72; CANR 3, 31,
134; CN 7; CPW; DAM DRAM, NOV,
POP; FW; INT CANR-31; MTCW 1, 2

French, Paul
See Asimov, Isaac

Freneau, Philip Morin 1752-1832 .. **NCLC 1,
111**
See also AMWS 2; DLB 37, 43; RGAL 4

Freud, Sigmund 1856-1939 .... **TCLC 52**
See also CA 115; 133; CANR 69; DLB 296;
EW 8; EWL 3; LATS 1:1; MTCW 1, 2;
NCFS 3; TWA

Freytag, Gustav 1816-1895 .... **NCLC 109**
See also DLB 129

Friedan, Betty (Naomi) 1921- .... **CLC 74**
See also CA 65-68; CANR 18, 45, 74; DLB
246; FW; MTCW 1, 2; NCFS 5

Friedlander, Saul 1932- .... **CLC 90**
See also CA 117; 130; CANR 72

Friedman, B(ernard) H(arper)
1926- .... **CLC 7**
See also CA 1-4R; CANR 3, 48

Friedman, Bruce Jay 1930- ...... **CLC 3, 5, 56**
See also CA 9-12R; CAD; CANR 25, 52,
101; CD 5; CN 7; DLB 2, 28, 244; INT
CANR-25; SSFS 18

Friel, Brian 1929- .... **CLC 5, 42, 59, 115; DC
8; SSC 76**
See also BRWS 5; CA 21-24R; CANR 33,
69, 131; CBD; CD 5; DFS 11; DLB 13;
EWL 3; MTCW 1; RGEL 2; TEA

Friis-Baastad, Babbis Ellinor
1921-1970 .... **CLC 12**
See also CA 17-20R; 134; SATA 7

Frisch, Max (Rudolf) 1911-1991 ... **CLC 3, 9,
14, 18, 32, 44; TCLC 121**
See also CA 85-88; 134; CANR 32, 74; CD-
WLB 2; DAM DRAM, NOV; DLB 69,
124; EW 13; EWL 3; MTCW 1, 2; RGWL
2, 3

Fromentin, Eugene (Samuel Auguste)
1820-1876 .... **NCLC 10, 125**
See also DLB 123; GFL 1789 to the Present

Frost, Frederick
See Faust, Frederick (Schiller)
See also TCWW 2

Frost, Robert (Lee) 1874-1963 .. **CLC 1, 3, 4,
9, 10, 13, 15, 26, 34, 44; PC 1, 39;
WLC**
See also AAYA 21; AMW; AMWR 1; CA
89-92; CANR 33; CDALB 1917-1929;
CLR 67; DA; DA3; DAB; DAC; DAM
MST, POET; DLB 54, 284; DLBD 7;
EWL 3; EXPP; MTCW 1, 2; PAB; PFS 1,
2, 3, 4, 5, 6, 7, 10, 13; RGAL 4; SATA
14; TUS; WP; WYA

Froude, James Anthony
1818-1894 .... **NCLC 43**
See also DLB 18, 57, 144

Froy, Herald
See Waterhouse, Keith (Spencer)

Fry, Christopher 1907- .... **CLC 2, 10, 14**
See also BRWS 3; CA 17-20R; CAAS 23;
CANR 9, 30, 74, 132; CBD; CD 5; CP 7;
DAM DRAM; DLB 13; EWL 3; MTCW
1, 2; RGEL 2; SATA 66; TEA

Frye, (Herman) Northrop
1912-1991 .... **CLC 24, 70; TCLC 165**
See also CA 5-8R; 133; CANR 8, 37; DLB
67, 68, 246; EWL 3; MTCW 1, 2; RGAL
4; TWA

Fuchs, Daniel 1909-1993 .... **CLC 8, 22**
See also CA 81-84; 142; CAAS 5; CANR
40; DLB 9, 26, 28; DLBY 1993

Fuchs, Daniel 1934- .... **CLC 34**
See also CA 37-40R; CANR 14, 48

Fuentes, Carlos 1928- .. **CLC 3, 8, 10, 13, 22,
41, 60, 113; HLC 1; SSC 24; WLC**
See also AAYA 4, 45; AITN 2; BPFB 1;
CA 69-72; CANR 10, 32, 68, 104; CD-
WLB 3; CWW 2; DA; DA3; DAB; DAC;
DAM MST, MULT, NOV; DLB 113;
DNFS 2; EWL 3; HW 1, 2; LAIT 3; LATS
1:2; LAW; LAWS 1; LMFS 2; MTCW 1,
2; NFS 8; RGSF 2; RGWL 2, 3; TWA;
WLIT 1

Fuentes, Gregorio Lopez y
See Lopez y Fuentes, Gregorio

Fuertes, Gloria 1918-1998 .... **PC 27**
See also CA 178; 180; DLB 108; HW 2;
SATA 115

Fugard, (Harold) Athol 1932- . **CLC 5, 9, 14,
25, 40, 80; DC 3**
See also AAYA 17; AFW; CA 85-88; CANR
32, 54, 118; CD 5; DAM DRAM; DFS 3,
6, 10; DLB 225; DNFS 1, 2; EWL 3;
LATS 1:2; MTCW 1; RGEL 2; WLIT 2

Fugard, Sheila 1932- .... **CLC 48**
See also CA 125

Fukuyama, Francis 1952- .... **CLC 131**
See also CA 140; CANR 72, 125

Fuller, Charles (H.), (Jr.) 1939- .... **BLC 2;
CLC 25; DC 1**
See also BW 2; CA 108; 112; CAD; CANR
87; CD 5; DAM DRAM, MULT; DFS 8;
DLB 38, 266; EWL 3; INT CA-112;
MTCW 1

Fuller, Henry Blake 1857-1929 .... **TCLC 103**
See also CA 108; 177; DLB 12; RGAL 4

Fuller, John (Leopold) 1937- .... **CLC 62**
See also CA 21-24R; CANR 9, 44; CP 7;
DLB 40

Fuller, Margaret
See Ossoli, Sarah Margaret (Fuller)
See also AMWS 2; DLB 183, 223, 239

Fuller, Roy (Broadbent) 1912-1991 ... **CLC 4,
28**
See also BRWS 7; CA 5-8R; 135; CAAS
10; CANR 53, 83; CWRI 5; DLB 15, 20;
EWL 3; RGEL 2; SATA 87

Fuller, Sarah Margaret
See Ossoli, Sarah Margaret (Fuller)

Fuller, Sarah Margaret
See Ossoli, Sarah Margaret (Fuller)
See also DLB 1, 59, 73

Fuller, Thomas 1608-1661 .... **LC 111**
See also DLB 151

Fulton, Alice 1952- .... **CLC 52**
See also CA 116; CANR 57, 88; CP 7;
CWP; DLB 193

Furphy, Joseph 1843-1912 .... **TCLC 25**
See Collins, Tom
See also CA 163; DLB 230; EWL 3; RGEL
2

Fuson, Robert H(enderson) 1927- .... **CLC 70**
See also CA 89-92; CANR 103

Fussell, Paul 1924- .... **CLC 74**
See also BEST 90:1; CA 17-20R; CANR 8,
21, 35, 69, 135; INT CANR-21; MTCW
1, 2

Gray, Simon (James Holliday)
1936- .... **CLC 9, 14, 36**
See also AITN 1; CA 21-24R; CAAS 3;
CANR 32, 69; CD 5; DLB 13; EWL 3;
MTCW 1; RGEL 2

Gray, Spalding 1941-2004 .... **CLC 49, 112; DC 7**
See also CA 128; 225; CAD; CANR 74;
CD 5; CPW; DAM POP; MTCW 2

Gray, Thomas 1716-1771 .... **LC 4, 40; PC 2; WLC**
See also BRW 3; CDBLB 1660-1789; DA;
DA3; DAB; DAC; DAM MST; DLB 109;
EXPP; PAB; PFS 9; RGEL 2; TEA; WP

Grayson, David
See Baker, Ray Stannard

Grayson, Richard (A.) 1951- .... **CLC 38**
See also CA 85-88, 210; CAAE 210; CANR
14, 31, 57; DLB 234

Greeley, Andrew M(oran) 1928- ...... **CLC 28**
See also BPFB 2; CA 5-8R; CAAS 7;
CANR 7, 43, 69, 104; CMW 4; CPW;
DA3; DAM POP; MTCW 1, 2

Green, Anna Katharine
1846-1935 .... **TCLC 63**
See also CA 112; 159; CMW 4; DLB 202,
221; MSW

Green, Brian
See Card, Orson Scott

Green, Hannah
See Greenberg, Joanne (Goldenberg)

Green, Hannah 1927(?)-1996 .... **CLC 3**
See also CA 73-76; CANR 59, 93; NFS 10

Green, Henry .... **CLC 2, 13, 97**
See Yorke, Henry Vincent
See also BRWS 2; CA 175; DLB 15; EWL
3; RGEL 2

Green, Julien (Hartridge) 1900-1998
See Green, Julian
See also CA 21-24R; 169; CANR 33, 87;
CWW 2; DLB 4, 72; MTCW 1

Green, Julian .... **CLC 3, 11, 77**
See Green, Julien (Hartridge)
See also EWL 3; GFL 1789 to the Present;
MTCW 2

Green, Paul (Eliot) 1894-1981 .... **CLC 25**
See also AITN 1; CA 5-8R; 103; CANR 3;
DAM DRAM; DLB 7, 9, 249; DLBY
1981; RGAL 4

Greenaway, Peter 1942- .... **CLC 159**
See also CA 127

Greenberg, Ivan 1908-1973
See Rahv, Philip
See also CA 85-88

Greenberg, Joanne (Goldenberg)
1932- .... **CLC 7, 30**
See also AAYA 12; CA 5-8R; CANR 14,
32, 69; CN 7; SATA 25; YAW

Greenberg, Richard 1959(?)- .... **CLC 57**
See also CA 138; CAD; CD 5

Greenblatt, Stephen J(ay) 1943- ...... **CLC 70**
See also CA 49-52; CANR 115

Greene, Bette 1934- .... **CLC 30**
See also AAYA 7; BYA 3; CA 53-56; CANR
4; CLR 2; CWRI 5; JRDA; LAIT 4; MAI-
CYA 1, 2; NFS 10; SAAS 16; SATA 8,
102; WYA; YAW

Greene, Gael .... **CLC 8**
See also CA 13-16R; CANR 10

Greene, Graham (Henry)
1904-1991 .... **CLC 1, 3, 6, 9, 14, 18, 27,
37, 70, 72, 125; SSC 29; WLC**
See also AITN 2; BPFB 2; BRWR 2; BRWS
1; BYA 3; CA 13-16R; 133; CANR 35,
61, 131; CBD; CDBLB 1945-1960; CMW
4; DA; DA3; DAB; DAC; DAM MST,

NOV; DLB 13, 15, 77, 100, 162, 201,
204; DLBY 1991; EWL 3; MSW; MTCW
1, 2; NFS 16; RGEL 2; SATA 20; SSFS
14; TEA; WLIT 4

Greene, Robert 1558-1592 .... **LC 41**
See also BRWS 8; DLB 62, 167; IDTP;
RGEL 2; TEA

Greer, Germaine 1939- .... **CLC 131**
See also AITN 1; CA 81-84; CANR 33, 70,
115, 133; FW; MTCW 1, 2

Greer, Richard
See Silverberg, Robert

Gregor, Arthur 1923- .... **CLC 9**
See also CA 25-28R; CAAS 10; CANR 11;
CP 7; SATA 36

Gregor, Lee
See Pohl, Frederik

Gregory, Lady Isabella Augusta (Persse)
1852-1932 .... **TCLC 1**
See also BRW 6; CA 104; 184; DLB 10;
IDTP; RGEL 2

Gregory, J. Dennis
See Williams, John A(lfred)

Grekova, I. .... **CLC 59**
See Ventsel, Elena Sergeevna
See also CWW 2

Grendon, Stephen
See Derleth, August (William)

Grenville, Kate 1950- .... **CLC 61**
See also CA 118; CANR 53, 93

Grenville, Pelham
See Wodehouse, P(elham) G(renville)

Greve, Felix Paul (Berthold Friedrich)
1879-1948
See Grove, Frederick Philip
See also CA 104; 141, 175; CANR 79;
DAC; DAM MST

Greville, Fulke 1554-1628 .... **LC 79**
See also DLB 62, 172; RGEL 2

Grey, Lady Jane 1537-1554 .... **LC 93**
See also DLB 132

Grey, Zane 1872-1939 .... **TCLC 6**
See also BPFB 2; CA 104; 132; DA3; DAM
POP; DLB 9, 212; MTCW 1, 2; RGAL 4;
TCWW 2; TUS

Griboedov, Aleksandr Sergeevich
1795(?)-1829 .... **NCLC 129**
See also DLB 205; RGWL 2, 3

Grieg, (Johan) Nordahl (Brun)
1902-1943 .... **TCLC 10**
See also CA 107; 189; EWL 3

Grieve, C(hristopher) M(urray)
1892-1978 .... **CLC 11, 19**
See MacDiarmid, Hugh; Pteleon
See also CA 5-8R; 85-88; CANR 33, 107;
DAM POET; MTCW 1; RGEL 2

Griffin, Gerald 1803-1840 .... **NCLC 7**
See also DLB 159; RGEL 2

Griffin, John Howard 1920-1980 ..... **CLC 68**
See also AITN 1; CA 1-4R; 101; CANR 2

Griffin, Peter 1942- .... **CLC 39**
See also CA 136

Griffith, D(avid Lewelyn) W(ark)
1875(?)-1948 .... **TCLC 68**
See also CA 119; 150; CANR 80

Griffith, Lawrence
See Griffith, D(avid Lewelyn) W(ark)

Griffiths, Trevor 1935- .... **CLC 13, 52**
See also CA 97-100; CANR 45; CBD; CD
5; DLB 13, 245

Griggs, Sutton (Elbert)
1872-1930 .... **TCLC 77**
See also CA 123; 186; DLB 50

Grigson, Geoffrey (Edward Harvey)
1905-1985 .... **CLC 7, 39**
See also CA 25-28R; 118; CANR 20, 33;
DLB 27; MTCW 1, 2

Grile, Dod
See Bierce, Ambrose (Gwinett)

Grillparzer, Franz 1791-1872 .... **DC 14;
NCLC 1, 102; SSC 37**
See also CDWLB 2; DLB 133; EW 5;
RGWL 2, 3; TWA

Grimble, Reverend Charles James
See Eliot, T(homas) S(tearns)

Grimke, Angelina (Emily) Weld
1880-1958 .... **HR 2**
See Weld, Angelina (Emily) Grimke
See also BW 1; CA 124; DAM POET; DLB
50, 54

Grimke, Charlotte L(ottie) Forten
1837(?)-1914
See Forten, Charlotte L.
See also BW 1; CA 117; 124; DAM MULT,
POET

Grimm, Jacob Ludwig Karl
1785-1863 .... **NCLC 3, 77; SSC 36**
See also DLB 90; MAICYA 1, 2; RGSF 2;
RGWL 2, 3; SATA 22; WCH

Grimm, Wilhelm Karl 1786-1859 .. **NCLC 3,
77; SSC 36**
See also CDWLB 2; DLB 90; MAICYA 1,
2; RGSF 2; RGWL 2, 3; SATA 22; WCH

**Grimmelshausen, Hans Jakob Christoffel
von**
See Grimmelshausen, Johann Jakob Christoffel von
See also RGWL 2, 3

**Grimmelshausen, Johann Jakob Christoffel
von** 1621-1676 .... **LC 6**
See Grimmelshausen, Hans Jakob Christoffel von
See also CDWLB 2; DLB 168

Grindel, Eugene 1895-1952
See Eluard, Paul
See also CA 104; 193; LMFS 2

Grisham, John 1955- .... **CLC 84**
See also AAYA 14, 47; BPFB 2; CA 138;
CANR 47, 69, 114, 133; CMW 4; CN 7;
CPW; CSW; DA3; DAM POP; MSW;
MTCW 2

Grosseteste, Robert 1175(?)-1253 . **CMLC 62**
See also DLB 115

Grossman, David 1954- .... **CLC 67**
See also CA 138; CANR 114; CWW 2;
DLB 299; EWL 3

Grossman, Vasilii Semenovich
See Grossman, Vasily (Semenovich)
See also DLB 272

Grossman, Vasily (Semenovich)
1905-1964 .... **CLC 41**
See Grossman, Vasilii Semenovich
See also CA 124; 130; MTCW 1

Grove, Frederick Philip .... **TCLC 4**
See Greve, Felix Paul (Berthold Friedrich)
See also DLB 92; RGEL 2

Grubb
See Crumb, R(obert)

Grumbach, Doris (Isaac) 1918- . **CLC 13, 22,
64**
See also CA 5-8R; CAAS 2; CANR 9, 42,
70, 127; CN 7; INT CANR-9; MTCW 2

Grundtvig, Nicolai Frederik Severin
1783-1872 .... **NCLC 1**
See also DLB 300

Grunge
See Crumb, R(obert)

Grunwald, Lisa 1959- .... **CLC 44**
See also CA 120

Gryphius, Andreas 1616-1664 .... **LC 89**
See also CDWLB 2; DLB 164; RGWL 2, 3

Guare, John 1938- .... **CLC 8, 14, 29, 67; DC
20**
See also CA 73-76; CAD; CANR 21, 69,
118; CD 5; DAM DRAM; DFS 8, 13;
DLB 7, 249; EWL 3; MTCW 1, 2; RGAL
4

Guarini, Battista 1537-1612 .... **LC 102**

Howe, Irving 1920-1993 .... **CLC 85**
See also AMWS 6; CA 9-12R; 141; CANR
21, 50; DLB 67; EWL 3; MTCW 1, 2

Howe, Julia Ward 1819-1910 .... **TCLC 21**
See also CA 117; 191; DLB 1, 189, 235;
FW

Howe, Susan 1937- .... **CLC 72, 152; PC 54**
See also AMWS 4; CA 160; CP 7; CWP;
DLB 120; FW; RGAL 4

Howe, Tina 1937- .... **CLC 48**
See also CA 109; CAD; CANR 125; CD 5;
CWD

Howell, James 1594(?)-1666 .... **LC 13**
See also DLB 151

Howells, W. D.
See Howells, William Dean

Howells, William D.
See Howells, William Dean

Howells, William Dean 1837-1920 ... **SSC 36;**
TCLC 7, 17, 41
See also AMW; CA 104; 134; CDALB
1865-1917; DLB 12, 64, 74, 79, 189;
LMFS 1; MTCW 2; RGAL 4; TUS

Howes, Barbara 1914-1996 .... **CLC 15**
See also CA 9-12R; 151; CAAS 3; CANR
53; CP 7; SATA 5

Hrabal, Bohumil 1914-1997 ...... **CLC 13, 67;**
TCLC 155
See also CA 106; 156; CAAS 12; CANR
57; CWW 2; DLB 232; EWL 3; RGSF 2

Hrotsvit of Gandersheim c. 935-c.
1000 .... **CMLC 29**
See also DLB 148

Hsi, Chu 1130-1200 .... **CMLC 42**

Hsun, Lu
See Lu Hsun

Hubbard, L(afayette) Ron(ald)
1911-1986 .... **CLC 43**
See also CA 77-80; 118; CANR 52; CPW;
DA3; DAM POP; FANT; MTCW 2; SFW
4

Huch, Ricarda (Octavia)
1864-1947 .... **TCLC 13**
See also CA 111; 189; DLB 66; EWL 3

Huddle, David 1942- .... **CLC 49**
See also CA 57-60; CAAS 20; CANR 89;
DLB 130

Hudson, Jeffrey
See Crichton, (John) Michael

Hudson, W(illiam) H(enry)
1841-1922 .... **TCLC 29**
See also CA 115; 190; DLB 98, 153, 174;
RGEL 2; SATA 35

Hueffer, Ford Madox
See Ford, Ford Madox

Hughart, Barry 1934- .... **CLC 39**
See also CA 137; FANT; SFW 4; SUFW 2

Hughes, Colin
See Creasey, John

Hughes, David (John) 1930- .... **CLC 48**
See also CA 116; 129; CN 7; DLB 14

Hughes, Edward James
See Hughes, Ted
See also DA3; DAM MST, POET

Hughes, (James Mercer) Langston
1902-1967 ..... **BLC 2; CLC 1, 5, 10, 15,**
35, 44, 108; DC 3; HR 2; PC 1, 53;
SSC 6; WLC
See also AAYA 12; AFAW 1, 2; AMWR 1;
AMWS 1; BW 1, 3; CA 1-4R; 25-28R;
CANR 1, 34, 82; CDALB 1929-1941;
CLR 17; DA; DA3; DAB; DAC; DAM
DRAM, MST, MULT, POET; DFS 6, 18;
DLB 4, 7, 48, 51, 86, 228; EWL 3; EXPP;
EXPS; JRDA; LAIT 3; LMFS 2; MAI-
CYA 1, 2; MTCW 1, 2; PAB; PFS 1, 3, 6,
10, 15; RGAL 4; RGSF 2; SATA 4, 33;
SSFS 4, 7; TUS; WCH; WP; YAW

Hughes, Richard (Arthur Warren)
1900-1976 .... **CLC 1, 11**
See also CA 5-8R; 65-68; CANR 4; DAM
NOV; DLB 15, 161; EWL 3; MTCW 1;
RGEL 2; SATA 8; SATA-Obit 25

Hughes, Ted 1930-1998 . **CLC 2, 4, 9, 14, 37,**
119; PC 7
See also Hughes, Edward James
See also BRWC 2; BRWR 2; BRWS 1; CA
1-4R; 171; CANR 1, 33, 66, 108; CLR 3;
CP 7; DAB; DAC; DLB 40, 161; EWL 3;
EXPP; MAICYA 1, 2; MTCW 1, 2; PAB;
PFS 4, 19; RGEL 2; SATA 49; SATA-
Brief 27; SATA-Obit 107; TEA; YAW

Hugo, Richard
See Huch, Ricarda (Octavia)

Hugo, Richard F(ranklin)
1923-1982 .... **CLC 6, 18, 32**
See also AMWS 6; CA 49-52; 108; CANR
3; DAM POET; DLB 5, 206; EWL 3; PFS
17; RGAL 4

Hugo, Victor (Marie) 1802-1885 .... **NCLC 3,**
10, 21; PC 17; WLC
See also AAYA 28; DA; DA3; DAB; DAC;
DAM DRAM, MST, NOV, POET; DLB
119, 192, 217; EFS 2; EW 6; EXPN; GFL
1789 to the Present; LAIT 1, 2; NFS 5,
20; RGWL 2, 3; SATA 47; TWA

Huidobro, Vicente
See Huidobro Fernandez, Vicente Garcia
See also DLB 283; EWL 3; LAW

Huidobro Fernandez, Vicente Garcia
1893-1948 .... **TCLC 31**
See also Huidobro, Vicente
See also CA 131; HW 1

Hulme, Keri 1947- .... **CLC 39, 130**
See also CA 125; CANR 69; CN 7; CP 7;
CWP; EWL 3; FW; INT CA-125

Hulme, T(homas) E(rnest)
1883-1917 .... **TCLC 21**
See also BRWS 6; CA 117; 203; DLB 19

Humboldt, Wilhelm von
1767-1835 .... **NCLC 134**
See also DLB 90

Hume, David 1711-1776 .... **LC 7, 56**
See also BRWS 3; DLB 104, 252; LMFS 1;
TEA

Humphrey, William 1924-1997 .... **CLC 45**
See also AMWS 9; CA 77-80; 160; CANR
68; CN 7; CSW; DLB 6, 212, 234, 278;
TCWW 2

Humphreys, Emyr Owen 1919- .... **CLC 47**
See also CA 5-8R; CANR 3, 24; CN 7;
DLB 15

Humphreys, Josephine 1945- ..... **CLC 34, 57**
See also CA 121; 127; CANR 97; CSW;
DLB 292; INT CA-127

Huneker, James Gibbons
1860-1921 .... **TCLC 65**
See also CA 193; DLB 71; RGAL 4

Hungerford, Hesba Fay
See Brinsmead, H(esba) F(ay)

Hungerford, Pixie
See Brinsmead, H(esba) F(ay)

Hunt, E(verette) Howard, (Jr.)
1918- .... **CLC 3**
See also AITN 1; CA 45-48; CANR 2, 47,
103; CMW 4

Hunt, Francesca
See Holland, Isabelle (Christian)

Hunt, Howard
See Hunt, E(verette) Howard, (Jr.)

Hunt, Kyle
See Creasey, John

Hunt, (James Henry) Leigh
1784-1859 .... **NCLC 1, 70**
See also DAM POET; DLB 96, 110, 144;
RGEL 2; TEA

Hunt, Marsha 1946- .... **CLC 70**
See also BW 2, 3; CA 143; CANR 79

Hunt, Violet 1866(?)-1942 .... **TCLC 53**
See also CA 184; DLB 162, 197

Hunter, E. Waldo
See Sturgeon, Theodore (Hamilton)

Hunter, Evan 1926- .... **CLC 11, 31**
See McBain, Ed
See also AAYA 39; BPFB 2; CA 5-8R;
CANR 5, 38, 62, 97; CMW 4; CN 7;
CPW; DAM POP; DLB 306; DLBY 1982;
INT CANR-5; MSW; MTCW 1; SATA
25; SFW 4

Hunter, Kristin
See Lattany, Kristin (Elaine Eggleston)
Hunter

Hunter, Mary
See Austin, Mary (Hunter)

Hunter, Mollie 1922- .... **CLC 21**
See McIlwraith, Maureen Mollie Hunter
See also AAYA 13; BYA 6; CANR 37, 78;
CLR 25; DLB 161; JRDA; MAICYA 1,
2; SAAS 7; SATA 54, 106, 139; SATA-
Essay 139; WYA; YAW

Hunter, Robert (?)-1734 .... **LC 7**

Hurston, Zora Neale 1891-1960 .... **BLC 2;**
CLC 7, 30, 61; DC 12; HR 2; SSC 4,
80; TCLC 121, 131; WLCS
See also AAYA 15; AFAW 1, 2; AMWS 6;
BW 1, 3; BYA 12; CA 85-88; CANR 61;
CDALBS; DA; DA3; DAC; DAM MST,
MULT, NOV; DFS 6; DLB 51, 86; EWL
3; EXPN; EXPS; FW; LAIT 3; LATS 1:1;
LMFS 2; MAWW; MTCW 1, 2; NFS 3;
RGAL 4; RGSF 2; SSFS 1, 6, 11, 19;
TUS; YAW

Husserl, E. G.
See Husserl, Edmund (Gustav Albrecht)

Husserl, Edmund (Gustav Albrecht)
1859-1938 .... **TCLC 100**
See also CA 116; 133; DLB 296

Huston, John (Marcellus)
1906-1987 .... **CLC 20**
See also CA 73-76; 123; CANR 34; DLB
26

Hustvedt, Siri 1955- .... **CLC 76**
See also CA 137

Hutten, Ulrich von 1488-1523 .... **LC 16**
See also DLB 179

Huxley, Aldous (Leonard)
1894-1963 .... **CLC 1, 3, 4, 5, 8, 11, 18,**
35, 79; SSC 39; WLC
See also AAYA 11; BPFB 2; BRW 7; CA
85-88; CANR 44, 99; CDBLB 1914-1945;
DA; DA3; DAB; DAC; DAM MST, NOV;
DLB 36, 100, 162, 195, 255; EWL 3;
EXPN; LAIT 5; LMFS 2; MTCW 1, 2;
NFS 6; RGEL 2; SATA 63; SCFW 2;
SFW 4; TEA; YAW

Huxley, T(homas) H(enry)
1825-1895 .... **NCLC 67**
See also DLB 57; TEA

Huygens, Constantijn 1596-1687 .... **LC 114**
See also

Huysmans, Joris-Karl 1848-1907 ... **TCLC 7,**
69
See also CA 104; 165; DLB 123; EW 7;
GFL 1789 to the Present; LMFS 2; RGWL
2, 3

Hwang, David Henry 1957- .... **CLC 55, 196;**
DC 4, 23
See also CA 127; 132; CAD; CANR 76,
124; CD 5; DA3; DAM DRAM; DFS 11,
18; DLB 212, 228; INT CA-132; MTCW
2; RGAL 4

Hyde, Anthony 1946- .... **CLC 42**
See Chase, Nicholas
See also CA 136; CCA 1

Johnson, E. Pauline 1861-1913 .... **NNAL**
See also CA 150; DAC; DAM MULT; DLB 92, 175

Johnson, Eyvind (Olof Verner) 1900-1976 .... **CLC 14**
See also CA 73-76; 69-72; CANR 34, 101; DLB 259; EW 12; EWL 3

Johnson, Fenton 1888-1958 .... **BLC 2**
See also BW 1; CA 118; 124; DAM MULT; DLB 45, 50

Johnson, Georgia Douglas (Camp) 1880-1966 .... **HR 3**
See also BW 1; CA 125; DLB 51, 249; WP

Johnson, Helene 1907-1995 .... **HR 3**
See also CA 181; DLB 51; WP

Johnson, J. R.
See James, C(yril) L(ionel) R(obert)

Johnson, James Weldon 1871-1938 .. **BLC 2; HR 3; PC 24; TCLC 3, 19**
See also AFAW 1, 2; BW 1, 3; CA 104; 125; CANR 82; CDALB 1917-1929; CLR 32; DA3; DAM MULT, POET; DLB 51; EWL 3; EXPP; LMFS 2; MTCW 1, 2; PFS 1; RGAL 4; SATA 31; TUS

Johnson, Joyce 1935- .... **CLC 58**
See also BG 3; CA 125; 129; CANR 102

Johnson, Judith (Emlyn) 1936- .... **CLC 7, 15**
See Sherwin, Judith Johnson
See also CA 25-28R; 153; CANR 34

Johnson, Lionel (Pigot) 1867-1902 .... **TCLC 19**
See also CA 117; 209; DLB 19; RGEL 2

Johnson, Marguerite Annie
See Angelou, Maya

Johnson, Mel
See Malzberg, Barry N(athaniel)

Johnson, Pamela Hansford 1912-1981 .... **CLC 1, 7, 27**
See also CA 1-4R; 104; CANR 2, 28; DLB 15; MTCW 1, 2; RGEL 2

Johnson, Paul (Bede) 1928- .... **CLC 147**
See also BEST 89:4; CA 17-20R; CANR 34, 62, 100

Johnson, Robert .... **CLC 70**

Johnson, Robert 1911(?)-1938 .... **TCLC 69**
See also BW 3; CA 174

Johnson, Samuel 1709-1784 .... **LC 15, 52; WLC**
See also BRW 3; BRWR 1; CDBLB 1660-1789; DA; DAB; DAC; DAM MST; DLB 39, 95, 104, 142, 213; LMFS 1; RGEL 2; TEA

Johnson, Uwe 1934-1984 .. **CLC 5, 10, 15, 40**
See also CA 1-4R; 112; CANR 1, 39; CD-WLB 2; DLB 75; EWL 3; MTCW 1; RGWL 2, 3

Johnston, Basil H. 1929- .... **NNAL**
See also CA 69-72; CANR 11, 28, 66; DAC; DAM MULT; DLB 60

Johnston, George (Benson) 1913- .... **CLC 51**
See also CA 1-4R; CANR 5, 20; CP 7; DLB 88

Johnston, Jennifer (Prudence) 1930- .... **CLC 7, 150**
See also CA 85-88; CANR 92; CN 7; DLB 14

Joinville, Jean de 1224(?)-1317 ..... **CMLC 38**

Jolley, (Monica) Elizabeth 1923- ..... **CLC 46; SSC 19**
See also CA 127; CAAS 13; CANR 59; CN 7; EWL 3; RGSF 2

Jones, Arthur Llewellyn 1863-1947
See Machen, Arthur
See also CA 104; 179; HGG

Jones, D(ouglas) G(ordon) 1929- ..... **CLC 10**
See also CA 29-32R; CANR 13, 90; CP 7; DLB 53

Jones, David (Michael) 1895-1974 .... **CLC 2, 4, 7, 13, 42**
See also BRW 6; BRWS 7; CA 9-12R; 53-56; CANR 28; CDBLB 1945-1960; DLB 20, 100; EWL 3; MTCW 1; PAB; RGEL 2

Jones, David Robert 1947-
See Bowie, David
See also CA 103; CANR 104

Jones, Diana Wynne 1934- .... **CLC 26**
See also AAYA 12; BYA 6, 7, 9, 11, 13, 16; CA 49-52; CANR 4, 26, 56, 120; CLR 23; DLB 161; FANT; JRDA; MAICYA 1, 2; SAAS 7; SATA 9, 70, 108; SFW 4; SUFW 2; YAW

Jones, Edward P. 1950- .... **CLC 76**
See also BW 2, 3; CA 142; CANR 79, 134; CSW

Jones, Gayl 1949- ...... **BLC 2; CLC 6, 9, 131**
See also AFAW 1, 2; BW 2, 3; CA 77-80; CANR 27, 66, 122; CN 7; CSW; DA3; DAM MULT; DLB 33, 278; MTCW 1, 2; RGAL 4

Jones, James 1921-1977 ...... **CLC 1, 3, 10, 39**
See also AITN 1, 2; AMWS 11; BPFB 2; CA 1-4R; 69-72; CANR 6; DLB 2, 143; DLBD 17; DLBY 1998; EWL 3; MTCW 1; RGAL 4

Jones, John J.
See Lovecraft, H(oward) P(hillips)

Jones, LeRoi .... **CLC 1, 2, 3, 5, 10, 14**
See Baraka, Amiri
See also MTCW 2

Jones, Louis B. 1953- .... **CLC 65**
See also CA 141; CANR 73

Jones, Madison (Percy, Jr.) 1925- ...... **CLC 4**
See also CA 13-16R; CAAS 11; CANR 7, 54, 83; CN 7; CSW; DLB 152

Jones, Mervyn 1922- .... **CLC 10, 52**
See also CA 45-48; CAAS 5; CANR 1, 91; CN 7; MTCW 1

Jones, Mick 1956(?)- .... **CLC 30**

Jones, Nettie (Pearl) 1941- .... **CLC 34**
See also BW 2; CA 137; CAAS 20; CANR 88

Jones, Peter 1802-1856 .... **NNAL**

Jones, Preston 1936-1979 .... **CLC 10**
See also CA 73-76; 89-92; DLB 7

Jones, Robert F(rancis) 1934-2003 .... **CLC 7**
See also CA 49-52; CANR 2, 61, 118

Jones, Rod 1953- .... **CLC 50**
See also CA 128

Jones, Terence Graham Parry 1942- .... **CLC 21**
See Jones, Terry; Monty Python
See also CA 112; 116; CANR 35, 93; INT CA-116; SATA 127

Jones, Terry
See Jones, Terence Graham Parry
See also SATA 67; SATA-Brief 51

Jones, Thom (Douglas) 1945(?)- ..... **CLC 81; SSC 56**
See also CA 157; CANR 88; DLB 244

Jong, Erica 1942- .... **CLC 4, 6, 8, 18, 83**
See also AITN 1; AMWS 5; BEST 90:2; BPFB 2; CA 73-76; CANR 26, 52, 75, 132; CN 7; CP 7; CPW; DA3; DAM NOV, POP; DLB 2, 5, 28, 152; FW; INT CANR-26; MTCW 1, 2

Jonson, Ben(jamin) 1572(?)-1637 . **DC 4; LC 6, 33, 110; PC 17; WLC**
See also BRW 1; BRWC 1; BRWR 1; CD-BLB Before 1660; DA; DAB; DAC; DAM DRAM, MST, POET; DFS 4, 10; DLB 62, 121; LMFS 1; RGEL 2; TEA; WLIT 3

Jordan, June (Meyer) 1936-2002 .. **BLCS; CLC 5, 11, 23, 114; PC 38**
See also AAYA 2; AFAW 1, 2; BW 2, 3; CA 33-36R; 206; CANR 25, 70, 114; CLR 10; CP 7; CWP; DAM MULT, POET; DLB 38; GLL 2; LAIT 5; MAICYA 1, 2; MTCW 1; SATA 4, 136; YAW

Jordan, Neil (Patrick) 1950- .... **CLC 110**
See also CA 124; 130; CANR 54; CN 7; GLL 2; INT CA-130

Jordan, Pat(rick M.) 1941- .... **CLC 37**
See also CA 33-36R; CANR 121

Jorgensen, Ivar
See Ellison, Harlan (Jay)

Jorgenson, Ivar
See Silverberg, Robert

Joseph, George Ghevarughese .... **CLC 70**

Josephson, Mary
See O'Doherty, Brian

Josephus, Flavius c. 37-100 .... **CMLC 13**
See also AW 2; DLB 176

Josiah Allen's Wife
See Holley, Marietta

Josipovici, Gabriel (David) 1940- ...... **CLC 6, 43, 153**
See also CA 37-40R; 224; CAAE 224; CAAS 8; CANR 47, 84; CN 7; DLB 14

Joubert, Joseph 1754-1824 .... **NCLC 9**

Jouve, Pierre Jean 1887-1976 .... **CLC 47**
See also CA 65-68; DLB 258; EWL 3

Jovine, Francesco 1902-1950 .... **TCLC 79**
See also DLB 264; EWL 3

Joyce, James (Augustine Aloysius) 1882-1941 .... **DC 16; PC 22; SSC 3, 26, 44, 64; TCLC 3, 8, 16, 35, 52, 159; WLC**
See also AAYA 42; BRW 7; BRWC 1; BRWR 1; BYA 11, 13; CA 104; 126; CD-BLB 1914-1945; DA; DA3; DAB; DAC; DAM MST, NOV, POET; DLB 10, 19, 36, 162, 247; EWL 3; EXPN; EXPS; LAIT 3; LMFS 1, 2; MTCW 1, 2; NFS 7; RGSF 2; SSFS 1, 19; TEA; WLIT 4

Jozsef, Attila 1905-1937 .... **TCLC 22**
See also CA 116; CDWLB 4; DLB 215; EWL 3

Juana Ines de la Cruz, Sor 1651(?)-1695 ...... **HLCS 1; LC 5; PC 24**
See also DLB 305; FW; LAW; RGWL 2, 3; WLIT 1

Juana Inez de La Cruz, Sor
See Juana Ines de la Cruz, Sor

Judd, Cyril
See Kornbluth, C(yril) M.; Pohl, Frederik

Juenger, Ernst 1895-1998 .... **CLC 125**
See Junger, Ernst
See also CA 101; 167; CANR 21, 47, 106; DLB 56

Julian of Norwich 1342(?)-1416(?) . **LC 6, 52**
See also DLB 146; LMFS 1

Julius Caesar 100B.C.-44B.C.
See Caesar, Julius
See also CDWLB 1; DLB 211

Junger, Ernst
See Juenger, Ernst
See also CDWLB 2; EWL 3; RGWL 2, 3

Junger, Sebastian 1962- .... **CLC 109**
See also AAYA 28; CA 165; CANR 130

Juniper, Alex
See Hospital, Janette Turner

Junius
See Luxemburg, Rosa

Just, Ward (Swift) 1935- .... **CLC 4, 27**
See also CA 25-28R; CANR 32, 87; CN 7; INT CANR-32

NOV; DLB 173, 212; DLBY 1980; EWL
3; FW; INT CANR-13; LAIT 5; MAWW;
MTCW 1, 2; NFS 6; RGAL 4; SATA 53;
SSFS 3

Kinnell, Galway 1927- ..... **CLC 1, 2, 3, 5, 13,
29, 129; PC 26**
See also AMWS 3; CA 9-12R; CANR 10,
34, 66, 116; CP 7; DLB 5; DLBY 1987;
EWL 3; INT CANR-34; MTCW 1, 2;
PAB; PFS 9; RGAL 4; WP

Kinsella, Thomas 1928- .... **CLC 4, 19, 138**
See also BRWS 5; CA 17-20R; CANR 15,
122; CP 7; DLB 27; EWL 3; MTCW 1, 2;
RGEL 2; TEA

Kinsella, W(illiam) P(atrick) 1935- . **CLC 27,
43, 166**
See also AAYA 7, 60; BPFB 2; CA 97-100,
222; CAAE 222; CAAS 7; CANR 21, 35,
66, 75, 129; CN 7; CPW; DAC; DAM
NOV, POP; FANT; INT CANR-21; LAIT
5; MTCW 1, 2; NFS 15; RGSF 2

Kinsey, Alfred C(harles)
1894-1956 .... **TCLC 91**
See also CA 115; 170; MTCW 2

Kipling, (Joseph) Rudyard 1865-1936 . **PC 3;
SSC 5, 54; TCLC 8, 17; WLC**
See also AAYA 32; BRW 6; BRWC 1, 2;
BYA 4; CA 105; 120; CANR 33; CDBLB
1890-1914; CLR 39, 65; CWA 2; DA;
DA3; DAB; DAC; DAM MST, POET;
DLB 19, 34, 141, 156; EWL 3; EXPS;
FANT; LAIT 3; LMFS 1; MAICYA 1, 2;
MTCW 1, 2; RGEL 2; RGSF 2; SATA
100; SFW 4; SSFS 8; SUFW 1; TEA;
WCH; WLIT 4; YABC 2

Kirk, Russell (Amos) 1918-1994 .. **TCLC 119**
See also AITN 1; CA 1-4R; 145; CAAS 9;
CANR 1, 20, 60; HGG; INT CANR-20;
MTCW 1, 2

Kirkham, Dinah
See Card, Orson Scott

Kirkland, Caroline M. 1801-1864 . **NCLC 85**
See also DLB 3, 73, 74, 250, 254; DLBD
13

Kirkup, James 1918- .... **CLC 1**
See also CA 1-4R; CAAS 4; CANR 2; CP
7; DLB 27; SATA 12

Kirkwood, James 1930(?)-1989 .... **CLC 9**
See also AITN 2; CA 1-4R; 128; CANR 6,
40; GLL 2

Kirsch, Sarah 1935- .... **CLC 176**
See also CA 178; CWW 2; DLB 75; EWL
3

Kirshner, Sidney
See Kingsley, Sidney

Kis, Danilo 1935-1989 .... **CLC 57**
See also CA 109; 118; 129; CANR 61; CD-
WLB 4; DLB 181; EWL 3; MTCW 1;
RGSF 2; RGWL 2, 3

Kissinger, Henry A(lfred) 1923- ..... **CLC 137**
See also CA 1-4R; CANR 2, 33, 66, 109;
MTCW 1

Kivi, Aleksis 1834-1872 .... **NCLC 30**

Kizer, Carolyn (Ashley) 1925- ... **CLC 15, 39,
80**
See also CA 65-68; CAAS 5; CANR 24,
70, 134; CP 7; CWP; DAM POET; DLB
5, 169; EWL 3; MTCW 2; PFS 18

Klabund 1890-1928 .... **TCLC 44**
See also CA 162; DLB 66

Klappert, Peter 1942- .... **CLC 57**
See also CA 33-36R; CSW; DLB 5

Klein, A(braham) M(oses)
1909-1972 .... **CLC 19**
See also CA 101; 37-40R; DAB; DAC;
DAM MST; DLB 68; EWL 3; RGEL 2

Klein, Joe
See Klein, Joseph

Klein, Joseph 1946- .... **CLC 154**
See also CA 85-88; CANR 55

Klein, Norma 1938-1989 .... **CLC 30**
See also AAYA 2, 35; BPFB 2; BYA 6, 7,
8; CA 41-44R; 128; CANR 15, 37; CLR
2, 19; INT CANR-15; JRDA; MAICYA
1, 2; SAAS 1; SATA 7, 57; WYA; YAW

Klein, T(heodore) E(ibon) D(onald)
1947- .... **CLC 34**
See also CA 119; CANR 44, 75; HGG

Kleist, Heinrich von 1777-1811 ...... **NCLC 2,
37; SSC 22**
See also CDWLB 2; DAM DRAM; DLB
90; EW 5; RGSF 2; RGWL 2, 3

Klima, Ivan 1931- .... **CLC 56, 172**
See also CA 25-28R; CANR 17, 50, 91;
CDWLB 4; CWW 2; DAM NOV; DLB
232; EWL 3; RGWL 3

Klimentev, Andrei Platonovich
See Klimentov, Andrei Platonovich

Klimentov, Andrei Platonovich
1899-1951 .... **SSC 42; TCLC 14**
See Platonov, Andrei Platonovich; Platonov,
Andrey Platonovich
See also CA 108

Klinger, Friedrich Maximilian von
1752-1831 .... **NCLC 1**
See also DLB 94

Klingsor the Magician
See Hartmann, Sadakichi

Klopstock, Friedrich Gottlieb
1724-1803 .... **NCLC 11**
See also DLB 97; EW 4; RGWL 2, 3

Kluge, Alexander 1932- .... **SSC 61**
See also CA 81-84; DLB 75

Knapp, Caroline 1959-2002 .... **CLC 99**
See also CA 154; 207

Knebel, Fletcher 1911-1993 .... **CLC 14**
See also AITN 1; CA 1-4R; 140; CAAS 3;
CANR 1, 36; SATA 36; SATA-Obit 75

Knickerbocker, Diedrich
See Irving, Washington

Knight, Etheridge 1931-1991 ... **BLC 2; CLC
40; PC 14**
See also BW 1, 3; CA 21-24R; 133; CANR
23, 82; DAM POET; DLB 41; MTCW 2;
RGAL 4

Knight, Sarah Kemble 1666-1727 .... **LC 7**
See also DLB 24, 200

Knister, Raymond 1899-1932 .... **TCLC 56**
See also CA 186; DLB 68; RGEL 2

Knowles, John 1926-2001 ... **CLC 1, 4, 10, 26**
See also AAYA 10; AMWS 12; BPFB 2;
BYA 3; CA 17-20R; 203; CANR 40, 74,
76, 132; CDALB 1968-1988; CLR 98; CN
7; DA; DAC; DAM MST, NOV; DLB 6;
EXPN; MTCW 1, 2; NFS 2; RGAL 4;
SATA 8, 89; SATA-Obit 134; YAW

Knox, Calvin M.
See Silverberg, Robert

Knox, John c. 1505-1572 .... **LC 37**
See also DLB 132

Knye, Cassandra
See Disch, Thomas M(ichael)

Koch, C(hristopher) J(ohn) 1932- .... **CLC 42**
See also CA 127; CANR 84; CN 7; DLB
289

Koch, Christopher
See Koch, C(hristopher) J(ohn)

Koch, Kenneth (Jay) 1925-2002 .... **CLC 5, 8,
44**
See also CA 1-4R; 207; CAD; CANR 6,
36, 57, 97, 131; CD 5; CP 7; DAM POET;
DLB 5; INT CANR-36; MTCW 2; PFS
20; SATA 65; WP

Kochanowski, Jan 1530-1584 .... **LC 10**
See also RGWL 2, 3

Kock, Charles Paul de 1794-1871 . **NCLC 16**

Koda Rohan
See Koda Shigeyuki

Koda Rohan
See Koda Shigeyuki
See also DLB 180

Koda Shigeyuki 1867-1947 .... **TCLC 22**
See Koda Rohan
See also CA 121; 183

Koestler, Arthur 1905-1983 ... **CLC 1, 3, 6, 8,
15, 33**
See also BRWS 1; CA 1-4R; 109; CANR 1,
33; CDBLB 1945-1960; DLBY 1983;
EWL 3; MTCW 1, 2; NFS 19; RGEL 2

Kogawa, Joy Nozomi 1935- ...... **CLC 78, 129**
See also CA 101; CANR 19, 62,
126; CN 7; CWP; DAC; DAM MST,
MULT; FW; MTCW 2; NFS 3; SATA 99

Kohout, Pavel 1928- .... **CLC 13**
See also CA 45-48; CANR 3

Koizumi, Yakumo
See Hearn, (Patricio) Lafcadio (Tessima
Carlos)

Kolmar, Gertrud 1894-1943 .... **TCLC 40**
See also CA 167; EWL 3

Komunyakaa, Yusef 1947- .. **BLCS; CLC 86,
94, 207; PC 51**
See also AFAW 2; AMWS 13; CA 147;
CANR 83; CP 7; CSW; DLB 120; EWL
3; PFS 5, 20; RGAL 4

Konrad, George
See Konrad, Gyorgy

Konrad, Gyorgy 1933- .... **CLC 4, 10, 73**
See also CA 85-88; CANR 97; CDWLB 4;
CWW 2; DLB 232; EWL 3

Konwicki, Tadeusz 1926- .... **CLC 8, 28, 54,
117**
See also CA 101; CAAS 9; CANR 39, 59;
CWW 2; DLB 232; EWL 3; IDFW 3;
MTCW 1

Koontz, Dean R(ay) 1945- .... **CLC 78, 206**
See also AAYA 9, 31; BEST 89:3, 90:2; CA
108; CANR 19, 36, 52, 95; CMW 4;
CPW; DA3; DAM NOV, POP; DLB 292;
HGG; MTCW 1; SATA 92; SFW 4;
SUFW 2; YAW

Kopernik, Mikolaj
See Copernicus, Nicolaus

Kopit, Arthur (Lee) 1937- ...... **CLC 1, 18, 33**
See also AITN 1; CA 81-84; CABS 3; CD
5; DAM DRAM; DFS 7, 14; DLB 7;
MTCW 1; RGAL 4

Kopitar, Jernej (Bartholomaus)
1780-1844 .... **NCLC 117**

Kops, Bernard 1926- .... **CLC 4**
See also CA 5-8R; CANR 84; CBD; CN 7;
CP 7; DLB 13

Kornbluth, C(yril) M. 1923-1958 .... **TCLC 8**
See also CA 105; 160; DLB 8; SFW 4

Korolenko, V. G.
See Korolenko, Vladimir Galaktionovich

Korolenko, Vladimir
See Korolenko, Vladimir Galaktionovich

Korolenko, Vladimir G.
See Korolenko, Vladimir Galaktionovich

Korolenko, Vladimir Galaktionovich
1853-1921 .... **TCLC 22**
See also CA 121; DLB 277

Korzybski, Alfred (Habdank Skarbek)
1879-1950 .... **TCLC 61**
See also CA 123; 160

Kosinski, Jerzy (Nikodem)
1933-1991 .... **CLC 1, 2, 3, 6, 10, 15, 53,
70**
See also AMWS 7; BPFB 2; CA 17-20R;
134; CANR 9, 46; DA3; DAM NOV;
DLB 2, 299; DLBY 1982; EWL 3; HGG;
MTCW 1, 2; NFS 12; RGAL 4; TUS

Lainez, Manuel Mujica
See Mujica Lainez, Manuel
See also HW 1

Laing, R(onald) D(avid) 1927-1989 . **CLC 95**
See also CA 107; 129; CANR 34; MTCW 1

Laishley, Alex
See Booth, Martin

Lamartine, Alphonse (Marie Louis Prat) de
1790-1869 .... **NCLC 11; PC 16**
See also DAM POET; DLB 217; GFL 1789
to the Present; RGWL 2, 3

Lamb, Charles 1775-1834 ..... **NCLC 10, 113;**
WLC
See also BRW 4; CDBLB 1789-1832; DA;
DAB; DAC; DAM MST; DLB 93, 107,
163; RGEL 2; SATA 17; TEA

Lamb, Lady Caroline 1785-1828 ... **NCLC 38**
See also DLB 116

Lamb, Mary Ann 1764-1847 .... **NCLC 125**
See also DLB 163; SATA 17

Lame Deer 1903(?)-1976 .... **NNAL**
See also CA 69-72

Lamming, George (William) 1927- ... **BLC 2;**
CLC 2, 4, 66, 144
See also BW 2, 3; CA 85-88; CANR 26,
76; CDWLB 3; CN 7; DAM MULT; DLB
125; EWL 3; MTCW 1, 2; NFS 15; RGEL
2

L'Amour, Louis (Dearborn)
1908-1988 .... **CLC 25, 55**
See Burns, Tex; Mayo, Jim
See also AAYA 16; AITN 2; BEST 89:2;
BPFB 2; CA 1-4R; 125; CANR 3, 25, 40;
CPW; DA3; DAM NOV, POP; DLB 206;
DLBY 1980; MTCW 1, 2; RGAL 4

Lampedusa, Giuseppe (Tomasi) di
.... **TCLC 13**
See Tomasi di Lampedusa, Giuseppe
See also CA 164; EW 11; MTCW 2; RGWL
2, 3

Lampman, Archibald 1861-1899 ... **NCLC 25**
See also DLB 92; RGEL 2; TWA

Lancaster, Bruce 1896-1963 .... **CLC 36**
See also CA 9-10; CANR 70; CAP 1; SATA
9

Lanchester, John 1962- .... **CLC 99**
See also CA 194; DLB 267

Landau, Mark Alexandrovich
See Aldanov, Mark (Alexandrovich)

Landau-Aldanov, Mark Alexandrovich
See Aldanov, Mark (Alexandrovich)

Landis, Jerry
See Simon, Paul (Frederick)

Landis, John 1950- .... **CLC 26**
See also CA 112; 122; CANR 128

Landolfi, Tommaso 1908-1979 .... **CLC 11, 49**
See also CA 127; 117; DLB 177; EWL 3

Landon, Letitia Elizabeth
1802-1838 .... **NCLC 15**
See also DLB 96

Landor, Walter Savage
1775-1864 .... **NCLC 14**
See also BRW 4; DLB 93, 107; RGEL 2

Landwirth, Heinz 1927-
See Lind, Jakov
See also CA 9-12R; CANR 7

Lane, Patrick 1939- .... **CLC 25**
See also CA 97-100; CANR 54; CP 7; DAM
POET; DLB 53; INT CA-97-100

Lang, Andrew 1844-1912 .... **TCLC 16**
See also CA 114; 137; CANR 85; CLR 101;
DLB 98, 141, 184; FANT; MAICYA 1, 2;
RGEL 2; SATA 16; WCH

Lang, Fritz 1890-1976 .... **CLC 20, 103**
See also CA 77-80; 69-72; CANR 30

Lange, John
See Crichton, (John) Michael

Langer, Elinor 1939- .... **CLC 34**
See also CA 121

Langland, William 1332(?)-1400(?) ..... **LC 19**
See also BRW 1; DA; DAB; DAC; DAM
MST, POET; DLB 146; RGEL 2; TEA;
WLIT 3

Langstaff, Launcelot
See Irving, Washington

Lanier, Sidney 1842-1881 . **NCLC 6, 118; PC**
50
See also AMWS 1; DAM POET; DLB 64;
DLBD 13; EXPP; MAICYA 1; PFS 14;
RGAL 4; SATA 18

Lanyer, Aemilia 1569-1645 .... **LC 10, 30, 83;**
PC 60
See also DLB 121

Lao-Tzu
See Lao Tzu

Lao Tzu c. 6th cent. B.C.-3rd cent.
B.C. .... **CMLC 7**

Lapine, James (Elliot) 1949- .... **CLC 39**
See also CA 123; 130; CANR 54, 128; INT
CA-130

Larbaud, Valery (Nicolas)
1881-1957 .... **TCLC 9**
See also CA 106; 152; EWL 3; GFL 1789
to the Present

Lardner, Ring
See Lardner, Ring(gold) W(ilmer)
See also BPFB 2; CDALB 1917-1929; DLB
11, 25, 86, 171; DLBD 16; RGAL 4;
RGSF 2

Lardner, Ring W., Jr.
See Lardner, Ring(gold) W(ilmer)

Lardner, Ring(gold) W(ilmer)
1885-1933 .... **SSC 32; TCLC 2, 14**
See Lardner, Ring
See also AMW; CA 104; 131; MTCW 1, 2;
TUS

Laredo, Betty
See Codrescu, Andrei

Larkin, Maia
See Wojciechowska, Maia (Teresa)

Larkin, Philip (Arthur) 1922-1985 ... **CLC 3,**
5, 8, 9, 13, 18, 33, 39, 64; PC 21
See also BRWS 1; CA 5-8R; 117; CANR
24, 62; CDBLB 1960 to Present; DA3;
DAB; DAM MST, POET; DLB 27; EWL
3; MTCW 1, 2; PFS 3, 4, 12; RGEL 2

La Roche, Sophie von
1730-1807 .... **NCLC 121**
See also DLB 94

La Rochefoucauld, Francois
1613-1680 .... **LC 108**

Larra (y Sanchez de Castro), Mariano Jose
de 1809-1837 .... **NCLC 17, 130**

Larsen, Eric 1941- .... **CLC 55**
See also CA 132

Larsen, Nella 1893(?)-1963 .... **BLC 2; CLC**
37; HR 3
See also AFAW 1, 2; BW 1; CA 125; CANR
83; DAM MULT; DLB 51; FW; LATS
1:1; LMFS 2

Larson, Charles R(aymond) 1938- ... **CLC 31**
See also CA 53-56; CANR 4, 121

Larson, Jonathan 1961-1996 .... **CLC 99**
See also AAYA 28; CA 156

La Sale, Antoine de c. 1386-1460(?) . **LC 104**
See also DLB 208

Las Casas, Bartolome de
1474-1566 .... **HLCS; LC 31**
See Casas, Bartolome de las
See also LAW

Lasch, Christopher 1932-1994 .... **CLC 102**
See also CA 73-76; 144; CANR 25, 118;
DLB 246; MTCW 1, 2

Lasker-Schueler, Else 1869-1945 ... **TCLC 57**
See Lasker-Schuler, Else
See also CA 183; DLB 66, 124

Lasker-Schuler, Else
See Lasker-Schueler, Else
See also EWL 3

Laski, Harold J(oseph) 1893-1950 . **TCLC 79**
See also CA 188

Latham, Jean Lee 1902-1995 .... **CLC 12**
See also AITN 1; BYA 1; CA 5-8R; CANR
7, 84; CLR 50; MAICYA 1, 2; SATA 2,
68; YAW

Latham, Mavis
See Clark, Mavis Thorpe

Lathen, Emma .... **CLC 2**
See Hennissart, Martha; Latsis, Mary J(ane)
See also BPFB 2; CMW 4; DLB 306

Lathrop, Francis
See Leiber, Fritz (Reuter, Jr.)

Latsis, Mary J(ane) 1927-1997
See Lathen, Emma
See also CA 85-88; 162; CMW 4

Lattany, Kristin
See Lattany, Kristin (Elaine Eggleston)
Hunter

Lattany, Kristin (Elaine Eggleston) Hunter
1931- .... **CLC 35**
See also AITN 1; BW 1; BYA 3; CA 13-
16R; CANR 13, 108; CLR 3; CN 7; DLB
33; INT CANR-13; MAICYA 1, 2; SAAS
10; SATA 12, 132; YAW

Lattimore, Richmond (Alexander)
1906-1984 .... **CLC 3**
See also CA 1-4R; 112; CANR 1

Laughlin, James 1914-1997 .... **CLC 49**
See also CA 21-24R; 162; CAAS 22; CANR
9, 47; CP 7; DLB 48; DLBY 1996, 1997

Laurence, (Jean) Margaret (Wemyss)
1926-1987 . **CLC 3, 6, 13, 50, 62; SSC 7**
See also BYA 13; CA 5-8R; 121; CANR
33; DAC; DAM MST; DLB 53; EWL 3;
FW; MTCW 1, 2; NFS 11; RGEL 2;
RGSF 2; SATA-Obit 50; TCWW 2

Laurent, Antoine 1952- .... **CLC 50**

Lauscher, Hermann
See Hesse, Hermann

Lautreamont 1846-1870 .. **NCLC 12; SSC 14**
See Lautreamont, Isidore Lucien Ducasse
See also GFL 1789 to the Present; RGWL
2, 3

Lautreamont, Isidore Lucien Ducasse
See Lautreamont
See also DLB 217

Lavater, Johann Kaspar
1741-1801 .... **NCLC 142**
See also DLB 97

Laverty, Donald
See Blish, James (Benjamin)

Lavin, Mary 1912-1996 . **CLC 4, 18, 99; SSC**
4, 67
See also CA 9-12R; 151; CANR 33; CN 7;
DLB 15; FW; MTCW 1; RGEL 2; RGSF
2

Lavond, Paul Dennis
See Kornbluth, C(yril) M.; Pohl, Frederik

Lawes Henry 1596-1662 .... **LC 113**
See also DLB 126

Lawler, Ray
See Lawler, Raymond Evenor
See also DLB 289

Lawler, Raymond Evenor 1922- .... **CLC 58**
See Lawler, Ray
See also CA 103; CD 5; RGEL 2

Lawrence, D(avid) H(erbert Richards)
1885-1930 .... **PC 54; SSC 4, 19, 73;**
TCLC 2, 9, 16, 33, 48, 61, 93; WLC
See Chambers, Jessie
See also BPFB 2; BRW 7; BRWR 2; CA
104; 121; CANR 131; CDBLB 1914-
1945; DA; DA3; DAB; DAC; DAM MST,
NOV, POET; DLB 10, 19, 36, 98, 162,

MacCarthy, Sir (Charles Otto) Desmond
1877-1952 .... TCLC 36
See also CA 167

MacDiarmid, Hugh .... CLC 2, 4, 11, 19, 63;
PC 9
See Grieve, C(hristopher) M(urray)
See also CDBLB 1945-1960; DLB 20;
EWL 3; RGEL 2

MacDonald, Anson
See Heinlein, Robert A(nson)

Macdonald, Cynthia 1928- .... CLC 13, 19
See also CA 49-52; CANR 4, 44; DLB 105

MacDonald, George 1824-1905 .... TCLC 9,
113
See also AAYA 57; BYA 5; CA 106; 137;
CANR 80; CLR 67; DLB 18, 163, 178;
FANT; MAICYA 1, 2; RGEL 2; SATA 33,
100; SFW 4; SUFW; WCH

Macdonald, John
See Millar, Kenneth

MacDonald, John D(ann)
1916-1986 .... CLC 3, 27, 44
See also BPFB 2; CA 1-4R; 121; CANR 1,
19, 60; CMW 4; CPW; DAM NOV, POP;
DLB 8, 306; DLBY 1986; MSW; MTCW
1, 2; SFW 4

Macdonald, John Ross
See Millar, Kenneth

Macdonald, Ross ..... CLC 1, 2, 3, 14, 34, 41
See Millar, Kenneth
See also AMWS 4; BPFB 2; DLBD 6;
MSW; RGAL 4

MacDougal, John
See Blish, James (Benjamin)

MacDougal, John
See Blish, James (Benjamin)

MacDowell, John
See Parks, Tim(othy Harold)

MacEwen, Gwendolyn (Margaret)
1941-1987 .... CLC 13, 55
See also CA 9-12R; 124; CANR 7, 22; DLB
53, 251; SATA 50; SATA-Obit 55

Macha, Karel Hynek 1810-1846 .... NCLC 46

Machado (y Ruiz), Antonio
1875-1939 .... TCLC 3
See also CA 104; 174; DLB 108; EW 9;
EWL 3; HW 2; RGWL 2, 3

Machado de Assis, Joaquim Maria
1839-1908 .... BLC 2; HLCS 2; SSC 24;
TCLC 10
See also CA 107; 153; CANR 91; DLB 307;
LAW; RGSF 2; RGWL 2, 3; TWA; WLIT
1

Machaut, Guillaume de c.
1300-1377 .... CMLC 64
See also DLB 208

Machen, Arthur .... SSC 20; TCLC 4
See Jones, Arthur Llewellyn
See also CA 179; DLB 156, 178; RGEL 2;
SUFW 1

Machiavelli, Niccolo 1469-1527 ... DC 16; LC
8, 36; WLCS
See also AAYA 58; DA; DAB; DAC; DAM
MST; EW 2; LAIT 1; LMFS 1; NFS 9;
RGWL 2, 3; TWA

MacInnes, Colin 1914-1976 .... CLC 4, 23
See also CA 69-72; 65-68; CANR 21; DLB
14; MTCW 1, 2; RGEL 2; RHW

MacInnes, Helen (Clark)
1907-1985 .... CLC 27, 39
See also BPFB 2; CA 1-4R; 117; CANR 1,
28, 58; CMW 4; CPW; DAM POP; DLB
87; MSW; MTCW 1, 2; SATA 22; SATA-
Obit 44

Mackay, Mary 1855-1924
See Corelli, Marie
See also CA 118; 177; FANT; RHW

Mackay, Shena 1944- .... CLC 195
See also CA 104; CANR 88; DLB 231

Mackenzie, Compton (Edward Montague)
1883-1972 .... CLC 18; TCLC 116
See also CA 21-22; 37-40R; CAP 2; DLB
34, 100; RGEL 2

Mackenzie, Henry 1745-1831 .... NCLC 41
See also DLB 39; RGEL 2

Mackey, Nathaniel (Ernest) 1947- .... PC 49
See also CA 153; CANR 114; CP 7; DLB
169

MacKinnon, Catharine A. 1946- .... CLC 181
See also CA 128; 132; CANR 73; FW;
MTCW 2

Mackintosh, Elizabeth 1896(?)-1952
See Tey, Josephine
See also CA 110; CMW 4

MacLaren, James
See Grieve, C(hristopher) M(urray)

Mac Laverty, Bernard 1942- .... CLC 31
See also CA 116; 118; CANR 43, 88; CN
7; DLB 267; INT CA-118; RGSF 2

MacLean, Alistair (Stuart)
1922(?)-1987 .... CLC 3, 13, 50, 63
See also CA 57-60; 121; CANR 28, 61;
CMW 4; CPW; DAM POP; DLB 276;
MTCW 1; SATA 23; SATA-Obit 50;
TCWW 4

Maclean, Norman (Fitzroy)
1902-1990 .... CLC 78; SSC 13
See also AMWS 14; CA 102; 132; CANR
49; CPW; DAM POP; DLB 206; TCWW
2

MacLeish, Archibald 1892-1982 ... CLC 3, 8,
14, 68; PC 47
See also AMW; CA 9-12R; 106; CAD;
CANR 33, 63; CDALBS; DAM POET;
DFS 15; DLB 4, 7, 45; DLBY 1982; EWL
3; EXPP; MTCW 1, 2; PAB; PFS 5;
RGAL 4; TUS

MacLennan, (John) Hugh
1907-1990 .... CLC 2, 14, 92
See also CA 5-8R; 142; CANR 33; DAC;
DAM MST; DLB 68; EWL 3; MTCW 1,
2; RGEL 2; TWA

MacLeod, Alistair 1936- .... CLC 56, 165
See also CA 123; CCA 1; DAC; DAM
MST; DLB 60; MTCW 2; RGSF 2

Macleod, Fiona
See Sharp, William
See also RGEL 2; SUFW

MacNeice, (Frederick) Louis
1907-1963 .... CLC 1, 4, 10, 53; PC 61
See also BRW 7; CA 85-88; CANR 61;
DAB; DAM POET; DLB 10, 20; EWL 3;
MTCW 1, 2; RGEL 2

MacNeill, Dand
See Fraser, George MacDonald

Macpherson, James 1736-1796 .... LC 29
See Ossian
See also BRWS 8; DLB 109; RGEL 2

Macpherson, (Jean) Jay 1931- .... CLC 14
See also CA 5-8R; CANR 90; CP 7; CWP;
DLB 53

Macrobius fl. 430- .... CMLC 48

MacShane, Frank 1927-1999 .... CLC 39
See also CA 9-12R; 186; CANR 3, 33; DLB
111

Macumber, Mari
See Sandoz, Mari(e Susette)

Madach, Imre 1823-1864 .... NCLC 19

Madden, (Jerry) David 1933- .... CLC 5, 15
See also CA 1-4R; CAAS 3; CANR 4, 45;
CN 7; CSW; DLB 6; MTCW 1

Maddern, Al(an)
See Ellison, Harlan (Jay)

Madhubuti, Haki R. 1942- ... BLC 2; CLC 6,
73; PC 5
See Lee, Don L.
See also BW 2, 3; CA 73-76; CANR 24,
51, 73; CP 7; CSW; DAM MULT, POET;
DLB 5, 41; DLBD 8; EWL 3; MTCW 2;
RGAL 4

Madison, James 1751-1836 .... NCLC 126
See also DLB 37

Maepenn, Hugh
See Kuttner, Henry

Maepenn, K. H.
See Kuttner, Henry

Maeterlinck, Maurice 1862-1949 ..... TCLC 3
See also CA 104; 136; CANR 80; DAM
DRAM; DLB 192; EW 8; GFL 1789 to
the Present; LMFS 2; RGWL 2,
3; SATA 66; TWA

Maginn, William 1794-1842 .... NCLC 8
See also DLB 110, 159

Mahapatra, Jayanta 1928- .... CLC 33
See also CA 73-76; CAAS 9; CANR 15,
33, 66, 87; CP 7; DAM MULT

Mahfouz, Naguib (Abdel Aziz al-Sabilgi)
1911(?)- .... CLC 153; SSC 66
See Mahfuz, Najib (Abdel Aziz al-Sabilgi)
See also AAYA 49; BEST 89:2; CA 128;
CANR 55, 101; DA3; DAM NOV;
MTCW 1, 2; RGWL 2, 3; SSFS 9

Mahfuz, Najib (Abdel Aziz al-Sabilgi)
.... CLC 52, 55
See Mahfouz, Naguib (Abdel Aziz Al-
Sabilgi)
See also AFW; CWW 2; DLBY 1988; EWL
3; RGSF 2; WLIT 2

Mahon, Derek 1941- .... CLC 27; PC 60
See also BRWS 6; CA 113; 128; CANR 88;
CP 7; DLB 40; EWL 3

Maiakovskii, Vladimir
See Mayakovski, Vladimir (Vladimirovich)
See also IDTP; RGWL 2, 3

Mailer, Norman (Kingsley) 1923- . CLC 1, 2,
3, 4, 5, 8, 11, 14, 28, 39, 74, 111
See also AAYA 31; AITN 2; AMW; AMWC
2; AMWR 2; BPFB 2; CA 9-12R; CABS
1; CANR 28, 74, 77, 130; CDALB 1968-
1988; CN 7; CPW; DA; DA3; DAB;
DAC; DAM MST, NOV, POP; DLB 2,
16, 28, 185, 278; DLBD 3; DLBY 1980,
1983; EWL 3; MTCW 1, 2; NFS 10;
RGAL 4; TUS

Maillet, Antonine 1929- .... CLC 54, 118
See also CA 115; 120; CANR 46, 74, 77,
134; CCA 1; CWW 2; DAC; DLB 60;
INT CA-120; MTCW 2

Maimonides 1135-1204 .... CMLC 76
See also DLB 115

Mais, Roger 1905-1955 .... TCLC 8
See also BW 1, 3; CA 105; 124; CANR 82;
CDWLB 3; DLB 125; EWL 3; MTCW 1;
RGEL 2

Maistre, Joseph 1753-1821 .... NCLC 37
See also GFL 1789 to the Present

Maitland, Frederic William
1850-1906 .... TCLC 65

Maitland, Sara (Louise) 1950- .... CLC 49
See also CA 69-72; CANR 13, 59; DLB
271; FW

Major, Clarence 1936- ... BLC 2; CLC 3, 19,
48
See also AFAW 2; BW 2, 3; CA 21-24R;
CAAS 6; CANR 13, 25, 53, 82; CN 7;
CP 7; CSW; DAM MULT; DLB 33; EWL
3; MSW

Major, Kevin (Gerald) 1949- .... CLC 26
See also AAYA 16; CA 97-100; CANR 21,
38, 112; CLR 11; DAC; DLB 60; INT
CANR-21; JRDA; MAICYA 1, 2; MAIC-
YAS 1; SATA 32, 82, 134; WYA; YAW

Maki, James
See Ozu, Yasujiro

Makine, Andrei 1957- .... CLC 198
See also CA 176; CANR 103

Malabaila, Damiano
See Levi, Primo

Malamud, Bernard 1914-1986 .. **CLC 1, 2, 3, 5, 8, 9, 11, 18, 27, 44, 78, 85; SSC 15; TCLC 129; WLC**
See also AAYA 16; AMWS 1; BPFB 2; BYA 15; CA 5-8R; 118; CABS 1; CANR 28, 62, 114; CDALB 1941-1968; CPW; DA; DA3; DAB; DAC; DAM MST, NOV, POP; DLB 2, 28, 152; DLBY 1980, 1986; EWL 3; EXPS; LAIT 4; LATS 1:1; MTCW 1, 2; NFS 4, 9; RGAL 4; RGSF 2; SSFS 8, 13, 16; TUS

Malan, Herman
See Bosman, Herman Charles; Bosman, Herman Charles

Malaparte, Curzio 1898-1957 .... **TCLC 52**
See also DLB 264

Malcolm, Dan
See Silverberg, Robert

Malcolm, Janet 1934- .... **CLC 201**
See also CA 123; CANR 89; NCFS 1

Malcolm X .... **BLC 2; CLC 82, 117; WLCS**
See Little, Malcolm
See also LAIT 5; NCFS 3

Malherbe, Francois de 1555-1628 .... **LC 5**
See also GFL Beginnings to 1789

Mallarme, Stephane 1842-1898 ...... **NCLC 4, 41; PC 4**
See also DAM POET; DLB 217; EW 7; GFL 1789 to the Present; LMFS 2; RGWL 2, 3; TWA

Mallet-Joris, Francoise 1930- .... **CLC 11**
See also CA 65-68; CANR 17; CWW 2; DLB 83; EWL 3; GFL 1789 to the Present

Malley, Ern
See McAuley, James Phillip

Mallon, Thomas 1951- .... **CLC 172**
See also CA 110; CANR 29, 57, 92

Mallowan, Agatha Christie
See Christie, Agatha (Mary Clarissa)

Maloff, Saul 1922- .... **CLC 5**
See also CA 33-36R

Malone, Louis
See MacNeice, (Frederick) Louis

Malone, Michael (Christopher)
1942- .... **CLC 43**
See also CA 77-80; CANR 14, 32, 57, 114

Malory, Sir Thomas 1410(?)-1471(?) . **LC 11, 88; WLCS**
See also BRW 1; BRWR 2; CDBLB Before 1660; DA; DAB; DAC; DAM MST; DLB 146; EFS 2; RGEL 2; SATA 59; SATA-Brief 33; TEA; WLIT 3

Malouf, (George Joseph) David
1934- .... **CLC 28, 86**
See also CA 124; CANR 50, 76; CN 7; CP 7; DLB 289; EWL 3; MTCW 2

Malraux, (Georges-)Andre
1901-1976 .... **CLC 1, 4, 9, 13, 15, 57**
See also BPFB 2; CA 21-22; 69-72; CANR 34, 58; CAP 2; DA3; DAM NOV; DLB 72; EW 12; EWL 3; GFL 1789 to the Present; MTCW 1, 2; RGWL 2, 3; TWA

Malthus, Thomas Robert
1766-1834 .... **NCLC 145**
See also DLB 107, 158; RGEL 2

Malzberg, Barry N(athaniel) 1939- ... **CLC 7**
See also CA 61-64; CAAS 4; CANR 16; CMW 4; DLB 8; SFW 4

Mamet, David (Alan) 1947- .. **CLC 9, 15, 34, 46, 91, 166; DC 4, 24**
See also AAYA 3, 60; AMWS 14; CA 81-84; CABS 3; CANR 15, 41, 67, 72, 129; CD 5; DA3; DAM DRAM; DFS 2, 3, 6, 12, 15; DLB 7; EWL 3; IDFW 4; MTCW 1, 2; RGAL 4

Mamoulian, Rouben (Zachary)
1897-1987 .... **CLC 16**
See also CA 25-28R; 124; CANR 85

Mandelshtam, Osip
See Mandelstam, Osip (Emilievich)
See also EW 10; EWL 3; RGWL 2, 3

Mandelstam, Osip (Emilievich)
1891(?)-1943(?) .... **PC 14; TCLC 2, 6**
See Mandelshtam, Osip
See also CA 104; 150; MTCW 2; TWA

Mander, (Mary) Jane 1877-1949 ... **TCLC 31**
See also CA 162; RGEL 2

Mandeville, Bernard 1670-1733 .... **LC 82**
See also DLB 101

Mandeville, Sir John fl. 1350- ...... **CMLC 19**
See also DLB 146

Mandiargues, Andre Pieyre de .... **CLC 41**
See Pieyre de Mandiargues, Andre
See also DLB 83

Mandrake, Ethel Belle
See Thurman, Wallace (Henry)

Mangan, James Clarence
1803-1849 .... **NCLC 27**
See also RGEL 2

Maniere, J.-E.
See Giraudoux, Jean(-Hippolyte)

Mankiewicz, Herman (Jacob)
1897-1953 .... **TCLC 85**
See also CA 120; 169; DLB 26; IDFW 3, 4

Manley, (Mary) Delariviere
1672(?)-1724 .... **LC 1, 42**
See also DLB 39, 80; RGEL 2

Mann, Abel
See Creasey, John

Mann, Emily 1952- .... **DC 7**
See also CA 130; CAD; CANR 55; CD 5; CWD; DLB 266

Mann, (Luiz) Heinrich 1871-1950 ... **TCLC 9**
See also CA 106; 164, 181; DLB 66, 118; EW 8; EWL 3; RGWL 2, 3

Mann, (Paul) Thomas 1875-1955 . **SSC 5, 80, 82; TCLC 2, 8, 14, 21, 35, 44, 60; WLC**
See also BPFB 2; CA 104; 128; CANR 133; CDWLB 2; DA; DA3; DAB; DAC; DAM MST, NOV; DLB 66; EW 9; EWL 3; GLL 1; LATS 1:1; LMFS 1; MTCW 1, 2; NFS 17; RGSF 2; RGWL 2, 3; SSFS 4, 9; TWA

Mannheim, Karl 1893-1947 .... **TCLC 65**
See also CA 204

Manning, David
See Faust, Frederick (Schiller)
See also TCWW 2

Manning, Frederic 1882-1935 .... **TCLC 25**
See also CA 124; 216; DLB 260

Manning, Olivia 1915-1980 .... **CLC 5, 19**
See also CA 5-8R; 101; CANR 29; EWL 3; FW; MTCW 1; RGEL 2

Mano, D. Keith 1942- .... **CLC 2, 10**
See also CA 25-28R; CAAS 6; CANR 26, 57; DLB 6

Mansfield, Katherine .... **SSC 9, 23, 38, 81; TCLC 2, 8, 39, 164; WLC**
See Beauchamp, Kathleen Mansfield
See also BPFB 2; BRW 7; DAB; DLB 162; EWL 3; EXPS; FW; GLL 1; RGEL 2; RGSF 2; SSFS 2, 8, 10, 11; WWE 1

Manso, Peter 1940- .... **CLC 39**
See also CA 29-32R; CANR 44

Mantecon, Juan Jimenez
See Jimenez (Mantecon), Juan Ramon

Mantel, Hilary (Mary) 1952- .... **CLC 144**
See also CA 125; CANR 54, 101; CN 7; DLB 271; RHW

Manton, Peter
See Creasey, John

Man Without a Spleen, A
See Chekhov, Anton (Pavlovich)

Manzano, Juan Francisco
1797(?)-1854 .... **NCLC 155**

Manzoni, Alessandro 1785-1873 ... **NCLC 29, 98**
See also EW 5; RGWL 2, 3; TWA

Map, Walter 1140-1209 .... **CMLC 32**

Mapu, Abraham (ben Jekutiel)
1808-1867 .... **NCLC 18**

Mara, Sally
See Queneau, Raymond

Maracle, Lee 1950- .... **NNAL**
See also CA 149

Marat, Jean Paul 1743-1793 .... **LC 10**

Marcel, Gabriel Honore 1889-1973 . **CLC 15**
See also CA 102; 45-48; EWL 3; MTCW 1, 2

March, William 1893-1954 .... **TCLC 96**
See also CA 216

Marchbanks, Samuel
See Davies, (William) Robertson
See also CCA 1

Marchi, Giacomo
See Bassani, Giorgio

Marcus Aurelius
See Aurelius, Marcus
See also AW 2

Marguerite
See de Navarre, Marguerite

Marguerite d'Angouleme
See de Navarre, Marguerite
See also GFL Beginnings to 1789

Marguerite de Navarre
See de Navarre, Marguerite
See also RGWL 2, 3

Margulies, Donald 1954- .... **CLC 76**
See also AAYA 57; CA 200; DFS 13; DLB 228

Marie de France c. 12th cent. - ..... **CMLC 8; PC 22**
See also DLB 208; FW; RGWL 2, 3

Marie de l'Incarnation 1599-1672 ...... **LC 10**

Marier, Captain Victor
See Griffith, D(avid Lewelyn) W(ark)

Mariner, Scott
See Pohl, Frederik

Marinetti, Filippo Tommaso
1876-1944 .... **TCLC 10**
See also CA 107; DLB 114, 264; EW 9; EWL 3

Marivaux, Pierre Carlet de Chamblain de
1688-1763 .... **DC 7; LC 4**
See also GFL Beginnings to 1789; RGWL 2, 3; TWA

Markandaya, Kamala .... **CLC 8, 38**
See Taylor, Kamala (Purnaiya)
See also BYA 13; CN 7; EWL 3

Markfield, Wallace 1926-2002 .... **CLC 8**
See also CA 69-72; 208; CAAS 3; CN 7; DLB 2, 28; DLBY 2002

Markham, Edwin 1852-1940 .... **TCLC 47**
See also CA 160; DLB 54, 186; RGAL 4

Markham, Robert
See Amis, Kingsley (William)

Markoosie .... **NNAL**
See Patsauq, Markoosie
See also CLR 23; DAM MULT

Marks, J.
See Highwater, Jamake (Mamake)

Marks, J
See Highwater, Jamake (Mamake)

Marks-Highwater, J
See Highwater, Jamake (Mamake)

Marks-Highwater, J.
See Highwater, Jamake (Mamake)

Markson, David M(errill) 1927- .... **CLC 67**
See also CA 49-52; CANR 1, 91; CN 7

Marlatt, Daphne (Buckle) 1942- .... **CLC 168**
See also CA 25-28R; CANR 17, 39; CN 7; CP 7; CWP; DLB 60; FW

Marley, Bob .... **CLC 17**
See Marley, Robert Nesta
Marley, Robert Nesta 1945-1981
See Marley, Bob
See also CA 107; 103
Marlowe, Christopher 1564-1593 . **DC 1; LC 22, 47; PC 57; WLC**
See also BRW 1; BRWR 1; CDBLB Before 1660; DA; DA3; DAB; DAC; DAM DRAM, MST; DFS 1, 5, 13; DLB 62; EXPP; LMFS 1; RGEL 2; TEA; WLIT 3
Marlowe, Stephen 1928- .... **CLC 70**
See Queen, Ellery
See also CA 13-16R; CANR 6, 55; CMW 4; SFW 4
Marmion, Shakerley 1603-1639 .... **LC 89**
See also DLB 58; RGEL 2
Marmontel, Jean-Francois 1723-1799 .. **LC 2**
Maron, Monika 1941- .... **CLC 165**
See also CA 201
Marquand, John P(hillips) 1893-1960 .... **CLC 2, 10**
See also AMW; BPFB 2; CA 85-88; CANR 73; CMW 4; DLB 9, 102; EWL 3; MTCW 2; RGAL 4
Marques, Rene 1919-1979 .. **CLC 96; HLC 2**
See also CA 97-100; 85-88; CANR 78; DAM MULT; DLB 305; EWL 3; HW 1, 2; LAW; RGSF 2
Marquez, Gabriel (Jose) Garcia
See Garcia Marquez, Gabriel (Jose)
Marquis, Don(ald Robert Perry) 1878-1937 .... **TCLC 7**
See also CA 104; 166; DLB 11, 25; RGAL 4
Marquis de Sade
See Sade, Donatien Alphonse Francois
Marric, J. J.
See Creasey, John
See also MSW
Marryat, Frederick 1792-1848 .... **NCLC 3**
See also DLB 21, 163; RGEL 2; WCH
Marsden, James
See Creasey, John
Marsh, Edward 1872-1953 .... **TCLC 99**
Marsh, (Edith) Ngaio 1895-1982 .. **CLC 7, 53**
See also CA 9-12R; CANR 6, 58; CMW 4; CPW; DAM POP; DLB 77; MSW; MTCW 1, 2; RGEL 2; TEA
Marshall, Garry 1934- .... **CLC 17**
See also AAYA 3; CA 111; SATA 60
Marshall, Paule 1929- .. **BLC 3; CLC 27, 72; SSC 3**
See also AFAW 1, 2; AMWS 11; BPFB 2; BW 2, 3; CA 77-80; CANR 25, 73, 129; CN 7; DA3; DAM MULT; DLB 33, 157, 227; EWL 3; LATS 1:2; MTCW 1, 2; RGAL 4; SSFS 15
Marshallik
See Zangwill, Israel
Marsten, Richard
See Hunter, Evan
Marston, John 1576-1634 .... **LC 33**
See also BRW 2; DAM DRAM; DLB 58, 172; RGEL 2
Martel, Yann 1963- .... **CLC 192**
See also CA 146; CANR 114
Martha, Henry
See Harris, Mark
Marti, Jose
See Marti (y Perez), Jose (Julian)
See also DLB 290
Marti (y Perez), Jose (Julian) 1853-1895 .... **HLC 2; NCLC 63**
See Marti, Jose
See also DAM MULT; HW 2; LAW; RGWL 2, 3; WLIT 1

Martial c. 40-c. 104 .... **CMLC 35; PC 10**
See also AW 2; CDWLB 1; DLB 211; RGWL 2, 3
Martin, Ken
See Hubbard, L(afayette) Ron(ald)
Martin, Richard
See Creasey, John
Martin, Steve 1945- .... **CLC 30**
See also AAYA 53; CA 97-100; CANR 30, 100; DFS 19; MTCW 1
Martin, Valerie 1948- .... **CLC 89**
See also BEST 90:2; CA 85-88; CANR 49, 89
Martin, Violet Florence 1862-1915 .. **SSC 56; TCLC 51**
Martin, Webber
See Silverberg, Robert
Martindale, Patrick Victor
See White, Patrick (Victor Martindale)
Martin du Gard, Roger 1881-1958 .... **TCLC 24**
See also CA 118; CANR 94; DLB 65; EWL 3; GFL 1789 to the Present; RGWL 2, 3
Martineau, Harriet 1802-1876 ...... **NCLC 26, 137**
See also DLB 21, 55, 159, 163, 166, 190; FW; RGEL 2; YABC 2
Martines, Julia
See O'Faolain, Julia
Martinez, Enrique Gonzalez
See Gonzalez Martinez, Enrique
Martinez, Jacinto Benavente y
See Benavente (y Martinez), Jacinto
Martinez de la Rosa, Francisco de Paula 1787-1862 .... **NCLC 102**
See also TWA
Martinez Ruiz, Jose 1873-1967
See Azorin; Ruiz, Jose Martinez
See also CA 93-96; HW 1
Martinez Sierra, Gregorio 1881-1947 .... **TCLC 6**
See also CA 115; EWL 3
Martinez Sierra, Maria (de la O'LeJarraga) 1874-1974 .... **TCLC 6**
See also CA 115; EWL 3
Martinsen, Martin
See Follett, Ken(neth Martin)
Martinson, Harry (Edmund) 1904-1978 .... **CLC 14**
See also CA 77-80; CANR 34, 130; DLB 259; EWL 3
Martyn, Edward 1859-1923 .... **TCLC 131**
See also CA 179; DLB 10; RGEL 2
Marut, Ret
See Traven, B.
Marut, Robert
See Traven, B.
Marvell, Andrew 1621-1678 .... **LC 4, 43; PC 10; WLC**
See also BRW 2; BRWR 2; CDBLB 1660-1789; DA; DAB; DAC; DAM MST, POET; DLB 131; EXPP; PFS 5; RGEL 2; TEA; WP
Marx, Karl (Heinrich) 1818-1883 .... **NCLC 17, 114**
See also DLB 129; LATS 1:1; TWA
Masaoka, Shiki -1902 .... **TCLC 18**
See Masaoka, Tsunenori
See also RGWL 3
Masaoka, Tsunenori 1867-1902
See Masaoka, Shiki
See also CA 117; 191; TWA
Masefield, John (Edward) 1878-1967 .... **CLC 11, 47**
See also CA 19-20; 25-28R; CANR 33; CAP 2; CDBLB 1890-1914; DAM POET; DLB 10, 19, 153, 160; EWL 3; EXPP; FANT; MTCW 1, 2; PFS 5; RGEL 2; SATA 19

Maso, Carole 19(?)- .... **CLC 44**
See also CA 170; GLL 2; RGAL 4
Mason, Bobbie Ann 1940- ... **CLC 28, 43, 82, 154; SSC 4**
See also AAYA 5, 42; AMWS 8; BPFB 2; CA 53-56; CANR 11, 31, 58, 83, 125; CDALBS; CN 7; CSW; DA3; DLB 173; DLBY 1987; EWL 3; INT CANR-31; MTCW 1, 2; NFS 4; RGAL 4; RGSF 2; SSFS 3, 8, 20; YAW
Mason, Ernst
See Pohl, Frederik
Mason, Hunni B.
See Sternheim, (William Adolf) Carl
Mason, Lee W.
See Malzberg, Barry N(athaniel)
Mason, Nick 1945- .... **CLC 35**
Mason, Tally
See Derleth, August (William)
Mass, Anna .... **CLC 59**
Mass, William
See Gibson, William
Massinger, Philip 1583-1640 .... **LC 70**
See also DLB 58; RGEL 2
Master Lao
See Lao Tzu
Masters, Edgar Lee 1868-1950 ...... **PC 1, 36; TCLC 2, 25; WLCS**
See also AMWS 1; CA 104; 133; CDALB 1865-1917; DA; DAC; DAM MST, POET; DLB 54; EXPP; MTCW 1, 2; RGAL 4; TUS; WP
Masters, Hilary 1928- .... **CLC 48**
See also CA 25-28R, 217; CAAE 217; CANR 13, 47, 97; CN 7; DLB 244
Mastrosimone, William 19(?)- .... **CLC 36**
See also CA 186; CAD; CD 5
Mathe, Albert
See Camus, Albert
Mather, Cotton 1663-1728 .... **LC 38**
See also AMWS 2; CDALB 1640-1865; DLB 24, 30, 140; RGAL 4; TUS
Mather, Increase 1639-1723 .... **LC 38**
See also DLB 24
Matheson, Richard (Burton) 1926- .. **CLC 37**
See also AAYA 31; CA 97-100; CANR 88, 99; DLB 8, 44; HGG; INT CA-97-100; SCFW 2; SFW 4; SUFW 2
Mathews, Harry 1930- .... **CLC 6, 52**
See also CA 21-24R; CAAS 6; CANR 18, 40, 98; CN 7
Mathews, John Joseph 1894-1979 .. **CLC 84; NNAL**
See also CA 19-20; 142; CANR 45; CAP 2; DAM MULT; DLB 175
Mathias, Roland (Glyn) 1915- .... **CLC 45**
See also CA 97-100; CANR 19, 41; CP 7; DLB 27
Matsuo Basho 1644-1694 .... **LC 62; PC 3**
See Basho, Matsuo
See also DAM POET; PFS 2, 7
Mattheson, Rodney
See Creasey, John
Matthews, (James) Brander 1852-1929 .... **TCLC 95**
See also DLB 71, 78; DLBD 13
Matthews, (James) Brander 1852-1929 .... **TCLC 95**
See also CA 181; DLB 71, 78; DLBD 13
Matthews, Greg 1949- .... **CLC 45**
See also CA 135
Matthews, William (Procter III) 1942-1997 .... **CLC 40**
See also AMWS 9; CA 29-32R; 162; CAAS 18; CANR 12, 57; CP 7; DLB 5
Matthias, John (Edward) 1941- .... **CLC 9**
See also CA 33-36R; CANR 56; CP 7

Matthiessen, F(rancis) O(tto)
1902-1950 .... **TCLC 100**
See also CA 185; DLB 63

Matthiessen, Peter 1927- ... **CLC 5, 7, 11, 32, 64**
See also AAYA 6, 40; AMWS 5; ANW;
BEST 90:4; BPFB 2; CA 9-12R; CANR
21, 50, 73, 100; CN 7; DA3; DAM NOV;
DLB 6, 173, 275; MTCW 1, 2; SATA 27

Maturin, Charles Robert
1780(?)-1824 .... **NCLC 6**
See also BRWS 8; DLB 178; HGG; LMFS
1; RGEL 2; SUFW

Matute (Ausejo), Ana Maria 1925- .. **CLC 11**
See also CA 89-92; CANR 129; CWW 2;
EWL 3; MTCW 1; RGSF 2

Maugham, W. S.
See Maugham, W(illiam) Somerset

Maugham, W(illiam) Somerset
1874-1965 .. **CLC 1, 11, 15, 67, 93; SSC 8; WLC**
See also AAYA 55; BPFB 2; BRW 6; CA
5-8R; 25-28R; CANR 40, 127; CDBLB
1914-1945; CMW 4; DA; DA3; DAB;
DAC; DAM DRAM, MST, NOV; DLB
10, 36, 77, 100, 162, 195; EWL 3; LAIT
3; MTCW 1, 2; RGEL 2; RGSF 2; SATA
54; SSFS 17

Maugham, William Somerset
See Maugham, W(illiam) Somerset

Maupassant, (Henri Rene Albert) Guy de
1850-1893 . **NCLC 1, 42, 83; SSC 1, 64; WLC**
See also BYA 14; DA; DA3; DAB; DAC;
DAM MST; DLB 123; EW 7; EXPS; GFL
1789 to the Present; LAIT 2; LMFS 1;
RGSF 2; RGWL 2, 3; SSFS 4; SUFW;
TWA

Maupin, Armistead (Jones, Jr.)
1944- .... **CLC 95**
See also CA 125; 130; CANR 58, 101;
CPW; DA3; DAM POP; DLB 278; GLL
1; INT CA-130; MTCW 2

Maurhut, Richard
See Traven, B.

Mauriac, Claude 1914-1996 .... **CLC 9**
See also CA 89-92; 152; CWW 2; DLB 83;
EWL 3; GFL 1789 to the Present

Mauriac, Francois (Charles)
1885-1970 .... **CLC 4, 9, 56; SSC 24**
See also CA 25-28; CAP 2; DLB 65; EW
10; EWL 3; GFL 1789 to the Present;
MTCW 1, 2; RGWL 2, 3; TWA

Mavor, Osborne Henry 1888-1951
See Bridie, James
See also CA 104

Maxwell, William (Keepers, Jr.)
1908-2000 .... **CLC 19**
See also AMWS 8; CA 93-96; 189; CANR
54, 95; CN 7; DLB 218, 278; DLBY
1980; INT CA-93-96; SATA-Obit 128

May, Elaine 1932- .... **CLC 16**
See also CA 124; 142; CAD; CWD; DLB
44

Mayakovski, Vladimir (Vladimirovich)
1893-1930 .... **TCLC 4, 18**
See Maiakovskii, Vladimir; Mayakovsky,
Vladimir
See also CA 104; 158; EWL 3; MTCW 2;
SFW 4; TWA

Mayakovsky, Vladimir
See Mayakovski, Vladimir (Vladimirovich)
See also EW 11; WP

Mayhew, Henry 1812-1887 .... **NCLC 31**
See also DLB 18, 55, 190

Mayle, Peter 1939(?)- .... **CLC 89**
See also CA 139; CANR 64, 109

Maynard, Joyce 1953- .... **CLC 23**
See also CA 111; 129; CANR 64

Mayne, William (James Carter)
1928- .... **CLC 12**
See also AAYA 20; CA 9-12R; CANR 37,
80, 100; CLR 25; FANT; JRDA; MAI-
CYA 1, 2; MAICYAS 1; SAAS 11; SATA
6, 68, 122; SUFW 2; YAW

Mayo, Jim
See L'Amour, Louis (Dearborn)
See also TCWW 2

Maysles, Albert 1926- .... **CLC 16**
See also CA 29-32R

Maysles, David 1932-1987 .... **CLC 16**
See also CA 191

Mazer, Norma Fox 1931- .... **CLC 26**
See also AAYA 5, 36; BYA 1, 8; CA 69-72;
CANR 12, 32, 66, 129; CLR 23; JRDA;
MAICYA 1, 2; SAAS 1; SATA 24, 67,
105; WYA; YAW

Mazzini, Guiseppe 1805-1872 .... **NCLC 34**

McAlmon, Robert (Menzies)
1895-1956 .... **TCLC 97**
See also CA 107; 168; DLB 4, 45; DLBD
15; GLL 1

McAuley, James Phillip 1917-1976 .. **CLC 45**
See also CA 97-100; DLB 260; RGEL 2

McBain, Ed
See Hunter, Evan
See also MSW

McBrien, William (Augustine)
1930- .... **CLC 44**
See also CA 107; CANR 90

McCabe, Patrick 1955- .... **CLC 133**
See also BRWS 9; CA 130; CANR 50, 90;
CN 7; DLB 194

McCaffrey, Anne (Inez) 1926- .... **CLC 17**
See also AAYA 6, 34; AITN 2; BEST 89:2;
BPFB 2; BYA 5; CA 25-28R, 227; CAAE
227; CANR 15, 35, 55, 96; CLR 49;
CPW; DA3; DAM NOV, POP; DLB 8;
JRDA; MAICYA 1, 2; MTCW 1, 2; SAAS
11; SATA 8, 70, 116, 152; SATA-Essay
152; SFW 4; SUFW 2; WYA; YAW

McCall, Nathan 1955(?)- .... **CLC 86**
See also AAYA 59; BW 3; CA 146; CANR
88

McCann, Arthur
See Campbell, John W(ood, Jr.)

McCann, Edson
See Pohl, Frederik

McCarthy, Charles, Jr. 1933-
See McCarthy, Cormac
See also CANR 42, 69, 101; CN 7; CPW;
CSW; DA3; DAM POP; MTCW 2

McCarthy, Cormac ...... **CLC 4, 57, 101, 204**
See McCarthy, Charles, Jr.
See also AAYA 41; AMWS 8; BPFB 2; CA
13-16R; CANR 10; DLB 6, 143, 256;
EWL 3; LATS 1:2; TCWW 2

McCarthy, Mary (Therese)
1912-1989 .. **CLC 1, 3, 5, 14, 24, 39, 59; SSC 24**
See also AMW; BPFB 2; CA 5-8R; 129;
CANR 16, 50, 64; DA3; DLB 2; DLBY
1981; EWL 3; FW; INT CANR-16;
MAWW; MTCW 1, 2; RGAL 4; TUS

McCartney, (James) Paul 1942- . **CLC 12, 35**
See also CA 146; CANR 111

McCauley, Stephen (D.) 1955- .... **CLC 50**
See also CA 141

McClaren, Peter .... **CLC 70**

McClure, Michael (Thomas) 1932- ... **CLC 6, 10**
See also BG 3; CA 21-24R; CAD; CANR
17, 46, 77, 131; CD 5; CP 7; DLB 16;
WP

McCorkle, Jill (Collins) 1958- .... **CLC 51**
See also CA 121; CANR 113; CSW; DLB
234; DLBY 1987

McCourt, Frank 1930- .... **CLC 109**
See also AMWS 12; CA 157; CANR 97;
NCFS 1

McCourt, James 1941- .... **CLC 5**
See also CA 57-60; CANR 98

McCourt, Malachy 1931- .... **CLC 119**
See also SATA 126

McCoy, Horace (Stanley)
1897-1955 .... **TCLC 28**
See also AMWS 13; CA 108; 155; CMW 4;
DLB 9

McCrae, John 1872-1918 .... **TCLC 12**
See also CA 109; DLB 92; PFS 5

McCreigh, James
See Pohl, Frederik

McCullers, (Lula) Carson (Smith)
1917-1967 .... **CLC 1, 4, 10, 12, 48, 100; SSC 9, 24; TCLC 155; WLC**
See also AAYA 21; AMW; AMWC 2; BPFB
2; CA 5-8R; 25-28R; CABS 1, 3; CANR
18, 132; CDALB 1941-1968; DA; DA3;
DAB; DAC; DAM MST, NOV; DFS 5,
18; DLB 2, 7, 173, 228; EWL 3; EXPS;
FW; GLL 1; LAIT 3, 4; MAWW; MTCW
1, 2; NFS 6, 13; RGAL 4; RGSF 2; SATA
27; SSFS 5; TUS; YAW

McCulloch, John Tyler
See Burroughs, Edgar Rice

McCullough, Colleen 1938(?)- .. **CLC 27, 107**
See also AAYA 36; BPFB 2; CA 81-84;
CANR 17, 46, 67, 98; CPW; DA3; DAM
NOV, POP; MTCW 1, 2; RHW

McCunn, Ruthanne Lum 1946- .... **AAL**
See also CA 119; CANR 43, 96; LAIT 2;
SATA 63

McDermott, Alice 1953- .... **CLC 90**
See also CA 109; CANR 40, 90, 126; DLB
292

McElroy, Joseph 1930- .... **CLC 5, 47**
See also CA 17-20R; CN 7

McEwan, Ian (Russell) 1948- .... **CLC 13, 66, 169**
See also BEST 90:4; BRWS 4; CA 61-64;
CANR 14, 41, 69, 87, 132; CN 7; DAM
NOV; DLB 14, 194; HGG; MTCW 1, 2;
RGSF 2; SUFW 2; TEA

McFadden, David 1940- .... **CLC 48**
See also CA 104; CP 7; DLB 60; INT CA-
104

McFarland, Dennis 1950- .... **CLC 65**
See also CA 165; CANR 110

McGahern, John 1934- ... **CLC 5, 9, 48, 156; SSC 17**
See also CA 17-20R; CANR 29, 68, 113;
CN 7; DLB 14, 231; MTCW 1

McGinley, Patrick (Anthony) 1937- . **CLC 41**
See also CA 120; 127; CANR 56; INT CA-
127

McGinley, Phyllis 1905-1978 .... **CLC 14**
See also CA 9-12R; 77-80; CANR 19;
CWRI 5; DLB 11, 48; PFS 9, 13; SATA
2, 44; SATA-Obit 24

McGinniss, Joe 1942- .... **CLC 32**
See also AITN 2; BEST 89:2; CA 25-28R;
CANR 26, 70; CPW; DLB 185; INT
CANR-26

McGivern, Maureen Daly
See Daly, Maureen

McGrath, Patrick 1950- .... **CLC 55**
See also CA 136; CANR 65; CN 7; DLB
231; HGG; SUFW 2

McGrath, Thomas (Matthew)
1916-1990 .... **CLC 28, 59**
See also AMWS 10; CA 9-12R; 132; CANR
6, 33, 95; DAM POET; MTCW 1; SATA
41; SATA-Obit 66

Merwin, W(illiam) S(tanley) 1927- ... **CLC 1, 2, 3, 5, 8, 13, 18, 45, 88; PC 45**
  See also AMWS 3; CA 13-16R; CANR 15, 51, 112; CP 7; DA3; DAM POET; DLB 5, 169; EWL 3; INT CANR-15; MTCW 1, 2; PAB; PFS 5, 15; RGAL 4

Metastasio, Pietro 1698-1782 .... **LC 115**
  See also RGWL 2, 3

Metcalf, John 1938- .... **CLC 37; SSC 43**
  See also CA 113; CN 7; DLB 60; RGSF 2; TWA

Metcalf, Suzanne
  See Baum, L(yman) Frank

Mew, Charlotte (Mary) 1870-1928 .. **TCLC 8**
  See also CA 105; 189; DLB 19, 135; RGEL 2

Mewshaw, Michael 1943- .... **CLC 9**
  See also CA 53-56; CANR 7, 47; DLBY 1980

Meyer, Conrad Ferdinand
  1825-1898 .... **NCLC 81; SSC 30**
  See also DLB 129; EW; RGWL 2, 3

Meyer, Gustav 1868-1932
  See Meyrink, Gustav
  See also CA 117; 190

Meyer, June
  See Jordan, June (Meyer)

Meyer, Lynn
  See Slavitt, David R(ytman)

Meyers, Jeffrey 1939- .... **CLC 39**
  See also CA 73-76, 186; CAAE 186; CANR 54, 102; DLB 111

Meynell, Alice (Christina Gertrude Thompson) 1847-1922 .... **TCLC 6**
  See also CA 104; 177; DLB 19, 98; RGEL 2

Meyrink, Gustav .... **TCLC 21**
  See Meyer, Gustav
  See also DLB 81; EWL 3

Michaels, Leonard 1933-2003 ..... **CLC 6, 25; SSC 16**
  See also CA 61-64; 216; CANR 21, 62, 119; CN 7; DLB 130; MTCW 1

Michaux, Henri 1899-1984 .... **CLC 8, 19**
  See also CA 85-88; 114; DLB 258; EWL 3; GFL 1789 to the Present; RGWL 2, 3

Micheaux, Oscar (Devereaux)
  1884-1951 .... **TCLC 76**
  See also BW 3; CA 174; DLB 50; TCWW 2

Michelangelo 1475-1564 .... **LC 12**
  See also AAYA 43

Michelet, Jules 1798-1874 .... **NCLC 31**
  See also EW 5; GFL 1789 to the Present

Michels, Robert 1876-1936 .... **TCLC 88**
  See also CA 212

Michener, James A(lbert)
  1907(?)-1997 .. **CLC 1, 5, 11, 29, 60, 109**
  See also AAYA 27; AITN 1; BEST 90:1; BPFB 2; CA 5-8R; 161; CANR 21, 45, 68; CN 7; CPW; DA3; DAM NOV, POP; DLB 6; MTCW 1, 2; RHW

Mickiewicz, Adam 1798-1855 . **NCLC 3, 101; PC 38**
  See also EW 5; RGWL 2, 3

Middleton, (John) Christopher
  1926- .... **CLC 13**
  See also CA 13-16R; CANR 29, 54, 117; CP 7; DLB 40

Middleton, Richard (Barham)
  1882-1911 .... **TCLC 56**
  See also CA 187; DLB 156; HGG

Middleton, Stanley 1919- .... **CLC 7, 38**
  See also CA 25-28R; CAAS 23; CANR 21, 46, 81; CN 7; DLB 14

Middleton, Thomas 1580-1627 ...... **DC 5; LC 33**
  See also BRW 2; DAM DRAM, MST; DFS 18; DLB 58; RGEL 2

Migueis, Jose Rodrigues 1901-1980 . **CLC 10**
  See also DLB 287

Mikszath, Kalman 1847-1910 .... **TCLC 31**
  See also CA 170

Miles, Jack .... **CLC 100**
  See also CA 200

Miles, John Russiano
  See Miles, Jack

Miles, Josephine (Louise)
  1911-1985 .... **CLC 1, 2, 14, 34, 39**
  See also CA 1-4R; 116; CANR 2, 55; DAM POET; DLB 48

Militant
  See Sandburg, Carl (August)

Mill, Harriet (Hardy) Taylor
  1807-1858 .... **NCLC 102**
  See also FW

Mill, John Stuart 1806-1873 .... **NCLC 11, 58**
  See also CDBLB 1832-1890; DLB 55, 190, 262; FW 1; RGEL 2; TEA

Millar, Kenneth 1915-1983 .... **CLC 14**
  See Macdonald, Ross
  See also CA 9-12R; 110; CANR 16, 63, 107; CMW 4; CPW; DA3; DAM POP; DLB 2, 226; DLBD 6; DLBY 1983; MTCW 1, 2

Millay, E. Vincent
  See Millay, Edna St. Vincent

Millay, Edna St. Vincent 1892-1950 ..... **PC 6, 61; TCLC 4, 49; WLCS**
  See Boyd, Nancy
  See also AMW; CA 104; 130; CDALB 1917-1929; DA; DA3; DAB; DAC; DAM MST, POET; DLB 45, 249; EWL 3; EXPP; MAWW; MTCW 1, 2; PAB; PFS 3, 17; RGAL 4; TUS; WP

Miller, Arthur 1915- ...... **CLC 1, 2, 6, 10, 15, 26, 47, 78, 179; DC 1; WLC**
  See also AAYA 15; AITN 1; AMW; AMWC 1; CA 1-4R; CABS 3; CAD; CANR 2, 30, 54, 76, 132; CD 5; CDALB 1941-1968; DA; DA3; DAB; DAC; DAM DRAM, MST; DFS 1, 3, 8; DLB 7, 266; EWL 3; LAIT 1, 4; LATS 1:2; MTCW 1, 2; RGAL 4; TUS; WYAS 1

Miller, Henry (Valentine)
  1891-1980 .... **CLC 1, 2, 4, 9, 14, 43, 84; WLC**
  See also AMW; BPFB 2; CA 9-12R; 97-100; CANR 33, 64; CDALB 1929-1941; DA; DA3; DAB; DAC; DAM MST, NOV; DLB 4, 9; DLBY 1980; EWL 3; MTCW 1, 2; RGAL 4; TUS

Miller, Hugh 1802-1856 .... **NCLC 143**
  See also DLB 190

Miller, Jason 1939(?)-2001 .... **CLC 2**
  See also AITN 1; CA 73-76; 197; CAD; CANR 130; DFS 12; DLB 7

Miller, Sue 1943- .... **CLC 44**
  See also AMWS 12; BEST 90:3; CA 139; CANR 59, 91, 128; DA3; DAM POP; DLB 143

Miller, Walter M(ichael, Jr.)
  1923-1996 .... **CLC 4, 30**
  See also BPFB 2; CA 85-88; CANR 108; DLB 8; SCFW; SFW 4

Millett, Kate 1934- .... **CLC 67**
  See also AITN 1; CA 73-76; CANR 32, 53, 76, 110; DA3; DLB 246; FW; GLL 1; MTCW 1, 2

Millhauser, Steven (Lewis) 1943- .... **CLC 21, 54, 109; SSC 57**
  See also CA 110; 111; CANR 63, 114, 133; CN 7; DA3; DLB 2; FANT; INT CA-111; MTCW 2

Millin, Sarah Gertrude 1889-1968 ... **CLC 49**
  See also CA 102; 93-96; DLB 225; EWL 3

Milne, A(lan) A(lexander)
  1882-1956 .... **TCLC 6, 88**
  See also BRWS 5; CA 104; 133; CLR 1, 26; CMW 4; CWRI 5; DA3; DAB; DAC; DAM MST; DLB 10, 77, 100, 160; FANT; MAICYA 1, 2; MTCW 1, 2; RGEL 2; SATA 100; WCH; YABC 1

Milner, Ron(ald) 1938-2004 ..... **BLC 3; CLC 56**
  See also AITN 1; BW 1; CA 73-76; CAD; CANR 24, 81; CD 5; DAM MULT; DLB 38; MTCW 1

Milnes, Richard Monckton
  1809-1885 .... **NCLC 61**
  See also DLB 32, 184

Milosz, Czeslaw 1911- ...... **CLC 5, 11, 22, 31, 56, 82; PC 8; WLCS**
  See also CA 81-84; CANR 23, 51, 91, 126; CDWLB 4; CWW 2; DA3; DAM MST, POET; DLB 215; EWL 3; MTCW 1, 2; PFS 16; RGWL 2, 3

Milton, John 1608-1674 ..... **LC 9, 43, 92; PC 19, 29; WLC**
  See also BRW 2; BRWR 2; CDBLB 1660-1789; DA; DA3; DAB; DAC; DAM MST, POET; DLB 131, 151, 281; EFS 1; EXPP; LAIT 1; PAB; PFS 3, 17; RGEL 2; TEA; WLIT 3; WP

Min, Anchee 1957- .... **CLC 86**
  See also CA 146; CANR 94

Minehaha, Cornelius
  See Wedekind, (Benjamin) Frank(lin)

Miner, Valerie 1947- .... **CLC 40**
  See also CA 97-100; CANR 59; FW; GLL 2

Minimo, Duca
  See D'Annunzio, Gabriele

Minot, Susan 1956- .... **CLC 44, 159**
  See also AMWS 6; CA 134; CANR 118; CN 7

Minus, Ed 1938- .... **CLC 39**
  See also CA 185

Mirabai 1498(?)-1550(?) .... **PC 48**

Miranda, Javier
  See Bioy Casares, Adolfo
  See also CWW 2

Mirbeau, Octave 1848-1917 .... **TCLC 55**
  See also CA 216; DLB 123, 192; GFL 1789 to the Present

Mirikitani, Janice 1942- .... **AAL**
  See also CA 211; RGAL 4

Mirk, John (?)-c. 1414 .... **LC 105**
  See also DLB 146

Miro (Ferrer), Gabriel (Francisco Victor)
  1879-1930 .... **TCLC 5**
  See also CA 104; 185; EWL 3

Misharin, Alexandr .... **CLC 59**

Mishima, Yukio ... **CLC 2, 4, 6, 9, 27; DC 1; SSC 4, TCLC 161**
  See Hiraoka, Kimitake
  See also AAYA 50; BPFB 2; GLL 1; MJW; MTCW 2; RGSF 2; RGWL 2, 3; SSFS 5, 12

Mistral, Frederic 1830-1914 .... **TCLC 51**
  See also CA 122; 213; GFL 1789 to the Present

Mistral, Gabriela
  See Godoy Alcayaga, Lucila
  See also DLB 283; DNFS 1; EWL 3; LAW; RGWL 2, 3; WP

Mistry, Rohinton 1952- ... **CLC 71, 196; SSC 73**
  See also BRWS 10; CA 141; CANR 86, 114; CCA 1; CN 7; DAC; SSFS 6

Mitchell, Clyde
  See Ellison, Harlan (Jay)

Mitchell, Emerson Blackhorse Barney
  1945- .... **NNAL**
  See also CA 45-48

Nosu, Chuji
See Ozu, Yasujiro

Notenburg, Eleanora (Genrikhovna) von
See Guro, Elena (Genrikhovna)

Nova, Craig 1945- .... **CLC 7, 31**
See also CA 45-48; CANR 2, 53, 127

Novak, Joseph
See Kosinski, Jerzy (Nikodem)

Novalis 1772-1801 .... **NCLC 13**
See also CDWLB 2; DLB 90; EW 5; RGWL
2, 3

Novick, Peter 1934- .... **CLC 164**
See also CA 188

Novis, Emile
See Weil, Simone (Adolphine)

Nowlan, Alden (Albert) 1933-1983 ... **CLC 15**
See also CA 9-12R; CANR 5; DAC; DAM
MST; DLB 53; PFS 12

Noyes, Alfred 1880-1958 ...... **PC 27; TCLC 7**
See also CA 104; 188; DLB 20; EXPP;
FANT; PFS 4; RGEL 2

Nugent, Richard Bruce 1906(?)-1987 ... **HR 3**
See also BW 1; CA 125; DLB 51; GLL 2

Nunn, Kem .... **CLC 34**
See also CA 159

Nussbaum, Martha 1947- .... **CLC 203**
See also CA 134; CANR 102

Nwapa, Flora (Nwanzuruaha)
1931-1993 .... **BLCS; CLC 133**
See also BW 2; CA 143; CANR 83; CD-
WLB 3; CWRI 5; DLB 125; EWL 3;
WLIT 2

Nye, Robert 1939- .... **CLC 13, 42**
See also BRWS 10; CA 33-36R; CANR 29,
67, 107; CN 7; CP 7; CWRI 5; DAM
NOV; DLB 14, 271; FANT; HGG; MTCW
1; RHW; SATA 6

Nyro, Laura 1947-1997 .... **CLC 17**
See also CA 194

Oates, Joyce Carol 1938- .. **CLC 1, 2, 3, 6, 9,**
11, 15, 19, 33, 52, 108, 134; SSC 6, 70;
WLC
See also AAYA 15, 52; AITN 1; AMWS 2;
BEST 89:2; BPFB 2; BYA 11; CA 5-8R;
CANR 25, 45, 74, 113, 129; CDALB
1968-1988; CN 7; CP 7; CPW; CWP; DA;
DA3; DAB; DAC; DAM MST, NOV,
POP; DLB 2, 5, 130; DLBY 1981; EWL
3; EXPS; FW; HGG; INT CANR-25;
LAIT 4; MAWW; MTCW 1, 2; NFS 8;
RGAL 4; RGSF 2; SSFS 17; SUFW 2;
TUS

O'Brian, E. G.
See Clarke, Arthur C(harles)

O'Brian, Patrick 1914-2000 .... **CLC 152**
See also AAYA 55; CA 144; 187; CANR
74; CPW; MTCW 2; RHW

O'Brien, Darcy 1939-1998 .... **CLC 11**
See also CA 21-24R; 167; CANR 8, 59

O'Brien, Edna 1932- ..... **CLC 3, 5, 8, 13, 36,**
65, 116; SSC 10, 77
See also BRWS 5; CA 1-4R; CANR 6, 41,
65, 102; CDBLB 1960 to Present; CN 7;
DA3; DAM NOV; DLB 14, 231; EWL 3;
FW; MTCW 1, 2; RGSF 2; WLIT 4

O'Brien, Fitz-James 1828-1862 ..... **NCLC 21**
See also DLB 74; RGAL 4; SUFW

O'Brien, Flann .... **CLC 1, 4, 5, 7, 10, 47**
See O Nuallain, Brian
See also BRWS 2; DLB 231; EWL 3;
RGEL 2

O'Brien, Richard 1942- .... **CLC 17**
See also CA 124

O'Brien, (William) Tim(othy) 1946- . **CLC 7,**
19, 40, 103; SSC 74
See also AAYA 16; AMWS 5; CA 85-88;
CANR 40, 58, 133; CDALBS; CN 7;
CPW; DA3; DAM POP; DLB 152; DLBD
9; DLBY 1980; LATS 1:2; MTCW 2;
RGAL 4; SSFS 5, 15

Obstfelder, Sigbjoern 1866-1900 .... **TCLC 23**
See also CA 123

O'Casey, Sean 1880-1964 .... **CLC 1, 5, 9, 11,**
15, 88; DC 12; WLCS
See also BRW 7; CA 89-92; CANR 62;
CBD; CDBLB 1914-1945; DA3; DAB;
DAC; DAM DRAM, MST; DFS 19; DLB
10; EWL 3; MTCW 1, 2; RGEL 2; TEA;
WLIT 4

O'Cathasaigh, Sean
See O'Casey, Sean

Occom, Samson 1723-1792 .... **LC 60; NNAL**
See also DLB 175

Ochs, Phil(ip David) 1940-1976 .... **CLC 17**
See also CA 185; 65-68

O'Connor, Edwin (Greene)
1918-1968 .... **CLC 14**
See also CA 93-96; 25-28R

O'Connor, (Mary) Flannery
1925-1964 .... **CLC 1, 2, 3, 6, 10, 13, 15,**
21, 66, 104; SSC 1, 23, 61, 82; TCLC
132; WLC
See also AAYA 7; AMW; AMWR 2; BPFB
3; BYA 16; CA 1-4R; CANR 3, 41;
CDALB 1941-1968; DA; DA3; DAB;
DAC; DAM MST, NOV; DLB 2, 152;
DLBD 12; DLBY 1980; EWL 3; EXPS;
LAIT 5; MAWW; MTCW 1, 2; NFS 3;
RGAL 4; RGSF 2; SSFS 2, 7, 10, 19;
TUS

O'Connor, Frank .... **CLC 23; SSC 5**
See O'Donovan, Michael Francis
See also DLB 162; EWL 3; RGSF 2; SSFS
5

O'Dell, Scott 1898-1989 .... **CLC 30**
See also AAYA 3, 44; BPFB 3; BYA 1, 2,
3, 5; CA 61-64; 129; CANR 12, 30, 112;
CLR 1, 16; DLB 52; JRDA; MAICYA 1,
2; SATA 12, 60, 134; WYA; YAW

Odets, Clifford 1906-1963 ..... **CLC 2, 28, 98;**
DC 6
See also AMWS 2; CA 85-88; CAD; CANR
62; DAM DRAM; DFS 3, 17, 20; DLB 7,
26; EWL 3; MTCW 1, 2; RGAL 4; TUS

O'Doherty, Brian 1928- .... **CLC 76**
See also CA 105; CANR 108

O'Donnell, K. M.
See Malzberg, Barry N(athaniel)

O'Donnell, Lawrence
See Kuttner, Henry

O'Donovan, Michael Francis
1903-1966 .... **CLC 14**
See O'Connor, Frank
See also CA 93-96; CANR 84

Oe, Kenzaburo 1935- .. **CLC 10, 36, 86, 187;**
SSC 20
See Oe Kenzaburo
See also CA 97-100; CANR 36, 50, 74, 126;
DA3; DAM NOV; DLB 182; DLBY 1994;
LATS 1:2; MJW; MTCW 1, 2; RGSF 2;
RGWL 2, 3

Oe Kenzaburo
See Oe, Kenzaburo
See also CWW 2; EWL 3

O'Faolain, Julia 1932- .... **CLC 6, 19, 47, 108**
See also CA 81-84; CAAS 2; CANR 12,
61; CN 7; DLB 14, 231; FW; MTCW 1;
RHW

O'Faolain, Sean 1900-1991 ...... **CLC 1, 7, 14,**
32, 70; SSC 13; TCLC 143
See also CA 61-64; 134; CANR 12, 66;
DLB 15, 162; MTCW 1, 2; RGEL 2;
RGSF 2

O'Flaherty, Liam 1896-1984 .... **CLC 5, 34;**
SSC 6
See also CA 101; 113; CANR 35; DLB 36,
162; DLBY 1984; MTCW 1, 2; RGEL 2;
RGSF 2; SSFS 5, 20

Ogai
See Mori Ogai
See also MJW

Ogilvy, Gavin
See Barrie, J(ames) M(atthew)

O'Grady, Standish (James)
1846-1928 .... **TCLC 5**
See also CA 104; 157

O'Grady, Timothy 1951- .... **CLC 59**
See also CA 138

O'Hara, Frank 1926-1966 .... **CLC 2, 5, 13,**
78; PC 45
See also CA 9-12R; 25-28R; CANR 33;
DA3; DAM POET; DLB 5, 16, 193; EWL
3; MTCW 1, 2; PFS 8; 12; RGAL 4; WP

O'Hara, John (Henry) 1905-1970 . **CLC 1, 2,**
3, 6, 11, 42; SSC 15
See also AMW; BPFB 3; CA 5-8R; 25-28R;
CANR 31, 60; CDALB 1929-1941; DAM
NOV; DLB 9, 86; DLBD 2; EWL 3;
MTCW 1, 2; NFS 11; RGAL 4; RGSF 2

O Hehir, Diana 1922- .... **CLC 41**
See also CA 93-96

Ohiyesa
See Eastman, Charles A(lexander)

Okada, John 1923-1971 .... **AAL**
See also BYA 14; CA 212

Okigbo, Christopher (Ifenayichukwu)
1932-1967 .... **BLC 3; CLC 25, 84; PC 7**
See also AFW; BW 1, 3; CA 77-80; CANR
74; CDWLB 3; DAM MULT, POET; DLB
125; EWL 3; MTCW 1, 2; RGEL 2

Okri, Ben 1959- .... **CLC 87**
See also AFW; BRWS 5; BW 2, 3; CA 130;
138; CANR 65, 128; CN 7; DLB 157,
231; EWL 3; INT CA-138; MTCW 2;
RGSF 2; SSFS 20; WLIT 2; WWE 1

Olds, Sharon 1942- .. **CLC 32, 39, 85; PC 22**
See also AMWS 10; CA 101; CANR 18,
41, 66, 98, 135; CP 7; CPW; CWP; DAM
POET; DLB 120; MTCW 2; PFS 17

Oldstyle, Jonathan
See Irving, Washington

Olesha, Iurii
See Olesha, Yuri (Karlovich)
See also RGWL 2

Olesha, Iurii Karlovich
See Olesha, Yuri (Karlovich)
See also DLB 272

Olesha, Yuri (Karlovich) 1899-1960 . **CLC 8;**
SSC 69; TCLC 136
See Olesha, Iurii; Olesha, Iurii Karlovich;
Olesha, Yury Karlovich
See also CA 85-88; EW 11; RGWL 3

Olesha, Yury Karlovich
See Olesha, Yuri (Karlovich)
See also EWL 3

Oliphant, Mrs.
See Oliphant, Margaret (Oliphant Wilson)
See also SUFW

Oliphant, Laurence 1829(?)-1888 .. **NCLC 47**
See also DLB 18, 166

Oliphant, Margaret (Oliphant Wilson)
1828-1897 .... **NCLC 11, 61; SSC 25**
See Oliphant, Mrs.
See also BRWS 10; DLB 18, 159, 190;
HGG; RGEL 2; RGSF 2

Oliver, Mary 1935- .... **CLC 19, 34, 98**
See also AMWS 7; CA 21-24R; CANR 9,
43, 84, 92; CP 7; CWP; DLB 5, 193;
EWL 3; PFS 15

Olivier, Laurence (Kerr) 1907-1989 . **CLC 20**
See also CA 111; 150; 129

Olsen, Tillie 1912- ... **CLC 4, 13, 114; SSC 11**
See also AAYA 51; AMWS 13; BYA 11;
CA 1-4R; CANR 1, 43, 74, 132;
CDALBS; CN 7; DA; DA3; DAB; DAC;

DAM MST; DLB 28, 206; DLBY 1980; EWL 3; EXPS; FW; MTCW 1, 2; RGAL 4; RGSF 2; SSFS 1; TUS

Olson, Charles (John) 1910-1970 .. **CLC 1, 2, 5, 6, 9, 11, 29; PC 19**
See also AMWS 2; CA 13-16; 25-28R; CABS 2; CANR 35, 61; CAP 1; DAM POET; DLB 5, 16, 193; EWL 3; MTCW 1, 2; RGAL 4; WP

Olson, Toby 1937- .... **CLC 28**
See also CA 65-68; CANR 9, 31, 84; CP 7

Olyesha, Yuri
See Olesha, Yuri (Karlovich)

Olympiodorus of Thebes c. 375-c. 430 .... **CMLC 59**

Omar Khayyam
See Khayyam, Omar
See also RGWL 2, 3

Ondaatje, (Philip) Michael 1943- .... **CLC 14, 29, 51, 76, 180; PC 28**
See also CA 77-80; CANR 42, 74, 109, 133; CN 7; CP 7; DA3; DAB; DAC; DAM MST; DLB 60; EWL 3; LATS 1:2; LMFS 2; MTCW 2; PFS 8, 19; TWA; WWE 1

Oneal, Elizabeth 1934-
See Oneal, Zibby
See also CA 106; CANR 28, 84; MAICYA 1, 2; SATA 30, 82; YAW

Oneal, Zibby .... **CLC 30**
See Oneal, Elizabeth
See also AAYA 5, 41; BYA 13; CLR 13; JRDA; WYA

O'Neill, Eugene (Gladstone) 1888-1953 ... **DC 20; TCLC 1, 6, 27, 49; WLC**
See also AAYA 54; AITN 1; AMW; AMWC 1; CA 110; 132; CAD; CANR 131; CDALB 1929-1941; DA; DA3; DAB; DAC; DAM DRAM, MST; DFS 2, 4, 5, 6, 9, 11, 12, 16, 20; DLB 7; EWL 3; LAIT 3; LMFS 2; MTCW 1, 2; RGAL 4; TUS

Onetti, Juan Carlos 1909-1994 .... **CLC 7, 10; HLCS 2; SSC 23; TCLC 131**
See also CA 85-88; 145; CANR 32, 63; CD-WLB 3; CWW 2; DAM MULT, NOV; DLB 113; EWL 3; HW 1, 2; LAW; MTCW 1, 2; RGSF 2

O Nuallain, Brian 1911-1966
See O'Brien, Flann
See also CA 21-22; 25-28R; CAP 2; DLB 231; FANT; TEA

Ophuls, Max 1902-1957 .... **TCLC 79**
See also CA 113

Opie, Amelia 1769-1853 .... **NCLC 65**
See also DLB 116, 159; RGEL 2

Oppen, George 1908-1984 ..... **CLC 7, 13, 34; PC 35; TCLC 107**
See also CA 13-16R; 113; CANR 8, 82; DLB 5, 165

Oppenheim, E(dward) Phillips 1866-1946 .... **TCLC 45**
See also CA 111; 202; CMW 4; DLB 70

Opuls, Max
See Ophuls, Max

Orage, A(lfred) R(ichard) 1873-1934 .... **TCLC 157**
See also CA 122

Origen c. 185-c. 254 .... **CMLC 19**

Orlovitz, Gil 1918-1973 .... **CLC 22**
See also CA 77-80; 45-48; DLB 2, 5

Orris
See Ingelow, Jean

Ortega y Gasset, Jose 1883-1955 ...... **HLC 2; TCLC 9**
See also CA 106; 130; DAM MULT; EW 9; EWL 3; HW 1, 2; MTCW 1, 2

Ortese, Anna Maria 1914-1998 .... **CLC 89**
See also DLB 177; EWL 3

Ortiz, Simon J(oseph) 1941- .... **CLC 45; NNAL; PC 17**
See also AMWS 4; CA 134; CANR 69, 118; CP 7; DAM MULT, POET; DLB 120, 175, 256; EXPP; PFS 4, 16; RGAL 4

Orton, Joe ...... **CLC 4, 13, 43; DC 3; TCLC 157**
See Orton, John Kingsley
See also BRWS 5; CBD; CDBLB 1960 to Present; DFS 3, 6; DLB 13; GLL 1; MTCW 2; RGEL 2; TEA; WLIT 4

Orton, John Kingsley 1933-1967
See Orton, Joe
See also CA 85-88; CANR 35, 66; DAM DRAM; MTCW 1, 2

Orwell, George ...... **SSC 68; TCLC 2, 6, 15, 31, 51, 128, 129; WLC**
See Blair, Eric (Arthur)
See also BPFB 3; BRW 7; BYA 5; CDBLB 1945-1960; CLR 68; DAB; DLB 15, 98, 195, 255; EWL 3; EXPN; LAIT 4, 5; LATS 1:1; NFS 3, 7; RGEL 2; SCFW 2; SFW 4; SSFS 4; TEA; WLIT 4; YAW

Osborne, David
See Silverberg, Robert

Osborne, George
See Silverberg, Robert

Osborne, John (James) 1929-1994 .... **CLC 1, 2, 5, 11, 45; TCLC 153; WLC**
See also BRWS 1; CA 13-16R; 147; CANR 21, 56; CDBLB 1945-1960; DA; DAB; DAC; DAM DRAM, MST; DFS 4, 19; DLB 13; EWL 3; MTCW 1, 2; RGEL 2

Osborne, Lawrence 1958- .... **CLC 50**
See also CA 189

Osbourne, Lloyd 1868-1947 .... **TCLC 93**

Osgood, Frances Sargent 1811-1850 .... **NCLC 141**
See also DLB 250

Oshima, Nagisa 1932- .... **CLC 20**
See also CA 116; 121; CANR 78

Oskison, John Milton 1874-1947 .... **NNAL; TCLC 35**
See also CA 144; CANR 84; DAM MULT; DLB 175

Ossian c. 3rd cent. - .... **CMLC 28**
See Macpherson, James

Ossoli, Sarah Margaret (Fuller) 1810-1850 .... **NCLC 5, 50**
See Fuller, Margaret; Fuller, Sarah Margaret
See also CDALB 1640-1865; FW; LMFS 1; SATA 25

Ostriker, Alicia (Suskin) 1937- .... **CLC 132**
See also CA 25-28R; CAAS 24; CANR 10, 30, 62, 99; CWP; DLB 120; EXPP; PFS 19

Ostrovsky, Aleksandr Nikolaevich
See Ostrovsky, Alexander
See also DLB 277

Ostrovsky, Alexander 1823-1886 .. **NCLC 30, 57**
See Ostrovsky, Aleksandr Nikolaevich

Otero, Blas de 1916-1979 .... **CLC 11**
See also CA 89-92; DLB 134; EWL 3

O'Trigger, Sir Lucius
See Horne, Richard Henry Hengist

Otto, Rudolf 1869-1937 .... **TCLC 85**

Otto, Whitney 1955- .... **CLC 70**
See also CA 140; CANR 120

Otway, Thomas 1652-1685 ... **DC 24; LC 106**
See also DAM DRAM; DLB 80; RGEL 2

Ouida .... **TCLC 43**
See De la Ramee, Marie Louise (Ouida)
See also DLB 18, 156; RGEL 2

Ouologuem, Yambo 1940- .... **CLC 146**
See also CA 111; 176

Ousmane, Sembene 1923- ... **BLC 3; CLC 66**
See Sembene, Ousmane
See also BW 1, 3; CA 117; 125; CANR 81; CWW 2; MTCW 1

Ovid 43B.C.-17 .... **CMLC 7; PC 2**
See also AW 2; CDWLB 1; DA3; DAM POET; DLB 211; RGWL 2, 3; WP

Owen, Hugh
See Faust, Frederick (Schiller)

Owen, Wilfred (Edward Salter) 1893-1918 ... **PC 19; TCLC 5, 27; WLC**
See also BRW 6; CA 104; 141; CDBLB 1914-1945; DA; DAB; DAC; DAM MST, POET; DLB 20; EWL 3; EXPP; MTCW 2; PFS 10; RGEL 2; WLIT 4

Owens, Louis (Dean) 1948-2002 .... **NNAL**
See also CA 137, 179; 207; CAAE 179; CAAS 24; CANR 71

Owens, Rochelle 1936- .... **CLC 8**
See also CA 17-20R; CAAS 2; CAD; CANR 39; CD 5; CP 7; CWD; CWP

Oz, Amos 1939- ...... **CLC 5, 8, 11, 27, 33, 54; SSC 66**
See also CA 53-56; CANR 27, 47, 65, 113; CWW 2; DAM NOV; EWL 3; MTCW 1, 2; RGSF 2; RGWL 3

Ozick, Cynthia 1928- .... **CLC 3, 7, 28, 62, 155; SSC 15, 60**
See also AMWS 5; BEST 90:1; CA 17-20R; CANR 23, 58, 116; CN 7; CPW; DA3; DAM NOV, POP; DLB 28, 152, 299; DLBY 1982; EWL 3; EXPS; INT CANR-23; MTCW 1, 2; RGAL 4; RGSF 2; SSFS 3, 12

Ozu, Yasujiro 1903-1963 .... **CLC 16**
See also CA 112

Pabst, G. W. 1885-1967 .... **TCLC 127**

Pacheco, C.
See Pessoa, Fernando (Antonio Nogueira)

Pacheco, Jose Emilio 1939- .... **HLC 2**
See also CA 111; 131; CANR 65; CWW 2; DAM MULT; DLB 290; EWL 3; HW 1, 2; RGSF 2

Pa Chin .... **CLC 18**
See Li Fei-kan
See also EWL 3

Pack, Robert 1929- .... **CLC 13**
See also CA 1-4R; CANR 3, 44, 82; CP 7; DLB 5; SATA 118

Padgett, Lewis
See Kuttner, Henry

Padilla (Lorenzo), Heberto 1932-2000 .... **CLC 38**
See also AITN 1; CA 123; 131; 189; CWW 2; EWL 3; HW 1

Page, James Patrick 1944-
See Page, Jimmy
See also CA 204

Page, Jimmy 1944- .... **CLC 12**
See Page, James Patrick

Page, Louise 1955- .... **CLC 40**
See also CA 140; CANR 76; CBD; CD 5; CWD; DLB 233

Page, P(atricia) K(athleen) 1916- ...... **CLC 7, 18; PC 12**
See Cape, Judith
See also CA 53-56; CANR 4, 22, 65; CP 7; DAC; DAM MST; DLB 68; MTCW 1; RGEL 2

Page, Stanton
See Fuller, Henry Blake

Page, Stanton
See Fuller, Henry Blake

Page, Thomas Nelson 1853-1922 .... **SSC 23**
See also CA 118; 177; DLB 12, 78; DLBD 13; RGAL 4

Pagels, Elaine Hiesey 1943- .... **CLC 104**
See also CA 45-48; CANR 2, 24, 51; FW; NCFS 4

Pavese, Cesare 1908-1950 .... **PC 13; SSC 19; TCLC 3**
See also CA 104; 169; DLB 128, 177; EW 12; EWL 3; PFS 20; RGSF 2; RGWL 2, 3; TWA

Pavic, Milorad 1929- .... **CLC 60**
See also CA 136; CDWLB 4; CWW 2; DLB 181; EWL 3; RGWL 3

Pavlov, Ivan Petrovich 1849-1936 . **TCLC 91**
See also CA 118; 180

Pavlova, Karolina Karlovna
1807-1893 .... **NCLC 138**
See also DLB 205

Payne, Alan
See Jakes, John (William)

Paz, Gil
See Lugones, Leopoldo

Paz, Octavio 1914-1998 . **CLC 3, 4, 6, 10, 19, 51, 65, 119; HLC 2; PC 1, 48; WLC**
See also AAYA 50; CA 73-76; 165; CANR 32, 65, 104; CWW 2; DA; DA3; DAB; DAC; DAM MST, MULT, POET; DLB 290; DLBY 1990, 1998; DNFS 1; EWL 3; HW 1, 2; LAW; LAWS 1; MTCW 1, 2; PFS 18; RGWL 2, 3; SSFS 13; TWA; WLIT 1

p'Bitek, Okot 1931-1982 .... **BLC 3; CLC 96; TCLC 149**
See also AFW; BW 2, 3; CA 124; 107; CANR 82; DAM MULT; DLB 125; EWL 3; MTCW 1, 2; RGEL 2; WLIT 2

Peacock, Molly 1947- .... **CLC 60**
See also CA 103; CAAS 21; CANR 52, 84; CP 7; CWP; DLB 120, 282

Peacock, Thomas Love
1785-1866 .... **NCLC 22**
See also BRW 4; DLB 96, 116; RGEL 2; RGSF 2

Peake, Mervyn 1911-1968 .... **CLC 7, 54**
See also CA 5-8R; 25-28R; CANR 3; DLB 15, 160, 255; FANT; MTCW 1; RGEL 2; SATA 23; SFW 4

Pearce, Philippa
See Christie, Philippa
See also CA 5-8R; CANR 4, 109; CWRI 5; FANT; MAICYA 2

Pearl, Eric
See Elman, Richard (Martin)

Pearson, T(homas) R(eid) 1956- .... **CLC 39**
See also CA 120; 130; CANR 97; CSW; INT CA-130

Peck, Dale 1967- .... **CLC 81**
See also CA 146; CANR 72, 127; GLL 2

Peck, John (Frederick) 1941- .... **CLC 3**
See also CA 49-52; CANR 3, 100; CP 7

Peck, Richard (Wayne) 1934- .... **CLC 21**
See also AAYA 1, 24; BYA 1, 6, 8, 11; CA 85-88; CANR 19, 38, 129; CLR 15; INT CANR-19; JRDA; MAICYA 1, 2; SAAS 2; SATA 18, 55, 97; SATA-Essay 110; WYA; YAW

Peck, Robert Newton 1928- .... **CLC 17**
See also AAYA 3, 43; BYA 1, 6; CA 81-84, 182; CAAE 182; CANR 31, 63, 127; CLR 45; DA; DAC; DAM MST; JRDA; LAIT 3; MAICYA 1, 2; SAAS 1; SATA 21, 62, 111; SATA-Essay 108; WYA; YAW

Peckinpah, (David) Sam(uel)
1925-1984 .... **CLC 20**
See also CA 109; 114; CANR 82

Pedersen, Knut 1859-1952
See Hamsun, Knut
See also CA 104; 119; CANR 63; MTCW 1, 2

Peele, George .... **LC 115**
See also BW 1; DLB 62, 167; RGEL 2

Peeslake, Gaffer
See Durrell, Lawrence (George)

Peguy, Charles (Pierre)
1873-1914 .... **TCLC 10**
See also CA 107; 193; DLB 258; EWL 3; GFL 1789 to the Present

Peirce, Charles Sanders
1839-1914 .... **TCLC 81**
See also CA 194; DLB 270

Pellicer, Carlos 1897(?)-1977 .... **HLCS 2**
See also CA 153; 69-72; DLB 290; EWL 3; HW 1

Pena, Ramon del Valle y
See Valle-Inclan, Ramon (Maria) del

Pendennis, Arthur Esquir
See Thackeray, William Makepeace

Penn, Arthur
See Matthews, (James) Brander

Penn, William 1644-1718 .... **LC 25**
See also DLB 24

PEPECE
See Prado (Calvo), Pedro

Pepys, Samuel 1633-1703 ... **LC 11, 58; WLC**
See also BRW 2; CDBLB 1660-1789; DA; DA3; DAB; DAC; DAM MST; DLB 101, 213; NCFS 4; RGEL 2; TEA; WLIT 3

Percy, Thomas 1729-1811 .... **NCLC 95**
See also DLB 104

Percy, Walker 1916-1990 .... **CLC 2, 3, 6, 8, 14, 18, 47, 65**
See also AMWS 3; BPFB 3; CA 1-4R; 131; CANR 1, 23, 64; CPW; CSW; DA3; DAM NOV, POP; DLB 2; DLBY 1980, 1990; EWL 3; MTCW 1, 2; RGAL 4; TUS

Percy, William Alexander
1885-1942 .... **TCLC 84**
See also CA 163; MTCW 2

Perec, Georges 1936-1982 .... **CLC 56, 116**
See also CA 141; DLB 83, 299; EWL 3; GFL 1789 to the Present; RGWL 3

Pereda (y Sanchez de Porrua), Jose Maria de 1833-1906 .... **TCLC 16**
See also CA 117

Pereda y Porrua, Jose Maria de
See Pereda (y Sanchez de Porrua), Jose Maria de

Peregoy, George Weems
See Mencken, H(enry) L(ouis)

Perelman, S(idney) J(oseph)
1904-1979 .. **CLC 3, 5, 9, 15, 23, 44, 49; SSC 32**
See also AITN 1, 2; BPFB 3; CA 73-76; 89-92; CANR 18; DAM DRAM; DLB 11, 44; MTCW 1, 2; RGAL 4

Peret, Benjamin 1899-1959 .... **PC 33; TCLC 20**
See also CA 117; 186; GFL 1789 to the Present

Peretz, Isaac Leib
See Peretz, Isaac Loeb
See also CA 201

Peretz, Isaac Loeb 1851(?)-1915 ...... **SSC 26; TCLC 16**
See Peretz, Isaac Leib
See also CA 109

Peretz, Yitzkhok Leibush
See Peretz, Isaac Loeb

Perez Galdos, Benito 1843-1920 ..... **HLCS 2; TCLC 27**
See Galdos, Benito Perez
See also CA 125; 153; EWL 3; HW 1; RGWL 2, 3

Peri Rossi, Cristina 1941- .. **CLC 156; HLCS 2**
See also CA 131; CANR 59, 81; CWW 2; DLB 145, 290; EWL 3; HW 1, 2

Perlata
See Peret, Benjamin

Perloff, Marjorie G(abrielle)
1931- .... **CLC 137**
See also CA 57-60; CANR 7, 22, 49, 104

Perrault, Charles 1628-1703 .... **LC 2, 56**
See also BYA 4; CLR 79; DLB 268; GFL Beginnings to 1789; MAICYA 1, 2; RGWL 2, 3; SATA 25; WCH

Perry, Anne 1938- .... **CLC 126**
See also CA 101; CANR 22, 50, 84; CMW 4; CN 7; CPW; DLB 276

Perry, Brighton
See Sherwood, Robert E(mmet)

Perse, St.-John
See Leger, (Marie-Rene Auguste) Alexis Saint-Leger

Perse, Saint-John
See Leger, (Marie-Rene Auguste) Alexis Saint-Leger
See also DLB 258; RGWL 3

Persius 34-62 .... **CMLC 74**
See also AW 2; DLB 211; RGWL 2, 3

Perutz, Leo(pold) 1882-1957 .... **TCLC 60**
See also CA 147; DLB 81

Peseenz, Tulio F.
See Lopez y Fuentes, Gregorio

Pesetsky, Bette 1932- .... **CLC 28**
See also CA 133; DLB 130

Peshkov, Alexei Maximovich 1868-1936
See Gorky, Maxim
See also CA 105; 141; CANR 83; DA; DAC; DAM DRAM, MST, NOV; MTCW 2

Pessoa, Fernando (Antonio Nogueira)
1888-1935 ..... **HLC 2; PC 20; TCLC 27**
See also CA 125; 183; DAM MULT; DLB 287; EW 10; EWL 3; RGWL 2, 3; WP

Peterkin, Julia Mood 1880-1961 ...... **CLC 31**
See also CA 102; DLB 9

Peters, Joan K(aren) 1945- .... **CLC 39**
See also CA 158; CANR 109

Peters, Robert L(ouis) 1924- .... **CLC 7**
See also CA 13-16R; CAAS 8; CP 7; DLB 105

Petofi, Sandor 1823-1849 .... **NCLC 21**
See also RGWL 2, 3

Petrakis, Harry Mark 1923- .... **CLC 3**
See also CA 9-12R; CANR 4, 30, 85; CN 7

Petrarch 1304-1374 .... **CMLC 20; PC 8**
See also DA3; DAM POET; EW 2; LMFS 1; RGWL 2. 3

Petronius c. 20-66 .... **CMLC 34**
See also AW 2; CDWLB 1; DLB 211; RGWL 2, 3

Petrov, Evgeny .... **TCLC 21**
See Kataev, Evgeny Petrovich

Petry, Ann (Lane) 1908-1997 .. **CLC 1, 7, 18; TCLC 112**
See also AFAW 1, 2; BPFB 3; BW 1, 3; BYA 2; CA 5-8R; 157; CAAS 6; CANR 4, 46; CLR 12; CN 7; DLB 76; EWL 3; JRDA; LAIT 1; MAICYA 1, 2; MAICYAS 1; MTCW 1; RGAL 4; SATA 5; SATA-Obit 94; TUS

Petursson, Halligrimur 1614-1674 .... **LC 8**

Peychinovich
See Vazov, Ivan (Minchov)

Phaedrus c. 15B.C.-c. 50 .... **CMLC 25**
See also DLB 211

Phelps (Ward), Elizabeth Stuart
See Phelps, Elizabeth Stuart
See also FW

Phelps, Elizabeth Stuart
1844-1911 .... **TCLC 113**
See Phelps (Ward), Elizabeth Stuart
See also DLB 74

Philips, Katherine 1632-1664 . **LC 30; PC 40**
See also DLB 131; RGEL 2

Philipson, Morris H. 1926- .... **CLC 53**
See also CA 1-4R; CANR 4

Polanski, Roman 1933- .... **CLC 16, 178**
    See also CA 77-80
Poliakoff, Stephen 1952- .... **CLC 38**
    See also CA 106; CANR 116; CBD; CD 5;
    DLB 13
Police, The
    See Copeland, Stewart (Armstrong); Sum-
    mers, Andrew James
Polidori, John William 1795-1821 . **NCLC 51**
    See also DLB 116; HGG
Pollitt, Katha 1949- .... **CLC 28, 122**
    See also CA 120; 122; CANR 66, 108;
    MTCW 1, 2
Pollock, (Mary) Sharon 1936- .... **CLC 50**
    See also CA 141; CANR 132; CD 5; CWD;
    DAC; DAM DRAM, MST; DFS 3; DLB
    60; FW
Pollock, Sharon 1936- .... **DC 20**
Polo, Marco 1254-1324 .... **CMLC 15**
Polonsky, Abraham (Lincoln)
    1910-1999 .... **CLC 92**
    See also CA 104; 187; DLB 26; INT CA-
    104
Polybius c. 200B.C.-c. 118B.C. ...... **CMLC 17**
    See also AW 1; DLB 176; RGWL 2, 3
Pomerance, Bernard 1940- .... **CLC 13**
    See also CA 97-100; CAD; CANR 49, 134;
    CD 5; DAM DRAM; DFS 9; LAIT 2
Ponge, Francis 1899-1988 .... **CLC 6, 18**
    See also CA 85-88; 126; CANR 40, 86;
    DAM POET; DLBY 2002; EWL 3; GFL
    1789 to the Present; RGWL 2, 3
Poniatowska, Elena 1933- . **CLC 140; HLC 2**
    See also CA 101; CANR 32, 66, 107; CD-
    WLB 3; CWW 2; DAM MULT; DLB 113;
    EWL 3; HW 1, 2; LAWS 1; WLIT 1
Pontoppidan, Henrik 1857-1943 .... **TCLC 29**
    See also CA 170; DLB 300
Ponty, Maurice Merleau
    See Merleau-Ponty, Maurice
Poole, Josephine .... **CLC 17**
    See Helyar, Jane Penelope Josephine
    See also SAAS 2; SATA 5
Popa, Vasko 1922-1991 .... **CLC 19**
    See also CA 112; 148; CDWLB 4; DLB
    181; EWL 3; RGWL 2, 3
Pope, Alexander 1688-1744 ...... **LC 3, 58, 60,**
    64; PC 26; WLC
    See also BRW 3; BRWC 1; BRWR 1; CD-
    BLB 1660-1789; DA; DA3; DAB; DAC;
    DAM MST, POET; DLB 95, 101, 213;
    EXPP; PAB; PFS 12; RGEL 2; WLIT 3;
    WP
Popov, Evgenii Anatol'evich
    See Popov, Yevgeny
    See also DLB 285
Popov, Yevgeny .... **CLC 59**
    See Popov, Evgenii Anatol'evich
Poquelin, Jean-Baptiste
    See Moliere
Porete, Marguerite c. 1250-1310 .. **CMLC 73**
    See also DLB 208
Porphyry c. 233-c. 305 .... **CMLC 71**
Porter, Connie (Rose) 1959(?)- .... **CLC 70**
    See also BW 2, 3; CA 142; CANR 90, 109;
    SATA 81, 129
Porter, Gene(va Grace) Stratton .. **TCLC 21**
    See Stratton-Porter, Gene(va Grace)
    See also BPFB 3; CA 112; CWRI 5; RHW
Porter, Katherine Anne 1890-1980 . **CLC 1,**
    3, 7, 10, 13, 15, 27, 101; SSC 4, 31, 43
    See also AAYA 42; AITN 2; AMW; BPFB
    3; CA 1-4R; 101; CANR 1, 65; CDALBS;
    DA; DA3; DAB; DAC; DAM MST, NOV;
    DLB 4, 9, 102; DLBD 12; DLBY 1980;
    EWL 3; EXPS; LAIT 3; MAWW; MTCW
    1, 2; NFS 14; RGAL 4; RGSF 2; SATA
    39; SATA-Obit 23; SSFS 1, 8, 11, 16;
    TUS

Porter, Peter (Neville Frederick)
    1929- .... **CLC 5, 13, 33**
    See also CA 85-88; CP 7; DLB 40, 289;
    WWE 1
Porter, William Sydney 1862-1910
    See Henry, O.
    See also CA 104; 131; CDALB 1865-1917;
    DA; DA3; DAB; DAC; DAM MST; DLB
    12, 78, 79; MTCW 1, 2; TUS; YABC 2
Portillo (y Pacheco), Jose Lopez
    See Lopez Portillo (y Pacheco), Jose
Portillo Trambley, Estela
    1927-1998 .... **HLC 2; TCLC 163**
    See Trambley, Estela Portillo
    See also CANR 32; DAM MULT; DLB
    209; HW 1
Posey, Alexander (Lawrence)
    1873-1908 .... **NNAL**
    See also CA 144; CANR 80; DAM MULT;
    DLB 175
Posse, Abel .... **CLC 70**
Post, Melville Davisson
    1869-1930 .... **TCLC 39**
    See also CA 110; 202; CMW 4
Potok, Chaim 1929-2002 ... **CLC 2, 7, 14, 26,**
    112
    See also AAYA 15, 50; AITN 1, 2; BPFB 3;
    BYA 1; CA 17-20R; 208; CANR 19, 35,
    64, 98; CLR 92; CN 7; DA3; DAM NOV;
    DLB 28, 152; EXPN; INT CANR-19;
    LAIT 4; MTCW 1, 2; NFS 4; SATA 33,
    106; SATA-Obit 134; TUS; YAW
Potok, Herbert Harold -2002
    See Potok, Chaim
Potok, Herman Harold
    See Potok, Chaim
Potter, Dennis (Christopher George)
    1935-1994 .... **CLC 58, 86, 123**
    See also BRWS 10; CA 107; 145; CANR
    33, 61; CBD; DLB 233; MTCW 1
Pound, Ezra (Weston Loomis)
    1885-1972 ... **CLC 1, 2, 3, 4, 5, 7, 10, 13,**
    18, 34, 48, 50, 112; PC 4; WLC
    See also AAYA 47; AMW; AMWR 1; CA
    5-8R; 37-40R; CANR 40; CDALB 1917-
    1929; DA; DA3; DAB; DAC; DAM MST,
    POET; DLB 4, 45, 63; DLBD 15; EFS 2;
    EWL 3; EXPP; LMFS 2; MTCW 1, 2;
    PAB; PFS 2, 8, 16; RGAL 4; TUS; WP
Povod, Reinaldo 1959-1994 .... **CLC 44**
    See also CA 136; 146; CANR 83
Powell, Adam Clayton, Jr.
    1908-1972 .... **BLC 3; CLC 89**
    See also BW 1, 3; CA 102; 33-36R; CANR
    86; DAM MULT
Powell, Anthony (Dymoke)
    1905-2000 .... **CLC 1, 3, 7, 9, 10, 31**
    See also BRW 7; CA 1-4R; 189; CANR 1,
    32, 62, 107; CDBLB 1945-1960; CN 7;
    DLB 15; EWL 3; MTCW 1, 2; RGEL 2;
    TEA
Powell, Dawn 1896(?)-1965 .... **CLC 66**
    See also CA 5-8R; CANR 121; DLBY 1997
Powell, Padgett 1952- .... **CLC 34**
    See also CA 126; CANR 63, 101; CSW;
    DLB 234; DLBY 01
Powell, (Oval) Talmage 1920-2000
    See Queen, Ellery
    See also CA 5-8R; CANR 2, 80
Power, Susan 1961- .... **CLC 91**
    See also BYA 14; CA 160; CANR 135; NFS
    11
Powers, J(ames) F(arl) 1917-1999 ..... **CLC 1,**
    4, 8, 57; SSC 4
    See also CA 1-4R; 181; CANR 2, 61; CN
    7; DLB 130; MTCW 1; RGAL 4; RGSF
    2
Powers, John J(ames) 1945-
    See Powers, John R.
    See also CA 69-72

Powers, John R. .... **CLC 66**
    See Powers, John J(ames)
Powers, Richard (S.) 1957- .... **CLC 93**
    See also AMWS 9; BPFB 3; CA 148;
    CANR 80; CN 7
Pownall, David 1938- .... **CLC 10**
    See also CA 89-92; 180; CAAS 18; CANR
    49, 101; CBD; CD 5; CN 7; DLB 14
Powys, John Cowper 1872-1963 ... **CLC 7, 9,**
    15, 46, 125
    See also CA 85-88; CANR 106; DLB 15,
    255; EWL 3; FANT; MTCW 1, 2; RGEL
    2; SUFW
Powys, T(heodore) F(rancis)
    1875-1953 .... **TCLC 9**
    See also BRWS 8; CA 106; 189; DLB 36,
    162; EWL 3; FANT; RGEL 2; SUFW
Prado (Calvo), Pedro 1886-1952 ... **TCLC 75**
    See also CA 131; DLB 283; HW 1; LAW
Prager, Emily 1952- .... **CLC 56**
    See also CA 204
Pratchett, Terry 1948- .... **CLC 197**
    See also AAYA 19, 54; BPFB 3; CA 143;
    CANR 87, 126; CLR 64; CN 7; CPW;
    CWRI 5; FANT; SATA 82, 139; SFW 4;
    SUFW 2
Pratolini, Vasco 1913-1991 .... **TCLC 124**
    See also CA 211; DLB 177; EWL 3; RGWL
    2, 3
Pratt, E(dwin) J(ohn) 1883(?)-1964 . **CLC 19**
    See also CA 141; 93-96; CANR 77; DAC;
    DAM POET; DLB 92; EWL 3; RGEL 2;
    TWA
Premchand .... **TCLC 21**
    See Srivastava, Dhanpat Rai
    See also EWL 3
Preseren, France 1800-1849 .... **NCLC 127**
    See also CDWLB 4; DLB 147
Preussler, Otfried 1923- .... **CLC 17**
    See also CA 77-80; SATA 24
Prevert, Jacques (Henri Marie)
    1900-1977 .... **CLC 15**
    See also CA 77-80; 69-72; CANR 29, 61;
    DLB 258; EWL 3; GFL 1789 to the
    Present; IDFW 3, 4; MTCW 1; RGWL 2,
    3; SATA-Obit 30
Prevost, (Antoine Francois)
    1697-1763 .... **LC 1**
    See also EW 4; GFL Beginnings to 1789;
    RGWL 2, 3
Price, (Edward) Reynolds 1933- ... **CLC 3, 6,**
    13, 43, 50, 63; SSC 22
    See also AMWS 6; CA 1-4R; CANR 1, 37,
    57, 87, 128; CN 7; CSW; DAM NOV;
    DLB 2, 218, 278; EWL 3; INT CANR-
    37; NFS 18
Price, Richard 1949- .... **CLC 6, 12**
    See also CA 49-52; CANR 3; DLBY 1981
Prichard, Katharine Susannah
    1883-1969 .... **CLC 46**
    See also CA 11-12; CANR 33; CAP 1; DLB
    260; MTCW 1; RGEL 2; RGSF 2; SATA
    66
Priestley, J(ohn) B(oynton)
    1894-1984 .... **CLC 2, 5, 9, 34**
    See also BRW 7; CA 9-12R; 113; CANR
    33; CDBLB 1914-1945; DA3; DAM
    DRAM, NOV; DLB 10, 34, 77, 100, 139;
    DLBY 1984; EWL 3; MTCW 1, 2; RGEL
    2; SFW 4
Prince 1958- .... **CLC 35**
    See also CA 213
Prince, F(rank) T(empleton)
    1912-2003 .... **CLC 22**
    See also CA 101; 219; CANR 43, 79; CP 7;
    DLB 20
Prince Kropotkin
    See Kropotkin, Peter (Aleksieevich)

Remizov, Aleksei (Mikhailovich)
1877-1957 .... **TCLC 27**
See Remizov, Alexey Mikhaylovich
See also CA 125; 133; DLB 295

Remizov, Alexey Mikhaylovich
See Remizov, Aleksei (Mikhailovich)
See also EWL 3

Renan, Joseph Ernest 1823-1892 . **NCLC 26, 145**
See also GFL 1789 to the Present

Renard, Jules(-Pierre) 1864-1910 .. **TCLC 17**
See also CA 117; 202; GFL 1789 to the Present

Renault, Mary .... **CLC 3, 11, 17**
See Challans, Mary
See also BPFB 3; BYA 2; DLBY 1983; EWL 3; GLL 1; LAIT 1; MTCW 2; RGEL 2; RHW

Rendell, Ruth (Barbara) 1930- .. **CLC 28, 48**
See Vine, Barbara
See also BPFB 3; BRWS 9; CA 109; CANR 32, 52, 74, 127; CN 7; CPW; DAM POP; DLB 87, 276; INT CANR-32; MSW; MTCW 1, 2

Renoir, Jean 1894-1979 .... **CLC 20**
See also CA 129; 85-88

Resnais, Alain 1922- .... **CLC 16**

Revard, Carter (Curtis) 1931- .... **NNAL**
See also CA 144; CANR 81; PFS 5

Reverdy, Pierre 1889-1960 .... **CLC 53**
See also CA 97-100; 89-92; DLB 258; EWL 3; GFL 1789 to the Present

Rexroth, Kenneth 1905-1982 .... **CLC 1, 2, 6, 11, 22, 49, 112; PC 20**
See also BG 3; CA 5-8R; 107; CANR 14, 34, 63; CDALB 1941-1968; DAM POET; DLB 16, 48, 165, 212; DLBY 1982; EWL 3; INT CANR-14; MTCW 1, 2; RGAL 4

Reyes, Alfonso 1889-1959 .... **HLCS 2; TCLC 33**
See also CA 131; EWL 3; HW 1; LAW

Reyes y Basoalto, Ricardo Eliecer Neftali
See Neruda, Pablo

Reymont, Wladyslaw (Stanislaw)
1868(?)-1925 .... **TCLC 5**
See also CA 104; EWL 3

Reynolds, John Hamilton
1794-1852 .... **NCLC 146**
See also DLB 96

Reynolds, Jonathan 1942- .... **CLC 6, 38**
See also CA 65-68; CANR 28

Reynolds, Joshua 1723-1792 .... **LC 15**
See also DLB 104

Reynolds, Michael S(hane)
1937-2000 .... **CLC 44**
See also CA 65-68; 189; CANR 9, 89, 97

Reznikoff, Charles 1894-1976 .... **CLC 9**
See also AMWS 14; CA 33-36; 61-64; CAP 2; DLB 28, 45; WP

Rezzori (d'Arezzo), Gregor von
1914-1998 .... **CLC 25**
See also CA 122; 136; 167

Rhine, Richard
See Silverstein, Alvin; Silverstein, Virginia B(arbara Opshelor)

Rhodes, Eugene Manlove
1869-1934 .... **TCLC 53**
See also CA 198; DLB 256

R'hoone, Lord
See Balzac, Honore de

Rhys, Jean 1890-1979 .... **CLC 2, 4, 6, 14, 19, 51, 124; SSC 21, 76**
See also BRWS 2; CA 25-28R; 85-88; CANR 35, 62; CDBLB 1945-1960; CD-WLB 3; DA3; DAM NOV; DLB 36, 117, 162; DNFS 2; EWL 3; LATS 1:1; MTCW 1, 2; RGEL 2; RGSF 2; RHW; TEA; WWE 1

Ribeiro, Darcy 1922-1997 .... **CLC 34**
See also CA 33-36R; 156; EWL 3

Ribeiro, Joao Ubaldo (Osorio Pimentel)
1941- .... **CLC 10, 67**
See also CA 81-84; CWW 2; EWL 3

Ribman, Ronald (Burt) 1932- .... **CLC 7**
See also CA 21-24R; CAD; CANR 46, 80; CD 5

Ricci, Nino (Pio) 1959- .... **CLC 70**
See also CA 137; CANR 130; CCA 1

Rice, Anne 1941- .... **CLC 41, 128**
See Rampling, Anne
See also AAYA 9, 53; AMWS 7; BEST 89:2; BPFB 3; CA 65-68; CANR 12, 36, 53, 74, 100, 133; CN 7; CPW; CSW; DA3; DAM POP; DLB 292; GLL 2; HGG; MTCW 2; SUFW 2; YAW

Rice, Elmer (Leopold) 1892-1967 ...... **CLC 7, 49**
See Reizenstein, Elmer Leopold
See also CA 21-22; 25-28R; CAP 2; DAM DRAM; DFS 12; DLB 4, 7; MTCW 1, 2; RGAL 4

Rice, Tim(othy Miles Bindon)
1944- .... **CLC 21**
See also CA 103; CANR 46; DFS 7

Rich, Adrienne (Cecile) 1929- ... **CLC 3, 6, 7, 11, 18, 36, 73, 76, 125; PC 5**
See also AMWR 2; AMWS 1; CA 9-12R; CANR 20, 53, 74, 128; CDALBS; CP 7; CSW; CWP; DA3; DAM POET; DLB 5, 67; EWL 3; EXPP; FW; MAWW; MTCW 1, 2; PAB; PFS 15; RGAL 4; WP

Rich, Barbara
See Graves, Robert (von Ranke)

Rich, Robert
See Trumbo, Dalton

Richard, Keith .... **CLC 17**
See Richards, Keith

Richards, David Adams 1950- .... **CLC 59**
See also CA 93-96; CANR 60, 110; DAC; DLB 53

Richards, I(vor) A(rmstrong)
1893-1979 .... **CLC 14, 24**
See also BRWS 2; CA 41-44R; 89-92; CANR 34, 74; DLB 27; EWL 3; MTCW 2; RGEL 2

Richards, Keith 1943-
See Richard, Keith
See also CA 107; CANR 77

Richardson, Anne
See Roiphe, Anne (Richardson)

Richardson, Dorothy Miller
1873-1957 .... **TCLC 3**
See also CA 104; 192; DLB 36; EWL 3; FW; RGEL 2

Richardson (Robertson), Ethel Florence Lindesay 1870-1946
See Richardson, Henry Handel
See also CA 105; 190; DLB 230; RHW

Richardson, Henry Handel .... **TCLC 4**
See Richardson (Robertson), Ethel Florence Lindesay
See also DLB 197; EWL 3; RGEL 2; RGSF 2

Richardson, John 1796-1852 .... **NCLC 55**
See also CCA 1; DAC; DLB 99

Richardson, Samuel 1689-1761 ...... **LC 1, 44; WLC**
See also BRW 3; CDBLB 1660-1789; DA; DAB; DAC; DAM MST, NOV; DLB 39; RGEL 2; TEA; WLIT 3

Richardson, Willis 1889-1977 .... **HR 3**
See also BW 1; CA 124; DLB 51; SATA 60

Richler, Mordecai 1931-2001 .... **CLC 3, 5, 9, 13, 18, 46, 70, 185**
See also AITN 1; CA 65-68; 201; CANR 31, 62, 111; CCA 1; CLR 17; CWRI 5; DAC; DAM MST, NOV; DLB 53; EWL 3; MAICYA 1, 2; MTCW 1, 2; RGEL 2; SATA 44, 98; SATA-Brief 27; TWA

Richter, Conrad (Michael)
1890-1968 .... **CLC 30**
See also AAYA 21; BYA 2; CA 5-8R; 25-28R; CANR 23; DLB 9, 212; LAIT 1; MTCW 1, 2; RGAL 4; SATA 3; TCWW 2; TUS; YAW

Ricostranza, Tom
See Ellis, Trey

Riddell, Charlotte 1832-1906 .... **TCLC 40**
See Riddell, Mrs. J. H.
See also CA 165; DLB 156

Riddell, Mrs. J. H.
See Riddell, Charlotte
See also HGG; SUFW

Ridge, John Rollin 1827-1867 ...... **NCLC 82; NNAL**
See also CA 144; DAM MULT; DLB 175

Ridgeway, Jason
See Marlowe, Stephen

Ridgway, Keith 1965- .... **CLC 119**
See also CA 172

Riding, Laura .... **CLC 3, 7**
See Jackson, Laura (Riding)
See also RGAL 4

Riefenstahl, Berta Helene Amalia 1902-2003
See Riefenstahl, Leni
See also CA 108; 220

Riefenstahl, Leni .... **CLC 16, 190**
See Riefenstahl, Berta Helene Amalia

Riffe, Ernest
See Bergman, (Ernst) Ingmar

Riggs, (Rolla) Lynn
1899-1954 .... **NNAL; TCLC 56**
See also CA 144; DAM MULT; DLB 175

Riis, Jacob A(ugust) 1849-1914 ..... **TCLC 80**
See also CA 113; 168; DLB 23

Riley, James Whitcomb 1849-1916 .... **PC 48; TCLC 51**
See also CA 118; 137; DAM POET; MAI-CYA 1, 2; RGAL 4; SATA 17

Riley, Tex
See Creasey, John

Rilke, Rainer Maria 1875-1926 .... **PC 2; TCLC 1, 6, 19**
See also CA 104; 132; CANR 62, 99; CD-WLB 2; DA3; DAM POET; DLB 81; EW 9; EWL 3; MTCW 1, 2; PFS 19; RGWL 2, 3; TWA; WP

Rimbaud, (Jean Nicolas) Arthur
1854-1891 ... **NCLC 4, 35, 82; PC 3, 57; WLC**
See also DA; DA3; DAB; DAC; DAM MST, POET; DLB 217; EW 7; GFL 1789 to the Present; LMFS 2; RGWL 2, 3; TWA; WP

Rinehart, Mary Roberts
1876-1958 .... **TCLC 52**
See also BPFB 3; CA 108; 166; RGAL 4; RHW

Ringmaster, The
See Mencken, H(enry) L(ouis)

Ringwood, Gwen(dolyn Margaret) Pharis
1910-1984 .... **CLC 48**
See also CA 148; 112; DLB 88

Rio, Michel 1945(?)- .... **CLC 43**
See also CA 201

Rios, Alberto (Alvaro) 1952- .... **PC 57**
See also AMWS 4; CA 113; CANR 34, 79; CP 7; DLB 122; HW 2; PFS 11

Ritsos, Giannes
See Ritsos, Yannis

Ritsos, Yannis 1909-1990 .... **CLC 6, 13, 31**
See also CA 77-80; 133; CANR 39, 61; EW 12; EWL 3; MTCW 1; RGWL 2, 3

Ritter, Erika 1948(?)- .... **CLC 52**
See also CD 5; CWD

Rivera, Jose Eustasio 1889-1928 ... **TCLC 35**
See also CA 162; EWL 3; HW 1, 2; LAW

Rivera, Tomas 1935-1984 .... **HLCS 2**
See also CA 49-52; CANR 32; DLB 82;
HW 1; LLW 1; RGAL 4; SSFS 15;
TCWW 2; WLIT 1

Rivers, Conrad Kent 1933-1968 .... **CLC 1**
See also BW 1; CA 85-88; DLB 41

Rivers, Elfrida
See Bradley, Marion Zimmer
See also GLL 1

Riverside, John
See Heinlein, Robert A(nson)

Rizal, Jose 1861-1896 .... **NCLC 27**

Roa Bastos, Augusto (Antonio)
1917- .... **CLC 45; HLC 2**
See also CA 131; CWW 2; DAM MULT;
DLB 113; EWL 3; HW 1; LAW; RGSF 2;
WLIT 1

Robbe-Grillet, Alain 1922- .... **CLC 1, 2, 4, 6,
8, 10, 14, 43, 128**
See also BPFB 3; CA 9-12R; CANR 33,
65, 115; CWW 2; DLB 83; EW 13; EWL
3; GFL 1789 to the Present; IDFW 3, 4;
MTCW 1, 2; RGWL 2, 3; SSFS 15

Robbins, Harold 1916-1997 .... **CLC 5**
See also BPFB 3; CA 73-76; 162; CANR
26, 54, 112; DA3; DAM NOV; MTCW 1,
2

Robbins, Thomas Eugene 1936-
See Robbins, Tom
See also CA 81-84; CANR 29, 59, 95; CN
7; CPW; CSW; DA3; DAM NOV, POP;
MTCW 1, 2

Robbins, Tom .... **CLC 9, 32, 64**
See Robbins, Thomas Eugene
See also AAYA 32; AMWS 10; BEST 90:3;
BPFB 3; DLBY 1980; MTCW 2

Robbins, Trina 1938- .... **CLC 21**
See also CA 128

Roberts, Charles G(eorge) D(ouglas)
1860-1943 .... **TCLC 8**
See also CA 105; 188; CLR 33; CWRI 5;
DLB 92; RGEL 2; RGSF 2; SATA 88;
SATA-Brief 29

Roberts, Elizabeth Madox
1886-1941 .... **TCLC 68**
See also CA 111; 166; CLR 100; CWRI 5;
DLB 9, 54, 102; RGAL 4; RHW; SATA
33; SATA-Brief 27; WCH

Roberts, Kate 1891-1985 .... **CLC 15**
See also CA 107; 116

Roberts, Keith (John Kingston)
1935-2000 .... **CLC 14**
See also BRWS 10; CA 25-28R; CANR 46;
DLB 261; SFW 4

Roberts, Kenneth (Lewis)
1885-1957 .... **TCLC 23**
See also CA 109; 199; DLB 9; RGAL 4;
RHW

Roberts, Michele (Brigitte) 1949- .... **CLC 48,
178**
See also CA 115; CANR 58, 120; CN 7;
DLB 231; FW

Robertson, Ellis
See Ellison, Harlan (Jay); Silverberg, Robert

Robertson, Thomas William
1829-1871 .... **NCLC 35**
See Robertson, Tom
See also DAM DRAM

Robertson, Tom
See Robertson, Thomas William
See also RGEL 2

Robeson, Kenneth
See Dent, Lester

Robinson, Edwin Arlington
1869-1935 .... **PC 1, 35; TCLC 5, 101**
See also AMW; CA 104; 133; CDALB
1865-1917; DA; DAC; DAM MST,
POET; DLB 54; EWL 3; EXPP; MTCW
1, 2; PAB; PFS 4; RGAL 4; WP

Robinson, Henry Crabb
1775-1867 .... **NCLC 15**
See also DLB 107

Robinson, Jill 1936- .... **CLC 10**
See also CA 102; CANR 120; INT CA-102

Robinson, Kim Stanley 1952- .... **CLC 34**
See also AAYA 26; CA 126; CANR 113;
CN 7; SATA 109; SCFW 2; SFW 4

Robinson, Lloyd
See Silverberg, Robert

Robinson, Marilynne 1944- ...... **CLC 25, 180**
See also CA 116; CANR 80; CN 7; DLB
206

Robinson, Mary 1758-1800 .... **NCLC 142**
See also DLB 158; FW

Robinson, Smokey .... **CLC 21**
See Robinson, William, Jr.

Robinson, William, Jr. 1940-
See Robinson, Smokey
See also CA 116

Robison, Mary 1949- .... **CLC 42, 98**
See also CA 113; 116; CANR 87; CN 7;
DLB 130; INT CA-116; RGSF 2

Rochester
See Wilmot, John
See also RGEL 2

Rod, Edouard 1857-1910 .... **TCLC 52**

Roddenberry, Eugene Wesley 1921-1991
See Roddenberry, Gene
See also CA 110; 135; CANR 37; SATA 45;
SATA-Obit 69

Roddenberry, Gene .... **CLC 17**
See Roddenberry, Eugene Wesley
See also AAYA 5; SATA-Obit 69

Rodgers, Mary 1931- .... **CLC 12**
See also BYA 5; CA 49-52; CANR 8, 55,
90; CLR 20; CWRI 5; INT CANR-8;
JRDA; MAICYA 1, 2; SATA 8, 130

Rodgers, W(illiam) R(obert)
1909-1969 .... **CLC 7**
See also CA 85-88; DLB 20; RGEL 2

Rodman, Eric
See Silverberg, Robert

Rodman, Howard 1920(?)-1985 .... **CLC 65**
See also CA 118

Rodman, Maia
See Wojciechowska, Maia (Teresa)

Rodo, Jose Enrique 1871(?)-1917 .... **HLCS 2**
See also CA 178; EWL 3; HW 2; LAW

Rodolph, Utto
See Ouologuem, Yambo

Rodriguez, Claudio 1934-1999 .... **CLC 10**
See also CA 188; DLB 134

Rodriguez, Richard 1944- .... **CLC 155; HLC
2**
See also AMWS 14; CA 110; CANR 66,
116; DAM MULT; DLB 82, 256; HW 1,
2; LAIT 5; LLW 1; NCFS 3; WLIT 1

Roelvaag, O(le) E(dvart) 1876-1931
See Rolvaag, O(le) E(dvart)
See also CA 117; 171

Roethke, Theodore (Huebner)
1908-1963 .... **CLC 1, 3, 8, 11, 19, 46,
101; PC 15**
See also AMW; CA 81-84; CABS 2;
CDALB 1941-1968; DA3; DAM POET;
DLB 5, 206; EWL 3; EXPP; MTCW 1, 2;
PAB; PFS 3; RGAL 4; WP

Rogers, Carl R(ansom)
1902-1987 .... **TCLC 125**
See also CA 1-4R; 121; CANR 1, 18;
MTCW 1

Rogers, Samuel 1763-1855 .... **NCLC 69**
See also DLB 93; RGEL 2

Rogers, Thomas Hunton 1927- .... **CLC 57**
See also CA 89-92; INT CA-89-92

Rogers, Will(iam Penn Adair)
1879-1935 .... **NNAL; TCLC 8, 71**
See also CA 105; 144; DA3; DAM MULT;
DLB 11; MTCW 2

Rogin, Gilbert 1929- .... **CLC 18**
See also CA 65-68; CANR 15

Rohan, Koda
See Koda Shigeyuki

Rohlfs, Anna Katharine Green
See Green, Anna Katharine

Rohmer, Eric .... **CLC 16**
See Scherer, Jean-Marie Maurice

Rohmer, Sax .... **TCLC 28**
See Ward, Arthur Henry Sarsfield
See also DLB 70; MSW; SUFW

Roiphe, Anne (Richardson) 1935- .. **CLC 3, 9**
See also CA 89-92; CANR 45, 73; DLBY
1980; INT CA-89-92

Rojas, Fernando de 1475-1541 ... **HLCS 1, 2;
LC 23**
See also DLB 286; RGWL 2, 3

Rojas, Gonzalo 1917- .... **HLCS 2**
See also CA 178; HW 2; LAWS 1

Roland, Marie-Jeanne 1754-1793 .... **LC 98**

**Rolfe, Frederick (William Serafino Austin
Lewis Mary)** 1860-1913 .... **TCLC 12**
See Al Siddik
See also CA 107; 210; DLB 34, 156; RGEL
2

Rolland, Romain 1866-1944 .... **TCLC 23**
See also CA 118; 197; DLB 65, 284; EWL
3; GFL 1789 to the Present; RGWL 2, 3

Rolle, Richard c. 1300-c. 1349 ...... **CMLC 21**
See also DLB 146; LMFS 1; RGEL 2

Rolvaag, O(le) E(dvart) .... **TCLC 17**
See Roelvaag, O(le) E(dvart)
See also DLB 9, 212; NFS 5; RGAL 4

Romain Arnaud, Saint
See Aragon, Louis

Romains, Jules 1885-1972 .... **CLC 7**
See also CA 85-88; CANR 34; DLB 65;
EWL 3; GFL 1789 to the Present; MTCW
1

Romero, Jose Ruben 1890-1952 .... **TCLC 14**
See also CA 114; 131; EWL 3; HW 1; LAW

Ronsard, Pierre de 1524-1585 . **LC 6, 54; PC
11**
See also EW 2; GFL Beginnings to 1789;
RGWL 2, 3; TWA

Rooke, Leon 1934- .... **CLC 25, 34**
See also CA 25-28R; CANR 23, 53; CCA
1; CPW; DAM POP

Roosevelt, Franklin Delano
1882-1945 .... **TCLC 93**
See also CA 116; 173; LAIT 3

Roosevelt, Theodore 1858-1919 ..... **TCLC 69**
See also CA 115; 170; DLB 47, 186, 275

Roper, William 1498-1578 .... **LC 10**

Roquelaure, A. N.
See Rice, Anne

Rosa, Joao Guimaraes 1908-1967 ... **CLC 23;
HLCS 1**
See Guimaraes Rosa, Joao
See also CA 89-92; DLB 113, 307; EWL 3;
WLIT 1

Rose, Wendy 1948- . **CLC 85; NNAL; PC 13**
See also CA 53-56; CANR 5, 51; CWP;
DAM MULT; DLB 175; PFS 13; RGAL
4; SATA 12

Rosen, R. D.
See Rosen, Richard (Dean)

Rosen, Richard (Dean) 1949- .... **CLC 39**
See also CA 77-80; CANR 62, 120; CMW
4; INT CANR-30

Rosenberg, Isaac 1890-1918 .... **TCLC 12**
See also BRW 6; CA 107; 188; DLB 20,
216; EWL 3; PAB; RGEL 2

Rosenblatt, Joe .... **CLC 15**
See Rosenblatt, Joseph

Rybakov, Anatoli (Naumovich)
1911-1998 .... **CLC 23, 53**
See Rybakov, Anatolii (Naumovich)
See also CA 126; 135; 172; SATA 79;
SATA-Obit 108
Rybakov, Anatolii (Naumovich)
See Rybakov, Anatoli (Naumovich)
See also DLB 302
Ryder, Jonathan
See Ludlum, Robert
Ryga, George 1932-1987 .... **CLC 14**
See also CA 101; 124; CANR 43, 90; CCA
1; DAC; DAM MST; DLB 60
S. H.
See Hartmann, Sadakichi
S. S.
See Sassoon, Siegfried (Lorraine)
Sa'adawi, al- Nawal
See El Saadawi, Nawal
See also AFW; EWL 3
Saadawi, Nawal El
See El Saadawi, Nawal
See also WLIT 2
Saba, Umberto 1883-1957 .... **TCLC 33**
See also CA 144; CANR 79; DLB 114;
EWL 3; RGWL 2, 3
Sabatini, Rafael 1875-1950 .... **TCLC 47**
See also BPFB 3; CA 162; RHW
Sabato, Ernesto (R.) 1911- .... **CLC 10, 23;**
HLC 2
See also CA 97-100; CANR 32, 65; CD-
WLB 3; CWW 2; DAM MULT; DLB 145;
EWL 3; HW 1, 2; LAW; MTCW 1, 2
Sa-Carneiro, Mario de 1890-1916 . **TCLC 83**
See also DLB 287; EWL 3
Sacastru, Martin
See Bioy Casares, Adolfo
See also CWW 2
Sacher-Masoch, Leopold von
1836(?)-1895 .... **NCLC 31**
Sachs, Hans 1494-1576 .... **LC 95**
See also CDWLB 2; DLB 179; RGWL 2, 3
Sachs, Marilyn (Stickle) 1927- .... **CLC 35**
See also AAYA 2; BYA 6; CA 17-20R;
CANR 13, 47; CLR 2; JRDA; MAICYA
1, 2; SAAS 2; SATA 3, 68; SATA-Essay
110; WYA; YAW
Sachs, Nelly 1891-1970 .... **CLC 14, 98**
See also CA 17-18; 25-28R; CANR 87;
CAP 2; EWL 3; MTCW 2; PFS 20;
RGWL 2, 3
Sackler, Howard (Oliver)
1929-1982 .... **CLC 14**
See also CA 61-64; 108; CAD; CANR 30;
DFS 15; DLB 7
Sacks, Oliver (Wolf) 1933- .... **CLC 67, 202**
See also CA 53-56; CANR 28, 50, 76;
CPW; DA3; INT CANR-28; MTCW 1, 2
Sackville, Thomas 1536-1608 .... **LC 98**
See also DAM DRAM; DLB 62, 132;
RGEL 2
Sadakichi
See Hartmann, Sadakichi
Sa'dawi, Nawal al-
See El Saadawi, Nawal
See also CWW 2
Sade, Donatien Alphonse Francois
1740-1814 .... **NCLC 3, 47**
See also EW 4; GFL Beginnings to 1789;
RGWL 2, 3
Sade, Marquis de
See Sade, Donatien Alphonse Francois
Sadoff, Ira 1945- .... **CLC 9**
See also CA 53-56; CANR 5, 21, 109; DLB
120
Saetone
See Camus, Albert
Safire, William 1929- .... **CLC 10**
See also CA 17-20R; CANR 31, 54, 91

Sagan, Carl (Edward) 1934-1996 .... **CLC 30,**
112
See also AAYA 2; CA 25-28R; 155; CANR
11, 36, 74; CPW; DA3; MTCW 1, 2;
SATA 58; SATA-Obit 94
Sagan, Francoise .... **CLC 3, 6, 9, 17, 36**
See Quoirez, Francoise
See also CWW 2; DLB 83; EWL 3; GFL
1789 to the Present; MTCW 2
Sahgal, Nayantara (Pandit) 1927- .... **CLC 41**
See also CA 9-12R; CANR 11, 88; CN 7
Said, Edward W. 1935-2003 .... **CLC 123**
See also CA 21-24R; 220; CANR 45, 74,
107, 131; DLB 67; MTCW 2
Saint, H(arry) F. 1941- .... **CLC 50**
See also CA 127
St. Aubin de Teran, Lisa 1953-
See Teran, Lisa St. Aubin de
See also CA 118; 126; CN 7; INT CA-126
Saint Birgitta of Sweden c.
1303-1373 .... **CMLC 24**
Sainte-Beuve, Charles Augustin
1804-1869 .... **NCLC 5**
See also DLB 217; EW 6; GFL 1789 to the
Present
Saint-Exupery, Antoine (Jean Baptiste
Marie Roger) de 1900-1944 .... **TCLC 2,**
56; WLC
See also BPFB 3; BYA 3; CA 108; 132;
CLR 10; DA3; DAM NOV; DLB 72; EW
12; EWL 3; GFL 1789 to the Present;
LAIT 3; MAICYA 1, 2; MTCW 1, 2;
RGWL 2, 3; SATA 20; TWA
St. John, David
See Hunt, E(verette) Howard, (Jr.)
St. John, J. Hector
See Crevecoeur, Michel Guillaume Jean de
Saint-John Perse
See Leger, (Marie-Rene Auguste) Alexis
Saint-Leger
See also EW 10; EWL 3; GFL 1789 to the
Present; RGWL 2
Saintsbury, George (Edward Bateman)
1845-1933 .... **TCLC 31**
See also CA 160; DLB 57, 149
Sait Faik .... **TCLC 23**
See Abasiyanik, Sait Faik
Saki .... **SSC 12; TCLC 3**
See Munro, H(ector) H(ugh)
See also BRWS 6; BYA 11; LAIT 2; MTCW
2; RGEL 2; SSFS 1; SUFW
Sala, George Augustus 1828-1895 . **NCLC 46**
Saladin 1138-1193 .... **CMLC 38**
Salama, Hannu 1936- .... **CLC 18**
See also EWL 3
Salamanca, J(ack) R(ichard) 1922- .. **CLC 4,**
15
See also CA 25-28R, 193; CAAE 193
Salas, Floyd Francis 1931- .... **HLC 2**
See also CA 119; CAAS 27; CANR 44, 75,
93; DAM MULT; DLB 82; HW 1, 2;
MTCW 2
Sale, J. Kirkpatrick
See Sale, Kirkpatrick
Sale, Kirkpatrick 1937- .... **CLC 68**
See also CA 13-16R; CANR 10
Salinas, Luis Omar 1937- ... **CLC 90; HLC 2**
See also AMWS 13; CA 131; CANR 81;
DAM MULT; DLB 82; HW 1, 2
Salinas (y Serrano), Pedro
1891(?)-1951 .... **TCLC 17**
See also CA 117; DLB 134; EWL 3
Salinger, J(erome) D(avid) 1919- .. **CLC 1, 3,**
8, 12, 55, 56, 138; SSC 2, 28, 65; WLC
See also AAYA 2, 36; AMW; AMWC 1;
BPFB 3; CA 5-8R; CANR 39, 129;
CDALB 1941-1968; CLR 18; CN 7; CPW
1; DA; DA3; DAB; DAC; DAM MST,
NOV, POP; DLB 2, 102, 173; EWL 3;

EXPN; LAIT 4; MAICYA 1, 2; MTCW
1, 2; NFS 1; RGAL 4; RGSF 2; SATA 67;
SSFS 17; TUS; WYA; YAW
Salisbury, John
See Caute, (John) David
Sallust c. 86B.C.-35B.C. .... **CMLC 68**
See also AW 2; CDWLB 1; DLB 211;
RGWL 2, 3
Salter, James 1925- .. **CLC 7, 52, 59; SSC 58**
See also AMWS 9; CA 73-76; CANR 107;
DLB 130
Saltus, Edgar (Everton) 1855-1921 . **TCLC 8**
See also CA 105; DLB 202; RGAL 4
Saltykov, Mikhail Evgrafovich
1826-1889 .... **NCLC 16**
See also DLB 238:
Saltykov-Shchedrin, N.
See Saltykov, Mikhail Evgrafovich
Samarakis, Andonis
See Samarakis, Antonis
See also EWL 3
Samarakis, Antonis 1919-2003 .... **CLC 5**
See Samarakis, Andonis
See also CA 25-28R; 224; CAAS 16; CANR
36
Sanchez, Florencio 1875-1910 .... **TCLC 37**
See also CA 153; DLB 305; EWL 3; HW 1;
LAW
Sanchez, Luis Rafael 1936- .... **CLC 23**
See also CA 128; DLB 305; EWL 3; HW 1;
WLIT 1
Sanchez, Sonia 1934- .... **BLC 3; CLC 5, 116;**
PC 9
See also BW 2, 3; CA 33-36R; CANR 24,
49, 74, 115; CLR 18; CP 7; CSW; CWP;
DA3; DAM MULT; DLB 41; DLBD 8;
EWL 3; MAICYA 1, 2; MTCW 1, 2;
SATA 22, 136; WP
Sancho, Ignatius 1729-1780 .... **LC 84**
Sand, George 1804-1876 ..... **NCLC 2, 42, 57;**
WLC
See also DA; DA3; DAB; DAC; DAM
MST, NOV; DLB 119, 192; EW 6; FW;
GFL 1789 to the Present; RGWL 2, 3;
TWA
Sandburg, Carl (August) 1878-1967 . **CLC 1,**
4, 10, 15, 35; PC 2, 41; WLC
See also AAYA 24; AMW; BYA 1, 3; CA
5-8R; 25-28R; CANR 35; CDALB 1865-
1917; CLR 67; DA; DA3; DAB; DAC;
DAM MST, POET; DLB 17, 54, 284;
EWL 3; EXPP; LAIT 2; MAICYA 1, 2;
MTCW 1, 2; PAB; PFS 3, 6, 12; RGAL
4; SATA 8; TUS; WCH; WP; WYA
Sandburg, Charles
See Sandburg, Carl (August)
Sandburg, Charles A.
See Sandburg, Carl (August)
Sanders, (James) Ed(ward) 1939- .... **CLC 53**
See Sanders, Edward
See also BG 3; CA 13-16R; CAAS 21;
CANR 13, 44, 78; CP 7; DAM POET;
DLB 16, 244
Sanders, Edward
See Sanders, (James) Ed(ward)
See also DLB 244
Sanders, Lawrence 1920-1998 .... **CLC 41**
See also BEST 89:4; BPFB 3; CA 81-84;
165; CANR 33, 62; CMW 4; CPW; DA3;
DAM POP; MTCW 1
Sanders, Noah
See Blount, Roy (Alton), Jr.
Sanders, Winston P.
See Anderson, Poul (William)
Sandoz, Mari(e Susette) 1900-1966 .. **CLC 28**
See also CA 1-4R; 25-28R; CANR 17, 64;
DLB 9, 212; LAIT 2; MTCW 1, 2; SATA
5; TCWW 2

Schrader, Paul (Joseph) 1946- .... **CLC 26**
See also CA 37-40R; CANR 41; DLB 44
Schreber, Daniel 1842-1911 .... **TCLC 123**
Schreiner, Olive (Emilie Albertina)
1855-1920 .... **TCLC 9**
See also AFW; BRWS 2; CA 105; 154;
DLB 18, 156, 190, 225; EWL 3; FW;
RGEL 2; TWA; WLIT 2; WWE 1
Schulberg, Budd (Wilson) 1914- .. **CLC 7, 48**
See also BPFB 3; CA 25-28R; CANR 19,
87; CN 7; DLB 6, 26, 28; DLBY 1981,
2001
Schulman, Arnold
See Trumbo, Dalton
Schulz, Bruno 1892-1942 .. **SSC 13; TCLC 5,**
51
See also CA 115; 123; CANR 86; CDWLB
4; DLB 215; EWL 3; MTCW 2; RGSF 2;
RGWL 2, 3
Schulz, Charles M(onroe)
1922-2000 .... **CLC 12**
See also AAYA 39; CA 9-12R; 187; CANR
6, 132; INT CANR-6; SATA 10; SATA-
Obit 118
Schumacher, E(rnst) F(riedrich)
1911-1977 .... **CLC 80**
See also CA 81-84; 73-76; CANR 34, 85
Schumann, Robert 1810-1856 ...... **NCLC 143**
Schuyler, George Samuel 1895-1977 .... **HR 3**
See also BW 2; CA 81-84; 73-76; CANR
42; DLB 29, 51
Schuyler, James Marcus 1923-1991 .. **CLC 5,**
23
See also CA 101; 134; DAM POET; DLB
5, 169; EWL 3; INT CA-101; WP
Schwartz, Delmore (David)
1913-1966 ... **CLC 2, 4, 10, 45, 87; PC 8**
See also AMWS 2; CA 17-18; 25-28R;
CANR 35; CAP 2; DLB 28, 48; EWL 3;
MTCW 1, 2; PAB; RGAL 4; TUS
Schwartz, Ernst
See Ozu, Yasujiro
Schwartz, John Burnham 1965- .... **CLC 59**
See also CA 132; CANR 116
Schwartz, Lynne Sharon 1939- .... **CLC 31**
See also CA 103; CANR 44, 89; DLB 218;
MTCW 2
Schwartz, Muriel A.
See Eliot, T(homas) S(tearns)
Schwarz-Bart, Andre 1928- .... **CLC 2, 4**
See also CA 89-92; CANR 109; DLB 299
Schwarz-Bart, Simone 1938- . **BLCS; CLC 7**
See also BW 2; CA 97-100; CANR 117;
EWL 3
Schwerner, Armand 1927-1999 .... **PC 42**
See also CA 9-12R; 179; CANR 50, 85; CP
7; DLB 165
Schwitters, Kurt (Hermann Edward Karl
Julius) 1887-1948 .... **TCLC 95**
See also CA 158
Schwob, Marcel (Mayer Andre)
1867-1905 .... **TCLC 20**
See also CA 117; 168; DLB 123; GFL 1789
to the Present
Sciascia, Leonardo 1921-1989 .. **CLC 8, 9, 41**
See also CA 85-88; 130; CANR 35; DLB
177; EWL 3; MTCW 1; RGWL 2, 3
Scoppettone, Sandra 1936- .... **CLC 26**
See Early, Jack
See also AAYA 11; BYA 8; CA 5-8R;
CANR 41, 73; GLL 1; MAICYA 2; MAI-
CYAS 1; SATA 9, 92; WYA; YAW
Scorsese, Martin 1942- .... **CLC 20, 89, 207**
See also AAYA 38; CA 110; 114; CANR
46, 85
Scotland, Jay
See Jakes, John (William)

Scott, Duncan Campbell
1862-1947 .... **TCLC 6**
See also CA 104; 153; DAC; DLB 92;
RGEL 2
Scott, Evelyn 1893-1963 .... **CLC 43**
See also CA 104; 112; CANR 64; DLB 9,
48; RHW
Scott, F(rancis) R(eginald)
1899-1985 .... **CLC 22**
See also CA 101; 114; CANR 87; DLB 88;
INT CA-101; RGEL 2
Scott, Frank
See Scott, F(rancis) R(eginald)
Scott, Joan .... **CLC 65**
Scott, Joanna 1960- .... **CLC 50**
See also CA 126; CANR 53, 92
Scott, Paul (Mark) 1920-1978 ...... **CLC 9, 60**
See also BRWS 1; CA 81-84; 77-80; CANR
33; DLB 14, 207; EWL 3; MTCW 1;
RGEL 2; RHW; WWE 1
Scott, Ridley 1937- .... **CLC 183**
See also AAYA 13, 43
Scott, Sarah 1723-1795 .... **LC 44**
See also DLB 39
Scott, Sir Walter 1771-1832 .... **NCLC 15, 69,**
110; PC 13; SSC 32; WLC
See also AAYA 22; BRW 4; BYA 2; CD-
BLB 1789-1832; DA; DAB; DAC; DAM
MST, NOV, POET; DLB 93, 107, 116,
144, 159; HGG; LAIT 1; RGEL 2; RGSF
2; SSFS 10; SUFW 1; TEA; WLIT 3;
YABC 2
Scribe, (Augustin) Eugene 1791-1861 . **DC 5;**
NCLC 16
See also DAM DRAM; DLB 192; GFL
1789 to the Present; RGWL 2, 3
Scrum, R.
See Crumb, R(obert)
Scudery, Georges de 1601-1667 .... **LC 75**
See also GFL Beginnings to 1789
Scudery, Madeleine de 1607-1701 .. **LC 2, 58**
See also DLB 268; GFL Beginnings to 1789
Scum
See Crumb, R(obert)
Scumbag, Little Bobby
See Crumb, R(obert)
Seabrook, John
See Hubbard, L(afayette) Ron(ald)
Seacole, Mary Jane Grant
1805-1881 .... **NCLC 147**
See also DLB 166
Sealy, I(rwin) Allan 1951- .... **CLC 55**
See also CA 136; CN 7
Search, Alexander
See Pessoa, Fernando (Antonio Nogueira)
Sebald, W(infried) G(eorg)
1944-2001 .... **CLC 194**
See also BRWS 8; CA 159; 202; CANR 98
Sebastian, Lee
See Silverberg, Robert
Sebastian Owl
See Thompson, Hunter S(tockton)
Sebestyen, Igen
See Sebestyen, Ouida
Sebestyen, Ouida 1924- .... **CLC 30**
See also AAYA 8; BYA 7; CA 107; CANR
40, 114; CLR 17; JRDA; MAICYA 1, 2;
SAAS 10; SATA 39, 140; WYA; YAW
Sebold, Alice 1963(?)- .... **CLC 193**
See also AAYA 56; CA 203
Second Duke of Buckingham
See Villiers, George
Secundus, H. Scriblerus
See Fielding, Henry
Sedges, John
See Buck, Pearl S(ydenstricker)

Sedgwick, Catharine Maria
1789-1867 .... **NCLC 19, 98**
See also DLB 1, 74, 183, 239, 243, 254;
RGAL 4
Seelye, John (Douglas) 1931- .... **CLC 7**
See also CA 97-100; CANR 70; INT CA-
97-100; TCWW 2
Seferiades, Giorgos Stylianou 1900-1971
See Seferis, George
See also CA 5-8R; 33-36R; CANR 5, 36;
MTCW 1
Seferis, George .... **CLC 5, 11**
See Seferiades, Giorgos Stylianou
See also EW 12; EWL 3; RGWL 2, 3
Segal, Erich (Wolf) 1937- .... **CLC 3, 10**
See also BEST 89:1; BPFB 3; CA 25-28R;
CANR 20, 36, 65, 113; CPW; DAM POP;
DLBY 1986; INT CANR-20; MTCW 1
Seger, Bob 1945- .... **CLC 35**
Seghers, Anna .... **CLC 7**
See Radvanyi, Netty
See also CDWLB 2; DLB 69; EWL 3
Seidel, Frederick (Lewis) 1936- .... **CLC 18**
See also CA 13-16R; CANR 8, 99; CP 7;
DLBY 1984
Seifert, Jaroslav 1901-1986 . **CLC 34, 44, 93;**
PC 47
See also CA 127; CDWLB 4; DLB 215;
EWL 3; MTCW 1, 2
Sei Shonagon c. 966-1017(?) .... **CMLC 6**
Sejour, Victor 1817-1874 .... **DC 10**
See also DLB 50
Sejour Marcou et Ferrand, Juan Victor
See Sejour, Victor
Selby, Hubert, Jr. 1928-2004 ..... **CLC 1, 2, 4,**
8; SSC 20
See also CA 13-16R; 226; CANR 33, 85;
CN 7; DLB 2, 227
Selzer, Richard 1928- .... **CLC 74**
See also CA 65-68; CANR 14, 106
Sembene, Ousmane
See Ousmane, Sembene
See also AFW; EWL 3; WLIT 2
Senancour, Etienne Pivert de
1770-1846 .... **NCLC 16**
See also DLB 119; GFL 1789 to the Present
Sender, Ramon (Jose) 1902-1982 ...... **CLC 8;**
HLC 2; TCLC 136
See also CA 5-8R; 105; CANR 8; DAM
MULT; EWL 3; HW 1; MTCW 1; RGWL
2, 3
Seneca, Lucius Annaeus c. 4B.C.-c.
65 .... **CMLC 6; DC 5**
See also AW 2; CDWLB 1; DAM DRAM;
DLB 211; RGWL 2, 3; TWA
Senghor, Leopold Sedar 1906-2001 ... **BLC 3;**
CLC 54, 130; PC 25
See also AFW; BW 2; CA 116; 125; 203;
CANR 47, 74, 134; CWW 2; DAM
MULT, POET; DNFS 2; EWL 3; GFL
1789 to the Present; MTCW 1, 2; TWA
Senior, Olive (Marjorie) 1941- .... **SSC 78**
See also BW 3; CA 154; CANR 86, 126;
CN 7; CP 7; CWP; DLB 157; EWL 3;
RGSF 2
Senna, Danzy 1970- .... **CLC 119**
See also CA 169; CANR 130
Serling, (Edward) Rod(man)
1924-1975 .... **CLC 30**
See also AAYA 14; AITN 1; CA 162; 57-
60; DLB 26; SFW 4
Serna, Ramon Gomez de la
See Gomez de la Serna, Ramon
Serpieres
See Guillevic, (Eugene)
Service, Robert
See Service, Robert W(illiam)
See also BYA 4; DAB; DLB 92

Shiel, M(atthew) P(hipps)
1865-1947 .... **TCLC 8**
See Holmes, Gordon
See also CA 106; 160; DLB 153; HGG;
MTCW 2; SFW 4; SUFW
Shields, Carol (Ann) 1935-2003 ...... **CLC 91,
113, 193**
See also AMWS 7; CA 81-84; 218; CANR
51, 74, 98, 133; CCA 1; CN 7; CPW;
DA3; DAC; MTCW 2
Shields, David (Jonathan) 1956- ..... **CLC 97**
See also CA 124; CANR 48, 99, 112
Shiga, Naoya 1883-1971 ..... **CLC 33; SSC 23**
See Shiga Naoya
See also CA 101; 33-36R; MJW; RGWL 3
Shiga Naoya
See Shiga, Naoya
See also DLB 180; EWL 3; RGWL 3
Shilts, Randy 1951-1994 .... **CLC 85**
See also AAYA 19; CA 115; 127; 144;
CANR 45; DA3; GLL 1; INT CA-127;
MTCW 2
Shimazaki, Haruki 1872-1943
See Shimazaki Toson
See also CA 105; 134; CANR 84; RGWL 3
Shimazaki Toson .... **TCLC 5**
See Shimazaki, Haruki
See also DLB 180; EWL 3
Shirley, James 1596-1666 .... **DC 25; LC 96**
See also DLB 58; RGEL 2
Sholokhov, Mikhail (Aleksandrovich)
1905-1984 .... **CLC 7, 15**
See also CA 101; 112; DLB 272; EWL 3;
MTCW 1, 2; RGWL 2, 3; SATA-Obit 36
Shone, Patric
See Hanley, James
Showalter, Elaine 1941- .... **CLC 169**
See also CA 57-60; CANR 58, 106; DLB
67; FW; GLL 2
Shreve, Susan
See Shreve, Susan Richards
Shreve, Susan Richards 1939- .... **CLC 23**
See also CA 49-52; CAAS 5; CANR 5, 38,
69, 100; MAICYA 1, 2; SATA 46, 95, 152;
SATA-Brief 41
Shue, Larry 1946-1985 .... **CLC 52**
See also CA 145; 117; DAM DRAM; DFS
7
Shu-Jen, Chou 1881-1936
See Lu Hsun
See also CA 104
Shulman, Alix Kates 1932- .... **CLC 2, 10**
See also CA 29-32R; CANR 43; FW; SATA
7
Shuster, Joe 1914-1992 .... **CLC 21**
See also AAYA 50
Shute, Nevil .... **CLC 30**
See Norway, Nevil Shute
See also BPFB 3; DLB 255; NFS 9; RHW;
SFW 4
Shuttle, Penelope (Diane) 1947- .... **CLC 7**
See also CA 93-96; CANR 39, 84, 92, 108;
CP 7; CWP; DLB 14, 40
Shvarts, Elena 1948- .... **PC 50**
See also CA 147
Sidhwa, Bapsy (N.) 1938- .... **CLC 168**
See also CA 108; CANR 25, 57; CN 7; FW
Sidney, Mary 1561-1621 .... **LC 19, 39**
See Sidney Herbert, Mary
Sidney, Sir Philip 1554-1586 . **LC 19, 39; PC
32**
See also BRW 1; BRWR 2; CDBLB Before
1660; DA; DA3; DAB; DAC; DAM MST,
POET; DLB 167; EXPP; PAB; RGEL 2;
TEA; WP
Sidney Herbert, Mary
See Sidney, Mary
See also DLB 167

Siegel, Jerome 1914-1996 .... **CLC 21**
See Siegel, Jerry
See also CA 116; 169; 151
Siegel, Jerry
See Siegel, Jerome
See also AAYA 50
Sienkiewicz, Henryk (Adam Alexander Pius)
1846-1916 .... **TCLC 3**
See also CA 104; 134; CANR 84; EWL 3;
RGSF 2; RGWL 2, 3
Sierra, Gregorio Martinez
See Martinez Sierra, Gregorio
Sierra, Maria (de la O'LeJarraga) Martinez
See Martinez Sierra, Maria (de la
O'LeJarraga)
Sigal, Clancy 1926- .... **CLC 7**
See also CA 1-4R; CANR 85; CN 7
Siger of Brabant 1240(?)-1284(?) . **CMLC 69**
See also DLB 115
Sigourney, Lydia H.
See Sigourney, Lydia Howard (Huntley)
See also DLB 73, 183
Sigourney, Lydia Howard (Huntley)
1791-1865 .... **NCLC 21, 87**
See Sigourney, Lydia H.; Sigourney, Lydia
Huntley
See also DLB 1
Sigourney, Lydia Huntley
See Sigourney, Lydia Howard (Huntley)
See also DLB 42, 239, 243
Siguenza y Gongora, Carlos de
1645-1700 .... **HLCS 2; LC 8**
See also LAW
Sigurjonsson, Johann
See Sigurjonsson, Johann
Sigurjonsson, Johann 1880-1919 ... **TCLC 27**
See also CA 170; DLB 293; EWL 3
Sikelianos, Angelos 1884-1951 .... **PC 29;
TCLC 39**
See also EWL 3; RGWL 2, 3
Silkin, Jon 1930-1997 .... **CLC 2, 6, 43**
See also CA 5-8R; CAAS 5; CANR 89; CP
7; DLB 27
Silko, Leslie (Marmon) 1948- .... **CLC 23, 74,
114; NNAL; SSC 37, 66; WLCS**
See also AAYA 14; AMWS 4; ANW; BYA
12; CA 115; 122; CANR 45, 65, 118; CN
7; CP 7; CPW 1; CWP; DA; DA3; DAC;
DAM MST, MULT, POP; DLB 143, 175,
256, 275; EWL 3; EXPP; EXPS; LAIT 4;
MTCW 4; NFS 4; PFS 9, 16; RGAL 4;
RGSF 2; SSFS 4, 8, 10, 11
Sillanpaa, Frans Eemil 1888-1964 ... **CLC 19**
See also CA 129; 93-96; EWL 3; MTCW 1
Sillitoe, Alan 1928- .. **CLC 1, 3, 6, 10, 19, 57,
148**
See also AITN 1; BRWS 5; CA 9-12R, 191;
CAAE 191; CAAS 2; CANR 8, 26, 55;
CDBLB 1960 to Present; CN 7; DLB 14,
139; EWL 3; MTCW 1, 2; RGEL 2;
RGSF 2; SATA 61
Silone, Ignazio 1900-1978 .... **CLC 4**
See also CA 25-28; 81-84; CANR 34; CAP
2; DLB 264; EW 12; EWL 3; MTCW 1;
RGSF 2; RGWL 2, 3
Silone, Ignazione
See Silone, Ignazio
Silver, Joan Micklin 1935- .... **CLC 20**
See also CA 114; 121; INT CA-121
Silver, Nicholas
See Faust, Frederick (Schiller)
See also TCWW 2
Silverberg, Robert 1935- .... **CLC 7, 140**
See also AAYA 24; BPFB 3; BYA 7, 9; CA
1-4R, 186; CAAE 186; CAAS 3; CANR
1, 20, 36, 85; CLR 59; CN 7; CPW; DAM
POP; DLB 8; INT CANR-20; MAICYA
1, 2; MTCW 1, 2; SATA 13, 91; SATA-
Essay 104; SCFW 2; SFW 4; SUFW 2

Silverstein, Alvin 1933- .... **CLC 17**
See also CA 49-52; CANR 2; CLR 25;
JRDA; MAICYA 1, 2; SATA 8, 69, 124
Silverstein, Shel(don Allan)
1932-1999 .... **PC 49**
See also AAYA 40; BW 3; CA 107; 179;
CANR 47, 74, 81; CLR 5, 96; CWRI 5;
JRDA; MAICYA 1, 2; MTCW 2; SATA
33, 92; SATA-Brief 27; SATA-Obit 116
Silverstein, Virginia B(arbara Opshelor)
1937- .... **CLC 17**
See also CA 49-52; CANR 2; CLR 25;
JRDA; MAICYA 1, 2; SATA 8, 69, 124
Sim, Georges
See Simenon, Georges (Jacques Christian)
Simak, Clifford D(onald) 1904-1988 . **CLC 1,
55**
See also CA 1-4R; 125; CANR 1, 35; DLB
8; MTCW 1; SATA-Obit 56; SFW 4
Simenon, Georges (Jacques Christian)
1903-1989 .... **CLC 1, 2, 3, 8, 18, 47**
See also BPFB 3; CA 85-88; 129; CANR
35; CMW 4; DA3; DAM POP; DLB 72;
DLBY 1989; EW 12; EWL 3; GFL 1789
to the Present; MSW; MTCW 1, 2; RGWL
2, 3
Simic, Charles 1938- .... **CLC 6, 9, 22, 49, 68,
130**
See also AMWS 8; CA 29-32R; CAAS 4;
CANR 12, 33, 52, 61, 96; CP 7; DA3;
DAM POET; DLB 105; MTCW 2; PFS 7;
RGAL 4; WP
Simmel, Georg 1858-1918 .... **TCLC 64**
See also CA 157; DLB 296
Simmons, Charles (Paul) 1924- .... **CLC 57**
See also CA 89-92; INT CA-89-92
Simmons, Dan 1948- .... **CLC 44**
See also AAYA 16, 54; CA 138; CANR 53,
81, 126; CPW; DAM POP; HGG; SUFW
2
Simmons, James (Stewart Alexander)
1933- .... **CLC 43**
See also CA 105; CAAS 21; CP 7; DLB 40
Simms, William Gilmore
1806-1870 .... **NCLC 3**
See also DLB 3, 30, 59, 73, 248, 254;
RGAL 4
Simon, Carly 1945- .... **CLC 26**
See also CA 105
Simon, Claude (Eugene Henri)
1913-1984 .... **CLC 4, 9, 15, 39**
See also CA 89-92; CANR 33, 117; CWW
2; DAM NOV; DLB 83; EW 13; EWL 3;
GFL 1789 to the Present; MTCW 1
Simon, Myles
See Follett, Ken(neth Martin)
Simon, (Marvin) Neil 1927- ... **CLC 6, 11, 31,
39, 70; DC 14**
See also AAYA 32; AITN 1; AMWS 4; CA
21-24R; CANR 26, 54, 87, 126; CD 5;
DA3; DAM DRAM; DFS 2, 6, 12, 18;
DLB 7, 266; LAIT 4; MTCW 1, 2; RGAL
4; TUS
Simon, Paul (Frederick) 1941(?)- ..... **CLC 17**
See also CA 116; 153
Simonon, Paul 1956(?)- .... **CLC 30**
Simonson, Rick ed. .... **CLC 70**
Simpson, Harriette
See Arnow, Harriette (Louisa) Simpson
Simpson, Louis (Aston Marantz)
1923- .... **CLC 4, 7, 9, 32, 149**
See also AMWS 9; CA 1-4R; CAAS 4;
CANR 1, 61; CP 7; DAM POET; DLB 5;
MTCW 1, 2; PFS 7, 11, 14; RGAL 4
Simpson, Mona (Elizabeth) 1957- ... **CLC 44,
146**
See also CA 122; 135; CANR 68, 103; CN
7; EWL 3

Simpson, N(orman) F(rederick)
1919- .... **CLC 29**
See also CA 13-16R; CBD; DLB 13; RGEL
2

Sinclair, Andrew (Annandale) 1935- . **CLC 2, 14**
See also CA 9-12R; CAAS 5; CANR 14, 38, 91; CN 7; DLB 14; FANT; MTCW 1

Sinclair, Emil
See Hesse, Hermann

Sinclair, Iain 1943- .... **CLC 76**
See also CA 132; CANR 81; CP 7; HGG

Sinclair, Iain MacGregor
See Sinclair, Iain

Sinclair, Irene
See Griffith, D(avid Lewelyn) W(ark)

Sinclair, Mary Amelia St. Clair 1865(?)-1946
See Sinclair, May
See also CA 104; HGG; RHW

Sinclair, May .... **TCLC 3, 11**
See Sinclair, Mary Amelia St. Clair
See also CA 166; DLB 36, 135; EWL 3; RGEL 2; SUFW

Sinclair, Roy
See Griffith, D(avid Lewelyn) W(ark)

Sinclair, Upton (Beall) 1878-1968 ..... **CLC 1, 11, 15, 63; TCLC 160; WLC**
See also AMWS 5; BPFB 3; BYA 2; CA 5-8R; 25-28R; CANR 7; CDALB 1929-1941; DA; DA3; DAB; DAC; DAM MST, NOV; DLB 9; EWL 3; INT CANR-7; LAIT 3; MTCW 1, 2; NFS 6; RGAL 4; SATA 9; TUS; YAW

Singe, (Edmund) J(ohn) M(illington)
1871-1909 .... **WLC**

Singer, Isaac
See Singer, Isaac Bashevis

Singer, Isaac Bashevis 1904-1991 .. **CLC 1, 3, 6, 9, 11, 15, 23, 38, 69, 111; SSC 3, 53, 80; WLC**
See also AAYA 32; AITN 1, 2; AMW; AMWR 2; BPFB 3; BYA 1, 4; CA 1-4R; 134; CANR 1, 39, 106; CDALB 1941-1968; CLR 1; CWRI 5; DA; DA3; DAB; DAC; DAM MST, NOV; DLB 6, 28, 52, 278; DLBY 1991; EWL 3; EXPS; HGG; JRDA; LAIT 3; MAICYA 1, 2; MTCW 1, 2; RGAL 4; RGSF 2; SATA 3, 27; SATA-Obit 68; SSFS 2, 12, 16; TUS; TWA

Singer, Israel Joshua 1893-1944 .... **TCLC 33**
See also CA 169; EWL 3

Singh, Khushwant 1915- .... **CLC 11**
See also CA 9-12R; CAAS 9; CANR 6, 84; CN 7; EWL 3; RGEL 2

Singleton, Ann
See Benedict, Ruth (Fulton)

Singleton, John 1968(?)- .... **CLC 156**
See also AAYA 50; BW 2, 3; CA 138; CANR 67, 82; DAM MULT

Siniavskii, Andrei
See Sinyavsky, Andrei (Donatevich)
See also CWW 2

Sinjohn, John
See Galsworthy, John

Sinyavsky, Andrei (Donatevich)
1925-1997 .... **CLC 8**
See Siniavskii, Andrei; Sinyavsky, Andrey Donatovich; Tertz, Abram
See also CA 85-88; 159

Sinyavsky, Andrey Donatovich
See Sinyavsky, Andrei (Donatevich)
See also EWL 3

Sirin, V.
See Nabokov, Vladimir (Vladimirovich)

Sissman, L(ouis) E(dward)
1928-1976 .... **CLC 9, 18**
See also CA 21-24R; 65-68; CANR 13; DLB 5

Sisson, C(harles) H(ubert)
1914-2003 .... **CLC 8**
See also CA 1-4R; 220; CAAS 3; CANR 3, 48, 84; CP 7; DLB 27

Sitting Bull 1831(?)-1890 .... **NNAL**
See also DA3; DAM MULT

Sitwell, Dame Edith 1887-1964 ..... **CLC 2, 9, 67; PC 3**
See also BRW 7; CA 9-12R; CANR 35; CDBLB 1945-1960; DAM POET; DLB 20; EWL 3; MTCW 1, 2; RGEL 2; TEA

Siwaarmill, H. P.
See Sharp, William

Sjoewall, Maj 1935- .... **CLC 7**
See Sjowall, Maj
See also CA 65-68; CANR 73

Sjowall, Maj
See Sjoewall, Maj
See also BPFB 3; CMW 4; MSW

Skelton, John 1460(?)-1529 ..... **LC 71; PC 25**
See also BRW 1; DLB 136; RGEL 2

Skelton, Robin 1925-1997 .... **CLC 13**
See Zuk, Georges
See also AITN 2; CA 5-8R; 160; CAAS 5; CANR 28, 89; CCA 1; CP 7; DLB 27, 53

Skolimowski, Jerzy 1938- .... **CLC 20**
See also CA 128

Skram, Amalie (Bertha)
1847-1905 .... **TCLC 25**
See also CA 165

Skvorecky, Josef (Vaclav) 1924- ...... **CLC 15, 39, 69, 152**
See also CA 61-64; CAAS 1; CANR 10, 34, 63, 108; CDWLB 4; CWW 2; DA3; DAC; DAM NOV; DLB 232; EWL 3; MTCW 1, 2

Slade, Bernard .... **CLC 11, 46**
See Newbound, Bernard Slade
See also CAAS 9; CCA 1; DLB 53

Slaughter, Carolyn 1946- .... **CLC 56**
See also CA 85-88; CANR 85; CN 7

Slaughter, Frank G(ill) 1908-2001 ... **CLC 29**
See also AITN 2; CA 5-8R; 197; CANR 5, 85; INT CANR-5; RHW

Slavitt, David R(ytman) 1935- ..... **CLC 5, 14**
See also CA 21-24R; CAAS 3; CANR 41, 83; CP 7; DLB 5, 6

Slesinger, Tess 1905-1945 .... **TCLC 10**
See also CA 107; 199; DLB 102

Slessor, Kenneth 1901-1971 .... **CLC 14**
See also CA 102; 89-92; DLB 260; RGEL 2

Slowacki, Juliusz 1809-1849 .... **NCLC 15**
See also RGWL 3

Smart, Christopher 1722-1771 . **LC 3; PC 13**
See also DAM POET; DLB 109; RGEL 2

Smart, Elizabeth 1913-1986 .... **CLC 54**
See also CA 81-84; 118; DLB 88

Smiley, Jane (Graves) 1949- ...... **CLC 53, 76, 144**
See also AMWS 6; BPFB 3; CA 104; CANR 30, 50, 74, 96; CN 7; CPW 1; DA3; DAM POP; DLB 227, 234; EWL 3; INT CANR-30; SSFS 19

Smith, A(rthur) J(ames) M(arshall)
1902-1980 .... **CLC 15**
See also CA 1-4R; 102; CANR 4; DAC; DLB 88; RGEL 2

Smith, Adam 1723(?)-1790 .... **LC 36**
See also DLB 104, 252; RGEL 2

Smith, Alexander 1829-1867 .... **NCLC 59**
See also DLB 32, 55

Smith, Anna Deavere 1950- .... **CLC 86**
See also CA 133; CANR 103; CD 5; DFS 2

Smith, Betty (Wehner) 1904-1972 .... **CLC 19**
See also BPFB 3; BYA 3; CA 5-8R; 33-36R; DLBY 1982; LAIT 3; RGAL 4; SATA 6

Smith, Charlotte (Turner)
1749-1806 .... **NCLC 23, 115**
See also DLB 39, 109; RGEL 2; TEA

Smith, Clark Ashton 1893-1961 .... **CLC 43**
See also CA 143; CANR 81; FANT; HGG; MTCW 2; SCFW 2; SFW 4; SUFW

Smith, Dave .... **CLC 22, 42**
See Smith, David (Jeddie)
See also CAAS 7; DLB 5

Smith, David (Jeddie) 1942-
See Smith, Dave
See also CA 49-52; CANR 1, 59, 120; CP 7; CSW; DAM POET

Smith, Florence Margaret 1902-1971
See Smith, Stevie
See also CA 17-18; 29-32R; CANR 35; CAP 2; DAM POET; MTCW 1, 2; TEA

Smith, Iain Crichton 1928-1998 .... **CLC 64**
See also BRWS 9; CA 21-24R; 171; CN 7; CP 7; DLB 40, 139; RGSF 2

Smith, John 1580(?)-1631 .... **LC 9**
See also DLB 24, 30; TUS

Smith, Johnston
See Crane, Stephen (Townley)

Smith, Joseph, Jr. 1805-1844 .... **NCLC 53**

Smith, Lee 1944- .... **CLC 25, 73**
See also CA 114; 119; CANR 46, 118; CSW; DLB 143; DLBY 1983; EWL 3; INT CA-119; RGAL 4

Smith, Martin
See Smith, Martin Cruz

Smith, Martin Cruz 1942- .. **CLC 25; NNAL**
See also BEST 89:4; BPFB 3; CA 85-88; CANR 6, 23, 43, 65, 119; CMW 4; CPW; DAM MULT, POP; HGG; INT CANR-23; MTCW 2; RGAL 4

Smith, Patti 1946- .... **CLC 12**
See also CA 93-96; CANR 63

Smith, Pauline (Urmson)
1882-1959 .... **TCLC 25**
See also DLB 225; EWL 3

Smith, Rosamond
See Oates, Joyce Carol

Smith, Sheila Kaye
See Kaye-Smith, Sheila

Smith, Stevie .... **CLC 3, 8, 25, 44; PC 12**
See Smith, Florence Margaret
See also BRWS 2; DLB 20; EWL 3; MTCW 2; PAB; PFS 3; RGEL 2

Smith, Wilbur (Addison) 1933- .... **CLC 33**
See also CA 13-16R; CANR 7, 46, 66, 134; CPW; MTCW 1, 2

Smith, William Jay 1918- .... **CLC 6**
See also AMWS 13; CA 5-8R; CANR 44, 106; CP 7; CSW; CWRI 5; DLB 5; MAI-CYA 1, 2; SAAS 22; SATA 2, 68, 154; SATA-Essay 154

Smith, Woodrow Wilson
See Kuttner, Henry

Smith, Zadie 1976- .... **CLC 158**
See also AAYA 50; CA 193

Smolenskin, Peretz 1842-1885 .... **NCLC 30**

Smollett, Tobias (George) 1721-1771 ... **LC 2, 46**
See also BRW 3; CDBLB 1660-1789; DLB 39, 104; RGEL 2; TEA

Snodgrass, W(illiam) D(e Witt)
1926- .... **CLC 2, 6, 10, 18, 68**
See also AMWS 6; CA 1-4R; CANR 6, 36, 65, 85; CP 7; DAM POET; DLB 5; MTCW 1, 2; RGAL 4

Snorri Sturluson 1179-1241 .... **CMLC 56**
See also RGWL 2, 3

Snow, C(harles) P(ercy) 1905-1980 ... **CLC 1, 4, 6, 9, 13, 19**
See also BRW 7; CA 5-8R; 101; CANR 28; CDBLB 1945-1960; DAM NOV; DLB 15, 77; DLBD 17; EWL 3; MTCW 1, 2; RGEL 2; TEA

NOV; DLB 145; DNFS 2; EWL 3; HW 1, 2; LAIT 5; LATS 1:2; LAW; LAWS 1; MTCW 1, 2; RGWL 2; SSFS 14; TWA; WLIT 1

Varnhagen von Ense, Rahel
1771-1833 .... **NCLC 130**
See also DLB 90

Vasari, Giorgio 1511-1574 .... **LC 114**

Vasiliu, George
See Bacovia, George

Vasiliu, Gheorghe
See Bacovia, George
See also CA 123; 189

Vassa, Gustavus
See Equiano, Olaudah

Vassilikos, Vassilis 1933- .... **CLC 4, 8**
See also CA 81-84; CANR 75; EWL 3

Vaughan, Henry 1621-1695 .... **LC 27**
See also BRW 2; DLB 131; PAB; RGEL 2

Vaughn, Stephanie .... **CLC 62**

Vazov, Ivan (Minchov) 1850-1921 . **TCLC 25**
See also CA 121; 167; CDWLB 4; DLB 147

Veblen, Thorstein B(unde)
1857-1929 .... **TCLC 31**
See also AMWS 1; CA 115; 165; DLB 246

Vega, Lope de 1562-1635 .... **HLCS 2; LC 23**
See also EW 2; RGWL 2, 3

Vendler, Helen (Hennessy) 1933- ... **CLC 138**
See also CA 41-44R; CANR 25, 72; MTCW 1, 2

Venison, Alfred
See Pound, Ezra (Weston Loomis)

Ventsel, Elena Sergeevna 1907-2002
See Grekova, I.
See also CA 154

Verdi, Marie de
See Mencken, H(enry) L(ouis)

Verdu, Matilde
See Cela, Camilo Jose

Verga, Giovanni (Carmelo)
1840-1922 .... **SSC 21; TCLC 3**
See also CA 104; 123; CANR 101; EW 7; EWL 3; RGSF 2; RGWL 2, 3

Vergil 70B.C.-19B.C. ... **CMLC 9, 40; PC 12; WLCS**
See Virgil
See also AW 2; DA; DA3; DAB; DAC; DAM MST, POET; EFS 1; LMFS 1

Vergil, Polydore c. 1470-1555 .... **LC 108**
See also DLB 132

Verhaeren, Emile (Adolphe Gustave)
1855-1916 .... **TCLC 12**
See also CA 109; EWL 3; GFL 1789 to the Present

Verlaine, Paul (Marie) 1844-1896 .. **NCLC 2, 51; PC 2, 32**
See also DAM POET; DLB 217; EW 7; GFL 1789 to the Present; LMFS 2; RGWL 2, 3; TWA

Verne, Jules (Gabriel) 1828-1905 ... **TCLC 6, 52**
See also AAYA 16; BYA 4; CA 110; 131; CLR 88; DA3; GFL 1789 to the Present; JRDA; LAIT 2; LMFS 2; MAICYA 1, 2; RGWL 2, 3; SATA 21; SCFW; SFW 4; TWA; WCH

Verus, Marcus Annius
See Aurelius, Marcus

Very, Jones 1813-1880 .... **NCLC 9**
See also DLB 1, 243; RGAL 4

Vesaas, Tarjei 1897-1970 .... **CLC 48**
See also CA 190; 29-32R; DLB 297; EW 11; EWL 3; RGWL 3

Vialis, Gaston
See Simenon, Georges (Jacques Christian)

Vian, Boris 1920-1959(?) .... **TCLC 9**
See also CA 106; 164; CANR 111; DLB 72; EWL 3; GFL 1789 to the Present; MTCW 2; RGWL 2, 3

Viaud, (Louis Marie) Julien 1850-1923
See Loti, Pierre
See also CA 107

Vicar, Henry
See Felsen, Henry Gregor

Vicente, Gil 1465-c. 1536 .... **LC 99**
See also DLB 287; RGWL 2, 3

Vicker, Angus
See Felsen, Henry Gregor

Vidal, (Eugene Luther) Gore 1925- .. **CLC 2, 4, 6, 8, 10, 22, 33, 72, 142**
See Box, Edgar
See also AITN 1; AMWS 4; BEST 90:2; BPFB 3; CA 5-8R; CAD; CANR 13, 45, 65, 100, 132; CD 5; CDALBS; CN 7; CPW; DA3; DAM NOV, POP; DFS 2; DLB 6, 152; EWL 3; INT CANR-13; MTCW 1, 2; RGAL 4; RHW; TUS

Viereck, Peter (Robert Edwin)
1916- .... **CLC 4; PC 27**
See also CA 1-4R; CANR 1, 47; CP 7; DLB 5; PFS 9, 14

Vigny, Alfred (Victor) de
1797-1863 .... **NCLC 7, 102; PC 26**
See also DAM POET; DLB 119, 192, 217; EW 5; GFL 1789 to the Present; RGWL 2, 3

Vilakazi, Benedict Wallet
1906-1947 .... **TCLC 37**
See also CA 168

Villa, Jose Garcia 1914-1997 .... **AAL; PC 22**
See also CA 25-28R; CANR 12, 118; EWL 3; EXPP

Villa, Jose Garcia 1914-1997
See Villa, Jose Garcia

Villa, Jose Garcia 1914-1997 .... **AAL; PC 22**
See also CA 25-28R; CANR 12, 118; EWL 3; EXPP

Villard, Oswald Garrison
1872-1949 .... **TCLC 160**
See also CA 113; 162; DLB 25, 91

Villaurrutia, Xavier 1903-1950 .... **TCLC 80**
See also CA 192; EWL 3; HW 1; LAW

Villaverde, Cirilo 1812-1894 .... **NCLC 121**
See also LAW

Villehardouin, Geoffroi de
1150(?)-1218(?) .... **CMLC 38**

Villiers, George 1628-1687 .... **LC 107**
See also DLB 80; RGEL 2

Villiers de l'Isle Adam, Jean Marie Mathias Philippe Auguste 1838-1889 ... **NCLC 3; SSC 14**
See also DLB 123, 192; GFL 1789 to the Present; RGSF 2

Villon, Francois 1431-1463(?) . **LC 62; PC 13**
See also DLB 208; EW 2; RGWL 2, 3; TWA

Vine, Barbara .... **CLC 50**
See Rendell, Ruth (Barbara)
See also BEST 90:4

Vinge, Joan (Carol) D(ennison)
1948- .... **CLC 30; SSC 24**
See also AAYA 32; BPFB 3; CA 93-96; CANR 72; SATA 36, 113; SFW 4; YAW

Viola, Herman J(oseph) 1938- .... **CLC 70**
See also CA 61-64; CANR 8, 23, 48, 91; SATA 126

Violis, G.
See Simenon, Georges (Jacques Christian)

Viramontes, Helena Maria 1954- .... **HLCS 2**
See also CA 159; DLB 122; HW 2; LLW 1

Virgil
See Vergil
See also CDWLB 1; DLB 211; LAIT 1; RGWL 2, 3; WP

Visconti, Luchino 1906-1976 .... **CLC 16**
See also CA 81-84; 65-68; CANR 39

Vitry, Jacques de
See Jacques de Vitry

Vittorini, Elio 1908-1966 .... **CLC 6, 9, 14**
See also CA 133; 25-28R; DLB 264; EW 12; EWL 3; RGWL 2, 3

Vivekananda, Swami 1863-1902 .... **TCLC 88**

Vizenor, Gerald Robert 1934- .... **CLC 103; NNAL**
See also CA 13-16R, 205; CAAE 205; CAAS 22; CANR 5, 21, 44, 67; DAM MULT; DLB 175, 227; MTCW 2; TCWW 2

Vizinczey, Stephen 1933- .... **CLC 40**
See also CA 128; CCA 1; INT CA-128

Vliet, R(ussell) G(ordon)
1929-1984 .... **CLC 22**
See also CA 37-40R; 112; CANR 18

Vogau, Boris Andreyevich 1894-1938
See Pilnyak, Boris
See also CA 123; 218

Vogel, Paula A(nne) 1951- ... **CLC 76; DC 19**
See also CA 108; CAD; CANR 119; CD 5; CWD; DFS 14; RGAL 4

Voigt, Cynthia 1942- .... **CLC 30**
See also AAYA 3, 30; BYA 1, 3, 6, 7, 8; CA 106; CANR 18, 37, 40, 94; CLR 13, 48; INT CANR-18; JRDA; LAIT 5; MAICYA 1, 2; MAICYAS 1; SATA 48, 79, 116; SATA-Brief 33; WYA; YAW

Voigt, Ellen Bryant 1943- .... **CLC 54**
See also CA 69-72; CANR 11, 29, 55, 115; CP 7; CSW; CWP; DLB 120

Voinovich, Vladimir (Nikolaevich)
1932- .... **CLC 10, 49, 147**
See also CA 81-84; CAAS 12; CANR 33, 67; CWW 2; DLB 302; MTCW 1

Vollmann, William T. 1959- .... **CLC 89**
See also CA 134; CANR 67, 116; CPW; DA3; DAM NOV, POP; MTCW 2

Voloshinov, V. N.
See Bakhtin, Mikhail Mikhailovich

Voltaire 1694-1778 . **LC 14, 79, 110; SSC 12; WLC**
See also BYA 13; DA; DA3; DAB; DAC; DAM DRAM, MST; EW 4; GFL Beginnings to 1789; LATS 1:1; LMFS 1; NFS 7; RGWL 2, 3; TWA

von Aschendrof, Baron Ignatz
See Ford, Ford Madox

von Chamisso, Adelbert
See Chamisso, Adelbert von

von Daeniken, Erich 1935- .... **CLC 30**
See also AITN 1; CA 37-40R; CANR 17, 44

von Daniken, Erich
See von Daeniken, Erich

von Hartmann, Eduard
1842-1906 .... **TCLC 96**

von Hayek, Friedrich August
See Hayek, F(riedrich) A(ugust von)

von Heidenstam, (Carl Gustaf) Verner
See Heidenstam, (Carl Gustaf) Verner von

von Heyse, Paul (Johann Ludwig)
See Heyse, Paul (Johann Ludwig von)

von Hofmannsthal, Hugo
See Hofmannsthal, Hugo von

von Horvath, Odon
See von Horvath, Odon

von Horvath, Odon
See von Horvath, Odon

von Horvath, Odon 1901-1938 .... **TCLC 45**
See von Horvath, Oedoen
See also CA 118; 194; DLB 85, 124; RGWL 2, 3

von Horvath, Oedoen
See von Horvath, Odon
See also CA 184

Warner, Sylvia (Constance) Ashton
See Ashton-Warner, Sylvia (Constance)
Warner, Sylvia Townsend
1893-1978 .. **CLC 7, 19; SSC 23; TCLC 131**
See also BRWS 7; CA 61-64; 77-80; CANR 16, 60, 104; DLB 34, 139; EWL 3; FANT; FW; MTCW 1, 2; RGEL 2; RGSF 2; RHW
Warren, Mercy Otis 1728-1814 ..... **NCLC 13**
See also DLB 31, 200; RGAL 4; TUS
Warren, Robert Penn 1905-1989 .. **CLC 1, 4, 6, 8, 10, 13, 18, 39, 53, 59; PC 37; SSC 4, 58; WLC**
See also AITN 1; AMW; AMWC 2; BPFB 3; BYA 1; CA 13-16R; 129; CANR 10, 47; CDALB 1968-1988; DA; DA3; DAB; DAC; DAM MST, NOV, POET; DLB 2, 48, 152; DLBY 1980, 1989; EWL 3; INT CANR-10; MTCW 1, 2; NFS 13; RGAL 4; RGSF 2; RHW; SATA 46; SATA-Obit 63; SSFS 8; TUS
Warrigal, Jack
See Furphy, Joseph
Warshofsky, Isaac
See Singer, Isaac Bashevis
Warton, Joseph 1722-1800 .... **NCLC 118**
See also DLB 104, 109; RGEL 2
Warton, Thomas 1728-1790 .... **LC 15, 82**
See also DAM POET; DLB 104, 109; RGEL 2
Waruk, Kona
See Harris, (Theodore) Wilson
Warung, Price .... **TCLC 45**
See Astley, William
See also DLB 230; RGEL 2
Warwick, Jarvis
See Garner, Hugh
See also CCA 1
Washington, Alex
See Harris, Mark
Washington, Booker T(aliaferro)
1856-1915 .... **BLC 3; TCLC 10**
See also BW 1; CA 114; 125; DA3; DAM MULT; LAIT 2; RGAL 4; SATA 28
Washington, George 1732-1799 .... **LC 25**
See also DLB 31
Wassermann, (Karl) Jakob
1873-1934 .... **TCLC 6**
See also CA 104; 163; DLB 66; EWL 3
Wasserstein, Wendy 1950- ... **CLC 32, 59, 90, 183; DC 4**
See also CA 121; 129; CABS 3; CAD; CANR 53, 75, 128; CD 5; CWD; DA3; DAM DRAM; DFS 5, 17; DLB 228; EWL 3; FW; INT CA-129; MTCW 2; SATA 94
Waterhouse, Keith (Spencer) 1929- . **CLC 47**
See also CA 5-8R; CANR 38, 67, 109; CBD; CN 7; DLB 13, 15; MTCW 1, 2
Waters, Frank (Joseph) 1902-1995 .. **CLC 88**
See also CA 5-8R; 149; CAAS 13; CANR 3, 18, 63, 121; DLB 212; DLBY 1986; RGAL 4; TCWW 2
Waters, Mary C. .... **CLC 70**
Waters, Roger 1944- .... **CLC 35**
Watkins, Frances Ellen
See Harper, Frances Ellen Watkins
Watkins, Gerrold
See Malzberg, Barry N(athaniel)
Watkins, Gloria Jean 1952(?)- .... **CLC 94**
See also BW 2; CA 143; CANR 87, 126; DLB 246; MTCW 2; SATA 115
Watkins, Paul 1964- .... **CLC 55**
See also CA 132; CANR 62, 98
Watkins, Vernon Phillips
1906-1967 .... **CLC 43**
See also CA 9-10; 25-28R; CAP 1; DLB 20; EWL 3; RGEL 2

Watson, Irving S.
See Mencken, H(enry) L(ouis)
Watson, John H.
See Farmer, Philip Jose
Watson, Richard F.
See Silverberg, Robert
Watts, Ephraim
See Horne, Richard Henry Hengist
Watts, Isaac 1674-1748 .... **LC 98**
See also DLB 95; RGEL 2; SATA 52
Waugh, Auberon (Alexander)
1939-2001 .... **CLC 7**
See also CA 45-48; 192; CANR 6, 22, 92; DLB 14, 194
Waugh, Evelyn (Arthur St. John)
1903-1966 .. **CLC 1, 3, 8, 13, 19, 27, 44, 107; SSC 41; WLC**
See also BPFB 3; BRW 7; CA 85-88; 25-28R; CANR 22; CDBLB 1914-1945; DA; DA3; DAB; DAC; DAM MST, NOV, POP; DLB 15, 162, 195; EWL 3; MTCW 1, 2; NFS 13, 17; RGEL 2; RGSF 2; TEA; WLIT 4
Waugh, Harriet 1944- .... **CLC 6**
See also CA 85-88; CANR 22
Ways, C. R.
See Blount, Roy (Alton), Jr.
Waystaff, Simon
See Swift, Jonathan
Webb, Beatrice (Martha Potter)
1858-1943 .... **TCLC 22**
See also CA 117; 162; DLB 190; FW
Webb, Charles (Richard) 1939- .... **CLC 7**
See also CA 25-28R; CANR 114
Webb, Frank J. .... **NCLC 143**
See also DLB 50
Webb, James H(enry), Jr. 1946- ...... **CLC 22**
See also CA 81-84
Webb, Mary Gladys (Meredith)
1881-1927 .... **TCLC 24**
See also CA 182; 123; DLB 34; FW
Webb, Mrs. Sidney
See Webb, Beatrice (Martha Potter)
Webb, Phyllis 1927- .... **CLC 18**
See also CA 104; CANR 23; CCA 1; CP 7; CWP; DLB 53
Webb, Sidney (James) 1859-1947 .. **TCLC 22**
See also CA 117; 163; DLB 190
Webber, Andrew Lloyd .... **CLC 21**
See Lloyd Webber, Andrew
See also DFS 7
Weber, Lenora Mattingly
1895-1971 .... **CLC 12**
See also CA 19-20; 29-32R; CAP 1; SATA 2; SATA-Obit 26
Weber, Max 1864-1920 .... **TCLC 69**
See also CA 109; 189; DLB 296
Webster, John 1580(?)-1634(?) ...... **DC 2; LC 33, 84; WLC**
See also BRW 2; CDBLB Before 1660; DA; DAB; DAC; DAM DRAM, MST; DFS 17, 19; DLB 58; IDTP; RGEL 2; WLIT 3
Webster, Noah 1758-1843 .... **NCLC 30**
See also DLB 1, 37, 42, 43, 73, 243
Wedekind, (Benjamin) Frank(lin)
1864-1918 .... **TCLC 7**
See also CA 104; 153; CANR 121, 122; CDWLB 2; DAM DRAM; DLB 118; EW 8; EWL 3; LMFS 2; RGWL 2, 3
Wehr, Demaris .... **CLC 65**
Weidman, Jerome 1913-1998 .... **CLC 7**
See also AITN 2; CA 1-4R; 171; CAD; CANR 1; DLB 28
Weil, Simone (Adolphine)
1909-1943 .... **TCLC 23**
See also CA 117; 159; EW 12; EWL 3; FW; GFL 1789 to the Present; MTCW 2
Weininger, Otto 1880-1903 .... **TCLC 84**

Weinstein, Nathan
See West, Nathanael
Weinstein, Nathan von Wallenstein
See West, Nathanael
Weir, Peter (Lindsay) 1944- .... **CLC 20**
See also CA 113; 123
Weiss, Peter (Ulrich) 1916-1982 .. **CLC 3, 15, 51; TCLC 152**
See also CA 45-48; 106; CANR 3; DAM DRAM; DFS 3; DLB 69, 124; EWL 3; RGWL 2, 3
Weiss, Theodore (Russell)
1916-2003 .... **CLC 3, 8, 14**
See also CA 9-12R, 189; 216; CAAE 189; CAAS 2; CANR 46, 94; CP 7; DLB 5
Welch, (Maurice) Denton
1915-1948 .... **TCLC 22**
See also BRWS 8, 9; CA 121; 148; RGEL 2
Welch, James (Phillip) 1940-2003 ..... **CLC 6, 14, 52; NNAL; PC 62**
See also CA 85-88; 219; CANR 42, 66, 107; CN 7; CP 7; CPW; DAM MULT, POP; DLB 175, 256; LATS 1:1; RGAL 4; TCWW 2
Weldon, Fay 1931- . **CLC 6, 9, 11, 19, 36, 59, 122**
See also BRWS 4; CA 21-24R; CANR 16, 46, 63, 97; CDBLB 1960 to Present; CN 7; CPW; DAM POP; DLB 14, 194; EWL 3; FW; HGG; INT CANR-16; MTCW 1, 2; RGEL 2; RGSF 2
Wellek, Rene 1903-1995 .... **CLC 28**
See also CA 5-8R; 150; CAAS 7; CANR 8; DLB 63; EWL 3; INT CANR-8
Weller, Michael 1942- .... **CLC 10, 53**
See also CA 85-88; CAD; CD 5
Weller, Paul 1958- .... **CLC 26**
Wellershoff, Dieter 1925- .... **CLC 46**
See also CA 89-92; CANR 16, 37
Welles, (George) Orson 1915-1985 .. **CLC 20, 80**
See also AAYA 40; CA 93-96; 117
Wellman, John McDowell 1945-
See Wellman, Mac
See also CA 166; CD 5
Wellman, Mac .... **CLC 65**
See Wellman, John McDowell; Wellman, John McDowell
See also CAD; RGAL 4
Wellman, Manly Wade 1903-1986 ... **CLC 49**
See also CA 1-4R; 118; CANR 6, 16, 44; FANT; SATA 6; SATA-Obit 47; SFW 4; SUFW
Wells, Carolyn 1869(?)-1942 .... **TCLC 35**
See also CA 113; 185; CMW 4; DLB 11
Wells, H(erbert) G(eorge) 1866-1946 . **SSC 6, 70; TCLC 6, 12, 19, 133; WLC**
See also AAYA 18; BPFB 3; BRW 6; CA 110; 121; CDBLB 1914-1945; CLR 64; DA; DA3; DAB; DAC; DAM MST, NOV; DLB 34, 70, 156, 178; EWL 3; EXPS; HGG; LAIT 3; LMFS 2; MTCW 1, 2; NFS 17, 20; RGEL 2; RGSF 2; SATA 20; SCFW; SFW 4; SSFS 3; SUFW; TEA; WCH; WLIT 4; YAW
Wells, Rosemary 1943- .... **CLC 12**
See also AAYA 13; BYA 7, 8; CA 85-88; CANR 48, 120; CLR 16, 69; CWRI 5; MAICYA 1, 2; SAAS 1; SATA 18, 69, 114; YAW
Wells-Barnett, Ida B(ell)
1862-1931 .... **TCLC 125**
See also CA 182; DLB 23, 221
Welsh, Irvine 1958- .... **CLC 144**
See also CA 173; DLB 271

Wicker, Tom .... CLC 7
See Wicker, Thomas Grey

Wideman, John Edgar 1941- ... **BLC 3; CLC 5, 34, 36, 67, 122; SSC 62**
See also AFAW 1, 2; AMWS 10; BPFB 4; BW 2, 3; CA 85-88; CANR 14, 42, 67, 109; CN 7; DAM MULT; DLB 33, 143; MTCW 2; RGAL 4; RGSF 2; SSFS 6, 12

Wiebe, Rudy (Henry) 1934- .. **CLC 6, 11, 14, 138**
See also CA 37-40R; CANR 42, 67, 123; CN 7; DAC; DAM MST; DLB 60; RHW

Wieland, Christoph Martin
1733-1813 .... **NCLC 17**
See also DLB 97; EW 4; LMFS 1; RGWL 2, 3

Wiene, Robert 1881-1938 .... **TCLC 56**

Wieners, John 1934- .... **CLC 7**
See also BG 3; CA 13-16R; CP 7; DLB 16; WP

Wiesel, Elie(zer) 1928- .... **CLC 3, 5, 11, 37, 165; WLCS**
See also AAYA 7, 54; AITN 1; CA 5-8R; CAAS 4; CANR 8, 40, 65, 125; CDALBS; CWW 2; DA; DA3; DAB; DAC; DAM MST, NOV; DLB 83, 299; DLBY 1987; EWL 3; INT CANR-8; LAIT 4; MTCW 1, 2; NCFS 4; NFS 4; RGWL 3; SATA 56; YAW

Wiggins, Marianne 1947- .... **CLC 57**
See also BEST 89:3; CA 130; CANR 60

Wigglesworth, Michael 1631-1705 .... **LC 106**
See also DLB 24; RGAL 4

Wiggs, Susan .... **CLC 70**
See also CA 201

Wight, James Alfred 1916-1995
See Herriot, James
See also CA 77-80; SATA 55; SATA-Brief 44

Wilbur, Richard (Purdy) 1921- ..... **CLC 3, 6, 9, 14, 53, 110; PC 51**
See also AMWS 3; CA 1-4R; CABS 2; CANR 2, 29, 76, 93; CDALBS; CP 7; DA; DAB; DAC; DAM MST, POET; DLB 5, 169; EWL 3; EXPP; INT CANR-29; MTCW 1, 2; PAB; PFS 11, 12, 16; RGAL 4; SATA 9, 108; WP

Wild, Peter 1940- .... **CLC 14**
See also CA 37-40R; CP 7; DLB 5

Wilde, Oscar (Fingal O'Flahertie Wills)
1854(?)-1900 .... **DC 17; SSC 11, 77; TCLC 1, 8, 23, 41; WLC**
See also AAYA 49; BRW 5; BRWC 1, 2; BRWR 2; BYA 15; CA 104; 119; CANR 112; CDBLB 1890-1914; DA; DA3; DAB; DAC; DAM DRAM, MST, NOV; DFS 4, 8, 9; DLB 10, 19, 34, 57, 141, 156, 190; EXPS; FANT; LATS 1:1; NFS 20; RGEL 2; RGSF 2; SATA 24; SSFS 7; SUFW; TEA; WCH; WLIT 4

Wilder, Billy .... **CLC 20**
See Wilder, Samuel
See also DLB 26

Wilder, Samuel 1906-2002
See Wilder, Billy
See also CA 89-92; 205

Wilder, Stephen
See Marlowe, Stephen

Wilder, Thornton (Niven)
1897-1975 .. **CLC 1, 5, 6, 10, 15, 35, 82; DC 1, 24; WLC**
See also AAYA 29; AITN 2; AMW; CA 13-16R; 61-64; CAD; CANR 40, 132; CDALBS; DA; DA3; DAB; DAC; DAM DRAM, MST, NOV; DFS 1, 4, 16; DLB 4, 7, 9, 228; DLBY 1997; EWL 3; LAIT 3; MTCW 1, 2; RGAL 4; RHW; WYAS 1

Wilding, Michael 1942- ...... **CLC 73; SSC 50**
See also CA 104; CANR 24, 49, 106; CN 7; RGSF 2

Wiley, Richard 1944- .... **CLC 44**
See also CA 121; 129; CANR 71

Wilhelm, Kate .... **CLC 7**
See Wilhelm, Katie (Gertrude)
See also AAYA 20; BYA 16; CAAS 5; DLB 8; INT CANR-17; SCFW 2

Wilhelm, Katie (Gertrude) 1928-
See Wilhelm, Kate
See also CA 37-40R; CANR 17, 36, 60, 94; MTCW 1; SFW 4

Wilkins, Mary
See Freeman, Mary E(leanor) Wilkins

Willard, Nancy 1936- .... **CLC 7, 37**
See also BYA 5; CA 89-92; CANR 10, 39, 68, 107; CLR 5; CWP; CWRI 5; DLB 5, 52; FANT; MAICYA 1, 2; MTCW 1; SATA 37, 71, 127; SATA-Brief 30; SUFW 2

William of Malmesbury c. 1090B.C.-c. 1140B.C. .... **CMLC 57**

William of Ockham 1290-1349 ..... **CMLC 32**

Williams, Ben Ames 1889-1953 ..... **TCLC 89**
See also CA 183; DLB 102

Williams, C(harles) K(enneth)
1936- .... **CLC 33, 56, 148**
See also CA 37-40R; CAAS 26; CANR 57, 106; CP 7; DAM POET; DLB 5

Williams, Charles
See Collier, James Lincoln

Williams, Charles (Walter Stansby)
1886-1945 .... **TCLC 1, 11**
See also BRWS 9; CA 104; 163; DLB 100, 153, 255; FANT; RGEL 2; SUFW 1

Williams, Ella Gwendolen Rees
See Rhys, Jean

Williams, (George) Emlyn
1905-1987 .... **CLC 15**
See also CA 104; 123; CANR 36; DAM DRAM; DLB 10, 77; IDTP; MTCW 1

Williams, Hank 1923-1953 .... **TCLC 81**
See Williams, Hiram King

Williams, Helen Maria
1761-1827 .... **NCLC 135**
See also DLB 158

Williams, Hiram Hank
See Williams, Hank

Williams, Hiram King
See Williams, Hank
See also CA 188

Williams, Hugo (Mordaunt) 1942- ... **CLC 42**
See also CA 17-20R; CANR 45, 119; CP 7; DLB 40

Williams, J. Walker
See Wodehouse, P(elham) G(renville)

Williams, John A(lfred) 1925- . **BLC 3; CLC 5, 13**
See also AFAW 2; BW 2, 3; CA 53-56; 195; CAAE 195; CAAS 3; CANR 6, 26, 51, 118; CN 7; CSW; DAM MULT; DLB 2, 33; EWL 3; INT CANR-6; RGAL 4; SFW 4

Williams, Jonathan (Chamberlain)
1929- .... **CLC 13**
See also CA 9-12R; CAAS 12; CANR 8, 108; CP 7; DLB 5

Williams, Joy 1944- .... **CLC 31**
See also CA 41-44R; CANR 22, 48, 97

Williams, Norman 1952- .... **CLC 39**
See also CA 118

Williams, Sherley Anne 1944-1999 ... **BLC 3; CLC 89**
See also AFAW 2; BW 2, 3; CA 73-76; 185; CANR 25, 82; DAM MULT, POET; DLB 41; INT CANR-25; SATA 78; SATA-Obit 116

Williams, Shirley
See Williams, Sherley Anne

Williams, Tennessee 1911-1983 . **CLC 1, 2, 5, 7, 8, 11, 15, 19, 30, 39, 45, 71, 111; DC 4; SSC 81; WLC**
See also AAYA 31; AITN 1, 2; AMW; AMWC 1; CA 5-8R; 108; CABS 3; CAD; CANR 31, 132; CDALB 1941-1968; DA; DA3; DAB; DAC; DAM DRAM, MST; DFS 17; DLB 7; DLBD 4; DLBY 1983; EWL 3; GLL 1; LAIT 4; LATS 1:2; MTCW 1, 2; RGAL 4; TUS

Williams, Thomas (Alonzo)
1926-1990 .... **CLC 14**
See also CA 1-4R; 132; CANR 2

Williams, William C.
See Williams, William Carlos

Williams, William Carlos
1883-1963 .... **CLC 1, 2, 5, 9, 13, 22, 42, 67; PC 7; SSC 31**
See also AAYA 46; AMW; AMWR 1; CA 89-92; CANR 34; CDALB 1917-1929; DA; DA3; DAB; DAC; DAM MST, POET; DLB 4, 16, 54, 86; EWL 3; EXPP; MTCW 1, 2; NCFS 4; PAB; PFS 1, 6, 11; RGAL 4; RGSF 2; TUS; WP

Williamson, David (Keith) 1942- ..... **CLC 56**
See also CA 103; CANR 41; CD 5; DLB 289

Williamson, Ellen Douglas 1905-1984
See Douglas, Ellen
See also CA 17-20R; 114; CANR 39

Williamson, Jack .... **CLC 29**
See Williamson, John Stewart
See also CAAS 8; DLB 8; SCFW 2

Williamson, John Stewart 1908-
See Williamson, Jack
See also CA 17-20R; CANR 23, 70; SFW 4

Willie, Frederick
See Lovecraft, H(oward) P(hillips)

Willingham, Calder (Baynard, Jr.)
1922-1995 .... **CLC 5, 51**
See also CA 5-8R; 147; CANR 3; CSW; DLB 2, 44; IDFW 3, 4; MTCW 1

Willis, Charles
See Clarke, Arthur C(harles)

Willy
See Colette, (Sidonie-Gabrielle)

Willy, Colette
See Colette, (Sidonie-Gabrielle)
See also GLL 1

Wilmot, John 1647-1680 .... **LC 75**
See Rochester
See also BRW 2; DLB 131; PAB

Wilson, A(ndrew) N(orman) 1950- ... **CLC 33**
See also BRWS 6; CA 112; 122; CN 7; DLB 14, 155, 194; MTCW 2

Wilson, Angus (Frank Johnstone)
1913-1991 . **CLC 2, 3, 5, 25, 34; SSC 21**
See also BRWS 1; CA 5-8R; 134; CANR 21; DLB 15, 139, 155; EWL 3; MTCW 1, 2; RGEL 2; RGSF 2

Wilson, August 1945- ... **BLC 3; CLC 39, 50, 63, 118; DC 2; WLCS**
See also AAYA 16; AFAW 2; AMWS 8; BW 2, 3; CA 115; 122; CAD; CANR 42, 54, 76, 128; CD 5; DA; DA3; DAB; DAC; DAM DRAM, MST, MULT; DFS 3, 7, 15, 17; DLB 228; EWL 3; LAIT 4; LATS 1:2; MTCW 1, 2; RGAL 4

Wilson, Brian 1942- .... **CLC 12**

Wilson, Colin 1931- .... **CLC 3, 14**
See also CA 1-4R; CAAS 5; CANR 1, 22, 33, 77; CMW 4; CN 7; DLB 14, 194; HGG; MTCW 1; SFW 4

Wilson, Dirk
See Pohl, Frederik

Wilson, Edmund 1895-1972 .. **CLC 1, 2, 3, 8, 24**
See also AMW; CA 1-4R; 37-40R; CANR 1, 46, 110; DLB 63; EWL 3; MTCW 1, 2; RGAL 4; TUS

Literary Criticism Series
Cumulative Topic Index

This index lists all topic entries in Gale's *Children's Literature Review* (CLR), *Classical and Medieval Literature Criticism* (CMLC), *Contemporary Literary Criticism* (CLC), *Drama Criticism* (DC), *Literature Criticism from 1400 to 1800* (LC), *Nineteenth-Century Literature Criticism* (NCLC), *Short Story Criticism* (SSC), and *Twentieth-Century Literary Criticism* (TCLC). The index also lists topic entries in the Gale Critical Companion Collection, which includes the following publications: *The Beat Generation* (BG), and *Harlem Renaissance* (HR).

Topic Index

NCLC Cumulative Nationality Index

AMERICAN

Adams, John **106**
Alcott, Amos Bronson **1**
Alcott, Louisa May **6, 58, 83**
Alger, Horatio Jr. **8, 83**
Allston, Washington **2**
Apess, William **73**
Arnold, Matthew **126**
Audubon, John James **47**
Barlow, Joel **23**
Bartram, William **145**
Beecher, Catharine Esther **30**
Bellamy, Edward **4, 86, 147**
Bird, Robert Montgomery **1**
Boker, George Henry **125**
Boyesen, Hjalmar Hjorth **135**
Brackenridge, Hugh Henry **7**
Brentano, Clemens (Maria) **1**
Brown, Charles Brockden **22, 74, 122**
Brown, William Wells **2, 89**
Brownson, Orestes Augustus **50**
Bryant, William Cullen **6, 46**
Calhoun, John Caldwell **15**
Channing, William Ellery **17**
Child, Lydia Maria **6, 73**
Chivers, Thomas Holley **49**
Cooke, John Esten **5**
Cooke, Rose Terry **110**
Cooper, Susan Fenimore **129**
Cooper, James Fenimore **1, 27, 54**
Cranch, Christopher Pearse **115**
Crèvecoeur, Michel Guillaume Jean de **105**
Crockett, David **8**
Cummins, Maria Susanna **139**
Dana, Richard Henry Sr. **53**
Delany, Martin Robinson **93**
Dickinson, Emily (Elizabeth) **21, 77**
Douglass, Frederick **7, 55, 141**
Dunlap, William **2**
Dwight, Timothy **13**
Emerson, Mary Moody **66**
Emerson, Ralph Waldo **1, 38, 98**
Field, Eugene **3**
Foster, Hannah Webster **99**
Foster, Stephen Collins **26**
Frederic, Harold **10**
Freneau, Philip Morin **1, 111**
Garrison, William Lloyd **149**
Hale, Sarah Josepha (Buell) **75**
Halleck, Fitz-Greene **47**
Hamilton, Alexander **49**
Hammon, Jupiter **5**
Harris, George Washington **23**
Hawthorne, Nathaniel **2, 10, 17, 23, 39, 79, 95**
Hawthorne, Sophia Peabody **150**
Hayne, Paul Hamilton **94**
Holmes, Oliver Wendell **14, 81**
Horton, George Moses **87**
Irving, Washington **2, 19, 95**
Jacobs, Harriet A(nn) **67**

James, Henry Sr. **53**
Jefferson, Thomas **11, 103**
Kennedy, John Pendleton **2**
Kirkland, Caroline M. **85**
Lanier, Sidney **6, 118**
Lazarus, Emma **8, 109**
Lincoln, Abraham **18**
Longfellow, Henry Wadsworth **2, 45, 101, 103**
Lowell, James Russell **2, 90**
Madison, James **126**
Melville, Herman **3, 12, 29, 45, 49, 91, 93, 123**
Mowatt, Anna Cora **74**
Murray, Judith Sargent **63**
Osgood, Frances Sargent **141**
Parkman, Francis Jr. **12**
Parton, Sara Payson Willis **86**
Paulding, James Kirke **2**
Pinkney, Edward **31**
Poe, Edgar Allan **1, 16, 55, 78, 94, 97, 117**
Rowson, Susanna Haswell **5, 69**
Sedgwick, Catharine Maria **19, 98**
Shaw, Henry Wheeler **15**
Sheridan, Richard Brinsley **5, 91**
Sigourney, Lydia Howard (Huntley) **21, 87**
Simms, William Gilmore **3**
Smith, Joseph Jr. **53**
Solomon, Northup **105**
Southworth, Emma Dorothy Eliza Nevitte **26**
Stowe, Harriet (Elizabeth) Beecher **3, 50, 133**
Taylor, Bayard **89**
Tenney, Tabitha Gilman **122**
Thoreau, Henry David **7, 21, 61, 138**
Timrod, Henry **25**
Trumbull, John **30**
Truth, Sojourner **94**
Tyler, Royall **3**
Very, Jones **9**
Warner, Susan (Bogert) **31, 146**
Warren, Mercy Otis **13**
Webster, Noah **30**
Webb, Frank J. **143**
Whitman, Sarah Helen (Power) **19**
Whitman, Walt(er) **4, 31, 81**
Whittier, John Greenleaf **8, 59**
Wilson, Harriet E. Adams **78**
Winnemucca, Sarah **79**

ARGENTINIAN

Echeverria, (Jose) Esteban (Antonino) **18**
Hernández, José **17**
Sarmiento, Domingo Faustino **123**

AUSTRALIAN

Adams, Francis **33**
Clarke, Marcus (Andrew Hislop) **19**
Gordon, Adam Lindsay **21**
Harpur, Charles **114**
Kendall, Henry **12**

AUSTRIAN

Grillparzer, Franz **1, 102**
Lenau, Nikolaus **16**
Nestroy, Johann **42**
Raimund, Ferdinand Jakob **69**
Sacher-Masoch, Leopold von **31**
Stifter, Adalbert **41**

CANADIAN

Crawford, Isabella Valancy **12, 127**
De Mille, James **123**
Haliburton, Thomas Chandler **15, 149**
Lampman, Archibald **25**
Moodie, Susanna (Strickland) **14, 113**
Richardson, John **55**
Traill, Catharine Parr **31**

CHINESE

Li Ju-chen **137**

COLOMBIAN

Isaacs, Jorge Ricardo **70**
Silva, José Asunción **114**

CUBAN

Avellaneda, Gertrudis Gómez de **111**
Casal, Julián del **131**
Manzano, Juan Francisco **155**
Martí (y Pérez), José (Julian) **63**
Villaverde, Cirilo **121**

CZECH

Macha, Karel Hynek **46**

DANISH

Andersen, Hans Christian **7, 79**
Grundtvig, Nicolai Frederik Severin **1**
Jacobsen, Jens Peter **34**
Kierkegaard, Søren **34, 78, 125**

ENGLISH

Ainsworth, William Harrison **13**
Arnold, Matthew **6, 29, 89**
Arnold, Thomas **18**
Austen, Jane **1, 13, 19, 33, 51, 81, 95, 119, 150**
Bagehot, Walter **10**
Barbauld, Anna Laetitia **50**
Barham, Richard Harris **77**
Barnes, William **75**
Beardsley, Aubrey **6**
Beckford, William **16**
Beddoes, Thomas Lovell **3, 154**
Bentham, Jeremy **38**
Blake, William **13, 37, 57, 127**
Bloomfield, Robert **145**
Borrow, George (Henry) **9**
Bowles, William Lisle **103**
Brontë, Anne **4, 71, 102**
Brontë, Charlotte **3, 8, 33, 58, 105, 155**

457

ISBN 0-7876-8639-5

9 780787 686390